PUBLICATIONS OF

THE COLONIAL SOCIETY
OF MASSACHUSETTS

VOLUME XCVII

THE MINUTES OF THE DARTMOUTH, MASSACHUSETTS MONTHLY MEETING OF FRIENDS 1699–1785

* * *

VOLUME I:
MEN'S MINUTES 1699–1773

THE MINUTES OF
THE DARTMOUTH, MASSACHUSETTS
MONTHLY MEETING OF FRIENDS
1699–1785

* * *

VOLUME I:

MEN'S MINUTES 1699–1773

THOMAS D. HAMM

EDITOR

BOSTON · 2022

COLONIAL SOCIETY OF MASSACHUSETTS

IN COOPERATION WITH

THE DARTMOUTH HISTORICAL AND ARTS SOCIETY

DISTRIBUTED BY

THE UNIVERSITY OF VIRGINIA PRESS

Dedication
To
DAN SOCHA

Printed from the Income of the Sarah Louisa Edes Fund

CONTENTS

VOLUME ONE

CONTENTS

VOLUME TWO

ILLUSTRATIONS

FOREWORD

DURING THE PAST 130 YEARS, the Colonial Society has published many church records, but they have all been either Congregational or Anglican, so this volume marks a new departure. The south coast of Massachusetts, adjoining the Rhode Island border, was throughout the seventeenth and eighteenth centuries a safe haven for those seeking to avoid too close scrutiny by either provincial authorities or the Congregational establishment in Boston. Thus, this borderland provided a refuge for Native Americans, freed Blacks, and religious dissidents, especially Quakers who faced severe penalties both in the Plymouth Colony, and later after 1691 in the Massachusetts Bay Colony.

The Dartmouth Monthly Meeting was the first group of Friends to gather for organized worship in the region. Being a 'worship group' within the Rhode Island Monthly Meeting, they did not begin recording their own minutes until being "set off" as their own Monthly Meeting in 1699. Since then, they have collected and preserved their records well into the twenty-first century. Constituting over six thousand manuscript pages, these volumes include not only the usual births, deaths, and marriages, but also the business records of their monthly meetings, a list of removals, and an eighteenth -century hand-written Book of Discipline, outlining the guiding principles of Quaker life and practice. Recognizing that a continuous set of records over such a long span of time was indeed a remarkable survival, the Dartmouth Historical and Arts Society set about digitizing and transcribing these manuscripts, and the Colonial Society of Massachusetts has now joined in the effort to make these records better known and more available by publishing the minutes of both the Men's and Women's Monthly Meetings from 1699 through the end of the American Revolution.

The well-regarded Quaker scholar, Thomas Hamm of Earlham College, generously provided a scholarly introduction for the records, together with appropriate annotations, that clarify for non-Quaker readers some of the group's most distinctive practices and highlight aspects of the documents that social historians will find particularly intriguing: the prominent role of women within Quaker meetings, marriage and courtship practices, offenses against "plainness," growing concern over abolition, and the delicate negotiations necessary with local government concerning taxes and military service.

In the sometimes sleepy world of local historical societies, the Dartmouth Historical and Arts Society is a remarkably energetic and ambitious organization. I would even venture to say unique in the scale and usefulness of its undertakings. Under the dynamic leadership of President Robert E. Harding and Project Manager Daniel Socha, the group devised a highly sophisticated program to transcribe these records, while still maintaining appropriate checks to insure accuracy. I highly recommend that interested readers visit their website www.dartmouthhas.org to examine many of the other fascinating documents that could not be included in this book.

The Colonial Society is particularly grateful to the Dartmouth at Smith's Neck Monthly Meeting for permission to publish this portion of their archives. Elton Hall, the long-time curator of the Colonial Society and a Dartmouth resident first made the Colonial Society aware of the DHAS efforts, and Bob Harding readily saw the value that bringing out a portion of these records under the Colonial Society's imprint might have for the project. Since joining forces with the CSM, Bob has been tireless, never shying away from even the most tedious tasks necessary to assist in this cooperative endeavor. Andrea Marcovici was particularly helpful in effecting the difficult transition of files from the DHAS website to a format that could be put into print. Jean Schnell (www.jeanschnell.com) provided the evocative photographs that accompany the text. Paul Hoffmann is responsible for the book's handsome design. Puritan Press of Hollis, New Hampshire, efficiently handled the printing and binding, and Kate Mertes compiled the index.

JOHN W. TYLER, *Editor of Publications*
COLONIAL SOCIETY OF MASSACHUSETTS

A BRIEF HISTORY: THE "QUAKER PROJECT" OF THE DARTMOUTH HISTORICAL AND ARTS SOCIETY

IF GEORGE FOX, the moving force whose vision, energy, and leadership inspired and directed the religious movement that became known as the "Society of Friends," had not required his followers to keep very specific records and minutes of their activities and built systems to enforce their faithful execution at the monthly meeting level, there would be no records to preserve and transcribe.

Likewise, if Donald Lines Jacobus, described by genealogist Milton Rubicam as "the man who more than any other single individual elevated genealogy to the high degree of scholarship it now occupies," had not established the modern standards of sourcing and citation in genealogy that have been so widely followed, we might not have appreciated the great value of the Friends' records to genealogical research.

Among the founding members of the Dartmouth Historical and Arts Society (DHAS) in 2011 were families with long pedigrees connected with the Society of Friends, and especially the Dartmouth Monthly Meeting. One of the founders, Marcia Cornell Glynn, has been a long-time member of the Board of Directors and still remains an Honorary Member of the Board. She played a key role in educating the DHAS about the important role played by Dartmouth Friends in historically significant events in our area, in Massachusetts, and, actually, in the country at large. Her brother, Russell Cornell, lately deceased, was not only an active DHAS member but also a 'weighty' elder in the Dartmouth Monthly Meeting (DMM).

In July 2017, Glynn delivered an illustrated lecture to a substantial collection of Dartmouth history buffs and Friends, at the venerable Apponegansett meeting House in Russells Mills, a village within the town of Dartmouth. She noted that the original town of "Old Dartmouth" (to distinguish it from the present town) now includes a city and four towns: New Bedford, Dartmouth. Westport, Fairhaven, and Acushnet and that in colonial times the Religious Society of Friends was the predominate religious affiliation of its residents. Her lecture generated substantial interest and local discussion, especially within the Dartmouth Historical and Arts Society.

Just a year after her talk, on July 22, 2018, Katherine Plant, a director of DHAS, spoke at the yearly meeting of the Dartmouth Monthly Meeting. Kathy was supported with slides and a PowerPoint presentation prepared by DHAS President, Robert E. Harding, and the lecture was video-taped by another director, Dan Socha, the group's webmaster and technical leader. Anne Lopoulos, a leader of the Dartmouth Monthly Meeting, chaired the meeting and introduced Kathy. Several years prior, an unfortunate experience with another local museum and historical society had caused the Dartmouth Monthly Meeting to remove their collection of delicate record books from that museum's custody for fear that frequent and unsupervised use by museum patrons entailed too much risk. Nevertheless, the Monthly Meeting was well aware of the need to find another way by which these fragile, environmentally sensitive records might be consulted. Participants in the meeting from both groups agreed that perhaps the DHAS might assist the Monthly Meeting by arranging for the records to be "digitized." A digital record would eliminate the need for frequent handling. After a review of the concept by the Monthly Meeting, formal papers were drawn up granting the DHAS permission to undertake the project.

Two DHAS leaders had extensive professional experience and practical knowledge with information systems design and data processing in business. After extensive discussions within the Board of Directors, Dan Socha, assisted by Bob Harding, took the lead in creating a process to get the job done. Early in the process, DHAS received significant and much appreciated guidance from Jane Fletcher Fiske, a veteran transcriber of colonial records and respected genealogist. This timely input started the undertaking off on the right foot by developing fundamental guidelines for transcription that prevented many time-consuming errors.

Although the process created to digitize, transcribe, review, quality-check, and post material on the DHAS website was entirely a DHAS creation, it is a 'generic system' that could also be used for similar collections of historical records. Thus, the process was thoroughly documented to preserve it for future utilization. Like most complex information systems, this one is composed of several 'sub-systems', each one contributing to the final results. But for our purposes here the details are less important than the overall goal: digitizing original records and preparing computer-ready transcriptions, faithful to the original manuscripts.

DHAS director Dan Socha went quickly to work, collecting the record books from the DMM and beginning the tedious process of scanning and creating image files. Dan's process was well described by local journalist Chloe Shelford writing in *Dartmouth Week* on December 25, 2018:

> When he decided to digitize the archive, Socha began researching how the experts—libraries, universities, and the government—scanned large historical doc-

uments, and built his own version of what those organizations use. His camera is mounted to a contraption that can be moved both up and down and forward and back over a table lit with clamp lights. "These are my really high-end lights from Home Depot," joked Socha. For larger documents, like maps, Socha will take photos of overlapping sections of the document and knit them together on his computer. All the photos are very high resolution (and very large files), which are transferred immediately to the computer. So Socha manually reduces the file size as much as possible without losing quality.

Simultaneously, Dan and Bob (with assistance from a growing cadre of project volunteers) set about designing and fitting together all of the subsystems needed to insure the faithful capture and transcription of the handwritten records into an accurate record that could be stored and searched via computers.

The Dartmouth Quaker records have a special value to genealogists and historians for specific reasons that can be briefly summarized as follows: (1) They are 'primary' sources, recorded at the time the events occurred by reliable clerks of the DMM, (2) Because of the Friends' particular custom of patiently repeating issues and waiting for general acceptance by the whole meeting, some events are often repeated over multiple months (and sometimes in both the Women's and the Men's minutes); these repetitious entries provide multiple opportunities to insure the correct spelling of names and the details of most of the incidents chronicled. (3) All the minutes are dated, thus placing them accurately within a timeline, and (4) The Quaker requirement for 'certificates of removal' when individuals or families moved from the jurisdiction of one monthly meeting to another (whether for marriage, visiting, preaching, or permanent relocation) yield very detailed information about patterns of geographic migration, since they specify locations, people, and specific times.

After careful planning and systems design, recruitment of a team, the parceling out of various roles, and training participants, this very ambitious project, took off at a steady pace, and, one by one, various volumes of the DMM record books were processed to completion, which included posting the transcribed version on the DHAS website along with images of the original manuscripts. Each and every volunteer, as well as the various professional firms engaged, accomplished their tasks with careful coordination by Project Manager, Dan Socha.

While we at DHAS were, as a team, pulling on the oars with a steady rhythm and making remarkable progress, we encountered a tragedy that shook us to the core. Dan, our project leader and technical expert discovered that he had a serious, life threatening illness. Dan played so many key roles on the project team, and within DHAS more generally, that this sudden news faced us with several immediate problems that needed thoughtful attention. Dan and president Bob Harding had a brief time to make some hasty plans to cope with the inevitable, fast-approaching reality.

Fortunately among the many capable and talented volunteers on the project team, there was one in particular with a very high level of relevant experience and skill who volunteered to take over his key role as Project Manager: Andrea Marcovici. Andrea has done a wonderful job, and the project has not missed a beat in the transition. Likewise, many of the other roles that Dan performed have gradually been filled by other volunteers within the organization. This has been a testimony not only to our resilience, but also to our esteem and love for our friend Dan Socha, to whom we dedicate this work.

As they are completed, all of the transcribed DMM records are being made available to the public at: https://dartmouthhas.org/quaker-transcriptions.html. The DHAS has also established contractual arrangements with the Colonial Society of Massachusetts and the New England Historic Genealogical Society to publish different subsets of the DMM Quaker Records Project. A fully searchable form of the eighteenth century records can be seen at www.colonialsociety.org/publications, and the removal records are available at https://www.americanancestors.org/search/databasesearch/2796/dartmouth-ma-quaker-records-1699-1920. As time permits, the DHAS intends to explore even more ways to distribute additional results in further publications.

ROBERT E. HARDING, *President*
DARTMOUTH HISTORICAL AND ARTS
SOCIETY

ACKNOWLEDGMENTS

THE RELIGIOUS SOCIETY OF FRIENDS, Dartmouth Meeting, has diligently documented their religious life for over 250 years. This large body of work might have been lost to history if not for the dedicated group of volunteers who brought these records into the digital age for research and preservation.

The following members of the Project Management Team (in alphabetical order) were responsible for digitizing records, fund raising, process design, developing transcription guidelines, implementation of the project, and quality assurance: Sally M. Aldrich, Robert E. Harding, Richard W. Gifford, Andrea L. Marcovici, Marian J. Ryall, and Daniel H. Socha.

Editors D. Jordan Berson, Steven Fitzroy, Kenneth Howland, Judith Lund, Andrea Marcovici, Tyler Pelletier, Diane Pereira, Barbara Silvia, Rebecca Smith, Susan Socha, and Emma Sylvia were responsible for reviewing and editing the transcriptions as they were received from the vendors Digital Divide Data and GoTranscript. Their work was critical in producing an exact match in order to insure that the transcriptions did not deviate from the handwritten records.

This work could not have happened without the generous donations of our benefactors: Dartmouth Friends of the Elderly, Dartmouth Friends Monthly Meeting – Smiths Neck, Ruth Ekstrom, Marland Family, Christopher McKeon, New England Yearly Meeting – Obadiah Brown Benevolent Fund, Kathy and Don Plant, Stat Southcoast, and Nancy Sutton.

Many guides, facilitators and consultants have aided our efforts along the way. This list will, without doubt, be incomplete, but must include our Colonial Society of Massachusetts, as well as its editor and gracious guide in this publishing project John Tyler. John's unfailing patience and thoughtful suggestions have facilitated our efforts from start to finish. DHAS board member and former Smith Neck Meeting pastor, the Rev. Pamela Cole and long time DHAS member, Burney Gifford have provided key insights and communications connections within the Quaker network, which have greatly facilitated our work. Likewise, Andy Grannell, former Allen's Neck Monthly Meeting pastor, now active in Portland, Maine, Quaker circles was instrumental in aiding our navigation of the various organizations of the Society of Friends. Very early in the life of the project a ZOOM meeting with Robert Cox (now deceased) Executive

Director of University of Massachusetts Amherst's, Special Collections & University Archives, which houses many original record books of the monthly meetings that make up the New England Yearly Meeting, was helpful and aided much of our early decision-making.

Also, we are grateful to the many different individuals within the NEYM organization who have answered our questions, helped us with communicating to the wider world of New England Friends and, in general, been totally supportive of our efforts.

Last but not least, to all the Board Members of DHAS and all of our members and friends who have been our constant source of support and encouragement over these long days of work on this substantial project, for all the ways you have contributed to the welfare of our little non-profit and its big ambitions—we are sincerely and deeply appreciative.

QUAKERISM IN DARTMOUTH

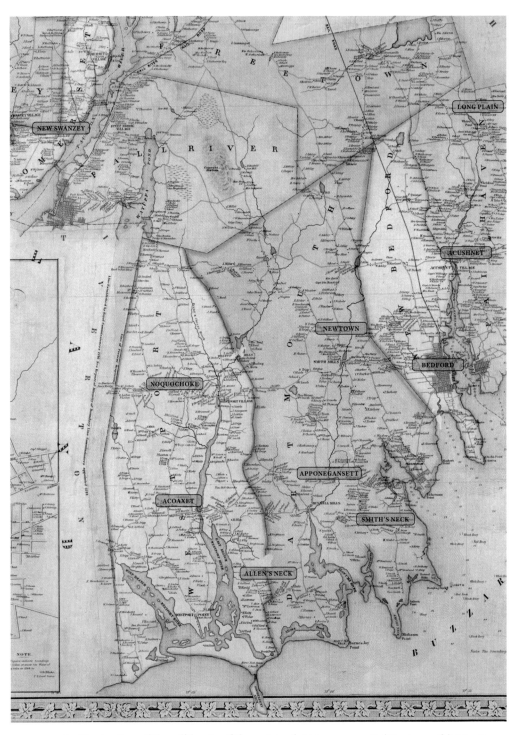

FIG. 1: *An illustration of the offshoots of the original Apponegansett (Dartmouth) Meeting superimposed on "A Map of Bristol County Massachusetts: based on the trigonometrical survey of the state," by Henry Francis Walling, 1852. Courtesy of the Norman B. Leventhal Map Center, Boston Public Library.*

INTRODUCTION

QUAKERISM IN DARTMOUTH

WITH THESE TWO VOLUMES, the Colonial Society of Massachusetts makes available the first minute books of the Dartmouth Monthly Meeting of Friends. Quakers were outliers in colonial New England. A self-defined "peculiar people," they embraced a vision of Christianity that their neighbors generally regarded as at best strange, at worst dangerously heretical. The years of suffering, even martyrdom, for their faith were largely behind them by the time that Dartmouth Friends formed their monthly meeting in 1699. But even a superficial reading of these records will show how different from their neighbors Friends remained, with their opposition to war, repudiation of judicial oaths, and the very existence of a women's meeting for business.

QUAKER ORIGINS

QUAKERISM WAS ONE of the radical sects that emerged from the English Civil War in the 1640s. The central figure was George Fox (1624-1691), the offspring of a Leicestershire yeoman family with strong Puritan views. By his own account, Fox was an unusually godly young man. The competing, and irreconcilable, claims of the religious groups around him deeply troubled Fox. Seeking the true Christian church, in 1643 he set off on a kind of spiritual pilgrimage, traveling around southern England, seeking out both clergy and laypeople with reputations for godliness, hoping that they would show him the true way. But, as Fox remembered, "there was none that could speak to my condition." So in his early twenties, he wandered up into the north of England. There Fox had a series of experiences that would become the foundation for the group that first called itself Children of the Light, later Friends of the Light, ultimately the Religious Society of Friends. "Quaker" was originally an insulting nickname, but as sometimes happens, Friends took it up.[1]

Fox's outlook put him on the extreme left wing of English spirituality in the 1640s and 1650s. Fox based his preaching on what he called "openings," what today we would call revelations, experiences in which Fox was confident that God had spoken

---

1. H. Larry Ingle, *First among Friends: George Fox and the Creation of Quakerism* (New York: Oxford University Press, 1994), 3-53, 54.

directly to him. Fox argued that divine revelation had not ceased when the last book of the Bible was written, because the same Holy Spirit that had inspired the writers of the Scriptures was still available to humans. Fox found biblical images and metaphors of *light* especially important. Most radically, he concluded that all human beings have within them a certain measure of divine light, "the Light of Christ inwardly revealed." If humans are obedient to it, it will lead them into lives acceptable to God, with heaven as their reward. But if they ignore the promptings of that Light, it will be extinguished and they will be lost. Fox repudiated the idea of a trained ministry. In his eyes, all Christians were called to be ministers. "To be bred at Oxford or Cambridge" did not do this, only inspiration from God. From this insight, Fox drew two radical conclusions. One was that God inspired women as well as men, that women had just as much right to speak and preach and pray publicly as men. The second shaped Quaker worship. Since the true ministry came through divine inspiration, and God could inspire anyone, Quaker worship had no set rituals, nor did a pastor preside over it. Instead, Friends gathered and waited in silence, confident that if God had a message for the group, God would inspire someone to speak. Fox's understanding of Scripture also led him to an extreme spiritual understanding of the sacraments. Quakers did not baptize with water or observe any form of outward communion. The only true baptism, Fox argued, was the baptism of the Holy Spirit. Communion was experienced in the fellowship of believers.[2]

Quaker distinctiveness, or "peculiarity," the term that Friends usually applied to themselves, did not stop here. Quakers broke with many of the customs of deference and hierarchy that characterized English society in the seventeenth century. They eschewed these practices because they saw them as puffing up human vanity. Quaker men did not remove their hats in the presence of their "betters," even when hauled into court. Friends refused to use titles like "Mister" or "Mistress" or "Your Honor," instead addressing other people by their full names or simply as "friend." The Quaker "plain language" of addressing others as "thee" or "thou" also reflected such convictions. In seventeenth-century English grammar, "thee" and "thou" were the singular forms of "you," comparable to "I" and "we" or "she" and "they." It was a mark of respect and courtesy to show respect to a superior, however, by addressing that individual as "you." It was rude and disrespectful for a child to call a parent "you"; likewise with servants and masters. Such practices gave Friends the reputation of being dangerous social revolutionaries.[3]

2. The best accounts of early Quaker thought are Hugh Barbour, *The Quakers in Puritan England* (New Haven: Yale University Press, 1964); and Rosemary Moore, *The Light in Their Consciences: Early Quakers in Britain, 1646-1666* (University Park: Pennsylvania State University Press, 2000).

3. William C. Braithwaite, *The Beginnings of Quakerism* (London: Macmillan, 1923), 486-99.

Historians debate how many of these beliefs and practices were unique to Friends. Certainly other radical groups between 1640 and 1660 blasted social and economic inequality, or allowed women to preach, or rejected normal practices of deference and civility. But Friends brought all of them together in a unique mixture. And many of their contemporaries found this threatening.[4]

Other facets of Quaker faith and practice were unsettling to contemporaries. Some Friends, including Fox, felt led to attend the services of other churches, evaluate the sermons and proceedings, and, if they found them inadequate, interrupt with their own critiques. Some Friends felt led to "go naked as a sign": to appear unclothed in a public place as a witness, sometimes to show their own spiritual innocence (like Adam and Eve in Eden before the Fall, they were "naked and not ashamed"); sometimes as a means of self-mortification; sometimes as a way of showing the "spiritual nakedness of the opposers of Friends." And Friends had a gift for vituperation and invective. In an age when religious debates routinely involved charges of blasphemy and satanic influences, Friends gave as good as they got. It speaks volumes that when Fox, in 1659, published his longest book, a critique of every anti-Quaker work issued up to that time, its title was *The Great Mystery of the Great Whore Unfolded: and Antichrist's Kingdom Revealed unto Destruction.*[5]

Quakers were aggressive evangelists. A sect that barely existed in 1650 had by 1660 spread to all parts of England and Wales and was making headway in Ireland and in English colonies in the Caribbean and North America. Adherents may have numbered as many as fifty thousand. One woman Friend actually embarked for Constantinople to preach to the sultan of the Ottoman Empire. By 1659, officials in London were nervous that Quakerism was spreading even in the army. Such anxieties were one factor in moving political and military leaders toward the restoration of the monarchy in the spring of 1660. Thus opposition to Quakerism was often ferocious. Typical was one of the earliest attacks on Friends, by Francis Higginson, a Puritan pastor in Westmorland with many ties to Massachusetts, *A Brief Relation of the Irreligion of the Northern Quakers.* Quakers were "Satan's seeds-men." Hundreds of Friends found themselves thrown into jail, charged with blasphemy or vagrancy. When James Nayler, a Yorkshire Friend who in the 1650s rivaled Fox as a preacher, felt led in Bristol

---

4. See, for example, Christopher Hill, *The World Turned Upside Down: Radical Ideas during the English Revolution* (Harmondsworth, Eng.: Penguin, 1972), 231-58; and Barry Reay, *The Quakers and the English Revolution* (New York: St. Martin's, 1985).

5. Barbour, *Quakers in Puritan England,* 127-59; Raymond Brown and Alan P. F. Sell, "Quakers and Dissenters in Dispute," in *The Quakers 1656-1723: The Evolution of an Alternative Community,* ed. by Richard C. Allen and Rosemary Moore (University Park: Pennsylvania State University Press, 2018), 124-47; Andrew Bradstock, *Radical Religion in Cromwell's England: A Concise History from the English Civil War to the End of the Commonwealth* (London: I. B. Tauris, 2011), 104-07.

to imitate Jesus's Palm Sunday entry into Jerusalem, he was branded, pilloried, and imprisoned by order of Parliament, and narrowly escaped execution.[6]

QUAKERISM IN NEW ENGLAND

GIVEN THIS REPUTATION, it is unsurprising that when two Quaker women, Mary Fisher and Ann Austin, arrived in Boston in July 1656, authorities there promptly clapped them into jail, confiscated and burned their books, had their bodies examined for marks of witchcraft, and then expelled them. Two days after Austin and Fisher were shipped out of Boston, eight more Quakers appeared. Authorities also imprisoned them, and, eleven weeks later, banished them. The Massachusetts General Court rushed to pass a law imposing a fine of one hundred pounds on any shipmaster who knowingly landed a Quaker in Massachusetts. Importing or possessing a Quaker book brought a fine of five pounds.[7]

Few things attracted Quakers as much as persecution. Over the next few years, what one historian labeled a "Quaker Invasion" took place, as Friends felt led to Massachusetts both to proselytize and to bear witness against the colony's "spirit of persecution." Authorities responded with more repressive legislation. A 1657 statute was even more severe, as historian Arthur J. Worrall summarizes: it "provided a fine of 100 pounds for importing Quakers and a fine of 40 shillings for each hour Massachusetts residents entertained Quakers knowingly, with imprisonment until payment. Each Quaker entering the colony after previous punishment was to have one ear cut off, a second ear on repeating the offense, and his tongue bored through with a hot iron for a third offense." But more Friends appeared in 1658, including three men who had already been expelled once and consequently lost an ear. So in the fall of 1658 the General Court passed its most draconian law. Nonresident Quakers entering Massachusetts and convicted of sharing Quaker beliefs were to be banished on pain of death. As signs of sympathy were appearing among local residents who did not necessarily embrace Quakerism themselves, trials were to be by a special court of assistants. A few residents of Salem who had become Friends were ordered banished if they did not return to orthodoxy.[8]

These measures were futile as well. So between October 1659 and March 1661 four Friends were hanged in Boston after being found guilty of returning after having

---

6. Thomas D. Hamm, *The Quakers in America* (New York: Columbia University Press, 2003), 18-22; Rosemary Allen, "Seventeenth-Century Context and Quaker Beginnings," in *The Oxford Handbook of Quaker Studies,* ed. by Stephen W. Angell and Pink Dandelion (New York: Oxford University Press, 2013), 26-28.

7. Arthur J. Worrall, *Quakers in the Colonial Northeast* (Hanover, N.H.: University Press of New England, 1980), 9-10.

8. Ibid., 10-11; Richard P. Hallowell, *The Quaker Invasion of Massachusetts* (Boston: Houghton Mifflin, 1884).

been banished. Three were English: Marmaduke Stevenson, William Robinson, and William Leddra. The fourth, Mary Dyer, was a former resident of Boston who had been banished two decades earlier as an ally of Anne Hutchinson. And dozens of Friends remained in jail.[9]

Meanwhile, Friends in England were publicizing the sufferings of their brothers and sisters in Massachusetts, most notably through George Bishop's book *New England Judged*. When Charles II was restored to the throne in the spring of 1660, Massachusetts authorities suspected that the monarch, who had no reason to love Puritans, would be looking for opportunities to strike back. So they released twenty-eight imprisoned Friends. Bishop and another leading English Friend, Edward Burrough, were granted an audience by the king, telling him that there was "a vein of blood open" in his colony of Massachusetts because of the persecution of Friends there. "I will stop that vein," Charles responded, and sent an order to Massachusetts to cease executions. To add insult to injury, Charles entrusted delivery to Samuel Shattuck, a Quaker convert from Salem who had been earlier been banished on pain of death. But the end of executions did not mean the end of persecution. Massachusetts passed a new law ordering Quakers to be whipped out of the colony.[10]

The experiences of Friends in Massachusetts between 1656 and 1661 were central to the formation of a New England Quaker identity. The growth of New England Quakerism would come at the peripheries. Converts to Quakerism in the Bay Colony were relatively few, limited almost entirely to Salem and towns in the northern part of Essex County. Another Quaker community developed in Dover, New Hampshire. And the Plymouth Colony, which was independent of Massachusetts before 1692, would see Quaker communities grow between 1660 and 1700.[11]

QUAKERISM COMES TO DARTMOUTH

THE PLYMOUTH COLONY was generally not as exacting in its Puritanism as Massachusetts. Governor William Bradford apparently inclined toward leniency, but he died in 1656, just as the Quaker "invasion" began, and his successor, Thomas Prence, was less tolerant. Plymouth's official position was to resist Quakerism, but by means less horrific than those the leaders of Massachusetts employed. Arthur J. Worrall sums up: "Plymouth authorities, though ordering the occasional whipping,

9. Worrall, *Quakers in the Colonial Northeast*, 12-14. Charles Dyer, a grandson of Mary, was later a member of Dartmouth Monthly Meeting. See his marriage to Mary Lapham in 1709.

10. Hugh Barbour and J. William Frost, *The Quakers* (Westport, Ct.: Greenwood, 1988), 52-53; Rufus M. Jones, *The Quakers in the American Colonies* (London: MacMillan, 1923), 94-99; George Bishop, *New England Judged, Not by Man's, but by the Spirit of the Lord, and the Summe Sealed up of New England's Persecutions, Being a Brief Relation of the Sufferings of the People Called Quakers in Those Parts of America, Etc.* (London: Robert Wilson, 1661).

11. Barbour and Frost, *The Quakers*, 52-53.

never indulged in corporal punishment to the same degree as did Massachusetts, did not banish its own people (although it encouraged their migration), did not execute Friends, and did not mutilate either Quaker missionaries or their converts." The imposition of test oaths, which Quakers refused to take, and fines for "harboring a "Quaker rantor or other Notoriouse heretiques" were the first steps. Later came threats of whippings and fines for attending or hosting Quaker gatherings. Nevertheless, Friends found some followers in the Plymouth Colony, especially in Marshfield, Scituate, and Sandwich. Christopher Holder, a Friend from England who was one of the victims of the Boston authorities, preached in Sandwich in 1657, and soon afterwards Friends began to hold meetings in the homes of William and Ralph Allen, the ancestors of many Dartmouth Friends.[12]

The origins of Quakerism in Dartmouth were also closely tied to its neighbor to the west, Rhode Island. Roger Williams's colony, established as a haven from persecution in the rest of New England, unsurprisingly became a major Quaker center. Among Quaker converts were followers and allies of Anne Hutchinson, whose antinomianism anticipated Quaker beliefs in critical ways. They mostly lived in Portsmouth and Newport. Williams himself had little use for Quaker theology and engaged in public debates with Quaker leaders. (George Fox and Williams fought a heated pamphlet war.) Williams saw Quakers as being as narrow and dogmatic as Puritans. But he remained committed to liberty of conscience. Friends steadily increased in numbers and influence in the colony. By the end of the century, Quakers had leading roles in Rhode Island's government, and continued prominent in it until the American Revolution.[13]

It is not clear who the first Quakers in Dartmouth were. Local historian Ann Gidley Lowry describes them as "Howlands, Allens, Slocums, Smiths and Tuckers." To these should be added the Laphams. The Howlands came from Marshfield, the Allens from Sandwich, and the Smiths from the town of Plymouth in the Plymouth Colony. The Tuckers had fled Massachusetts. The Laphams and Slocums came from Rhode Island.[14]

12. Worrall, *Quakers in the Colonial Northeast*, 15-17; Ann Gidley Lowry, *Quakers and Their Meeting House at Apponegansett: Paper Read at Meeting of the Old Dartmouth Historical Society, August 14, 1940* (N.p., 1940), unpaginated; Walter Spooner Allen, "The Family of George Allen, the Immigrant, and Its Connection with the Settlement of Old Dartmouth," *Old Dartmouth Historical Sketches*, 18 (1907), 12-22. Christopher Holder's daughter Mary (Holder) Slocum (1662-1737) was a member of Dartmouth Monthly Meeting. See William A. Wing, "Peleg Slocum of Dartmouth and His Wife Mary Holder," ibid., 3 (1903), 4-6.

13. Worrall, *Quakers in the Colonial Northeast*, 18-20, 31-41; Jones, *Quakers in the American Colonies,* 171-212; Sydney V. James, *Colonial Rhode Island: A History* (New York: Charles Scribner's Sons, 1975), 39-47, 186-88; David D. Hall, *Anne Hutchinson: Puritan Prophet* (Saddle River, N.J.: Pearson, 2010); David S. Lovejoy, "Roger Williams and George Fox: The Arrogance of Self-Righteousness," *New England Quarterly*, 66 (June 1993), 199-225; Robert J. Lowenherz, "Roger Williams and the Great Quaker Debate," *American Quarterly*, 11 (Summer 1959), 157-65.

14. Lowry, *Quakers and Their Meetinghouse*, unpaginated.

By the time that Dartmouth Monthly Meeting was established in 1699, Friends had settled on a clear organization and hierarchy of authority. At the base was the individual congregation. It was usually referred to as a meeting for worship or a particular meeting. Friends eschewed the label "church" for individual congregations, feeling that that should be applied to the universal body of believers. At various times, Dartmouth Monthly Meeting included Apponegansett, Acushnet, Newtown, Acoaxet, Rochester, New Bedford, Centre, New Swansey, Nosequchuck, and Smith's Neck particular meetings. One or more of these combined in the preparative meeting. (Dartmouth was unusual in having preparative meetings that sometimes included more than one congregation or particular meeting.) The preparative meeting would meet monthly for business purposes. At times a preparative meeting might be transferred to another monthly meeting. In 1740, for example, Rochester Preparative Meeting was taken away from Dartmouth and joined to Sandwich Monthly Meeting. Rochester Friends had aroused concern at times by their lack of participation in Dartmouth Monthly Meeting affairs, and apparently it was concluded that it would be more convenient for them to be part of Sandwich.[15]

Preparative meetings took their name from the fact that they prepared business for consideration by the monthly meeting. Men Friends offered a description of their function in First Month 1706: "to Consider of the afairs amongst friends and see what may be convenient to be recommended to the monthely meeting so that the monthely meeting may not be Incumbred with a multitude of unneesesearey buseness." Matters "convenient" usually involved membership, or, more often, reports of members who had deviated from the standards expected of Quakers. The monthly meeting was (and remains) the basic business unit for Quakers. Usually, before 1900, a monthly meeting was made up of two or more preparative meetings. When a preparative meeting, or combination of preparatives, was judged large enough to constitute its own monthly meeting, then the monthly meeting would be divided, with the new monthly meeting being "set off" from the older one. In 1766, for example, Dartmouth set off Acoaxet Preparative Meeting as Acoaxet Monthly Meeting. (The name was changed to Westport, to coincide with the name of the town, in 1812.) This can be a confusing process when tracking individuals, as usually no list of the "set off" members was made. They simply disappear from the records of their old monthly meeting and appear in the those of the new one. As examination of the Dartmouth

---

15. Rosemary Moore, "Gospel Order: The Development of Quaker Organization," in *The Quakers 1656-1723*, ed. by Allen and Moore, 54-75; *Souvenir of the Bi-Centennial of the Dartmouth Monthly Meeting of the Society of Friends, Massachusetts* (N.P.: Franklyn Howland, 1899), 13-14; Carol Hagglund, "Disowned without Just Cause: Quakers in Rochester, Massachusetts, during the Eighteenth Century" (Ph.D. diss., University of Massachusetts, 1980), 132-38.

Monthly Meeting minutes shows, monthly meetings received people into membership either by transfer from another monthly meeting, or by conversion, "convince-
ment," as Friends called it. Monthly meetings also could deprive erring members of
their membership. The usual term for this was *disownment*. Monthly meetings were
charged with keeping records of births and deaths, and they oversaw marriages of
members. Monthly meetings also were responsible for property matters, appointing
trustees to hold title to meetinghouse lands and burial grounds. They cared for poor
and needy members. And they raised money for various purposes, including dues or
"stock" paid to the quarterly and yearly meeting. Monthly meetings did not necessarily observe political boundaries—they might extend across town, county, or even
provincial lines.[16]

Two or more monthly meetings made up a quarterly meeting. As the name suggests, these were meetings for business held four times a year. For the period of these
records, Dartmouth Friends were part of Rhode Island Quarterly Meeting, reflecting
their proximity and longstanding connections with Friends in Newport. Quarterly
meetings exercised oversight over monthly meetings by evaluating their answers to
queries about the state of affairs in the monthly meetings. They handled appeals of
disownments. And they confirmed or disallowed the appointment of elders and the
recording of ministers.[17]

The highest level of authority for Friends was the yearly meeting, which determined rules and regulations for the body and issued statements on spiritual issues.
New England Friends often claim that their yearly meeting is the oldest in the world,
with its first sessions taking place in 1661. But surviving records begin in 1672, when
George Fox himself was present. In the eighteenth century it was often referred to as
the "Yearly Meeting for Rhode Island." Yearly meeting sessions were held in Newport,
where the "Great Meetinghouse," constructed in 1699, is now a museum. Well into
the eighteenth century, in addition to the annual business sessions, Friends held an
annual "general meeting," which was centered on worship. Several of these were held
within Dartmouth Monthly Meeting's bounds.[18]

Theoretically, yearly meetings were independent of each other. But Quaker practices bound them closely together and helped preserve uniformity on essential matters of faith and practice, with a few exceptions, until the 1820s. American Friends
usually deferred to the leadership of English Friends. By the 1750s, Philadelphia

16. Moore, "Gospel Order," 54-75; *Souvenir*, 14.
17. Moore, "Gospel Order," 54-75; Jones, *Quakers in the American Colonies*, 141-42.
18. Jones, Quakers in the American Colonies, 143-45; For the 1661 claim, see http://scua.library.umass.
edu/new-england-yearly-meeting/

Yearly Meeting had emerged as the first among American equals, and its epistles and advices were also given close attention by Friends in New England.[19]

Despite persecution, Quakerism took root and grew in New England. From five monthly meetings in 1695, by 1772 the New England Yearly Meeting had grown to thirteen in New Hampshire, Massachusetts, and Rhode Island. As examination of Dartmouth records after 1740 will show, New England Friends would be central to the expansion of Quakerism in New York. By the time of the American Revolution, about 30 percent of all Massachusetts Quakers were members of Dartmouth Monthly Meeting.[20]

DARTMOUTH MONTHLY MEETING
IN THE QUAKER WORLD

ONE FINDS REGULAR references to Friends beyond Dartmouth in the Dartmouth records. Not only institutions but shared faith and practice tied Friends together.

Over the course of the eighteenth century, the structures of leadership that Friends elsewhere embraced were emerging in Dartmouth Monthly Meeting. Before 1700, Friends with "a gift in the line of the ministry" or preaching were usually called "public Friends." After 1700 they were increasingly referred to as ministers. Friends recognized a gift in ministry not through ordination—Friends regarded that as implying that human action somehow conferred a gift in ministry. Instead, Friends "recorded" ministers, making a record of a gift divinely bestowed. No public Friends or ministers are identified as being recorded by Dartmouth Monthly Meeting before 1750, although we know from other records that Nicholas Davis, Peleg Slocum and Stephen Wilcox were public Friends. The most prominent was Davis (1690-1755), "an able skillful minister of the gospel, dividing the word of truth aright; zealous against obstinate offenders, but to those under affliction, his words were as healing balsam, and his speech as dew on the tender grass." The process is implied, however, by disownment of Deborah Wilber in Eighth Month 1772. The women's minutes noted that she had "Some times has Appeared Publickly as a Minister tho' never fully Approved of as a Minister amongst friends." By 1736 the monthly meeting was also appointing elders, Friends who were charged with the oversight of the ministry in meeting, encouraging speaking that edified hearers and discouraging, even silencing, speaking that did not. The first named are James Barker and Abraham Tucker, although women served as

---

19. Elizabeth Cazden, "'Within the Bounds of Their Circumstances': The Testimony of Inequality among Eighteenth-Century New England Friends," in *Quakerism in the Atlantic World, 1690-1830*, ed. by Robynne Rogers Healey, (University Park: Pennsylvania State University Press, 2021), 44-64.

20. Barbour and Frost, *The Quakers,* 54; Alice Sue Friday, "The Quaker Origins of New Bedford, 1765-1815" (Ph.D. diss., Boston University, 1991), 239.

elders as well. A third category of appointments was of overseers or visitors, whose functions are discussed below.[21]

The official roles that Friends gave to women were one of the most distinctive aspects of Quakerism. Women were recorded ministers and served as elders and overseers. Male and female Friends held separate meetings for business. Generally, the minutes of the business meetings of women Friends are the oldest written records we have of organized groups of women in colonial America. Men handled matters involving men, and women those involving women Friends. The two meetings did not have equal powers. Men dealt with matters of property and relations with the town and provincial governments, although women Friends had their own funds, or "stock," that they collected and disbursed. Thus the women's minutes of Sixth Month 1737 show that Ruth Tucker and Phebe Tucker were appointed to "balance the accounts of this meeting." And while the men did not require the approval or unity of women Friends to disown a member, the disownment of female Friends by the women's monthly meeting required the approval of the men.[22]

One function of the monthly meeting was to grant certificates of removal to Friends moving beyond the monthly meeting's bounds. In the monthly meeting's early days, at least, there was an expectation that Friends would consult with the monthly meeting before undertaking such actions. Thus the men's minutes of Tenth Month 19, 1709, show that there were "some agetations" about Samuel Mott selling out and moving to Newport. It was the "sience [sense] of this meeting" that "It will not be for his Advantag in aney wise," and so the men refused to grant a certificate. Likewise Dartmouth Friends recorded the arrival of Friends moving within their bounds. The certificates were issued only after inquiry to make sure that the subjects were not leaving behind unpaid debts and could be recommended as consistent members. Illustrative is a the process in the men's monthly meeting in First Month 1733, when John Lapham and family moved to Smithfield Monthly Meeting:

> *The friends that wer appointed to See into John Laphams*
> *Sircumstances relating to his removing to Smith*
> *field to live gives this meeting an account that*

---

21. Michael P. Graves, "Ministry and Preaching," in *Oxford Handbook of Quaker Studies,* ed. by Angell and Dandelion, 277-83; *Souvenir,* 21; William C. Braithwaite, *The Second Period of Quakerism* (London: Macmillan, 1921), 542-44. For Nicholas Davis, see *A Collection of Memorials Concerning Divers Deceased Ministers and Others of the People Called Quakers, in Pennsylvania, New-Jersey, and Parts Adjacent, from Nearly the First Settlement Thereof to the Year 1787. With Some of the Last Expressions and Exhortations of Many of Them* (Philadelphia: Joseph Crukshank, 1787), 165-67. The men's minutes of 11th Mo. 17, 1736 refer to "the Elders of Rochester meeting."

22. For women Friends generally in this period, see Rebecca Larson, *Daughters of Light: Quaker Women Preaching and Prophesying in the Colonies and Abroad, 1700-1775* (New York: Knopf, 1999).

they find nothing but things are Clear and that he is
like to remove in good order. and this meeting
appoints yᵉ Same friends to draw up a few lines by
way of Certificate to yᵉ monthly meeting at Smithfield
of him and his wifes unity with friends here

Other monthly meetings carefully scrutinized certificates. Thus in Eighth Month 1769 the men recorded that Smithfield Monthly Meeting was dissatisfied with what it had received regarding Samuel Howland, Jr. They had "discover[ed] a Shortness in the Certificate Respecting the Settlement of his owtward Affares." It appears to have been the practice to read the certificates aloud in the monthly meeting. Thus the women's minutes for Sixth Month 20, 1757, show that "Patience Easty Certificate was read and friends had unity with it: also Sarah Cornwell Certificate was read and friends accepted it and She is taken under the Care of this meeting." The men's meeting issued certificates for men, the women's for women. Before 1740, removals from Dartmouth were mainly within Massachusetts and Rhode Island. After 1740, there was a steady increase in certificates directed to monthly meetings in New York: Oblong, Nine Partners, and Saratoga.[23]

References to the quarterly meeting appear regularly, as both men and women Friends appointed representatives to attend the sessions. One finds many minutes about epistles being prepared for the quarterly meeting. Their contents are never recorded, but it appears that they contained answers to the queries. These were questions which quarterly meetings, and ultimately the yearly meeting, used to assess the spiritual state of the yearly meeting. New England Yearly Meeting agreed on a set in 1700. Quaker historian Rufus M. Jones described their function as "calling for an examination of the life from at least a dozen moral and spiritual view-points." But Dartmouth Friends found the constant examination trying at times. At the monthly meeting of Fourth Month 2, 1785, men Friends united with a proposal from women Friends asking: "whether the answering the Queries once a year only, would not be more useful, or at least, that some of the Principal ones only be answer'd at Each Quarter."[24]

Although London Yearly Meeting did not exercise formal authority over other yearly meetings, Dartmouth Friends were aware of it and noted its epistles and advices. The first reference, in the men's minutes of Fifth Month 21, 1718, is illustrative. Friends had read "some minits of ye yearly meeting at London 1717 concerning tomb stones distinguishing apparel for the dead and bowing and Cryings which minits are ordered

---

23. Friday, "Quaker Origins of New Bedford," 233-34.
24. Jones, *Quakers in the American Colonies*, 145-46.

to be read on a first day meeting for worship." And they occasionally called for its aid. In Third Month 1717 they asked a Friend traveling to England to inform Friends there about a law for the maintenance of ministers that Dartmouth Friends found threatening, apparently in the hope that they would lobby for its repeal. Likewise Dartmouth Friends noted and read epistles from other yearly meetings, almost always New York and Philadelphia. When women Friends opened their own monthly meeting minute book, they copied into it lengthy epistles and statements from George Fox and English and Irish Friends.[25]

One of the ways that Dartmouth Friends maintained ties with the larger Quaker world was through the regular visits of ministers from other monthly and yearly meetings, in some cases even from England. Rufus Jones describes the impact that they had: "They believed, and their listeners believed, that they were 'divinely sent messengers.' They came into the homes of the native Friends and supplied them with the facts, the news, the personal drama, of the wider Society of which they formed a fragment. By word of mouth those of all sections heard of the progress of events, the issues before the Society, the spread of 'Truth' as they called it, and they learned to know, in their isolated spot, the main problems of the whole movement, which they this in some measure shared." The names of some of the most prominent Quaker ministers of the eighteenth century appear as attending a session of Dartmouth Monthly Meeting: John Churchman, John Griffith, Rachel Wilson, Susanna Lightfoot, Warner Mifflin, David Sands, and William Hunt. And these are only those present for a monthly meeting. Many others were among Dartmouth Friends at other times. Dartmouth Friends aided these visitors, as when in Eighth Month 1762 they ordered the meeting treasurer "to pay Jonathan Hussey thirty Shillings for Shoeing a traveling Friends Horse."[26]

The number of visits from traveling ministers, and the sheer volume of the monthly meeting's minutes, increased substantially after 1750. This reflects another current in the larger Quaker world, what historians of Quakerism have labeled the "Reformation" of the eighteenth century. Beginning in the 1730s, influential Friends, first in Philadelphia Yearly Meeting, then in London Yearly Meeting, and then in other yearly meetings, became concerned by what they perceived as declining spiritual life, growing worldliness, and lax enforcement of the Discipline. And in the 1770s, we find Dartmouth Friends showing their commitment to this vision of reformation,

---

25. See, generally, Frederick B. Tolles, *Quakers and the Atlantic Culture* (New York: Macmillan, 1960). For the influence of London Yearly Meeting, see Elizabeth Cazden, "'Within the Bounds of Their Circumstances,'" 44-64.

26. Jones, *Quakers in the American Colonies*, 139-40. See also Larson, *Daughters of Light*, 172-231. For an example of a prominent minister visiting Dartmouth not mentioned in the minutes, see *The Works of John Woolman. In Two Parts* (London: James Phillips, 1775), 127.

particularly rigorous enforcement of the Discipline. They acknowledged their "Coolness and want of true Zeal for the cause of Truth" and their "indifferency." They renewed efforts "for the revival of our antient Discipline" through "Stirring up the Careless Lukewarm Indolent members to Love and good works." Between 1760 and 1779 the number of disownments doubled.[27]

Dartmouth Friends were aware of Friends elsewhere and their needs and tried to offer aid. In 1705 they contributed to the construction of a meetinghouse in Salem, and in 1707, 1709, and 1760 toward one in Boston. In 1744 they paid 26 pounds toward building meetinghouses in Taunton and Westerly, and between 1758 and 1760 gave over 200 pounds for building the new Friends meetinghouse in Providence. The minutes of Ninth Month 1724 show that Friends contributed 20 pounds to aid "John Handson a friend Living at Dover to the eastward of Boston who has of Late had his Wife and Seaveral Children Carried away by the Indians, and also his bedding and other Cloathing."[28]

CONTOURS OF QUAKER LIFE

BY THE END OF THE SEVENTEENTH CENTURY, as Dartmouth Friends were holding their first monthly meetings for business, Quakerism was changing. It was entering into a period, which would last for over a century, of what historians have labeled quietism. The evangelistic zeal of the first generation was fading. Increasingly Friends focused instead on internal discipline and purity, both as individuals and as a corporate body. Converts were still made, but, for the most part, Friends depended on retaining the children of members to keep up their numbers.[29]

Friends had relatively few officials. Both the men's and women's meetings had clerks, whose duty was to preside at meetings for business. Friends did not vote. It was the role of the clerk, after a full discussion of the matter before the meeting, to discern what the sense of the meeting was. This was not necessarily the view of the majority. Instead, it reflected what the clerk perceived as the will of God on a particular matter. One finds an occasional reference to majority rule. At the men's monthly meeting held Twelfth Month 1730/1731, a committee appointed to arbitrate a difference between two Friends reported that it could not agree. The monthly meeting decided "that the Majority of sd Comtee. Shall determine the matter." The minutes

27. Dartmouth Monthly Meeting Men's Minutes, 4th Mo. 1, 1775, 9th Mo. 18, 1780; Dartmouth Monthly Meeting Women's Minutes, 11th Mo. 16, 1778; Friday, "Quaker Origins of New Bedford," 130. For this subject generally, see Jack D. Marietta, *The Reformation of American Quakerism, 1748-1783* (Philadelphia: University of Pennsylvania Press, 1984).

28. Lowry, *Quakers and Their Meeting House at Apponegansett*, unpaginated.

29. Robynne Rogers Healey, "Quietist Quakerism, 1692-c.1805," in *Oxford Handbook*, ed. by Angell and Dandelion, 47-62.

do not record discussions or debates, only conclusions. But occasionally they convey some sense of the emotional tone of a meeting, as on Eleventh Month 18, 1754, when the clerk recorded that there was "Considerable of agitation." While anyone was welcome to attend meetings for worship, meetings for business were supposed to be "select," closed to non-members as well as Friends no longer in good standing. Thus on Third Month 17, 1730, when Nathan Soule, who had refused to abide by the decision of an arbitration committee appeared, it was the judgment of Friends that he "ought not to sit in monthly meetings as a member thereof until he hath made acknowledgement to friends Sattisfaction." Before 1785, the men's meeting had but four clerks: John Tucker from 1699 to 1751, Isaac Smith 1751-1762, Job Russell 1762-1774, and William Anthony Jr. 1774-1785. The first clerk of the women's monthly meeting mentioned in the records is Hepzibah Hussey in 1770.[30]

The Dartmouth minutes are records of the monthly meeting business meetings, but they do give us hints of what took place in the Sunday (or in Quaker parlance First Day) and midweek meetings for worship, usually when Friends perceived that something was amiss. In Twelfth Month 1705 two Friends were appointed to speak with Hannah Jenny about offering vocal prayers that were "out of the unity of the meeting," meaning that Friends found them improper or disturbing. Similarly, when in 12th Month 1742 Friends judged that Abigail Kirby "appear[ed] in publick Testimony Contrary to the advice of the monthly meeting" John Howland and Adam Mott were appointed "to Labour with her to persuade her to be silent." Five years later when Peace Wood attended meeting and "uttered things which . . . we can no ways Joyn with," a committee of seven Friends was appointed to talk with her. Their efforts were unsuccessful, since in 6th Month 1749 the men's monthly meeting recorded that while there had "been much Labour and pains bestowed upon Peace Wood to bring her to a Sence of her outgoings but all Seems to work no effect on her," it disowned her. In 1757 Peace apologized, however, and was restored to membership. Sometimes Friends were troubled as much by the manner of presentation as by the substance. In 4th Month 1766, the monthly meeting took up the case of Stephen Wilcox, who had "Appeared in this Meeting in a very Passionate Manner, Casting heavy Reflections on us, Saying that he believed we Should have fewer Testimones [*sic*] Amongst us, And that it was Pitty we Shou[l]d have any Except it be Some to Reprimand us for our Wickedness, and Stamping on the floor in a passionate manner and Grief and Sorrow of the Sincere in heart." We also find confirmation of Dartmouth's observance of the Quaker custom of standing when someone felt moved to offer prayer. To remain seated was considered an insult to the person who had offered the prayer. So when

---

30. *Souvenir,* 17; Pink Dandelion, *An Introduction to Quakerism* (Cambridge: Cambridge University Press, 2007), 217-19.

Hannah Gifford and Elizabeth Gifford refused to rise when Ann Gifford prayed in 1772, women Friends sent committees to labor with them. We find but one reference to sleeping in meeting, in the men's minutes in Second Month 1784, which implies that either Dartmouth Friends heeded frequent exhortations to avoid drowsiness, or it did not trouble them.[31]

The Dartmouth minutes do give a sense of the doctrinal and theological vision of Friends. Central is the idea of "that of God in every one," the Inward Light. Thus when they disowned Ebenezer Allen in Sixth Month 1706, they concluded that his misconduct stemmed from "for want of keeping In true Subjection to that princeple he made profesion of: towith the Sp[i]rit of truth In his own heart w^hich Sperit will lead all them that are obediant to it out of Everey thing that is Contrary to the nature of it and Inconsistant with it." Similarly, when they proceeded against John Howland in Twelfth Month 1712, they explained his "vain conversation" as the fruit of his "not herkning to friends nor to The teachings of ye Grace of God which would teach him and all me[n] to Live soberly in this present world." In Ninth Month 1773, judging Abner Russell the father of a "Bastard Child," they concluded that he was "not giving heed to the grace of God in his own heart, a Measure whereof is given to Every man to profit withal." In Second Month 1775, when women Friends were considering Content Tucker for membership, they did so after finding "a Good principle in her." Yet occasionally a Calvinist tone creeps into the minutes. Striking is the disownment of Holder Slocum for gaming, horse racing, and not attending meetings in Second Month 1768. Although repudiating him, they hoped that he would repent, but only "if it be Consistant with Divine pleasure."

Satan was real to Dartmouth Friends. When William Soule was "So much overcome With Strong drink So that he hath abused and beat his wif Seaverall times . . . and threatned her with hard Speeches to that degree that it is thought it not Safe for her to live with him," Friends disowned him in Sixth Month 1732. They recorded that he had "given Way to the temptation of the Wicked one." When Benjmain Davol was disowned for premarital sex in Third Month 1765, he was judged as having "Given way to the Insinuations of the Evil one." Peace Shearman explained her having a child too soon after marriage in 9th Month 1769 "by Giving way to the Tem[p]tation of the Adversary."

Only once does a case of Dartmouth Friends confronting outright heresy appear in these records. On First Month 15, 1742, the men's monthly meeting appointed a committee to deal with William Ricketson, who "of Late Entertained Certain Eronious

---

31.Dartmouth Monthly Meeting Men's Minutes, 12th Mo. 18, 1705, 12th Mo. 20, 1742, 2nd Mo. 20, 1747, 6th Mo. 21, 1749, 9th Mo. 19, 1757, 4th Mo. 21, 1766; Dartmouth Monthly Meeting Women's Minutes, 8th Mo. 17, 19th Mo. 1772.

notions Contrary to our principles." Two months later, the monthly meeting concluded that further labor with Ricketson would be pointless and concluded to disown him. The actual statement of disownment on Fifth Month 19 detailed his heresy. He had "given Way to strange and wrong notions." The first was that "Adam was in a better State after he had transgressed against the Command of God than he was before he was in before," The second was that "from Adam to the Coming of Christ in the flesh the wickedest of Men brought as much honour to God as the Righteous." Although Ricketson was apparently argumentative in advocating his ideas, no reference appears in the minutes to any other Friend embracing them. In Fourth Month 1766, Daniel Tripp, whom Oblong Monthly Meeting in New York had disowned for marrying out of meeting, was apparently causing problems in Dartmouth. Oblong Friends reported that he had "Set up a Separate Meeting" there, but he apparently had no impact at Dartmouth.[32]

Quakers saw themselves as called by God out of "the world" to be a "peculiar people," manifesting by certain distinctive practices, their "walk" and "conversation," the highest forms of Christian conduct. The nature of Quaker membership was evolving in the first decades of Dartmouth Monthly Meeting's existence. Friends generally regarded the children of Friends as being members at birth, and by the 1740s this had been regularized as "birthright membership." Such Friends retained it for the rest of their lives unless they forfeited it through misconduct. Friends saw membership as involving reciprocal obligations. Members individually committed themselves to abide by the Discipline, the meeting to help them in this and other ways. Thus in Ninth Month 1709, the men's minutes show that it was the sense of the meeting that Robert Gifford being "a friends Child: is under the care and Custety of this meeting and ought to be visited as a friend." Birthright membership meant that in every generation young people reached adulthood with no desire to be Quakers, did things that were at odds with Quaker rules, and faced disciplinary proceedings.[33]

Throughout the eighteenth century, some inhabitants of Dartmouth were "convinced of Truth," and requested to be received into membership. This began with a committee interviewing them to gauge their sincerity and understanding of Quaker beliefs. If the report was favorable, then the meeting almost always accepted the committee's recommendation. Typical is the language found in the women's minutes for Eleventh Month 19, 1781: "The Friends that hath had the matter under their care concerning the Sencerity of Patience Austins request, Inform they have had Several

---

32. William Ricketson's views echo those of the Ranters of the 1640s and 1650s. See A. L. Morton, *The World of the Ranters: Religious Radicalism in the English Revolution* (London: Lawrence & Wishart, 1970), 76-79.

33. Braithwaite, *Second Period of Quakerism*, 459.

Sollid opportunities with her and She appears Sinceare therein, and they think well of her being received,~ This meeting accepts of Said report and do Receive her into membership and under the care of this meeting."[34]

One frustrating characteristic of Friends in this period was their indifference to statistics. While keeping voluminous records, they showed no interest in counting just how many members they had. One estimate gives Dartmouth Monthly Meeting about 1,250 members in 1777. A visiting Friend in 1758 estimated 800 people at a meeting he had attended. Another visitor in 1766 thought 2,000 attended a meeting at Apponegansett when he preached. Nor can we easily estimate the numbers affiliated with given particular preparative meetings. Rochester town records show 37 Quaker households there in the 1730s.[35]

A significant proportion of the minutes of both the men's and women's meetings concern marriages, both those "in meeting" and out, the latter a violation of the rules. The minute books give a good sense of the process of marriage under the care of the meeting. When two Friends wished to marry, they appeared before both the men's and women's monthly meetings and declared their intention to wed. A committee, usually of two, was appointed separately by the two meetings to ascertain the "clearness" of the man and woman. This was not a form of premarital counseling. The committee made no judgments about compatibility. Instead, they made sure that both parties were free of engagements or commitments to others, and presumably were sensitive to hints about a need for haste in marrying because a baby was on the way. For younger Friends, the consent of parents and guardians was also required—the age at which this was dispensed with is unclear. But if Friends thought a parental objection unreasonable, they ignored it. Thus when in 1730 Eliashib Smith and Audrey Gifford wished to marry and her father Christopher Gifford objected, Dartmouth Friends asked the quarterly meeting for guidance. When it responded that "his reason against their proceeding in marriage is of no weight or vallue," the couple was allowed to proceed. If the investigation revealed no impediments, then the couple appeared before the men's and women's monthly meetings, reaffirmed their intention to marry, and were given permission to do so. This was usually referred to as "passing meeting." The marriage would usually take place at the conclusion of a regular midweek meeting for worship. A certificate would have been prepared in advance and those present invited to sign as witnesses. The certificate in its entirety would also be copied into the monthly meeting record of marriages.[36]

34. For people who attended worship regularly but never became members, see Friday, "Quaker Origins of New Bedford," 186-87.

35. Hagglund, "Disowned without Just Cause." 287-88; *Souvenir*, 15.

36. For the Gifford case, see Dartmouth Monthly Meeting Men's Minutes, 8th Mo. 2, 1730. The most

Most monthly meeting business involved dealing with members who had violated Quaker rules. These regulations were embodied in what Friends called "The Discipline." New England Friends had first codified their version in 1708, although they made occasional additions to it, such as forbidding gravestones in 1712 and the wearing of periwigs in 1722. Generally, its provisions followed the lead of Friends in London, although there were exceptions. Monthly meetings had their own manuscript copies. Men Friends paid eighteen pounds and ten shillings to have their copy transcribed in Fifth Month 1763. A year later, in Tenth Month 1764, appointing a "Standing Committee," the men noted that they acted "pursuant to the late Book of Discipline in page 138." In 1766, when Coaxet Monthly Meeting was set off from Dartmouth, Dartmouth Friends agreed to bear the cost of making a copy for them. Thriftily, when changes were made, the whole book was not recopied. In Seventh Month 1772, when the monthly meeting "Received a Transcript of Several matters Concluded on as Rules of our Society at our Last yearly meeting," it appointed two Friends "to Place the Above Said rules under Proper heads in our Book of Discipline." New England Yearly Meeting was the first to put its Discipline into print, in 1785.[37]

At the front line of enforcing the Discipline were the meeting officers variously referred to in the minutes as "visitors," "inspectors," and finally "overseers." It appears that the original expectation was that these Friends would be proactive. At the monthly meeting held Third Month 22, 1704, six men were "chosen to Inspect into the lives and Conversations of friends for the half year insuing." That meant visiting families individually. Friends usually accepted such oversight. The visitors reported in Eighth Month 1708 "in their accounts of their visits to this meeting: that they find friends Caind [kind] and do take their: labour of love In visiting them Caindly [kindly]." Three years later, in Seventh Month 1711, the visitors reported to the women's monthly meeting they "for ye most part were Kindly Excepted; & where any thing was amiss & spoken to there seems to be a Spirit of Condecention ~ Signifying yt they would

---

detailed treatment of the process of Quaker marriages in this period is J. William Frost, *The Quaker Family in Colonial America: A Portrait of the Society of Friends* (New York: St. Martin's, 1973), 150-86. See also Mary E. Austin, "Courtship and Marriage of Ye Old Time Quakers," *Old Dartmouth Historical Sketches*, 34 (1912); and Barry Levy, *Quakers and the American Family: British Settlement in the Delaware Valley* (New York: Oxford University Press, 1988). Dartmouth historians note that after 1700 marriages in the Friends meetings were also entered in the town records, even though Friends denied civil government any authority over marriage.

37. Worrall, *Quakers in the Colonial Northeast*, 77-78; *The Book of Discipline, Agreed on by the Yearly-Meeting of Friends for New-England: Containing Extracts of Minutes, Conclusions and Advices of That Meeting, and of the Yearly-Meetings of London, Pennsylvania and New-Jersey and New-York: Alphabetically Arranged* (Providence: John Carter, 1785). For the Discipline in this period, see Andrew Fincham, "Friendly Advice: The Making and Shaping of Quaker Discipline," in *Quakerism in the Atlantic World*, ed. Healey, 65-88. The Dartmouth records include a copy of "Christian and Brotherly Advices Given forth from Time to Time by the Yearly Meeting for London." See https://dartmouthhas.org/uploads/1/0/0/2/100287044/book_of_disipline_1_p_1-125_signed.pdf

indeavour it should be soe no more." But it was sometimes thankless work. In the women's monthly meeting First Month 17, 1729, the visitors reported: "their visits in a general way were kindly accepted but in Some families so but were Rather reflected upon." In Second Month 1768, the men's minutes show: "This Meeting hath Made Trial for a Choice of Visitors, and finding the work of Great Importance, but no friend finding the weight of that Service laid on them at present," it could make no appointment. Eventually Friends were found for the work, but they faced criticism. In First Month 1773, two of them complained that David Smith had called them "fals men." Only in Third Month 1785 did the monthly meeting offer overseers a job description:

> As the service of the Overseers is not
> pointed out to them, in any manner particular
> in the Minute of their appointment, the follow-
> ing is concluded to be a necessary addition for
> that purpose, viz, They are desired to meet to-
> gether frequently by themselves, in as retired a man-
> ner as may be, and endeavour to center down to their
> own Gifts and Measures in order to get under a due
> Sense of the Weight of the Work assigned them; and
> under this Engagement of mind to keep up a careful
> Watch and Inspection over themselves and the several
> Members of this Meeting to see that the Cause
> and Testimony of Truth be kept up and maintain-
> ed and where any shall appear faulty or defective
> or walk disorderly, tenderly to treat and Labour with
> them, in order to discover to them the Evil of their
> ways; but if such cannot be reclaimed and
> they appear manifestly Guilty of the Matter in
> charge, that then Information in Writing be
> brought to the Meeting of the State of the
> Fact and Circumstances attending it and they
> are particularly desired to watch and guard
> against, and discourage, that backbiting,
> slandering spirit so prevalent among us, ma-
> king report to this Meeting of the progress
> of their Service from Time to Time.

When the overseers learned of a transgression of the Discipline, they made some sort of investigation that normally involved visiting the offender. Doubtless cases where suspicions proved unfounded never made it into any record. And at times, overseers tried to prevent transgressions, as when they heard that a member was contemplating marrying out of meeting. But if an accusation or rumor proved to have some basis, then the overseers reported it to the preparative meeting. It, in turn, weighed the case, and if it concluded that the complaint was justified, reported it to the monthly meeting. The monthly meeting then appointed a committee of at least two Friends, sometimes more, to "labor" with the offender and bring him or her to see the fault and make an acknowledgement of wrongdoing to the meeting for it. Both the men's and women's minutes contain numerous examples. The offender was expected to appear in person and read the document. And acceptance was not automatic. Thus when Mary Wing submitted a paper in Sixth Month 1753, the monthly meeting judged it not "ful enough." She tried again in the next month, but the monthly meeting still chose to "Suspend the matter till we have Some further Proof of her Sincerity." When the monthly meeting accepted an acknowledgement, the process was not complete until it had been read again at the close of a meeting for worship.

If the labors of the committee were unsuccessful and the offender proved obdurate, then the monthly meeting would proceed to disownment. A formal statement would be drawn up, laying out the offense and the attempts of Friends to bring about repentance, culminating with the declaration that the offender was no longer a member of "our Society." Illustrative is the disownment of Stephen Wilcox in 1770:

> *Whereas Stephen Wilcox of Dartmouth in the County of Bristol*
> *in the Province of the Massachusetts Bay in New England, Having*
> *been Educated under the Care of friends, and has long made*
> *Profession with us, and in times past bore a Publick Testimony*
> *which was Acceptable Among us, Yet Nevertheless with Sorrow we*
> *find that thro' the Prevailence of the Adversary, and disregarding*
> *the divine Principal of Life in his own heart, he has So deviated*
> *from the way of Truth, and the Profession he has made as to*
> *fall into Several Reproachful Evils & disorders, particularly*
> *in that he being Intrusted by a Friend of Falmouth to Carry Some*
> *money to William Smith and Converted the Same to his own use*
> *whereby he betrayed his Trust, and very Much deceived the S,ᵈ*
> *friend, for the want of which money the Said Wᵐ Smith hath*
> *Exhibited his Complaint to this meeting, and likewise the*
> *Said Stephen is found in the Neglect of that Indispensable duty*
> *of attending Religious Meetings of Divine Worship and discipline*
> *And friends having in Great love & tenderness toward him Re-*
> *-peatedly Visited him & Labour'd with him in order to discover to*
> *him the Evil of his ways, and Reclaim him from his outgoings*
> *But our Labour of Love not obtaining the desired Effect to*
> *the Satisfaction of this Meeting, Therefore for the Clearing of [Truth erased]*

the precious Truth and friends from the Reproach of Such Evils and
defective Members this Meeting is Concerned to Give this forth as
a Testimony Against him, and do hereby Publickly disown the
Said Stephen Wilcox from being a member of our Society, and
from under the Care of this meeting, Sincerely desiring (if
it be Consistant with Divine pleasure) that he may yet Return
from the Evil of his ways, and by an unfeigned Repentance
and Reformation, be Restored to the way of Truth & Salvation.
Given forth by our Monthly Meeting of friends held in Dartm.ᵒ
the 19ᵗʰ of the 3,ᵈ month 1770,
And Signed in & by order of Said Meeting by Job Russell Clerk

Several features of this statement are noteworthy. First, Stephen's misconduct is explained as the result of allowing "the Adversary" to prevail, instead of heeding "the divine Principal of Life in his own heart." Second, the specific offenses are named. Third, the public is assured that Friends have made efforts to make Stephen see the error of his ways. Finally, it is made clear that Stephen is not being cast out just because he is a sinner, but rather that it is done to uphold the reputation of Friends, "for the Clearing of the precious Truth and friends from the Reproach of such Evils and defective Members." Disownments could be appealed to the quarterly and yearly meeting, but appeals were rare, and reversals even rarer.

Some of the offenses that brought disownment would have brought sanctions in other religious bodies. Thus in Twelfth Month 1774, women Friends proceeded against Elizabeth Tucker for the "Reproachful Evil of taking Spirituous Liquor to excess." In Third Month 1766, the overseers complained that Benjamin and Francis Allen "hath Allowed of fiddling and dancing in their Houses." A decade later, in Second Month 1776, Benjamin Shearman was proceeded against for going to "a place of frallicking." Friends likewise testified against those who engaged in horse racing, fighting, theft, slander and defamation, "vile speech," and any form of dishonesty. Friends showed little tolerance for premarital sex. They kept track of the time between marriage and the birth of the first child and proceeded when it was clear that conception was prior to marriage. And they likewise disowned women who bore bastard children and men who were proved to be the fathers of them.

More Friends, however, lost their membership because they offended against distinctive Quaker rules and practices. By far the most common reason for disownment by Dartmouth Friends was marriage without the consent of the meeting, or "marriage out of unity." This might be to a non-Quaker or to another Friend in a non-Quaker ceremony, usually by a justice of the peace. It was equally an offense for parents to consent to such marriages, or for any Friend to attend the ceremony. We get a glimpse into how Friends tried to convince doubters of the rightness of Quaker positions in the report of Friends appointed to labor with Jabez Barker, Jr., who in 1771 allowed the double wedding of his daughters to take place in his house. They had "a Long Conferrance with him on that subject. Endeavouring (according to our Abilities) to Convince him of his Error therein we likewise Shew^d [showed] him a Coppy of part of a minute made in our yearly meeting in the year 1708. Which we think is very Clear against Such Conduct as his, yet he would by no means Condemn the Same, nor yet own that he had broaken any order of Friends, but used many Words tending to Justifie himself therein."[38]

The other Quaker "peculiarity" that preoccupied Friends was their "testimony against all wars and fighting." Pacifism had not been a firm doctrine for the first generation of Friends. But by the early eighteenth century, it was the rule that Friends could not bear arms, even in self-defense, or provide material support for soldiers and armies. Some cases were clear. Friends could not train with the militia, or stand guard, or do anything that involved submitting themselves to military discipline. Likewise they could not voluntarily supply goods for military use. Conscientious Friends submitted to fines or even went to jail rather than violate this testimony of Friends. Such cases were more common in wartime, but militia musters were also held in peacetime, and Friends found themselves fined or imprisoned then as well. Nicholas Lapham's account of his experiences during Queen Anne's war, recorded in the men's minutes of Ninth Month 19, 1711, is unusually vivid:

> I being Empressed [Impressed] this Last Summor 1711 in an
> expeditian to go to Canada to war wch I refused
> for Concience sake for I beleive y^t I ought not
> To take up ye Carnal sword against any ~~peo~~ Nation
> or people & some time after I was had to James
> Sissons before Colenal [Colonel] Church & there was
> an Order writ & read to mee wherein I was
> Commanded to go to Rocksbury [Roxbury] & Commit my selfe
> to Colenall [Colonel] William Dudley wch I Could not find
> freedom To do neighther: & after that I was
> Warned go to the Castle Island Lying near
> To Boston to take up armes wch I refused also
> and one [on?] ye 16th Day of ye 6th Month Leightenant [Lieutenant]
> John Akin came to my house wth severall with
> him ~~&~~ for aid & S^d akin Took Mee by force
> & Dragged mee out of my House & then

38. Marietta, *Reformation*, 66-67; Dartmouth Monthly Meeting Men's Minutes, 12th Mo. 25, 1771.

Commanded his aid [aide] to assist him wch they Did &
Took mee and set mee on Horce Back [horseback] & held
Mee on & Carried mee to Timothy Maxfields
& then committed mee to the Custidy of John
Briggs Insign [Ensign] who carried mee ye next Day
To Bridg[e]water & ye next Day to the Castle wch was
the Last Day of ye week being near night I was had
Before ye Captain of ye Castle & he asked mee
Whither I would take up armes I told him
That I should not take up ye Carnal weapon
John Commanded the officer to take Care of mee
til Second Day and then I was brought before
ye Captain of ye Castle again the 2^d Day morning & he
asked Me whither I would work there I told him
no for wch I was put into a Close place Called y^e
Hole or Dungeon & there to be kept without
Victuals or Drink but was Let out again the same
Day near sun set & there was still kept at ye Castle
& often urged to work but could not although told
that If I would work y^t [that] I Should be released in a little
time but If not I might be put aboard some man
of war but I Could not med[d]le ᵼ & at ye end of 4
Weeks & 2 dayes I was released & brought of [off?] & set
at Liberty without paying or giving any Money.

But not all Friends were equally committed. In wartime especially, there were always some who chose to bear arms or pay war taxes.[39]

By the early eighteenth century, Friends increasingly distinguished themselves by their commitment to "plainness." Just what it meant to be a "plain Friend" is incapable of precise definition, but Friends were agreed that it meant avoiding "worldly," fashionable dress, and using the "plain language" of thee and thy to single persons. So in First Month 1721 men Friends took up the case of Benjamin Soule "who is gone from the order of friends into the fassion of ye world in his apparel." Twelve years later, in Tenth Month 1733, they testified against Henry Tucker who had "let him selfe into a Liberty that is not agreeable to our Holy Profession in wearing divers sorts of Perriwigs and his hat set up on three sides like the vain Custom of ye World and also Speaking of words not agreeable to our profession." In Third Month 1756, Christopher

---

39. Peter Brock, *The Quaker Peace Testimony 1660 to 1914* (York, Eng.: Sessions, 1990), 24-61; Meredith Baldwin Weddle, *Walking in the Way of Peace: Quaker Pacifism in the Seventeenth Century* (New York: Oxford University Press, 2001), 132-33, and passim.

Gifford Jr. was refused permission to lay his marriage intentions before the meeting because of "his wearing fashionabl Cloaths." Women Friends were likewise sensitive to these transgressions, although the nature of them is frustratingly vague. Typical is the notation in the women's minutes for Eighth Month 21, 1780, that Mary Smith was "dressing and fashioning herself out of Plainess that our principles leads to."[40]

A source of periodic difficulty for Friends was their refusal to take oaths or swear in court. Friends justified this stance by citing the injunction of Christ as found in Matthew 5:34. Their position was that Christians should speak the truth at all times, under all circumstances, and oaths implied that people spoke truth only when sworn. In Third Month 1702, Dartmouth Friends noted that the provincial oath requirement prevented Friends from serving on juries as well as in other official roles. Parliament in 1696 had allowed Friends to offer affirmations instead of oaths, but this act did not apply to the colonies. Only in 1744 did Massachusetts, after petitions from Dartmouth Friends, follow suit. Even then it did not apply to provincial offices, effectively disqualifying Friends from holding them, or in criminal cases.[41]

The theme besides enforcing the rules that emerges from the minutes is that of community. Friends submitted themselves to live by a Discipline that other Friends would enforce because they believed that it was for their spiritual good. And in turn Friends aided each other when necessary. At the monthly meeting of Seventh Month 1706, the meeting agreed to a "contribuation" to Isaac Vinson of Rochester, whose house had burned. The monthly meeting had overseers of the poor who were charged with reporting regularly.[42] Friends did not allow poor and aged members to become public charges; meetings were responsible for them. Thus in Twelfth Month 1747, the men's meeting noted that Anne Shaw, an aged Friend, was "not capable of helping her selfe as need Requires" and had asked the meeting's aid. It appointed three Friends "to take some account of what she has to help her selfe withal and to see that she has a suitable place to Resid at and to have the oversight of all things necessary." Sometimes the meeting intervened to defend the disadvantaged. In Second Month 1712, two Friends were appointed to "take care" that the widow Sarah Allen's son did not sell property on which she was dependent "with out good provision for her lively hood." Dartmouth Friends were Yankees, however, and were like their non-Quaker neighbors in occasionally disputing who was responsible for poor Friends. Thus in

---

40. See J. William Frost, "From Plainness to Simplicity: Changing Quaker Ideals for Material Culture," in *Quaker Aesthetics: Reflections on a Quaker Ethic in American Design and Consumption*, ed. by Emma Jones Lapsansky and Anne A. Verplanck (Philadelphia: University of Pennsylvania Press, 2003), 16-40.

41. Worrall, *Quakers in the Colonial Northeast*, 104-05; Braithwaite, *Second Period*, 183-84.

42. Dartmouth Monthly Meeting Men's Minutes, 10th Mo. 2, 1761. For the larger context, see Ruth Wallis Herndon, *Unwelcome Americans: Living on the Margins in Early New England* (Philadelphia: University of Pennsylvania Press, 2001).

Third Month 1769 a report was made of an ongoing dispute with Sandwich Monthly Meeting whether it or Dartmouth should care for a poor Friend named Rachel Soule.

Friends gave attention to the young. From time to time the monthly meeting referred to schools, as in Eighth Month 1723 when two Friends were appointed to "look for a friend School master that is capable to read write and cypher." Half a century later, this was still a concern, when men Friends on Ninth Month 20, 1779, following an admonition from the quarterly meeting, appointed a committee "on the weighty Subject of Erecting Schools for the better Education of our youths." From time to time the minutes mention "Youth's Meeting." But one wonders if these occasions were devoted largely to warning young people against temptations and diversions. The men's minutes, for example, show that in Eighth Month 1711 three Friends were appointed "to Draw up a Testimony against friends Children going together and wres[t]ling on first Dayes." A year later, in Tenth Month 1712, the visitors reported mournfully that they had "visited some famelyes of friends and they find things out of Ordor amongst some of friends children and of Some of them they have hope but of other Some they have but lettel or no hope."[43]

Friends did not always live in harmony. Doubtless most personal disputes were resolved informally, but occasionally the meeting's intervention was requested. The Discipline was clear—when Friends could not resolve differences themselves, they were obligated to ask the meeting to arbitrate rather than resorting to the courts. Often the sources of difficulty are left vague in the minutes. The men's minutes of Third Month 1704 are a good example: "Jonathan Devel William Soul John Lapham Jnr William wood and Judah Smith and Robert Gifford are chosen to hear and determin the deference [between] nathaneel howland and John Peckham and Jacob Mott Increase allin and Stephen Willcock are chosen to hear and determin the deferance between Eliezar Smith and Nathaneel howland." To refuse to abide by the findings of an arbitration was a disownable offense, as this case from Third Month 1771 shows:

> *The Greatest part of the Committee Appointed to Inquire into the*
> *Complaint of Benjᵃ, Thoˢ and Peleg Shearman Against Humphry*
> *Smith report as followeth, which is accepted*
> *According to appointment of the Monthly Meeting we had*
> *Humphry Smith & the Shearmans together to Inspect into the Controversy*
> *Subsisting between them, and have to Inform, that firstly Sᵈ Smith*
> *Queried if Gospel order had been kept to, and by Inquiring we found that*
> *before they Entered their Complaint to the meeting one of the overseers*

---

43. For the "Youth's Meeting," see the men's minutes for 4ᵗʰ Mo. 21, 1708 and 6ᵗʰ Mo. 17, 1776 and the women's minutes for 1ˢᵗ Mo. 17, 1718. For Quakers and education, see Jones, *Quakers in the American Colonies*, 166-67.

taking a friend with him went to S^d Smith with Thos Shearman on the
affair, which appear'd to us according to Good order, then S^d Smith
Demanded a Coppy of the Complaint which after Consideration we
Thought best for him not to have without he would promise to make
no use thereof in the Law, which promise he Refused, Then we offer'd that
a friend Should wait with him as long as he thought Proper to peruse
and Consider the Complaint, and he might Call in friends to advise with
but not Suffer any Coppy to be taken, and then Give us an Answer
which offer S^d Smith Refused Complying with- Then we refer'd S^d
Smith to Give us Some reasons . . . why he Refused to Leave the
the affair to men, by he declined giving us any, for we found the Shear-
-mans would Leave it to men by them Equally Chosen or the Meeting might
Choose them and they would be bound to abide Judgment, and the Shearmans
Say there is a Number of Judicious Neighbours are Ready to Say that Smiths
Evidence in Court Contradicts the Known matters of fact but yet they
offer'd to Settle the whole affare by friends as aforesaid, and we have
made Much Inquiry in Regard to its touching Titles of Land and find
that Said Smiths and Shearmans written Titles Jointly Concur and the dispute
is only in Settling the Line, and our Judgment is that where friends hold
Land under Vouchers not to Compel them to Leave to Arbitration, but
in this Controversy we find that the Shearmans are willing that a num-
-ber of Surveyors Should take Said Smiths Deed and by the Return
therein, Run the Line as they shall think Just & Right, and they will
be bound to abide by the Same, which Appears to us that the Shearmans
Contend, for no Land that S^d Smith holds under a Voucher, therefore our
Judgment is that Said Smith ought to Leave the Controversy to men
or Render Sufficient Reason why, which he declines — —

Occasionally disputes were more personal. The women's minutes of Fourth Month 1782 tell of some vague difficulty between Silvester Howland (a woman) and Sarah Howland. It was resolved with both promising not "in any wise to hurt each other Cherrecter." As a mark of their sincerity, they asked that "all Evidences, or other things committed to writeing respecting the above difficulty . . . be committed to the fire."

Quaker families were not free of problems, which these records occasionally reveal. Inheritance disputes took place. In Third Month 1732, the men's meeting rendered its judgment in a disagreement between "John Whitely and his wives Children." In Ninth Month 1759, meeting arbitrators were called on to "determine the Contraversy between William Sisson and his brother Jonathan." The arbitrators decided, after consulting the brothers' father's will, that William was to pay Jonathan one pound fourteen shillings two pence and one farthing annually toward the support of their sister Hannah. Marital problems, if they became public enough, became a matter for the meeting. In Fifth Month 1763, Friends disowned Abigail (Allen) Macumber. It was bad enough that she had "married in the common way of other people" rather than in meeting, but she now refused to live with her husband. At least one case of domestic violence involved a woman assaulting a man. Women Friends testified against Elisabeth Howland in Eighth Month 1777 on finding that she had "fallen into bodily Strife with her father-in-law Isaac Howland and abused him."

FRIENDS AND THE LARGER WORLD

THE PREVIOUS SECTION described how the Quaker refusal to bear arms or swear oaths brought difficulties with town, county, and provincial authorities from time to time. But this was not the only way that Friends refused to conform to the expectations of the larger society.

Dartmouth Friends lived with the reality that Congregationalism was the established church of Massachusetts. A 1692 statute, amended in 1693, required every town to have a "learned orthodox minister, or ministers." If a town refused to make such an appointment, a quarter sessions court could do so. And all residents of the town, dissenters included, were taxed for the support of these ministers.[44]

Dartmouth was a stronghold of Quakers and Baptists, and the town ignored the 1692 and 1693 laws. So in 1702 the General Court, noting that "in some few towns and districts within this province, divers of the inhabitants are Quakers, and other irreligious averse to the publick worship of God and to a learned and orthodox ministry," took another tack. The Court of General Sessions "was empowered to appoint freeholders to assess for the selectmen and require town constables to collect the tax." Four years later, the General Court gave itself the power to appoint orthodox ministers for the recalcitrant towns, and in 1708 sent Rev. Samuel Hunt to Dartmouth. His salary of 50 pounds was added to the provincial taxes due from the town.[45]

For Friends, refusal to pay "priest's wages" was a matter of conscience. Others in Dartmouth shared Quaker reservations. In 1703, Philip Cummings, a local constable, had been jailed because of his refusal to collect this particular tax; he died a prisoner. In 1708, two Friends, Thomas Taber Jr. and Deliverance Smith, who were both town selectmen and assessors, were sent to jail for refusing to assess the tax. An appeal to Governor Joseph Dudley and Friends in London, however, brought their

44. Worrall, *Quakers in the Colonial Northeast*, 112-13.

45. Ibid., 118-19; William G. McLoughlin, *New England Dissent 1630-1833: The Baptists and the Separation of Church and* State (2 vols., Cambridge: Harvard University Press, 1971), 166; Dartmouth Monthly Meeting Men's Minutes, 6th Mo. 16, 1708.

release by Dudley's order. There the matter rested until 1722, when the General Court added 100 pounds to Dartmouth's provincial assessment to pay the Rev. Mr. Hunt's salary. Dartmouth's selectmen, Philip Taber and John Akin (the former a Friend), refused to assess the tax. Instead, the town meeting voted to raise 700 pounds for the selectmen's legal expenses and to send an appeal to the king. It also named a Friend, Nathaniel Howland, as the town's minister, knowing that he would refuse a salary. In fact, Taber and Akin spent eighteen months in jail before the Crown overturned the law. In 1728 and 1732, Massachusetts relented to the extent of exempting Friends and Baptists from church rates.[46]

Other denominations occasionally appear in the Dartmouth records, usually in the context of their drawing Friends away. Friends did not consider the worship of other churches to be wrong in itself. But other churches had ministers who received at least minimal support for their preaching. To attend their services even casually was to compromise Friends' testimony in favor of a "free Gospel ministry." Friends did not recognize a right to resign one's membership. A desire to do so would have been treated as evidence of disunity, itself an offense. So it was that in Ninth Month 1761, men Friends noted with alarm: "We understand that Elihu Bowen that took a distaste Against Friends Principles and is Joined to the Baptists, or is about to Join with them." Paid ministry was not the only thing that Friends found unacceptable about other denominations. In Fourth 1776 the men's minutes show a report from the overseers that Peleg Gifford, Jr., "hath been to a Baptice meeting and undertook to Emitate them in Singing which we think very unbecoming to one of our profession." Apparently such behavior appeared more frequently during the American Revolution. In Seventh Month 1777 women Friends joined the men in appointing a committee "to treat and labour with those families that are inclining to freequant or attend Such meetings as are not in Unity with friends."

Native Americans continued to live in and around Dartmouth in the eighteenth century, and they appear occasionally in these records. In Eighth Month 1703, the men's meeting appointed two Friends to investigate Ebenezer Allen's treatment of an Indian called Jeremiah. Two months later they reported that Allen "did beat and abuse the Sd Indian as the report was." Friends "long laboured In Love and much tenderness to show him . . . his rashness and Eror" and Allen finally expressed contrition. In Sixth Month 1730 "one Thomas Cesar an Indian" submitted a written application

46. Worrall, *Quakers in the Colonial Northeast*, 119-23; William G. McLoughlin, "The Dartmouth Quakers' Struggle for Religious Liberty, 1692-1734," *Quaker History*, 78 (Spring 1989), 1-23; Lowry, *Quakers and Their Meeting House at Apponegansett*, unpaginated. McLoughlin is mistaken in making Taber a Baptist, as he regularly appears in the Dartmouth minutes. See McLoughlin, *New England Dissent*, I, 175, 181. For Philip Cummings, see https://dartmouth.theweektoday.com/article/new-video -tour-features-one-dartmouths-oldest-houses/32155

for membership. The next month two Friends appointed to make "Enquiry" into his "life and Conversation" reported that they had found "nothing but that it hath been Orderly" and he was received into membership. In Seventh Month 1733 the men recorded that it had paid ten pounds in doctor's bills for Thomas and had collected more to meet the needs of his family.

Africans also appear in the Dartmouth records. Like their neighbors, some Dartmouth Friends were enslavers until the time of the American Revolution. Some early Quakers expressed qualms about slavery. George Fox, visiting Barbados in 1672, where many Friends held slaves, urged Friends to treat them kindly. In 1688, Friends in Germantown, Pennsylvania, sent an antislavery statement to Philadelphia Yearly Meeting, and other Friends including Elihu Coleman, of neighboring Nantucket, attacked slavery as incompatible with Christianity. Before 1750, however, most Friends did not openly question enslavement, but instead embraced the concept of "Christian slavery"—that master and slave could live together in a mutually beneficial relationship, with masters treating their slaves kindly and fairly. Friends in Newport and Providence were actively involved in the slave trade.[47]

The first appearance of a slave in the Dartmouth records is horrifying, and Dartmouth Friends found it disturbing enough that they called a special monthly meeting to deal with it on Third Month 30, 1711. Abigail Allen, the wife of the Ebenezer who had abused the Indian Jeremiah, had consented to and encouraged "the Creuell and unmercyfull whipping or beating of her negro manservant he being striped naked and hanged up by the hands," the abuse almost certainly causing his death. Friends disowned her, pronouncing her actions "not only UnChrist[i]an but inheuman" and were "Consarned to tes[t]efy to the world that wee do ut[e]rly desowne all Such actions and all who are found In them and perticurly the person above named." Seven months later, she asked to be readmitted to membership, but Friends were unconvinced that she was sufficiently contrite. Not until 1714, when Abigail submitted a paper in which she confessed her "hardness of heart," did she regain membership.[48]

Whether the Allen case affected subsequent events is unclear, but in First Month 1716 "some friends" asked the men's meeting whether "it be agreeable to truth to purchase slaves and keep them term of Life." The meeting referred the question to the

---

47. For early Quaker views of slavery, see Thomas E. Drake, *Quakers and Slavery in America* (New Haven: Yale University Press, 1950), 1-47; and Brycchan Carey, *From Peace to Freedom: Quaker Rhetoric and the Birth of American Antislavery, 1657-1761* (ibid., 20212). For Friends and "Christian slavery," see Katharine Gerbner, *Christian Slavery: Conversion and Race in the Protestant Atlantic World* (Philadelphia: University of Pennsylvania Press, 2018), 49-73.

48. Dartmouth Monthly Meeting Men's Minutes, 3rd Mo, 30, 10th Mo. 17, 1711, 1st Mo. 15, 1714. For differing views of the impact of this case, see Donna McDaniel and Vanessa Julye, *Fit for Freedom, Not for Friendship: Quakers, African Americans, and the Myth of Racial Justice* (Philadelphia: Quaker Press, 2009), 13.

quarterly meeting. That autumn, in the monthly meeting of Tenth Month, after the "matter relating to purchasing slaves" was "agetated," "the most of ye meeting" concluded "that it would be most agreeable to our holy profession to forbear for time to come to be any wayes concerned in purchasing any slaves." Again the question went to the quarterly meeting, and thence to the yearly meeting. But the yearly meeting was not ready for radical action. It issued a mild statement urging Friends "to wait for the wisdom of God how to discharge themselves in that weighty affair," and advised them not to import more slaves, but did not forbid it. Thereafter the subject disappears from the Dartmouth records for forty-three years.[49]

Meanwhile, New England Yearly Meeting was slowly moving toward a stronger antislavery stance. In 1743 and 1744, it discussed slavery and warned Friends against buying imported slaves. By 1760, following the lead of London and Philadelphia yearly meetings, it warned against involvement in the slave trade. Ten years later, it made selling a slave an offense against the Discipline and appointed a committee to encourage members to liberate their slaves. Three years later, the yearly meeting took the final step of ordering members to liberate those they were enslaving, except those who could not otherwise care for themselves.[50]

Dartmouth Friends followed yearly meeting policy. In 1760, they investigated reports Jedidiah Wood had had sold two Indian children to Nova Scotia. Four years later, they confronted Isaac Howland Jr. not only about marrying out of unity but his "Practice of the Slave Trade," disowning him when he refused to make a satisfactory acknowledgement. Early in 1772, the monthly meeting appointed a committee "to visit those that Posess Slaves." In Seventh Month, they reported despite their earnest efforts, six Friends were still enslavers. Three agreed to emancipate those they held, but three were recalcitrant. The monthly meeting labored with them for the next four years, apparently out of a conviction that keeping them in membership made it more likely they would ultimately do the right thing. As late as 1784, however, the monthly meeting found "two cases that remain in an unsettled way." The Massachusetts Supreme Court had ruled in 1781 that slavery was incompatible with the state's constitution, but recent research suggests that the process of abolition both began earlier and continued longer than has been previously understood.[51]

After emancipation was complete at Dartmouth, Friends grappled with its

49. Dartmouth Monthly Meeting Men's Minutes, 1st Mo. 19, 10th Mo. 17, 1716, 5th Mo. 15, 7th Mo. 19, 8th Mo. 21, 1717; Drake, *Quakers and Slavery*, 30-32.

50. Drake, *Quakers and Slavery*, 63-64, 78-79.

51. Dartmouth Monthly Meeting Men's Minutes, 5th Mo. 20, 1765, 4th Mo. 7, 7th Mo. 20, 1772, 1st Mo. 17, 6th Mo. 20, 9th Mo. 19, 28, 1774, 9th Mo. 23, 11th Mo. 27, 1776, 1st Mo. 19, 1777, 12th M. 20, 1784; . See Gloria Whiting, "Emancipation without Courts or Constitution: The Case of Revolutionary Massachusetts," *Slavery & Abolition* (Nov. 2020), 41:458-78

implications. In 1777, the monthly meeting asked the quarterly meeting's advice about buying slaves in order to liberate them. The quarterly meeting gave its blessing, so long as the liberator consulted with Friends. In 1783, for reasons that are unclear, the monthly meeting followed quarterly meeting instructions in appointing a committee to visit "those who have heretofore held Slaves among us, and those that have been so held." The committee reported that they had done so, and "Endeavoured In Love and tenderness to Impress their minds with a Sense of Religious duty, and laboured for a proper & Suitable Adjustment of the matter." But Friends were apparently not committed to full equality. In January 1784, "being informed that the Black people that attended Our meeting for Worship have at sometimes not been suitably provided with Seats," it appointed a committee to do so.[52]

REVOLUTION

THE AMERICAN REVOLUTION affected Dartmouth Friends. From other sources, we know that it disrupted the maritime economy. It brought invasion by British forces. It offered temptations in the form of privateering and "prize goods." And it brought problems not only in the form of the usual challenges Friends faced in wartime but also in adjustment to a new government.[53]

Exactly two months after the confrontations at Lexington and Concord, at the monthly meeting of Sixth Month 19, 1775, Dartmouth faced its first case of military service. "We are informed that Joseph Trafford is Inlisted in to the war or militia and been Labor'd with by one of the overseers," the men recorded. Trafford had refused to change course, so "for the Clearing of truth" they disowned him. Still, Friends apparently remained hopeful that the conflict would not prove too disruptive, as in Eighth Month they gave certificates to Friends in England for John Howland and John Williams, who were "about to go there on account of business."

As in past wars, some Dartmouth Friends felt it right to take up arms. A shipping center, Dartmouth offered dual temptations, not only serving in the militia or the Continental Army, but also joining the crews of privateers. So in First Month 1777 Friends acted quickly against Rhalf Allen when they learned that he had "Inlisted & gone on bord of a Vessell of War." Friends continued to deal with such cases until the end of the war, showing little sympathy with those who felt it right to fight. When Stephen Mott enlisted in the spring of 1777, Friends recorded that they had tried to "Reclaim him from the Evil of his ways." Two months later, they disowned William

---

52. Ibid., 2nd Mo. 17, 4th Mo. 21, 1783, 1st Mo 28, 1784.

53. A detailed treatment of the experience of Dartmouth Quakers in this period is Friday, "Quaker Origins of New Bedford," 122-475.

Russell for "Inlist[ing] into the wars," which they deemed "Reproachfull to our Society." At times arms-bearing Friends elaborated their misconduct. Early in 1779, the overseers reported that Peleg Gifford Jr. had "appear'd in a War Like manner with his Gun in order to Stand Wach with others of the Militia and also been found with others Shoouting at a Turkey set up for that purpos."[54]

The monthly meeting also took a firm stand against supplying anything that might be used for warlike purposes. When in Tenth month 1775 the overseers reported that Josiah Wood "hath been in the Practice of firing up and mending Guns for the Use of war," they sent a committee to labor with him. Initially "he gave them Incouragement of Desisting," and even submitted an acknowledgement, but in Third Month 1776 the meeting learned that "he Still continues in the practice of mending guns in this time of public Commotion." This time he refused to make satisfaction, and the monthly meeting disowned him. Other Friends were more conscientious. Early in 1776 John Williams appeared and confessed that "he Some time past Inconsiderately fixed and sold Some straps for the use of Solder[s]s in [carrying] their warlike Stores but going uneasy therein Desisted from Suppl[y]ing them in any such matters." The meeting accepted his acknowledgement.[55]

Generally, the war appears less often in the minutes of the women's monthly meeting. A woman Friend reported that she had not been able to attend quarterly meeting early in 1777 because of the "great Commotions." But one aspect of Quaker behavior during the war that women Friends closely monitored was the temptation to indulge in the use of "prize goods."[56]

A feature of eighteenth-century naval warfare was privateering: governments giving private ship owners and captains "letters of marque" to capture enemy merchant ships. The ships and their cargoes would be sold, often at bargain prices, and the proceeds divided among the owners and crews. Friends had a longstanding testimony against dealing in "prize goods" as the fruits of war. Nevertheless, some Friends gave in to temptation. Sugar was a special problem, and women Friends faced it as much as men, doubtless because they were the usual purchasers. When confronted, some Friends acknowledged that they had "Insideratly Purchashed Or pertook . . . of those goods called prize goods taken by War and Violence." But others refused and were disowned. In one case, six Dartmouth Friends were accused of joining others "in purchasing and Owning a Vessel that was Taken in the War, or by way of Violence." The

---

54. Dartmouth Monthly Meeting Men's Minutes, 1st Mo. 20, 2nd Mo 17, 4th Mo. 21, 6th Mo. 16, 8th Mo. 17, 10th Mo. 20, 1777, 10th Mo. 19, 11th Mo. 16, 1778, 4th Mo. 19, 5th Mo. 26, 9th M. 20, 11th Mo. 14, 1779, 3rd Mo. 20, 1780, 8th Mo. 19, 1782, 4th Mo. 21, 1783.

55. Ibid., 10th Mo. 16, 1775, 1st Mo. 15, 2nd Mo. 19, 4th Mo. 15, 1776.

56. Dartmouth Monthly Meeting Women's Minutes, 1st Mo. 20, 1777.

Friends answered that they were "Ignorant that She was Such a Vessel." Although the report of the committee to investigate is missing from the minutes, it appears that the meeting accepted the explanation, as the matter was dropped. The meeting was less tolerant of the conduct of Weston Smith, whom it disowned at the end of the war for having sailed on a vessel "which took a Vessel by Force of Armes," even though he had been "precaussioned" by Friends before he embarked.[57]

The overthrow of royal government presented Dartmouth Friends with other problems. Once the war began, Friends withdrew from town affairs. Local patriots were prone to regard them as Tories; Dartmouth's Congregational minister, Rev. Samuel West, questioned whether pacifists were really Christians. On the other hand, such a reputation did not protect against depredations at British hands. In September 1778 a British squadron descended on the town, destroying ships in the harbor and plundering and burning onshore. At least one Friend, Elihu Mosher, was taken prisoner. Unsurprisingly, in the next year at least thirty Quaker families left for New York.[58]

The draft was not as much of a problem for Dartmouth Friends as might have been anticipated. The new state militia law exempted Friends who had been members before April 19, 1775, although occasionally Friends fell afoul of special calls for troops. In 1779 Seth Huddleston of Dartmouth went to jail rather than serve.[59] But there were two other problems, oaths and taxes.

Oaths were an old headache for Friends. A 1778 Massachusetts law required all elected officials to take an oath of loyalty. Friends objected that that required them to take sides, and New England Yearly Meeting ordered Friends to refuse it. That meant that Friends could not hold any elective office, although they continued to send petitions to Boston.[60]

A number of Dartmouth Friends were caught up in the one schism to affect New England Yearly Meeting in the eighteenth century. The war meant the imposition of taxes to fund it. Friends had no objection to taxes in principle and did not cease paying them with the overthrow of royal government. But taxes imposed specifically to fund the war were a problem. And in 1780, desperate to raise more men for the Continental Army, Massachusetts passed a new law, requiring Quakers to pay a fine or

---

57. For examples of purchasing prize goods, see ibid., 11th Mo. 27, 1776, 1st Mo. 30, 2nd Mo. 7, 3rd Mo. 17, 4th Mo. 21, 1777, 2nd Mo. 22, 1778; and Dartmouth Monthly Meeting Men's Minutes, 11th Mo. 17, 1776, 1st Mo. 0, 1777, 2nd Mo. 17, 3rd Mo. 17, 4th Mo. 21, 6th Mo. 16, 1777. For the ship case, see ibid., 3rd Mo. 15, 4th Mo. 19, 1779. For the Smith case, see ibid., 5th Mo. 19, 1783. For privateering, see Fred J. Cook and William L. Verrell, *Privateers of Seventy-Six* (Indianapolis: Bobbs-Merrill, 1976).

58. Friday, "Quaker Origins of New Bedford," 205-07, 263-65, 279; Dartmouth Monthly Meeting Men's Minutes, 9th Mo. 21, 1778.

59. Arthur J. Mekeel, *The Quakers and the American Revolution* (York, Eng.: Sessions, 1996), 257; Friday, "Quaker Origins of New Bedford," 238-42, 260.

60. Friday, "Quaker Origins of New Bedford," 251.

provide a substitute when drafted. If substitutes were not supplied, then the town was subject to a fine of 300 pounds. Meanwhile, officials would collect fines from refusing Quakers by seizing their property. Most Dartmouth Friends chose to suffer distraint rather than yield.[61]

Even before the imposition of the "Quaker tax," a Friend in the neighboring town of Rochester had proposed a different course. Timothy Davis in 1776 had published a pamphlet in which he argued that Christ's injunction to "render unto Caesar the things that are Caesar's" meant that Friends should pay taxes of all kinds. Unlike the Free Quakers in Newport and Philadelphia, who actively supported the Revolution, Davis was a pacifist. He simply believed that paying taxes even specifically used for war was consistent with Quaker principles. New England Yearly Meeting disagreed, and Davis was disowned in 1778. He and his supporters responded by separating to form what they called the New Society of Friends. While most of the seceders came from Sandwich Monthly Meeting, Davis found support in Dartmouth, as a series of disownments for attending "separate meetings" beginning in 1779 shows.[62]

Dartmouth Monthly Meeting thus emerged from the Revolution battered but intact. It had survived invasion, internal divisions, and the suspicion and hostility of neighbors. If the minutes of the monthly meetings of men and women are reliable evidence, Friends there had upheld Quakerism in all of its distinctive features, no matter how trying or unpopular they might be. And they remained committed to doing so. Significantly, at the last monthly meeting recorded in the first book of women's records, four Friends were "appointed to Labour with the Members of this meeting for the Reviveal of Plainness," and to remove "other defects."[63]

ACKNOWLEDGMENTS

HISTORIANS AND GENEALOGISTS everywhere should be grateful to the Dartmouth Historical and Arts Society, which has digitized and made available Dartmouth Monthly Meeting records 1699-1968. Their web site should be consulted to see the original minute books published here, as well as birth, death, and marriage records. They have been expertly transcribed under the direction of Andrea Marcovici. Robert E. Harding, the president of the Dartmouth Historical and Arts Society, was uniformly encouraging. Aaron Rubinstein, Head, Special Collections and University Archives, at the

---

61. Ibid., 331-36; Mekeel, *Quakers and the American Revolution,* 260-61.

62. Mekeel, *Quakers and the American Revolution,* 168-69, 335-36; Dartmouth Monthly Meeting Men's Minutes, 6th Mo. 19, 8th Mo. 20, 9th Mo. 18, 11th Mo. 20, 12th Mo. 18, 1780, 5th Mo. 21, 7th Mo. 16, 1781; Dartmouth Monthly Meeting Women's Minutes, 9th Mo. 20, 1779, 6th Mo. 19, 10th Mo. 16, 1780, 2nd Mo. 19, 1781. The most detailed account of Davis and his group is Hagglund, "Disowned without Just Cause," 217-48.

63. Dartmouth Monthly Meeting Women's Minutes, 5th Mo. 24, 1782.

W.E.B. Du Bois Library at the University of Massachusetts, Amherst, which houses the New England Yearly Meeting archives, rapidly supplied a copy of minutes of the Meeting for Sufferings in 1782. My colleague Michael Birkel of the Earlham School of Religion suggested parallels between William Ricketson and the Ranters.

BOOK I: 1699–1727

att a mans meeting in the Town of Dartmouth the 6
Day of the 11 month 169⅔ at the House of John Lapham
are under written Peleg Slocum Jacob Mot Abraham
Tucker and John Tucker the day and year above written
undertakes to build a meeting House for the people of
God in Scorn Called Quakers 35 foot long 30 foot wide
and 14 foot Stud To worship and Serve the true and
Living God in according as they are persuaded in Contience
they Ought to Do and for no other use Intent or
Purpos but as afores and when one or more of us
Decease then Imediately the Survivers Chose others in our
room together with the Consent of the asembly of the
said people So to be and Remain to us and them for Ever
as afores and when D House Which D House Shall be
Compleatly finished at or before the 10 Day of the 8 month
next Insuing the date heref In witness here to wee
Subscribe our names with our own hands
And for the use of the said Society of people towards
the building of D House of our free will Contribute to
as followeth

John Tucker — — — — — 10 — 00 — 00
Peleg Slocum — — — — 15 — 00 — 00
John Lapham — — — — 05 — 00 — 00
Nathanael Howland — 05 — 00 — 00
Abraham Tucker — — 10 — 00 — 00
Increas Allen — — — 05 — 12 — 00
Ebenezer Allen — — 05 — 00 — 00
Eleazer Slocum — — 03 — 00 — 00
Jacob Mott — — — — 03 — 00 — 00
Benjamin Howland — 02 — 00 — 00
Richard Evens — — — 01 — 00 — 00
Judah Smith — — — 01 — 00 — 00

FIG. 2: *The opening page of the records of the Apponegansett Friends Monthly Meeting Records, 1699. Courtesy of the Dartmouth at Smith's Neck Monthly Meeting.*

At a monthly meeting of friends

(1699) At a mens meeting in the Town of **Dartmouth** held
Day of the 11 month[1] 1698/9 at the House of **John Lapham**
we underwritten **Peleg Slocum Jacob Mott Abraham
Tucker** and **John Tucker** the day and year above written
undertakes to build a meeting House for the people of
God in scorn Called Quakers 35 foot long 30 foot wide
and 14 foot studs; To worship and serve the true and
Living God in according as they are persuaded in Continu[?]
they ought to Do and for no other use Intent or
Purpos but as aforesd and when one or more of us
decease then imediately the survivers chose others in our
room together with the consent of the assembly of the
said people so to be and Remain to us and then for Ever
as aforesd ~~and when sd Houle~~ Which sd House shall be
Compleatly finished at or before the 10 day of the 8 month
next insuing the date herof in witness here to we ~~
Subscribe our names with our own hands.
And furthe we of the said society of people towards
the building of sd house of our free will Contribute
as followeth

John Tucker – – – – – 10-00-00
Peleg Slocum – – – – – 15-00-00
John Lapham – – – – – 05-00-00
Nathanael Howland – 05-00-00
Abraham Tucker – – – 10-00-00
Increas Allen – – – – – 03-12-00
Ebenezer Allen – – – – 05-00-00
Eleazer Slocum – – – – 03-00-00
Jacob Mott – – – – – – 03-00-00
Benjamin Howland – –02-00-00
Richard Evens – – – – 01-00-00
Judah Smith – – – – – 01-00-00

At A Monthly Meeting of friends at the house of
Peleg Slocumb in Dartmouth the 26th of the 4m 1699
It was A good that there should be A further Contri-

1. Like Puritans, Friends eschewed the usual names for the months of the year as honoring pagan gods. Thus "11 month" etc.

bution towards the defraying the Charge of boulding the
Meeting house: and there was subscribd – – – 12£–18ˢ–00ᵈ

At A Monthly Meeting of friends holdon at the house
of **Peleg Slocumb** in Dartmouth the 24ᵗʰ of the 5ᵐ 1699.
John Hodly and **Mary Slocumb** did lay there intention
of mariag before this meeting and the meeting Chose-
John Layspham & Jacob Mott to make inquiry about their – –
Clearnes Concerning mariage and bring in their answers
to the next monthly meeting

At A Monthly Meeting of friends holdon at the house of – –
Peleg Slocumb in Dartmouth the 24ᵗʰ of the 6ᵐ 1699
and this meeting Called upon **John Lapham & Jacob Mott**
for to give in their answer Concerning **John Hodly** and
Mary Slocumb their Clearness Concerning Mariage
their answer is that they find nothing that may hinder
their proseding: and **John Hodly & Mary Slocumb** also
Came this second time still signifiing their intention of
and desired their answer & this meeting finding nothin
that may hinder their intention: they had their answer
that they might prosed to take oath other in ~~the~~ mariag
according to the good order of truth:
and **Valintine Hudolstun [Hudleston] & Nathaniel Howlan[d]** ar Chosd
to atend the quarterly meeting at Rhodeisland.
An acount of the quarterly meetings at Rhodeisland
is the first third day of the first month and the first
third day of the 4ᵐ and the first third day of the 7ᵐ
and the first third day of the 10ᵐ

At A Monthly Meeting of friends holdon at the house of **Peleg**
Slocumb in Dartmouth the 18ᵗʰ of the 7ᵐ 1699
there was inquiri made if there was any business &
there was propounded something Concerning suffer-
-ing for not training and it was agreed that they shoud
try for som thing from under the Clarks hand & bring the
return to the next monthly meeting[2]

[blank space]

2. A 1693 Massachusetts statute required adult men "to train, to watch under arms, and to be impressed
for service." Apparently the monthly meeting hoped that if members liable for such service presented
certificates that they were Friends in good standing authorities might excuse them. See Arthur Worrall,
Quakers in the Colonial Northeast (Hanover, N.H.: University Press of new England, 1980), 132-33.

At A Monthly Meeting of friends ∧holdon at the house of ~~the~~
Peleg Slocumb in Dartmouth the 13th of the 9m 1699
it is agreed that our fourth day meeting next before our
monthly meeting is to be Cept [kept] at **Cockest [Acoaxet]**[3] one day at **Stephen**
Willcocks next at **Jeams [James] Tripp**s and so by turn Continuing
this insuwing number

At A Monthly Meeting of friends holden at the house of
Peleg Slocumb in Dartmouth the 11th of the 10m 1699
there was inquiri made whether there was any busines & no busines appeared

At A Monthly Meeting of friends holdon at the house of
Peleg Slocumb in **Dartmouth** the 8th of the 11m 1699
and there was Contributed sixteen shiling & eightpence
whereof fiften shiling was paid fo a book for the uuse
of the meeting for the recording births mariages and
deaths of friends

At A Monthly Meeting of friends holdon at the house of
Peleg Slocumb in Dartmouth the 5th of the 12m 1699
John Lapham junior & Mary Russel did lay their intention
of mariage before this meeting – –
and **Nathaniel Howland** and **Abraham Tucker** ar Chos
to Enquire in to their Clearness Concerning marriage
and bring in their answer to the next monthly meeting

(1700) At A Monthly Meeting of friends holdon at the house of
Peleg Slocumb in **Dartmouth** the 4th of the 1m 1700
and this meeting Called upon **Nathaniel Howland** and
Abraham Tucker for to give in their answer Concerning
John Lapham junr & Mary Russel their Clearness Concerning
mariag their answer is that they find nothing that may
hinder their prosedings **and John Lapham junor & Mary Russel**
also came this second time still signifiing their intention
in mariag and desire their answer and this meeting
finding nothing that may hinder intention they had their
answer that they might proseed to take each other in
mariage according to the good order of truth
and **Stephen Willcock & John Tucker** are Chose to atend
the quarterly meeting

3. Over the years, clerks spelled the Wampanoag place name Acoaxet (the modern town of Westport, Massachusetts) in a variety of ways. This is the only place in the transcription where the modern spelling will be inserted in square brackets.

At A monthly meeting of friends holdon at the house of
Peleg Slocumb in Dartmouth the 1ᵗʰ of the 2ᵐ 1700
it is agreed that the fourth day meeting at **Coakset**
Shall continue there tell [till?] the meeting see Cause to
removed[?] it

At A monthly meeting of friends holdon at the house of –
Peleg Slocumb in **Dartmouth** the 29ᵗʰ of the 2ᵐ 1700
it is further agreed that their [there] be a further contribution
towards the finis[h]ing of our meeting house: –
and there was subscribed – – – – –   £   s   d
                                              8—12—00

At A Monthly Meeting of friends holdon at the house of
Peleg Slocumb in **Dartmouth** the 27ᵗʰ of the 3ᵗʰ month 1700)
there was Chose **Vollintin [Valentine] Huddlston** & **John Lapham** to
attend the quarterly meeting and **Jacob Mott** &
John Tucker to attend the yearly meeting

At A monthly meeting of friends holdon at the house
of **Peleg Slocumb** in **Dartmouth** the 24ᵗʰ of the [*illegible*] 4ᵐ 1700)
there was inquiry mad[e] whether there was any busines
to this meeting and the answer was none – – – – –

At A Monthly Meeting of friends holdon at the house
of **Peleg Slocumb** in **Dartmouth** the 22ᵗʰ of the 5.ᵐᵒ 1700)
and no busines apeared – – – – –

At A monthly meeting of friends holdon at the house
of **Peleg Slocumb** in **Dartmouth** the 19ᵗʰ of the 6ᵐᵒ 1700)
and no busines did appear – – – – –

At A monthly meeting of friends holdon at the house of
Peleg Slocumb in **Dartmouth** the 16ᵗʰ of the 7ᵐᵒ 1700)
and no busines did appear – – – – –

At A monthly Meeting of friends holdon at the house
of **Peleg Slocumb** in **Dartmouth** the 14ᵗʰ of the 8ᵐᵒ 1700)
and no busines did appear – – – – –

(1700) At A Monthly Meeting of friends holdon at the house of
Peleg Slocumb in **Dartmouth** the 11ᵗʰ of the 9ᵐᵒ 1700) the [ma
rryings?] of **Hugh Copothit** ~~from~~ from **flushin [Flushing⁴]** was Red [read?]

At A Monthly Meeting of friends holdon at the house of
Peleg Slocumb in **Dartmouth** the 9ᵗʰ of the 10ᵐᵒ 1700)

4. Flushing Monthly Meeting in New York included New York City Friends.

inquiri was made if there was any busines and the answer
was none

At A Monthly Meeting of friends holdon at the house of
Peleg Slocumb in **Dartmouth** the 6ᵗʰ of the 11ᵐᵒ 1700)
Abraham Booth and **Abigail Howland** did lay their intention
of Mariage before this meeting and they were desired
to wait tell [till] the next monthly meeting for their answer and
Peleg Slocumb & **Stephen Wilcock** was Chose to inspect into
their Clearness & bring in their answer to the next – –
monthly meeting

At A Monthly Meeting of friends holdon at the house of
Peleg Slocumb in **Dartmouth** the 3ᵗʰ of the 12ᵐᵒ 1700)
Abraham Booth & **Abigail Howland** appeared the second
time &ₐ desired their answer and things being clear their
answer was that they might take each other when they
see time Conveniant in the good order of truth – – – – –

(1701) At A Monthly Meeting of friends holdon at the house
of **Peleg Slocumb** the 3ᵗʰ of the 1ᵐ 1701)
and no business did appear – – – – –

At A Monthly Meeting of friends holdon at the house
of **Peleg Slocumb** in **Dartmouth** the 31ᵗʰ of the 1ᵐᵒ 1701)
it is agreed that our meeting begin at the Eleventh
hower [hour]

At A Monthly Meeting of friends holdon at the house
of **Peleg Slocumb** in **Dartmouth** the 28ᵗʰ of the 2ᵐᵒ 1701)
and no business did appear – – – – –

At A Monthly Meeting of friends holdon at the house
of **Peleg Slocumb** in **Dartmouth** the 26ᵗʰ of the 3ᵐᵒ 1701)
and **Nathaniel Howland** & **John Tucker** was Chose to
attend the quarterly meeting and **Peleg Slocumb**
& **Jacob Mott** was Chose ₐᵗᵒ attend the yearly meeting – –
Next

At A monthly meeting holdon at the house of
Peleg Slocumb in **Dartmouth** the 23ᵗʰ of the 4ᵐᵒ 1701)
and no busines did appear – – – – –

At A monthly meeting holden at the house of **Peleg**
Slocumb in **Dartmouth** the 21ᵗʰ of the 5ᵐᵒ 1701)
and no business appeared – – – – –

At A monthly meeting holden at the house of **Peleg
Slocumb** in **Dartmouth** the 18th of the 6<u>mo</u> 1701)
and **Jacob Mott** & **Stephen Wilcock** was Chose to attend
the quarterly meeting next – – – – –

At A monthly meeting of friend holden at the hous of – –
Peleg Slocumb in **Dartmouth** the 15th of the 7<u>mo</u> 1701)
this meeting has given out two sertificates one to **Peleg
Slocumb** and one to **Stephen Wilcock** – – – – –

At A monthly meeting of friends holden at the house of
Peleg Slocumb in **Dartmouth** the 13th of the 8<u>mo</u> 1701)
and no business appeared – – – – –

At A monthly meeting of friends holden at the house of
Peleg Slocumb in **Dartmouth** the 10th of the 9<u>mo</u> 1701)
and no busines appeared – – – – –

At A monthly meeting of friends holden at the house of
Peleg Slocumb in **Dartmouth** the 8th of the 10<u>mo</u> 1701)
and no business appeared

At A monthly meeting of friends holden at the house
of **Peleg Slocumb** in **Dartmouth** the 5th of the 11<u>mo</u> 1701)
and no business appeared

At a monthely meeting of friends held at **Peleg Slocom**s
house in **Dartmouth** the 2nd of the 12th month 1701)
Wee have received three papers in answer to ~
george keaths great Sheet[5] and two other books frinds
in **philadelphia** at a monthely meeting of friends held at the
the 2nd of the first month (Hous of **Peleg Slocum** in **Dartmouth**
        1702   **Jacob mott** and **Peleg Slocum** are chose to atend the

5. George Keith (1638-1716), a Scot, was educated as a Presbyterian minister but converted to Quakerism in 1663 and emerged as an influential Quaker preacher and writer. He emigrated to New Jersey in 1684 and to Philadelphia in 1689. There he became involved in a bitter controversy with leading Friends, whom he accused of departing from essential Christian doctrines. Friends disowned him and he was ordained an Anglican priest. He then produced a series of attacks on Quaker theology and individual Friends. See Hugh Barbour and J. William Frost, *The Quakers* (Westport, Ct.: Greenwood, 1988), 343-44; and Jon Butler, "'Gospel Order Improved,' The Keithian Schism and the Exercise of Quaker Ministerial Authority in Pennsylvania," *William and Mary Quarterly* , 3rd Ser., 31 (July 1974), 431-52. The "great Sheet" is probably Keith's *A Serious Call to the Quakers Inviting Them to Return to Christianity*, published as a broadside in London in 1700. See Joseph Smith, *A Descriptive Catalogue of Friends' Books, or Books Written by Members of the Society of Friends, Commonly Called Quakers, from Their First Rise to the Present Time, Interspersed with Critical Remarks, and Occasional Biographical Notices, and Including All Writings by Authors before Joining, and by Those After Having Left the Society, Whether Adverse or Not, as Far as Known* (2 vols., London: Joseph Smith, 1867), II, 38-39.

(1702) At a monthely meeting of friends held at the house of
Peleg Slocom in **Dartmouth** the 30th of the first month <u>1702</u>
and inquiry being made and no business appeared – – – – –

At a monthely meeting of friends held at the hous of **Peleg Slocum**
In **Dartmouth** the 7th[?] of the 2<u>mo</u> 1702
Inquirey being made if their was [*illegible*] bussiness to this meeting
And the answer was no business

A[t] a monthely meeting of friends held at the house of **Peleg**
Slocum iⁿ Dartmouth the 28th of the 3<u>mo</u> <u>1702</u>
where as their is a concarne [concern] about friends serving in office
as Jureymen and other officeses whereas at present wee can
not be admitted to Sarve [serve] with out Swaring it is therefor agreed
by this meeting that friends should make their Redress to the
Jenerale [General] Court at **boston** for releife[6] – –
And **Benjamin howland** and **Stephen Willcock** are
chosen to atend the next qu'ly meeting and **Jacob Mott** and
John Tucker are chose to attend the yearly meeting. – – – – –

At a monthely meeting of friends held at the house of **Peleg**
Slocum in **Dartmouth** the 22nd of the 4<u>mo</u> 1702
Nathanel howland and **John Tucker** was chose for to goe
to deliver our petition to the govᵉnor at **boston** – –
And **Isaac newson**[?] and **Timothey Davise**[?] appeared for ~~
　　Sepecan [Sippican?][7] meeting – –
And **william wood** and **Elizer Smith** are Chose to make in=
　　quirey into **James tripp** his clearness concarning marriadg and
to bring in their answer to the next monthely meeting – – – – –

At a monthely meeting ~~at~~ freinds held at the home of **peleg**
Slocum in **Dartmouth** the 20th of the 5mo 1702
　　and the mee[t]ing reckned with **Thomas brigs** ʲⁿʳ[?] for keeping the meeting house and paid him for the same – –
And the making up the accounts with the meeting is referd
to the next monthely meeing – – – – –

6. In 1696, Parliament had given English Friends the right to offer affirmations instead of oaths, but the law did not apply to the colonies. This may have been the relief Dartmouth sought. Regardless, their petition was unsuccessful. See William C. Braithwaite, *The Second Period of Quakerism* (London: Macmillan, 1921), 183-84; and Worrall, *Quakers in the Colonial Northeast,* 104.

7. The Sippican Meeting was located on land in what was then the town of Rochester, but is now the modern town of Marion, Massachusetts.

At a monthely meeing of friends held at the house of **Peleg
Slocum** in **Dartmouth** the 17ᵗʰ of the 6ᵐᵒ 1702. – –
Jacob Mott and **Peleg Slocum** was chose for to atend the
quarterly meeting next

At a monthely meeting of friends held at ᵗʰᵉ ʰᵒᵘˢᵉ ᵒᶠ **Peleg Slocum**
in **Dartmouth** the 14ᵗʰ of the 7ᵐᵒ 1702 – –
Nathanel howland and **John Tucker** are Chosen to
goe to the Asembley for to spake to our pertition – – – – –

At a monthely meeting of freinds held at the house of **Peleg Slocum**
in **Dartmouth** the 12ᵗʰ of the 8ᵐᵒ 1702
the yearly meeting Epistle from our freinds in **london** [*illegible*]
rend[?] to the comfort of friends – – – – –

At a monthly meeting of friends held at the house of **Peleg
Slocom** in **Dartmouth** the 9ᵗʰ of the 9ᵗʰ mo. 1702 – –
Ralph Chapman and **Deliverance Slocum** layed
their Intention of marrige be fore this meeting and
they was desired to wait til the next meeting for this answᵉʳ
And **william Soul** and **Benjamin howland** was chose
to see into their clearnes and to bring in theys[?] answer to
the next monthley meeting – –
And **Benjamin howland** and **John Tucker** was chosen to
atend the quarterly meeting next – – – – –

At a monthly meeting of freinds held at the house of **peleg
Slocum** in **dartmouth** the 7ᵗʰ:10ᵐᵒ 1702
Ralph Chapman and **Deliverance Slocum** appeared the
Second time for their answer ᵃⁿᵈ things being clear their answᵉʳ
was that they might take Each other when they see con-
veniant in the order of truth – –
And this meeting refers the mat[t]er concarning the bu[i]lding
a mee[t]ing hous of Providence to the next monthely meeting – – – – –

At a monthely meeting of friend held at the house of **Peleg
Slocum** in **Dartmouth** the 4ᵗʰ of the 11ᵗʰ ᵐᵗʰ 1702 – –
Jacob mott and **Eliazar Slocum** are Chosen to agree with
Rhoad Island meeting About bu[i]lding a meeting house at
Providence – –
And **Deliveranc Smith William Soul Eliezar Smith** ~~and~~
And **Abraham Tucker** are chose to agree with a carpendor
to bu[i]ld an addition to the meeting house – – – – –

At a monthely meeting of freinds held at the house of **Peleg Slocu**ᵐ
in **Dartmouth** the **first** day of the 12ᵗʰ ᵐᵗʰ 1702/3 – –
Nathanel Chase and **Abigal Shearman** did lay thir Intention
of marrig before the mee[t]ing and they wer desired to wait
for thir answer untel the next monthly meeting – –
And **Nathanel howland** and **Eliazer Slocum** was Chosen
to Inspect into their clearness and bring in their answer to
the next monthely meeting – – – – –

(*1703*) At a monthely meeting of friends held at the house of
Peleg Slocum in **Dartmouth** the **first** day of the 1[?] mo 1703
Peleg Slocum Stephen Willcock and **John Tucker** are
chosen to atend the quarterly meeting next – –
And **Nathanel howland** and **Elizear Slocum** brought in
their answer consarning **nathanel Chace** and **Abigal
Shearman** that they find nothing that may hinder their In
tentions of marrig and the afores^d **Nathanel Chase** and
Abigal Shearman appeared the second time desiring an answer
and things being Clear the answer of the monthly was that they
might proceed to tak[e?] Each other in the order of truth

At a monthely meeting of freinds held at the house of **Peleg
Slocum** in **Dartmouth** 29ᵗʰ[?] of the first mo^th 1703 – –
and inquirey being made no business appeared – – – – –

At a monthely meeting of friends held at the house of **Peleg Slocum**
in **Dartmouth** the 26ᵗʰ[?] of the second month 1703
and thir [there] was no business – – – – –

At a monthly meeting of friend held at the hous of **Peleg Slocum**
in **Dartmouth** the 24ᵗʰ of the 3ʳᵈ m^th 1703 – –
and our monthely meeting is ordered to be ceept[?] [kept?] at our
meeting hous – –
And **Jacob mott nathanal howland** and **John Tucker** are
chosen to Atend the quarterly meeting and year-ly meet

At a monthely meeting of friends held at our meeting hous
in **Dartmouth** the 21ˢᵗ of the 4ᵗʰ m^th 1703 – –
Joseph Russell jnr[?] and **marey Tucker** layd their Intentions of marrig befor this meeting – –
and they wer desiered to tarey [tarry?] for their answer tel the
next monthely meeting.
Eliezar Slocum and **Nathanel howland** a^re? chosen to Inspect

Into their Clearness and bring in their answer to the next
monthely meeting – –
nine shillings and four-penc rceived for books and 10 books=
remains

At a monthely meeting of friends held at our meeting house
In **Dartmouth** the 19th of the 5th m th 1703 – –
Joseph Russell jnr[?] and **Marey Tucker** came the second
time for their answer as to their former Intintion of marrig
and things being clear they had their answer that they
might prosed to take Each other in the good order of truth.
And **Jacob Mott John tucker** and **Benjamin howland**
are chose to Inspect into the lives and conversations of such
as profes truth – – – – –

At a monthely meeting of freinds held at our meeting house
In **Dartmouth** the 16th of the 6th m th 1703
Stephen Willcock and **nathanel howland** are chosen to
Attend the quarterly meeting next
And **Eliezar Slocum** and **Eliezar Smith** are chose to attend the
yearly meeting at **Salam** [**Salem**] next.
And the business cosarning **Ebenezer Allin** [w]ho not being her[e] is Refered
to the next monthely meeting and **John Lapham william
wood** are Chose to Inspect into the [*illegible*] and Conversation
of freinds for this folowing month
[*4 line illegible insertion*]

At a monthely meeting of freinds held at our meeting house in
Dartmouth the 11th of the 8th m th 1703 – –
John Lapham and **Deliverance Smith** are Chosen to Enspect=
into the report consarning **Ebenezar Allin**s beating and abus=
ing of an Indian and bring in their answer to the next monthey meeting.
and **John Tucker** and **nathanel howland** are chose to spake
with **Thomas Brigs** about his being ofended with Some for report
ing that he keept a rude house and to bring in their answer
to the next monthely meeting and they are allso apoynt=
ed to Enspect Into the lives and conversations of friends
for this folowing month – – – – –

At a monthely meeting of friends held at our meeting house in
Dartmouth the 8th of the 9th m th 1703.
William Bourn and **hannªh Shearman** did lay their In=
tention of marrag be for this meeting and they wer desired to

wait untel the next monthley meeting for their answer – –
Benjamin howland and **Nathanel howland** are chosen to
Inspect into their clearness and bring in their answer
to the next monthely meeting.
Peleg Slocom and **Increes allin** are chosen to Inspect in
to the lives and conversations of friends for the folowing
month – – – – –

At a monthely meeting of friends held at our meeting house in
Dartmouth the 5th of the 10th m̲th 1703 – –
and the friends that was chosen to wit **John Lapham**
and **Deliverance Smith** to Inspect in to the deferance be
tween **Ebenezer allin** and an Indian called **Jeremiah**
was called to give in their answer and their answer is
that they find that **Ebenezer allin** did beat and abuse the
Sᵈ Indian as the report was.
and after freinds had long laboured In Love and much ten=
derness to show him the sᵈ **allin** his rashness and Eror
he did at last condem it and say that he was sorey for it – –
Peleg Slocum and **Abraham Tucker** are Chosen to attend
the quartorly meeting.

At a monthely meeting of friends held at our meeting house In
Dartmouth the **third day** of the 11th m̲th 1703 – –
William Wood Deliverance Smith and **John Tucker**
are Chosen to Inspect into the lives and conversations
of friends for this folowing month.

At a monthely meeting of friends held at our meeting house in
Dartmouth the one and thirtyeth day of the 11th[?] m̲th 1703 – –
and their was no business appeared – – – – –

At a monthely meeting of friends held at our meeting house in **Dartmouth**
the twenty third of the twelveth month 1703 – –
Peleg Slocum nathaneel howland and **Increas allien** are to
attend the next quartorly meeting – –
and **Eliezer Slocum Benjamin howland** and **John Tucker**
are chosen to furder Inspect into the business betwixt **Josiah=
merehow** and **John fish** and bring in their answer to the next
monthely meeting. – –
William Wood nathaneel howland and **Eliezar Slocom** are
chosen to Inspect into the lives and conversations of freinds for

this month Insuing[8] – –
And the business consarning **Thomas gachel** is refered to the next
monthly meeting that if aney freind have aney thing upon his
mind to labour furder with him thay may have time to clear
themselves and truth[?] of him. – – – – –

(1704) At a monthly meeting of friends held at our meeting house in **Dartmouth**
the 27th of the first month 1704 – –
this meeting hath made up their accounts with **Eleiezer=
Smith** for his work about the meeting house and have
payed him – –
And **John Russell** and **Rebeckah Ricketson** did lay their
Intention of marrige before this meeting, and they was desired to
tarey untel the next monthely meeting for their answer – –
nathaneel howland and **william Soul** are chosen for to In=
spect into their Clearness and bring in their answer to the
next monthely meeting – –
and to Inquier into **henrey tucker** his clearness consarning
marrig and bring in their answer to the next monthely meeting – –
and **Stephen willcock Deliverance Smith** and **Benjamin
howland** are chosen for to go to **John fish** and his wife to lab=
our furder with them to shew them their shortness In speak=
ing rash words to **Josiah merehow** – – – – –

At a monthly meeting of friends held at our mee[t]ing house in **Dartmouth**
the 24th of ye second month 1704 – –
John Russell and **Rebeaca Reketson** came for their answer and
things being clear the meetings answer was that they – –
might prosceed according to their Intentions and take each other
In the order of truth
and **John Tucker** and **Benjamin howland** are chosen to draw
up something consarning **thomas gatchel** his disorderly walk
ing – – – – –

At a monthely meeting of freinds held at our meeting house
in **Dartmout[h]** the 22 [illegible] of third month 1704 – –
Jonathan Devel [Davol] william Soul John Lapham Jnr william wood
and **Judah Smith** and **Robert gifford** are chosen to hear and
and determin the deferance between **nathaneel howland** and
John Peckham – –
and **Jacob Mott Increase allin** and **Stephen Willcock** are chosen to

8. These Friends apparently filled the roles later known as overseers.

hear and determin the deferance between **Eliezar Smith** and **Nathaneel howland** – –
And **Peleg Slocumb** and **John Tucker** chosen to atend the quartor^{ly}
meeting next – –
and **nathaneel howland** and **John Tucker** are chosen to atend
the yearl[y] meeting at **Rhoad Island**
And **Peleg Slocum Incres Allin Benjanin howlan John Tucker
James tripp** and **william wood** are chosen to Inspect into the lives
and Conversations ^{of} freinds for the half year Insuing, – –
And **Jacob mott Increase Allin** and **Stephen Willcock** have Ended the
deferance between **Eliezar Smith** and **nathanieel howland** – – – – –

At a monthely meeting of friends held at our meeting house in
Dartmouth the 19th of ye 4th mth 1704 – –
Eliashib Smith and **dinah Allin** of **Sandwich** did lay their In=
tention of marrige befor the meetin
And **Benjamin allin** and **deborah Russell** did lay their Inten
tion of marrige before the meeting. and they wer all desired to
stay untel the next monthely meeting for their answer – –
and **William Soul** ^{and John Lapham Jnr [?]}are chosen to Inspect Into their Clearness
and bring in their answer to the next monthely meeting – –
John lapham william Soul Deliverance Smith [*illegible*] **Jacob
mott Eliezar Slocom** and **william wood** ar chosen to hear
the deferance between **Ebenezer allien** and **Nathaneel howlan**^d
And to End the Same – –
and the six freinds above named have heard determined and
Ended the above said deferance between **Ebenezer allin** and
and **nathaneel howland** – – – – –

At a monthley meeting of friends held at our meeting house
in **Dartmouth** the 17th of the 5th mth. 1704 – –
and the six friends that was chosen last third month
to hear and determined the deferance between **nathaneel
howland** and **John Peckham** and their answer is that
they have heard determined and Ended s^d deferance – – – – –

At a monthely meeting of fr^{ds} held at our meeting hous
in **Dartmouth** the twenty first day of the 6th mth 1704
Peleg Slocum and **John Tucker** are chosen to atend
Salam [Salem] yearly meeting – –
and **Stephen willcock** and **Benjamin howland** are
chosen to attend the quarterly meeting next at **rhoad Island**

And **Eliashib** smith and **Dinah Allin** [**Allen**] and **Benjamin Allin** [**Allen**]and **deborah**
Russell came to this meeting and desired answer to their former In
tentions signefieing they wer still of the same mind – –
and friends finding things clear the answers to them all was
that they might proseed to take each other in marrig according
to the good order of truth – –
and that when young people first lay their Intintion of marrig
befor the monthely meeting that they have their parents consent first – –
and **John tucker** and **Eliezar Slocom** are chosen to agree with
a friend to keep the meeting house this insuing year – –
And **Eliezer Slocom** and **nathaneel howland** ar chosen to
furder labour with **John Summers** to Shew him his Errour
ahere faloweth a coppey of the abovesaid **dinah allins** [**Allen**] sertifeca^te
from our freind^s at **Sandwich** – –
Whereas **Dinah Aallin** [**Allen**] desired of this meeting a cirtificate of her
clearness from any man concerning marriage these are to
signifie to aney men and womans meeting where these
may come that **Dinah Allien** [**Allen**] aforesaid is as fare as wee can
understand clear from aney[?] Ingagement in marriege
to aney man.
this from our men and womens meetings at **william Allins**
In **sandwich** this 5 day of **6 m**th **1704**

		Marey Wing
William Allin [Allen]	John Goodsped	Bathsheba Allin
Robert Harpar	Priseila Allin	Lydia Dillingham
Zacriah Jenkens	Mary Gifford	Rest Perry
John Wing	Mary Hoxly	Debroah Wing
James Mills	Abiah Jenkins	Dorethy Butler
Daniel Allin	Marey bowerman	Sarah Cilla

At a monthely meeting of fr^ds held at our meeting house in
Dartmouth the 18th of ye 7th month 1704 – –
Eliezer Smith and **Benjamin Howland** are chosen to – –
attend the yearly meeting at **Situate**– –
William Soul Nathaneel Howland Stephen Willcock
And and **John tucker** are chosen to writ answer to
the lettar that was sent from old **England** to this
meeting Consarning **John Summors**. – –
And **John Lapham John Richmand Deliverance Smith**
Stephen Willcock and **Peleg Slocum** are chosen to
speke with **Ebenezer Allin** [**Allen**] concarning his desorder[?]=

ly Speches at the town house – –
Peleg Slocum and **John tucker** ar chosen to labour furder
with **John fish** and his wife for to condem their spekinig [speaking?]
to **Josiah merehow** [**Merihew**] as they Did concarning a bill – – – – –

At a monthly meeting of freinds held at our meeting house
In **Dartmouth** the 20ᵗʰ day of the 9ᵗʰ m̲t̲h̲ 1704 – –
the defferance about **John fish** is rfered to the nex meeting
whereas their is a defferance between **Ebenezer Allin** [**Allen**]
and **Nathaneel Howland**. the meeting mak[e]s Choice
of **Jonahan Devel** [**Davol**] **William Wood John lapham Juʳ**
Judah Smith Stephen Willcock [**Wilcox**] and **Eliezer Slocom** [**Slocum**]
to End all defferances ᵇᵉᵗʷᵉᵉⁿ them lands Excepted and bring
In thir answer to the next monthly meeting – –
and the meeting Desired our freinds **Richard Eastes** [**Estes**] and his
brother **Mathew Estes** to Spake with **Danil Zacharies** to
know the charge which he hath ben at about the prison=
ers – –
and **Eliezer Slocom** and **Nathaneel Howland** are Chosen
to attend the quartorly meeting next – –
Benjamin Howland and **William Wood** are Chosen to
End the defferance between **Christepher Gifford** and
Richard kerby and between **Christepher Gifford** and
his wife and **John kerby** and bring in their answer
to the next monthely meeting

At a monthely meeting held at our meeting hous In **dartmouth**
the 18ᵗʰ of the 10ᵗʰ m̲t̲h̲ 1704 – –
the buseness about **John fish** and his wife is refered to
the next monthely meeting – –
and the Judgment concarning **Ebenezer Allin** [**Allen**] and
Nathaneel Howland is Referend [Referred?] to the next month=
ly meeting – –
friends at **Cokset** have desired to have the first day meeting
for this wentor [winter] amongst themselves Except the first day
befor[e] the monthely ᵐᵉᵉᵗⁱⁿᵍ and it is granted and their weekly
mee[t]ing to be on the fift[h] day of the week

At a monthely meeting held at our meeting house In **dartmouth**
the 15ᵗʰ of the 11ᵗʰ m̲t̲h̲ 1704
This meeting haveing received a letter from **Richard** and

Mᵃᵗhew Estes Consarning what **Daniel Zacharies**[?] hath ben
out about the priseners [prisoners] and he hath keept no account so
this meeting desiers [desires] the priseners to draw up an acount
and bring it into the next monthly meeting⁹ – –
and **James burril** [Burrel] and **mehetable Russell** widow did lay
their Intentions of marriag[e] befor[e] the meeting – –
and they were desired to wait tel the next monthly meᵉting
for their answer – –
and **peleg Slocum** and **John Tucker** are Chosen to I[n]spect
into their Clearness and bring in their ᵃᶜᶜᵒᵘⁿᵗ to the next monthly meeting – –
and this meeting doth take up with what **John fish** and
wife hath given. In condeming what they said to **Josiah**
Merehow about a bill and that it be pased by and no more
said about it – –
and **Eliezer Slocom** and **John lapham** the younger are Chose
to Inspect Into **John Smith**s Clearness in order that he ~~
may have a Sertfecate [Certificate] both of his life and Conversation
and allso of his Clearness Consarning marriage – – – – –

at a monthly meeting o freinds held at our meeting house
In **Dartmouth** the 19ᵗʰ of the 12ᵗʰ mᵗʰ 1704 – –
James Burril and **Mehetable Russell** widow came
befor this meeting for answer to their Intentions and[?]
befor the last monthly meeting signefieing they were
Stil of the Same mind. – –
And friends finding things clear they had ther an=
swer that they might prᵒceed and take Each other in
the Order of Truth.
and allso care hath ben taken for her former husbands ~~chi~~
Child and the Estate Secured for him – –
And **petter** [Peter] **Easton** of **newport** on **Rhoad Island** and **Content**
Slocum of **Dartmouth** did lay their Intintions of marriaᵍᵉ
before the meeting and they was desired to stay until
the next monthely meeting for an answer – –
William Soul [Soule, Sowle] and **John Lapham Juʳ** are Chosen to
Inspect into their Clearness. And bring In their answer
to the next monthely meeting – –
and **peleg Slocum** and **Benjamin Howland** are Chisen

9. Prisoners had to provide for many of their own needs, such food or fuel. Apparently the monthly meeting wanted accounts, perhaps to pay help pay some of their costs.

FIG. 3: *The first meeting house for Apponegansett was built in 1699. The existing structure dates from 1791.*
© *Copyright Jean Schnell*

to Atend the quartorly meeting next. and **Elizer** [**Elezer**?] **Smith**
and **peleg Slocum** ar chosen to atend the yearly meet
ing at **Sandwich**. – – – – –

Coppey of **John Smith**s Cirteficate – –
these are to satesfy all freinds where these may com[e]
that our friend **John Smith** haveing a desir[e] for some
time to goe to Sea. and now haveing a sutab[l] [suitable?] opertunety
for an Employ with our friend **Mathew Eastes** [**Estes**] – –
the S[d] **John Smith** Did lay his design befor our last ~~
monthely meeting. that he might have the meetings
Conscent and freinds haveing Considred of it and Seeing ~~noth~~
nothing that may Justly hender him he haveing Such
an opertunety for an Imploy for a livelyhood – –
and wee can give this furder testmony cocarning [concerning] him: that he hath
ben a man of a sober life and Conversation amongst us

and hath walked as becometh the truth. – –
and allso that he is Clear from all women Conserning – –
marriage

[*middle third of page is blank*]

(*1705*) ~~At our meeting house I~~ At a monthely meeting held at
our meeting house In **Dartmouth** the 19th of the first m̲th 1705 – –
Petter [Peter] Easton and **Content Slocum** apeared the Second
time before this meeting to receive answer to their pro=
p°sials laid before the last monthly meeting – –
an Inquirey being made Into their Clearness and nothing
appearing to hender their Intentions the meeting givs
them an answer that they might prosceed to take
Each other In the order of truth – –
and **Increas Allin [Increase Allen] william wood** and **James burril [Burrel]**
are Chosen to inquire[?] into the lives and Conversations o friends for this
Insuing month
and her[e] faloweth the coppey of **petter Estons [Peter Eastons]** Certificate from the
monthely meeting at **Rhoad Island** – –
whereas **peater [Peter] Easton** of **newport** on **Rhoad Island** Son of ~~
weston and **Rebecah Clark** of Said **newport** hath as wee un=
derstand by the Approbation of his Sd parents desired a Certificate
of us to say the monthely meeting of Disapline he being in ~~
persuance of marriage as wee understand with **Content** the
daughter of **peleg Slocom [Slocum]** and **marey [Mary?]** his wife of **Dartmouth**
these are therfore to Certifie all whom it may concern
that wee haveing made Enquirey according to truth and find
nothing to the contrary but that he is clear of Entanglement with
aney women so fare as wee know Except said **Content**. and
as for his Conversation for time past hath been sober according
to truth and Semes [seems] well Inclind and freequents freinds meet=
ings both of worship and of Disapline and wee have ~
nothing to object against his Enclination according to
his proposal and wee desir his welfare and Remaine
your friend in the truth.
Signed by order and apoyntment of our monthely mens
meeting at **newport** on **Rhoad Island** the 27th of the
twelvth month 174/5 [*sic*] – –

Danil Gould	Tho Cornell	Thomas hicks
Jacob Mott	John Borden	Samuell Hicks
Walter Clark	William Barker	John Hedley
John Allin [Allen]	William Anthony	William freeborne
John Easton seenor	Preserved fish	Samuell Easton

At a monthely meeting of friends held at our meeting house
In **Dartmouth** the 16th of the Second month 1705 – –
James Burril Increes Allin [**Increase Allen**] **William Wood** are Chosen
to Inspect into the lives and Conversations of them that
prophes [profess?] truth

At a monthely meeting of frinds held at our meeting house
In **Dartmouth** the twenty first day of the thurd month 1705 – –
James Burriel Increes Allin and **William Wood** are
Chosen to mak[e] Inquirey Into the lives and Conversations
of them that prophes truth
And whereas their is a Complaint **by Christepher Giford** [**Christopher Gifford**]
    to this
meeting Consarning **William Macumber**s Ronging [wronging] him.
Where upon the meeting made shoyce [choice] of **John Tucker**
peleg Slocum and **Deliverance Smith** to hear and In=
spect Into the truth of the above said Comeplaint and give
In their Answer to the next monthely meeting – –
And the six friends that was Chosen to End the deferance be=
tween **Ebenezer Allin** [**Allen**] and **nathaneel Howland** have given
In their determination that **Ebenezar Allin** is to blame Con=
carning Sd Deferance and **Nathaneel Howland** was to blame
for not rateing himself for money that he had at youce [use] – –
And **peleg Slocum Stephen Willcock** [**Wilcox**] and **John Tucker**
are Chosen to attend the next yea[r]ly meeting – –
and **Ebenezer Allin** not being Satesfied with the Judgment
of the ~~meeing~~ meeting doth apele [appeal] to the quartorly meeting
for a furder hearing which is granted – –
and that all the papers that **Ebenezer allin** [**Allen**] hath given
In Concarning Said deferance are to be delivered to **John** =
Tucker for him to Deliver to the quortorly meeting as their
may be ocasion – – – – –

At a monthely meeting of friends held at our meeting haus In
Dartmouth the 18th of the 4th mth 1705
the three freinds was Called upon that was Chosen to In=

spect Into the Conversations of them that prophese [profess?]
truth and their answer is they find nothing but that
things are weel – –
and the Same are Conteneued [Continued] for this Ensuing month
And **peleg Slocum Stephen Willcock** and **John** =
Tucker are Chosen to make Sarch [search?] whuther: – –
Christpher gifford hath hade gospel order and dew [due?] ad=
monition given him; and if they find that he hade
then they are to Draw up his Condemnation against
the next monthly meeting – –
and **peleg Slocum Deliverance Smith John Tucker**
John Lapham William Soul [Soule] and **Eliezar Slocom** [Slocum]
are Chosen to hear and [Determine?] the Deferance be ~~
tween **William Macumber**[?] [*crease in ms.*] and **Chrstepher Gifford**
and give in their answer [to?] the next monthly meeting – –
And **peleg Slocum** and **Benjamin Howland** are Chosen
to goe to **Sepecan** to know the Re[a]son whey they have not
atended the montheley meeting and give in their answer
to the next monthly meeting – – – – –

At a monthely meeting held at our meeting house In
Dartmouth the 16th of the 5th m̲t̲h̲ 1705 – –
the three frinds that was Chosen the last monthly meeting
[to?] Inspect into the lives and conversations of friends – –
was Called upon and their answer was that they find nothing
but that things are preaty weell – –
And the same three freinds are Continiued for this Insuing month
and **peleg Slocum Stephen Willcock James Burriel** [Burrel] and
John Tucker are Chosen to Enquire In to **Jacob Mott**s Clear=
ness In order that he may have a Certificate drawn against
the next monthly meeting – –
And the two friends that was Chosen the last monthely to
go to **Sepecan** are Stil Continued to preform the Sam[e] Sarvice

At a monthely meeting of friends held at our meeting house In
Dartmouth the [?]th day of the 6 m̲t̲h̲ 1705 – –
Edward perrey [Perry] of **Sandwich** and **Eliphel Smith** the dau
daughter of **Eliezar Smith** of **Dartmouth** did lay their In=
tenti[o]ns of marriage befor this meeting and friends desired
them to wait untel the next monthly meeting for their
answer – –

and **Eliezer Slocum** are Chose to Inquier In to their Clear
ness and bring In their answer to the next monthely meeting – –
and **William Wood Eliezer Slocum** and **John Tucker**
are Chosen to Enspect Into the lives and Conversations
of friends for this Insuing month
and **abraham Tucker** and **benjamin Howland** are
Chosen to atend the quorterly meeting – –
Eliezar Slocum and **John Tucker** are Chosen to attend the yearly meeting [...ouse?; *illegible*] – – – – –

At a monthely meeting of friends held at our meeting house
In **Dartmout[h]** the Seventeenth day of Seventh month 1705 – –
Stephen Willcock [Wilcox] and **John tucker** are Chose to know
the Reason why Some of our freinds at **rochester** have
desarted our meeting of disepline and give In their answer
to the next monthely meeting – –
and **Edward perrey [Perry]** and **Eliphel Smith** appeared the
Second time In order to receive answer to their proposials
laid before the last monthely meeting Signefing they was
Stel of the Same mind.
and Inquirey being made according to the order of truth
and nothing appearing to hender their Intentions they
had their answer from this meeting that they might
proceed according to their Intentions and take Each other
In the order of truth
And **William Wood Eliezar Slocum** and **John Tucker**
are Chosen to In Spect into the Lives and Conversations
o[f] friends for this Ensuing month – –
Stephen Willcock Eliezar Slocum and ~~J nn~~ – –
John Tucker are Chosen to atend **Situate [Scituate]** meeting – –
hear faloweth the coppy of **Edward perreys** Sertinecate[?] [Certificate]
concarning his clearness in ma—age [marriage]
to our freinds and Brethren at **Dartmouth** wee
Send greeting
Where as our friend **Edward perrey [Perry]** appeared at our
last monthely meeting and Did desir[e] of us a Cirtifi=
cate of his Clearness in marrige in ordor their unto ~~
freinds apoynted two friends to Inquire into his Clear=
ness and haveing made Inquiery and do:not find
nothing but that he is Clear from aney Intanglment

withth [*sic*] aney women heere.

their for these are to Signifye that wee have unity with
him and Desir his welfare. and Remain your freinds
and bretheren In the unchangable truth.

Sandwich the Seventh of the 7th month <u>1705</u>

William Allin [Allen]	**Richard landars**	**Abiah[?] Jenkins**
ludwick Hoxie	[*illegible*] **Wing**	**lydia Dillingham**
Danil Allin	[*illegible*] **perry**	[*illegible*] **holway**
John Dilingham	**Willi[am?] Wing**	**Rest[?] perrey [Perry]**
Stephen harper	[*illegible*] **allin**	**Dorethey butlar[?]**
thomas Bowerman	**Mary hoxie**	**Experance Bowerman**
	hannah gifford	

At a monthely meeting of friends held at our meeting
house In **Dartmouth** the 11th of the 8th m̲th̲ 1705 – –
Stephen Willcock and **John Tucker** are Still
Continued to Spake with **Sepecan** friends according
to the apoyntment of the last monthely meeting – –
and a paper allso was Read in this meeting Concarning
Bu[i]lding of a meeting house at **Salam.** Wʰerein they desir[e]
Som asisstance from our monthely meeting where up=
on this meeting toock it in to their Considration In
order to return freinds an Answer as Soon as
conveniatly freinds Can. – –
And it is proposed that friends Should have a ~~
Colection Every monthely meeting for to defray
the nesesarey Charges that may arise amongst freinds
and **peleg Slocum Stephen Willco[c]k [Wilcox]** and **Benjamin
Howland** are Chosen and added to **John Tucker** to
peruse the monthely meeting minits and what
they Shall think Convienient to order them to be
Cometted to Record – –
John tucker William Wood and **Eliazer Slocum**
are Chosen to Inspect into the lives and conversa=
tions of fr[ien]ds

At a monthely meeting of friends held our meeting
house In **Dartmouth** the 19th of the 9th m̲th̲ <u>1705</u>
and whereas it was proposed the last monthely ~~
meeting that freinds Should have a monthely Colect=
ion and this meeting Considring the proposals

and finding it Conveniant and nesescerey do agree
that their Should be a Colection Everey Monthely ~~
meeting – –
and their is Colected –   –   –   –   –   –   – 0$^£$ – 13^S – 00^d
And it is agreed by this meeting that **Stephen** ~~
Willcock Abraham Tucker William Soul [**Soule**] **John** =
Lapham Ju^r and **John Tucker** are Chosen to geat [get?]
a deed of our meeting house and land of **peleg** ~~
Slocum a gainst the next monthely meeting – –
and **Benjamin Howland** is Chosen to keep the
Colection of frinds and to Disburst it as this meeting
may see Cause – –
and it is agreed that freinds on the other side **Coxset** river
should have their meeting as they had it the last ~
winter – – – – –

At a monthely meeting of freinds held at our meeting
house in **Dartmouth** the 17th of y^e 10th mth 1705
their was Colected –   –   –   –   –   –   – 0$^£$ – 11^S – 08^d
and the friends that was Chosen to Inspect in to the lives
and Conversations of them that profess truth was Called
upon to give an account how they find thing and ~~
their answer is that they find things prety weell – –
And this meeting hath an account of a deferance ~~
between **John Sumers** [**Summers**] and **Jonathan Devel** [**Davol**] and that
the S^d **Summers** refuseth to End it according to the good
ordor of truth – –
w^{h}ere upon the meeting Chose **James Burril** [**Burrel**] and **Eliezar**
Slocum to advise **John Summers** to Submett to the ordor
of truth and put an End to S^d Deferanc against the next monthely
meeting – –
Increas Allin [**Increase Allen**] **Eliezar Slocum** and **John tucker** are ~~
Chosen to Enspect in to the lives and C[on]versations of
freinds for the month Insuing – – – – –

At a monthely meeting held at our meeting house
in **Dartmouth** the one and twenty day of the 11th mth 175/6 [*sic*] –
the three freinds were called over that was chosen the last
monthely meeting to Inspect into the lives and Con=
versations of friends and their answer is thy find –
things not well – –

And **John Lapham James Burrill** are chosen and
added to the former two friends to labour to put things
In order against the next monthly meeting – –
and the former three friends are stil Contenued to In=
spect in to the lives and Conversations of them ~~
prophes truth for this Insuing month – –
and **John Wing** and **Nathaneel Howland** are Chosen
to procur a coppey of **Christepher Gifford**s Condemnation
from the mon[thely meeting?] at **Sandwich** if their be aney to
be had – and their was Colected –   –   –   –   –   –   – 0–13 –07 –

At a monthely meeting of freinds held at our meeting house
In **Dartmouth** the 18th of the 12th mth 1705
their was Colected –   –   –   –   –   –   – 0ᴸ –10ˢ –05ᵈ
peleg Slocum and **Benjamin Howland** are apoynted to
See what friends are freely willing to Contribut toward
the bu[i]lding of a meeting house at **Salam** [**Salem**] – –
Increas Allin [**Allen**] **Elizar Slocom** [**Slocum**] and **John tucker** are ~~
Chosen to Inspect into the lives and Conversations of freinds
for the month Insuing – –
Increas Allin [**Allen**] and **Deliverance Smith** are Chosen to
attend the yearly meeting at **Sandwich** – –
and **Stephen Willcock** [**Wilcox**] and **Nathaneel Howland** are
Chosen to attend the quorterly meeting next – –
John tucker and **Benjamin howland** are Chosen to
Speak with **Hannah Jeney** [**Jenny, Jenne**] concarning her ofering
her Self in prᵃyer out of the unity of the meeting – – – – –

(1706) At a monthly meeting of freinds held at our meeting
house ~~the first mth~~ In **Dartmouth** the 18th of the first mth 1706
thir was colected –   –   –   –   –   –   – 0ᴸ–06ˢ–06ᵈ
it's agree and it is agreed that friends Should have a preparetive
d that meeting one [on?] the forth day of the week faling out next
their sho befor the monthely meeting after the time of worsh=
uld be
a preparit ip : is over to Consider of the afairs amongst friends
ive and see what may be conveniant to be recomended to
meeting the monthely meeing that so the monthely meeting
may not be Incumbred with a multitud of ~~un~~
unnesesearey buseness – –
and to chuse two or three waighty freinds to present
the nesescearey buseness to the monthey mee[ti?]ng as

may be given them in charg by the preparitive ~~~
meeting – –
And **James Burril** and **Eliezar Slocum** are chosen – –
to Inquir in to the Complaint of **Christepher gifford** ~~
and see if things be out of order to Labour to have them
amended and bring in their answer to the next monthly meeting – – – – –

At a monthly meeting of friends held at our meeting
house In **Dartmouth** the 15th of the Second mont[h] 1706
~~ther~~ their was colected – – – – – – – 0£–09s–00d
the two friends that was Chose to atend **Sandwich**
yearly meeting was Called upon and they give us to
under stand that the Sd yearly meeting desir[e]s this meet=
ing to makeup one Subscription to wards the bu[i]lding a
meeting house at **Salam [Salem]** ten[?] pounds – –
and it is concluded that freinds Should Considr of it untel
the next monthely meeting – –
and the meeting agrees to lend **William Macumber Ju**r Shilings twelve
in money out of the monthely meeting Stock and he is to repay
it again on or befor the third Second day in the Eight month
next – –
Stephen Willcock [Wilcox] Eliezar Slocum Deliverance Smith ~
and **John Tucker** are Chosen to Speak with **Ebenezer** =
Aallin [Allen] Consarning his goeing to Law with a brother before
unblievers and Bring in his Answer to the next
monthely meeting – –
Eliezar Slocum and **William Soul [Soule]** are Chose to Spake
with **William Chase** Concarning his delivering things by
way of testemony In our publick asembley of Worship
on the first day of the week Contarary to Sound doctrin[e]
and In Case he will not Condemn it then to make it known
to the mee[t]ing where he doth belong – – – – –

At a monthely meeting of friends held at our meeting
house In **Dartmouth** the 20th of the third month 1706
and their was colected – – – – – – – 0£–09s–09d
and it is concluded to make our Subscription towards
the bu[i]lding of **Salam** meeting house teen [sic] pounds – –
and the four friends that was Chosen the last monthely
meeting to Spake with **Ebeneze[r] Allin [Allen]** brought in his
answer that he doth Justify himself In going to law

with **Nathaneel Howland** for he said that he had gon[e]
as fare with him as the law of God did require it he
did understand ~~is it~~ —— what that is
and for as much as the above said **Ebenezer Allin** [**Allen**] ~~and~~
and **Nathaneel Howland** was under dealings of the
last yearly meeting at **Rhoad Island** this meeting
doth refer him to the next yearly meeting at **Rohad Island**
for the proof of his aforesaid answer – –
And **John lapham** and **John Tucker** are Chosen to Spake
with **Ebenezer Allin** [**Allen**] Concerning his having his
Daughter in marriage to one of the World Conterary to
the good order of truth and bring in their answer the next
monthely meeting – –
and **Eliezer Slocum** and **John Tucker** are Chosen to
Spake with **Eliezar Smith** Concerning his refraining
of our meeting – –
Stephen Willcock and **John Tucker** are Chosen
to atend the next quarterly and yearly meeting at
Rhoad Island – –
And the maner of Estableshing of our meeting house
and Land is refere'd to the quartorly meeting next –
and the matter concarning **William Chaces** [**Chase**] delivering
of Doctren wich is unsound is allso refered to the – –
abovesaid ~~gu~~ quartorly meeting – –
and it's agreed that the meeting that was kept on the
other side **Coxset river** for the winter Seson on the
first day of the weeck Should be at the meeting ~~
house for the Summer

At our monthely meeting of friends held at our meet=
ing house In **Dartmouth** the 24th of the 4th mth 1706 – –
their was colected –　 –　 –　 –　 –　 –　 – 00£–08s–06d
and **Stephen Willcock Benjamin Howland** and
Eliezar Slocum and **John Tucker** are Chosen to ~~
Spak with **Ebenezer Allin** [**Allen**] Concarning his going
to Law with **nathaneel Howland** and bring in
their answer to the next monthely meeting – –
and **John Lapham** and **John Tucker** brought in ~
their answer that **Ebenezer allin** [**Allen**] will not make ~~
Satisfaction for his giveing and marreing his daugh

tor ^{to one} out of the unity of friends – –
And **Eliezar Slocom** [**Slocum**] and **John Tucker** brought in ~
their answer that they have laboured with **Eliezer**
Smith according to order and he has Condemed his
[*illegible*] and for [*illegible*] [*crease in ms.*] Carfull [*careful*] – – – – –

At a monthly meeting of friends held at our meeting
house In **Dartmouth** the 15th of the 5th <u>m</u>th 1706 – – – – –
their was Colected –   –   –   –   –   –   – 0[£] –10^s –09^d
and the friends that was Chosen the last monthely
mee[t]ing to Spake with **Ebenezer Allin** [**Allen**] Consarning his
going to law Contrary to truth brought in their ~~
answer that he will not be recla[i]med but doth
willfuly presest [persist?] to his on [own?] hurt and to the great ~~
truble of the Church In Justefyeing him Self In his
Desorderly prosceedings
where fore friends haveing largely laboured with
him and finding themselves Clear are Constrained
to Caus[e] his Condemnation to be drawn up and Signed
by this meeting for the Clearing of truth and freinds
of his Desorderly Walking – –
And **Elizar Slocum** and **John tucker** are Chosen
to read to **Ebenezer allin** [**Allen**] his Condemnation and if he
will Condemn his out goeings to the Satesfaction of
friends then the Condemnation given by this meeting
is not to be read in publick – –
but if he refuseth then the Judgment to be openly
Read the next first day Come week[s?] in the latter
End of our publick meeting of worship – –
and **peleg Slocum** and **Benjamin Howland** are
Chosen to go to **Rochester** to know the re[a]son why ~
they have not Atended the monthely meeting and
bring in their answer to the next monthely meeting – –
and this meeting mak[e]s Choyce of **peleg Slocum** ~
Stephen Willcock [**Wilcox**] **Icreas Allin** [**Increase Allen**] and **John Tuck**^{er}
to See into the lives and Conversations of freinds
for the quortor of a year I[n]suing – – – – –

At a monthly meeting of friends held at our meeting house
In **Dartmouth** the 19th of the 6 <u>m</u>th 1706 <u>and</u> Colected 2[£] –04^s –0^d
Eliezar Slocom and **John Tucker** give In their answ^{er}

that they have Read the Judgment of the last monthe-
ly meeting to **Ebenezer Allin** [**Allen**] and he refusing to make
Satesfactin the aforsade Judgment [*words illegible due to tear*] publick
according to order of the last monthely meeting as faloweth
Where as **Ebenezer Allin** [**Allen**] of **Dartmouth** In the County of **bristol
new England** haveing for maney years frequented the ~~~
mee[t]ing of us the people [*illegible*] Called quakers and
Semed to Joyne in Sosietay [Society] with us but for want of keeping
In true Subjection to that princeple he made profesion of: to
with the Sp[i]rit of truth In his own heart wʰich Sperit
will lead all them that are obediant to it out of Everey thing
that is Contrary to the nature of it and Inconsistant with
it he hath given way to his own Inclinations and hath
gon[e] to law before unbelivers with one that is In Socyaty [Society]
with us and not withstanding; all the faithfull labour
of love and Earnest Endevours of us his freinds as a ~~~
Sociaty of people to perswade him to the Contrary he ~~
hath willfully presested [persisted?] to the griefe of us his friends and
Scandall of that holey prenciple he made profecion of
for which Cause wee find ourselves Concarned to testefye
to the world that wee do utterly desown all such actions
and all who are found In them and perticalerly the persoⁿ
above named and as it is our Christian Duty to pray ~~
for all people wee do hartely Desir[e] allmighty God to
open his understanding, if it be his will, to give him
to Se[e] his out going that he may find a place of trew
repentance: before the time of his visetation be over – –
given forth by our monthely meeting In **dartmouth** the
fifteenth day of the fift[h] month 1706
Signed In behalf of Sᵈ meeting by

John Tucker	**William Soul** [Soule]	**William Wood**
peleg Slocumb [Slocum]	**John lapham Juʳ**	**James Burrel**
Benjamin Howland	**Judah Smith**	**Abraham tucker**
Eliezar Slocumb	**William Macumber**	**nicholas howland**
Stephen Willcock	**Henrey Howland**	**Samuell Mott**

and **Peleg Slocum** and **Benjamin Howland** was Called
upon to know whether thy had Spoken with **Rochest**[e]**r**
freinds according to apoyntment and they Sigenify that
had laboured with them and they did own themselves
to Short and Slack In their duty In that they did not ~~
atend the monthely meeting as they ought to have

don[e] and for time to com[e] they Said they hoped to be mor[e]
Carfull [carefull] – –
And **Eliezar Slocum** is Chosen to go with **thomas macumber**
to know the truth of what the S^d **macumber** did say and
do[?] In the takeing his Ingagement before the Justice and
return the answer to the next monthly meeting – –
and where as **Robert gifford** and **Mathew Wing** Did Set
their hands to a paper to forwarn the Seclect [Select] men
from making aney rates upon their Estaats [Estates] Except ~~they~~
they was qualefieed [qualified] as the Law derects and the
sience [sense?] of the meeting is that what they have don[e] is
Contrary to truth

At a monthely meeting of freinds held at our meeting
house In **Dartmouth** the 16th of the 7th m^th <u>1706</u>
and their was Colected –   –   –   –   –   –   – 00^£ –10^s –04^d
And it is agreed that their Should be a Contributation to help
Isaac Vinson of **Rochester** his house being Accedantually [Accidently]
burned and to Bring it In to **John Tucker**s by the next
fift[h] day com weeck– –
and **John Tucker** and **John Lapham Ju^r** is Chosen
to Carrey the Same to the S^ad **Vinson** – –
peleg Slocum and **James Burril** [Burrel] is Chosen to attend the
Quarterly meeting next – –
John Tucker Stephen Willcock [Wilcox] **Benjamin Howland**
and **James Burril** are Chosen to goe to **thomas macom=**
ber to see if he will give the mee[t]ing Satesfaction for
his Spakeing or acting things not agreeable to truth
and give in their answer to the next monthely ~~~
meeting– –
and the meeting adjourns untel the next fourth day Com
Week – –
And it is agreed that wee should have a colection to help to
defray the charg[e] that our freinds have ^ben at In **old England**
to get that Law Repeal[e]d that was made In **Conetecut**
Coleney [Connecticut Colony] against friends[10] – –

10. The law in question had been made in 1656. It imposed a fine on those who sheltered Quakers,
banned circulation of Quaker books, and ordered Quakers jailed or banished. In October 1705, the
Privy Council in London ordered its repeal after lobbying by English Friends and with the support of
Massachusetts Governor Joseph Dudley. See J. Hammond Trumbull, ed., *The Public Records of Connecticut
Prior to the Union with New Haven Colony, May 1665* (Hartford: Brown and Parsons, 1850,), 283-84; and
Charles J. Hoadly, *The Public Records of Connecticut, from August, 1689 to May, 1706* (Hartford: Case,
Lockwood and Brainard, 1868), 546.

and **John tucker** is Chose to geet [get] the deed of our meeting house
and Land Recorded In the County Records and the meeting
to pay the Charge – –
And it is agreed that their Should be a peace [piece] of Land of Six
Roods [Rods] Square fenced In with Stone wall for a buring [burying]
ground – – – – –

At a monthely meeting of friends held at our meeting house In
Dartmouth the one and twanteth day of the 8th m^th 1706
and their was Colected –   –   –   –   –   –   – £00–10s–01d
and It is agreed that their should be a furder Colection to wards the
Releife of our freind at **Rochester** who hath lost his hous[e] by
fire as is mentioned In the last monthely meeting ^minit and to
bring it in to **John tuckers** by the next monthely mee[t]ing – –
and where as It was ag^reed at the last monthely meeting that
their Should be a Colection to help to defray the Charge of
Repealing of a Law made against friends in **Conetecut**
Coleney and This meeting doth allso agree that **benjamin** ~~~
Howland Should pay five pounds out of the meetings Stock
toward the defraying of the afords^d Charge – –
and **William Chase** hath given this meeting Satesfaction
Concarning the Doctrin[e] that was Delivered by him amongst
us at our meeting house some time sence which was un=
sound, and his confesion to be reed amongst us in a publick
meeting the next first Day by **John tucker** or some other freind– –
and the meeting adjourns tel the next forth day Com week
John tucker and **Stephen Willcock** hath given In their answer
that that they have laboured with **thomas macumber** accord=
ing to the order of the last montely meeting and he gives
no satesfaction – –
and friends are yet Concarned to labour furder with him
And so the mattar is refered to the next monthely meeting
And **John tucker** and **Stephen Willcock** are Chosen to Spake
with **Mathew Wing** and **Robert Gifford** to Shew them
their Shortnes[s] In set[t]ing their hands to a paper to for warne
the Select men from rateing their Estat[e]s Except they was
quolefied as the Law derects which is Contrary to the ~~
princeples of truth

At a monthely meeting of friends held at our meeting house
In **Dartmouth** the 18th day of the 9th m^th 1706 – –
And their was Colected –   –   –   –   –   –   – 0£–08s–11d

and Received of **William Macumber Jun**^r three Shilings
of the twelve Shillings in money lent him the last
Second month and **peleg Slocum** ~~is~~ to pay the rest – –
And **Benjamin Howland** hath Sent five pounds in money
to **Boston** according to the order of the last monthely meeting
and it is agreed that **Cokset** freinds should have their first days
meeting on the other Side the river for this wintor all Except
the first day befor Each monthely meeting
and their weekley meeting is oredred [ordered?] to be at the
meeting house the fourth day befor the monthely
and this meeting hath ben much Consarned about **thomas
Macombe**^rs denying his holding up his hand when he
gave Evidance In the Cace between **Josaph [Joseph] hix** and him
Self and the friends that was appoynted to deal with
him give in this answer that the S^d **macomber** doth Juste=
fy him Self against five Evidences given in wrig^hting a=
gainst him[11] – –
And **John tucker peleg Slocum[d?] Stephen Willcock [Wilcox]** and
Eliazer Slocum are Chosen to draw up the aboveSd
thomas macombers Condemnation and Read it to him
be for the next monthely meeting – –
and **John Tucker** and **Stephen Willcock** give In their
answer Concerning **mathew Wing** and **Robart gifford**
that they Condemn their signing the afor mentioned paper

---

at a monthely meeting held at our meeting house In **Dartmouth**
the 16th day of the 10th mth 1706 – – their was Colected – –[£]00 –11^s–09^d
and this meeting after abundance of Labour In love
and much tenderness to wards **Thomas macumber** to
Shew him his out goings but he Refusing [?] to hear
the meeting is furder Conscarned to Cause a paper of
Condemnation to be Drawn up against him for the ~~
Clearing of truth and freinds and to declare to the world
that he is non [not?] of us and have Chose **peleg Slocum**
and **Eliezer Slocum** to Reed it to him be for it be ~~
read in publick against him and give in their answ^{er}
to the next monthely meeting – –
And **William Soul [Soule]** and **peleg Slocum** are Chosen
to atend the Quarterly meeting next – –
and this meeting doth advise that all friends bring

11. Apparently Macomber had held his hand in such a way as to suggest an oath, which would have been a violation of the Discipline.

their Children and Sarvents as of ten as well they
Can:to meeting on the week days and to monthely meetings as
well as first days meetings and to keep to the
hour appoynted – –
and **John tucker** and **william Soul** are Chosen to
make up the acoumts [accounts] with **Benjamin Howland** Con
sarning the monthely meeting Colection and bring
In their acoumts to the nex[t] monthely meeting – –
and so the meeting adjourns untell the first fourth
day in the 11th mth next – –
the meeting being mett according to adjournment
the first day of the Eleventh month – 1706/7 – – – – –

At a monthely meeting held at our meeting house In **Dartmouth**
the 20th of the 11th month 1706/7 and their was Colected – £00–15s–06d
and **peleg Slocum** and **William Soul** mak[e]s their return
from the Quartorly meeting that the quartorly meeting
according to our Request: have granted us at youths ~~
meeting to be keept the first Sixt[h] day In the Second fift[h]
Eight[h] and Eleventh months which will fal[l] out the ~~
Sixt[h] day next be for Each Qurly meeting at **Rhoad Island** – –
John Tucker and **William Soul** are called upon
Consarning their makeing up the accomts with ~~~
Benjamin Howland Concarning our colection and it
not being done Its refered to the next monthely meeting
and where as their is a deferanc presented to the meeting
Concarning **Jonathan Devel [Davol]** and **John Summors [Summers]** – –
the meeting mak[e]s Choyse of **Deliverance Smith Nathanell**
Howland Eliezer Slocum and **John tucker** to hear and
determin[e] Sd Deferance and give their answer to the next
monthely meeting – –
and **Stephen Willcock** and **William Wood** are Chosen to
Spake with **James Tripp** Consarning his being over ~~
taken In drink and Bring their Answer to the next monthly=
ly meeting – –
James Buril [Burrel] Eliezer Slocum and **Benjamin Howland**
are Chosen to labour with **peleg Slocum** that he may
Joyn with friends and Sign a deed In the method that
thomas Stoary hath Sent to us and bring In their
Answer to the next monthely meeting – – – – –

At a monthely meeting of friends held at our meeting
house In **Dartmouth** the 17th of the 12th mth 176/7 [*sic*] – –
their was Colected – – – – – – – – £00 –10s –05d
Increas[e] Allin [Allen] and **Eliezar Slocum** are Chosen overseers
of the monthely meetings of Busieness that if aney should
present them selves at Sd meetings that are not members
of them then to Inquire of them their buseness and if they
cannot give a Satesfactory answer: then to Desir[e] them In love
to With Draw
William Wood and **Stephen Willcock** gives In their – ~
Answer that they have Spoken with **Jeames [James] Tripp** ~
and he is willing to condemn his being overtaken In
drink to the Satesfaction of freinds – –
and the above sd two frie[nds?] **william wood** and **Stephen
willcock** ar[e] Continued to goe with **Jeams [James] Tripp** to see that he doth
Condemn it where it was don[e] – –
and **Benjamin Howland Eliezar Slocum** and **Samuell Mott**
are Chosen to Spake with **Eliezar Smith** Consarning his report=
ing of things out of the monthely meeting the which is Incon=
sistant with truth: and Consarning his out runings upon
other acounts and bring In their answer to the next monthly
meeting – – – – –

(1707) At a monthely meeting of friends held at our meeting hous[e] In
Dartmouth the 17th of the first month 1707 – –
and their is Colected – – – – – – – £00 –09s–10d
And the Buseness Consarning **James tripp** is Referred
to the next monthly meeting – –
william Soul [Soule] and **John tucker** hath made up the accounts
with **Benjamin Howland** Concarning the monthely meet=
ings Colection and have belanced the accounts and their
Remains In Stock with what hath ben Colected at this
meeting forty two Shillings – –
And **Samuell Mott** and **Benjamin howland** are Chosen to
to Shew **Eliezer Smith** his Shortness In accusing **Elizar =
Slocum** and **William Wood** for gooing Contrary to the
monthely meetings ordor In goeing together to **Seconet [Sakonnet]**
when **Eliezer Slocom** was Chosen to goe with **Thomas** ~~
macomber thether [thither?] and make their Return to the next
monthly meeting – –

and **Stephen Willcock** [**Wilcox**] and **John Tucker** are chosen to
Attend the next Quartorly meeting – –
And **Benjamin Howland** is ordered to pay **Judah Smith**
twenty Shellings ^{out of the meeting Stock} to wards his keeping of the meeting
house
and this meeting doth order the four freinds that was Chose
to vewe [view?] the monthely meeting minits that they make
Choyse of a man to Record the meeting buseness and the
meeting to pay him for his sarvice – – – – –

At a monthely meeting of freinds held at our meeting
In **Dartmouth** the 21ˢᵗ of the Second month 1707 –––
their was Colecte[d] –   –   –   –   –   –   – £00 – 11ˢ – 00ᵈ
and where as **Stephen Willcock** and **William Wood** were
Chosen the last twelveth[?] month to goe with **James tripp**
to see that he did condemn his being overtake In drink In
the place where it was don[e] and their answer is that he
has Condemed it to the satesfaction of friends – –
And **Benjamin Howland** and **Samuell Mott** brought In
their Answer that they have laboured with **Eliezer Smith**
to Shew him his misstak [mistake] Concarning **william Wood**
and **Eliezar Slocom** According to order of the last monthly
meeting – –
and their answer is that he refuseth to hear – – – – –

At a monthely meeting of freinds held at our meeting
house In **Dartmouth** the 19ᵗʰ of the thurd month 1707 – –
and thier was Colected –   –   –   –   –   –   – £00 –09ˢ –05ᵈ
and **John Tucker Eliezar Slocum** and **Benjamin** =
Howland are Chosen to furder Labour with **Eliezar** =
Smith to come to be Reconsiled to the meeting – –
and bring In their answer to the next monthely ~~~
meeting – –
and **Benjamin Howland** is ordred to let **John Lapham Juʳ**
have twelve Shillings out of the Colection to pay
the doctor for what he did for **Debroah** [**Deborah?**]: **Landars** in
the time of her Seckness – –
and it is ordered that the first day meeting at **acoxset**]
Is to be at our meeting house for the Summer – –
And **Eliezer Slocum** and **John tucker** are Chosen
to Spake with **Rochester** friends to know the ~~

Re[a]son ~~to know the~~ why they have not attended the
monthely meeting of late – –
and Bring In their Answer to the next monthely
meeting – –
and where as the yearley meeting at **Rhoad Island**
hapneth to be on the Same day that our next month=
ly meeting Should be on their for [therefore] the S^d meeting Is
adjourned until the fourth Second day In the 4 month
next

At a monthly meeting held at our meeting house In
Dartmouth the 23th of the 4th m^th 1707 Colected -^£0 -09^s -01^d
peleg Slocumb [**Slocum**] and **William Sloule** [**Soule**] are Chosen
to attend the Quarterly meeting at **Rhoad Island**
And it's agreed that **rochestor** friends have a preparitive
meeting after their meeting of worship on the first
day of the week befor[e] the monthly meeting – –
And the freinds that was Chose for to labour with
Eliezer Smith ware Called up on and their answer
Is that he refuseth to give the meeting setesfaction for
his desorderly proseedings against the monthly meeting =
and **John tucker** is Chosen to Drawup **Eliezer Smith**
his Condemnation In order that it may be reed to him
before it be reed in publeck and **William Soule Eliezer
Slocum** and **Samuell Mott** are Chosen to Reed the Sade
Condemnation to the s^d **Eliezer Smith** and bring In their
Answer to the next monthely meeting – – – – –

At a monthely meeting of friends held at our meeting
house In **Dartmouth** the one and twenteth Day of the
fift month 1707 – this was colected –   –   –   –   –   –   – 0^£ – 08^s – 01^d
And the friends that was Chosen the last monthely
meeting to Reed **Eliezer Smith** his Condemnation
to him was Called upon and their answer is that **Eliezer
Smith** is willing to Condemn his reporting of things
out of the monthly meeting as faloweth – –
friends I have well Considied the matter of that which I
could out of the meeting to **John Aken** and I do hastily
repent for the Same and desir forgiveness both of god and
and his people that wee may come In to love and unity
as we have for: **Eliezar Smith** – –

And furder **Eliezar Smith** hath given Satesfaction to
the monthely meeting ^conserning his wronging the meeting by ~~wri~~
wrighting the which he doth Condemn as faloweth
where In I have given aney ocasion by wrighting
to the meeting to greive aney sensear hearted friend or
freinds for which I am hartely sorrey and desir for=
giveness: **Eliezar Smith**
And **Stephen Willcock Benjamin Howland** and
John Lapham Ju^r are chosen to spake with **Thomas
Macomber** Concarning his abuseing **Ruth Smith**
with words and to End s^d ^deferance it they can and bring In
their Answer to the next montheley meeting – –
and the friends that was chosen to Inspect into the con=
versation of friends was called upon and their answer
is that **Merebah Slocumb** the Daughter of **Eliezar
Slocumb** is about to marrey to one contrarey to her.
parince [parents'] consent and the advice of friends – –
where upon the meeting made choice of **James** [~~Burr~~]
Burril and **Judah Smith:** to Spake with **Meribah
Slocumb** consarning her disorderly proceedings and [to]
Bring In their Answer to the next monthly meeting
and the bounding out the buring ground is referd to the
next monthely meetig – – – – –

At a monthly meeting of friends held at our meeting house
In **Dartmouth** the 18th day of the 6th m^th 1707 –
and their was Colected –   –   –   –   –   –   – 00^£ – 06^s – 08^d
And **Isaac Barker** and **Elisebeth Slocumb** did lay their [sd?]
Intention of marrige before the meeting –
and they was Desired to Stay untel the next monthely
meeting for their Answer – –
John Tucker and **William Soule** are apoynted to Enspect
Into their Clearness and bring In their Answer to the next
monthly meeting – –
and the friends that was chosen to Spake with **Thomas -
Macumber** concerning his abusing **Ruth Smith** with
words was called upon and their Answer was that
Thomas Macumber does condemn those words which he
Spoak to **Ruth Smith** – –
and the friends that was Chosen to Spake with **Merebah**

Slocumb concarning her disoderly proseeding towards [sd]
marrige Contrary to the order of friends: being Called up =
on: give In their answer that they had ben with her and
have laboured with her according to the good order of [sd]
truth In love and much tenderness and have recieved
no Satesfactory answer from her – –
and for as much as the sᵈ **Merebah** hath preceeded [cross out]
no further at the present the matter is refered untel further
ocasion – –
and **John Tucker** and **William Soul** are Chose to bound
out the bureing yard bay the next monthly meeting –
and **Judah Smith** is paid for his keeping the meeting hous
and **John Tucker** and **Eliezer Slocumb** are chose to agree
with a friend to keep the meeting house for the Insuinɡ
year – – – – –

At a monthly meeting of friends held at our meeting hous
In **Dartmouth** the 15ᵗʰ Day of the 7ᵗʰ mᵗʰ 1707 –
their was Colected –   –   –   –   –   –   – 00£ – 08ˢ – 05ᵈ
And the two friends that was Chose to Enspect Into
the Clearness of **Isaac Barker** and **Elisebeth Slocumb**
Concarning marriage. being Called upon and they give
their answer that they find thing are not clear – –
And so the matter is refered to the next monthely meeting
that thing s may be cleared to the Satesfaction of friends – –
And **Judah Smith** hath taken the meeting house to keep
to the Insuing year and the year begun the last monthly
meeting and If it prove to harde for him then **John** =
Tucker and **Eliezar Slocumb** are to be helpfull to him in that
Service
And **Isaac Barker** desirs that this meeting would be help
full to him to Clear that mattar that hinders his proceed=
ing In marrige – –
and In order their unto the meeting made Choice of [sd?]
William Soule Nathanell Howland John Lapham Juʳ
and **Benjamin Howland** to asist him and bring In
their answer to the next monthly meeting – –
And **John Tucker Peleg Slocumb** and **Stephen Willcock**
are Chosen to Attend the Quarterly meeting at **Rohad**=
Island next – –

And the matter concarning chusing of two friends for
to Spake to people to come orderly In to meeting as ~~so~~
soon as Convenianbly they can after th^ey come to the [sd?]
meeting house and not to stand talking and Spending
away their time with out doors as the maner of some
hath ben to their own hurt and to the truble of freinds
Is rfered to the next monthly meeting – – – – –

At a monthly meeting of friends held at our meeting
house In **Dartmouth** the 21th day of the 8th m^th 1707
their was Colected –   –   –   –   –   –   – 00^£ – 10^s – 00^d
And the four friends that was Chose the last
monthly meeting for to be helpfull to **Isaac Barker**
Concarning what did hender him from haveing his
Answer relating to marrige at the last monthly [sd?]
meeting give In their Answer that the matter y[?]
Ended and truth Cleared – –
And **Isaac Barker** and **Elisebeth Slocumb** came be=
for this meeting desiering an answer to their former
Intentions of marrige Signifieing they was Still of
the Same mind – –
and things being clear they had their answer that
they might take Each other in the order of truth – –
William Soule and **Benjamin Howland** are Chose
to See **Isaac Barker** and **Elisebeth Slocumb** Solomnize
their marrige in the good order of truth – –
And **John Lapham** and **John tucker** are Chose to Spake to
friends and people that frequent our meetings that they
Come In to meeting and not to hold discorses without In the
time of meeting – – – – –

At a monthly meeting of friends held at our meeting house
In **Dartmouth** the 17th day of the 9th m^th 1707 –
their was colected –   –   –   –   –   –   – 00^£ – 12^s –00^d
Benjamin Howland and **William Soul** was called up=
on to give In their answer whether **Isaac Barker** and [unknown symbol?]
Elizebeth Slocumb hath Solominized their marrige In
the order of truth – –
And they answer that thay se their marrige acomplished
according to order – –
And it is agreed that friends at **Cokset** shall have their

meeting on the first days amongst themselves all Except
the first day before the monthly meeting – –
and then they are ordered to com to the meeting here[?]
And it is agreed that freinds should have a Subscription
of four pounds which was proportioned on our meeting
by the qw⁻ᵗ meeting towards the acomplishing the charge
of friends meeting house In **Boston**: and if the subscrip=
tion doth not amount to the above sd four pounds then
the sume is to be made up out of the monthly meeting
Stock – –
and their is subscribed this day –   –   –   –   –   –   – 02$^£$ – 16^s – 00^d
pᵉ**leg Slocumb Stephen Willcock** and **John tucker**
are Chosen to goe to **Rochester** to be helpfull to friends
their and to Instruct them In the order of truth by reeding[?]
the orders their of unto them or otherwise as need may require – – .
And **John Tucker** is Chose to see the money colected
for **boston** meeting house transported to **Sandwich**
Quarterly meeting – – – – –

---

at a monthly meeting of friends held at our meeting house
In **Dartmouth** the 15ᵗʰ day of the 10ᵗʰ <u>mth</u> 1707 – –
their was Colected –   –   –   –   –   –   – 00$^£$ – 07^s – 00^d
peleg Slocumb Stephen Willcock and **John tucker** was
Calle upon to give in their account whether they had ben
At **Rochester** according to Apoyntment of the last month
ly meeting and they answer that they have be their: and they
find things not well their amongst friends for which [~?]
ocasion the meeting doth stil continue the Same three [~?]
friends and aded unto them **Benjamin Howland Eliezar**
Slocumb and **Increase Allin** to furder labour with them
to shew them their shortness In not attending the monthly meeting and not obsarving the order therof – –
And **John thicker** and **Judah Smith** ar appoynted to
Drawout the queries and minits of the yearly meeting
that are sutable to be reed amongst the youth – –
And the meeting is adjourned untel the next fourth
day com two weeks – – – – –

---

the meeting being meet according to adjournment -
the 31ᵗʰ day of the 10ᵗʰ <u>mᵗʰ</u> 1707 –
And the money Colected the last monthly meeting

was accoring to order Delivered to **Sandwich** Qu^{rt}
meeting In order to be sent to **Edward Shippey** –
and the friends that was Chose to goe to **rochester**
report that they hav ben their and friends their have
given some Satesfaction and Signefie that they shall
Indevor to be mor deligent to attend the monthely ~
meetings for the time to come[12]– –
Some deferanc presented to this meeting between **John**
tucker and **thomas macumber** –
Nathaneel Howland and **Eliezer Slocumb** are chose
to hear s^d Deferance and labour to reconsile the matar
if they can. and make report to the next monthly
meeting how they find things – –
John tucker and **peleg Slocumb** are chosen to
attend the Qu-^{t} meeting next – – – – –

At a monthly meeting of friends held at our meeting
house In **Dartmouth** the 19th day of the 11th m^{oh} 1707
their was Colected –   –   –   –   –   –   – 00$^£$– 08^s – 10^d
And the friends that was chosen the last monthely
meeting to see to make up the Deferance between
John tucker and **thomas Macumber** and they report
that s^d **macumber** is to blame and refuseth to make
Satesfaction: and It is agreed by this meeting that **tho=**
Macumber shall pay the twelve Shillings demand^{dc}
And make Satesfaction for his Contrediction about It – –
and the Same freinds are continued and **John Lapham**
is added unto them to tel him the meetings Judgment – –
and this meeting doth thinks it best to further labour with
hannah Jeney concarning her appearing In publick asembelys
In prayer and her Disorederly ^{singing} and preaching out of the unot^y
of friends – –
John tucker and **Eliezer Slocumb** are Chosen to labour
with her and make their return to the next monthely
meeting – – – – –

At a monthely meeting of friends held at our meeting house
In **Dartmouth** the 16th of the 12th mth 1707 – –
their was colected –   –   –   –   –   – 00$^£$ – 09^s – 06^d

---

12. Rochester Friends were erratic in their participation in the affairs of Dartmouth Monthly Meeting. The reasons are unclear. See Carol Hagglund, "Disowned Without Just Cause: Quakers in Rochester, Massachusetts, during the Eighteenth Century" (Ph.D. diss., University of Massachusetts, 1980), 132–37.

the two freinds that was chosen the last monthely
meeting to Spake to **hannah Jeney** give In their answer
that they have ben with her and She Desirs time of con=
sidration untel the monthly meeting befor the Qur^ly
meeting next wi^hch is granted – –
And this meeting orders **Benjamin Howland** to make up
what the wemen have colected twenty shillings which
is 4 shillings and 6 pence and pay **Judah Smith** for his keeping
the charge of the meeing house half a year – –
And this meeting agrees to the Quarterly meeting minits
to Chuse Visetors to goe with the over seers to viset the
famelyes of friends once In the quartor – –
Increas Allin John tucker peleg Slocumb and **william
wood** are chosen over seers and **Stephen Willcock** and
Eliezar Slocumb are Chosen visetors for **Dartmouth**
meeting and **Savery Cleffton** for **Rochester** meeting

(1708) At a monthly meeting of friends held at our meeting
house In **Dartmouth** the 15th of the first month 1708
their was Colected –　–　–　–　–　–　– 00^£ – 08^s – 11^d
Dartmouth meeting Called **Judah Smith** and **benjam^in
Howland** Appeared: ^Ro^**chester** meeting called and not
Appeared – –
And the friends that was Chosen to furder labour ~~
with **thomas macumber** gives In their acount that
he refuseth to make aney Satesfaction and the meeting
being Clear as to furder Dealings with s^d **Macumber**
do Appoynt **Eliezar Slocumb** and **Nathaneel Howland**
to draw up his Condemnation – –
and the friends that was to Spake with **hannah J^eney**
hath ben with her and she refars her self to the ~~
Qu^rt meeting of ministors – –
And the meeting adviseth that freinds go forwards and
finesh their subscription to wards the fencing In the burring
ground by the latter End of the forth month next – –
And It is all so advised that all freinds bring In the berths
and Deaths of their Children as Soon as Conveniantly they
can: to be recorded – –
And the meeting is adjourned unte the first six day In
the next month – –
And the meeting being meet according to adjournment

Elizer Slocumb and **Nathaneel Howland** gives In their
acount that they have drawnup **thomas macumber**s ~~
Condemnation according to order w^hich was perused and
signed by this meeting – –
And **William Wood** and **William Soule** are Chosen ~~
to Reed it to him and if he stil refuseth to make Sates
faction then to reed his Condemnatisn In publick
the next first day befor the monthly meeting after
the time of worship is over – –
John tucker and **peleg Slocumb** are Chosen to attend
the Qu^rt meeting next – – – – –

At amonthely meeting of friends held at our meeing
house In **Dartmouth** the 19th day of the Second m^th 1708
their was Colected – – – – – – – 00 – 12 – 02
Dartmouth meeting Called **Judah Smith** and **Benjamin
Howland** appeared **Rochestor** Called **John Summers** appeared – –
Thomas Macumbers Condemnation was Reed as faloweth – –
Where as **Thomas Macumber** of **Dartmouth** In the
County of Bristol In **New England** – –
haveing for some years freequented the meetings of us
the people In Scorn Called Quakers: and Semed to Joyne
In Sosiaty with us. but for want of keeping In true sub
Jection to that princaple he made profesion of to wit
the sperit of truth In his own heart wich sperit will
Lead all them that are obediant to it out of Everey thing
that is Contrarey ^to the nature of It and Inconsestant with
It. he hath given way to this covetious mind and hath
Denied to pay his Debt: but hath denyed that it is dew though
It is proved dew by soficant Evedance: and allso the s^d ~~
thomas macumber hath ben found contradicting him=
self for to Excuse himself at one time saying they could
not make up the acomts and another time said that
he had money of his owne implyeing that he had no
need to be In ~~De~~debted but for four shillings and six pence:
And notwithstanding at that time It is proved that he
was asked if he had aney money and he Answered no
w^hich he hath allso denyed and the s^d **thomas macum**^ber
at another time said the accounts was but nin shillings
Between them. but for want of keepeing In Subje=
ction to that Devine principle of truth In his owne

heart and not harkening to the Counsell and advice of
his freinds who laboured with him to Reclame him from
those Evils he was found In; But in a willfull stredron ~
temper he slited their advice allthoug given him In – –
done from time to time there for is theis given forth to
clear the blesed truth and us the people of god called
Qakers of all such Disorderly Walkers -&- wee are constrained
And doe give this as a testimony against him the s^d **tho=**
macumber and he is Denyed by us untel he repent
And Amend which wee Earnestly Desier for his souls
sak given forth by our monthly meeing held by ~~
Adjournment In **Dartmouth** within the County above s^d
the second day of the second month 1708 – –
signed In behalf of said meeing by

Eliezar Slocumb	**peleg Slocumb**
Benjamin Howland	**James Burriell**
Stephen Willcock	**Nathanel Howland**
John Lapham	**William Wood**
John Tucker	**John Lapham Jur**
William Soule	**Eliezar Smith**
Judah Smith	

And **peleg Slocumb** and **John tucker** gives In their
Account that they have attended the Qa^r meeting ac=
cording to order – –
Some Deferance between **peleg Slocumb** and **Eliezar**
Slocumb and Some persons were appoynted to hear ~~and~~
the Said Deferance which they did. but **peleg** refuseth
to stand to their Determination or to refer him self furder
where upon **Increas Allin** and **Abraham tucker**
was: Chosen to labour further with him and tel him
that he must Either Stand to the Judgement allredey
given or refer himself to the monthly meeting – –
and bring in their answer to the nex monthely ~
meeting – –
and the Qu^{rt} meeting made choise of **peleg Slocumb**
and **John tucker** to Attend the yearly meeting

At a monthely meeting of friends held at our
meeing house In **Dartmouth** the 17th day of the 3rd mth 1708
Their was Collected –   –   –   –   –   –   – £ – 10[?] – 02
Dartmouth Weekley meting Called **Judah Smith**

And **Benjamin Howland** appeared **Rochester** Called
Isaac Vinson appeared – –
Abraham Tucker and ~~Eliezar Slocumb~~ **Increas Allin** [**Allen**] brought
In their Answer to this meeting wich is that **peleg**
Slocum and his brother **Eliezar** is agreed as to that
part depending between them: but for as much ^{pelege} as
and **Eliezar** and **William Soule** did Invest one ~
arbetratory power: In **John tucker** and Some others
to hear and Determin S^d Deferance wich depended
and they the S^d **John tucker** and others. having ~
Agred:: **but pelege** refusing to Stand to their awarde
Did unadvisedly proceed In bringing S^d Deferance to
the town meeting over the heads of the arbetraters
and with out the C^onsent of this meeting the which
Is Estemed Disorder: and **Peleg** not willing to be con=
vinced of the disorderlyness their of: nor willing
to come under the Judgment of the meeting for
the same: but like to Intertain hard thoughts, of the ~~
meeting. thinking they do Asume aperogative beyond
what (y) nesesery, therfor this meeting and **peleg**
doth agree to Chnge the falowings friends to hear the
whol matter: and If they see cause to make aney ~
alteration In the former arbetration by **John tucker**
and partners: they may: but if not then that It shall
stand as agreed by them the s^d arbetrators: and allso
that the falowing persons: doe determin what Satesfact=
ion: **peleg** ought to give to this meeing for his disord=
erly proseedings over the head of the meeting: and
that If **William Soule** and **Eliezar Slocumb** has con
sented that **Peleg** Should proseed as he has don then
that they shall allso give Satesfactio to y^e meeting for
their so doing: but and if S^d persons here after none
noted think that the meeing or [those?] other frds
have Inqured ye s^d ~~persons~~ **Peleg** then Regulate and
determin In that allso:
the persons nominated to determin betwext the ~
above s^d persons: are
Joseph Wanton: **William Barker**: and **Thomas Corn**^{well}
Willm Anthony and **Abraham Anthoney Juner** or
aney two of the later three: or the major part of them

to meet with **Peleg Slocumb** and the arbetrators:
at the house of **Pelege Slocumb** next six day In the morning
and this meeting doth agree that the first day ~~~
meeting at **Coxset** shall be at the meeting house for
this Summer as formerly – –
**Stephen Willcock: Benjamin Howland: John
Tucker: William Soule:** and **Judah Smith** or aney
one of the last two are Chosen to peruse the mon=
thly meetings minits In order that what is ~~
neseserey may be recorded – –
Stephen Willcock and **William Wood** are appoynted
to procure two hands to ~~mana~~ goe with friends
to **Nantucket** to mannege the boat: and the month
ly meeting to pay them for their service – – – – –

At a monthly meeting of freinds held at our meeting
house In **Dartmouth** the twenty first day of the 4 mth 1708
their was Colected –   –   –   –   –   –   – 00$^£$ – 07^s – 00^d [?]
Stephen Willcock and **William Wood** are called up
one to give In their account concarning the twoo: ~~men~~
men that they procured to goe with friends: to ~
Nantucket: and their answer was that they have had
no account foram the meen as yet: so they are desiared
to do It against the next monthly meeting – –
And **Benjamin Howland** and **Abraham tucker** are
Chose to Spake with **Peleg Slocumb** to know w^{h}ether
he will give the meeting another deed of the meeting
hous Land: after another form: and **Abraham Cha^{se}**
is desired to asest them: and bring In their answer
to the next monthelly meeting:
And this meeting Agrees that the fourth days meeting
that happeneth In the week: that the youths meeting
is In: is omited: that the youths meeting maye be
the more fully attended – –
And the friends that was appoynted: the last monthly
meeting: to hear and Determin the Deferance: betw^{en}
Peleg Slocumb and his brother **Eliezar** and **William
Soule:** and allso to hear and Determin the Deferanc^e
Btween s^d **Pelege** and the meeting: give In their ~
Answer to this meeting which is as foloweth – –
persuant ^{to} the Agreement of last monthly meeting: held

at **Dartmouth** the 7ᵗʰ of the 3ᵐᵒ 1708 – –
Wee: **Joseph Wanton thomas Cornell William Barker**
and **Abraham Anthoney Juner** Being asested by **Patrck**
Henderson: Did apear at **Peleg Slocumb**s house: where wee
meet with **Peleg Slocumb Eliezar Slocumb** and **William Soule**:
Who did first authoriz: the following Arbetrators (viz)
John tucker Benjamin Howland William Wood and
Judah Smith woʰm allso wee have hade present: with
us: and after large conferance with them yᵉ sᵈ **Peleg** and
Eliezer Slocumb and **William Soule** and: **John tucker** and
the rest of the Arbetrators: they and Everey of them
mutaly agreeing and Declaring befor us that they and
Everey of them shall and will stand to: and In Everey
parte preform fullfill and keep: wat shall by us be agreed
upon in Every Respect as Shall be here after: declared
under our hands: – –
And for as much as on Principall parte of the difference – ~
depending is betwext **Peleg Slocumb** and his Brother **Elazer**
Slocumb both of the **town of Darmouth** and **County of**
Bristol In **New England**: It is mutualy Agreed betwext ~~
them that they and Everey of them yᵉ sᵈ **Peleg** and **Eliezar**
Slocumb: Shall and will from time to time: them their
heirs Exceutors administorators and asigns: preform full=
fill and keep: all and Every part: of the agreement: ~
which by us the Sᵈ **Joseph Wanton** and partners shall be
hear after Declared under our hands: and if they the sᵈ ~
Peleg and **Eliezar**: or Either of them their heirs or asigns:
shall at aney time after the decˡaration of our agreement
made and done betwext them and on be half of them their
heirs and asigns: they or aney of them desenting from or
refusing: to stand to what shall be Determined: and Declared
betwext them: then such and Every of them see Desenting
to forfitt the Sume of one hundred pounds: to be paid ~~t~~o
the Determination heare after declared Respecting
this mattar, to all which the sᵈ **Peleg** and **Elizar** doth
Agree: for them selves their heirs: and asigns: to Stand
to Establesh for Ever: Except they or their asigns: mut=
ualy agree to have and hould other wife, and as ~~
further confermation their of has her unto Interchang:
ably yet their hands and seals this 21 day ³mo 1708

witneses present
Stephen Willcock   **Peleg Slocumb•**
Issac Barker   **Elizar E**h25**. Slocumb•**
                                                               mark

And for as much as **William Soule** of the **town of** ~
Dartmouth and the **Cunty of Bristol** In **New England** Is
one princip^{e}ly concerned In the mater depending to
be Determined by us the S^d **Joseph Wanton** and partners
It is therfor Agreed that the S^d **Will**m **Soule** his heirs ~
Exceutors and administorators and asigns Shall be bound
under the penalty of one hundred pounds: to stand: to
fullfill and keep: the agreements award and Determi=
nation   him onehis part wich shall be herafter
Declared under our hands: and the S^d Sume of one
hundred pounds: to be payed by him his heirs or asigns
to Such persons: Legaly serving for the Same: for – –
Just Dameges done to them through the nonprefor=
mance of him the S^d **Will**m **Soule**: his heirs Executors
or asigns to which the S^d **Wll**m **Soule**: doth Covenan^t
and Agree: and as a further Confarmation hereof
has here unto Set his hand and Seal this 21 first
day of the third month 1708 – –
witneses presents
                                                      William Soule •

Stephen Willcock
Isaac Barker

to all people to whome these presents $_\wedge$^{may} come know
ye that where as there has ben some differance ocasion[-]
ed through unadvised management: depending for
some time betwixt **Peleg Slocumb Elizar Slocumb** and
William Soule where upon they did make choice ~~of~~
to be heard and determined their in [therein] by **John Tucker,**
Benjamin Howland Judah Smith and **William**
Wood: and accordingly they the sd **John Tucker** and
partners heard and awarded: but **Peleg** to forwardly
desenting from their agreement: for some slender ~
Reasons not necessary not here to mention: and ~
the sd mater being Reported to the monthly meeting:
and being under their consideration: did at last month=

ly meeting held at **Dartmouth** ye **17**th **3 month 1708** – –
Apoynt that wee the sd **Joseph Wanton** and partners
should over hale the sd mater here and determin the
sd differance: – –
And now by virtue of the power invested in us not
only by the monthly meeting but allso: by theece [these]
Persons Emeadietly concarned: Wee doe awarde and
determin for them their heirs and administ– –
rators and assigns that their shall be a drift way: ~
with gatts [gates] suficent throug **Elizer Slocumb**s Land.
Accordind as it was laid out by the town: In bredth
About: Eight Rods: leading down to the End of the ~
Beach and so to the landing place: and to contenew [continue]
for the uss [use] of ₍such₎ who has or may at aney [any] time here=
after have ocation [occasion] to ride leade ₍cart₎ or drive aney or all=
sorts of creturs [creatures] such as aney people shall have ocas=
ion ride lead cart or drive as aforsd [aforesaid] – –
And that there be an open high way from the sd ~
Eliezar Slocumbs land through **Pelege Slocumb**s ~
Land and thence to the **Souls** land and from thence
to **Ebenezer Allin**s [**Allen**] land until it comes to **Josiah Allin**s [**Allen**]
land and then betwixt **Josiah Allin**s [**Allen**] land and the sd
Souls land and sea until it enters the comon [common] or undivided
land: and that the sd high way shall all along be alowed [allowed]
at least two Rods in width   provided that where it joyns
upon the sd **Allin**s [**Allen**] land: the sd two Rode [sic] in width: shall
be taken out of the sd **Souls** land: and allso what part
of sd high way leads throug **Peleg Slocumb**s land: shall
be suficently fenced and so maintained: by them their heirs
and assigns for Ever-: that is to say one Equale half there
of to be fenced and maintained by **Peleg** and his heirs and
assigns: and the other half by **Eliezar** and his heirs and
assigns – –
It is allso agreed that their shall be a drift way thro
ugh the sd **Souls** land ~~and~~ with gatts [gates]: and as wide as
may be ajudged nesesery by the town or select men ~
for all sorts of gathers to pass and repass: whether
rideing leadind cart and or driving &c – –
and for as much as formerly their was a comon
high way laid out throug **Peleg Slocumb**s land ~

where his now dwelling house stands which can't
be altered but by the town agreement, if now the town
see cause to disannul: and shut or cause to be shut up:
and noe more ocopyd as such the sd high way leading by his house then and under that consideration
their shall be a drift way leading through his land
lying on the other side of or from his house: in the
place where he shewed **John Tucker** of and some ~
others: with gatts [gates] and of a conveniant breth: beseting[?]
to ride leade cart or drive aney or all sorts of cattle or – –
creturs: passing and repassing as they may have ocasion
and it is furder agreed that if at aney time hereafter
the town should se [see] cause to Re Establish and cause to
be opened and occopyed the sd high way or if aney person
or persons should at any time here after [*illegible*] the
opning and occopying of sd high way by law sute [suit]
or other wise then and under that consideration
Shall be lawfull for the S^d **Peleg Slocumb Slocumb**
to shut up: and occopy the S^d drift way as he his heirs
or asigns Shall see Cause – –
Thus wee though good to awarde and determin
accordind to the best of our understanding given
under our hands: In **Peleg Slocumb**s house
the 21 day of the 3mo 1708 – –
before It is absolutely delivered by us **Joseph Wanton**

Wee doe further ag^{r}re that the	**thomas Cornell**
drift way leading th^{r}ough the	**William Barker**
Souls land shall not Exceed	**Abraham Anthoney J**^{ur}

In width above four Rods
and allso that the drift
way leading throug **Pelege**
Slocumbs home lot shall
not Exceed four Rods In width
wee do allso agree that all these proceedings by us In
these affairs should be Carfully Recorded In the
monthely meeting Book: and yet notwith=
standing that these same being y^e oregenall: Shall
be carfully pined and preserved In the S^d monthley
meeting Book

Pursuant to the minut of last monthely meeting

Espeacly that part depending betweext **Peleg Slocumb**
and friends: wee do think that **Pelegs** proceedings: under
Several Considerations has been not so orderly and becom=
=ing as it ought to be: and In perticular his Refusing to
Stand to the awarde of **John tucker** and partners In the
mater depending beetwext him his brother and **William
Soule**: and allso: In his absenting from the monthely meet=
=ing when he knew that the S^d mater would be – –
Agetated In the meeting: and allso his unadvised way
of presenting s^d mater to the town meeting: all which
we. doe disaprove and plaC Judgment upon: and under ar
Consideration: of these things wee have delt with **Pelege**:
And he Segnefys to us that he is Sorey for Such mis=
steps: and wee considring that throw the thickness
of his hearing: he did not so rightly a^prehend nor un=
derstand the mater In Its proceedings: the which
the which might have laid him under several
Disadvanteges: there fore wee desier and think It most
Expediant under Several Considrating Espeacely seeing
that he has: Come to an acknowledgment to us:
therfor It is our Sence and Judgment that from
hence forth the Church be noe further trobled with
S^d mater: but that **Pelege** and freinds doe live In love
And Unity as be cometh Bretheren – –

given under our hand   **Joseph Wanton**
this 21: of the third month <u>1708</u>   **Thomas Cornell**
                                      William Barker
                                      Abraham Anthony Ju^r

And the meeting Is adjourned untel the next fourth
day Come two weeks – – – – –

the meeting being meet according to adjournment
the 7th day of the 5th month <u>1708</u>
Stephen Willcock and **Benjamin Howland** was
Appoynted for to atend the Quarterly meeting at
Rhoad Island next

At a monthely meeting of friends held at our <u>1708</u>
meeting house In **Dartmouth** the 15th of the: 5th <u>mo</u>
And their was Colected –   –   –   –   –   –   – 0^£ – 09^s – 03^d
And this meeting orders **Benjamin Howland** to pay
out of our Stock to **Thomas Hathaway** Eight Shillings

for the hier of horses for friends – –

And six shillings to **Daniel Wood** for goeing to **Nantucket**
with friends – –

And **Stephen Willcock Samuell Mott** and **Benjamin
Howland** are appoynted to give **William Ricketson** and
Merebah Slocumb their answer Consarning their
laying their Intentions of marriage befor the monthely meeting
and make their return to the next monthly meeting – –

And the freinds that was Chosen the last monthely
meeting: for to Speak with **Peleg Slocumb** for to know
whether he would give another deed of the meeting
house Land after another method and they Report
that S^d **Slocumb** is not willing – –

Where upon the meeting made choyce of **Benjamin =
Howland Eliezer Slocumb William Wood Judah =
Smith** and **Samell Mott** for trustees to have a deed made
to them from the former trustees In the method that
Thomas Story Sent to us for the better securing the
S^d land – –

and **Benjamin Howland** is Chosen to get a deed Drawn
by the next monthly meeting – –

And freinds are desired to finesh the fenceing the
bureing ground by the next monthly meeting – – – – –

At a monthly meeting of friends held at our meeting
house In **Dartmouth** the 16th of the 6th mo^th 1708 – –
their was Colected –   –   –   –   –   –   – 0^£ – 12^s – 03^d

And the three freinds that was Chosen the last
monthly meeting for to give **William Ricketson**
And **Meribah Slocumb** the Reason why they
could not be prmetted to lay their Intention of
marriage: before the laast monthely meeting: and
they make report: to this meeting: that the s^d ~
William Ricketson and **Merebah Slocumb**: are
willing to take up with the good order of the meet=
ing: and to come through the same– –

And the Eight Shillings which **Benjamin Howland**
was ordered to pay to **Thomas Hathaway** the
last monthly meeting was paid according to order – –

And allso the six Shillings was: paid to **Daniel Wood**:
as ordered – –

And **George Thomas** of **portsmouth** on **Rhoad Island**

And **Martha Tucker** of **Dartmouth** laid their Inten=
tions marriage before this meeting – –
allso **Samuell Howland** of **freetown** and **marcy**
Merehew of **Dartmouth** did laye their Intention
of marriage befor this meeting – –
And **William Ricketson** and **Marebah Slocumb**
both of **Dartmouth** did likewise lay their Intention
of marriage be fore S^d meeting – –
Stephen Willcock and **Benjamin Howland** are
Chosen to Inspect and Inquire Into: all: their Clear=
ness Consarning marriage: and to bring In their ~
Answer to the next: monthely meeting – –
And It is agreed and ordered by this monthly meeting
that all freinds that have or hereafter may have ~~
ocasion to lay their Intentions of marrige before the
monthly meeting that they or some freind on their behalf
Shall Aquaint the preparitive meeing their with
before they present It to the monthly meeting – –
And **John Tucker** and **Eliezar Slocumb** are Chosen
to agree with a friend for to keep the meeting ~~
house for the Insuing year – –
and to see that the friend that keept the meeting
house the last year be paid for his sarvice – –
And **Benjamin Howland** hath goten a deed drawn
according to order and It is aproved of by this meeting – –
And ordered to be signed and Acknowleged and ~~
And Recorded –
And **John Tucker** is appoynted to get the same Accomplished – – – – –

At a monthly meeting of friends held at our meeting
house In **Dartmouth** the 20th day of the 7th moth 1708
their was Colected –   –   –   –   –   –   – £0 – s06 – 11^d
and **John Sumers** apered for **rochester** meeting –
And the two friends are Called upon namely ~~
Stephen Willcock and **Benjamin Howland** to
give In their answer how they find things consarning
the Clearness of the six friends that Did lay their
Intentions of marriage before the last monthly meeting: – –
and they report that they have made ~~req~~ Inquierey
And they find nothing that my Justely hinder
their Intentions – –

and the six friends: to wit: **Samuell Howland** and ~
Marcy Merehow: and **William Recketson** and ~
Merebah Slocumb: and **George Thomas** and **Martha
Tucker** all appeared the Second time desiring an ~~
Answer they all signefying that they still Intended marriag
and nothing appearing to hinder their Intentions they
all had ther answers that they might proceed to
take Each other In the good order of truth – –
and **Benjamin Howland** and **John Lapham** are chosen
to See **Samuell Howland** and **Marcy Merehow** ~~Solomnize
their marriage In the order of truth: and **John Tucker**:
and **William Wood** are Chosen to See **George Thomas** and
Martha Tucker: acomplish their mariage In the good:
order of truth – –
and **Increas Allin** [**Allen**] and **William Soule** are Chosen to
See **William Recketson** and **Merebah Slocumb**
Solomnize their marriage In the order of truth – –
and **Stephen Willcock** and **Eliezar Slocumb** are Chosen
to attend the Quartorly meeting at **Rhoad Island** next – –
And this monthely meeting refers the buseness Consarning
the Rate which is required of this town by the Jenerel
Court or: Assembley at **boston**: part of which rate is
soposed to be for the: mantainance: of ahierling ~~
priest: to the Quartorly at **Rhoad Island** next – –
for their Advice – –
and **John Tucker**: is appoynted to goe to **Boston** ~~to~~
to carrey a petition on the behalf of friends to the
Goveᴿnor and Counsel to desier them to omet the make
-ing and gathering: that part of sᵈ rate: wich is soposed
for a priest: the which part friends canot be active In
Either makeing or paying the Same It being contrarey
to that princaple of truth which wee mak ~~
profesion of – –
here faloweth the coppeys of **Samuell Howland** of **free
Town** In the **County of Bristol** and **George Thomas**
of **Portsmouth** on **Rhoad Island** their Setificates Con=
Sarning marriage – –
to our freinds and Brethren In **Dartmouth** or Else where ~~
whom It may Consarn: where as **Samuell Howland** of **free
Town** being withIn yᵉ Sircuit of our monthly meeting: haveing

a desire to marrey amongst friends: sometime past did Request
or desier A Sitificate of our s^d meeting of his Clearness relateing
Marriage: of which weehave thus Considred and have
proceeded according to the good order of truth: and find
nothing to obiect or hender: his s^d proceedings their in: wee
kept [?] your freinds and Brothers in: of this our monthly meeting
held at **new port** on **Rhoad Island** this 7th of the 7th mo^th 1708
Signed In the behalf of s^d meeting:
by **John bourden [Borden]**: Thomas Rodman: Frances Brayton
Joseph Wanton: William Anthony: Richard Borden:
William – Barker: Samuell hicks: Samuell thurston:
Joseph Anthony Ju^r: Samuell Easton: Thomas hicks:
John h^ewlet Thomas Cornell Ju^r – –
the coppey of **George Thomas**: his Certificate here
faloweth

from our monthly meeting held at **N**ewport on **Rhoad**=
Island the 7th of the 7th mo^th 1708 – –
to our friends and Brethren at **Dartmouth** is the
Salutation of our love to you all: In the unity: and ~~
felloship: of the Spirit: of truth – –
these are to sertifi you that our friend **Georg Thomas**
Did desier: of our last monthly meeting A Certificate of his
life and Conversation and Clearness Rlating marriage which
S^d meeting according to the good order of truth Established A
Amongst us: did appoynt two friends: to Inquier In to:
And they make Report unto: this meeting: that they have
Inquired and find nothing; but that he hath ben: of: a
good conversation: and is In unity with us and is allso
Clear from aney person Relating: Marrige: Excepting
Martha Tucker: so far as wee know: whose groth and
prosperety wee: sencearly Desier may be continued to the
End: In the blessed truth:
Signed by order and on behalf of this meeting: by

Jacob Mott: **John Borden**:   **Jacob Mott Junr**:
Thomas Rodman: **Gilse Slocum**:   **gidian freebourn**:
Joseph Wanton: **William Anthony**:   **William Barker**
Frances Brayton: **John Coggeshall**:   **Thomas Cornell** ^Ju
John Hewlet: **John Stanton Ju^r**:   **Richard Bourder**
Samuell Hicks: **Thomas Hicks**:   **Ephraim Hicks**:
Samuell Thurston   **Josep Anthoney Ju**:   **Samuel Easton**

and the meeting is adjourned untell the fourth ^{day} be for the
Quartorly meeting next –
the meeting being meet; according to Adjournment
the 6th day of the 8th moth 1708 – –
the visitors: Brings In their accounts of their visits
to this meeting: that they find freinds Caind[?] and do
take their: labour of love In visiting them Cain^coly[?]

---

the monthly meeting that Should have ben held the
In the 8th month is held by adjournment the first day
of the 9th moth 1708 – –
And their was Colected –   –   –   –   –   –   – £00 – 11^s – 03^d
And the friends that was Chosen the last monthly
meeting: to see the marriages Solomnized In the
good Order of truth: – –
was Called upon: and they answered that they did:
see the marriages Acomplished In the good Order
of truth – –
And **John Tucker** hath ben at **boston** with a petition
to the governor and Counsel: as apoynted:
but he could not get an Answer as yet: whether: the
will Omet the Sixty pounds that is soposed for the
ministers rate: or not[13] – –
and **John tucker** signifies to this meeting that
he is not willing to receive aney money for his
Service: In going to **boston** to the governor and Counsel
on the be half of freinds and others – – – – –

At a monthly meeting of freinds held at our meeting
house In **Dartmouth** the 15th day of the 9th moth 1708 -
their was colected –   –   –   –   –   –   – £00 – 09^s – 10^d
Dartmouth meeting called: **Benjamin Howland**
and **Judah Smith** appeared – –
Rochester meeting Called and not appeared – –
and the two friends that was appoynted at the
last preparitive meeting: for to Inquier of **Jonathan
Ricketson**: Consarning: his laying the Intention of
his marriage: before this meeting – –

13. In November 1706 the Massachusetts General Court passed a law granting it the right to appoint a Congregational minister for all towns lacking one and impose rates for his pay. Dartmouth's magistrates refused to obey and were jailed. Governor Joseph Dudley, who was sympathetic to Quakers, ordered their release. See Alison Gilbert Olson, Making the Empire Work: London and American Interest Groups, 1690-1790 (Cambridge: Harvard University Press, 1992), 85-86.

And they haveing Spoken with him doe make report
to this meeting: that h sayeth that he doth not Intend
to lay his Intention of marriage be for the monthly
meeting: but saith the he thinks it no sin to be
married other wise – –
and **John Tucker John Lapham Ju**r: and **Judah Smith**
are Appoynted to furder labour with him: his short=
ness: and bring In their answer to the next monthly meeting – –
And the friends: on the other sid **Coxeset: river** desier that
they may have: their meeting for the winter seson as formerly – –
which is granted – –
and the bureing ground being fenced In: their remains
dew to **John Lapham Ju**r: six Shillings: and **Benjamin
Howland** is ordered to pay him out of the monthely
meeting Stock – – – – –

At a monthly meeting: of friend held at our meeing:
house: In **Dartmouth**: the 20th day of the 10th moth 1708 -
their was colected –   –   –   –   –   –   – 00£ – 01s- 01d
Dartmouth meeting Called **William Soule** and
Judah Smith appeared – –
Rochester meeting Called and none apeared – –
and the friends that was appoynted the last monthly
meeting to furder labour: with **Jonathan Ricketson** ~~
to shew him his: Shortness: In not being willing to ~~
lay the Intentions of his marriege: be fore the meeting:
they make report to this meeting that his answer is that
he sees no harme In marriing acording to the Costome
of the world: – –
and Saith that at present he doth not In tend to be
married In the order of friends – –
And **John Lapham Ju**r and William Wood are Chose to atend the quarter=
ly meeting at **Rhoad Island** next – –
and **Benjamin Howland** is ordered to pay **Judah Smith**
ten Shillings out of the Stock for his keeping the meeting
house one quarter of a year14 – –
and **Benjamin Howland** is allso ordered to pay **John Tucker**
nine Shillings and six pence for his Desburstements about
the recording the deeds of the meeting house land – –
and our friend **Deliverance Smith** being one of the Select

14. The stock was the meeting treasury.

men or asesors of the town: was seized by **Samuell**
Gallop – Sheirif of **Bristol** [Bristol County, Mass.]: by an order of the Jeneral
Court at **Boston**: and Comeeted prisoner to the County
Goal at **Bristol**:
Becaus he could not for Conscians Sake assese the
Sume of Sixty pounds Enaxed to the Queens taxe ~~
which Sume was soposed as afore mentioned and now
It is Evident: to be for the mantanince of a hierling ~~
minestor:
and friends haveing unity with him in his ~~
Suffererings – –
doe appoynt **Benjamin Howland** and **Judah Smith**
to procur a hand to manneg the S^d **Deliveranc Smith**s
buseness whilst he is a prisonar on the account of
truth and friends – –
and Ingage him his wages: and the monthly meeting
to reImbrerst the same:
and the meeting is adjourned untel the Seventh
day of the Eleventh month next – – – – –

And the meeting being mett according to adjourn=
ment the 7th of the 11th mo^th 1708
the visetors Being Called [?] gives In their ~~
accounts to this meeting of their viseting of freinds
familyes and they make reporte that they find things
prety well In Some familes but In other some things
are not will – –
John Tucker and **Judah Smith** are appoynted to draw
an Epestle to the quarterly meeting at **Rhoad Island**
gieveing an account of the affairs of truth amongst us – – – – –

At a monthely meeting of friends held at our
meeting house In **Dartmouth** the 17th of the 11th mo^th 1708/9
their was Collected –   –   –   –   –   –   – 00^£ – 09^s – 08^d
Dartmouth meeting Called **William Soul** and **Eliezar**
Slocumb appeared – –
Rochester meeting Called and not Appeared ~~
and **Benjamin Howland** and **Judah Smith** make
report to this meeting that according to order of ~
last monthly meeting they have hired **James**
Russell to look after **Deliverance : Smith**s busness – –

for one month – –
And this meeting agrees to lend as much money out
of the Stock: as will pay the s^d **Russell**: for his months
work: and orders **Benjamin Howland** to let him
have It – –
And **Benjamin Howland** and **Judah Smith** are Still
Continued for to See that **Deliverance Smith** dont want
a hand to look after his buseness he being Stel a prisoner
on truths account
And **John Tucker** is appoynted by this meeting to go to
Boston: to the Jeneral Court: to See if he Cane geet aney releaf for our friends
who now remain prisoners with the s^d **Deliverance**
Smith in the Country Goal at **Bristol** – –
and the meeting is to helpe him to money to bare his Expences – –
And **Stephen Willcock** and **Eliezar Slocumb** are Chosen
to visit friends at **Rochester**: to See how things are among^st
them and make their return to the next monthly meeting – –
Nathanell Howland and **William Soule**: are : Chosen
to viset the prisoners: and see what they want and take
Care that their wants may be Suplyed – –
William Wood Eliezar Slocumb and **Henery Howland**
are Chose to go to **robart gifford** and labour with him to
shew him his Desorder In refusing to pay his proportion
of the Queens tax: and that freinds cannot stand by him In
so Doeing

At a monthly meeting of friends held at our meeting
In **Dartmouth** the 2i first day of the 12th mo^th 1708/9
and their was Colected –   –   –   –   –   –   – 00^£ 11^s – 01^d
And wher as It was Recomended: to this meeting
that Some freinds or friendly people at: **aCushanack** [Acushnet][15]
Desiers that their may be: a meeting of worship appoy^n
ted amongst them once In a month – –
and after some debate upon the mater freinds did
unanemosly agree: that their Request might be
Answered thinking it might be for the honour of
god and for the promortion of truth amongst them:
and so recomends It to the Quarterly meeting

15. As with Acoaxet, these records contain a variety of spellings for the Wampanoag place name indicating the modern town of Acushnet, adjacent to New Bedford, Massachusetts. The insertion of the proper spelling in square brackets will not be repeated.

for their : Concurance and Asestance their In – –
And **William Soul** and **Judah Smith** ar Appoynted
to Draw up a Certificate for our Antiant friend
Hugh Coperthit: of **flushing**: Consarning his ~~
Sarvice and labour of love amongst us – –
allso aComfertable Epestle was red here from our
Antiant freinds and bretheren from their yearly
meeting held at **london** last thurd month – –
And an Epestle allso from the Quarterly meeting
was Read amongst us and Caindly Excepte [kindly accepted] – –
And by reson that the last monthely meeting
minits: Could not be hade; where In was ~~
Several refers to this meeting the Clarke not being
at home – –
their fore the meeting Adjourns until the ~~
Second: fourth day in the first month next – – – – –
this meeting Being meet accourding to adjourne=
(1709) ment the 9ᵗʰ day of the first month 1709 – –
and this meeting orders **Benjamin Howland** to pay
James Russell for his second months works out
of the meeting Stock
And **John Tucker** gives this meeting an acount
thaat he hath ben at **boston** as ordered and the ~~
Jeneral Court hath granted an order to the Sherif of
of **Bristol**: to Relleise the prisoners they paying him
the fees: wich they Could not do:
therefore they are still continued prisoners – –
Stephen Willcock and **Eliezer Slocumb** according to
Appoyntment: have ben at **Rochester** and they give
an account that freinds their are not so well as they
Could wish: but hope that things may be better – –
And the friends appoynted: to Spake with **Robart Gifford**
gives In their answer that he hath given Satesfaction
and hath paid his rate – –
and the prisoners: to wit **Deliverance Smith**: and
Thomas Taber Junʳ are Released and Come home
but the manner of their Commetment and their
Release shall be more largely Declared here ~~
after under the hand of one of them – – – – –

(1709) At a monthely meeting of friends held at our meet=
ing house In **Dartmouth** the 21ˢᵗ day of the 1ˢᵗ moth 1709
the Colection was –   –   –   –   –   –   – £ 0- 08ˢ – 06ᵈ
Dartmouth meeting: Called **Benjamin Howland** and
Judah Smith appeared – –
Rochester meeting Called and not Appeared – –
and **Benjamin Howland** gives this meeting an
account that he hath pay'd **James Russell** for one
months work twenty Eight Shillings – –
as ordered by the last monthly meeting
and **Judah Smith**: hath made up the accounts
with **Benjamin Howland** as ordered: and
their remains In the Stock –   –   –   –   –   –   – 02ᵉ – 04ˢ – 09ᵈ
And **Charles Dyer** the Sone of **Charls Dyer** of **Newport**
on **Rhoad Island** and **Marcy lapham** daughter of
John lapham of **Dartmouth** – –
Did lay ther Intention of marriage: before this meeting
and they were Desiered ~~they~~ to tarrey until the next
monthly meeting for their Answer – –
And **John Tucker** and **William Wood** are Apoynted to see
In to their Cleanness relating marrige and Bring In their – –
Answer to the next monthly meeting – –
And **William Wood** Desiers the aprebation of the meeting
for to put out one of his Children an apprentice to **nicholas**
Howland and this meeting both agree and Consent to
the Same – –
and the Sufering: of **William Wood** for not training
was Read and aproved and ordered: to be recommended ~
to the quarterly meeting
And this meeting Is Adjourned untel the 6ᵗʰ day of the
Second month – – – – –
the meeting being meet according to Adjournment the
Sixt day of the Second month 1709 – –
and this meeting hath recived an account of **Deliverance**
Smith Consarning his late Imprisonment and the meeting
Recomends: the Same to the quarterly meeting – –
John Tucker and **Benjamin Howland** : are Chosen: to
Atend the quᵃterly meeting next at Rhoad Island
this meeting hat received an account of the visetors
as faloweth – –

these are to Satesfie the monthly meeting that wee
have visited the most of friends famielys here but
by reason of my not being weell: wee have ~~nt~~ not ~~
preformed a Jeneral Visit but so far as wee have
ben wee find things preti well: Except Some that
are not so rightly Consarned as they ought to be
and those need a great deal of labour to bring them
to obsarve the orders of friends – – – – –

At a monthly meeting of freinds held at our meeting
house In **Dartmouth** the 18th day of the second <u>mo</u>th 1709 – –
Dartmouth meeting Called **Judah Smith** and **John
Tucker** appeared
Rochester: meeting called **John Sumers** Appeared – –
And the buseness consarning **Charls Dyer** and
Marcy lapham is refered to the next monthly meeting – –
Allso a meeting of worship is Established at **Cushanet** [**Acushnet**]
by the quarterly meeting as requested
and is to be keept the last first day In Every month
And the Quarterly meeting of ministers: haveing – –
laboured with **Hannah Jenney**: and advised her to
be Silent: In meetings of worshp:
but shee: not takeing up with their advice: they
Reffer: here to our monthly meeting: to Deele with
her as they may see meet: In the wisdom of god – –
And **Benjamin Howland** and **John Tucker** are
Chosen: to Spake with the Sd **Hannah Jeney**: to
let here know: that freinds have no : unity with
here preaching praying and singing: In publick
meetings: and if Shee will stil go on conterarye to
the advice of freinds: then freinds will be constrained
for to give forth: a publick testimony against here
proceeding In that Case – –
and **thomas taber Ju**r: being a friendly man and a
late prisoner with our friend **Deliverance Smith** – –
and he behaveing him selfe as becometh the truth
which he sufered for In the time of his Imprison=
- ment and freinds haveing unity with him: In
his Suferings – –
do think It their Christian duty to Contrebut some=
thing to wards the suport of his fameley In

the time of his late Imprisonment – –
And the Epestle from the qua^r meeting was read
to our comfort and Satesfaction – –
and here followeth ^{a coppey} of **Deliverance Smiths** letter
which he sent: to the monthly meeting giveing
an acount of the manner of his Imprisonmente
and sufferings – – – – –

[Two blank pages]

At a monthly ^{meeting} of friends held at our meeting house In
Dartmouth the sixteenth of the third month – – 1709
their was Collected –   –   –   –   –   –   – 0£ – 09ˢ – 03ᵈ
Dartmouth weekly meeting called: **Judah Smith** and
Benjmin Howland appeared; **Rochester** meeting
Called and not appeared – –
And the buseness consarning **Charls Dyer** and **Marcy =
Lapham** is rᵉfered to the next monthely meeting – –
and this meeting orders **Benjamin Howland** to let:
Thomas Cornell have ten Shillings out of the meeting
Stock: to help to Defray :the Charge of friends pasege
to **nantucket**
And the first day at **aCokset**: is Concluded to be at the
meeting house for this summer – –
And this meeting understands by **John Summers** :and
~~TIM~~ **Timothey Davice** [**Davis**]: that friends at **Rochester** are
neglegent : In not atending their preparitive meeting
According to order – –
where for: **Stephen Willcock**: and **Benjamin Howland**
are Appoynted to viset them: and stir them up:
to Deligancy: In their meetings: and to obsarve the
good orders of truth established amongst friends – –
and this meeting orders **Benjamin Howland** to
pay: **Judah Smith** Eight Shillinᵍs out of the Stock
for his Recording the minits of the monthly meetin

At amonthly meeting of friends held at our meeting
house In **Dartmouth** the twenteth of the fourt: month 1709
their was Colected –   –   –   –   –   –   – 0£ - 12ˢ - 04ᵈ
Dartmouth weekly meeting called **Judah Smith** and
William Soule appeared: &

Rochester weekly meeting called and : not appeared
and the Bussnes consarning **Charls Dyer** and **marcy**
Lapham is refered to the next monthly meeting – –
John Tucker and **Benjamin Howland** are Chosen to
attend the Quarterly meeting next – –
the visitors being called upon: they give In the folowing
account friends wee have pᵣeformed a Jeneral visit in the
fameles of friends: thᵣough out the weekly meetings In **Dartm**ᵒᵘᵗʰ
and wee find that our labour of [love?] was [?] sarvice to
some: and things ᴶᵉⁿᵉʳᵃˡʸ are prety well amongst friends – –
Eliezer Slocum, Increas Allin – –
And **Benjamin Howland** and **Judah Smith** are chosen
to wright an Epestle to the Quarterly meeting giveing
an acount of the afairs of truth amongst us – – – – –

At a monthly meeting of friends held at our meeting
house In **Dartmouth** the 18ᵗʰ day of the fift month 1709 -
their was Colected –   –   –   –   –   –   – oˡ-09ˢ-04ᵈ
Dartmouth meeting called **William Soule** and **Judah**
Smith apeared **RoChester** meeting called **Saverey**
Cleffton [Clifton] Appeared – –
and It is desired by this meeting that all freinds who
have ben Imprest this yea[r] that they bring In their ~
acounts how they have stood : In truths testemony againsᵗ
waring and fighteing and also how they came to be
Released from the sᵈ Impress – to the next monthly
meeting – –
Benjamin Howland and **John Lapham Ju**ʳ are
Chosen visitors and aded to the two that was formerly
appoynted – –
and **Henrey Howland :** is agreed: with to make up the
gape Into the burieing ground : and to be paid out of
the monthly meeting Stock – –
and It is ordered that **Benjamin Howland** ~~shoud~~should
pay ᵗᵒ **John Lapham** twenty shillings out of our
stock: for his keeping the meeing house
and tis recomended to theis meeting by **rochester** freinds
that they may have the meeting that is keept at **John**
Summers : removed to **John Wings:** and allso a weekly
meeting setled amongst them – –
and this meeting refers It to the next monthely

meeting : for a full result In the matter – –
and **mathew Wi[n]g** gives this meeting an account of
his being Imprest as foloweth
to the monthly meeting In **Dartmouth:** friends these
are to sartifie the meeting: that I have ben Imprest and
hired a man to goe In my roome : but upon Consideration
I was condemned In my self for so doing and I am sorey
for the same and I hope I shall doe so no more – –

mathew Winge

At a monthely meeting of friend held at our meeting
house In **Dartmouth** the fifteenth of the 6th : m̲th̲ 1709
there was colected –   –   –   –   –   –   – 0l-06s-08d
Dartmouth meeting called **William Soule** and **Judah**
Smith appeared: **rochester** meeting called and not Apeared – –
and It is ordered that **Benjamin Howland** should pay five
Shillings to his brother **Henrey** for makeing the gate
and posts for the buring yard – –
Charls Dyer and **Mary Lapham** appeared the second
time: Sigenefying still their Intention of marrige and
nothing appearing to hinder their Intention he haveing
a SerifiCate from the monthly meeing whereunto he
did belong : a Coppey of which here foloweth – –
from our monthly mens meeting of freinds held at **new**
port on **Rhoad Island** ye 14th day of the 4th month 1709
to our friends at **Dartmouth:** is the Saleutaton of our Dear
love In the truth: and where as **Charls Dyre** son of ~
Charles Dyer : of **newport :** Deceased desired a certificate of us
he being as wee understand In persuance of marriage ~
with **marey** the Daughter of **John Lapham** and **marey**
his wife of **Dartmouth :**
these are theirfore : to certifie whom it may concarn that
we have made: Inquiery : Concarning him and do finde
nothing but that he is clear of intanglement as to mariag
so for as we know with any here amongst us : and
and as to his convesation of late has seemed to be sober: and
well Inclind: and frequents friends meetings and
wee have nothing against :his proceeding in marriag
so Desiring his prosperety: and growth in the truth
we conclud: signed by order and In be half of:
our monthly meeting by _____

thomas Cornell Clark of ye meeting

they had their answer : that they might take : each
other In Conveniant tim In the Desente order
of truth – –
and **William Wood** and **John Tucker** are appoynted
to sea that the marriage is Solemnized In the good -
order of truth _____
and the bussenes concarning the setelement of a weekley
meeting at **rochester** is ref^{e}red to the next monthely meeting
and **Nathanell Howland** and **William Soule** was called up =
on: to give In their accounts of what they have Des^{b}urted to =
wards the Suport of the late prisoners on the meetings
account and they say they have desbursted nothing on the
meetings account – –
John Tucker and **Eliezer Slocumb** are called upon to give
In their account: Concarning this Care about the meeting
house the last year – –
and their Answer is: that their is dew to them ten ~
shillings: and this meeting orders **Benjamin Howland**
to paye it to them out of our Stock – –
and **John Tucker** and **Eliezer Slocum** are still continued
for to take care of the meeting house for the Insuing
year – –
and It^{i}s ordered that **Benjamin Howland** should
pay **Judah Smith** :twelve shillings for recording
the monthly meetings minits: out of the monthly
meeting Stock – –
and this meeting hath subscribed teen pounds to:
to wards the building of friends meeting in **Boston**
and this meeting hath received an account form our
freinds In wrighting: which was **Imprest** this year
which was read to the satesfaction: of the meeting
and ordered to be recorded: as foloweth – – – – –

to the monthely meeting of freinds In **Dartmouth**
holden the fiftenth day of the sixt month 1709 – –
Dear friends and bretheren: thinking It our Christan duty
and acording to the good order of truth: to give you this
folowing: account
friends: on the 9th day of the third month last in this
present year: we whose nanes [names] are under wretten
three of us being at the town house In **Dartmouth** ~
were Impresed by **John Akin** leuthenat of the train

band; In to the Queens Service to goe to **Canadya** [**Canada**][16] !
and he required us to appear the next day at the hous
of **Josiah Allin** [**Allen**] to receive furder order: and acordingly we
went to S^d allins and when wee came our furder order ~
was to be Exercised In a warlike postour.
and we told S^d **Akin** that we could not In conciance
act In aney warlike postur: nor use carnal weapons to ~
destroy mens lives: who said He took notice of our answer
and told us wee might go home untel furder order
which we Did and remained at or about home untel the 18th
^day of the month: and then being ordered to appear be fore Colenel
Byfield wee went with **William Soule:** (who was Impres
by the above s^d **Akin:** the 11th of the Same month to goe to
Caniday In her majestys service) and ordered to appear
at the town house In **Bristol** [**Bristol, Mass., now R.I.**]: on the 18th day of the s^d 3th m^th
so wee went to **Joseph Wanton**s where: we meet with
our friend **William Wood** who was going with his son **Will=**
iam Wood to **Bristol**: for **Robart Brownel** came the 11th day of
the third month 1709: and Imprest his son to go to **Canady**
In the Queens service:
after wards: **Nathanell Soule** warned him to appear at
the the town house In **Bristol** on the 18th day of the
s^d third month: then we considred the matter and ~
thought It might be best: for **William Wood** to leave
his Son their and goe and Spake In his sons bhalf
which he did: then wee went to **Bristol** together
and Appeared befor Colonol **Byfield:** who asked: us
some questions: to which wee answered that wee
Could nout for Consiance Sake act In a War lick ~
posture to Destroy mens lives: for In So doing we shou^d
ofend god and In cur his Displeasur: and when **William**
Wood Juner was called his father spoke In his behalf
then Colenol **Byfield :** asked him if his sone was
a Quaker too: he said it is against his mind to goe to
ware and he would not kill a man for the world
then one that sat by: said **Byfield** said take him:
then he [sat?] down **William**'s name In his Book
then he put us all: under the Comand of Capt ~
Joseph Brown: and charged us to march with him

16. Hereinafter the correct spelling is not inserted.

to **Rocksburie** [**Roxbury, Massachusetts.**] by the 25th of sad [said] month: which
　charge wee
could not obay: but after ward he being more modrate
Desiered us to goe down not In aney warlike posture but
to take our own time: So as to meet Capt. **Brown** at the ~
Governors at **roxburey** the Sd 25th of the month which
we finding freedom to doe accordingly went thether and
laid our cause before the governeur **Joseph Dudly** who was
verey kind to:us and gave us our liberty to go home with out
Demanding aney money of us: or wee paying him aney In
which liberty through the goodness of god wee still remain
your friends

　　　　　　　John Tucker:　　**William Wood**
　　　　　　William Soule:　　**John Lapham Jr**
　　　　　　　　　　Deliverance Smith

---

an other paper from **nathaneell Howland** to friends -
-ing of the people
called Quakers In **Dartmouth:** that on the 9th day of the
third month 1709
I was Imprest by **John Akin** Into the queens sarvice
an allso warned me to appear at **Josiah Allins** on the
next day to receive furder order: which I did then
he said his order was to Exersise me In a warlike postour
with others that was Imprest: untel he had furder order then
I tould him it was against my consiance ~~in~~ to aCt In
SuCh a way to go out to war to destroy mens lives or
words to that purpos: which he said he took notiCe of
and Said I might go home untel furder order: then
after ward I was warned to go with sd **akin** to the
town house In **Bristoll** [**Bristol, Mass., now R.I.**] the 18th day of the sd third
month: and accordingly: I went with him tel we
came to brother **Daniell** at the ferrey: then the said ~
Akin called mee aside and released mee from the
Impres with out my paying aney fine or promesing
aney – –

　　　　　　　　　　Nathanell Howland

At a monthly meeting of : friends held at our meeting
house in **Dartmouth** the 19th day of the 7th mth 1709 – –
their was Colected –　 –　 –　 –　 –　 –　 – 0l-10s-09d

Dartmouth weekly meeting called: **Judah Smith**
and **John Lapham Ju^nr** appeared – –
Rochester weekly meeting: called and not appeared
William Wood and **John Tucker** hath brought In
their answer: to this meeting: that **Charls Dyer**
and **Marcy Lapham** Did Solemnise their marrige
In the good order of truth – –
And the busenes: Concarning the Settleing of a weekly
meeting amongst friends: at **Rochester** is refer^d
to the next monthly meeting: by reson their is
no representitive from their meeting – –
and In as much as their is no : friends from the
preparative meeting at **Rochester**: this meeting
Doth appoynt **Benjamin Howland** and **Eliezar**
Slocum : to visit them: and stur them up In
their Duty deligently to attend the monthly meeting – –
and **John Tucker** : and **William Wood** are chosen
to attend the quarterly meeting next – –
and **Stephen Willcock** : and **William Wood** gives
this meeting: to understand: that they have spoken
with **Thomas Wait**: ConCarning his Comeing
amongst freinds: to take ^a wife: and he Saith he
is willing to Submet to the good order of truth – –
and **John tucker** is appoynted : to give **thomas**
Wait a few lines: to freinds at **nantucket** Signifying that he is In good unity with friends: here
of this meeting – –
and the minits of the last yearly meeting was read
at this meeting and Caindly [kindly] approved of by the meeting
and the meeting is adjourned untel the 12th day of the
Eight month ~~next~~
the monthly meeting being meet according to Adjournment
the 12th day of the 8th mo^th 1709 – –
the visitors give in their account to this meeting
that they find: things prety well Jeneraly amongst
freinds Except Some perticular familys things are
no well: but friends are in hopse that In time they
may come to be better – –
and **John Tucker** and **Judah Smith** are chosen to
wright an :Epestle: to the Quarterly meeting: next

giveing an account of the afairs of truth amongst
us – – – – –

At a monthly meeting of friends held at our meeting
house In **Dartmouth** the 17th day of the 8th moth 1709 – –
their was colected – – – – – – – 0^l-09^s-5^d
Dartmouth weekly meeting called **Judah Smith** and
John Lapham Junr appeared – –
Rochester meeting called and not appeared – –
James Russell :and **Rebecah Howland** Did lay their
Intention of marrige before this meeting: and they
wer Desired to wait untel the next monthly meeting for an answer – –
and **Benjamin Howland** and **John Lapham** are
chosen: to Inquier In to their Clearness: and bring
In their answer to the next monthly meeting: how
they find things – –
And **Eliezar Slocum** reports: to this meeting that
he hath ben at **Rochester** according to apoyntment
and hath spoken with friends their: and they signify
that they condemn their Slackness and hope for time
to come they shall be more Deligent In attending the
~~weekly~~ monthly meeting – –
and **John tucker** and **William Wood** make report to
to this meeting that they have attended the quarterly
meeting: according to appoyntment: and **John tucker**
and **Judah Smith**: have written an Epestle to the
Quarterly meeting as ordered – – – – –

At a monthly meeting of friends held at our meeting
house In **Dartmouth** the 21 first of the 9$\underline{th}$ mth 1709 – –
their was colected – – – – – – – 0^l-04^s-11^d
Dartmouth weekly meeting called **Judah Smith**
and **John Lapham** appeared – –
Rochester meeting called and not appeared – –
and the two friends that was chosen the last ~
monthly meeting to Inspect into the clearness of
James Russell and **Rebecah Howland** concarning
marriage: was called upon: and their answers is that:
they have made Inquirey and find nothing that
may hinder their Intention of marriage – –

James Russell and **Rebecah Howland** Apeared the ~
Second time: before the meeting: Desiering an answer
to their proposals of marriage laid before the last monthly =
meeting: Signifying that they both Still Intended marriage
and friends finding things Clear they had their answer
that they might proceede: to take Each other In marriage
In the good order of truth – –
and **Benjamin Howland** : and **John Lapham Ju**^{r} is
Appoynted to see the marriage acomplished In the decent
order of truth – –
and the teen pounds: Subscribed to wards the building of
the meeting house at **boston**: was colected at this meeting: and Delivered to **Thomas Cornell** In order to
be sent to **boston** for the Use above sd – –
and where as **Elizabeth** the Daughter of **hisekiah** – –
Smith and of **marcy** his wife: hath walked Desorderly
In marring with one of the world: Contrary to the
good order of truth Estableshed amongst us: and
the advice of friends: and friends being clear of
her this meeting maks choyce of **John tucker** and **Increas**
Allin to Draw up a paper of condemnation concarning her
and bring It into the next monthly meeting – –
and where as It^s proposed to this meeting by the visitors whether
Robart Gifford is accounted a friend In unity or not – –
and it is the sience [sense] of the meeting that **robart Gifford** bing [being]
a friends Child: is under the Care and Custety of this meet-
ing and ought to be viseted as a friend – –
and it is agreed that friends at **Coxset** should have ther meeting: on the first Day of the weeke: on the other side the river
for this winter as formerly – –
allso we recived an Epestle from the last quarterly
meeting at **rhoad Island**: which was read and kindly
Excepte [accepted]: where by we underStand: that the monthly
meeting at **Rhoad Island** is altered and is to be held on
the last third Day in Everey month – – – – –

At a monthly meeting of friends held at our
meeting house In **Dartmouth** the 19th of the 10th: mth 1709
their was colected –   –   –   –   –   –   – 0^l-13^s-06^d
Dartmouth weekly meeting called **Judah S**^{m}**ith**
and **John Lapham** Appeared – –

Rochester weekly called and **Joseph Wing** Appeared – –
And **Benjamin Howland** and **John Lapham** ~~w~~
was Called upon: to know whether they Did See
James Russell and **Rebeca Howland** Consemat
their marriage In the order of truth – –
And their answer is: that they were at the marria^g
and they know not: but that things was Carried
on prety well – –
And **John green** of **Warwick** and **Marcy Allen** the
Daughter of **Increas Allien** of **Dartmouth** Did lay their
Intentians of marr be for this meeting and they
was Desiered to wait for an Answer until the next monthly
meeting – –
And where as **John Tucker** and **Increas Allin** was
Appoynted by the last Monthly meeting: to Draw up
a paper of Condemnation Concarning **Elizebeth Tripp**
and their being nothing done: this meeting doth still
continoue them to do It against the next monthly
meeting – –
And **John Tucker** an **william wood** is appoynted
to attend the Quarterly meeting at **Rhoad Island**
next – –
And the visitors of this meeting hath given In ~~ther~~
their Accounts of their visiting of friends and they
signefy that things are prety ~~w~~ well In some
fameleys: but In other some things are not ~
well but wee hope that In time things may be
better – –
And **Benjamin Howland** and **John Lapham**
Is Appoynted: to se In to the Clearness of **John: green**
and **Marcy Allin** concarning marriage and bring
In their Answer to the next monthly meeting – –
And **Nathaneel Howland** hath requested: the liberty
of this meeting: to set up a Stable on the meeting
house land: which is granted – –
And **Judah Smith** is apoynted to make up the monthely
meetings Accounts with **Benjamin Howland** and
make Returne to the next monthly meeting – –
And this meeting Is adjourned untel the next
the next forth Day come week which will be the

28th day of this Instant – –
and the meeting being meet according to Adjurn=
ment the 28th of the 10th month 1710 – –
And where as some agetations hath be concarning
Samuell Mott his seling of his habetation and
removeing to **newport** on **Rhoad Island** to live
and It is the sience [sense] of this meeting: that It will not
be for his Advanteg In aney wise: so canot give
our consent their to at the present – –
and **John tucker** and **Judah Smith** is Appoynted
to Draw up an Epestle to the next quartorly meet=
ing giveing an account of the afairs of truth amongst
us – –
And **Rochester** preparetive meeting hath requested
of the monthly meeting: that they may have a
weekly meeting^ for worship Established amongst them and
to be keept on the fift Day of the week at **John wing**s
and allso that they may have their preparetive meet=
ing on the fift day of the week before the monthly
meeting after the meeting of worship is Ended – –
and that they have a monthly meeting of worship on
the first day at **John Wing**s once In four weeks: all which is
grante[d] and alowed by this meeting – – – – –

At a monthly meeting of friends held at our meeting
house In **Dartmouth** the 16th Day of the 11th month 1709
their was Colected –   –   –   –   –   –   – 0£-10s-06d
Dartmouth weekly meeting called **Benjamin =
Howland** and **Eliezar Slocum** appeared – –
Rochester weekly meeting called and not all
Appeared – –
John Green and **Marey Allin** [**Allen**] apeared before
this meeting Desiering an Answer to their ~
proposals of marriage layed before the last month
ly meeting saying they was still of the same mind
the said **John green** [**Greene**] haveing his mothers concent In that
matter and allso a Certificate from the monthly meeting
where unto he did belong: the coppey of which are
here Insarted – –
from our monthly meeting for buseness at **Estgreenwich** [**East Greenwich**]
the 19th day of the 10th month 1709 In the coloney of

Rhoad Island to yᵉ monthly meeting of bisness of friends
at **Dartmouth** Greetingst – –
whereas our friend **John Greene** haveing Desiered a Sertifyca^te
from our monthly meeting these may therefore In~
form you that he has made a profestione [profession] of the bles[s]ed
Truth with us for some Considrable time and that
his life and conversatin has ben Answerable theire
unto he being In good unity with us hear [here] being
of some service amongst us And furder wee do signyfi
that concerning marreag we have taken care at our
monthly meeting And do find nothing to the ~~en~~
contrary but that he is clear from all here as conc[e]rn=
ing marriage – –
Signed by order and In behalf of our sd meeting
by
Benjamin Barton :   Robert Wesgate   Abner Spencer
Samuel Perrey :   Samuell Aldrich
Zacriah Jenkens :   Thomas Arnold
Thomas Rodman Juʳ: ────────────
here foloweth a coppey of his mothers consent – –
                In the Coloney of **Rhoad Island**
Potawomet [Potowomut] in **Warwick [RI]** the 11ᵗʰ of the 11ᵗʰ month <u>1709</u>
to the monthly meeting of friends at **Dartmouth**
these are to Inform you yᵗ [that] as to yᵉ proceedings of my son
John Green Concerning marrieg hee has my free ~~consent~~
consent their unto
from your wellwishing friend: **Elizebeth Green**
And the said **Marey: Allin [Mary Allen]** allso haveing her perance [parents]
Consent: the meeting give them their Answer – that
they might take Each other In the good order of truth
And **Benjamin Howland** and **John Lapham** is appoynted to se[e] them Consumate their marriage In the good
order of truth – –
And **Jabush Barker** and **Rebecah Russell** did lay
their Intentions of marriage be for this meeting – –
and they was desiered to wait untel the next monthly
meeting for an answer – –
nathaneel Howland and **James Burriell [Burrel]** are Chosen
to Inspect Into their Clearness concarning marriage
and make return to the next monthly meeting – –

And where as **John Tucker** and ~~Eliezar Slocum~~
Increas Allin [**Increase Allen**] was continued the last monthly meet=
ing to draw up a paper of condemnation concarning
Elizebet [**Elizabeth**] **Tripp** and It not being fully acomplished
to the Satesfaction of friends:
they are still continued: and **Benjamin Howland**
and **Elizear** [**Eliezer**] **Slocum** are Appoynted and added to
them for the full Acomplishing the same – –
and the meeting adjourns untel the 25 fift of this
Instant – – – – –

the meeting being met according ₐ^to adjournment the 25 fift of the 11th mo^th <u>1709</u>
the four friends appoynted to Draw up the condemna
tion concarning **Elizebeth tripp** ~~her cond~~ have don
It and presented It to this meeting: and the meeting
~~the meeting~~ seeth cause to refer It to the next month
ly meeting: befor it goes forth In publick – –
and **Judah Smith** is called upon to give an account ~
whethe he hath mad[e] up the monthly meetings accom[p]^ts
with **Benjamin Howland** and It is not don so hee
Is conteuned stell to do it and make return to the next
monthly meeting – –
And **John tucker** is Appoynted to give **Rochester** friends
an account In wrighting that their request as to Setle=
ing their: meetings was granted the last

At a monthly meeting of friends held at our meeting
house In **Dartmouth** the 20th day of the 12th month 1709 – –
the Colection was –   –   –   –   –   –   – £l[?]-08^s-08^d
Dartmouth weekly ₐ^meeting called **Judah Smith** and **John=
Lapham** Appeared – –
Rochester weekly called **Savory Clefton** [**Clifton**]
Appeared – –
and the two freinds that was apoynted the last month
ly meeting ₐ^do give In their answer: that **John Green** and
Marey Allin [**Mary Allen**] did acomplish their marriage In the order
of the meeting – –
And the matter concarning **Jabush Barker** and
Rebecah Russell is refered to the nex[t] monthly ~
meeting – –
and the accounts not as yet being made up with

Benjamin Howland concarning the collection:
Ju[d]ah Smith is still Continued to do It and make
return to the next monthly meeting – –
And John tucker hath given Rochester^ freinds an account
of the setling of their meetings as appoynted – –
and this meeting makes choice of William Wood
Eliezer Slocum John Lapham and William Soule
to peruse what Elizabeth tripp sent In to the monthly
meeting Concarning her Joyning In marrige out of the
good order established amongst us – –
and give In thir Judgment whether that be sefesiant [sufficient]
to clear truth which shee sent In to the monthly meeting
or whether the monthly ought to give forth a
publick testimony against her – –
Dartmouth weekly meeting ~~meeting~~ called no buseness
rochester weekly meeting called and John wing son of
John Wing of Rochester appeared at this meeting
Desiaring a certifycate of his Clearness as to marriage
And Saverey Clifton and Timothey Davice [Davis] are
Chose to Inquier Into his Clearness as to marrege
and bring In their Answer to the next monthly
meeting – –
and was received the Epistle from the last Quartorly
meeting the which was read at this meeting and
was caindly [kindly] Excepted [accepted] – –
the freinds above Chosen to Consider and advise with
some women friends about the matter Relating ~
Elizebeth tripp: Do give their advice that a paper
of Condemnation go forth publickly against her
which this meeting doth think well of – –
And do order John Tucker to Read publickly the said
Condemnation on a first day after meeting or se[e]
It done by the next monthly meeting and make
return their of – – – – –

(1710) At a monthly meeting of friends held at our meeting
house In Dartmouth the 27th day of the first: mth 1710 – –
the Colection was –　 –　 –　 –　 –　 –　 – 0£-09s-02d
Dartmouth weekly meeting Called Judah Smith
and John Lapham appeared – –
Rochester weekly meeting called John wing jur apeared – –

Judah Smith hath made up the monthly meetings
Accounts with **Benjamin Howland** as appoynted
And their remains In the Stock –   –   –   –   –   –   – 02ᶠ-14ˢ-09ᵈ
And **Jabush Barker** and **Rebecah Russell** came
the second time for their Answer as to takeing Each other
In marriage and things appearing Clear they had their
Answer that they might take Each other In the good order
of truth – –
and **nathaneel Howland** and **James Burill** [Burrel] are Chosen
to see them Solomnize their marriage In the good order
Established ~~In the good ord~~ Amongst us – –
and **Joseph Chace** sone of **William** ᶜʰᵃᶜᵉ of **Swansey** and
Abigall [Abigail] **tucker** of **Dartmouth** did lay their Intentions
of their marriag before this meeting and they was
Desired to wait untel the next monthly meeting for
an Answer – –
and **John tucker** and **Stephen Willcock** [Wilcox] are Chosen to
make Inquierey In to ther clearness and bring In their
~~clear~~ answer to the next monthly meeting – –
and this meeting apoynts **Benjamin Howland** to
pay **Judah Smith** what is dew [due] to him for recording
the monthly meeting minits – –
and make return to the next monthly meeting
what is done[17] – –
and **John tucker** makes report to this meeting that
he hath Read **Elizebeth Tripps** condemnation as
Apoynted the last monthly ~~monthly~~ meeting – –
which is as foloweth; whare as friends ware Informed
that **Elizebeth Smith** the daughter of **Hizekiah** [Hezekiah] **Smith**
and of **Marey** his wife that Shee did Intend to marrey
out of the order of friends their for freinds did labour
with her to show her: her Shortness their In but Shee
Did not take their advice but was married contrarey
to the good order of friends
their for we who are Called Quakers: Can do no les but
to Clear our salves [ourselves] and the bles[s]ed truth that we make
profesion of but to signify to the world that we have no
unity with such marriages nor with the said **Elizebeth**
In her so marr[y]ing: out of the good order of truth

17. References to payments for making and copying Quaker records are rare.

Estableshed amongst friends.

Signed by order and In behalf of our monthly men
and womens meeting held at **Dartmouth** the 20th day
of the twelfth: month 1709 or 10: by

Ruth Tucker	: Marey Smith	: Savrey Cleffton [Savory Clifton]
Rachel Allin [Allen]	: Marey Lapham Ju^r	: Stephen Willcock [Wilcox]
Hannah Soule	: hope merehow	: Judah Smith
Hannah tucker	: John tucker	: william wood
marey Slocum	: John Lapham Ju^r	: Henrey tucker
Sarah gifford	: Increas Allin [Increase Allen]	: Josiah merehow [Merihew]
Dorcase [Dorcas] Earl – –		

and **Judah Smith** and **John tucker** is appoynted to
Draw up an Epestle to the quartorly meeting next – –
And **John tucker: William: wood** and **Elizar [Eliezer] Slocum**
Is Chosen to attend the quartorly meeting next – –
and **William Soule** desiers the Aprabation of the meet^ing
to put his sone an aprantice [apprentice] to ~~Nicholas Howland~~
John Russell w^hich the meet[ing] hath unity with

At a monthly meeting of freinds held at our meet=
ing house In **Dartmouth** the 15th of the 2 m^th 1710 – –
Dartmouth weekly meeting Called **Judah Smith**
and **william Soule** appeared – –
Rochester weekly meeting Called **Isaac Benson** Appeared – –
and their was Colected –   –   –   –   –   –   – 0^£-12^s-09^d
and Inquirey being made whether **Jabush Barker**
And **Rebecah Russell** had Solomnized their
marriage In the good order of truth and the answ^er
was that they had acomplished It according
to order – –
And the buseness Concarning **Joseph Chase** and
Abigal Tucker things not being Clear
relating their Intention of marriage they are refered
to the next monthly meeting for their answer – –
and **Benjamin Howland** is still Continued to pay **Judah**
Smith for Recording the monthly meeting and he Is:
Desiered to do It against the next monthly meeting – –
and the freinds that was appoynted to draw up an Epestle
to the Quartorly meeting have done It according to order
and the freinds that was Chosen to Attend the quartorly

meeting: make report that they have attended yᵗ [that]
meeting According to appoyntment – – – – –

At a monthly mans meeting of friends held ate our meeting
house In **Dartmouth** the 15ᵗʰ day of the 3ᵗʰ: mº 1710 – –
the Colection was –   –   –   –   –   –   – 0ᶠ-10ˢ-03ᵈ
Dartmouth weekly meet called **Judah Smith** and:
william Soule: appeared – –
Rochester weekly meeting Called **John Summers** apearᵉᵈ
and the buseness Concarning **Joseph Chase** and **Abigal=**
Tucker is refered to the next monthly meeting: because
the sd **Joseph Chase** hath not a Certifycate from the
monthly meeting to which he doth belong – –
and **Benjamin Howland** hath paid **Judah Smith**
for Recordding the monthly meeting minits:
twelve Shillings: as ordered the last monthly meeting ~
and **Thomas Smith** at **pensalvenia** [**Pennsylvania**] the sone of ~
Eliezar Smith of **Dartmouth** Desiered of this monthly ᵐᵉᵉᵗⁱⁿᵍ
A Certifycate of his Clearness as to marriage: In order
their unto this meeting appoynted **Deliverance Smith**
and **William Wood:** to Inquire In to his Clearness
and If they find things Clear then they are appoynteᵈ
to Draw up a Certifycate for him and make their returⁿ
to the next monthly meeting – –
and the quartorly meeting Epestle Was read at this
meeting and Excepted and alowed and the meeting
agrees to com to a Subscription: for to defray part of the
Charge of **Kingstown** meeting: ʰᵒᵘˢᵉ as Requested by the
last Quartorly meeting: and the Sume: requested
Is four pounds – –
and it is agreed that the first day meeting on the
other side **Coxet** river should: be at the meeting ~
house for this Summer according to former ~~agree~~
agreement – –
william wood John lapham James Bourrell [**Burrel**] and
Increase Allien [**Allen**] are appoynted to go with some ~
women friends: to conseder whether their ought
to be a paper of publick Condemnation to be given
forth against **Abigal Howland** the daughter of
Benjamin Houland [**Howland**] for marr[y]ing out of the order
of truth – –

and the freinds above Chosen have Considred the
mater concarning the above named **abigal howland**
and give In their Judgment that their ought to be
a paper of condemnation drawn up and given forth
against her – –
and the Same freinds are appoynted to draw
It up against the next monthly meeting – – – – –

At a monthly meeting of freinds held at the
meeting house In **Dartmouth** the 19th of the 4th moth 1710
the Colection was –   –   –   –   –   –   – 0ℓ-10s-03d
Dartmouth weekly meeting Called: **Judah Smith** and
william Soule Appeared – –
Rochester weekly meeting called: **Elisha wing** appeared
And **Joseph: Chasce [Chase]** and **Abigal Tucker** came to this
meeting: and Desiered an Answer to their former proposials
of marriage layd before the monthly meeting signifyeing
they still Intended marriage – –
And nothi[n]g Apearing to hender their Intentions and the
Said **Joseph Chasce [Chase]** haveing a Certifycate from the monthly
to which he doth belong:
they had their answer that they might take Each other In the
good order or truth – –
and **John tucker** and **Stephen Willcock [Wilcox]** are Chosen to see
their marriage acomplished In the good order of truth – –
A Certifycate was: given forth by this meeting: to **Thomas
Smith** at **pensalvenia** of his Clearness Concarning ~~marg~~ marriage – –
and **John tucker** is appoynted to signe the above said
Certifycate In the behalfe of the said monthly meeting ~
and **Ruth Smith** Desiered a Certifycate of this monthly
meeting Signifying that Shee had a Concarne [concern] upon
her mind to visit her Children In **pencelvenia**]: and
freinds haveing unity with her Concarne apoynted
Judah Smith and **John tucker** to Draw a Certifycate
for her and Signe It in behalf of the meeting – –
william wood John tucker and **Stephen Willcock [Wilcox]** are
Chosen to atend the Quartorly meeting next – –
and **Benjamin Howland** is ordered to let **John tucker**
have twenty Shillings for keeping the meeting house – –
and the friends thet was Chosen the last monthly =
meeting to Draw up a paper of Condemnation: against

Abigal Howland have done It: and it was Read and ~
Aproved by this meeting – –
And **John tucker** is appoynted to reed the Same publick=
ly on the first day at the braking up of the meeting
of worship ————— Some time befor the next monthly meeting – –
of which these folowing is a Coppey – –
this is given forth to clear our Holy profession by us
the people Called Quakers – –
Where as **Jonathan Ricketson** and **Abigaile Howland**
being born of believing parance [parents] and they being Likely
to marrey Contrarey to the good Order of truth Estableshed
amongst us: wee haveing advised them to the Contrarey
but they taking no advice from us haveing acomplished
It Contrarey to our Order for which we disowne them
to be of our Society and Communion Signed by order
of our monthly meeting at **Dartmouth** yᵉ 19ᵗʰ day of the 9ᵗʰ mᵒ 1710
by

Hannah tucker	pheby [Phebe] tucker	John tucker
Hanah [Hannah] Soule	hope merehow [Merihew]	Stephen willcock [Wilcox]
Ruth tucker	marey [Mary] Smith	Judah Smith
marey [Mary] Slocum	Increase Allin [Allen]	Henrey [Henry] tucker
Rachel Allin [Allen]	James Burrill [Burrel]	Josiah Merehow [Merihew]
Ruhamah Smith	william wood	Abraham tucker
marey [Mary] Lapham	John Lapham	Eliezar [Eliezer] Slocum

and the meeting is adjourned until the first
sixt day of the fift month next – – – – –

the meeting being meet According to Adjournment
the 7ᵗʰ day of the fift month 1710 – –
and the Visetors brought In their account to this
meeting of their visiting freinds famelyes belonging
to the monthly meetings and they make Report
that they have preformed a Jeneral visit: and find
things In the Jeneral amongst freinds pretty well
but In some famelyes not well but hope that things
In time may come to be better – –
And **Stephen willcock [Wilcox] william wood** and **John
tucker** is appoynted to Draw up and [sic] Epestle to the
quartorly meeting next: giveing an account how
things are amongst us – –

And It is refered for the advice: and Judgment of the
Quartorly meeting – –
whether If a friend shall give his Child In marriage
to one of the world after that freinds have laboured
with him and advised him to the Contrary and he
Shall presest [persist] to the accomplishing the Same then
whether a paper of Condemnation under his own hand
may be taken up with for Satesfaction or whether ~
a paper of Condemnation ought not to go forth against
him from the monthly meeting – – – – –

At a monthly meeting of freinds held at our meeting house In
Dartmouth the 17th of the 5th month –   –   –   –   – 1710 – –
the Colection was –   –   –   –   –   –   – 0ᴸ-09ˢ-09ᵈ
Dartmouth weekly meeting Called **Benjamin Howland**
and **Judah Smith** Appeared – –
Rochester weekly meeting called and not apeared – –
and the freinds that was appoynted to see **Joseph Chace** [**Chase**]
And **Abigal tucker**s marriage acompleshed acording to
order make report that It is not yet acomplished and
the Same freinds are Still Continued to see It and bring
In their answer to the next monthly meeting – –
and the friends that was appoynted to Draw a Certifycate
for ruth Smith have don It as ordered – –
forruth and **John tucker** mak[e]s report to this meeting that he
hath Read **Jonathan Riketsons** [**Ricketsons**] and **Abigal Howland**s
Condemnation according to appoyntment of last month
ly meeting – –
and **John tucker** and **william wood** have attended
the quartorly meeting as appoynted – –
and **Benjamin Howland** is Called upon to know whether
he hath paid **John tucker** as appoynted the last ~
meeting and It is not don so he is Still Continued to
do It and make returne to the next monthly meeting
and the friends that was apoynted to wright an
Epestle to the quartorly meeting make Report that
they have done It – –
and this meeting received a letter from **Walter**
Newberey [**Newberry**]: with Eighty two Books of our freind
patrick Henderson which he wret [wrote] In answer

to a Scandlas [scandalous] book of: **Cotton Mathers**[18] – –
the Books Coms to –   –   –   –   –   –   – 02$^\pounds$-15^s-00^d

At a monthly meeting of freinds held at our meeting
house In **dartmouth** the 21: first day of the 6th m^o 1710 – –
the Colection was –   –   –   –   –   –   – 0$^\pounds$-12^s-00^d
Dartmouth weekly meeting Called **James Burrill [Burrel]** and
Eliezar Slocum appeared – –
Rochester weekly meeting called **Elisha Wing** apeared
And **Stephen Willcock [Wilcox]** and **John tucker** give In
their acount to this meeting that they did See
Joseph Chace [Chase] and **Abigal Tucker** Acomplish their
marriage In the order of truth – –
and **Benjamin Howland** hath paid **John tucker**
according to apoyntment – –
and the Books which was recived the last month=
ly meeting of **Wallter Nubery [Walter Newberry]**: are paid for and
John tucker is apoynted to see the money transport^{ed}
to the sd **Wallter Nubery** – –
John tucker and **Eliezar Slocum** are apoynted
to procur a friend to keep the meeting house for
the Insuing year – –
and where as friends being senceble that **John fish**
was about to Joyne his daughter In marriage ~
with one of the world Cantrary to the good order
Establshed amongst us: freinds went to him and
advised him to the Contrary labouring much with
him to Shew him the Eill [evil] Consequence that
might folow – –
but not with standing freinds Care and advice
he hath presested [persisted] to the acomplishing the same – –
where aupon the meeting made Choyce of **Benjamin**
Howland and **Eliezar Slocum** to Draw up a paper of
Condemnation for the Clearing of truth and freinds
of the said **John fish:** his desorderly walking – –
and make their return to the next ᵐmonthly meeting – –

18. Patrick Henderson was an Irish Friend. His book was *Truth and Innocence, the Armour and Defence of the People Called Quakers, against the Wiles of Satan and His Emissaries: Being an Answer to Part of a Book, Entituled,* The Man of God Furnished, *Put Forth by Several, Who Call Themselves Ministers of the Gospel in the Churches of New-England. Wherein That Part, viz., Is Fairly Examined and Detected* (London, J. Sowle, 1709). One chapter of *The Man of God Furnished* was "Armour against the Wiles of Quakerism."

And **Eliezar Slocum** and **Benjamin Howland**
are Chosen to Speake with **Hezekiah Smith**: con=
Carning his Disorderly Carrege In the monthly
meeting when the meeting was wrightly Con=
Carned about his daughters marreing out of the order
of truth – –
and **John tucker** did Signefy to this meeting that he
had a concarn rested up^{on} his mind for some time
to travel to the westward to viset freinds In those
parts and freinds haveing unity with his Con=
carne did make Choyce of **Judah Smith** and
John Lapham to wright a Certifycate for him and sign
It In the be half of said meeting[19] – –
and **Eliezar Slocum** and **Benjamin Howland** make report
that they have Spoken with **Hezekiah Smith** and he
hath Condemned his disorderly Carrege to the satesfactin
of the meeting – – – – –

At a monthly meeting of friends held at our meeting hous[e]
In **Dartmouth** the 8th day of the seventh month 1710 – –
their was Colected for the use of freinds – – – – – – – 0$^{£}$-05^{s}-6^{d}
Dartmouth meeting Called **Judah Smith** and **William Soul** [**Soule**]
Appeared – –
Rochester weekly meeting Called none appeared – –
and **John Tucker** is still Continued to Bring a recept for
the money which he had to pay for **patrick**s books – –
Eliezer Slocum maks Return to this meeting that **John -
lapham** is to keep the mee[t]ing house as usall – –
and **Eliezer Slocum** and **Benjamin Howland** have drawn
up a Condemnatision [*sic*] against **John fish:** for giveing his
Daughter In marrige to one of the world – –
and It is as foloweth – –
whereas **John fish** of **Dartmouth** In the County of **Bristol**
In **new England:** hath gon from the principle of truth which
he hath made pr[o]fesion of and Joyning him selfe with the sp[i]rit
of Eror: and hath given his daughter In marrige to one of the
world: notwithstanding friends advised him to the Contrarey labouring
with him In time to Shew him the [full?] Consequence that might

---

19. Any Friend traveling as a minister was expected to carry a certificate proving membership and the unity of Friends of his or her monthly meeting. See Rebecca Larson, *Daughters of Light: Quaker Women Preaching and Prophesying in the Colonies and Abroad* (New York: Alfred A. Knopf, 1999), 109.

follow yet he hath willfully proceeded to the accomplishing
the same Contrarey to the advice of freinds: and the good order ~
Established amongs[t] us – –
therefore fri[e]nds are Concarned to testify in publick that they have
no unity with the s^d **John fish**:
but do deny him to be In younion and Communion with us – –
given forth form [from] our monthly meeting the 8th day of the 7th mth <u>1710</u>
Signed In behalf of s^d meeting by – –

Increas Allin [Increase Allen]	**Eliezar Smith**	**Abraham tucker**
Hizekiah [Hezekiah] **Smith**	**John lapham**	**Charles Dyer**
Stephen Willcock [Wilcox]	**James burrill** [Burrel]	**Josiah Merehew** [Merihew]
nathaneel howland	**Eliezer Slocum**	**Benjamin Howland**
Judah Smith	**william wood** – –	

and **Deliverance Smith** is appoynted to read It on a
first day after meeting at our meeting house and make return to
the next monthly meeting – –
John Lapham and **Judah Smith** make report that they have
Drawn up **John Tuckers** sertifycate as apoynted – –
Eliezar Slocum John Lapham and **Judah Smith** was appoynted
to attend the quortorly meeting next – –
the freinds that was formerly appoynted to v[i]ew the month
ly meeting minits – –
was Called upon and they give In their answer that they have
Don It and ordered them to be Recorded – –
this meeting doth appoynt **Timothey Davis** to assist **Savrey Cleffton** [Savory Clifton]
In the Service of visiting – –
William Soul [Soule] is appoynted to procur a pot to make fire[?] In and
Cols [coals?] to burn In it – –
Judah Smith Eliezar Slocum and **John Lapham** was appoyn=
ted to draw up an account to send to the quortorly meeting – –
this meeting is adjourned untell our youths meeting which will
be the sixt day of the Eight month next – – – – –

the meeting being meet according to adjournment the sixt
of the Eight month 1710 – –
the visitors give this meeting an account that they have not
made so Jeneral a viset as they ought to have done: yet by what
hath ben don we understand that things are pretty well
amongst friends – –
william Soul is appoynted to wright to freinds at **Rochester**
to stur [stir?] them up in deliqancy[?] and let them ~~kne~~ know that the month

ly meeting takes notic[e] of their neglect – – – – –

at a monthly meeting of friends held at our meeting house In
Dartmouth the 16th day of the Eight month 1710 – –
their was Colected –   –   –   –   –   –   – 0£-06s-06d
Dartmouth weekly meeting Called **william wood** and **Benjamin
Howland** apeared
Rochester weekly meeting Called and not appeared – –
the freind that was app°ynted to read the paper Concarning **John
fish** makes report to this meeting that he hath don It according
to order – –
and the freinds appoynte to atend the quortorly meeting make report
that they have atended the said meeting as ordered – –
the friends Appoynted to draw an account to the quortorly meeting
have don It as ordered by the last monthly meeting – –
william Soul [**Soule**] maks report to this meeting that he hath provided a
pot and coals according to order – –
and **william Soul** hath written to freinds at **rochester** as ordered
and whereas the quortorly meeting of ministers[?] have returned
Nathanel Howland to this monthly meeting to deal with him as In the
wisdom of truth they may think fit – –
Consarning his appearing In publick mee[t]ings of worship In prayer
and testamony to the burden of friends – –
this meeting refers It to the ~~Cos~~? weighty Considration of freinds untell
the next monthly meeting – –
Eliezar Slocum and **Benjamin Howland** is appoynted to Spake with
the said **nathanel** and let him know the mind of the quortorly meeting – –
and make return to the next monthy meeing – –
and the Epestle from the quortorly meeting In the fift month was re[a]d
and Excepted at this meeting – – – – –

At a monthly meeting of friends held at our meeting house In **Dartmouth**
the twenteth of the 9th month – – 1710 – – their was Colected 0£-10s-05d
Dartmouth weekly mee[t]ing Called **Benjamin Howland** and ~~Wi~~
william Soul appeared – –
Rochester weekly meeting Called **timothey Davise** [**Timothy Davis**] appeared – – –
this meeting orders **Benjamin Howland** to pay: **william Soul** Seventeen
Shillings and three pence for the pot and ~~a~~ Coals which he provided
for the Service of the meeting – –
and the matter Consarning **Nathanel Howland**s baring a publick
testimony amongst freinds is refered to the Consideration of the
next monthly meeting – –

and the freinds on the other side of **Coxet** river desiers that they
may have their meetings upon the first day of the week as formerly
which is granted – –
Joseph wing sone of **John wing** of **Rochester** desiered a Certificate
from this meeting Consarning his Clearness as to marrige – –
william Soul and **Savrey Clefton** [**Clifton**] was Chosen to Inspect In to ther
Clearness and bring In their answer to the next monthly meeting – –
and the Epestle from the last quortorly meeting was read and Excepted – – – – –

at a monthly meeting held at our meeting house In **Dartmouth** the
~~the 18~~ the 18th day of the 10th month <u>1710</u> – – their was Cᵒlected 0ᶠ-10ˢ-10ᵈ
Dartmouth weekly meeting ~~mee~~ Called **Judah Smith** and **william**
Wood appeared – –
Rochester weekly meeting Called **John Summers** ᴶʳ[?] appeared – –
the matter of deferance [difference] with **Nathanel Howland** Consarning his
Apearing In publick testimony amongst freinds In their publick meetings – –
Is refered to the next quortorly meeting for business – – and **Benjamin:** ᴴᵒʷˡᵃⁿᵈ
hath paid **william Soul** [**Soule**] according to appoyntment of the last
monthly meeting – –
the freinds that was appoynted the last monthly meeting to In
spect Into the Clearness of **Joseph wing** with respect to marrig – –
~~and~~ give their answer that they have made Inquirey and find no=
thing that may hender his proseding In marrig – –
and the visitors of **Dartmouth** weekly meeting is Called upon to give
their account how things are In freinds famileys: and they give
this meeting an account that **Thomas waight** [**Wait**] is about to take a
wife out of the order of freinds – –
John Tucker and **Judah Smith** is appoynted to Spake with him
Consarning that matter and bring their answer to the next monthly meeting
Benjamin Howland is ordered to pay **mathew Allin** [**Allen**] twelve Shillings
for the Use of his mare to the Eastward – –
the Visitors give their account that they ʰᵃᵛᵉ preformed a general visit
so far as they well can and their visits was kindly Excepted
but they find things not so weelle [well?] as they Could wⁱsh – –
Judah Smith and **william Soul** is appoynted to draw up an
Account to the quortorly meeting next – –
william Soul Benjamin Howland and **Judah Smith** is
appoynted to attend the quortorly meeting next – – – – – –

~~In~~ at a monthly meeting of freinds held at our me[e]ting house In
Dartmouth ᵗʰᵉ 15th day of the 11th month 1710 – – their was Colected 0ᶠ-11ˢ-08ᵈ

Dartmouth weekly meeting Called **Judah Smith and william wood**
appeared – – **Rochester** weekly meeting called not apeared – –
Judah Smith and **John tucker** gives this account that they have
Spoken with **thomas weight** [**Wait**] as appoynted the last monthly
meeting Consarning his going to take a wife out of the good ~
order of truth ᵃⁿᵈ hath laboured muuch with him ⁱⁿ ˡᵒᵛᵉ to Shew him
the Il [ill] Concequance that might follow: but he did not Seeme to
ᵗᵃᵏᵉ up with their advice – –
their for the matter is refered untel furder ocasion – –
william Soul and **Judah Smith** have drawn up an account to
the quortorly meeting [*blot*] **william Soul Benjamin Howland** and **Judah
Smith** make: rᵉport that they have atended the quortorly meeting as ordered

---

At a monthly meeting of freinds held at our meeᵗing house In **Dartmouth**
the 19ᵗʰ day of the 12ᵗʰ month 1710 – – their was Colected 0ᵋ-07ˢ-10ᵈ
Dartmouth weekly meeting Called **william Soul** and **william wood** appeared
Rochester weekly meeting called and none appeared – –
this meeting is Informed **thomas weight** [**Wait**] hath accomplished his marrige
out of the good order Established amongst us: where upon this meeting is
Consarned to give out a publick testimony against his proseding – –
and orders **John tucker** to Read the same on a first day before the
next monthly meeting: which is as foloweth – –
whereas **thomas wait** of **Dartmouth** In the County of **Bristol** In the
province of the **Masechusets Bay** Ind **new England** did for some time past
Com to our monthly meeting and Did Desiar to be In unity with freinds
and to be married amongst freinds In the good order Estabelished amongst
us. where upon freinds Couceld [counseled?] him under the[*blot*] Care and admonition
of the Church: but he declining from that which he Semed to have a
desier after: and went about to take a wife out of the good order of freinds
whereupon freinds laboured with him to perswade him to the Contrary
and to Show him the Ill consequence that might follow – –
but he refused to take the advice of freinds: and went on to the acomplish
ing; the Same Contrarey to the good order Estableshed amongst us – –
theirfore this meeting is Consarned to give forth a publick testimony ~
against the abovesaid **thomas Wait** and do disowne him to be one In
Sosiety withe us – –
given forth at our monthly meeting the 19ᵗʰ day of the 12ᵗʰ month 1710
Signed In behalf of Said meeting by

John Tucker	william wood	Stephen Willlcock [Wilcox]
Eliezar Slocum	John Lapham	nathanel Howland
Judah Smith	Benjamin Howland	nicholas Howland

Increas Allin [Allen]   James Burrill [Burrel]   Henrey Tucker
william Soul [Soule]   Abraham Tucker   william wood Jun[r]

(1711) at a monthly meeting of freinds helde at our meeting house In
Dartmouth the 26[th] day of the first month 1711 – – their was Colected 0[£]-08[s]-0[d]
Dartmouth weekly meeting Called **william Soule** and **Benjamin Howland**
app[e]ared – – **Rochester** weekly meeting Called non appeared – –
John tucker gives this meeting an [a]ccount that he hath Read
thomas waits Condemnation as appoynted – –
william wood and **John Lapham** is appoynted to attend the quor=
torly meeting next – –
Judah Smith and **Benjamin Howland** is appoynted to draw up an
account to the quortorly meeting – – the visitors Called to give an acount
how they find things In freinds famelys as to the afairs of truth – –
and their answer is that they find things prety well amongst freinds
Judah Smith is appoynted to make up the monthly meetings account
with **Benjamin Howland** and bring the account to the next ~
monthly meeting – – – – –

at a monthly meeting: of freinds held at our meeting house In **Dartmouth** the 6th of
the second month 1711 – – their was Colected for the use of friends 0[£]-09[s]-08[d]
Dartmouth weekly meeting Called **Judah Smith** and **william Soul** [Soule] appeared
Rochester weekly meeting Called and none appeared – –
william wood and **John Lapham** has attended the quortorly meeting
Judah Smith and **Benjamin Howland** hath drawn up an account to
the quortorly meeting as appoynted – –
Judah Smith has made up the monthly meetings account with
Benjamin Howland and their remains In the Stock 05[£]-02[s]-05[d]
and this meeting agrees that the orders Estabeleshed amongst freinds
Shall be Read at our monthly meeting once a quortor or oftenor – –
this meeting maks Choyce of **John tucker Stephen Willcock** [Wilcox] and
Elizer [Eliezer] **Slocum** to go to visit **rochestor** preparitive meeting and
to know the re[a]son why they have neglected to attend the monthly
Meeting: and bring In their answer to the next monthly meeting – –
the Epestle from the last quortorly meeting was Read and weell
Excepted – – **Benjamin Howland** and **william wood** is appoynted
to asist the women freinds In makeing Inquirey Consarning **abigal allins** [Abigail Allens]
allowing or incoreging [encouraging] the Creuel [cruel] and unmercyfull Beating
   or whi[p]ping
of her negro mansarvant – – – – –

At a monthly meeting of friends held In **Dartmouth** the twenty first day

of the third month 1711 – – their was Colected –　–　–　–　–　–　– 0$^£$-09^s-03^d
Dartmouth weekly meeting Called **Judah Smith** and **william wood**
Appeared – – **Rochester** weekly meeting Called **Elisha wing** appeared – –
It is agreed that the first day meetings at **Coxset** shall be for this
Somer [summer]: the first first day in Every month – –
Some Deferance [difference] presented to this meeting between **Charls** [Charles] **Dyer**
and **John Lapham** $_{and}$ **Nicholas Lapham** – –
Abraham tucker Judah Smith william Soul[e] **Benjamin Howland**
and **william wood** were Chosen: to hear and determan the Said
Deference – –
Stephen Willcock [Wilcox] and **John tucker** maks report that they have
visited **Rochester** weekly meeting as appoynted: and they find things
not well amongst them: and that was the reson [reason] that they have – –
neglacted the monthly meeting – –
the deferance consarning **Charls** [Charles] **Dyer** and **John** and **Nicholas**
lapham is refered to the $_{next}$ monthly meeting for an: answer – –
Judah Smith Benjamin Howland and **John tucker** is appoynted
to draw up **Abigal Allin**s [Abigail Allens] Condemnation – –
rochestor meeting gives an account that things are not so well a
mongst them as they should be: yet they think it best to labour
furdor [further] to get them amended – –
and the meeting adjourns untill the nex fourth day com week

---

the meeting being meet according$_{ing}$ to the adjournment the 30th of the 3 moth ^{1711} – –
hath given forth a paper of **Abigal Allin**s Condemnation and
orders **John tucker** to read It or Cause It to be Read In publick on: a
first day before the next monthyly meeting – – as foloweth – –
where as **Abigall Allin** [Abigail Allen] the wife of **Ebenezar Allen** of the
towne of **Dartmouth** In the County of **Bristol** In **new England**
having for many years freequented the meetings of us the
people Called Quakers and was Joyned In Sosieaty with us
But fore want of keeping In treue Salection[?] to that prenciple
Shee made profesion of: to wit the Spirit of truth In her own
heart which Sperit will lead all them [who?] obedient unto It
out of Everey thing that is Contrary against[?] the[?] natur of It and is In
Consist[e]nt with[?]; Shee hath ben given over to hardness of
heart to Such a degree that she hath ben not only consenting
but Incoraging the Creuell and unmercyfull whip[p]ing or
beating of her negro mansarvant he being strip[p]ed naked and
hanged up by the hands In his masters house and thir [~~beat..~~]
beating or whiping of him so unmercyfully that it is to be feard

that it was in some measur[e] the oc[c]asion of his death that
followed Soon after: [the?] [which?] wee do account is not only
unChrist[i]an but unheuman [inhuman] for which Cause we find our
selves Consarned to testefy to the world that wee do ut[e]rly ~
desowne all Such actions and all who are found In them
and perticurly the person above named – –
and as it is our Christ[i]an duty to pray for all people wee do
hartyly Desire allmighty god to open her ~~Spirit~~ understanding
if it be his will to give her to See her outgoings that Shee
may find a place of true repentance before the time of her viset=
tatsion [visitation?] be over – –
given by our men and womens monthly meeting held by
adjournment the 30th day of the third month 1711 – –
Signed In behaff of Said meeting by

Ruhamah Smith	**Judah[?] Howland**	**Judah Smith**
Sarah [J?] allin [Akin?]	**[...an?] Earle**	**Increase Allin**
marey lapham	**marey Smith**	**Eliezar Smith**
Rachell Allin [Allen]	**Ruth Smith**	**william wood**
Hannah tucker	**Ruth tucker**	**Deliverance Smith**
Hannah Soul [Soule]	**John tucker**	**Eliezar Slocum**
Benjamin howland	**william Soul**	**Stephen Willcock**

At a monthly meeting of feinds [friends] held at our meeting In **Dartmouth**
the Eighteenth of the fourth month 1711 – – their was colected – – £0 –06s–02d
Dartmouth weekly meeting Called **Judah Smith** and **william Soul** appeared
Rochester weekly meeting Called and not appeared – –
the paper of **Abigall Allins** [**Abigail Allens**] Condemnation was Read according
to order –– the Deferance [Difference] between **John Lapham nicholas lap
ham** and **Charl[e]s Dyer** is Ended – –
William Soul Abraham tucker and **william wood** are Chosen
to attend the Quortorly meeting next – –
william wood is appoynded [appointed] to get a lock for the meeting house
door and to be paid out of the Stock – –
and the meeting : adjourns untel the first Sixt[h] day in the fift month
the meeting being meet according to adjournment the Sixt[h] day
of the fift[h] month 1711 – –
Benjamin Howland is ordered to pay **william wood** Eighte[e]n pence
for the lock for the meeting house door – –
the visitors gives this meeting an account that they have not
visited the familyes of freinds this last Quortor – –
Judah Smith and **John tucker** are appoynted to draw up an

account to the Quortorly meeting next – – – – –

At a monthly meeting of freinds held at our meeting house In – –
Dartmouth the 17th day of the fift[h] month 1711 – – their was Colected – £0 –09s –3d
Dartmouth weekly meeting called **Eli[e]zar Slocum** and **william Soul**
appeared – – **Rochester** weeckly meeting Called **Elisha Wing** appeared – –
William **wood** and **William Soul** giv[e]s an acount that they
have attended the quortorly meeting as ordered – –
Judah Smith and **John tucker** have drawn up an acount to the
Quortorly meeting as appoynted – –
their hath ben three yearly meeting Epestles read In this meeting
for to stur up freinds to faithfullness In keeping up truths ~~~~
testimony : against wars and larning [learning] to ware [war] or paying for aney ~~suck~~
such thing – –
thise meeting doth advise the visitors that they be deligant [diligent] in
visiting the fameleys of freinds and advise them that they be
Carefull to bare a faithfull testimony against wars and larning [learning]
of war and against paying of money for aney Such thing – –
and the matter Consarning **John mendol** [**Mendall**] is refered to the next
monthly meeting – –
the Quortorly meeting Epestle was Read and was caindly [kindly] Excepted
and do agree with their proposals Consarning Sending to **England**
for some of **George Fox** his primers for Children to larne to
read In: and the money to be taken out of our Colection and Sent
to the Quortorly meeting[20] – – – – – –

at a monthly meeting of friends held at our meeting house In
Dartmouth the 20th of the 6th month 1711 – – their was Colected – – £0-05s-08d
Dartmouth weekly meeting Called **Judah Smith** and – –
william wood appeared – – **Rochester** weekly meeting
Called **timothey Davis** appeared – –
the mattar Conserning **John Mendol** is refered to the next
monthly meeting – –
the freinds chosen by the last preparitive meeting of **Dartmouth**
to go to **Increas[e] Allins** [**Allens**] daughtor **Susana** to know whether the
report be true of her being with Child – –
the freinds appoynted make report they have ben with her
and shee acknowledges that shee is with Child and tak[e]s all
the blame and shame to her self an Clears her parents – –

20. The "primer" was G[eorge] F[ox] and E[llis] Hookes], *Instructions for Right Spelling, and Plain Directions for Reading and Writing True English, Etc. With Several Delightful Things Very Useful and Necessary for Young and Old to Read and Learn* (London: T. Sowle, 1706). It was first published in 1673.

this meeting finding an n^esesety to Draw up a Condemnation
against her for it ~~wich~~ which being Read and signed here
is ordered to be read publickly on a first day at this meeting
house by **william soul** and make return to the next -
monthly meeting:
which condemnation is as foloweth – –
to all people to whom this may come for the clearing of the
truth
where as **Susanah allin [Allen]** daughter of **Increas Allin [Allen]** of **Dartmouth**
not with standing she was educated amongst freinds yet
not herkning [harkening] to ye Spirit of God in her one [own?] heart nor
advice of her parents and friends but giving way to y^e
enemy and her one [own?] lusts: is with Child as her selfe
acknowledgeth
these may signifie we have no unity therewith:
but Do utterly abhor & testify against all such
ungodly actions & the Spirit that Leads there unto
& disown her for ye same but desire ye Lord may
Give her a Sence of ye Evil of her doings &
hearty Sorrow & repentance & forgiveness for y^e
same:
from our monthly men and womens meeting
held at **Dartmouth** ye 20th of the 6th month 1711

Stephen Wilcock	**Hannah Tucker**
Peleg Slocumb	**Sarah Allen**
Benjamin Howland	**Ruhema Smith**
Joseph Russell	**Hassadiah Russell**
John Russell	**Rachel Allen**
William Wood ju	**Mary Slocumb**
Adam Mott	**Hannah Cadman**
Increas[e] Allen	**Susanna Wilcock [Wilcox]**
Nathaniell Howland	**Mary Smith**
William Wood	**Eliezabeth Russell**
Eliezer Slocumb	**Ruth Tucker**
Judah Smith	**Mary Lapham**
William Soule	**Mary Layton**
Josiah Merehew	**Hope Merehew [Merihew]**
Abram Tucker	**Sarah Landers**
John Lapham	**Phebe Tucker**

And **John Tucker** & **Eliezer Slocumb** [**Slocum**] is appoin
ted to procure a friend to keep the meeting house
for yᵉ ensuing year – –
and this meeting Desires all friends yᵗ [that] was empres [impressed]
sed this present year may bring in a true account
to the next monthly meeting how they have born up
Truths testimony in yᵗ Case – –
This meeting being informed that some friends
or their children or boath have given money to
Encourage people to go to war or to excuse them
selves or children from being empressed to go to war
— The visiters are Desired to make diligent
Enquiry therein and deal wᵗʰ all such & make Re
port thereof to our next monthly Meeting – – – – –

at a monthly meeting of friends held at our
Meeting House in **Dartmouth** yᵉ 17ᵗʰ of the 7ᵗʰ
Month 1711 – –
There was ‸ᶜᵒllected for yᵉ use of friends £00 – 4ˢ= 10ᵈ
Dartmouth weekly meeting Called **Judah Smith** &
William Wood appeared – – **Rochester** weekly meeting
Called none appeared – –
& **Susanna Allen** her Condemnation was read
one a first Day as Ordered – –
Judah Smith & **Josiah Merehew** [**Merihew**] hath given
in their accounts Concerning their being empres
sed to yᵉ sattisfaction of this Meeting – –
& some other friends yᵗ were empressed not
being here – therefore it is refered until yᵉ next
Monthly meeting for them to Give in their accounts – –
Judah Smith Stephen Willcock [**Wilcox**]
& **John Tucker** – – is appointed to Draw up
something to Clear yᵉ truth from yᵉ skandal yᵗ may
be Cast upon it by reason of some friends Children
Running together & wres[t]ling on a furst Day – –
And this meeting is adjourned until yᵉ first 6 day
of yᵉ 8ᵗʰ month – – – – –

This meeting being meet according to Adjournment
yᵉ 4ᵗʰ of yᵉ 8ᵗʰ MO – – 1711 – –
The 3 friends yᵗ was Chose to Draw up a Testimo

ny against friends Childrens going together &
wres[t]ling on first Dayes is not yet Done but it is
Desired yᵗ it may be done against the next
Monthly meeting in order yᵗ it may be Signed – –
& yᵉ visiters being Called upon to give in their accounts
of their visiting of friends famlyes & how they
find things amongst yᵐ [them] & they report yᵗ they find yᵐ
Loving took their vissits kindly & whare they
saw anything out of order they speak to it & it
was also well taken & promised to endeaver yᵗ it
may be amended & some things not well but
Hope Care will be taken about it – –
William Wood & **Joh[n] Tucker** is appointed to
attend yᵉ quarterly Meeting next – –
Judah Smith & **John Tucker** are appointed to
Draw up an account Shewing yᵉ quarterly
meeting how things are amongst us – –
William Wood is appointed to Take yᵉ Care of yᵉ
50 Shillings yᵗ was agreed on at yᵉ last quarterly
Meeting for us to send for Books & deliver it
to yᵉ quarterly Meeting – –
John Tucker & **Deliverance Smith** are
appointed to Speak wᵗʰ **Daniel Shepherd**
& to give him to understand yᵉ order of friends
& what he must expect if he Come in unity
wᵗʰ us & be a member of this meeting – – – – –

Att a monthly meeting of friends held at
our meeting house in **Dartmouth** yᵉ 14ᵗʰ of yᵉ
8ᵗʰ month 1711 – – There was Collected £00 = 06ˢ = 09ᵈ
Dartmouth weekly meeting Called **William Wood**
& **Judah Smith** appeared – –
Rochester Weekly meeting Called Not appeared – –
& yᵉ friends yᵗ was Chose yᵉ Last Monthly meeting
to Draw up a Judgment against friends Children
& servants going to wres[t]ling is Done & is
as followeth – –
And **John Tucker** is appointed to read the
same on a furst day at the end of yᵉ meeting
of worship – –
Whereas Wee have been Informed yᵗ several

friends Children with other have been together
on a first Day of yᵉ Week a wrestling wᶜʰ hath
brought Trouble and reproach upon us & yᵉ
Truth wᶜʰ we profess – –
& now for yᵉ Clearing of our Inocency [innocence]; we Declare
Against all Lewedness & vanity in such especially
as are under our Care whom we do not allow to
Run together on yᵉ first Dayes of yᵉ Week
nor any other times to be found in wrestling
& what evils else of yᵉ Like Tendancy to draw
out yᵉ Mind Contrary to Godlyness and further
for yᵉ Preventing of yᵉ above vanityes & evils we
Caution advise & warn all parents of Children
Masters & Mistresses of famlyes yᵗ are in So
ciety with us yᵉ People Called Quakers first to
use Their Authority in wisdom & Truth wᵗʰ their
Children & servants & if they can not Reclaim
yᵐ then we as a Society of Church being sesonably made
acquainted there with Shall by Gods assistance
use our utmost endeavers to Reclaim them
Which if we cannot Do then shall not only testify
against such practises but also against yᵉ Person
or pearsons so offending and declare publickly yᵗ they
are not of us – –
Signed by order – & in behalf of our Monthly
meeting held at our meeting House the 15ᵗʰ
of the 8ᵗʰ month 1711
by **John Tucker**

Nathaniell Howland	**Thomas Taber jun**
William Wood	**John Lapham**
Increas[e] Allen	**Josiah Merrehew [Merihew]**
Peleg Slocumb [Slocum]	**Stephen Willcock [Wilcox]**
Benjamin Howland	**Judah Smith**
Eliezer Slocumb	**Jabez Barker**
James Burrill [Burrel]	**Charles Dyre [Dyer]**
William Soule	**Nicholas Lapham**

John Tucker and **Judah Smith** hath given yᵉ quarter
ly meeting an account how things are amongst us
as appointed – –
John Tucker & **William Wood** Report that they

have attended ye quarterly meeting as appointed – –
and **William Wood** hath delivered y^e money to the
Quarterly meeting as appointed- y^e Matter Concerning
Daniell Shepherd is refered to the next monthly meeting

at a Monthly Meeting of friends held at
our Meeting ho[u]se in **Dartmouth** y^e 19th Day of y^e
9th Mo 1711 – – There was Collected £00 – – 09^s = 06^d
Dartmouth weekly Meeting Called **William**
Wood appeared – – **Rochester** Weekly
meeting Called Not appeared – –
Nicolas Lapham hath given in his account how
he Came clear of his being empressed [impressed] to this
meetings Content & **John Tucker Juner** also
hath given in his account to Content
And is as followeth
I being Empressed this Last Summor 1711 in an
expeditian to go to **Canada** to war wch I refused
for Concience sake for I beleive y^t I ought not
To take up ye Carnal sword against any ~~peo~~ Nation
or people & some time after I was had to **James**
Sissons before Colenal [Colonel] **Church** & there was
an Order writ & read to mee wherein I was
Commanded to go to **Rocksbury** [**Roxbury**] & Commit my selfe
to Colenall [Colonel] **William Dudley** wch I Could not find
freedom To do neighther: & after that I was
Warned go to the **Castle Island** Lying near
To **Boston** to take up armes wch I refused also
and one [on?] ye 16th Day of ye 6th Month Leightenant [Lieutenant]
John Akin came to my house wth severall with
him & for aid & S^d **akin** Took Mee by force
& Dragged mee out of my House & then
Commanded his aid [aide] to assist him wch they Did &
Took mee and set mee on Horce Back [horseback] & held
Mee on & Carried mee to **Timothy Maxfield**s
& then committed mee to the Custidy of **John**
Briggs Insign [Ensign] who carried mee ye next Day
To **Bridg[e]water** & ye next Day to the **Castle** wch was
the Last Day of ye week being near night I was had
Before ye Captain of y^e **Castle** & he asked mee
Whither I would take up armes I told him

That I should not take up yᵉ Carnal weapon
John Commanded the officer to take Care of mee
til Second Day and then I was brought before
yᵉ Captain of yᵉ **Castle** again the 2ᵈ Day morning & he
asked Me whither I would work there I told him
no for wᶜʰ I was put into a Close place Called yᵉ
Hole or Dungeon & there to be kept without
Victuals or Drink but was Let out again the same
Day near sun set & there was still kept at yᵉ **Castle**
& often urged to work but could not although told
that If I would work yᵗ [that] I Should be released in a little
time but If not I might be put aboard some man
of war but I Could not med[d]le ~~w~~ & at yᵉ end of 4
Weeks & 2 dayes I was released & brought of [off?] & set
at Liberty without paying or giving any Money

Nicholas Lapham

Here follows a Coppy of **John Tucker Juner**s paper which
he gave in also at yᵉ said monthly meeting – –
I being empressed [impressed] yᵉ Last sum[m]er in an expeditian to
Canada to War but I was Counted to [too] young by Colenal [Colonel]
Church & so not put upon that expeditian
but afterwards one [on?] a first Day of yᵉ Week after
Meeting Leightenant [Lieutenant] **Akin** having an order from
Colenal [Colonel] **Benjamin Church** to Carry yᵉ men that said
Akin had empressed to go to the **castle** Whereupon said
John Akin Commanded mee to go but I refused to go
with him then he Commanded **Thomas Briggs** &
Jonathan Talman [**Tallman**] to Lay hold on me but they Did
not but Let me alone till the sixt[h] day following
wᶜʰ was yᵉ 16ᵗʰ Day of yᵉ 6ᵗʰ month 1711 · · ·
& then **John Briggs** & **Thomas Cornil** [**Cornell**] son of
Stephen Cornil came to my father[s] House in the
Morning & took me by force & set me on
Horce back & carried mee to **Bridg[e]water** that
day & yᵉ next Day to yᵉ **Castle** [**Castle Island**] which was yᵉ Last
Day of the Week being near night I was Had
before the Captain of yᵉ **Castle** & he asked mee
Whither I would take up armes & I told him
No so he Commanded the officer to take Care
of mee till Second Day & then I was brought

before yᵉ Captain of yᵉ **Castle** again the Second Day
Morning & he asked Mee Whither I would
Work there I Told him I would Consider of it
& he said I must not stand there to Consider
of it but must go to work or go into yᵉ Hole
& consider of it there & I went to work
about halfe an Hour & then & I went up to him
and told him that I Could work no More there
and he Said I Should go into yᵉ hole and there
Lye while I would work but yᵉ officers Came to
Mee the next Day & asked mee Whither I would
Work & I said no and they said yᵗ I must
Go into the hole but they Did not put mee in
but threat[e]ned to put mee in or Carry mee
aboard some Man of war but I Could not
Med[d]le & at the end of 4 weeks & 2 Dayes
I was Released & brought off & set at Liber
ty without giving of any money – –

                              John Tucker juner

John Tucker & **Judah Smith** are appointed
to Speak with **Daniell Shepherd juner**
& give in their accou[n]t to yᵉ next monthly
meeting
This meeting orders yᵗ **Benjamin Howland**
Should pay **Joshua Easton** 8 Shillings & 7ᵈ
for yᵉ Mending a glass at yᵉ Meeting House
& the friends that was to see that thee
Meeting House seats were finnished are
Desired to speak with the Carpenter & see
Whither he will finnish yᵐ [them] in any reᵃsonable
Time & make return to yᵉ next Monthly
Meeting – –
And **Coxet** friends Desires that they may
have their first Dayes meeting for the winter
Season as us[u]al which is granted – – – – –

A[t] a Monthly Meeting of friends held at
our Meeting house in **Dartmouth** the
17ᵗʰ Day of the 10ᵗʰ Month 1711
There was Collected 9 Shillings & seaven [seven] pence
Dartmouth Weekly Meeting Called

William Wood appeared – **Rochester** Weekly
Meeting Called none appeared – –
John Tucker & **Judah Smith** [Is?] still
Continued to speak with **Daniell Shepherd**
– – **Benjamin Howland** hath paid 8 Shillings
& seaven pence as ordered yᵉ Last Monthly
Meeting – –
yᵉ friends yᵗ was to Speak with yᵉ Carpenter
Reports that he will finnish yᵉ seates
this Winter – –
~~Eliezer Slocumb~~ A paper being presen
ted to this meeting from **Abigall** [Abigail] **Allen**
Wherein Shee signifies that Shee Desires to
Come into unity with friends & yᵉ sence of
this meeting is that shee should wait
till friends have a sence that shee is fitt
to be ˣcepted [accepted] – –
and **Eliezer Slocumb** [Slocum] and **William Soule**
are appointed to give ~~Her~~ the mind of yᵉ
meeting – – **Stephen Willcock** [Wilcox] &
John Tucker are appointed to attend
the quarte[r]ly meeting next – –
& yᵉ visiters are called to give in yᵉ account
how they find things among friends
And thire account is as followeth
that they have not but that things are pretty
well among friends but they have not
been out to visit friends famlyes this Last
quarter – –
John Tucker & **Abram** [Abraham?] **Tucker** are appoin
ted to Draw an accoount to yᵉ Quarterly
Meeting – –

att a monthly meeting Of friends held at
our Meeting ho[u]se in **Dartmouth** yᵉ 29ᵗʰ Day of
the 11ᵗʰ Month 1711 – –
There was Collected 9 Shilling & 2ᵈ
Dartmouth Weekly meeting Called
William Wood Judah Smith appeared
Rochester Weekly meeting Called not
appeared — **John Tucker** hath Spoken with

Daniell Shepherd Juner as appointed
& he Desires to sit in the monthly meeting
of business W^ch is granted He observing y^e
order there established – –
Abigall Allen hath had ye mind of ye Last
Monthly meeting & Shee saith that Shee
is Willing to give what sattisfaction thee
Meeting Desireth & it is ye mind of this
meeting that Shee Condemn those things
in perticuler for Which Shee was Denied
in writing to be exposed as far as friends
Thinke fitt and then wait till by her good fruits
Shee Manifests to ye Meeting that She has
Really Come in by amendment of Life – –
Eliezer Slocumb [**Slocum**] & **John Tucker** is to let her
have a coppy of this Minnit – –
William Wood is ad[d]ed to the other two friends to
Have the over sig[h]t of our monthly meetings
for business that none sitt in them but Such as
are allowed – –
the epistle from the Last quarterly meeting
was read and kindly accepted – – – – –

Att a monthly meeting of friends held att
our Meeting House in **Dartmouth**
the 18th Day of ye 12th month 1711/12 – –
there was Collected 4^s- **Dartmouth** Weekly
Meeting Called **Judah Smith John Lapham**
appeared — **Rochester** Weekly Meeting Called
None appeared – –
~~Eliezer Slocumb~~ & ~~William Wood gives this~~
~~meeting~~ **John Tucker Eliezer Slocumb**
hath Spoken with **Abigall** [**Abigail**] **Allen** & given her
the mind of ye Meeting ~~and~~ With a Coppy of
y^E Minnit as appointed – –
a Small book of **James Burrills** [**Burrels**] Late of
Dartmouth deceased was presented to This
Meeting for ye Approbation of ye Meeting for
the printing ye same[21] – –
William Soule & **Benjamin Howland**

21. No record has been found of the publication of this work.

& **John Tucker** & **Deliverance Smith** are
appointed to peruse the same & make return
to the next Monthly meeting – –
Abram Tucker and **John Tucker** are appointed to let
Rochester Preparitive Meeting know that y^e
Monthly Meeting hath had no ~~ne~~ no account
from them this severall Monthly meetings
& to write to y^e visiters there that they perform
A generall vissitt against y^e next preparitive Meeting – – – – –

(*1712*) Att a monthly meetin[g] of friends held at our
meeting house in **Dartmouth** the 17th Day of the
first month 1712 – –
Collected & received for Book[s?] $^£$oo[?] =15$^{[s?]}$ = oo^d
Dartmouth Weekly meeting Called **Judah Smith**
& **William Wood** appeared **Rochester** Weekly
Meeting Called **Elisha Wing** appeared – –
& y^e friends that were chosen to peruse the
Book that was presented to y^e Last monthly meet
ing in writing reports that they find nothing
but that it may be printed And this Meeting
Recommends ye S^d Book to the quarterly Meet
ing for their perusal and Concurance therein – –
Abram Tucker & **John Tucker** make report that they
have Writ to **Rochester** proparetive Meet
ing and to ye visiters as appointed ye buisieness [business]
of **Dartmouth** meeting Called y^e
The friends that was appointed to see the
addition of ye meeting house ^{a}Compleated Saith
that it is done ~~e~~ and their is Due to y^m [them] four
teen pence & this meeting orders **Benjamin**
Howland to pay it out of the Stock – –
A paper was signed at this meeting concerning
Deborah Smiths proceeding in marriage Contrary
to the order of friends and is as followeth – – – – –

[bottom quarter of page is blank as well as top half of the next]

John Tucker is appointed to read ye same on a
first Day at ye Latter end of the meeting before
the next monthly meeting – –

From **Rochester** no buisieness – –

The visitter Called to give in the account of their
visiting **Rochester** gives an account y^t [that] things
are pretty well and encouraging – –

Dartmouth vissiters gives their account that
things in the generall are pretty well some perticu
lers not so well as we desire – –

And this meeting is adjourned till the 4th day of the
2^d— month next – –

This meeting being meet according to adjournment

The 4th Day of the 2^d month – 1712 – –

**Benjamin Howland Eliezer Slocumb [Slocum] & William
Wood** are appointed to attend the quarterly meeting – –

Judah Smith & John Tucker are appointed to Draw
up an account to the Quarterly meeting next
Shewing how things are amongst us – –

Deliverance Smith is appointed to make
up the monthly meeting account with **Benjamin
Howland** and make return to the next Monthly
Meeting – – – – –

At a Monthly mee[t]ing held at our meeting house in **Dartmouth**
the 21^{fst} of the second month 1712 – – their was Colected – £0-11^s-0^d

Dartmouth weekly meeting Called **Judah Smith** and $^{(and\ one\ and\ four\ pen[ce?])}$ $_{for\ Book[?]}$
William Wood ap[p]eared – –

Rochester weekly meeting Called and non[e] appeared – –

Judah Smith and **John tucker** have drawn up the account
to the quortorly meeting as appoynted – –

Benjamin Howland William Wood and **Eliezar Slocumb**
have attended the quortorly meeting as appoynted – –

John tucker reports that he hath Read **Deborah Smith**s ~
that is now **Debroah Allins [Allens]** Condemnation as appoynted – –

Deliveranc[e] Smith is s[t]ill Continued to make up [to?] The monthly =
meetings account with~~t~~ **Benjamin Howland** – –

the buseness of **Dartmouth** weekly meeting Called – –

Abraham tucker and **John tucker** are appoynted to
take [care?] that the widow **Sarah Allins [Allens]** sone [son] doth not
Sell the Inheretance that ^{shee} is to have ^{her} liveing out of
with out good provision for her lively hood ~~

During her life – –

this meeting agrees to bu[i]ld a stabel [stable] twenty foot

one way and teen [ten?] foot the other way for the Use of
traveling friends and **Abraham tucker** and **John =
tucker** are appoynted to get the work don[e] and ~~
finished by the last of the seventh month <u>1712</u>
and they have liberty to Joyn a stable to It for their
own Use – – **Joseph Russell Jur** ^{is} to get a pasege [passage] for
John Oxley to go to **nantucket** and the meeting is to
pay the charge – –
the quortorly ^{mee[t]ing} Epistle was read and kindly Excepted

---

At a monthly meeting of friends held at our meeting house
In **Dartmou[t]h** the 19th day of the third month 1712 – – –
Dartmouth weekly meeting Called **william wood** and ~~
Judah Smith appeared – –
rochester weekly meeting Called **Savery Clefton** [**Savory Clifton?**] appeared ––
their was Col[l]ected for the Use of friends –   –   –   –   –   – [£]0–05^s–03^d
Deliverance Smith hath made up the meetings accounts
with **Benjamin Howland** as apoynted and their remains
In the stock –   –   –   –   –   –   – [£]07–08^s–03^d
John tucker and **Abraham tucker** according to the order of the
Last monthly meeting makes Report that they have taken sefisiant
Care for a Sutable mantainence for the widow **Sarah Aallin** [**Allen**]
Josep[h] Russell Jur makes report that the meeting has no thing
to pay for **John Oxleys** paseg [passage] to **nantucket** – –
the fri^ends one [on?] the other side **Coxset** river desir[e]s that they ~~
may have a meeting amongst them two first days In a month
which is granted for this summer – –
and the meeting Is ordered to be at **James tripps** the first ––
first day In Everey month and at **William Woods** [the?] second
first day In Eerey [every] month – –
Rochester meeting Called no buseness
our next monthly meeting is adjourned untel the fo[u]rth
second day In the fo[u]rth month next – –

At a monthly meeting of freinds held at our meeting house
In **Dartmouth** the 23th [*sic*] day of the 4th month 1712 – – –
th^eir was Col[l]ected for the use of freinds –   –   –   –   – [£]0–09^s-00^d
Dartmouth weekly meeting Called **Judah Smith** and **william
Wood** appeared – –
Rochester weekly meeting Called not appeared – –
John tucker hath provided a passeg for freinds to goe to
Nantucket as appoynted by the last preparitive meeting ––

John tucker and **william Wood** are appoynted to attend
the Quorterly meeting next – –
Judah Smith and **John tucker** are Appoynted to Draw
up an ac[c]ount to the Quortorly meeting Shewing ~~
how the testemony of truth Is keept up amongst us – –
John tucker Judah Smith John Russell Stephen willcock [Wilcox]
and **Abraham tucker** are appoynted to have the over
sight of freinds Buring [Burying] ground and to see that It be keept
Cl⁽ᵉ⁾ar of brush and that freinds burey In order and that none
be bur[i]ed their but freinds and Such as freinds Al[l]ow off [of] – –
the visitors g⁽ⁱ⁾ve their Account that they have not visited
the familyes of friends sence the last Quortorly meeting
but they Signify that for the time to Come they will be
more Deligant [diligent] – – – – –

At a Monthly meeting of friends held at our meeting house
in **Dartmouth** the twenty first day of the fift[h] month ∸ – 1712
their was Col[l]ected for the Use of friends –   –   –   –   – ᶠ0– 05ˢ-07ᵈ
Dartmouth weekly meeting Called **Judah Smith** and ~~
William Wood Ap[p]eared – –
Rochester weekly meeting Called and not Ap[p]eared – –
and freinds had a paseig [passage] to **nantucket** and back again
with **Jonathan Hathaway** and he wanted not take ~~
aney thing for their passeg – –
william wood and **John tucker** have attended the quortorly
meeting as appoynted – –
Judah Smith and **John tucker** have drawn up an account
to the Quortorly meeting as Appoynted– –
this meeting being Informed that **Benjamin Russell** hath
taken an oath to serve In the place of a Constable – –
Contrarey to the Com[m]and of Christ: for which he signe=
fyes he is sorey [sorry] — and the Judgment of the meeting is
that he should Condemn It be fore the Justice where he
toock It
Deliverance Smith and **Eliezar Slocumb** [Slocum] are appoynt
ed to see It don[e] and make return to the next – –
monthly meeting

At a monthly ᵐᵉᵉᵗⁱⁿᵍ of freinds held at our meeting house In – –
Dartmouth the 18ᵗʰ day of the 6ᵗʰ month 1712
their was Col[l]ected for the Use of freinds –   –   –   –   – ᶠ0-05ˢ-05ᵈ

Dartmouth weekly meeting Called **william Wood** and ~~
Judah Smit[h] Appeared – –
Rochestor weekly meeting Called **nicholas Davis** appeared – –
Eliezer Slocumb and **Deliverance Smith** hath spoken with
Benjamine Russell as appoynted – –
and he sayes that he Cannot Condemn his taking the oath
of a Constable be fore the Justece not yet – –
some Deferance presented to this meeting be tween **hizekiah** [**Hezekiah**]
Smith and his brother **Deliverance Smith** – –
this meeting makes Choyse of **thomas taber Junr Elizer** ~~
Slocumb william Soul[e] nicholas Howland and **Henrey** =
tucker to hear and determin[e] said Deferance and make
return to the next monthly meeting – –
the quartorly meeting Epestle was read amongst us and
was well Excepted– – – – –

At a monthly meeting of friends held at our meeting house
In **Dartmouth** the 15th day of the seventh month 1712– –
their was Col[l]ected for the use of friends –   –   –   –   –   – £0–05^s–06^d
Dartmouth weekly meeting Called **Judah Smith** and ~~w~~ **William**
Soul[e] Appeared – –
Rochester weekly meeting Called not Appeared – –
The friends that were Chose to hear & Ditermin the
Differance b_etwixt **Hezekiah Smith** and **Deliverance**
Smith hath given their Award: and it is ordered to
be Delivered to the parties Concerned – –
The visiters gives this meeting an Account that
they have visited y^e famlyes of friends and in
Some famlyes things pretty well and there
visits kindly accepted and in some others not well
but [²]~~their~~ visits rejected – –[blot]–
and **Sarah Allen** hath ye Consent of this meeting
to remove with her son into the **Narraganset**
Countrey and hath given her a sertificate in order
thereto – and its ~~left~~ to the visiters to Labour
with **John Howland** concerning his going to
Marry Contrary to the order of truth – –
John Lapham & **William Wood** and **John Tucker**
are appointed to attend the quarterly meeting next – –
Judah Smith & **John Tucker** are appointed to
draw up an account to the quarterly meeting – – – – –

At a monthly meeting of friends held at our meet
ing house in **Dartmouth** the 20th of th 8th month
1712 — there was Collected –   –   –   –   –   –   – 00-02=10
Dartmouth Weekly meeting Called **William Wood**
and **John Lapham** appeared – –
Rochester Weekly meeting Called **Elisha Wing**
appeared — **John Tucker William Wood** and
John Lapham have attended the quarterly meeting
as appointed **John Tucker** and **Judah Smith** hath
Drawn up an account to the quarterly Meeting
— **Charles Dyre** Desires a sertefycate from
this meeting which is refered to the next
Monthly meeting – –
The account from **Rochester** peroparetive
Meeting is that Things are pretty well amongst
friends — **Abram Tucker** and **John Tucker** is
Still Continued to get the stable finnished
by the next monthly meeting

At a monthly meeting of friends held at our
Meeting House in **Dartmouth** the 17th of ye
9th month 1712 — there was Collected – 00=05-10
Dartmouth weekly meeting Called **Judah Smith**
William Wood appared – –
Rochester weekly meeting called and none appeared – –
and freinds have had some conferance consarning giev=
ing **Charls Dyer** a sertifycate and nothing apearing against him
the meeting appoynts **Judah Smith** and **John Tucker**
to Draw one against the next monthly meeting – –
Abraham Tucker and **John Tucker** are stil continued
to get the stable finished – –
and friends one the other side of **aCoxset river** are
alowed to have their meetings their as formerly – –
John Tucker and **Eliezer Slocumb** are appoynted to
agree with afreind to keep the meeting house the Insu-
=ing year – – – – –

At a monthly meeting of friends held at **Dartmouth**
the 15th day of the 10th month 1712 – –
their was Colected for the Use of friends –   –   –   – 0lb-10s-01d
Dartmouth weekly meeting Called **William Wood**
and **Judah Smith** Apeared – –

Rochester weekly meeting Called **John Summers**
Appeared — and the friends appoynted have drawn
up a sertifycate for **Charles Dyer** whih is alowed and
~~an~~ signed by this meeting – –
and **Benjamin Howland** is ordered to pay **Judah**
Smith twenty shillings for keeping the meeting house
John Lapham Judah Smith and **William Wood** are
Appoynted: to Draw up a paper of Condemnation
against **John Howland:** for his marring contrarey
to the ordor of: truth – –
the visitors gives an account that they have viseted
several freinds fameleys and they find things prety
well — **William Wood** and **Sephen Willcock** are appoynted to attend the
quortorly meeting next – –
and **Rochester** meeting desires the monthly meeting to
Aseste them In the setlement of and securety of thire
meeting house land — and **Thomas Taber** and **John Tucker**
are Appoynted to aseste them – –
Judah Smith and **John Tucker** are appoynted to draw
up an account to the quortorly meeting – –
this meeting is adjourned til the next fourth day
come week – – – – –

the meeting being meet according: to adjournment the
twenty forth of the 10th month 1712 – –
the visitors give their acount that they have visited
some famelyes of freinds and they find things out of
Ordor amongst Some of freinds children and of Some
of them they have hope but of other Some they have
but lettel or no hope – –
Stephen Willcock Deliverance Smit and **Judah**=
Smith are appoynted to labour with them to bring
them to a sight and sence of their out goings and make
return of their doings to the next monthly meeting
and this meeting rfers **John Howland**s Condemnation
Drawn up at the monthly meeting held the 15th =
of the 10th month 1712 to the quortorly meeting
for their advice whether a publick testimoney ought
to go forth against the said **Howland** or not – –
Some friends of this meeting being desatesfyed think
ing It ought not to go forth against him – –

and **Thomas Taber Ju^r** proposed to this meeting that they
may have an other meeting of worship their once
In a month – which is refered to the next monthly
meetings Considratinon – – – – –

At a monthly meeting of friends held at our Meeting
House in **Dartmouth** the 15th Day of y^e 11th month 1712/13
there was Collected for the use of friends 00-08=01
Dartmouth Weekly meeting Called **Judah Smith** and
William Wood appeared — **Rochester** Weekly meeting
Called **Elisha Wing** appeared – –
and **Benjamin Howland** hath paid **Judah Smith**
twenty Shillings as appointed – –
Deliverance Smith and **Stephe Wilcock** and
Judah Smith hath Spoken With the young men as
appinted by the Last monthly meeting and the young
men Do not Justefy them selves in their being at
John Akinses at an unseasonable time and they
Hope they shall Do so no more –– –
and this meeting Doth according to the Request of
friends at **Cushnot** grant that they shall have
another meeting of Worship there which is to be
those who first Day in every month except it be when
it falls out to be that first Day next before the
monthly meeting of business – –
William Wood and **Stephen Willcock** hath attended
the quarterly meeting as appinted – –
the Epistle from the quarterly meeting was read
amongst us & was kindly accepted and ye epistle from
The yearly meeting in **London** was read amongst us
and was kindly accepted – –
John Tucker is appointed to get the yearly meeting
Minnits Coppied out for **Rochester** meeting – –
William Soule is appinted to Read **John Howland**
his Condemnation one a first Day of the week before
the next Monthly meeting – – – – –

At a monthly meeting of friends held ħ at our meet
ing house in **Dartmouth** the 16th of the 12th month
1712/13 There was Collecte for the use of friends 00-10=01
Dartmouth Weekly meeting Called **Judah Smith**

and **William Wood** appeared — **Rochester** Weekly
Meeting Called **Nicolas Davis** appeared – –
John Howlands Condemnation was read as appinted
and is as followeth – –
From our monthly meeting held at **Dartmouth**
The 15th of y^e 10th month 1712 — This is given forth
for the Clearing of Truth and friends – –
Whereas **John Howland** the Son of **Nathaniell
Howland** hath been a man of a vain Conversation
and not as becomes ye Truth and friends have Laboured
With him from time to time to bring him to
a sight of those vanities which Doth not become our
holy profession but he not herkning to friends nor to
The teachings of ye Grace of God which would teach him
and all mee to Live soberly in this present world
and he refused to take the Counsel and advice given
him by friends but took him a wife out of the order
of truth established amongst friends all w^{ch} [which] hath
been greatly to ye trouble and greif of faithful
friends therefore this Meeting Doth deny him to be
one of us – :
Signed in behalf of said meeting by

John Tucker	William Wood juner	Josiah Merehew
Stephen Willcock	Judah Smith	Nicolas Lapham
William Wood	Eliezer Slocumb	Jabez Barker
Abram Tucker	Peleg Slocumb	Henry Tucker
John Lapham	Increas Allen	————————

John Tuker is still continued to get a yearly meeting
minnits Drawn out for **Rochester** meeting – –
William Soule Deliverance Smith and **Eliezer Slocumb**
are Still Continued for to Speak further with
Benjamin Russell to know what he Can Do for y^e clear
ing of y^e Testimony of truth Concerning his taking
The place of a Constable and that he attend the next
monthly meeting

(1713) At a Monthly Meeting of friends held at our
Meeting house in **Dartmouth** the 16th of y^e 1st month
1713 there was collected for y^e use of friends 00-06=01
Dartmouth weekly meeting Called **William Wood**

and **Judah Smith** appeared – –
Rochester Weekly Meeting Called not appeared – –
John Tucker hath Drawn out the yearly meeting
minnits for **Rochester** as appointed – –
and the Matter Concerning **Benjamin Russell**
is Refered to yᵉ adjournment – –
Whereas it was recommended to this meeting yᵗ [that]
there is a report spread abroad yᵗ our friend
Valentine Huddelstone did take an oath in yᵉ
Case of his giving evidence at **Bristol** Cort Last part
— **Benjamin Howland John Tucker** and **Deliverance**
Smith are appointed to assist **Valentine Huddelstone**
Concerning the said report and to Draw up something
that May Clear truth and friends – –
Benjamin Howland is appointed to pay **John Tucker**
for Drawing out the abovesᵈ minnits – –
and upon the request of yᵉ vissiters the Meeting
adjournes until the first sixth day of yᵉ 2ᵈ month

This Meeting being meet according to adjournment
The 3ᵈ Day of the 2ᵈ month 1713 – –
our visiters gives this meeting their account that
they have visited most of yᵉ famlyes of friends &
there visits was kindly accepted and things pretty
Well as far as they saw & where things had been out
or order wee have Laboured in Love to bring them
to a sight of it – –
Something Done to wards **Valentine Huddlestone**
his giving in his evidence Contrary to yᵉ order of friends
— and this meeting refers to yᵉ quarterly meeting
Whither it may be agreeable wᵗʰ [with] yᵉ testimony of truth
for a friend to hold up his hand when he is Called
to give evidence to yᵉ truth of what he knows
In any Case Before Atherity or otherwis – –
Benjamin Howland William Wood and **John Tucker**
are appointed to attend yᵉ quarterly meeting next
— **Judah Smith** and **John Tucker** are appointed to
Draw out an account to yᵉ quarterly meeting – – – – –

At a monthly meeting of friends held at our
meeting house in **Dartmouth** the 20ᵗʰ day of yᵉ
2ᵈ month: 1713 — there was Collected 00-04=00

Dartmouth Weekly meeting Called **Judah Smith** &
William Wood appeared – **Rochester** weekly
Meeting called none apeared – –
That matter Concerning **Benjamin Russell**s
Giving his paper of his Condemning of his taking his -
place of a Constable by an oath is refered – –
and it is advised by this meeting y^t every friend
that is master of a famly Doth Take Care of
his famly y^t [that] they be not concerned in writing
of lie bills and to Labour to find out them y^t [that]
has been Concerned in such Papers – –
and y^t [that] friends take care to bring their Children
to meeting on first days or keep them at home
Benjamin Howland hath paid 00-04=00 for Drawing out
y^e yearly meeting minnits for **Rochester** meeting – –
Valentine Huddlestones paper was read and it is y^e
judgment of this meeting y^t [that] he read it at y^e next
Quarter Sessions or cause it to be read if there
be not a bar and take a friend or two wth [with] him – –
y^e friends y^t was appointed to Draw an account
to ye quarterly meeting have done it – –
William Wood hath attended ye quarterly meeting – –
William Wood and **Judah Smith** and **John Tucker** are
appointed to Dispose of the [primendars?] & return
ye money into y^e Stock the Little ones 5^{sx} y^e great ones
at 11^{sx} — The quarterly meeting Epistle was read
and kindly accepted – – – – –

At a monthly meeting of friends held at our meet
ing house in **Dartmouth** the 18th Day of y^e 3^d month
1713 ther was Collected for the use of friends 00-08=00
Dartmouth weekly meeting Called **Judah Smith** & **William
Wood** appeared
Rochester weekly meeting Called none appeared – –
Nathaniell Chace having the honey taken out of a hive
of bees by wch Cause y^e said hive of bees was Left
Some time in y^e Last winter and suspecting
some friends children to have a hand in taking
of s^d honey therefore **William Wood John Lapham**
and **Judah Smith** & **Jabez Barker** and **Henry Tucker**
are appointed to make enquiry and search into

the truth as far as they can and make return
of their Doings to yᵉ next monthly meeting – –
Deliverance Smith is appointed to makeup
The monthly meetings accounts with **Benjamin
Howland** and make return to yᵉ next monthly
Meeting and whereas **Elezer Slocumb** Desires
To be suspended from being a visiter it is re
fered to yᵉ next monthly Meeting for a further Consideration – –
And yᵉ meeting at **Coxset** is to be two first
Days there in a month for this Summer & to be
the 2 first first Dayes in every month – – – – –

At a monthly meeting of friends held at
our meeting house in **Dartmouth** the 22ᵈ Day
of the 4ᵗʰ month 1713 – –
there was Collected for yᵉ use of friends 00-09=00
Dartmouth Weekly meeting Called **Judah Smith**
and **William Wood** appeared – –
Rochester weekly meeting Called none
appeared —— **Deliverance Smith** hath
made up the account of yᵉ Collection of the
monthly meeting and there is remaining in th
Stock ten pounds eight shillings and two pence
— the fine friends that was appointed to make
Search into yᵉ truth of **Nathaniell Chace** his
suspecting some of friends Children having
a hand in taking of yᵉ honey out from his
bees they make return to this meeting that
they cannot as yet find out the truth of yᵗ [that] matter
Wherefore **Thomas Taber juner** and **Josiah Merehew**
is added to yᵐ to make further Inquiry into
The truth of yᵗ matter and make return of their Doings
to the next monthly meeting
Stepehn Willcock & **John Tucker** are appointed to attend
the quarterly meeting next — the visiters gives this
meeting an account that they have not visited
the famlyes of friends this Last quarter – –
Judah Smith and **John Tucker** are appointed to Draw
up an account to the quarterly meeting next – – – – –

At a monthly meeting of friends held at our

meeting house in **Dartmouth** the 20th Day of the
5th month 1713 there was Collected – – – – – 00-03=07
Dartmouth Weekly meeting Called **Judah Smith** and
William Wood appeared – –
Rochester weekly meeting Called and none appeared
The friends that was Chose to make enquiery into
the matter Concerning **Nathaniell Chace** his loosing
hi honey out of a hive Do bring in the following
account – –
Friends according to the Desire of ye Last monthly
meeting we have endeavered to speak wth [with] **George Howland**
the Son of **Nathaniell Howland** and the witnesses
face to face but was prevented speaking with him
by his father who said his Son was under him and he
withheld him from us saying he would take the
Matter into his own hands and examin
his Son and the witnesses him selfe for the
Meeting had taken wrong steeps and had Concerned
Them Selves with business that Did not belongue
to them – – – – – – –

        William Wood   Judah Smith
        Thomas Taber jun.   Josiah Merehew
        John Lapham   Jabez Barker

And whereas **Nathaniel Howland** did charge the
Meeting with Taking wrong steeps in ye matter
Said **Howland** has acknowledged his Shortness to
the Sattisfaction of the meeting – –
And whereas **George Howland** Son of s^d
Nathaniel Howland was a pearson suspected
for taking ye honey **Nathaniell Howland** and
Nathaniel Chace do give an account to this
meeting that the matter is made up between
them and Sattisfaction is made – –
and the persons chose to attend ye quarterly meet
ing Do give an account that they were not
There and there were no account sent – –
and this meeting advises that friends restrain
their Children and searvants from going into Com
panies on first Dayes before or after Meeting
but go home in good order – –

And whereas several reports are brought to
this meeting of friends Children geting together
in companies on first Dayes and being Disorderly
William Wood Stephen Willcock and **John Tucker**
were appointed to inquire into yᵉ truth thereof
and make report to the next monthly meeting – –
The Last quarterly meeting Epistle was Read and
kindly accepted – – – – –

At a monthly meeting of friends held at our
Meeting house in **Dartmouth** the 17ᵗʰ Day of
the 6ᵗʰ month 1713 there was Collected 00-05=08
Dartmouth Weekly meeting Called **William Wood**
and **William Soule** appeared
Rochester weekly meetin Called **Elisha Wing** appeared
Whereas **William Wood Stephen Willcock** and **John Tucker**
have not made inquiry concerning some of friends
Children being out of order some time past on first
Dayes they are still continued to make inquiry in to
that matter – – It is concluded by this meeting
to answer the request of yᵉ quarterly meeting to
raise fower pounds and ten shillings in money to
wards the building of **Dover** Meeting House and yᵉ
Subscribers to bring in their money to the next month
ly meeting – – no business from **Rochester**
But friends in Love and unity – – – – –

At a monthly meeting of friends held at our
meeting house in **Dartmouth** the 21ˢᵗ Day of yᵉ 7ᵗʰ month
1713 there was Collected for the use of friends 00-03=05
Dartmouth weekly meeting Called **John Lapham** and
Judah Smith appeared – – **Rochester** Weekly meet
ing Called ~~none~~ **Savery Clifton** appeared – –
it is the Conclution of this meeting that whereas
Valentine Huddlestone hath neglected the proforming
the meetings order Concerning his Confering his fault – –
at **Bristol** that unless he Doth lack some faithful
friend wᵗʰ [with] him and Do it before next monthly meet
ing that Judgment must go forth against him – –
Stephen Willcock and **William Wood** do give an account
to this meeting that they have enquired into yᵉ Report
Concerning friends Children being Disorderly on yᵉ first Dayes

of yᵉ week and the young men do partly Denie the
things they were Charged wᵗʰ and in Some respects
Confess their faults – –
This meeting orders **Benjamin Howland** to pay 02ˡ-07ˢ=6ᵈ
out of the Stock unto **William Wood** for to Carry to
the quarterly meeting for **Dover** meeting house
William Wood and **Thomas Taber Juner** are Chose
to attend the quarterly meeting and **Judah Smith**
and **John Lapham** are appointed to Draw up an
account to yᵉ quarterly meeting – – – – –

At a monthly meeting of friends held at our
Meeting house in **Dartmouth** yᵉ 19ᵗʰ of y 8ᵗʰ month 1713
Dartmouth weekly meeting called **Judah Smith**
and **John Lapham** appeared – –
Rochester Weekly meeting Called and none appear
ed — the matter concerning **Valentine Huddlestone**
Is refered to yᵉ next monthly meeting
William Wood and **Increas Allen** are appointed
to go to **Valentine Huddlestone** and his wife
and Inquire into the truth of yᵉ report concer
ning her burning her husbands paper which yᵉ
Monthly meeting ordered to be read at **Bristol** Cort
William Wood and **Thomas Taber juner** have attended
the quarterly meeting and **Judah Smith** and **John
Lapham** have Drawn up an account to the
quarterly meeting – –
and we receive yᵉ Epistle from yᵉ Last quarterly
Meeting wᶜʰ was read and kindly accepted – –
and it is Concluded yᵗ [that] friends on yᵉ other side of
Coxet river should hould their first Dayes meet
ings for yᵉ winter season as formerly – –
The matter Concerning stiring up the visiters or
making a new Choice is referd to yᵉ next monthly meet
ing – the Collection was –   –   –   –   –   –   – 00-08-00

at a monthly meeting of friends held at our meeting
house in **Dartmouth** the 16ᵗʰ day of the 9ᵗʰ month 1713
there was Collected for the use of friends –   –   –   – 00ˡᵇ-19ˢ=07ᵈ
Dartmouth weekly meeting Called **Judah Smith** and
William Wood appeared – –
Rochester Weekly meeing Called none appeared – –

The matter Concerning **Valentine Huddlestone** is
refered to yᵉ next monthly meeting and **Increas
Allen** and **Eliezer Slocumb** are ordered to Speak wᵗʰ [with]
him and let him know that this meeting desires him
to be at yᵉ next monthly meeting in order to give
friends better Sattisfaction concerning his progress in
the matter at **Bristol** – –
and also to let his wife know that friends are troubled
at her standing to Justefy her burning the paper and
Desire her to consider of yᵉ matter that so shee may
give better sattisfaction – –
and the matter Concerning the visiters being consid
ered it is Concluded that they go on wᵗʰ [with] the work of
WiVisiting and **John Tucker** is aded to yᵐ [them]
John Tucker and **Eliezer Slocumb** ar Continued to
take care of yᵉ meeting house as formerly – – – – –

at a Monthly meeting of friends held at our
Meeting house in **Dartmouth** the 21ˢᵗ of yᵉ 10ᵗʰ month 1713
there was Collected –   –   –   –   –   –   – 00ˡᵇ-09ˢ=11d
Dartmouth Weekly meeting Called **William Wood**
and **John Lapham** appeared – –
Rochester Weekly meeting Called none appeared
Eliezer Slocumb gives an account to this meeting
that he has spoke wᵗʰ **Valentine Huddleston** and his
wife as ordered by the Last monthly meeting and he
signifies that the season was such that he could not
well attend yᵉ meeting therefore yᵉ matter concerning
him is refered to yᵉ next monthly meeting – –
Eliezer Slocumb and **William Wood** are appointed
to attend yᵉ Quarterly Meeting next – –
The visitters gives an account yᵗ they have visited
most of the famlyes of friends and that in some
famlyes they find things pretty well and in some
famlyes some things not very well: where they
give some admonition which they think was well
Taken – – **John Tucker** and **Judah Smith** are
appointed to Draw up an account to yᵉ Quarterly
Meeting – – **Edward Wing** & **Desire Smith**
Did lay their Intentions of marrage with each other
Before this meeting and they were desired to wait

for their answer til the next monthly meeting – –
Benjamin Howland and **Henry Tucker** are appointed
to See in to their Clearness and bring in their
answer to yᵉ next monthly meeting – –
Benjamin Howland is appointed to pay twenty shillings
to **John Tucker** for keeping yᵉ meeting house – – – – –

Att a monthly meeting of friends held at our meeting
House in **Dartmouth** the 18ᵗʰ of the 11ᵗʰ mo 1713
There was Collected for yᵉ use of friends 00ˡᵇ-07ˢ=03ᵈ
Dartmouth Weekly meeting Called **William Wood**
and **John Lapham** appeared – –
Rochester weekly meeting Called **Stephen Wing** appeared
Edward Wing and **Desire Smith** did appear at this
Meeting for their answer as to marrage and they
had their answer that they might take each other
in the order of truth Some time between this and the
next monthly meeting – –
John Tucker and **William Wood** are appointed to see
the marrage accomplished in yᵉ Good order of truth – –
The matter Concerning **Valentine** and his Wife is
refered to yᵉ next monthly meeting – –
John Tucker hath Drawn an account to the Quarterly
meeting as appointed – –
William Wood and **Eliezer Slocumb** have atten
ded yᵉ quarterly meeting – –
Abigall Allens Paper of acknowledgment the publish
ing of it is refered to the Consideration of yᵉ next
monthly meeting – – – – –

At a monthly meeting of friends held at our meeting
house in **Dartmouth** the 15ᵗʰ of yᵉ 12ᵗʰ month 1713
There was Collected for yᵉ use of friends 00ˡᵇˢ=10ˢ=03ᵈ
Dartmouth weekly meeting Called **William Wood** appear
ed — **Rochester** Weekly meeting Called **Elisha Wing**
appeared — **John Tucker** and **William Wood** gives an
account that **Edward Wing** and **Desire Smith** Did
take each other in the order of truth – –
The matter Concerning **Valentine Huddlestone**s
Wife is refered to yᵉ next meeting – –
Those that were to build the stable have finished
their work and Do give the account of their Charge

to be seaven pounds nineteen shillings – –
And **Benjamin Howland** is ordered to pay s^d 07^{lbs}=19^s=00^d
to **John Tucker** out of y^e Collection – –
And that matter Concerning **Abigall Allen**
is refered to the next monthly meeting for a
further Consideration – –
The Quarterly meeting Epistle was read at this
Meeting and is ordered to be read Publickly on
a first Day at the Breaking up of the meeting
of worship

(1714) At a monthly meeting of friends held at our
meeting house in **Dartmouth** the 15th of the
first month 1714 – –
There was Collected for the use of friends 00^l=06^s=11^d
Dartmouth Weekly meeting Called **William
Wood** and **Judah Smith** appeared – –
Rochester Weekly meeting Called **Nicolas Davis**
appeared – – **Abigall Allen**s paper of her own
acknowledgment is received by this meeting
and is as followeth

leave a To — The monthly meeting to be held in **Dartmouth** the 18th day
vacancy of the 3^d month 1713 = Whereas I have seen incouraging
and Consenting to the beating of my Negro Servant beyond
what I now think was convenient for wch I have been condemned
selfe: and am much troubled for the same and Do acknowledg
I was off my wach at that time and so hav hardness of heart got
in which and if I had kept to the Spirit of truth I had not
Incouraged and consented to as aboves^d ; so for the clearing of truth
and the testimony thereof I give in these Lines Desiring that y^e
Lord and his people might pass it by and that I might come into
unity wth his people again – –

                          Abigall Allen

John Tucker Is ordered to read it or order it to be read
on a first Day before the next monthly meeting
and she to come into unity with friends again by her
good Conversation – –
Benjamin Howland hath paid **John Tucker** 07^l=19^s=00^d
as appointed by the Last monthly meeting – –
and this meeting hath an account from the propa
retive meeting that **Henry Howland** hath taken a

wife out of the order of truth and this meeting is
Concerned to give a publick Testimony against him
and is as followeth – –
Whereas **Henry Howland** of **Dartmouth** in the
County of Bristol in the **Province of the Massachu
sets Bay** in **New England:** having for seaveral years
been esteamed a member of our monthly meeting
of **Dartmouth** afores^d and been accounted one in
unity w^th [with] us yet hath of Late Contrary to the advice
of friends and the Good orders established among y^m [them] pro
ceeded to take a wife for wch reason this monthly meet
ing is Concerned to give forth this as a testimony against
his so Proceeding and to Disown him for being one
In unity wth us
Given forth at our monthly meeting is S^d **Dartmouth**
The 15th Day of the 1 month 1714 Signed in behalf of
s^d Meeting by

Peleg Slocumb	—	**Benjamin Howland**	—	**Josiah Merehew**
Increas Allen	—	**Thomas Taber juner**	—	**John Tucker**
William Wood	—	**Nicolas Davis**	—	**Jabez Barker**
Eliezer Slocumb	—	**John Lapham**	—	**William Wood jun**
Nathaniel Howland	—	**Judah Smith**	—	**Nicolas Lapham**

John Tucker is appointed to read the same or Cause it to
be read — **William Wood** and **John Tucker** are appoin
ted to attend ye quarterly meeting next – –
Judah Smith & **John Tucker** are appointed to Draw
up an account to the Quarterly meeting – –
And the vissitters at **Rochester** gives an account
that they have visited ye famlyes of friends there
an things ore as well as Can be well expected among
Them — and this meeting is adjourned until the
fourth Day next before ye Quarterly meeting – – – – –

The meeting being meet according to adjournment
the 7th Day of the 2^d month 1714 – –
Leave a vacancy The visiters are Called to give an account of their
visiting and their answer is as followeth

[*The bottom half of the page is blank*]

At a monthly meeting of friends held at our meeting
House in **Dartmouth** the 19th Day of the 2d month 1714
There was Collected for ye use of friends 00lb-06sh=08d
Dartmouth weekly meeting Called **William Wood** and
Judah Smith appeared — **Rochester** Weekly meet
ing Called none appeared — and the matter
Concerning **Vallentine Huddlestone** is Refered to
to the next monthly meeting – –
John Tucker hath read **Abigall Allen** her own
Condemnation as appointed – –
And **Henry Howland**s Condemnation was read – –
William Wood and **John Tucker** hath attended ye
Quarterly meeting and **Judah Smith** and **John Tucker**
hath Drawn an account to ye quarterly meeting – –
Christopher Giffords charge against **Richard Kirby**
being enquired into and wee Cannot find but that
the matter is already ended by men of their own chusing – –
the quarterly and yearly meetings Epistles were
read and kindly accepted – – – – –

At a monthly meeting of friends held at our meet
ing House in **Dartmouth** the 17th of the 3rd mo: 1714
There was Collected for ye use of friend — 00lb=03sh=8d
Dartmouth weekly meeting Called **William Wood**
and **Judah Smith** appeared – –
Rochester weekly meeting Called none appeared
Benjamin Howland Judah Smith and **John Tucker**
are appointed to speak wth **Valentine Huddlestone**
Concerning his neglecting answerining the advice
of friends in Condemning his takin his oath in
Bristol Court and make return of their
Doings to ye next monthly meeting – –
and the meeting of worship on ye first Day
at **Coaksit** is ordered to Be keept there Constantly
accept the first Day next Before ye monthly meet
ing — **Thomas Taber juner** is appointed to
be helpful to peruse ye monthly meeting minnits
and fitt ym for to be recorded –

At a monthly meeting of friends held at our
Meeting house in **Dartmouth** the 21st Day of
the 4th month 1714 – There was Collected

for the use of friends 00^{lb}-09^s=07^d
Dartmouth weekly meeting Called **William
Wood** and **Judah Smith** appeared – –
Rochester Weekly meeting Called **Timothy Davis**
and **Benjamin Boarman** appeared – –
And **Valentine Huddlestone** hath Condemned
his so Longue Neglecting His Condemning his
Taking an Oath at **Bristol Court**
Joseph Russell and **John Tucker** is ap
pointed To be helpful To traviling friends
for a Passage to **Nantucket**
And the Visiters being Called upon to
Give an account of their visiting of friends
famlyes — They Signefy to this meeting that
they have not made aney progress in that work
this Last Quarter – –
Judah Smith Timothy Davis and **John Tucker**
are appointed to attend y^e Quarterly meeting
next — **Judah Smith** and **John Tucker** are to Draw
up an account to the Quarterly meeting shewing
how the affairs of truth is amongst us – –
Benjamin Howland is appointed to pay to **John Tucker**
out of the Stock 00^l=12s=04^d for keeping the meeting house

Att a monthly meeting of friends held at our meet
ing House in **Dartmouth** the 19th day of y^e 5th month 1714
There was Collected for the use of friends 00^l-04^s=00^d
Dartmouth Weekly meeting Called **William Wood**
and **Judah Smith** appeared – –
Rochester weekly meeting Called none appeared
Judah Smith and **John Tucker** hath Drawn up an
account to the quarterly meeting and they
have attended y^e Quarterly meeting as appointed
And **Benjamin Howland** hath paid to **John Tucker**
twelve shillings and 4 pence as ordered by the Last
meeting — Whereas this meeting hath been Infor
med that **William Soule juner** and **Gilles Slocumb**
and **Daniel Shepherd juner** hath been Disorderly
in their voyage to the yearly meeting at **Nantucket**
this meeting Doth appoint **Eliashib Smith** and
Joseph Russell juner wth ye Visiters to inspect

into the s^d report how they find things to the next month
ly meeting — And the Epistle from the Last
Quarterly meeting was read and Kindly accepted – –
Judah Smith is appointed to make up the monthly
meeting account with **Benjamin Howland** and bring in
the account to the next monthly meeting – –
and it is agreed that the money sent for by the quarterly
Meeting shall be raised for four shilling Land
for the use of **Boston** meeting house – – – – –

At a monthly meeting of friends held at
our meeting house in **Dartmouth** the 10th Day
of the 6th month 1714 – –
There was Collected for the use of friends 00^l-05^s=07^d
Dartmouth Weekly meeting Called **Judah Smith**
and **William Wood** appeared – –
Rochester Weekly meeting Called **Joseph Wing**
appeared and the friends that was appointed
to make inquiery concerning y^e Disorder of
William Soule Juner and **Giles Slocumb** and
Daniel Shepherd Juner and they find that the
report Concerning **Daniel Shepherd** is falie but
for ye other two things are not clear as yet and
the friends that was before appointed are still
Continued to further Inspect into the truth of
s^d report and make return to the next monthly meeting – –
and **Judah Smith** hath made up the monthly meet
ings account w^th **Benjamin Howland** and their
remains in the Stock three pounds thirteen shil
lings and three pence – –
And this meeting hath made a Subscription in part
of pay for the Land that **Walter Newberry** bought
of **William Mumford** at **Boston** for the use
of friends meeting house – –
and this meeting Desires the visiters to visit the
famlyes of friends by the next monthly meeting

At a monthly meeting of friends held at our meet
ing house in **Dartmouth** the 20th of the 7th month 1714
There was Collected for the use of friends 00^l-05^s-01^d
Dartmouth Weekly meeting Called **William Wood**
appeared — **Rochester** Weekly meeting Called none appeared – –

And the Matter Concernin **William Soule juner**
and **Giles Slocumb** is refered to the next monthly
meeting — **John Tucker** and **William Wood** are appoin
ted to attend the next quarterly meeting **John Tucker**
and **Judah Smith** are appointed to Draw up an
account to the quarterly meeting – –
John Tucker is appointed to receive the Collecton
agread upon at the Last monthly meeting and to
Carry the money to yᵉ Quarterly meeting – –
the visiters gives an account that they have visit
ed the most of the famlyes of friends and for the
most part they find things pretty well — and where
we found things not well Wee Did advise that it
should be amended —

At a monthly meeting of friends held at our
Meeting House in **Dartmouth** the 18ᵗʰ Day of the
8 month 1714 — There was Collected 00ˡ-03ˢ=08ᵈ
Dartmouth Weekly meeting Called **William Wood**
and **John Lapham** appeared – –
Rochester Weekly Meeting Called and none appeared
and the matter Concerning **William Soule juner**
and **Giles Slocumb** is Refered to the next month
ly meeting — **William Wood** and **John Tucker**
have attended the Quarterly meeting – –
and **John Tucker** hath Carried the money to the
Quarterly meeting as appointed
John Tucker and **Judah Smith** have Drawn up an
Account to the quarterly meeting as appointed
Eliezer Slocumb and **John Tucker** are ordered
to take Care of the meeting house for the ensuing year

At a monthly meeting of friends held at our meet
ing house in **Dartmouth** the 15ᵗʰ of the 9ᵗʰ month 1714
there was Collected for the use of friends 00ˡ-06ˢ=05ᵈ
Dartmouth weekly meeting Called none appeared
Rochester weekly meeting Called **Nicolas Davis**
appeared – –
And the matter Concerning **William Soule** and **Giles
Slocumb** is refered to the next monthly meeting – –
A paper presented to this meeting from the pre
paritive meeting at **Rochester** signifying that

Benjamin Hilliard and Hannah Davis have
proceeded in marrage Contrary to the order of truth
John Tucker and Stephen Willcock are appointed
to Speak with them if they Can with conveniency
and to shew them the evil of their proceeding – –
and to See how the young womans parents have
Kept them selves clear in that matter – – – – –

At a monthly meeting of friends held at our meet
ing House in Dartmouth the 20th of the 10 mo 1714
there was Collected for the use of friends 00l-02s=03d
Dartmouth weekly meeting Called William Wood &
Judah Smith appeared – –
Rochester weekly meeting Called Stephen Wing ap
peared — William Wood Judah Smith and
William Baker are appointed to Speak wth William
Soule juner and Giles Slocumb and let them
know that if they will not give the monthly meeting
Sattisfaction for their outgoings then the Testimo
ny of truth will go against them – –
Stephen Willcock and John Tucker hath Spoken with
Benjamin Hilliard and Hannah Davis Concerning
their marrying Contrary to the Good order of truth
and Did tell them the Disadvantage of it but they seem
ed to incline to their own way – –
and we also Spoke wth Timoth Davis and his Wife and
by what they said to us they were pretty clear con
cerning that matter – –
and Elisha Wing is appointed to read Benjamin Hilliard
and Hannah Hilliard their Condemnation on a first
Day at the end of the meeting – –
Which is as followeth — Whereas Benjamin
Hilliard and Hannah Davis now Hannah Hilliard
the Daughter of Timothy Davis and Sarah his wife
of Rochester Boath of ym being under ye Care of friends
have proceeded in marriage Contrary to ye advise of
friends and ye Good order Established amongst us
the Society of people Called Quakers for wch [which] their so
Doing we Do disown ym and their practis and wee De
sire ye Lord may give ym a sight of their out goings
and a heart of repentance – –

Given forth by our monthly men and womens meet
ings in **Dartmouth** the 20th of ye 10th month 1714

Peleg Slocumb	**Benjamin Howland**	**Ruth Tucker**
Nathaniel Howland	**Josiah Merehew [Merihew]**	**Phebe Tucker**
John Tucker	**Judah Smith**	**Mary Lapham**
William Soule	**Stephen Wing**	**Mary Smith**
Jabes Barker	**Joanna Mott**	**Elezabeth Russell**
John Lapham	**Mary Slocumb**	**Hannah Soule**
William Wood	**Hannah Tucker**	
Stephen Willcock	**Rachel Allen**	

And whereas **Hannah Born** now **Hannah Akin** hath
proseeded in marrage to one of the world Contrary
to the good order Established among friends thi meet
ing is Concerned to give forth a condemnation against
her wch is as followeth – –
Whereas **Hannah Born** now **Akin** of ye town
of **Dartmouth** in the **County of Bristol** in ye
Province of ye Massachusets Bay in **New England**
The said **Hannah Akin** hath been in time past
one in society wth us the people Called Quakers
and Did Marry a man in unity wth frnds and also
married him ye good order established amongst
us: But for want of keeping to Truth and to ye
Good order thereof according to her former proceedings
in Taking of her former Husband but now hath Left us
& her practis whilst amongst us and Let out her mind
to a man not in Society wth us and married him
Contrary to the Good order of friends although advi
sed By friends to ye contrary
Therefore this meeting is Concerned to give
forth a Publick testimony against the above
said **Hannah Akin** and Do Disown her to be
one in Society wth us.
Given forth by our monthly men & womens
Meeting held at our meeting House in **Dartmouth**
the 20th of ye 10th month 1714

John Tucker	**Jabes Barker**	**Rachel Allen**
Joseph Russell	**Abraham Tucker**	**Ruth Tucker**
Benjamin Howland	**Nathaniel Howland**	**Mehetabell Wing**
William Wood	**John Russell**	**Eliezabeth Russell**

William Soule	Nicolas Lapham	Mary Lapham
John Lapham	Joanna Mott	Phebe Tucker
Stephen Willcock	Mary Slocumb	Mary Smith
Stephen Wing	Hannah Tucker	Hannah Soule
Josiah Merehew [Merihew]		

Stephen Willcock John Lapham and **John Barker** are
Appoynted to atend the quarterly meeting next – –
Judah Smith and **John Tucker** are appoynted to draw
up an account to the Quarterly meeting next – –
And the visiters gives an account that they have not vis=
etted freinds the last quortor — But hope that they shall give
a Jeneril visit by the next quortorly meeting – –
and **William Soul** [**Soule**]is appoynted to read **Hannah Akin** her
Condemnation before the next monthly meeting – – – – –

At a monthly meeting o friends held at our meeting house
In **Dartmouth** the 24th of the Eleventh month – – 1714
their was Colected for the use of friends – 0^{lb}-04^{s}-00^{d}
Dartmouth weekly meeting called **William Wood** and
Judah Smith appeared
Rochester weekly meeting called **Elisha Wing** appeared
those freinds appoynted the last monthly meeting to Spake with
William Soule ju^{r} and **Gils Slocumb**: have spoke with
them — and they have Each of them sent In a paper
to this meeting where In they acknowlidg that they have
ben disorderly In their Conversation and desiar to be for
given and say they hope to be more carefull for time to
Come: but friends being doubtfull of their sencerety do
at present: refer the matter for forther tryall to See
whether their futer conversation will be answerable
to their pretence – –
John Lapham and **Jabez Bark** [**Barker**] did attend the Quar
torly meeting as they were appoynted – –
and **John Tucker** and **Judas Smith** have draw up
and sent an account to the quortorly meeting – –
and **William Soul** [**Soule**] did read **Hannah Akin** her condem=
-nation as appoynted – –
and **Elisha Wing** did read **Benjamin Hilyerd**s and **Hannh
Hilyerd**s Condemnation as apoynted – –
and where as **Marcy Smith** is married contrarey to the order
of truth and this meeting agrees that condemnation shall

go against her and **Thomas Taber** and **John Tucker** are
Appoynted to draw her Condemnation against the next
monthly meeting – –
and **Benjamin Howland** has paid **John Tucker** twelve
shillings for keeping the meeing house – – – –

At a monthly meeing held at our meeting in **Dartmouth** the
the twenty first day of the twelvth month – – 1714
their was colected for the use of friends – 06^{lb}-05^s-07^d
Dartmouth weekly meeting called **Judah Smith** and
William Wood appeared – –
Rochester weekly called **Savery Clefton [Clifton]** appeared – –
Nicolas Davis and **Marey Summer** did lay their intent
-ions of marrige before this meeting
and they was desired to wait for their answer until
the next monthly meeting – –
and they was desired to wait for their answer until
the next monthly meeting – –
and **Saverey Clefton** and **John Tucker** ar Chosen to See Into their
Clearness and bring in their answer to the next monthly meeting
Thomas Tucker Ju^r and **John Tucker** hath drawn up
Hizekiah Smiths daughter **Marcy** her Condemnation
and It is signed by this meeting – and is as followeth – –
Whereas **Mary** the Daughter of **Hezekiah**
Smith and **Mary** his wife of **Dartmouth**
in the **Countey of Bristol** in **New England**
Having been one and under ye Care of our
Meeting yet hath of Late Contrary to the
Good order Established among friends and without
the knowledg of her father proceeded in marrage
to the reproach of the truth professed amongst us
and to the greif of the sober minded we are
Therefore concerned to give our Testimony against
the said Disorderly and unbecoming action and Do
Disown the said **Mary** now the Wife of **Thomas**
Trafford to be one of us the people Called Quakers
Desireing that she may Come to a sight of her
outgoing and return if it be the Will of the Lord
given forth by our Monthly Meeting of men and women
Held at our Meeting House in **Dartmouth** the 21
Day of the 12 month 1714

Peleg Slocumb

John Tucker

Abram Tucker

John Summers

Increas Allen

Eliezer Slocumb

Stephen Willcock

Savery Clefton [Clifton]

Nicholas Davis

Benjamin Howland

Henry Tucker

William Soule

William Wood

John Lapham

William Wood

Joseph Russell

Judah Smith

Jabes Barker

Thomas Taber jun

Thomas Hathaway

Joanna Mott

Mary Slocumb

Rachel Allen

Hannah Tucker

Hephziba Hathaway

Mary Lapham

Eliezabeth Summers

Susanna Willcock

Mary Lapham

Phebe Tucker

Mary Russell

Mary Smith

Mary Laton

Juner[Lawton]

Juner Tabitha Wait

Abigal Chace

Ruth Tucker

———————

And **William Soule** is appinted to read the
Same on a first Day at the end of a meeting
before the next monthly meeting – –
Benjamin Howland and **John Tucker** are ap
pointed to Speak with **Nathaniel Smith**
Concerning his telling the Justis that his
Sister **Mary** had her fathers Consent to be
Married to **Thomas Trafford** and that they
was Lawfully Published and bring in their
answer to the next monthly meeting – –
The Quarterly meeting Epistle Was read at
this meeting and was kindly accepted – –
and it is Desired that friends may tak it
into their Consideration how or what method
friends that Travil into forreign parts how
they may return that the meeting to whom
They belongue may be senceable that they have
beheaved them selves according to truth – –
and it is advised that the visiters go forward
in their visiting of friends famlyes and
give their account to the next monthly

meeting how they find things – –
and Whereas there has been some Difrance
of Late amongst some for blonging to this
meeting about the Laying out of The Ceder
Swamps and it has been so mannaged that
as is thought by this Meeting so as to bring
A reproach upon f^{rds} [friends] and a Dishonour
to ye Truth Professed amongst us it is
Therefore Concluded to Chuse some friends
to enquire into that Matter and Where they
Find that any have been of from their wach to
endever to bring them to a sence of it so that if
it be possible to bring friends into love & unity
and to give an account to ye next monthly meet
ing how they find things relating to ye matter & where
any Cannot be brought in the judgment of those friends
to a sight of their faults they are to Let y^m [them] know
that this meeting Desires y^m to be at the next
monthly meeting in order to Sattisfie the meeting
& **Benjamin Howland Stephen Willcock** and **William
Soule** are Chose on that account
And the next monthly meeting is adjourned
to the 4th Second Day of the Next Month
Att a Monthly Meeting of friends

(1715) Held at our meeting House in **Dartmouth**
The 28 Day of the first month 1715
there was Collected for the use of friends oo^{lb}-oo^{sh}=oo^d
Dartmouth Weekly meeting called **William Wood**
and **Judah Smith** appeared – –
Rochester weekly meeting Called none appeared
Nicolas Davis and **Mary Summers** Came for
their answer as to taking each other in marrage
and nothing appearing to Hinder their said in
tentions they had their answer that they may
Take each other in the Good order established
amongst f^{rds} – –
And **Benjamin Borman** and **Hannah Wing**
did Lay their intentions of marrage before this
Meeting and they were Desired to wait for their
answer till the next monthly meeting – –

Savery Clifton and **John Lapham** are appointed
to inspect into their clearness and bring in their
answer to the next monthly meeting – –
Savery Clifton and **John Tucker** are Chosen to
see **Nicolas Davis** and **Mary Summers** solemnize
their Marrage in the Good order of truth – –
And **Mary Trafford** her Condemnation was read – –
Benjamin Howland and **William Soule** according
to appointment brought in an account in rela
tion to the Difrance about ye Ceder Swamps wch is
ordered to be recorded & is as followeth – –
To the monthly meeting of Friends held in **Dart**
mouth the 28th of the first month 1715
We whose names are under writen have enquired
Into that Diforance amongst friends Concerning the
Ceder Swamps and they have in General man
her acknowledged to each other their shortness in
So Doing to our Great Sattisfaction and mutal
Cumfort and they have forgiven each other and are
come into Love and unity again and so wee pray
The Lord to keep them and us in that Spirit to
the end of our Dayes – –

> Benjamin Howland
> William Soule

Eliezer Slocumb William Wood and **John**
Tucker are chosen to attend the Quarterly meet
ing next – – **John Tucker** and **Judah Smith** are
appointed to Draw up an account to the Quarterly
Meeting – and this meeting is adjourned til the next
fourth Day come Week

The meeting being met according to adjournment
the first Day of the 2^d month 1715 – –
Benjamin Howland and **John Tucker** makes report to
this meeting that they have spoke with **Nathaniel Smith**
concerning his going before the Justis and ther signefying
that his sister **Mary Smith** had had her Parents
consent to marry wth **Tho. Trafford** wch was no such
thing & he hath condemned the same and said he is
sorry for so doing and Hopes he shall do so no more – –
And this meeting hath sent 17 Shillings and three pence

for 14 Books sent by the Quarterly meeting

At a monthly meeting of friends held at our meeting
house in **Dartmouth** the 18th Day of the 2d mo 1715
There was Collected for the use of friends 00lb-04s=00d
Dartmouth Weekly meeting Called **John Lapham**
and **Judah Smith** appeared
Rochester weekly meeting Called **Nicolas Davis** ap
peared — **Savery Clifton** and **John Lapham** makes
report to this meeting that they find nothing but that
Benjamin Boarman and **Hannah Wing** may pro
ceed in marrage & they appeared this meeting
for their answer & they had there answer that
they might proceed to take each other in mar
rage in the order of truth – –
Thomas Taber Juner and **Joseph Wing** are ap
pointed to see their marrage accomplished
According to order — **John Tucker** and **Judah
Smith** hath Drawn up an account to the Quar
terly meeting and **John Tucker** and **William Wood**
Hath attended ye Quarterly meeting – –
And **John Tucker** has Carried the money for to
pay for the books as appointed – –
And this meeting received the Epistle from
The Last Quarterly meeting – – – – –

At a monthly meeting of friends held at our
Meeting house in **Dartmouth** the 16th Day of
the 5th month 1715 – –
There was Collected for the use of frds 00l-05s=00d
Dartmouth Weekly meeting Called **William Wood**
and **Judah Smith** appeared – –
Rochester Weekly meeting Called **Elisha Wing** appeared
The friends Chose to see the marrages Solemni
sed in the good order of truth at **Rochester** have
Been at Said Marrages and makes report
That they were accomplished according to order
and at this meeting there was a Subscribtion
made towards the building of **Salem** meeting
House and friends are Desired to bring in their
Money to the next monthly meeting – –
It is advised that friends be Careful of their

Children that go abroad to yearly Meetings
that they bring no Dishonour to the Truth
Professed by us – – – – –

At a monthly meeting of friends held at our meet
ing house in **Dartmouth** the 20th day of ye 4th month 1715
Dartmouth Weekly meeting Called **William Wood** and
Judah Smith appeared
Rochester Weekly meeting Called **Joseph Wing** appeared
And the Subscribtion that was made the Last monthly
Meeting for **Salem** Meeting House is brought in to
This meeting in order to be sent to the Quarterly
Meeting next and the Sum is –   –   –   –   –   – 07^l=03^s=00^d
Stephen Willcock and **John Tucker** are appointed to
attend the Quarterly meeting next and carry y^e money
Gathered for **Salem** meeting House – –
The visiters are Called to give in their accounts
of their visiting of friends famlyes and they signefy
to this meeting that they have not been out
upon that servis since the Last Quarter – –
And this meeting advies the visiters for time
to come to be more Dilegent in their Service
of visiting that so the monthly meeting may have
a better account how things are amongst us once
a Quarter — This meeting orders **Benjamin**
Howland to Let **Judah Smith** have 25 shillings out
of the stock for keeping the meeting House – –
Thomas Taber jun,^{r} and **Jo,**^{n} **Tucker** are appointed
to Draw up an account to the Quarterly
meeting **Benjamin Howland** and **Deliverance**
Smith are appointed to git the Meeting House
Land laid out – – – – –

At a monthly meeting of friends held at our
meeting in **Dartmouth** the 18th Day of y^e 5th mo 1715
There Was Collected for the use of friends 0^l-05^s=8^d
Dartmouth Weekly meeting Called **William Wood**
and **Deliverance Smith** appeared – –
Rochester Weekly meeting Called none appeared
Benjamin Howland hath paid **Judah Smith**
twenty five shillings as appointed – –
John Tucker hath Carried the Money to the

Quarterly meeting as ordered – –
Tho, Taber Juner and **John Tucker** did Draw an
account to the Quarterly meeting as they
were appointed – –
And **Deliverance Smith** and **Jon Russell** are
ordered to procure a quantity of Land and
Git it Laid out for the benefit of the fire Wood – – – – –

At a monthly meeting of friends held at
our meeting House in **Dartmouth** the 15th day
of the 6th month 1715 – –
There was Collected for the use of frnds [friends] 00lb-05sh=00d
Dartmouth Weekly meeting Called **William Wood**
and **Jon Lapham** appeared – –
Rochester Weekly meeting Called not appeared
The yearly meeting Epistle from the ministers
Was read in this meeting and also the Epistle from
the Quarterly meeting and boath Well accepted – –
Deliverance Smith Was appointed to make up
The monthly meeting accompts With **Benjamin**
Howland

At a monthly meeting of friends held at
our meeting House in **Dartmouth** the 19th d of
the 7th month 1715
There Was Collected for the use of friends 00lb-05sh=06d
Dartmouth weekly meeting Called **William Wood** and
Judah Smith appered — **Rochester** weekly meeting
Called **Nathan Summers** appeared – –
Deliverance Smith has made up the monthly meet
ing account wth [with] **Benjamin Howland** as appointed – –
the Last monthly meeting and there remains in
the stock foure pounds seaven shillings an three pence
This meeting makes Choice of **William Wood** to be
a visiter — A repoart is made to this meeting
Concerning the Disorderly Walking of **William Soule**
juner and **Peleg Slocumb juner** and **Eliezer Slocumb juner**
Deliverance Smith Judah Smith and **Henry Tucker**
are appointed to inspect into the truth of said report
and make return how they find things to the next
monthly meeting — **Stephen Wilcock** and **William**
Wood are appointed to attend the quarterly meeting

next — **William Wood** brings in an account of
one hundred and seaventeen pounds of Chees taken
from him for his sons not training by **William
Bowdish** Clark of the Western millitary Company
in **Dartmouth** under **Nathaniel Soule** Leightenant
the chees is esteemed worth forty four shillings
for three pounds Demanded – –
The meeting is adjourned to the 12th Day of ye next month

The meeting being meet according to adjournment
the 12th Day of the 8th month 1715 – –
the visiters gives this meeting an account that
They have visited the most of the famlyes of
friends but not all and they find that some
friends Chilldren are much out of order and
some famlyes pretty well – –
John Tucker and **Abram Tucker** are Chose to
Draw an account to the Quarterly meeting – – – – –

At a monthly meeting of friend held at our meet
ing hose in **Dartmouth** the 17th Day of the 8th m 1715
There was Collected for the use of friends 00^l=5^s=0^d
Dartmouth weekly meeting Called **Judah Smith**
appeared — **Rochester** Weekly meeting Called not appered
James Barker and **Eliezabeth Tucker** did Lay their
intention of marrage with each other before this
meeting and they was Desired to wait until the
next monthly meeting for their answer – –
John Lapham Josiah Merehew [**Merihew**] are appointed
to make Equiry into their Clearnese and make
Return to the next monthly meeting – –
Deliverance Smith Judah Smith and **Henry
Tucker** they are Still Continued to enquire whi
ther the report be true concerning the three
young men or not – –
Stephen Willcock and **William Wood** Did attend
the Quarterly meeting as they were appointed
Abram Tucker and **Jo^n Tucker** did send an
account to the Quarterly meeting – –
Deliverance Smith and **Benjamin Howland** are
appointed to git some addition of seats made
In the Galleryes of the meeting House if they

Can against the yearly meeting[22] – –
and the monthly meeting to pay the Charge

At a monthly meeting of friends held at our meet
ing House in **Dartmouth** the 21st Day of ye 9th month 1715
Dartmouth Weekly meeting Called **William Wood** and
John Lapham appeared — **Rochester** weekly meeting
Called **Nicolas Davis** appeared – –
James Barker and **Eliezabeth Tucker** came for their
answer their answer was that they might proceed
to take each other in marrage in the order
of truth — **John Tucker** and **William Wood**
are appointed to see that they accomplish their
Marrage according to order and make the return
to the next monthly meeting – –
A paper presented to this meeting by **Robert Tripp**
signefying that **William Bowdish** took from him
a steer worth 50 shillings for neglecting to train
nine Dayes which is allowed to be presented to the
Quarterly meeting – –
A report to this meeting concerning some friends
being somewhat out of order and **Deliverance Smith**
Benjamin Howland and **John Lapham** and **Thomas Taber**
are appointed to inspect into the truth of the sᵈ report
A paper presented to this meeting from **Rochester** signefy
ing that **Patience Clefton** [**Clifton**] hath hath had a child
with out a husband — **John Tucker Tho, Taber** are
appointed to Draw her condemnation – – – – –

At a monthly meeting of friends held at our meet
ing House in **Dartmouth** the 19th day of the 10th mo - 1715
There was Collected for the use of friends 00ˡ-04ˢ=00ᵈ
Dartmouth weekly meeting Called **William Wood** and
Judah Smith appeared — **Rochester** weekly meeting Called
None appeared — **William Wood** and **John Tucker**
Gives an account that **James Barker** and **Eliezabeth**
Tucker Did take each other in marrage in the
Order of truth — The friends that was chose
The Last meeting to inspect into the truth of
The report that was reported of **Eliezer Smiths**

---

22. This was not for the yearly meeting for business, but rather for one of the annual general meetings for worship.

Not beheving him selfe according to our profession
is refered to the next monthly meeting – –
Thomas Taber Juner and **John tucker** hath Drawn
up **Patience Clefton** her Condemnation as ordered
And it was signed at this meeting and **Elisha Wing**
is ordered to read it at **Rochester** on a first Day
at the end of the meeting of Worship – –
It is agreed at this meeting that there shall be
a meeting House built on the other side of **Cokset**
river 28 foot wide and 34 foot longue and 16 or 17
foot studd — and there is nothing Done as to
visiting the Last Quarter – –
John Tucker William Wood and **Stephen Willcock**
are chose to attend the Quarterly meeting next
John Tucker and **Abram Tucker** are chose to
Draw up an account to the Quarterly meeting
John Tucker and **Eliezer Slocumb** are appointed
to procure ~~the~~ friend to keep the meeting
House the ensuing year – –
And the next monthly meeting is adjourned
until the fourth second Day in the next month

11 mo= At a monthly meeting of friends held at our meeting
house in **Dartmouth** the 23 Day of the 11th month 17 15/16 — collected 10£-[?]
Dartmouth meeting called **William Wood** and **Judah Smith**
appeared: The friends that were appointed to attend the quarter
=ly meeting have attended according to order
Abraham Tucker and **John Tucker** have drawn up the account
to the Quarterly meeting as appointed
And the Epistle from the from the Quarterly meeting in ye 8th month and the
Epistle from the Last Quarterly meeting was boath of them read and
kindly accepted. And **Patience Clifton** her condemnation was Read as
ordered and is as followeth – –
Whereas **Patience Clifton** the Daughter of **Savorie Clifton** and
Dorothy his wife of **Rochester** in the county of **Plymouth** in **New England**
having been educated among friends and under the Care of our meeting
hath by giving way to the evil one fallen into the unclean sin of
fornication (being of Late delivered of a bastard child) to the dishonour
of God the reproach of ^the truth and grief of all those amongst us who sincerely
Desire ye prosperety of Zion: We are therefore concerned to give forth
this as a publick testimony against that wicked and detestable action

and do Deny the said **Patience Clifton** to be one of us the people of God called Quakers Desiring that if it be the will of God Shee may through unfeigned Repentance obtain pardon for this her great wickedness and all other her outgoings – –

Given by our men and womens monthly meeting of friends held at our meeting house in **Dartmouth** the 19th of ye 10th month 1715 :

John Tucker	Hezekiah Smith	
Abraham Tucker	Henry Tucker	Ruth Tucker
Eleazer Slocum	Thomas Hathaway	Rachel Allen
William Wood	Joseph Taber	Hannah Tucker
Stephen Willcock	Josiah Merihoo	Elisabeth Russell
John Lapham	Wm Wood jun	Mary Lawton
Joseph Russell	Jabez Barker	Mary Smith
Deliverance Smith	Eliashib Smith	Mary Lapham
James Tripp	John Russell	
Judah Smith	Nicolas Lapham	

and **James Tripp** is Imployed by this meeting to build a meeting house for the use of friends on the west side of **Coakset River** tharty foot long twenty eight foot wide and 16 or 17 foot studd

and the monthly meeting to defray the charge and it is concluded that the house abovesd should be finished by the 15th day of the 8th month next And **Benjamin Howland** is ordered to pay **Jabez Barker** for bords that was used about the meeting house 1£-03s=0d out of the stock-

The friends that was chose to inspext into the disorder of some friends bring in their account as followeth– –

Dartmouth the 20th of the 11th month 1715/16

We being chosen by the monthly meeting in the 9th month 1715 to enquire concerning **Eleazer Smith** and **Thomas Smith** their un =seamly words and behavier at **Seth Ropes** & we do find that **Thos Smith** in his words and actions was too light and ary for one professing truth which he readily owned but as to their being in drink we dont find they were and we do advize him for time to come that he be careful that he do not ^speak nor act so as to bring a reproach upon the Truth and the professor of it and we do advize that **Hezekiah Smith** and **John Lapham** and all friends to be careful in Reporting anything of friends, and not to strain things beyond what they are but to Consider which will be most for the honour of the Truth Whither to speak or to keep silent   – **Deliverance Smith**
                                              Benjamin Howland

The business of **Rochester** meeting called

FIG. 4: *Although the first Westport (Acoaxet) Meeting House was finished in 1716, the present structure dates from 1813.* © *Copyright Jean Schnell*

and an account was brought to this meeting of several friends that
are deceased at **Rochester** of late In order to be recorded

12 mo= At a monthly meeting of friends held at our meeting house in **Dartmouth**
the 20ᵗʰ Day of the 12ᵗʰ month 1715/16 –
Dartmouth meeting called **Judah Smith** and **Deliverance Smith** appeared
Rochester meeting called none appeared
This ^meeting hath concluded to come to a subscription to pay for the building of
the meeting house at **Acoxet.** and **Benjamin Howland** hath paid
Jabez Barker 1ᶠ-03ˢ-00ᵈ as appointed at the Last meeting – –
And this meeting has appointed **Stephen Willcocks** and **Tho. Taber** ⁱᵘⁿ
to purchase a piece of Land to set the meeting house upon on the
west side of **accoxet River** – –
And this meeting advises the visiters to dillegence in their service
So that there may be a full account given to the next monthly meeting

~~At a monthly meeting of friends held at our meeting house in Dartmouth~~
~~the 19ᵗʰ day of the 1st month 1715/16—~~
~~There was collected for the~~

And **Abraham Tucker** and **John Tucker** are appointed to Receive the
Collection for **accoxet** meeting house and to pay it out as there may be
need and for as much as it difficult to git small mony it is agreed
to have our collection once a Quarter: and to collect for the
Quarter past next monthly meeting

1716　At a monthly meeting of friends held at our meeting house in
Dartmouth the 19th day of the 1st month 1715/16

1 mo= There was collected for the use of friends 13 shillings – –
Dartmouth meeting called **Deliverance Smith** and **Judah Smith** appeard
Rochester meeting called and none appeard
The visiters were called upon to Give in their accounts which they
did and is as followeth — That they have visited the most of friends
famlyes under their care and their visits for the most part were
kindly accepted and in some friends famlies they find things pretty
well and in some others not so well as they could Desire
where they gave such advice as they thought suitable to their condition
Eleazer Slocum and **Thomas Taber** ⁱᵘⁿ are appointed to attend
the Quarterly meeting next
and **John Tucker** & **Thos Taber** ⁱᵘⁿ are appointed to Draw up an account
to the Quarterly meeting how things are among friends relating
to Truth – –
And it being proposed by some friends to this meeting whither it
be agreable to truth to purchase slaves and keep them term of
Life wᶜʰ is refered to yᵉ considration of the Quarterly meeting
Benjamin Howland and **Deliverance Smith** brought in their account
of their charge in their building of the new gallery wᶜʰ is 01ᶠ-18ˢ=04ᵈ
which **Benjamin Howland** is ordered to pay out of yᵉ stock
he is also ordered to pay **Judah Smith** 13ˢ out of the stock toward
keeping the meeting house which sum yᵉ said **Benjamin Howland**
forthwith paid

2m= At a monthly meeting of friends held in **Dartmouth** the
16 day of yᵉ 2ᵈ month 1716
Dartmouth meeting called **Judah Smith** and **Williᵐ Wood** appeared
Rochester meeting called & none appeared:
And **Eleazer Slocum** and **Thomas Taber** ᴵᵘⁿ hath (~~attend the quar~~
~~=terly meeting as appointed~~) Drawn up an account to the
Quarterly meeting as appointed
And the Widow **Mary Divel** desired the advise of this meeting
concerning the putting her son an aprentis to **Robert Tripp** to Learn
the trade of a tanner which this meeting doth agree too

And the Quarterly meeting Epistle was read and kindly accepted
The business of the preparitive meeting is that friends be careful
to make their wills for the settlement of their Estates in time

3 mo= At a monthly meeting the 21st day of the 3.d month 1716
Dartmouth weekly meeting called **Judah Smith** and **William Soule** appeared
Rochester weekly meeting called none appeared
The business of **Dartmouth** meeting called and there is no business
presented from the preparitive meeting

4 mo= At a monthly meeting of friends held in **Dartmouth** the 18th day of
the 4th month 1716 there was collected for the use of friends 1£-0s=0d
Dartmouth weekly meeting called **William Wood** and **Judah Smith**
appeared: **Rochester** meeting called **Stephen Wing** appeared
The business of **Dartmouth** meeting called and the business of **Rochester**
And whereas there is occation of the choise of some friends to be
chose to take a deed of some land to set **Coakset** meeting house upon
the meeting makes choice of **Stephen Willcocks William Wood**
Henry Tucker and **Tho.s Taber** Jun and **Joseph Taber** to be the person to
take sd deed
and **Eleazer Slocum** and **William Wood** are appointed to attend the
Quarterly meeting next: and **John Tucker** and **Tho.s Taber** Jun are
appointed to draw up an account to the quarterly meeting

5 mo= At a monthly meeting of friends held at our meeting house
in **Dartmouth** the 16th day of ye 5th month 1716
Dartmouth meeting called **Judah Smith** and **William Wood** appeared
Rochester meeting called **Nicholas Davis** appeared
and the two friends that was appointed to attend the Quarterly
meeting hath attended as appointed.
And **John Tucker** makes report to this meeting that there was
an account Drawn up and sent to the Quarterly meeting – –
The business of **Dartmouth** meeting **Called** and the business of
Rochester meeting called : from **Dartmouth** meeting no business
a paper presented to this meeting signefying that **John**
Sumers hath gone about to take a woman of ye world to wife
Contrary to the good ord.er Established among friends and **Stephen**
Willcock Thomas Taber jurn and **John Tucker** are appointed to speak with
sd **Sumers** to know whither he will condem his outgoing and clear
Truth or not and make return of their doings to ye next monthly
meeting and the Quarterly meeting epistle was Read at
this meeting and kindly accepted – –

_6 mo_= At a monthly meeting of friends held at our meeting house in
         Dartmouth yᵉ 20ᵗʰ day of yᵉ 6ᵗʰ month 1716 –
         Dartmouth meeting called **William Wood** and **Judah Smith** appeared
          Rochester meeting called **Elisha Wing** appeared
         And **Benjamin Howland** and **Judah Smith** is appointed to see the
         young cupple declare their intentions of mariage before the month
         =ly meetings in order: **Eleazer Slocum** ᴶᵘⁿ and **Deborah Smith** the
         daughter of **Delverance Smith** boath of **Dartmouth** did lay their
         intentions of marriage and they were desired to wait till yᵉ next
         monthly meeting for their answer and **Benjamin Howland** and
         Judah Smith are appointed to inquire into the clearness wᵗʰ
         respect to marriage and make Return to the next monthly meet
         =ing: and those appointed to speak with John Sumers do bring in
         an account that they have been with him and he justifies his
         actions wherefore this meetᵗng Concludes that he still Remains under dealing

_7 mo_= At a monthly meeting of friends held at our meeting house in
         Dartmouth yᵉ 17 ᵈᵃʸ of the 7ᵗʰ month 1716 – –
         There was collected for yᵉ use of friends –   –   –   – 00ᵉ:-13ˢ:-00ᵈ
         Dartmouth meeting called **William Wood** and **Judah Smith** appear
         =ed: **Rochester** meeting Called and none appeared
         The two friends that was chosen the Last monthly meeting to
         inspect into the two young friends clearness as to mariage make
         Report that they find nothing but that **Eleazer Slocum** ᴶᵘⁿ and
         Deborah Smith might proceed and **Eleazer Slocum** ᴶᵘⁿʳ and **Deborah**
         Smith came for their answer ~~concer~~ concerning their taking
         each other in marriage and they had their answer that they
         might take each other in yᵉ Good order of truth and **Benjamin**
         Howland and **Judah Smith** is appointed to see yᵉ mariage ~~solem~~
         Solemnized in yᵉ good order ^of truth and make return to yᵉ next
         monthly meeting. The business of **Dartmouth** meeting called
         James Tucker desires a sertificate from this meeting and
         Jabez Barker and **Josiah Merihoo** is appointed to make enquiry
         into his clearness Concerning mariage and conversation and
         make report how they find things to yᵉ next monthly meeting
         and provide a sertificate accordingly and this meeting
         orders **Benjam^in Howland** to pay **Judah Smith** 25 Shillings
         out of the monthly meeting Stock for keeping the meeting house
         And this meeting is adjourned till yᵉ first sixt day of the week in
         the 8ᵗʰ month next
         This meeting being met according to adjournment this 5ᵗʰ day

of yᵉ 8ᵗʰ month 1716 the visiters gives this meeting an account
that they have visited pretty Generally the famlies of friends
belonging to this meeting and in a general way they find
things pretty well as far as they said
And **Abraham Tucker** & **John Tucker** is appointed to draw an account
(Shewing how things are amongst us Relating to truthˢ affairs)
To yᵉ Quarterly next: and **Increase Allen** and
Abraham Tucker is appointed to attend yᵉ Quarterly meeting next

8 mo=   At a monthly meeting of friends held at out meeing house
in **Dartmouth** the 15ᵗʰ day of yᵉ 8ᵗʰ month 1716
Dartmouth meeting called **Judah Smith** appeared
Rochester meeting called & none appeared : the business of
Dartmouth meeting called and **Benjamin Howland** and
Judah Smith do make report to this meeting that yᵉ marriage
between **Eleazer Slocum** ʲᵘⁿ and **Deborah Smith** hath been solem
=nized in the good order of truth: and **Abraham Tucker** and
John Tucker hath signified yᵗ they Did draw up an account to
yᵉ quarterly meeting as ordered.
And **Increase Allen** hath attended yᵉ Quarterly meeting as
ordered: And **James Tucker** has a certificate signed rela
ting to his clearness wᵗʰ respect to marriage

9 mo=   At a monthly meeting held at our meeting house in
Dartmouth yᵉ 19ᵗʰ day of yᵉ 9ᵗʰ month 1716:
Dartmouth meeting called **William Wood** and **Judah Smith**
appeared : **Rochester** meeting called: The minnits of yᵉ
yearly meeting Recommended to the Quarterly meeting and
So to yᵉ monthly meeting was read by request of yᵉ prepa
=ritive meeting Last and yᵉ Quarterly meeting minnits was
Read and kindly accepted
Rochester no business

10 mo=   At a monthly meeting held at our meeting house in **Dartmouth**
by friends, the 17ᵗʰ day of yᵉ 10ᵗʰ month 1716 **Dartmouth** meeting called
William Wood and **Judah Smith** appeared:
Rochester meeting called **Stephen Wing** appeared
The business of **Dartmouth** meeting called and **John Tucker** and
Eleazer Slocum are chosen to take care of **Dartmouth** meeting house
For the ensuing year and yᵉ visiters were called upon to give an account
of their visiting friends fam^ilies and they give no account of any
thing done in that service yᵉ Last Quarter.

The business of **Rochester** called and they give an account that
John Summers hath taken a wife contrary to yᵉ good order esta
=blished amongst friends and this meeting Doth conclude that Judg
=ment must go forth against him for that and also for his other
disorders wherein he hath gone out of the good order of truth
And **John Tucker** and **Thomas Taber junʳ** are appointed to Drw up a
paper of condemnation in order to be signed at yᵉ next monthly
meeting. And **Stephen Wing** is chosen to be a visiter for **Rochester**
weekly meeting
The matter relating to purchasing slaves Recommend to yᵉ
Quarterly meeting being agetated in yᵉ meeting it is concluded by
the most of yᵉ meeting that it would be most agreable to our holy
profession to forbear for time to come to be any wayes concerned in
purchasing any slaves
And **Eleazer Slocum William Wood** & **Thoˢ Taber junʳ** are appointed
to attend yᵉ Quarterly meeting and **John Tucker** & **Thomas Taber junʳ**
are appointed to draw up an acount to yᵉ Quarterly meeting
how yᵉ affaires of Truth are amongst us.

---

11 mo= At a monthly meeting of friends held at our meeting house in
Dartmouth yᵉ 21ˢᵗ day of yᵉ 11ᵗʰ month 17 16/17
Dartmouth meeting called **William Wood** and **Judah Smith** appear
=ed **Rochester** meeting called **Stephen Wing** appeared
The business of **Dartmouth** meeing called this meeting hath signed
a condemnation against **John Summers** his proseeding in mariage
Contrary to yᵉ good order of truth as established among friends
And **Thomas Taber junr** is or ordered to read it in **Rochester** meeing
of worship on a first day of yᵉ week or cause it to be read:
This meeting has conculuded to make a subscribtion to pay
 3ᵉ Due for yᵉ Land where on **Coakset** meeting house stands
And **Benjamin Howland** is ordered to pay 12ᵉ 6ᵈ out of yᵉ meet
=ing stock to **John Tucker** for keeping yᵉ meeting house
The business of **Rochester** meeting called and they give an account
that **Benjamin Clifton** and **Sarah Davis** have published their
intentions of marriage contrary to yᵉ good order of friends and
John Tucker and **Stephen Willcocks** are desired to go and Labour
with yᵐ to shew them yᵉ danger of their proceedings

12: mo At a monthly meeting of friend held at our meeting house
in **Dartmouth** yᵉ 18ᵗʰ day of yᵉ 12ᵗʰ month 17 16/17:
Dartmouth meeting called **William Wood** and **Eleazer Slocum**

appeared: **Rochester** meeting called none appeared:
And **Thomas Taber** Junr has signifyed that he has Read
John Summers his condemnation as ordered and is as
followeth:
Whereas **John Summers** of **Rochester** in the county of
Plymouth in **New England** hath for some years made profession
of ye Blessed truth as it is held and professed amongst us the people
Called Quakers and having been by the ordering providence of
God deprived of his wife by her decease hath shown a hafty desire
to obtain another Contrary to ye Good order and chast comendable
custom among friends in so much that in a few months he did
proceed so far wth one not of our proffession to bublished according
to the custom of ye contry which action though he proceeded no
furtherein therein yet did stand to justifie obstinately Refusing
and trampling upon the advice of friends that throgh ye Godly care
of ye monthly meeting were sent to advise him concerning that
matter and now of Late hath farther appeared in slight and contempt
of ye good order established amongst ^us friends
Therefore we are concerned to give this forth as a testimony
against his out goings denying him to be one in unity with us the
people ^of god called ^of god Qukers desiring if it be the will of God he may come
to a sence of his out going and through unfeigned repentance
Return and find mercy
Given forth at our monthly meeting of friends held at our meeting
House in **Dartmouth** ye 21st day of ye 11th month 17 16/17

Stephen Willcock	John Tucker
John Lapham	Peleg Slocum
Tho- Taber junr	Valentine Huddlestone
Benjamin Howland	Abraham Tucker
Judah Smith	Nathaniel Howland
Thomas Hathaway	Eleazer Slocum
Josiah Merihoo	William Wood
William Soule	Deliverance Smith

And **Benjamin Howland** hath paid 12 shillings and 6 pence as ordered
at the last monthly meeting: and **Stephen Willcock** and **John
Tucker** hath beea at at **Rochester** as desired the last monthly
meeting but **Benjamin Clifton** and **Sarah Davis** had accomplished
their mariage before they came there and they could not conve
=niently speak wth them: so that matter is refered to ye next
monthly meeting

The business of **Dartmouth** meeting called
Whereas **John Kees** sent in a paper to this meeting concerning
his not proceeding in marriage with **Rachel Allen** which this
meeting for something therein mentioned doth not approve of
nor accept for sattisfaction: And **John Tucker** and **Thos Taber** ju^r
is appointed to signify ye reason thereof in behalfe of ye meeting

(1717) At a monthly of friends held at our meeting house in –
1:mo **Dartmouth** the: 18:th day of y^e— 1st month: 1717:
There was collected for ye use of friends —— 0[£]–12^s–06^d
Dartmouth meeting called **Eleazer Slocum** and ~~**Judah Smiths**~~
appeared: **Rochester** meeting called and none appeared
And ye business concer^ning **Benjamin Clifton** and **Sarah**
Davis is Refered to ye next monthly meeting
The business of **Dartmouth** meeing called and this meeting is
ajourned till y^e first sixt Day in y^e 2^d month next
This meeting being met according to ajournment:
this 5th day of y^e 2^d month: 1717:
the visitters being called upon to give in their account
Concerning their visiting friends famelies and their
account is as followeth y^t they have visited the fami
=lies of friends belonging to this meeting in a pretty general
way and they dont find but things are pretty well for the
most part and they think their visits for the most part
well accepted
And **William Wood** and **Eleazer Slocum** is appointed to
attend y^e Quarterly meeting next: and **Abraham Tucker**
and **John Tucker** is appointed to draw up an account to y^e
Qurterly meeting next.
And this meeting is ajourned till y^e 10 of the 2^d month 1717
This meeting being met accord to ajournment
this 10th day of y^e 2d month 1717:
Some suffering allowed at this meeting of **Peleg Slocum**
And **Abraham Tucker** and **John Tucker** at **Chilmark**

2:mo= At a monthly meeting of friends held at our meeting
house in **Dartmouth** y^e 15th day of the 2^d month 1717
Dartmouth meeting called **Judah Smith** and **Eleazer Slocum**
appeared: **Rochester** — meeting called none appeared
The business Concerning **Benjamin Cliffton** and **Sarah**
Davis is Refered to the y^e next monthly meeting.
~~And **William Wood** and **Eleazer Slocum**~~

And **John Tucker** and **Abraham** have drawn up an
account and sent it to yᵉ quarterly meeting as appoint-
=ted And **William Wood** and **Eleazer Slocum** hath
attended the Quarterly meeting as appointed
This meeting hath received and epistel from yᵉ quarter
=ly meeting Dated yᵉ 11ᵗʰ of the 11ᵗʰ month: 1716
and from yᵉ Quarterly meeting yᵉ 12:ᵗʰ of yᵉ 2:ᵈ month 1717
and they was boath read and kindly accepted
The business of **Dartmouth** meeting Called and **Deliverance**
Smith hath brought the returne of the survey of
yᵉ Land whereon friends meet ing house stands in
Ponaganset vilage and is ordered to be recorded in yᵉ packigers
Records and friends to pay for yᵉ Recording

3:mo= At a monthly meeting of friends held at our meeting house in
Dartmouth the: 20ᵗʰ day of yᵉ 3ᵈ month : 1717:
Dartmouth meeting called **William Wood** and **Josiah Smith** appeared
Rochester meeting called **Elisha Wing** appeared
and **Eleazer Slocum** and and **Deliverance Smith** and **Judah Smith**
is appointed to speak wᵗʰ **Timothy Davis** and his wife to know whither
they have kept yᵐselves clear in their testimony in the marriage
of their daughter **Sarah Davis** with **Benjamin Clifton** contrary to
the good order established amongst friends and also to speak wᵗʰ yᵉ abovesd
Benjamin Clifton and **Sarah** to know how it hath been that they
have proceeded in marriage Contrary to yᵉ good order of friends
and the friends to make return to yᵉ next monthly meeting how
they find things:
And this meeting makes choice of **Griffin Owen** and **Peleg Slocum**
and **Eleazer Slocum** to Draw up some account to **Walter Newbury**
concerning a Late act for yᵉ maintainance of ministers and Desire
him to take yᵉ sd act along with him to old **England** and delier it to
John Whiteing or some other friends yᵗ he shall think suitable:
And our freinds **Griffin Owen** and **John Saltkite**[?] was at this meeting
and their service was kindly accepted and they shewed ther
certificates and they was well approved.[23]

4 mo= At a monthly meeting of friends held at our meeting house
in **Dartmouth** the 24ᵗʰ day of yᵉ 4ᵗʰ month 1717:

23. John Salkeld (1672-1739) was a native of Cumberland, England. A minister, he emigrated to
Chester County, Pennsylvania about 1705, where he lived until his death. See "John Salkeld," *Friends
Miscellany*, 3 (9ᵗʰ Mo. 1832), 66-70.; *The Salkeld Family of Pennsylvania, from John Who Emigrated in 1705,
to the Fourth Generation, So Far as Is Known* (n.p., 1867), 1-2.

There was collected for the use of friends –   –   –   – 01$^£$=05^s=01^d

Dartmouth meeting called **Judah Smith** and **Deliverance Smith**
appeared: **Rochester** meeting called. and none appeared

Edward Wing and **Sarah Tucker** did signify to this meeting their
intentions of taking each other in marriage if y^e Lord permitt
and **Josiah Merihoo** and **Henry Tucker** is appointed to see into
their clearness and bring in the^ir answer how the find things to
the next monthly meeting.

And whereas **Eleazer Slocum Deliverance Smith** and **Judah Smith**
have not been wth **Timothy Davis** and his wife and **Benjamin**
Clifton and his wife according to ye order of the Last monthly
meeting they are continued to Do sd business and to bring in their
account to ye next monthly meeting:

The visiters being called upon say that little has been done in
visiting y:^{e} Last Quarter:

John Tucker and **Tho- Taber jun^r** are appointed to draw up an account
to y:^{e} Quarterly meeting **John Tucker** and **Stephen Willcocks** and
Eleazer Slocum are appointed to attend y^e Quarterly meeting
and the (~~meeting have the~~) meeting have made up the accompts
with **Benjamin Howland** and there remains in y^e stock: 1$^£$=02^s=11^d
and this dayes collection which is aforesd –   –   –   – 1 = 03 = 0

And **Benjamin Howland** is to pay 22 Shillings to **Wm Wood**
for mony that he paid toward y^e Land whereon **Coakset** meeing
house stand; which he forth with paid:

And **Benjamin Howland** is also ordered to pay 21 Shillings out of
the Stock to **Eleazer Slocum** for keeping y^e meeting house

---

5 mo= At a monthly meeting of friends held at our meeting house
in **Dartmouth** the 15th day of y^e 5th month 1717:

Dartmouth meeting called **Eleazer Slocum** and **Judah Smith**
appeared: **Rochester** meeting caled **Elisha Wing** appeared

Edward Wing and, **Sarah Tucker** ~~ap~~ Came before this meeting
~~for their answer~~ and desired the meetings answer with respect
to their intentions of mariage which they laid before the Last
monthly meeting and the meeting answers that they^{ings} being
Clear they may proceed in the good order of truth between this
and the next monthly meeting

And **Benjamin Howland** and **Eleazer Slocum** and **John Tucker**
are appointed to see it accomplished:

And **Eleazer Slocum Deliverance Smith** and **Judah Smith** have
been with **Timothy Davis** and **Benjamin Clifton** as appointed and

have discoursed them concerning the sd **Cliftons** taking his wife
out of yᵉ order of truth as it is established amongst friends and
said **Benjamin Clifton** justefies him selfe in his taking his Wife
and this meeting makes chore of **Tho: Taber junr** and **John Tucker**
to draw up their condemnation against next monthly meeting
and **John Tucker** hath drawn up an account to the Quarterly
meeting ——————— as appointed ———————
And **Stephen Wilcocks** and **John Tucker** hath attended yᵉ Quarterly
meeting as appointed and **Benjamin Howland** has paid 21ᶠ: out of
the meetings stock to **Eleazer Slocum** for keeping the meeting
house as ordered. The friends of **Rochester** preparetive meeting
deisre the assitance of this meeting toward the orderly setling
the Land whereon their meeting house stands and the house also and
the^ir burying ~~ground~~ place: and the meeting advises that they have as
soon as may be the sd house and lands made over to some perticular
friends in the usual method among friends in such cases and the per
=sons nominated by the meeting are **Savory Clifton Stephen Wing**
Nicolas Davis Thoˢ Hathaway: and **Joseph Taber** and **John Tucker** and
Tho- Taber Junʳ are ordered to be helpful to them in accomplishing the
work: and the Epistle from **London** yearly meeting and our last
quarterly meeting were read and kindly accepted and the matter
in the Quarterly meeting epistle concerning slaves is refered to
the next monthly meeting:
And this meeting Doth agree to come to further subscrption to
=wards yᵉ defraying the charge of **Coakset** meeting house
and whereas **James Howland** is about to take a wife out of
the good order of truth to yᵉ trouble of friends, the meeting appoints
Benjamin Howland and **Eleazer Slocum** to Let him know yᵉ mind of
the meeting and to advise him in the matter:

_6mo=_ At a monthly meeting of friends held at our meeting house
In **Dartmouth** yᵉ 19ᵗʰ day of yᵉ 6 month 1717
Dartmouth meeting called **Deliverance Smith** and **Judah Smith**
appeared: **Rochester** meeting called **Elisha Wing** appeared
nothing being done concerning **Rochester** meeting house and Land
about it it is refered to next monthly meeting and **John Tucker**
and **Benjamin Howland** do give account that **Edward Wing** and
Sarah Tucker have taken each other in marriage according to
yᵉ Good order of truth: The business relating to **James Howlands**
taking a wife out of yᵉ order as friends is refered to the next
monthly meeting and yᵉ matter relating to Slaves refered from

yᵉ quarterly meeting to yᵉ Consideration of this meeting being
spoken to it is refered to yᵉ next monthly meeting
And **Stephen Wilcocks Deliverance Smith Benjamin Howland
Abraham Tucker** and **Thoˢ Taber Junʳ** are ordered to draw up
something relating to that matter for the meeting to sign if
they approve of it and the condemnation of **Benjamin Clifton**
and his wife is signed and **Elisha Wing** is appointed to read it at
the conclution of their meeting of worship on a first Day-
And the friends of **Coakset** vilage having Desired to have a meeting
of worship every first day it is allowed that they may for time to
come have a meeting according to their desire and **John Summers**
of **Rochester** having signifyed to this meeting his desire to come in
=to unity again wᵗʰ friends and hath sent a paper to this meeting
to signify yᵉ same the meeting hath appointed **John Tucker** an
Elisha Wing to speak with him in order to know his sincerity
and make report to yᵉ next monthly meeting – –
And some friends sufferings being sent from **Rochester** are read
and approved to be sent to yᵉ Quarterly meeting

_7 mo:_ At a monthly meeting of friends held at our meeting house
in **Dartmouth** yᵉ 16:ᵗʰ day of yᵉ 7ᵗʰ month 1717
Dartmouth meeting Called **William Wood** and **Benjamin Howland**
appeared: **Rochester** meeting called **Stephen Wing** appeared
Eleazer Slocum and **Thoˢ Taber Junʳ** are chose to draw up a
condemnation against **James Howland**s Disorderly walking
proceeding in marriage and present it to yᵉ next monthly meeting
to be signed: and **Elisha Wing** has Read **Benjamin Clifton** and his
Wives condemnation: which is a followeth -
Whereas **Benjamin Clifton** the son of **Savory Clifton** of
Rochester in the county of **Plymouth** in **New England** and
Sarah Davis daughter of **Timothy Davis** of sd **Rochester** being
boath friends children yet have proceeded in mariage to each other
contrary to yᵉ good order established among friends on that account
and contrary to their parents consent especially yᵉ parents of
the said **Benjamin Clifton** – –
Therefore we are concerned to give forth this as a publick
testimony against their disorderly proceedings denying ^them to be of
us the people called Quakers desiring that if it be the will of God
they may come to a sense of their out goings and find money
Given forth at our monthly meeting of friends held at our meeting
House in **Dartmouth** the 19ᵗʰ day of yᵉ 6ᵗʰ month 1717

Increase Allen	Henry Tucker	Mary Lapham
Peleg Slocum	Nicolas Lapham	Hannah Tucker
John Tucker	Nathaniel Howland	Rachel Allen
Joseph Russell	Benjamin Howland	Mary Laton
Stephen Willcock	Judah Smith	Mehetabel Burrel
Elisha Wing	Joseph Russell: Ju<u>nr</u>	Mary Lapham Jun<u>r</u>
William Wood	Ruth Tucker	Phebe Tucker
John Lapham	Mary Slocum	Mary Russell
Deliverance Smith	Hephzibah Hathaway	Mary Smith

And **John Tucker** and **Elisha Wing** not having spoke wth **John Sum**
=**mers** as ordered the Last monthly meeting it is refered to the next
monthly meeting the friends appointed to draw up something
Relating to Slaves to send to y^e Quarterly meeting have done it
and it being read the meeting doth approve of it and appoint
John Tucker and **Thomas Taber Jun**^r to Sign it in behalfe of ye meeting
and **Thomas Taber Jun**^r and **Stephen Willcock** is ~~appointed to attend y^e~~ ^ordered
    to give the
Quarterly meeting an account how the affairs of truth are
amongst us and it is proposed to offer to ye quarterly meeting whither
it may not be well for friends not to sue any at Law or suffer them
selves to be sued without the advice of ye monthly meeting they belong to
it it can be or otherwise the advice of some substantial friends[24]
The collection is refered to ye next monthly meeting – – – – –

_8 mo_ At a monthly meeting ^of friends held at our meeting house in **Dartmouth**
the 21st day of ye 8th month 1717
Dartmouth meeting called **William Wood** appeared
Rochester meeting called none appeared
Daniel Goddard of **Marshfield** and **Mary Tripp** the daughter
of **James Tripp** have laid their intentions of mariage before this
meeting and they are desired to wait till ye next monthly meet
for their answering
And **William Wood** and **Stephen Willcock** are ordered to inquire
into their clearness with respect to mariage and give an
account to y^e next monthly meeting:
Elisha Wing and **John Tucker** is still continued to speak with
John Summers: And **Thomas Taber ju**^{nr} hath attended y^e Quar
=terly meeting as appointed and **Tho**^s **Taber jun**^r and **John Tucker**
hath signed a paper relating to slaves as appointed:

24. It was an established rule that one Friend could not sue another without authorization of the
monthly meeting. Dartmouth Friends proposed extending this to lawsuits against non-Friends.

And **John Tucker** and **Thomas Taber Jun**ʳ hath drawn up an
account to yᵉ Quarterly meeting as appointed:
And **James Howlands** condemnation is refered to yᵉ next month
=ly meeting and the same persons wᵗʰ **Benjamin Howland** are
ordered to draw it up against sd meeting The Quarterly
meeting Epistle was read and kindly accepted

9ᵗʰ mo: At a monthly meeting of friends held at our meeting house
in **Dartmouth** yᵉ 18ᵗʰ day of yᵉ 9ᵗʰ month 1717.
Dartmouth meeting called **William Wood** and **Judah Smith**
appeared: **Rochester** meeting called **Elisha Wing** appeared
There was Collected for yᵉ use of friend – – 1ᶠ-04ˢ=04ᵈ
The friends that were appointed yᵉ last monthly meeting to
inquire into **Daniel Goddard**s and **Mary Tripp**s Clearness as to
marriage do make report that they find nothing but that they
may proceed and said **Goddard** has brought a certificate from
the monthly meeting of friends at **Pembrook**²⁵ wᶜʰ signifies
their allowance of his proceeding and his clearness as to
marriage he also brought a few lines from his father and
mother wᶜʰ signifies their consent to his present proceedings
And yᵉ said **Daniel Goddard** and **Mary Tripp** presented them selves
before this meeting desiring friends answer as to their intentions
Laid before yᵉ last monthly meeting and they were answered that
nothing appearing to hinder they might proceed in the order
of truth and **William Wood** and **John Tucker** are appointed to see
it accomplished accordingly.
And **Isaac Howland** yᵉ Son of **Benjamin Howland** and
Hannah Allen yᵉ daughter of **Ebenezer Allen** did lay their in
=tentions of mariage before this meeting and they are desired
To wait till yᵉ next monthly meeting for their answer and
Deliverance Smith and **Judah Smith** are appointed to inquire
into their clearness with respect to mariage and give account
to yᵉ next monthly meeting
And **John Tucker** and **Elisha Wing** are still continued to speak
wᵗʰ **John Summers**: and **James Howland**s condemnation is drawn
up approved and signed and **John Tucker** is ordered to read it or
cause it to be read between this and next monthly – –
The business of **Dartmouth** prepariative meeting called
Rochester prepariative meeting business called no business
presented: and there being a paper presented to this meeting

25. I.e., Pembroke, Massachusetts. The misspelling is not noted hereafter.

from **John Summers** and it being read **Nathaniel Howland**
and **Deliverance Smith** and Tho⁵ **Taber Jun**ͬ are appointed to
write an answer to it and send it to him as soon as may be

_10: mo:_ At a monthly meeting held at our meeting house in **Dartmouth**
the 16ᵗʰ day of yᵉ 10ᵗʰ month 1717:
There was collected for yᵉ use of friends 16 shillings
Dartmouth meeting called **Judah Smith** appeared: **Rochester**
meeting Called and none appeared – –
And **Isaac Howland** and **Hannah Allen** having laid their intenti
=ons of marriage before yᵉ Last monthly meeting did now present
them selves desiring yᵉ meetings answer and the meeting not
having so good an account of yᵉ young womans having: ~~having having~~
her parents consent as ought to be do answer them that they may
proceed in yᵉ good order of truth between this and yᵉ next monthly meet
=ing provided that they then bring an account of her parents consent
James Howlands Condemnation has been read according to yᵉ order of
the Last monthly meeting and is as followeth_____
Whereas **James Howland** the son of **Nathaniel Howland** and **Rose**
his wife of **Dartmouth** in the county of **Bristol** in yᵉ province of yᵉ
Massachusets Bay in **New England** hath from his childhood been
Educated amongst friends his father and mother being both of yᵉ
people called quakers yet hath in slight of friends and the good
advice and counsel by them given him and in contept of the good
Order established among friends proceeded to take a wife in the common
way of other people we are therefore concerned to give this forth a pub
=lick testimony against said Disorderly action and do deny the said **James
Howland** to be one of us yᵉ people called qukers truly desiring that he
may return and find mercy wᵗʰ God and tenderly all friends Children
to beware of giving way to the inducements of Satan Least they be
led forth to scorn friends and yᵉ testimony of yᵉ Blessed Truth as it
has been delivered through great tribulations even to the sealing of it
with the blood of many faithful witnesses surely wo will be the portion
∴ of these that can Slightly trample ~~upon~~ thereon and by whome the testimo
=ny of the Blessed truth may fall in the Street in any perticuler unless
by true and unfeigned repentance they return to God which that
every disorderly and disobedient one may do is our sincere desire
given forth at our monthly meeting of friends held at our meeting
house in **Dartmouth** yᵉ: 18ᵗʰ day of yᵉ: 9ᵗʰ month 1717:

| **John Tucker** | **Benjamin Howland** | **Tho**⁵ **Smith** |
| **Abraham Tucker** | **Josiah Merihoo** | **W**ᵐ **Soule** |

Peleg Slocum	Elisha Wing	Thoˢ Taber Junʳ
Stephen Willcock	Thomas Hathaway	Henry Tucker
William Wood	Joseph Russell	Jabez Barker

And **Deliverance Smith** and **Josiah Smith** are appointed to see
the abovesaid cupple that **Isaac Howland** and **Hannah Allen**
accomplish their marriage in the good order of truth
And **John Tucker** and **Stephen Willcock** are appointed to attend the
Quarterly meeting next the visiters of **Dartmouth** meeting being
Called upon they give no account: and **John Tucker** and **Eleazer
Slocum** are ^appointed to take care of the meeting house for yᵉ year following
And **John Tucker** and **Thos Taber junʳ** are appointed to draw upon
account to yᵉ Quarterly meeting
and whereas **Daniel mosher** makes a complaint to this meeting
that **Nathaniel Howland** has wronged him This meeting makes
Choice of **Deliverance Smith Jabez Barker** and **Wᵐ Soule** to
heare the matter and make up the differance if they can and
if they cannot to make report to the next monthly meeting
The friends appointed to see **Daniel Goddard** and **Mary Tripp**
solemnize their mariage in the Good order of truth
say that it was so accomplished as far as they said – – – – –

1717/18 At a monthly meeting of friends held at our meeting house in **Dartmouth**
11:mo: the 20ᵗʰ day of yᵉ: 11ᵗʰ month: 177/18: **Dartmouth** meeting called **Judah Smith**
and **William Wood** appeared: **Rochester** meeting called none appeared
Deliverance Smith and **Judah Smith** being called upon to give an
account how **Isaac Howland** and **Hannah Allens** marriage was carri
=ed on and they say in Good order as far as they know:
And **John Tucker** hath attended yᵉ Quarterly meeting as appointed
Thomas Taber Juⁿ and **John Tucker** did Draw up an account to yᵉ Quarter
=ly meeting as appointed: the men that were chosen to make
inspection into yᵉ Differance between **Daniel Mosher** and **Nathaniel
Howland** makes report to this meeting that yᵉ sd **Mosher** refuses
to Lave the whole differance to them Therefore they thought not
best to meddl therewith: The business of **Dartmouth** preparitive
meeting called but no business presented the Epistle from yᵉ Quar
=terly meeting was read and kindly accepted

12 mo: At a monthly meeting of friends held at our meeting house
in **Dartmouth** yᵉ 17ᵗʰ day of th 12 month 1717/18: **Dartmouth** meeting
Called **Benjamin Howland** and **Judah Smith** appeared:
Rochester meeting Called and **Nicolas Davis** appeared
Daniel Shepherd junʳ and **Mary Shearman** yᵉ Daughter of

William Shearman have Laid their intentions of mariage before
this meeting also **William Soule ju^{nr}** and **Rachel Allen** ye Daughter
of **Increase Allen** have likewise laid their intentions of mariage
before the meeing and they are all desired to wait till ye next
monthly meeting for their answer and **Eleazer Slocum** and
Henry Tucker are appointed to see into **Wm Soule**s and **Rachel
Allen**s Clearness with respect to mariage and **Judah Smith**
and **John Lapham** to see into ye clearness of the other cupple in
that respect: **Darmouth** business called and there is no further
business: **Rochester** business called and no business presented

1 mo: At a monthly meeting of friends held at our meeting house in
Dartmouth ye 17 day d̶ of the 1st month 1717/18
There was collected for the use of friends — 14 Shillings and 6 pence
whereas **Daniel Shepherd** and **Mary Shearman** did the Last
monthly meeting lay their intentions of marriage and were to
have their answer at this meeting but the young woman being
ill it is refered to ye next monthly meeting.
William Soule jun and **Rachel Allen ju^{nr}** presented them selves
the 2^d time during their answer with respect to their intention.
of marriage laid before the last monthly meeting and the meeting
answered that nothing appearing to hinder they may proceed
to take each other in marriage in ye good order of truth
Dartmouth meeting called **Deliverance Smith** and **Judah Smith**
appeared. **Rochester** meeting called **Elisha Wing** appeared
The business of **Dartmouth** meeting called **Eleazer Slocum**
and **Henry Tucker** are appointed to see the marriage between
Wm Soule and **Rachel Allen** accomplished in ye good order of truth
and they ar permited to selemnize their marriage on ye next
4th day of ye week although it be a meeting day by cource but
not to be allowed as a president for time to come – –
The visiters being called upon do give account that nothing
had been done in that service the last quarter – –
And **Stephen Willcocks** and **Benjamin Howland** are appointed
to attend ye Quarterly meeting next
And a matter being presented from ye preparitive meeting of
Dartmouth concerning ye puting off the hat or standing uncovered
in laying the intentions of marriage and receiving their answers
and the meeting being generally of ye mind that it ought not to
be and the meeting refers it to ye consideration of ye Quarterly
Meeting: also from said ^preparitive meeting a query whither our marriages

among friends be good without a Justice of yᵉ Peace and whither
friend be obliged to invite a Justice to their marriages and if a
Justice be invited to come and it so happen that he cannot or
will not come whither friends are obliged to go to another which
matter is also refered to yᵉ next Quarterlymeeting[26]:
The business of **Rochester** meeting called and they ^⁻ᵛⁱˢⁱᵗᵉʳˢ give account
that they have visited the famlies of friends and things for the
most part are pretty well amongst them -
And then was presented some Sufferings of friends from **Rochester**
which was approved to be sent to yᵉ Quarterly meeting
and this meeting is ajournd till yᵉ sixth day next before yᵉ quarterly
meeting ───────────────────────────────────
This meeting being meet according to ajournment this 4ᵗʰ day
of yᵉ 2ᵈ month 1718:
The visters gives the following account that they have visited
the famlies of friends belonging to **Dartmouth** meeting and for
the most part as far as they said things are pretty well and **Thoˢ**
Taber junʳ and **John Tucker** and **Nathaniel Howland** or eighter two
of them are appointed to draw up an account to the Quarterly meeting – –
And **William Wood** and **John Tucker** are appointed to attend the
Quarterly meeting next
───

_2 mo:_　At a monthly meeting of friends held at our meeting house in
Dartmouth yᵉ 21ˢᵗ of yᵉ 2ᵈ month 1718
Dartmouth meeting called **William Wood** and **Benjamin Howland** appeared
Rochester meeting called none appeared
Daniel Shepherd and **Mary Shearman** appeared before this meeting
for their answer as to their intentions of marriage and equiry being
made into their clearness and nothing appearing to hinder their sᵈ
intentions they had their answer that they might proceed in marriage
to each other in yᵉ good order of truth:
And **Stephen Willcocks** and **William Wood** and **John Tucker** hath atten
=ded yᵉ Quarterly meeting as appointed and **John Tucker** hath drawn
up an account to the Quarterly meeting as appointed and **Judah Smith**
and **John Lapham** are appointed to see **Daniel Shepherd** and **Mary**
Shearmans marriage solemnized in the good order of truth and make
return to the next monthly meeting: The Epistle of yᵉ Last Quarter

26. Concerns about the legality of Quaker marriages went back to the 1650s, but by the eighteenth
century the question had generally been resolved in favor of Friends. See Rufus M. Jones, _The Quakers in_
the American Colonies (London: Macmillan, 1911), 147. Dartmouth historians note that at least through
1720, one of the witnesses to marriages in meeting was often a Congregationalist justice of the peace from
Little Compton: Joseph Church, Benjamin Church, or Job Almy.

=ly meeting was read among us and kindly accepted: and the friends that
were appointed to see that **Wᵐ Soule** and **Rachel Allen** did Solemnize
their marriage in the good order of truth makes report that they were
there and they saw nothing but that it was performed in good order
And **Wᵐ Soule** is appointed to draw a deed of Land that yᵉ meeting
bought of **Deliverance Smith** and there was Collected 10 shillings
and ^it was ordered to be paid to **James Tripp** towards the build the meeting house

3:mo: At a monthly meeting of friends held at our meeting house in
Dartmouth yᵉ 19ᵗʰ day of yᵉ 3ᵈ month 1718 —
Dartmouth meeting called **Judah Smith** and **Benjamin Howland**
appeared: **Rochester** meeting called **Elisha Wing** appeared – –
Judah Smith and **John Lapham** being called upon to give in their
account how things was managed at **Daniel Shepherd** and
Mary Shearmans marriage and their answer is that it was
managed in the order of truth as far as they saw
the business of **Rochester** meeting called and no business presented

4 mo: At a monthly meeting of friends held at our meeting house
in **Dartmouth** the 23ᵈ day of yᵉ 4ᵗʰ month 1718
Dartmouth meeting called **Josiah Merihoo [Merihew]** and **Henry Tucker**
appeared: **Rochester** meeting called **Stephen Wing** appeared
and there was collected for yᵉ use of friends 1:04:6
The business of **Dartmouth** meeting called **Deliverance Smith**
John Tucker and **Benjamin Howland** are appointed to attend the
Quarterly meeting next: and **Judah Smith** and **John Tucker** is
appointed to Draw an account to the quarterly meeting next
the business of **Rochester** meeting called but no business presented
The Epistle of yᵉ yearly meeting from **London** held in **London** in yᵉ
year 1717 was read at this meeting and kindly accepted

5 mo: At a monthly meeting of friends held at our meeting house in
Dartmouth yᵉ 21 day of the 5ᵗʰ month 1718 —
dartmouth meeting called **Benjamin Howland** and **Judah Smith**
appeared — **Rochester** meeting called **Elisha Wing** appeared
The business of **Dartmouth** meeting called and **John Tucker** and
Benjamin Howland hath attended yᵉ Quarterly meeting as
appointed and **John Tucker** and **Judah Smith** did draw up an
account to yᵉ Quarterly meeting as they were appointed
The epistle from the Quarterly meeting was read to good Sattisfactiₒₙ
also some minits of yᵉ yearly meeting at **London** 1717 concerning
tomb stones distinguishing aparel for the dead and bowings and

Cryings which minits are ordered to be read on a first day meet
ing after worship by **John Tucker** or some one who he may
appoint - and there was a subscribtion made by friends at
this meeting in answer to the desire of the Quarterly meeting
who ordered our monthly meeting to raise ten pounds for yᵉ
service of truth and **John Tucker** is ordered to receive the mony
and convey it to yᵉ next quarterly meeting of friends
no business from **Rochester** to this meeting:
Benjamin Howland is ordered to pay 30 shillings out of the meet
-ings Stock to **John Tucker** and **Eleazer Slocum** for keeping the
meeting house

6 mo:　At a monthly meeting of friends held at our meeting
house in **Dartmouth** the 18ᵗʰ day of yᵉ 6ᵗʰ month 1718
Dartmouth meeting called **William Wood** and **Judah Smith**
appeared – –
Rochester meeting called **Stephen Wing** appeared
John Tucker has caused the munits to be read according to yᵉ
order of the Last monthly meeting
~~The visiterˢ being called upon~~
The business of **Dartmouth** being called the visiters are desired
to visit the families of friends between this and the next monthly
meeting: from **Rochester** no business presented

7 mo:　At monthly meeting ^of friends held at our meeting house in **Dartmouth**
the 15ᵗʰ day of the 7ᵗʰ month 1718– –
there was collected for the use of friends – – 0ᶠ-17ˢ=0ᵈ
Dartmouth meeting called **Benjamin Howland** and **Judah Smith**
appeared — **Rochester** meeting called **Elisha Wing** appeared
Joseph Mosher the Son of **Nicholas Mosher** and **Mehetabel**
Smith did lay their intentions of taking each other in mariage
and **Benjamin Howland** and **Deliverance** ^Smith are ^appointed to see into their clearness
in respect to mariage and also that they have their parants
Consent: And **Benjamin Howland** hath paid to **John Tucker** and
Eleazer Slocum 30 Shillings as ordered: the Subscribtion of 10 £
agreed upon at yᵉ monthly meeting in the 5ᵗʰ month last is
finnished – –
The business o **Rochester** ^meeting called and they have gathered forty
Shillings for the use of friends and sent it by **Elisha Wing** and it
is ordered to be sent to yᵉ Quarterly meeting next by **John Tucker**: ~~and~~
And **William Wood Elisha Wing** and **John Tucker** is appointed to attend
yᵉ Quarterly meeting next: and **Judah Smith** and **John Tucker**

are appointed to draw up an account to the Quarterly meeting
next and this meeting desires to have an account what is done
concerning the buying and keeping of Slaves

8 mo:　At a monthly meeting of friends held at our meeting house
in **Dartmouth** the 20ᵗʰ day of yᵉ 8ᵗʰ month 1718 – –
dartmouth meeting called **Benjamin Howland** and **Josiah Merihoo [Merihew]**
appeared – – **Rochester** meeting called none appeared – –
The friends that were chosen to make inquiry in to **Joseph Mosher** ʲᵘʳ
and **Mehetabel Smith**s Clearness from all others in relation to mariage
and also the consent of parents gives account that they find nothing
to hinder their proceedings in that affair: and they the said **Joseph
Mosher** and **Mehetabel Smith** presenting them selves before this
meeting desiring their answer they had their answer that
they might proceed to take each other in the Good order of truth
and **Benjamin Howland** and **Deliverance Smith** are appointed to
See the mariage solemnized in the good order of truth
and bring in their answer how they find things to the next monthly meeting
And **John Tucker** and **Judah Smith** hath drawn an account to
the Quarterly meeting as appointed and **John Tucker** hath
carried yᵉ twelve pounds of yᵉ Quarterly meeting as appointed
and **Benjamin Howland** is ordered to pay 26 shillings for mend
=ing and making glass for yᵉ meeting house – – – – –

9 mo:　At a monthly meeting of friends held at our meeting house
in **Dartmouth** yᵉ 17ᵗʰ day of yᵉ 9ᵗʰ month:1718:
Dartmouth meeting called **Benjamin Howland** and **William Wood**
appeared: **Rochester** meeting called and none appeared:
Adam Mott and **Apphia Hathaway** have laid their intentions
of mariage before this meeting **Henry Tucker** and **Thoˢ Taber** ʲᵘⁿʳ
are appointed to inquire into their clearness with respect to
mariage and make report to yᵉ next monthly meeting:
Benjamin Howland and **Deliverance Smith** makes report to this
meeting that they have attended yᵉ mariage of **Joseph Mosher**
and **Mehetabel Smith** and it was performed in the order of
Truth as far as they saw – – – – –

10 mo:　At a monthly meeting of friends held at our meeting house
in **Dartmouth** the 15ᵗʰ day of the 10ᵗʰ month 1718 =
Dartmouth meeting called **Eleazer Slocum** and **Jabez Barker**
appeared: **Rochester** meeting called **Elisha Wing** appeared
There was Collected for yᵉ use of friends – 0ᶠ-09ˢ=06ᵈ
Adam Mott and **Apphia Hathaway** presented them selves

before this meeting desiring y^e meetings answer with respect
to their proceeding in mariage and inquiry having been made and
things on boath sides appearing clear the meeting allowes that
they may proceed to take each other in mariage in the good order
of truth between this and the next monthly meeting and **Henry
Tucker** and **Thomas Taber ju^{nr}** are appointed to see it accom
=plished accordingly and make report to y^e next monthly meeting
And the visiters being called upon have no account to give
and y^e meeting advises that they be careful to visit the fami
lies of friends so that there may be a full account to give to
the Quarterly meeting in y^e 2.^d month next:
And **William Wood** and **Stephen Willcox** and **Elisha Wing** are appoin
=ted to attend y:^e Quarterly meeting next – –
and **John Tucker** and **Thos Taber jun^r** are appointed to draw
up an account to the quarterly meeting concerning the
affairs of truth amongst us
The business of **Rochester** meeting called it is Signifyed from
their proparitive meeting that **Benoni Uin [Youen]** of **Rochester**
has signified to them his intentions of proceeding mariage with
Hasadiah Landers of **Sandwich** friends do therefore make choice
of **Elisha Wing** and **Stephen Wing** to inquire into his conversation
and clearness with respect to mariage and make report to
the next monthly meeting:

11:mo At a monthly meeting friends held at our meeting house in
Dartmouth the 19th day of ye 11:th month:1718/19:
Dartmouth meeting called **Henry Tucker** appeared:
Rochester meeting Called and none appeared – –
William Wood and **Elisha Wing** hath attended y:^e Quarterly
Meeting as appointed: and **John Tucker** hath drawn an account
to y^e quarterly meeting:
And it is desired that friends take care to git the deed acknowledged
and concerning **Adam Mott** and **Benoni Uin** relating to mari
=age see the next month minits:
And **John Tucker** and **Henry Tucker** is appointed to take care
of the meeting house y:^e ensuing year ^and the year to beginn at y:^e
Last monthly meeting and the meeting to pay the charge:
we received the Epistle from the last Quarterly meeting which
was read and kindly accepted:

12:mo= At a monthly meeting of friends held at our meeting house in
Dartmouth y:^e 16:th of y^e 12th: 1718/19:

Dartmouth meeting called **Judah Smith** and **Henry Tucker** appeared
Rochester meeting called **Stephen Wing** appeared – –
Thomas Taber ju^(nr) gives account to this meeting that the mariage
between **Adam Mott** and **Apphia Hathaway** was performed in the
good order of truth – –
and the friends appointed to inquire into **Benoni Uin** Conversation
and clearness with respect to mariage do make report ~~the~~
to this meeting that they find nothing to ye contrary but that he
may proceed: and the meeting hath given him a sertificate
directed to ye monthly meeting at **Sandwich** according to s^d report
The business of **Dartmouth** meeing called it being proposed from
Dartmouth preparitive meeting whither it be agreable to
truth to fetch timber of from another mans lot that was
fallen ^thereon before the lot was laid out without leave of the owner of
said lot it is concluded by the full consent of y^e: s^d meeting
that no friend ought to fetch any such Timber without leave
first obtained of y^e: owner of such lands: for **Rochester** no business

1718/19: At a monthly meeting of friends held at our meeting house in
1 _mo_: **Dartmouth** the 16th day of y^e: 1st month: 171 18/19:
There was collected for y^e: use of friends: 1^£-11^s-6^d
Phneas Chace of **Tiverton** and **Desire Wing** of **Rochester** the
Daughter of **John Wing** of **Rochester** deceased: have laid their inten
tions mariage before this meeting who are desired to wait till the
next monthly meeting for their answer:
And **Nathan Barlow** having desired a f certificate of his clear
=ness with respect to mariage and conversation: and **Elisha Wing**
and **Nicolas Davis** are appointed to inquire into the same and
give an account thereof to y^e: next monthly meeting
The business of **Dartmouth** meeting Called **William Wood** and **Judah**
Smith being appointed to present y^e: business the visiters do
give account that they have pretty generally visited y^e: fami
lies of friends and as far as they saw things are pretty well
for ye most part and friends generally in unity
And **William White** having offered some contribution towards the
finnishing **Coakset** meeting house this meeting makes choice of
John Tucker William Wood and **Stephen Willcocks** to signify the order
of friends to him on such occations and to give account to the
next monthly meeting whither he be minded to become one with us
And **James Tripp** the Son of **James Tripp** having a design of
proceeding in mariage contrary to the order of friends and he

appointed by the preparitive meeting about it and he not
giving a positive answer this ^meeting appoints **Nathanil Howland** and
Deliverance Smith to Labour farther with him and give account
to the next monthly meeting
Rochester meeting Called **Nicholas Davis** appeared and no
farther business presented: only **Elisha Wing** and **Nicholas
Davis** are appointed to inquire into **Phineas Chace** and **Desire
Wing**s clearness with respect to mariage and conversation
and make report to y^e: next monthly meeting and **Nicolas
Davis** and **John Tucker** and **Thos Taber ju^nr** are chose to attend
the Quarterly meeting and also to draw an account to ye house

_2^d mo_ At a monthly meeting of friends held at our meeting house in
Dartmouth the 20th day of the 2^d month 1719:
Dartmouth meeting called **Benjamin Howland** and **Judah Smith**
appeared: **Rochester** meeting called **Elisha Wing** appeared – –
Phineas Chace and **Desire Wing** not appearing not appearing for
their answer it is refered till y^e: next monthly meeting
That matter concerning speaking w^th **William White** is refered
for an account till y^e: next monthly meeting:
And the friends appointed to speak with **James Tripp Junr**
concerning his marying out of the order of friends do give account
that he had accomplished his mariage before they had oppertunity
to speak with him friends are therefore concerned to condemn s^d
Disorderly practice and to deny the said **James Tripp Junr** to be one
of us the people called Qukers and **Thomas Taber Ju^nr** is appointed
to draw up a paper of friends Denying him and present it to the
next monthly meeting to be signed – –
The persons chose to attend the Quarterly meeting did attend s^d meeting
also **John Tucker** and **Thomas Taber jun^r** did draw up an account to the
Quarterly meeting as ordered: The business of **Dartmouth** meeting
Called no business appeared: **Rochester** no business – –
and friends have signed a certificate signifying **Nathan Barlow**es
Clearness relating to mariage: This day the accounts were made
up and ballanced with **James Tripp** Concerning the building of
Coakset meeting house and there remains 40 shillings in **John
Tucker**s hands of the subscription for s^d meeting house – – – – –

_3^d mo:_ At a monthly meeting of friends held at our meeting house
in **Dartmouth** ye 18:^th day of the 3^d: month 1719:
Dartmouth meeting called **Abraham Tucker** and **Josiah Merihoo [Merihew]**
appeared: **Rochester** meeting called **Stephen Wing** appeared

the friends appointed to speak with **Wᵐ White** do give account that
he desires some time of consideration and the condemnation of
James Tripp Junʳˢ disorderly walking and proceeding in mariage
is presented to the meeting which is as followeth
according to yᵉ order of the Last monthly meeting and being
accepted and signed **Deliverance Smith** is ordered to read it
or cause it to be read on a first day at **Coaxet** meeting
House at the end of the meeting for worship between this and
the next monthly meeting
Dartmouth business called no business appeared:
Rochester business called none presents only some sufferings
presented from **Rochester** which are accepted and ordered to
be sent to the yearly meeting – –
the business relating to **Phineas Chace** his proceeding in mariage
is refered to yᵉ: next monthly meeting by reason of yᵉ: yearly
meeting falling ^out to be on the 3ᵈ-2ᵈ: day of yᵉ: next month the
next monthly meeting and preparitive meeting is ajourned one week
Later than usual

4ᵗʰ mo= At a monthly meeting of friends held at our meeting house in **Dartmouth**
the 22ᵈ: day of yᵉ: 4ᵗʰ :1719: **Dartmouth** meeting Called **William Wood**
and **Judah Smith** appeared: **Rochester** meeting called – –
Savery Clifton appeared
There was Collected for the use of friends – – 1- 07 = 0
Deliverance Smith being called upon to know whither he
hath read **James Tripp junʳˢ** Condemnation and he answers
that he hath not done it and so he is continued still to
read yᵉ same according to yᵉ order of yᵉ Last monthly
meeting the sufferings that ^was presented —— was presented ^ from Rochester to yᵉ yearly
meeting at **Rhoad Island** as appointed – –
The business of **Dartmouth** meeting called **William Wood**
Thomas Taber junʳ and **John Tucker** are appoind to attend
the Quarterly meeting next: **Deliverance Smith** and
John Tucker are appointed to draw up an account to yᵉ:
Quarterly meeting: **Phineas Chace** and **Desire Wing**
appeared at this meeting desiring their answer relating
to their taking each other in mariage and nothing
appearing to hinder their said intentions they had their
answer ^that they might proceed in taking each other in the good
order of truth and **Savery Clifton** and **John Tucker** is
appointed to see it performed as above sᵈ and make return

to the next monthly meeting:

The business of **Rochester** meeting Called and their was
a paper prsented signifying their love but no business
one thing omited: viz: the visiters being called upon to know
how they find things under their care and answer was made
that nothing was done in respect of visiting friends
famlies the last Quarter

5:th mo= At a monthly meeting of friends held at our meeting
House in **Dartmouth** y:e 20:th day of y:e 5:th month 1719
Dartmouth meeting called **William Wood** and **Judah Smith**
appeared: **Rochester** meeting called **Elisha Wing** appeared
James Tripp jun.:r Condemnation hath been read according
to order - **John Tucker** and **William Wood** have attended the
quarterly meeting = and **John Tucker** and **Deliverance Smith**
have drawn up an account to the Quarterly meeing:
and **John Tucker** gives account that **Phineas Chace**
and **Desire Wing** have performed their mariage in the
Good order of truth as far as they saw
The business of **Dartmouth** meeting Called it is proposed
to this meeting that **Thomas Smith** hath a desire to go to y:e
westward to visit his relations ^and friends and desires the consent of
this meeting therein and a few lines of their unity in way
of S:d Certificate:
And **John Tucker** and **Tho::s Taber ju.:r** are ordered to draw a
certificate accord^ing to s:d request and present it to the next
monthly meeting to be signed
And **Peleg Slocum** having signified that their is an intention
of mariage between his son **Giles Slocum** and **Elisabeth**
Wanton the daughter of **John Wanton** of **Newport** and
desires a certificate of this meeting of his sons clearness
on that account w:th others: and **Eliezer Slocum** and **Henry**
Tucker are appointed to inquire into the same and make
report to the next monthly meeting how they find things
and it being requested it is granted that **William Wood**
James Tripp Robert Tripp Daniel Goddard and **Hannah Cadman**
may build a stable of 20 foot squair on friends meeting house
land at **Cokset** only it is advised that **Stephen Willcock** and
James Tripp do set of ^such a piece of Land as they may think suit
=able for a burying place and the bounds and quantity thereof
to be given in to the next monthly meeting

The business of **Rochester** meeting called no business
there is no epistle from yᵉ: Quarterly meeting
Ruth Lawtons condemnation is given forth and signed and
John Tucker is appoind to read it or cause it be read at
Cokset meeting house on a first day after yᵉ meeting of

6ᵗʰ:mo: At a monthly meeting of friends held at our meeting house
the 17:ᵗʰ day of yᵉ: 6 month :1719
Dartmouth meeting Called **Benjamin Howland** and
Deliverance Smith appeared:
Rochester meeting called **Elisha Wing** appeared
Tho:ˢ Smith hath a certificate granted him and signed at
this meeting signifying our consent in his going to **Pensilvan**ᵢₐ
to visit his friends and relations there:
Also **Giles Slocum** hath a certificate signed signifying his
clearness in regard of marriage:
And the friends appointed to set out the burying ground
on yᵉ: meeting house land at **Cokset** do give account that
they have alloted the South east corner of said lot to ly six
rods in length north and south and fowr rods wide at yᵉ south
end and three rods wide at the north end for a burying place
and **Ruth Lawton**s ^condemnation hath been read according to the order of
the Last monthly meeting which is as followeth
Whereas **Ruth Lawton** of **Dartmouth** in the **County of Bristol** in
New England having been educated ~~in~~ among friends her
mother being one in unity with us the people called Quakers
and her selfe made some pretended shew of Love to friends
and the blessed truth professed amongst us yet by giving way to
a Reprobate mind hath gone out into Stubborness and disobedience to
her parets by keeping company w:ᵗʰ a lacivious person and at last
to the commiting of that unclean sin of fornication as appears
by her having a bastard child to the dishonour of god reproach to
truth and skandal to the professors thereof
Now though it is matter of sorrow and grief to all the sincere
hearted amongst us that any of our youth should thus fall into
the snares of the Devil to the wounding of their soules yet are
we constrained to give this forth as a testimony against such
fowl and wicked practices denying the said **Ruth Lawton** to be
one of us the people called Quakers heartily desiring that if it
be the will of God she may by taking the shame to her selfe
through Godly ^sorrow and sincere repentance find pardon and acceptance w:ᵗʰ him

Given forth at our monthly meeting held in **Dartmouth**
the 20:th day of the 5:th month 1719: and Signed by

John Tucker:	**Tho:s Taber ju**nr**:**	**Rose Howland**
Abraham Tucker:	**John Lapham:**	**Mary Slocum**
Peleg Slocum:	**Josiah Merihoo: [Merihew]**	**Ruth Tucker**
Increase Allen:	**Joseph Russell ju**nr**:**	**Mary Howland**
Judah Smith:	**Robert Tripp:**	**Tabitha White**
Nathaniel Howland:		**Abigal Allen**
William Wood:	**Mary Lawton**	**Mary Lapham**
Stephen Willcock:	**Rachel Allen**	**Mary Russell**
Elisha Wing	**Hannah Cadman**	**Mary Smith**
		Ruth Smith – –

And there being some of ye dying sayings of **Gearshom
Smith** presented to this meeting which are thought to
be of service to be read at a publick meeting and **Deliverance
Smith** is ordered to read it at a convenient time
The business of **Rochester** meeting Called and no business
appeared: and **John Tucker** having signefied his design of
traviling into y^e western parts to visit friends and his
Relations: friends have given him a certificate signifying
their unity therein

7th mo: At a monthly meeting of friends held at our meeting house
in Dartmouth the 21:st day of y^e: 7:th month 1719
There was Collected for the use of friends =
Dartmouth meeting called **W.**m **Wood** and **Judah Smith**
appeared: **Rochester** meeting called **Elisha Wing** appeared
The business of **Dartmouth** meeting called: **Benjamin Howland
William Wood** and **Deliverance Smith** are appointed to attend
the Quarterly meeting The visiters being called upon
do give account that they have visited friends famlies
under their care and as far as they saw things are for
the most part pretty well and where they saw things amiss
they have taken care that it be mended and the persons
appointed to attend y^e Quarterly meeting are ordered to
draw up an account to the Quarterly meeting:
And it being presented to this meeting from the prepa=
ritive meeting of **Dartmouth** that there is a report that
William Soule has brought a scandal on truth and friends
by Bargaining in an underhand way wth **Ruben Allen** and
others this meeting makes choice of **Elisha Wing Benjamin**

Howland Thomas Taber jun.ʳ William Wood and Deliverance Smith
and Henry Tucker to to inquire into the ground of said report
and they or the major par part of them to determine and judge
of the whole matter and make report to the next monthly
meeting: Rochester business called and none appeared
the collection is refered to yᵉ: next monthly meeting

At a monthly meeting held at our meeting house in
Dartmouth the 19ᵗʰ day of the 8ᵗʰ month 1719
Dartmouth meeting called Deliverance Smith and Judah
Smith appeared: Rochester meeting called Elisha Wing
appeared: there was collected for the use of friends – 1ˡ-00ˢ=00ᵈ:
The friends appointed to attend the Quarterly meeting
8:ᵗʰ mo: Last have attended it and did Draw up an account to the
Quarterly meeting as ordered:
The friends appointed to judge in the matter between
William Soule and Trustrum Allen have given in their
Judgment and is as followes:
We whose names are under written being appointed by the
monthly meeting held at our meeting house in Dartmouth the
21:ˢᵗ day of the 7ᵗʰ: month:1719: to hear and give judgment
in a matter brought to sᵈ meeting by Trustrum Allen
about the Estat of Josiah Allen late of Dartmouth decesed
We have heard the matter debated between them do conclude
and it is our Judgment that William Soules going to away
privately without the advice of friends was disorderly
and that he ought to condemn it: and as to his far
gaining in an under hand way wᵗʰ Benjamin Allen and
others we fear that Wᵐ Soule was not so upright
As he ought to ^have been in the prosicution of that business
and the matter being doubtful to us we leave it to yᵉ Lord
who will judge every man according to his deeds and whereas
we have taken notice of seaveral hard speaches that have
passed between Wᵐ Soule and Trustrum Allen wherein we
judge they were both to blame we do advise them for time
to come to Live in love for he that sayes he Loves God and
hates his Brother is a lyar for he that loves not his brother
whome he hath seen how can he Love God whome he hath
not seen but he who loves God loves his Brother

Benjamin Howland	:	Deliverance Smith
William Wood	:	Elisha Wing
Henry Tucker	——	Thomas Taber Junʳ

The business of **Dartmouth** meeting called it being
reported to this meeting that **Robert Tripp** and **Alice
Anthony** have proceeded in mariage contrary to the
order of friends **William Wood** is appointed to inquire into
the truth of s^d Report and give account to the next
monthly meeting there being also a report that **George
Soule** and **Lydia Howland** have published their intention
of mariage contrary to ye order of friends **Deliverance
Smith** and **Judah Smith** are ap^pointed to inquire into s^d
report and give an account the next monthly meeting
Rochester meeting called and no business presented
The Epistles from y^e: Quarterly meetings in the 5:^th month
Last past and the last quarterly meeting are read in this
meeting and kindly accepted: **Trustrum Allen** appealed
from the judgment of friends to y^e: to the next Quarterly
meeting: **Deliverance Smith** is appointed to make
the monthly meeting accounts with **Benjamin Howland**

9th mo: At a monthly meeting of friends held at our meeting
House in **Dartmouth** y^e: 16th day of y:^e 9:^th 1719:
Dartmouth meeting called **Henry Tucker** appeared
Rochester meeting called **Nicolas Davis** appeared
John Summers j^unr and **Rest Davis** y^e: daughter of **Timothy
Davis** Laid their intentions of mariage before this meeting
and **Savory Clifton** and **Stephen Wing** are appointed to
see into their clearness on that account ^thereof and give account
thereof to y^e: next monthly meeting in order that they may
Then have their answer – –
And whereas it appears that **Robert Tripp** and **Alice
Anthony** have proceeded in mariage contrary to the good
order of friends and that **George Soule** and **Lydia Howland**
have done y^e: like **Thomas Hathaway** and **Tho:^s Taber j^unr**
are appointed to draw up a paper for each of their condem
=nations to be ready in order to be signed at the next month
=ly meeting: and **Deliverance Smith** has made up the
monthly meetings accounts w^th **Benjamin Howland**
and there remains in the Stock – – 06^l=05^s=10^d
Stephen Willcox having Signified his disign of Traviling
to **Sandwich** and them parts to visit friends this meeting
has given him a certificate Signifying their unity therewth

10th mo: At a monthly meeting of friends held at our meeting

House in **Dartmouth** the 21ˢᵗ day of yᵉ 10ᵗʰ month 1719:
There was collected for yᵉ: use of friends – – 01ˡ=06ˢ=01ᵈ
Dartmouth meeting called **William Wood** and **Judah Smith**
appeared – – **Rochester** meeting called **Stephen Wing**
appeared: **John Summers Jun:ʳ** and **Rest Davis** appeared
for their answer and the friends appointed giving account
that they find nothing to hinder their proceeding in
mariage The meeting answers that they may proceed
to take each other in mariage in the good order of truth
between this and yᵉ: next monthly meeting and **Stephen
Wing** and **Savory Clifton** are appointed to See their
Mariage Solemnized accordingly and make report
thereof to the next monthly meeting – –
And the friends appointed to draw up **Robert Tripp** and
his wives condemnation for their disorderly proceeding
in mariage and also for **George Soule** and his wife for
the Like cause have done it and they are signed in order
to be read and **Deliverance Smith** is ordered to read
Robert Tripp and his wives Condemnation or cause it to
be read at **Coakset** meeting on a first day at the conclu
=tion of the time of worship: and **John Tucker** is ordered
to do the like by the other at **ponaganset** meeting and
both to make return thereof to the next monthly meeting
Benjamin Howland is ordered to pay.30 ˢʰⁱˡᵍ: out of yᵉ: monthly
meeting stock to **John Tucker** for keeping the meeting house
which he accordingly paid for the year past:
The visiters give no account of visiting – –
Rochester business called no business presented
John Tucker and **Thomas Taber junr** are appointed
to draw up an account to the next Quarterly meeting
and **Stephen Willcocks** and **Thos Taber junʳ** are appointed
to attend the Quarterly meeting next:
And a concern lying on this meeting concerning friends
wearing of wiggs is refered to be proposed to the next
Quarterly meeting:
And it is ordered that the meeting at **Cushnot** be
held every first day except they day before the monthly
meeting till the first of the 3:ᵈ month next

11ᵗʰ mo: At a monthly meeting ^of friends held at our meeting house
in **Dartmouth** the 18:ᵗʰ day of yᵉ: 11:ᵗʰ 1719:

Dartmouth meeting called **Judah Smith** and **Wᵐ Wood**
appeared: **Rochester** meeting called **Stephen Wing** appeard
Stephen Wing and **Savory Clifton** gives account that
John Summers junʳ: and **Rest Davis** have accomplished
their marriage according to the good order established
among friends **George Soule** and his wives condemnation
has been read according to yᵉ order of the last monthly
monthly meeting and is as followeth

Whereas **George Soule** Son of **William Soule** and **Hannah**
his wife and **Lydia Howland** the Daughter of **Benjamin**
Howland and **Judeth** his wife. both of **Dartmouth** in the
County of Bristol in **New England** having been educated
amongst friends their parents being all of yᵉ: people
Called Quakers have of Late proceeded in marriage to
Each other contrary to the good order established amongst
us on that account: we do therefore give this forth as
a publick Testimony against sᵈ Disorderly proceeding
and also do deny the sᵈ **George Soule** and **Lydia** his wife
to be of us the peole called Quakers Sincerely desiring
if it be the will of God they may come to a Sight and
Sence of this and all other their outgoings and by an
unfeigned repentance find acceptance with the Lord
and his people Signed at our monthly meeting
at **Dartmouth** yᵉ: 21:ˢᵗ of the 10:ᵗʰ month 1719

John Tucker	**Ruth Tucker**
Abraham Tucker	**Rachel Allen**
Eliezer Slocum	**Hannah Tucker**
William Soule	**Elisabeth Russell**
William Wood	**Mary Lawton**
Stephen Willcock	**Mehetabel Burrel**
Deliveranc Smith	**Phebe Tucker**
Joseph Russell junʳ.	**Mary Lapham**
Nathaniel Howland	**Mary Smith**
Benjamin Howland	**Rose Howland**
John Lapham	**Mary Lapham**
Henry Tucker	**Mary Smith**
Peleg Slocum	

And **Robert Tripp** and his wives condemnation not
being read: **Deliverance Smith** is Still continued
to do it between this and the next monthly meeting

And **John Tucker** and **Thos Taber junr**: have Drawn
up an account to the quarterly meeting – –
According to the order of the Last monthly meeting
and it not being sent it is ordered to be sent with
the account to ye: next Quarterly meeting
Stephen Willcox has attended ye: quarterly meeting
according to order – –
And a complaint being brought to this meeting
that our friend **Tho:s Coalman [Coleman]** of **Scituate** has of
Late commenced a sute in law against our friend
Richard Kirby contrary to the order of friends and
the advice of the apostle wherefor **John Tucker**
Nathaniel Howland and **Tho.s Taber junr** are ordered
to signify to sd **Thomas Coleman** that sd act is disorder
=ly and to ~~desire~~ ^advise him to desist from proceeding any farther
in sd matter and also to give an account to **Scituate**
monthly meeting of his sd proceeding to go to Law with
his Brother that thay may take care to prevent farther
proceeding therein: The Epistle from ye: Quarterly
meeting was read and kindly accepted – –
The meeting orders **Benjamin Howland** to pay 1l=19s=03d
out of the monthly meeings stoock to **John Russell** for
the meeting house hand irons which wth 2l=10s=09d: paid by the
womens meeting make ye: full price

12:mo:　At a monthly meeting of friends held at our meeting
house in **Dartmouth** ye: 15th day of ye: 12th: month 1719/20 – –
Dartmouth meeting called **William Wood** and **Judah Smith**
appeared: **Rochester** meeting called none appeared
Deliverance Smith has read **Robert Tripp** and his
wives condemnation as ordered: and is as followeth
Whereas **Robert Tripp** and **Alice Anthony** both of **Dartmouth**
in the **County of Bristol** in **New England** having been educated
among friends and as to appearance have walked in a degree
comformable to the good order established among us yet of
late in contradiction to the good shew that they have
formerly made and the greif and trouble of friends they
have refused the good and wholesome order among them
relating to marriage having lately been married to each
other from among friends thereby giving advantage to the
light and airy wanton people to make a skoff and devition

of friends and the blessed truth professed amongst us – –
We are therefore concerned to give this forth as a publick
testimony against their deisorderly walking and to deny
the said **Robert Tripp** and **Alice** his Wife to be of us the people
called Quakers sincerely desiring if it be the will of God
they may come to a sight and sence of their out going
and come into unity with the people of God – –
Signed at our monthly meeting held at **Dartmouth**
the 21st: of the 10th: month 1719 – –

John Tucker	:	Deliverance Smith	:	Rachel Allen
Abraham Tucker	:	Thomas Hathaway	:	Hannah Tucker
Benjamin Howland	:	Henry Tucker	:	Ruth Tucker
Eliezer Slocum	:	Joseph Russell:junr	:	Hannah Soule
William Wood	:	Thomas Taber:junr	:	Elizabeth Russell
Nathaniel Howland	:	Josiah Merihoo [Merihew]	:	Mary Lapham
Stephen Willcock	:	Hezekiah Smith	:	Mehetabel Burril
John Lapham	:	Peleg Slocum	:	Mary Russell
Judah Smith	:	William Soule	:	Phebe Tucker
				Mary Lapham junr
				Mary Smith – –
				Rose Howland – –

The friends that were ordered to signify to the monthly
meeting of **Scituate** the proceeding of **Thomas Coleman** against
Richard Kirby have done it
Benjamin Howland has paid 1l-19s=03d to **John Russell**
according to the order of the Last monthly meeting
The business of **Dartmouth** meeting called
And it being requested the next preparitive and
monthly meeting be a[d]journed one week longer than
the usual time it is ordered that it ˄should be so and it appearing
that there is due to **Judah Smith** the Sum of 3£:18s:08d
for recording the monthly meeting minits
Benjamin Howland is ordered to pay it out of the
monthly meeting Stock – –
And whereas **William Soule** by ye judgment of some friend[s?]
appointed by the monthly meeting held in the 7th month
last past to hear to hear and give judgment in a matter
brought against him by **Trustrom [Tristram?] Allen** did judg[e] that
he ought to condemn his going to the westward privately
without the advice of friends he has now condemned it

and is as followes
I Do acknowledg[e] that my going to the westward and
not first acquainting friends thereof was Contrary
to the order of friends and I am Sorry that it hap[pe]ned
so and hope that I shall be more careful for the
Time to come ————————————— **William Soule**

1720: At a monthly meeting ˄of friends held at our meeting house
1ˢᵗ mo: in **Dartmouth** yᵉ 28ᵗʰ day of yᵉ 1ˢᵗ month 1720:
There was Collected for yᵉ use of friends £1=16ˢ=02ᵈ
Dartmouth meeting called **William Wood** and **Judah Smith**
appeared: **Rochester** meeting called **Elisha Wing** ˄and Jon Wing appeared
Benjamin Howland has paid the Sum of £3:18ˢ:08ᵈ
to **Judah Smith** according to yᵉ order of the last monthly
meeting: The business of **dartmouth** meeting called
James Tripp demanded 17ˢ=2ᵈ for the expence towards **coakset**
meeting house which **Benjamin Howland** paid out of the
˄monthly meeting Stock by order of the meeting
The visiters of **Dartmouth** meeting called upon do give
account that they have visited the most of friends
fam[i]lies belonging to their care and find things for
the most part pretty well and where things were not
well they gave advice that it might be amended
and friends Seem to take their vis[i]ts kindly: and
Rochester meeting business called and their visiters give
account that they have visited friends fam[i]lies
And find things amongst them pretty well
and **Elisha Wing Deliverance Smith** and **Thoˢ Taber junʳ**
are appointed to attend the quarterly meeting next
And **John Tucker** and **Thoˢ Taber junʳ** are appointed to
draw up an account to the Quarterly meeting

2ᵈ mo: At a monthly meeting of friends held at our meeting
House in **Dartmouth** the 18ᵗʰ day of the 2ᵈ month 1720
Dartmouth monthly meeting called **William Wood** and
Judah Smith appeared – –
Rochester meeting called none appeared – –
Elisha Wing Deliv˄**erance Smith** and **Thoˢ Taber junʳ**
have attended the quarterly meeting according to the
appointment of the last monthly meeting – –
and **John Tucker** and **Thoˢ Taber junʳ** have drawn up
an account to the Quarterly meeting as ordered

The business of **Dartmouth** meeting called:
and **Beriah Goddard** of **James Town** and **Ann Smith**
the daughter of **Deliverance Smith** of **Dartmouth**
have laid their intentions of ^taking each other in mar[r]iage and they are
desired to wait till the next monthly meeting for
their answer: and **Eliezer Slocum** and **William Wood** are
appointed to Inquire into their Clearness on that account
and make return to the next monthly meeting – –
And whereas **Nathan Soule** has offered to contribute
somet[h]ing towards finnishing **coakset** meeting House
William Wood and **James Tripp** and **John Tucker** are
desired to speak with him and to let him know how
friends can receive on such occations
according to the request of the Quarterly meeting
friends have made a subscribtion for **Salem** meeting
House which **John Tucker** is Desired to receive and
Carry it in to the yearly meeting
And in Compliance to the advice of the quarterly meet=
=ing with respect to renewing of visiters by a new choice
this meeting makes choice of **Eleazer Slocum Benjamin**
Howland Deliverance Smith Thos Taber jun^r
and John Tucker – –
And whereas **Sarah Wing** the Daughter of our friend
Elisha Wing of **Rochester** hath fallen into that fowl Sin
of fornication as appears by her own confession:
this meeting has given forth a condemnation against
her to read publickly at the end of friends meeting of
worship at **Cushnot** and **Thomas Taber Junr** is ordered to
read it between this and the next monthly meeting

3^d _mo:_   At a monthly meeting of friend[s] held at our meeting
House in **Darthmouth** [_sic_] the 16th day of the 3^d month 1720 :
Dartmouth meeting Called **William Wood** and **Judah**
Smith appeared:
Rochester meeting called **Elisha Wing** appeared
the young cupple that appeared and laid their intentions
of marriage the last monthly meeting not appearing
for their answer it is refered to y^e next monthly
meeting: And the friends that were ordered to let
Nathan Soule know the mind of this meeting wth respect
to his offering to contribute towards the finnishing of
Coakset meeting house haveing Spoken with him and given

=his answer to this meeting and the meeting having Considred
of it do order the same friends to let him know that he
is desired to wait some time in the counsel of God to be
Confirmed in the principles of Truth.

And **Thos Taber junr** has read **Sarah Wing**s Condemnation
according to the order of the Last monthly meeting
which is as followeth _____

Whereas **Sarah Wing** the Daughter of **Elisha Wing**
of **Rochester** in the County of **Plymouth** in **New England**
her parents being friends and She educated in the way of
Truth yet to the dishonour of God reproach of the Blessed truth
professed amongst us and greif of friends She has by giving way
to the temptation of Satan and her own wicked inclination
fallen into that foul Sin of fornication as appears by her
own Conffession: we Do therefore give this forth as a publick
Testimony against Sd wicked and unclean action denying the
Sd **Sarah Wing** to be one of us the people Called Quakers
Sincerely desiring if it be the Will of God She may come to
a Sight and Sence of this her Sin and all other her Sins
and by an unfeigned repentance find mery

Given forth at our monthly meeting of friends held in
Dartmouth the 18th day of ye 2d month 1720:

John Tucker	
Abraham Tucker	
Peleg Slocum	**Mary Slocum**
William Wood	**Hannah Tucker**
⫶ **Eliezer Slocum**	**Hannah Cadmon** [Cadman]
Nathaniel Howland	**Rachel Allen**
Judah Smith	**Ruth Smith**
Benjamin Howland	**Abigal** [Abigail] **Allen**
Deliverance Smith	**Hope Merihoo** [Merihew]
William Soule	**Mary Lawton**
James Tripp	**Rose Howland**
Thomas Hathaway	**Phebe Tucker**
Stephen Willcock [Wilcox]	**Mary Lapham**
Henry Tucker	**Mary Russell**
Thomas Taber junr	**Ruth Tucker**
Jabez Barker	**Mary Smith**
John Lapham	**Dinah Smith**
Josiah Merihoo [Merihew]	
Eliashib Smith _____	

no business from the preparitive meetings – –
In order to answer the desire of the Quarterly meeting on
the account of friends wearing of wiggs: **John Tucker**
Benjamin Howland Deliverance Smith and **Tho⁵ Taber jun**ʳ
are ordered to Draw up Something on that account to be
ready at the next monthly meeting

_4:mo:_ At a monthly meeting of friends held at our meeting
house in **Dartmouth** the: 20ᵗʰ day of the 4ᵗʰ month 1720:
Dartmouth meeting called **Wᵐ Wood** and **Judah Smith** appear[e]d
Rochester meeting called none appeared.
Beriah Goddard and **Ann Smith** appearing for their answer
and the meeting having inquired into their clearness and
finding nothing but that they may proceed the meeting ther[e]fore
answers that they may proceed to take each other in marriage
In the good order of Truth between this and the next
monthly meeting and **John Tucker** and **William Wood** are
appointed to See their marriage accomplished accordingly
and **John Tucker** has received the Subscription for **Salem**
meeting house and delivered it in to yᵉ yearly meeting
according to order – –
The friends that were ordered by the Last monthly
meeting to signify the mind of yᵉ meeting to **Nathan**
Soule having done it and he signifies that he has considered
of the matter and sees nothing but that he can comply
to the orders of friends in all Respects :
And the friends that were ordered to: (by the Last monthly
meeting: Draw up something on the account of wiggs
having done it: it is accepted and ordered to be sent to the
Quarterly meeting in the account
Deliverance Smith and **Eleazer Slocum** and **William Wood**
=are ordered to attend the Quarterly meeting next
And **John Tucker** and **Thomas Taber jun**ʳ are appointed
to draw up an account to the Quarterly meeting

_5:mo:_ At a monthly meeting of friends held at our
meeting house in (**Dartmouth** on the 18ᵗʰ day of yᵉ 5ᵗʰ mo 1720
Dartmouth meeting called **Deliverance Smith** and
Judah Smith appeared
Rochester meeting called **Stephen Wing** appeared
John Tucker and **Wᵐ Wood** gives account that they
marriage between **Beriah Goddard** and **Ann Smith**

has been accomplished in the good order of truth
Eleazer Slocum and **W<u>m</u> Wood** gives account that they
have attended ye Quarterly meeting:
John Tucker and **Thomas Taber jun^r** have drawn up an account
to ye Quarterly meeting according to order:
The Epis[t]le from the quarterly meeting was read and
kindly accepted:
No business from **Rochester** preparitive meeting:

6: mo:　At a monthly meeting of friends held at our meeting
house in **Dartmouth** the 15th day of the 6th month 1720
Dartmouth meeting called **William Wood** and **Judah Smith**
appeared: **Rochester** meeting called **Elisha Wing** appeared
John Walker jun^r of **Marshfield** and **Sarah Summers** of
Rochester have laid their intentions of marriage before
this meeting and they are desired to wait till the next
monthly meeting for their answer :
The business of **Dartmouth** meeting called and it is desired
that the visiters be stir[r]ed up to visit the families of
friends between this and the next monthly meeting:
The business of **Rochester** meeting called and no business
Except that of ye intention of marriage
and **Elisha Wing** and **Stephen Wing** are appointed to
inquire into their clearness wth respect to marriage
and to give in their account to the next monthly _{meeting}

7:mo:　At a monthly meeting of friends held at our meeting
house in **Dartmouth** the 19th day of the 7th month: 1720:
Dartmouth meeting Called **William Wood** and **Judah Smith**
appeared: there was Collected for y^e use of friends: $0^£=16^s=00^d$
Rochester meeting Called **Nicolas Davis** appeared – –
John Walker and **Sarah Summers** not appearing for
their answer it is refered to the next monthly meeting
The business of **Dartmouth** meeting called and **Benjami[n]**
Howland is ordered to pay 35 Shillings out of y^e monthly
meeting stock to **John Tucker** and **Henry Tucker** for keep
=ing the meeting house for halfe a year that is past – –
which he forthwith paid – –
And **Benjamin Howland** and **Deliverance Smith**
are appointed to seat the up[p]er gallery:
The business of **Rochester** meeting called no business
This meeting is a[d]journed to the 7th day of y^e 8th month next

This meeting being met according to a[d]journment
the visiters gave in their account that they have made
a pretty General visit of the families of friends
belonging to this monthly meeting and find things for the
most part pretty well as far as they saw and to some
they gave advice as they thought needful
And that their visits were kindly accepted
John Tucker and **Thos Taber junr** are ordered to draw
up an account to the Quarterly meeting **John Tucker**
Nicolas Davis and **Wm Wood** are appointed to attend
the Quarterly meeting

At a monthly meeting of friends held at our meeting
House in **Dartmouth** ye 17th of ye 8th month 1720:
Dartmouth meeting called **William Wood** and **Judah**
Smith appeared : **Rochester** meeting called
Stephen Wing appeared: **John Walker** and **Sarah**
Summers having formerly laid their intentions of
marriage before this meeting and now appearing
for their answer and all things appearing

8th mo:

Clear the meeting answers that they may proceed to
take Each other in marriage in the good order of
Truth between this and the next monthly meeting and
Stephen Wing and **Thos Taber junr** are appointed to See
the marriage Solemnized _____
Also **Samuel Wing** the Son of **Daniel Wing** of **Sandwich**
and **Dorothy Clifton** the daughter of **Savory Clifton**
of **Rochester** have laid their intentions of marriage
before this meeting who are desired to wait till ye
next monthly [meeting?] for their answer and **Elisha Wing** and
Stephen Wing are appointed to inquire into their
Clearness and make report to the next monthly meet
=ing **John Tucker** and **Thomas Taber junr** have drawn
an account to the Quarterly meeting and **John Tucker**
and **Wm Wood** have attended the Quarterly meeting
according to order _____ ·
The business of **Dartmouth** meeting Called and a
differance between **James Howland** and **Jedediah Allen**
being laid before this meeting the meeting makes choice
of **Jabez Barker John Russell Robert Kirby** and **Josiah**
Meriho [**Merihew**] or either three of them to end the Sd Differance

and it is the mind of this meeting that the S^d parties
do become bound to each other in Suitable bonds in the
judgment of those appointed to end S^d Differance
to Stand to their award
from Rochester no farther business _____
The Epistle from the Quarterly meeting was read to
friends Sattisfaction

9th mo: At a monthly meeting of friends held at our meeting house
in **Dartmouth** the 21st day of the 9th month :1720
Dartmouth meeting called **William Wood** and **Judah Smith**
appeared: **Rochester** meeting called **Savory Clifton** appeared
Samuel Wing and **Dorothy Clifton** not appearing for their
answer it is refered to the next monthly meeting
Stephen Wing and **Thos Taber jun^r** give account that the
marriage between **John Walker** and **Sarah Summers**
was accomplished according to the good order of truth
Benjamin Russell and **Abigal Howland** the daughter of
Nicholas Howland have laid their intentions of marriage
before this meeting who were desired to wait till the next
monthly meeting for the[i]r answer
Also **Joseph Tucker** and **Mary Howland** Daughter of S^d
Nicolas Howland have laid their intentions of marriage
before this meeting who are Likewise desired to wait
till the next monthly meeting for their answer
And **Deliverance Smith** and **Henry Tucker** are ordered
to inquire into the clearness of the first couple with
respect [to?] marriage and conversation
And **Jabez Barker** and **John Lapham** are ordered [to?] inquire
into the clearness of the other couple with respect [to?] mar[r]iage
and Conversation and each to make report to ye next
monthly meeting: And whereas there is a report that
Sarah Howland the daughter of **Nathaniel Howland** is
married out of the order of friends and ~~contrary to~~
without the consent of her parents **Thomas Taber jun^r**
is ordered to the truth of S^d report and give an account
to the [?] next monthly meeting _____
And the matter between **James Howland** and **Jedediah
Allen** not being fully finnished it is refered to the
next monthly meeting

10 mo: At a monthly meeting of friends held at our meeting
House in **Dartmouth** yᵉ 19ᵗʰ day of the 10ᵗʰ month 1720
Dartmouth meeting called **Eleazar Slocum** and **Judah Smith**
appeared: There was collected for the use of friends- £1:-13ˢ:-06ᵈ
Rochester meeting called **Stephen Wing** appeared
Samuel Wing and **Dorothy Clifton** appeared desiring the meet
=ings answer with respect to: their ~~taking each other~~
Intentions of marriage laid before this meeting at our
monthly meeting in the 8ᵗʰ month Last past and nothing
appearing to hinder their proceeding the meeting answers
that they may proceed to take each other in the good order
of truth between this and the next monthly meeting
And **Elisha Wing** and **Stephen Wing** are appointed to see
it accordingly accomplished _____
Also **Benjamin Russel** [Russell] and **Abigal Howland** having laid
their intentions [of?] marriage before our Last monthly meeting
and now appearing for their answer the meeting answers
that they may proceed to take each other in the good order
of truth between this and the next monthly meeting
and **Deliverance Smith** and **Henry Tucker** are appointed
to see it accordingly accomplished
And **Joseph Tucker** and **Mary Howland** having Likewise laid
their intentions of marriage before the last monthly meeting
and now appearing for their answer the meeting answers
that they may proceed to take each other in the good order of
truth between this and the next monthly meeting
and **Jabez Barker** and **William Wood** are appointed to see it
accordingly accomplished
Thomas Taber jnʳ: being appointed to inquire Concerning
Sarah Howlands being married out of the order of friends he
gives account that he understands that She is married
and Sᵈ **Taber** is appointed to draw a Condemnation against
her for her disorderly proceeding
And the friends appointed to accom[m]odate the differance
between **James Howland** and **Jedediah Allen** have finnished yᵉ
matter – – The business of **Dartmouth** meeting called
Benjamin Howland is ordered to pay 7ˢ and 9ᵈ to **Antipas
Hathaway** for mending the meeting House Glass – –
William Wood and **Thomas Taber junʳ** are appointed to attend
the Quarterly meeting and **John Tucker** and **Thoˢ Taber juʳ** is

to Draw an account to the Quarterly meeting
Benjamin Howland is ordered to pay £1:15ˢ:0ᵈ: to **Deliverance Smith**
out of the Stock and to pay to him Selfe 5 Shillings
and whereas **Rober[t?] Tripp** has Signified his Desire of being
received into unity with friends Some time past and was
Desired to wait a while and now friends being desir[o]us to
know how his mind Stands and how his conversation has
been **John Tucker Wᵐ Wood** and **Thomas Taber Junʳ** are to
se[e] into the matter
Deliverance Smith is ordered to make up the monthly meeting
accounts wᵗʰ **Benjamin Howland**
from **Rochester** meeting no business

---

11 mo: At a monthly meeting of friends held at our meeting
House in **Dartmouth** the 16ᵗʰ day of yᵉ 11ᵗʰ month 1720:
Dartmouth meeting called **Deliverance Smith** and **Judah Smith**
appeared: **Rochester** meeting called **Nicolas Davis** appeared
Daniel Weeden of **James Town** and **Joanna Slocum** the Daughter
of **Eliezer Slocum** have Laid their intentions of marriage
before this meeting who are desired to wait till the next
monthly meeting for their answer and **Benjamin Howland**
and **Deliverance Smith** are ordered to inquire into their
Clearness with respect to mar[r]iage and Conversation and give
account to the next monthly meeting
Stephen Wing gives account that the marriage between
Samuel Wing and **Dorothy Clifton** was performed in the good
order of truth as Established among ~~them~~ friends
And **Deliverance Smith** and **Henry Tucker** give the like ₐaccount
of **Benjamin Russel [Russell]** and **Abigal Howland**s marriage
and **Wᵐ Wood** and **Jabez Barker** do also give the same account
of **Joseph Tucker** and **Mary Howland**s marriage
and **Deliverance Smith** not haveing made up the monthly
meeting accounts wᵗʰ **Benjamin Howland** he is ordered
to Do it by the next monthly meeting **Benjamin Howland**
has paid 7ˢ and 9ᵈ to **Antipas Hathaway** and £1=15ˢ: to **Deliverance Smith** _____
And: 5 Shillings to himselfe according to the order of the
last monthly meeting: **John Tucker** and **Wᵐ Wood** give
account that they have Spoke wᵗʰ **Robert Tripp** according
to the order of the Last monthly meeting and he signifies
that he is still Desirous to come into unity wᵗʰ friends
William Wood and **Thoˢ Taber junʳ** have attended the Quarterly

meeting as they were ordered:

Sarah Akins condemnation is drawn up and Signed and
Deliverance Smith is ordered to read it at the end of yᵉ
meeting of worship between this and the next monthly
meeting: No business from yᵉ preparitive meetings – –

_12ᵗʰ mo:_ At a monthly meeting of friends held ~~he~~ at our meet
=ing House in **Dartmouth** yᵉ 20ᵗʰ day of yᵉ 12ᵗʰ month 1720/21
Dartmouth meeting called **Wᵐ Wood** and **Judah Smith** appeared
Rochester meeting called **John Wing** appeared:
Daniel Weeden and **Joanna Slocum** appeared Desiring the
meetings answer relating to their intentions of marriage
Laid before yᵉ last monthly meeting and nothing appearing
to hinder their proceedings: the meeting answers that they
may proceed to take each other in marriage in the good
order of truth: and **Benjamin Howland** and **Deliverance
Smith** are ordered to se[e] it accordingly accomplished and give
account to the next monthly meeting – –
Deliverance Smith has made up the monthly meetings
accounts wᵗʰ **Benjamin Howland** and finds that
there remaines in the Stock £0 – 09ˢ = 09ᵈ
Deliverance Smith has read **Sarah Akin**s Condemnation
according to the order of the Last monthly meeting
and is as followeth
Whereas **Sarah** the Daughter of **Nathaniel Howland** and
Rose his wife of **Dartmouth** in the county of **Bristol** in
New England having been Educated amongst friends not
regarding the fear of God the honour of her parents nor the
good order established amongst friends hath Stubbornly and
willfully against the mind of her father and mother kept com
=pany (with a man) from time to time that they did
not allow of and at last in the Same obstinate Spirit hath
procceded in mar[r]iage with him out of the unity of friends
to the grief of her parents and trouble of friends – –
We are therefore concerned for the clearing of friends to give this
forth as a publick testimony against all disobedience to parents and
disorderly walking and perticularly against the abovesᵈ actions
of the Said **Sarah** now the wife of **Timothy Akin** of **Dartmouth**
Denying her to be one of us the people called Quakers yet Sincerely
desiring if it be the will of God She may come to a Sight and
Sence of this and all other her outgoings and by an unfeigned repen

=tance and amendment of life so walk as to find mercy with
the Lord - - - - - given forth at our monthly meeting of friends
held in **Dartmouth** the 16th day of the 11th month 1720/21 Signed at Sd meeting by

Nathaniel Howland	Henry Tucker	Mary Slocum
John Tucker	John Lapham	Hannah Tucker
Benjamin Howland	Josiah Merihoo [Merihew]	Rachel Allen
Eleazer Slocum	Joseph Taber	Hannah Soule
William Wood	Thomas Taber jur	Mary Smith
Stephen Willcock [Wilcox]	Judah Smith	Phebe Tucker
James Tripp	———————————	Dinah Smith
Deliverance Smith	Ruth Tucker	Mary Russel[1]

The business of **Dartmouth** meeting called
it being proposed whither it may be profitable to have part
of our yearly meeting held at **coakset** meeting house which
is refered to the next monthly meeting for farther conside
=ration this meeting advises that the visiters take care
to visit the families of friends so as an account may be
given to the next monthly meeting
Rochester meeting called no business

Whereas there is a complaint from the monthly meeting
of **Rhoad Island** that **Benjamin Slocum** the Son of **Eleazer**
Slocum is accused for gitting a young ~~on~~ woman with child
that belongs to their meeting ther[e]fore **William Wood** and
and **Thomas Taber junr** are ordered to Speak with him and
advice him if he be guilty to go and marry her otherwise
to go with them to the young woman to clear him Selfe
If he can to her face and **John Tucker** is ordered to
inform the monthly meeting of **Rhoad Island** how far
this monthly meeting has proceeded in the matter
and by reason of the falling of **Sandwich** ^yearly meeting our
next monthly and preparitive meetings are a[d]journed one week

_1721_
_1st mo:_ At a monthly meeting of friends held at our meeting
House in **Dartmouth** the 27th day of the 1mo 1721
Dartmouth meeting called |<u>**Elisha Wing**</u> appeared for **roches**ter
Deliverance Smith and **Henry Tucker** appeared
There was Collected for the use of friends £1 = 08s = 00d
Benjamin Howland and **Deliverance Smith** gives account
that the marriage between **Daniel Weeden** and **Joanna**
Slocum hath been accomplished in the good order of truth

the proposal relating to the hold in part of our yearly
meeting at **coakset** is refered to the consideration of the
Quarterly meeting and whither to have the meeting devided [divided]
or another day added
The visiters gives account that the[y?] have been with
Benjamin Soule who is gone from the order of friends
into the fassion of yᵉ world in his apparrel who Signifyed
that he is resolved to have his own way and refuses to
be advised by them: the meeting therefore appoints **Judah Smith**
and **Henry tucker** to Speak with and to Let him know that
if there be no reformation the meeting must proceed to
deny him: And whereas the persons ordered to Speak
with **Benjamin Slocum** and **Dinah Burrel** face to face
have not done it the Same friends or one of ˄them is ordered
Still to do it and to git Some friends of **Rhoad Island**
meeting to go with them.
Dartmouth ~~meeting~~ ˄business Called and **Holder Slocum** having
Signifyed his desire of ~~a certificate~~ proceeding in
marriage with **Hannah Hull** of **James town** and Desires
a certificate of his clearness from others therefore
Jabez Berker [Barker] and **Henry Tucker** are appointed to inquire
into his clearness on that account and of his conversation
and make report to the next monthly meeting – –
And **Joseph Slocum** Signifies to this meeting the like design
with **Susanna Wanton** the daughter of **John Wanton** therefore
Josiah Merihoo [Merihew] and **John Lapham** are to make inquiry of
his clearness and conversation and make report how they find
things to yᵉ next monthly meeting. **Rochester** business called
and none presented this meeting is a[d]journed till yᵉ first 6ᵗʰ day
of the next month – –
This meeting being met according to a[d]journment this 7ᵗʰ of yᵉ
2ᵈ month 1721 the visiters gives this meeting an account
that they have visited the families of friends belonging to
this meeting and their visits were kindly accepted for the
∴ most part and things pretty well generally but in some fami
=lies not well where they gave advise thaat such things might
be amended **Wᵐ Wood Deliverance Smith** and **Thoˢ Taber junʳ**
are appointed to attend the Quarterly meeting next
~~And John Tucker are appointed to Draw up an account to~~
~~the Quarterly meeting~~

And **Thomas Taber** and **John Tucker** are appointed to draw
up an account to the Quarterly meeting

2ᵈ mo: At a monthly meeting of friends held at our meeting house in
Dartmouth the 17ᵗʰ day of yᵉ 2ᵈ month 1721:
dartmouth meeting called ~~called~~ **William Wood** & **Judah Smith**
appeared: **Rochester** meeting called none present – –
the friends appointed to speak wᵗʰ **Benjamin Soule** not having
both spoken with him they are continued to do it between this
and the next monthly meeting – –
And the friends appointed to See **Benjamin Slocum** and
Dinah Burril [**Burrel**] face to face not having yet accomplished the
Same **Wᵐ Wood** and **Stephen Willcocks** [**Wilcox**] are ordered to see them
together and hear what they can Say and give account to the
next monthly meeting – –
William Wood and **Thomas Taber junʳ** have attended the Quarter
=ly meeting as appointed – –
Thomas Taber junʳ and **John Tucker** hath drawn up an account
of the affairs of this meeting and Sent it to the Quarterly
meeting as appointed: – –
It is proposed to this meeting that **Jedediah Allen** the Son
of **Increas[e] Allen** desires a certificate from our monthly
meeting of his clearness in relation to marriage and
Judah Smith and **Henry Tucker** are appointed to make
inquiry into his clearness and conversation and make report
how they find things to the next monthly meeting – –
Christopher Gifford junʳ having desired a certificate on the
account of his design of proceeding in marriage wᵗʰ
Mary Borden the daughter of **Richard Borden** of **Tiverton**
William Wood and and **Henry Tucker** are ordered to mak[e]
inquiry into his clearness and conversation and make
report to the next monthly meeting – –
Desire Howland the daughter of **Benjamin Howland** having
charged **John Slocum** the Son of **Eleazer Slocum** wᵗʰ gitting
of her with child **John Tucker** and **Wᵐ Wood** are to endea
ver to have them face to face to hear what each of them
can say in the matter – –
and the visiters having given account to this meeting
that **Increas Allen junʳ** has a design of marrying his
Cousin as appears by his keeping company with **Lydia Allen**
the daughter of **Joseph Allen**. the meeting orders **Judah Smith**

and **Deliverance Smith** to advise him to forbear keeping
her company on any such account and that if he do
still persist friends must deny him – –
Robert Tripp and his wife having given this meeting
Sattisfaction for their out goings for which they wer[e] denyed
by a writing under their hands which this meeting orders
said **Robert** to read at the end of the meeting of worship
at **Coakset** on a first day or cause it to be read in his presents [presence]
The Epistle from yᵉ Quarterly meeting was read
and kindly accepted – – – – –

_3ᵈ mo:_　At a monthly meeting of friends held at our meeting
house in **Dartmouth** the 15ᵗʰ day of the 3ᵈ month :1721:
Dartmouth meeting Called **William Wood** and **Judah Smith**
appeared: **Rochester** meeting called **Stephen Wing** appeared
The friends appointed to Speak with **Benjamin Soule** Concerning
his disorderly walking not having yet done it they are Still continued
and desired to do it between this and the next monthly meeting
Stephen Willcock [**Wilcox**] and **William Wood** with seaveral friends of
Rhoad Island have Seen **Benjamin Slocum** and **Dinah Burril** [**Burrel**]
face to face and She Confidently charged him to be the father of
her child and he as confidently denied it but by seaveral
curcumstancial evidences the matter looking doubtful on his
side it is refered for further Consid[e]ration – –
The friends chose to speak with **John Slocum** and **Desire Howland**
~~face~~ not having oppertunity to do it are Still continued to
endeaver to have an oppertunity before the next monthly
meeting and speak with them as appointed – –
The friends appointed to Speak with **Increas Allen jun**ʳ
and to advise him to forbear keeping company wᵗʰ his Cousin
Lydia Allen wᵗʰ the design of marrying her have done it
and he Signifyed to them that he is minded to proceed notwith
=standing the order and advice of friends: and he being present
at Sᵈ meeting the meeting advises him to forbear and not to
go out of unity wᵗʰ friends in such a disorderly proceeding – –
Robert Tripp hath read his and his wives acknowledgment
of their outgoing (his wife being present) according to the
last monthly meeting – –
Certificates were given to **Jedediah Allen** and **Christopher
Gifford jun**ʳ of their clearness in order to mar[r]iage – –
Stephen Willcocks had a certificate from this meeting of

friends unity with his design of Traviling Eastward to visit
friends: the meeting makes choice of **John Tucker Elisha
Wing Stephen Wing William Wood Deliverance Smith**
and **Thomas Taber jun**ʳ to be visiters for the year following
and till there be another Choice – – – – –

4ᵗʰ mo: At a monthly meeting of friends held at our meeting house in
Dartmouth the 19ᵗʰ day of the 4ᵗʰ month :1721:
There was collected for the use of friends – £1= 11ˢ = 00ᵈ
Dartmouth meeting called **William Wood** and **Judah Smith**
appeared: **Rochester** meeting called none appeared – –
Thomas Borden the Son of **Richard Borden** of **tiverton**
and **Mary Gifford** the daughter of **Christopher Gifford** of
Dartmouth have laid their intentions of marriage before
this meeting who are desired to wait till the next
monthly meeting for the[i]r answer and **William Wood**
and **John Lapham** are appointed to inquire into their
clearness with respect to marriage and Conversation and
make return to the next monthly meeting – –
The friends appointed to Speak wᵗʰ **Benjamin Soule** concerning
his disorderly walking have Spoke wᵗʰ him and he signifies
to them that he is not senceable of any harm there is
in his fash[i]onable cloathing and until he sees the evil of it
he Shall not refrain it: Therefore the meeting desires
the Same friends or one of them to let him know that
it is the mind of this meeting that he appear at the next
monthly meeting and give better Sattisfaction – –
The friends appointed to Speak wᵗʰ **John Slocum** and
Desire Howland face to face having not had oppertunity
are Continued to do it between this and the next monthly
meeting: and the meeting orders his father to give him
notice that he meet the Sᵈ friends at **Benjamin Howland**s
in the evening after the youths meeting next and to let
them know whither his Son will attend them or not
before the time of meeting – –
Our friend **Stephen Willcock** [**Wilcox**] having performed his visit
Eastward hath returned his certificate to this meeting – –
It is proposed to leave to the considratidration [consideration] of the
Quarterly meeting whither if one that is under the care of
friends be about to proceed in any thing contrary to the order
of friends and he be by friends advised to forbear and the

person refuse to hear but Signifies that he or she will
proceed whither friends may forthwith proceed to deny such
a one or whither friends must wait to See the thing
accomplished first – –
Deliverance Smith John Tucker and **Thomas Taber jun**ʳ
are appointed to attend the Quarterly meeting and they or
Eighther two of them to draw up an account to the Quarterly
meeting and Sign it in behalfe of the meeting – –
Benjamin Howland is ordered to pay 3ˢ to **Deliverance Smith** and
14ˢ to **Thomas Taber jun**ʳ for mon[e]y by them lent to the meeting
and 12ˢ to **John Lapham** for keeping the meeting house:
which with what the Women have paid is the Whole Sum for
halfe a year: he is also ordered to pay 2ˢ to **Wᵐ Wood** all
which was forthwith paid. – – – – –

5ᵗʰ mo: At a monthly meeting of friends held at our meeting house
in **Dartmouth** yᵉ 17ᵗʰ day of yᵉ 5ᵗʰ month 1721 – –
Dartmouth meeting Called **William Wood** and **Judah Smith**
appeared: **Rochester** meeting Called **Elisha Wing** appeared
Benjamin Soule not appearing to give this meeting Sattisfaction
according to the order of the last monthly meeting: this meeting
desires his father or one of the friends that were before
appointed to let him know that it is the mind of this meeting
that he appear at the next monthly meeting in order thereto – –
The friends appointed to See **John Slocum** and **Desire Howland**
face to face have Done it but not having mad[e] a thorow progress
therein it is refered to the next monthly meeting – –
and the Same friends are to go through with it and then give
in their account – –
John Tucker and **Deliverance Smith** have drawn up an
account to the Quarterly meeting and attended Sᵈ meeting
as ordered – –
Thomas Borden and **Mary Gifford** appearing for their answer
and all things being Clear the[y] had their answer that they might
proceed to take each other in the good order of truth between this
and the next monthly meeting – –
And **Wᵐ Wood** and **John Lapham** are appointed to See it
accordingly accomplished – –
The business of **Dartmouth** meeting Called no business
The business of **Rochester** meeting Called no business – –
The Epistle from our last yearly meeting was read to friends

Sattisfaction: and as the request of the Quarterly meeting
relating to a yearly meeting Stock this meeting Complies wth it
And in order thereto have made a Subscribtion and friends
are desired to pay in what they Subscribe to **John Tucker** in
order to ₐbe carryₐed to the Quarterly meeting – –
The Quarterly and yearly meeting haveing given judgment
against **Wm Soule** as appears by their seaveral Judgme[n]ts
sent down to us with the Quarterly meeting Epistle and
their advice tha[t] we See it accomplished S^d **William Soule** is
desired to put him Selfe in a way to perform it by the next
monthly meeting – –
And friends being desired by the Quarterly meeting as [?]
advice from the Yearly meeting to consider what may be
the best way to suppress the extravigancie of friends
wearing of wiggs it is left to friends consideration till y^e
next monthly meeting – – – – –

_6^th mo:_ At a monthly meeting of friends held at our meeting
house in **Dartmouth** the: 21st day of the 6th month: 1721:
Dartmouth meeting called ~~W^m~~ **Judah Smith** appeared =
Rochester meeting called **Stephen Wing** appeared – –
Benjamin Soule appeared at this meeting and not giving
Sattisfaction it is refered to the next meeting for conside
=ration and further proₐsicution – –
William Wood and **John Lapham** give account that the
marriage between **Thomas Borden** and **Mary Gifford** was
accomplished in the good order of friends – –
The friends appointed to Se[e] **John Slocum** and **Desire Howland**
face to face and hear what they could Say do give in their
account which is as follows – –

               [_bottom quarter of page is blank_]

And the Said **John Slocum** not clearing him Selfe to friends
Sattisfaction and being found in a falsehood in his talk about
it is the mind of this meeting that he be denied by friends
Therefore **John Tucker** and **Thos Taber jun^r** are appointed to
draw up a condemnation against him: and one against **Desire
Howland** in order to be Signed at next monthly meeting – –
The matter relating to **Wm Soule** is refered to next
monthly meeting – –
John Tucker and **Thos Taber jun^r** are appointed to draw
up Something relating to wiggs and bring to the next

monthly meeting – –

Dartmouth preparitive meeting business called and it
appearing that **Increas[e] Allen** has married his K[i]nswoman
contrary to the order of the yearly meeting this meeting
orders **John Tucker** and **Thomas Taber jun**ʳ to draw up a
Condemnation to be Signed and read at the next monthly
meeting — **Rochester** meeting Called no business – –
The visiters are desired to visit friends families and give
account to the next monthly meeting – – – – –

_7ᵗʰ mo:_ At a monthly meeting of friends held at our meeting house
in **Dartmouth** yᵉ 18ᵗʰ day of the 7ᵗʰ month 1721 – –
Dartmouth meeting called **William Wood** and **Judah Smith**
appeared: **Rochester** meeting called **Elisha Wing** appeared
Whereas **Benjamin Soule** the Son of **William Soule** is gone
out into the fassions of the world in his apparrel and has
been often advised (both by the visiters and by friends appoin
=ted by the meeting and also by the monthly meeting he being
present) to reform yet he obstinately refuses to hear but
Signefies that he will go on in his own way therefore this
meeti[ng] Doth declare the Said **Benjamin Soule** to be from
under yᵉ Care of friends – –
At **William Soule**s request the matter between him and
the **Allen**s is refered to the next monthly meeting – –
The friends appointed to draw up something Conccerning
wiggs have done it and it being approved: ~~and Signed John Tucke~~
is ordered to be sent up to the Quarterly meeting wᵗʰ yᵉ account
The Condemnation against **John Slocum** being drawn up
approved and Signed **John Tucker** is ordered to read it or cause it
to be read as usual between this and yᵉ next monthly meeting
Also **Desire Howland**s condemnation is Drawn approved and
Signed and **John Tucker** is appointed to read it or cause it to be
read as usual between this and the next monthly meeting
The Condemnation of **Increase Allen jun**ʳ: is drawn up and
Signed and read and is as followeth – –
Whereas **Increase Allen** the Son of **Increase Allen** of **Dartmouth**
in the **County of Bristol** hath proceeded to take his near Kins
Woman in marriage contrary to the order of friends and
the advice of this meeting to him given: Therefore this meeting
Doth declare the Said **Increase Allen jun**ʳ: is not in unity with
us the people Called Quakers given forth and Signed at our

monthly meeting held in **Dartmouth** the 18th of ye 7th: month: 1721
Signed at Said meeting by – –

John Tucker	**Elisha Wing**	
William Wood Thos: Taber junr:		**Jabez Barker**
Increase Allen	**John Lapham**	**Benjamin Howland**
Nicolas Davis	**Henry Tucker**	

And there being two friends children whose parents are first
Cousins by blood who have desired to lay their intentions of
marriage before this meeting and friends being thoughtful that
Such a proceding is contrary to the order of friends but not
being fully Sattisfied Do refer it to the Consideration of the
Quarterly meeting what may be thought proper to be done
in such a case[27]: The visiters of **Dartmouth** meeting have done
nothing on the account of visiting the famllies of friends
The visiters of **Rochester** meeting do give account that they
have visited the families of friends belonging to their ~~ea~~
meeting and find things among friends relating to truth
for the most part pretty well – –
There being some friends Sufferings brought from **Rochester**
they are approved and ordered to be Sent to ye Quarterly meet
=ing – – and **Deliverance Smith** and **Thos Taber junr:** are
appointed to draw an account to the Quarterly meeting – –
and they and **Elisha Wing** are appointed to attend the sd
meeting: This meeting is ajourned til the afternoon after
the youths meeting next. The meeting being met according
to ajourment the visiters give account that they have visit
=ed the most of friends families belonging to our meeting
And find that their visits were generally kindly accepted and
things for the most part pretty well – – – – –

8:th mo: At a monthly meeting of friends held at our meeting house
in **Dartmouth** the 23d day of the 8:th month 1721 – –
Dartmouth meeting called **Judah Smith** and **John Lapham**
appeared = **Rochester** meeting Called none appeared – –
And the differance between **William Soule** and the **Allens**
is refered to the next monthly meeting – –
And **John Tucker** hath read **John Slocum** and **Desire Howlan**
Condemnations as appointed which are as followeth
Whereas **John Slocum** the Son of **Eleazar Slocum** of **Dartmout**

---

27. New England Friends by 1728 had settled on a policy of discouraging marriages of second and even
third cousins, but not forbidding them. See J. William Frost, *The Quaker Family in Colonial America: A
Portrait of the Society of Friends* (New York: St. Martin's, 1973), 161.

in the county of **Bristol** in **New England** is accused by
Desire Howland the daughter of **Benjamin Howland** of S^d
Dartmouth with gitting her with child which fact although
the S^d **John Slocum** doth deny yet it hath been proved that
he was falce in his plea for vindication So that he hath not
cleared him Selfe to the Sattisfaction of this meeting – –
Therefore we do deny the S^d **John Slocum** to be one of us the
people Called Quaker desiring if it to be the will of God that
he may Senceablely come to Light of all his outgoings and by
true repentance find mercy with the Lord – –
given forth at our monthly meeting held in **Dartmouth**
the 18th day of the 7th month 1721 and Signed at S^d meeting by

John Tucker	Increase Allen	Thomas Taber jun^r:
William Wood	John Lapham	Benjamin Howland
Elisha Wing	Henry Tucker	Jabez Barker
Judah Smith	Nathaniel Howland	

Here follows **Desire Howland**s Condemnation – –
Whereas **Desire Howland** the daughter of **Benjamin Howland**
of **Dartmouth** in the county of **Bristol** in **New England**
hath fllen into that wicked and Skandalous Sin of fornication
as appears by her being delivered of late of a Bastard child
begotten of her body to the dishonour of God reproach of
the blessed truth professed amongst us and grief of friends
These are therefore given forth as a publick Testimony
Against all Such unclean and detestable actions: denying
the Said **Desire Howland** to be one of us the people called
Quakers yet desiering if it be the will of God She may come
to a light and Sence of the evil of her doings and by unfeign
=ed repentance find mercy – –
Signed at our men and womens meeting held at at
Dartmouth the:18th of y^e 7th month 1721

John Tucker	Henry Tucker	Rachel Allen
William Wood	John Lapham	Hannah Tucker
Increas Allen	Elisha Wing	Mary Laton
Judah Smith		Hannah Soule
Nicolas Davis	Ruth Tucker	Mary Lapham
Benjamin Howland	Mary Slocum	Mary Russell
Mary Smith	Phebe Tucker	Rebekah Russell

And **Thomas Taber jun^r** and **Deliverance Smith** hath drawn
up an account to the Quarterly meeting as appointed and

also attended S^d meeting as as appointed – –

The business of **Dartmouth** meeting Called no business
and the ~~bu~~ Epistle from our Quarterly meeting Last was
read and kindly accepted – – – – –

9th mo: At a monthly meeting of friends held at our meeting house
in **Dartmouth** the 20th day of the 9th month 1721 – –
Dartmouth meeting Called **William Wood** and **Judah Smith** appear^ed
Rochester meeting Called none appeared – –
Nathan Soule hath contributed towards building **Coakset** meeting
house five pounds – This meeting hath Laboured with **William
Soule** that he would fulfil the judgment of the yearly meeting
and he doth refuse to fulfil the Same – –
The business of **Dartmouth** meeting called this meeting being
informed that **William Soule**s Daughters **Hannah** and **Mary Soule**
are married Contrary to the order of friends **Thomas Taber jun^r**
and **John Tucker** are appointed to draw up their condemnations
in order to be Signed at the next monthly meeting and this
meeting cannot see that **William Soule** hath been clear in
his Testimony against their proceedings which is refered to the
Consideration of the next monthly meeting

10th mo: At a monthly meeting of friends held at our meeting
house in **Dartmouth** the 18th day of ye 10 month 1721:
Dartmouth meeting Called **William Wood** and **Judah Smith**
appeared. **Rochester** meeting called none appeared:
Abraham Tucker jun^r and **Elisabeth Russell** daughter of
John Russell boath of **Dartmouth** have declared before this
meeting their intentions of taking each other in marriage
and they were desired to wait for their answer til the next
monthly meeting: And **Deliverance Smith** and **Jabez
Barker** are appointed to See into their clearness and make
return to the next monthly meeting how they find things
The business concerning **William Soule** his refusing to
conform to the Quarterly^ and yearly meetings judgments is agreed
to be refered to the Quarterly meeting next – –
And the matter concerning **William Soule**s bearing
his testimony against his daughters proceeding in marriage
Contrary to truth is refered to the next monthly meeting
And **Henry Tucker** and **John Tucker** is appointed to keep
the meeting house for the insuing year – –
John Tucker William Wood and **Henry Tucker** are appointed

to attend the Quarterly meeting: **John Tucker** and **Judah
Smith** are appointed to draw an account to the Quarterly
meeting – – and **Henry Tucker** is appointed to read
Mary Soule and **Hannah Soule**s Condemnation on a
first day: between this and the next monthly meeting
And **John Tucker** is ordered to pay **James Tripp** thirty Shilling
upon the account of **Coaxet** meeting house and the Quarterly
Collection is refered to the next monthly meeting – – – – –

11 At a monthly meeting of friends held at our meeting house
in **Dartmouth** the 15:th day of the 11:th month 1721/22
Dartmouth meeting called **William Wood** and **Judah
Smith** appeared collected for the use of friends 1£ – 02s – 11d
Rochester meeting called none appeared – –
Abraham Tucker jun:r and **Elisabeth Russel** appeared
before this meeting, for their answer concerning their take
=ing each other in marriage and nothing appearing to hinder
their proceeding they had their answer they might pro
=ceed to take each other in marriage in the good order of
truth in And **Deliverance Smith** and **Jabez Barker** are
appointed to See them Solemnize their marriage in the good
order of truth and make return to the next monthly meeting
John Tucker hath payed **James Tripp** thirty Shillings according
to the order of the Last monthly meeting – –
William Wood and **Henry Tucker** have attended the Quarterly
meeting as appointed: **John Tucker** and **Judah Smith** have
drawn up an account to ye Quarterly meeting:
And **Henry Tucker** hath read **Hannah** & **Mary Soule**'s Condem
=nations as appointed which are as followeth:
Whereas **Hannah Soul** the daughter of **William Soule** of
Dartmouth in the County of **Bristol** in **New England** having
had her Education amongst us the people of God called Quakers
but for want of keeping to the principle of Truth hath
proceeded in marriage Contrary to the good order Established
amongst us the abovesd people although advised to the Contrary
Therefore we do deny the Said **Hannah** now the wife of
Joseph Hollie jun:r to be one of us the people called Quakers
Desiring that if it be the will of God that She may senceablely
Come to a Sight of her out goings and by true repentance
find mercy with the Lord and Come into unity with his
people: Given forth at our monthly meeting of men and

women held in Dartmouth the 18:ᵗʰ day of the 10ᵗʰ month 1721

	Nathaniel Howland	Hannah Tucker
Peleg Slocum	John Lapham	Ruth Tucker
Stephen Willcox	Henry Tucker	Phebe Tucker
William Wood	John Tucker	Mary Laton
		Mehetabel Burril
		Dinah Smith

Whereas **Mary Soule** the daughter of **William Soule** of
Dartmouth in the County of **Bristol** in **New England** – –
hath had her education amongst us the people of God Called
Quakers but for want of keeping to the principle of truth
hath proceeded in marriage contrary to the good order established
amongst us the abovesd people although advised to the Contrary
Therefore we do deny the said **Mary** now that wife of **William**
Page to be one of us the people called Quakers – –
Desiring that if it be the will of God the[y] may Senceablebly
come to a Sight of all her outgoings and by true repentance
find mercy with the Lord – –
Given forth at our monthly meeting of men and women
held in **Dartmouth** the 18:ᵗʰ day of the 10ᵗʰ month 1721: – –

Stephen Willcox	Judah Smith	Hannah Tucker
Peleg Slocum	Henry Tucker	Ruth Tucker
William Wood	John Tucker	Mary Latham
Nathaniel Howland	Jabez Barker	Mary Russell: Phebe Tucker
John Lapham		mary Smith: dinah Smith mary Laton: mehetabel burril

And we received the Epistle from the Quarterly meeting
which was read and kindly accepted – –
and the matter Concerning **William Soule** and the **Allins**
is refered to the next monthly meeting – –
and **Judah Smith** is appointed to read the munits [minutes] to him
Benjamin Howland is appointed to pay to **John Tucker**
and **Henry Tucker** or eighther of them 1ᶠ = 15ˢ = 08ᵈ for keping
the meeting house the Last year – –
This meeting is informed that **Peleg Smith** and **Mary:**
Howland both of **Dartmouth** have proceeded in marriage
with each other contrary to the order of friends and
Thomas Taber juonʳ and **John Tucker** are appointed draw
their condemnation against the next monthly meeting

_12 mo:_　At a monthly meeting of friends held at our meeting

House in **Dartmouth** the 19th day of the 12th month 1721/2
Dartmouth meeting called **William Wood** and **Judah Smith**
appeared: **Rochester** meeting Called **Elisha Wing** and **Nicolas**
Davis appeared: The marriage between **Abraham Tucker junr**
and **Elisabeth Russell** not being accomplished the friends
appointed to see it done are Still continued and are to give in
their account to next monthly meeting – –
Benjamin Howland has paid 1:£ = 15:s for keeping the meeting house
according to the order of the Last monthly meeting – –
The business of **Dartmouth** meeting called: ~~it being proposed~~
The visiters are advised to perform a general visit of friends
families between this and ye next monthly meeting – –
Deliverance Smith is appointed to make up the monthly
meeting accompts with **Benjamin Howland** and bring it to the
monthly meeting next – –
John Tucker and **Thomas Taber junr** have Drawn a Condem
=nation against **Peleg Smith** and his wife for their disorderly
proceeding in marriage: which is accepted and Signed and
and **He[n]ry Tucker** is ordered to read it or cause it to be read
at the conclution of the meeting of worship on a first day
between this and ye next monthly meeting – –
Rochester meeting business called and their meeting presents
a paper from **Hannah Hillier** wherein she acknowledgeth
her outgoing in her disorderly marriage and desires to come
into unity with friends: also **Sarah Clifton** of said meeting
did send a paper some time past of the Like nature and this
meeting having Comfortable hopes of their Sincerity doth
accept of their that is ye Sd **Hannah Hillier** and **Sarah**
Cliftons acknowledgments and of them as friends in unity
w:th this meeting: and **Elisha Wing** is appointed to read
their Sd acknowledgments in the meeting of worship at
Rochester at ye end of the meeting – –
And there being a differance brought to this meeting between
Joseph Allen and **Nathaniel Howland** of one partie and
Thrustrom of the other partie concerning ye estate of **Josiah**
Allen deceased and Sd **Joseph Allen** and **Nathaniel Howland**
did offer to leave it to the meeting and to be bound to Stand
to ye award of Such as the meeting Should appoint to diter
=mine the Same but sd **Thrustrom Allen** refused to have it
unless he might have Liberty to appeal to ye Quarterly meeting

which this meeting thinks not propper in Such a case
and therefore doth refuse to act in the matter – –
The matter relating to **Wᵐ Soule** is refered to next
monthly meeting: our next preparitive meeting and
monthly meeting is ajourned one week longer than yᵉ
usual time – – – – –

1722 At a monthly meeting of friends held at our meeting
1 mo: House in **Dartmouth** yᵉ 26ᵗʰ day of yᵉ 1ˢᵗ month: 1722:
There was collected for the use of friends – – 1ˡ – 04ˢ : 00ᵈ – –
Dartmouth meeting called **Judah Smith** and **Wᵐ Wood**
appeared: **Rochester** meeting called **John Wing** appeared
The friends appointed to Se the marriag between **Abraham**
Tucker and **Elisabeth Russell** Solemnized in the good order
of truth do Say that they attended yᵉ Solemnizeing of sᵈ
marriage and that it was accomplished in the good order
of truth for ought they know – –
The ~~friends appointed~~ visiters being called upon do give
account that they have visited yᵉ most of friends families
and and find things in a general way pretty well as far
as they saw: **Deliverance Smith** not haveing made
up the monthly meeting accompts wᵗʰ **Benjamin Howland**
he is still continued to do it by the next monthly meeting
Henry Tucker has read **Peleg Smith** and his wives and ^condemnation accor
=ding to yᵉ order of the Last monthly meeting & is as followeth
Whereas **Peleg Smith** yᵉ Son of **Deliverance Smith**
of yᵉ Town of **Dartmouth** in yᵉ Coun[ty] of **Bristol** in **New**
England and **Mary Howland** the Daughter of **Nathaniel**
Howland of sᵈ **Dartmouth** being the children of friends
and have been [e]ducated in the way of truth
Yet of Late although they have been perticularly exhorted
and advised to the contrary by friends have preceeded in
marriage out of the good order of us the people called
Quakers we do therefore deny yᵉ said **Peleg Smith** and **Mary**
his wife to be of us the ^sᵈ people ~~called~~ Sincerely desireing
that if it be the will of god that they may come to a true
Sence of their outgoings and by their circunspect walking
before God and amongst us his people be received into the
fold where the great Shepherd is giving rest and peace to
to them that are his – –
Given forth and Signed at our monthly meeting held in

Dartmouth y:ᵉ 19 of y:ᵉ 12ᵗʰ month 1722/21

Nathaniel Howland

John Tucker	**Jabez Barker**	**Phebe Tucker**
Judah Smith	**Joseph Russell** junʳ.	**Mary Russell**
William Wood	**William Wood** junʳ.	**Mary Laton**
Elisha Wing		**Mary Smith**
Thomas Taber junʳ:	**Ruth Tucker**	**Dinah Smith**
Abraham Tucker	**Mary Slocum**	**Mehetabel Burril**
John Lapham	**Hannah Tucker**	
Nicolas Davis		

Elisha Wing has read the acknowledments of **Hannah
Hillier** and **Sarah Clifton** as ordered – –

John Tucker is ordered to pay 3ˡ – 10ˢ to **Jame Tripp** towards
the finnishing of **Coakset** meeing [meeting] house which is mony in
his hands belonging to y:ᵉ meeting – –

The judgment of y:ᵉ yearly meeting relating to **Wᵐ Soule**
being considered of it is concluded that Judgment must go forth
in as much as he refuses to comply therewith: and **Henry
Tucker** and **Thomas Taber** junʳ are appointed to draw up
a Condemnation against him the sᵈ **Wᵐ Soule** and present
it to the next monthly meeting and if it be approved to
be signed – –

The business of **Dartmouth** meeting Called
And whereas Seaveral Friends are owners of Slaves which
may desire to take each other in marriage and no direct
method established among friends in that case as we know
of it is refered to the Qurterly meeting to consider of
and propose a rule for the time to come in that matter
if they think fit — **Rochester** meeting business called
none presented: **Stephen Willcox William Wood** and
Thomas Taber jun.ʳ are appointed to ~~draw~~ attend y:ᵉ
Quarterly meeting **John Tucker** and **Tho:ˢ Taber** junʳ are
appointed to draw an account to the Quarterly meeting

At a monthly meeting of friends held at our meeting house
in **Dartmouth** y:ᵉ 23:ᵈ day of the 2.ᵈ month 1722:
Dartmouth meeting called **Deliverance Smith** and **Judah Smith**
appeared – – **Rochester** meeting called none appeared – –
John Tucker gives account that he has paid 3:ˡ 10ˢ to **James
Tripp** according to yᵉ order of Last monthly: he has also paid
3 pounds & 5 Shillings to y:ᵉ Quarterly meeting it bein this

meetings Collection towards a yearly meeting Stock – –
and was Concluded upon at our monthly meeting in the 5:ᵗʰ
month last: **Deliverance Smith** has made up the accompt
w:ᵗʰ **Benjamin Howland** according to order and finds that
there remaines in the in the monthly meeting Stock 3:ˡ 01ˢ: 08ᵈ
Isaac Wood and **Mary Potter** the daughter of **Nathaniel Potter**
both of **Dartmouth** have laid their intentions marriage
before this meeting and **James Tripp** and **Robert Kirby** are
appointed to make inquiry into their clearness with respect
to marriage and conversation and give account thereof
to the next monthly meeting – –
Stephen Willcox William Wood and **Thomas Taber jun**ʳ have
drawn an account to the Quarterly meeting according to ᵒʳᵈᵉʳ
William Soules Condemnation is read approved and Signed
and **Thomas Taber** is ordered to read it at the end of the time
of worship on a first day between this and the next monthly meetⁱⁿᵍ
And **William Wood John Tucker Stephen Willcocks**
Nathaniel Howland Joseph Taber and **Thomas Taber jun**ʳ
are appointed visiters for the ensuing year and till there
be a new choice – –
The Epistle from the Quarterly meeting was was read
and kindly accepted – – – – –

3ᵈ *mo:* At a monthly meeting of friends held at our meeting house
in **Dartmouth** the 21:ˢᵗ of y:ᵉ 3:ᵈ month 1722:
Dartmouth meeting called **Deliverance** and **Judah Smith**
appeared: **Rochester** meeting Called **Elisha Wing** appeared
Isaac Wood and **Mary Potter** appeared for their answer
relating to their intentions of marriage laid before yᵉ
Last monthly meeting and nothing appearing to hinder
they have their answer that they may proceed to take
each other in marriage in the good order of truth between
this and the next monthly meeting and **James Tripp** and
Robert Kirby are appointed to Se their marriage accom-
=plished and give an account thereof to the next monthly meeting – –
Seth Russell the Son of **Joseph Russell** and **Hannah Allen**
the Daughter of **Increas Allen** both of **Dartmouth** – –
Laid their intentions of marriage before this meeting
and **Deliverance Smith** and **Henry Tucker** are appointed
to inquire into their clearness with respect to marriage
and Conversation and give account to the next mo.ly meeting

Thomas Taber jun[r] has read **William Soule**s condemnation
which is as followeth – –
Whereas **William Soule** of **Dartmouth** in the County of
Bristol in **New England** who for many years past hath professed
him selfe to be one of the people called Quakers and hath been
in Some measure esteemed in unity with them yet by giving
way to much of a craving mind after the things of this
world did of Late in a hiden and undiscovered way purchse
part of the estate of **Josiah Allen** deceased to y[e] damage of
those to whome it did belong and with whome he so bargained
and did take the Sum of thirty pounds to release S[d] bargain
for all which the judgments of the Quarterly meeting and yearly
meetings: to which S[d] matters have ben refered have gon against
William Soule judging that he ought publickly to Condemn his
s[d] proceedings and to return the s[d] Sum of thirty pounds to the persons
from whome he had received the Same all which the S[d] **William**
Soule doth refuse to perform although this meeting hath waited
Long and endeavered from time to time to perswade him thereto
we do therefore condemn the s[d] proceedings of of the s[d] **Wm Soule**
with his obstinate refusal to comply with the judgments of s[d]
meetings and do deny him to be one of us the people called Quakers
yet desiring Sincerely that if it be the will of God he may come
to a Sence of his outgoing and by makeing amends to those
he has wronged and a circumspect walking before God find
mercy with him and Come into unity with his people – –
Given forth and Signed at our monthly meeting held in **Dartmouth**
the 23:[d] day of y:[e] 2[d] month 1722: – – **Judah Smith** – –

Thomas Taber jun[r]	**John Lapham**	**Nathaniel Howland**
John Tucker – –	**Stephen Willcock**	**Joseph Russel jun**[r]
William Wood	**Henry Tucker**	**William Wood jun**[r]

no business from y[e] weekly meetings – – – – –

---

4 mo: At a monthly meeting of friends held at our meeting house
in **Dartmouth** y:[e] 18th day of the 4th month 1722 – –
Dartmouth meeting called **William Wood** and **Judah Smith**
appeared: **Rochester** meeting Called **Elisha Wing** appeared
James Tripp and **Robert Kirby** give account that the
marriage between **Isaac Wood** and **Mary Potter** was Solemnised
in the good order of truth – –
Seth Russel and **Hannah Allen** appeared for their answer
and nothing appearing to hinder their answer is that they

proceed to take each other in marriage in the good order
of truth in Some Convenient time between this and the
next monthly meeting and **Deliverance Smith** and **Jabez**
Barker are appointed to See it accordingly accomplished
Peleg Slocum jun^r desiring a certificate of his clearness
relating to marriage **John Lapham** and **Jabez Barker**
are appointed to inquire into y:ᵉ same and and give account
thereof to next monthly meeting – –
William Wood Elisha Wing and **Deliverance Smith** are appoin^{ted}
To attend the Quarterly meeting **John Tucker** and **Tho**^s **Taber** ju
are ordered to draw up an account to yᵉ Quarterly meeting
no business from **Rochester** – – – – –

At a monthly meeting of friends held at our meeting house
in **Dartmouth** the 16:th day of y:ᵉ 5th month 1722:
Dartmouth meeting Called **William Wood** and **Judah Smith**
appeared: **Rochester** meeting Called **Stephen Wing** appeared
Deliverance Smith and **Jabez Barker** give account that
that ^{they were at ye Solemnzeing} yᵉ marriage between **Seth Russell** and **Hannah**
Allen and saw nothing but that it was performed in the
good order of truth: **James Shearman** and **Grizel Meriho [Merihew]**
Laid their intentions of marriage before this meeting who
are desired to wait till the next monthly meeting for their
answer and **John Lapham** and **Henry Tucker** are appointed
to inquire into their Clearness on that account and make
Report to next monthly meeting – –
Peleg Slocum jun^r has had a certificate of his clearness
with respect to marriage: **William Wood** and **Deliverance**
Smith have attended the Quarterly meeting and **John Tucker**
and **Thomas Taber** have drawn and Sent an account according
to order: **Stephen Willcock** desiring a certificate on y:ᵉ
account of his desire of proceeding in marriag wth **Judeth**
Barnet of **Nantucket**: **William Wood** and **Thomas Taber jun**^r
are appointed to inquire into his clearness and make report
to yᵉ next monthly meeting – –
no business from **Rochester** The Epistle from the Quarterly
meeting was read and kindly accepted: **David Irishes** certificate
from the monthly meeing of friends on **Rhoad Island** was read
giving a good account of his Conversation and the
unity they have with his Testimony – – – – –

6 mo: At a monthly meeting of friends held at our meeting house in
　　　Dartmouth the 20:th day of y:e 6:th month 1722:
　　　Dartmouth meeting Called **William Wood** and **Judah Smith** appeared
　　　Rochester meeting Called **Elisha Wing**^ and Nicolas Davis appeared – –
　　　James Shearman and **Grizel Meriho [Merihew]** appeared for their answer
　　　and nothing apearing to hinder they had their answer that
　　　they might preceed in taking each other in marriage in the
　　　good order of truth in Some Convenient time between this
　　　and the next monthly meeting – –
　　　And **Henry Tucker** and **John Lapham** are appointed to Se
　　　it accomplished in the good order of truth and make report
　　　to the next monthly meeting – –
　　　Dartmouth weekly meeting called and no business presented
　　　Rochester meeting Called **Nicolas Davis** desires a certificate
　　　to vavil [*sic:* travel?] in the Servis of truth which is granted – –
　　　and a certificate is granted to **Stephen Willcock** (at this
　　　meeting) as to his clearness in respect to marriage

7 mo: At a monthly meeting of friends held at our meeting house in
　　　Dartmouth y:e 17:th day of the 7:th month 1722:
　　　Dartmouth meeting Called **William Wood** and **Judah Smith**
　　　present: **Rochester** meeting Called **Elisha Wing** present
　　　Henry Tucker and **John Lapham** being Called upon make
　　　Report that the marriage between **James Shearman**
　　　and **Grizel Meriho [Merihew]** was decently accomplished in the
　　　Order of truth: Collected at this meeting and delivered to
　　　Benjamin Howland 17 Shillings and 6 pence – –
　　　Benjamin Wing son of **Matthew Wing** of **Dartmouth** and
　　　Content Tucker Daughter of **Abraham Tucker** of s:d.Town laid
　　　their intentions of marriage to Each other before this meeting
　　　they were Desired to wait until y:e next monthly meeting
　　　for their answer & **John Lapham** and **Josiah Merriho [Merihew]** are
　　　appointed to inquire into their Clearness and Conversation
　　　of s:d **Wing** and make report to y:e Next monthly meeting – –
　　　Our worthy friend **Robert Jordan** of **Virginia** being at this
　　　meeting his Certificate from the monthly meeting of **Chap**
　　　tank Nansemum [Chuckatuck, Nansemund] y:e 12:th d of 2:d month 1722 was
　　　　　Read to our mutual
　　　Sattisfaction: s:d S. Certificate was ~~allowed~~ also approved by
　　　the halfe year meeting held at **Maryland West river** y:e 16:th

of the 3:ᵈ month 1722[28]: This day being far spent this meeting
is ajourned unto the first sixth day of the 8:ᵗʰ month and
the business of this meeting which is not accomplished is
refered to the adjourment:
This meeting being met according to adjournment this 5ᵗʰ day
of yᵉ 8:ᵗʰ month 1722 **John Tucker** and **Deliverance Smith**
are appointed to draw up an account to y:ᵉ Quarterly
meeting: **Stephen Willcock** and **Henry Tucker** are appointed
to attend yᵉ Quarterly meeting – –
The visiters gives this meeting an account that they have
visited the families of friends belonging to this meeting and
find things Generally pretty well – – – – –

8ᵗʰ mo: At a monthly meeting of friends held at our meeting
House in **Dartmouth** y:ᵉ 15:ᵗʰ day of the 8:ᵗʰ month 1722:
Dartmouth meeting called **Deliverance Smith** and
Nathaniel Howland appeared: **Rochester** meeting Called
none appeared – –
Benjamin Wing and **Content Tucker** appeared at this
meeting for their answer and nothing appearing to hinder
they had their answer that they might proceed to take each
other in marriage in the order of friends and **John Tucker**
and **Josiah Merriho [Merihew]** are appointed to se it accomplished in the
Same and make return to the monthly meeting – –
And **John Laton** son of **George Laton** of **Dartmouth** and **Patience
Kirby** Daughter of **Robert Kirby** of sᵈ **Dartmouth** Signifyed their
intentions of ^taking each other in marriage and they were desired to wait ill the
next monthly meeting for their answer and **William
Wood** and **Matthew Wing** are appointed to inquire into their
clearness and conversation and make report to yᵉ next
monthly meeting how they find things – –
it hath been Signifyed to this meeting that **William Russell**
Son of **Jonathan Russell** of **Dartmouth** desires a certificate of
his Clearness in Respect to marriage and conversation and
Benjamin Howland and **John Lapham** are appointed to
to make inquiry into the Same and make return to the
Next monthly meeting how they find things – –

28. Robert Jordan (1693-1742) was a minister from Nansemond County, Virginia, who traveled
widely in North America and visited England. See *A Collection of Memorials Concerning Divers Deceased
Ministers and Others of the People Called Quakers, in Pennsylvania, New-Jersey, and Parts Adjacent, from
Nearly the First Settlement Thereof to the Year 1787. With Some of the Last Expressions and Exhortations of
Many of Them* (Philadelphia: Joseph Crukshank, 1787), 109-18.

Stephen Willcock and Henry Tucker have attended y:ᵉ Quarter
=ly meeting as appointed and John Tucker hath drawn an
account to Quarterly meeting as appointed and the
Epistle of the Quarterly meeting was read at this meeting
and kindly accepted: John Tucker and Wᵐ Wood are
appointed to Speak wᵗʰ Stephen Willcock concerning ~~the~~
his Leaving his family this winter – – – – –

At a monthly meeting of friends held at our meeting house in
Dartmouth the 19:ᵗʰ day of the 9:ᵗʰ month 1722:
Dartmouth meeting Called Judah Smith and Josiah Meriho [Merihew]
appeared Rochester meeting called none appeared.
John Laton and Patience Kirby appeared at this meeting
for their answer as to taking each other in marriage
and nothing appearing to hinder their sᵈ intentions they had
the Consent of this meeting to take each other in the good order
of truth in Some Convenient time between this and the next
monthly meeting: and Wᵐ Wood and Matthew Wing are
appointed to Se it accomplished in the good order of truth and
make return to the next monthly meeting how they find things
The business of Dartmouth meeting Called no business presented
Deliverance Smith and John Tucker is appointed to draw up
a certificate for W:ᵐ Russell and Sign it in behalf of the
monthly meeting: John Tucker and Josiah Merihoo [Merihew] makes report
to this meeting that Benjamin Wing and Content Tucker have
accomplished their marriage in the order of truth, as far
as the[y] Saw – – – – –

10ᵗʰ mo: At a monthly meeting of friends held at our meeting house
in Dartmouth y:ᵉ 17:ᵗʰ day of y:ᵉ 10:ᵗʰ month 1722: collected: 2ˡ: 01ˢ: 0
Dartmouth meeting Called Deliverance Smith and Benjamin
Howland present: Rochester meeting Called Stephen Wing appearᵈ
The friends appointed to See John Laton and Patience Kirby
Solemnize their marriage makes report that it as accom
=plished in y:ᵉ Good order of truth   Deliverance Smith and
John Tucker hath drawn ~~an account to the Quarterly meeting~~
a certificate for Wᵐ Russell and Signed it according to
the order of y:ᵉ Last monthly meeting – –
The business of Dartmouth meeting called this meeting orders
Benjamin Howland to pay 2 pounds and 4 shillings to
John Tucker and Henry Tucker for keeping the meeting house and

repareing the Chimney the year past: And **John Tucker** and
Henry Tucker are appointed to keep yᵉ meeting house the ensuing
year: The business of **Rochester** meeting Called an account in
writing from their preparitive meeting was presented to this
meeting that they have no business but their Love – –
Deliverance Smith and **Henry Tucker** are appointed to attend
the Quarterly meeting next – –
John Tucker and **Deliverance Smith** are appointed to draw
up an account to the Quarterly meeting: and **Stephen**
Willcock desires some lines from this meeting of his unity
with this meeting and and of friends unity w:ᵗʰ his removeing
to **Nantucket** which is granted and **Deliverance Smith** and
John Tucker are appointed to draw it and Sign it in behalf
of the monthly meeting – – – – –

11ᵗʰ mo:
At a monthly meeting of friends held at our meeting house in
Dartmouth y:ᵉ 21:ˢᵗ day of y:ᵉ 11ᵗʰ month 1722:
Dartmouth meeting Called **Wᵐ Wood** and **Judah Smith** present
Rochester meeting Called **Nicolas Davis** present – –
Benjamin Howland hath paid 2ˡ: 4ˢ: to **John Tucker** and
Henry Tucker as appointed y:ᵉ Last monthly meeting – –
and **Henry Tucker** hath attended y:ᵉ Quarterly meeting
as appointed: And **Deliverance Smith** and **John Tucker** hath
drawn upon account to the same according to order:
John Tucker and **Deliverance** have drawn up some lines for
Stephen Willcock according to the order of yᵉ Last monthly meeting
The Quarterly meeting Epistle was read at this meeting
and Kindly accepted – – – – –

12:th mo:
At a monthly meeting of friends held at our meeting
House in **Dartmouth** y:ᵉ 18:ᵗʰ day of y:ᵉ 12ᵗʰ month 1722/23
Dartmouth meeting Called **William Wood** and **Judah Smith**
present: **Rochester** meeting called **Savery Clifton** present
The business of **Dartmouth** meeting Called
This meeting orders **Benjamin Howland** to pay **Joseph Russel ju**
junʳ one Shilling for recording the return of the Survey of
the meeting house Land in **aponaganset** vilage
The business of **Rochester** meeting Called and they give us
an account that they have no business to present at this
time: The next monthly meeting is adjourned till yᵉ 4ᵗʰ
second day in the first month next

<u>1ˢᵗ mo:</u> At a monthly meeting of friends held at our meeting
  1723 House in **Dartmouth** y:ᵉ 25:ᵗʰ day of the first month 1723
        Dartmouth meeting called **Judah Smith** and **Deliverance**
        Smith appeared: **Rochester** meeting Called **Nicholas Davis**
        appeared: **Benjamin Howland** hath paid **Josep Russell Junʳ**
        one Shilling f the Recording the returne of the Survey
        of the meeting house Land
        An Epistle was read at this meeting from **Old England**
        and it is Desired that all friends be careful to observe
        the good advice therein Given and as for that Concerning
        Chusing of friends to attend the sessions it is refered to
        the Quarterly meeting: The friends Chose to attend the
        Quarterly meeting are **Nicolas Davis William Wood** and
        John Tucker: This meeting is adjourned til the first Sixth
        day in the 2:ᵈ month – –
        This meeting being met according to adjournment the
        5:ᵗʰ day of y:ᵉ 2:ᵈ month 1723: The visiters being Called
        upon gives this meeting an account that they have
        visited y:ᵉ families of friends belonging to this meeting in
        a pretty General way and have had pretty good Sattisfaction
        In their service though they find not all things So well as
        they Could Desire: **John Tucker** and **Henry Tucker** are appointed
        to draw up an account to the Quarterly meeting next – –

At a monthly meeting of friends held at our meeting house in
Dartmouth the 15:ᵗʰ day of y:ᵉ 2:ᵈ month 1723:
Dartmouth meeting Called **Judah Smith** and **Benjamin**
Howland present: **Rochester** meeting Called **Nicolas Davis**
appeared **John Tucker** and **Henry Tucker** have drawn
up an account and Sent it to Quarterly meeting – –
as appointed: and **John Tucker** and **Wᵐ Wood** hath
attended the Quarterly meeting as appointed – –
The business **Dartmouth** meeting Called and **Deliverance**
Smith is appointed to make up the monthly meetings
accompts w:ᵗʰ **Benjamin Howland** and make return
to y:ᵉ next monthly meeting how the accompt is – –
And **Stephen Wing** and **David Irish** are appointed
visiters for **Rochester** meeting for the Insuing year
And for **Dartmouth** meeting **Joseph Taber Thomas Hatha=**
=way John Tucker Deliverance Smith William Wood and

Matthew Wing are chosen visiters for the Insuing year
or til others be chosen. The Epistle from y:ᵉ Last Quarterly
meeting was read at this meeting and kindly accepted

3:ᵈ mo: At a monthly meeting of friends held at our meeting
house in **Dartmouth** yᵉ 20:ᵗʰ day of of the 3:ᵈ month 1723
Dartmouth meeting Called **Judah Smith** appered
Rochester meeting Called **Stephen Wing** appeared
Deliverance Smith is still continued to make up the
monthly meetings accomt w:ᵗʰ **Benjamin Howland**
and make return to the next monthly meeting – –
The business of **Dartmouth** meeting Called no business
The business of **Rochester** meting called none presented

4ᵗʰ mo: At a monthly meeting of friends held at our meeting
House in **Dartmouth** the 24ᵗʰ day of yᵉ 4ᵗʰ month 1723
There was collected for the use of friends 1£ – 07ˢ – 06ᵈ
Dartmouth meeting Called **William Wood** and **Deliverance
Smith** appeared: **Rochester** meeting Called **Savory Clifton** and
Nicolas Davis appeared: **Deliverance Smith** hath made the
monthly meetings accompts wᵗʰ **Benjamin Howland** and there
Remaines in the Stock 5£ – 18ˢ – 11ᵈ
The business of **Dartmouth** meeting Called **William Wood** and
Nicolas Davis are appointed to attend yᵉ Quarterly meeting
next: and **John Tucker** and **Deliverance Smith** are appointed
to draw an Epistle to the quarterly meeting aforesᵈ – –
The business of **Rochester** meeting Called and they signify in
writeing that they have no business to this meeting:

5ᵗʰ mo: At a monthly meeting of friends held at our meeting house
in **Dartmouth** yᵉ 15:ᵗʰ day of yᵉ 5:ᵗʰ month 1723:
Dartmouth meeting Called **Wᵐ Wood** and **Judah Smith** appeard
Rochester meeting Called none appeared – –
William Wood hath attended yᵉ Quarterly meeting
the Quarterly meeting Epistle was read at this meeting
and kindly accepted – – – – –

6 mo: At a monthly meeting of friends held at our meeting house
in **Dartmouth** the 19:ᵗʰ day of yᵉ 6 month 1723 – –
Dartmouth meeting Called **William Wood** and **Judah Smith**
appeared **Rochester** meeting called **Nicolas Davis** appeared
the business of **Dartmouth** meeting Called
This meeting hath agreed that we should endeavor to git

a friend Skool master to teach our children to read and
write and **James**^ ᵀʳⁱᵖᵖ ~~Barker~~ and **Deliverance Smith**
are appointed to See to git one and make return to the
next monthly meeting The business of **Rochester** meeting
Called and no business
A paper was presented to this meeting by the women friends
signed by **Elisabeth Tripp** Signifying her trouble for not taking of
The advice of friends in her marriage which is accepted and
ordered to be read on a first day at the end of the meeting of worship
and **Deliverance Smith** is ordered to read the Same

[blank quarter of page]

7 mo: At a monthly meeting of friends held at our meeting house
in **Dartmouth** the 16:ᵗʰ day of yᵉ 7:ᵗʰ month 1723 – –
There was Collected for the use of friends 1ᵏ – 01ˢ – 00ᵈ
Dartmouth meeting Called **Judah Smith** and **Josiah Merrihoo** [Merihew]
appeared: **Rochester** meeting Called **Stephen Wing** appeared
The business of **Dartmouth** meeting Called – –
Nicolas Davis William Wood and **John Tucker** are appointed to
attend the Quarterly meeting next
The business of Rochester meeting Called: The visiters of
Rochester meeting gives account that they have visited the
families of friends belonging to their meeting and their
visits were kindly accepted and where they thought needful
they gave advise: And this meeting orders **Benjamin Howland**
To pay to **John Lapham** 1ᵏ – 15ˢ – 00 for keeping the meeting house
one pound of sᵈ mony we received of the Women – –
and **benjamin Howland** is to pay 4 Shillings to **Eleazer Slocum**
for giting [getting] the deed of the land belonginging [*sic*] to the meeting house
And this meeting is adjourned till yᵉ first day in yᵉ 8ᵗʰ month next
This meeting being met according to adjournment
This 4ᵗʰ day of the 8ᵗʰ month 1723 The visiters gives this
Meeting an account ₐᵗʰᵃᵗ they have made Some progress in the viseting
friends families belonging to this meeting and found things
pretty well as far as they Said
And **John Tucker** and **Henry Tucker** are appointed to draw
up an account to yᵉ Quarterly meeting next

8:ᵗʰ mo: At a monthly meeting of friends held at our meeting
house in **Dartmouth** yᵉ 21:ˢᵗ day of yᵉ 8:ᵗʰ month 1723:
Dartmouth meeting called **Judah Smith** and **Benjamin Howland**
appeared: **Rochester** meeting called none appeared – –

The business of **Dartmouth** meeting Called **Nicolas Davis** and
John Tucker hath attended yᵉ Quarterly meeting as appointed
And **John Tucker** and **Henry Tucker** have drawn up an
account to yᵉ Quarterly meeting as appointed – –
Henry Tucker and **James Barker** are appointed to look for
a friend School master that is capable to read write and
cypher and to know upon what termes and to make return
to our next monthly meeting of their proceedings therein
And **Deliverance Smith** hath read **Elisabeth Tripps** acknow=
=ledgment of her out going in her marriage Contrary to the
Good order of truth as appointed:
Samuel Howland Son of **Nicolas Howland** deceased: and **Sarah
Soule** Daughter of **Wᵐ Soule** deceased both of **Dartmouth** did
declare their intentions of marriage ‸ʷⁱᵗʰ ᵉᵃᶜʰ ᵒᵗʰᵉʳ before this meeting
and they was Desired to wait til yᵉ next monthly meeting
for their answer and **Judah Smith** and **Eliashib Smith** are
appointed to [*sic*] their clearness in respect to marriage and
Conversation and mak report to yᵉ next monthly meeting

9ᵗʰ mo: At a monthly of friends held at our meeting house in
Dartmouth the 18:ᵗʰ day of yᵉ 9:ᵗʰ month 1723:
Dartmouth meeting Called **William Wood** and **Judah Smith**
appeared: **Rochester** meeting Called none appeared:
Judah Smith and **Eliashib Smith** makes [*sic*] have made Inquiery
into **Samuel Howland**s clearness as appointed and they find nothing
to hinder their proceedings in marriage and yᵉ sᵈ **Samuel Howland**
and **Sarah Soule** appearing in this meeting desireing answer
and nothing appearing to hinder they had their answer that they
might proceed to take eacher [*sic*] in marriage in yᵉ good order
of truth in Some Convenient time before next monthly meetᵢₙg
And **Eliashib** [**Smith**] and **John Lapham** are appointed to See that
they perform yᵉ Same in the order of friends and make return
to yᵉ next monthly meeting – –
The business of **Dartmouth** meeting Called **Henry Tucker** and
James Barker hath Spoke with **George Howland** as appointed
by the preparitive meeting to perswade him not to go out of
the good order of truth in his marriage and his father hath
advized him to marry in the order of truth and he refuses
as yet – – – – –

10 mo At a monthly meeting of friends held at our meeting House in
Dartmouth yᵉ 16:ᵗʰ day of yᵉ 10ᵗʰ month 1723:

There was collected for the use of friends 1$^£$=05^s=03^d:
Dartmouth meeting Called **William Wood** and **Judah Smith**
present: **Rochester** meeting Called **Stephen Wing** appeared
John Lapham reports to this meeting that he was at y^e – –
marriage of **Samuel Howland** and H̶ **Sarah Soule** and it was
proformeed [performed] in prettey good order – –
The business of **Dartmouth** meeting Called and the meeting
orders **Benjamin Howland** to pay 1 pound 15 ^{s} outo [sic] of the
meetings Stock to John Tucker ‸& Henry Tucker for keeping the meeting house
the Last half year past – –
And **John Tucker** and **Henry Tucker** are chose to keep the
meeting house the insuing year: and **William Wood Deliverance**
Smith and **Henry Tucker** are appointed to attend ye Q[u]arterly
meeting next: And **John Tucker** and **Deliverance Smith**
are appionted to draw up an Epistle to ye Quarterly meeting
The business of **Rochester** meeting called: none presented:
The Epistle from the Quarterly meeting was read and kindly accepted – – – – –

11:th mo: At a monthly meeting of friends held at our meeting House in
Dartmouth the 20th day of the 11:th month 1723/24:
Dartmouth meeting Called **Judah Smith** appeared
Rochester meeting Called **Elisha Wing** appeared. **Benjamin**
Howland hath paid 1$^£$ – 15^s : 00^d out of y^e Stock to **John Tucker** and
Henry Tucker as appointed
And **Deliverance Smith** and **Henry Tucker** hath attended the
Quarterly meeting as appointed: And **Deliverance Smith**
and **John Tucker** hath drawn up an account to y^e Quarterly
meeting as ordered:
The business of **Dartmouth** meeting Called and **Benjamin Howland**
is ordered to pay to **Henry Tucker** 1$^£$: 07^s: 06^d out of the Stock
for mending the glass: the business of **Rochester** meeting called
answer was made no business
The Epistle of y^e Quarterly meeting was read in this meeting
and Kindly accepted – – – – –

12:th mo: At a monthly meeting of friends held at our meeting house in
Dartmouth the 17th day of the 12th month 1723/24:
Dartmouth meeting Called **Judah Smith** and **Benjamin Howland**
present: **Rochester** meeting Called none appeared:
Benjamin Howland ‸hath paid: 1$^£$ = 07^s = 06^d as appointed to **Henry Tucker**
at y^e Last monthly meeting:
The business of **Dartmouth** meeting Called:

[blank space for five lines]

John Tucker jun^r is appointed to assist his father in writeing
in the business of the monthly meeting – – – – –

1724
1 mo:
At a monthly meeting ∧$^{of \ friends}$ held at our meeting house in **Dartmouth**
the 16:th day of y^e first month 1723/24 – –
Dartmouth meeting called **William Wood** and **Judah Smith**
appeared **Rochester** meeting Called none appeared:
Barnabas Howland and **Rebekah Lapham** did lay their intent$_{ions}$
of marriage before this meeting ~~before this meeting~~ and they was
Desired to wait til y^e next monthly meeting for their answer
and **Deliverance Smith** and **Henry Tucker** is appointed to
inquire into their Clearness in respect to marriage and Conversa$_{tion}$
and bring in how they find things to y^e next monthly meeting
And the friends appointed at the Last monthly meeting gives
This meeting an account that friends hath in a general
way paid their province tax as was Desired y^e Last mo:^{ly} meeting
And there was Collected for y^e use of friends 1$^£$ = 04^s = 00^d:
Wm Wood and **John Tucker** are appointed to attend the
Quarterterly [sic] meeting: **John Tucker** and **Deliverance Smith**
are ordered to draw up ∧^{an} account to the quarterly meeting
and this meeting is adjourned til the first 6th day in the next month
This meeting being met according to adjournment this 3:^{d} day of ye 2:^{d}
month 1724: our visiters gives this meeting an account
that they have visited ye families of friends belonging to
this meeting in a pretty General way and their visits generally
was well accepted: and in Some families they found nothing
to ye Contrary but things was well but in Some others not
well where they gave suitable advice and are in hopes for
the time to come that they will be better

2:^{d} mo:
At a monthly meeting of friends held at our meeting
house in **Dartmouth** the 20:th day of ye 2:^{d} month 1724:
Dartmouth meeting Called **William Wood** and **Judah Smith**
present: **Rochester** meeting Called **Nicolas Davis** appeared
Deliverance Smith and **Henry Tucker** hath inquired into
Barnabas Howlands Clearness wth respect to marriage
and finding nothing to hender their intentions and
The s^d **Barnabas Howland** and **Rebecca Lapham**
appearing at this meeting for their answer they had
their answer that they might proceed to take each other
in marriage in the good order of truth and **Deliverance**

Smith and **Henry Tucker** are appointed to See it accordingly accomplished
William Wood Elisha Wing and **John Tucker** have
attended the Quarterly meeting as appointed
And **John Tucker** he and **Deliverance Smith** hath sent
and account to the Quarterly meeting as appointed:
The business of **Dartmouth** meeting Called
Joseph Taber Joseph Russell jun^r **John Tucker Henry
Tucker William Wood** and **Robert Kirby** are Chosen
visiters fo[r] the year insuing: **John Tucker** and **Henry
Tucker** are appointed to draw up **George Howland**s
Condemnation and bring it to ye next monthly meeting
The business of **Rochester** meeting Called and their visiters
for the insuing year are **Elisha Wing** and **Savory Clifton**
The Quarterly meeting Epistle was read and kindly accepted

3^d mo:　At a monthly meeting of friends held at our meeting
House in **Dartmouth** the 18:^th day of the 3:^d month 1724:
Dartmouth meeting Called **Judah Smith** appeared:
Rochester meeting Called **Nicolas Davis** appeared:
Henry Tucker and **John Tucker** hath drawn up **George
Howland**s Condemnation as appointed
Deliverance Smith and **Henry [Tucker?]** doth make report to
this meeting that the marriage between **Barnabas
Howland** and **Rebecca Lapham** was orderly Carried on
as far as they saw: **Henry Tucker** is appointed to
Read **George Howland**s Condemnation on a first at the
end of the meeting of Worship: between this and the
next monthly meeting: **Rochester** meeting Called no business

4th mo:　At a monthly meeting of friends held at our meeting
House in **Dartmouth** the 22:^d day of the 4th month 1724
Dartmouth meeting Called **William Wood** and **Judah Smith**
present: **Rochester** meeting Called **Stephen Wing** present
Henry Tucker hath read **George Howland**s Condemnation
as appointed and is as followeth – –
Whereas **George Howland** the Son of **Nathaniel Howland** of the
Town of **Dartmouth** in the County of **Bristol** in **New England**
deceased: the Said **George Howland** being a friends Child and hath
been Educated in the way of truth yet of Late although he hath
been exhorted and advised to ye Contrary by friends hath
proceeded in marriage out of the good order established amongst

us the people Called Quakers

We do therefore deny the Said **George Howland** to be one of us
yᵉ sᵈ people Sincerely desireing that he may Come to a true
Sence of his out going and by his circumspect walking before
God and amongst his people be received into the fold where
the great Shepherd is giving rest and peace to them that
are his: Given forth and Signed at our monthly meeting
held in **Dartmouth** the 18:ᵗʰ day of the 3:ᵈ month 1724:

Henry Tucker

John Lapham	**Joseph Taber**	**William Wood: junʳ**
Benjamin Howland	**Thomas Hathaway**	**Adam Mott**
Judah Smith	**Savory Clifton**	**Nicholas Lapham**
Josiah Merrihoo [Merihew]	**Nicholas Davis**	**Deliverance Smith**

Amos Taber Son of **Joseph Taber** of **Dartmouth** and **Elisabeth
Lapham** daughter of **John Lapham** of Sᵈ **Dartmouth** have
laid their Intentions of marriage to each other before this
meeting and was desired to wait til the next monthly meeting
for their answer and **Eliashib Smith** and **Henry Tucker** are
appointed to inquire into their clearness in respect to marriage
and Conversation and make return to yᵉ next monthly
meeting how they find things

The business of **Dartmouth** meeting Called **William Wood**
Nicolas Davis and **John Tucker** are appointed to attend
the Quarterly meeting next: and **John Tucker** and **Henry
Tucker** are appointed to draw upon account to yᵉ Quarterly
meeting: Rochester meeting no business:

5: mo: At a monthly meeting of friends held at our meeting house
In **Dartmouth** the 20ᵗʰ day of yᵉ 5:ᵗʰ month 1724
Dartmouth meeting Called **William Wood** and **Judah Smith**
appeared: **Rochester** mee[t]ing Called **Elisha Wing** present
William Wood and **John Tucker** hath attended yᵉ Quarterly
meeting as appointed: and **John Tucker** and **Henry
Tucker** hath drawn up an Epistle to the Quarterly meeting
as ordered: **Amos Taber** and **Elisabeth Lapham** appeared
at this meeting Desireing their answer as to their
takeing each other in marriage and nothing appearing
to hinder their sᵈ proceedings they had their answer
that they might proceed to take each other in marriage
in the good order of truth in Some Convenient time
before the next monthly meeting:

And **Deliverance Smith** and **Henry Tucker** are appoin
=ted to See their marriage Solemnised in the Good order
of truth and make return to the next monthly meeting
The business of **Dartmouth** meeting Called no business presented
No business from **Rochester** to this meeting:
The Quarterly meeting Epistle was read at this meeting
and well accepted: This meeting hath received 12 Small
Books of Caution to friends families set out by the
yearly meeting in **London** which was here Disposed for
the use of friends:

6 mo: At a monthly meeting of friends held at our meeting
House in **Dartmouth** the 17:th day of yᵉ 6:th month: 1724:
Dartmouth meeting Called **William Wood** and **Judah Smith**
appeared: **Rochester** meeting Called none appeared
There was Collected for the use of friends 0ᶠ = 08ˢ = 00
Deliverance Smith attended yᵉ ₍marriage₎ ~~Quarterly meeting~~
of **Amos Taber** and **Elisabeth Lapham** and doth make
Report to this meeting that it was Solemnised in the
Good order of truth
Jonathan Wood and **Peace Davis** have Laid their intentions
of marriage before this meeting and are desired to wait
till the next monthly meeting for their answer and
Robert Kirby and **John Russell** are appointed to make
Inquiry into their clearness wᵗʰ respect to marriage and Conversation
and make report to yᵉ next monthly meeting
And **Thomas Smith** Son of **Thomas Smith** of **Providence** in the
Colony of **Rhoad Island** and **Providence plantations** in **New England**
and **Sarah Russell** Daughter of **Joseph Russell junʳ** of **Dartmouth**
In yᵉ County of **Bristol** in **New England** have laid their intentions
of takeing each other in marrige before this meeting and are
Desired to wait till yᵉ next monthly meeting for their answer
And **Nathan Jene [Jenne]** Son of **Mark Jene [Jenne]** and **Pricilla Taber** Daughter
of **Thomas Taber** deceased both of **Dartmouth** have laid their
Intentions of marriage before this meeting and are Desired to
wait till yᵉ next monthly meeting for their answer
and **Thomas Hathaway** and **Nicolas Davis** are appointed to
make inquiery into their Clearness wᵗʰ respect to marriage
and Conversation and make return to yᵉ next monthly meeting

At a monthly meeting of friends held at our meeting House in
In **Dartmouth** yᵉ 21:ˢᵗ day of 7:th month 1724:

There was Collected for yᵉ use of friends 1ᶠ = 00ˢ = 06ᵈ
Dartmouth meeting Called **Judah Smith** & **William Wood**
present: **Rochester** meeting Called and **Stephen Wing** appeard
Jonathan Wood and **Peace Davis** appearing for their answer
and nothing appearing to hinder they had their answer that
they might proceed to take each other in marriage ˄in ye good order of truth in Some
Convenient time before the monthly meeting ~~mee~~ next:
and **James Tripp** and **Robert Kirby** are appointed to See their
marriage Solemnised in like order and make return to
the next monthly meeting:
And **Nathan Jene [Jenne]** and **Pricilla Taber** came to this meeting
for their answer as to taking each other in marriage and
things being inquierd into and nothing appearing to hinder
their intentions they had their answer that they might proceed
to take each other in marriage in the good order of truth
in Some Convenient time between this and the next monthly
meeting: and **Thomas Hathaway** and **Joseph Taber** are appointed to
See their marrige Solemnised in the good order of truth
and make report to yᵉ next monthly meeting how things
are Carried on
And **Simeon Gifford** Son of **Robert Gifford** of yᵉ town of
Dartmouth in the County of **Bristol** in **New England**
and **Susanna Jenkins** Daughter **Zachary Jenkins** of
KingsTown in the Colony of **Rhoad Island** and **Providence**
plantations in **New England** deceased have laid their
Intentions of takeing each other in marriage before this
meeting and are Desired to wait til yᵉ next monthly meet
=ing for their answer: and **William Wood** and **Robert Kirby**
are appointed to make inquiry into their Clearness
wᵗʰ Respect to marriage and Conversation and make
Return to yᵉ next monthly meeting
And **John Tucker** is appointed to Draw up a certificate
for **Daniel Goddard**:
And There was a paper presented to this meeting Signed
by **George Soule** being an acknowledgmen[t] of his outgoings
in his Disorderly marriage and another from his wife
Lidia Soule of yᵉ Same tenour which was both read
in this meeting and approved and they the Sᵈ **George**
Soule and his wife **Lidia Soule** to Come into unity and be
under the Care of friends their Sᵈ acknowledgements are as followeth

To the monthly meeting of friends to be held in **Dartmouth**
the 21 day of yᵉ 7:ᵗʰ month 1724: Whereas I did in the year 1719
proceed in marriage Contrary to yᵉ Good order and advice of friends
amongst whome I was brought up and had my Education and
for the abovesᵈ Disorderly proceedings I was Justly Denyed to
be one in unity with them the people Called Quakers Whome
I Do beleive to be the Church of God: Truth hath appeared to
me so lovely that it Causeth me to have a mind to be reconsiled
and to Condemn my outgoings in not keepin to yᵉ Good order of
the Church and advice of friends in that weighty consideration
of Marriage and as for my trespases I Desire God to forgive me
and that friends would pass it by and receive me into unity again

George Soule

To the monthly meeting of men and women friends in **Dartmouth**
to be held the 21ˢᵗ day of yᵉ 7ᵗʰ month 1724:
Whereas in the year 1719: I proceeded in marriage Contrary to the
good order of truth and advice of friends among whome I have been
brought up and had any Education and for my Disorderly proceeding
I was Justly denied to be one in unity wᵗʰ them the peple of
God Called Quakers Wherein I frely do acknowledg my fault
and I Do desire ~~to be one in unity~~ that God would forgive me
my trespases and that friends would pass it by and I to come
under the Care of friends again

Lidia Soule – –

And **Nicolas Davis Joseph Taber Joseph Russell** junʳ and
Henry Tucker are appointed to attend yᵉ Quarterly meeting
And **John Tucker** and **Henry Tucker** are appointed to Draw
up an account to yᵉ Quarterly meeting – – – – –

_8:ᵗʰ mo:_ At a monthly meeting of friends held at our meeting house
in **Dartmouth** the 19:ᵗʰ day of yᵉ 8:ᵗʰ month: 1724:
Dartmouth meeting Called **James Barker** and **Henry Tucker**
appeared: **Rochester** meeting Called none appeared:
Thomas Smith junʳ of **Providence** and **Sarah Russell** daughter
of **Joseph Russell** junʳ of **Dartmouth** Came to this meeting
and desired their answer as to yᵉ takeing each other in
marriage and nothing appearing to hinder their intentions
The sᵈ **Smith** having a certificate from **Providence** ~~of~~
monthly meeting of his Clearness they had their answer
that they might proceed to take each
other in marriage in Some Convenient time before the

next monthly meeting and **Deliverance Smith** and
Henry Tucker are appointed to See their marriag in
Like manner Solemnized:
Robert Kirby makes report to this meeting that he hath
attended the marriage of **Jonathan Wood** and **Peace Davis**
and it was performed in the order of truth as far as he Saw
And **Joseph Taber** makes report to this meeting that
he was at the marriage of **Nathan Jene [Jenne]** and **Pricilla
Taber** and it was Solemnized in the order of truth as
far as he saw: **John Tucker** and **Henry Tucker** hath
Drawn up an account to yᵉ Quarterly meeting as appointed
and **Joseph Taber** and **Henry Tucker** hath attended yᵉ
Quarterly meeting as appointed – –
And **John Lapham** and **John Tucker** are appointed to assist
the women in Drawing Something up to Clear Truth of
The disorderly proceeding of **Daborah [Deborah] Smith** the daughter
of **Hezekiah Smith** of **Dartmouth** her proceeding in
marriage Contrary to the good order established amongst
friends: And **Eliashib Smith** and **Josiah Merihoo [Merihew]** are
appointed to Labour with **Edward Wing** to see whither he
will make Sattisfaction for his refusing to take up with
the advice of friends in that case between **William Hart**
and him selfe and to advise him to appear at our next
monthly meeting and they to make return to the Same
of their doings in that Case:

9:ᵗʰ mo: At a monthly meeting of friends held at our meeting house
in **Dartmouth** the 16:ᵗʰ day of yᵉ 9:ᵗʰ month 1724:
Dartmouth meeting Called **William Wood** & **Judah Smith**
appeared **Rochester** meeting Called **Elisha Wing** appeared
Henry Tucker ~~and~~ doth make report to this meeting that
Thomas Smith and **Sarah Russels [Russells]** marriage was consimated
in the good order of truth.
A paper was presented to this by order of the preparitive
meeting Signed by **Jonathan Ricketson** and his wife **Abigal
Ricketson** which was read Considered and approved and
Deliverance Smith is appointed to read yᵉ Same publickly
on a first day at the end of the meeting of worship and
is as followeth
To the monthly meeting of friends to be held in **Dartm**ₒᵤₜₕ

the 16th day of ye 9:th month 1724: Whereas we in the
year 1710 proceeded in marriage Contrary to the good orders of
Friends whereof we do Condemn our outgoings and Count our
selves Justly Denied and we Do Desire that God would forgive
us and that friends would pass it by so that we may be in
unity with them again   **Jonathan Ricketson**

                                      Abigal Ricketson

And here was Signed a condemnation against **Daborah Read**
now wife of **Thos Read** Concerning her going out of the good
order of friends in marriage and is as followeth

Whereas **Deborah** ~~Read~~ **Smith** Daughter of **Hezekiah**
Smith of **Dartmouth** in the County **Bristol** in **New England**
having been Educated among friends her parents professing
them selves to be of the people called Quakers hath of Late
proceeded in marriage Contrary to the good order established
amongst us on that account we do therefore give this forth
as a publick testimony against sd disorderly proceeding
and also do deny the Said **Deborah** ~~Read~~ now wife of **Thomas**
Read to be of us the people Called Quaker Sincerely desireing
that if it be the will of God Shee may Come to a Sight and
Sence of her out goings in all respects and by an unfeigned
repentance find acceptance with the Lord and His People
Signed at our meeting held in **Dartmouth** the 16th day of the
ninth month 1724:   Mary Lapham

John Tucker	**Henry Tucker**	**Elisabeth Russell**
Benjamin Howland	**Joseph Russell Junr**	**Mehetabel Burril [Burrel]**
John Lapham	**Peleg Slocum**	**Phebe Tucker**
Nicolas Davis	**Jabez Barker**	**Mary Russell:**
Judah Smith	**Mary Slocum**	**Mary Laton [Lawton]**

And **Henry Tucker** is appointed to read the Same ~~sd~~
publickly on a first day at the end of the meeting of Worship
And it is agreed ~~that~~ at this meeting that our meeting house
Should be enlarged and to have it finnished before next
Yearly meeting: And a Subscribtion of 20 pounds is agreed
upon at this meeting for **John Handson [Hanson]** a friend Living at
Dover to the Eastward of **Boston** who has of Late had his
Wife and Seaveral Children Carried away by the Indians
and also his beding and other Cloathing and **John Tucker**
is appointed to receave the mony and send it by the first
oppertunity – – – – –

10:th mo: At a monthly meeting of friends held at our meeting house
In **Dartmouth** the 21st day of the 10th month 1724:
Dartmouth meeting Called **Judah Smith** and **William Wood**
appeared: **Rochester** meeting Called **Nicolas Davis** appeared
Jedediah Wood and **Keziah Summers** having laid their intenti
=ons of marriage before this meeting and was Desired to wait
til the next monthly meeting for ther answer
and **Nicolas Davis** and **John Lapham** are appointed to make
inquiry into their Clearness and make return to the next
monthly meeting and **David Irish junr** and **Jeneverath**
Summers haveing laid their intentions of marriage before
this meeting was desired to wait until ye next monthly
meeting for their answer and **Thomas Hathaway** and **Joseph**
Taber are appointed to make inquiery into their clearness
and make return to the next monthly meeting
And there was Collected for the use of friends 0£ – 12s = 06d:
Deliverance Smith hath read **Jonathan Ricketson** and his
wives [*sic*] acknowledgments according to the order of ye last monthly
meeting and **Henry Tucker** hath read **Deborah** now wife of
Thomas Read her Condemnation as appointed:
and there was Collected at this meeting 10£: pounds for **John**
Hanson and **John Tucker** is appointed to send it to **Benjamin**
Bagnel [**Bagnall**] in **Boston:**
Henry Tucker John Russell and **John Tucker** are appointed
as trustees to make an addition to our meeting House:
John Tucker and **Henry Tucker** are appointed to oversee
the meeting house the insuing year
And **Benjamin Howland** is appointed to pay to **John Tucker**
one pound and ten Shillings: and **William Wood** and **Eliashib**
Smith are appointed to attend the Quarterly meeting next
and **Benjamin Howland** and **Deliverance Smith** are appointed
to draw up an account and Send it to the quarterly meeting

11:th mo: At a monthly meeting of friends held at our meeting house in **Dartmouth**
The 18:th day of the 11:th month 1724/5
Dartmouth meeting Called **Judah Smith** and **William Wood** appeared
Rochester meeting Called **John Wing** appeared
David Irish and **Jeneverah Summers** came for their answer and
all things appearing Clear they had their answer that they might
proceed to take each other in marriage in the good order of truth in
Some Convenient time between this and next monthly meeting

And **Thomas Hathaway** and **Joseph Taber** are appointed to Se[e] their
marriag[e] Selemnized [Solemnized] in the good order of truth
Nicolas Davis and **Hannah Wood** Daughter of **William Wood**
of **Dartmouth** in the County of **Bristol** in **New England**
have laid their intentions of taking each other in marriage
and are Desired to wait until the next monthly meeting for
their answer and **John Wing** and **Joseph Taber** are appointed
to make inspection into their clearness and make return
to yᵉ next monthly meeting: And **John Tucker** hath Sent the
mony to **Benjamin Bagnel** as appointed:
Benjamin Howland has paid 1£ = 10ˢ = 00 as to **John Tucker** as appoinₜₑd
And **Deliverance Smith** hath drawn up a Epistle and Sent
it to the Quarterly meeting as ordered: **Eliashib Smith**
hath attended the Quarterly meeting as appointed
This meeting is Still Dissattisfied with **Edward Wing** and
Eliashib Smith is appointed to advise him to appear at our
next monthly meeting: The Quarterly meeting Epistle
was Read at this meeting and kindly accepted:

_12:ᵗʰ mo:_ At a monthly meeting of friends held at our meeting house
in **Dartmouth** the 15:ᵗʰ day of yᵉ 12ᵗʰ month 1724/25
Dartmouth meeting Called **Judah Smith** and **Benjamin**
Howland present **Rochester** meeting Called **Stephen Wing** present
Jedediah Wood and **Keziah Summers** Came for their answer
and friends haveing made inquiery and finding nothing to
hinder they had their answer that they might proceed to take
Each other in marriage in the good order of truth in Some
Convenient time between this and the next monthly meeting
and **James Tripp** and **John Tucker** ˏʲᵘⁿʳ are Chose to See it Consimated
in the abovesᵈ order: and make report to the next monthly
meeting: And **Nicolas Davis** and **Hannah Wood** came to this
meeting for their answer and friends haveing made inquiery
into their clearness and finding nothing to hinder they had
Their answer that they might proceed to take each other
in marriage in Some Convenient time between this and the
next monthly meeting and **Judah Smith** and **Josiah Merihoo** [Merihew]
are Chose to See their marriage Solemnized in the good order
of truth and make return to the next monthly meeting:
Joseph Taber makes return to this meeting that **David Irish**
Jeneverah Summers their marriage was performed in the
Good order of truth:

A letter was presented to this meeting from **George Cornel** [**Cornell**]
and **Deliverance Smith** and **Henry Tucker** is to write an
answer to **George Cornel**: **Edward Wing** appeared at this
meeting as was Desired and Saith he is Sorry that he did not
take the advice of friends: **Deliverance Smith** is appointed
To make up the monthly meetings accounts with **Benjamin
Howland**: **John Howland** doth give in an acknowledgment
to this meeting of his ou[t]going in his marriage and it was
accepted and **Deliverance Smith** is appointed to read it
on a first day between this and the next monthly meeting
The business of **Rehester** [**Rochester**] meeting Called and none presented:

<u>1725</u>   At a monthly meeting of friends held at our meeting house
<u>1:ˢᵗ mo</u>   in **Dartmouth** the 15ᵗʰ day of yᵉ 1:ˢᵗ month 1725:
Dartmouth meeting Called **Wᵐ Wood** and **Judah Smith**
appeared = **Rochester** meeting Called **Elisha Wing** appeared
John Tucker junʳ = makes report to this meeting that the mar
=riage of **Jedediah Wood** and **Keziah Summers** was performed
in the good order of truth: And **Judah Smith** and **Josiah Merrihoo** [**Merihew**]
doth make report to this meeting that the marriage between
Nicolas Davis and **Hannah Wood** was Selemnized in the good
order of truth: **Deliverance Smith** hath read **John Howland**s
acknowledgment of his out going in marriage as appointed
William Wood and **Josiah Merihoo** [**Merihew**] are appointed to make inquiry
into **Francis Tripps** clearness with respect to marriage and
Conversation and write him a certificate if the[y] find nothing to
hinder his proceedings **Elisha Wing Deliverance Smith** and **Thoˢ**
:   **Hathaway** are appointed to attend the Quarterly meeting next
and this meeting is adjourned til the fir[st] 6 day in yᵉ 2:ᵈ month next
This meeting being met according to adjour[n]ment this: 2:ᵈ of yᵉ 2ᵈ m: 1725
The visiters gives this meeting an account of their Service in the
visiting the families of friends and they find nothing but that
things for the most part pretty well and their visits well accepted
And **John Tucker** and **Henry Tucker** are appointed to draw up an
Epistle to the Quarterly meeting – – – – –

<u>2:ᵈ mo</u>:   At a monthly meeting of friends held at our meeting House in
Dartmouth the 19:ᵗʰ day of the 2ᵈ month 1725:
Dartmouth meeting Called **William Wood and Judah Smith** present
Rochester meeting Called **Nicolas Davis** present
Simeon Gifford Son of **Robert Gifford** of **Dartmouth** in the County
of **Bristol** in **New England** and **Susanna Jenkins** Daughter of

Zachary Jenkins of **Kingston** in the Colony of **Rhoad Island** and
Providence plantations in **New England** deceased appeared at this
meeting for their answer as to their intentions of taking each
other in marriage and nothing appearing to hinder they had
their answer that they might proceed to take each other in
marriage in the good order of friends in Some Convenient
time between this and the next monthly meeting and
Wᵐ Wood and **Robert Kirby** are appointed to See it in Like
manner performed and make return to the next monthly
meeting: And **Elisha Wing** hath attended yᵉ Quarterly
meeting as appointed: And **John Tucker** hath drawn up an
account to the Quarterly meeting as appointed
The Epistle of our yearly meeting was read at this meeting
and well accepted: – – – – –

_3:ᵈ mo:_ At a monthly meeting of friends held at our meeting house in
Dartmouth the 17:ᵗʰ day of yᵉ 3:ᵈ month 1725:
Dartmouth meeting Called **Wᵐ Wood** and **Benjamin Howland**
present: **Rochester** meeting Called **Nicolas Davis** ap˄ᵖeared
William Wood makes report to this meeting that the
marriage between **Simeon Gifford** and **Susanna Jenkins** was
accomplished in the Good order of friends.
It is agreed at this meeting that there should be ad[d]ed to **Cushnot**
one meeting more in a month and when it So happens that
there is five first dayes then there is two to be ad[d]ed:
and them that are added to be kept at **Joseph Tabers**:
This meeting makes a new Choice of visiters for **Rochester**
Savory Clifton and **Elisha Wing**: for **Dartmouth Thomas Hathaway**
Benjamin Allen Eliashib Smith John Lapham William Wood
and **Robert Kirby**: This meeting is adjourned until the first
fourth day in the fourth month next
This meeting being met according to adjournment
this 2:ᵈ day of the 4:ᵗʰ month 1725:
The accounts of Some Sufferings of **Peleg Slocum** and
John Tucker haveing their creatures taken away of from
Their Islands ˄called Elisabeths Islands by Distraint by **John Mayhu** [**Mayhew**] Constable
 of **Chilmark**
was presented to this meeting Taken from **Peleg Slocum** eighty
Sheep for the Priests rate and towards the building a
Presbyterian meeting house yᵉ said Sheep was Sold for 34ᶠ= 00 = 00
Demand was 26: pounds 12 Shilling and 11 pence:

And taken from **John Tucker** on yᵉ Like occation one
Horce Sold for 10ᵉ: and one heffer Sold for 2 pounds ten Shillings
demand was 7ᵉ –: 15ˢ =: 04ᵈ all taken in yᵉ year 1724:
the abovesᵈ sufferings was perused and ordered to be sent to the
~~Quarterly~~ ʸᵉᵃʳˡʸ meeting at **Rhoad Island**

4ᵗʰ mo: At a monthly meeting of friends held at our meeting house
in **Dartmouth** yᵉ 21:ˢᵗ day of the 4:ᵗʰ month 1725:
There was Collected for the use of friends 3ᵉ: 03ˢ = 09ᵈ:
Dartmouth meeting Called **Wᵐ Wood** and **Judah Smith**
present: **Rochester** meeting Called **Elisha Wing** present
Wᵐ Wood and **Deliverance Smith** and **Elisha Wing** are
appointed to attend the Quarterly meeting next
and **John Tucker** and **Henry Tucker** are appointed to draw
an Epistle to the Quarterly meeting next
And it is agreed that friends Come to a Subscribtion to
help the prisoners that Suffered imprisonment at **Bristol**
for not makeing the rates for **Samuel Hunt** a presbyterian
minister: The prisoners names are **John Akin Philip Taber**
Jacob Taber and **Beriah Goddard** and ~~bring in~~ bring in the
Subscribtion to the next monthly meeting – – – – –

5ᵗʰ mo: At a monthly meeting of friends held at our meeting House
in **Dartmouth** the 19ᵗʰ day of yᵉ 5ᵗʰ month 1725:
Dartmouth meeting Called **William Wood** and **Judah Smith**
appeared: **Rochester** meeting Called **Nicolas Davis** appeared
And **Deliverance Smith** and **William Wood** hath attended the
Quarterly meeting as appointed and **John Tucker** hath sent
an Epistle to yᵉ Quarterly meeting and the quarterly meeting
Epistle was read and kindly accepted and the request therein
agreed to be answered: And this meeting hath signed a Condem
=nation against **Content Briggs** for her going out of the unity
of friends in her marriage: and is as followeth:
Whereas **Content Howland** Daughter of **Nathaniel Howland**
deceased and **Rose Howland** his widow of **Dartmouth** in the county
of **Bristol** in **New England**: having been Educated amongst friends
her parents professing them Selves to be of the people Called
Quakers hath of Late proceeded in marriage Contrary to the
good order established amongst us on that account we do therefore
Give this forth as a publick Testimony against the Said disorderly
proceeding and also do deny yᵉ said **Content** now wife of
Weston Briggs to be of us the people Called Quakers Sincerely

Desireing that if it be the will of god Shee may Come to a sight
and Sence of this and all other her outgoings and by an
unfeigned repentance find mercy with the Lord and his
people: Signed at our monthly meeting held in **Dartmouth**
the 19:th day of the 5:th month 1725
~~John Tucker : Benjamin Howland : Deliverance Smith~~
William Wood · **Josiah Merihoo [Merihew]** · **Peleg Slocum**
Joseph Taber · **John Lapham** · **Jabez Barker** · **Judah Smith**
Deliverance Smith · **Eliashib Smith** · **James Barker**
Nicolas Davis · **Jonathan Wood** – –
Mary Slocum · **Hannah Tucker** · **Rachel Allen** · **Dinah Smith**
MaryLaton[Lawton] · **HopeMerihoo[Merihew]** · **MaryLapham** · **PhebeTucker**
Mary Smith · **Hannah Howland** · **Ruth Tucker** · **Rebecca Barker**
And **Henry Tucker** is appointed to read it at the Conclution of the
meeting of worship on a first day before the next monthly meeting
No business presented from **rochester** meeting – – – – –

6th: *mo:* At a monthly meeting of friends held at our meeting house
in **Dartmouth** yᵉ 16th day of yᵉ 6th month 1725:
Dartmouth meeting Called **Wᵐ Wood** and **Benjamin Howland**
appeared: **Rochester** meeting Called **Nicolas Davis** appeared
And **Henry Tucker** hath read **Content Brigg**es Condemnation
as appointed. This meeting hath gathered yᵉ 10 pounds
according to the request of yᵉ Quarterly meeting and
Joseph Russell junʳ: is to send the mony to Providence to
Samuel Aldrage
Deliverance Smith hath made up the monthly meetings
accompts w:th **Benjamin Howland** as appointed and there
Remains in the Stock 8£: 07ˢ: 10ᵈ
The business of **Dartmouth** meeting Called and no business appeared

7th *mo:* At a monthly meeting of friends held at our meeting
House in **Dartmouth** y:ᵉ 20th day of y:ᵉ 7th month 1725:
Dartmouth meeting Called **William Wood** and **Benjamin**
Howland appeared: **Rochester** meeting Called **Elisha Wing** present
Joseph Russell junʳ: hath sent yᵉ 10[lb?] for the building of Providence
meeting house as appointed:
There was Collected at this meeting for y:ᵉ use of friends 13ˢ = 0ᵈ
Henry Tucker and **John Lapham** and **Nicholas Davis** are
appointed to attend y:ᵉ Quarterly meeting **Deliverance Smith**
and **Judah Smith** is appointed to draw an account to yᵉ quarterly meeting

8ᵗʰ mo: At a monthly meeting of friends held at our meeting
House in **Dartmouth** y:ᵉ 18:ᵗʰ day of y:ᵉ 8:ᵗʰ month 1725:
The Several meetings thereto Called upon for **Dartmouth**
Benjamin Howland and **Judah Smith** appeared for **Rochester**
none appeared
Nicholas Davis and **Henry Tucker** hath attended y.ᵉ Quarterly
meeting as appointed: and **Deliverance Smith** and **Judah Smith**
hath drawn up an account and sent it to y.ᵉ Quarterly
meeting as appointed: The business of **Dartmouth** meeting
Called and y:ᵉ Quarterly meeting Epistle was read and
at this meeting and well accepted:
And **Isaac Smith** desires lines of recommendation from
this meeting upon y.ᵉ account of his traviling to the west
ward which is granted and **John Tucker** is to sign it in
behalfe of the meeting

9:ᵗʰ mo At a monthly meeting of friends held at our meeting house in
Dartmouth the 15th day of yᵉ 9ᵗʰ month 1725:
The Seaverall meetings thereto belonging Called upon for **Dartmouth**
William Wood and **John Lapham** present for **Rochester**
Elisha Wing present: The business of **Dartmouth** meeting
Called: It is agreed that our old meeting House should be enlarged
and finnished against our next yearly meeting – –
And **Henry Tucker** and **John Russell** are chose to See it finnishₑ𝑑
in order: and it is also agreed ^at this meeting that friends Come to a Subsirb_tion
to defray the Charge of our petetioning to England for friends
case from Suffering under y:ᵉ Presbyterian ministers – –
This meeting being informed that **Seth Allen** y:ᵉ Son of
Ebenezer Allen deceased of **Dartmouth** in the **County of Bristol**
in **New England** doth desire a Certificate of his clearness as
to marriage: **Eliashib Smith** and **John Russell** is appointed to
See into his Clearness and Conversation and bring in how
they find things to y:ᵉ next monthly meeting – –
A paper being presented by the womens meeting concerning
Desire howlads out goings which was read and accepted
and is as followeth – –
To y:ᵉ monthly meeting of friends to be held in **Dartmouth**
The 15:ᵗʰ day of y:ᵉ 9ᵗʰ month 1725:
Whereas I was Educated and brought up among friends
but for want of keeping to y.ᵉ principle of truth ~~in my~~
and friends in time past but have committed sin an iniqui_ty

which was a disgrace to me and a dishonour to truth and
friends for which I was justly denied to be one in Society
w:th them the people Called Quakers and for my trans
=gression and Sin I have been often Sorry and troubled for it
and now do desire that the Lord would forgive mee my Sin
and that friends would pass it by and receive me under
their Care again – –

Desire Howland

and **Henry Tucker** is ordered to read the above written
acknowledgement on a first day at the end of the meeting of
worship between this and the next monthly meeting
This meeting is adjourned til next fourth day come week
This meeting being mett according to adjournment this
24th day of y:e 9:th month 1725:
it being proposed that friends hath an offer of Some
Land at **Cushnet** to build a meeting house upon and
Nicholas Davis and **John Tucker** are appointed to vew
and See whither it be a place Convenient and know
the termes that we may have it upon and make return
to ye next monthly meeting
And there was Collected at this meeting for ye use of friend,
18 Shillings and 6 pence – – – – –

_10th mo:_　At a monthly meeting of friends held at our meeting
House in **Dartmouth** y:e 20th day of y:e 10th month 1725
The Seaveral meetings ther unt belonging Called upon for
Dartmouth Benjamin Howland and **Judah Smith** present
for **Rochester Elisha Wing** present: **Eliashib Smith**
and **John Russell** makes report to this meeting that
they have made enquiery into **Seth Allen**, Clearness as to
marriage and they find nothing but that he is Clear
from any intanglement here and he doth promise to
the order of friends in his Conversation and **John Tucker**
is ~~to~~ appointed to Draw a Certificate for Sd **Allen** and Sign
it in behalfe of y:e ^monthly meeting. and **Henry Tucker** hath read
Desire Howlands acknowledgment of her out goings
according to y:e order of the last monthly meeting
And **Nicholas Davis Joseph Taber** and **Thomas Hathaway**
hath vewed the land at **Cushnot** as appointed but have
not agreed w̲th̲ ye owner which is referd to y:e next
monthly meeting: == The business of **Dartmouth** meeting

Called this meeting orders **Benjamin Howland** to pay
2 pounds out of y:ᵉ Stock to **John Tucker** & **Henry Tucker**
for keeping the meeting House for y:ᵉ year past – –
and **John Tucker** & **Henry Tucker** are Chose to keep the
meeting house for the year ensuing:
And **Henry Tucker** and **Elisha Wing** are appointed to attend
the quarterly meeting and **John Tucker** and **Henry Tucker**
appointed to draw up an Epistle to y:ᵉ Quarterly meeting
The business of **Rochester** meeting called and no business presented

_11ᵗʰ mo:_ At a monthly meeting of friends held at our meeting House in
Dartmouth the 17:ᵗʰ day of y:ᵉ 11:ᵗʰ month 17 ²⁵/₂₆:
The Seaveral meetings there unto belonging Called upon for
Dartmouth Deliverance Smith and **Josiah Merihoo** present
for **Rochester Nicholas Davis** present – –
John Lapham junʳ of **Dartmouth** ~~of~~ In the Country
of **Bristol** in **New England** and **Desire Howland** Daughter
of **Benjamin Howland** of Sᵈ **Dartmouth** Laid their intentions
of ^taking each other in Marriage before this meeting and was desired to wait
til y:ᵉ next monthly meeting for their answer and
Josiah Merihoo and **Joseph Russell** junʳ are appointed to
inquire into their clearness and make return to the
next monthly meeting how they find things – –
Benjamin Howland hath paid **John Tucker** & **Henry Tucker**
forty Shillings as appointed and **Elisha Wing** and **Henry
Tucker** hath attended y:ᵉ Quarterly meeting as appointed
The business of **Rochester** meeting Called no business presented
The Epistle y.ᵉ Quarterly meeting was read and well accepted

_12ᵗʰ mo:_ At a monthly meeting of friends held at our meeting house
in **Dartmouth** y:ᵉ 21ˢᵗ day of y.ᵉ 12ᵗʰ month 17 ²⁵/₂₆:
The overseers Called upon for **Dartmouth William Wood**
and **Deliverance Smith** present: for **Rochester**
Nicolas Davis present: **John Lapham** junʳ: and **Desire
Howland** appeared at this meeting for their answer and
things being inquired into and nothing appearing to hinder
their Intentions they had their answer that they were
permited to take ~~a~~ each other in marriage and **Joseph
Russell** and **Josiah Merihoo** are appointed to See it accomplishₑd
and they are permitted to take each other on a week day
after y:ᵉ meeting of worship is over – –

George Smith Son of **Deliverance Smith** and **Elisabeth**
Allin [Allen] Daughter of **Increase Allin** deceased both of **Dartmouth**
Laid their intentions of ^takeing each other in marriage before this meeting and they
was Desired to wait for their answer til the next monthly
meeting and **Henry Tucker** and **John Russell** are appointed to
inquire into their Clearness with respect to marriage and
Conversation and make return to yᵉ next monthly meeting
how they find things:
And **Thomas Hathaway**s house being burnt it is proposed
to this meeting whither it may be best to have the meeting
kept that was formerly at **Thoˢ Hathaway,** and it is
Concluded that it be kept for this winter where he now dwells
Rochester preparetive meeting hath sent us five pounds
for the use of friends: – – – – –

_1726:_　At a monthly meeting of friends held at our meeting house
_1ˢᵗ mo:_　in **Dartmouth** y:ᵉ 21:ˢᵗ day of y:ᵉ 1ˢᵗ month 17 ²⁵/₂₆
The Seaveral meeting therunto belonging Called upon
for **Dartmouth William Wood** and **Deliverance Smith** present
for **Rochester** none appeared:
George Smith and **Elisabeth Allin** appeared at this meting
for their answer and things appearing Clear they had their
answer that they might proceed to take each other in
marriage in the good order of truth in Some Convenient time
before yᵉ next monthly meeting and **Henry Tucker** and **John**
Russell are appointed to See it in Like manner performed
And **John Tippits [Tibbets?]** of **Grnnage [Greenwich]** in the **Colony of Rhoad Island**
and Providence plantaons in New England and **Sarah Soule**
the Daughter of **George Soule** of **Dartmouth** in y:ᵉ County of
Bristol in **New England** deceased: have laid their intentions
of taking each other in marriage before this meeting
and were desired to wait for their answer til the next
monthly meeting And **Josiah Merihoo [Merrihew]** and **Joseph Russell**
make report to this meeting that they have attended the
marriage between **John Lapham junʳ** and **Desire Howland**
And they Said nothing but things was orderly performed
And **John Tucker** and **Deliverance Smith** ar appointed to draw
an Epistle to y:ᵉ Quarterly meeting next and **John Tucker**
and **William Wood are** appointed to attend yᵉ Same
and this meeting is adjourned til yᵉ first day of y:ᵉ 2:ᵈ month next

2:ᵈ mo: At a monthly meeting of friends held at our meeting
House by adjournment the first day of y:ᵉ 2ᵈ month 1726
The visiters give in their account that they have visited
friends families and they find things pretty well for the
most part as far as they saw – – – – –

At a monthly meeting of friends held at our meeting
House in **Dartmouth** the 18ᵗʰ day of y:ᵉ 2ᵈ month 1726:
The **Seaveral** meetings thereunto belonging Called upon
for **Dartmouth Deliverance Smith** and **John Lapham**
present for **Rochester Nicolas Davis** present
John Tucker hath drawn an epistle to yᵉ Quarterly meeting
as appointed and also attended yᵉ same
And **John Tippits [Tibbets]** and **Sarah Soule** Came to this meeting for
Their answer and nothing appearing to hinder their intentions
and y:ᵉ Sᵈ **John Tippits** haveing a Certificate from the monthly
meeting where he belongs they had their answer that they
might proceed to take each other in marriage in the good
order of truth in Some Convenient time before next
monthly meeting and **W:ᵐ Wood** and **James Tripp** are
appointed to See it accordingly performed and make return
to yᵉ next monthly meeting – –
And **John Russell** y:ᵉ Son of **John Russell** Late of **Dartmouth**
deceased and **Joanna Tucker** daughter of **Abraham Tucker**
of Sᵈ **Dartmouth** deceased Signefied to this meeting their
intentions of taking each other in marriage: to this meeting
and they was desired to wait til the next monthly meeting
for their answer and **Eliashib Smith** and **John Lapham**
Are appointed to make inquiery into their Clearness and make
return to yᵉ: next monthly meeting how they find things
& there was Collected for y:ᵉ use of friends £1 = 02ˢ : 6ᵈ
& there was Collected by **Rochester** friends to defend our case
in **Old England** against the hireling Priests £3 = 0ˢ ⁼ 0ᵈ
and by friends in **Dartmouth** – –   2 = 5 =0

3ᵈ mo: At a monthly meeting of friends held at our meeting
House in **Dartmouth** y:ᵉ 16:ᵗʰ day of y:ᵉ 3ᵈ month 1726:
The **Seaveral** meetings thereto belonginging Called upon
for **Dartmouth Wᵐ Wood** and **Deliverance Smith** present
for Rochester **Stephen Wing** present – –
John Russell and **Joanna Tucker** appeared at this meeting
for their answer as to taking each other in marriage

inquiery being made into their clearness and nothing
appearing to hinder their intentions they had their answer
that they might proceed to take each other in marriage
in the good order of truth and **John Lapham** and
Eliashib Smith are appointed to See it accomplished in
like manner and make return to y:ᵉ next monthly
meeting: And **James Tripp** and **Wᵐ Wood** hath attended
John Tippits [Tibbets] and **Sarah Soule**s marriage and they make
report that it was Solemnized in yᵉ good order of truth
The business of **Dartmouth** meeting Called
This meeting doth agrea to raise mony to defray the
Charge of enlargeing our meeting house
Rochester meeting Called and no business presented

4ᵗʰ _mo:_   At a monthly meeting of friends held at our meeting
House in **Dartmouth** y:ᵉ 20:ᵗʰ day of y:ᵉ 4ᵗʰ: month 1726
Dartmouth meeting Called **W:ᵐ Wood** and **Judah Smith** present
:   **Rochester** meeting Called **Elisha Wing** present
Eliashib Smith and **John Lapham** makes report to
this meeting that the marriag between **John Russell**
And **Joanna Tucker** was Solemnized in y:ᵉ good order of
Truth: The business of **Dartmouth** meeting Called:
This meeting doth appoint **John Tucker** and **Deliverance
Smith** to draw up an Epistle to y:ᵉ Quarterly meeting
And **W:ᵐ Wood Elisha Wing** and **Nicolas Davis** are appoin_ted_
to attend y:ᵉ Quarterly meeting:
And this meeting Doth make a new Choice of visiters
and **W:ᵐ Wood John Tucker John Lapham Joseph Taber**
and **Joseph Russell junʳ**: are Chosen visiters for y:ᵉ insuing
year: The business of **Rochester** meeting Called and
Elisha Wing and **Savory Clifton** are Continued visiters
for y:ᵉ year insuing

5ᵗʰ _mo:_   At a monthly meeting of friends friends held at our meet=
=ing House in **Dartmouth** y:ᵉ 18ᵗʰ Day of y:ᵉ 5:ᵗʰ month 1726:
The Seavearal meetings thereunto belonging Called upon
for **Dartmouth W:ᵐ Wood** present: for **Rochester Elisha
Wing** present: **John Tucker** and **Deliverance Smith** hath
Sent an Epistle to y:ᵉ Quarterly meeting as appointed
and **W:ᵐ Wood** and **Nicolas Davis** hath attended y:ᵉ Quarterly
meeting as appointed:
And there was Collected for the use of friends – – £0 – 19ˢ = 05ᵈ

The business of **Dartmouth** meeting Called the Quarterly
meeting Epistle was read at this meeting and well accepted
And the: 16: pounds as is therein desired to be raised and
paid by the yearly meeting at **Rhoad Island** is agreed to
This meeting being informed that **Abigal Wing** daughter
of **Matthew Wing** Late of **Dartmouth** deceased hath proceeded
in marriage Contrary to the good order of friends and
John Tucker is appointed with y:ᵉ women to Draw up her
Condemnation in order to be Signed at y:ᵉ next monthly
meeting: **Rochester** meeting business Called and none presented

_6 mo:_ At a monthly meeting of friends held at our meeting
House in **Dartmouth** yᵉ 15ᵗʰ day of yᵉ 6ᵗʰ month 1726
Dartmouth meeting Called **Benjamin Howland** and **John
Lapham** appeared: **Rochester** meeting Called **Elisha Wing**
present and **Abigail Wing**s condemnation being Signed
Henry Tucker is appointed to read it in Some Convenient
time between this and yᵉ next monthly meeting:
The business of **Rochester** meeting Called & no business presenₜₑd

_7ᵗʰ mo:_ At a monthly meeting of friends held at our meeting
House in **Dartmouth** y:ᵉ 19:ᵗʰ day of yᵉ 7:ᵗʰ month 1726
The Seaveral meetings thereunto belonging Called upon for
Dartmouth W:ᵐ **Wood** and **Deliverance Smith** present
for **Rochester Elisha Wing** present
Henry Tucker hath read **Abigal** now wife of **David
Durfie [Durfee]** her Condemnation and is as followeth:
Seth Celly son of **Jeremy Celly** of **yarmouth** in the County
of **Barnstable** in **New England** and **Mehetabel Wing** daughter
of **Elisha Wing** of **Rochester** in y:ᵉ County of **Plymouth** in
New England having laid their intentions of takeing each
other in marriage before this meeting they were desired
to wait till y:ᵉ next monthly meeting for their answer
and **Nicolas Lapham** Desires a certificate as to his clearness
in respect to marriage and Conversation and **Judah Smith**
and **Adam Mott** is appointed to enqure into y.e Same and
make report to y:ᵉ next monthly meeting:
Nicholas Davis desires a certificate of friends unity in his
Concern to travil to visit friends in yᵉ western parts
which is refered to y.ᵉ next monthly meeting
W:ᵐ **Wood Elisha Wing** and **John Tucker** is appointed to
See to the Settlement of his affairs that all thing may

be well: a paper being presented to this meeting from y:ᵉ
Preparitive meeting signed by **Peleg Smith** and **mary** his
wife Concerning their Disorderly proceeding in marriage
Contrary to y:ᵉ order of friends which was accepted and
Ordered to be read publickly on a first day at the Conclute
of the meeting of worship and they to come under the
Care of friends and yᵉ monthly meeting and **Henry Tucker**
is appointed to read the Same which is as followeth
Darthmouth yᵉ 14:ᵗʰ of yᵉ 7:ᵗʰ month 1726 to – –
To the preparative meeting to be held this Day
Friends whereas contrary to yᵉ minds of our parents
and y.ᵉ advice of friends we proceeded in marriage out
of y:ᵉ good order of truth for which and all other our out
Goings we have been often times heartily sorry and do
here in acknowledg our falts and take yᵉ blame to our
Selves that truth and friends may be clear and desire
that God would forgive us and that friends would pass it
By and receive us under their care again

       Peleg Smith
       Mary Smith

And this meeting is adjourned until y:ᵉ 2ᵈ: 4ᵗʰ day in yᵉ 8ᵗʰ
month next – –
This meeting being mett accord to adjournment this 12ᵗʰ day
of y:ᵉ 8:ᵗʰ month 1726: The visiters being Called upon to
give in their account of their visiting y:ᵉ families
of friends their account is that they have made some
progress in that service and that things was pretty well
for yᵉ most part as far as they Saw:
And **Nicolas Davis** and **John Tucker** is appointed to draw
up an account to y.ᵉ Quarterly meeting and to attend yᵉ Same

8ᵗʰ mo: At a monthly meeting of friends held at our meeting
House in **Dartmouth** y:ᵉ 17ᵗʰ day of y:ᵉ 8ᵗʰ month 1726
Dartmouth meeting Called **Deliverance Smith** and
John Lapham present: **Rochester** meeting Called none appearₑd
Nicolas Davis Desires a certificate of friends unity of
as to his traveling to y:ᵉ next monthly meeting:
and **W:ᵐ Wood Elisha Wing** and **John Tucker** are appoin
ted to See to y:ᵉ Settlement of his affaires as
And **W:ᵐ Wood Jun:ʳ** Desires a certificate of friends
unity with his traviling wᵗʰ **Nicolas Davis** into the

Western parts and **Holder Slocum** and **John Tucker**
is appointed to see into his clearness:
And **Judah Smith** and **Adam Mott** haveing made inquiry
into **Nicolas Lapham** Clearness wth respect to
marriage and Conversation and finding nothing to hinder
and his request is granted :and **Seth Celle [Kelly]** and **Mehetabel
Wing** not appearing at this meeting for their answer it
is referred to y:^{e} next monthly meeting – – – – –

9:th mo: At a monthly meeting of friends held at our meeting house
in **Dartmouth** y:^{e} 21st: day of ye 9th month 1726
the Seaveral meeting there unto ^belonging called upon
For **Dartmouth Deliverance Smith** and **John Lapham** present
for **Rochester Elisha Wing** present
Seth Celle and **Mehetabel Wing** came to this meeting for
their answer which is granted that they might proceed to
take each other in marriage in Some Convenient time
between this and ye next monthly meeting and **Nicolas
Davis** and **Stephen Wing** are appointed to see their marriage
Consimated in y:^{e} good order of truth
The Epistle from ye Quarterly meeting was read and kindly
accepted: and **Deliverance Smith** is appointed to keep the
Quarterly Collection and **John Tucker** and **Deliverance
Smith** is appointed to make up the monthly meeting
accounts w:th **Benjamin Howland**

10th mo: At a monthly meeting of friends held at our meeting
House in **Dartmouth** y:^{e} 19:th day of ye 10th month 1726
The Seaverl meetings thereunto belonging called upon
for **Dartmouth Deliverance Smith** and **John Lapham** present
for **Rochester Elisha Wing** present – –
Nicolas Davis and **Stephen Wing** makes report to this
meeting that **Seth Celle** and **Mehetabel Wings** marriage
was Solemnized in y^{e} good order of truth
John Tucker and **Deliverance Smith** have made up the
accounts with **Benjamin Howland** as appointed and
there remains in y:^{e} Stock – – £10 = 01^{s} = 09^{d}:
And **Henry Tucker** and **John Tucker** are appointed to
oversee the meeting house for y:^{e} insuing year
and **John Tucker** and **Henry Tucker** are appointed to
draw an Epistle to y:^{e} Quarterly meeting next and
also to attend y.^{e} Same: And **John Lapham** is aded to

John Russell to oversee y.ᵉ burying ground:
This meeting orders **Deliverance Smith** to pay **John** and
Henry Tucker £2 = 10ˢ = 00ᵈ for Looking after the meeting
house the year past: There was Collected at this meeting
for the use of friends – – £1 = 15ˢ = 06ᵈ:

11:ᵗʰ mo: At a monthly meeting of friends held at our meeting
House in **Dartmouth** y:ᵉ 16ᵗʰ day of y:ᵉ 11ᵗʰ month 17 ²⁶/₂₇
The Seaveral meeting thereunto belonging Called upon
for **Dartmouth Deliverance Smith** and **Wᵐ Wood**
present: for **Rochester Stephen Wing** present
John Tucker and **Henry Tucker** hath drawn an Epistle
to yᵉ Quarterly meeting as appointed and **Henry Tucker**
and **John Lapham** hath attended y:ᵉ Quarterly meeting
Archipas Hart ~~an~~ Son of **W:ᵐ Hart** of **Dartmouth**
in the **County** of **Bristol** in **New England** and **Sarah
Clifton** Daughter of **Savory Clifton** of **Rochester** in yᵉ
County o **Plymmouth** in **New England** Laid their inten-
=tions of marriage before this meeting and were desired
to wait until the next monthly meeting for
their answer and **Adam Mott** and **Henry Tucker**
are appointed to inquire into their clearness with respect
to marriage and Conversation and make return to the
next monthly meeting: and **Deliverance Smith** hath
paid £2 = 10ˢ = 00 to **John Tucker** and **Henry Tucker**
as ordered: And the Epistle from yᵉ Quarterly meeting
was read and kindly accepted

At a monthly meeting of friends held at our meeting
House in **Dartmouth** the 20:ᵗʰ day of yᵉ 12ᵗʰ month 17 ²⁶/₂₇
The **Seaveral** meeting thereto belonging Called upon for
Dartmouth Deliverance Smith and **John Lapham** present
for **Rochester Nicolas Davis** and **Elisha Wing** present
Archipas Hart and **Sarah Clifton** appeared at this meet
ing for their answer in respect to taking each other in
marriage and nothing appearing to hinder their sᵈ
intentions they had their answer that they might pro
ceed to take each other in marriage in yᵉ good order
of truth in Some Convenient time between this and
the next monthly meeting and **Elisha Wing** and **Stephen
Wing** are appointed to See it in Like manner accomplished

This meeting being informed by the women that **Alice Soule**
The Daughter of **Wᵐ Soule** Late of **Dartmouth** deceased hath
Gone out of the good order of truth in marriage: Therefore
Deliverance Smith and **John Tucker** are appointed to assist
the women in Drawing up her Condemnation – - -
This meeting doth appoint **John Russell** to provide 2 broad
hoes and one Shovel and a mattock and a spade for the use
of friends: **Rochester** meeting Called & no business presented
The ∧next monthly meeting is adjourned til the 4:ᵗʰ 2:ᵈ day in y:ᵉ first month
This meeting being mett according to adjournment this 27ᵗʰ day

1ˢᵗ mo: of the first month 1727 – –

1727: The Seaveral meetings thereto belonging Called upon for
Dartmouth Deliverance Smith and **W:ᵐ Wood** present
for **Rochester Nicolas Davis** present upon Consideration
that Seaveral friends by reason of earnest business
could not well attend this meeting is adjourned til tomorrow
at the usual time of meeting
This meeting being met according to adjournment this 28ᵗʰ
day of the first month 1727: **Elisha Wing** and **Stephen
Wing** makes report to this meeting that **Archipas Hart** and
Sarah Cliftons marriage was accomplished in y:ᵉ good order of
truth: there was Collected at this meeting for y:ᵉ use of friends
one pound ten Shillings and two pence:
John Tucker and **Deliverance Smith** hath drawn up **Alice
Soule**s Condemnation and **Henry Tucker** is appointed to
read the Same on a first day after the meeting of worship
~~in~~ Some time between this and the next monthly meeting
W:ᵐ Wood Nicolas Davis and **Adam Mott** are appointed
to ~~draw up an Epistle to~~ ~~attend y:ᵉ~~ Quarterly meeting next **John Tucker** and
Nicolas Davis are appointed to draw up an account to yᵉ ₘₑₑₜᵢₙg Quarterly

At a monthly meeting of friends held at our meeting house
in **Dartmouth** y:ᵉ 17th day of y:ᵉ 2:ᵈ month 1727 – –

2ᵈ mo: The Seaveral meetings thereto belonging Called upon
For **Dartmouth W:ᵐ Wood** and **Deliverance Smith** present
For **Rochester** none appeared: **Wᵐ Wood Nicolas davis**
and **Adam Mott** hath attended y:ᵉ Quarterly meeting
as appointed and **Nicolas Davis** and **John Tucker** hath
drawn up an account to y:ᵉ Quarterly meeting as appoinₜₑd
And **Henry Tucker** hath read **Alice Soule**s Condemnation
as appointed and is as followeth

Nicolas Davis Deliverance Smith Henry Tucker and
John Tucker are chose to agree with Stephen West jun^r:
~~and inform~~ for Land at acushnet to Set a meeting house
to ye next monthly meeting: Wm Wood Deliverance Smith
and Henry Tucker are appointed to Speak with Preserved
Merihoo [Merrihew] and Sarah Taber alias Merihoo to know Whither
the report of her haveing a child and laying of it to
the Said Merihoo be true and make return to the
next monthly meeting of the their Doings.
The Epistle from the Quarterly meeting was read
at this meeting and well accepted

At a monthly meeting of friends held at our meeting house
in Dartmouth ye 15th day of ye 3:^d month 1727:
3^d mo: The Seaveral meetings thereto belonging called upon
for Dartmouth Deliverance Smith and John Lapham present
for Rochester Nicolas Davis present – –
Those friends that was chosen at ye Last monthly meeting
to agree with Stephen West jun^r at Cushnot for Land to set a
meeting house upon an a burying place make report to this
meeting that they have agreed with him: and this meeting
makes choice of Henry Tucker to git it Laid out and git a
Return of the Same and make return to y:^e next month
=ly meeting of his doings therein – –
This meeting thinks best that all friends that hath occation
to acquaint y:^e preparitive meeting w:th their Intentions
of marriage do appear there in their own persons – –
Preserved Merihoo [Merrihew] and Sarah his wife their condemnation
is Signed and Deliverance Smith is appointed to read it
on a first day after the meeting or worship between this
and y:^e next monthly meeting
This meeting hath raised 8 pounds to be aded to y:^e 9 pounds
already in hand: Deliverance Smith hath paid Samuel
Willis 2 pounds 8 Shillings for bricks – – – – –

At a monthly meeting of friends held at our meeting
House in Dartmouth y:^e 19:th day of ye 4th month 1727:
4th mo: The Seaveral meetings thereunto belonging Called upon
for Dartmouth deliverance Smith and John Lapham
for Rochester none appeared:
Deliverance Smith hath read Preserved Merihew and
his wive condemnation as appointed and is as followeth

Thomas Akins Son of **John Akins** of **Dartmouth** in yᵉ
County of **Bristol** in **New England** and **Abigal Allen** daughter
of **Ebenezer Allen** deceased of Sᵈ **Dartmouth** hath Laid
their intentions of marriage before this meeting and are
desired to wait for their answer until yᵉ next monthly
meeting: **Henry Tucker** hath got yᵉ Land laid out to build a
meeting house upon and a burying place as appointed and it
Is refered to y:ᵉ next monthly meeting for further consideration
and **Deliverance Smith** and **Josiah Merihoo [Merrihew]** are appointed to See
into **Thomas Akins** and **Abigal Allens** Clearness with respect
to marriage and Conversation and make return to y:ᵉ next
monthly meeting: **Deliverance Smith** and **Henry Tucker** are
appointed to attend yᵉ Quarterly meeting: and **John Tucker** is
appointed to draw up an Epistle to yᵉ Same – –
There was Collected at this meeting for the use of friends: £1 = 06ˢ = 12ᵈ

At a monthly meeting of friends held at our meeting
House in **Dartmouth** yᵉ 17:ᵗʰ day of y:ᵉ 5:ᵗʰ month 1727:
5ᵗʰ mo: The Seaveral meetings thereunto belonging Called upon for
Dartmouth W:ᵐ Wood and **Deliverance Smith** present
for **Rochester** none appeared
Thomas Akins and **Abigal Allen** came to this meeting
for their answer and their answer was that they might
proceed to take each other in marriage in Some Convenient
time between this and y:ᵉ next monthly meeting and **John
Russell** and **John Lapham** are appointed to See their marriage
Concimated in the good order of truth and make return to yᵉ
next monthly meeting: **John Wing** ~~and ma~~ ye Son of
John Wing of **Sandwich** in **New England** and **Mary Tucker**
daughter of **Henry Tucker** of **Dartmouth** have Laid their Inten
=tions of takeing each other in marriage before this meeting
and were desired to wait until y.ᵉ next monthly meeting for
their answer: There is a subscribtion agreed upon at this
meeting to pay for yᵉ finnishing of this meeting house and for
the purchaseing of Land to build a meeting house upon and
a burying place at **Cushnot** – –
John Tucker Deliverance Smith and **Adam Mott** are chosen
visiters for **Ponaganset** for yᵉ ensuing year: and for
Cushnet Joseph Taber for **Coakset Wᵐ Wood**: for **Rochester**
Elisha Wing and **Savory Clifton**: This meeting makes
choice of **Nicolas Davis Joseph Taber Joseph Russell junʳ**

Adam Mott and John Tucker junᵣ to have yᵉ deed made to
of yᵉ Land at Cushnot to buld a meeting house upon as
above written and to git a deed for the same – –
The Epistle from yᵉ Quarterly meeting was read at this
meeing and kindly accepted – – – – –

At a monthly meeting of friends held at our meeting house
In Dartmouth y:ᵉ 21ˢᵗ day of y:ᵉ 6:ᵗʰ month 1727:

6th mo: The Seaveral meetings thereunto belonging Called upon for
Dartmouth Deliverance Smith and John Lapham present
for Rochester Nicolas Davis present: John Russell and John
Lapham makes report to this meeting that Thoˢ Akins and
Abigal Allens marriage was Concimated in yᵉ good order
of truth John Wing and Mary Tucker came to this meeting
for their answer & their answer was that they might take
Each other in marriage in the good order of truth in Some
Convenient time before the next monthly meeting and
James Barker and Adam Mott are appointed to See their
Marriage Concimated in y:ᵉ good order of truth and make
report to yᵉ next monthly meeting Rochester no business

omitted page the 128 the account that Rochester visiters gave in
which is as followeth – –
To yᵉ monthly meeting of friends to be held in Dartmouth yᵉ 28ᵗʰ of
the first month 1727: We have visitors yᵉ families of friends
in a general way. and we find things for the most part pretty well
but some things we found out of order and are in Concern and
Labour for amendment—and we have been for the most part
Received in Love and we hope our Labour may be of service

Elisha Wing
Savory Clifton

10:mo: At a monthly meeting of friends held at our meeting house
1727 in Dartmouth the 18th day of ye 10th month 1727
The seaveral meetings thereunto belonging Called upon
For Dartmouth Deliverance Smith and John
Lapham present. For Rochester Elisha Wing
There was Collected at this meeting for the use
of friends — — — . — — — — — — — — o — 11 = 01
John Tucker and Henry Tucker are chose to oversee
the meeting the Ensuing year : and James Barker
is chosen in the room of Nicholas Davis to have the
deed of the land made to that was bought of Stephen
West Junr at Acushonet to build a meeting house
upon : And this meeting orders Deliverance Smith
to pay fifteen Shillings towards ye aforesd Land
And this meeting orders Deliverance Smith to pay
John Tucker and Henry Tucker forty Shillings for
keeping the meeting House : And Elisha Wing and
John Lapham are Chose to attend ye Quarterly meeting
And John Tucker is appointed to draw an Epistle to ye same

11:mo: At a monthly meeting of friends held at our meeting
1727 house in Dartmouth ye 15 of ye 11 month 1727
The seaveral meetings there to belonging Called upon
For Dartmouth Deliverance Smith and Josiah Merihew
present — For Rochester none appeared
Elisha Wing and John Lapham hath attended the
Quarterly meeting as appointed : And John Tucker and
Elisha Wing hath drawn an Epistle to ye same
And the Epistle from ye Quarterly meeting was read at
this meeting and well accepted : And Jonathan
Tabers Condemnation is Referred for further Considerat-
on

12 mo At a monthly meeting of friends held at our meeting
17 27/28 house in Dartmouth ye 19 day of ye 12 month 1727/8
The seaverall meetings thereunto belonging Called
upon : for Dartmouth Deliverance Smith and John
Lapham present : For Rochester Elisha Wing present

FIG. 5: *Page nine of the records of the Apponegansett Friends Monthly Meeting Records, 1727. Courtesy of the Dartmouth at Smith's Neck Monthly Meeting.*

The Records of The
Discipline of Friends,
In The Monthly Meeting of **Dartmouth**
Containing a Register of the Several
Transactions, In the Affairs of the
Church;
From the Tenth Month A D 1727, Old
Stile, To the Ninth Month A D 1762 New
Stile, Inclusive;

10:mo: At a monthly meeting of friends held at our meeting house
  1727   in **Dartmouth** the 18th day of yᵉ 10th month 1727
      The Seaveral meetings thereunto belonging Called upon
      for **Dartmouth Deliverance Smith** and **John
      Lapham** present for **Rochester Elisha Wing**
      There was Collected at this meeting for the use
      of friends –   –   –   –   –   –   – 0 – 11=01
      John Tucker and **Henry Tucker** are chose to oversee
      the meeting the Ensuing year: and **James Barker**
      is Chosen in the room [place] of **Nicholas Davis** to have the
      deed of the land made to that was bought of **Stephen
      West Junʳ** at **Acushonet** to build a meeting house
      Upon: And this meeting orders **Deliverance Smith**
      to Pay fifteen Shillings towards yᵉ aforesd Land
      And this meeting orders **Deliverance Smith** to pay
      John Tucker and **Henry Tucker** forty Shillings for
      keeping the meeting House: and **Elisha Wing** and
      John Lapham are Chose to attend yᵉ Quarterly meeting
      And **John Tucker** is appointed to draw an Epistle to yᵉ Same

11:mo: At a monthly meeting of friends held at our meeting
  1727   house in **Dartmouth** yᵉ 15 of yᵉ 11 month 1727
      The Seaveral meetings thereto belonging Called upon
      for **Dartmouth Deliverance Smith** and **Josiah Merihw** [**Merihew**]
      Present - For **Rochester** none appeared
      Elisha Wing and **John Lapham** hath attended the
      Quarterly meeting as appointed and **John Tucker** and

Elisha Wing hath drawn an Epistle to yᵉ Same
And the Epistle from yᵉ Quarterly meeting we read at
This meeting and well accepted: And Jonathan
Tabers Condemnation is Refered for further Consideratiₒₙ

12 mo
1727/28
At a monthly meeting of friends held at our meeting
house in Dartmouth yᵉ 19 day of yᵉ 12 month 1727/8
The Seaverall meetings thereunto belonging called
upon: for Dartmouth Deliverance Smith and John
Lapham present: for Rochester Elisha Wing present
And Jonathan Tabers Condemnation is referred until the
next monthly meeting. And Abraham Tucker Deliver
a certificate from this meeting in relation to his
Clearness as to marriage and conversation and
Josiah Merrihew and Elishib Smith are appointed
to see into it and make report to yᵉ next monthly meeting
And Ebenezer Slocum also delivers another
upon the same account Which John Russell and
John Lapham are appointed to see into and make return
to yᵉ next monthly meeting And Henry Tucker and Adam Mott are appointed to
assist the women in drawing up Hester Taber now
wife of William Palmer her condemnation for her
outgoing in marrying Contrary to yᵉ good order
Established among friends
No business from Rochester and the next monthly
meeting is adjourned until ye third fourth day in the
next month and Judah Smith and Abraham Tucker is
appointed to make up the meetings accounts with
Deliverance Smith

1:mo:
1728
At a monthly meeting of friends held at our meeting
house in Dartmouth yᵉ 20 day of yᵉ 1 month 1728 – –
The several meetings thereto belonging Called upon
for Dartmouth Deliverance Smith and John Lapham
present for Rochester none present
The friends that were appointed to see into the Abraham
Tuckers Clearness as to any intanglement in marriage
find none enet to Hannah Hull of Rhode Island
and to his conversati['on' is inserted above the line] pretty orderly
As also the friends appointed to see into Ebenezer
Slocums Clearness they report that they find nothing
of any intanglement with any person Except with

Bathsheba Hull of **Rhoad Island**: and as to his Conver
- sation not so orderly as could desire but for time to
come he promises to reform
And **John Tucker** and **Adam Mott** are appointed to draw
up each of them a certificate and sign them in behalfe
of yᵉ monthly meeting: And **John Tucker** and **Judah Smith**
hath made up the monthly meetings accounts with
Deliverance Smith and the remains in ye Stock 3=07=0 [6?]
And it is referred to yᵉ Quarterly meetings judgment
whither the monthly meeting ought not to sign a
Condemnation against **Jonathan Taber**s proceeding
in marriage Contrary to ye order of friends
or to take his own Condemnation which is here also presented
 Our visitors being called upon gives their account
that they have done nothing in that service
And **John Tucker** and **John Lapham** are appointed to
attend the Quarterly Meeting and to Draft an
Epistle to yᵉ same and sign it. And our Collection
is referred to the next monthly meeting
And the matter concerning **Hester Tabor** refered
to the Next monthly meeting

2:mo: At a monthly meeting of friends held at our
1728 Meeting house in Dartmouth the 15 day of ye 2 m 1728
the several meetings thereunto belonging called
upon. For **Dartmouth William Wood** and **Deliver**[‘ance’ squeezed below the line]
Smith present for **Rochester Stephen Wing** present
John Tucker and **john Lapham** hath drawn up
Abraham Tucker and **Ebenezer Slocum**s Certificates
and **John Tucker** hath signed them in behalf of
the monthly meeting as appointed: and **John Tucker**
and **John Lapham** hath drawn up an Epistle to the
Quarterly meeting and attended the same as appointed
Collected at this meeting for the use of friends 1-11=07
And the matter concerning **Hester taber** not being
done **Henry Tucker** and **Adam Mott** are still continued
to draw up her condemnation: And **John Tucker** and
Delivrance Smith are appointed to view the
monthly meeting minutes in order that they may be
put upon record
And **Isaac Smith** is appointed to Record them And

this meeting orders **Deliverance Smith** to pay
John Tucker 10 shillings and **Adam Mott** 2 shillings
And **John Whitely** and **Abigail Allen** hath laid their
intentions of taking each other in marriage before
this meeting and are desired to wait until the next
Monthly meeting for their answer and to settle
their estates so that their children may not be dam
nifyed by their marrying and **Deliverance Smith**
and **John Lapham** are appointed to assist them
The Quarterly meeting Epistle was read at this
meeting and kindly accepted
No business from **Rochester**

3:mo: At a monthly meeting of friends held at our
1728 meeting house in **Dartmouth** the: 20 day of yᵉ 3 mo:1728
The several meetings thereunto belonging Called
upon for **Dartmouth Deliverance Smith** and
John Lapham present for **Rochester Stephen Wing**
present **Deliverance Smith** according to order hath
paid **John Tucker** -10 shillings and **Adam Mott** 2ˢ
as appointed: And **Deliverance Smith** and **John Lapham**
are still continued to assist **John Whitely** and
Abigall Allen in setling their estates before they
have their answer and whereas **Deborah Read**
hath in time past gone out of ye unity of friends in
marry [sic] Contrary to the advise of friends doth now
give in a paper of acknowledgment Condemning of
her outgoings and **Deliverance Smith** is appointed
to read it on a first day between this and the next
monthly meeting. And this meeting orders **Deliverance
Smith** to pay to **John Tucker** and **Henry Tucker** forty
shillings for keeping the meeting house which is done
according to order and **Jonathan Taber**s acknowledg
-ment of his outgoings is referred until the next
monthly meeting
And **Joseph Taber** is appointed to Read **Hester Palmers**
Condemnation which is as followeth – – – – –

[the rest of the page is blank]

The business of **Rochester** called and none presented
and this meeting adjourns the next monthly meeting
until the fourth second day in the next month

4:mo: At a monthly meeting of friends held in our
1728   meeting house the 24 day of the 4 month 1728 – –
       The seaveral meeting thereto belong[ing] called upon for
       Dartmouth William Wood and **Deliverance Smith**
       present for **Rochester Elisha Wing** present
       And there was collected for the use of friends: 2=05=08
       and **Deliverance Smith** is still continued to read
       Deborah Reads acknowledgment and **Jonathan
       Taber**s acknowledgment for his outgoings in marriage
       was read and accepted: and **Joseph Taber** hath read
       Hester Palmers Condemnation as appointed
       and **Elisha Wing** and **William Wood** are appointed to attend
       the Quarterly meeting and **Elisha Wing** and **John Tucker** is
       appointed to draft an Epistle to the same
       and **John Whitely** and **Abigail Allen** having settled their
       estates this meeting gives them their answer that
       they are permitted to take each other in marriage in
       some convenient time between this and the next
       monthly meeting and **Deliverance Smith** and **John
       Lapham** are appointed to see their marriage Solemnized
       in the Good order of truth and make return to yᵉ next
       monthly meeting. And this meeting makes a new choice of
       visitors for **Dartmouth John Howland James Barker** and
       Adam Mott[;] for **Rochester Elisha Wing** and **Stephen Wing**
       and at this meeting **John Russell** Jun: **John Howland James
       Barker Adam Mott** and **John Tucker** jun ^ was chose to have yᵉ deed
       of the meeting house land made to [left blank]

5:mo: At a monthly meeting of friends held at our meeting house
1728: in **Dartmouth** the 15 day of the 5 month 1728
       the seaveral meeting thereto belonging called upon for
       Dartmouth John Lapham and **Eliashib Smith** present
       for **Rochester** none appeared – – –
       And **Deliverance Smith** is still continued to read **Deborah
       Read**s acknowledgment and **William Wood** attended the
       Quarterly meeting as appointed and **John Tucker** and
       Elisha Wing hath drawn an account to yᵉ same as

appointed and **John Lapham** makes report to this meeting
that he was at yᵉ marriage of **John Whitely** and **Abigall
Allen** and found nothing but that it was accomplished
in good order. And this meeting agrees to come to a
subscription of: 10: pounds for **Richard Patridg** for
service which he hath done for friends in **England**

6: *mo:*   At a monthly meeting of friends held at our meeting
1728:   House in **Dartmouth** ye 19 Day of 6 month 1728
the seaveral meetings thereunto belonging called upon for
Dartmouth Deliverance Smith and **John Lapham** present
Rochester Elisha Wing present and **Deliverance
Smith** hath read **Deborah Reads** acknowledgment
as appointed and **John Lapham** and **Isaac Howland** is
appointed to make enquiry into **Benjamin Smith** clearance
as to marriage and conversation and draw up a Certficate
according as they shall find it
And **William Wood Junʳ** hath a mind to travil Westward
and requires a certificate and **John Tucker** is appointed to
draw one up and sign it in yᵉ behalf of this meeting
Rochester meeting Called and no business presented

7:*mo:*   At a monthly meeting of friends held at our meeting
1728:   House in **Dartmouth** the 16: day of the 7 month. . 1728:
Dartmouth meeting called none appeared by appointment
Rochester meeting Called none appeared
There was collected for the use of friends – – 1 08=00
John Tucker and **Deliverance Smith** are appointed to
attend the Quarterly meeting and Draw up an account
to yᵉ same: There hath happened some Difference between
Jonathan Merrihoo and his brother **Josiah** which **John
Russell Isaac Howland Henry Tucker Adam Mott** and
John Howland are appointed to hear and determine
And make return to the next monthly meeting
This meeting is adjourned until the first [sixt?] day in
the next month.
This mee[t]ing being meet according to adjournment
the visiters brings in their account that they have
visited the most of friends families of friends in **Apo
naganset vilage** and their visits were accepted in
love but where things were amiss they were in
hopes they might be better

8 mo: At a monthly meeting of friends held at our meeting
1728: House in **Dartmouth** on the 21 day of the 8 month 1728
The Seaverall meetings thereunto belonging Called
upon for **Dartmouth Eliashib Smith** and **Joseph
Russell Junr** present for **Rochester Nicholas Davis**
present **John Tucker** and **Deliverance Smith** hath
Drawn an Epistle to the Quarterly meeting as appointed
but it hap[pe]ned that they could not well attend it
Abraham Russell and **Dinah Allen** having laid their
Intentions of taking each other in marriage: They are
to wait until the next monthly meeting for their answ[er]
and **Josiah Merihoo [Merihew]** and **John Russell** are appointed to
make inquiry into the young mans clearness and make
Return to ye next monthly meeting
The differance between **Josiah Merihoo [Merihew]** and his brother
Jonathan not being ended the Same friends are still
Continued to end ye Same and bring in their account
to the next monthly meeting
And **Dorothy Wing** of **Rochester** being about to Remove
to **Sandwich** to Live Disires a certificate of this meeting
which **Elisha Wing** and **Nicholas Davis** is appointed
to draw up in order to be Signed at our next month
-ly meeting and this meeting orders **Deliverance Smith**
to pay **Henry Tucker** 11 Shillings for mending the
meeting House glass and the House where it was burnt
And **Joseph Taber** ˏ^John Walker and **Elisha Wing** are appointed to
Labour with **Samuel Wing** of **Rochester** to Show him
the Evil of his inclinations to take a young woman to
wife that is not a believer in the principles of truth
Friends the people Called Quakers: and make return to
the next monthly meeting of their doings therein

9:mo: At a monthly meeting of friends held at our meet
1728: ing House in **Dartmouth** ye 18 day of the 9 month 1728—
Dartmouth meeting Called **Wm Wood** and **Eliashib
Smith** present **Rochester** meeting Called **Elisha Wing**
and **Nicholas Davis** appeared
Whereas **Abraham Russell** and **Dinah Allen** laid their
Intentions of taking each other in marriage before
the last monthly meeting now they Came
for their answer and friends finding nothing to
hinder their intention their answer was that they

might proceed to take each other in marriage in
some Convenient time between this and the next
monthly meeting and **John Russell** and **Josiah Merrihoo** [Merihew]
are appointed to see their marriage S[c]onsummated
ind the gooder of truth
And **Edward Wing** and **Patience Ellis** having laid their
intention of taking each other in marriage before
this meeting they are Desired to wait until the next
monthly meeting for their answer and **Henry Tucker**
and **Eliashib Smith** are appointed to Enquire into
their Clearness and make report to the next monthly
Meeting. And **James Russell** and **Mary Howland** having laid
their Intentions of taking Each other in marriage before this
Last monthly meeting they are desired to wait until
our next monthly meeting for their answer and
John Howland and **James Barker** is appointed to make
Enquiry into their Clearness and make return to the
next monthly meeting
And **Deliverance Smith** unto **Henry Tucker** 11 Shillings
as ordered The friends that were appointed to Speak
with **Samuel Wing** are Still Continued to Labour with
him and bring in an account their Doings to the next
monthly meeting
and **John Tucker** is appointed to assist the women in
Drawing up a Condemnation against **Hannah** now
wife of **William Wood Juner** for proceeding Contrary to
the advise of friends in her marriage

10:mo: At a monthly meeting of friends held at our meeting
1728: House in **Dartmouth** the 16 day of the 10 month 1728
The Seaveral meetings thereto belonging Called upon
fo[r] Dartmouth **Eliashib Smith** and **Adam Mott** presen[t]
for **Rochester** none appeared by appointment
There was Collected at this meeting for ye: use of friend[s]
one pound and 2 pence
John Russell and **Josiah Merihoo** [Merihew] being Called upon to
give in their account Concerning **Abraham Russell**
and **Dinah Allens** marriage Signify that they Saw nothing
but that it was S[c]onsumated in the good order of Truth
Edward Wing and **Patience Elliss** [Ellis] Came to this meeting

for their answer in Referance to their taking each
other in marriage and they had their answer that they
might proceed to take each other in marriage in
Some Convenient time between this and the next month=
ly meeting and **Henry Tucker** and **Eliashib Smith** are
appointed to See their marriage Consumated in the
good order of truth and make Return to yᵉ next
monthly meeting. and **James Russell** and **Mary Howland**
Came to this meeting for their answer and their
answer was that they might proceed to take each
other in marriage in Some Convenient time between
this and the next monthly meeting.
And **John Howland** and **James Barker** is appointed to
See their marriage Selemnized in the good order established among friends and make return to the next monthly
meeting: Receivd of the women in mon[e]y 2 : 14 : 00
which was paid to **John Tucker** for keeping yᵉ meeting House
This meeting agreas [agrees] to ~~Come to a Subscribtion~~ build a
Meeting House at **Acushnot** near the bizness of friends
meeting House at **Pembrook** And **Thomas Hathaway Joseph
Taber Jacob Taber** and **Henry Tucker** are appointed to See
it done as Soon as Can be with Conveniency
And **Nicholas Davis Henry Tucker** and **Joseph Russell
Junʳ**: are appointed to attend the Quarterly meeting
and to draw up an Epistle to the Same and **John Tucker**
to assist them and **John Tucker** and **James Barker** are
appointed to oversee the meeting House the Ensuing year
And **Hannah Wood**s Condemnation was Signed at this
meeting and is as followeth. ~~and~~————————————

20 d.   At a monthly meeting of friends held at our meeting house
11 mo: in **Dartmouth** the 20 day of the 11 month 1728:
1728:   The Seavral meetings thereunto belonging Called upon
    for **Dartmouth Adam Mott** and **James Barker** present
    for **Rochester** none appeared by appointment
    Henry Tucker and **Eliashib Smith** make Report to this meeting
    That they were at the marriage of **Edward Wing** and **Patince** [**Patience**]
    Ellis and Saw nothing but that it was Carried on in the good
    order of truth: And **John Howland** and **James Barke**r also
    Signifies to this meeting that **James Russell** and **Mary Howland**s

marriage was Consumated in the Good order of truth
John Tucker and **Henry Tucker** hath drawn up an Epistle
to yᵉ Quarterly Meeting and **Henry Tucker** and **Nicholas Davis**
hath attended the Quarterly meeting as appointed
This meeting orders **Deliverance Smith** to pay **John Lapham**
Six Shillings for keeping the meeting House
And **John Tucker** and **Henry Tucker** are appointed to assist
the women in Drawing up **Hope Smith**s Condemnation
for her out goings and **Hannah Wood**s Condemnation is
Read according to order The Epistle from the Quarterly
meet was read and kindly accepted

12:mo: At a monthly meeting of friends held at our meeting
1728/9 House in **Dartmouth** the 17 day of the 12 month 1728/29
The Seaveral meetings thereunto belonging Called upon for
Dartmouth Eliashib Smith and **Adam Mott** present for
Rochester Stephen Wing present
Deliverance Smith hath paid **John Lapham** 6 Shillings as
appointed **John Tucker** and **Henry Tucker** hath Drawn up
Hope Smiths Condemnation and yᵉ 2[?] Signing of it is Refered
until the next monthly meeting and **Henry Tucker** and
Adam Mott are Chose to Purge the Monthly meetings of
Such persons that is not under the Care of friends
And this meeting doth agrea [agree] and are Come to a Subscribtion
for the building of **Acushonet** meeting House

1 mo: At a monthly meeting of friends held at our meeting House
1729: in **Dartmouth** the 17 day of the 1 month 1729
The Seaverall meetings thereunto belonging Called upon
For **Dartmouth Willim Wood** and **Adam Mott** present
for **Rochester Elisha Wing** present
There was Collected at this meeting for yᵉ use of friends £1:05ˢ:02ᵈ
Hope Smiths Condemnation is Signed as appointed and
Jabez Barker is appointed to Read it in Some Conve
nient time between this and the next monthly meeting
after our meeting of worship and is as followeth
Whereas **Hope** the Daughter of **Deliverance Smith**
and **Mary** his Wife of **Dartmouth** in the **County of Bristol**
in **New England** having been educated among friends
Not Regarding the fear of God the honour of her parents
Nor of friends, hath by giving way to the evil one and
her own wicked inclinations Committed that great Sin

of fornication which wicked action we the people ‸ of God Called
Quakers do deny all Such wicked actions and do give this
forth as a publick Testimony against the abovesd **Hope Smith**
her ungodly and wicked action yet Si[n]cerely ~~Desireing~~
and truly Desireing that if it be the will of God Shee
May Come to a Sight and Sence of her out goings and
by an unfeigned Repentence and amendment of life
To walk as to find mercy with the Lord
Given forth at our monthly meeting held in **Dartmouth**
the 17 day of the 1 month 1729:

John Tucker
William Wood
Henry Tucker　　　　　　　**Ruth Tucker**
John Lapham　　　　　　　**Hannah Tucker**
James Barker　　　　　　　**Mehetabel Burril** [?]
Deliverance Smith　　　　　**Phebe Tucker**
Adam Mott　　　　　　　　**Mary Lapham**
Elisha Wing　　　　　　　**Elisabeth Barker**
Isaac Howland　　　　　　**Rose Howland**
Nicholas Lapham　　　　　**Mary Howland**
John Howland　　　　I acknowledg the above written
Nicholas Davis　　　　to be Equal and Just
Jabez Barker　　　　　　　　**Hope Smith**

The business of **Dartmouth** meeting Called the visiters
being Called upon to give in their accounts of their
Care in visiting friends families and their account
is as followeth
To the monthly meeting that is to be held in **Dartmouth**
the 17 day of the first month 1729
We the Subscribers Give the monthly meeting the
following account that we have visited most of the
families of friends in **Dartmouth** and in most families
we were kindly ~~accepted~~ Received and they Expressed a
Great deal of Sattisfaction in our visits and when we
gave them our advice in Love and tenderness they
owned that it was the truth and hoped that it would
be of good Service to them and their Children and
hoped they Should be more Careful for the time to Come
So that we believe that truth gaines ground in Some
families: but in other Some we received but

a Cool reception and hard Reflections to our great Sorrow
and trouble: but where things were amiss and out of
order we did not Spare ~~to~~ Labour and Pains in true love
~~that things~~ to have them Mended, but we Must leave
the Effect to yᵉ Only Wise God who has all power in his
hand So we have no more to Communicate to your Consideration but remain your friends

John Howland　　　　　　**Phebe Tucker**
Nicholas Davis　　　　　　**Mary Howland**
James Barker ————————

John Tucker Elisha Wing and **Adam Mott** are Chosen
to attend the Quarterly meeting and **John Tucker** and
Elisha Wing are appointed to draw an Epistle to the
Same: The business of **Rochester** meeting Called and
whereas **Samuel Wing** hath refused to take friends
advise: this meeting makes Choice of **Elisha Wing**
Joseph Taber and **John Tucker** to Draw up a Condemnation
against him and bring it to our next monthly meeting
in order to be Signed

2:mo: At a monthly meeting of friends held at our meeting
1729: House in **Dartmouth** the 21 day of yᵉ 2 month 1729
The Seaveral meetings thereto belonging Called upon
For **Dartmouth William Wood** and **Deliverance Smith**
present for Rochester none appeared
Jabez Barker hath read **Hope Smith**s Condemnation
as appointed **John Tucker** and **Elisha Wing** hath attended
the Quarterly meeting and drawn up an Epistle to the
Same as appointed The Epistle from the Quarterly
was read at this meeting and kindly accepted – – – – –

3: mo: At a monthly meeting of friends held at our meeting
1729 house in **Dartmouth** the 19 day of yᵉ 3 month 1729
The Seaveral meeting thereto belonging Called upon
for **Dartmouth John Howland** and **Jabez Barker** presen[t]
for **Rochester Savory Clifton** present
Nicholas Davis and **Ruth Tucker** did lay their Intentions of taking each other in marriage before this
Meeting and **Savory Clifton** and **Jabez Barker** are
appointed to inquire into their Clearness as to marriage
and Conversation and make return to the next
monthly meeting how they find things

John Tucker and Elisha Wing hath drawn up Samuel
Wings Condemnation as appointed and it is approved and
Signed and Elisha Wing and is appointed to Read the
Same in Some Convenient time between this and the
next monthly meeting on a first day after the meet-
ing of worship at Rochester meeting house
or Cause it to be done
And the next monthly meeting is adjourned until the 4
Second day in the 4 month next

4 mo: At a monthly meeting of friends held at our meeting house
1729: in Dartmouth the 23 day of the 4 month 1729
The Seaverall meetings thereunto belonging Called upon
for Dartmouth none appeared by appointment
for Rochester Elisha Wing present
Collected for the Use of friends – – £1 -11ˢ = 08ᵈ
Whereas Nicholas Davis and Ruth Tucker Laid their
Intentions of taking each other in marriage before the
Last monthly meeting Now they Came for their Answer
and their answer was that they might proceed to take
each other in marriage in the good order of truth in Some
Convenient time between this and the next monthly meeting
and John Howland and James Barker are appointed to
See their marriage Consumated and make return to the
Next monthly meeting; and Elisha Wing is Still Conti-
nued to read Samuel Wings Condemnation
And John Tucker and Isaac Howland are appointed to
make up the meetings accounts with the Treasurer – –
John Tucker and Nicholas Davis is appointed to take
Some Method to procure a friend School Master
And this meeting makes a new Choice of visiters
(viz) John Tucker and Adam Mott for Aponaganset
and Joseph Taber and Joseph Russell Junʳ for Cushnot
For Coakset William Wood and Eliashib Smith
For Rocheste[r] Savory Clifton and Elisha Wing
John Tucker Elisha Wing and Adam Mott are
appointed to atte[n]d yᵉ Quarterly meeting and Draw an
Epistle to the Same: and this meeting ords [orders] Deliverance
Smith to pay to John Tucker and James Barker for
keeping the meeting House – – £2- 10ˢ- 00ᵈ
And Mary Traffords acknowledgment was read at this

Meeting and accepted and is as followeth

Dartmouth the 15 day of the 2 month 1729

to the monthly meeting of friends to be held at **Dartmouth**

the third Second day of this instant

Friends whereas in time past I proceeded in marriage

Contrary to the Advice of frie^nds and the good order practiced

among them, which disorderly proceedings brought trouble to

friends and proved a great grief to my parents.

Now Friends I Condemn the abovesd Disorderly proceedings

as wrong and a breach of Good order; for which disorderly

proceeding I am heartily Sorry and pray that you would

Remitt mine Offence So far as pertains to you,

with Sincere Desires that you would Receive me under

your Care and for the time to Come have an Eye

over me for Good which is the hearty Desire of

Your friend – – **Mary Trafford**

---

5 mo: At a monthly meeting of friends held at our meeting

1729: House in **Dartmouth** the 21 day of the 5 month 1729

The Seaverall meetings thereunto Called upon

for **Dartmouth** Wm **Wood** and **Adam Mott** present

for **Rochester Nicholas Davis** present

John Howland and **James Barker** makes report to

this meeting that **Nicholas Davis** and **Ruth Tucker**s

marriage was Consumated in the Good order of truth

John Tuck [**Tucker**] and **Isaac Howland** is appointed to make

up accounts with the Executor of our treasurer

Deliverance Smith deceased:

John Tucker hath attended the Quarterly meeting

and Drawn up an Epistle to the Same as appointed

And this meeting makes Ch[o]ice of **Adam Mott** to be our

Treasurer in the Room of our friend **Deliverance**

Smith deceased: The Epistle from the Quarterly

meeting was read at this meeting and kindly accepted

And this meeting agrees to Come to a Subscribtion of

four pounds to renew the yearly meeting Stock

---

6 mo: At a monthly meeting of friends held at our meeting

1729: House in **Dartmouth** the 18 day of the 6 month 1729

The Seaveral meetings thereto belonging Called upon

for **Dartmouth William Wood** and **Henry Tucker** present

for **Rochester** none appeared by appointment

John Tucker and Isaac Howland are Still Continued
to make up the accounts with the Executor of ye treasur[er]
There is a deed drawn up and Signed according to appointment
for the meeting House Land at **Cushnot:**

7 mo: At a monthly meeting of friends held [at] our meeting
1729: House in **Dartmouth** the 15 day of ye 7 Month 1729:
The Seaverall meetings thereto belonging Called upon
for **Dartmouth Eliashib Smith** and **John Howland** present
for **Rochester Nicholas Davis** present
Whereas the Last Quarterly meeting Sent for fower [four]
pounds to renew the yearly meeting Stock which this
meeting hath Gathered and **John Howland** ˏis appointo to Carry the
Same to ye next Quarterly meeting
Rochester meeting Called and no business presented
John Tucker William Wood John Howland and **Nicholas
Davis** are appo[i]nted to attend the ~~Quarter~~ the Quarterly
meeting next and to Draw an Epistle to the Same
and this meeting is adjourned til ye first Sixth day
in the next month
This meeting being met according to adjournment this
third day of the 8 month 1729: the visiters being Called
upon to give in their account of how they find things.
under their Care in friends fam[i]lies they give the
following account that they have visited in a pretty
Generall way the families of friends that are
under their Care and things pretty well for the most
part so far as they Saw but in Some families not
So well as they desire and this meeting agreas [agrees] that
when the ˏbooks (viz) **Robert Barclays** apollegies that are
near ready to Come out of the press that when they
are ready then they Shall have the remainder of the
Mony for printing them[1]

8 mo: At a monthly meeting of friends held at our meeting House
1729 In **Dartmouth** the 20 day of the 8 month 1729:

1. Robert Barclay's *An Apology for the True Christian Divinity, as the Same Is Held Forth, and Preached by the People, Called in Scorn, Quakers; Being a Full Explanation and Vindication of Their Principles and Doctrines, by Many Arguments, Deduced from Scripture and Right Reason, and the Testimonys of Famous Authors, Both Antient and Modern, with a Full Answer to the Strongest Objections Usually Made against Them, Presented to the King* was first published in 1678. Friends regarded it as the authoritative statement of their beliefs. The New England Yearly Meeting sponsored a printing by James Franklin in Providence in 1729.

The Seaverall meetings ther[e]to belonging Called upon
For **Dartmouth Eliashib Smith** present
for **Rochester Savory Clifton** present
The 4 pounds that was gathered the Last monthly meeting
for Renewing the yearly meeting Stock was Carried and
Delivered to the Quarterly meeting as appointed
John Tucker Wᵐ Wood and **Nicholas Davis** hath attended
the Quarterly meeting and Drawn an account to yᵉ Same
according to appointment And this meeting doth Still
Continue those friends that was to git a friend School mas-
ter and that he Shall be a Grammer according to former
Advice and this meeting to be at the Charge thereof
No business from **Rochester** presented
The Epistle from yᵉ Quarterly meeting was Read at this
Meeting and kindly accepted

9 mo: At a monthly meeting of friends held at our meeting
1729 House in **Dartmouth** the 17 day of the 9 month 1729
The Seaverall meetings thereto belonging Called upon
for **Dartmouth Joseph Taber** and **Joseph Russell Junʳ** presen[t]
for **Rochester Nicholas Davis** present
Benjamin Taber and **Susanna Lewis** desires this meeting[s?]
approbation in taking each other in marriage
and they are desired to wait until our next monthly
meeting for their answer And **Nicholas Davis** and
Adam Mott are appointed to make Enquiry into
their Clearness with respect to marriage and Conversation and make return to the next monthly meeting
And **Wᵐ Wood Junʳ**: Desires a Certificate from this
Meeting of his Clearness in marriage and Conversation
And **Jabez Barker** and **Adam Mott** are appointed to enquire
into the Same and make ~~re~~ report to the next monthly
Meeting how they find things Relating to that Affair
and **Elisabeth Willcox [Wilcox]** daughter of **Stephen Willcox [Wilcox]**
having gone out of the Order of friends in having a
Child and She being not married This meeting doth
appoint **John Tucker** and **William Wood** to assist the
women in Drawing up her Condemnation
No business presented from **Rochester**

10 mo: At a monthly meeting of friends held at our meeting house
1729: in **Dartmouth** the 15 day of the 10 month 1729

The Seaverall meetings therto belonging Called upon
for **Dartmouth William Wood** and **Adam Mott** present
for **Rochester John Wing** present
Ebenezer Shearman and **Wait Barker** having laid
their Intentions of taking each other in Marriage before
this meeting they are desired to wait until our next
for their answer and **Joseph Russell junᵣ** and **Henry
Tucker** are appointed to Enquire into their Clearness and
Conversation and make Report to the next monthly
meeting: and **Thomas Lapham** and **Abigall Wilber** [Wilbur] laid
their Intentions of taking Each other in marriage before
this meeting and **Eliashib Smith** and **Adam Mott** is appointed to make inquiry into their Clearness and Conversation
and make report to our next monthly meeting
Nicholas Davis and **Adam Mott** having made Enquiry into
Benjamin Taber and **Susanna Lewis**es Clearness and Conver-
Sation make report to this meeting that they find nothing to
hinder their proceedings: and this meeting Receiv'd forty
Shillings of the women: and there was Collected by this
meeting for the use of friends – – – – 01 - 05 = 00
John Tucker and **Isaac Howland** hath made up this meetings
accounts with the Executor of the Treasurer and there
Remains in the Stock Seaven pounds and Six Shilling: 7 = 06 = 00
and this mony is all Disposed of Except one pound ten Shillings
and Six pence which is put in to the Treasurers hands
Eliashib Smith and **Adam Mott** is appointed to take Care of
the meeting House: **Joseph Taber Jacob Taber** and **Thoˢ Hathaway**
is appointed to oversee the burying Ground at **Cushnot**. **John Tucker**
Joseph Russell Junᵣ and **Henry Tucker** are appointed to attend -
the Quarterly meeting and Draw up an Epistle to yᵉ Same
and **Adam Mott** and **Isaac Smith** is appointed to peruse the
monthly meeting munits with **John Tucker** in order that
they may be put on Record and **Isaac Wood** is appointed to
Read **Elisabeth Willcox** [Wilcox] her Condemnation which is as
Followeth:

[top half of page is blank]

~~11 mo:~~
~~1729/30~~ And this meeting orders those friends that are appointed
to attend the Quarterly meeting to pay the remainder part
of the mony for **Robert Barclay**s appollegies and bring

them to our next monthly meeting and yᵉ meeting to pay
them the mony again
Rochester meeting Called and no business presented

11 mo: At a monthly meeting of friends held at our meeting
1729/30 house in **Dartmouth** the 19 day of the 11 month 1729/30
The Seaverall meetings thereto belonging Called upon
for **Dartmouth Adam Mott** present
for **Rochester Nicholas Devis [Davis]** present
Henry Tucker makes report to this meeting that he hath
made Enquiry into **Ebenezer Shearman**s Clearness as
to marriage and Conversation and finds nothing to hinder
his proceedings: **Ebenezer Shearman** and **Wait Barker**
Came to this meeting for their answer
And there answer was that they might proceed to
take each other in marriage in the good order of truth
and **Adam Mott** and **Eliashib Smith** is appointed to See it
done and make report to the next monthly meeting
And likewise **Benjamin Taber** and **Susanna Lewis** Came
to this meeting for their answer and their answer was
that they may proceed to take each other in marriage
in the good order of truth in Some Convenient time
between this and the next monthly meeting and
Nicholas Davis and **John Walker** is appointed to See
their marriage Consumated and in the Good order of
truth and make Return to the next monthly meeting
And **Thoˢ Lapham** and **Abigal Wilber [Wilbur]** Came to this meeting
for their answer Enquiry being made into their
Clearness and Conversation and nothing appearing
to hiender their proceedings their answer was that
they might proceed to take each other in marriage in
the good order of truth and **John Russell** and **Nicholas
Lapham** is appointed to See the Same Consumated in the
abovesd order and make report to our next monthly meeting: **Joseph Russell junʳ** hath attended yᵉ Quarterly
meeting as appointed and **John** and **Henry Tucker**
hath drawn an Epistle to the Same

12 mo: At a monthly meeting of friends held at our meeting
1729/30 House in **Dartmouth** the 16 day of the 12 month 1729/30
The Seaverall meetings thereto belonging Called upon for
Dartmouth Wᵐ Wood present for **Rochester Nicholas Davis**

Nicholas Davis and John Walker that they attended Benja[n]
Tabers marriage and that it was Carried on in good order
as far as they Saw. And likewise Adam Mott and Eliashib
Smith makes report to this meeting that they attended
Ebenezer Shearmans marriage and that it was Consumated in good order. and John Russell and Nicholas Lapham
makes report to this meeting that they attended Tho[s] Lapham
Marriage and they Saw nothing but that it was Carried
on in Good order: David Joy and Mary Taber Laid their
intentions of taking each other in marriage before
this meeting and they are desired to wait until our
next for their answer and Joseph Taber and Joseph
Russell jun[r]: are appointed to make Enquiry into
Their Clearness and Conversation and bring in their account
to the next monthly meeting. Rochester business Called & none present[ed]

1 mo: At a monthly meeting of friends held at our meeting House
1730: In Dartmouth the 16 day of the 1 month 1730
The Seaverall meetings thereto belonging Called upon for Dartmou[th]
William Wood and Adam Mott present for Rochester none appeared
Moses Shearman and Meribah Wood laid their Intentions of taking
each other in marriage before this meeting and are desired to wait
til the next monthly meeting for their answer and Jabez Barker
and John Lapham are appointed to make Enquiry into their
Clearness and Conversation and make return to our next
Monthly meeting how they find things
and Likewise Gideon Gifford and Elisabeth Allen laid their intentions of taking Each other in marriage before this meeting
and are desired to wait until our next monthly meeting
for their answer and Adam Mott and Eliashib Smith are
appointed to make Enquiry into their th Clearness and Conver-
Sation and make return to our next how they find things
And our friends Mary [R?]ennal and Mary Lewis from
Pensalvania was here and their Certificates was read
to this meetings Sattisfaction
And there was Collected at this meeting – – 2 – 10 = 06
William Wood Jun[r] desireing a Certificate this meeting doth
grant him one: and this meeting is adjourned until the
first Sixth day in next month
This meeting being mett according to adjournment this first
Sixth day in the 2d month 1730

The Visiters brings in their account of their visits which
is as followeth: We have visited the famlies of friends in a
pretty Generall way that is under our Care and in Some
families things pretty well as far as we Saw and in other
Some not well where we gave advice which did seam to
be well taken: **John Tucker Joseph Russell jun^r Henry Tucker**
and **Adam Mott** are Chose to attend the Quarterly meeting
and draw an Epistle to the Same

2 *mo:*   At a monthly meeting of friends held at our meeting House
1730   in **Dartmouth** the 20 day of y^e: 2 month 1730
The Seaverall meetings thereto belonging Called upon for
Dartmouth Joseph Taber and **Adam Mott** present for
Rochester none appeared by appointment
John Tucker Henry Tucker Joseph Russell jun^r and **Adam
Mott** attended the Quarterly meeting as appointed and
drew an Epistle to y^e. Same as ordered
and **David Joy** and **Mary Taber** Came to this meeting for
their answer in relation to their taking each other in marriage and Enquiry being made into their Clearness and
nothing appearing to hinder their proceedings in that affair
they had their answer that they might proceed to take
Each other in marriage in the Good order of truth
in some Convenient time between this and y^e. next month
ly meeting and **Joseph Taber** and **Joseph Russell jun^r** is appointed to see their marriage Consummated and make
return to the next monthly meeting
and Likewise **Moses Shearman [Sherman]** and **Meribah Wood** Came
for their answer and their answer was that they
might take each other in marriage in the Good order
of truth in some Convenient time between this and the
next monthly meeting and **Jabez Barker** and **John
Lapham** are appointed to see their marriage Solemnized
in the aforesd order and make return to the next
monthly meeting and: **Gideon Gifford** and **Elisabeth Allen**
Came for their answer and their answer was that
they might take each other in marriage in the good order
of truth in some Convenient time between this and the next
monthly meeting and **Eliashib Smith** and **Adam Mott** is
appointed to see it Consummated in the aforesd order and
make return to the next monthly meeting: and **Jonathan**

Smith and his wife their Certificate was read at this
meeting and is as followeth

From our monthly meeting held at **Providence** the 8 day
of the 2 month 1730.

To friends at **Dartmouth** Greeting: &c

Dear friends after the Sallutation of our Love these are to
Ceartify you that whereas **Jonathan Smith** and his wife
desired a few lines from this meeting for your Sattisfaction
of what station they stood in when they went from us these
therefore are to inform you tho they had sayt it in
Some things in time past yet since their Conversation has been
such as demonstrated a reformation and a Return towards friends
so that they were received and under the Care of this meeting when
they went from us and we recommend them as such to you desireing
your Care over them for their preservation in the truth

Signed by

		Benjamin Pain
Josiah Owen	Seth Aldrich	Nathaniel Gibson
Samuel Aldrich	Moses Aldrich	Benjamin Taste [Tabre?]
Thomas Smith	Joseph Arnold	Stephen Swett

And the Epistle from the Quarterly meeting was read at this
Meeting and kindly accepted

---

3 mo: At a monthly meeting of friends held at our meeting House in
<u>1730</u>   **Dartmouth** the 18 day of the 3 month 1730
the Seaverall meetings thereto belonging Called upon for **Dartmouth**
William Wood and **Adam Mott** present for **Rochester** none appeared
Joseph Taber gives this meeting an account that **David Joy**
and **Mary Taber**s marriage is Consummated in the good order of
truth; and Likewise **John Lapham** gives an account that
Moses Shearman and **Meribah Wood**s marriage was
Consummated in in the good order of truth
and likewise **Eliashib Smith** gives this meeting an account
that **Gideon Gifford** and **Elisabeth Allen**s marriage was
Consummated in the good order of truth – –
Isaac Smith and **Mary Willcox [Wilcox]** Laid their intentions of taking
Each other in marriage before this meeting and weare desired to
wait until our next monthly meeting for their answer and
John Lapham and **Henry Tucker** are Chosen to enquire into
their Clearness Respecting marriage and Conversation and
bring in an account to yᵉ. next monthly meeting have they find things
and whereas **Amoz [Amos] Taber** hath ~~hath~~ married Contrary to the

advise of friends this meeting makes Choice of **John Tucker** and
Jabez Barker to draw up his Condemnation and bring it to our
next monthly meeting in order to be Signed
and **Adam Mott** is appointed to get a new book to Record the
monthly meeting munits [minutes] in and this meeting orders **Adam Mott**
to pay **Isaac Smith** 2ᶠ: 15ˢ for Recording the monthly meeting munits

4 mo: At a monthly meeting of friends held at our meeting house
1730 the: in **Dartmouth** the 22 day of yᵉ 4 month 1730 – – .
The Seaverall meetings thereto belonging Called upon for
Dartmouth William Wood and **Adam Mott** present for
Rochester none appeared by appointment
Isaac Smith is appointed to be assisting to **John Tucker** in
the place and Stead of **John Tucker Junᵉʳ** late deceased
John Lapham and **Henry Tucker** gives this meeting an account
that they find nothing to hinder **Isaac Smith** and **Mary Willcox [Wilcox]**
in Respect to marriage
Isaac Smith and **Mary Willcox** Came for their answer
and their answer was that they might take each other in
marriage in some Convenient time between this and the next
monthly meeting and **John Lapham** and **Henry Tucker** are
appointed to see the same Consumated and in the good order
of truth and to bring in their account to our next
Joseph Borden of **Tiverton** and **Abigil [Abigail] Russell** of **Dartmouth**
laid their intentions of marriage before this meeting and are
desired to wait for their answer until our next
W: Visiters nominated for **Rochester Elisha Wing** and
John Wing, for **Cushnet Nicholas Davis** and **Joseph Taber**
For **Dartmouth Ponaganset John Tucker John Howland**
James Barker and **Adam Mott**. For **A Coakset William**
Wood and any one of the above named for **Ponaganset**
John Tucker Adam Mott Elisha Wing and **Henry Tucker**
are appointed to attend the Quarterly meeting and Draw
up an account to yᵉ. Same
The Suffering of friends at **Rochester** whereof an account
was presented to this meeting which is accepted
This meeting orders that **Adam Mott** take 50 Shillings
out of the Stock for halfe a year keeping the meeting house

5 mo: At a monthly meeting of friends held at our meeting
1730 House in **Dartmouth** the 20 day of the 5 month 1730:
Dartmouth meeting Called **William Wood** and **Henry**

Tucker present: **Rochester** meeting Called none appeared
John Lapham and **Henry Tucker** gives this meeting an accou$_{nt}$
that they was at the marriage of **Isaac Smith** and
Mary Willcox
And Said nothing but that it was Carried on in the good order
of truth; **John Tucker** and **Elisha Wing** have attended the Quarterly meeting; and Drawn up an account to y^e. Same: according
to the order of the Last monthly meeting.
The Epistle from y^e. Quarterly meeting was read at this
meeting and kindly accepted:
And **Joseph Borden** and **Abigail Russell** appeared at this meeting for their answer in relation to their taking each other
in marriage: and things appearing Clear they had their
answer that they might proceed to take each other in
marriage in the good order of truth in some Convenient
time between this and the next monthly meeting and
John Howland and **Adam Mott** are appointed to See their
marriage Consumated in abovesd [abovesaid] order and make
return to the next monthly meeting
There was Collected at this meeting for the use of friends 3$^£$=00^s=6^d
Adam Mott hath paid 2$^£$=15^s=0^d: to **Isaac Smith** for the Recording
the monthly meeting munits: [minutes]
And **Amos Taber**s Condemnation was Signed at this meeting and **Jabez Barker** is ordered to read it at **Cushnet**
meeting on a first day at thend of the meeting of worship

6 mo: At a monthly meeting of friends held at our meeting House
1730:   in **Dartmouth** the 17 day of the 6 month 1730
     Dartmouth meeting Called **William Wood** and **Adam**
     Mott present: **Rochester** meeting Called **Elisha Wing** and
     Stephen Wing present:
     John Howland and **Adam Mott** gives this meeting an
     account that they was at the marriage of **Joseph Borden**
     and **Abigail Russell** and Saw nothing but that it was Con-
     sumated in the Good order of truth
     Jabez Barker hath read **Amos Taber**s Condemnation
     according to y^e. order of the last monthly meeting
     and is as followeth – –
     Whereas **Amos Taber** Son of **Joseph Taber** of **Dartmouth**
     in the **County of Bristol** in y^e. **Province of ye Massachusets**
     bay in **New England** hath from his Childhood been Educated
     among friends; his father and mother both of them the

people Called Quakers – –
yet he in disregard to friends and the Good advice given him
to the Contrary (who Laboured with him in love)
Gone Contrary to their advice and proceeded in marriage
with a woman of an unclear Conversation having had a
bastard Child some time before
which proceedings hath been to the great greif of his father
and the trouble of friends: for which Disorderly proceedings
we are therefore Concerned to give this forth as a
publick Testimony against such disorderly proceedings: and
do deny the sd **Amos Taber** to be one of us the people Called
Quakers: Truly Desireing that he may return and find
Mercy with the Lord
Tenderly advising all friends Children to beware of keeping
bad and vain company least they are drawn into things
that are evil and Dishonour the blessed truth we profess
and Disgrace themselves
Signed by order of sd meeting   **Joseph Russell Ju^r**

John Tucker	**Henry Tucker**	**Jedediah Wood**
William Wood	**Judah Smith**	**Peter Allen**
Joseph Taber	**Adam Moot**	**Eliashib Smith**
Joseph Russell	**William Wood Ju^r**	**Joseph Tucker**
John Lapham	**Jonathan Wood** ———	

And whereas there was a paper presented to the Prepa=
ritive meeting Signed by one **Thomas Cesar** an Indian
signifying his Desire to be under the Care and in unity With
friends. This meeting makes Choise of **John Tucker** and
William Wood to make Enquiry into his Life and Conver=
sation to know whither it be agreable to our principle
and bring in their account to y^e next monthly meeting
and **Adam Mott** hath paid **Jabez Barker** 2=10=0:
out of the meetings Stock for halfe a year keepin the
Meeting House
Rochester meeting business Called and no business presented
and whereas **Adam Mott** was one of the overseers
of our monthly meeting and Desireing to be Excused from
that Servise: this meeting makes Choice of **John Howland**
to Serve in his room – – – – –

7 mo: At a monthly meeting of friends held at our meeting
1730: house in **Dartmouth** the 21 day of the 7 month 1730

The Seaveral meetings thereto belonging Called upon
For **Dartmouth Joseph Russell jun**ʳ present
for **Rochester Stephen Wing** present
And **John Tucker** and **William Wood** gives this meeting an
account that they have mad [made] Enquiry into the life and
Conversation of **Thomas Case** and find nothing but that
it hath been Orderly and this meeting thinks fit to receive
him under their Care
And whereas Friends of **Cushnet** hat[h] Signified to our
preparitive meeting of their desire to have a meeting of
worship setled there on every first day as well the first day
preceeding our monthly meeting as other first days
which is Granted
And whereas the Stable that was built to put Travilars
Horces in being very much out of Repare this meeting
appoints **Jabez Barker** to repare it and bring in his account
to the next monthly meeting
And this meeting agreaeth to Come to a Subscribtion towards
the finnishing of **Cushnot** meeting House
And whereas **Eliashib Smith** having Signified to our prepa=
ritive meeting of his desire of Laying his intentions of
Marriage with **Adry Gifford** and the matter appearing
Something Diffecult by reason of his not having her fathers
Consent which matter this meeting thinks propper to refer
to the Consideration of yᵉ Quarterly meeting next for their
Judgment And **Elisha Wing Joseph Russell jun**ʳ and **John Tucker**
to attend the Quarterly meeting and to draw an account to
the Same – –
And **Keziah Wood** Wife of **William Wood jun**ʳ her Certificate
was read at this meeting and accepted and she to be
under the Care of this meeting.
And the visiters of **Rochester** gives this meeting an account
that they have visited the families of friends belonging to their
Care and yᵉ accᵗ: is as followeth
To the monthly meeting to be held in **Dartmouth** the 21 day of
the 7 month 1730: These may inform that we have visited
the families of friends belonging to our meeting at **Rochester**
and we were received in love and things for the most part
was pretty well Excepting some few things not so well as
we Could Desire but upon Reproof there was promise of

Reformation　　　　　　　　　　　　　　　**John Wing**
　　　　　　　　　　　　　　　　　　　　　Elisha Wing
And this meeting is adjourned until the first sixth day in yᵉ 8ᵗʰ month next
This meeting being met according to adjournment this 2 day of
of the 8ᵗʰ month 1730: The visiters of **Aponaganset** and **Coakset**
weekly meetings gives this meeting an account That they
have visited yᵉ families of friends for the most part under
their Care and things for yᵉ: most part pretty well as far as
they Saw but not all together well

8: 1730　At a monthly meeting of friends held in **Dartmouth** the 11 Day of
the 8 month 1730: **Dartmouth** meeting Called **John Lapham** and
Adam Mott present: **Rochester** meeting Called **Elisha Wing**
present: **Jebez Barker** gives this meeting an account
that he has worked about the Stable that he was appointed
to Repaire and his wor and the nailes that used about it
Comes to 13 Shillings and **Adam Mott** is ordered to pay it out
of the meetings Stock
Butler Wing Son of **Elisha Wing** of **Rochester** and **Bethsheba**
Clifton daughter of **Lavery Clifton** of sᵈ town have Laid their
Intentions of taking each other in marriage: before this meet
=ing and are desired to wait til yᵉ next monthly meeting for
their answer: and **Stephen Wing** and **John Wing** are appoin=
ted to Enquire into their Clearness respecting marriage
and Conversation and make report to the next monthly
meeting: And the Epistle from yᵉ Quarterly meeting was
read at this meeting and kindly accepted
And the matter Concerning **Eliashib Smith** and **Audry Gifford**
that was refered to the Quarterly meeting the Judgment of
the Quarterly meeting is that whereas her father **Christopher**
Gifford his reason against their proceeding in marriage is of
no weight or vallue that friends may admit of their pro=
ceeding in marriage to each other
Joseph Russell junʳ: hath attended the Quarterly meeting
as appointed and **John Tucker** hath drawn an account
to the Same according to the Order of the Last monthly
meeting: And whereas it was proposed to the Consideration
of this meeting whither ~~th~~ it might not be proppor for
The monthly meeting to be at the Charge of housing Travilers
Horces that Comes to Labour in the Gospel among us
which this meeting thinks to be very well and agreas to

And whereas there was a Complaint to the visiters from **Jacob Soule** (which was
presented to this meeting) Concerning **Nathan Soules** Son **George**
that he hath begotten his daughter with Child absented himselfe
and it is the mind of this meeting that **Nathan Soule** should do his
Endeaver to git his Son home and that he and the young woman
should have a hearing face to face before Som Sollid friends both
men and women that may be unconcerned and the sd **Nathan
Soule** to give an account to the next monthly meeting
of what he hath done in the matter

9 mo: At a monthly meeting of friends held at our meeting House in
1730 **Dartmouth** the: 16 day of the 9 month 1730
Dartmouth meeting Called **William Wood** and **Adam Mott** present
Rochester meeting Called **Elisha Wing** present:
The friends that were appointed to See into **Butler Wing** and
Bethsheba Cliftons Clearness have sent an account to this meet
=ing in writing that they have mad inquirey and find nothing to
the Contrary but that he may proceed in marriage with
Bethsheba Clifton
And **Butler Wing** and **Bethsheba Clifton** appeared at this meet=
ing for their answer in relation to ther taking Each other in
marriage and things appearing Clear they had their answer
that they might proceed to take each other in marriage in
Some Convenient time between this and the next monthly
meeting, and **Stephen Wing** and **John Wing** are appointed to see
their marriag Consumated in the good order of truth and
make return to the next monthly meeting
And **Adam Mott** hath paid **Jabez Barker** 13 Shillings out of
the monthly meetings Stock as appointed
And **Nathan Soule** gives this meeting an account that he hath
Spoken with his Son **George** and that he is willing to have a hear=
ing with the young woman provided that **Jacob Soule** would
become bound not to take that advantage to prosecute him in yᵉ Law
And **Jacob Soule** hath Complained to yᵉ Visiters that **Nathan
Soule** was instrumental or Some Ways Incouraging in his
absenting him selfe so as not to be brought to Justice in the
matter relating to his daughter
This meeting makes Choice of **Henry Tucker Eliashib Smith
John Howland Thomas Smith** and **Isaac Howland**
To talk with **Nathan Soule** and **Jacob Soule** face to face to
see how things are and to bring in their account to the next

monthly meeting

And there was a paper Signed at this meeting and in behalf of
the meeting in order to send to our present Governor **Jonathan
Belcher** Signifying our willingness to Comply with giving him
his Sallery according to the Kings Instructions and **Henry Tucker**
is appointed to Carry and to make return to the next monthly
meeting

10: mo: At a monthly meeting of friends held at our meeting House
1730 in **Dartmouth** the 21 day of the 10 month 1730

Dartmouth meeting Called upon **Henry Tucker** and **John Howland**
present **Rochester** meeting Called **Nicholas Davis** present
The friends that were appointed to See **Butler Wing** and
Bethsheba Cliftons marriage Solemnized not being present
it is refered to the next monthly meeting

Henry Tucker makes report to this meeting that he hath not
been to Carry the Letter to the Governor: he is still Continu=
=ed to do it and make return to the next monthly meeting

And **Stephen Wing** and **Margrate Clifton** both of **Rochester**
did lay their intentions of taking Each other in marriage
before this meeting and were desired to wait for their an=
swer until the next monthly meeting and **Elisha Wing**
and **Joseph Tabor** are appointed to see into their Clearness
and make report to the next monthly meeting

And **Stephen Willcox** Son of **Stephen Willcox** and
Mary Thomas both of **Dartmouth** Laid their Intentions
of taking each other in marriage before this meeting
and were desired to wait for their answer til the next
monthly meeting

And the friends that were appointed to talk with **Nathan**
and **Jacob Soule** have given in an account in writing to this
meeting of their doings therein

And this meeting Chooseth **Henry Tucker** and **James Barker**
to overse the meeting House for the year Insuing

There was Collected at this meeting for yᵉ use of friends 1= 06 =04
and there was 1- 15= 0 given by the womens meeting
Towards keeping the meeting House

And this meeting orders **Adam Mott** to pay **Jabez Barker** 2£=10ˢ=00ᵈ
out of the meetings Stock for halfe a years kepping the meeting
house: And this meeting appoints **John Tucker Henry Tucker**
Elisha Wing and **Thomas Smith** to attend the Quarterly meeting

next and to Draw an Epistle to the Same

And this meeting agreas to come to a Subscribtion for **Joshua**
a friend belonging to **Yarmauth** the being in a Low Condition
as to his worldly affaires

And it was proposed whither it might not be propper to do
Something towards Giting a School master to teach friends
Children which is refered to the next monthly meeting

11 mo: At a monthly meeting of friends held at our meeting House
1730/31   in **Dartmouth** yᵉ 18 day of the 11 month 1731/30

Dartmouth meeting Called **Adam Mott** and **Isaac Howland**
present: Rochester meeting Called **John Wing** appeared
John Wing and **Stephen Wing** Give this meeting an account
that they were at the marriag of **Butler Wing** and **Bethsheba
Clifton** and Saw nothing but that it was Carried on in the Good
order of friends.

And **Elisha Wing** hath Sent an account to this meeting that
he hath made Inquiry into yᵉ Clearness and Conversation
of **Stephen Wing** and finds nothing to hinder his proceedings
in Respecting marriage

And **William Wood** and **Adam Mott** makes report to this
meeting that they have enquired into the life and Conversation of **Stephen Willcox** and find nothing to hinder his
proceedings.

And **Stephen Wing** and **Margrate Clifton** appeared at this
desireing an answer in relation to their taking each other
in marriage and had their answer that they might proceed
to take each other in marriage in the good order of truth
in Some Convenient time between this and the next
Monthly meeting and **Joseph Taber** and **John Walker** are appoited
to See their marriage Consumated in the above sᵈ order and
Make return to the next monthly meeting.

And **Stephen Willcox** and **Mary Thomas** Came to this meeting
Came to this meeting for their answer as to their takin each
other in marriage and their answer was that they might
proceed to take each other in marriage in the Good order of
friends in Some Convenient time between this and the next
Monthly meeting and **William Wood** and **Adam Mott** are appoin-
=ted to see their marriage Solemnized in the above Good order
and make report to the next monthly meeting.

And **Richard Smith** Son of **Judah Smith** and **Dorothy Potter** daughter

of **Stoakes Potter** deceased both of **Dartmouth**, laid their intentions
of taking each other in Marriage before this meeting
And were desired to wait until the next monthly meeting for their
answer and **Isaac Howland** and **John Russell** are appointed to
inquire into his Clearness and Conversation and make return
to the next monthly meeting how they find things
And **Henry Tucker** makes report to this meeting that he hath Sent
the Letter which the Monthly Meeting ordered to be sent to the
Governour; by **Samuel** There a **Mendon** friend
the friends that were appointed to attend the Quarterly
Meeting have attended it and drawn an Epistle to the Same
According to Order
The Epistle at from the Quarterly Meeting was read at
this meeting and well accepted
And **William Wood Jun**ʳ and his wives Marriage Certificate
was read at this meeting to friends Satisfaction
Stephen Willcox desires Leave of this meeting of Worship
which this meeting allowes of
And whereas the Comᵗᵉᵉ: that was Chose to hear **Nathan Soule**
and **Jacob Soule** Concerning the Difference between them
not having made a final Issue of the Same **John Tucker**
John Tucker Jabez Barker and **John Russell** are aded to them
to Judg and Determine the matter and make return to the
next monthly meeting: no business from **Rochester**

12
month:
1730/1

At a monthly meeting of friends held at our meeting
House in **Dartmouth** the 15 day of the 12 month 1730/31
Dartmouth meeting Called **William Wood** and **Adam Mott**
present: **Rochester** meeting Called **Stephen Wing** present
Joseph Taber and **John Walker** gives this meeting an account
that they Was at the marriage of **Stephen Wing** and **Margrat**
Clifton and that it was Carried on in Good order as far as they saw
And **Adam Mott** Gives this meeting an account that he was at
the marriage of **Stephen Willcox** and **Mary Thomas** and Saw
nothing but that it was performed in good order
John Russell and **Isaac Howland** Give this meeting an account
that they have made Enquiry into the Clearness and Conversation
of **Richard Smith** and find nothing to hinder his proceeding
in marriag with **Dorothy Potter** according to their Intentions
and **Richard Smith** and **Dorothy Potter** Came to this meeting
for their answer in relation to their taking each other

in marriage and had their answer that they might proceed
to take each other in Marriage in the Good order of friends
in Some Convenient time between this and the next
monthly meeting and **John Russell** and **Isaac Howland** are
appointed to See their Marriage accomplished in the aforesd
order and make return to the next monthly meeting
and **Eliashib Smith** and **Audry Gifford** did lay their inten
=tions of taking each other in marriage before this Meeting
and were desired to wait til the next monthly meeting
for their answer

And **Adam Mott** and **Joseph Tucker** to See into his Clearness
respecting marriage and Conversation and make return to the next
Monthly Meeting

And **Humphry Smith** Son of **Deliverance Smith** deceased and
Mary Willcox Daughter of **Jeremiah Willcox** both of **Dartmouth**
did Lay their intentions of taking Each other in marriage before
this meeting and were desired to wait til yᵉ next monthly meeting
for their answer and **Isaac Howland** and **Nicholas Lapham** are
appointed to Enquire into the young mans Clearness and make
Report to the next monthly meeting

and **Nathaniel Curby** Son of **Robert Curby** and **Abigall Russell**
Daughter of **James Russell** both of **Dartmouth** did lay their inten-
tions of taking each other in marriage before this meeting and
Were desired to wait for their answer until yᵉ next monthly
Meeting and **Wᵐ Wood** and **Jedidiah Allen** are appointed to make
Enquiry into his Clearness Respecting marriage and Conversation
and make report to the next monthly meeting

and **Eliashib Smith** and **Isaac Smith** are appointed to mak up
the monthly meeting accompts with yᵉ treasurer and bring in
their account to the next monthly meeting

And whereas the Comᵗᵉᵉ: nominated at the Last monthly meeting
to Judg upon **Nathan** and **Jacob Soules** difference, not all agreing
in Judgment this meetings Judgment is that the Majority of sᵈ
Comᵗᵉᵉ: Shall determine the matter

Which they Quickly did and brought in their Judgment which
was that he the sᵈ **Nathan Soule** Should Come to the next
monthly meeting and acknowledg to the meeting that he
was to blame in the above mentioned promised

and **Richard Smith** Desires Leave of this meeting that he
may Solemnize his marriage on a fourth Day after the meeting
of worship

1 mo: At a monthly meeting of friends held at our meeting House
1730/31 in **Dartmouth** the 15 day of yᵉ 1 month 1730/31

Dartmouth meeting Called **William Wood** and **Adam Mott**
present **Rochester** meeting Called **Nicholas Davis** present
John Russell and **Isaac Howland** give this meeting an account
that they were at **Richard Smith** and **Dorothy Potters** marriage
and Saw nothing but that it was performed in good order
Adam Mott and and **Joseph Tucker** Signifies to this meeting that
they enquired into the Conversation and Clearness of **Eliashib
Smith** in relation to marriage and find nothing to hinder his
proceedings in that affair
Nicholas Lapham and **Isaac Howland** gives an account
that they have made Inquiry into the Clearness and Conversation of **Humphry Smith** and find nothing to hinder his proceed=
ing in marriage according to ~~their inte~~ his intentions.
And **William Wood** hath made inquiry into yᵉ Clearness and
Conversation of **Nathaniel Curby** and finds nothing to hinder his
proceedings in relation to marriage
Eliashib Smith and **Audry Gifford** appeared at this meeting
and desired the meetings answer in relation to their taking
each other in marriage and their answer was that they
might proceed to take each other in marriage in the good
order of truth in Some Convenient time between this and the
next monthly meeting and **John Howland** and **John Russell**
are appointed to see their marriage Consumated and mak re=
turn to the next monthly meeting
Humphry Smith and **Mary Willcox** Came to this meeting
for their answer and their answer was that they might
proceed to take each other in marriage in the good order
of truth and **William Wood** and **Henry Tucker** are appointed
See their marriage Sollemnized in the above sᵈ order and
make return to the next monthly meeting
And **Nathaniel Curby** and **Abigail Russell** Came to this meet
ing for their answer in Relation to their taking Each other
in marriage and their answer was that they might proceed
to take each other in marriage in Some Convenient time
between this and the next monthly Meeting in the good order
of truth: and and **Thomas Smith** and **John Russell** are appointed
to See their marriage Consumated in yᵉ aforesd order and
make return to yᵉ next monthly meeting

Eliashib Smith and Isaac Smith have made up the monthly
meetings accompts with Adam Mott and there remains
in the Stock – – :2 -15 =01

The matter Concerning Nathan Soule is refered to the
next monthly meeting

And John Tucker James Barker and Adam Mott are
appointed to attend yᵉ Quarterly meeting next and to draw
up an account to yᵉ Same

There was Collected at this meeting – – :2£ -01ˢ =05ᵈ
and Rochester visiters gives this meeting an account
that they have visited the families of friends belonging to
their Care and find things indifferent well

and Cushnot visiters gives an account that they have visited
the families of friends that belong to their Care and find
things pretty well Considering their Circumstances
and this meeting is adjourned until the youths meeting next

This meeting being met according to adjournment this
2:ᵈ day of the 2:ᵈ month 1731

The visiters being Called upon belonging to Ponaganset
and Coaxet they give no account of visiting the families
of friends under their Care

And it is ordered that Adam Mott Should take twenty
Shillings out of the Stock for Service done for friends

---

2 mo: At a monthly meeting of friends held at our meeting House in
1731   Dartmouth the 18 day of the 2 month 1731

The Seaverall meetings thereto belonging Called upon for Dartmouth
Henry Tucker and Adam Mott present
for Rochester none appeared

John Russell and John Howland gives this meeting an account
that they were at Eliashib Smith and Audrey Giffords marriage
and Saw nothing but that it was orderly performed

Henry Tucker makes report to this meeting that Humphrey Smith
and Mary Willcoxes marriage was Solemnized in the Good order
of truth. And John Russell and Thomas Smith makes report to
this meeting that Nathanael Curby and Abigal Russells marriage
was Solemnized in the Good order of Truth

And the matter Concerning Nathan Soule is refered to yᵉ next
Monthly meeting

And John Tucker Adam Mott and James Barker hath attended
the Quarterly meeting and Drawn up an Epistle to yᵉ Same

as appointed
The business of **Dartmouth** meeting Called and yᵉ friends that
was appointed to See after **Robert Barclays** apollegies are ordered
to bring in their accounts to yᵉ next monthly meeting how things
are respecting that matter
And the Epistl from yᵉ Qurterly meeting was read at this
Meeting and well accepted

3 mo: At a monthly meeting of friends held at our meeting House in
1731: **Dartmouth** the 17 day of yᵉ 3 month 1731
the Seaverall meetings therunto belong Called upon for **Dartmouth**
Adam Mott present: for **Rochester** none present:
and the matter Concerning the account of **Robert Barclays**
appollegies is refered to the next monthly meeting
And **Nathan Soule** appeared at this meeting and Refuseth to
take up with friends advice and Judgment which is refered
to the next monthly meeting
And this meeting is adjourned until the 2:ᵈ fourth day in the
next month
This meeting being mett according to adjournment this 9ᵗʰ day
of yᵉ 4 month 1731 but no business was presented in order to be
done

At a monthly meeting of friends held at our meeting House in
Dartmouth the 21 day of the 4 month 1731
Dartmouth meeting Called **Henry Tucker** and **Adam Mott** present
Rochester meeting Called and **Stephen Wing** appeared
and Concerning the account of **Robert Barclays** appollegies
is refered to yᵉ next monthly meeting
and **Nathan Soule** appeared at this meeting and Still refuseth
to take up with friends judgment, it is therefore the
judgment of this meeting that **Nathan Soule** ought not to sit
in monthly meetings as a member thereof until he hath
made acknowledgment to friends Sattisfaction
Our Dear friend **Ruth Jones** from **Pensilvania** was at this meet
ing and her Certificate was read to friends Sattisfaction
and **Adam Mott** hath paid **Henry Tucker** and **James Barker**
3 pounds of the meetings Stock towards keeping yᵉ meeting House
And our former Visiters for the year past are Still Continued
for the Service of visiting friends families for yᵉ year Ensuing
And **John Tucker** is added to them
and **John Tucker** and **William Wood** are appointed to attend the

Quarterly meeting next and to draw an Epistle to the Same
The yearly meeting from **London** baring date yᵉ 18 of the 5 month
:1730 was read at this meeting to friends Sattisfaction

5 *mo:* At a monthly meeting of friends held at our meeting House in
1731 **Dartmouth** the 19 day of the 5 month 1731
The Seaverall meetings thereto belonging Called upon for
Dartmouth **Adam Mott** and **Jabez Barker** present
And **Savery Clifton** for **Rochester**
and the account of **Rober Barclays** appollegies not being ready
it is refered to the next monthly meeting
John Tucker and **William Wood** have attended yᵉ Quarterly
Meeting: and Drawn an account to the Same
The Epistle from the Quarterly meeting was read at this meeting
to friends Sattisfaction: and friends of this meeting agreas to Come
to a Subscribtion of 6 pounds for the Quarterly meeting Stock
as it was requested by the Quarterly Meeting and to bring it in
at the next monthly meeting
and whereas there was an account Sent from **Rochester**
preparitive meeting to this meeting that the widow **Sarah**
Clifton now wife of **John Rose** hath gone out of the good
order Established among friends and married one that is no
friend, for which disorderly proceedings this meeting is Concer=
=ned for the Clearing of truth to draw up a Condemnation
against her and **John Tucker** and **Isaac Smith** are apponted
to draw one and present it to the next monthly meeting
in Order to be Signed
and there was a Condemnation Signed at this meeting against
Hannah Chace daughter of **Nathaniel Chace** for Commiting
fornication and **Henry Tucker** is appointed to read it between
This and the next monthly meeting on a first day at the end
of the meeting of worship on a first day at **Aponaganset**
Meeting House

6 *mo:* At a monthly meeting of friends held at our meeting House
1731 in **Dartmouth** the 16 day of the 6 month 1731
The Seaverall meetings thereunto belonging Called upon
for **Dartmouth John Howland** and **Adam Mott** present
for **Rochester Elisha Wing** present
and nothing being done toward the account of **Robert Barclays**
appollegies it is refered to the next monthly meeting
The Subscribtion mentioned at the last monthly meeting

for the yearly meeting Stock was paid in at this meeting and
delivered into **John Tuckers** hands in order for **Thoˢ Leach**
And **John Tucker** and **Isaac Smith** have drawn up **Sarah Clifton**
now wife of **John Rose** her Condemnation and presented to this
meeting which is allowed and Signed and **Elisha Wing** is ordered
to read it at **Rochester** meeting House on a first day after the
Meeting of Worship between this and the next monthly meeting
and make return to the Same

And **Henry Tucker** hath read **Hannah Chaces** Condemnation
according to order which is as followeth

Whereas **Hannah Chace** Daughter of **Nathaniel Chace** of
Dartmouth in the **County of Bristol** in **New England** having been
Educated among friends (yet to the Dishonour of God reproach
of the blessed truth professed amongst us and to the grief of friends)
hath by giving way to the Temtations of Satan and her own
Wicked inclination fallen into that Wicked and Scandalus Sin
of fornication as appears by her being delivered of Late of a
bastard Child

We do therefore give this forth as a publick testimony against
s^d wicked and unclean action Denying the s^d **Hannah Chace**
to be one of us the people Called Qukers heartily desireing
that if it be the Will of God she may by taking Shame to her
selfe through Godly Sorrow and Sincere Repentance find
Mercy with the Lord

Given forth at our monthly meeting of men and women
friends held in **Dartmouth** the 19:^th day of the 5:^th month <u>1731</u>
and Signed by

John Tucker	**Joseph Tucker**	**Elisabeth Barker**
W:^m Wood	**Adam Mott**	**Rebecca Russell**
Tho:^s Hathaway	<u>**Nicholas Lapham**</u>	**Rebecca Barker**
Savorie Clifton	**Mehetabel Burril**	**Jean Smith**
Joseph Russell	**Ruth Tucker**	**Rebecca Slocum**
Henry Tucker	**Mary Russell**	**Abigal Whitely**
Joseph Russell jun^r	**Phebe Tucker**	**Grisel Sherman**
Eliashib Smith	**Mary Lapham**	
Tho:^s Smith	**Sarah Taber**	

7 mo: At a monthly meeting of friends held in **Dartmouth** at friends
<u>1731</u> Meeting Huse on the 20 day of y^e: 7 month 1731
     Dartmouth Meeting Called **Henry Tucker** and **Adam Mott**
     present **Rochester** meeting Called **Stephen Wing** present

and the account of **R. B**: appollegies is refered to yᵉ next monthly
Meeting and **Elisha Wing** not having read **Sarah Rose** as
Condemnation he is Still Continued to do it and make return
to the next monthly meeting

Anthony Arnold Son of **John Arnold** of **Providence** in the
Colony of **Rhoad Island** in **New England** and **Sarah Fish** Daughter
of **John Fish** of **Dartmouth** in **New England** did lay their intenti-
=ons of taking each other in marriage before this meeting
And were desired to wait for their answer until the next
monthly meeting: and **Henry Tucker** and **Adam Mott** are
appointed to Make enquiry into the young mans Clearness
and make return to yᵉ next Monthly Meeting

and Friends of **Acushnot** proposed at this meeting that they
have a mind to build a stable upon the meeting house land
at **Acushnot** to put friends horses in which this meeting
agreas to

There was Collected at this meeting House for the use of
friends – – £02 05ˢ 08ᵈ

and this meeting is adjourned until yᵉ first fourth day in the
eighth month next

This meeting being met according to adjournment this
6 day of the 8 month 1731

Adam Mott Joseph Russell junʳ and **Henry Tucker** are appoin-
=ted to attend the Quarterly Meeting next and Draw up an
Epistle to the Same and **John Tucker** to assist them

8 mo: At a monthly meeting of friends held at our meeting House
1731   in **Dartmout**h the 18 day of the 8 month 1731:
The Seaveral meetings thereunto belonging Called upon
for **Dartmouth Adam Mott** present: for **Rochest**er
John Wing present
and the matter Concerning the appollegies is refered to
the next monthly meeting
The Friends that were appointed to draw up an account
to yᵉ Quarterly meeting have done it but could not attend it
by reason of the Weather being So Stormy that they Could
not git over the ferry
And **Anthony Arnold** and **Sarah Fish** Came for their
answer to this meeting and nothing appearing to hinder
their Intentions they had their answer that they might
proceed to take Each other in marriage in the order of

truth and **Adam Mott** and **Thomas Smith** are appointed
to se it performed in the above s^d order and make return
to the next monthly meeting
and **Seth Hilliar** and **Dorcas Davis** boath of **Rochester** did
lay their Intentions of taking Each other in marriage
before this meeting and are desired to wait until the next
Monthly meeting for their answer and **John Wing** and
Stephen Wing are appointed to see into their Clearness
and make return to the next Monthly Meeting
And **Elisha Wing** hath read **Sarah Rose** her condemnation
which is as followeth.
Whereas **Sarah Clifton** Widow of **Benjamin Clifton**
Late of **Rochester** in the County of **Plymouth** in **New England**
and now Wife of **John Rose** hath of Late gone out of the good
order established among ~~friends~~ us the people of God Called
Qukers and was married by a Presbyterian Minister So Called
to one that is not in unity with us
Notwithstanding she was once before Condemned by Friends for
Commiting an offence of the same nature tho not of so high a
degree for which afterwards she did make Some Shew of
repentance and sent in a paper to our monthly meeting
Signifying her sorrow for the same and desiring that friends
would pass it by and that she might Come under friends Care and
in unity with them again which was Granted: yet now through
Willful Disobedience and slight of ye Good order Established among
us as plainly appears by her keeping Company in an hidden and
unadvisable manner with one whose principles is avers to
ours and friends having discharged their duty in advising her
to the Contrary as Soon as they had oppertunity after they
heard of it and yet she hath proceeded to marry out of the
good order of friends. Therefore we are Concerned to give this
forth as a publick Testimony against her Obstinate and
Willful proceedings denying the s^d **Sarah Clifton** now **Rose** to be
one of us the people Called Qukers
Desireing if it be the Will of God she may Come to a sight
and sence of her out goings and so Come to unfeigned repentance
And find mercy with the Lord and Com into unity with
his people
Given forth at our monthly meeting held in **Dartmouth**
the 16 day of the 6 month 1731: and signed by order and in

behalfe of s^d meeting by   **John Tucker** Clerk

                                    of s^d meeting

And the Epistle from the Quarterly meeting was read at
this meeting and well accepted

And the meeting hath signed a Certificate for **Thomas Lapham**
and his wife Recommending them to the monthly meeting held
at **Smithfield** in the Colony of **Rhoad Island** and **Providence**
plantations in **New England**

9 mo: At a monthly meeting of friends Held at our meeting House in
1731   **Dartmouth** the 15 day of the 9 month 1731

        Dartmouth Meeting Called **Tho:^s Smith** and **Adam Mott** present

        Rochester meeting Called **Savory Clifton** appeared

and nothing being towards the account of ye appollegies it is refered
to the next monthly meeting

and **Seth Hilliar** and **Dorcas Davis** appeared at this meeting
for their answer in relation to their taking each other in
marriage and nothing appearing to hinder their proceeding
in that affair they had their answer that they might proceed
to take each other in marriage in the good order of truth
in same Convenient time between this and the
next monthly meeting

And **William Wood** and **Adam Mott** are appointed to
see their marriage Consumated in the afores'd order and
make return to the next monthly meeting

and **John Russell jun:^r** of **Dartmouth** son of **John Russell**
and **Patience Tucker** the Daughter of **Henry Tucker** of
s^d **Dartmouth** have Laid their Intentions of taking each
other in marriage before this meeting and were desired
to wait until y^e next monthly meeting for their answer
and **Eliashib Smith** and **George Soule** are appointed to see
into the young mans Clearness in referance to mar:
=riage and Conversation and make return to the
next monthly meeting

And **Tho:^s Smith** and **Adam Mott** makes report to this
Meeting that they was at the Solemnizing of **Anthony**
Arnold and **Sarah Fishes** marriage and Saw nothing
but that it was accomplished in y^e Good order Established
among friends

And it was thought propper at this meeting that Some
friend Should be Chosen to Git the meeting House Glas mend

=ed and **John Russell** is appointed to git it done and make
return to the yᵉ next monthly meeting
Rochester meeting and no business presented

10: mo: At a monthly meeting of friends held at our meeting
1731: House in **Dartmouth** the 20 day of the 10 month 1731
Dartmouth meeting Called **Jabez Barker** and **James
Barker** present: **Rochester** meeting Called and none appear.ᵈ
The friends that were appointed to inspect into
John Russell junʳ: Clearness makes report that they have
Made Enquiry and find nothing to Hinder their proceedings
and **John Russell** and **Patience Tucker** appeared at this
meeting desireing their answer in relation to their
taking each other in marriage and nothing appearing
to hinder they had their answer that they might proceed
to take each other in marriage in the good order of truth
and **James Barker** and **Abraham Tucker** are appointed
to see their marriage Consumated and make return to
the next monthly meeting
and **Adam Mott** makes report to this meeting that he was
at the marriage of **Seth Hillier** and **Dorcas Davis** and saw
nothing but that it was Carried on in the good order of truth – –
And **Timothy Ricketson** the Son of **Jonathan Ricketson**
and **Bethsheba Willbor** Daughter of **Benjamin Willbor**
both of **Dartmouth** did Lay their intentions of taking
Each other in marriage before this meeting – –
And are desired to wait until the next monthly meeting
for their answer: and **John Howland** and **Eliashib Smith**
are appointed to see into the young mans Clearness respecting
Marriage and Conversation and make return to the next
Monthly Meeting
and nothing being done towards yᵉ amount of yᵉ Appollegies
it is refered to the next monthly meeting
and **Abraham Tucker** and **Joseph Tucker** are appointed to
oversee the Meeting House for the year Ensuing
And **John Howland** and **Adam Mott** are appointed to attend
the Quarterly Meeting next and Draw an Epistle to yᵉ same
and this meeting orders **Adam Mott** to pay one pound sixteen
Shillings to **Henry Tucker** and **James Barker** for Keeping the
Meeting House th year past
and there was Collected at this meeting for yᵉ use of friends £1=19ˢ =8ᵈ

And **Adam Mott** paid **H:T**: and **J. B** one pound sixteen
Shillings as ordered

11 mo:　At a monthly meeting of friends held at our meeting House
1731:　in **Dartmouth** the 17 day of 11 month 1731
　　　　Dartmouth meeting Called **Nicholas Lapham** present
　　　　Rochester meeting Called **John Wing** present
　　　　and **Abraham Tucker** gives this meeting an account that
　　　　the marriag between **John Russell** and **Patience Tucker**
　　　　was performed in the Good order of truth as far as he saw
　　　　and there was an account of **Rober Barclays** appollegies
　　　　brought in at this meeting and there remains yet ~~to~~
　　　　Ten of s^d books belonging to this Meeting
　　　　the business of **Rochester** Called and it was proposed that
　　　　Whereas **John Walker** of **Rochester** being in a low helpless
　　　　Condition and having thoughts of selling his farm to put him
　　　　selfe in a way to sustain his family and Desires the advise
　　　　and Counsel of friends in that affair and this meeting
　　　　makes Choice of **John Tucker Benjamin Allen** and
　　　　Nicholas Davis to go and enquire into his affairs and make
　　　　Return to the next monthly meeting
　　　　And this meeting is adjourned until the next fourth day Come Week
　　　　day of the 11 month 1731/32 **Timothy Ricketson** and **Bethsheba**
　　　　Willbor appeared at this meeting and Desired their answer in
　　　　relation to their taking each other in marriage and things
　　　　appearing Clear they had their answer that they might
　　　　proceed to take each other in marriage in the good order
　　　　Established among friends in Some Convenient time between
　　　　this and the next monthly meeting
　　　　And **John Howland** and **Jabez Barker** are appointed to see
　　　　their marriage Consumated in the good order of truth and
　　　　Make return to the next monthly meeting
　　　　John Howland and **Adam Mott** hath drawn up a Epistle to the
　　　　Quarterly Meeting and **Adam Mott** hath attended y^e same
　　　　And the Quarterly meeting Epistle was read at this meeting
　　　　and well accepted

12 mo:　At a monthly meeting of friends held at our meeting House
1731/32:　In **Dartmouth** the 25 day of the 12 month of 1731\32
　　　　Dartmouth meeting Called **James Barker** and **Adam Mott**
　　　　present: **Rochester** Meeting Called **Stephen Wing** present

Thomas Yenin the son of Benoni Yenin of Rochester
and Abigail Wood daughter of William Wood of Darmouth
Signified to this meeting their intentions of taking each other
In marriage and they were desired to wait until the next
monthly meeting for their answer and Elisha Wing Stephen
Wing and Jedediah Allen are appointed to enquire into the
young mans Clearness as to Marriage and Conservation
and make return to yᵉ: next monthly meeting
And the friends that were appointed to John Walkers
Circumstances makes report that they have been down
to Rochester and their judgment is that it would be well
for friends to extend their Charity and help him a little
as they find fredom which this meeting agreas to
And John Howland and Jabez Bearker makes report to
this meeting that they were at the Solemnizeing of
Timothy Ricketson and Bethsheba Willbor marriage and
that things wer Carried on in Good order as far as they saw
and this meeting adjourne the next Preparitive and month
=ly meeting one week Longer than the usual Corse by reason
of Sandwich yearly meeting
And Adam Mott gives this meeting an account that he
hath bought a book to record the minits of yᵉ monthly
Meeting in and it Cost £1-08ˢ=08ᵈ and this meeting orders
him to take one pound and ten shillings out of yᵉ stock
for the cost of yᵉ Book and trouble in procureing of it
and this meeting orders Adam Mott to pay one pound sixteen
shillings out of the stock for meending the meeting House glass

1 mo: At a monthly meeting of friends held at our Meeting House
1732: in Dartmouth yᵉ: 27 day of the first month 1732
Dartmouth meeting Called James Barker and John Russell
prent: Rochester meeting Called Elisha Wing present
The friends that were appointed to Enquire into Thomas
Yenins Clearness makes report that they have made Enquiry
And Thomas Yenin [Youen] and Abigail Wood appeared at this
meeting and Desired their answer in relation to their
taking each other in marriage and they had their answer
that they might proceed to take each other in marriage
in the good order of truth in some Convenient time between
this and the next monthly meeting and Jedediah Allen
and Robert Tripp are appointed to see their Marriage

accomplished in the above s^d order and make return to
the next Monthly Meeting

And **John Borden** the son of **Richard Borden** of **Tiverton**
in the County of **Bristol** in **New England** and **Hannah**
Russell widow of **Seth Russell** Late of **Dartmouth** deceas^d
have laid their intentions of taking Each other in marriage
before this meeting and were desired to wait til the
next monthly meeting for their answer and he to
produce a Certificate from the monthly meeting where
he belongs of his Clearness respecting marriage and
Conversation and this meeting appoints **John Tucker**
Benjamin Allen and **James Barker** to see how matters
are like to be setled among the widows Children that
they be not wronged nor injured (of what Propperly belongs
to them) by their mothers second Marriage

And **Adam Mott** hath taken one pound ten shillings
out of the Stock and hath paid one pound sixteen shillings
out of the Stock to **John Russell** as ordered

and **John Russell** gives this meeting an account that he
hath made as many Tools for the meetings use as Comes
to £2-05^s=00^d and **Adam Mott** is ordered to pay it out of
the meetings Stock

And there was Collected at this meeting for the use of
friends　　　　　　　　　　　　　　　　1-17=06

John Tucker Joseph Russell jun^r and **Elisha Wing** are
appointed to attend the Quarterly Meeting next and Draw
an Epistle to the Same

And this meeting is adjourned until the last fourth day
before the Quarterly meeting

This meeting being met according to adjournment this 12
day of the 2 month 1732

The visiters of this meeting being Called upon gives this
meeting an account that they have done nothing towards
the visiting of friends families

And the visiters of **Rochester** sent an account in
writeing to this meeting which is as followeth

To the Monthly meeting to be holden at **Dartmouth** the 27 day
of ye first month 1732 These may inform that we have
visited the families of friends in a Generall Way and we
find for past things among friends are pretty well

Excepting some few things not so well as we desired but
we laboured for amendment and we are not without
hopes and they received us in love and learned to receive
our visits kindly   **John Wing**
                                                     Elisha Wing

And the visiters of **Acushnot** gives this meeting an
account that they have visited some of the families of
friends belonging to their Care and that their visits were
well accepted according to their judgment

2 *mo:* At a monthly Meeting of friends Held at our meeting
1732: House In **Dartmouth** yᵉ: 17 day of the 2 month 1732:
Dartmouth meeting Called **Adam Mott** and **Joseph Tucker**
present. **Rochester** meeting Called none appeared
Robert Tripp gives this meeting an account that he was
at the solemnizeing of the marriage between **Thoˢ: Yenin**
and **Abigal Wood** and saw nothing but that it was Carried
on in Good order
The friends that were Chose to take Care Concerning
Hannah Russells Children that they might not be wronged
by their mothers second marriage have taken Care about
it and gives this meeting an account that that things
are like to be Carried on Well and Well setled
And at this meeting **John Borden** and **Hannah Russell**
Came for their answer and things appearing Clear-
he the sᵈ **Borden** producing a Certificate from the monthly
meeting where he belongs of his Clearness as to marriage
and Conversation: This meeting Gives them their answer
that they might proceed to take each other in marriage
In the Good order of truth in Some Convenient time
between this and the next monthly meeting
and **Benjamin Allen** and **Joseph Russell junʳ**: are appointed
to see their Marriage Solemnized in the above sᵈ order
and make Return to yᵉ next monthly meeting
And **Adam Mott** and Gives this meeting and account
that he hath paid **John Russell**   2-05=00
according to the order of the last monthly meeting
The friends that were appointed to attend the Quarterly
Meeting have attended it and also Drawn an account
to the same according to order
And where as the friends of **Acushnot** vilage have

Signified that they have a desire to have a weekeday
meeting setled in their vilage one or two days in a
Month and this meeting having taken it into Conside=
=ration have granted that they may have two week day
Meetings in a month setled among them and it is left
their judgement to se the days and also the time of
day when to meet
And whereas ther was a Differance prsented to this meeting
between **John Whitely** and his wives Children this meeting
therefore makes Choice of **Eliashib Smith James Barker John
Howland** and **George Soule** to judge and determine the matter
between them and make return to the next monthly
Meeting
And the Quarterly Meeting Epistle was read at this meeting
and kindly accepted

---

3 mo At a monthly meeting of friends held at our meeting
1732: House in Dartmouth the 15 day of the 3 month 1732
the Seaverall meetings thereunto belonging Called upon
for **Dartmouth John Tucker** present for **Rochester
Stephen Wing** present
The friends that wer appointed to see **John Borden** and
Hannah Russells marriage Consumated Gives this meeting
an account that it was Carried on pretty orderly
And **Acushnot** friends having met and Considered
the matter Concerning what two days in a month
might be most suitable to establish in their vilage
for meetings of worship they Conclude upon the first
and the last fourth days in every month Which this
Meeting agreas to
and the friends that were appointed to determine
the differance between **John Whitely** and his wives
Children have agreed and brought in their judgment
Which is as followeth
We whose names are underwritten being appointed by the
Monthly meeting to hear and Determine yᵉ: Differance
between **John Whitely** and his sons in Law² relating to the
Goods or moveable Estate that of right appears to be the
Childrens: Which sd **Whitely** and his wife took without
consent of sᵈ Children: and of his Complaint of their

2. Here "sons-in-law" means stepsons.

not paying him according to former agreement.
We have heard them, and it is our Judgment that the
said **John Whitely** shall shall Return them Goods
or moveable Estate: or the vallue of them to her
Daughters which she gave them to:
Likewise it is our Judgment that ye: Thirty pounds
Mentioned in the articles shall be void; and that all
His sons in Law that are under the care of our
Monthly meeting Shall pay the mony to **John Whitely**
yearly and every year which is due by bond to his
wife　　　　Given under our hands this fifteenth
day of the third month 1732　　　　　**Eliashib Smith**
　　　　　　　　　　　　　　　　　　　James Barker
　　　　　　　　　　　　　　　　　　　John Howland
　　　　　　　　　　　　　　　　　　　Georg Soule

4 Mo: At a monthly meeting of friends held at our Meeting
1732: House in **Dartmouth** the 19 day of the 4 month 1732.
Dartmouth meeting called **Eliashib Smith** and **Nicholas**
Lapham present---
—**Rochester** meeting Called and **John Wing** present.
—There was collected at this meeting – – £ -17 = 00
—**John Tucker Adam Mott James Barker** and
John Howland are chosen visitors for the year
Ensuing for **Aponaganset** vilage – –
—and **Nicholas Davis** and **Joseph Taber** for **Acushnet**
and **William Wood** for **Acoaxet** – –
—and **Stephen Wing** and **John Wing** for **Rochester**.
—And whereas there was a complaint brought
in to this meeting Concerning **William Soule** his
walking disorderly in abusing his wife revelling
and drunk[en]ness in an ungodly manner notwith=
=standing the good advise and godly care that friends
Have taken with him from time to time he
Doth still persist in his perntious [pernicious] ways therefore
it is the judgement of this meeting for the Clearing
of truth to give forth a publick testimony against
him the sd **William Soule** – –
—and also there is a Complaint from **Rochester**
that **Rest Summers** widow of **John Summers** junʳ
hath gone out of the order of friends and married

to one that is no friend Notwithstanding friends
have taken care and advised her to the Contrary
Therefore this meeting is concerned to give forth
a testimony against her and **John Tucker** and
Jabez Barker are appointed to draw up both
their Condemnations and this meeting is adjourned
until the next fourth day come week. – –
—This meeting being met according to adjournment
this 28 day of the 4th month 1732. – –
William Soules Condemnation is drawn up
and brought to this meeting and approved and
John Tucker hath signed it in ye behalfe of
this Meeting and **Isaac Wood** is ordered to read
it or Cause to be read at **Accoaxet** Meeting
House on a first day at the end of the meeting
of worship and make return to the next
Monthly meeting – –
And also **Rest Summers** now **Randal** her Condemnation is
Signed at this meeting by **John Tucker** by order and in behalfe
of sd meeting and **Elisha Wing** is appointed to read it or cause
it to be read at **Rochester** Meeting House on a first day at
the end of the meeting of worship and make return to the
next monthly meeting – –
—and **John Tucker**[,] **Thomas Smith** and **Adam Mott** are appointed
to attend the quarterly meeting next and Draw an Epistle
to the same – –
—and this meeting orders **Adam Mott** to pay **John Shepherd**
three pounds out of the meetings stock for halfe a years
keeping the Meeting House – –
—And whereas there was a paper of acknowledgment read
at this meeting signed by **Humphrey Smith** and his wife
Signifying their sorrow for falling into that which is con-
=trary to and also a skandal to our holy profession it is
the mind of this meeting that they both should be present
and be to read the same or cause it to be read at the
End of the meeting of worship on a first day at **aponagan**
=**set** meeting house – –

At a monthly meeting of friends Held at our meeting House
in **Dartmouth** the 17 day of the 5 month 1732. **Dartmouth**
meeting called **Joseph Russell jn**r and **Eliashib Smith** present

Rochester meeting called **Stephen Wing** present
And we not knowing whether **William Soule**s Condemnation
is read it is refered to ye next monthly meeting
And **Elisha Wing** hath read **Rest Randal**s Condemnation
which is as followeth

[top half of page is blank]

John Tucker and **Adam Mott** hath attended yᵉ Quarterly
Meeting And Drawn an Epistle to yᵉ Same
And **Adam Mott** hath paid **John Shepherd** three pounds out
of yᵉ Stock as ordered – – – –

6 mo: 1732: At a monthly meeting of friends Held at our meeting
House in **Dartmouth** the 21ᵈ of yᵉ 6 month 1732
Dartmouth meeting Called **Isaac Howland** and **George Soule**
present **Rochester** meeting called and none appeard
Isaac Wood hath read **William Soule**s Condemnation
which is as followeth – –
Whereas **William Soule** Son of **William Soule** late of
Dartmouth deceased in the County of **Bristol** in the
Province of yᵉ **Massachuset[t]s Bay** in **New England** hath
had his Education among friends the people Called Quakers
And Was married among them yet hath in slight friends
and good advice and counsel given to him by them he being
Under the Care of our monthly meeting friends hath
visited him from time to time to perswade him to
leave of keeping bad Company and his bad Conversation
but he hath neglected their advice and slighted their
Counsel and hath given Way to the temptation of
the Wicked one to that degree that he hath been
often times So much overcome With Strong drink
So that he hath abused and beat his wif Seaverall times
as hath been Credibly reported and threatned her with hard
Speeches to that degree that it is thought it not Safe for her
to live with him
We are therefore Concerned to give this forth as a publick
Testimony against Such disorderly actions and do Deny the said
William Soule to be one of us the people Called Quakers
Truly Desiring that he may return and find mercy With God
Given forth at our monthly meeting held by adjournment
the 28ᵗʰ of yᵉ 4 month 1732 Signed by order and in behalfe

of said meeting by – – **John Tucker**: Clerk
The Quarterly Meeting Epistle was read at this meeting
and kindly accepted

7m:1732 At a monthly meeting of friends held at our meeting
House in **Dartmouth** yᵉ 18 day of yᵉ 7ᵗʰ month 1732 – –
Dartmouth meeting Called **James Barker** and **Isaac
Howland** present: **Rochester** meeting Called none present
There was Collected at this meeting for yᵉ use of friends 05ᶠ-50ˢ=06ᵈ
And this meeting appoints **John Tucker** and **Joseph Russell jur**
to see after yᵉ deed of **Acushnot** meeting House Land
And it was advised at this meeting that all friends that
are heads of families be Careful that their Children
and Servants beheave them selves sober and orderly
at meetings of Worship for there hath been notice taken
that Some of our young people are to much out of
order in their behaviour in meetings in whispering
and laughing and runing out of meetings which makes
disturbance and very disagreable in a people professing
Godlyness
And this meeting is adjourned until yᵉ first sixth day in
the eighth month next
This meeting being meet according to adjournment this
sixth day of the eighth month 1732
The visiters of **Aponagansett Village** gives this meeting an
account that they have visited the families of friends
under their care in some degree but not all by reason
of Disappointment but so far as they went their visits
did seem to be well accepted and for the most part
things pretty weel accord˄ing to their observation
And the visiters of **Accushnot Vilage** gives an account that
they have visited yᵉ families of friends for yᵉ most part belong
ing to their Care: and had good Sattifaction in their visits and
have good Grounds to believe that Truth gains ground in some
families
And **John Tucker** and **Joseph Russell juʳ** are appointed to
attend yᵉ Quarterly Meeting and to draw an Epistle to yᵉ Same

8 mo: At a monthly Meeting of friends held at our meeting
1732 House in **Dartmouth** yᵉ 16ᵗʰ of yᵉ 8ᵗʰ month 1732
The severall meetings thereto belonging Called upon for
Dartmouth Thomas Smith present – –

for **Rochester Elisha Wing** present

And yᵉ matter Concerning **Hump[h]ry Smith** and his Wife
is refered to yᵉ next monthly meeting

And the matter concerning the deed of yᵉ land that belongs
to **Accushnot** meeting House is refered to the next
monthly meeting

And **John Tucker** and **Josep[h] Russell** juʳ have attended the
Quarterly meeting and Drawn an Epistle to yᵉ same

And **William Sanford** of **Dartmouth** son of **William
Sanford** of **Portsmouth** on **Rhoad Island** and **Rebeckah
Howland** of **Dartmouth** aforesd have laid their intention
of taking each other in marriage before this meeting
and are desired to wait until yᵉ next monthly meeting
for ther answer And **John Howland** and **Jabez Barker**
are appointed to inquire Concerning the young
mans Clearness respecting marriage and conver
sation and make return to the next monthly meeting

And the Epistle from yᵉ Quarterly meeting was
read at this meeting and kindly accepted

And whereas **Peter Allen** is accused of commit
ting fornication with **Content Smith** which he doth
deny therefore this meeting doth appoint **Joh[n] Howland**
and **James Barker** to go with the Women friends and
hear the sd **Allen** and **Content Smith** discourse together
to see what they can find out concerning yᵉ matter
and make return to yᵉ next monthly meeting

9 m　At a monthly meeting of friends held at our meeting House
1732　in **Dartmouth** the 20ᵗʰ day of yᵉ 9ᵗʰ month 1732

Dartmouth Meeting Called **James Barker** and **Adam Mott**
present **Rochester** meeting Called and none appeared

John Howland and **Jabez Barker** makes report to the meeting
that they have made Inquiry into yᵉ Clearness and Conversation
of **Wᵐ Sanford** and find nothing to hinder his proceedings in his
Intended Marriag wᵗʰ **Rebekah Howland**

And **William Sanford** and **Rebeckah Howland** appeared at
this meeting and desired their answer in relation to their
taking each other in marriage and their answer was
that they might proceed to take each other in marriage
observing the good order of truth in yᵉ performance thereof
and **Jabez Barker** and **John Howland** are appointed to

See their marriage Solemnized in the abovesd order and
make return to the next monthly meeting
And Whereas **Humphry Smith** and his wife doth refuse
or neglect to take up with friends judgment in readin their
acknowledgment it is the mind of this meeting that judgment
must go forth against them if the will persist in it and
John Howland and **Joseph Tucker** are appointed to [let]
them know the mind of yᵉ meeting and bring in their
account to the next monthly meeting
and Concerning yᵉ deed of **Accushnot** meeting House land
it is refered to yᵉ next monthly Meeting
And yᵉ Matter Concerning **Peter Allen** is refered to
the next monthly meeting
And this meeting appoints **Eliashib Smith** and **Isaac Smith**
to make up accompts with ~~wi~~ the Tresurer in yᵉ
Meetings behalf
And **John Whitely** not taking up with friends judgment
between him and his wives children this meeting appo[i]n[t]
John Russell and **George Soule** to let him know that if
he doth persist in it friends must proceed to deny him
and bring in their account to yᵉ next monthly meeting
And **Adam Mott** is appointed to pay to **Isaac Smith** £2=25ˢ=00[d]
for Recording the Monthly Meeting Munits [minutes]
And Whereas **William Russell** the son of **Joseph Russell Juʳ**
hath gone out of the way and Married (one that is not a believer
in friends Principles) out of the good order of truth for
which disorderly proceedings friends are concerned to give
forth a Testimony against him and **Joh[n] Tucker** and
Isaac Smith are appointed to draw up his Condemnation
And present it to yᵉ next Monthly Meeting

10 m:⎱
1732:⎰ At a monthly meeting of friends held at our meeting
House in **Dartmouth** the 18ᵗʰ day of yᵉ 10ᵗʰ Month 1732
Dartmouth meeting Called **James Barker** and **Joseph
Tucker** present
Rochester meeting called **Elisha Wing** present
Jabez Barker and **Joh[n] Howland** gives this meeting
an account that yᵉ marriage of **William Sanford** and
Rebeckah Howland Was Solemnized in yᵉ Good order
of truth according to the best of their observation
Richard Craw and **Joanna Shearman** did Signify

to this meeting that they have an intention of
taking each other in marriage and are desired to wait
until the next monthly meeting for their answer
And **William Willcox [Wilcox]** and **Dorothy Allen** did lay their
intentions of taking each other in marriage before this
meeting and were desired to wait til yᵉ next monthly
meeting for their answer and **Thomas Smith** and
George Soule ar[e] appointed to inquire into yᵉ young
mans Clearness Respecting marriage and Conversation
and make return to yᵉ next monthly meeting
And **Jabez Barker** and **John Russell** are appointed
to se into **Richard Craws** Clearness on yᵉ Same account
and accordingly to make return
Eliashib Smith and **Isaac Smith** have made up this meet$_{ings}$
accompts wᵗʰ yᵉ Tresurer and we find by their account
that he hath disbu[r]sted £2=11ˢ=1ᵈ of his own mony upon the
y̶ᵉ̶ meetings accounts and no mony in yᵉ Stock
And **Joseph** ~~Russell~~ **Tucker** gives this meeting an account
that he hath let **Humphry Smith** know the mind of the
Meeting and the Sd **Humphry Smith** doth Condecend to take
up with the Meetings advice in reading his acknowledgment
or to git Some body to do it according to yᵉ meetings Judgment
and desires yᵉ meeting to allow him two months' time to do it in
which this meeting agreas to
There was Collected at this meeting 3 pounds 5 Shillings and 6ᵈ
And whereas **Peter Allen** hath owned before Severall
Witnesses that he was falce in denying that which he was
Charged wᵗʰ by **Content Smith** it is yᵉ ~~Judgment~~ Mind of this
meeting that Judgment should go forth against boath him
and yᵉ sd **Content Smith** and **Jabez Barker** and **Isaac Smith**
are appointed to draw up their Condemnation and bring
it to yᵉ next monthly meeting in order to be signed
And the friends that was chose to Speak wᵗʰ **John Whitely**
gives this meeting an account that they have let
him know yᵉ meetings mind and he doth Still refuse to
take up with friends Judgment. Therefore it is yᵉ mind
of this Meeti[ng] that the Sd **JOHN WHITELy** should
not be reckned as one under yᵉ care of this meeting.
until he Shall make Sattisfaction to yᵉ monthly meet$_{ing}$
And **Adam Mott** hath paid two pounds five Shillings

to **Isaac Smith** according to yᵉ ord‸ᵉʳ of yᵉ last monthly meeting

John Tucker Elisha Wing and **Thomas Smith** are appoinₜₑd

to attend‸ᵉᵈ the Quarterly meeting next and to draw

an Epistle to yᵉ Same

John Tucker and **Isaac Smith** hath drawn up **Wᵐ Russell**s

Condemnation which this meeting doth approve of

and **John Tucker** hath Signed it by order of this meeting

and **John Tucker** is appointed to read the Same or cause it

to be read at **Aponaganset** meeting House on a first day at

the end of yᵉ meeting for worship between this and the next

Monthly meeting

And **Joseph Tucker** and **Abraham Tucker** are appointed

to overse yᵉ meeting House for the year Ensuing

And **Adam Mott** hath taken 2 pounds Eleven Shillings

and a penny by the meetings order out of ye Collection being

What was due to him for mony that he had disbu[r]sted of his

own upon the meetings account

And **Benjamin Shearman** hath lent this meeting the

Sum of two pounds and ten Shillings

And this meeting orders **Adam Mott** to pay 3 pounds

to **Joseph Tucker** and **Abraham Tucker** for halfe a̶

keeping yᵉ meeting house halfe a year wᶜʰ is done

No business from **Rochester**

---

11 Mo⎫ At a monthly meeting of friends held at our meeting house
1732/3⎭ in **Dartmouth** the 15ᵗʰ day of yᵉ 11 month 1732/3

Dartmouth meeting Called **James Barker** and **Isaac**

Howland present

Rochester meeting Called and none appeared

John Russell and **Jabez Barker** gives this meeting

an account that they have made Inquiry into **Richard**

Craws Clearness respecting marriage and conversation

and find nothing to hinder his Intended marriage

And **Thomas Smith** and **George Soule** also gives this meet

ing an account that they have made inquiry into

William Willcox [Wilcox]es Clearness and find nothing to hinder

his intended marriage

And **Richard Craw** and **Joanna Shearman** appeared

at this meeting desireing their answer in relation

to their taking each other in marriage and their answer

was that they might proceed to take each other in

Marriage in Some Convenient time between this and
the next monthly meeting observing yᵉ Good order of
Truth in the performance thereof and **Jabez Barker**
and **John Russell** are appointed to see their marriage
Sollemnized and make return to yᵉ next monthly meet_ing
And **William Willcox [Wilcox]** and **Dorothy Allen** appeared at
this meeting desiring their answer and their answer
was that they might proceed to take each other in
marriage in Some Convenient time between this and
the next monthly meeting observing the good order
Truth in that affair and **Joseph Russell Juʳ** and **John
Howland** are appointed to See their marriage Consu
mated and make return to yᵉ next monthly meeting
And **Ichabod Kirby** Son of **Robert Kirby** and **Rachel Allen**
daughter of **Joseph Allen** did lay their intentions of taking each
other in marriage before this meeting and are desired to
wait til yᵉ next monthly meeting for their answer
and **John Russell** and **George Soule** are appointed
to inquire into yᵉ young mans clearness respecting
marrige and Conversation and make return to the next
monthly meeting
And **William Russell**s Condemnation hath been read
according to yᵉ order of yᵉ last monthly meeting
and is as followeth
Whereas **William Russell** the Son of **Joseph Russell Juʳ**
of **Dartmouth** in the county of **Bristol** in the Province
of yᵉ **Massachuset[t]s Bay** in **New England** – –
hath ˏfrom his childhood been Educated amongst friends his father and mother
being both of the people called Quakers yet hath in Slight
of friends and the good advice and Counsel by them
given to him and also contrary to his father and
mothers consent proceeded in marriage out of the good
order Established among Friends with one that is of another
perswation which disorderly proceeding is not only
Contrary to our orders but contrary to yᵉ Scriptures
of Truth wher the Apostle adviseth the Believers
not to be unequally yoaked with unbelievers
which disorderly proceeding hath been a great grief
and trouble to his parents and to all sincere friends
that are Concerned for his good

And for the clear of Truth and that all may know
that we have no unity with Such Obstinate disorder
and mixt marriages we can do no less than give
this forth as a publick Testimony against him the sd
William Russell Denying him to be one of us yᵉ people
Called Quakers truly desiring that he may return
and find mercy with God Tenderly advising all young
peple (viz) Friends Children to beware of giving
way to yᵉ inducements of Satan lest they be led forth to scorn
friends and the Testimony of yᵉ blessed truth as it hath been
delivered through great tribulations
Even to the sealing of y̶ᵉ it with the Blood of many faithful
Witnesses: Surely we will be the portion of those can so
Slightily trample upon it and ₍ᵗᵒ those by whome the Testimony
of yᵉ Blessed Truth may fall in the Streets by any perticular
Unless by true and unfeigned repentance to God
which that every disorderly and disobedient one may do
is our Sincere desire
Given forth at our monthly meeting of friends held
at our meeting House in **Dartmouth** the 18ᵗʰ of the
10ᵗʰ month 1732
And Signe by order and in behalfe of sd Meeting by

John Tucker Clerk

And **Jabez Barker** and **Isaac Smith** hath drawn up
Peter Allen and **Content Smith**s Condemnation which ₍is approved₎
and **John Tucker** hath Signed it in behalf of yᵉ meeting
and is also appointed to read it or cause it to be read at
Ap[p]onaganset meeting house at the end of yᵉ meeting
for worship on a first day between this and yᵉ next monthly ₍meeting₎
And the friends that were appointed to attend.
the Quarterly meeting have done it and drawn
an Epistle to the Same as ordered and the Epistle
from the Quarterly meeting was read at this
Meeting and well accepted
And this meeting hath received forty Shillings of the
women and paid it to **Benjamin Shearman** for
a part of what the monthly meeting borrowed of him

---

12 m⎫ At a monthly meeting of friends held at our meeting
1732/3⎭ House in **Dartmouth** the 19ᵗʰ day of yᵉ 12ᵗʰ month 1732/3
Dartmouth meeting called **John Howland** present

Rochester meeting Called **John Wing** present
John Russell and **Jabez Barker** makes report to this
meeting that **Richard Craw** and **Joanna Shearman**s
marriage was consumated in good order as according to
their observation
Joseph Russell ju^r and **John Howland** gives this meeting
an account that they was at the marriag of **William
Willcox** [**Wilcox**] and **Dorothy Allen** and Saw nothing but that
it was performed in good order
John Russell and **George Soule** makes report to this
meeting that they have made inquiry into the Clearness
and Conversation of **Ichabod Kirby** and find nothing to
hinder his proceedings in his intended marriage w^th **Rachel Allen**
And **Ichabod Kirby** and **Rachel Allen** appeared at this
Meeting desiring their answer in relation to their taking
each other in marriage and their answer was that they
might proceed to take eacher [*sic*] in marriage in the good
order of Truth in Some Convenient time between this
and the next monthly meeting and **John Russell** and
George Soule are appointed to See their marriage
Solemnized as aforesd and make re[t]urn to ye next month_{ly}
Meeting.
And **Peter Allen** and **Content Smith**s Condemnation
hath been read and is as followeth.
Whereas **Peter Allen** of **Dartmouth** Son of **Zechariah** [**Zachariah**]
Allen deceased and **Content Smith** Daughter of **Judah Smith**
of **Dartmouth** aforesd having given way to the Temptations
of Satan and have fallen into ye Sin of fornication
as appears by the sd **Content Smith** having a bastard
Child and he the sd **Peter Allen** owning the child to
be his he the sd **Peter Allen** having for Some time
made Pr[o]fession of the Truth with us the people called
Quakers and She ye Sd **Content Smith** having been
Educated amongst us her father and mother being
both of us ye People called Quakers: which
Wicked action is to ye dishonour of God and a reproa_{ch}
of the blessed Truth they made profession off.
We are Concerned therefore to give this forth as
a publick Testimony against Such Scandelus
practices and do disown the sd **Peter Allen** and

Content Smith to be in unity with us the people
Called Quakers truly desiring that if it be yᵉ will of
God that they may come to unfeigned Repentance
and find mercy.
Given forth at our monthly meeting of friends
held in **Dartmouth** the 15ᵗʰ day yᵉ 11ᵗʰ month 1732/3
And Signed by order and in the behalfe of
sd Meeting by

John Tucker Clerk

John Lapham jnʳ hath Signified to this meeting that
he hath a mind to Remove with his family to **Smith
field** in **Rhoad Island** Colony to Live and Desires ~~a few
lines by way of Certificate~~ Friends Concurrance
in that affair and **John Russell Jabez Barker** and
George Soule are appointed to See into his surcumstances
in the matter and make return to yᵉ next monthly
Meeting: and the next preparitive and monthly Meeting
are adjourned one week longer than the usual Course
by reason of **Sandwich** yearly meeting

---

1 mo⎫
1733⎭   At a monthly Meeting of friends held at our
Meeting House in **Dartmouth** on the 26ᵗʰ Day of yᵉ
first month 1733 **Dartmouth** meeting called **Adam
Mott** and **Isaac Howland** present
Rochester meeting Called and none appeared
There was Collected at this Meeting for yᵉ use of
Friends – – £01 - 08ˢ - 00[d]
Edward Wing Son of **John Wing** deceasd and **Rebekah
Slocum** did lay their intentions of taking each other
in marriage before this meeting and were desired
to wait until yᵉ next monthly meeting for their answer;
And **John Tucker Adam Mott** and **John Russell** are
appointed to See how things are like to be Setled
and whither the widows children are like to be
wronged by their mothers marrying.
John Russell and **George Soule** makes report to this
meeting that they were at the Marriage of **Ichabod
Kirby** and **Rachel Allen** and Saw nothing but that
it was decently Carried on
The friends that wer appointed to See into **John Laphams**
Sircumstances relating to his removing to **Smith**

field to live gives this meeting an account that
they find nothing but things are Clear and that he is
like to remove in good order. and this meeting
appoints yᵉ Same friends to draw up a few lines by
way of Certificate to yᵉ monthly meeting at **Smithfield**
of him and his wifes unity with friends here
And this meeting hath paid **Benjamin Shearman**
the mony that they borrowed of him
The Visiters of **Ap[p]onagansett** Village have given this meeting
an account of their Service in the visiting the families of friends
John Tucker Adam Mott John Howland and **Joseph Tucker**
are appointed to attend yᵉ Quarterly Meeting next and
to Draw an Epistle to yᵉ Same
And **Humphry Smith** hath Complied with yᵉ meetings judgmen[t]
in reading his paper of acknowledgment of his and his wifes
outgoings
And **Jabez Barker** and **James Shearman** are Chosen to
assist yᵉ Women in drawing up **Mary Smith** Condem
nation for her disorderly marriage and present it to the
next monthly meeting in order to be Signed

---

2 m⎫
1733⎭   At a monthly meeting of friends held at our meeting
House in **Dartmouth** on the 16ᵗʰ day of the 2ᵈ month1733
Dartmouth meeting Called **John Russell** and **Thomas Smith**
present: **Rochester** meeting Called and none appeared
Edward Wing and **Rebeckah Slocum** not appearin for
their answer it is refered to yᵉ next monthly meeting
Joh[n] Tucker Adam Mott and **John Howland** have attended the
Quarterly meeting and Drawn an Epistle to the Same
Jabez Barker is appointed to read **Mary Goddard**s Condem
nation at a monthly meeting befor yᵉ men and women ₚₐᵣₜ[?]
The Quarterly meeting Epistle was read at this
Meeting an[d] kindly accepted

---

3 m⎫
1733⎭   At a monthly meeting of friends held at our meeting
House in **Dartmouth** the 21 day of the 3 month 1733
Dartmouth meeting Called **James Barker** and **Adam Mott**
present **Rochester** meeting Called and none apeared
and **Edward Wing** not appearing at this meeting for his answer
it is refered to yᵉ next monthly meeting
and **Jabez Barker** is appointed to read **Mary Goddard**s Condem

nation at the next monthly meeting befor yᵉ men and
Wom[en] part

4 m⎱
1733⎰
At a monthly meeting of friends held at our meeting
House in **Dartmouth** the 18ᵗʰ day of the 4ᵗʰ month 1733
The Severall meetings thereto belonging called upon
for **Dartmouth Adam Mott** and **Thomas Smith** present
for **Rochester Savory Clifton** present
There was Collected this meeting for yᵉ use of friends :1-17-04
Jabez Barker hath read **Mary Goddard**s Condemnation
as appointed and is as followeth
Whereas **Mary Smith** daughter of D[e]liverance **Smith**
Late of **Dartmouth** deceased and **Mary** his wife hath had
her Education amongst the people Called Quakers her
father and mother were both of sd people notwithstand
ing she hath of late gone and married out of yᵉ order of
sd people though She hath been advised to yᵉ Contrary
by her mother and other friends Concerned therefore
this meeting is concerned to give this forth as a Testimony
against such disorderly proceedings and do deny the sd
Mary now Wife of **John Goddard** to be one in unity with
us the people Called Quakers desireing that if it be the
Will of yᵉ Lord she may Come to a Sight of her outgoings
And find mercy with the Lord
Signed by order and in behalfe of the monthly meeting
held at **Dartmouth** on the 15ᵗʰ of yᵉ 2ᵈ month 1733
by   **John Tucker** Clerk
Edward Wing and **Rebeckah Slocum** appeared at this
Meeting desiring their answer in relation to their taking
each other in marriage and things being enquired
into and nothing appearing to hinder they had their
answer that they might proceed to take each other
in marriage in yᵉ Good order of Truth in Some Convenient
time between this and the next monthly meeting
And **Henry Tucker** and **Adam Mott** were appointed to
See their marriage Consumated in the abovesd order
and make return to the next monthly meeting
the visiters Chose for this year are for **Acushnot**
Benjamin Allen and **Joseph Russell** juʳ and for
Ap[p]onagansett John Tucker John Howland and
James Barker and for **Acoaksett** Wᵐ **Wood Joseph Tripp** [*carryover line*]

and **Jonathan Wood**
Nicholas Davis John Tucker and **Adam Mott** are appoin
ted to attend yᵉ Quarterly meeting next and to draw
an Epistle to yᵉ Same
Our Dear Friends **Mungo Benley** [Beuley?] and **Samuel Stephens**
from **Ireland** were here and ther Certificates was
read to yᵉ good Sattifaction of this meeting
and this meeting orders **Adam Mott** to pay to the overseers of
yᵉ Meeting House the Sum 3 pounds for halfe a years
keeping yᵉ meeting House

5 m⎱
1733⎰ At a monthly meeting of Friends held at our meeting House
in **Dartmouth** the 16ᵗʰ day of the 5ᵗʰ 1733
Dartmouth meeting Called **John Howland** and **James Barker**
present **Rochester** meeting Called and none appeared
Henry Tucker and **Adam Mott** makes report to this meeting
that they was at **Edward Wing** and **Rebeckah Slocum**s marriage
and saw nothing but that it was performed in good order
The friends that were appointed to attend yᵉ Quarterly
meeting have attended it and drawn an account to the
Same according to order
And yᵉ Quarterly meeting Epistle was read at this meeting
and well accepted

6 m⎱
1733⎰ At a monthly meeting of friends held at our meeting
House in **Dartmouth** the 20ᵗʰ day of yᵉ 6ᵗʰ month 1733
The severall meetings thereto belonging Called upon for
Dartmouth Eliashib Smith and **John Howland** present
Rochester meeting Called and none appeared
The visiters of **Acoakset** have given in an account to
this meeting that they have in a generall way visited the
families of friends under their care and that they had
Good Sattisfaction in their visits and that Truth prevales
with some to a good degree
and this meeting is adjourned until this day 2 weeks
This meeting being meet according to adjournment
this 3ᵈ day of the 7ᵗʰ month 1733 and no business presented

7 mo⎱
1733⎰ At a monthly meeting held at our meeting House
in **Dartmouth** on the 17ᵗʰ day of yᵉ 7ᵗʰ month 1733:
The several meetings thereto belonging called upon
for **Dartmouth Adam Mott** and **Joseph Russell** juʳ present

For **Rochester Stephen Wing** present
There was Collected at this meeting 11 pounds two shillings
and 8 pence whereof 10 pounds to pay the doctor for
what he hath done for **Thomas Cezer** and the rest to
be disbu[r]sted to Supply the necesity of yᵉ sd **Cezar** the
mony being put into ~~James Barkers~~ **Abraham Tucker**s
hands who with **James Barker** are chose to se into his and
his families affairs and to Supply their necesity as need
Shall require and to bring their accounts to yᵉ monthly ₘₑₑₜᵢₙg
Joseph Benson the son of **Joseph Benson** of **Rochester**
and **Experience Barlow** daughter of **Shubal Barlow**
of **Rochester** aforesd did lay their intentions of taking
each other in marriage before this meeting and were
desired to wait til yᵉ next monthly meeting for their
answer and **Savory Clifton** and **Stephen Wing** are appointed
to inspect into yᵉ young mans Clearness respecting
marriage and Conversation and make return to the
next monthly meeting
And **Josep[h] Lapham** hath Signified to this meeting that
he desires a few lines by way of Certificate to the monthly
meeting in **Smithfield** and this ~~and~~ meeting appoints
John Russell and **George Soul** [Soule] to draw up one Relating to
his Clearness Respecting Marriage and Conversation
and bring it to the next monthly meeting
And **James Barker** and **Joseph Tucker** are chose to
be assistants with **John Tucker** to have the oversight
of Testimonies
And **John Tucker Joseph Russell** juʳ and **James Barker**
are Chose to attend yᵉ Quarterly meeting next
and to draw an Epistle to yᵉ Same
and our Collection for to Supply yᵉ Stock is refered
to the next monthly meeting
And this meeting is adjourned until yᵉ first 6 day in yᵉ next ₐmonth
This meeting being met according to adjournment
this 5ᵗʰ day of the 8 month 1733
The visiters of **Aponganset** hath given in their account
that they have visited the most part of yᵉ families
of friends under their care and that for as far as
they went they found things pretty well
and the visiters of **Acuchnot** have done nothing this

Quarter as to that service

And from **Rochester** we have receiv,d no account

---

8 m⎫
1733⎭ At a monthly meeting of friends held at our meeting
House in **Dartmouth** the 8ᵗʰ month 1733
Dartmouth meeting called **Adam Mott** present
Rochester Meeting Called **Savory Clifton** present
Savory Clifton and **Stephen Wing** makes report to this
meeting that they have made inquiry into **Joseph Benson**s
Clearness Respecting marriage and Conversation
And find nothing to hinder his proceedings in his inte[n]ded marriage
and **Joseph Benson** and **Experience Barlow** appeared at this
meeting desireing their answer in relation to their taking
each other in marriage and they had their answer that
they might proceed to take each other in marriage in the
good order of truth in Some convenient time between this
and yᵉ next monthly meeting and **Savory Clifton** and
Stephen Wing are appointed to See their marriage
Sollemnized and make return to yᵉ next monthly meeting
There was a Certificate drawn up and presented to this
meeting for **Joseph Lapham** and **John Tucker** hath Signed
it by order and in the behalfe of this meeting
And **John Tucker** and **Joseph Russell** juʳ hath attended
the Quarterly meeting and drawn an Epistle to yᵉ Same
And Whereas **Henry Tucker** the Son of **Henry Tucker**
Having been out of order in divers respects and much
Labour hath been bestowed upon him in love to Endeavour
to a Sight of his outgoings but he doth still seem to persist
and make no acknowledgment to friends Sattisfaction
This meetings Therefore thinks best to draw a Condemnaₜᵢₒₙ
against him and **John Tucker** and **Isaac Smith** are
appointed to draw it up and bring it to the next monthly meeting in order to be signed
There was Collected at this meeting for yᵉ use of friends £1-14ˢ-11ᵈ
And Whereas **Mary Merihew** [**Merrihew**] daughter of **Josiah Merihew** [**Merrihew**]
hath gone out of yᵉ order established amongst friends and
married one that is not a friend Contrary to the abovesd
good order and to yᵉ advice of friends that laboured with
her to perswade her to yᵉ contrary this meeting
therefore thinks fit to draw up a Condemnation
against her and **John Tucker** and **Isaac Smith** are

appointed to draw it and bring it to the next month
ly meeting in order to be signed

---

9 m⎫ At a monthly meeting of friends held at our meeting
1733⎭ House in **Dartmouth** the 19ᵗʰ of yᵉ 9ᵗʰ month1733:
Dartmouth meeting called **James Barker** and **John Howland**
present: **Rochester** meeting called **Stephen Wing** present
Stephen Wing gives this meeting an account that **Joseph**
Benson and **Experience Barlow**s marriage was performed
in good order.
The friends that were appointed to draw up **Henry Tucker**
juʳ his Condemnation have done it and this meeting doth
approve of it and **John Tucker** hath signed it by order and
in behalfe of this meeting
And **Jabez Barker** is appointed to read it on a first day at
the end of yᵉ meeting for Worship between this and the next
monthly meeting at **Aponaganset** meeting House
And **Mary Merihew [Merrihew]** ₐnow Kirbys Condemnation was presented to this
meeting and is approved by the meeting and **Jabez Barker**
hath read it in this meeting and is as followeth
Whereas **Mary Merihew [Merrihew]** Daughter of **Josiah Merihew [Merrihew]**
of **Dartmouth** in yᵉ County of **Bristol** in the province of
the **Massachuset[t]s Bay** in **New England** hath had her Education
among friends the People called Quakers but for want of
keeping to yᵉ Spirit of Truth and her Education hath joyned
her Selfe in marriage with one that is not under our
Care and is also under a Skandalus report of being
father to a Bastard Child:
Although She hath been Laboured with in order to perswade her to the Contrary by friends that wished her well
but She hath still Slighted their advice and Counsel
to the trouble of Honest friends we are therefore Concer
ned to give this forth as a Testimony against Such disorder
ly proceedings and do denie the sd **Mary** now wife ₐof **Richard**
Kirby to be one in Unity with us yᵉ people Called Quakers
Desireing that if it be yᵉ will of God She may through
unfeigned Repentance Come to See her outgoings
and find Mercy. Given for[th] at our monthly Meeting
held at our meeting House in **Dartmouth** the 19ᵗʰ day
of the 9ᵗʰ month 1733 and Signed by order and in
behalfe of Sd meeting by – – **John Tucker** Clerk

And **Holder Slocum** desires a Certificate of his
Clearness respecting marriage and Conversation
and **John Russell** and **Jabez Barker** are appointed
to inquire into yᵉ matter and draw up one if think
fit and make return to yᵉ next monthly meeting

---

10 m)
1733 ∫
At a monthly meeting of friends held at our
meeting House in **Dartmouth** the 17ᵗʰ day of yᵉ 10ᵗʰ m: 1733
The Severall meetings thereto belonging called upon
for **Dartmouth Thomas Smith** and **Adam Mott** present
For **Rochester** none appeared
There was Collecte[d] at this meeting for yᵉ use of friends £2-00ˢ-00ᵈ
and **Jabez Barker** hath read **Henry Tucker** Condenation
Which is as followeth
Whereas **Henry Tucker** ₍Son of Henry Tucker₎ and **Phebe** his wife of **Dartmouth**
in the County of **Bristol** in yᵉ Province of yᵉ **Massachuset[t]s Bay**
in **New England** hath had his Education among Friends but for
want of keeping to the Spirit of Truth and yᵉ Good order
Established among friends hath gone from his Education and
let him selfe into a Liberty that is not agreable to our
Holy Profession in wearing divers sorts of Perriwiggs and
his hat set up on three sides like the vain Custom of yᵉ World
and also Speaking of words not agreable to our profession
And for these his outgoings he hath been laboured with and
Advised to Condemn and forsake the Same but he hath not
done it to yᵉ Sattisfaction of yᵉ monthly meeting but Still
goes on in his vain Conversation to the grief of the
Sincere hearted among us Therefore for the Clearing of
Truth of Such Reproachful things we are Concerned to
give this forth as a publick ~~Testimony~~ Condemnation
against him yᵉ sd **Henry Tucker** denying him to be one
in Unity with us the People called Quakers Sincerely
desiring that if it may be yᵉ will of God that he may Come
to a Sence of his outgoings and by unfeigned Repentance
find mercy with the Lord
Given forth at our monthly meeting Held in **Dartmouth**
the 19ᵗʰ day of yᵉ 9ᵗʰ month 1733
And Signed in the behalfe of Said meeti[ng] by

John Tucker Clerk

Henry Hedly [Hedley] son of **John Hedly [Hedley]** deceasᵈ and **Rachel Shearman**
daughte[r] of **Daniel Shearman** deceasᵈ did lay their intentions

of taking each other in marriage before this meeting
and were desired to wait until the next monthly meeting
for their answer and **Thomas Smith** and **Joseph Russell ju^r**
are appointed to make inquiry into his clearness
Respecting marriage and Conversation and make
return to ye next monthly meeting
And whereas ye Roof of the meeting House being grown Leaky
it is concluded by this meeting that **John Howland**
And **John Shepherd** should be the undertakers to procure the
Shingles and to Do ye Work so as to have it finished by the
Latter end of ye next summer
The friends that were appointed to draw up a Certificate
for **Holder Slocum** have done it and **John Tucker** hath
Signed it by order of this meeting
John Tucker Nicholas Davis and **Thomas Smith** are appoin_{ted}
to attend ye Quarterly Meeting next and draw an Epistle
to the Same
And **Joseph Tucker** and **Abraham Tucker** are appointed
to oversee ye meeting House for the year insuing
and **Adam Mott** hath paid three pounds to ye overseers
for keeping ye meeting house halfe a year.

---

11 m⎫ At a monthly meeting of friends held at our meeting
1733/4⎭ house in **Dartmouth** the 21 day of ye 11 month 1733/4
Dartmouth meeting Called **Jabez Barker** and **Adam**
Mott present. **Rochester** meeting Called **John Wing** present
Thomas Smith and **Joseph Russell ju^r** makes report to
this meeting that they have mad[e] inquiry into **Henry**
Hedlys [Hedleys] Clearness respecting marriage and Conversation
and find nothing to hinder his proceedings in his intended
marriage with **Rachel Shearman**.
And **Henry Hedly** [Hedley] and **Rachel Shearman** appeared at
this meeting desiring their answer in relation to their
taking each other in marriage and they had their answer
that they might proceed to take each other in marriage
in the Good order of Truth in Some Convenient time
between this and ye next monthly meeting and **Thomas Smith**
and **Joseph Russell Ju^r** are appointed to See their marriage
Consumated and make return to ye next monthly meeting
And **Thomas Smith** hath attended ye Quarterly meeting and
drawn an Epistle to the Same

And yᵉ Quarterly meeting Epistle was read at this meeting
and kindly accepted　　No business from **Rochester**

12 m⎫
1733/4⎭ At a monthly meeting of friends held at our meeting
House in **Dartmouth** the 18ᵗʰ day of yᵉ 12ᵗʰ month 1733/4
Dartmouth meeting called **Adam Mott** and **John Howland**
Rochester meeting called **Savory Clifton** and **John Wing** present
Joseph Russell Juʳ and **Thomas Smith** gives this meeting an account
that the marriage of **Henry Hedly** [**Hedley**] and **Rachel Shearman** was
performed in yᵉ Good order of truth as far the [they?] Saw
Benjamin Wing the Son of **John Wing** and **Mary Hilliar** [**Hiller**?] daughter
of **Jabez Hilliar** [**Hiller**?] both of **Rochester** have laid their intentions
of taking each other in marriage before this meeting and
were desired to wait til yᵉ next monthly meeting for their
answer and **Savory Clifton** and **Stephen Wing** are appointed
to Inquire into yᵉ young mans Clearness respecting marriage
and Conversation and make return to yᵉ next monthly meeting
And Whereas **Caleb Russell** son of **Joseph Russell juʳ** hath
Signified that he intends marriage with **Rebekah Borden**
of **Tiverton** and desires a Certificate of his Clearness
Respecting marriage and Conversation and **Nicholas Davis**
and **Benjamin Allen** are appointed to make inquiry and
and to draw one if they find things clear and present it
to yᵉ next monthly meeting in order to be Signed
And **John Tucker** and **James Barker** are appointed
by this meeting to take Care and do their endeaver as
far as may be Consistunt with Truth that no disorderly
person or any that may come with an evil eye do not
sit in our meetings of Discipline
And Whereas **Peleg Slocum** deceas.ᵈ hath as we understand
Given ten pounds to the use of our monthly meeting
this meeting appoints **John Tucker** to git the mony and
bring it to the monthly meeting and this meeting adjourns
the monthly meeting next to the fourth day of yᵉ week
following the second day as it used to be on by Course

1 m⎫
1734⎭ At a monthly meeting of friends held at our meeting
House in **Dartmouth** the 20ᵗʰ day of the first month 1734
The Severall meetings thereto belonging Called upon
for **Dartmouth Thomas Smith** and **James Barker** present
For **Rochester John Wing** present
The friend that were to see into **Benjamin Wing**s Clearness

have Signified that they have done it and find nothing to
hinder his proceedings in his intended marriage
And **Benjamin Wing** and **Mary Hillier** appeard at this
meeting desireing an answer in relation to their taking
each other in marriage and their answer was that
that they might proceed to take each other in marriage
in Some Convenenient time between this and the next
monthly meeting in the good order of truth and
Joseph Taber and **Savory Clifton** are appointed to see
their marriage Solemnized in yᵉ above sᵈ order and make
return to the next monthly meeting
The friends that were appointed to draw up a Certificate
for **Caleb Russell** have done it and **John Tucker** hath
signed it in behalfe of yᵉ meeting
There was Collected at this meeting for yᵉ use of friends 2£-09ˢ=06ᵈ
The friends appointed to attend yᵉ Quarterly meeting
are **John Tucker Elisha Wing** and **Adam Mott**
The Visiters of **Accoakset** hath given in their account
to this meeting that they have visited the families of
friends belonging to their care and that their visits
was taken kindly and in Some families where things
was out of order they Laboured with them in Love
that they might do better
And the visiters of of **Rochester** have given in
their account to this meeting of their visiting friends
families belonging to their care
and this meeting is adjourned until the 4ᵗʰ day of
the week that the Quarterly meeting is on
~~The visitors of Cushnot vilage hav~~
This meeting being mett according to adjournment
this 10ᵗʰ day of yᵉ 2ᵈ month 1734
The visiters of **Acushnot** village have given in their
account of their Service in that affair
And the visiters of **Aponaganset** gives no account

2 m: At a monthly meeting of friends held at our meeting
1734 House in **Dartmouth** the 15:ᵗʰ day of yᵉ 2ᵈ month 1734
Dartmouth meeting called **William Wood** and **Jabez Barker**
present from **Rochester** none appeared
There was an account sent from **Rochester** that the
marriage between **Benjamin Wing** and **Mary Hilliar** was

accomplished in the Good order of Truth
John Tucker and **Adam Mott** hath attended yᵉ Quarterly
Meeting and drawn an Epistle to yᵉ Same
and yᵉ Epistle from yᵉ Quarterly meeting was read at this
Meeting and kindly accepted

3m: At a Monthly meeting of friends held at our meeting House
1734 in **Dartmouth** the 20:ᵗʰ day of yᵉ 3:ᵈ month 1734
The Severall meetings thereto belonging called upon for
Dartmouth William Wood and **Adam Mott** present
From **Rochester Elisha Wing** present
Our Friend **Zachariah Nikson** of **North Carolina** was at
this meeting and his Certificate was read to friends Satisfaction[3]
And the next preparitive and monthly meeting are
adjourned one week longer than they are by Cource by
reason of yᵉ yearly meeting

4 m: At a monthly meeting of friends hed at our meeting House
1734 in **Dartmouth** the 24:ᵗʰ day of yᵉ 4:ᵗʰ month 1734
The Severall meetings thereto belonging Called upon for
Dartmouth James Barker and **Adam Mott** preesent
for **Rochester** none appeared
There was Collected at this meeting £1-15ˢ =06ᵈ
and this meeting orders **Adam Mott** to pay to the overseers
of yᵉ meeting house 2 pounds out of yᵉ Stock which with
twenty Shillings that was paid in by the wome makes
3 pounds that was owe for halfe a years keeping yᵉ meeting
House Which is done
And whereas **Ellen Taber D**aughter of **Joseph Taber**
hath gone out of yᵉ good order Established among friends
and married to one that is not a friend this meeting
having Considered the matter it is refered to yᵉ next
monthly meeting for further Consideration
The visiters chosen for this year are for **Aponaganset**
John Tucker James Barker John Howlan and **Adam Mott**
and for **Accushnot Benjamin Allen** and **Joseph Russell Ju**
and for **Accoakset Joseph Tripp** and **Jonathan Wood**
and yᵉ choice of visiters for **Rochester** is refered to
the next monthly meeting

3. Zachariah Nixon (1684-1739) of Pasquotank Monthly Meeting, North Carolina. See William Wade Hinshaw, ed., *Encyclopedia of American Quaker Genealogy* (6 vols., Ann Arbor: Edwards Brothers, 1936-1950), I, 110.

And we have an account that **Susanna Smith** is
gone out of the good order of friends and married to
one that is her near kinsman which is refered to
the Consideration of the next monthly meeting
And **John Tucker Adam Mott** and **Joseph Russell Jur**
are appointed to attend the Quarterly meeting next
and to Draw an Epistle to yᵉ Same
And the matter Concerning **Ellen Taber** is refered
to yᵉ next monthly meeting
And Whereas there was no Friends from **Rochester**
at this meeting this meeting orders **John Tucker**
and **Adam Mott** to write to **Rochester** preparitive
meeting that they attend the next monthly meeting[4]

5th mo: At a monthly Meeting of friends held at our
1734 meeting House in **Dartmouth** yᵉ 15:ᵗʰ day of yᵉ 5ᵗʰ m: 1734
Dartmouth meeting Called **John Howland** and **Joseph
Tucker** present **Rochester** Meeting Called and none present
James Green the Son of **Jabez Green** of **Warwick**
in the Colony of **Rhoad Island** and **Hannah Tucker**
the Daughter of **Abraham Tucker** deceased did lay
their intentions of taking each other in Marriage
before this meeting and were desired to wait til the
next monthly meeting for their answer
And **William Lake and Joanna Butler** Did lay their
intentions of taking each other in marriage before
this meeting and were desired to wait til the next
monthly meeting for their answer and **John Howland**
and **Jabez Barker** are appointed to make Enquiry into
the young mans Clearness respecting marriage and
Conversation and make return to the next monthly
Meeting
And the matter Concerning **Ellen Taber** is refered
to yᵉ next monthly meeting and whereas there was
no friends from **Rochester** at this meeting this meeting
orders **John Tucker** and **Adam Mott** to write to
Rochester Preparitive meeting that they attend
the next monthly meeting
In order to give an account who it may be propper to Chuse
visiters for **Rochester**

4. The previous six lines are crossed out in the manuscript.

And the Matter Concerning **Susanna Smith** is refered to
the next monthly meeting

And **John Tucker** and **Joseph Russell** hath attended the
Quarterly Meeting and Drawn an Epistle to the Same

And this meeting hath received of **Holder Slocum** the
Sum of 10 pounds Which Was Given to the meeting by his
father **Peleg Slocum** in his Last Will and Testament
Which Was paid by order of the meeting to **Joseph Taber**
for Shingles

6 mo At a monthly meeting of Friends held at our meeting
1734 House in **Dartmouth** the 19th day of the 6th mouth 1734
The Severall meetings thereto belonging Called upon
for **Dartmouth Tho: Smith** and **Joseph Tucker** present
for **Rochester Savory Clifton** present

The friends that were appointed to Enquire into **William
Lake**s Clearness make report that they have inspect
=ed into the matter and find nothing to hinder his
intended marriage

and **James Green** and **Hannah Tucker** appeared
at this meeting Desiring an answer in relation to
their taking each other in marriage and nothing
appearing to hinder they had their answer that
they might proceed to take each other in marriage
in Some Convenient time between this and the next
Monthly meeting observing the good order of truth in
the performance thereof and **John Russell** and **Adam
Mott** are appointed to See their marriage Consummated
into Good order and make return to yᵉ next Monthly meeting

And **Wᵐ Lake** and **Joanna Butler** appeared at this
Meeting Desiring their answer in relation to their
taking each other in marriage and their answer
was that they might proced to take each other in
Marriage in Some Convenient time between this and
the next monthly meeting in the Good order of truth
and **John Howland** are appointed to to See their marriage
Solemnized in Sᵈ order and make return to the
next monthly meeting

And **William Ricketson** was at this meeting and the
Meeting having agetated matters with him Concerning
his Sons wearing a periwig and the Disorderly marriage

of his Daughter he desires some further time to Consider
of it and so it is refered to the next monthly meeting
And there was a condemnation Signed at this meeting
by **John Tucker** in the behalfe of yᵉ meeting against
Alice Smith for commiting fornication
and **John Tucker** is appointed to read it or git Some
body to read it on a first day at the end of yᵉ meeting of
Worship between this and the next monthly meeting
and **John Tucker** is appointed to Draw up a Condem=
nation against **Susanna Smith** for her Disorderly
marriage and also another against **Ellen Taber** for
the like offence and bring them to yᵉ monthly meeting
next in order to be Signed
And the Quarterly Meeting Epistle was read and
kindly accepted by this meeting

_7 mo_ At a monthly meeting of friends held at our
_1734_ Meeting House in **Dartmouth** on the 16ᵗʰ day of yᵉ 7ᵗʰ
Month 1734 **Dartmouth** meeting Called **John Howland**
and **James Barker** present **Rochester** Meeting Called
Elisha Wing present **John Russell** gives this meeting
an account that **James Green** and **Hannah Tucker**
marriage was Carried on and accomplished in good
order as far as he saw
and **Jabez Barker** and **John Howland** gives this
Meeting an account that they was at the marriage
of **William Lake** and **Joanna Butler** and Saw nothing
but that it was carried on Decently and in good order
And **William Ricketson** appeared at this meeting
and hath made the meeting Satisfaction as to his
Daughters disorderly marriage and as for his sons
wearing a perriwig he doth Signifie that he will do
his Endeaver to persuade him to Desist
And **Alice Smith**s condemnation hath been
read according to order and is as followeth
Whereas **Alice Smith** the Daughter of **Deliverance Smith**
late of **Dartmouth** deceased in the **County of Bristol** in the
Province of the Massachustes Bay in **New England** and **Mary** his
widow the afore metioned **Alice Smith** having been Educated
among Friends the people Called Quakers but for want
of keeping to Education and to the Spirit of Truth hath by

giving way to yᵉ evil one fallen into the unclean sin
of fornication (being delivered of a bastard child) to the
Dishonour of God the reproach of the blessed Truth
and grief of all those amongst us that sincerely
desires the prosperity of Zion: we are therefore
Concerned to give this forth as a publick Testimony
against that wicked and detestable action and Do Denie
the Sᵈ **Alice Smith** to be one of us the people of God called
Quakers Desiring that if it be yᵉ will of God She may
through unfeigned repentance obtain pardon for
this her great wickedness and all other her outgoings
Given forth at our monthly meeting held in **Dartmouth**
the 19ᵗʰ day of yᵉ 6ᵗʰ month 1734: and Signed by order and
in behalfe of sᵈ meeting by   **John Tucker**
                                     Clerk of sᵈ Meeting
And **Susanna Smith** and **Ellen Tabers** Condemnations
were not brought to this meeting therefore it is refered
to the next monthly meeting
John Tucker Elisha Wing and **Nicholas Davis** are
appointed to attend yᵉ Quarterly meeting next and
to Draw an Epistle to the Same
And Whereas **Benjamin Powers** hath Signified that
hath a mind to travil westward ad Desires a few
lines of Recommendation Concerning how his life
and Conversation hath been Since he hath been
among us therefore **Joseph Russell** juʳ and **Joseph Tucker**
are appointed to inspect into the matter and if they
find things clear to Draw up Something and bring it
to the next monthly meeting in order to be signed

8 mo At a monthly meeting of friends held at our meeting
1734 House in **Dartmouth** the 21 day of yᵉ 8ᵗʰ month 1734
Dartmouth meeting called **James Barker** and **Adam Mott**
present
Rochester Meeting Called **Elisha Wing** present
Beriah Goddard and **Unice West** laid their intentions
of taking each other in marriage before this meeting
and were desired to wait til the next monthly meeting
for their answer and **Joseph Tripp** and **William Wood**
are appointed to See into **Beriah Goddard**s Clearness Concerning
Marriage and Conversation and to bring in their account

to the next monthly meeting

And **James Cornell** and **Abigail Tripp** appeared and
Laid their intentions of taking each other in marriage
before this meeting and were desired to wait until the
next monthly meeting for their answer and **Robert
Tripp** and **Jonathan Wood** are Chose to make inquiry into
James Cornells Clearness and make return to the next
monthly meeting

And **Joseph Merihoo** and **Edith Whitely** did Lay their
Intentions of taking each other in marriage before this
Meeting and were Desired to wait till the Next monthly
meeting for their answer and **Eliashib Smith** and
Adam Mott are appointed to mak inquiry into **Joseph
Merrihoo**s Clearness relating to marriage and Conver-
sation and make return to the next monthly meeting

And **Jabez Barker** and **Isaac Smith** are appointed
to make inquiry into **John Perry**s Clearness concerning
Marriage and Conversation and to draw up how they
find things and bring it to the next monthly meeting

And **Jedidiah Wing** of **Rochester** hath Signified to this meeting
that he desires a Certificate and this meeting hath
Chosen **Savory Clifton** and **John Wing** to make inquiry into
his Clearness as to marriage and Conversation and to draw
up how they find things and bring it to the next monthly
meeting And there was Collected at this meeting for the
use of Friends one pound twelve Shillings and three pence

And **Susanna Smith** Condemnation was read in this
meeting and is as followeth

Whereas **Susanna Smith** daughter of **Judah Smith** Late
of **Dartmouth** deceasd in the County of **Bristol** in the Province
of the **Massachusets Bay** in **New England** having had her Education
among friends her parents being friends but for want
of keeping to the Spirit of truth and the good order Established
among friends hath of Late given way to her own
inclination and hath married out of the Good order of
Friends and married her mothers Sisters Son though
advised to the Contrary by Friends

We are therefore concerned to give this forth as a
Testimony against disorderly walkers and in particular
against the above **Susanna** nw wife of **Stephen**

Colvin Denying her to be one in unity with us the people
Called Quakers yer Desiring that she may Come to a sight and ^her Sence of
her out goings and to a true and unfeigned repentance so
as to find mercy with the Lord
Given forth at our monthly meeting held in **Dartmouth**
the 21 day of the 8th month 1734: and Signed by order and
in behalfe of Said meeting by **John Tucker** – Clerk
And **Jabez Barker** is appointed to read **Ellen Taber**s Condemnation at **Cushnet** meeting house on a first day after meeting.

9 mo At a monthly meeting of friends held at out meeting House
1734 in **Dartmouth** on the 18th of the 9th month 1734
The Severall meetings thereto belonging Called upon for
Dartmouth John Howland and **Adam Mott** present
for **Rochester Elisha Wing** present
William Wood and **Joseph Tripp** gives this meeting an account
that they have have inquired into the Clearness and
Conversation of **Beriah Goddard** and find nothing to hinder
his intended marriage and the friends that were appointed
to See into the Clearness and Conversation of **Joseph Merihoo**
gives an account that they find nothing to hinder his
intended marriage also **Robert Tripp** and **Jonathan Wood** give
this meeting an account that they have made inquiry into
James Cornells Clearness and find nothing to hinder his
intended marriage
And **Beriah Goddard** and **Unice West** appeared at this meeting
Desiring an answer as to their taking each other in marriage
and their answer was that that they might proceed to
take each other in marriage in the good order of truth in
Some Convenient time between this and the next month
ly meeting and **Joseph Russell ju**r and **Joseph Taber** are
appointed to See their marriage Consummated in the
above order and make return to the next monthly meeting
And **James Cornell** and **Abigail Tripp** appeared at this
Meeting Desiring their answer as to their taking each
other in marriage and their answer was that they
might proceed to take each other in marriage in the
Good order of Truth in Some Convenient time between
this and the next monthly meeting and **Robert Tripp**
and **Jonathan Wood** are appointed to See their marriage
Solemnized in the Good order and make return to the

next monthly meeting
And **Joseph Merrihoo** and **Edith Whitely** appeared at this
meeting Desiring their answer and their answer was
that that they might proceed to take each other in
Marriage observing of Good order of truth in the performance thereof and **Eliashib Smith** and **Adam Mott** are
appointed to See Solemnizing thereof and make return
to the next monthly meeting
And **Henry Chase** Son of **Abraham Chase** of **Tiverton**
and **Mary Tripp** Daughter of **Abiel Tripp** of **Dartmouth**
Did lay their intentions of taking each other in marriage before this meeting and were Desired to wait for
their answer till the next monthly meeting
And ther was a Certificate Signed at this meeting
for **Jedediah Wing** and this meeting appoints **Eliashib
Smith** and **Isaac Smith** to make up accounts with the
Treasurer; and this meeting hath Cleared the accounts
with **Joseph Taber** Concerning the Shingles,
and **Jabez Barker** not having read **Ellen Tabers**
Condemnation he is still continued to do it between this
and the next monthly meeting
And Whereas **Pave Russell** and **Rebekah Ricketson** being
Friends Children and yet have gone out of the Good order
Established among friends in marriage therefore this
meeting appoints **Jabez Barker** ^and **James Barker** to Labour with him
to See if he is willing to Condemn his outgoings and make
return to the next monthly meeting
And there was a Certificate Signed at this meeting for
John Perry

_10 mo 1734_ At a monthly meeting of friends held at our meeting
House in **Dartmouth** the 16 day of the 10 month 1734
The Severall meetings thereto belonging Called uppon
for **Dartmouth John Howland** and **Adam Mott** present
for **Rochester Elisha Wing** present
Joseph Taber and **Joseph Russell** ju^r Gives this meeting an
account that the marriage of **Beriah Goddard** and
Unice West was Carried on in good order as far as they saw
and the Friends that were appointed to See **James Cornells**
Marriage Consumated gives an account that is
perforformed in Gooder as far as they saw

And also the friends that was to See **Josep Merrihoo**
Marriage Solemnized in Good order according to their judgment
And **Henry Chase** and **Abigail Tripp** appeared at this
meeting Desiring their answer in relation to their
taking each other in marriage and their answer saw
that they might proceed to take each other in marriage
in Some Convenient time between this and the next
monthly meeting observing the Good order of Truth in the
performance thereof and **Joseph Tripp** and **Jonathan Wood**
are appointed to see the their marriage Solemnized and
make return to the next monthly meeting
And **Rufus Greene** ~~and~~ of **Warwick** son of **Jabez Greene**
and **Martha Russell** Daughter of **Joseph Russell ju**ʳ
Did Lay their Intentions of taking each other in marriage
before this meeting and were Desired to wait until the
next monthly meeting for their answer
And there was Collected at this meeting for the use
of friends two pounds Eight Shillings and ten pence
And **Eliashib Smith** and **Isaac Smith** have made up the
accounts with the Treasurer and find there is due to
him　　　　　　　　　　　　　　£1-07-07–
And **Jabez Barker** hath read **Ellen Taber**s Condem
nation which is as followeth
Whereas **Ellen Taber** Daughter of **Joseph Taber** of **Dartmouth**
in the County of **Bristol** in the Province of the **Massachusets**
Bay in **New England** Having been Educated among Friends
the People Called Quakers but not regarding the Spirit
of Truth in her heart nor the advice of her Father nor
the advice of friends hath Stubbornly and Willfully kept
Company with one that is no ~~soit~~ a man that is ~~of a~~
not of our Society and hath joined with him in marriage
Contrary to the practice and Good order of friends
as also Contrary to the advice of the Apostle Paul given
to the Corinthians 2 Corinth. 6 Chapter and 14ᵗʰ verse
where it is said be ye not unequally yoaked together
with unbelievers for what fellowship hath righteousness
with unrighteousness and what communion hath
hath light with Darkness: We are therefore Concerned
to for the Clearing of the Truth and Friends to give this
forth as a Publick Testimony against all Disorderly walking and perticularly against the above s[ai]d **Elen** now

Wife of **Peter Craper [Crapo]** Denying her to be one of us
the people Called Quakers yet Sicerely Desiring that
if it be the will of God she may come to a sight and sence
of her outgoings and by unfeigned Repentance ~~found~~
and amendment of Life to walk or to find mercy with
the Lord.
Given forth at our monthly meeting ^of friends held in **Dartmouth**
the 21st day of the 8th month 1734
and Signed by order and in behalfe of sd meeting
by   **John Tucker**: Clerk[5]

At a monthly meeting of friends held at out meeting House in **Dart
mouth** the 20th Day of the 11th month 173⁴/₅
Dartmouth meeting Called **Adam Mott** present
Rochester meeting Called and none appeared. **Henry Chase**
and **Mary Tripps** marriage hath been orderly accomplished
according to information
And **Rufus Greene** and **Martha Russell** appeared at this meeting
and had their answer in relation to their taking Each other
In marriage which was that they might proceed to take
Each other in marriage in some Convenient time between
this and the next monthly meeting according to the Good
order of truth and **John Lapham** and **Jabez Barker** are
appointed to see their marriage Consummated in the
above sd order and mak return to the next monthly meeting
The Friends that were appointed to attend the Quarterly
meeting and Draw an Epistle to the Same have done it
according to order.
Ther was a paper presented to this meeting by **Peleg
Huddleston** Signifying his desire of Coming under the Care
of Friends Which this meeting find freedom to accept
and he to be under our Care
Ther was aCondemnation Signed at this meeting
against **Mary Hathhan [Hathaway]** for her out goings and **Joseph
Russell** juʳ is appointed to read it or cause it to be read
at **Cushnet** meeting House on a first day after the meeting
of Worship between this and the next monthly meeting
There was also a Condemnation Signed at this meeting
against **Paul Russell** and **Rebecca Ricketson** now wife
of sd **Paul Russell** for their Disorderly marriage

5. Written at the bottom of the page:' began to record 1745'

which is as followeth

Whereas **Paul Russell** son of **James Russell** of **Dartmouth**
in the County of **Bristol** in the Province of **Massachusets**
Bay in **New England** and **Rebecca Ricketson** daughter of
Jonathan Ricketson of the Town and County above sd the
sd **Paul Russell** and **Rebecca Ricketson** having been Educated
amongst the people of God called Quakers and now having
gone out of the good order Established amongst the sd people
in marriage then advised to the Contrary and now for
the Clearing of the Truth from such disorderly proceedings
We Do disown the sd **Paul Russell** and **Rebecca** now Wife
of sd **Paul Russell** to be in unity with us the people
Called Quakers

At a Monthly meeting of friends held at our meeting
House in **Dartmouth** on the 17th Day of the 12th moth
173⁴/₅ The Severall meeting therein to belonging
Called upon for **Dartmouth James Barker** and
Adam Mott present for **Rochester** ~~none~~ Elisha Wing appeared
John Lapham and **Jabez Barker** hath Signified
to this meeting that they was at the marriage of
Rufus Green and **Martha Russell** and that it was
Sollemnized in the Good order of truth as far as they
Saw. And **Mary Hathaways** Condemnation hath
been read according to the order of the last monthly
meeting and is as followeth

Whereas **Mary Hathaway** Daughter of **Thomas Hathaway**
of **Dartmouth** in the County of **Bristol** in the province
of the **Massachusets Bay** in **New England** having had
her Education among friends the people Called
Quakers but for want of keeping to her Education
and to the Spirit of Truth in her own heart hath
given way to the Temptations of the Wicked one that
She hath kept Company with one that is an unbe
liever as to our principles to that Degree that she
hath Committed the sin of fornication and also
married to him all which is Contrary to the Scripture
of Truth and to our holy profession to the Dishonour
of God and grief of the Honest hearted amongst us
we are therefore Concerned to give this forth as a
publick Testimony against that wicked action and

do deny her the Said **Mary** now wife of **Thomas Kempton**
to be one in unity with us the People Called Quakers
Desireing if it be the will of God she may through unfeigned
Repentance obtain Pardon for this her wickedness
and all her other outgoings Given forth at our monthly
meeting held in **Dartmouth** the 20 day of the 11ᵗʰ month 173⁴/₅
and Signed by order and in behalfe of sd meeting by

John Tucker – Clerk

(1735) At a monthly meeting of Friends held at our meeting house in
Dartmouth on the 19ᵗʰ day of the 1 month 1735 the Severall
meetings thereto belonging Called upon for **Dartmouth**
John Howland and **James Barker** present for **Rochester**
Elisha Wing present
There was Collected at this meeting for the use of friends £2 05s 3d
And Whereas **William Lake** and his wife hath sent in a
paper to this meeting Condemning their outgoings
Friends having considered the matter it is the mind of
this meeting that it may be accepted if he the Sd **Lake**
will read it or git Some body to do it publickly on a first
Day at the End of the meeting of Worship at **Ponagansett**
meeting House between this and the next monthly
meeting. And this meeting is adjourned til the first Sixth
day in the 2ᵈ month
This meeting being met according to adjournment this
4 day of the 2ᵈ month 1735 There was Some Sufferings
of Friends of **Coakset** Vilage for their refusing to praize[?]
presented to this meeting which this meeting doth
accept in order that they may be sent to the next
Quarterly meeting The visiters belonging to our
monthly meeting have given in their accounts that
they have in a generall way visited the Families of
Friends and for the most part find things pretty well and
where they found things not well they Laboured for
a reformation that Friends appointed to attend the
Quarterly meeting are **John Tucker Elisha Wing**
John Howland and **James Barker** and to Draw an
Epistle to the Same

At a monthly meeting of friends held at our meeting
House in **Dartmouth** on the 21 day of the 2 month 1735
the Severall meetings therto belonging Called upon for

Dartmouth **James Barker** and **Adam Mott** present
for **Rochester** none appeared
And **William Lake** hath read his paper of acknowledge
ment according to the order of the Last monthly meeting
which was followeth[6]

[*the next page is blank*]

The friends that were apponted to attend the Quarterly meeting
have done it and Drawn an Epistle to the Same as ordered
The Epistle from the Quarterly meeting was read at this
meeting and kindly accepted

At the monthly meeting of Friends held at our meeting
House in **Dartmouth** on the 19th Day of the 3 month 1735
the meetings thereto belonging Called upon for **Dartmouth**
John Howland and **James Barker** present for **Rochester**
Elisha Wing present
And whereas there was a Complaint brought to this
meeting against **Thomas Hathaway** Concerning his
keeping Company at divers unseasonable times with
Woman of a Disgraceful Character this meeting having
Discoursed and Laboured with him Concerning the
matter and he not giving any resonable Satisfaction
it is the mind of this meeting for the Clearing of the
Truth that a Condemnation Should go forth against him
and **John Tucker Elisa Wing** and **Isaac Smith** are
appointed to draw one and present it to the next
monthly meeting
And **Nicholas Davis** hath preseted an account
of his Suffering upon the account of his sons not
training which is accepted in order to go to Quar
terly meeting

At a monthly meeting of friends held at our meeting
House in **Dartmouth** on the 16 day of the 4 month
1735 the Severall meetings therto belonging Called
upon for **Dartmouth Eliashib Smith** and **Jabez**
Barker present for **Rochester** none appered
and it was Concluded this meeting being adjourned till
the 23 day of this instant
This meeting being met according to adjournment

6. In the ms., the record of the monthly meeting for the 16th day of the 8th month 1738 appears here. In this edition it has been repositioned in the proper chronological order. [See p. 392.]

this 23 day of the 4 month 1735 The friend that
were appointed to Draw up **Thomas Hathaway**s
Condemnation have done and this meeting doth
approve it and have ordered **Jacob Taber** to read
or Cause it to be read at **Cushnet** meeting house
on a first day at the end of the meetin for worship
and make return to the next monthly meeting
Collected at this meeting for the use of friends 1-16-09
The Friends appointed to attend the Quarterly meeting
are **John Tucker Adam Mott** and **Joseph Tucker** and
also to draw an Epistle to the Same
And this meeting orders **Adam Mott** to pay to the over
seers of the meeting house 30 Shillings towards keeping
the meeting House the halfe year past which is done

At a monthly meeting of friends held at our meet
ing House in **Dartmouth** on the 21 day of the 5 month
1735 The Severall meetings thereto belonging Called
upon for **Dartmouth John Howland** and **James Barker**
present for **Rochester Elisha Wing** present
And **Thomas Hathaway**s Condemnation hath been
read and is as followeth
Whereas **Thomas Hathaway** of **Dartmouth** in the **Coun**
ty of Bristol in the **Province of the Massachusets Bay**
in **New England** hath made profession with us the people
Called Quakers for some time past nevertheless for
want of a Watchful Care hath of Late fallen into
Severall Scandalous and reproachful things which
we have Carefully and Diligently inquired into
and maturely Considered the matter and his difence
therein and he not Clearing himselfe to our Satis
faction we therefor do Deniy him to be one of our
Communion Sincerely desireing that if it be the
Will of God he may Come to a Sight and Sence of his
out goings and to an unfeigned repentance
Given forth at our monthly meeting held in
Dartmouth the 23 of yᵉ 4 month 1735
and Signed by order and in behalfe of Sᵈ meeting
by   **John Tucker** Clerk
And **John Tucker** and **Adam Mott** hath attended
the Quarterly meeting and Drawn an Epistle to
the same. And the Epistle from the Quarterly

meeting was read at this meeting and kindly
accepted There was Collected and brought into
this meeting by the women the Sum of 20 Shillings
Which was delivered to the Treasurer for the meetings use
it was Concluded at this meeting to come to a Subscription
to raise the Sum of 20 pounds to supply the yearly meeting stock
and other necesary Churges arising among ourselves
of which Subscription there is nine pounds 3 shilling & 6 pence
paid in and Delivered to **Adam Mott**
And this meeting orders **Adam Mott** to pay to the overseers
of the meeting house £1 -10ˢ-00ᵈ which which is done
and also this meeting orders the Treasurer to pay to **Jonathan
Wood** the Sum of 40 shillings towards the support of **Deborah
Landers** and also to pay to **John Shepherd** 4 pounds for
Work done towards repairing the meeting House which he
hath done and there remains yet due to sᵈ **Shepherd** the
Sum of 3 pounds 5 shillings and 6 pence

At a monthly meeting of friends held at our meeting
House in **Dartmouth** on yᵉ 18 day of the 6 month 1735
the Severall meetings thereto belonging Called upon for
Dartmouth James Barker and **John Howland** present for
Rochester none appeared
The Visiters Chosen for **Coakset** village are **William
Wood** and **Joseph Tripp** and for **Ponagansett John
Tucker Adam Mott Joseph Tucker** and **Barnabus
Howland** and for **Cushnot Benjamin Allen** and **Joseph
Russell** juʳ. And whereas **William Russell** yᵉ Son of **Joseph
Russell** juʳ hath Signifyed that he desires a Certificate of
his Clearness respecting marriage and Conversation this
meeting appoints **Benjamin Allen** and **John Howland**
to inquire into yᵉ matter and if they find things Clear to
draw one and bring it to yᵉ next monthly meeting
and whereas this meeting hath received a paper Signed
by **Meribah Shearman** Signifying her Sorrow for her
outgoings which this meeting having Considered it is
their mind that she shoul take the paper and read it
or cause it to be read at the end of the meeting of worship
on a first day between this and the next monthly meeting
and she to be present
And this meeting orders **Adam Mott** to pay to pay **John
Shepherd** four pounds nineteen Shillings and Six pence

it being the sum in full of what the meeting ows him upon
his own account and the glaziere which is done
and this meeting is adjourned till the next forth day
come week
This meeting being mett according to adjournment the
27 day of the 6 month 1735 there was a certificate brought
to this meeting for **Michael Smith** of his Clearness respecting
marriage and Conversation directed to the monthly meeting
at **Swansey** and Signed by **John Tucker** in behalfe of yᵉ meeting

At a monthly meeting of friends held at our meeting House
in **Dartmouth** on the 15ᵗʰ Day of the 7ᵗʰ month 1735
The Severall meetings thereto belonging Called upon for
Dartmouth James Barker and Adam Mott present
for **Rochester John Wing** present
Ther was a Certificate presented at this meeting for
William Russell and **John Tucker** hath Signed it in behalfe
of this meeting
Elisha Wing and **John Wing** are appointed visiters for
Rochester the visiters of **Coaksett** have given in an
account to this meeting of their Service in visiting friends
families and Signify that they find thing as well as Could be
Expected for the most part
Ther was Collected at this meeting for the use of friends £2-12ˢ=9ᵈ
This meeting orders **Adam Mott** to pay to **Jonathan Wood**
3 pounds 13 Shillings and nine pence for yᵉ Support of
Deborah Landers which is done
And this meeting is adjourned until the first fourth day
in the 8ᵗʰ month
This meeting being mett according to adjournment this 3ᵈ
day of the 8 month 1735: the visiters of **Ponagansett** village
have given in their account that they have visited the
families of friends under their care in a General Way
and also the visiters of **Rochester** have sent in their account
to this meeting of their service in that affair
The friends appointed to attend yᵉ Quarterly meeting
are **John Tucker William Wood Adam Mott** and **Joseph Tucker**
and to draw an Epistle to yᵉ Same

At a monthly meeting of Friends held at our meeting House in
Dartmouth on the 20ᵗʰ day of yᵉ 8 month 1735 the Severall
meetings thereto belonging Called upon for **Dartmouth** non [none]

appeared by appointment **Rochester** meeting Called and none
appeared **Meribah Shearman**s acknowledgment hath been
read as appointed
The friend appointed to attend the Quarterly meeting have done
it and Drawn an Epistle to the Same as appointed
and the Epistle from the Quarterly meeting was read at this
meeting and well accepted

At a monthly meeting of friends Held at our Meeting House
in **Dartmouth** on the 17th Day of ye 9th month 1735 the
Severall meetings thereto belonging Called upon for **Dartmouth**
John Howland and **Isaac Howland** present for **Rochester**
Elisha Wing present **Adam Mott** hath paid in the mony
that was raised to Supply the yearly meeting Stock which was
3 pounds and 10 Shillings according to the request of ye Quarterly
Meeting and Whereas thee hath been a report Concerning
David Akin that he hath acted that which is reproachful
in abusing **John Whitely** Which after having Discoused with
Sd **Akin** he doth acknowledge and Signifies that he Will
draw up something in order to make Sattisfaction against
the next monthly meeting

At a monthly meeting of friends held at our meeting
House in **Dartmouth** on the 15 day of ye 10th month 1735
the Severall meetings thereto belonging Called upon
for **Dartmouth James Baker** and **John Howland**
present for **Rochester Elisha Wing** present
There was Collected at this meeting for the use of Friends
one pound eighteen shillings
Luke Hart and **Mary Huddlestone** Did lay their inten
tions of taking each other in marriage before this
meeting and were desired to wait till ye next monthly
meeting for their answer and **Eliashib Smith** and **Adam**
Mott are appointed to inquire into the young mans
Clearness respecting marriage and Conversation and
make return to the next monthly meeting
David Akin hath given a paper of acknowledgment to
this meeting which at present are not free to take up
with for full Sattisfaction so ye matter is refered
The Friends appointed to attend the Quarterly meeting are
Adam Mott Elisha Wing and **Thomas Smith** and to Draw an
Epistle to the Same The Friends appointed to oversee the

Meeting House for the year insuing are **Joseph Tucker**
and **Abraham Tucker** and there was 40 Shillings brought
in by the women toward the support of **Deborah Landers**
which was delivered to **Joseph Tripp**
and it was Conclud that the next monthly meeting
Should Come to a further Collection upon the same account
and this meeting hath ordered that **Adam Mott** should
pay three pounds to the overseers for halfe a year
keeping the meeting house which is Done

At a monthly meeting of friends held at our
Meeting House in **Dartmouth** on the 19th day of ye 11
month 1735/6 the Severall meetings thereto belonging
Called upon for **Dartmouth James Barker** and **Adam
Mott** present for **Rochester Stephen Wing** present
Eliashib Smith and **Adam Mott** makes report to
this meeting that they have mad [made] inquiry into **Luke
Hart**s Clearness and find nothing to to hinder him
in his intended marriage
Luke Hart and **Mary Huddlestone** appeared at
this meeting for their answer relating to their
taking Each other in marriage and their answer
was that they might proceed to take each other in
marriage in Some Convenient time between this
and the next monthly meeting observing the good
order of truth in the performance thereof
and **Eliashib Smith** and **Adam Mott** are appointed
to see their Marriage Consumated in the aforesd
order and make return to the next monthly meeting
Adam Mott hath attended the Quarterly Meeting
and there was an Epistle drawn and sent as ordered
Eliashib Smith and **Isaac Smith** are appointed
to make up accompts with the Tresurer and bring
in their accounts to ye next monthly meeting
The Quarterly meeting Epistle was read at this
meeting and kindly accepted
And it was desired in the Epistle that our monthly
meeting Should Collect the Sum of 17 pounds which is refered
to the next monthly meeting

At a monthly meeting of Friends held at our meeting House
in **Dartmouth** on the 10 day of the 12 month 1735/6 the Severall

Meetings therto belonging Called upon for **Dartmouth**
Adam Mott and and **Abraham Tucker** present
for **Rochester Eliashib Wing** present
Nicholas Howland and **Zerniah Russell** did lay their
intentions of taking each other in marriage before
this meeting and were desired to wait till the next
monthly meeting for their answer and **John Lapham** and
Joseph Russell Juʳ: are appointed inquire into the
young mans Clearness respecting marriage and Conver
sation and make report to the next monthly meeting
Eliashib Smith makes report to this meeting that he
was at the marriage of **Luke Hart** and **Mary Huddleston**
and that it was Carried on in good order according to
his observation
and Whereas **Isaac Chase** hath been Disorderly in
his Conversation this meeting appoints **James Barker**
and **George Soule** to Labour with him in order to bring
him to a sight of his out goings and make return to
the next monthly meeting
Eliashib Smith and **Isaac Smith** have reckoned
with the treasurer and find that after accᵗˢ: ballanced
there remains in the Stock 11 Shillings

(1736) At a monthly meeting of friends held at our meeting
House in **Dartmouth** the 15ᵗʰ day of the first month 1736
The Severall meetings therto belonging Called upon
for **Dartmouth John Howland** and **James Barker**
present for **Rochester John Wing** Present
The Friends that were to inquire into **Nicholas Howland**
Clearness makes report that they find nothing to
to hinder his intended marriage
and **Nicholas Howland** and **Zeruiah Russell** appeared
at this meeting for their answer as to taking each other
in marriage and their answer was that they might
proceed to take each other in marriage in some Conve
nient time between this and the next monthly meeting
Observing the good ord of Truth in the performance thereof
and **John Lapham** and **Joseph Russell** are apponted to see
their marriag Consummated in the aforesᵈ order and
make return to the next monthly meeting
David Akin hath sent in a paper to this meeting

Signifying his Sorrow for the abuse offered to **John
Whitely** and it is the mind of this meeting that s^d **Akin**
shall Read s^d paper or Cause it to be read he being present
and at the end of the meeting of Worship one a first day
at **Ponagansett** meeting House between this and the
next monthly meeting
The visiters of **Rochester** and **Coaksett** have given in
their accounts of their visiting the families of friends
in a generall way under their Care
There was Collected at this meeting for ye use of friends 1-06-03
There was 2 papers presented to this meeting one from
William Rand and another from **Rest Randal** his
Wife Signifying their desire of to Come into unity with
friends and it is the mind of this meeting that Friends
should wait some for further proof of their Sincerity
and this meeting is adjorned til the first 6 day in
the second month next
This meeting being mett according to adjornment this
second day of ye 2^d month 1736
The visiters of **Cushnot** have given in their account
that they have visited friends families in under
their Care The visiters of **Ponagansett** have done
nothing this Qurter towards visiting friends families
The friends that were Chosen to speak with **Isaac Chase**
have done it and signify to this meeting that they Cannot
find that he hath any inclination to make Sattisfaction
Therefore this meeting appoints **Jabez Barker** and
Isaac Smith to draw up something against him and
bring it to the next monthly meeting and this meeting
and this meeting appoints **John Tucker John Howland**
And **Joseph Tucker** are appointed to attend the Quarterly
meeting and Draw an Epistle to the Same

At a monthly meeting of friends held at our meeting
House in **Dartmouth** on the 19th day of the 2^d month 1736
The Severall meetings thereto belonging Called upon for
Dartmouth James Barker and ~~Adam Mott~~ **John Howland** present
for Rochester ~~Savory Clifton present~~ none appeared
The Friends that were appointed to attended the Quarterly
meeting have done it and Drawn an Epistle to the Same
as ordered and **David Akins** paper was read as ordered

and is as followeth

To the monthly ~~monthly~~ meeting of friends to be holden
in **Dartmouth** on the 15th of the first month 1736
Friends I being of my Watch have abused **John Whitley**
for which I have been very sorry and Deeply bowed
in my spirit many times and have been since with
John Whitely and made him Sattisfaction for the
wrong done him and Desire that Friends would
pass it by and God to forgive me my trespass against
the truth   **David Akin**
Joseph Brownell and **Leah Lawton** did lay their
intentions of taking each other in marriage before
this meeting and were desired to wait til the next
monthly meeting for their answer and **William Wood**
and **Joseph Tripp** are appointed to inquire into their
Clearness Respecting marriage and Conversation
and make return to the next monthly meeting
and **Isaac Chase** his Condemnation was Drawn up
and brough to this meeting and accepted and **John
Tucker** hath Signed it in behalfe this meeting
And **Joseph Tucker** is appointed to read it on a first day at
the end of the meeting of Worship between this and the next
monthly meeting
and the Quarterly meeting Epistle was read at this
meeting and kindly accepted and **Amos Taber** hath sent
in a paper to this meeting Signifying his Sorrow for his
outgoings desiring that friends would receive him
under their Care Which this meeting accepts of

At a monthly meeting of friends held at our meeting house
in **Dartmouth** on the 17th day of ye 3d month 1736
The Severall meetings thereto belonging Calloneing Called
upon for **Dartmouth James Barker** and **Adam Mott**
present **Rochester** meeting Called **Savory Clifton** present
The Friends appointed to inquire into **Joseph Brownels**
Clearness makes report to this meeting that they have
made inquiry into the matter and find nothing to hinder
his proceedings in his intended marriage
and **Joseph Tucker** hath read **Isaac Chases** Condem
=nation which is as followeth

[Bottom of page blank]

And **Joseph Brownel** and **Leah Lawton** apeared at this
meeting for their answer and their answer was that
they might proceed to take each other in marriage in Some
Convenient time between this and the next monthly
meeting and **William Wood** and **Joseph Tripp** are appointed
to See their marriage Consummated and make return
to the next monthly meeting
and **John Lapham** and **Joseph Russell** gives this meeting
an account that **Nicholas Howland** and **Zruiah Russells**
marriage was performed in the good order of Truth
and **Joseph Brownel** hath Desired leave of this meeting
that he may accomplish his marriage on a meeting
day which this meeting doth Consent to

At a monthly meeting of friends held at our meeting
House in **Dartmouth** on the 21ᵈ: of the 4ᵗʰ month 1736
The Severall meetings thereto belonging Called upon
for **Dartmouth William Wood** and **James Barker** present
for **Rochester Savory Clifton** present
William Wood and **Joseph Tripp** gives this meeting an account
that **Joseph Brownel** and **Leah Lawtons** marriage was Solemniz,d
in good order
and Will**iam Bowd** the Son of **William Bowdish** and **Mary Hart**
the Daughter of **William Hart** hath laid their intentions
of taking each other in marriage before this meeting and
were desired to wait till the next monthly meeting for their
answer and **John Howland** and **Abraham Tucker** are
appointed to See into the young mans Clearness respecting
marriage and Conversation and make return to the
next monthly meeting
The visiters Chosen for this year are for **Coaksett William
Wood Joseph Tripp** and **Jonathan Wood** and for **Cushnot
Joseph Russell** juʳ and and **Benjamin Allen** and for
Rochester Elisha Wing and **John Wing**
There was Collected at this meeting for yᵉ use of friends 1-19=4
and this meeting orders the Treasurer to pay to the over
seers thirty shillings out of the Stock which with mony
that the women gave in was due for halfe a years keeping
the meeting House which mony was forthwith paid
and **Samuel Howland** hath sent in a paper to this meeting

Signifying his Sorrow for his outgoings in taking an Oath which is refered
to the Consideration of the next monthly meeting
An wheas **Barnabas Chase** hath gon out of the good
ord Established amongst us in marriage and Friends
have Laboured with him but he hath not regarded
it therefore this meeting appoints **Jabez Barker** and
Isaac Smith to Draw up a Condemnation against him
and bring it to the next monthly meeting
and whereas there was a Complaint brought to this
meeting against **William Wood** the son of **William Wood**
Concerning his mannagement abou a parcel of goats
that he sold to **David Stafford** which is refered
John Tucker James Barker Adam Mott Elisha Wing
and **Isaac Smith** are appointed to attend yᵉ Quarterly
meeting next and to Draw an Epistle to the same

At a monthly meeting of friends held at our meeting
House in **Dartmouth** on the 19ᵗʰ day of the 5ᵗʰ mo 1736
The severall meetings thereto belonging Called upon for
Dartmouth James Barker and **Abraham Tucker**
present for **Rochester** none appeared
John Howland and **Abraham Tucker** makes report to
this meeting that they have made inquiry into **William
Bowdish**es Clearness respecting marriage and Conversa
tion and find nothing to hinder his intended marriage
William Bowdish and **Mary Hart** appeared at this
meeting for their answer in relation to their taking
each other in marriage and their answer was that
they might proceed to take each other in marriage in
Some Convenient time between this and the next
monthly meeting observing the good order of Truth
in the accomplishment thereof and **John Howland**
and **Abraham Tucker** are appointed to see their
marriage Consummated and make return to the
next monthly meeting
and the paper that **Samuel Howland** sent in to the
last monthly meeting hath been read in this meet=
ing and Friends find fredom to accept of it for
for sattisfaction
And **Barnabas Chase** his Condemnation was brought to
this meeting and it is refered to the Quarterly meeting

Whither such Condemnations ought to be read publickly
or only in the monthly meeting
The Friends that were appointed to attend the Quarterly meeting
have attended it and Drawn an Epistle to yᵉ same
and the Epistle from the Quarterly meeting was read at
this meeting and well accepted
and it: [sic]

At a monthly meeting of Friends held at our
Meeting House in **Dartmouth** on the 16ᵗʰ day of yᵉ 6 month
1736 the Severall meetings thereto belonging called upon
for **Dartmouth Joseph Tucker** and **Abraham Tucker**
present for **Rochester Elisha Wing** present
John Howland and **Abraham Tucker** makes report to
this meeting that **William Bowdish** and **Mary Hart**s
marriage was Consummated in the good order of truth

At a monthly meeting of Friends held at our meeting
House in **Dartmouth** on the 20ᵗʰ day of the 7ᵗʰ month 1736
the Severall meetings thereto belonging Called upon for
Dartmouth James Barker and **Abraham Tucker** present
for **Rochester** none appeared
There was Collected at this meeting for the use Friends
2:00=06 The mony which Friends have subscribed toward
building of **Tiverton** meeting House was brought in to
this meeting in order to be sent by the represetitives
to yᵉ Quarterly meeting
and this meeting agreas to take an hundred books
so [?] written originally by **Moses West** whither Quar
terly meeting are about to git reprinted[7]
And **John Tucker Adam Mott** and **James Barker** and
John Howland are appointed to attend the Quarterly meeting went and to draw an Epistle to the same
and this meeting is adjourned til the first sixth day in the
next month

7. Moses West, *A Treatise concerning Marriage, wherein the Unlawfulness of Mixt-Marriages Is Laid Open from the Scriptures of Truth. Shewing That It Is Contrary to the Will of God, and the Practice of His People in Former Ages, and Theerefore of Dangerous Consequence, for Persons of Different Judgments in Matters of Religious Worship, tTo Be Joyned Together in Marriage. Written for the information and Benefit of Christian Professors in General, and Recommended More Particularly to the Youth of Either Sex amongst the People Called Quakers. To Which Is Added, by Way of Appendix, Sundry Piece of Advice, Extracted from Several of the Yearly Meeting's Epistles* (Leeds, Eng.: James Lister, 1736). First published in 1707, West's work had gone through six printings between 1726 and 1736. There is no record of a New England imprint, but an edition was printed in Philadelphia in 1738.

This meeting being met according to adjournment this
first day of yᵉ 8 month 1736 we received accounts
from the visiters of **Ponagansett** and **Coakset**] that they
have visited the families of friends in a pretty general way

At a monthly meeting of Friends held at our meeting house
in **Dartmouth** on the 18ᵗʰ day of yᵉ 8ᵗʰ month 1736
The severall meetings therto belonging Called for
Dartmouth John Howland and **Abraham Tucker**
present for **Rochester** none appeared
The Friend that were appointed to attend the Quarterly
meeting have attended it and Drawn an Epistle to yᵉ same
Recompense Kirby and **Rebecca Cornell** hath laid
their intention of taking each other in marriage
before this meeting and were desired to wait for
their answer til the next monthly meeting and
Jedidiah Allen and **John Russell** are appointed to
make inspection into the young mans Clearness
respecting marriage and Conversation and make
return to the next monthly meeting
Barnabas Chase his Condemnation was read at this
meeting and and ~~the meeting~~ **John Tucker** hath signed it in the
behalfe of this meeting and **John Tucker** is ordered
to read it or cause it to be read at the end of yᵉ meet
ing for worshsip on a first day between this and the next
monthly meeting
The Epistle from yᵉ Quarterly meeting was read at
this meeting and kindly accepted

At a monthly meeting of Friends held at our meeting
House in **Dartmouth** on the 15ᵗʰ day of the 9ᵗʰ month 1736
The severall meeting of Friends held at our meeting
House in **Dartmouth** on the 15ᵗʰ day of the 9ᵗʰ month 1736
The severall meetings therto belonging Called upon for
Dartmouth John Howland and **James Barker** present
for **Rochester** none appeared
John Russell makes report to this meeting that he
hath mad inquiry into the Clearness and Conversation
of **Recompence Kirby** and finds nothing to hinder his
his intended marriage and **Barnabas Chase** his Con
demnation hath not been read according to the order
of the last monthly meeting **John Tucker** is still

Continued to see it done between this and the next
monthly meeting
Recompence Kirby and **Rebecca Cornell** appeared
at this meeting for their answer
And their answer was that they might proceed to take
each other in marriage in Some convenient time between
this and the next monthly meeting Observing the Good
order of truth in the prosecution thereof and **John Russell**
and **Holder Slocum** are appointed to see their marriage
Consummated in the s^d good order and make return to
the next monthly meeting

At a monthly meeting of friends held at our meeting House
in Dartmouth on the 20th day of the 10th month 1736 the
severall meetings thereto belonging Called upon for
Dartmouth James Barker and **John Howland** present
for **Rochester Elisha Wing** present
John Russell and **Holder Slocum** gives this meeting an account
That **Recompence Kirby** and **Rebecca Cornell**s marriage
was sollemnized in the good order of Truth according to the
Good order of truth according to their judgment
Job Howland and **Naomy Chase** Did lay their intentions
of taking each other in marriage before this meeting
and were Desired to wait til the next monthly meeting
for their answer and **Jabez Barker** and **Isaac**
Smith are appointed to inspect into the young mans
Clearness respecting marriage and Conversation
and make return to the next monthly meeting
There was Collected at this meeting 1 pound 9 Shillings and 6^d
And **Barnabas Chse** his Condemnation hath been read
according to order and is as followeth
Whereas **Barnabas Chase** the Son of **Nathanael**
Chase and **Abigail** his wife of **Dartmouth** in the
County of Bristol in the **Province of the Massachusets**
Bay in **New England** being one that hath been under
the Care of frinds yet hath for severall years past
gone Contrary to the good orders Established amongst
us the people Called Quakers both in habit and con
versation and hath been Laboured with in love in
order to bring him to Something of a Conformity
but instead of taking up with such Wholesom Counsel

that hath from time to time been given him he
hath rather grown more Obstinate and hath of
Late fallen into the reprochful sin of fornication
For which Scandalous action with the rest of his outgoings we
Can done less for the Clearing of the Blessed Truth and the
Tes[t]imony thereof buth give forth this as a publick Tesimomony
against Such things and them that are found in the practi[ce?]
thereof and Do deny him the Sd **Barnabas Chase** to be one in
unity with us yet truly desireing that he may come to
a Sight of this with all other his outgoing and find mercy
with the Lord. Given forth at our monthly meeting
held in **Dartmouth** on the 18th day of the 8th month 1736
and Signed by order of sd meeting by **John Tucker** Clerk
The business of **Rochester** is refered to the next monthly
meeting and this meeting orders the tresurer to pay one
pound eleven Shillings to **Isaac Smith** for recording
the monthly meeting munits
And also to pay to the overseers 3 pounds for keeping
the meeting House the halfe year past which be forth
with paid: And we received twenty Shillings of ye Women
which was delivered to the Tresurer
The Friends appointed to attend ye Quarterly meeting
are **John Tucker Elisha Wing James Barker Thomas
Smith** and **Joseph Tucker**

At a monthly meeting of friends held at our
Meeting House in **Dartmouth** on the 17th day of the 11
Month 1736/7 The Severall meetings therto belonging
Called upon for **Dartmouth Abraham Tucker** and
Peleg Smith present for **Rochester** none appeard
The Friends that were appointed to inquire into
Job Howlands Clearness respecting marriage and
Conversation gives an account to this meeting that
they find nothing to hind[er] his inte[n]ded marriage
and **Job Howland** and **Naomy Chase** appeared at
this meeting desireing an answer in relation to their
taking each other in marriage And their answer
was that they might proceed to take eac[h] other in mar
riage in Some Convenient time between this and the
next monthly meeting observing the good order
of Truth as in the accomplishment thereof

And **John Howland** and **John Lupham [Lapham]** are appointed to see
their marriage Sollemnized in the abovsd order and make
return to the next monthly meeting

Joseph Tripp and **Abigal [Abigail] Wait** appeared at this meeting Signify
ing their Intentions of taking each other in marriage
and Were desired to waᶦt til yᵉ next monthly meeting for
their answer and **William Wood** and **Robert Tripp** are
appointed to inquire into **Joseph Tripp**s clearness respecting
marriage and Conversation and make return to the
next monthly meeting

And **Nicholas Davis** is appointed to advise the Elders
of **Rochester** meeting that they render an account of mat
ters to the next monthly meeting

The Friends appointed to attend the Quarterly meeting
have all attended it but **Thomas Smith** and there was an
Epistle drawn and Sent and we received an Epistle from
the Quarterly meeting which was read at this meeting
and well accepted

And **John Tucker Jabez Barker** and **James Barker**
are appointed to assist the Women in their orderly
proceeding against **Meribah Shearman** now wife of
John Roan and **Elisabeth Mosher** daughter of **Joseph
Mosher** for their Disorderly marrying

At a monthly meeting of friends held at our meeting
House in **Dartmouth** on the 21 day of the 12ᵗʰ month
1736/7 The Severall meetings thereto belonging Called
upon for **Dartmouth John Howland** and present
for **Rochester Elisha Wing** and **John Wing** present

John Lapham and **John Howland** gives this meeting
an account that **Job Howland** and **Naomy Chase**[es?]
marriage was Consummated in good order

The Friends appointed to inquire into **Joseph Tripp**s
Clearness makes report to this meeting that they
find nothing to hinder his proceeding in his intended
marriage And **Joseph Tripp** and **Abigail Wait** appeared
at this meeting desireing their answer in relation
to their taking each other in marriage and their answer
was that they might proceed to take each other in marriage
in Some Convenient time between this and the next monthly meeting
Observing the good order of Truth in the performance

Thereof and **William Wood** and **Robert Tripp** are appointed
to See their marriage Sollemnized and make repor[t] to
the next monthly meeting
And **Joseph Tripp** hath desired leave of this meeting to
accomplish his marriage week day meeting appointed
for worship which is granted

(*1737*) At a monthly meeting of friends held at our meeting ho[u]se
in **Dartmouth** on the 21 day of the first month 1737
The Severall meetings therto belonging Called upon
for **Dartmouth James Barker** and **Abraham
Tucker** present **Rochester** mee[t]ing Called **John
Wing** present **William Wood** gives this meeting an
account that the marriage of **Joseph Tripp** and
Abigail Wait was Consummated in the good
order of truth
This meeting hath received an account from
Rochester which is refered to the next monthly
meeting and there Was Collected at this meeting 2=06=06
There was Considerable of agetation at this meeting
Concerning **Thomas Smith**s asserting that **Henry Tucker**
was a false man and sd **Tucker** was at this meeting
doth assert that he is Clear of sd Charge therefor
it is the judgment of this meeting that sd **Smith**
Should make out his Charge or else to Condemn
his asserting of it
And this meeting is adjournd til the youths meeting.
This meeting being mett according to adjournment
this first day of the 2 month 1737
it was Concluded at this meeting in Consideration
of the papers that **William Randall** and his Wife sent
in to the monthly meeting in the 12 month 1735
And of the good report ~~that~~ Concerning them Since
that they Should be received under our Care
according their request
The visitters of **Ponagansett** and **Coaksett** have
given in their accounts of their Service in that
affair **John Tucker Elisha Wing** and **James Barker**
are appointe to attend yᵉ Quarterly meeting and
Draw an Epistle to the Same
And ther was an account brought this meeting by **John**

Lapham that he hath done Severall Services for the
meeting by order of yᵉ Overseers as much as Comes to two and
twenty Shillings and this meeting orders the Treasurer to
pay it out of the Stock

At a monthly meeting of friends held at our meeting house
in **Dartmouth** on the 18ᵗʰ day of the 2ᵈ month 1737 the Several
meetings therto belonging Called upon for **Dartmouth**
Isaac Howland and **Abraham Tucker** present
for **Rochester Nicholas Davis** present,
and **Meribah Shearman** now wife of **John Roan** her
Condemnation was read at this meeting and is as followeth
Whereas the Widow **Meribah Shearman** having had
her Education among friends and formerly having
been married amongst them having of late Contrary
to the good advice of Friends gone and married out of
the Good order Established amongst the people Called Qua
kers for which with her other outgoings we the sd
people do deny the sd **Meribah** now the wife of **John
Roan** to be one in unity with us the people Called
Quakers Desiring that she may Come to a sence of
her outgoings and find mercy with the Lord
The Friends that were appointed to attend the Quar
terly meeting have attended it and drawn an Epistle
to the Same as appointed and the Quarterly meeting
Epistle was read at this meeting and well accepted
and the matter concerning **Thomas Smith** and **Henry
Tucker** is refered to the next monthly meeting
and **Adam Mott** hath paid one pound two shillings
to **John Lapham** as appointed

At a monthly meeting of friends held at our
meeting House in **Dartmouth** on the 16 day of the
3ᵈ month 1737 the severall meetings thereto belong
ing Called upon for **Dartmouth Adam Mott** and
John Howland present **Rochester** meeting Called
Elisha Wing present
David Stafford Son of **Josiah Stafford** of Tiverton ˄ and Lydia Davel [Davol] did
lay their intentions taking each other in marriage
before this meeting and were desired to wait til
the next monthly meeting for their answer
There was two papers from **Rochester** presented to

this meeting one from **Aaron Griffith** and his wife ane [and]
One from **Simon Hathaway** and his wife acknowledg
ing their outgoings which are refered for further
Consideration.
And whereas there hath been Considrable of agita
=tion in this meeting Concerning **William Wood** the son
of **William Wood** his Cace and it was unanimously
Concluded at this meeting to Refer the Whole matter
to a Committe to Judge and Determine the matter
The Committe agreed upon are **Samuel Aldrich**
William Anthony and **John Earle**
And **Barnabas Howland Peleg Smith** and **Isaac
Smith** are appointed to represent the monthly meeting
to give the Com^tee a right information how things
have been Carried on in the matter
And the friends appointed to See into the matter
relating to **Thomas Smith** and **Henry Tucker** have
brought in their Judgment which is as followeth
We the Subscribers have taken the matter Left to us
into Due Consideration and we do not find the Charge
that **Thomas Smith** Expressed against **Henry Tucker**
to be fully proved but it evidently appears that
Henry Tucker did greatly Equivocate in his answer
to **John Akin** at thee Town meeting
Benjamin Allen James Shearman George Soule
Peleg Huddlestone Robert Tripp

At a monthly meeting of Friends held at our
Meeting House in **Dartmouth** on the 20th day of
the 4 month 1737 the Severall meetings thereto
belonging Called upon for **Dartmouth John Howland**
and ~~and~~ **Abraham Tucker** present for **Rochester**
David Stafford not coming for his answer at this
meeting it is refered to the next monthly meeting
and **Joseph Tripp** and **Robert Tripp** are appointed
to make inspection into his Clearness and make re
turn to the next monthly meeting
The Com^tte appointed to Judge and Determine
the matter between the monthly meeting and **William Wood**
have sent in their Judgment which is as followeth
We the Committe in pursuance to **Dartmouth** monthly meetings

request have mett on the account and heard the allegations
on both Sides Respecting a parcel of Goats that he **William Wood**
sold to **David Stafford** and **Timothy Ricketson** And Waitily Considered
the matter and pressing the Case very Close upon Sd **Wood**
that so he Seemed to be Smitten in his own Conscience
and therefore he has given a paper of Condemnation
which we here Inclose for your meeting And also we
appoint the Bearer hereof **Isaac Smith** to read Sd
paper at the next first day meeting after your monthly
meeting And this is what we thee Sd Com^tte have Determined
for Friends Sattisfaction in that Case as Aforesd
Newport Rhode Island the 11th of ye 4 month 1737
Samuel Aldrich   William Anthony   John Earll [Earle]
The visiters that Served the last year for **aponagansett**
are appointed to stand for that Service the Insuing year
and also the Same for ~~Coaksett~~ ^Cushnot that Served the last year
And **Joseph Tripp Jonathan Wood** and **Peleg Huddlestone**
are appointed visitters for **Coaksett** and for **Rochester**
Elisha Wing and **Joh[n] Wing**
The friends appointed to attend the Quarterly meeting
are **John Tucker Elisha Wing** and **John Howland**
The Epistle from the yearly meeting held in **London** in the
year 1736 was read at this meeting and it is the mind
of this meeting that Sd Epistle should be read on a first
day meeting between this and the next monthly
Meeting There was Collected at this meeting 2=09=05

At a monthly meeting of friends held at our meeting
House in **Dartmouth** on the 18th Day of the 5th month 1737
the Severall meetings thereto belonging Called upon for
John Howland and **Adam Mott** present for **Rochester** none
appeared The Friends that wer appointed to inspect
into **David Stafford**s Clearness have done it
And find nothing to hinder his proceedings in his intended
marriage and also Sd **Stafford** producing a Certificate
from **Rode Island** monthly meeting
And **David Stafford** and **Lydia Davel [Davol]** appeared at this
meeting desireing an answer in relation to their taking
Each other in marriage and their answer was that
they might proceed to take each other in marriage
in Some Convenient time between this and the next

monthly meeting observing the good order of Truth
in the performance thereof and **Joseph Tripp** and
Robert Tripp ar appointed to See their marriage Sollem
nized and make return to the next monthly meeting
annd **Isaac Smith** hath read **William Wood**s paper
according to order: which is as followeth
Whereas I **William Wood** of **Dartmouth** son of **William
Wood** for want of a watchful Care have brought
a Scandalous reproach upon my selfe the Holy Truth
and Friends that is in not keeping fully to my Words
and Contracts with **David Stafford** and **Timothy
Ricketson** in Looting of a parcel of Goats with the
Sd **Stafford** and **Ricketson** as aforesd which I am
Sorry for and Desire my well wishing friends may
find freedom to pass ~~at~~ ₍this my offence to them₎ by and that I may be more
Careful for the time to Come to give the like occation
pr me **William Wood** ju^r
The Friends appointed to attend the Quarterly meeting
Have attended it and Drawn an Epistle to the same
And this meeting hath ordered that a Letter to be
Sent down to the Governor in order to let him
know the Diffecult Sircumstance that we ly
under by reason of our Justices not giving us our
ingagements according to the Indulgannce as in
times past and **John Tucker** is ordered to do it and
Sign it in behalfe of the monthly meeting
The Epistle from the Quarterly meeting was read at
this meeting and well accepted
And **Thomas Smith** has Signified to this meeting that
he is Sorry that there has been So much discource
in the matter relating to **Henry Tucker** and him selfe
and hopes he shall be more Careful for the time to Come

At a monthly meeting of Friends held at our meeting House
in **Dartmouth** the 15th day of the 6th month 1737
The Severall meetings therto belonging Called upon for **Dartmouth**
John Lapham and **Isaac Howland** present for **Rochester**
Elisha Wing present The friends appointed to see **David
S[t]afford** and **Lydia Davels [Davol]** marriage Consummated gives
this meeting an account that it was accomplished in
go^od order according to their judgments

There was a Condemnation brought to this meeting
and Signed by order of sd meeting by **John Tucker** against
Elisabeth Mosher Daughter of **Joseph Mosher** and **John
Tucker** is appointed to read it or Cause it to be read
on a first day at the end of the meeting of Worship at
Ponagansett meeting House between this and the next
Monthly meeting

And **Henry Tucker** hath Sent in a paper to this meeting
Condemning his unwarrantable Discource at a Town
Meeting Expressing his Sorrow for the Same and it is
the mind of this meeting that he Should read it or
git Some body to do it at the end of the meeting of wor
ship on a first day between this and the next monthly
meeting. And **Adam Mott** is ordered to pay 3 pounds
and ten Shillings to the Overseers for halfe a years
keeping the meeting House which he forthwith paid

At a monthly meeting of Friends held at our meeting
House in **Dartmouth** on the 19th day of ye 7th month 1737
The Severall meetings thereto belonging Called uppon
for **Dartmouth James Barker** and **John Howland**
present for **Rochester John Wing** present
And **Elisabeth Mosher** now the wife of **Josiah Allen**
her Condemnation hath been read according to the
order of the Last monthly meeting and is as
followeth
　　　　　　　[top half of page is blank]
And there was Collected at this meetin for the use of
Friends 1=19–00
and the paper that **Henry Tucker** sent in hath been
read accord to order
The visiters of **Ponagansett** and **Coaksett** have given
in their accounts to this meeting of their proceed
ings on the account of visiting
And **Benjamin Wing** and **Experience Benson** of **Rochester**
have laid their intention of takinge each other in
marriage before this meeting and were desired to
Wait till the next monthly meeting for their answer
And **Elisha Wing** and **Stephen Wing** are appointed to
inquire into their Clearness as to marriage and
Conversation and make return to the next monthly

Meeting And also to see that things are Clear Concer
ning the widows Child that it be not wronged by her
Second marriage
The Friends appointed to attend the Quarterly meet
ing are
John Tucker James Barker and **John Howland** and to draw
an Epistle to the Same
The visiters of **Rochester** and **Cushnot** have not done any
anything in referance to visiting Friends families and they
are advised to perform their Service upon that account
and bring in the account soon as may be with Conveniency

At a monthly meeting of friends held at our meeting House
in **Dartmouth** on the 17 day of the 8ᵗʰ month 1737
The Severall meetings thereto belonging Called upon
for **Dartmouth Joseph Russell** and **James Barker** present
for **Rochester Elisha Wing** and **John Wing** present
And **Benjamin Wing** and **Experience Benson** appered
at this meeting for their answer in relation to their
taking Each other in marriage and their answer was
that they might proceed to take each other in marriage
in Some Convenient time between this and the next
monthly meeting observing the good order of Truth in the
performance thereof and **Elisha Wing** and **Savory Cliffton**
And Are appointed to See their marriage Consumma
ted and make return to the next monthly meeting
And **Joseph Smith** and **Elizabeth Davis** layd their
intentions of taking Each other in marriag before
this meeting and were desired to wait till the next
monthly meeting for their answer and **Joseph Tucker**
and **John Howland** are appointed to inquire into
the young mans Clearness respecting marriag and Conver
sation and make return to the next monthly meeting
John Tucker and **John Howland** hath attended the
Quarterly meeting and Drawn an Epistle to yᵉ Same
The Epistle from yᵉ Quarterly meeting was read
and kindly accepted

At a monthly meeting of friends held at our
meeting House in **Dartmouth** on the 21 day of the 9 month
1737 The Severall meetings therto belonging Called upon
For **Dartmouth John Howland** and **James Barker** present

for **Rochester Elisha Wing** present
We have received an account from **Rochester** that
Benjamin Wing and **Experience Benson**s marriag was
Consummated in the good order of truth **John Howland**
and **Joseph Tucker** gives this meeting an account that
they have mad[e] inspection into **Joseph Smith**s Clearness
as to marriage and Conversation and find nothing to hin
der his proceedings in his intended marriage
And **Joseph Smith** and **Elisabeth Davis** appeared at this
meeting desireing their answer and their answer
was that they might proceed to take each other in mar
riage in Some convenient time between this and the
next monthly meeting and **Joseph Taber** and **Isaac Smith**
Are appointed to see their marriage Consummated
and make return to the next monthly meeting
And **Joseph Barker** and **Rebecca Smith** did lay their
Intentions of taking each other in marriage before
this meeting and were desired to wait til the next month
ly meeting for their answer and **James Barker** and
Abraham Tucker are appointed to See into the young
mans Clearness and make return to the next monthly
meeting

At a monthly meeting of friends held at our meeting
House in **Dartmouth** on the 19th day of ye 10 month 1737
The Severall meetings thereto belong Called upon for
Dartmouth James Barker and **Abraham Tucker** present
Rochester meeting Called **Stephen Wing** present **Joseph
Taber** and **Isaac Smith** gives this meeting an account
that **Joseph Smith** and **Elisabeth Davis**es marriag was
Orderly performed
And **Joseph Barker** and **Rebecca Smith** appeared
at this meeting for their answer and their answer
was that they might proceed to take
each other in marriage in Some Convenient time
between this and the next monthly meeting observing the
good order of truth in the performance thereof –
And **James Barker** and **Abraham Tucker** are
appointed to see their marriag Consummated in sd good order
and make return to the next monthly meeting
And **Seth Shearman** and ~~**Rebecca**~~Ruth **Lapham** did lay their Inten

tions of taking Each other in marriage before this meeting
and were desired to wait till the next monthly meeting
for their answer and **John Russell** and **Isaac Howland** are
appointed to See into yᵉ young mans Clearness respecting
marriage and Conversation and make return to the
next monthly meeting
And **Ruben Davel** [**Davol**] and **Mary Ricketson** did lay their
intentions of taking each other in marriage before this
Meeting and were desired to wait till the next monthly
Meeting for their Answer and **John Russell** and **Robert
Tripp** are appointed [to] see into the young mans
Clearness respecting marriag and Conversation and make
return to the next monthly meeting
And the visiters of **Rochester** and **Cushnot** have given in
their accounts of their visiting friends families to this
meeting. There was Collected at this meeting 3:00:09
And this meeting orders the Tresurer to pay to the over
seers five pounds and four shillings for halfe a years
keeping the meeting House and for Some worke done —
about the House
And **Joseph Tucker** and **Abraham Tucker** are appointed
overseers to the meeting House for the year insuing
We received of the women twenty shillings which
went into the Stock and **Adam Mott** hath paid the £5=1ˢ=00ᵈ
according to order
The friends appointed to attend the Quarterly meeting
are **John Tucker Elisha Wing James Barker John Howland**
and **Joseph Tucker** and To Draw an Epistle to the Same

At a monthly meeting of friends held at our meeting
House in **Dartmouth** on the 16ᵗʰ day of the 11th month 1737/8
The Severall meetings thereto belonging Called upon for
Dartmouth Eliashib Smith and **John Lapham** present for
Rochester none appeared
The Friend that were appointed to inquire into **Seth Shearman**s Clearness
They give this meeting an account that find nothing
to hinder his proceeding in his intended marriage
And also the friend appointed to inspect into **Ruben
Davels** [**Davol**] Clearness gives this meeting an account that
they find nothing to hinder his proceedings in his intend
ed marriage And **Ruben Davel** [**Davol**] and **Mary Ricketson**

appeared at this meeting Desireing their answer in re
lation to their taking Each other in marriage and
their answer was that they might proceed to take each
other in marriage in Some Convenient time between
this and the next monthly meeting observing the good order
of truth in the performance thereof and **John Russell**
and **John Lapham** are appointed to see their marriage
Sollemnized in the abovesd order and make return to
the next monthly meeting

And **Seth Shearman** and **Ruth Lapham** appeared at this
meeting Desireing their answer and their answer was
that they might proceed to take each other in marriage
in Some Convenient time between this and the next
monthly meeting observing the Good order of Truth
in the accomplishing of it and **Jabez Barker** and **Isaac
Smith** are appointed to see their marriage Consumma
ted in the sd good order and make return to yᵉ next month
ly meeting And **Benjamin Russell** the Son of **Jonathan
Russell** and **Hannah Allen** the Daughter of **John Allen**
did Lay their intention of taking each other in marriage
before this meeting and were desired to wait till the
next monthly meeting for their answer

And **Adam Mott** and **Joseph Tucker** are appointed to
See into the young mans Clearness as to marriag and
Conversation and make return to the next monthly
meeting And **Abraham Tucker** gives this meeting an
account that the marriage of **Joseph Barker** and
Rebecca Smith was performed in the good order
of truth as far as he Saw

The friends that were appointed to attend the Quarterly
Meeting have attended it all except **John Tucker** and
Drawn an Epistle to the Same

And wherea[s] **James Russell** hath signifyed to this meeting
that his Son **James** has set up his publishment against
his Consent and Contrary to the order Established amongst
Friends Therefor **Jabez Barker** and **Isaac Smith** are
appointed to talk with his Son to know the reason of his
disorder and make report to the next monthly meeting

And **Ruben Davel [Davol]** and **Seth Shearman** hath desired
leave to Sollemnize their marriag on a weekday meeting
for worship which is granted

At a monthly meeting of Friends held at our meeting
House in **Dartmouth** on the 20th day of ye 12th month 1737/8
The Severall meetings therto belonging Called upon for
Dartmouth Adam Mott and **Abraham Tucker** present
for **Rochester** none appeared **Adam Mott** and **Joseph
Tucker** makes report to this meeting that they have
made inquiry into **Benjamin Russell**s Clearness and
find nothing to hinder his intended marriage
The Quarterly meetings Epistle was read at this meeting
and well accepted And **Benjamin Russell** and **Hannah
Allen** appeared at this meeting for their answer
And their answer was that they might proceed to
take each other in marriage in Some Convenient
time between this and the next monthly meeting and
Adam Mott and **Joseph Tucker** are appointed to See
their marriage Consummated in the good order of
truth and make return to the next monthly meeting
And **Jabez Barker** and **Isaac Smith** gives this
meeting an account that they wer at **Seth Shearm**an
and **Ruth Lapham**s marriage and Saw nothing but
that it was Sollemnized in the good order of Truth
And **John Russell** and **John Lapham** also Signifies
that **Ruben Davel [Davol]** and **Mary Ricketson**s marriage
was accomplished in good order
And whereas there is a report that **Abraham Tucker** the
Son of **Henry Tucker** is guilty of being the father of **Ruth
Slocum**s Child and he not Clearing him selfe to Friend Satis
faction it is the mind of this meeting that he [remain?] under
Dealing

(1738) At a monthly meeting of Friends held at our meeting house
in **Dartmouth** on the 20th day of the first month 1738
Dartmouth meeting Called **Isaac Howland** and **Georg[e] Soule**
present The Friends that were appointed to see **Benja**n
Russell and **Hannah Allen**s marriag Sollemnized makes
report to this meeting that it was accomplished in good
order according to their Judgments
And **Jacob Shearman** and **Margrate Prance [Prince]** was
at this meeting and laid their intention of taking
Each other in marriage and were desired to wait till
the next monthly meeting for their answer And **John**

Lapham and **Isaac Howland** are appointed to inspect
into the young mans Clearness and make return to
to the next monthly meeting
And this meeting is adjourned till the first day in the next mon_{th}
This meeting being mett according to adjournment this
first day of the 2ᵈ month 1738
An account of visiting Friends families both of **Coaksett**
and **Ponaganset** was presented to this meeting
John Tucker William Wood and **James Barker** are
appointed to attend the Quarterly meeting and to draw
an Epistle to the Same

At a monthly meeting of friends held at our meeting
House in **Dartmouth** the 17ᵗʰ day of the 2ᵈ month 1738
Dartmouth meeting Called **Joseph Tucker** present
Rochester meeting Called **Nicholas Davis** present
The Friends that were appointed to enquire into
Jacob Shearmans Clearness makes repor to this
meeting that they find nothing to hinder his intended mar
riage And **Jacob She[a]rman** and **Margrate Prance [Prince]**
appeared at this meeting for their answer
And their answer was that they might proceed to take each
other in marriage in Some Convenient time between this
and the next monthly meeting observing the good order of
Truth in the performance thereof and **John Lapham** and
Isaac Howland are appointed to see their marriage Consummated
and make return to the next monthly meeting
The Friends that were appointed to attend the Quarterly
meeting have attended it all except **James Barker**
and Drawn an Epistle to the Same according to order
And **Jacob Shearman** hath desired leave to Solemnize
his marriage on a week day meeting for worship
which is granted
And Whereas She that was the widow of **Edward Wing** hath
brought a Scandal upon her selfe and the blessed Truth
by having a Child So soon after her second marriage
Therfore **Eliashib Smith** and **Joseph Tucker** are appoin
ted to go with the women to See what She Can do towards
making Sattisfaction
And there was Collected at this meeting – – £2=02ˢ=09ᵈ
and **John Howland** is appointed git the books written

originally by **Moses West**

And whereas there is a Scandalous report of **Abraham
Thomas** Concerning his being the Father of a bastard
Child therefore **John Russell** and **George Soule** are
appointed to inquire into sd report and they are Sen[s]ible
that it is true to give advice as they may think most
propper in that case and make return to yᵉ next monthly _{meeting}

At a monthly meeting of Friends held at our meeting
House in **Dartmouth** on the 15ᵗʰ day of the 3ᵈ month 1738
The Severall meetings therto belonging Called upon for
Dartmouth James Barker and **John Howland** present
for **Rochester Elisha Wing** present
John Allen the Son of **Ebenezer Allen** and **Margrate
Soule** did lay their intentions of taking each other in
marriag before this meeting and were desired to wait
till the next monthly meeting for their answer
and **Robert Kerby [Kirby]** and
John Russell are appointed to inquire into the young
mans Clearness Respecting marriage and Conversation
and make return to the next monthly meeting
And **Joseph Havens** and **Rebecca Russell** did lay their
intentions of taking each other in marriage befor this
meeting and were desired to wait till the next monthly
meeting for their answer and **James Barker** and
Abraham Tucker are appointed to make inspection into
the young mans Clearness and make return to the
next monthly meeting
John Lapham and **Isaac Howland** gives this meeting an account
that **Jacob Shearman**s marriage was Consummated in
the Good order of Truth according to their judgments
and **Patience Wood** formerly Widow of **Edward Wing**
hath Sent in a paper to this meeting Signifying her
Sorrow for her outgoings and it is the mind of this meet
ing that She should take it and git somebody to read it
She being present at the end of the meeting of worship on
a first day between this and the next monthly meeting
And the friends that were appointed to Speak with
Abraham Thomas are Still Continued to Speake with
him and make return to the next monthly meeting

At a monthly meeting of friends held at our meeting House
in **Dartmouth** on the 19th day of the 4th month 1738
the Severall meetings thereto belonging Called upon
for **Dartmouth Eliashib Smith** and **James Barker**
present for **Rochester** meeting Called **Nicholas Davis**
present **Robert Kirby** gives this meeting an account
that he hath not herd any thing but that **John Allen**
is Clear in relation to marriag and Conversation
and **James Barker** and **Abraham Tucker** gives this
meeting an account that they have inquired into
Joseph Havens Clearness and find nothing to hinder
his intended marriage fo
And **John Allen** and **Margrate Soule** appeared at this meeting
for their answer in relation to their taking Each other in
marriage and their answer was that they might proceed to
take each other in marriage in Some Convenient time
between this and the next monthly meeting observing the
good order of Truth in the accomplishment thereof and
John Russell and **Robert Kirby** are appointed to see their
marriage Consummated in the sd good order and make return
to the next monthly meeting
And **Joseph Havens** and **Rebecca Russell** appeared at this
meeting Desireing their answer in relation to their taking
Each other in marriag and their answer was that they
might proceed to take each other in marriage in Some
Convenient time between this and the next monthly
meeting observing the good order of Truth in the accomplish
ment thereof and **James Barker** and **Abraham Tucker**
are appointed to See their marriage Consummated in
the aforesd good order and make return to ye next monthly meeting
the Epistle from the yearly meeting at **London** baring —
date 1737 Was read at this meeting to our good Sattisfaction
And the Widow **Elisabeth Tripp** being about to remove to
Rhod Island to live desire a few lines by way of Certificate
from our monthly meeting therefore this meeting appoints
Jabez Baker to draw one and bring it to the next
monthly meeting
The visiters Chose for this year are for **Coaksett William
Wood** and **Christopher Gifford** and for **Ponagansett Jedidiah
Allen Abraham Tucker Peleg Huddelstone [Huddlestone]** and **Peleg Smith**

And for **Cushnott Jacob Taber** and **Jonathan Taber**
and for **Rochester Elisha Wing** and **John Wing**
The Friend appointed to atte[n]d the Quarterly Meeting
are **John Tucker Elisha Wing James Barker** and
Joseph Tucker And to Draw an Epistle to the Same
There was Collected at this meeting for friends use 1-17-09
And this meeting orders the tresurer to ˏpay the Overseers
9 pounds, and 10 Shillings for the Last halfe years keeping the
Meeting House

At a monthly meeting of Friends held at our meeting House
in **Dartmouth** on the 17ᵗʰ day of yᵉ 5ᵗʰ month 1738
The Severall meetings thereof Called upon for **Dartmouth**
Eliashib Smith and **John Lapham** present
for **Rochester John Wing** present
And **John Russell** gives this meeting an account that
the marriag of **John Allen** and **Margrate Soule** was
Sollemnized in good order according to his judgment
And **Abraham Tucker** gives this meeting an account
that **Joseph Havens** his marriage was Carried on and
accomplished in the good order of Truth according to
his Judgment
The Friends that were appointed to attend the Quarterly
meeting have atteneᵈ it all but **Joseph Tucker** and drawn
an Epistle to the Same as appointed
And **Joseph Taber** hath Signified to this meeting that he
Desires a Certificate of his Clearness relating to marriag
and Conversation And **Joseph Russell ju**ʳ and **Benjamin**
Allen are appointed to inquire into the matter and
if they find things Clear to draw one and present it
to yᵉ next monthly meeting
And **Patience Woods** paper hath been read as ordered
There was a Certificate Signed at this meeting for
Elisabeth Tripp And **Jabez Barker** is appointed to draw
a Certificate for **William Lake**

At a monthly meeting of friends held at our meet
ing House in **Dartmouth** on the 21 day of the 6 month
1738 The Severall meetings thereunto belonging Called
upon for **Dartmouth John Howland** and **John Lapham**
present for **Rochester Nicholas Davis** present

Benjamin Allend and **Joseph Russell** doth Signify to this
Meeting that they have inquired into **Joseph Tabers**
Clearness as appointed and Find nothing but that he
is Clear and there was a Certificate Signed at this
Meeting for him
And ther was a Certificate Signed at this meeting for **William Lake**
and his Wife And **Jonathan Taber** hath Signifyed to this meeting
that he is not free to Serve as a visiter therefore this meeting
appoints **Nicholas Davis** in his room
And **Benjamin Wing** hath Signified to this meeting that he desires
a certificate of his Clearness respecting marriage and Conver
Sation and this meeting appoints **Jabez Barker** and **Jedidiah
Allen** to make inquiry into the matter and if they find things
Clear to Draw one and bring it to the next monthly meeting

At a monthly meeting of friends held at our meeting House
in **Dartmouth** on the 18th day of the 7th month 1738 the Severall
Meetings therto belonging Called upon for **Dartmouth James
Barker** and **Abraham Tucker** present for **Rochester**
none appeared
William Ricketson the Son of **William Ricketson** and **Hannah
Russell** the Daughter of **Benjamin Russell** did lay their in
tentions of taking Each other in marriage before this meeting
and were desired to wait till ye next monthly meeting for
their answer and **Jedidiah Allend [Allen]** and **Isaac Smith** are
appointed to make inquiry into the young mans Clearness
as to marriage and Conversation and make return to
the next monthly meeting
And there was a Certificate Signed at this meeting for
Benjamin Wing And there was Collected at this meeting
for the use of Friends 2 pound one Shilling and 3 pence
And this meeting is adjourned till the first 6 day in the 8th mo:
This meeting being mett according to adjournment this
6 day of the 8th month 1738 the visitters belonging
to this meeting have in a generall way given in their
accounts of their Service in visiting Friends families
and Signify that they met with pretty good Sattisfaction
for the most part
The Friends appointed to attend the Quarterly meeting
are **John Tucker Eliashib Smith** and **James Barker**
and to Draw an Epistle to the Same

[8]At a monthly meeting of Friends held at our meeting House
in **Dartmouth** on the 16th day of the 8 month 1738
the Severall meetings therein to belonging Called upon
for **Dartmouth James Barker** and **Joseph Tucker** present
for **Rochester Gideon Gifford** present
The Friends that were appointed to enquire into **William
Ricketson**s Clearness respecting marriage and Conversation
gives this meeting an account that they find nothing to hinder
his Intend marriage
The Friends appointed to attend the Quarterly meeting ~~are~~
have attended it and Drawn an Epistle of the Same
as ordered and the Quarterly meeting Epistle was read
at this meeting and well accepted
William Ricketson and **Hanna Russell** appeared at
this meeting for their answer and their answer was
that they might proceed to take each other in marriage
in Some Convenient time between this and the next
monthly meeting observing the good order of Truth
In the performance thereof and **Adam Mott** and **Jedidiah
Allen** are appointed to see their marriage Consumated
in the above sd good order and make return to the next
monthly meeting

At a monthly meeting of Friends held at our meeting
House in **Dartmouth** on the 20th of ye 9th month 1738
the Severall meetings therto belonging Called upon for
Dartmouth Adam Mott and **Jame[s] Barker** present
for **Rochester Elisha Wing** present
And whereas **Jacob Shearman** and his wife are about to move to
the **BeechWoods** to live he desires a few lines by way of
Certificate to the monthly meeting where he is like to
belong and **Abraham Barker** the Son of **James Barker**
being a Seafaring man also desires a Certificate and
Jabez Barker and **Isaac Smith** are appointed to
Draw up Certificates for them both And bring them
to the next monthly meeting
And the visiters have brought an account to this meeting
that **John Slocum** being about to marry out of the order
Established amongst us and that he doth Signify them that

8. The minutes of the 8th month 1738 are inserted here in correct chronological order from p. 92 of
the original manuscript

he intends to proceed and Doth not Seem to incline
to Come orderly And **Adam Mott** and **Abraham Tucker**
are appointed to Labour further with him and bring
in their account to the next monthly meeting

At a monthly meeting of Friends held at our meeting
House in **Dartmouth** on the 18th day of ye 10th month 1738
The Severall meetings thereto belonging Called upon for
Dartmouth James Barker and **Adam Mott** present
for **Rochester Stephen Wing** present
There was Collected at this meeting for the use of friends 1:16:3
the Friend that were appointed to Discourse with
John Slocum have done it and do not find that he
gives any incouragement to marry amongst us
And the matter is refered till the next monthly meeting
The Friends appointed to attend the Quarterly meeting
are **Elisha Wing Adam Mott John Howland** and
Abraham Tucker and to draw an Epistle to ye Same

At a monthly meeting of Friends held at our meeting
House in **Dartmouth** on the 15th of ye 11th month 1738
this meeting being Called **John Howland** and **Isaac Howland**
present **Rochester** meeting Called **Elisha Wing** present
There was 20 Shillings given by their women towards
keeping the meeting House
And **Stephen Peckom [Peckham]** and **Keturah Arthur** did lay their
intentions of taking each other in marriage before this
meeting and were desired to wait till the next monthly meet
ing for their answer and **Joseph Russell jur** and **Benjamin Allen**
are appointed to mak[e] inspection into his Clearness as to
marriage and Conversation and make return to the next
monthly meeting
At the request of **James Barker** the matter Concerning
John Slocum is refered to the next monthly meeting

At a monthly meeting of Friends held at our meeting
House in **Dartmouth** on the 19th day of the 12 month 1738/9
the Severall meetings therto belonging Called upon for
Dartmouth Eliashib Smith and **Adam Mott** present for
Rochester none appeared and there hath been inquiry made
Concerning **Stephen Peckoms [Peckham]** Clearness and the report is
that they find nothing to hinder his proceedings in his intended
marriage

And the Quarterly meetings Epistle was read at this meeting
and well accepted and agreable to the Directions of the
Quarterly meeting we have Concluded to come to a Subscrip
tion of 7 pounds towards the building of **Lecester [Leicester?]** meeting
House: **Stephen Peckom [Peckham]** and **Keturah Arthur** appeared
at this meeting for their answer in relation to their taking
Each other in marriage And their answer was that they might
proceed to take each other in marriage in Some Convenient
time between this and the next monthly meeting observing
the Good order of Truth in the accomplishment thereof
And **Joseph Russell** and **Benjamin Allen** are appointed to
See their marriage Consummated and make return to
the next monthly meeting
and there was a paper presented to this meeting from **John
Slocum** but friends are of the mind that it doth not
reach the matter in full there^fore **John Tucker** and **James
Barker** are appointed to Discource further with him
The matter Concerning **John Russell**s allowing his daughter
in his house out of the order of friends is refered to the
next monthly meeting

(1739) At a monthly meeting of Friends held at our meeting House
in **Dartmouth** on the 19 day of the 1 month 1739
The Severall meeting thereto belonging Called upon for **Dartmouth**
Henry Tucker present for **Rochester** none appeard
Collected at this meeting for the use of Friends 1:16:09
Joseph Russell and **Benjamin Allen** gives this meeting
an account that that **Stephen Peckom** and **Keturah
Arthur**s Marriage was Consummated in good order according to their
Judgment **John Cornell** hath Signified to this meeting
that he desires that he and his Children maybe under
the care of Friends for the time to Come
There hath been some discourse at this meeting Conserning
his Suffering his Daughter to married out of the order
of Friends and he seems to Justify the matter
Therefore this meeting appoints **John Howland** and
John Tucker to discourse further with him
And whereas **Abraham Tucker** the Son of **Henry Tucker**
Having been under dealing for some time and hath
done nothing to make Friends Sattisfaction it is the
mind of this meeting that **John Howland** Should acquaint

him that if he doth not do something in order to make
Sattisfaction that a Condemnation must go forth against
him and this meeting as adjourned till the 28th day of
this Instant

This meeting being mett according to adjournment this
28 day of the first month 1739 the visiter of **Coaksett**
and **Ponagansett** have given in their account that
they have visited friends Friends families under their
Care and find things pretty well for ye most part
and this meeting is adjourned till the 6 day of the 2 month

This meeting being mett according to adjournment
this 6 day of the 2d month 1739
The matter Concerning **John Slocum** and **Abigail
Willbore** is refered to the next monthly meeting
and whereas **Abraham Tucker** the Son of **Henry
Tucker** hath for some time past been unde a scandalus
report of being the father of a Bastard Child and been
under dealing Some Considerable time;
and he no ways Clearing himselfe to Friends Sattisfaction it is
the mind of this meeting that **John Tucker** – should Draw up a
Condemnation against him and bring it to the next monthly
meeting; And **Abraham Thomas** not having made Sattisfaction
Concerning the Scandalus report that was about him this meet
ing appoints **George Soule** and **Peleg Huddlestone** to desire him
to appear at the next monthly meeting
The Friends appointed to attend the Quarterly meeting and
draw an Epistle to the Same are **John Tucker William Wood**
and **John Howland**

Aat a monthly meeting of Friends held at our meeting House
in **Dartmouth** on the 16 day of the 2 month 1739
the Severall meetings therto belonging Called upon for **Dartmouth**
Joseph Russell and **Isaac Howland** present for **Rochester**
none appeared **Robert Hall** of **North Kingston** and **Isabel
Shearman** the Daughter of **Daniel Shearman** deceasd Did
lay their intentions of Taking Each other in marriage before
this meeting and were Desired to wait till the next monthly
meeting for their answer and **John Potter** of **Providence**
and **Hannah Barker** did lay their intentions of taking each
other in marriage before this meeting and were desired to
wait till the next monthly meeting for their answer

The matter concerning **John Slocum** is referd to the next
monthly meeting

Abigail Willbore hath sent in a paper to this meeting
Condemning her outgoings which this meeting accepts and
orders that she should read it or get some body to read it
at the end of the meeting of Worship on a first day between
this and the next monthly meeting she being present

And was a Condemnation presented to this meeting against
Abraham Tucker the Son of **Henry Tucker** which this meeting
hath Considered and **John Tucker** hath Signed it by order of this
meeting and **John Tucker** is ordered to read it or Cause it to
be read on first day after the meeting of worship between
this and the next monthly meeting

And **Abraham Thomas** was at this meeting and Desires
that Friends would wait a month longer and sinifies that
he hopes he shall Draw up something that may make Sattisfaction

And **John Tucker** and **John Howland** hath attended the Quarterly
Meeting and Drawn a Epistle to the Same

And we received an Epistle from the Quarterly meeting which
was read to the good Sattisfaction

At a monthly meeting of Friends held at our meeting
House in **Dartmouth** on the 21 day of the 3 month 1739
The Severall meetings therto belonging Called upon for
Dartmouth Eliashib Smith and **John Howland** present
for **Rochester Stephen Wing** present

Robert Hall and **Isabel Shearman** appeared at this meeting
Desireing their answer in relation to their taking each
other in marriage and their answer was that they might
proceed to take each other in marriage in Some Convenient
time between this and the next monthly meeting observing
the good order of truth in the in the performance thereof
and **Joseph Russell** and **Adam Mott** are appointed to See their
Marriage Sollemnized in S^d good order and make return
to ye next monthly meeting

And **John Potter** and **Hannah Barker** appeared at this
meeting Desireing their answer and their answer was
that they might proceed to take each other in marriage
in Some Convenient time between this and the next monthly
meeting observing the good order of truth in the accomplishment
thereof and **Eliashib Smith** and **John Howland** are appoin

ted to see their marriag Consummated in the aboves^d order
and make return to the next monthly meeting
And **Abigail Willbor**s paper not having been read it
is Desired that it might be done between this and
the next monthly meeting
And the matter Concerning **John Slocum** is refered till
the next monthly meeting
And the matter Concerning **Abraham Thomas** is refered
And whereas **Benjamin Tucker** hath desired a Certificate
of his Clearness as to marriage and Conversation this
meeting appoints **Benjamin Allen** and **John Howland**
to make inquiry into his Clearness and to Draw one
and bring to the next monthly meeting if they think
propper

At a monthly meeting of Friends held at our meeting
House in **Dartmouth** on the 18th day of the 4 month 1739
The Severall meetings therto belonging Called upon for **Dartmouth**
John Howland and **Joseph Tucker** present for **Rochester** none appeared
by appointment **Abraham Stafford** the Son of **Joseph Stafford**
of **Tiverton** and **Ruth Wood** the Daughter of **William Wood** of **Dartmouth**
did lay their intentions of taking Each other in marriage before
this meeting and were desired to wait till ye next monthly
meeting for their answer
Joseph Russell and **Adam Mott** gives this meeting an account
that **Robert Hall** and **Isabel Shearman**s marriage was
Consummated in the good order of Truth as far as they Saw
Eliashib Smith and **John Howland** gives this meeting an
account that **John Potter** and **Hannah Barker**s marriage
was Consummated in the good order of Truth according to
their Judgment
And **Abram Tucker**s Condemnation hath been read
and is as Followeth
Whereas **Abraham Tucker** the Son of **Henry Tucker**
of **Dartmouth** in the **County of Bristol** in the **Province**
of the Massachusets Bay in **New England** hath been brought
up among Friends the People Called Quakers out of late
hath been accused to be the Father of a bastard Child
and not Clearing himselfe of s^d accusation to the Sattisfaction
of Friends Therefore this meeting is Concerned to give
this forth as a Testimony against him the s^d **Abraham**

Tucker Denying him ~~the~~ to be one in unity with
us the people called Quakers; yet Desiring that he
may Come to a Sight and Sence of his outgoings and to
a true and unfeigned Repentance
Given forth at our monthly meeting held in **Dartmouth**
the 16:th day of the 2 month 1739
Signed by order and in behalfe of sd meeting by

                               John Tucker Clerk

The matter Concerning **Abigail Willbor** and **John
Slocum** is refered to the next monthly meeting
The Epistle from the yearly meeting in **London** bearing
date 1738 was read at his meeting to good Sattisfaction
The Visiters Chose for this year are for **Ponagansett
Peleg Smith Abraham Tucker John Howland** and **James
Barker** and for **Coaksett Jonathan Wood** and
Christopher Gifford jur:
For **Rochester Elisha Wing** and **Savory Clifton** and for
Cushnet Jacob Taber and **Benjamin Allen**
and this meeting hath given **Benjamin Tucker** a Certificate

---

At a monthly meeting of Friends held at our meeting
House in **Dartmouth** on the 16 day of the 5 month 1739
The Severall meetings thereto belonging Called upon for
Dartmouth John Howland and **James Barker** present
for **Rochester Elish Wing** present
And **Abraham Stafford** and **Ruth Wood** not appearing
at this meeting for their answer it is refered till the
next monthly meeting
And the paper that **Abigail Willbore** Sent in not being
read it is Still refered
And Whereas **John Wing** the Son of **John Wing** and **Hannah
Gifford** the Daughter of **Gideon Gifford** of **Rochester**
being near in relation one to the other have proceeded
in marriage Contrary to the good order Established among
us and also to the wholesome advice of their parents
and Friends given them in that affair it is the Con
clusion of this meeting that a Condemnation should go
forth against them and **Isaac Smith** is ordered to draw
up one and bring it to ye next monthly meeting
and **John Wing** is aded to **Elisha Wing** and **Savory Clifton**
to Serve as a visiter for ye year Insuing

And Whereas our Friends **Robert Mosher** and **John
Mosher** and **Joseph Brownell** being now under Con
finement upon Truth account this meeting appoints
Joseph Tripp and **Nathanael Potter** to See Concerning them
and their Families Sircumstance that they do not
Suffer too much and to be assisting in that affair and
bring in their accounts to the monthly meeting
and there was 1-04-0 overplus Concerning Some Subscrip
tion that hath been made which is ordered to into
the Stock
And this meeting orders the Treasurer to pay the overseers
the Sum of 3 pounds and 10 Shillings for halfe a year
keeping the meeting House

At a monthly meeting of Friends held at our meeting
House in **Dartmouth** on the 20 day of the 6 month 1739
The Severall meetings therto belonging Called upon for
Dartmouth Eliashib Smith and **Adam Mott** present for
Rochester Elisha Wing present
Abraham Stafford and **Ruth Wood** appeared at this meeting
for their answer in relation to their taking each other
in marriage and their answer was that they might
proceed to take each other in marriage in Some Convenient
tim between this and the next monthly meeting observing
the good order of Truth in the performance thereof and **Joseph
Tripp** and **Christopher Gifford** are appointed to see their
marriage Consummated in the aboves^d order and make
return to the next monthly meeting
The paper that **Abigail Willbore** Sent in hath been
read and is a followeth
To the monthly meeting of **Dartmouth** I am Sorry for
my outgoings in Breaking the good orders of Friends I hope
the Lord will ~~pass it~~ forgive me and that Friends would
pass it by and receive me under their Care it was not
the little Esteam that I had of friends that Caused me to to Leave
Them   **Abigail Willbore**
and the matter Concerning **Abraham Thomas** is refered
to the next monthly meeting
The matter Concerning **John Russell**s Suffering his daughter
to married out of the order of friends is refered to the
~~next monthly meeting~~^Consideration of ye Quarterly meeting

And **Adam Mott** hath paid 3 pound and ten Shillings
to the overseers as ordered

At a monthly meeting of friends held at our meeting
House in **Dartmouth** on the 17th day of the 7th month 1739
The Severall meetings therto belonging Called uppon for
Dartmouth Benjamin Allen and **Abraham Tucker**
present For **Rochester Stephen Wing** present
Joseph Tripp and **Christopher Gifford** gives this meeting
an account that that they was at the Sollemnizing of
the marriag of **Abraham Stafford** and **Ruth Wood** and
Saw nothing but that it was performed in good order
William Russell and **Elisabeth Willbore** did lay their
intentions of taking each other in marriage before this
meeting and were desired to wait till the next monthly
meeting for their answer
And **Isaac Howland** and **Peleg Smith** are appointed are
appointed to inquire into **William Russell**s Clearness
Respecting marriage and Conversation and make
return to the next monthly meeting
And **Joseph Taber** the Son of **Joseph Taber** and **Mary
Tinkham** the Daughter of **John Tinkham** did lay
their intentions of taking each other in marriage
before this meeting and were desired to wait till the next
monthly meeting for their answer and **Benjamin
Allen** and **Joseph Russell** are appointed to See into
the young mans Clearness respecting marriage and
Conversation and make return to the next monthly
meeting There was Collected at this meeting 1-15:03
The visiters of of **Rochester** and **Coaksett** have given
in their accounts of their Service in visiting friends
families and this meeting is adjourned till the first
6 day in the next month
This meeting being mett according to adjournment
this 5th day of the 8th month 1739 the visiters of **Cushnet**
have given in their account that they have in a
generall way visited the families of friends under
their Care and find things in a generall way pretty well
And the visiters of **Ponagansett** have given in their
account that they have been in the Service of visit
ing friends families and find things for the most

part pretty well as far as they Saw
There was a condemnation signed at this against
Abraham Thomas and **John Tucker** is appointed
to see that it be read at the End of the meeting
for worship on a first day between this and the
next monthly meeting
Joseph Brownell Robert Mosher and **John Mosher**
have given in an account in writing of their discharge
from prison

At a monthly meeting of Friends held at our meeting
House in **Dartmouth** on the 15th day of the 8th month 1739
the Severall meetings thereto belonging Called upon for
Dartmouth Benjamin Allen and **Isaac Howland** present
for **Rochester John Wing** present **Isaac Howland** and
Peleg Smith gives this meeting an account that they
find nothing to hind his proceedings in his intended marriage
And **Joseph Russell** and **Benjamin Allen** makes report
to this meeting that they have made inquiry into the
Clearness of **Joseph Taber ju^r:** and find nothing to hinder
his intended marriage
And **William Russell** and **Elisabeth Willbore** appeared at
this meeting for their their answer and their answer
was that they might proceed to take each other in mar
riage in Some Convenient time between this and the next
monthly meeting Observing the good order of Truth in the
accomplishment thereof and **Jedidiah Allen** and **Holder
Slocum** are appointed to See their marriage Consummated
and make Return to the next monthly meeting
And **Joseph Taber** and **Mary Tinkham** appeared at this
meeting for their answer and their answer was that
they might proceed to take each other in marriage in
Some convenient time between this and the next monthly
meeting and observing the good order of truth in the
performance thereof and **Benjamin Allen** and **Joseph
Russell** are appointed to See their marriage Sollemnized
in the good order of truth and make return to the next
monthly meeting
The Friends that were appointed to attend the Quarter
ly meeting have attended it according to the order of
the last monthly meeting

And **Abraham Thomas**es Condemnation hath been
read as ordered and is as followeth
Whereas **Abraham Thomas** of **Dartmouth** in the **County
of Bristol** in the **province of the massachusets Bay** in
New England being one that hath had his Education
Amongst us The People Called Quakers yet for want
of an upright and sircumspect walking hath gone from
his Education into many things which are not Consistant
with our holy profession and also hath been accused
with Comitting the Scandalus Sin of Fornication which
which he no ways Clearing him Selfe from and Friends
have long waited and laboured with him in order to
bring him to a Sight and Sence of his outgoings but as
yet nothing doth appear as Effectual in that respect
therefore it is thought best for the Clearing of the Truth
from Such Enormities and those that are found in
them to to give this forth as a publick testimony against
it Denying him the S^d **Abraham Thomas** to be one in
unity with us the aforeS^d people yet truly desiring
that he may Come to a Sight and Sence of his outgoings
and to unfeigned Repentance
Given for that our monthly meeting Held in **Dartmouth** by adjournment
on the 5th day of the 8th month 1739 and Signed by order
And in behalfe of S^d meeting **John Tucker**: Clerk
And **John Wing** and his wives Condemnation hath
been read as appointed
Whereas **John Wing** the Son of **John Wing** and **Hannah
Gifford** Daughter of **Gideon Gifford** of both of **Rochester**
in the **County of Plymouth** ine **Province of the Mas
sachusets Bay** in **New England** being Educated in
the way of Truth their Parents professing to be of us
the people Called Quakers yet for want of keeping
to their Education and a true Sircumspect walking
have gone out of unity with us and taken each other in
marriage in the common way of other people they being
also nearer in relation to each other than is allowed
to marry amongst us For which disorderly proceeding
Contrary to the advice of their Parents and other friends
that were Concerned for their their good
We can do no less than give this forth as a Publick

Testimony against them Denying the the S^d **John Wing**
and **Hannah** his wife to be now in unity with us
the people Called Quakers yet truly desiring that they may
Come to a Sight of all their outgoings and to unfeigned
Repentance Given forth at our monthly meeting held in
Dartmouth on the 20th: day of the 6 month 1739 - - -
and Signed by order S^d meeting by **John Tucker** Clerk-
The Friends that were appointed to attend the Quarterly meeting
are have attended it and Drawn an Epistle to the Same
as ordered and the Quarterly meeting Epistle was read
at this meeting and well accepted
and the matter between this meeting and **John Russell**
was made up at the Quarterly meeting to this meetings
Sattisfaction
and whereas **James Russell** the Son of **James Russell**
hath gon out of the way of friends in his marriag Contrary
to his Fathers Consent this meeting appoints **Isaac Howland**
and **Peleg Smith** to discourse with him to see Whither
he hath any mind to make Sattisfation
and **John Slocum** not having done any thing to friends
Sattisfaction for the Disorders that he hath been in
Holder Slocum is ordered to let him know that if he
doth not do something further Judgment must go forth
against him

At a monthly meeting of friends held at our meeting
House in **Dartmouth** on the 19th day of the 9th month 1739
The Severall meetings therto belonging Called upon for
Dartmouth none appeared by appointment
for **Rochester Nicholas Davis** present
Jedidiah Allen and and **Holder Slocum** gives this meeting
an account that **William Russell** and **Elisabeth Willbore**s
marriage was Consummated in the good order of
Truth according to their Judgments
Isaac Howland and **Peleg Smith** are Continued to
labour with **James Russell ju^r**: for his outgoings **Holder
Slocum** is Still Continued labour further with **John
Slocum**

At a monthly meeting held at our meeting House in
Dartmouth on the 17 day of the 10 month 1739 the Severall
meetings therto belonging Called upon for **Dartmouth**

for **Dartmouth John Howland** and **Adam Mott** present
none appeared for **Rochester**
John Slocum hath given in a paper to this meeting Condemn
ing his outgoing which hath been read and this meeting
takes up with it for Sattisfaction and is as followeth
To the monthly meeting to be held in **Dartmouth** on the
on the 17ᵗʰ day of the 10ᵗʰ month 1739
Dear I have gone out of the good order Established in marri
age and going to training which things I am Sorry for
and all the other my Conversation which the Testimony of truth is
against that I am Come to a Sight of and I do Desire
that you would pass it by as far as belongs to you and
that I might Still remain under your Care

John Slocum

And **Isaac Howland** and **Peleg Smith** are ordered to
Draw up **James Russell juʳ**, Condemnation if he doth
nothing him selfe and bring it to the next monthly meeting
And this meeting is adjourned till the first 6 day in the next month
This meeting bein mett according to adjournment
This 4ᵗʰ day of the 11ᵗʰ month 1739/40 **Abraham Tucker** and
Joseph Tucker are appointed to Oversee the meeting
House the year insuing
and **Adam Mott** hath paid 3 pound ten Shillings
as ordered to the overseers
Elisha Wing Joseph Tucker and **Peleg Smith** are appoin
ted to at attend the Quarterly meeting and Draw
an Epistle to the Same
There hath bee considerable of Discourse at this
at this Concernin the differance between the
visiters of this meeting and **Phebe Tucker** which
is refered to the next monthly meeting

At a monthly meeting of Friends held at our meet
ing House in **Dartmouth** on the 21 day of yᵉ 11ᵗʰ m 1739/40
Dartmouth meeting Called **Thomas Smith** and **John**
Shepherd present **Rochester** meeting Called and
none appeared **Peleg Cornell** the Son of **Thomas**
Cornell and **Mary Russell** daughter of **Joseph**
Russell did lay their intentions of taking each
other in marriage before this meeting
And were Desired to wait for their answer ill the next monthly

meeting and **George Soule** and **Benjamin Wing** were appointed
to inquire into the young mans Clearness respecting marriage
and Conversation and make return to the next monthly
meeting **Isaac Howland** and **Peleg Smith** not having Drawn
up **James Russell**s Condemnation are Still Continued to do it
against the next monthly meeting
The Friends that were appointed to attend the Quarterly meeting
have attended it and Drawn an Epistle to the Same as ordered
The Quarterly meeting Epistle hath been read at this
Meeting And well accepted There was 20 Shillings given by
the Women towards keeping the meeting House

At a monthly meeting of Friends held at our meeting
House in **Dartmouth** on the 18th day of ye 12th month 1739/40
The Severall meetings thereto belonging Called upon for
Dartmouth John Howland and **James Barker** present
for **Rochester** none appeared
George Soule gives this meeting an account that he
hath mad Inquiry into **Peleg Cornell**s Clearness and
finds nothing to hinder his intended marriage
Peleg Cornell and **Mary Russell** appeared at this meet
ing Desiring their Answer in relation to their taking
Each other in marriage and were answered that
the might proceed to take each other in marriage
in Some Convenient time between this and the next
monthly meeting Observing the good order of truth in the
accomplishment thereof and **John Howland Benjamin
Allen** are appointed to See their marriage Consummated
in the above Sd good order and make return to the next
and **David Smith** and **Jane Brown** appeared at this
meeting and did lay their intentions taking each other
in marriage before this meeting and were desired to
wait till the next monthly meeting for their answer
and **James Barker** and **John Shepherd** are appointed
to inquire into the young mans Clearness respecting mar
riage and Conversation and make return to the
next monthly meeting
And **James Russell Juner** hath hath given in a
Paper Condemning his outgoings in respect to his mar
riage and going to Training which this meeting accepts of
and he to remain under our Care

And this meeting hath received a paper Signed by **Eunice
Akin** Condemning her outgoings Which this meeting orders
that She Should git Some body to read at the end of the meet
ing of Worship on a first day She being present

(*1740*) At a monthly meeting of Friends held at our meeting
House in **Dartmouth** on the 17ᵗʰ day of the first
Month 1740 The Severall meetings thereunto belonging
Called upon for **Dartmouth John Howland** and **Abraham
Tucker** present For **Rochester Stephen Wing** present
James Barker and **John Shepherd** makes report to this meeting
that that they have made inquiry into **David Smith**s Clearness
Respecting marriage and Conversation and find nothing to
hinder his proceeding in his intended marriage
And the Friends appointed to ~~inquire into~~^see **Peleg Cornell**s
marriage Consummated gives this meeting an account
that it was orderly Carried on
David Smith and **Jane Brown** appeared at this meeting for
their answer in relation to their taking each other in marriage
and their answer was that they might proceed to take each
other in marriage in Some Convenient time between
this and the next monthly meeting Observing yᵉ good order
of Truth in the performance thereof And **John Howland** and
Isaac Smith are appointed to See their marriage Consumma
ted and make return to yᵉ next monthly meeting
And **George Allen** and **Rachel Smith** did lay their Intentions
of taking Each other in marriage before this meeting and
were desired to wait till yᵉ next monthly meeting for their
Answer and **Joseph Russell** and **Joseph Taber** are appointed to
to See into the young mans Clearness respecting marriage
and Conversation and make return to yᵉ next monthly meeting
There was Collected at this meeting for yᵉ use of Friends 2£:00ˢ:07ᵈ
And whereas there hath been a differance between this
meeting and **Phebe Tucker** this meeting appoints **Nicholas Davis
John Howland Jonathan Wood Barnabas Howland** and **Isaac Smith**
a Comᵗᵉᵉ with the women to hear and and Determine the matter
and make return to the next monthly meeting
And this meeting is adjourned till the youths meeting
On the 4ᵗʰ day of yᵉ 2ᵈ month 1740 Friends mett according to
adjournment **Benjamin Tripp** Son of **Joseph Tripp** hath Signified to
this meeting that he hath an intention of marriage with **Martha**

Luther of **Swansy** And desires a Certificate thefore this meeting
appoints **Christopher Gifford** and **Peleg Huddelstone** to enquire into
his Clearness as to marriage and Conversation and ~~ma~~
draw a Certificate if they find nothing to hinder
And this meeting appoints **John Tucker John Howland John Lapham**
And **James Barker** to attend the Quarterly meeting and Draw an
Epistle to the Same
The Visiters belonging to **Coaksett** and **Ponagansett** have
brought in their accounts of visiting to pretty good Satisfaction
for the most part

At a monthly meeting of friends held at our meeting House
in **Dartmouth** on the 21 day of the 2ᵈ month 1740
Dartmouth meeting Called **John Howland** and **Adam Mott**
present for **Rochester John Wing** present
Friends Having enquired into **George Allen** Clearness find
nothing to hinder his intended marriag with **Rachel Smith**
and **George Allen** and **Rachel Smith** appeared at this meeting
for their Answer and their answer was that they might
proceed to take Each other in marriage in Some Convenient
time between this And the next monthly meeting and
Adam Mott and **Joseph Tucker** are appointed to See their
marriage Consummated and make return to the next
monthly meeting. The Friends that were appointed to
attend yᵉ Quarterly meeting and Draw the Epistle have
done it according to order
And and hereas **Benjamin Tripp** desired a Certificate and
Friends Having made Enquiry and find nothing to Hinder
have granted the Same
And **William Hart** and **Mary Shepherd** did lay their Intention
of taking each other in marriage before this meeting
and were desired to wait til the next monthly meeting for
their answer and **Eliashib Smith** and **Adam Mott** are
appointed to Make Enquiry into his Clearness as to marriage
and Conversation and make return to the next monthly
Meeting And this meeting appoints **John Tucker** and
Isaac Howland to Labour with **Eleazer Smith** for his disorder
John Howland and **Isaac Smith** makes report to this meeting
that **David Smith** and **Jane Brown**s marriag was orderly
Carried on
The Com:ᵗᵗᵉ nominated to hear and Determine **Phebe Tucker**s

Case have taken up for Sattisfaction a Paper of Acknowledg
ment Signed by the S^d **Phebe Tucker** and hath appointed **Joseph
Tucker** to read it it publickly on a First day after the meeting
of Worship between this and the next monthly meeting

At a monthly meeting of Friends held at our meeting House
in **Dartmouth** on the 20th day of ye 3^d month 1740
Dartmouth meeting Called **John Howland** and **Adam Mott**
present, **Rochester** meeting Called and none appeared
Adam Mott and **Joseph Tucker** makes report to this
Meeting that **George Allen**s Marriage was Carried on in
good order the Friends that were appointed to Enquire into
William Harts Clearness makes report to this meeting
that they find nothing to Hinder his intended marriage
William Hart and **Mary Shepherd** appeared at this meeting
for their answer relating to their taking each other in
marriage And they had their Answer that they might proceed
to take Each other in marriage in Some Convenient time
between this and the next monthly meeting Observing the
good order of Truth in the accomplishment thereof
And **Eliashib Smith** and **Adam Mott** are appointed to See
their marriage Sollemnized and make return to the next
Monthly meeting
And **Joseph Tripp** and **Judeth Mosher** did lay their intentions
of taking each other in marriage before this meeting and
Jonathan Wood and **Benjamin Shearman** are appointed
to enquire into the young mans Clearness respecting mar
riage and Conversation and make return to the next
monthly meeting. The matter Concerning **Eleazer Smith**
is refered to ye next monthly meeting
And **Phebe Tucker**s paper of acknowledgement hath been read
according to order and is a followeth
To the monthly meeting of Friends in **Dartmouth**
Well Esteamed Friends Whereas my mannagement in
that affair of **Ruth Slocums** as it hath been resented hath
Caused a great uneasiness amongst Friends too acknowledge
that it was not so propper as it ought to have been
and in particular that of offoring her forty pounds.
more than her Lagacy which hath proved of a bad Consequence
and I Do acknowledge that my Conduct in the affair hath
brought a dishonour to the Truth which I do hereby Condemn

and am Sorry for it and hope to be more Careful for
the time to Come

Dated in **Dartmouth** the 4th day of 2 month 1740

At a monthly meeting of friends held   {**Phebe Tucker**
at our meeting House in **Dartmouth** on the 23^d Day of
the 4th month 1740 this meeting being Called **Eliashib Smith**
and **Adam Mott** appeared for **Dartmouth** for **Rochester**
none appeared

Eliashib Smith and **Adam Mott** gives this meeting an
account that **William Hart**s marriag was accomplished
in good order And **Jonathan Wood** and **Benjamin Shearman**
makes report to this meeting that they have made enquiry
into **Joseph Tripp**s Clearness respecting marriage and Con
versation And find nothing to hinder his intended marriage

Joseph Tucker and **Simeon Gifford** are appointed to enquire
into **Lot Tripp**s Clearness respecting marriage and
Conversation and if they find things Clear to Draw up
Some thing for him and bring it to the next monthly meeting

Joseph Tripp and **Judeth Mosher** appeared at this meeting
Desiring an answer as to their taking Each other
in marriage and their Answer was that they might
proceed to take Each other in marriage in Some Con
venient time between this and the next monthly
meeting observing the good order of Truth in the
performance thereof and **James Shearman** and
Isaac Smith are appointed to See their marriage
Sollemnized and make return to the next month
ly meeting

The Epistle from the yearly meeting held in **London**
in the year 1739 was read at this meeting to good
Sattisfaction And **Eleazer Smith** and his wife have
given in a paper to this meeting Condemning their
outgoings which this meeting accepts and orders that
they read it or git some body to do it on a first day at the
end of the meeting of Worship between this and the next
monthly meeting

There was Collected at this meeting £1:10^s=00^d

The matter Concerning Chusing an Elder for **Coakset**
meeting to assist **William Wood** is refered to the
Consideration of y^e next monthly meeting

And this meeting orders **Isaac Smith** to make up
the meetings accompts with **Adam Mott**
And **John Tucker Eliashib Smith John Howland** and
James Barker ar appointed to attend the Quarterly
meeting and Draw and Epistle to yᵉ Same
The Choice of visiters is refered to the next monthly meeting
And this meeting orders **Adam Mott** to pay to the over
seers five pounds one Shilling for keeping the meeting
House halfe a year and Some [otherges?]

5 mo: At a monthly meeting of Friends held at our meeting
1740 House in **Dartmouth** on the 21 day of the 5ᵗʰ month 1740
The Severall meetings therto belonging Called upon for
Dartmouth Isaac Howland and **Adam Mott** present
for **Rochester** none appeared
The Friends appointed to Draw up **Lot Tripp**s Certificate
have done it and **John Tucker** hath signed it by order
of this meeting the Friends that were appointed to See
Joseph Tripps marriage Consummated gives an account
that it was accomplished in good order according to their
Judgment
Daniel Russell and **Edith Howland** appeared at this meeting
and Lay,d their intentions of taking each other in marriage
and were Desired to wait till the next monthly meeting
for their answer And **Eliashib Smith** and **Adam Mott**
are appointed to See into the young mans Clearness
and make report to the next monthly meeting
Eleazar Smith and his wives acknowledgement hath
been read according to order and is as followeth
To the monthly meeting of Friends in **Dartmouth**
Well Respected Friends Whereas we through the Subtile
Insinuations of the Evil Spirit Which Worketh in the
Children of Disobedience have given Way to a dishonest
conversation as is manifest – by our having a child in a
short time after marriag which we do acknowledge
to be a Skandal to the blessed Truth and a reproach to the pro
fessors thereof aknowledging our outgoings and Condemning
ourselves hoping that god will forgive us in this respect
and all others wherein we have been amiss
And we Desire that you our Friends would have a Watchful

Care over us for the time to come

Eleazar Smith

Meribah Smith

Isaac Smith is Still Continued to make up the accompts
With the Treasurer
The Friend that wer appointed to ~~make up accom~~
attend the Quarterly meeting have most of them attended
it and Drawn an Epistle to the Same
The Quarterly meeting Epistle Was read out this meeting and
Well accepted the Choice of visiters is refered til yᵉ
next monthly meeting

6 mo: At a monthly meeting of friends held at our meeting
1740   House in **Dartmouth** on the 18 day of the 6ᵗʰ month 1740
     Dartmouth meeting Called **Adam Mott** and **Thomas Smith**
     present **Rochester** meeting Called none appeared
     the friend that were appointed to see into **Daniel**
     Russells Clearness gives this meeting an account that
     they find nothing to hinder his intended marriage
     And **Isaac Smith** hath made up this meetings accompts
     With **Adam Mott** and there remains in the Stock 3:09:06
     Daniel Russell and **Edith Howland** appeared at this
     Meeting for the answer relating to their taking each
     other in marriage and their answer was that they might
     proceed to take Each other in marriage in Some
     Convenient time between this and the next monthly
     Meeting observing the good order of truth in the perfor
     mance thereof and **Jedidiah Allen** and **George Soule**
     are appointed to see their marriage Consummated
     and make return to the next monthly meeting
     And **Daniel Russell** desired leave of this meeting to
     Sollemnize his marriage on a fourth day Which is
     granted
     The visiters Chose for this year ar for **Coaksett** are
     Joseph Tripp and **Nathanael Potter**
     And for **Ponansett Joseph Tucker Jedidiah Allen Abraham**
     Tucker Eliashib Smith Adam Mott and **Peleg Smith**
     And for **Cushnot Benjamin Allen** and **Jacob Taber**

7 mo: At a monthly meeting of Friends held at our meeting
1740   House in **Dartmouth** on the 15ᵗʰ day of the 7ᵗʰ month 1740

Dartmouth meeting Called **John Howland** and **Adam Mott**
present **George Soule** and **Jedidiah Allen** gives this meet
ing an account that **Daniel Russell**s marriage was
mannaged in good order as far as they Saw
Nathanal Bowdish and **Frances Lapham** did Lay
their intention of marriage before this meeting and
were desired to wait till the next monthly meeting
for their Answer and **John Howland** and **Abraham**
Tucker are appointed to enquire into **Nathanael**
Bowdishes Clearness respecting marriage and Conver
sation and make return to yᵉ next monthly meeting
and this meeting is adjourned till the first sixth day in
the eighth month next
This meeting being mett according to adjournment this
3ᵈ day of the 8ᵗʰ month 1740
The visiters of our Severall Weekly meetings have
given in their accounts of their service in in that
affair and they find things for the most part pretty well
John Tucker James Barker Adam Mott and **William**
Wood are appointed to attend the Quarterly meeting
and to Draw an Epistle to the Same

At a monthly meeting of Friends held at our meeting
House in **Dartmouth** on the 20ᵗʰ day of yᵉ 8ᵗʰ month 1740
this meeting being Called **John Howland** and **Abraham**
Tucker present
The Friends that were appointed to attend the Quar
terly meeting have attended it Some of them and
Drawn an Epistle to the Same
The Friends that were to inspect into **Nathanael**
Bowdishes Clearness makes report to this meeting
that they find nothing to hind his proceedings in his
Intended Marriage.
Nathanael Bowdish and **Frances Lapham** appeared at this
meeting for their answer in relation to their taking each
other in marriage And their answer was that they they
might proceed to take each other in marriage in Some
Convenient time between this and the next monthly
meeting observing the good order Established amongst
friends in the accomplishing thereof
And **Isaac Howland** and **Peleg Smith** are appointed

to See their marriage Consummated and make
return to the next monthly meeting
The Quarterly meeting Epistle was read at this
Meeting and well accepted

At a monthly meeting of Friends held at our meeting
House in **Dartmouth** on the 17th day of yᵉ 9ᵗʰ month 1740
Dartmouth meeting Called **James Barker** present
Isaac Howland and **Peleg Smith** gives this meeting an
account that **Nathanael Bowdish** and **Frances
Lapham**s marriage was Consummated in good
Order

At a monthly meeting of friends held at our meet
ing House in **Dartmouth** on the 15ᵗʰ day of the 10ᵗʰ month
1740 This meeting being Called **Abraham Tucker**
and **Joseph Tucker** present
There was Collected at this meeting for the use of
Friends with mony that the women gave in £2:11ˢ=02ᵈ
This meeting appoints **Adam Mott Thomas Smith
Joseph Tucker** and **James Barker** to attend the
Quarterly meeting and Draw an Epistle to yᵉ Same
Our ancient Friend **John Tucker** hath requested of
this meeting that **Isaac Smith** should be appointed in
his room to record the Deaths and births of Friends
which this meeting hath Consented to an **Isaac Smith**
is appointed for that purpos
And this meeting orders **Adam Mott to** pay to the glazier
for glazing done about the meeting House £2 – 12 – 00
and also to pay the overseers ~~~~~~~~~ 3 – 10 – 00
for halfe a years keeping the meeting House
And **Joseph Tucker** and **Abraham Tucker** are appoint
=ed overseers for yᵉ meeting House the year insuing

At a monthly meeting of Friends Held at our meet
=ing House in **Dartmouth** on the 19ᵗʰ day of the 11ᵗʰ month
1740: this meeting being Called **John Howland** and
Adam Mott present
The Friends appointed to attend the Quarterly meeting
were none of them there by reason of the Difficulty
of the Season
Adam Mott hath paid to the glazier ᶠ2:12ˢ as ordered

and £3:10ˢ:00 to the overseers
There was Collected at this meeting — £0:19ˢ=06ᵈ

At a monthly meeting of friends held at our meeting
House in **Dartmouth** on the 16 day of the 12ᵗʰ month 1740
This meeting being Called **Thomas Smith** present
This meeting appoints **Abraham Tucker Adam Mott**
and **Peleg Smith** to Labour with **Daniel Howland**
to Endeavour that he may Conform so as to be married
among friends.
And this meeting is adjourned till the 25ᵗʰ day
of this Instant
This meeting being meet according to adjournment
this 25ᵗʰ day of the 12ᵗʰ month 1740
Daniel Howland and **Mary Slocum** did lay their
Intentions of taking Each other in marriage before
this meeting and were desired to wait till the next
monthly meeting for their answer
And **Abraham Tucker** and **Peleg Smith** are app
ointed to See into yᵉ young mans Clearness respect
ing marriage and Conversation and make
return to the next monthly meeting

(1741) At a monthly meeting of Friends held at our meeting
House in **Dartmouth** on the 16 day of the first month
1741 **Dartmouth** meeting Called **James Barker** and
Abraham Tucker present
The Friend that were appointed to See into **Daniel
Howland**s Clearness
makes report to this meeting that they find nothing to
hinder his intended marriage
Daniel Howland and **Mary Slocum** appeared at this meet
ing for their answer in relation to their taking each
other in marriage and their answer was that they
might proceed to take each other in marriage in Some
Convenient time between this and the next monthly
meeting observing the good order of Truth in the
accomplishment thereof and **Adam Mott** and **Jedediah
Allen** are appointed to See thir marriage Consummated
and make return to the next monthly meeting
There was Collected at this meeting £1:06ˢ:00ᵈ
The Quarterly meeting Epistle was read at this meeting

and kindly accepted

And **James Tripp** hath Sent in a paper to this meeting
Signifying his Sorrow for his Disorderly marriage
and Desires to Come under the Care of Friends which
this meeting takes up with

And this meeting is adjourned til the first day in
the next month

This meeting being met according to adjournment
this 3ᵈ day of the 2ᵈ month 1741

The visiters of **Coakset** meeting have given in a Com
fortable account of their Service in that affair

Adam Mott John Howland and **James Barker** are
appointed to attend yᵉ Quarterly meeting next and
to Draw an Epistle to yᵉ Same

At a monthly meeting of friends held at our meeting
House in **Dartmouth** on the 20ᵗʰ day of yᵉ 2ᵈ month 1741

Dartmouth meeting Called **John Howland** and **Abraham
Tucker** present

The Friends appointed to see **Daniel Howland**s marriage
Consummated makes report to this meeting that it
Was performed but not so well in all respects as they
Desired. **William Gifford** and **Elisabeth Tripp** did lay their
Intentions of takeing each other in marriage before
this meeting and were desired to wait til the next
monthly meeting for their answer

And **Eliashib Smith** and **Jedidiah Allen** are appointed
to inquire into the young mans Clearness respecting
marriage and conversation and make return to
the next monthly meeting

The Friends appointed to attend the Quarterly meeting
have done it and Drawn an Epistle to the Same

And the Quarterly meeting Epistle was read at this
meeting and well accepted

At a monthly meeting of Friends held at our meeting
House in **Dartmouth** on the 18ᵗʰ day of the 3ᵈ month
1741 This meeting is adjourned til the 27ᵈ of this instant

This meeting being met according to adjournment
this 27 day of the 3ᵈ month 1741 this meeting being Called
John Howland and **Abraham Tucker** present

The friends appointed to See into **William Gifford**s

Clearness makes report to this meeting that they have
made inquiry into **William Gifford**s Clearness and find
nothing to hinder his proceedings in his intended marri_{age}
William Gifford and **Elisabeth Tripp** appeared at
this meeting for their answer in relation to their taking
Each other in marriage and their answer was that they
might proceed to take each other in marriage in Some Con
venient time between this and the next monthly meet
ing observing the good order of truth in the performance
thereof and **Jonathan Wood** and **Nathanael Potter** are
appointed to See their marriag Sollemnized and make
return to the next monthly meeting

At a monthly meeting of friends held at our meeting House
in **Dartmouth** on the 22ᵈ Day of the 4ᵗʰ month 1741
This meeting being Called **Jabez Barker** and **Peleg Smith**
present The yearly meeting Epistle from **London** was read
at this meeting to good Sattisfaction
The Friends appointed to See **William Gifford**s marriage
Consummated makes report to this meeting that it
was orderly accomplished
John Tucker John Howland and **James Barker** are
Appointed to attend the Quarterly Meeting and draw
an Epistle to the Same
And **Jabez Barker** and **Isaac Smith** are appointed
to draw a Certificate for **William Russell** and his wife
they being removed to **Oblong**⁹ to live and bring it to the next monthly meeting
And **Adam Mott** is appointed to pay to the overseers £3: 10ˢ: 00
for halfe a years keeping the meeting House which he hath done
There was a paper presented this meeting Signed by **Elisabeth**
Howland wife of **James Howland** juʳ which this meeting
accepts and orders that she should read the Same or git
Some body to do it publickly on a first day at the end of the
Meeting for worship she being present
And whereas **Thomas Akin** hath as we understand taken
the oath in common form which being Contrary to our
principles This meeting therfore appoints **John Tucker**
and **Adam Mott** to Discource with sd **Akin** in order
to bring him to a Sight of his out goings

---

9. The Oblong was a narrow but largely unsettled strip of land granted to New York, running from the northern border of Greenwich, Connecticut, to the southern boundary of Massachusetts. The Oblong Meeting House was first constructed in Pawling, New York in 1742.

At a monthly meeting of Friends held at our meeting
House in **Dartmouth** on the 20th day of the 5th month 1741
This meeting being Called **John Howland** and **Adam Mott**
present The Friends appointed have Drawn an Epistle
to the Quarterly meeting and **John Howland** hath
attended it The Quarterly meeting Epistle hath been read
at this meeting and kindly accepted
The visiters Chose for this year are for **Ponagansett**
ar **Joseph Tucker Abraham Tucker Jedidiah Allen**
and **Peleg Smith** for **Coaksett Jonathan Wood** and
Nathanael Potter
And For **Cushnot Jacob Taber** and **Benjamin Allen**
This meeting hath received a Certificate Signed by
Friends of **Sandwich** Concerning their unity with Eliphal Harper[?] ~~her~~
and her good Conversation whilst she abode wth them
Recommending her to our care which was red to the
good Sattisfaction of this meeting

At a monthly meeting of Friends held at our meeting House
in **Dartmouth** on the 17 day of ye 6 month 1741
This meeting being Called **Abraham Tucker** and **John Howland**
present And it is referred to the Consideration of the Quarter
ly meeting whither if any of our young Friends should go out and
marry in the Common way of other people that the visiters
dealing with them Should be Sufficient or whither the monthly
meeting proceed further in dealing with them before Denial

At a monthly meeting of Friends held at our meeting House
in **Dartmouth** on the 21 day of the 7 month 1741
This meeting being Called **James Barker** and **Adam Mott**
present **Abraham Tucker** and **Peleg Smith** are appointed
to Inspect into the Circumstances of **George Soule**s removal
and to Draw a certificate if they think propper
And **John Russell** and **Thomas Smith** is added to them for
that purpose And make report to the next monthly meeting
Eliashib Smith and **Josiah Merihoo [Merihew]** is chosen to inspect into
the Circumstance of **Richard Smith**s removal and to
make return to the next monthly meeting
And this meeting is adjourned til the youths meeting
This meeting being met according to adjournment this Second
day of the 8th month 1741 **John Tucker Joseph Russell** and
Adam Mott are appointed to attend the Quarterly Meeting

Next and to Draw an Epistle to the Same
The visiters of **Coaksett** have given in their account
of what they have done as to visiting Friends families
and that they had Generally pretty good Sattisfaction
There was Collected at this meeting — — - 0:16=03

At a monthly meeting of Friends held at our
Meeting House in **Dartmouth** on the 19 day of yᵉ 8 month
1741 This meeting being Called **John Howland** and **Abraham
Tucker** present The Friends appointed to attend the
Quarterly meeting have done it and drawn an Epistle
to the Same as appointed
The Quarterly meeting Epistle was read at this meeting
and well accepted
There was a Certificate Signed at this meeting for **George
Soule** and his wife and another for **Richard Smith** and
his wife in order to go to the monthly meeting at **Mama
roneck** in the Government of **New york**

At a Monthly meeting of Friends held at our meeting House
in **Dartmouth** on the 16 day of the 9 month 1741
This meeting being called **John Howland** and **Abraham
Tucker** present
John Gifford and **Bathsheba Lapham** did lay their intentions
of taking each other in marriage before this meeting
and were Desired to wait til the next monthly meeting for
their answer and **John Russell** and **Jedidiah Allen** are
appointed to Enquire into yᵉ young mans Clearness respect
ing marriage and Conversation and make return to the
next monthly meeting
There was an Epistle read in this meeting from the year
ly meeting in **Pensilvania** baring 1723 and there was
one Paragraf recommended therein which Friends are
desired Duly to Consider for the future the thing was that
if any Friend or any under the Care of friends should apply
themselves to any that under Culler [color] of any art shal pre
tend to find things lost or stolen that they should be speedily
dealt with[10]

At a monthly meeting of Friends held at our meeting House

10. This reference shows how even after the end of active witch hunting in New England, belief in magical arts continued to be a concern. For context, see Jon Butler, "Magic, Astrology, and the Early American Religious Heritage, 1600-1760," *American Historical Review*, 84 (April 1979), 317-46.

in **Dartmouth** on the 21 day of the 10ᵗʰ month 1741
This meeting being Called **Eliashib Smith** and **John Howland**
present The Friends appointed to Inspect into **John Gifford**s
Clearness gives this meeting an account that they have
Mad Enquiry and find nothing to hinder his proceedings in
his Intended marriage
And **John Gifford** and **Bathsheba Lapham** appeared at this
meeting for their [answer] relating to their taking Each other in mar
riage And their Answer was that they might proceed to take
Each other in marriage in Some Convenient time between
this and the next monthly meeting observing the good
order of Truth in the accomplishing thereof
And **John Russell** and **Abraham Tucker** are appointed
to See their marriage Consummated and make return
to the next monthly meeting
There was Collected at this meeting for yᵉ use of Friends
The Sum of £4:11:02 with what yᵉ women gave in
And this meeting orders the Tresurer to pay £3:10ˢ:00ᵈ for the
Last halfe years keeping the meeting
The Friends appointed to attend the Quarterly meeting are
James Barker Joseph Tucker and **Adam Mott** and to
Draw an Epistle to the Same The visiters of **Cushnot**
have given in their account of their service
and this meeting is adjourned til the youths meeting
This meeting being mett according to adjournment this
first day of the 11ᵗʰ month 1741
Joseph Tucker and **Abraham Tucker** are appointed to
oversee the meeting House the year Insuing
And **Adam Mott** hath paid the 3:10 as ordered
The visiters of **Apongansett** have given in their account
that they have done something relating to visiting friends
families

At a monthly meeting of Friends held at our meeting
House in **Dartmouth** on the 18ᵗʰ day of yᵉ 11ᵗʰ month 1741
This meeting being Called **Abraham Tucker** and **Adam
Mott** present **John Russell** gives this meeting an account
that **John Gifford**s marriage was Consummated in the
good order of Truth as far as [he?] Could understand
the Friends appointed to attend the Quarterly meeting
have all attended it but **Adam Mott** And Drawn an

Epistle to the Same
And **Silas Kerby** [**Kirby**] and **Elisabeth Russell** did lay their
Intentions of taking Each other in marriage befor
this meeting and wer desired to wait til the next
Monthly Meeting for their answer and **John Russell**
And **Jedidiah Allen** are appointed to Enquire into the
young mans Clearness respecting marriage and Conversa
tion and make return to the next Monthly Meeting
and the Quarterly meeting Epistle was read at this
meeting and well accepted

At a monthly meeting of Friends held at our meeting
House in **Dartmouth** on the 15ᵗʰ day of the 12ᵗʰ month 1741
this meeting being Called **James Barker** present **Francis
Allen** and **Rebeckah Tucker** did lay their intentions
of taking each other in marriage before this
meeting and were desired to wait til the next
monthly meeting for their answer and **James Barker**
and **John Howland** are appointed to See into the young
mans Clearness as to marriage and Conversation and
make return to the next monthly meeting
And whereas **Isaac Howland**s Daughter **Meribah**
hath gone out of the good order Established amongst us in
Contracting marriage with one that is not under the Care
of friends and her first Cousin the[re]fore this meeting appoints
Peleg Smith and **George Smith** to assist the Women in Labor
ing with her to see if they bring her to a Sight of her out
goings. And this meeting is adjourned til the 24ᵗʰ of this instant
This meeting being met according to adjournment this 24ᵗʰ
of the ~~first~~ 12ᵗʰ month 1741
We understand that **Seth Allen** hath gone out of the
good order Established amongst friends in marriage
therefore this meeting appoints **John Russell** and
Abraham Tucker to Speak with him to See if he doth
Any ways incline to make Sattisfaction and make return
to the next monthly meeting
And also **Abraham Wing** having Committed the like
offence **Eliashib Smith** and **Adam Mott** to Speak With
him and bring their account to the next monthly
Meeting

(*1742*)　At a monthly meeting of Friends held at our meeting House
In **Dartmouth** on the 15ᵗʰ day of the 1ˢᵗ month 1742
This meeting being Called **John Howland** and **Thomas
Smith** present The Friends appointed to see into **Silas
Kerby**s [**Kirby**] Clearness makes report to this meeting that
they find nothing to Hinder his proceedings in his intend
ed marriage
And **James Barker** gives this meeting an account
that he hath made Inquiry into **Fra[n]cis Allen**s Clearness
and finds nothing to Hinder his intended marriage
Silas Kerby [**Kirby**] and **Elisabeth Russell** appeared at this
meeting for their Answer relating to their taking Each
other in marriage and their answer was that theʸ
might proceed to take each other in marriage in
Some Convenient time between this and the next
monthly meeting observing the good order of Truth in the
accomplishment thereof
And **Isaac Howland** and **Peleg Smith** are appointed to
See their marriage Consummated in the abovesd order
and make return to the next monthly meeting
And **Francis Allen** and **Rebeckah** ~~Russell~~ ᵀᵘᶜᵏᵉʳ appeared
at this meeting for their Answer in Respect to their taking
Each other in marriage And their answer was that
they might proceed to take each other in marriage
In Some Convenient time betwe this and the next
monthly meeting observing the good order of truth
in the performance thereof And **John Howland** and
Joseph Tucker are appointed ~~in the performance
thereof to~~ see it accomplished orderly and make
return to the next monthly meeting
The Friends appointed to attend the Quarterly
Meeting are **Eliashib Smith James Barker** and **Joseph
Tucker** and to Draw an Epistle to the Same
there was Collected at this meeting for the use of Friends
one pound eight Shillings and nine pence
Abraham Tucker gives this meeting an account
that they have ˅ⁿᵒᵗ discoursed with **Seth Allen** therefore
they are Still Continued to do it and bring in their account
to the next monthly meeting
And this meeting hath received a paper from

Abraham Wing Signifying his Sorrow for this disorder
ly marriage which this meeting thinke best to Con
sider further of therefore the matter is refered
And whereas **David Akin** being about to remove
with his family to **Oblong** to live he Desires a Certi
ficate therefore this meeting appoints **Isaac Howland**
Peleg Smith and **George Smith** to make inquiry into
his Circumstances and Draw one accordingly if they
think propper
And whereas **William Ricketson** hath of Late Enter
tained Certain Eronious notions Contrary to our
principles this meeting appoints **Benjamin Allen**
Isaac Howland and **Peleg Smith** to Labour with
him in order to reclaim his Judgment in the premi
=ses And to let him know that if he will persist
in the Same Friends must proceed to Deny him
The Vis[i]ters of **Coakset** have give in an account ~~that they have~~
in writing of their Service in visiting friends families
And this meeting is adjourned til the youths meeting
This meeting being meet according to adjournment this 2ᵈ Day
of the 2ᵈ month 1742
John Howland ˄and **Adam Mott** are appointed with the rest that was
Chosen to attend the Quarterly Meeting

At a monthly meeting of Friends held at our meeting House
in **Dartmouth** on the 19ᵗʰ day of the Second month 1742
This meeting being Called **John Howland** and **Thomas Smith** presin[t]
Isaac Howland and **Peleg Smith** gives this meeting an account
that **Silas Kerbys** [**Kirby**] marriage was Consummated in
the good order of truth according to their Judgment
And **John Howland** gives this meeting an account that
he was at **Frances** [**Francis**] **Allens** marriage and Saw nothing
but that it was carried on in good order
And **Adam Mott** hath attended the Quarterly meeting
and there was an Epistle Drawn and sent
the Friends appointed to Discource with **Seth Allen**
not having done it they ar Still Continued to do it and
bring in their account to the next monthly meeting
The Friends appointed to draw **David Akins** Certificate
not having done are Still continued to do it and bring
it to the next monthly meeting

the Matter Concerning **William Ricketson** is refered to
the next monthly meeting
The Quarterly meeting Epistle was read at this meeting
and well accepted

At a monthly meeting of Friends held at our meet
ing House in **Dartmouth** on the 17th day of the 3d m[o]
1742 this meeting being Called **John Howland** present
There was a Condemnation drawn up and Signed at
this meeting against **Seth Allen** and **Jabez Barker**
is appointed to read it at the end of the meeting of
Worship on a first day between this and the next monthly
meeting: And there was a Certificate Signed at this
meeting for **David Akin** and Directed to Friends
Mamaronak
And Whereas there hath been a great deal of Labour bestow
ed upon **William Ricketson** in order to bring him to
a right Sence of his out goings but altogether
Seemingly to no Effect therefore this meeting appoints
John Tucker and **Isaac Smith** to Draw up a Condem
nation against him and bring it to the next monthly
Meeting

At a monthly meeting of Friends held at our meet
ing House in **Dartmouth** on the 21 day of ye 4 m 1742
This meeting being Called **John Russell** and **Thomas Smith**
present **Jabez Barker** hath read **Seth Allens** Con
demnation as appointed and is as followeth
Whereas, **Seth Allen** of **Dartmouth** in the County
of **Bristol** in the Province of ye **Massachusets Bay**
in **New England** hath of late married out of the
good order Established amongst us the people Called
Quakers and taken one that was not in unity
with us And also Seems to Justify fidling and Dancing
in his House which practice has always been Contrary
to our profession and Friends Have laboured with
him in love to reform him but he refused to hear them
therefore this meeting gives this forth as a Testimony
against Such practices Denying him the sd **Seth Allen**
to be one in unity with us the people Called Quakers
Sincerely desireing he may Come to a Sight of his out
goings and find mercy with the Lord

Signed by order and in the behalfe of sd meeting this 17th d
of the 4th month 1742 by **John Tucker** Clerk
And **Thomas Akin** was at this meeting And hath
made Something of acknowledgment as to his taking
the oath as mentioned Some time past and he desires
Still to remain under our Care which is granted
and **William Ricketson**s Condemnation was drawn
up and brought to this meeting and **John Tucker**
hath signed it by order and in the behalfe of this
meeting and is ordered to read it or git Some by [body?] to do it
on a first day after the meeting of Worship
between this and the next monthly meeting
And this meeting is adjourned til the first sixth day in the next
Month
This meeting being met according to adjournment this
2d Day of the 5th month 1742
This meeting received an Epistle from the yearly Meeting
at **London** and it was kindly accepted
And **Joseph Russell** and **Jabez Barker** was Chosen to
attend the Quarterly meeting and to draw an Epistle
to the Same

At a monthly meeting of friends held at our meeting
House in **Dartmouth** on the 19th of the 5th month 1742
This meeting being Called **John Howland Adam Mott**
present and **William Ricketson**s Condemnation hath
been read according to the order of the last monthly
meeting And is as followeth
Whereas **William Ricketson** of **Dartmouth** in
the County of **Bristol** in the Province of the **Massachuset[t]s**
Bay in **New England** being one that hath for many
years made profession with us the People Called
Quakers yet for want of keeping to the Spirit of truth
hath let in and given Way to strange and wrong notions
Contrary to our profession two of which articles
are as followeth firstly that **Adam** was in a better
State after he had transgressed against the Command
of God than he was in before Secondly that from **Adam**
to the Coming of Christ in the flesh the wickedest of
Men brought as much honour to God as the Righteous
these with many more Such like notions he doth Stand

to Justify though much labour hath been bestowed
upon him from time to time in order to bring him of
from his errors but he still rejects our Counsel
for which for the Clearing of our Holy profession
We give this forth as a publick Testimony against it
denying him the Sd **William Ricketson** to be one in unity
With us the people called Quakers truly desireing that
sight wherin hath mist the Way and that Good may Shew him
Mercy Given forth at our monthly meeting held in **dartmouth** on the
21 day of the 4 month 1742 and Signed by order and read
in behalfe of Sd meeting by   **John Tucker** Clerk
This meeting hath Collected with forty Shillings that the women
gave in the Sum of £4:12:0
Our friend **Hannah Jenkinson** was at this meetin and
her Certificate was read to good Sattisfaction
And the Quarterly meeting Epistle was read at this
meeting to good Sattisfaction
And this meeting orders **Adam Mott** to pay to the
Overseers of the meeting House the sum of £5:10ˢ:00ᵈ
for keeping the meeting House and for gutters to yᵉ windows
And whereas **Hannah Wing** Daughter of **Edward Wing**
deceased and **Meribah Howland** daughter of **Isaac
Howland** have both of them gone out of the good order
Established among Friends and married those
that were not under our Care therefor this meeting
appoints **Jabez Barker** and **Isaac Smith** to draw up
Something in order to Clear the truth of them and
bring it to the next monthly meeting
And **Jabez Barker** hath attended the Quarterly Meet
ing and drawn an Epistle to yᵉ Same
and this meeting hath received the Quarterly meeting
Epistle which was read and well accepted

At a monthly meeting of Friends ~~of~~ Held at our
Meeting House in **Dartmouth** on the 16 day of the 6ᵗʰ
month 1742 This meeting being Called **John Howland**
and **Adam Mott** present
The visiters Chosen for this year are for **Coakset**
Joseph Tripp and **John Mosher** for **Ponagansett**
Adam Mott Abraham Tucker Jedidiah Allen and
Peleg Smith And for **Cushnot Benjamin Allen** and

Joseph Russell
There was a Condemnation Signed at this meeting
against **Hannah Mosher**
And whereas **Meribah Briggs** hath Sent in a paper
Signifying her sorrow for her outgoings this meeting
appoints **Peleg Smith** and **George Smith** to go once more
with the women that advised with her before to
Endevor to know her Sincerity
And whereas **Eliphal Harper** being about to remove
to **Pensilvania** to live She desires a Certificate
And **Joseph Tucker** and **Isaac Smith** are appointed to assist
the women in making inquiry whither things are clear and
Draw up a Certificate for her if nothing be found to hinder
And **Benjamin Lapham** being removed to a place Called
Situate to live in **Rhoad Island** Government he desires
a Certificate therefore this meeting appoints **Isaac Howland**
and **Peleg Smith** to make inspection into the matter and if
they find things Clear to Draw one and bring it to the next
monthly meeting
Adam Mott hath paid £5:10ˢ:00ᵈ to yᵉ overseers as ordered

At a monthly meeting of friends held at our meeting
House in **Dartmouth** on the 20ᵗʰ day of the 7 month 1742
This meeting being Called **Adam Mott** and **John Howland**
present
There was a Certificate Signed at this meeting for
Benjamin Lapham
There was Collected at this meeting £1: 03ˢ: 03ᵈ
And this meeting is adjorned til the first 6ᵗʰ day in yᵉ next month
This meeting being met according to adjournment this
first day of the 8ᵗʰ month 1742
The visiters of **Ponaganset** and **Coakset** have given in
their account of the Service
And whereas **Francis Tripp** hath through ignorance
as he Saith taken the oath in Some time past he hath
Sent in a paper to this meeting Signifying his sorrow
for the trouble of Friends in that affair and his own
unwatchfulness which this meeting accepts of
The Friends appointed to attend the Quarterly meeting
are **John Howland Thomas Smith** and **Joseph Tucker**
and to Draw an Epistle to the Same

And this meeting hath Signed a Certificate for **Eliphal**
Harper

At a monthly meeting of Friends held at our meet
ing House in **Dartmouth** on the 18th day of the 8th month
1742 This meeting being Called **Abraham Tucker** present
Hannah Moshers Condemnation was read at this
and is as followeth
Whereas **Hannah Mosher** wife of **George Mosher**
and Daughter of **Edward Wing** and **Sarah** his wife
Dartmouth in the County of **Bristol** in the Province
of the **Massachuset[t]s Bay** in **New England** deseaced [deceased]
being one that was Educated in the way of Truth her
Father and Mother both professing with us the peo
ple Called Quakers yet for want of keeping to
her Education hath gone and married one that
under our Care in the Common way of other people
although advised to the Contrary for which her
Disorderly proceedings we can do no less than give
this forth as a Testimony against her denying her
the Sd **Hannah Mosher** to be one in unity with us
the aforesd People yet Sincerely desiring that She
may Come to a Sight and Sence of her out goings
and find mercy with the Lord
Given forth at our monthly meeting held in **Dartmouth**
on the 18th day of the 8th month 1742
And Signed by order of the Sd meeting by **John Tucker** Clerk
The Friends appointed to attend the Quarterly
Meeting have done it and Drawn an Epistle to
the Same The Quarterly meeting Epistle was read
at this meeting and kindly accepted
And whereas **Timothy Russell** the Son of **John Russell**
hath desired a Certificate of this meeting of his Clearness
relating to marriage and Conversation to the monthly
meeting at **Greenwich** he being about to marry a young
woman belonging to them parts and **Isaac Smith** and
Isaac Howland are appointed to inquire into the
Matter and Draw one if they find things Clear and bring
it to the next monthly meeting

At a monthly meeting of friends held at our meeting
House in **Dartmouth** on the 15th day of the 9th month 1742

This meeting being Called **John Howland** and **Abraham
Tucker** present The Friends appointed to Draw up
a Certificate for **Timothy Russell** have done it
and it was Signed at this meeting

At a monthly meeting of Friends held at our meeting
House in **Dartmouth** on the 20ᵗʰ day of the 10ᵗʰ month 1742
This meeting being Called **John Howland** and **Adam Mott**
Present: There was Collected at this meeting 2:18=06
and this meeting orders the Tresurer to pay to the overseers
the Sum of 3 pound ten Shillings for half a years keeping
the meeting House And this meeting hath received forty
Shillings of the Women towards keeping the meeting House
and **Adam Mott** hath paid the ₤3:10ˢ as above ordered
The Friends appointed to attend yᵉ Quarterly meeting
are **Benjamin Allen John Howland** and **Peleg Smith**
and to draw an Epistle to yᵉ same

At a monthly meeting of friends held at our meeting
House in **Dartmouth** on the 17ᵗʰ day of the 11ᵗʰ month 1742
this meeting being Called **James Barker** and **Isaac Howland**
present **John Howland** and **Peleg Smith** hath attended
the Quarterly meeting and Drawn an Epistle to the Same

At a monthly meeting of friends held at our meeting
House in **Dartmouth** on the 21 day of the 12ᵗʰ month 1742
This meeting being Called **John Howland** and **Abraham
Tucker** present the Quarterly meeting Epistle was
read at this meeting and well accepted
And Whereas **Holder Slocum**s daughte **Alice** is gone
and Married out of the good order Established amongst
friends this meeting therefore appoints **James Barker
Abraham Tucker** and **Jedidiah Allen** to talk with
Sd **Slocum** to See how clear he hath kept him Selfe
and to give Suitable advice as they may think propper
and make return to the next monthly meeting
and whereas **John Allen** hath Signifyed that he
hath a mind to move with his family into the
Western parts to live this meeting therefore
appoints **John Russell** and **Isaac Smith** with the
visiters to mak enquiry into his Circumstances
and if they think Suitable draw up a certificat for
him and bring it to the next monthly meeting

(*1743*) At a monthly meeting of Friends held at our
meeting House in **Dartmouth** on the 21st day of
the first month 1743
This meeting being Called **Adam Mott** and **Abraham
Tucker** present : **Peleg Gifford** and **Abigail Shepherd**
Did lay their intentions of taking each other
in marriage before this meeting and were desired
to wait til the next monthly meeting for their
answer and
There was Collected att this meeting for the
use of Friends two pounds nine Shillings and two pence
The Friends appointed to discource with **Holder Slocum**
have done it but not being fully Sattisfied the
matter is refered til the next monthly meeting
The visiters have given in their account in
Writing to this meeting
This meeting hath Signed a Certificate for **John Allen**
There was a paper read at this meeting Signed
by **Meribah Briggs** Signifying her Sorrow for
her out goings which this meeting accepts of and
She to remain under our Care
And whereas the Widow **Mary Davel** [**Davol**] hath a mind
to remove into the Western parts to live with
her Son in Law and desires a Certificate this meeting
therefore this meeting appoints **Jonathan Wood** and
John Mosher to inquire into her Circumstances
And Draw one if they think fit and bring it to
the next monthly meeting
And **James Barker Peleg Smith** and **Abraham Tucker**
are appointed to attend the Quarterly meeting
and to Draw an Epistle to the Same – – – – –

At a monthly meeting of friends held at our meeting in **Dartmo**uth
on the 18 day of the 2d month 1743 This meeting being Called
James Barker and **Peleg Smith** present **Peleg Gifford** and
Abigail Shepherd appeared at this meeting Desiring their answer
in relation to their taking each other in marriage and their an=
swer was that they might proceed to take each other in marriage observing the good order Established amongst friends
In the performance thereof and **John Howland** and **Henry
Hedly** are appointed to see their marriag Consummated in

Sd order and make return to yᵉ next monthly meeting
And **Peleg Smith** hath attended the Quarterly meeting and
there was an Epistle drawn and Sent
And **Thomas Smith** being Lately come home from **Pensilvania**
hath brought a certificate with him from the monthly meeting
In **New Garden** which Was read to our Sattisfaction And there
Was a Certificate brought to this meeting and Signed for the
Widow **Davel** [**Davol**] & this meeting hath had a Consideration upon
the paper that Was sent to the Last monthly meeting by **Thomas
Taber** And It is yᵉ Conclution of this meeting that It should be
accepted And he to remain under our Care
The Friends appointed to Speak with **Nathaniel Kerby** [**Kirby**] and his
Wife have done it but have not received full Sattisfaction
but are not without hopes therefore yᵉ matter is refered

At a monthly meeting of Friends held at our meeting House
In **Dartmouth** on yᵉ 16ᵗʰ Day of the 3ᵈ month 1743 **John Howland**
present **John Howland** and **Henry Hedly** gives this meeting an
account that **Peleg Gifford** and **Abigail Shepherd**s marriage
Was Consummated In good order as far as they Saw
Jabez Barker and **Isaac Smith** are chose to draw up a paper of
Condemnation against **Mary Wood** Widow of **Isaac Wood** Late decesed
for marrying out of yᵉ order Established amongst Friends

At a monthly meeting of [Friends] held at our meeting House In **Dartmouth**
on yᵉ 20 day of the 4 month 1743 This meeting being Called **John
Howland** and **Abraham Tucker** present
And whereas the Friends appointed to draw up **Mary Wood**s Condem
nation not having done it ar Still Continued to do it against yᵉ
next monthly meeting: Collected at this meeting – – – 2 – 06 – 00
And the Tresurer is ordered to pay to the overseers £5- 09ˢ- 08ᵈ for
yᵉ Last halfe years keeping yᵉ meeting House And for Some other
business done about sd House
And the Tresurer hath paid the abovesd mony to yᵉ overseers
The Friends appointed to attend yᵉ Quarterly Meeting are **James
Barker Thomas Smith** & **Joseph Tucker** and Draw an Epistle to
the Same

At a monthly meeting of Friends held at our meeting House
In **Dartmouth** on yᵉ 18ᵗʰ of yᵉ 5ᵗʰ month 1743 **Isaac Howland**
And **Peleg Smith** present **Jabez Barker** and **Isaac Smith** have drawn
up **Mary Wood**s Condemnation and it was read in this meeting

and is as followeth

Whereas **Mary Wood** Late wife of **Isaac Wood** deceas'd of **Dart**
=**mouth** In the County of **Bristol** In yᵉ Province of yᵉ **Massachuset[t]s Bay** In
New England And now wife of **Charles Brownell** being One that
in her first Husbands days made profession with us the
People Called Quakers but for want of having a due regard there-
-unto hath of Late married to one that is not in profession with
us Contrary to yᵉ good advice of Friends that hath from time to time
been Given for which disorderly proceeding we Can do no less but give
this forth as a Condemnation against her denying her yᵉ sd **Mary**
~~**Wood to**~~ Now the Wife of **Charles Brownell** aforesd to be one in
unity with us but truly desiring if it be the will of God She may
Come to a sence of her out goings And find mercy
Given forth at our monthly meeting held In **Dartmouth** on
the 18ᵗʰ day of the 5ᵗʰ month ~~And~~ 1743 and Signed by order of sd
Meeting by – – –   **John Tucker** Clerk.
And also **Alice Slocum**s Condemnation for the lik[e] offence was
drawn up and brought this meeting and Is as followeth
Whereas **Alice Slocum** daughter of **Holder Slocum** of **Dartmouth** in
yᵉ County of **Bristol** In yᵉ Province of yᵉ **Massachuset[t]s Bay** In **New England**
being one that hath had her Education among us the people Called
Quakers but for want of keeping to the Spirit of Truth In her Selfe
and taking the wholesom advice of Friends that hath been duely
given her hath let her mind out and married to one that is not in
Unity with us for which disorderly proceedings we Can do less but
give forth this as a Testimony against it denying her the sd **Alice**
now wife of **Job Almy** to be one in unity with us yet we do
Sincerely desire that she Come to unfeigned Repentance and
find mercy Given forth at our monthly meeting held in
Dartmouth on the 18 day of yᵉ 5ᵗʰ month 1743 and Signed by order=
of sd meeting by   **John Tucker** Clerk
The Friends appointed to attend the Quarterly meeting and Draw
an Epistle to the Same have done it as appointed
This meeting hath received an Epistle from the yearly meeting
in **London** which was read to good Sattisfaction baring date 1742
And the Quarterly meetings Epistle was read to good Sattisfaction

At a monthly meeting of Friends held at our meeting house In
Dartmouth on the 15ᵗʰ day of the 6 ₍month₎ 1743
This meeting being Called **Abraham Tucker** & **Joseph Tucker** present
The Visiters Chose for **Coakset** for this year are **William Wood Jonathan**

Wood & **John Mosher** And for **Ponaganset** the Sam[e] that
Served the Last year And the Same friend that Served the Last
year for **Cushnot** are Continued And Whereas **Robert Tripp** as we
understand hath been Guilty of Some Defraud toward the High Sheriff
of yᵉ County of **Bristol** And hath been Cited Several times to this Meet
ing but Refuses or Neglects to Come therefore this meeting appoints
Christopher Gifford Nathˡˡ Potter & **Joseph Tripp** to talk wᵗʰ him and
desire him to Come to yᵉ Next monthly meeting in order to make
the Meeting Sattisfaction or else he may Expect Judgment to go
forth against him. And **Robert mosher** and **Sarah Lawton** did lay
their Intentions of taking each other In marriage before this
Meeting and were desired to wait till the next monthly meeting
for their answer & **Joseph Tripp** and **Jonathan Wood** are appointed
to make Enquiry Into yᵉ young mans Clearness and
make return to yᵉ next monthly meeting

At a monthly meeting of Friends held at our meeting House in
Dartmouth on the 22 day of yᵉ 7ᵗʰ month 1743 This meeting being
Called **Adam Mott** & **Abraham Lawton** present
Robert Mosher and **Sarah Lawton** did Lay their Intentions of
taking Each other In marriage before this meeting and were
desired to wait till the next monthly meeting for their
answer and **Joseph Tripp** and **Jonathan Wood** are appointed
to make Enquiry into the young mans Clearness and make return
to yᵉ next monthly meeting[11]
And yᵉ visitters of **Coakset** have given In their account in
Writing. There was Collected at this meeting – – ᵉ1-09-00
And Whereas **Robert Tripp** hath not appeared but hath Sent
Some Excuce to this meeting **Joseph Tripp** is appointed to
Let him know that We Expect Some Sattisfaction at the
Next monthly meeting or else Judgment must go forth against
him And this meeting is adjourned till yᵉ first sixth day in next ₘₒₙₜₕ
This meeting being mett according to adjournment this
7ᵗʰ day of yᵉ 8ᵐ 1743 the **Coakset** visiter signifies that they
have visited the families of Friends for the most part under their
Care and find things for the most part as Well as they Could Expect
And we received no account from **Cushnot**
John Tucker John Howland Joseph Tucker & **Abraham Tucker**
are appointed to attend the Quarterly meeting and Draw an
Epistle to the Same

---

11. The preceding six lines repeat material included in the minutes of the previous monthly meeting

At a monthly meeting of friends held at our meeting
House In **Dartmouth** on the 17th day of the 8th month 1743
This meeting being Called **Jedidiah Allen** & **Isaac Smith**
present there was a Certificate read at this meeting Signed
by our friends at **Nantucket** Concerning their unity with
Jonathan Hussey & his wives removal from thence to
dwell amongst us which was well accepted
The Friends appointed to attend the Quarterly meeting have
done all Except **John Tucker** and Drawn an Epistle
to the Same as appointed
and the Quarterly meeting Epistle hath been read and
Well accepted
Robert Mosher and **Sarah Lawton** appeared at this meet
-ing for their answer and their answer was that they
might proceed to take each other In marriage In some
Convenient time between this & the next monthly meet
ing observing the good ord established amongst us In the
accomplishing thereof and **Jonathan Wood** and **Nathaniel
Potter** are appointed to See their marriage Consummated
annd make return to the next monthly meeting
Robert Tripp hath appeared at this meeting and Some
Sattisfaction & Signifies that he hopes that he Shall do
Something further at the next monthly meeting
And Whereas we understand that the books that the month
ly meeting Subscribed for are printed and the mony is
Wanting to pay for it therefore **John Howland** is appoin
ted to git the mony and procure the books for the monthly
meeting

At a monthly meeting of Friends held at our meeting
House In **Dartmouth** on the 21 day of the 9 month 1743
This meeting being Called **Thomas Smith** and **Abraham
Tucker** present **Nathll Potter** makes report to this meet
ing that **Robert Mosher** and **Sarah Lawton**s marriage
Consummated In the good order of Truth
And **Daniel Wood Jur.** and **Mary Wady** laid their Intention
of taking each other in marriage before this meeting and were
desired to wait till the next monthly meeting for their answer
John Howland and **James Barker** are appointed to See Into the
young mans Clearness Concerning marriage and Conversation
and make return to the next monthly meeting

and **Robert Tripp** hath made Sattisfaction to this meeting Concer
ning the matter about the high sheriff
The matter about the book is refered till next monthly meeting
And Whereas **Joseph Jennings** & his wife hath desired that they
and their famly might be taken under the Care of this meeting
this meeting agree to take them under their Care
And there hath been Some Conference about reparing the
meeting House Which is refered to next monthly meeting

At a monthly meeting of Friend held at our meeting House in
Dartmouth on the 19 day of the 10th month 1743
This meeting is adjourned till the first sixth day Ju the next month
This meeting being mett according to adjournment this 6th day
Day of the 11 month 1743 **Daniel Wood** & **Mary Wady** appeared
at this meeting for their answer & their answer was that
they might proceed to take each other in marriage In Some
Convenient time between this and the next monthly
meeting observing the Good order Established among Friends
In the accomplishment thereof & **James Barker** and **John**
Howland are appointed to See their marriage Consummated
in the abovesd order and make return to the next monthly
meeting And the matter Concerning the books is refered till next
monthly meeting There was Collected at this meeting 2ᵋ-03-04
also the Women gave forty Shillings – – – 2 -00-00
The Tresurer is ordered to pay to the overseers 4ᵋ-05-00
for halfe a years keeping the meeting house
And **Adam Mott Stephen Willcock** and **James Barker**
are appointed to attend the Quarterly meeting and
Draw an Epistle to the Same
And the Tresurer hath paid the 4ᵋ-5ˢ as ordered
And this meeting appoints **John Howland James Barker**
Thomas Smith Isaac Howland and **Joseph Tucker** a Comᵗᵗᵉ
to Consider after what manner to repair or add to the meeting
house and to go forward with it as they think propper
Joseph Tucker and **Abraham Tucker** are appointed to
to oversee the meeting House the year Insuing

At a monthly meeting of Friends held at our meeting House
on in Dartmouth the 16 day of the 11th month 1743
This meeting being Called **Thomas Smith** and **Isaac Howland**
present **John Howland** and **James Barker** gives this
meeting an account that **Daniel Wood and Mary Wadys**

Marriage was was Consummated In good order according
to their Judgment **Adam Mott** and **Stephen Willcock** hath
attended the Quarterly meeting & Drawn an Epistle to
the Same as appointed And the Quarterly meeting Epistle
Was read at this meeting & well accepted
And this meeting hath received the books Called **George Fox**es
primmers In number 150 and it is Concluded that they
may be Sold for 3 shilling a piece[12]

At a monthly meeting of Friends held at our meeting
House In **Dartmouth** on the 20ᵗʰ day of the 12 month 1743
This meeting being Called **John Howland** & **Abraham Tucker**
present **Daniel Gifford** son of **Timothy Gifford** and **Ann How
land** Daughther of **Isaac Howland** Did lay their Intentions of
taking Each other in marriage before this meeting and
Were Desired to wait till the next monthly meeting for
their answer and **Jedidiah Allen** & **John Russell** are ap
pointed to make Enquiry Into the young mans Clearness
as to marriag and Conversation and make return to
the next monthly meeting
And whereas **Abigail Kirby** doth proceed at times to
appear in publick Testimony Contrary to the advice of
of the monthly meeting Therefore **John Howland** and **Adam
Mott** are appointed to Labour further with her to
persuade to be silent
And Whereas **Sarah Brownell** daughter of **Joseph Brownell**
hath of late gone out of order and married with one that
is not under our care therefore this meeting orders
Jabez Barker and **Isaac Smith** to draw her Condemnation
And bring it to the next monthly meeting

(1744) At a monthly meeting of Friends held at our meeting House In
Dartmouth on the 19 day of the first month 1743/44 this meeting being
Called **John Howland** & **Adam Mott** present
Thomas Smith and **Experience Chase** did Lay their Intentions of
taking each other in marriage before this meeting and were desired
to wait till the next monthly meeting for their answer and
James Barker & **John Shephard** are appointed to Inspect into his
Clearness and make return to the next monthly meeting
and **John Park** of **Grotton** in the Colony of **Connecticut** and
Sarah Gifford Daughter did lay their intention of marriage

12. See above, Book 1, n. 19.

before this meeting and were Desired to wait till the next
monthly meeting for their answer and **Eliashib Smith** and **Stephen
Willcock** are appointed to see that things are Clear and bring
in their account to the next monthly meeting
The visitters of **Coakset** and **Cushnot** have goven in their
accounts In writing to this meeting of their Service
The Friends apointed to See Into **Daniel Gifford**s Clearness gives
this meeting an account that they find nothing to hinder
his proceedings
And **Daniel Gifford** and **Ann Howland** appeared at this meet
ing for their and their answer was that they might proceed
to take each other in marriage in Some Convenient time
between this and the next monthly meeting observing the
good order Established amongst us In the accomplishing thereof
And **Peleg Smith** and **George Smith** are appointed to See their
Marriage Consummated and make return to the next monthly
meeting. And the matter Concerning **Abigail Kerby** is refered
till the next monthly meeting
There was a paper of Condemnation Signed at this meeting
against **Sarah Brownell** and is as followeth – –
Whereas **Sarah Peckham** ~~now Brown~~ Daughter of **Joseph
Brownell** and now the wife of **Stephen Peckhan** ju^r of **Dartmouth**
In the County of **Bristol** in the Province of the **Massachussets Bay**
in **New England** being one that was Esteamed under the Care
of Friends yet for want of keeping to the principles of truth
as it is held and mainted amongst us the People Called Quaker
hath gone and married one that is not under our Care
out of the order Established amongst us although Duly advises
to the Contrary for which Disorderly Proceeding we find it
our Duty to give this forth as a Testimony against denying
The sd **Sarah Peckham** to be one in unity with us the aforesd
People Truly Desiring that she may Come to a Sence of her
Outgoing and find mercy Given forth at our monthly meet
ing held In **Dartmouth** on the 19 day of the first month 1743/4
Signed by order of sd meeting by   **John Tucker** Clerk
And this meeting Is adjournd till the months meeting
This meeting being mett according to adjournment this
this 6th day of the 2^d month 1744
The visiters ~~the on~~ In a Generall Way belonging to this
meeting have given in their accounts that they have

visited the families of Friends excepting that part between
the **mill River** and **Coakset River**
John Tucker Joseph Tucker & **John Howland** are appoited
to attend the Quarterly meeting and Draw an Epistle to the same

At a monthly meeting of Friends held at our meeting
House In **Dartmouth** on the 16 day of 2ᵈ month 1744
This meeting being Called **John Howland** & **Jedidiah Allen**
present The Friend appointed to See into **Thomas Smith** Clearness
makes report to this meeting that they find nothing to hinder
his Intended marriage & we understand that things are clear
relating to **John Park**
And **Thomas Smith** and **Experience Chase** appeared at this
meeting for their answer and their answer was that they
might proceed to take each other In marriage In some
Convenient time between this and the next monthly
meeting observing the Good order Established amongst Friend
In the accomplishment thereof
And **John Park** and **Sarah Gifford** likewise appeared at
this meeting desiring their answer and their answer was
that they might proceed as abov/d
And **Peleg** & **George Smith** gives this meeting an account
that **Daniel Gifford** and **Ann Howland**s Marriage Was Consum
mated in good order
And **Johnson Tucker** hath attended the Quarterly meeting
and there was an Epistle drawn and Sent as ordered
This meeting hath received an Epistle from the Quarterly
meetin which was read and well accepted
And the was Collected at this meeting – – 1ᶜ – 16ˢ – 08ᵈ
And there a Complant brought to this meeting against **Robert**
Rebert Tripp that he is Indebted to **William Davel**s blacksmith and
doth neglect to pay it Therefore this meeting doth appoint
Jedidiah Wood and **Christopher Gifford** to see into the matter
and make return to the next monthly meeting
And Whereas **Meribah Slocum** is about to remove to **Newport**
to Live and Desires a Certificate
Therefore this meeting appoints **John Howland** & **Adam Mott**
to prepare one and bring it to the next monthly meeting
And **Joseph Russell** and **John Howland** are appointed to see
Thomas Smith and **Experience Chase**s marriage Consumma
ted In the good order Established amongst friends

And **John Shepherd** & **Stephen Willcock** and appointed see
John Park and **Sarah Gifford**s marriage Consumated
as abovesd

At a monthly meeting of Friends held at our meeting
House In **Dartmouth** on the 21 day of the 3 month 1744
This meeting being Called **John Howland** & **Abraham Tucker**
present. **John Howland** gives this meeting an account
that he was at the Solemnizing of **Thomas Smith** and
Experience Chases marriage And Saw nothing but
that it was Carried on in Good order
And also **Stephen Willcock** Signifies that **Joseph Park** and
Sarah Giffords marriage was Carried on in good order
And **Robert Tripp** hath made up w^th **Wm Davel**
And there was a Certificat Signed at this meeting for
Meriber Slocum
And this meeting hath received a Certificate from friends
at **Pembrook** Concerning **Bethia Walker** recommend
ing her to our Care which is accepted

At a monthly meeting of Friends held at our meeting
House In **Dartmouth** on the 18th day of the 4 month 1744
This meeting being Called **John Howland** and **Peleg Smith**
present The Epistle from **London** yearly meeting baring
date 1743 was read at this meeting and well accepted
The Friends appointed to attend the Quarterly meeting are
Eliashib Smith John Howland & **Stephen Willcock**
There was Collected at this meeting – – 2^£ – 13^s – 02^d
And this meeting is adjourned till the monthly meeting
This meeting being met according to adjournment this 6 day
of the 5th month 1744 This meeting orders the treasurer to pay
the overseers the Sum of 4 pounds & five Shillings old Tenor
for the Last halfe years keeping the meeting house

At a monthly meeting of Friends held at our meeting House
In **Dartmouth** on the 16th day of the 5th 1744
This meeting being Called **Adam Mott** and **Abraham Tucker**
present - The Treasurer hath paid the 4 pound 5 shillings
as ordered **Eliashib Smith** and **Stephen Willcock** hath attend
ed the Quarterly meeting as appointed The Epistle from the
Quarterly meeting was read at this meeting & well accepted
And Whereas **Joseph Russell ju^r**; is about to marry out of the

Good order Established amongst us therefore this meeting
appoints **Adam Mott** and **George Smith** to advise with the
In order that he may refrain proceeding in that matter
And whereas **Abraham Wing** being removed to the **Oblong**
to live he desires a Certificate from this meeting therefore
this meeting appoints **Eliashib Smith** and **Adam Mott** to to make
Enquiry into the matter and Draw one if they think propper
and bring it to the next monthly meeting

At a monthly meeting of Friends held at our meeting House
In **Dartmouth** on the 20th day of the 6 month 1744 this meeting
being Called **John Howland** and **Adam Mott** present
Barnabas Mosher and **Bethiah Walker** did lay their Inten
tions of taking each other In marriage before this meeting
And were desired to wait till the next monthly meeting
for their answer and **Eliashib Smith** & **Josiah Merihew**
are appointed to enquire into the young mans Clearness
Respecting marriage and Conversation and make re
turn to the next monthly meeting
The matter Concerning **Abraham Wings** Certificate
is refered till the Next monthly meeting

At a monthly meeting of Friends held at our meeting
House In **Dartmouth** on the 17th day of the 7th month 1744
This meeting being Called **Joseph Tucker** and **Abraham
Tucker** present **Barnabas Mosher** and **Bethiah
Walker** appeared at this meeting for their ^answer and their
answer was that they might proceed to take each other
in marriag in Some Convenient time between this
and the Next monthly meeting Observing the good order
Established amongst Friends in the performance thereof
and **Eliashib Smith** and **Adam Mott** are appointed to see their
marriage Sollemnized In the abovesd order
The visitters of that part of **Ponaganset** to the westward of
the **Mill River** have given in their accounts to this meeting
that they Find that Several Friends have been out of order
in paying money towards upholding Warring & Fighting therefore
this meeting appoints **Isaac Howland Joseph Tucker** and
Peleg Smith to Labour with them to see if they can make
Sattisfaction for what they have done Contrary to our
principles in that Care and bring In their account to
the next monthly meeting. The Friends appointed to attend

the Quarterly meeting are **James Barker John Howland**
and **Adam Mott** and to Draw an Epistle to the Same
And the Collection is refered to the next monthly meeting

At a monthly meeting of Friends held at our meeting House
In **Dartmouth** on the 15 day of the 8th month 1744 This meeting
being Called **John Howland** and **Abraham Tucker** present
Eliashib Smith makes report to this meeting that **Barna
bus Mosher** and **Bethiah Walker**s marriage was Consum
mated In Decent order
And **Robert Kirby ju**r and **Abigail Allen** did lay their
Intentions of taking each other in marriage and
were Desired to wait till the next monthly meeting
for their answer and **John Russell** & **Jedidiah Allen**
are appointed to see Into the young mans Clearness
And **John Macumber** and **Desire Potter** did lay their
Intentions of taking Each other In Marriage before
this meeting & were Desired to wait till the next
monthly meeting for their answer and **Joseph Tripp** and
Jonatha^n Wood are appointed to Enquire Concerning the
young mans Clearness respecting marriag & Con
versation and make return to the next monthly meeting
And Whereas the Friends that were appointed to Labour
With those that having been out of order towards Propa
gating Warring and fighting not having done it it is refered
to the next monthly meeting
The Friends appointed to attend the monthly meeting have
done it and Drawn an Epistle to the Same as appointed
The Epistle from the Quarterly meeting was read at this
meeting and kindly accepted
And this meeting hath Concluded to come to a Subscription
towards paying the charg of the new addition to the
meeting house
And this meeting appoints **John Howland** and **Joseph
Tucker** to take the Charge of Gitting the Subscription and
paying of it out

At a monthly meeting of Friends held at our meeting
House In **Dartmouth** on the 19th Day of the 9th month 1744
This meeting being Called **John Howland** and **Abraham
Tucker** present
There was a Certificate Signed at this meeting for

Lydia Soule Signifying our kind reception of her visit
amongst us there was also another Signed at this
meeting for **Abraham Wing**
And **Robert Kerby** and **Abigail Allen** appered at this
meeting for their answer and their answer was that
they might proceed to take each other in marriage in
Some Convenient time between this and the next
monthly meeting observing the good order Established
amongst Friends in the performance thereof
And **John Russell** and **Jedidiah Allen** are appointed
to See their Marriage Consummated and make return
to the next monthly meeting
And **John Macumber** & **Desire Potter** appeared at
this meeting for their answer And their answer
Was that they might proceed to take each other in
marriage in some Convenient time betwee this and
the next monthly meeting observing the abovesd good
order in the performance thereof and **Joseph Tripp**
and **Jonathan Wood** are appointed to see their marriage
Consummated and make return to the next
monthly meeting
There was Collected at this meeting 2$^£$--01^s--02^d
The matter Concerning Some Friends not keeping
to their Testimony against fighting is refered
till the next monthly meeting
And Whereas **John Ricketson** and **Phebe Russell** having
Set up their Publishment of marriage out of the good
order Established amongst Friends This meeting appoints
Adam Mott & **Jedidiah Allen** to Endeavour to persuade
them to desist

10 <u>mo</u> 1744

At a monthly meeting of Friends held at <u>our</u> meeting
House In **Dartmouth** on the 17th day of the 10th month 1744
This meeting being Called **John Howland** & **Abraham Tucker**
present **John Russell** & **Jedidiah Allen** gives this meeting
an account that **Robert Kerby** and **Abigail Allens**
marriage hath been orderly Consummated
And **John Wood** and **Hannah Wing** did lay their Intentions
of taking each other in marriage before this meeting
and were Desired to wait till the next monthly meeting

for their answer and **Christopher Gifford** & **Nathaniel**
are appointed to enquire into the young mans Clearness
Respecting marriage and Conversation and make return
to the next monthly meeting
And **Samuel Lawry** and **Pernel Mott** did lay their Intenti
ons of taking each other in marriage before this meeting
and were desired to wait till the next monthly meeting
for their answer And **John Howland** and **Joseph Tucker**
are appointed to see Into the young mans Clearness
and make return to the next monthly meeting
And **Joseph Tripp** & **Jonathan Wood** gives this meeting an
account that **John Macumber** and **Desire Potters** marriage
was Consummated in good order
And **Ebenezer Slocum** hath made Sattisfaction to this
meeting Respecting his giving money for the propagation
of Waring and Fighting and as for the rest that have been
out of order in that affair the matter is refered till
the next monthly meeting and the Com.ᵗᵗ to Labour
further with them
There was Collected at this meeting – – – 2ᵉ – 02ˢ – 06ᵈ
and this meeting is adjourned until the first 6 day in next <u>month</u>
This meeting being met according to adjournment
this 4ᵗʰ day of the 11ᵗʰ month 1744
Stephen Willcock Thomas Smith and **Abraham Tucker**
are appointed to attend the Quarterly meeting next
and to Draw an Epistle to the Same
And **Joseph Tucker** and **Abraham Tucker** are appointed
overseers for the meeting House the year Insuing
John Tucker John Howland James Barker Joseph Tucker
and **Isaac Smith** are appointed to view the minutes in
order that all that are necessary may be put to record

At a monthly meeting of Friends held at our meeting
House in **Dartmouth** on the 22 day of the 11ᵗʰ month 1744
This meeting being Called **John Howland** and **Abraham**
Tucker present. The Friends appointed to attend the Quar
terly meeting have done it and Drawn an Epistle to the Same
And the Friends appointed to Enquire into **Samuel Sawdy**
Clearness makes report that they find nothing to hinder
his Intended marriage
And our Friend **Benjamin Farris** from the **Oblong** was

at this meeting Whose Labour in the Ministry among
us was very acceptable And his Certificate was
read to good Sattisfaction
And **Samuel Sawdy** and **Pernel Mott** appeared at
this meeting for their answer and their answer was
that they might proceed to take each other in
marriage in Some Convenient time between this
And the next monthly meeting observing good order
Established amongst Friends In the performance thereof
The matter Concerning those that have been out
of order In Propagating Waring and fighting is refered
till the next monthly meeting
And **John Howland** & **Joseph Tucker** are appointed to
See **Samuel Sawdy**s marriage Consummated
We have received the Quarterly meeting ^Epistle which was
read wherein it was desired that we should raise
a Sum on money for the defraying the Charge of
building of **Westerly** and **Taunton** meeting Houses
And whereas there hath been Several Friends children
married of Late out of the order Established among
Friends The matter is refered to the next monthly
Meeting

At a monthly meeting of Friends held at our
meeting House In **Dartmouth** on the 18th of the 12 m
1744 This meeting being Called **Abraham Tucker** present
The friends that were appointed to Enquire Into **John
Wood**s Clearness makes report that they find nothing
to hinder his Intended marriage
And **John Wood** and **Hannah Wing** appeared at this
meeting for their ^answer and their answer was that
they might proceed to take each other in marriage
In Some Convenient time between this and the next
monthly meeting observing the Good order Established
amongst friends In the Performance thereof and
Nathaniel Potter and **Christopher Gifford** are appointed
to See their marriag Consummated and make return
to the next monthly meeting
The making up the monthly meetings accompts
with the Tresurer is refered
A **Joseph Tucker** gives this meeting an account

that he was at **Samuel Sawdy**s marriage and
Saw nothing but that it was orderly accomplished
And **Nicholas Howland** hath sent In a paper
to this meeting Signifying his Sorrow for paying
mony toward the upholding Warring and fighting
which is accepted
And there was a Complaint brought against
Nicholas Lapham to this meeting that he doth refuse
to pay to **Timothy Potter** the mony that the Arbitra
tors awarded him Therefore this meeting appoints
John Russell George Smith and **Jonathan Smith**
to go to sd **Lapham** to know the reasons that he doth
not pay it and make return to the next monthly meeting
And **Brice Shepherd** son of **John Shepherd** hath
requested a Certificate of this meeting to the
monthly meeting at **Swansey** of his clearness
as to marriage and Conversation Therefore
this meeting appoints **Joseph Tucker** and **Henry
Hedly** to to make Enquiry Into the affair to draw
one accordingly
The matter Concerning those that have been
out of order in upholding Warring and Fighting
not being throughly finished is refered
And **Holder Slocum** hath been at this meeting and
made some acknowledgement as to his paying
money to uphold the ~~sevv~~
And whereas **Abigail Kerby** hath not made
Sattisfaction Therefore this meeting appoints
Jonathan Wood to take Some Friend or friends
to go with to advise her and see what she can do
and make return to the next monthly meeting
The Friends appointed to perue the munites have
gone through the greatest part of the business
And **Isaac Smith** is ordered to Record them
And Whereas **John Ricketson** and **Phebe Russell**
and **Joseph Russell ju^r** and **Judith Howland** have
gone out of the order Established amongst Friends
and married In the Common way of other People
Therefore this meeting appoints **John Tucker** and
Isaac Smith to Draw their Condemnations and

bring them to the next monthly meeting

At a monthly meeting held at our meeting House
In **Dartmouth** on the 18 day of the 1ˢᵗ month 1745
Dartmouth meeting Called **John Howland** and
Adam Mott present
The Friends appointed to See **John Wood** and **Hannah
Wing**s marriag accomplished gives this meeting an
account that it was Consummated according
to good order in their Judgment
And we have had the report of the Com.ᵗᵉᵉ that
was appointed to Discource with **Nicholas Lapham**
And it is this meetings Judgment that he the Sd **Lapham**
Should pay the money to **Timothy Potter** according
to the award of the Arbitrators without he can come
In with Sd **Potter** to have another hearing
And there was a Certificate Signed at this meeting
for **Brice Shepherd**
And whereas **James Tripp** is about to remove
to the **Oblong** to Settle desires a Certificate therefore
This meeting appoints **Christopher Gifford** and
Jedidiah Wood to Enquire Into his Sircumstances
and Draw one if they find things Clear and bring
it to the next monthly meeting
And **James Tucker Benjamin Howland** and **Jonathan
Ricketson** have made Some Sattisfaction as to their
being out of order in Propating Waring and fighting
and whereas **Daniel Howland** hath been dealt
with in that affair yet still doth remain obstinate
this meeting thinks best not only for that but
for many other disorders to set him aside and
do deny him to beine in unity with us or under
our care
And **Othniel Tripp** hath been at this meeting and Desire
to be under the Care of Friends and this meeting hath granted
his Request
And there was Collected at this meeting 2ᶜ-14ˢ-00
and this meeting orders the Tresurer to pay to the
overseers 4 pounds five shillings for the last halfe year
keeping the meeting House
The **Coakset** Visitters have given in their accounts

In writing to this meeting The Friends appointed to
Draw up **Joseph Russell ju.**^r and his wives and **John Ricketson**
and his wives Condemnations have done it and it is
refered to the next monthly meeting
And this meeting is adjourned til the first 6 day in next month
This meeting being met according to adjournment this
5th day of the 2^d month 1745 **John Howland Joseph Tucker**
and **Peleg Smith** are appointed to attend the Quarterly
meeting and Draw an Epistle to the Same – –
And **Thomas Smith** and **Isaac Smith** hath made up
the monthly meetings accompts with **aDam Mott** and
there remains in the Stock 3 pounds 14 Shillings
And this meeting hath Chosen **Abraham Tucker**
Tresurer In the room of **Adam Mott**
And as to what was requested in the Quarterly meet
ing Epistle Concerning Raising money to building meeting
Houses we are not in a way now to Comply with

---

15 - 2 ᵐᵒ At a monthly meeting of Friends held at our meeting
1745 House in **Dartmouth** on the 15th day of the 2^d month 1745
This meeting being Called **Stephen Willcock** and **Abraham**
Tucker present We received a Certificate from
the monthly ^meeting at **South Kingston** recommending **John**
Park to our Care which is accepted
The Friends appointed to attend the Quarterly ᵐᵉᵉᵗⁱⁿᵍ have done
it and Drawn an Epistle to the Same
And the Quarterly meeting Epistle hath been read
and agreable to the advice set forth in sd Epistle this
this meeting doth Conclude to Come to a Subscriptin
of 26 pounds for defraying the charge of **Westerly**
and **Taunton** meeting Houses The business refered
from last monthly meeting to this is refered to
the next
And **Timothy Ricketson** hath requested of this
meeting a few lines by Way of Certificate to the
monthly meeting at the **Nine Partners**[13] he being
about to remove there live with his wife and
famly And **Jonathan Wood** and **Ebenezer Slocum**
are appointed to make enquiry into his Sircumstances

13. The Nine Partners land grant was in Dutchess County, New York, adjacent to the Oblong. A meeting house was constructed there in the modern town of Millbrook, New York, during the 1740s.

and Draw one accordingly if they think propper
There was a certificate Signed at this meeting for
James Tripp

3 <u>mo</u>   At a monthly meeting of Friends held at our meeting
1745   House In **Dartmouth** on the 20 day of yᵉ 3ᵈ month 1745
This meeting being Called **John Howland** and **James**
Barker present **Jonathan Smith** makes report
to this meeting that according to the appointment
of the monthly meeting he hath acquainted **Nicholas**
Lapham with the mind of the meeting and he refuses
to take up with the meetings judgment therefore
the matter is refered to the next monthly meeting
and **James Barker** and **Abraham Tucker** to Labour
further with him and let him know that if he
Will not Comply with the meeting judgment must go
forth against him
William Anthony and his Wife Lately removing here
from **Swansey** brought a Certificaate from **Swansey**
monthly meeting of Friends which was read and accepted
too And **Joseph Russell ju.ʳ** and his wives Condemnation
Was read at this meeting and is as followeth
Whereas **Joseph Russell** son of **Joseph Russell** of **Dartmᵐᵒᵗʰ**
and **Mary** his wife and **Judith Howland** now **Russell** daughter
of **Barnabas Howland** and **Rebeckah** his wife of of
Dartmouth aforesd being Educated in the way of
Friends the people Called Quakers their parents
making profession with us the aforesd People
and being nearer in relation one to another than
are allowed to marry amongst us yet they have
kept Company and married out of yᵉ good order
Established amongst us to the grief of the honest hearted
And Contrary to the Wholesom advice and Counsel that
hath from time to time been given them Therefor for
the Clearing of our profession of Such disorders we find it
our Duty to give forth a Testimony against them denying
the sd **Joseph Russell** and **Judith** his wife to be in unity
the People Called Quakers Signed by order and in
behalf of sd meeting by   **John Tucker** Clerk
And **John Ricketson** and his wives Condemnation
was read at this meeting and is as followeth

Whereas **John Ricketson** son of **Jonathn Ricketson**
and **Abigail** his wif of **Dartmouth** in the County of
Bristol in the Province of yᵉ **Massachussets Bay** in **New
England** and **Phebe Russell** now **Ricketson** Daughter of
John Russell and **Rebekah** his wife of **Dartmouth** aforesd
being Eduacated amongst us the People Called Quakers their
Parents being of that denomination yet have let out
their affections so far as to be married in yᵉ Common
Way of other People they being nearer of him than is
allowed to marry amongst us they having been advised
and persuaded in Love to desist for which disorderly
proceedings we can do for the Clearing the Truth
which we profess but give forth a Testimony against
them denying them the sd **John Ricketson** and **Phebe**
his wife to be in unity withus the People Called Quakers
Signed by order and in behalfe of sd meeting by
John Tucker Clerk
And **Timothy Ricketsons** Certific=
ate is refered to next monthly meeting
And **Abraham Tucker** and **Barnabus Howland** are
added to the Com.ᵗᵗᵉ that was appointed to make up
accounts for building And reparin the meeting House
And whereas there hath been many that are
under the care of Friends that have been Lately
impressed to have armes this meeting appoints **Peleg
Smith Abraham Tucker Isaac Howland** and **Jonathan Wood
Christopher Gifford** and **John Mosher** to assist and
advise as the many be occation

At a monthly meeting of friends held at our meeting
House In **Dartmouth** on the 17ᵗʰ Day of the 4ᵗʰ m. 1745
This meeting is adjourned til the 24 day of this instant
This meeting being met according to adjournment
this 24ᵗʰ day of the 4ᵗʰ month 1745 **Eliashib Smith**
present The yearly meeting Epistle from **London**
baring Date 1744 was read in this meeting to good
Sattisfaction; **Beriah Goddard** and **Susanna Sisson**
did lay their Intentions of taking each other In marriage
before this meeting and were desired to wait til the
next meet monthly meeting for their answer and
Joseph Tripp and **Benjamin Shearman** are appointed

to Inspect into Sd **Goddard**s Clearness and make return
to the next monthly meeting
Our Quarterly Collection is refered til next monthly meeting
John Howland Stephen Willcock and **Peleg Smith** are
appointed to attend the Quarterly meeting next and
to Draw an Epistle to yᵉ Same
The Friends appointed to Discource with **Nicholas
Lapham** not having done it are still Continued to do
it as soon as may be And this meeting is adjourned
till the first 6 day in the next month
This meeting being met according to adjournment
this 5 day of yᵉ 5 month 1745
And Whereas **Nicholas Lapham** hath been much
Laboured with in order to reclam him wherein
hath been amiss refering to a cace depending between himselfe and **Timothy Potters** yet doth take
no notice so as to do anything to Friends Sattisfaction
Therefore this meeting appoints **Isaac Smith** ^doing something to Clear
the Truth of Such reproaches and bring it to the next
monthly meeting
And Wheres the meeting hath been at a great
Charge about the addition to the meeting house and
other necessary things We think propper tp apply
our Selves to the Quarterly meeting for Some relief
The Chusing visiters is refered to yᵉ next monthly
meeting
And **Isaac Smith** brings in an account of 5 pounds
and 16 Shillings due to him for Recording the monthly
meeting munites

---

5 ᵐᵒ 1745

At a monthly meeting of friends held at our meeting House
In **Dartmouth** on the 15 day of the 5 month 1745
This meeting being Called **John Russell** and **James Barker**
present. And **Beriah Goddard** and **Susannan Sisson** appeard
at this meeting for their answer and their answer was
that they might proceed to take each other In marriage
In Som Convenient time between this and the next
monthly meeting observing the good order Established
amongst Friends In the performance thereof And **Joseph Tripp**
and **John Mosher** are appointed to See their marriage

Consummated and make return to the next monthly
meeting There was Collected at this meeting – – 3$^£$ - 05^s - 02^d
This meeting orders the Tresurer to pay to the overse
ers 4 pounds and 5 Shillings for halfe a years keeping the
Meeting House **John Howland** and **Stephen Willcock** hath
attended y^e Quarterly meeting and Drawn an Epistle to
the Same as ordered
And the Quarterly meetings Epistle was read at this
meeting and well accepted
And **Isaac Smith** hath received to his Sattisfaction
For recording the munites
And **Adam Gifford** hath Signified to this meeting that
he desires a Certificate of his Clearness as to marriage
and Conversation to the monthly meeting at **RodeIsland**
Therefore this meeting appoints **Eliashib Smith**
and **Adam Mott** to make enquiry and Draw one if they
find things Clear and bring it to the next monthly
meeting There was a paper presented to this meeting
from **Susanna Shearman** wife of **William Shearman**
Signifying her sorrow for her outgoings which
this meeting accepts and **Isaac Smith** is ordered $^{\wedge\text{to read}}$
it at the end of a first day meeting
And whereas **John Lawton** hath as we understand
paid money toward the uphold in the Millitary
This meeting appoints **Jonathan Wood** and **Christopher
Gifford** to Labour with him to a sight
of what he that done amiss. The visitters chose for this
year for **Ponaganset** are **Abraham Tucker**
and **Peleg Smith** and the rest is refered til the
next monthly meeting

At a monthly meeting of Friends held at our meetinghouse
In Dartmouth on the 19 day of 6 month 1745
This meeting being called **John Howland** & **Abraham
Tucker** present The Treasurer 4 ^{L} 6 ^{s} to the over
seers as ordered And **Joseph Tripp** gives this meeting an
account that the marriage of **Beriah Goddard** and **Susanna
Sisson** and that it was accomplished in good order
Philip Allen & **Susanna Allen** Did Lay their Intentions
of marriage before this meeting and were Desired to
wait til ye next monthly meeting for their answer.

And **John Russell** and **Ebenezer Slocum** are appointed
to see into ye young mans Clearness respecting marriage
and conversation and make return to ye next monthly
Meeting. And whereas **Stephen Willcock** and **Peace Wood**
being about to travail into the Western parts upon
the account of ye ministry had each of them Certificates
Signed at the meeting
And there was a Certificate Signed at this meeting
for **Adam Gifford** and Directed to ye monthly meeting at
Rhode Island: And the ‸ former sojourner **Adam Mott** hath paid
3 pound 14 Shillings to our present Treasurer **Abraham
Tucker** being what remained in the Stock when account
was made up with **A Mott**
And this meeting hath received from **South Kingston** Concer
ning **Sarah Park** of her good Conversation whilst she was
there Recommending her to us which is accepted
And whereas **John Lawton** hath not made Satisfaction
to this meeting the matter is referred til the next monthly
meeting. The visitors chose for **Coakset** for this year
are **Jonathan Wood** and **John Mosher** and the chusing visi
tors for **Cushnot** is referred til next monthly meeting
And Whereas there is considerable of mony due upon
account of ye Charge of the meeting House this meeting
agrees to pay use from this day to **John Howland** and he
to Disburse it where it is due

At a monthly meeting of Friends held at our meeting
House in Dartmouth on the 16 day of the 7ᵗʰ month 1745
This meeting being called **John Howland** and **Abraham Tucker**
present. The Friends appointed to enquire into **Philip
Allen**s Clearness make report that they find nothing to
obstruct his proceeding in his intended marriage
And **Philip Allen** and **Susanna Allen** appeared at this meeting
for their answer and their answer was that they might
proceed to take each other in marriage in some convenient
time between this and the next monthly meeting observing
the Good order Established amongst Friends in yᵉ performance
thereof and **John Russell** and **Ebenezer Slocum** are appointed
to see their marriage Solemnized in sᵈ good order and make
return to the next monthly meeting.
And this meeting orders ye Treasurer to pay to **Isaac Smith**

the sum of 4l-08s-1od old tenor being the remainder of
the sum of his demand for recording the monthly
meeting minits

And **Paul Russell** hath sent a paper to this meeting
Signifying his Sorrow for the Disorder that he hath been
in times past Desiring to be under the Care of Friends
Which this meeting accepts & he to be under this meetings
care for the time to come.

And **Benjamin Allen** and **Jacob Taber** are chosen
visitors for **Cushnot** for the ensuing year.

And the meeting concludes to let the matter rest concern
ing **John Lawton**.

And whereas **Adam Mott** paid the mony for **Nicholas
Lapham** to **Timothy Potter** through a mistake which s^d
Lapham refuses to make up to **Mott** which is referred
to next monthly meeting.

And this meeting is adjourned til the first 6th day in next month.

This meeting being met according to adjournment this 4th day
of ye s^d month 1745.

The visitors of **Ponaganset** make report to this meeting
that they have made some progress in visiting Friends famil
ies and in the General things pretty well but in some
places not so well and there they labored for an amend[ment written above]

Thomas Smith Peleg Smith Barnabas Howland and
Joseph Tucker are appointed to attend the Quarterly
Meeting next and Draw an Epistle to the Same.

At a monthly meeting of Friends held at our meeting house
In Dartmouth on the 21st day of ye 8 month 1745
This meeting being called **John Howland** and **James Barker**
present **John Russell** gives this meeting an account that
he was at **Philip Allens** marriage and saw nothing but
that it was consummated in good order

And **Othniel Tripp** and **Abigail Jenkins** Did lay their
Intentions of taking each other in marriage before this
meeting and were Desired to wait till our next month
-ly meeti[ng] for their answer And **Jonathan Wood** and
John Mosher are appointed to see into **Othniel
Tripp**s Clearness and make return to the next month
-ly meeting. And **Lemuel Sisson** and **Deborah Wing**
Did also lay their Intentions of marriage before

this meeting and were Desired to wait till the next
for their answer And **John Howland** and **James Barker**
are appointed to see into the young mans Clearness
respecting marriage and Conversation and make return
to the next monthly meeting
And the Treasurer hath paid 4$^£$-08^s=10^d to **Isaac Smith**
according to the order of y^e last monthly meeting
And this meeting hath had some discource relating
to **Nicholas Lapham**s Case and it is the Judgment of
this meeting tha a Condemnation ought to go forth
against him and **Isaac Smith** is ordered to Draw one
and bring it to the next monthly meeting
The Friends appointed to atte^{n}d the Quarterly meeting
have Done all Excepting **Barnabas Howland** and
Drawn an Epistle to the Same as appointed
And the Quarterly meeting Epistle was read at this
Meeting and Well accepted

At a monthly meeting of Friends held at our meet
ing House in **Dartmouth** on the 18th Day of ye 9th month
1745 This meeting being present **James Barker**
And **Adam Mott** the Friend appointed to Enquire
into **Othniel Tripp** and **Lemuel Sisson**s Clearness
makes report that they find nothing to hinder their
Intended Marriages And **Othniel Tripp** and **Abigail
Jenkins** and **Lemuel Sisson** and **Deborah Wing** Came
to this meeting Desiring their answers and
answer was that they might proceed to marry
In Some Convenient time between this and the next
monthly meeting observing the good order Established
among Friends in the performance thereof And **Jonathan
Wood** and **John Mosher** are appointed to see **Othniel Tripp**
and **Abigail Jenkens** their marriag Consummated
Insd[in said?] good order and **John Howland** and **James Barker**
are appointed [to] See **Lemuel Sisson** and **Deborah Wing**s
marriage Consummated as aboves^d and all to make
return to ye next monthly meeting
And there was a condemnation Signed at this
meeting against **Nicholas Lapham** and **Isaac Smith** is
appointed to read it the End of a meeting on a first
day between this and ye next monthly meeting

And whereas it was proposed at this meeting whither
it might not be propper to settle a meeting at
Adam Motts or thereabouts this winter which hath
been considered and this meeting comes to a conclution
that there should be a meeting Settled there on Every
First Day of yᵉ Week for this winter excepting that first
preceeding the monthly meeting

At a monthly meeting of Friends held at our meet
ing House In **Dartmouth** on the 18ᵗʰ day of yᵉ 10ᵗʰ month 1745
Present **James Barker** and **Abraham Tucker**
Jonathan Wood and **John Mosher** give an account
that **Othniel Tripp** and **Abigail Jenkins** their marriage
Was Consummated In good order
And **John Howland** and **James Barker** gives an account
In the like manner Concerning **Lemuel Sisson** and
Deborah Wings marriage: And **John Howland** ʲⁿʳ and
Deborah Shepherd did lay their intentins of marriage
before this meeting and were desired to wait till
the next monthly meeting for their answer
and **James Barker** and **Abraham Tucker** – –
are appointed to make enquiry Into the young mans
Clearness and make return to the next monthly meet-
ing. **Nicholas Lapham**s Condemnation hath been read
as ordered and Is as followeth
Whereas **Nicholas Lapham** of **Dartmouth** in the County
of **Bristol** In the Province of the **Massachusetts Bay** in
New England being one that hath for many years made
profession with us the People Called Quakers being
accused and Complained of to our monthly meeting by
Timothy Potter of **Dartmouth** aforesd of Fraudelent
Dealing with him the sᵈ **Potter** therefore through Friends
Assistance the matter was Left to an Arbitration Each
party promising to stand too and fulfil the award which
Said **Lapham** Contrary to his Promise Doth refuse or
neglect to Do: Although much Labour hath been
bestowed to perswade to it but all to no purpos
Therefor for the Clear-ⁱⁿᵍ of the blessed truth which we
Profess and that all may know that we have no unity
with such fallacious and Fraudelent Dealing we

can do no less but give forth this as a publick Testimo
ny against it and Do Deny him the s^d **Nicholas Lapham**
to be one in unity with us the afores^d People
Yet truly desiring that he may Come to a sence of
his outgoings and find mercy
Given forth at our monthly meeting held In **Dart
mouth** on the 18th Day of the 9th month 1745
And Signed In and by order of s^d meeting by
                    John Tucker, Clerk
And there was collected at this meeting – – 1_[?]^£–12^s–00^d
And whereas **Abraham Barker** hath Desired a Certi
ficate of this meeting to the monthly meeting of **Rhoad
Island** of his clearness as to marriage and Conversation
therefor **Jabez Barker** and **Henry Hedly [Hedley]** ar[e] appoin
ted to make Enquiry and Draw one if they think fit
and bring it to the next monthly meeting – –
And whereas Friends of **Coakset** have requested of this
meeting that there might be a Preparitive meeting
settled amongst them which this meeting think reasonable
and their request Is granted
The Friends appointed to attend the ~~monthly~~ Quarterly meeting are
Jonathan Wood and **John Mosher** and to draw an
Epistle to the Same: The former overseers for the
Meeting House are continued for one year longer – – – – –

At a monthly meeting of Friends held at our meeting
House In **Dartmouth** on the 20th Day of ye 11th month 1745
James Barker and **Abraham Tucker** present
The Friends appointed to make enquiry into **John Howland**s
Clearness makes report that they find nothing to hinder
his intended marriage
John Howland and **Deborah Shepherd** appeared at this
meeting for their answer and their answer was that
they might proceed to take each other In marriage in
Some convenient time between this and the next month
ly meeting observing the good order Established amongst
Friends In the performance thereof and **James Barker**
and **Abraham Tucker** are appointed to see their
marriage Sollemnized In ye aboves^d order and make
return to the next monthly meeting

And **William Gifford** and **Patience Russell** Did lay
their Intentions of taking each other In marriage
before this meeting and were desired to wait till our
next monthly meeting for their answer and **Jedediah
Wood** and **John Mosher** are appointed [to] enquire Into the
young mans Clearness respecting marriage and Con
versation and make return to the next monthly meeting
And **Natha[n]iel Mosher** and **Ruth Mott** did lay their Inten
tions of marriage before this meeting and were desired
to wait till the next monthly meeting for their answer
And **Eliashib Smith** and **Joseph Tucker** are appointed to
Enquire Into the young mans Clearness and make return
to the next monthly meeting
The Friends appointed to attend the Quarterly meeting have
done it and Drawn an Epistle to the Same as ordered
And the Quarterly meeting Epistle hath been read and
well accepted
We have received an account and also seen the Discharge
from and the hand of the High Sherrif of **Bristol County**
Concerning **Philip Tripp** who hath suffered six months
Imprisonmen[t] for refusing to be concerned in warring
and fighting. There was forty shillings sent in to this
meeting by the women toward keeping the meeting house
And whereas we understand that **John Slocum** hath
been much out of order in keeping company and gaming
and Drinking to the Dishonour of our holy profession
Therefore this meeting appoints **Jabez Barker** and
Stephen Willcock to talk with s^d **Slocum** to see what
he can do for Satisfaction
And there hath been a report Concerning **Timothy
Ricketson** that hath put a bond into an Attorneys
hand in order to give it out when ye s^d bond hath been
already answered Therefor this meeting appoints
Christopher Gifford and **Ebenezer Slocum** to endeavour
to find out the Truth of the matter and let the monthly
meeting know how they find it
And **Increase Allen** hath sent in a paper to this meeting
Signifying his Sorrow for his outgoing in his Disorderly
marriage and Desires to come into unity again which
this meeting accepts and he to be under our Care

And this meeting ‸orders the Treasurer to pay to the overseers the Sum of 4£–05s–00d old Tenor for halfe a years keeping the meeting House

---

[page is blank]

At a monthly meeting of Friends held at our meeting House in **Dartmouth** on the 18th day of the 1 month 1745/46 **Adam Mott** and **Abraham Tucker** present for **Ponaganset** and **Jonathan Wood** & **Benjamin Shearman** for **Coakset**
There was collected at this meeting for ye use of Friends 2£–00s–0d and **Abram Tucker** hath paid the 4£–5s–0d as ordered
And **Jedidiah Wood** gives this meeting an account that the marriage of **William Gifford** and **Patience Russell** was con summated in good order
And whereas we have received no Sattisfaction from ~~This~~ **John Slocum** this meeting appoints **Ebenezer Slocum** to let him know that if he doth not do something to Friends Sattisfaction we must proceed to set him aside and he to make return to ye next monthly meeting
The Friends appointed to Discource with **John Chase** have done and the matter is refered to the next monthly meeting. And Whereas this meeting hath considered the ~~S~~Circumstance of **Abigail Kerby** [**Kirby**] and it is the mind of this meeting that she ought to condemn her appearing in publick before she had made acknowledgment for her outgoings and also to be silent in that respect till Friend are further Sattisfied and **Benjamin Shearman** Is ordered to let her know the mind of this meeting
And Whereas **John Lawton**s two Daughters have both gone out of our good order and married in the Common Way of other People Therefore this meeting orders **Isaac Smith** to Draw both their Condemnations and bring them to the next monthly meeting
and the visiters of **Coakset** have given in their account In writing to this meeting
And this meeting is adjourned til the first 6 day in ye 2d mo.
This meeting being met according to adjournment this 4 day of ye 2d month 1746: **Eliashib Smith** and **Joseph Tucker** gives this meeting an account that ~~the~~ **Nathanael Mosher** and **Ruth Mott**s marriage was consummated

In good order. The visiters of **Ponaganset vilage** gives
this meeting an account that they have made some
Progress in visiting Friends famlyes and that where they have
been they find things for the most part pretty well and where
things were amiss they laboured that there might be an amend
ment: **Josiah Akin** and **Judith Huddlestone** did lay their Inten
tions of marriage before this meeting and were desired to wait
until next monthly meeting for their answer and **Jabez**
Barker and **John Russell** are appointed to make Enquiry
In to the young mans Clearness and make return to the
next monthly meeting
And whereas our yearly meetings are generally very
large and full it is thought Propper that the meeting
that doth use to be held at **Coakset** on the fifth day of the
week be omitted and that the yearly meeting be held at
Coakset the three following Days as well as at **Ponaganset**
James Barker[,] **John Howland** and **Abraham Tucker** are
appointed to attend the Quarterly meeting and Draw an
Epistle to the Same

At a monthly meeting of Friends held at our meeting
House In **Dartmouth** on the 21 day of the 2ᵈ month 1746
John Howland and **James Barker** present for **Ponaganset**
for **Coakset**] **Benjamin Shearman** present
The Friends appointed to Enquire into **Josiah Akin**s
Clearness make report that they find nothing to hinder
his Intended marriage And the Friends appointed to see into
Meribeh Slocums sircumstances gives account that
affairs are settled to Sattisfaction
And **John Wanton** and **Meribeh Slocum** appeared at
this meeting for their answer and their answer was
that they might proceed to take each other In marriage
observing the good order Established amongst Friends in the
accomplishing thereof and **Jabez Barker** and **Joseph**
Tucker are appointed to see their marriage Sollemnized
In the abovesᵈ order and make return to yᵉ monthly
meeting next
And **Josiah Akin** and **Judith Huddlestone** apeared at this
meeting for their answer and their answer was that
they might proceed to take each other in marriage in
Some Convenient time between this and the next

monthly meeting observing the good od [order] Established
among Friends in the consummating thereof and
Jabez Barker and **John Russell** are appointed to
see their marriage Sollemnized and make return
to the next monthly meeting
And **Isaac Gifford** and **Mary Cornell** Did lay their In
tentions of taking each other in marriage before
this meeting and weve desired to wait till the next
monthly meeting for their answer And **Joseph Mosher**
and **William Sanford** are appointed to make Enqui
ry into **Isaac Giffords** Clearness and make return
to the next monthly meeting
And the matter concerning **John Slocum** is sus
pended and **John Russell** and **Holder Slocum** are
appointed to advise further with him to see if
they can bring him to Condemn his bad practices
and make return to the next monthly meeting
The Friends appointed [to] attend the Quarterly meeting
have done it and Drawn an Epistle to the Same
And the Quarterly meeting Epistle was read at
the meeting and well accepted.
And whereas there was a report brought to
this meeting that **William Wood** the son of **Willam Wood**
had spread a scandalous report of **Stephen Willcock**
Therefore this meeting appoints **Joseph Tucker**
and **Henry Hedly**[**Hedley**] & **Isaac Smith** to make enquiry in
to the matter and make return to ye next monthly meeting

At a monthly meeting of Friends held at
our meeting House In Dartmouth on the 19th Day of
the 3d month 1746 **Ponaganset** meeting called **John
Howland** present **Coakset** meeting Called **Christo
pher Gifford** and **James Cornell** present
John Russell and **Jabez Barker** gives this meeting an
account that **Josiah Akin** and **Judith Huddlestone**s mar
riage was orderly consummated. The Friends appointed
to enquire into **Isaac Giffords** clearness gives account
that they find nothing to hinder his Intended marriage
And **Isaac Gifford** and **Mary Cornell** appeared at this
meeting for their answer and their answer was
that they might proceed to take each other in mar

riage In Some Convenient time between this and
the next monthly meeting observing the good or
der Established amongst Friends in the performance
thereof and **Joseph Mosher** & **William Sanford** are
appointed to see their marriage Consummated in the
above to order and make return to ye next monthly meeting
And **Joseph Tucker** gives this meeting an account that
Joseph Wanton and **Meribeth Slocum**s marriage was
Consummated In good order and the matter concer
ning **John Slocum** is referred till the next monthly meeting
And **Rebeckah Lawton** now wife of **David Milk**
her Condenation was read at this meeting and
~~Signed and John Mosher~~ Is as followeth
Whereas **Rebekah Lawton** daughter of **John Lawton**
of **Dartmouth** In the County of Bristol In the Province of
the Massachusetts Bay In New England being one that
has been Educated amongst us the People Called Quakers
yet for want of keeping to her Education hath gone
into a liberty so as to keep company and marry with
a man that is not of our Communion out of the good
order Established among friends and contrary to the
advice of her Father and Friends Therefore for the
leaving of the blessed Truth of such obstinate
and Disorderly proceedings we can do no less than to
give this forth as a condemnation against her
Denying her s^d **Rebekah** now the wife of **David**
Milk to be one in unity with us the above People
yet sincerely desiring that she may come to a sence of
her outgoing and find mercy
Given forth at our monthly meeting held at Dartmouth
on the 19th day of 3 month 1746 and signed in and by order
of sd meeting by – – – – – **John Tucker** Clerk
And **Mary Lawton** now wife of **Jonathan Davol** her
condemnation was brought to this meeting and appro
ved and **John Mosher** is appointed to read it or see that
it is done between this and the next monthly meeting
And the matter between **William Wood** and **Stephen Willcock**
is made up and the matter between **William Wood** and **Adam**
Mott is referred til next monthly meeting
And whereas **Christopher Gifford** and **Ebenezer Slocum**

were chose to make Enquiry into a skandalous report
of **Timothy Ricketson Thomas Smith** and **George Smith**
are appointed [illegible] sd **Slocum** a comm^tte to Enquire further
and give in their Judgement in the matter
And whereas **Sarah Park** being gone to **Westerly** to
live desires a Certificate of this meeting This meeting
appoints **Isaac Smith** to Draw one and bring it the
the next monthly meeting

At a monthly meeting of Friends held at our meet
ing House In Dartmouth on the 16th day of ye 4 month 1746
Tho. Smith and **James Shearman** present and this
meeting is adjourned until the 23 of the 4 month 1746
This meeting being met according to adjournment
this 28 of the 4 month 1746
And **John Mosher** signifies to this meeting that **Mary
Davel[Davol]** Condemnation hath been read as ordered
And **William Sanford** gives this meeting an account that
Issac Giffords marriage was consummated in good order
And as to the matter between **Adam Mott** and **William
Wood** it is by the Parties agreed and approved by this
meeting that **Jabez Barker Peleg Smith** and **Ebenezer
Slocum** be a com^tee to hear and Determine the matter
the matter concerning **Timothy Ricketson** is referred
and the com^tte to make further inspection into ye matter
And this meeting hath received a certificate from
the monthly meeting at **Portsmouth** on **Rhode Island**
concerning **Ann Gifford** wife of **Adam Gifford** recom
mending her to our care which we accept with
Satisfaction: And **Edward Cornell** hath signified
his desire of coming under the care of friends
Which this meeting accepts and he to be under our care
Collected at this meeting 1–17–00
And this meeting orders the Treasurer to pay to ye overseers
a pound ten shillings for ye last halfe year keeping ye meeting house
And whereas we cannot find that **John Slocum** is
any ways reformed in his life and conversation this
meeting appoints **Isaac Smith** to Draw up his condemnati
on and bring it to the next monthly meeting And as
to the request of the Quarterly meeting towards our

coming to subscription for building **Swansey** meeting
House we donot find that we are in a way to do any
thing at present
And the yearly meeting Epistle from **London** was read to good
Satisfaction And **Thomas Smith Stephen Willcock** and
Peleg Smith are appointed to attend the Quarterly
meeting and Draw and Epistle to the same

At a monthly meeting of Friends held at our meeting
House in Dartmouth on the 21 of the 5 month 1746
Ponaganset meeting called **James Barker** and **John
Howland** present **Coakset** meeting called **Joseph Tripp**
and **Jonathan Wood** present
The matter concerning **Timothy Ricketson** is referred
to ye next monthly meeting And yᵉ Treasurer hath
paid the 4 pounds ten shillings as ordered
Thomas Smith and **Stephen Willcock** give an account
that they have attended the Quarterly meeting and
Drawn an Epistle to ye same as appointed
We received an Epistle from the Quarterly meeting
Which was read and well accepted
The matter Concerning **Adam Mott** and **William Wood**
is referred til next monthly meeting
And **Isaac Smith** hath Drawn **John Slocum**s condem
nation as appointed which is signed and **Jabez Barker**
is ordered to read it on a first day after meeting
and **Lemuel Sisson** and his wife hath sent in a paper
concerning their outgoing and **Benjamin Shearman**
is to see that it revised publickly after a first day meet
ing and **Eleazer Smith** hath sent in a paper to this
meeting condemning his going to tra[in]i[n]g which is accep
ted and this meeting approves of a meeting of Friends
to be held at **Josiah Merihews** for 4 months from this
time on the first day of the week
And **Jonathan Wood** hath Signified to this meeting that
hath a Concern to Travil as far as **Long Island** In the
Service of Truth and Desires a Certificate therefore
Christopher Gifford John Mosher and **Isaac Smith** are
are appointed to See Into his Sircumstances and Draw
one if they find things Clear things Clear and bring it to
the next monthly meeting

And the Chusing of visiters is refered to the next
monthly meeting

At a monthly meeting of Friends held at our meeting
House in **Dartmouth** on the 18 Day of yᵉ 6 month 1746
Ponaganset meeting Called **John Howland** and **Abraham
Tucker** present for **Coakset Jedidiah Wood** and
Benjamin Shearman The matter Concerning **Timothy
Ricketson** is refered to next monthlymeeting
And **Jabez Barker** hath read **John Slocum**s Con
demnation according to order and is as followeth
Whereas **John Slocum** the son of **Eleazer Slocum**
late of **Dartmouth** in the **County of Bristol** in the
Province of yᵉ **Massachusets Bay** in **New England** being
one that was Educated amongst the People Called Quakers
But for want of keeping to his Education and the
Spirit of Truth In his own Concience hath gone
into many things which are Contrary to our holy pro
fession in keeping Company and Drinking Strong drink to
Excess and gaming and Such like evil Practices and though
he hath been much Laboured with in order for a refor
mation yet nothing doth seem to work any Effect
upon him but he Still Doth persist in the abovsᵈ prac
:tices therefore for the Clearing of our holy profession
from Such Enormities we can do no less but give
forth this as a Publick Testimony against it Denying
him the Sᵈ **John Slocum** to be one in unity with us
the aboveSᵈ People yet truly Desiring that he may
Come to unfeigned repentance of all his out goings
Given forth at our monthly meeting held In **Dartmouth**
on the 21 day of the 5 month 1746 And Signed by order
of Sᵈ meeting by   **John Tucker** Clerk
And **Lemuel Sisson** and his wives Paper Condemning
their outgoings hath been read according to order and
Is as followeth
To the Monthly meeting of Friends to be held In **Dartmouth**
on the 21ˢᵗ of yᵉ 5ᵗʰ month 1746. Loving Friends Whereas
we have to our own Shame brought Dishonour
upon Friends and that holy Profession which we
Profess by having a Child born too soon after mar
riage for which we are Sorry and Desire Friends

Would pass by our outgoings: **Lemuel Sisson Deborah Sisson**
And **Nahanael Howland** the Son of **John Howland**
And **Joanna Howland** Widow of **William Howland**
And Daughter of **William Ricketson** Did lay their
Intentions of taking each other in marriage
before this meeting and were Desired to wait
until our next monthly meeting for their
answer and **Abraham Tucker** and **James Barker**
are appointed to Enquire into the young mans
Clearness and make return to the next monthly
meeting: And **Elisha Coggeshal** of **Newport** and
Elisabeth Russell Daughter of **Benjamin Russell**
Did lay their Intentions of marriage before this
meeting and were Desired to wait til the next
monthly meeting for their answer
The Friends appointed to make up the matter
between **William Wood** and **Adam Mott** have
done it and **William Wood** hath Sent in a Paper
Condemning his Spreading Some Skandalous
Reports of **Adam Mott**

7-1746   At a monthly meeting of Friends held at our meeting
House in **Dartmouth** on the 15th Day of the 7th mo: 1746
Ponaganset meeting Called **James Barker** and **Abraham
Tucker** present: for **Coakset Christopher Gifford** and
Othniel Tripp: The Friends appointed to see into
Nathaniel Howlands Clearness makes report that they
find nothing to hinder his proceeding In his intended
marriage: And **Nathanael Howland** and **Joanna
Howland** appeared at this meeting for their an
swer as did **Elisha Coggeshal** and **Elisabeth Russell**
And they had their answer that they might proceed
to marry observing the Good order Established among
Friends in the accomplishing thereof In Some Conve-
-nient time between this and the next monthly
meeting And **James Barker** and **Abraham** are
appointed to See **Nathanael Howland**s marriage
Orderly accomplished and **Stephen Willcock** and
Isaac Howland are Chose upon the like account
for **Elisha Coggeshal**
And **John Lawton** and and **Rebekah Allen** Did lay

Lay their Intentions of taking each other In mar
riage before this meeting and were desired to wait
til the next monthly meeting for their answer
And **Christopher Gifford** and **John Mosher** are
appointed to Enquire into **John Lawtons** Clear
-ness and make return to the next monthly
meeting The visiters Chose for this year for **Pona**
ganset are **Abraham Tucker James Barker**
Stephen Willcock and and **Peleg Smith** and for
Coakset Jonathan Wood and **John Mosher** and
for **Cushnot Jacob Taber** and **Benjamin Allen**
And we understand that **William Macumber Ju**ͬ
hath a Desire to Come under the Care of Friends
Therefore this meeting **Othnil Tripp** and
John Cornell to make Enquiry Into his Sircumstances
Whither it is as becomes the Truth and make return
to the next monthly meeting. And visiters of **Coakset**
Have given in their account in Writing of their
Service in visiting Friends famlies
The Friends appointed to attend the ~~monthly m~~
Quarterly meeting are **Stephen Willcock James**
Barker Joseph Tucker and **John Mosher** And to
Draw an Epistle to the Same And this meeting hath
agreed to come to a Subscription for **Swansey** meeting
House the Collection in refere to next monthly meeting

At a monthly meeting of Friends held at our meeting
House In **Dartmouth** on the 20th Day of the 8th month 1746
Ponaganset meeting Called **James Barker** and
Abraham Tucker present for **Coakset Christopher Gifford**
And **John Cornell** present The Friends appointed to
See Into **John Lawtons** Clearness gives this meeting an
account that they find nothing to hinder his intended
Marriage with **Rebekah Allen**
And **John Lawton** appeared at this meeting for
their answer and their answer was that they might
proceed to take each other in marriage in Some
Convenient Time between this and the next monthly
Meeting Observing the good order Established among
Friends In the accomplishment thereof and **Christopher**
Gifford and **Joseph Russell** are appointed to See that

the matter is accomplished in the order abovesᵈ and
make return to the next monthly meeting and
James Barker and **Abraham Tucker** gives this meeting
an account that **Nathanael Howland**s marriage was
Sollemnized orderly
And **Isaac Howland** and **Stephen Willcock** gives this meet
in an account that **Elisha Coggeshal** and **Elisabeth
Russell**s marriage was orderly Consummated
The Friends appointed to enquire into **William Macum
-ber**s Sircumstances makes report that they find nothing
but that he is of an orderly Conversation therefore
this meeting Doth Conclude that both he and his wife
be under the Care of this meeting for the time to Come
The Friends appointed to attend the Quarterly meet
ing have all Excepting **Stephen Willcock** and the
Epistle was Drawn and Carried
The Collection for **Swansy** meeting House is refered
to next monthly meeting And whereas there hath
been a report brought in to this meeting that
William Wood Son of **William Wood** hath been
very unjust in relation to a Piece of Gold that
received of a Friend In **Pensilvania** in order to
be Delivered to **Nathanael Starbuck** of **Nantucket**
Therefore this meeting appoints **John Howland**
Joseph Tucker and **Barnabus Howland** to en
-quire into the matter and talk with Sᵈ **Wood**
to See what they can bring him to do

9/1746　At a monthly meeting of Friends held at our
meeting House in **Dartmouth** on the 17 day of the 9ᵗʰ
month 1746 **Ponaganset** meeting Called **James
Barker** and **Abraham Tucker** present for
Coakset Benjamin Shearman and **John Mosher**
Joseph Russell gives this meeting an account
that **John Lawton** and **Rebekah Allen**s marriage
Was Consummated orderly
And **William Barker** and **Hannah Wood** Did
lay their intentions of taking each other in
marriage before this meeting and were desired
to wait til the next monthly meeting for their

answer and **John Howland** and **Stephen Willcock**
are appointed to See into the young mans Clear
ness and make return to the next monthly
meeting and as there hath been nothing done
relating to **William Wood**s cace it is refered
to the next monthly meeting
And **Abraham Tucker** is appointed With **John Howland**
and **Joseph Tucker** in that Service in the room of **Barna**
-bus Howland. And this meeting hath allowed that there
be a meeting kept at **Josiah Merihew**s for the Six Insuing
months. **Jonathan Wood** being returned from his
Journy in the Service of Truth hath brought Certifi
cates with him one from **Long Island** and another
from the **Oblong** to good Sattisfaction

At a monthly meeting of Friends held at our meet
ing House In **Dartmouth** on the 15 day of the 10ᵐ 1746
Ponaganset meeting Called **John Howland** and **Abra**
-ham Tucker present for **Coakset Jonathan Wood**
and **John Mosher** present The Friends appointed to
Enquire Into **William Barker**s Clearness gives
this meeting an account that find nothing to
hinder his proceedings in his intended marriage
William Barker and **Hannah Wood** appeared
at this meeting for their answer and their answer was that they might proceed to take each
other in marriage in Some Convenient time
between this and the next monthly meeting obser
ving the good order Established amongst Friends
In the performance thereof and ~~Benjamin Wing~~ **Christopher Gifford**
and ~~Peleg Huddlestone~~ **Nathaniel Potter**s are appointed to see their
marriage Consummated and make return to the
next monthly meeting
And **Jonathan Sisson** juʳ: and **Hannah Howland**
Did lay their intentions of taking each other in
marriage before this meeting and were Desired
to wait til the next monthly meeting for their
Answer and **Benjamin Wing** and **Peleg Huddlestone**
are appointed to See into the young mans Clear
-ness and make return to the next monthly meeting

And **Joseph Earl** Son of **John Earle** of **Swansey** and
Eunice Hathaway Daughter of **Richard Hathaway** did
Lay their intention of marriage before this meeting
And were Desired to wait til the next monthly meet
ing for their answer
And we understand that **William Wood** hath given
The Com.^{tte} encouragement that he will make
Sattisfaction to the Friend In Pensilvanis
There was Collected at this meetin for the use friends
of Forty Shillings which with forty Shillings that
the women brought in makes 4 pounds
Joseph Tucker and **Nathaniel Potter** are appointed
to attend the Quarterly meeting and Draw an Epistle
to the Same. And this meeting orders the Tresurer
to pay to the overseers the Sum of 4-10-0 for the
Last halfe years keeping the meeting House

11 At a monthly meeting of Friends held at our
1746 meeting House in **Dartmouth** on the 19th day of the
11 month 1740 **Ponaganset** meeting Called **James**
Barker and **Peleg Smith** present for **Coakset**
Christopher Gifford and **Jonathan Wood** present
Benjamin Wing and **Peleg Huddlestone** gives this
meeting an account that they find nothing to
hinder **Jonathan Sisson**s intended marriage
Jonathan Sisson and **Hannah Howland** Did ~~lay~~
~~their Inte~~ appear at this meeting for their
answer and their answer was that they might
proceed to take each other in marriage in Some
Convenient time between this and the next
monthly meeting observing the good order of
Friends in the accomplishment thereof and
Peleg Huddlestone and **Benjamin Wing** are appoin
-ted to see the marriage Consummated in the aboves^d
order and make return to the next
monthly meeting
And **Joseph Earle** and **Eunice Hathaway** had their answer in
like manner and **John Howland** and **Henry Hedly** are appoin
-ted to see their marriage Consummated in good order and
make return to the next monthly meeting
And **Adam Mott** and **Joseph Tucker** have attended the

Quarterly meeting and and Drawn an Epistle to the
Same as appointed And the Quarterly meeting Epistle
hath been read and well accepted
Thomas Smith and **Stephen Willcock** and **James Barker**
are appointed to make up the monthly meetings accounts
With the Tresurer The Friends appointed to See **William
Barker**s marriage Consummated Signify that it was
performed in good order

12

1746/7

At a monthly meeting of Friends held at our meeting
House in **Dartmouth** on the 16ᵗʰ day of the 12 month 1746/7
Ponaganset meeting Called **James Barker** and **Abraham
Tucker** present for **Coakset Edward Cornell** present
The Friends appointed to See **Jonathan Sisson** and **Hannah
Howland** And **Joseph Earle** and **Eunice Hathaway**s marriages
Consummated Signify that they was orderly accomplished
And **Richard Gifford** and **Elisabeth Cornell** Did Lay their
Intentions of taking each other in marriage before this
meeting as did also **Joshua Lapham** and **Hannah Shearman**
and were Desired to wait til the next monthly meeting
for their answers. And **Nathaniel Potter** and **Edward Cornell**
And **John Russell** and **Peleg Smith** are appointed to Enquire
Concerning the young mens clearness and make return
to the next monthly meeting
The Friends appointed to make up accompts with the
Tresurer not having done it it is refered to the next
monthly meeting

At a monthly meeting of Friends held at our meeting
House In **Dartmouth** on the 16ᵗʰ day of the first month 1746/7
Ponaganset meeting Called **John Howland** and **James
Barker** prent for **Coakset Jonathan Wood** and **Benja Shearman**
And Whereas we have had no account of the marriage
of **Jonathan Sisson** and **Hannah Howland** it is refered
to next monthly meeting[14]
And **Richard Gifford** and **Elisabeth Cornell** and **Joshua
Lapham** and **Hannah Shearman** appeared at this meet
-ing for their answers And their answer was that they
might proceed to marry in Some Convenient time be
tween this and the next monthly meeting observing

14. In the manuscript, an X is placed over the last three lines.

our good order in the Consummation thereof and
Nathanael Potter and **Edward Cornell** and **John Russell**
and **Peleg Smith** are appointed to See their marriages
Sollemnized and make return to the next monthly
meeting And the matter Concerning a Settlement with
the Tresurer not being finnished it is Refered until
next monthly meeting
There was Collected at this meeting for ye use of friends 2-08-00
And whereas there hath been a Scandalous report of
Timothy Ricketson which he hath never Cleared him
selfe of tho often requested by Friends to Do it therefore
for the Clearing the Truth which we Profess it is the
mind of this meeting that a Condemnation Should go
forth against him and this meeting appoints
Isaac Smith and **Thomas Smith** to draw it up and bring
It to the next monthly meeting And also to Draw up
another against **Joseph Havens**
And this meeting appoints **James Barker** and **Joseph
Tucker** with **John Russell** to be overseers of the bury
-ing Ground. And **Joseph Tripp Jonathan Wood** and
Christopher Gifford to be overseers of ye burying Grounds
at **Coakset** and for **Cushnot Benjamin Allen Joseph
Russell** and **Jacob Taber**
It was Discoused at this meeting whether it might
not be propper that there be another Day added to
our yearly meeting for the ministers and Elders to
meet together both for **Ponaganset** and **Coakset** which
is refered to the Consideration of ye monthly meeting
next. The Friends appointed to attend the Quarterly
meeting are **James Barker Adam Mott Joseph Tucker**
and **Peleg Smith.** And whereas **Benjamin Ricketson**
hath gone out of the way and married out of our
good order therefore this meeting appoints **John Russell**
and **Ebenezer Slocum** to talk with him to see whither
he Can Do any thing to make Sattisfaction

2   At a monthly meeting held at our meeting House In **Dartmouth**
1747   on the 20th Day of the 2 month 1747 **Ponaganset** meeting Called
John Howland present for **Coakset Christopher Gifford** and
Edward Cornell. James Tucker and **Ruth Tucker** and **Job Anthony**
and **Sarah Wing** And **John Walker** and **Margrate Mosher** Did

all Lay their Intentions of marriage before this meeting and
Were Desired to wait till the next monthly meeting for
answers. And **Josiah Merihew** and **Adam Mott** are appointed
to Enquire into **James Tucker** and **John Walker**s Clearness
respecting marriage and Conversation and make return to
The next monthly meeting and **John Russell** and **Peleg Hud
-dlestone** are appointed to Enquire Concerning **Job Anthony**s
Clearness and make return accordingly

And **Benjamin Wing** and **Peleg Huddlestone** have given
this meeting an account that that **Jonathan Sisson** and
Hannah Howlands marriage was Consummated In Good
order And **John Russell** and **Peleg Smith** gives the like account
Concerning **Joshua Lapham** and **Hannah Shearman**s marriage
the matter about making up with the tresurer is Still Continued
There was a Condemnation signed at this meeting against
Joseph Havens and it is ordered that **Isaac Smith** should read
It at the end of a first Day meeting between this and the
next monthly meeting

The Friends appointed to attend the Quarterly meeting
have all attended Except **Joseph Tucker** and Drawn an
to it as appointed. And the Quarterly meeting Epistle was
read at this meeting and Well accepted

There was also Condemnation Signed at this meeting
against **Timothy Ricketson** and **Isaac Smith** is ordered it at
the End of a first Day meeting And whereas **Thomas Hathaway**
hath Sent In a paper to this meeting Desiring to Come under
the Care of Friends This meeting appoints **John Howland**
and **Stephen Willcock** to go to Sᵈ **Hathaway** to See what Sence
they Can have of his Condition

And Whereas **Peace Wood** hath been in this our meeting
And uttered things which which we can no ways Joyn With
Therefore this meeting appoints **James Barke Peleg Smith**
John Howland Joseph Tucker ~~Jos~~ **Abraham Tucker** and **Isaac
Howland** and **Ebenezer Slocum** to talk with her and
bring their report to the next monthly meeting

At a monthly meeting of Friends held at our meeting
House In **Dartmouth** on the 18 day of yᵉ 3 month 1747
Ponaganset meeting Called **John Howland** and **Abraham
Tucker** present for **Coakset Robert Mosher** and **James
Cornell** present the Friends appointed to See Into **John**

Walkers and **James Tuckers** Clearness gives this meeting an account that
they find nothing to hinder their Intened marriages
And the friends appointed to See into **Job Anthonys**
Clearness Signify they find nothing to hinder his Intended
marriage. **James Tucker** and **Ruth Tucker Job Anthony**
and **Sarah Wing John Walker** and **Margrate Mosher**
appeared at this meeting for their Answer and their
answer was that they might proceed to marry In
Some Convenient time between this and the next
monthly meeting observing our good order in the
accomplishment thereof and **Josiah Merihew** and **Adam
Mott** are appointed to Se **John Walkers** marriage Solem
-nized in s^d order and make return to the next monthly
meeting And **James Barker** and **John Howland** are
appointed to See **James Tucker** marriage Sollemnized
In like manner and **John Russell** and **Peleg Huddlestone**
are appointed to See **Job Anthonys** marriage Consumma
-ted as abovesd and make return to the monthly meet
-ing next. The friends appointed to make up accompts
With the Tresurer have done it and there remains in
the Stock 4 pounds thirteen Shillings old tenor 4-13-0
And **Isaac Smith** hath read **Joseph Havens** and **Timothy
Ricketson**s Condemnations which is as followeth
Whereas **Joseph Havens** of **Dartmouth** in the **County of
Bristol** in the **Province of the Massachusets Bay** In **New
England** being one under the Care of Friends the people
Called Quakers yet for want of keeping to the Spirit of
Truth hath given Way to his own lustful inclinations
So far as to be guilty of the Sin of Fornication as appears
by an Indian Woman that was Delivered of a bastard
Child in the house where he resided and laying it to
him and he no ways clearing him selfe from s^d Scan
dal but immediately absconded So that Friends had
not oppertunity to Deal with him Nevertheless for the
Clearing the blessed Truth and that all may know that we
have no fellowship With Such Wicked and Detestable Practices
We can do no less but give this forth as a publick Testimony
Against it Denying him the S^d **Joseph Havens** to be one in unity
With us the abovesd People yet truly Desiring that if it be
the Will of God he may come to a Sight and Sence of this

his great evil and all other his outgoings and by unfeigned
repentance find mercy With the Lord
Given forth at our monthly meeting held In **Dartmouth**
on the 20ᵗʰ Day of the 2ᵈ month 1747 and Signed In and by order
of Sᵈ meeting by   **John Tucker** Clerk
Whereas **Timothy Ricketson** son of **Jonathan Ricketson**
of **Dartmouth** in the **County of Bristol** In yᵉ **Province of the
Massachusets Bay** In **New England** being one that was
under the Care of Friends yet as we apprehend through
a worldly and covetous Disposition he hath fallen
under a Scandalous report of Endeavouring to recover
mony that was Due upon a bond which was before
answered and although Friend have taken great pains
to git the matter Cleared up he Denying the fact yet
doth nothing to Clear him selfe any ways Sattisfactory as
he hath often promised and Friends have sent to him and
wated a long tim till we see no likelyhood that ever will
do anything to Clear the Truth of sᵈ reproach We therefore can do no less for the Clearing the Same from Such
and such like fallacious Practice but give forth a publick
Testimony against it Denying him the Sᵈ **Timothy Ricketson**
to be one in unty with us the People Called Quakers yet
Sincerely Desiring that he may Come to a sight of his
out goings and find mercy Given forth at our monthly
meeting held In **Dartmouth** on the 20ᵗʰ Day of the 2ᵈ month
1747 And Signed In and by ord of sᵈ meeting by
                              John Tucker Clerk
The matter Concerning **Benjamin Ricketson** is refered
to next monthly meeting
The Friends appointed to talk with **Thomas Hathaway**
have brought in their report and also another paper
Signed by Sᵈ **Hathaway** which this meeting accepts and
be to be under our Care and **Jacob Taber** is appointed
read sᵈ Paper on a first Day at the end of the meeting for
worship at **Cushnot** meeting House
And this meeting hath Condecended that there should
be a meeting held at **Josiah Merihew**s or thereabouts
As In time past for the Six ensuing months
The Friends appointed to Discource with **Peace Wood**
have Done it but can have no Sattisfaction therefore

they are Still Continued to Labour further With her
and make return to the next monthly meeting

At a monthly meeting of Friends held at our meeting
House In **Dartmouth** on the 15 day of yᵉ 4 month 1747
Ponaganset meeting Called **Abraham Tucker** present
for **Coakset John Cornell** and **Benjamin Shearman**
The Friends appointed to Se the orderly accomplishing
of **Job Anthony**s and **John Walker**s marriages gives
an account that they were orderly Consummated
And the matter Concerning **Benjamin Ricketson**
is refer,ᵈ to next monthly meeting
And this meeting appoints **Adam Mott Thomas Smith**
And **Joseph Russell** to attend the Quarterly meeting
And Draw an Epistle to the Same and this meeting
is adjourned till next for this Day week
At a monthly meeting held by adjournment on the
22ᵈ Day of the 4 month1747 **John Howland** and **James
Barker** gives this meeting an account that **James
Tucker** and **Ruth Tucker**s marriage was Consuma
-ted in order and **Jacob Taber** gives an account
that he hath read **Thomas Hathaway**s acknowledg
-ment as ordered
And this matter Concerning **Peace Wood** is refered until the
next monthly meeting The certificates of our travaling
Friends **John Griffith** and **David Farris** was read to good
Sattisfaction

At a monthly meeting of Friends held at our meeting
House In **Dartmouth** on the 20 day of the 5 month 1747
Ponaganset meeting Called **James Barker** and **Abraham
Tucker** present for **Coakset Christopher Gifford** present
The matter Concerning **Peace Wood** is refered to the
next monthly meeting And the matter Concerning
Benjamin Ricketson is refered til next monthly meeting
The Friends appointed to attend the Quarterly meeting
have Done it and Drawn an Epistle to it as appointed
And the Quarterly meetings Epistle hath been read
and well accepted. And **Adam Mot Abraham Tucker
Peleg Huddlestone** and **Peleg Smith** are Chosen visitters
for the year Ensuing for **Ponaganset** for **Cushnot**
Jacob Taber and **Benjamin Allen** and the Chusing vi

-sitters for **Coakset** is refer to next monthly meeting
And this meeting orders the tresurer to pay to the over
-seers the sum of 4-10-0 old tenor for the last halfe
years keeping the meeting House
There was Collected at this meeting 1ᵖ-18ˢ-04ᵈ old tenor

At a monthly meeting of Friends held at our meet
-ing house in **Dartmouth** on the 17ᵗʰ Day of the 6 mᵒ: 1747
Ponaganset meeting Called present **James Barker**
and **John Howland:** and **Othniel Tripp** and **Benjamin
Shearman** for **Coakset** The matter Concerning **Peace
Wood** is refered to next monthly meeting
And whereas **Benjamin Ricketson** hath done nothing
to Friends Sattisfaction
Therefore this meeting orders **Isaac Smith** to Draw
up a Condenation against him and bring it to the next
Monthly meeting And the Tresurer hath paid to the
Overseers 4ˡ-10ˢ-0ᵈ as ordered the visiters chose for
Coakset for this year are **Jonathan Wood Othniel
Tripp** and **Benjamin Shearman**
Collected at this meeting for yᵉ use of Friends 1-00-06

At a monthly meeting of Friends held at our meeting
House In **Dartmouth** on the 21 day of the 7 month 1747
Ponaganset meeting Called **John Howland** & **James
Barker** present for **Coakset Benjamin Shearman** present
And **Francis Barker** and **Sarah Howland** Did lay
their Intentions of marriage before this meeting
And Were Desired to Wat til the next monthly meeting
for their answer And **James Shearman** and **Isaac
Smith** are appointed to enquire into **Francis
Barkers** Clearness and make return to the next
monthly meeting And **David Gifford** and **Deborah
Hart** Did likewise Lay their Intentions and were desi
red to wait accordingly and **Eliashib Smith** and
Joseph Mosher are appointed to enquire into **David
Gifford**s Clearness and make return accordingly
There was Collected at this meeting for Friends use 2ˡ-07ˢ=10ᵈ
And Whereas **Peace Wood** hath made no Sattisfaction
Therefore this meeting Concludes to let the matter
rest for some time
And there was a Condemnatition Signed at this meet

ing against **Benjamin Ricketson** and is as followeth
Whereas **Benjamin Ricketson** Son of **Jonathan Rick**
etson and **Abigail** his Wife of **Dartmouth** in the **County**
of **Bristol** in the **Province of** yᵉ **Massachusets Bay** in **New**
England being one that was under the Care of Friends
The People Called Quakers his Father and Mother both
professing to be of our Society
yet for the want of a Due regard to his Education and the princi-
-ple of truth In himselfe hath gone out and married in
the Common Way of other people for which breach of
Our Good order after all propper Endeavor In Love
to reclaim him which hitherto hath seemed to prove
Ineffectual we can Do no less according to our ancient good
Custom but give forth a Condemnation against him
Denying him the sᵈ **Benjamin Ricketson** to be one in
unity with us the aforesᵈ People yet truly Desiring that
he may Come to a sence of his out goings and find mercy
Given forth at our monthly meeting held in **Dartmouth**
on the 21 day of the 7 month 1747 and Signed in and
by order of sᵈ meeting by **John Tucker** Clerk
And the visiters of **Coakset** have brought in their
accounts In writing to this meeting of their Service
In visiting Friends famlies
And whereas this meeting is Considerably in debt
for building an reparing the meeting House therefore
This meeting Desires the parties Concerned to bring
their accompts of the Whole in order that it may
be adjusted and this meeting is adjourned until the first
Sixth day in the 8 month next

At a monthly meeting held at our meeting House in
Dartmouth by adjournment on the 2 day of yᵉ 8ᵐ: 1747
The Friends appointed to attend the Quarterly meet
ing are **James Barker Joseph Tucker** and **Abraham Tucker**
And they to Draw the Epistle to the Quarterly meeting
At a monthly meeting of Friends held at our meeting
House in **Dartmouth** on the 13 day of the 8 month 1747
Ponaganset meeting Called **James Barker** and **John**
Howland present for **Coakset Jonathan Wood** and
Benjamin Tripp present. The Friends appointed to
Enquire into **Francis Barker** and **David Gifford**s

makes report that they find nothing to hinder
their intended marriages
Francis Barker and **Sarah Howland** and **David Gifford**
and **Deborah Hart** appeared at this meeting for their answer
and their answer was that they might proceed marry
In Some Convenient time between this and the next
monthly meeting observing the good order Established
among Friends in the accomplishment thereof
And **Elashib Smith** and **Joseph Mosher** and **James Shearman**
and **Isaac Smith** are appointed to See their marriages
Sonsummated in the abovesᵈ order and make return
to the next monthly meeting
And the Quarterly meeting Epistle was read at this
meeting and well accepted
And this meeting hath at the request of the Quarterly
meeting Collected the Sum of 5 pounds 12 Shillings for a
poor woman at **Situate** and the mony was Delivered to **Thomas Smith**

At a monthly meeting of Friends held at our meeting
House In **Dartmouth** on the 16 day of the 9ᵗʰ month 1747
Ponaganset meeting Called **John Howland** and **James Barker**
present **Coakset** meeting Called **Othniel Tripp** and
Benjamin Shearman present We have an account
that **Francis Barker** and **Sarah Howland** and **David**
Gifford and **Deborah Hart** their marriages were
Consummated In good order The Friend belonging to **Coakset**
have Collected and Sent into this meeting £1-01ˢ-6ᵈ
for the poor woman at **Situate** which in all makes
£6-13ˢ-6ᵈ old tenor and it is refered to yᵉ next monthly
meeting to see if we can Do Something more in that respect
And it is Concluded at this meeting that the meeting of
Worship should be kept at **Josiah Merihew**s for 6 months
longer as heretofore

At a monthly meeting of Friends held at our meeting
house In **Dartmouth** on the 21 day of the 10 month 1747
Ponaganset meeting Called present **Stephen Willcock**
And **Daniel Russell** for **Coakset Edward Cornell**
And **Benjamin Howland** and **Anne Briggs** Did lay
their Intentions of taking each other In marriage before
this meeting and were Desired to wait till the next
monthly meeting for their answer and **William**

Anthony and **John Russell** of **Mishoam**[15] are appointed
to Enquire into the young mans Clearness and make
return to the next monthly meeting
Adam Mott Jonathan Wood and **Stephe Willcock** are
appointed to attend the Quarterly meeting and Draw an
Epistle to the Same. Ther was Collecd at this meeting £2-01^s-04^d
And **Jabez Barker** and **James B Shearman** are appointed
to make up accompts with the Tresurer
And **Joseph Tucker** and **Abraham Tucker** are Continued
Overseers for the meeting House for ye Insuing year
And this meeting orders the Tresurer to pay £4-10^s-0^d old tenor
to **John Shepherd** for the Last halfe years keeping ye Meeting House
And as to the Request of the Quarterly meeting Concer
-ning our Collecting for **Swansey** meeting House since
things are so Chargeable and Difficult among our selves
not to Do anything as yet

At a monthly meeting of Friends held at our meeting
House In **Dartmouth** on the 18th Day of ye 11 month 1747/8
Benjamin Howland and **Anne Briggs** appeared at this
meeting for their answer and nothing appearing to hinder
they had ther answer that might proceed to take each other
in marriage In Some Convenient time between this and the
next monthly meeting Observing the good order Established
amongst Friends in the accomplishment thereof
And **James Barker** and **Stephen Willcock** are appointed to
See their marriage Consummated in good order
And **Joseph Brownell** and **Hannah Bowdish** and **Paul Russell** and **Elisabeth Bowdish**
and **William Sisson** and **Lydia Potter** Did lay their Intentions
of Marriage before this meeting And were Desired to wait
till the next monthly meeting for an answer
And **Jedidiah Wood** an **Nathanael Potter** and **Peleg Huddlestone**
and **Benjamin Wing** and **Jabez Barker** and **James Sherman**
are appointed to mak Enquiry into the young mens Clear
-ness as to marriage and conversation and make return
to the next monthly meeting
Jonathan Wood and **Stephen Willcock** hath attend the
Quarterly meeting and Drawn an epistle to ye same
We received the Quarterly meetin Epistle which was
read and well accepted: **Jabez Barker** and **James Shearman**

15. I.e. Mishaum Point on the south coast of the town of Dartmouth.

hath made up accompts with the tresurer and they find
3 pound one shilling in the Stock
And **Nathanael Potter** appears for **Coakset** –

At a monthly meeting of Friends held at our meeting
House in **Dartmouth** on the 15 day of yᵉ 12 mᵒ: 1747/8
Ponaganset meeting Called **James Barker** and
Barnabus Howland present for **Coakset Robert
Mosher** and **Edward Cornell**
There hath been Enquiry made according to order
Concerning the three Coupples that laid their Inten
tions of marriag befor yᵉ last monthly meeting
and we Dont understand that there is any thing appears
to hinder their proceeding in their Intended marriages
And they appearing for their answer they had their
answers that they might proceed to marry in Some
Convenient time between this and the next monthly
meeting Observing the good order established among
Friends in the accomplishing thereof And **James Barker**
and **John Howland** And **Joseph Tucker** and **Abraham Tucker**
And **Jonathan Wood** and **Edward Cornell** are appointed to
to see their marriages Consummated in the abovesᵈ order
and make return to the next monthly meeting
And **Jacob Mott** and **Anne West** Did lay their Intenti
ons of taking Each other In marriag before this meeting
And were Desired to wait till the next monthly meeting
for their answer And **Josiah Merihew** and **James Shear
man** are appointed to make Enquiry into the young
mans Clearness respecting marriage and Conversation
And make return to the next monthly meeting
James Barker and **Stephen Willcock** gives this meeting
an account that **Benjamin Howland** and **Anne Briggs**
their marriage was Consummated In good order
And whereas **Anne Shaw** being a person that hath
had her Conversation among Friends and being grown
Into years and not capable of helping her selfe as need
Requires She Doth therefore make her application to Friends
to take the oversight of her. Therefore this meeting
appoints **John Howland Peleg Smith** and **Stephen Willcock** [Wilcox]
to take some account of what she has to help her
selfe withal and to see that she has a suitable place

to Resid at and to have the oversight of all things neces
sary In the affair and Render an account to the month
ly meeting from time to time as the Sircumstances of
things may alter And we understand that the Chore
of the new building to the meeting House as to what
belonged to **John Howland** is made up

At a monthly meeting of Friends held at our meeting
House in **Dartmouth** on the 21 day of the first month 1748
Ponaganset meeting Called **John Howland** and **Stephen Willcock [Wilcox]**
present for **Coakset** and **Othniel Tripp** and **Jonathan Wood**
And **Josiah Merihew** and **James Shearman** gives this meeting
an account that they find nothing to hinder **Jacob Mott**s
proceedings in his Intended marriage. **Jacob Mott** and
Anne West appeared at this meeting for their answer
And their answer was that they might proceed to take
each other in marriage in Some Convenient time
between this and the next monthly meeting observing
our Good Order In the performance thereof And **John
Howland** and **Joseph Tucker** are appointed to se their
marriage Consummated in S^d order and make return
to the next monthly meeting. And **Samuel Howland**
and **Ruth Davel** Did lay their Intentions of marriage before
this meeting as Did also **Benjamin Allen** and **Eliphal
Slocum** and **Jonathan Smith** and **Silvia Howland**
And were Desired to wait for their answer till next
monthly meeting And **James Shearman** and **Isaac Smith**
and **Joseph Russell** and **John Howland** and **John Russell**
and **William Anthony** are appointed to See Into their
Clearness respecting marriage and Conversation
and make return to the next monthly meeting
The Friends appointed to see **Joseph Brownell** and **Paul
Russell** and **William Sisson**s marriages Consumated give
account to this meeting that they were Decently accomplished
Collected at this meeting for the use of Friends 2=10-00
And this meeting orders the Tresurer to pay 2-17-00
old Tenor to **Stephen Willcock** for brick that he pro-
cured about the meeting House
And **John Howland James Barker Jonathan Wood**
and **Nathanael Potter** are appointed to attend the
Quarterly meeting and Draw an Epistle to the Same

At a monthly meeting of Friends held at our meeing
House in **Dartmouth** on the 18 day of the 2 month 1748
Ponaganset meeting Called **James Barker** and **Abraham**
Tucker present for **Coakset Jonathan Wood** and **Oth**
-niel Tripp present The Friends apponted to Inspect Into
the Clearness of the three Cupples that laid their Inten
tions Last monthly meeting gives this meeting an
account that they find nothing to hinder their intended marriages
And they appearing for their answers they had
their answers that they might Proceed to marry
In Some Convenient time between this and the next
monthly meeting observing the good order Established
amongst Friends in the performance thereof
and **Isaac Smith** and **James Shearman** are appointed
to See **Samuel Howland** and **Ruth Davels [Davol]** marriage
accomplished in good order and **John Russell** and **Jabez**
Barker are appointed upon the Same account for
Benjamin Allen and **Eliphal Slocum. And Peleg Smith**
and **George Smith** for **Jonathan Smith & Silvia Howland**
and all to make return to ye next monthly meeting
The Friends Appointed to see **Jacob Mott** and **Anne**
Wests marriag Sollemnized makes report that
It was orderly performed
And three of ye Friends appointed to attend the
Quarterly meeting have done it and Drawn Epistle
to the Same. And the Quarterly meeting Epistle
was read at this meeting and well accepted
And this meeting orders the Tresurer to pay to **John**
Shepherd 2 pound 8 shillings & Six pence old Tenor for some
thing done about the meeting House, which is paid

At a monthly meeting of Friends, held at our meeting
House In **Dartmouth** on the 16 Day of the ye 3 month
1748 **Ponaganset** meeting Called **James Barker** and
Abraham Tucker present for **Coakeset Joseph Tripp**
and **Edward Cornell** The Friend appointed to see
the three marriages Sollemnized gives this meeting
an account that they were orderly Consummated
And this meeting doth Consent that the [there?] be a meet
-ing held at **Josiah Merihew**s or **Adam Mott**s or some
where thereabouts on the first Day of the Week

for the six ensuing month Excep on the first day
preceeding the monthly meeting.
And whereas **Jonathan Ricketson jur.** and **Jabez Barker Jur.** have married out of the good order Establishe[d] among us therefor this meeting orders **Adam Mott** and **Isaac Smith** to talk with Sd **Barker** to See whither he will Condemn his disorder
And **James Barker** and **Henry Hedly** are appointed to talk with **Jonathan Ricketson** upon yᵉ Same account
And whereas there hath been Several Friends impressed to go to Warr Therefore this meeting appoints **Abraham Tucker Peleg Smith Isaac Howland James Barker** and **Jedidiah Wood** a Comtee [committee] to act for the meeting in Way as me [may?] be Re=quisite until the next monthly meeting

---

At a monthly meeting of Friends held at our meeting House In **Dartmouth** on the 20th Day of the 4 month 1748
Ponaganset meeting Called **James Barker** and **Abraham Tucker** present. For **Coakset Benjamin Shearman** and **Edward Cornell** present
And Whereas there is Several of our Friends now under Confinement In **Taunton** Goal [gaol; jail] for refusing to be Concerned In Warring and fighting **Thomas Smith** and **Peleg Smith** are appointed to take the oversight of **Barnabas Howland** and **Seth Shearmans** families and See that thing Dont Suffer too much by reason of their Confinement And **Edward Cornell** is appoin=ted upon the Like account for **Othniel Tripp** –
The matter Concerning **Jabez Barker jur** and **Jona=than Ricketson jur** is refered until yᵉ next monthly meeting: Ou[r] Friends **Zechariah Farris** and **Robert Lewis** and **Nathanael Lewis** from **Pensilvania** was at this meeting and their Certificates were read to good Sattisfaction
And the yearly meeting Epistle from **London** was read at this meeting and kindly accepted
The Friends appointed to attend the Quarterly meeting and Draw an Epistle to yᵉ Same are **Jonathan Wood** and **Stephen Willcock [Wilcox]**
There was Collected at this meeting for the use of Friend 4£ – 08s = 00d old tenor

And the Tresurer is ordered to pay to **John Shepherd**
5 pound old tenor for for the last half years keep=
ing the meeting House which is Done

At a monthly meeting of Friends held at our
meeting House in **Dartmouth** on the 18th Day of ye 5 month
1748 **Ponaganset** meeting Called **James Barker**
and **Abraham Tucker** present for **Coakset**
Benjamin Shearman and **Jonathan Wood**
There was a paper Read at this meeting Signed by
Jonathan Ricketson jur which this meeting doth
not accept for full Sattisfaction, therefor the
matter is Continued for some time
And also **Jabez Barker Ju**r hath Sent in a paper
to this meeting Concerning his Disorderly marriage
Which this meeting accepts for Sattisfaction
and is as followeth
To the monthly meeting of Friends to be held in **Dartmouth** on ye 18th of the 5th month 1748
Loving Friends Whereas I have gone out of ye good
order Established among Friends in marriage and
also Contrary to my Parents advice which upon
Due Consideration if it was to Do again I think I
should not Do it and Do hereby acknowledge it to
be Disorderly and Desire that Friends would pass
by my offence against them And desire thir [their] Care
over me for the time to Come **Jabez Barker ju**r
And **Jonathan Wood** and **Stephen Willcock** [Wilcox] have
attended the Quarterly meeting and Drawn
an Epistle to the Same as appointed
The Epistle from the Quarterly meeting was read
at this meeting and well accepted
And whereas there is nine pounds old tenor Due
to Friends at **Boston** for Charge and trouble in
Sending a letter tending to the releif of Friends
Therefore **Joseph Tucker** and **Peleg Smith** are
appointed to See that the mony is paid as Soon
as may be with Conveniency
And this meeting is Complyance to ye advice of the
Quarterly meeting have agreed to Come to a Sub=
Scription towards the upper meeting House in **Westerly**

At a monthly meeting of Friends held at our
meeting House In **Dartmouth** on the 15th Day of the
6 month 1748 **Ponaganset** meeting Called
John Howland and **Abraham Tucker** present
for **Coakset Joseph Tripp** and **Jonathan Wood**
Giles Slocum and **Silvia Russell** and **Peleg Slocum**
and **Elisabeth Brown** Did lay their intentions
Of taking each other in marriage before this meeting
and were Desired to wait til the next monthly me[e]ting for their
answers: And **Joseph Tucker** and **Abraham Tucker** are appointed to Enquire Into ye young mens Clearness respecting marriage and Conversation and make return to the next
monthly meeting
And there was a Condemnation Signed at this meeting
against **Elisabeth Russell** Daughter of **James Russell** and
Isaac Smith is ordered to read it at the end of a first day
meeting The visitters Chose for this year are for **Coakset**
Joseph Tripp and **John Mosher** And for **Ponaganset Abraham**
Tucker and **Peleg Smith**
And Whereas this meeting thinks it propper to Choose
Some Friends to have an Inspection into the Sircumstances
of our Friends that are prisoners at **Taunton** and to
let this meeting know how it is and to provide such things
for them as necescity Shall require Therefore **Joseph**
Mosher is appointed to See Into that affair

At a monthly meeting of Friends held at our meeting
House In **Dartmouth** on ye 19th Day of the 7th month 1748
Ponaganset meeting Called **John Howland** & **James Barker**
present for **Coakset Joseph Tripp** and **John Mosher**
The Friends appointed to Enquire Into **Giles** and
Peleg Slocums Clearness gives this meeting an account
that they have done it and find nothing to hinder
their Intended marriages
And **Giles Slocum** and **Silvia Russell** and **Peleg**
Slocum and **Elisabeth Brown** appeared at this meet
ing for their answer and their answer was that they
might proceed to marry in Some Convenient time between [this]
and the next monthly meeting observing the good order
Established amongst Friends In the accomplishment
thereof and **Abraham Tucker** and **Stephen Willcock**

are appointed to See their marriage Sollemnized
And **Robert Barker** and **Joanna Russell** and **Walter
Easton** an **Meribeh Ricketson** and **William Howland**
and **Rebeckah Peckham** and **William Bennit [Bennet]** and
Hannah Taber Did lay their intentions of marriage
before this meeting and were desired to wat [wait] til the
next monthly [meeting?] And **Adam Mott** and **Nathan Davis**
are appointed to See Into **William Bennit**s Clearness
respecting marriage and Conversation and make
return to the next meeting
And **Hannah Peckham** Wife of **William Peckham**
hath Signified to this meeting that She Desires to
Come and under our Care which is granted
And **Isaac Smith** hath read **Elisabeth Russell**s
Condemnation as appointed
And the Widow **Joanna Russell** being about to
marry this meeting appoints **Humphry Smith**
Ebenezer Slocum and **Abraham Tucker** to Inspect
Into the matter Concerning the Estate that belonged
to her first Husband that things may be Settled so
that no Damage may occur upon the account of
her Second marriage to her Children
There was a Certificate read at this meeting
Directed from the monthly meeting at **Swansey**
Recommending **John Davis** and his Wife to our
Care which is accepted And Whereas **Humphry
Wady** Desires a Certificate to the monthly meeting
at **Shrewsbury** This meeting appoints **Thomas
Smith** and **Stephen Willcock [Wilcox]** to make Enquiry and
Draw one if they think propper and bring it to the
Next monthly meeting
The Friends appointed to attend the Quarterly
meeting are **Adam Mott** and **Joseph Tucker** and to
Draw an Epistle to the Same There was Collected
at this meeting 2 pound three shillings and two pence
And there was Collected by this meeting toward
the meeting House at **Westerly** 12 pound old tenor
And the visiters of **Coakset** have given in their
account in writing of their Service in visiting
Friends families

At a monthly meeting held at our meeting House In **Dartmouth** on the 17th Day of the 8th month 1748 **Ponaganset**
meeting Called **John Howland** and **Abraham Tucker** present
for **Coakset Joseph Tripp** and **Edward Cornell** present
Robert Barker and **Joanna Russell** And **Walter Easton**
and **Meribeh Ricketson** and **William Howland** and
Rebeckah Peckham and **William Bennit** and **Hannah
Taber** Came for their answer and they had their
answers that they might proceed to marry in the good
order Established amongst Friends In Some Convenient
time between this and the next monthly meeting
observing the good order Established among Friend in
the accomplishment thereof And **John Howland** and
Abraham Tucker are appointed to See **William Bennit**
and **Hannah Taber**s marriage Consummated as also
William Howlands and **Rebeckah Peckham**s In the aforesd
good order and make return to the next monthly
Meeting: And **Stephen Willcock** and **Isaac Smith**
are appointed to see **Robert Barker** and **Joann [Joanna] Russell**s
And **Walter Easton** and **Meribeh Ricketson**s mar-
riages Consummated in like manner and make
return to the next monthly meeting
The Friends appointed to See **Giles** and **Peleg Slocum**s
marriages Consummated gives this meeting an account
that the[y] were orderly accomplished
Tho the young people that were married not so orderly
In their Apparel as they ought to be
The friends appointed to Draw a Certificate for
Humphry Wady Signify that they find Somany [*sic*]
things In the Way that they Could not do it therefore
This meeting orders the Same Friends to write to
Sd **Wady** to Let him know the reason
The Friends appointed to attend the Quarterly meeting
have Done it and Drawn an Epistle to ye Same as
appointed And the Quarterly meeting Epistle was read
at this meeting and well accepted
The Friends appointed to Discource with **Peace Wood** have
done it and She hath made no Sattisfaction therefore
the matter is refered to the next monthly meeting

At a monthly meeting of Friends held at our meet
ing House In **Dartmouth** on the 21 day of the 9 month
1748: **Ponaganset** meeting Called **James Barker** and
Abraham Tucker present **Coakset** meeting Called
Nathaniel Potter and **Jedidiah Wood** present
John Howland and **Abraham Tucker** gives this
meeting an account that **William Bennit** and
Hannah Tabers marriage hath been orderly
Consummated. And **Stephen Willcock** and
Isaac Smith gives the Same account Concerning
Robert Barker and **Joanna Russell** and **Walter Easton**
and **Meribeh Ricketson**
And this meeting hath agreed that there be a meet
ing kept at **Josiah Merihew**s or **Adam Mott**s on the
first Days of the Week fir this Winter Season
And the matter Concerning **Peace Wood** is refered
to the next monthly meeting And **Jonathan Wood**
and **Nathanael Potter** are Chosen Visiters, for **Coakset**
And **Adam Mott** and **Henry Hedly** are Chosen Visitter
for that part of **Ponaganset** lying to the ~~East~~^Westward
of the meeting House River and to the Eastward of
Coakset River

At a monthly meeting of Friends held at our meet [*sic*]
meeting House in **Dartmouth** on the 19 day of the
10 month 1748 **Ponaganset** meeting Called **James
Barker** and **Abraham Tucker** present for **Coakset**
Benjamin Shearman and **Joseph Jennings** present
There was Collected at this meeting $2^£ -11^s- 4^d$ old tenor
And the matter Concerning **Peace Wood** is refered
until the next monthly meeting
And this meeting hath received of the Women
3 pounds old Tenor to go towards keeping the meet
ing House. And this meeting orders the Tresurer
to pay to the overseers five pounds old tenor
for the last halfe years keeping the meeting House
The Friends appointed to attend the Quarterly meeting are
Thomas Smith Adam Mott Stephen Willcock [Wilcox] and **Nathanael Potter**
and to Draw an Epistle to the Same And it is reported at
this meeting that **William Howland** and **Rebeckah Peckham**[s]
marriage hath been Consummated at **Cushnot** meeting Hous]

And **Joseph Tucker** and **Abraham Tucker** are appointed
overseers of the meeting House for yᵉ Insuing year
And the Tresurer hath paid the five pounds as ordered
to the overseers

At a monthly meeting of Friends held at our meeting
House In **Dartmouth** on the 16 Day of yᵉ 11 month 1748
Ponaganset meeting Called **John Howland** and **Stephen
Willcock** present **Coakset** meeting Called **Edward
Cornell** and **Jedidiah Wood** present
Adam Mott and **Nathanael Potter** hath attended
the Quarterly meeting as appointed and there was
an Epistle Drawn and Sent and the Quarterly meetings
Epistle was read at this meeting and well accepted
The matter Concerning **Peace Wood** is refered to
the next monthly meeting

At a monthly meeting held at our meeting House
In **Dartmouth** on the 20 Day of the 12 month 1748
Ponaganset meeting Called **Adam Mott** and **Abraham
Tucker** present for **Coakset Nathanael Potter**
And **Increas [Increase] Allen** and **Hannah Springer** Did lay
their intentions of taking each other in marriage
before this meeting and wer[e] Desired [to wait?] until the next
monthly meeting for their answer and **Holder Slocum**
and **Simeon Gifford** are appointed to See into the young
mans Clearness respecting marriage and Conversation
and make return to the next monthly meeting
And Whereas **Thomas Yeuin**[?] and his Wife hath Sig
nified to this meeting that they are about to remove
to the **Nine partners** in the Goverment of **New York**
And Desire a Certificate and Friends assistance
Therefore this meeting appoints **Nathaniel Potter**
And **Isaac Smith** to Enquire into the matter and
Do what is propper in that affair
And **Joseph Tucker** hath Signified that he hath 24
Shillings and 5 pence in his hands mony belonging
to the monthly meeting which he is ordered to
pay to the Tresurer And the matter Concerning **Peace
Wood** is refered to yᵉ next monthly meeting

At a monthly meeting of Friends held at our meet

ing House In **Dartmouth** on the 20 Day of yᵉ 1 mᵒ 1748/9
Pon[a]ganset meeting Called **John Howland** and **James**
Barker present for **Coakset Benjamin Shearman**
and **Jonathan Wood**. And **Simeon Gifford** makes
report to this meeting that there hath been Enquir[y?]
made into **Increas [Increase] Allen**s Clearness and nothing hath
been found to hinder his Intended marriage
And **Increas Allen** and **Hannah Springer** appear
ed at this meeting for their answer and their
answer was that they might proceed to take each
other in marriage In Some Convenient time
between this and the next monthly meeting obser
ving the good order established amongst Friends
In the accomplishment thereof And **John Russell**
and **Stephen Willcock** are appointed to See their mar
riage Consummated and make return to the next
monthly meeting
And **Benjamin Shaw** and **Elisabeth Potter** did lay
their Intentions of taking each other in marriage
before this meeting and were Desired to wait till
the next monthly meeting for their answer and
Jonathan Wood and **Benjamin Shearman** are
appointed to enquire into the young mans Clearness
respecting marriage and Conversation and make
return to the next meeting
and **Joseph Tucker** hath paid the 24ˢ and 5 pence as ordered
And there was Collected at this meeting 3ᵉ–1ˢ–6ᵈ old Tenor
The Friends appointed to attend the Quarterly meeting
and Draw an Epistle to the Same are **James Barker**
Stephen Willcock and **Adam Mott**: And this meeting
is adjourned til the youths meeting
This meeting being mett according to adjournment this
7ᵗʰ Day of the 2ᵈ month 1749 the visitters of **Aponaganset** vilage
have given in their account in writing to this meeting of their
Service in visiting friends families the substance whereof is
that they found things for the most part pretty well but in
Some places not so well and that a separating dividing Spirit
Doth Seem to much to predominate which they Endeavored
to Suppress and Discourage

At a monthly meeting of Friends held at our meeting

House In **Dartmouth** on the 17th Day of ye 2d month 1749
Ponaganset meeting Called **John Howland Joseph Tucker**
present **Coakset** meeting Called **John Cornell** & **Jonathan Wood**
present. **Jonathan Wood** and **Benjamin Shearman** makes
report to this meeting that they have made enquiry into
Benjamin Shaws Clearness and Do not find nothing but
that he is Clear Excepting apparell in that not so
orderly as they Could Desire. And **Benjamin Shaw** and
Elisabeth Potter appeared at this meeting for their answer
and their answer was that they might proceed to take each
In marriage In Some Convenient time between this and
the next monthly meeting observing the good order Establish
-ed among Friends in the performance thereof and **Jonathan Wood** and **John Cornell** are appointed to See their
marriage Consummated and make return to the next
monthly meeting. And **John Russell** makes report to
this meeting that **Increas [Increase] Allen** and **Hannah Springer**s
marriage was Consummated In good order
The Friends appointed to attend the Quarterly meeting
have Done it and Drawn an Epistle to the Same
And the Epistle from the Quarterly meeting hath been
read at this meeting and Well accepted
And Whereas **Benjamin Howland** Desires a Certificate
from this meeting to the monthly meeting at **Swansy**
of his Clearness respecting marriage and Conversation
this meeting appoints **James Shearman** and **Isaac Smith**
to make enquiry and Draw one if ˄they think propper and
bring it to the next monthly meeting
There was an account brought to this meeting from
Thomas Hathaway that he hath Received the Sum of 4 pound
14 Shillings and 5 pence of **Abraham Tucker** for mending
the Glass belonging to the meeting House
And whereas **Abigail Kerby [Kirby]** Doth persist Contrary
to the advice of Friends in way of publick Testimony it
Is refered to the Consideration of ye next monthly
meeting And also the matter Concerning **Peace Wood**
is refered to the next monthly meeting

At a monthly meeting of Friends held at our meeting
House In **Dartmouth** on the 15th Day of the 3d month 1749
Ponaganset meeting Called **Peleg Smith** present **Coakset**

meeting Called **Jonathan Wood** and **John Cornell** present
The Friends appointed to See **Benjamin Shaw** and **Elisabeth
Potter**s marriage Consummated gives this meeting an
account that It was accomplished in reasonable
good order There was a Certificate Signed at this
meeting for **Humphry Wady** and his Wife and famly
they being about to remove to **Shrewsbury**
And there was a Certificate Signed at this meeting
for **Benjamin Howland**
And **John Howland Joseph Tucker** and **Nathanael
Potter** are appointed to go in the meetings behalf to
Abigail Kerby and let her know that Friends are
Grieved that She goes on Contrary to their advice
In bearing a publick Testimony And that if She doth
persist therein She must be Set aside
And whereas this meeting hath been informed that
Peace Wood hath publickly Declared at a meeting
at **Coakset** that which tends much to breakin the
unity and Concord among Friends therefore this
meeting appoints **John Tucker John Howland Peleg
Smith** and **Abraham Tucker** to Discource with
S^d **Peace Wood** and endevour to Shew her wherein
She hath been out of the way and make return
to the next monthly meeting. And this meeting hath
granted there Should be a meeting kept for 6 months
Longer at **Josiah Merihew**s or **Adam Mott**s
Our Worthy Friends **Abraham Farrington** and **John Sykes**
was at this meeting from **WestSerley** [**Westerly**] whole Labour of love
we had good unity with and their Certificate were read to
good Sattisfaction The Friends appointed to attend the
Quarterly meeting are **James Barker** and **Abraham
Tucker** and they to Draw an Epistle to the Same

At a monthly meeting of Friends held at our meeting
House In **Dartmouth** on the 17th Day of the 5th month 1749
Ponaganset meeting Called **John Howland** and **James Barker**
present. **Coakset** meeting Called **Othniel Tripp** present
There was Collected at this meeting 6 pound 16 Shilling & 2^d
And the matter Concerning **Peace Wood** is refered until
the next monthly meeting
And this meeting orders the tresurer to pay 30 Shillings

old tenor to **John Russell ju^r** for the use of mony that
he lent to the monthly meeting the Principle being paid
by the yearly meeting. And this meeting order the Tre
-surer to pay to the overseers five pound old Tenor for
the Last halfe yers [years] keeping the meeting House
The Friends appointed to attend the Quarterly meeting
~~are~~ And Draw the Epistle have not Done it they not
being well The Quarterly meetings Epistle was
read at this meeting and well accepted
And the Tresurer hath paid the 5 pounds as ordered
and also the 30 Shillings to **John Russell ju^r**

At a monthly meeting of Friends held at our
Meeting House in **Dartmouth** on the 21 day of the 6 m:
1749 **Ponaganset** meeting Called **John Howland** and
Joseph Tucker present **Coakset** meeting Called
Christopher Gifford and **Nathanael Potter** present
And whereas the[ere] hath been much Labour and pains
bestowed upon **Peace Wood** to bring her to a Sence of her
outgoings but all Seems to work no Effect with her
Therefore it is the Judgment of this meeting that
She ought to be Set aside and **Isaac Smith** and **Peleg
Smith** are appointed to Draw up a Condemnation
against her and bring it to the next monthly
meeting
And this meeting appoints **Abraham Tucker**
And **Peleg Smith** to See that no Disorderly persons or
Such that are not under the Care of Friends Do
Sit in our meetings of Disapline [Discipline]

6   At a monthly meeting of Friends held at our meet
1749 -ing House in **Dartmouth** on the 18th Day of y^e 7^m: 1749
Ponaganset meeting Called **James Barker** and **Abraham
Tucker** present **Coakset** meeting Called **Edward
Cornell** present
The yearly meeting Epistle from **London** baring
Date the 4th month 1748 was read In this meet
=ing and well approved
Charles Slocum and **Sarah Allen** Did lay their
Intentions of taking each other in marriage
before this meeting as also Did **Philip Davel** [**Davol**]
and **Elisabeth Shearman** and were Desired to

wait until yᵉ next monthly meeting for their
answer and **Holder Slocum** and **John Russell** are
appointed to Enquire Concerning **Charles Slocum**s
Clearness as to marriage and Conversation
and **Nathanael Potter** and **Isaac Smith** are
appointed in that affair for **Philip Davel** – –
and all to make ~~ma~~ Return to yᵉ monthly meeting
And **Peace Wood**s Condemnation was brought
to this meeting and **John Tucker** hath Signed
it by order of yᵉ meeting
And **Edward Cornell** is ordered to Carry the Sd
Condemnation and let her have the perusal of
it and bring it to the next monthly meeting
The Friends appointed to attend the Quarterly
meeting are **Joseph Tucker Peleg Smith** and
Abraham Tucker and they to Draw an
Epistle to the Same And this meeting is adjour
-ned till the youths meeting
This meeting being meet according to adjourn
ment this 6 day of the 8 month 1749 – – – – –

At a monthly meeting of Friends held at our meeting House in
Dartmouth on the 16 Day of the 8 month 1749 **Ponaganset**
meeting Called **Isaac Howland** and **Stephen Willcock** present
Coakset meeting Called **Jonathan Wood** & **Edwᵈ Cornell** present
Nathanael Potter and **Isaac Smith** gives this meeting an account that they have made Enquiry into **Philip Davel**s
Clearness and find nothing to hinder his intended marriage
And **John Russell** gives this meeting an account that
he finds nothing to hinder **Charles Slocum**s intended
marriage: And **Charles Slocum** and **Sarah Allen**
And **Philip Davel** [**Davol**] and **Elizabeth Shearman** appeared
at this meeting for their answer and their answer
was that they might proceed to marry in Some
Convenien[t] time between this and the next month
-ly meeting observing the Good order established among
Friends In the Consummation thereof
And **John Russell** and **Stephen Willcock** are appointed [to?]
See **Charles Slocum** and **Sarah Allen**s marriage Con
summated in Sd good order And **James Shearman**
and **Isaac Smith** are appointed to See **Philip Davel**

And **Elisabeth Shearman**s marriag Consummated in
Sd good order and make return to the next monthly
meeting: And **Peace Wood**s Condemnation hath been
read at this meeting & is as followeth
Whereas **Peace Wood** wife of **Jonathan Wood** of **Dartmouth**
In the County of **Bristol** In the Province of the **Massachu-
set[t]s Bay** In **New England** Having been one that for
many years hath made profession with us the People
Called Quakers and hath born a publick Testimony
amongst us which hath been well approved of yet
In Some time past through a misled zeal She Delivered
many things at a monthly meeting in **Ponanset** which
Friends Could not Join with for which She was Seasonably
and tenderly dealt with time after time but She always
Justified it for which Friends proceeded to deny her
Publick Testimony. And Since that at a marriage at
Coakset She uttered publickly many thing Contrary to good order
both against the monthly meeting and against perticular
friends by name Declaring the marriage Certificate
to be Such that no Friend in the Order of God Could
Sign it which things doth Tend very much to Distur-
=bance and Seperation And She having been
Tenderly and lovingly dealt with by Sollid Friends
in order to bring her to a Sence of her outgoings
but She Still to the great Grief of the Honest hearted
amongst us Doth Justify her Selfe We Do think it
Propper to give forth this as a Testimony against
Denying the S^d **Peace Wood** to be one In unity with
us The abovesd People yet truly Desiring that She
may Come to a Sight of her ourtgoings [*sic*] and find mer
-cy with the Lord Signed In and by order of our
monthly meeting held in **Dartmouth** on the 18th day
of the 7th month 1749 by

        John Tucker Clerk – –

The Friends appointed to attend the Quarterly
meeting have done it all but **Peleg Smith** and
Drawn an Epistle to the Same as appointed
And whereas it was Signified in the Epistle that
8 pound ten Shillings was our proportion towards
the yearly meeting Stock which is refered to the

next monthly meeting as is also the request of
the monthly meeting at **Pembrook** towards the Sup
-port of an Ancient Woman there
Adam Mott Henry Hedly Abraham Tucker and
Peleg Smith are Continued visitters for **Ponaganset** and for that part of **Coakset** to the eastward
of **Coakset** river. And **Jonathan Wood** and **Nathaniel
Potter** are Still Continued visitters for **Coakset**

At a monthly meeting held at our meeting House
In **Dartmouth** on the 20 Day of the 9 month 1749
Ponaganset meeting Called **James Barker** present
for **Coakset Edward Cornell** and **Joseph Tripp ju**ʳ
John Russell gives this meeting an account
that he was at **Charles Slocum** and **Sarah
Allen**s marriage and Saw nothing but that
It was performed in good order And **James Shearman** and
Isaac Smith gives this meeting an account that **Philip Davel [Davol]**
and **Elisabeth Shearman**s marriage was Consummated in good
order. And **Francis Allen** and **Mary Ridington** Did lay
their Intentions of taking each other in marriage before
this meeting and were Desired to wait until the next
monthly meeting for their answer and **Henry Hedly**
and **Adam Mott** are appointed to Enquire into **Francis
Allen**s Clearness respecting marriage and Conversation
and make return to the next monthly meeting
The 8 pound 10 Shillings for the yearly meeting Stock is re
-fered to the next monthly meeting
And this meeting hath given Consent that ther Should
be a meeting kept for 6 months longer at **Josiah
Merihew**s. And Friends have agreed to come to a Sub
scription for the ancient Woman at **Pembrook** – – – – –

At a monthly meeting of Friends held at our meeting
House In **Dartmouth** on the 18ᵗʰ Day of yᵉ 10ᵗʰ month 1749
Ponaganset meeting Called **Abraham Tucker** and
Joseph Tucker present for **Coakset Joseph Tripp** and
Jedidiah Wood present
And **Francis Allen** and **Mary Ridington** appeared
at this meeting for their answer: And nothing
appearing to hinder they had their answer that they

might proceed to take each other in marriage in
Some Convenient time between this and the next month
-ly meeting Observing the good order Established amongst
Friends in the accomplishment thereof And **Adam
Mott** and **Henry Hedly** are appointed to See their mar
-riage Consummated in Sd good order and make return
to the next monthly meeting
And the 8 pounds 10 Shillings towards the yearly meeting
Stock is refered till the next monthly meeting
The Friends appointed to attend the Quarterly
meeting and Draw an Epistle to the Same are
Henry Tucker Adam Mott and **Joseph Tucker**
And there was Collec[te]d at this meeting 3 pounds for the use
of Friends. And this meeting orders the Tresurer to pay
5 pounds old Tenor to the overseers for keeping the
meeting House the last halfe year
And this meeting appoints **Joseph Tucker** and **Abraham
Tucker** overseers of the meeting House for the year
Insuing. And the tresurer hath paid yᵉ 5 pounds as ordered

At a monthly meeting of Friends held at our meet
ing House in **Dartmouth** on the 15 day of yᵉ 11ᵐ 1749
Dartmouth meeting Called **John Lapham** and
Abraham Tucker present **Coakset** meeting Called
Jonathan Wood and **Endward [Edward?] Cornell** present
And **Adam Mott** makes report to this meeting
that **Francis Allen** and **Mary Ridington**s marriage
was Consummated in good order accord to his Judgment
And **Joshua Cornell** and **Lusanna Gifford** Did lay
their intentions of marriage before this meeting
and were desired to wait until our next monthly
meeting for their answer and **Benjamin Wing** and
Jedidiah Wood are appointed to make Enquiry into
The young mans Clearness respe[c]ting marriage and
Conversation and make return to the next
monthly meeting and the 8 pound ten Shillings toward
the yearly meeting Stock is refered to next monthly
meeting The Friends appointed to attend yᵉ Quarterly
meeti[ng] and Draw the Epistle have ˄ᶰᵒᵗ done it by
reason of the hardness of yᵉ Season
and the Quarterly meetings Epistle was read at

this meeting and well accepted
And **Joseph Tucker** and **Peleg Smith** hath Settled
accounts with the Tresurer and find in the Stock 0ᵉ-1ˢ-4ᵈ
And whereas **David Shepherd** Desires a Certificate
from this meeting to the monthly meeting at **Sandwich**
of his Clearness Respecting marriage and Conversation
This meeting therefore appoints **Adam Mott** and
Joseph Tucker to make Enquiry and Draw one if
they find things Clear and bring it to the next
monthly meeting

At a monthly meeting of Friends held at our meeting House
in **Dartmouth** on the 19 day of the 12 month 1749 **Ponaganset** meet
ing Called **Joseph Tucker** and **Abraham Tucker** present
Coakset meeting Called **Jedidiah Wood** present
The Friends appointed to see into **Joshua Cornell**s Clearness
makes report that they find nothing to hinder his Intend
-ed marriage And **Joshua Cornell** and **Lusanna Gifford**
appeared at this meeting for their answer and their
answer was that they might proceed to take each other
in marriage in Some Convenient time between this
and the next monthly meeting observing the good order
Established amongst Friends in the Sollemnizing thereof
And **Nathanael Potter** and **Jedidiah Wood** are appointed
to see their marriage Consummated and make return
to the next monthly meeting
And **Job Gifford** and **Martha Willcock** [Wilcox] Did lay their Inten
-tions of taking each other in marriage before this
meeting and were Desired to wait until the next
monthly meeting for their answer and ~~Daniel Russell~~ John Russell
~~and Isaac Smith~~ and Jonathan Ricketson are appointed to see Concerning **Job**
Giffords Clearness and make return to the next month
-ly meeting And **Isaac Kelly** and **Judith Shearman**
Did also lay their intentions before this meeting and
were Desired to wait for their answer till yᵉ next
monthly meeting And there was a certificate Signed
at this meeting for **David Shepherd**
And **Josiah Akin** hath Signified to this meeting that
he is about to remove with his famly to the **Oblong**
to live and Desires a Certificate to the monthly meet
ing where he is like to belong And **Isaac Smith** and

Daniel Russell are appointed to make Enquiry and Draw
one if they think propper and bring it to the next
meeting And this meeting hath mad[e] a beginning
towards a Subscription for the yearly meeting Stock
And **Henry Tucker** hath taken it and to bring it to
the next monthly meeting And whereas there
hath been Something mentioned Concerning Friends
Suffering it is refered to next monthly meeting

At a monthly meeting of Friends held at our meeting House
In **Dartmouth** on the 19ᵗʰ Day of the 1 month 1749/50
Ponaganset meeting Called **Abraham Tucker** and
Peleg Smith present **Coakset** meeting Called
Jonathan Wood and **Joseph Tripp Juʳ** present **Nathanael
Potter** and **Jedidiah Wood** gives this meeting an ac
-count that **Joshua Cornell** and **Lusanna Gifford**s
marriage hath been Consummated in good order
as far as they Saw. And **Job Gifford** and **Martha
Willcock** [**Wilcox**] appeared at this meeting for their an
swer and their answer was that they might
proceed to take each other in marriage in Some
Convenient time between this and the next month
-ly meeting observing the good order Established
amongst Friends in the performance thereof
And **James Barker** and **Abraham Tucker** are ap
-pointed to see their marriage Consummated in Sd
Good order and make return to the next monthly
meeting And **Barnabas Howland** and **Penelope
Allen** Did lay their intentions of taking each other
in marriag before this meeting and were desired
to wait until yᵉ next monthly meeting for their
answer and **Joseph Tucker Humphry Smith** and
Ebenezer Slocum are appointed to see into
Barnabas Howlands Clearness and also to endevor
to Settle things that the[re] be no wrong Done to the
Widows Children by her Second marriage
And there was a Certificate Signed at this meet
ing for **Josiah Akin**
The visitters of **Ponaganset** have given in their
account to this meeting in writing
And the Subscription for the yearly meeting Stock

is finnished and **Henry Tucker** is ordered to Carry
it ˄to the Quarterly meeting
And there was Collected at this meeting 3£ –17ˢ -00ᵈ
old tenor which was delivered to the Tresurer
And whereas **Barnabas Howland Othniel Tripp**
Seth Shearman and **William Mosher** have[16]
Suffered 12 months Imprisonment for refusing to go to War
an account thereof is ordered to be sent to the Quarterly meet
-ing and that the Sheriff of the County was very kind to them
in the time of their Confinement
The Friends appointed to attend the Quarterly meeting are
Henry Tucker Joseph Tucker and **Jonathan Wood** and to Draw
an Epistle to the Same

At a monthly meeting of Friends held at our meeting
House in **Dartmouth** on the 17 Day of the Second month 1750
Ponaganset meeting Called **Isaac Howland** and **Abraham**
Tucker present **Coakset** meeting Called **Othniel Tripp**
and **Joseph Brownell** present The Friends appointed to
See Into **Barnabas Howland**s Clearness on Settling the
Widows affairs brings in an account that it is Done
And they find nothing to hinder their Intended marriage
And **Barnabas Howland** and **Penelope Allen** appeared
at this meeting for their answer as Did **Isaac Kelly** and
Judith Shearman and they had their answers that they
might proceed to marry In Some Convenient time
betw[een] this and the next monthly meeting observing
our Good order in th[e] accomplishing of them
And the Friends appointed to attend the Quarterly
meeting have done it and Drawn the Epistle as appoinₜₑd
And Whereas **Richard Gifford** being about to marry
out of the good order Established amongst Friends
this meeting appoints **Jedidiah Wood** and **Edward**
Cornell to Speak with Sd **Gifford** in order to perswade
him to Desist in that affair
And **John Russell** and **John Shepherd** are appointed
to See the marriages accomplished in good order
And **George Smith** hath brought a paper to this meet
-ing Signifying his Sorrow for allowing a disorderly
marriage which is refered

---

16. "Friends imprisoned" is written in pencil at the bottom of the manuscript page in later hand.

At a monthly meeting held at our meeting house in
Dartmouth on the 21 day of the 3 month 1750
Ponaganset meeting Called **Abraham Tucker** and
Peleg Smith present
Coakset meeting Called **Edward Cornell** and **Jedidiah
Wood** present And whereas **Richard Gifford** hath
gone and married with his former wives sister
Contrary to our good order and also Contrary to the
Law of this Province although he hath been from time
to time Laboured with not to proceed in that manner
Therefore **Isaac Smith** is ordered to Draw up a
Condemnation against him and bring it to the next
monthly meeting. And **John Russell** gives an ac
-count to this meeting that **Barnabas Howland**
and **Penelope Allen** and **Isaac Kelly** and **Judith
Shearman**s marriages was Consummated in good
order according to his Judgment
Our Worthy Friends **John Scarborough** and **James
Daniel** from **Salem** in **West Jersey** were at this
meeting and the Labour of Love well accepted
And their Certificates were read to good Sattisfaction
George Smith and his wife have given in a paper
Signifying their Sorrow for allowing a marriage
In their House Contrary to the order among Friends
Which this meeting accepts for Sattisfaction
And this meeting appoints **Abraham Tucker** an
Elder in the room of **James Barker** Deceased
And whereas **Caleb Hathaway** son of **Richard
Hathaway** hath Signified his Desire of coming under
Our care this meeting appoints **Adam Mott** and
Henry Hedly to Discource with him Concerning his
Complyance with Friends orders and make return
to the next monthly meeting
And this meeting hath Concluded that there be a
meeting kept at **Josiah Merihew**s for 6 months
longer after the former manner

At a monthly meeting of friends held at our
meeting House in **Dartmouth** on the 10 day of the
4 month 1750 **Ponaganset** meeting Called **Isaac
Howland** and **Abraham Tucker** present **Coakset**

meeting Called present **Robert Mosher** and
Othniel Tripp
Ther was a Condemnation against **Richard Gifford** brought
to this meeting which is refered to next monthly meeting
The Friends appointed to Discource with **Caleb Hathaway**
have Done it and they Signify that he hath given them
good Sattisfaction Therefore it is the Conclution of this
meeting he should be under our care for the time to come
The Friends appointed to attend the Quarterly meeting
~~have Done it~~ And Draw an Epistle to the Same are
Henry Tucker Nathanael Potter and **Adam Mott** and
there was Collected at this meeting for the use of Friends £2-16ˢ-06ᵈ
And whereas **Stephen Willcock** hath Signified to this meet
-ing that he lies under a Difficult Sircumstance by
reason of Some Debts that lyeth against him he not
being in a Capacity to Sattisfy the Same Therefor he
Doth Desire that Friends Would Contribute Something
to his necessity Therefore this meeting appoints
Humphry Smith Ebenezer Slocum and **Barnabus**
Howland to make enquiry into his affairs and bring
an account to the next monthly meeting
And whereas there there hath been some debate in
this meeting Whither if first Cousins marry together
it being Contrary to our orders that their Condemning
their offence may ever be received so as for them to
Come into unity again which is refered to the
Quarterly meeting
and this meeting orders the Tresurer to pay five
pounds old tenor to the overseers for the last halfe
years keeping the meeting House and the Epistle
from **London** baring Date 1749 Was read at this
to good Sattisfaction

At a monthly meeting of Friends held at our meeting
House in **Dartmouth** on the 16 Day of the 5 month 1750
Ponaganset meeting Called **Joseph Tucker** and **Abraham**
Tucker present **Coakset** meeting Called **Joseph Tripp** and
Benjamin Tripp present
Our Friends **Ann Schoolfield** and **Lydia Mendinghall**
Was at this meeting ~~and~~ from **Pensilvania** and their
Labour In the Truth Well accepted and their Certifi

-cates read to good Sattisfaction and there was a
Condemnation Signed at this meeting against
Richard Gifford and **Jedidiah Wood** is appointed
to read it at the end of a First day meeting at **Coakset**
between this and the next monthly meeting
And **Henry Tucker** and **Nathanal Potter** hath attend
-ed the Quarterly meeting as appointed and Drawn
an Epistle to the Same as appointed
And the Epistle from the Quarterly meeting hath
been read at this meeting and well accepted
It was Concluded at the Quarterly meeting that Frie[n]ds
might receive into unity again such first cousins that
have broken our good order in marriage upon true
Repentance and Suitable acknowledgment
The Friends appointed to See Into **Stephen Willcox**es affairs
have brought in their account and it is the advice
of this meeting that he should put himself in order
to pay his Just Debts by Selling his place or Some other
Suitable method and the former Com:^tte to be helpful
In assisting him by advice

At a monthly meeting of Friends held at our meeting
House in **Dartmouth** onth 20 day of ye 6 month 1750
Ponaganset meeting Called **Joseph Tucker** present
Coakset meeting Called and none appeared and this
meeting is adjourned until ye next 4th Day Come Week
This meeting being met according to adjournment rhis
29th Day of the 6 month 1750 **Samuel Howland S**on
of **Isaac Howland** And **Elisabeth Butler** did lay their
Intentions of taking each other in marriage before
this meeting and were desired to wait until the
next monthly meeting for their answer and **Caleb**
Russell and **Henry Hedly** are appointed to Enquire
into the young mans Clearness and make return
to the next monthly meeting
And this meeting hath received a Certificate from
the monthly meeting at **Pembrook**Concerning **Prince**
Barker and his wife recommending the to our Care
And **Jedidiah Wood** hath read **Richard Gifford**s Condemnation
as appointed which is as followeth
Whereas **Richard Gifford** there Son of **Christopher Gifford**

and **Mary** his his Wife of **Dartmouth** in the **County of Bristol** in
the **Province of the Massachusets Bay** in **New England** being one
being one that had his Education among Friends the people
Called Quakers yet for want of keeping to his education
and not regarding the wholesom orders Established amongst
Friends hath gone and married his former wives Sister
although much pains hath been taken by Friends to persuade him to Desist but yet Contrary to all the good ad-
-vice that hath been from time to time Duly given him
he hath willfully proceeded to accomplish his Desire in that
affair for which Willful and Publick offence we can
do no less but give forth this as a publick Condemnation
against him the S^d **Richard Gifford** Denying him to be one
in unity with us the abovesd People yet truly desiring
if it be the Lords Will that he may Come to a Sence of his
outgoings and to unfeigned
Given forth at our monthly meeting Held in **Dartmouth**
on the 15th Day of the 5th month 1750: and Signed in and
by order of s^d meeting by   **Isaac Smith**
And whereas **John Wing** and **Hannah** his Wife hath
made acknowledgment to this meeting Signifying their
Sorrow for for their going out of order Established
amongst s^d Friends in marriage which is accepted
And whereas **Luke Hart** hath made application to this
meeting he being under Difficult Sircumstance, and
Desires Some help of Friends which is refered to the
next monthly meeting
And **Adam Mott** and **Henry Hedly Abraham Tucker**
and **Peleg Smith** are Continued visitters for the ensuing
year and **Jonathan Wood** and **Nathanael Potter**
for **Coakset**

At a monthly meeting of Friends held at our meeting
House in **Dartmouth** the 17th of the 7th month 1750-
Ponaganset meeting Called **Isaac Howland** and **Isaac
Smith** present **Coakset** meeting Called **Othniel Tripp**
and and **Jedidiah Wood** present
The Friends appointed to See Into **Samuel Howland**
Clearness make report to this meeting they find nothing
to hinder his intended marriage
And **Samuel Howland** and **Elisabeth Butler** appeard

at this meeting for their answer and their answer
Was that they might proceed to take each other in
marriage in Some Convenient time between this
and the next monthly meeting observing the good
order Established amongst Friends in the accomplish
-ment thereof And **Jabez Barker** and **Stephen
Willcock** are appointed to See their marriag Consum
-mated and make return to the next monthly meet
-ing And **Philip Anthony** and **Mary Goddard** Did lay
their intentions of taking each other in marriage
before this meeting and were Desired ~~to lay~~ wait for their
answer until the next monthly meeting
John Wing and **Jemima Shepherd** and **John Sisson**
and **Sibil Huddleston** Did lay their Intentions of
marriag and were desired to wait accordingly
And **John Russell** and **Benjamin Wing** are appointed
to make Enquiry into **John Sisson** and **John Wing**s
Clearness respecting marriage and Conversation
and make return to the next monthly meeting
And **Samuel Chase** hath Sent in a Paper to this
meeting Desiring that Friends might receive him
Into unity Therefore this meeting appoints **Jabez
Barker Joseph Tucker Abraham Tucker** and **Peleg
Smith** ~~to~~ and **Ebenezer Slocum** to talk with s^d
Chase and Enquire into his Conversation and bring
In their Judgment and Sence of the matter to the
next monthly meeting
The Friends appointed to attend the Quarterly meet
-ing and Draw an Epistle to the Same are **Joseph
Tucker Abraham Tucker** and **Peleg Smith**
There hath been Considerable agetation at this meet
-ing refering to **Stephen Willcox**es Cace and it is the
Judgment of this meeting that as Speedily as may be
he put himselfe in away with the advice of the Com:^tte to pay his
Just Debts and to take their advice in all matters of Consequence
relating to that affair. And as there was a motion made
Concerning the meeting coming to a Subscription for s^d **Willcock**
It was the sence of this meeting that it is not propper

At a monthly meeting of Friends held at this our meeting
House In **Dartmouth** on the 15 Day of the 8 month 1750

Ponaganset meeting Called **Adam Mott** and **Isaac Howland**
present and for **Coakset** meeting **Jonathan Wood**
And ~~Jonathan~~ **John Russell** and **Benjamin Wing** reports
to this meeting that they have enquired into **John Wing** and
John Sisson Clearness as to marriage and Conversation
And find nothing to hinder their proceeding In their intended
marriage. And **John Wing** and **Jemima Shepherd John Sisson**
and **Sibil Huddleston Philip Anthony** and **Mary Godard** all
appeared at this meeting for their answers and their answers
was that they might proceed to marry in the good order of
Friends in Some Convenient time between this and the
next monthly meeting. And ~~Philip~~ **William Anthony** and **Peleg Smith**
are appointed to see **Philip Antony** and **Mary Goddard**s marriage
Consummated in the S^d Good order and make return to the
next monthly meeting
And **John Russell** and **Benjamin Wing** are appointed to see
John Sisson and **Sibil Huddlestone**s marriage Consummated
as afores^d and make return to ye next monthly meeting
And **Abraham Tucker** and **Stephen Willcox** are
appointed to see **John Wing** and ~~Ste~~ **Jemima Shepherd**s marriage
Consummated as afores^d and to make return as aforesd
And **Jabez Barker** and **Stephen Willcock** reports to this
meeting that they Saw **Samuel Howland** and **Elisabeth**
Butlers marriage Consummated as appointed
The matter Concerng **Samuel Chase** is refere to the
next monthly meeting and **Eliashib Smith Jossiah Merihew**
Joseph Mosher and **Henry Hedly** is added to the former
Com:^{tte} in the affair of **Samuel Chases**
The Friends appointed to attend the Quarterly meeting
and Draw an Epistle to the Same have Done it
And this meeting has received An Epistle from the
Quarterly meeting which was read and well accepted

At a monthly meeting of Friends held at our meeting
House In **Dartmouth** on the 19th Day of ye 9 month 1750
Ponaganset meeting Called **Joseph Tucker** and **Abraham**
Tucker present **Coakset** meeting Called **Jedidiah Wood**
and **Nathanael Potter** present
The Friends appointed to See the three Cupples mar-
-riages Consummated gives an account that they
Were all Consummated in good order

And **Nicholas Howland** and **Mary Sisson** Did lay their
Intention of taking each other in marriag before
this meeting and were desired to wait till the next
monthly meeting and were desired to wait till the next
monthly meeting for their answer and **Jonathan Wood**
and **Edward Cornell** are appointed to make Enquiry
Into the young mans Clearness respecting marriage
and Conversation and make return to the next month
-ly meeting There was Collected at this meeting 2 pound
12 Shillings and 6 pence
The matter Concerning **Samuel Chase** is refered till
the next monthly meeting And this meeting orders
the Tresurer to pay to **James Mitchel** of **Rode Island**
two and twenty Shillings old tenor for some charge that
he was at Concerning Friends passage to **Nantucket**
and this meeting Doth agree that there should be a meeting
kept as heretofore at **Josiah Merihew**s or thereabouts
for 6 months longer And whereas **Alice Smith**
hath sent in a paper to this meeting Signifying her
sorrow for her outgoings which is refered to the
Consideration of the next monthly meeting
And Whereas **Peleg Smith** hath Signified to this
meeting that he hath been at Considerable Charge
and trouble refering to his trust Concerning **Ann
Shaw** therefore he is Desired to bring in his account
To the next monthly meeting

At a monthly meeting of Friends held at our meeting House in
Dartmouth on the 17ᵗʰ Day of the 10ᵗʰ mon 1750 **Ponaganset**
meeting Called **Abraham Tucker** and **Peleg Smith** present
Coakset meeting Called **Christopher Gifford** and **Jonathan Wood**
present The Friends appointed See Into **Nicholas Howland**s Clear
-ness makes report to this meeting that they find nothing to hinder
his intended marriage
And **Nicholas Howland** and **Mary Sisson** appeared at this
meeting for their answer and their answer was that
they might proceed to take each other in marriage in
Some Convenient time between this and the next
monthly meeting observing the good order Established a-
mongst Friends in the Performance thereof and **John
Russell** and **Benjamin Wing** are appointed to see their

marriage Consummated in s^d order and make return
to the next monthly meeting
And there was Collected at this meeting for the use of
Friends six pound one shilling old Tenor
And this meeting is adjourned until the youth meeting
This meeting being met according to adjournment this
4 day of the 11 month 1750 The matter Concerning **Samuel
Chase** is refered till the next monthly meeting And the
matter Concerning **Alice Smith** is also refered
And there was two papers sent in to this meeting one
by **Abraham Slocum** and his wife the other by **Lusanna
Russell** Which are refered to ye next monthly meeting
And **Joseph Tucker** and **Abraham Tucker** are appointed
Overseers of the meeting House for the year Ensuing
And **Abraham Tucker** hath paid ten pounds old tenor
to **William Wood** for keeping the meeting House
Henry Tucker Adam Mott Joseph Tucker and **Nathanael
Potter** are appointed to at attend the Quarterly
meeting and Draw an Epistle to the Same
Peleg Smith hath brought in his account to this
meeting of his trouble relating to **Anne Shaw**
Which is refered for Consideration to the next
monthly meeting

At a monthly meeting of Friends held at our meeting
House in **Dartmouth** on the 21 Day of ye 11 month 1750
Ponoganset meeting Called **Joseph Tucker** and **Abraham
Tucker** present for **Coakset Edward Cornell** and
Jedidiah Wood present **Benjamin Wing** gives this
meeting an account that **Nicholas Howland**s mar-
-riage was Consummated In good order
And **James Haden** of **Newport** and **Deborah Brown**
Did lay their Intentions of taking each other in
marriage before this meeting as Did also **John Russell**
and **Catharine Williams** and were Desired to wait
for their answers until the next monthly meeting
And **Joseph Tucker** and **Adam Mott** are appointed
to Enquire Into **John Russell**s Clearness respecting
marriage and Conversation and make return to the
next monthly meeting
The Friends appointed to attend the Quarterly meeting

and Draw an Epistle to the Same have Done it as
appointed And the Paper that **Susanna Russell**
Sent in hath been read in this meeting and is
accepted And she is ordered to read it or git some
body to read it at the end of a first Day meeting
And **Abraham Slocum** and **Alice Smith**s papers
are refered to the next monthly meeting
And the matter Concerning **Samuel Chase**
is refered till next monthly meeting

At a monthly meeting of Friends held at our meet
-ing House in **Dartmouth** on the 18 day of the 12 month
1750 **Ponaganset** meeting Called **Adam Mott** and
Abraham Tucker present for **Coakset Jonathan
Wood** and **Othniel Tripp James Hayden** and
Deborah Brown appeared at this meeting for their
answer and their answer was that they might
proceed to take each other In marriage In some
Convenient time between this and the next month
ly meeting. And **Adam Mott** and **Abraham Tucker**
are appointed to See their marriag Consummated in the
good order of Friends
And the Com:^tte hath brought in their result concerning **Sam:^l
Chase** in Writing and it is the Conclution of this meeting that he be
under our Care. And Where **Caleb Russell** Desires Some lines
by Waw [Way] of Certificate of his Clearness in relation to marriage
and Conversation to the monthly meeting at **Nantucket**
Therefore this meeting appoints **Joseph Tucker** and **Abraham
Tucker** to Inspect into the matter and Draw one if they
find things Clear and bring it to the next monthly meeting
Abraham Slocum and **Alice Smith**s papers a refered to
the next monthly meeting
And the Quarterly meetings Epistle hath been read
at this meetin and well accepted

At a monthly meeting of Friends held at our meeting
House In **Dartmouth** on the 18th Day of ye 1 month 1750/51
Ponaganset meeting Called **Barnabas Howland**
and **Joseph Tucker** present for **Coakset Nathanel
Potter** and **Othniel Tripp** present. **Adam Mott** and
Abraham Tucker gives this meeting an account that
James Hayden and **Deborah Brown**s marriage hath been

Consummated in good order according to their observation
And whereas **John Chase** hath had a Scandalous accusation
of being Father to a bastard Child and the visitters have
Dealt with him from time to time but he hath not ta
-ken any Care as we Can learn to make any Sattisfaction
by Clearing himselfe or otherwise Therefore **Jabez
Barker** and **Isaac Smith** are appointed to take With s^d **Chase**
to see whither he will do any thing in that affair and
make return to the next monthly meeting
There was a Certificate brought to for **Caleb Russell**
And **Joseph Tucker** is ordered to Sign it in behalfe
of the monthly meeting
There was three papers read at this meeting one from
Alice Smith and one from **Abram Slocum** an his Wife
and one from **William Smith** and hos Wife Which are
accepted and they ordered to be read they being present
on a first day at at the end of the meeting of Worship
And whereas **Joseph Jenning** hath requested a
Certificate of this meeting to the monthly meeting
at the **Oblong** for himselfe and famly Therefore
this meeting appoints **Jonathan Wood** and
Nathanael Potter to make Enquiry into their
Sircumstances And Draw one if they find things
Clear and bring it to the next monthly meeting
And this monthly meeting hath Concluded to take
an Hundred of **Robert Barclays** Catechisms
And Whereas **Weston Kerby** as as we understand hath
married or is about to marry out of the good order
Established among friends Therefore this meeting
appoints **Othniel Tripp** and **Jedidiah** are appointed
to Speak With s^d **Kerby** And give such advice as they think
propper and make return to ye next monthly
meeting And whereas **Stoaks Potter** Son of **Nathaniel
Potter** hath Set up his Publishement out of ye order of
Friends this meeting appoints **Jonathan Wood** and
Othniel Tripp to talk With him and bring their
account to ye next monthly meeting
And this meeting is adjourned until ye youths meeting
This meeting being met according to adjournment
this fifth Day of ye 2^d: month 1751
This meeting appoints **Jonathan Wood Joseph Tucker**

And **Stephen Willcock** to attend the Quarterly
meeting and Draw an Epistle to the Same
And our Collection is refered till the next month
ly meeting And whereas **Stephen Willcock** hath
mad application to this meeting about Stting [Setting] a
House upon **Barnabas Earl**s land therefore this
meeting appoints **John Shepherd** in the room of
Ebenezer Slocum with other two that were
of the former Com:ᵗᵗᵉ to give Such advice and
Instruction as they think propper in the affair
The visitters being Called upon The Visitters
for **Ponaganset** have given in their account
in Writing and we have received no account
from **Coakset**. This meeting hath raised by way
of Subscription 18 pounds one shilling

At a monthly meting of Friends held at our meeting House
In **Dartmouth** on the 15 Day of the 2ᵈ: month 1751
Ponaganset meeting Called **Abraham Tucker** present for
Coakset Jedidiah Wood present And **Lusanna Russell**s
paper hath been read as ordered and Is as followeth
To the monthly meeting of Friends &c
These few lines may let you know the Exercise that I
have been under on my own account for by not
keeping to my Education I and the advice of Friends and
the Testimony of Testimony of Truth in my own heart
have given way so far to yᵉ temptations of yᵉ Enemy
as to fall into the henious Sin of fornication as is
made publick to the World for which offence I am
Sorry and Do Condemn it with all my heart
Hoping God will forgive me and Desire Friends
would pass by my offences and let me remain under
Dartmouth yᵉ 19 of yᵉ 9 month 1750

                              Susanna Russell

The Friends appointed to see into **John Russell** respecting
marriage and conversation signify that they find nothing to hinder his intended marriage and there
was a Certificate brought to this meeting Directed
to us from yᵉ monthly meeting at **Shrewsbury**
Signifying **Katharine Williams** her Clearness and
Orderly Conversation

And **John Russell** and **Katharine Williams** came
to this meeting for their answer and their answer
was that they might proceed to take each other in
marriage in Some Convenient time between this
and the next monthly meeting observing the good
order Established amongst Friends in yᵉ performance
thereof And **Adam Mott** and **Joseph Tucker** are
appointed to see their marriage consummated in
sᵈ order and make return to yᵉ next monthly
meeting And **Stoaks Potter** and **Rebeckah Shaw**
Did lay their Intentions of taking each other in
marriage before this meeting and were Desired to
wait til yᵉ next monthly meeting for their answer
And **Jedidiah Wood** & **Othniel Tripp** are appointed to
See Into the young mans Clearness and make
Return to the next monthly meeting
Ther was Collected at this meeting £2-14s=09d old tenor
The Friends appointed to talk with **Weston Kerby**
have done and Signify that he Doth Justify his
himselfe Therefor **Isaac Smith** is ordered to Draw
a Condemnation against him and bring it to
the next monthly meeting
And whereas the Friends appointed to talk with
John Chase not having done it this meeting
appoints **Adam Mott** and **Henry Hedly** to talk with
him to See if he hath any mind to make Sattisfaction
Stephen Willcock hath attended yᵉ Quarterly
meeting and Drawn an Epistle to yᵉ Same
And yᵉ Quarterly meeting Epistle hath been read
And well accepted
And **Joseph Tucker** and **Peleg Smith** are appointed
to make up accounts with yᵉ Tresurer
And whereas **Ebenezer Slocum** being about
to remove to **New Port** on **Rhode Island** to live
Doth request a Certificate to the monthly
meeting there therefore this meeting appoints
Peleg Smith and **Daniel Russell** to make En-
quiry into the affair and Drawn one if they
think propper and bring it to yᵉ next monthly
Meeting

At a monthly meeting of Friends held at our
meeting House In **Dartmouth** on the 20 day of
the 3 month 1751 for **Ponaganset Peleg Smith**
and **Abraham Tucker** present for **Coakset**
Jedidiah Wood and **Othniel Tripp** present
And **Stockes Potter** and **Rebeckah Shaw** came
to this meeting for their answer and their
answer was was that that they might proceed
to to take each other in mariage in Some
Convenient time between this and the next
monthly meeting observing the good order
Established amongst us in yᵉ performance thereof
And **Jedidiah Wood** and **Othniel Tripp** are appointed to
See their marriage Consummated In sᵈ order and make
return to the next monthly meeting
And **Job Cornell** and **Mary Davis** did Lay their intentions of taking each other in marriage before this
meeting and were Desired wait till yᵉ next monthly
meeting for their answer and **Othniel Tripp** and
Nathaniel Potter are appointed to See into yᵉ young
mans Clearness and make return to yᵉ next month
ly meeting & **Joseph Tucker** hath Signifyed to this meet
ing that **John Russel** and **Katharine Williams** their
marriage was Consummated In good order
And whereas the Widow **Elizabeth Hammond** hath
Writ to this meeting Disiring to Come under the Care
of Friends Therefore this meeting appoints **Adam**
Mott and **Henry Hedly [Hedley]** to go with some women Friends
to visit her and bring in their account to yᵉ next
monthly meeting
And Whereas **John Chase** hath been Dealt with from
time to time and we can find no inclination in him
to Clear him selfe to friends Sattisfaction this meet
ing therefore appoints **Jabez Barker** & **Isaac Smith**
to Draw up a Condemnation against him and bring
it to yᵉ next monthly meeting
The matter Concerning **Ebenezer Slocum**s Certificate
Is refered until yᵉ next monthly meeting
And **Weston Kerbies** Condemnation hath been read
at this meeting And **Joseph Tucker** and **Isaac Smith**

hath Signed it by order of the meeting
and is as followeth

Whereas **Weston Kerby** Son of **Nathaniel Kerby**
deceased and **Abigail** his wife of **Dartmouth** in the
County of Bristol in the **Province of Massachusets
Bay** In **New England** being one that hath been
Educated among Friends his Father and mother
being boath professors with us the People Called
Quakers yet for want of keeping to his education
hath of late gone and married and In the Common
Way of other People
Out of the good order Established amongst us altho
he hath been Seasonably and Lovingly dealt with
yet doth give no Encouragement of making any
Sattisfaction Therefore this meeting thinks prop
-per to give forth this as a Testimony against him
Denying him the S^d **Weston Kerby** to be one in unity
with us the aboves^d People yet Truly Desiring that
he may Come to a Sight of his outgoings & find mercy
Given forth at our monthly meeting held in
Dartmouth on the 20th Day of the 3 month 1751
And Signed In & by order of s^d meeting by

> **Joseph Tucker**
> **Isaac Smith**

And whereas the Friends appointed to make up
accompts With ye Tresurer not having Done it
They are Continued to do it and bring in their ac
count to ye next monthly meeting
And this meeting gives Leave that there be a
meeting kept as heretofore at **Isiah Merihew**s
or thereabouts for one year Longer
And this meeting hath appointed **Nathaniel
Potte** & **Benjamin Tripp** Son of **Joseph Tripp**
Trustees to take a new Deed of ye Land belong
ing to **Coakset** meeting House[17]
And Whereas **Joseph Brownell** hath gone out
and married out of ye good order of Friends
therefore this meeting appoints **Jonathan Wood**
And **Edward Cornell** to talk with him to See

---

17. The preceding sentence has been crossed over in the manuscript.

Whither he will make any acknowledgmen
At the monthly meeting the 24 day of the
4 month 1751 **Henry Tucker Adam Mott** and
Henry Hedly & **Nathaniel Potter** are appointed
to atten yᵉ Quarterly meeting and Draw an
Epistle to the Same

4
1751 At a monthly meeting held by adjournment on the
24ᵗʰ Day of 4ᵗʰ month 1751 The Friends appointed to See
into **Job Cornell**s clearness makes report that they
find nothing to hinder his intended marriage
And **Job Cornell** and **Mary Davis** appeared at this meet
ing for their answer & their answer was that
they might proceed to take each other In marriage
in Some Convenient time between this and the
next monthly meeting observing the good order
Established amongst Friends in the performance
thereof And **Nathaniel Potter** and **Othniel Tripp** are
appointed to See their marriage Consummated in sᵈ order and
make return to the next monthly meeting
The Friends appointed to See **Stokes Potter** and **Rebekah
Shaw**s marriag Consummated Signifies that it was
Done in good order the matter Concerning the Widw
Hammond is refered until yᵉ next monthly meeting
And **Jseph Tucker** hath mad up accompts with the Tre
-surer and there remains In yᵉ Stock Seven pound
one Shilling & three pence
There was a Certificate Signed at this meeting for
Joseph Jennings and his famly they being remvd
to yᵉ **Oblong** to live our Worthy Friends **Rebekah Harvey** and **Jane Ellis**
from **Pensilvania** were at this meeting and their
Certificats were read to good Sattisfaction and the
yearly meeting Epistle was read In this meeting to
good Sattisfaction And **William Sanford ju**ʳ hath
Sent in Some lines to this meeting Signifying his
Sorrow for marrying out of the meeting which
this meeting accepts for Sattisfaction And the matter
Concerning **Ebenezer Slocum**s Certificate is refered
until yᵉ next monthly meeting as is also the mat=
-ter Concerning **Joseph Brownel** and **John Chase**

At a monthly meeting of Friends held at our meet
-ing House In **Dartmouth** on ye 15th Day of ye 5 mo: 1751
Ponaganset meeting Called **Abraham Tucker** and
Peleg Smith present **Coakset** meeting Called
Othniel Tripp and **Nathaniel Potter** present
The Friends appointed to See **Job Cornell** and **Mary
Davise**s marriag Consummated gives this meeting
an account that that It was orderly accomplished
And **Thomas Hicks** and **Elisabeth Hamond** Did lay
Their intentions of taking each other in marriage
before this meeting and were Desired to wait
until ye Next monthly meeting for their answer
And **Benjamin Slocum** & **Phebe Wing** Did lay their
Intentions of marriage before this meeting and
were Desired to wait till ye next monthly meet
-ing for their answer And **Abraham Tucker** and
Adam Mott are appointed to Enquire Into the
young mans Clearness And make return to the
next monthly meeting
And **H**enry **Tucker** hath attended the Quarterly
meeting and there was an Epistle Drawn and
Sent And the Quarterly meeting epistle was read
at this meeting and kindly accepted And whereas
Joseph Brownell hath not as yet made Sattisfac
tion for his Disorder the matter is refered till
the next monthly meeting And the matter
Concerning **John Chase** is also refered
And Whereas **Samuel Chase** hath been at this
meeting Desiring to Come under the Care and
In unity With Friends which this meeting agreas to

At a monthly meeting of Friends held at our
meeting House In **Dartmouth** on the 19th Day of ye
6 month 1751 **Ponaganset** meeting Called **Adam
Mott** and **Peleg Smith** present for **Coakset**
Jedidiah Wood and **Edward Cornell** present
The Friends appointed to Enquire into **Benjamin
Slocum**s Clearness gives this meeting an account
that they find nothing to hinder his intended
marriage the matter Concerning **Joseph Brownell**
is refered until the next monthly meeting

And **Thomas Hicks** and **Elisabeth Hammond** appear
-ed at this meeting for their answer

As Did also **Benjamin Slocum** and **Phebe Wing** and they
had their answers that they might proceed to marry in
the good order Established amongst Friends in Some Con
venient time between this and the next monthly
meeting observing the good order established amongst
In yᵉ accomplishment thereof And **Adam Mott** and **John
Shepherd** are appointed to See **Benjamin Slocum** and **Phebe
Wing**s marriage Sollemnized in sᵈ good order and make
return to yᵉ next monthly meeting

And **Joseph Mosher** and **Joanna Mott** Did lay their
Intentions of taking Each other in marriage before
this meeting and were Desired to wait till our next
monthly meeting for their answer and **Eliashib
Smith** & **Abraham Tucker** are appointed to make
Enquiry Into **Joseph Mosher**s Clearness and make
return to the next monthly meeting

And this meeting Concludes to renew the Deeds of yᵉ
meeting House lands for **Coakset** and **Ponaganset**
and **Cushnot** The Friends appointed to take yᵉ Deeds

Deeds are for **Coakset William Gifford** And **Benjamin**
of trust **Tripp** & **Joseph Tripp** Sons of **Joseph Tripp**
And for **Ponaganset Nicholas Howland Daniel
Russell David Smith** & **William Barker** and for
Cushnot Caleb Russell Bartholome Taber and
Francis Allen & **Benjamin Allen** juʳ:

And **John Chase**s Condemnation hath been read and
Signed by order of yᵉ meeting by **Isaac Smith** and is
as followeth

Whereas **John Chase** the Son of **Nathaniel Chase** and
Abigail his wife of **Dartmouth** in the **County of Bristol**
In the **Province of** yᵉ **Massachusets Bay** in **New England**
Having been under the Care of Friends the People
Called Quakers and having fallen under Some Disa-
-greable reports and been under Dealing upon that
account and not Clearing him self to Friends Sattis
faction and also as a further aggrevation hath
of late married out of the good order Established
among Friends for all which his Disorderly

Proceedings we can Do no less than Set him aside
Denying him the S^d **John Chase** to be in unity with us
the aboves^d People yet Sincerely desiring that he may
Come to a Sight of his outgoings and find mercy
Given forth at our monthly meeting held in **Dartmouth**
on the 19th Day of ye 6 month 1751 And Signed In &
by order of S^d meeting by   **Isaac Smith**

At a monthly meeting of Friends held at our meet
ing House in **Dartmouth** on ye 16 Day of ye 7th mo 1751
Ponaganset meeting Called **Henry Tucker** and **William
Barker** present and for **Coakset Christopher Gifford**
and **Othniel Tripp** present
The Friends appointed to Enquire into **Joseph Moshers**
Clearness make report that they find nothing to hin-
der his Intended Marriage & **Joseph Mosher** & **Joanna
Mott** appeared at this meeting for their answer
And their answer was that they might proceed to
take each other in marriage in Some Convenient
time between this and the next monthly meeting
observing the good order Established amongst Friends
In ye performance thereof and **Eliashib Smith** and
Abraham Tucker are appointed to See their marriage
Consummated in ye aboves^d good order and make
return to ye next monthly meeting
And the Friends appointed ~~to (Enquire Concerning~~
Benjamin Slocums Clearness makes report that they
~~find nothing to hinder his~~ proceedings ~~in his intended
marriage)~~ See **Benjamin Slocum** and **Phebe Wing**s
marriage Consummated in good order gives this
meeting an account that it was according to their
observation And **Jonathan Barney** and **Hannah
Russell** Did lay their intentions of taking each other
in marriage in marriage before this meeting and
were Desired to wait till ye next monthly meeting
for their answer
There was Collected at this meeting 4£-12^s 0^d old tenor
The Friends appointed to attend the Quarterly meeting are
Abraham Tucker Peleg Smith and **William Barker** and
to Draw an Epistle to ye Same And ye matter Concerning
Joseph Brownell is refered till ye next monthly meeting

And **Isaac Smith** is Chosen Clerk to yᵉ monthly meeting
for this year. And **Anne Almy** hath Sent in a paper
to this meeting Condemning her outgoings which is re
fered to yᵉ next monthly meeting And there was Collec
ted Eeight pounds fourteen Shillings old tenor towards
the yearly meeting Stock at **London**

At a monthly meeting of Friends held at our meeting
House In **Dartmouth** on the 21 day of yᵉ 8 month 1751
Ponaganset meeting Called **Joseph Tucker** present **Coakset**
meeting Called **Jonathan Wood** & **Jedidiah Wood** present
and **Abraham Tucker** gives this meeting an account
That **Joseph Mosher** and **Joanna Mott**s marriage was
Consumated in good order
And **Jonathan Barney** and **Hannah Russell** appeared
at this meeting for their answer and their answer
was that they might proceed to take each other in mar
-riage In Some Convenient time between this and yᵉ
next monthly meeting observing yᵉ good order Established
amongst Friends In yᵉ performance thereof And **Stephen
Willcock** and **Abraham Tucker** are appointed to See their
marriage Consummated In sᵈ order and make return to yᵉ
next monthly meeting The Friends appointed to attend
the Quarterly meeting and Draw an Epistle to yᵉ Same
have Done it And yᵉ Quarterly meeting Epistle hat been
read and weell accepted and yᵉ matter Concerning
Joseph Brownell is refered till nxt month meeting
And our Friend **Lydia Soule** from yᵉ Nine Partners
In yᵉ Government of the **New Yourk** was at this meeting
And her Certificate was read to good Sattisfaction
There was Collected at this meeting 3 pounds 8 Shillings OT
And **Stephen Willcox** And **David Smith** are appointed to
Draw up a Certificate for **Lydia Soule**
And there hath been Some Discource in this meeting
Concerning Chusing Chusing visittors which is refered to
the next monthly meeting And **Abraham Tucker** hath
paid 6 pound 10 Shillings old Tenor for yᵉ last ½ yers keeping yᵉ
meeting house
And this meeting is adjourned until the fourth Day
After yᵉ yearly meeting
This meeting being met according to adjournment this

30th Day of ye 8 month 1751 There was a Certificate
Signed at this meeting for **Lydia Soule**

~~And~~ At a monthly meeting of Friends held at our
meeting House In **Dartmouth** on the 18th Day of the
9th month 1751 **Ponaganset** meeting Called **Barnabas
Howland** & **William Barker** present And for **Coakset
Nathll** [Nathaniel] **Potter** and **Edwd Cornell** present
And **Stephen Willcock** [Wilcox] gives this meeting an account
that **Jonathan Barney** and **Hannah Russell**s marriage
Was Consummated in good order
And **Benjamin Smith** and **Susannah Wood** Did
Lay their Intentions of marriage before this meeting
and Were Desired to wait till the next monthly
meeting for their answer And **John Russell juner**
And **Daniel Russell** are appointed to See into the
young mans Clearness and make return to the
next monthly meeting
And Whereas **Joseph Brownell** hath been dealt
with from time to time but we can find no encli
nation in him to make up the matter Therefor
this meeting appointed to Draw up a Condemnation
Against him and bring it to ye next monthly meetin
And **Rebekah Kerlye**s [Kirby] Condemnation was brought
to this meeting & **Isaac Smith** hath Signed it by order
of ye meeting And **Edwd Cornell** is appointed to read
it or git Some body to Do it on a first day at the
end of ye meeting for worship at **Coakset** meeting House
And make return to ye next monthly
The visitters Chose for this year for **Ponaganset Abraham
Tucker** and **Peleg Smith** and for **Coakset Jonathan Wood**
and **Nathaniel Potter** And **Holder Slocum** is appointed
to Let **Increase Allen junr** know that it is the mind
of this meeting that he that Comply with the Judgment
of the Comtte in the Cace relating between himselfe &
Barnabas Howland And Whereas **Robert Tripp** Desires
a few lines by way of Certificate for him selfe and his
famly to the monthly meeting at **Smithfield** therefore
this meeting appoints **Edward Cornell** and **Jedidiah
Wood** to Do it
And **Ann Almy**s paper is refered until the

next monthly meeting

At a monthly meeting of Friends held at our meeting
House in **Dartmouth** on the 16 Day of yᵉ 10 month 1751
Ponaganset meeting Called **Abraham Tucker** & **Peleg Smith**
present for **Coakset James Cornell** and **Benjamin Tripp**
present The Friends to See into **Benjamin Smith**s Clearness
gives this meeting an account that they find nothing to hinder
his intended marriage And **Benjamin Smith** and **Susannah
Wood** appeared at this meeting for their answer and they
had their answer that they might proceed to take each
other In marriage in Some Convenient time between
this and the next monthly meeting observing our good
Order In yᵉ acco[m]plishment thereof And **James Shearman**
and **Isaac Smith** are appointed See their marriage Consummated in Sd good order & make return to yᵉ next
monthly meeting And **Rebekah Kerby**es [**Kirby**] Condemnati
on hath been read according to order & is as followeth
Whereas **Rebekah Kerby** [**Kirby**] Daughter of **Nathaniel Kerby** [**Kirby**]
Late of **Dartmouth** in yᵉ County of **Bristol** In the Province
of yᵉ **Massachuset[t]s Bay** In **New England** Deceased & **Abigail** his
Wife being one that hath had her Education amongst us
the People Called Quakers her Father & Mother being
both Friends but yet for want of keeping to
her Education & yᵉ Spirit of truth in her Selfe hath
given way to the Insinuations of yᵉ Enemy So as to fall
Into the Scandalous Sin of fornication And although
timely Care hath been taken to bring her to a Sence
of her outgoings yet th[e]re appears no Sign of Repentance
Therefore for yᵉ Clearing of yᵉ Blessed Truth from Such
Enormities we Cand Do no less but give forth this as
a Publick Testimony against her Denying her the Sd
Rebekah Kerby [**Kirby**] to be one in unity with us the abovesd
People yet truly Desiring that if it be the will of God
She may Come to a Sight and Sence of her out
goings and find mercy
Given forth at our monthly meeting of men and Women
held In **Dartmouth** on the 18 day of yᵉ 9 month 1751
And Signed by order of Sd meeting by **Isaac Smith** Clerk
The matter Concerning **Increase Allen jur** is refered
till yᵉ next monthly meeting

And **Edward Cornell** and **Daniel Russell** are appointed
to git yᵉ Deeds of the Lands belonging to yᵉ meeting
Housee finished And **Adam Mott** and **Henry** are appoin[ted]
visitters with yᵉ other two for **Ponaganset**
There was Collected at this meeting 4 pound 3 Shillings OT[18]
And This meeting accepts of **Ann Almy**es acknowledg
ment for Sattisfaction and **Isaac Smith** is ordered read
it at Some Convenient time She being present
Adam Mott Abraham Tucker and **Jonathan** [*sic*] are
appointed to attend yᵉ Quarterly meeting and Draw
an Epistle to yᵉ Same And **Joseph Brownell**s Condem
nation hath been read And **Isaac Smith** hath Sidned [signed]
it by order of yᵉ monthly meeting And is as followeth
Whereas **Joseph Brownell** of **Dartmouth** in the County
of **Bristol** in the Province of yᵉ **Massachusets Bay** in **New
England** being one that hath made Profession for these
many years with us the People Called Quake[r]s yet for
Want of Steady to his profession hath of Late Contrary
to our good order married in the Common Way of other
People for which breach of our wholesom order we
Cand Do no other for the Clearing of yᵉ blessed Truth
but give forth this as a Testimony against him having
Cleared our Selves in Advice and Counsel in that
affair And Do Deny him the Sd **Joseph Brownell**
to be one in unity with us yet truly Desiring that he
may Come to a Sence of his out going and find mercy
Given forth at our monthly meeting held In **Dartmouth**
on the 16 Day of the 10 month 1751 And Signed by
order & in behalfe of Sd meeting by **Isaac Smith** Clerk
And this meeting hath Signed a Certificate for **Robert
Tripp** And the Tresurer hath paid **Wᵐ Wood** yᵉ Sum of
6 pounds & 10 Shillings for the Last ½ years keeping
the meeting House

At a monthly meeting of Friend held at our meet
ing House In **Dartmouth** on yᵉ 20ᵗʰ Day of the 1ᵗʰ month
1752 ₍new stile [style]₎ **Ponaganset** meeting Called **John Russell** present
Coakset meeting Called **Christopher Gifford** and **Joseph
Tripp** present the Friends held at our appointed to
See into **Benjamin Smith**s Clearness & **Susanna**

18. I.e., Old Tenor, the provincial currency

Woods marriage Consummated gives this meeting
an account that it was orderly performed
Increas[e] Allen juʳ was at this meeting and Signifies that
he takes up with the Com^ttes Judgment relating to a cace
between himselfe and **Barnabas Howland**
The Friends appointed to attend yᵉ Quarterly meeting
have Done it and Drawn an Epistle to yᵉ Same
And the Epistle from yᵉ Quarterly meeting was read
at this meeting and well accepted And whereas it is
reckoned propper that there Should be three over
seers to yᵉ burying ground belonging to yᵉ meeting
of Friends at **Ponaganset** this meeting appoints
Abraham Tucker in yᵉ room of **James Barker**
Decesed with **John Russell** & **Joseph Tucker** for that
Service And **James Shearman** is Chosen Tresurer
In the room of **Abraham Tucker**
And **Joseph Tucker** is appointed to make up accounts
With the former Tresurer

At a monthly meeting of Friends held at our
meeting House In **Dartmouth** on yᵉ 17ᵗʰ Day of yᵉ 2ᵈ
month 1752 **Ponaganset** meeting Called **Adam
Mott** and **Abraham Tucker** present **Coakset**
meeting Called **Nathaniel Potter** and **William
Gifford** present And **William Tripp** and **Lydia
Shearman** Did lay their intentions of taking each
other in marriage before this meeting and were
Desired to wait till yᵉ next monthly meeting for
their answer And **Nathaniel Potter** and **Jedidiah
Wood** are appointed to make Enquiry Into the young
mans Clearness And make return to yᵉ next mon
thly meeting And whereas **Joshua Lapham** is re-
moved with his fam[i]ly to **Smithfield** in **Rod [Rhode] Island**
Goverment to Live Doth desire a Certificate
from this meeting to the monthly meeting there
and this meeting appoints **Jabez Barker** and **Isaac
Smith** to make Enquiry and Draw one accordingly
and bring it to yᵉ next monthly meeting And **John
Shepherd** & **David Smith** are Chosen to Settle
with yᵉ former Com^tte relating to **Ann Shaw**

At a monthly meeting of Friends held at our meet

-ing House in **Dartmouth** on yᵉ 16 Day of yᵉ 3 month
1752 **Ponaganset** meeting Called **Abraham Tucker**
and **Joseph Tuc[k]er** present **Coakset** meetin Called
Nathaniel Potter and **Jonathan Wood** present
The Friends appointed to See into **William Tripp**s
Clearness makes report that they find nothing to
hinder his intended marriage And **William Tripp**
and **Lydia Shearman** appeared at this meeting for
their answer and thir answer was that they might
proceed to take each other in marriage in Some
Convenient time between this and the next
monthly meeting observing the good order Esta
blished among Sd Friends in the performance therof
and **Isaac Smith** and **Henry Hedly** are appointed to
Se their marriage Sollemnized In yᵉ abovsd order
and make return to yᵉ next monthly meeting
And **Isaac Cornell** & **Priscilla Mosher** Did lay
their Intentions of marriage before this meeting
and were desired to wait till yᵉ next monthly
meeting for their answer and **Jonathan Wood** and
Jedidiah Wood are appointed to Enquire Concer
-ning the young mans Clearness And make re
-turn to yᵉ next monthly meeting
And **Joseph Tucker** hath made up accounts with
the former Tresurer and ther remains in the
Stock 5 pound one Shilling & three pence
And **Joshua Lapham** had a Certificate Signed at
this meeting — And **Stephen Willcock** [Wilcox] **Jonathan Wood**
Nathaniel Potter Henry Tucker & **Jedidiah Wood**
are appointed to attend yᵉ Quarterly meeting
and Draw an Epistle to yᵉ Same
Collected at this meeting 3-8-10 old tenor
and the Tresurer is ordered to pay to **Thomas**
Hathaway for glazing £8-15ˢ -0ᵈ old tenor
And this meeting Concludes to Come to a Subscrip
-tion for the yearly meeting Stock in **London**
and this meeting is adjourned until the
youths meeting next
This meeting being met according to adjournment this 3ᵈ –
Day of yᵉ 4 month 1752 and no business presented

At a monthly meeting of friends held at our meeting
House in **Dartmouth** on the 20th Day of the 4 month
1752 **Ponaganset** meeting ~~House in Dartmouth on the~~
Called **Joseph Tucker** and **Abraham Tucker** present for
Coakset meeting Called **John Cornell** and **Edwd Cornell** pre_{sent}
The Friends appointed to See into **Isaac Cornell**s Clear
ness gives this meeting an account that they find
nothing to hinder his intended marriage and **Isaac
Cornell** ~~gives~~ and **Priscilla Mosher** appeared at this
meeting for their answer and their answer was
that they might proceed to take each other in marriage in Some Convenient time between this and the
next monthly meeting observing ye Good order Esta
blished amongst Friends in ye performance thereof
And **Abraham Tucker** and **Joseph Tucker** are appointed to See their marriage Sollemnized in sd order and
make return to ye next monthly meeting
The Friends appointed to See **William Tripp** and **Lydia
Shearman**s marriage Consummated gives this meet
ing an account that it was orderly accomplished
The Friends appointed to attend ye Quarterly mee[t]ing
and Draw an Epistle to ye Same have done it all but
on The Tresurerer not having paid ye mony orderd
to **Thomas Hathaway** he is Desired to Do it between
this and ye next monthly meeting
And ye Epistle from ye Quarterly meeting hath been
read in this meeting & well accepted
The matter Concerning **Ann Shaw** not being finnish
ed is refered to ye next monthly meeting
this meeting hath Come to a further Subscription
towards the **London** yearly meeting Stock and the Sum
Subscribed is 12 pound old tenor
And Whereas **Samuel Tripp** hath Spoken for a Certi
ficate from this meeting to ye monthly meeting at
Sandwich therefore this meeting appoints **Joseph** and
Abraham Tucker are appointed to Draw one if they find
things Clear and bring it to ye adjournment of this meeting
And this meeting is adjourned till the next fourth
Day Come week
At a monthly meeting held by adjournment on the

29 of yᵉ 4ᵗʰ month 1752 There Was a Certificate Signed
at this meeting for **Samuel Tripp**

At a monthly meeting of Friends held at our meet
ing House in **Dartmouth** on the 18 day of the 5 month
1752 **Ponaganset** meeting Called **Abraham Tucker**
present **Coakset** meeting Called **Jedidiah Wood** and
Robert mosher present The Friends appointed to
See **Isaac Cornell** and **Priscilla Mosher**s marriage
Consummated gives this meeting an account that
it was orderly performed according their judgment
and the matter Concerning **Ann Shaw** is refered
till yᵉ next monthly meeting
And whereas **Daniel Wood** Son of **Jonathan Wood**
Desires a few lines by way of Certificate of his
Clearness as to marriage and Conversation from
this meeting to yᵉ monthly meeting
 at **Swanzey** therefore this meeting ap
points **Christopher Gifford** and **Edward Cornell** to
make Enquiry and if they find things Clear to Draw
one and bring it to yᵉ next monthly meeting
And there was a paper presented to this meeting
Signed by **William Wood juʳ** and **Mary** his Wife
Signifying their Sorrow for their outgoings wich
is refered to yᵉ next monthly meeting

At a monthly meeting of Friends held at our meet
in **Dartmouth** on the 22ᵈ Day of the 6 month 1752
Ponaganset meeting Called **James Shearman** and
Jonathan Ricketson present **Coakset** meeting Called
~~James Shearman~~ none appeared; our friend
William Horne of **Darby** in **Pensilvania** was at
this meeting and his Certificate was read to good
Sattisfaction there was a Certificate Signed at this
meeting for **Daniel Wood** & **William Wood** and his
Wives ₍paper₎ is refered till the next monthly meeting
The Friends appointed to attend the ~~monthly~~ Quarterly meeting
are **Henry Tucker Nathaniel Potter Abraham Tucker**
Abraham ~~Tucker~~ Russell and they to draw an Epistle
to the Same There was Collected at this meeting for the
use of Friends 2ᵉ–19ˢ–08ᵈ old Tenor

At a monthly meeting held at our meeting House in
Dartmouth on the 20 Day of the 7 month 1752 **Pona
ganset** meeting Called **Abraham Tucker** and **Adam
Mott** for **Coakset Christopher Gifford** and **Nathaniel Potter**
The Friends appointed to attend the Quarterly meeting
Have Done it and Drawn an Epistle to the Same as appoin
ted and the Quarterly meeting Epistle hath been read at
this meeting and well accepted and we have received
an Epistle from yᵉ yearly meeting in **London** baring
Date yᵉ 3 month ~~1752~~ 1751 which was read and kindly
accepted And **William Wood** and his wives paper hath
Considered and this meeting accepts of it for Sattisfaction
And Desire that he would git Some Friend to read it they
being present at the end of yᵉ meeting for worship on
a first Day And the matter Concerning **Ann Shaw** is
refered till yᵉ next monthly meeting And there
Was Collected at this meeting 5ᵉ - 03ˢ - 08ᵈ old tenor
And whereas the Common Stable being out of repair
This meeting appoints **George Smith** to take Care and
Repair the Same

At a monthly meeting of Friends held at our meeting
House in **Dartmouth** on the 17ᵗʰ Day of yᵉ 8 month 1752
Ponaganset meeting Called **Adam Mott** & **Abraham
Tucker** present **Coakset** meeting Called **Nathaniel
Potter** and **Othniel Tripp** present
And **John Wood** of **Little Compton** and **Jerusha Taber**
Did lay their intentions of taking each other in mar
riage before this meeting and were desired to wait
till yᵉ next monthly meeting for their answer
And **Jonathan Wood** and **Nathaniel Potter** are appointed
to Enquir Concerning ~~the young~~ **John Wood**s Clearness
as to marriage and Conversation and make return
to the next monthly meeting
And the Tresurer hath paid 7 pound old tenor to
John Shepherd for the Last halfe years keeping the
meeting House And whereas **Abraham Slocum** hath
requeste a few lines by way of Certificate to yᵉ monthly
meeting at **Rhode Island** this meeting appoints **Isaac
Howland** and **William Anthony** to make Enquiry and
Draw one if they think propper and bring it to yᵉ

FIG. 6: *The Long Plain Meeting House in Acushnet is the original structure first built in 1759.*
© *Copyright Jean Schnell*

next monthly meeting & yᵉ matter Concerning **Ann
Shaw** not being Compleated is refered till yᵉ next
monthly meeting
And **Joseph Tucker Peleg Smith** and **Daniel Russell**
are appointed to attend the Quarterly meeting
next and Draw a Epistle to yᵉ Same

At a monthly meeting of Friends held at our
meeting House in **Dartmouth** on the 16 Day of the
10 month 1752 **Ponaganset** meeting Called **Jabez
Barker** and **Smith** [*sic*] present for **Coakset Christopher
Gifford** and **Edward Cornell** present The Friends appoin
ted to See into **John Wood**s Clearness makes report
they find nothing to hinder his Intended marriage
And **John Wood** and **Jerusha Taber** appeared at this
meeting for their answer and their answer was
that they might proceed to take each other in mar
-riage in Some Convenient time between this and

the next monthly meeting observing the good order
Established amongst Friends in yᵉ performance there
-of and **Caleb Russell** and **Isaac Smith** are appointed
to See their marriage ~~Convenient~~ Consummated
in sd order and make return to yᵉ next monthly meet_ing_
And **Philip Tripp** and **Sarah Wood** Did lay their
Intentions of taking each other in marriage before
this meeting and were desired to wait till the next
monthly meeting for their answer and **Christopher**
Gifford and **Edward Cornell** are appointed to Enquire
Into yᵉ young mans Clearness and make return
to the next monthly meeting
The Signing of **Abraham Slocum**s Certificate is
refere till the next monthly meeting
And **Joseph Tucker** and **Daniel Russell** hath attended the Quarterly meeting and Drawn Epistle to yᵉ Same as appointed
And the Quarterly meeting Epistle hath been read at this
meeting and well accepted
Our Friend **Samuel Spencer** of **Abington** in **Pensilva-**
-nia was at this meeting Whose Testimony and Labour
of Love ˄ᵂᵃˢ well accepted & his Certificate was read to good
Sattisfaction And Whereas **John Lapham** being about
to remove to **Providence** to live and Desires a Certi-
-ficate therefor this meeting appoints **Peleg Smith** and
George Smith to make Enquiry into his Circumstances
And Draw one accordingly

At a monthly meeting of Friends held at our meeting
House in **Dartmouth** on yᵉ 20ᵗʰ day of yᵉ 11ᵗʰ mo: 1752
Ponaganset meeting Called **John Russell** present
Coakset meeting Called **Christopher Gifford** and **Joseph**
Tripp juʳ present & **Caleb Russell** gives this meeting an
account that **John Wood** and **Jerusha Taber**s marriage
was Consummated in good order The Friends appointed
to See into **Philip Tripp**s Clearnes[s] makes report that
they find nothing to hinder his intended marriage
And **Philip Tripp** and **Sarah Wood** appeared at this meet
ing for thir answer and their answer was that they
might proceed to take each other in marriage in Some
Convenient time between this and yᵉ next monthly
meeting ~~for their answer~~ observing yᵉ Good order Established

among Friends In the performance thereof
And **Prince Howland** and **Deborah Slocum** did lay their Inten
tions of taking each other in marriage before this meeting
and were Desired to wait till yᵉ next monthly meeting
for their answer and **Joseph Tucker** & **Abraham Tucker**
are appointed to make Enquiry into yᵉ young mans
Clearness And make return to yᵉ next monthly meet
-ing And **Christophe Gifford** and **Edward Cornell** are appoin-
-ted to ~~Enquire~~ [see] ~~into~~ **Philip Tripp** and **Sarah Wood**s marriage
Consammated in yᵉ abovesd good order and make return
to yᵉ next monthly meeting And this meeting hath
received two Certificates one for **John Wing** And another
for his Wife Signed by the monthly meeting of **Rhode
Island** Recommending them to our Care
James Shearman hath paid to **Thomas Hathaway** £8-15ˢ-00ᵈ
old tenor as ordered – –
And there was a Certificate Signed at this meeting
for our Travailing Friend **Samuel Spencer** and
another for **John Lapham**

At a monthly meeting of Friends held at our meet
-ing House In **Dartmouth** on yᵉ 18ᵗʰ Day of yᵉ 12 month
1752 **Ponaganset** meeting Called **John Shepherd**
and **Caleb Russell** present **Coakset** meeting Called
Jonathan Wood and **Christopher Gifford** present the
Friends appointed to See **Philip Tripp** and **Sarah Wood**s
marriag Sollemnized makes report that it was
orderly accomplished: And **Abraham Tucker** and
Joseph Tucker gives this meeting an account that
they find nothing to hinder ᶺ **Prince Howland** his Intended marriage
And **Prince Howland** and **Deborah Slocum** appeared
at this meeting for their answer and their answer
Was that they might proceed to take each other in
marriage in Some Convenient time between this
and the next monthly meeting And **Joseph Tucker**
and **Abraham Tucker** are appointed to See their
marriage Consummated In the Good order Established
amongst Friends And make return to yᵉ next month
-ly meeting And **John Russell** and **Deborah Hunt** did lay
their Intentions of taking each other in marriage
before this meeting And were Disired to wait till

the next monthly meeting for their answer and
Joseph Tucker and **Peleg Smith** are appointed to
Enquire Into **John Russell**s Clearness and make return
to the next monthly meeting
And **Thomas Hathaway** and **Lois Taber** Did lay their in-
-tentions of taking each other in marriage before this
meeting And were Desired to wait till yᵉ next monthly
meeting for their answer and **Jonathan Hussey** and
Caleb Russell are appointed to make Enquiry Concern
-ing the young mans Clearness and make return
to the next monthly meeting
The Friends appointed to attend the Quarterly meeting
Have done it and Drawn an Epistle to yᵉ Same
And the Quarterly meeting Epistle hath been read
at this meeting and well accepted And the Tresurer
hath paid 7 pound old Tenor to the overseers[19]
At a monthly meeting of Friends held at our meeting House in
Dartmouth on the 19ᵗʰ Day of yᵉ 2d mo[20]
Jonathan Wood Adam Mott and **Abraham Tucker** and to Draw
an Epistle to the Same And this meeting orders the Tresurer[21]
to pay to the overseers 7 pound old Tenor for yᵉ Last halfe years
keeping yᵉ meeting House ~~in Dartmouth~~
And there was Collected at this meeting £6 -05ˢ -04ᵈ old Tenor

---

At a monthly meeting of Friends held at our meeting
House In **Dartmouth** on the 15ᵗʰ Day of yᵉ 1ˢᵗ month 1753
Ponaganset meeting Called **John Shepherd** and **Daniel Russell**
present for **Coakset Jedidiah Wood** and **William Gifford**
present The Friends appointed to enquire Concerning **Thomas**
Hathaways Clearness makes report that they find nothing
to hinder his Intended marriage
And the Friend appointed uppon yᵉ Same account
For **John Russell** give an account that they find things
Clear And ~~Jonathan~~ **John Russell** and **Deborah Hunt**
And **Thomas Hathaway** and **Lois Taber** appeared at this
meeting for their answers ˄ and their answers Was that they might proceed
to marry in the gooder [*sic*] Established among Friends
In Some Convenient time between this and yᵉ next

19. The preceding five lines in the manuscript are crossed out with a large X
20. The preceding two lines are crossed out with a large X.
21. The preceding two lines are crossed out with a large X.

monthly meeting and **Isaac Howland** and **Peleg Smith**
are appointed to See **John Russell** and **Deborah Hunt**s
marriage Consummated In sd order & make return to yᵉ
next monthly meeting And **Caleb Russell** and **Jonathan
Hussey** are appointed upon yᵉ Same account for **Thomas
Hathaway** and **Lois Taber** & to mak return as abovesd
The Friends appointed to attend the Quarterly meeting
and Draw an Epistle to yᵉ Same have done it as ordered
And the Tresurer hath paid 7 pound old Tenor to yᵉ overseers

At a monthly meeting of Friends held at our meeting
House In **Dartmouth** on the 19ᵗʰ Day of yᵉ 2ᵈ month 1753
Ponaganset meeting Called **Abraham Tucker** and
Peleg Smith present for **Coakset Othniel Tripp** and
Christopher Gifford Joseph Tucker and **Abraham Tucker**
gives this meeting an account that **Prince Howland**
and **Deborah Slocum**s marriage was orderly Consummated
The Friends appointed to See **John Russell** and **Deborah
Hunt**s marriage Solle[m]nized makes report that it was
Done in good order And **Jonathan Huss [Hussey]** gives this meet-
ing an account that **Thomas Hathaway** and **Lois Taber**s
marriage was Consummated in good order
And whereas it is thought necessary that our
burying yard Should be Enlarged This meeting appoints
**Henry Tucker Abraham Tucker James Shearman
Joseph Tucker** and **George Smith** a Comᵗᵗᵉ to conc__tnd[?]
how it Shall be Done and to See that it is Done
And this meeting appoints **Joseph Tucker Abraham** ˄ᵀᵘᶜᵏᵉʳ
Adam Mott and **Isaac Smith** to view yᵉ monthly
meeting munites in order that they may go on record

At a monthly meeting of Friends held at our meeting
House In **Dartmouth** on the 19ᵗʰ Day of the 3ᵈ month 1753
Ponaganset meeting Called **John Shepherd** & **Abraham
Tucker** present for **Coakset John Cornell** & **Edward
Cornell** present · And **Isaac Smith** is Chose Clerk for
To the monthly meethly meeting for this year or till
Another be Chosen in his room
And **Jabez Barker** and **Isaac Smith** are ordered to make
up the meetings accounts with the Treasurer
The Friends appointed to view the munits have Done it

And **Isaac Smith** is ordered to put them upon Record
And whereas **John Shepherd Jur** hath made application
to this meeting for a Certificate to yᵉ monthly at
Sandwich of his Clearness in relation to marriage and
Conversation therefore this meeting appoints **David Smith**
And **Jonathan Hussey** to make Inquiry and Draw one
accordingly and yᵉ Treasurer is ordered to pay to **George
Smith** Eleven pound old tenor for reparing the Common
Stable there was Collected at this meeting ten pound four
and Six pence old tenor The Friends appointed to attend
the Quarterly meeting are **Peleg Smith Joseph Tucker** and
Abraham Tucker and ~~Abraham~~ to Draw an Epistle to yᵉ Same
and this meeting agreas that the meeting be held as usual
at **Isiah** [**Isaiah**] **Merihew**s or thereabouts for one year longer
And the Treasurer hath paid the 11 pounds as ordered

At a monthly meeting of Friends held at our meeting House in
Dartmouth on the 16 Day of yᵉ 4ᵗʰ month 1753 **Ponaganse**[t] meeting
Called **John Shepherd** present for **Coakset** none appeard
Benjamin Russell son of **John Russell** and **Ann Smith** Did lay their
Intentions of marriage before this meeting and were Desired to wait
till yᵉ next monthly meeting for their answer and **Isaac Howland**
And **William Anthony** are appointed to make Inquiry into the
young mans Clearness and make return to yᵉ next monthly meeting
The Friends appointed to make up accounts with the Treasurer
have done it and find that he hath Disbusted [Disbursed] 12 Shillings & 1 peny
upon the meetings account & nothing In yᵉ Stock
The Friends appointed to attend yᵉ Qurterly meeting hav done
it & Drawn an Epistle to yᵉ Same as appointed the Friends
appointed to Draw **John Shepherd**s Certificate have Done it
and it is Signed by order of this meeting The visitters Chose
for this year are **Abraham Tucker Peleg Smith Adam Mott**
& **Henry Hedly** And Whereas **Ebenezer Shearman** and his
famly are about to remove to yᵉ **Oblong** or **nine partners**
to Dwell and Desires a Certificate This meeting appoints
David Smith & **Jonathan Hussey** to make Inquiry and Se whither
matters are Clear and Draw one accordingly the Choosing
Visitters for **Coakset** is refered till yᵉ next monthly
meeting And whereas there hath been a Scandalous report
Spread abroad Concerning **John Wing** and his wife this
Meeting appoints **Isaac Howland James Shearman**

Abraham Tucker Peleg Smith Daniel Russell & Caleb Russell
to Inquire into ye matter & make report to ye next
monthly meeting meeting of Friends held at our meeting House
in **Dartmouth** on the 21 day of the 5th month 1753 **Ponaganset**
meeting Called **Adam Mott** and **Abraham Tucker** present
for **Coakset Christopher Gifford** and **Jedidiah Wood**
And **Benjamin Russell** & **Ann Smith** appeared at this meeting
for their answer and things appearing Clear they had their
answer that they might proceed to take each other in mar
riage in Some Convenient time between this and the next
monthly meeting observing the good order Established among
Friends in the accomplishing thereof And **William Anthony**
and **Barnabas Howland** are appointed to See their marriage
Consummated and mak return to the next monthly meeting
And **Josiah Wood** and **Hannah Tucker** did Lay their
Intentions of marriage before this meeting and were
Desired to wait till ye next monthly meeting for their
answer and **Jabez Barke [Barker]** & **John Russell** are appointed
to make Inquiry into the young mans Clearness respecting
marriage and Conversation & make return to next
monthly meeting There was a Certificate brought and Signed
Att this meeting for **Ebenezer Shearman**
The Choosing Vistters for **Accoakst** is refered till ye next
monthly meeting And **Abraham Howland** hath sent a
Paper to this Signifying his Sorrow for his outgoing in marriage
and Apparel which is refered for further Consideration
And this meeting is adjourned till ye next fourth Day Come Week
This meeting being mett according to adjournment
this 30th Day of ye 5 month 1753
The Comtte appointed to bring their report Concerning
John Wing and his wife have done it and it is the judg
meent of this meeting that there ought to go forth a publick
Condemnation against him & **Mary Wing** wife of sd
John Wing and **Jabez Barker James Shearman** are ordered
to Do it and bring it to the next monthly meeting

At a monthly meeting of friends held at our meeting House
In **Dartmouth** on the 18th day of ye 6 month 1753
Ponaganset meeting Called **Peleg Smith** & **Stephen Willcock [Wilcox]**
present for **Coakset** none appeared by appointment
Josiah Wood & **Hannah Tucker** appeared at this meeting

for their answer and their answer was that they might
proceed to take each other in marriage In Some Convenient
time between this and the next monthly meeting obser
ving the good order Established amongst Friends in the
performance thereof

And **Jabez Barker** & **John Russell** are appointed to See their marriage
Consummated and make return to yᵉ next monthly meeting

And **John Taber** and **Sarah Walker** Did lay thir intentions
of taking each other in marriage before this meeting And
were Desired to wait till yᵉ next monthly meeting for
their answer And **Abraham Russell** & **Caleb Russell** are
appointed to mak Inquiry into **John Taber**s Clearness And
make return to the next monthly meeting The Friends
appointed to See **Benjamin Russell** & **Ann Smith**s marriage
Consummated gives this meeting an account that it was
done according to good order And yᵉ Choosing visitters for
Coakset is refered till next monthly meeting

Ther was Collected at this meeting 4ᵉ -02ˢ -4ᵈ old tenor

The prossecution of Friends Judgment against **Mary Wing**
is Suspended by reason of a paper she Sent which Friends
not thinking ful enough this meeting appoints **Jonathan Wood**
Stephen Willcock [Wilcox] & **George Smith** to go to sd **Mary Wing** to
See if she Can Sincerely ack[n]owledge according to the tenor
of yᵉ Judgment of yᵉ Committee and also to Endeavour that
John Wing do Something to Sattisfy Friends accord to the
Tenor of yᵉ aforesd Judgment

And this meeting orders ₍the Tresurer to pay to₎ **Daniel Russell** 1ᵉ -10ˢ -0ᵈ old Tenor

And this meeting is adjourned till yᵉ youths meeting

This meeting being mett according to adjournment this
6 day of yᵉ 7ᵗʰ month 1753

Peleg Smith Stephen Willcock [Wilcox] **John Russell** & **Abraham
Russell** are appointed to attend the Quarterly meeting
and Draw an Epistle to the Same and **Mary Wing** hath
Sent in a Paper to this meeting which we think full
enoug[h] to answer yᵉ Judgment of yᵉ Comᵗᵉᵉ
but is thought propper that She Should Condemn
her endeavouring to & cover the things which She has
now Confessed And the matter Concerning **John Wing**
is refered till the next monthly meeting

At a monthly meeting of Friends held at our meeting house
In **Dartmouth** on the 16 day of the 7 month 1753 **Pon[ag]anset**
meeting Called **Josep[h] Tucker** and **Abraham Tucker** present
for **Coakset** & **Nathaniel Potter** present & **Jedidiah Wood**
John Russell gives this meeting an account that **Josiah**
Wood & **Hannah Tucker**s marriage was Consummated in
good order the Choosing visitters for **Coakset** is refered
till the next monthly meeting The Friends appointed to
attend the Quarterly meeting have done it all except
Stephen Willcock [**Wilcox**] and Drawn an Epistle to the Same as ord
ered And the Quarterly meeting Epistle hath been read in
this meeting and well accepted and as to the matter mentioned
in the Epistle Concerning **Kingston** meeting House it is referd
to the monthly meeting and the yearly meeting Epistle from
London Dated 1752 was read in this meeting and Kindly accep
ted And **John Ricketson** and his wife hath sent in a paper
to this meeting Signifying their Sorrow for their Disorderly
proceeding in marriage which is refered for further
Consideration And **Mary Wing** hath Sent in a paper to
this meeting Confessing her out goings which this
meeting orders to be read publickly at yᵉ end of first Day
meeting for worship and it is Concluded that friends do not
receive her in full unity but to Suspend the matter till we
have Som further proof of her Sincerity
And the matter Concerning **John Wing** is refed to yᵉ next
monthly meeting And **John Taber** & **Sarah Walker** appeared
at this meeting for their answer and their answer was
that they might proceed to take each other in marriage
in Some Convenient time between this and the next month
ly meeting observing good order established among friends
in the accomplishment thereof And **Abraham Tucker**
and **Caleb Russell** are appointed to See their marriage
Consummated And **Humphry Smith** is ordered to let
Jonathan Nickols [**Nichols**] Know the proc[blot]dings of our monthly
meeting with **Mary Wing**

At a monthly meeting of Friends held at our meeting house
in **Dartmouth** on the 20 Day of yᵉ 8 month 1753 **Ponaganset**
meeting Called **Isaac Howland** and **George Smith** present
for **Coakset Jedidiah Wood** and **Othniel Tripp**

And **Othniel Tripp** and **Nathaniel Potter** are Chosen Visitters
for **Coakset** and as to the matter Concerning a Subscription
for **Kingston** meeting House it is refer to next monthly meeting
and **Mary Wing**s Paper hath been read as ordered
And is a[s] followeth
To the monthly meeting of Friends to be held In **Dartmouth** on the 16 Day
of the 7 month 1753 Respected Friends and others whome it may Concern
these are to inform that although I have had my Education among Friends yet by
giving way to a Craving mind have been too far misled so as to be guilty
of altering a Receipt given by **Jonathan Nickols [Nichols]** from Sixteen to Sixty
pounds and altering ye book to make it agrea wth ye Receipt: & have Endea
vou[r]ed to Evade and Cover ye Same which has brought a Scandal upon
my selfe and my Friends for which unwise management I am heartily
Sorry and Do Condemn it hoping God may forgive me and Friends pass it by
and I Still to remain under their Care   **Mary Wing**
It was Concluded by the Sd moonthly meeting that altho she hath given
In the foregoing paper that we do not Receive her as yet
as a friend In unity that is full unity as yet
but Suspend the matter till we have Some further
Proof of her Sincerity
And **Ann Almy**es paper of acknowledgment hath been Read
Caleb Russel[l] gives this meeting an account that **John Taber**s
marriage was Consummated in good order
And whereas **John Ricketson** and his wife and **Abraham**
Howland and **William Mosher** have Sent in papers Condemning
their outgoings in marry out of the order of Friends which have
been read and and this meeting accepts them and they to be under
the Care of this meeting
And the matter Concerning **John Wing** is refered to the next
monthly meeting

At a monthly meeting of Friends held at our meeting House
in **Dartmouth** on the 17th Day of ye 9 month 1753 **Ponaganset**
meeting Called **Adam Mott** present for **Coakset Jonathan Wood**
and **Nathaniel Potter** And **Daniel Wing** and **Lydia Shepherd**
Did lay their intentions of marriage before this meeting and
were Desired to wait til ye next monthly meeting for their
answer and **John Russell** and **Jabez Barker** are appointed to in
quire into the young mans Clearness and make return to the next
monthly meeting There was Collected at this meeting 5^£ -6^s -6^d old tenor
There was 10^£ -13^s -0^d old tenor Subscribed at this meeting towards

charge of **Kingston** meeting House And yᵉ tresurer is ˄ordered to pay 7 pound old
tenor to **John Shepherd** for the last halfe ye[a]r keeping the meeting
House
And Whereas **John Wing** hath been under Dealing and friends
have taken great pains with him & he Doth not make
Sattisfaction therefore this meeting orders **Isaac Smith**
to Draw up a paper of Denyal against him & bring it to
the next monthly meeting
And **Joseph Tucker** & **Abraham Tucker** & **Jonathan Wood**
are appointed to attend the Quarterly meeting and to Draw
Epistle to yᵉ Same
And the Visitters were Called upon but no account ready

At a monthly meeting of Friends held at our meeting
House In **Dartmouth** on yᵉ 15 Day of yᵉ 10 month 1753
Ponaganset meeting Called **John Shepherd** and **Isaac Smith**
present **Coakset** meeting Called & none appeared by
appointment **Daniel Wing** & **Lydia Shepherd** Came to this
meeting for their answer and their answer was that
they might proceed to take each other in marriage in
Some Convenient time between this And the next monthly
meeting ob[s]erving yᵉ good order among Friends in the
performance thereof
And **Solomon Hoxie** of **Sandwich** and **Jemima Shearm[an]**
Did Lay their intentions of marriag befor this meeting
And were Desire to wait til yᵉ monthly meeting
for their anser And **John Russell** and **Jabez Barker**
are appointed to Se **Daniel Wing**s ~~Clear~~ marriage Consum
mated and make report to yᵉ monthly meeting next
And yᵉ Treasurer hath paid 7 pounds old tenor to **John**
Shepherd as ordered
And **Humphry Smith** Signifies that he hath read
the paper that **Mary Wing** Sent in to **Jonathan Nickols** [Nichols]
and Sd **Nickols** [Nichols] Desires a Coppy of it which is left to yᵉ
Consideration of yᵉ next monthly meeting
And yᵉ matter Concerning **John Wing** is refered to yᵉ
next monthly meeting
And yᵉ Friends appointed to attend yᵉ Quarterly meeting
and Draw an Epistle to the Same have done it
And the Quarterly meeting Epistle hath been read and
Well accepted and as to their request concerning our

doing Something towards repairing **Warwick** [**Rhode Island**?] meeting House
It is Left to the Consideration of yᵉ next monthly meeting
And the matter Concerning **John Wing** is refered to yᵉ next
monthly meeting
And whereas **Benjamin Tripp** Son of **Joseph Tripp** being removed
to **Rhode Island** to Dwell with his famly Desires a Certificate
from this meeting Therefor this meeting appoints **Jedidiah
Wood** & **Christopher Gifford** to Draw one and bring it to yᵉ next
monthly meeting

At a monthly meeting of friends held at our meeting
House in **Dartmouth** on the 19ᵗʰ day of the 11ᵗʰ month 1753
Ponaganset meeting Called **Adam Mott** and & **Abraham Tucker**
present for **Coakset Christopher Gifford** & **Jedidiah Wood**
And **John Russell** gives this meeting an account that he
Was at **Daniel Wing** and **Lydia Shepherd**s marriage and
Saw nothing but that it was orderly Consummated
And it is the mind of this meeting that it is not propper
that **Jonathan Nickols** [**Nichols**] Should have a Coppy of **Mary Wing**s
paper as yet
And there was a Certificate Signed at this meeting for
Benjamin Tripp And whereas **John Wing** Desires an
Appeal to yᵉ Quarterly meeting which is Granted
And as to the Subscription for **Warwick** [**Rhode Island**?] meeting house
it is refered till yᵉ next monthly meeting

At a monthly meeting of friends held at our meeting House
In **Dartmouth** on the 17ᵗʰ Day of yᵉ 12 month 1753
Ponaganset meeting Called **Abraham Tucker** & **Peleg Smith**
present for **Coakset Christopher Gifford** & **James Cornell**
Solomon Hoxie and **Jemima Shearman** Came to this
meeting for their answer and their answar was that
they might proceed to take each other in marriage
in Some Convenient time between this & yᵉ next mon
thly meeting observing the Good order Established among
Friends In the performance thereof
And **Thomas Davis** of **Freetown** and **Hannah Wood** widow
of **John Wood** Late of **Dartmouth** deceased And **Isaac Wood**
and **Ruth Barker** Did lay their intentions of marriage before
this meeting and were desired to wait till yᵉ next monthly
meeting for their answers
And **Christopher Gifford** and **Nathaniel Potter** are appointed

to See Into **Isaac Woods** Clearness and make report to the next
monthly meeting And the Treasurer is ordered to pay to
John Shepherd 13 pound 12 Shillings old tenor
And **Humphry Smith Edward Cornell** & **Nathanil Potter**
are appoint^ted to See into the widow **Hannah Wood**/ Sircum
stances whether ther be likely to happen any Damage
to her Children by her Second marriage
There was Collected at this meeting 13£ old Tenor
And **Joseph Tucker** & **Abraham Tucker** are appointed
to See **Solomon Hoxie** & **Jemima Shearman**s marriage
Consumated and make report to the next monthly meeting
And this meeting is adjourned till the youths meeting
This meeting being met according to adjournment this
4th Day of the 1st month 1754 **Abraham Tucker** ~~Peleg~~
~~Smith~~ **Jonathan Wood James Shearman** & **Caleb Russell**
are appointed to attend the Quarterly meeting & Draw
an Epistle to the Same

At a monthly meeting of Friends held at our meeting
House in **Dartmouth** on the 21st Day of the first month 1754
Ponaganset meeting Called **Abraham Tucker** & **Peleg Smith**
for **Coakset Jedidiah** ^Wood & **Edward Cornell**
The Friends appointed to Inquire into **Isaac Woods** Clearness
Signify that they find nothing to hinder his intended
marriage The friends appointed to attend the Quarterly
meeting have most of them attended it and Drawn an
Epistle to the Same And the Epistle from the Quarterly meeting
was recid and kindly accepted
Isaac Wood and **Ruth Barker** appeared at this meeting
for their answer & their answer was that they might
proceed to take each other in marriage in Some conve
nient time between this and the next monthly meet
ing observing the good order Established among friend
In the accomplishing thereof And **Adam Mott** and
Joseph Tucker are appointed to See their marriage Consum
mated and make return to the next monthly meeting
Thomas Davis and **Hannah Wood** not coming for their answer
it is refered til the next monthly meeting And the Friends appointed
to See **Solomon Hoxies** marriage Sollemnized Signify that it was
accomplished according to order
The Visitters chose for **Ponaganset** for this year are **Abraham Tucker**

And **Peleg Smith** And the Treasurer hath paid 13$^{£}$–12^{s} as ordered

At a monthly meeting held at our meeting house in **Dartmouth**
on the 18 day of the 2^{d} month 1754 **Ponaganset** meeting called
Abraham Tucker & **Peleg Smith** present for **Coakset Christopher
Gifford** and **Edward Cornell Joseph Tucker** gives this meeting
an account that **Isaac Wood** & **Ruth Barkers** marriage was
Consumated in good order
And **Philip Trafford** & **Naomy Allen** Did lay their Intentions
of marriage before this meeting as Did also **John Gidley** and
Susannah Tripp and were desired to wait till the next monthly
meeting for their answer And **Nicolas Howland** and **Daniel
Russell** are appointed to See into the young mans Clearness
And make return to the next monthly meeting
and **Thomas Davis** and **Hannah Wood** not coming for their
answer it is refered to next monthly meeting
And whereas there was a Complaint brought in to this
meeting by the visitters Concerning **John Wing**s Charge against
Thomas Briggs that sd **Briggs** had Spoken falsely and he could
Prove it which the visitters have laboured with him the sd
Wing to make out his Charge or suitable acknowledgment
which he Doth refuse or neglect to Do Therefore this meeting
appoints **Holder Slocum Benjamin Howland William Barker
Nathaniel Howland** & **Paul Russell** to Discource with sd
Wing to Se what he will do in the affair
And they also to Labour with him in order to bring him to
a Sence and acknowledgment of his harsh Rough and Disor
derly Speeche & behaviour in the monthly meeting

At a monthly meeting of friends held at our meeting
House In **Dartmouth** on the 18th day of the 3^{d} month 1754
Ponaganset meeting Called **Joseph Tucker** & **Abraham Tucker**
present for **Coakset Robert Mosher** & **Philip Tripp** present
The Friends appointed to See into **Philip Trafford** & **John Gidley**s
Clearness Signify that they find nothing to hinder their
Intended marriages And **Philip Trafford** and **Naomy Allen**
and **John Gidley** and **Susannah Tripp** appeared at this
meeting Desiring their answer
And their answer was that thy might proceed to marry
In Some Convenient time between this and the next monthly
meeting observing the good order Established amongst
Friends In the performance thereof

And **Nicolas Howland** and **Daniel Russell** are appointed
to See their marriage Consummated in sd order and
make return to the next monthly meeting
And **Jacob Taber ju^r** and **Lydia Howland** Did lay
their intentions of marriage before this meeting and
were Desired to wait till the next monthly meeting
for their answer and **Abraham Russell** and **Caleb
Russell** are appointed to Inquire into the young mans
Clearness & make return to the next monthly meeting
Thomas Davis and **Hann Wood** not coming for their answer
it is refered to next monthly meeting
There was Raised and brought into this meeting a
Subscription of 22 pounds 3 Shillings for reparing **War
Wick** meeting House and **Joseph Tucker** hath Recev,d it
and ordered to Carry it to the Quarterly meeting
The Friends appointed to attend the Quarterly meeting
are **Adam Mott Joseph Tucker** and **William Barker**
And they to Draw an Epistle to the Same
and this meeting is adjourned to the youths meeting

At a monthly meeting held by adjournment on the
5th Day of the 4 month 1754 And whereas **John Wing**
having appealed from the Judgment of this meeting
to the Quarterly meeting this meeting appoints **Abraham
Tucker** and **Peleg Smith** to go to the Quarterly meeting to
answer to Sd appeal and the Com^tte appointed to Labour
with **John Wing** have Done it and brought their account
that he hath no ways made out his Charge against
Thomas Briggs Therefore this meeting orders **Isaac Smith**
to Draw up his Denyal and bring it to the next monthly meeting
At a monthly meeting of friends held at our meeting
House in **Dartmouth** on the 15 Day of the 4th month 1754
Ponaganst meeting Called **Daniel Russell** & **Caleb Russell** present
for **Coakset Christopher Gifford** & **Edward Cornell** present the
Friends appointed to See **Philip Trafford** & **Naomy Allen** and **John Gidley**
and **Susannah Tripps** marriage Sollemnized Signify that it was
done in good order
And the Friends appointed to See into **Jacob Tabers** Clearness
Signify that they find nothing to hinder his intent marriage
And **Jacob Taber** & **Lydia Howland** appeared at this meeting
for their answer & their answer was that they might

proceed to take each other in marriage in some Convenient
time between this & the next meeting observing the
good order Established among Friends In the performance thereof
And **Abraham** & **Caleb Russell** are apointed to See their mar
riage Consummated in Sd order & make rturn to the
next monthly meeting
And **Joseph Tucker** hath Carried the Subscription as
appointed & Delivered it at the Quarterly meeting
The Friends appointed to attend the Quarterly meeting have
done it as ordered and the Quarterly meeting Epistle hath
been read and well accepted And **Abraham Tucker** and
Peleg Smith have attended the Quarterly meeting on the
account of **John Wings** appeal have done it but nothing
is Done in that affair by reason that **John Wing** Could
not attend it by reason of the indisposition of his famly therefore
the Same friends are still Continued for that Service to
the next Quarterly meeting
The Friends of **Coakset** have requested leave of this meeting
to Repair their meeting House which is granted and this
meeting is adjourned until the next 4th day Come week
This meeting being met according to adjournment this
24th of the 4th mon 1754
Thomas Davis & **Hannah Wood** appeared at this meeting
for their answer and their answer was that they might
proceed to take each other in marriage in Some Con
venient time between this and the next monthly
meeting observing the good order Established amongst
Friends in the performance thereof and **Abraham Tucker**
and **John Russell** are appointed to See their marriage Consum
mated and make return to the monthly meeting next -
And the matter Concerning **John Wing** is Refered to the
next monthly meeting

5/1754 At a monthly meeting of Friends held at our meeting
House in **Dartmouth** on the 20th Day of the 5th month 1754
Ponaganset meeting Called **Abraham Tucker** and **Peleg
Smith** present and for **Coakset Jonathan Wood**
And **Caleb Russell** gives this meeting an account that
Jacob Taber & **Lydia Howland**s marriage was Consumma
ted In good order
And **Abraham Tucker** & **John Russell** gives this meeting

an account that that **Thomas Davis** and **Hannah Wood**
marriage hath been Sollemnised according to order
And whereas Some Friends thinks it necessary that
a meeting House be built near **Josiah Merihews** this meeting
appoints **Jonathan Wood John Russell Benjamin Wing**
Peleg Smith and **Caleb Russell** a Com^tte to go and have
a right understanding of the matter and if they think it
propper that one should be built to Conclude upon the
place and Dimentions of the House and bring in their
account to the next monthly meeting
And **Adam Mott** and **Henry Hedly** are Chosen Visitters
for the year Insuing for that part of this village lying
to the Westward of **Pascamanst River**
And whereas **John Wing** hath Desired an appeal from
this meetings Judgment in the Cace between sd **Wing**
Thomas Briggs which is granted

At a monthly meeting of Friends held at our meeting
House in **Dartmouth** on the 17 day of the 6 month 1754
Ponaganset meeting Called **Thomas Smith** & **Jabez Barker**
present And this meeting is adjourned until the Second
4th Day of this Instant
At a monthly meeting held In **Dartmouth** by adjourment
on the 24 Day the 6 month 1754 **Coakset** meeting Called
Christopher Gifford present
The Friends appointed to attend the Quarterly meeting
and D the Epistle are **Abraham Tucker Peleg Smith**
Christopher Gifford & **Nathaniel Potter**
And whereas this meeting thinks it propper that there
that ther be an addition to the Com^tte that were
Appointed to see about build a meeting House near **Josiah Merihews**
This meeting appoints **Holder Slocum Nathaniel Potter David Smith**
and **Benjamin Wing** upon that account and bring in their
Judgment to the next monthly meeting

At a monthly meeting of Friends held at our meeting House in
Dartmouth on the 15th Day of the 7th month 1754 **Ponaganse[t]** meeting
Called **Wm Barker** & **Job Russell** present for **Coakset** none appear-ed
The Friends appointed to attend the Quarterly meeting have
Don it & Drawn the Epistle as ordered
The Com^tte appointed about the meeting House at **New Town**

Signify that they have picked upon a place near sd **Merihews**
and bounded it out in **Josiah Merihews** Land Supposed to be about
an acre which sd **Merihew** doth Promice that he will give
to Friends for that use And **David Smith John Russ the 3ᵈ** and
Joseph Smith Nathaniel Howland Barnabas Mosher and
Bartholomew Taber are appointed to take sd Deed of the
Land and make return to the next monthly meeting
And the Quarterly meeting Epistle hath been read and well
accepted And this meeting Concludes to come to a further
Subscription for **Warwick** meeting House
And we understand that the Quarterly meeting hath Con
firmed our Judgment against **John Wing**
And the yearly meetings Epistle from **London** was read
in this meeting to good Sattisfaction
There was Collected at this meeting 4ᵉ -10ˢ old tenor
And whereas we understand that **Josep[h] Merihew** in mar
rying one not under the Care of Friends and also having
Child soon after marriage therefore this meeting appoints
Joseph Mosher & **Joseph Tucker** to talk with him and
bring in their account to the next monthly meeting
And this meeting hath receive 14 small Books which
are to go about and returne to this monthly meeting
every month
And **Isaac Smith** is Still Continued to Draw up **John
Wing** Denyal & bring it to the next monthly meeting

At a monthly meeting of Friends held at our meeting
House in **Dartmouth** on the 19 Day of the 8 month 1754
Ponaganset meeting Called **Joseph Tucker** & **Abraham Tucker**
present for **Coackset Jonathan Wood** and **Ichabod Kerby**
And whereas **Joseph Merihew** hath ~~her~~ Sent in a paper to
This meeting Signifying his Sorrow for his outgoings
which this meeeting orders Sd **Merrihew** to Read or git
Somebody to read it he being present at the End of the
meeting for worship on a first Day between this and the
next monthly meeting
And **Isaac Smith** hath Drawn up **John Wing** Denyal
And whereas he hath Sent in a paper to this meeting
In Consideration of which the matter is refered to
the next monthly meeting
And whereas **Ichabod Eady [Eddy]** hath Signified that he

hath a Desire to Come under the Care of Friends this
meeting **Jonathan Wood** & **Christopher Gifford** to
Talk with sd **Eady** and See if he is willing to Conform to
Friends principles and make report to the next monthly meeting
And there was Collected at this meeting 1ᶠ -4ˢ -7ᵈ old tenor
The Com^tte appointed to take the Deed of the Land to build a
meeting House on near **Josiah Merihews** have Done it

At a monthly meeting meeting of Friends held at our
meeting House In **Dartmouth** on the 16ᵗʰ day of the 9 month
1754 **Ponaganset** meeting Called **Joseph Tucker** and
Abraham Tucker present for **Coakset Christopher**
Gifford & **Jonathan Wood** and **Joseph Merihews** paper
hath been read as ordered and is as followeth
To the monthly meeting of Friends to be held in
Dartmouth on the 19ᵗʰ Day of the 9 month 1754
well Esteamed Friends the are to inform you ~~that~~
of my msconduct it being much out of Good order
for although I have had my Education among Friends
yet through unwatchfulness have given way Se far
to the Lust of the flesh as to Commit fornication and
Have married out of the order of Friends all which hath
brought a great Scandal upon the blessed truth that
I hav made profession of which great Disorder I do
heartily Condemn and am Sorry for and Desir God
may forgive me and friends to pass it by So far as to
Remain under their Care

Joseph Merihew

And whereas this meeting hath Considered the matter Concerning
The Paper that **John Wing** Sent in this meeting thinks propper
That **Joseph Tucker** & **Jonathan Wood** & **Abraham Tucker** should
go to sd **Wing** to See if the Can have a Sence that he is Sincere
and also to See if he will add to sd paper what they think propper
The Friends appointed to talk with **Ichabod Eady** have done
it and had pretty good Sattisfaction and this meeting Conclud
That be under our Care, for the time to come
The Friends appointed to attend the Quarterly meeting are
Joseph Tucker Peleg Smith Jonathan Wood & **John Russell the** 2ᵈ
There was Collected this meeting 3 pound one Shilling old tenor
And whereas **Benjamin Howland** Desire a Certificate of
his Clearness as to marriage & Conversation to the monthly

meeting at **Rode Island** therefore this meeting appoints
George Smith and **William Anthony** to make Inquiry & Draw
one if they think propper & bring on it to the next monthly
meeting Ther was 17$^£$-18 Shillings paid in it bein the Subscription
for **Richmond** & **Warwick** meeting Houses and it was Delivered
to **John Russell** In ord to go to the Quarterly meeting
And this meeting orders the Tresurer to pay to to **John Shepherd**
2 pounds & 10 Shillings old tenor
And Whereas we understand that **Obadiah Mosher** hath
Set up his publishment in ordder to marry out of the
good order Established among Friends therefore this meet
ing orders **Jonathan Wood Christopher Gifford** and **Othniel Tripp**
to talk with sd **Obadiah** and give him Such advice as they think
propper in the affair And the Tresurer hath paid the 2 pound
ten Shillings as ordered
And this meeting is adjourned until the youth meeting
This meeting being met according to adjournment this 4th day
of the 10th month 1754 There was Subscribed for the building of
a meeting House at Newtown four hundred & one pound ten
Shillings old tenor it is Supposed that the Sd House will Cost 1000 pound
In **Rhoad Island** Currency the house is to be thirty foot scuare
And nine foot post

At a monthly meeting of Friends held at our meeting House in
Dartmouth on the 21 day of the 10 month 1754 **Ponaganset**
meeting Called **Abraham Tucker** presen -
For **Coakset Jonathan Wood** and **Christopher Gifford**
And **John Wing** hath Sent in a paper to this meeting and
it is the Judgment of this meeting not to accept it for full
Sattisfaction at present but let the matter rest a while
Three of the Friends appointed to attend the Quarterly meet
ing have Done it and drawn an Epistle to the Same and
the Quarterly meeting Epistle hath been read and well
accepted And **Hannah Briggs** hath Sent in a paper to
this meeting Condemning her Disorderly marriage which
is refered to the next monthly meeting
And **Jonathan Wood** and **Othniel Tripp** are Chosen visitters
for **Coakset** for this year The Friends appointed to talk with
Obadiah Mosher have Done it but he hath gone on and
married out of our order Therefore **Othniel Tripp** is ordered
to let him know that if he Doth not do Something to Sattisfy

Friends at the nect monthly meeting that Judgment must
go forth against him And there was a Certificate Signed
at this meeting for **Benjamin Howland** Son of **Isaac Howland**
And this meeting appoints **Joseph Smith** & **Barnabas Mosher**
to take the Care of Doing Something towards building the meeting
at ~~Coakset~~ **Newtown** and go on with it as they think propper
according to the Subscriptions

At a monthly meeting of Friends held at our meeting House
In **Dartmou[th]** on the 18 Day of the 11 month 1754 **Ponaganset**
meeting Called **John Russell** & **Nathaniel Bowith** present
for **Coakset John Mosher** & **Othniel Tripp** The matter
Concerning **Hannah Briggs** is refered until the next month
ly meeting And **Othniel Tripp** Signifies that he hath let
Obadiah Mosher know the mind of of the meeting and he Doth
not Seem to Incline to make Sattisfaction therefore this
meeting appoints **Isaac Smith** to Draw up a Paper of Denyal
against him and bring it to the next monthly meeting
there was two Certificates Signed at this meeting one for
Mary More ^and Mary Weeks[?] and the other for **Henry Chase** Directed to
the monthly meeting at **Oblong** or **Nine Partners** in the
Government of **New York**
And this meeting hath agread to Come to a further further
Subscription towards **Richmond** meeting House
And there hath been Considerable of agetation at this meeting
Concerning **John Wing**
And it is the result of this meeting that **Isaac Smith** Should Draw a
paper of Denyal against him and bring it to the next monthly meeting

At a monthly meeting of friends held at our meeting House in
Dartmouth on the 16 Day of the 12 month 1754 **Ponaganset** meeting
Called **Adam Mott** and **Joseph Tucker** present for **Coakset**
Christopher Gifford present And **Benjamin Wing ju͟r** & **Bathsheba**
Potter Did lay their intentions of marriage before this meeting
and were Desired to wait until the next monthly meeting
for their answer and **Joseph Tripp Ju͟r** and **James Cornell**
are appointed to See into the young mans Clearness and
make return to the next monthly meeting
There wa[s] paper of Denial brought to this meeting against
Obadiah Mosher which was read and **Isaac Smith** hath Signed
it by order of this meeting And there was Collected at this
meeting Seven pound and Shillings old **Rhoad Island** tenor

The matter Concerning **Hannah Briggs** is refered until the
next monthly meeting

The Friends appointed to attend the Quarterly meeting ar[e]
Jonathan Wood Joseph Tucker William Sanford & **Caleb Russell**
And to Draw an Epistle to the Same

And whereas **Adam Mott** hath Signified that he hath thoughts
of travailing with **Nicholas Davis** into the **Jersies** therefore
this meeting appoints **Joseph Tucker Abraham Tucker**
and **Isaac Smith** to Inquire Into his Sircumstance and
prepare a Certificate for him if they find things Clear

And **Joseph Tucker** & **Abraham Tucker** ar Chosen over
seers for the year Insuing

And this meeting orders the Tresure to pay **John Shepherd**
the Sum of eight pound ten Shillings **Rhoad Island** money
for the Last halfe years keeping the meeting House and Some
Work which he Did about it

At a monthly meeting of Friends held at our meeting House
In **Dartmouth** on the 20th Day of the first month 1755
Ponaganset meeting Called **Abraham Tucker** & **Peleg Smith**
present **Coakset** meeting Called **Christopher Gifford** and **James
Cornell** present and this meeting hath accepted of **Hannah
Briggs**es paper & She to remain under our Care

And **Benjamin Wing** and **Bathsheba Potter** appeared at this
meeting for their answer and their answer was that they
might proceed to take each other in marriage in Some Con
venient time between this and the next monthly meeting
observing the good order Established among Friends in the
accomplishment thereof And **James Cornell** and **Joseph
Tripp** are appointed to See their marriage Consummated
In sd Good order And **Walter Cornell** & **Ruth Wood** Did lay
their intentions of marriage before this meeting and
were Desired to wate until the next monthly meeting
for their answer and **Christopher Gifford** and **Ichabod
Kerby** are appointed to inquire Concerning the young mans
Clearness & make return to the next monthly meeting
Jonathan Wood and **Caleb Russell** hath attended the
Quarterly meeting as appointed and Drawn an Epistle to
the same And the Quarterly meeting Epistle ~~to the Same~~
hath been read and well accepted

And **Isaac Smith** is is appointed to make up accounts with

The Treasurer And we understand that **Abner Ricketson**
hath gone out of the way in several Respects enticing a
young woman Contrary to her Parents so as to take her
away without their Consent and marry her before a
Justice of Peace and not only So but had a child Soon after
marriage And we also understand that **John Ricketson**
was assisting in the affair and went with him to the justice
when he went to be married and was one that gave bond
to Indemnify the Justice
And **Gideon Howland** Son of **Barnabas Howland** hath
sent in a paper to this meeting Signifying ^his Sorrow for his outgoing
and having a Child Soon after marriage which is refered
for Consideration And **James Shearman Isaac Smith**
and **George Smith** are appointed to Discou[r]ce with **Abner**
Ricketson and **John** concerning their Disorde above sd
And make return to the next monthly meeting
And whereas **Joseph Potter** son of **Nathaniel Potter**
Deceased hath Set up his publishment in order marry
out of the order of Friends this meeting appoints **Joseph Tripp**
and **James Cornell** to talk with him to see if he will Do any thing
in order to Reform and Come amongst friends
And **Isaac Smith** hath received the Sum in full of his Demands
for Recording the monthly meeting munites it being 14£–13s–00d
Rhodd Island old tenor
And **William Barker** and **Jonathan Hussey** ^are appointed to in
quire into the Conversation of **John Wing** of late Since he
hath Sent in his last paper

At a monthly meeting of Friends held our meeting House
In **Dartmouth** on the 17 day of the 2d month 175[5] **Ponaganset**
meeting **Called Abraham Tucker** and **Peleg Smith** present
for **Coakset Francis Tripp** & **Joseph Tripp** present
the Friends appointed to see into **Walter Cornell**s Clearness
Signify they find nothing to hinder his intended marriage
And **Isaac Smith** hath mad up the meetings accounts with
the Treasurer and there remains in the Stock –7s–4d
and **James Cornell** and **Joseph Tripp** Signifies that **Benjan**
Wing and **Bathsheba Potter**s marriag was Consummated
in preetty good order
And **Walter Cornell** and **Ruth Wood** appeared at this
meeting for their answer and their answer was that

they might proceed to take each other in marriage in
Some Convenient tim between this & the next monthly
meeting observing the good order Established amongst
Friends in the performance thereof and **Christopher
Gifford** and **Joseph Tripp** are appointed to See their marriage
Consummated & make return to the next monthly meeting
And **John Ricketson** hath sent in a paper to this meeting
Signifying his Sorrow for his breach ^of order which is refered
to the next monthly meeting And whereas we Cannot
find any Reformation in **Abner Ricketson** we Judge it to
be our Duty to give forth a Denyal against him and **Isaac
Smith** is appointed to draw it and bring it to the next monthly
meeting and also sd **Abner**s wife being under the Same Sircum
stance Friends thinks proper to the Denyal should go out
against them both
The Friends appointed to talk with **Joseph Potter** have Done it
yet he hath gone on and married out of our good order there
for **Isaac Smith** is ordered to clear our professioion of him
And whereas the Friends appointed to Inquire into **John
Wing**s into Conversation gives an account to this meeting
that it is such that Cannot be Justified therefore this meeting
thinks propper that a Judgment should go forth against him
And appoints **Isaac Smith** to Draw up something upon that
account and bring it to the next monthly meeting
And whereas **Stephen Willcock** being under Diffecult Sir
cumstances in relation to Land that he sold to **John Wing**
Therefore this meeting appoints **Humphry Smith** to take Such
Suitable measured as he may think propper in the Cace
And make return to the next monthly meeting
And Whereas **John Kerby** Son of **Ichabod Kerby** hath Set up
his publishment in order to marry out of the good order esta
blished among Friends thefore this meeting orders **Christopher
Gifford** & **Jedidiah Wood** to Labour further with him the visitter
having already Done their Duty in that affair

At a monthly meeting of Friends held at at our meeting
House in **Dartmouth** on the 17th Day of the 3 month 1755
Ponaganset meeting Called **Adam Mott** present for **Coakset**
John Mosher present The Friends appointed to see **Walter Cornell**s
and **Ruth Woods** marriage Consummated Signify that it was
performed in good order and this meeting hath further Considred

John Ricketsons paper and have accepted it for Sattisfaction
And **Abner Ricketson** & his wives paper of Denyal and **Joseph
Potter**s paper were read at this meeting and **Joseph Tucker** is
appointed to read **Abner Ricketson** and his wives Denyal
at the end of a meeting for worship on a fir[s]t Day between this
and the next monthly meeting
The visitters of Ponaganset village have given in an account
of their Service in visitting Friends famlies which Seameth
to be to pretty good Sattisfaction And **Ruth Anthony** wife
of **John Anthony** hath Sent in a paper Signifying her Sorrow
for her Disorderly proceedings Desiring to remain under our
Care which this meeting accepts and **Humphry Smith** Signifies
that the Care is gone against **Stephen Willcock** relating to
John Wings affair
And **Humphry Smith** is Still Continued to Do what he thinks propper
In the Cace The Friends appointed to Labour further with **John Kerby**
not having Done it are Continued & to bring their account to the
next monthly meeting And **Gideon Howland**s paper hath been
Considered at this meeting friends Do accept and he to read it or
git Some body to Do it at the end of a meeting for worship on a
first Day between this and the next monthly meeting he being
present And **Philip Trafford** and his wife have sent in a paper
to this meeting Condemning their outgoings which is refered
And whereas **John Wing** hath Sent in a paper which Doth seem
to be pretty well worded therefor the meeting hath Suspended
the Condemnations going forth against him one month longer
to See whither his Conversation Shall prove agreable
And our Collection is refered until the next monthly and
And this meeting hath Signed a Certificate for **Adam Mott**
And this meeting is adjourned untill the youth meeting
This meeting being met according to adjournment the 4 day of
the 4th month 1755 The Choosing of Visitters is refer to the
next monthly meeting The Friends appointe to attend the month
ly meeting are **Joseph Tucke Jonathan Wood Abraham Tucker**
and **Peleg Smith** and they to Draw the Epistle to the Same

At a monthly meeting of Friends held at our meeting House
In **Dartmouth** on the 21 Day of the 4 month 1755
Ponaganset meeting Called **Abraham Tucker** & **Peleg Smith**
present and for **Coakset Jedidiah Wood** present
And **Abner Ricketson** & his wives Denyal hath been read as

as ordered And is as followeth

And the Friends appointed to Discouce with **Joh Kerb[y]** Signify
That they have Done it and Doth not Seem to have any in
Clination to Condemn it therefore is is the mind of this meet
ing that a Condemnation Should go forth against him and
Isaac Smith is ordered to Draw up one and bring it to
the next monthly meeting

And **Gideon Howland**s Paper hath been read accord
ing to order And there was Collected at this meeting
4 pound five Shillings & 3 Pence old Tenor

And whereas **Lydia Kerby** Daughter of **Nathaniel Kerby**
Deceased hath been guilty of having a bastard Child for
which She hath been under Dealing and She no ways incli
ning to to Condem it it is the judgment of this meeting
that a paper of Denial Should go forth against her and
Isaac Smith is ordered to Draw up one and bring it to the
next monthly meeting And the matte Concerning **John
Wing** is refered to the next monthly meeting and **Daniel
Russell** and **Isaac Smith** are appointed to talk with **Philip
Trafford** and See whether they Can have any Sence that
he is Sincere in Condemning his outgoings

The Friends appointed to attend the Quarterly meeting
have Done it all except **Peleg Smith** and Drawn the
Epistle as ordered And the Quarterly meetings Epistle
hath been read ~~as orde~~ And well accepted

At a monthly meeting of Friends held at our meeting
House in **Dartmouth** on the 19 Day of the 5 month 1755
Ponaganset meeting Called **Joseph Tucker** & **Peleg Smith**
present for **Coakset Jedidiah Wood** present

And **Thomas Cornell** and **Mary Russell** Did lay their inten
tions of marriage before this meeting and were Desired
to wait until the next monthly meeting and **Jonathan
Wood** and and **Daniel Russell** are appointed to Se into see
Into **Thomas Cornell**s Clearness and make returns to the
next next monthly meeting And **Isaac Smith** not
Having Drawn **John Kerby**es Denyal he is Continued to
Do it against next monthly meeting

And there was a Condemnation brought to this meeting against
Lydia Kerby and **Isaac Smith** hath Sig^ned it by order of this meeting
And **John Mosher** is appointed to read it on a first day at the end of

the meeting for worship at Coakset meeting House and we under
stand that **Peter Davel** hath a mind to Come under the Care of
Friends therefore **Jonathan Wood** & **Othniel Tripp** are appointed
to go to his House and See further Concerning him & his famly
And Friends have accepted of **Philip Trafford** & his wives acknow
ledgment And he is ordered to read it or git Some body to read it
he being present at the end of a meeting for worship on a first
day And the matter Concerning **John Wing** is Suspend a while
Longer Att a monthly meeting of friends held at our meeting
House in **Dartmouth** on the 16 day of the 6 month 1755 **James
Shearman** & **Jonathan Hussey** present and this meeting
is adjourned till Day Week

This meeting being meett according to adjournment this 23 day
of the 6 month 1755 the Friends appointe to Inquire Into
Thomas Cornells Clearness makes report to this meeting that they
find nothing to hinder his Intended marriage And **John Mosher**
hath Read **Lydia Kerby**es Denial as apponted and is as followeth
And **Thomas Cornell** and **Mary Russell** appeared at this
meeting for their answer and their answer was that
they might proceed to take each other in marriage in
Some Convenient time between this and the next
monthly meeting observing the good order established
among friends in the accomplishment thereof and
Peleg Smith & **Daniel Russell** are appointed to See their
marriag Consumated in sd order and make return to the
next monthly meeting
This meeting orders the Treasurer to pay to pay to the over
seers nine pound **Rhoad Island** Currancy for the last halfe
years keeping the meeting House
The friends appointed to attend the Quarterly meeting
are **Abraham Tucker Abraham Russell William Barker**
and **Daniel Russell** and to Draw an Epistle to the Same and
Isaac Smith hath Drawn ~~an~~ **John Kerbys** Denyal which
This meeting accepts and **Isaac Smith** hath Signed it by
order of the meeting The matter Concerning **Peter Davol**
is refered until the next monthly meeting

At a monthly meeting of Friends held held at our meeting House
in **Dartmouth** on the 21 Day of the 7 month 1755 **Ponganset**
meeting Called **Abraham Tucker** and **Peleg Smith** present for
Coakset Jonathan Wood & **Ichabod Eady** present

And **Danel Russell** gives this meting an account that
Thomas Cornell and **Mary Russell**s marriage was Consuma
ted In Good order and the Treasurer hath paid the 9 pound
to the overseers as ordered three of the Friends appointed
to attend the Quarterly meeting have Done it and Drawn
the Epistle as appointed and **Philip Trafford** and his wives
paper hath been read as ordered
And friends having further Considred the matter concerning
Peter Davel find fredom to accept him under our Care
And the yearly meeting Epistle from **London** hath bee read
in this meeting to good Sattisfaction And the Quarterly
meetings Epistle hath been read to this meetings Sattisfaction
And **Abraham Tucker** & **Peleg Smith** are appointed visitters
for **Ponaganset** for this year And **William Barker** and
Nathaniel Howland are appointe to assist them
And **Jonathan Wood Othniel Tripp** & **Joseph Tripp** are
appointed visitters for **Coakset** and **Paul Russell** and **Nath¹
Howland** are appointed to See into the affair of **Newtown** meeting
House and what Charges have arisen and bring in thei account
to the next monthly meeting

8/1755   At a monthly meeting of Friends held at our meeting House in **Dartmouth**
on the 18 day of the 8 month 1755 **Ponganset** meeting Called **Joseph Tucker**
and **Abraham Tucker** present for **Coakset Christopher Giffor[d]** & **Joseph
Tripp Timothy Gifford** & **Martha Tucker** Did Lay their intentions of
marriage before this meeting & were Desired to wait till the next
monthly meeting for their answer and **Holder Slocum** & **Daniel Russell**
are appointed to make Inquiry into the young mans Clearness & make
return to the next monthly meeting
And we understand that there is 155 pound 11 Shillings Due upon
account of the Charge of **NewTown** meeting House and **Humphry Smith**
Is appointed to git in the Subscriptions for the Same and pay out
whre it is Due

At a monthly meeting of Friends held at our meeting House in
In **Dartmouth** on the 5ᵗʰ Day of the 9 month 1755 **Ponaganset**
meeting Called **Isaac Howland** and **Abraham Tucker** present
And for **Coakset Othniel Tripp** & **Jonthan Wood** The Friends appoin
ted to See into **Timothy Gifford**s Clearness Signify they find nothing
to hinder his Intended marriage And **Timothy Gifford** and **Martha
Tucker** appeared at this meeting for their answer & their
answer was that they might proceed to take each other in mar

riage In Some Convenient time between this & the next
monthly meeting observing our gooder in the accomplishing thereof
And **Holder Slocum Daniel Russell** are appointed to See their
marriage Consummated in sd order and make return to the
next monthly meeting
And there was a paper of Denyal Signed at this meeting against
John Wing and **Isaac Smith** is ordered to to Read it on a first day
at the end of the ^end of meeting for worship at **Ponaganset** meeting House
between this and the next ~~meeting house~~ monthly meeting
The Friends appointed to attend the Quarterly meeting are
Jonathan Wood. Peleg Smith & **William Barker** and they Draw
an Epistle to the Same
And the visitters have been Called upon to give answer to
Some Queries Recommeⁿded to us by the Quarterly meeting
but were not able to give Distinct & Sattisfactory answers
and they was likewise Called upon to give an account of their
Service in visits friends families but they Signfy that they have
no formal account

At a monthly meeting of Friends held at our meeting House
In **Dartmouth** on the 20 Day of the 10 month 1755 **Ponaganset**
meeting Called **Peleg Smith** present for **Coakset** none appeared
And this meeting is adjourned till the first day in the 11 month 1755
This meeting being meet according to adjournment this 5 day
of the 11 month 1755 The Frends apponted to See into **Timothy
Gifford** & **Martha Tucker**s marriage that it Should be Carried
on in good order not being here it is refered to the next
monthly meeting And **Isaac Smith** hath read **John Wing**s
paper of Denial and is as followeth
Whereas **John Wing** of **Dartmouth** in the **County of Bristol**
In the **Province of the Massachusets Bay** In **New England** and
Now Resident In **Rhoad Island** being one that hath made
Profession with us the People Called Quakers yet for want
of a wathful Care over him Selfe hath let him Selfe into
an undue Liberty in his Discource in particular in his
Saying that **Samuel Look** was an old Rogue and he would
Indite him and also in Saying that he give his attest that
he receive a Receip Signed by **Jonathan Nickols** for Sixty
pounds which hath proved to be falce which Things being
of a fraudulous Nature and much Labour hath been bestowed
upon him to bring to a sight of his outgoings but nothing

Effectual hath been Done by him to make Sattisfaction
Therefore the ^ monthly meetings Judgment was that a paper of Denial
ought to go forth against him but upon his Sending in Some
papers the matter hath been Suspended for some time for
proof of his S^incerity but nothing to us appearing in that
nature it is the Judgment of this meeting that he ought
to be Set aside and Do give this forth as a Publick Testimony
against him Denying the Sd **John Wing** to be one to be one in
unity with us the abovesd people yet truly Desiring that
he may Come to a Sence of his out goings & find mercy
Given forth at our monthly meeting held In **Dartmouth**
on the 15 of the 9ᵗʰ month 1755 And Signed by order and in sd
meeting by

                Isaac Smith Clerk

The Friends appointed to attend the Quarterly and Draw an
Epistle to the Same have Done it as ordered and the
Quarterly Epistle hath been read in this meeting and
well accepted And our Collection is refered till next
monthly meeting

At a monthly meeting ~~month~~ of Friend held at our meet
ing House in **Dartmouth** on the 17ᵗʰ Day of the 11 month 1755
Ponaganset meeting Called **Abraham Tucker** and **Peleg Smith** present for **Coakset**] meeting Called **Ichabod Eady** and **Jedidiah Wood**
Daniel Russell Signifies that **Timothy Gifford** & **Martha Tucker**s
marriage was orderly Consummated
At whereas The Friends of **Newtown** meeting Desires leave of
this meeting to have week Day ^Day meeting Settled amongst them
which this meeting agres and that it be on each fifth Day in
Every week except the fifth preceeding the monthly meeting
for the three Winter months Insuing Our Friend **Adam**
Mott having Returned from his Religeous visit to the **West**
wood and returned our Certificate and also produced Several
Certificates from where his Service hath been to our good
Sattisfaction there was Collected at this meeting for the
use of Friends two pound nineteen Shillings **Rhoad Island** money

---

At a monthly meeting of Friends held at our meeting House
In **dartmouth** on the 15ᵗʰ Day of the 12 month 1755 **Ponaganset**
meeting Called **Abraham Tucker** & **Peleg Smith** present for **Coakset**
Jonathan Wood & **Christopher Gifford** present
And whereas **Peleg Gifford** is removed with his famly to

Wareham to Dwell and Desire a Certificate to the monthly
meeting at **Sandwich** Therefore this meeting appoints
Joseph Tucker & **Nathaiel Howland** to Enquire into his Sircum
stances & Draw one and bring it to the next meeting if
they think Propper And whereas **William Barker** Desires
a Certificate to the monthly meeting at **Rhoad Island** in relation
to marriage & Conversation therefore this meeting appoin[ts] the
abovesd two Frinds to make Inquiry and Draw one if they
think propper and bring it to the next monthly meeting
The of **Ponaganset** Visitters being Called upon they give an
account that they have visitted the greatest part of Friends
famlies under their Care and find things pretty well in
Some places & where they found things amiss they gave such
advice as they thought Suitable And also they have mad answer
to the Queries according to order which are reccommended
to the Quarterly meeting And the visitters for **Coakset** have
been Called upon but their answer was that they had not done
any thing The Friends appointed to attend the Quarterly
meeting and Draw an Epistle to the Same are **Joseph Tucker**
Adam Mott & **John Russell Jun**[r]
There was Collected at this meeting for the use of Friends
Six pounds **Rhoad Island** money And this meeting orders
The Tresurer to pay to the overseers nine pounds **Rhoad]**
Island money for the Last halfe years keeping the meet
ing house And this meeting orders it being their mind that
on monthly meeting Days it might be better to meet at
eleven of y[e] Clock that for the time to Come that Friends
obseve & meet that time on monthly meeting Days

At a monthly meeting of Friends held at our meeting
House in **Dartmouth** on the 19th Day of y[e] 1 month 1756
Ponaganset meeting Called **Abraham Tucker** and
Peleg Smith present for **Coakset John Mosher** and **Joseph**
Tripp present The friends appointed have Drawn a
Certificate for **Peleg Gifford** and brought it to this meet
ing which is Signed as also another for **W**[m] **Barker**
and **Joseph Tucker** & **Adam Mott** hath attend the Quarterly
meeting & Drawn an Epistle as ordered and the Quarterly
meeting Epistle hath been read at this meeting and well
accepted And the Tresurer has paid the nine pounds to the
Overseers as ordered and **Benjamin Russell** Son of **John** y[e] 2[d]

hath Sent a paper to this meeting Concerning his paying mony
towars the wars which is accepted
And whereas **Mary Slocum** Daughter of **Holder Slocum**
hath gone out of the way & married out of our Good order
Therefor this meeting orders **Isaac Smith** to Draw ~~ore~~
ore assist yᵉ Women Frinds In Drawing up a paper of
Denial against her and bring it to yᵉ monthly meeting

At a monthly meeting of Friends held at our meeting House
In **Dartmouth** on the 16 Day of yᵉ 2 month 1756
Ponaganset meeting Called **Abraham Tuck** & **Peleg Smith**
present For **Coakset Jonathan Wood** & **Peter Davel** present
And whereas **Jethro Hathaway** hath Sent a paper in to this
meeting Signifying his Desire to be under yᵉ Care of Friends
Which we have Considred and and Concluded that he be
under our Care for the time to Come
There was a paper of Denial brought to this meeting
agaist **Mary Slocum** and **Isaac Smith** hath Signed it by
order of this meeting and is ordered to read it at the
End of a meeting for worship on a first Day between this
and the next monthly meeting

At a monthly meeting of Friends held at our meeting house In **Dartmouth**
on the 15 Day of yᵉ 3 month 1756 **Ponaganset** meeting Called **Abraham
Tucker** & **Peleg Smith** present for **Coakset Jonathan Wood** and **Ichabod
Eady** present and **Isaac Smith** hath read **Mary Slocum** now **Tuckers**
Denial as appointed and is as followeth
Whereas **Mary Slocum** now wife of **William Duker** and Daughter
of **Holder Slocum** & **Rebekah** his Wife of **Dartmouth** in the **County of
Bristol** In the **Province of** yᵉ **Massachusets Bay** In **New England** being
One that had her education amongst Friends the People Called Qukers
yet by giving way to her own Evil inclinations hath kept Company
and married one very Contrary to her Father & mothers Consent
and not only So but hath had a Child in a short time after marriage
And Friends having Cleared them Selves as to their Duty in advising
and Dealing with her & no sign of Repentance apearing We Can
do no less for the Clearing the Blessed Truth of from such obstinate
and Scandalous Proceedings but give forth this a publick Testimony
against it Denying the sᵈ **Mary Tucker** to be one in unity with us
the abovesᵈ People but Truly Desiring if it be the Will of God she
may Come to a Sense of her out goings and unfeigned Repentance
Given forth at our monthly meeting held in **Dartmouth** on

the 16 Day of ye 2^d month 1756 And Signed in and by order of
S^d meeting by   Isaac Smith Clerk
And **Gershom Smith** & **Phebe White** Did Lay their Intention
of taking Each other In marriage before this meeting and
Wer Desired to wait until ye next monthly meeting for
their answer And **James Shearman** & **Daniel Russell** are
are appointed to Inquire into ye young mans Clearness
and make return to ye next monthly meeting
The visitters both of **Ponaganset** & **Coakset** have given in
Their accounts of their Service in visitting Friends families
and Signify that where they found things not well they
gave Such advice as they thought most propper
And the Queries have been read and answers Given by
the Visitters which is ordered to be Carried to the Quarterly meeting
The Friends appointed to attend the Quarterly meeting are
Adam Mott Abraham Tucker Jonathan Wood & **Peleg Smith**
and to Draw the Epistle to the Same
There was Collected at this meeting five pound ten Shilling
four **Rhoad Island** money
And this meeting thinks proper to grant that there be still Con
tinued a week Day meeting at **New Town** as heretofore as long
as the monthly meeting shall think propper And we understand
That **Christopher Gifford Juner** hath made an attempt to
Lay his intentions of marriage before the ~~monthly~~ prepari
tive meeting at **Coakset** & was not admitted by reason of
his wearing fashonabl Cloaths therefore we understand
that he is about to marry from among Friends this meeting
appoints **Daniel Russell Ichabod Eady** & **Joseph Tripp** to Speak
With the young man and See if there be any hopes of reclam
ing him

At a monthly meeting of Friends held at our meeting House
In **Dartmouth** on the 19 Day of ye 4 month 1756 **Ponaganset**
Meeting Called **Abraham Tucker** present for **Coakset Jonathan**
Wood And **Jonathan Mosher** present And **Gershom Smith** and
Phebe White ~~Did lay their Intentions of marriage~~
Came to this meeting for their answer and nothing appearing
to hinder they had their answer that they might proceed to take
Each other in marriage in Some Convenient time between
this and the next monthly meeting Observing ye Good ord Esta
-blishe among Friends In ye performance thereof and

Daniel Russell & **Joseph Tripp** are appointed to See their
marriage Consummated in s^d order & make return to the
monthly meeting next

And **Samuel Wing** & **Elizabeth Barker** and **Deliverance
Smith** and **Hannah Smith** Did Lay their Intentions
of marriage before this meeting and were Desired to Wait
until ye next monthly meeting for their answers
and **Barnabas Howland** and **John Russell** are appointed
to inquire into **Deliverance Smith**s Clearness and **Jonathan
Hussey** and **David Smith** are appointed to Inquire into
Samuel Wings Clearness and make report to ye next
monthly meeting The Friends appointed to attend the
Quarterly meeting have Done it all Except **Abraham
Tuker** and Drawn a Epistle to ye Same as appointed

And **Abiel Macomber** and **Rest Davel** Did Lay their inten
-tions of marriage befor this meeting and were Desired to
wait until the next monthly meeting for their answer
And **John Mosher** and **Othniel Tripp** are appointed to Inquire into
the young mans Clearness and make return to the next monthly
meeting And **Samuel Wing** and **Elisabeth Barker** and **Deliverance
Smith** & **Hannah Smith** appeared at this meeting for their answer
And their answers was that they might proceed to marry In Some
Convenient time between this and the next monthly meeting
Observing the good order Established amongst Friends in the perfor
-mance thereof and **Barnabas Howland** & **John Russell** are appoin
-ted to See their marriage Consumated ^22

The Friends appointed to talk with **Christopher Gifford ju^r** not having
oppertunity to Do it except **Ichabod Eady** to whom he signified that
he was off the mind of marrying among Friends and we understand
that he is married out of ye unity of Friends And **Peleg Huddlestone**
and **Daniel Russell** are appointed to Discource with S^d **Gifford** to See if
he is willing to to make any Sattisfaction for his Disorder

And whereas **John Tucker** hath Signified to this meeting that he
Desires a Certificate to the monthly meeting at **Rhoad Island** of
his Clearness as to marriage & Conversation therefore this meet
-ing appoints **James Shearman** & **Isaac Smith** to make Inquiry
and Draw one if they think fit

And whereas **Francis Tripp** hath had a Desire to lay his Inten
tions but this meeting but Friends thinks it is too much hurrying to be Decent

---

22 The previous nine lines are crossed out with a large X.

Therefore it refered to yᵉ next monthly meeting for Consideration
And **Jabez Barker** & **Isaac Smith** are ordered to make up this
meetings accompts with the Tresurer

At a monthly meeting of friends held our meeting House in **Dart**
-**mouth** on the 17 Day of the 5 month 1756 **Ponaganset** meeting
Called **James Shearman** & **George Smith** present for **Coakset**
Othniel Tripp & **Joseph Tripp** present The Friends appointed to
the three young mens Clearness that laid their Intentions
before the last monthly meeting Signify they find nothing to
hinder their proceedings in marrage and **Daniel Russell** and
Joseph Tripp gives this meeting that **Gershom Smith** and **Phebe**
Whites marriage was Consummated in good order
and **Deliverance Smith** and **Hanna Smith** and **Samuel Wing**
and **Elzabeth Barker** and **Abiel Macumber** and **Rest Davel**
Came to this meeting for their answers and each Coupple had
their answers that they might proceed to marry
in marriage in the good order Establi
-shed among Friends In Some Convenient time between this
and the next monthly meeting And the Same Friends that
were appointed to See into their Clearness to See their
marriages Consummated In sᵈ order and make return to
the next monthly meeting And there was a Certificate Signed
at this meeting for **John Tucker Jabez Barker** and **Isaac**
Smith hath made up the monthly meetings accompts with
the Tresurer and there remains in the Stock Six Shillings
and eleven pence **Rhoad Island** old tenor And the Quarterly
meeting Epistle hath been read at this meeting and well
accepted The Friends appointed to attended the Quarterly
meeting have Done it according to order
The Friends appointed to talk with **Christopher Gifford Ju**ʳ
not having Done it are Still Continued to Do it and make
return to the next monthly meeting
And **Francis Tripp** & **Content Griffeth** Did lay their intentions
of marriage before this meeting & were Desired to wait till
the next monthly meeting for their answer and **Jedidiah**
Wood & **John Mosher** are appointed to inquire Into **Francis**
Tripps Clearness & make return to yᵉ next monthly meeting

At a monthly meeting of Friends held at our meeting house
In **Dartmouth** on the 22 Day of the 6 month 1756 **Ponan**
-**set** meeting Called **James Shearman** & **Peleg Smith** present

for **Coakset Othniel Tripp** & **Jonathan Wood** present
The Friends appointed to See into **Francis Tripps** Clearness
Signify they find nothing to hinder his Intended marriage
And **Francis Tripp** & **Content Griffeth** appeared at this
meeting for their answer & their answer was they might
proceed to take each other in marriage in Some Convenient
time between this & the next monthly meeting observing the
Good order Established amongst friends in the accomplishing
thereof And **Peleg Smith** & **Barnabas Howland** ar appointed
to See their marriage Consummated and make return to the
next monthly meeting And **Christopher Davel** & **Mehetabel
Allen** Did lay their Intentions of marriage fore this meeting
and wer Desired to wait till the next monthly meeting for
their answer and the Friends appointed at the last monthly
to See the marriages Solemnized Signify that they were Con
-summated in good order
And whereas **Christopher Davel** Spent the greatest part of his time last
Winter hereaways **Othniel Tripp** & **Joseph Tripp** are appointed to make
Inquiry into his Clearness and bring in their account to the next monthly
meeting The Friends appointed to Discource With **Christopher Gifford ju**^{r}
Signify that they have Dan it and he Seems to have no Inclination
to make Sattisfaction Therefore this meeting orders **Isaac Smith** to
Draw up a paper of Denial against him and being it to the next
monthly meeting **Joseph Tucker Jonathan Wood** & **Peleg Smith** are
appointed to attend the Quarterly meeting and Draw ye Epistle are
Joseph Tucker Jonathan Wood & **Peleg Smith** And whereas **Prince
Barker** Desires a Certificate for him Selfe & family to the monthly
meeting at **Pembrooke** Therefor this meeting appoints **Isaac How
-land** and **Peleg Smith** to Draw one if they find it propper and bring
It to the next monly meeting

At a monthly meeting of Friends held at out meeting House in
Dartmouth on the 9 Day of ye 7 month 1756 **Ponaganset** meeting
Called **William Barker** & **John Russell** present for **Coakset Othniel
Tripp** & **Jonathan Wood** the Friends appointed to See into **Francis
Tripp** & **Content Griffith**s marriage that it was Consummated
In Good ord Signify that it was orderly performed
And **Christopher Davel** & **Mehetabel Allen** appeared at this
meeting for their answer and their answer was that they
might proceed to take Each other In marriage In Some Con
-venient time between this & the next monthly meeting

observing the good orde Established among friends in the
performance thereof and **John Russell** and **Daniel Russell**
are appointed to See their marriage Solemnized in s^d
order & make return to the next monthly meeting
And the yearly meetins Epistle from **London** was read at this
meeting to Good Sattisfaction And **Peleg Smith** hath attended
the Quarterly meeting & Drawn the Epistle as ordered
And the Epistle from the Quarterly meeting hath bee read
and well accepted And **Christopher Gifford Ju^r** paper of Denyal
hath been read in this meeting and accepted and **Isaac
Smith** hath Signed it by order of this meeting
and there was a Certificate Signed at this meeting for
Prince Barker and the Choosing of visitters is refered
till the next monthly meeting
And **Barnabas Howland Caleb Russell** and **John Russel the 3^d** are
appointed and added to the visitters of **Ponaganset** to give Such
propper advice & Counsel as may be Necisary to Such Friends as
are brought into Troubl upon the account of military affairs
And **Peleg Huddlestone** are appointed upon the Same account
for **Coakset** There was Collected at this meeting 6£–10^s–02^d
Rhoad Island old tenor And the Treasurer is ordered to pay
to the keeper of our meeting House 9 pound **Rhoad Island** tenor

At a monthly meeting of friends held at our meeting House
on the 16 Day of ye 8 month 1756 **Ponaganset** meeting Called
Abraham Tucker & **James Shearman** present for **Coakset**
Jonathan Wood and **John Mosher** present **Daniel Russell** makes
Report to this meeting this meeting that that **Christopher Davel**
and **Mehetabel Allen**s marriag hath been Consumated orderly
the visitters appointed for this year are **Abraham Tucker
Peleg Smith Nathanael Howland William Barker** and for
Coakset Jonathan Wood Othniel Tripp John Mosher & **Joseph
Tripp** and **Adam Mott** & **Barnabas Howland** are added & appointed
as visitters with the other **Ponaganset** visitters

At a monthly meeting of Friends held at our meeting House
In **Dartmouth** on the 20 Day of ye 9 month 1756 **Ponaganset**
meeting Called **Adam Mott** & **John Russell** present for **Coakset**
John Mosher & **Peter Davel** And **Jedidiah Allen** & **Eunice Wood**
Did lay their intentions of marriage before this meeting and
wer Desired to wait until the next monthly meeting for their
Answer the 9 pounds **Rhoad Island** Currancy that was ordered

to be paid to **Jonathan Hussey** is paid as ordered
And **Nicholas Howland Daniel Russell** are appointed to see
Into **Jedediah Allen**s Clearness & make report to the next
monthly meeting The Friends appointed to attend the Quarterly
meeting are **Jonathan Wood Joseph Tucker** & **Joh Mosher** and
They to Draw an Epistle to Same Collected at this meeting
2 pound 16 Shillings & 10 pence **Rhoad Island** Currancy and this
meeting is adhourned until yᵉ first Sixth day in yᵉ next month
This meeting being met according to adjournment this first
day of the 10 month 1756 The visiters of **Ponaganset** being Called
upon Signify that they have not mad any progress in visitting
friends families this Last Quarter
Neighther made answer to the Qeries **Coakset** visitters Signify that they have
visitted Frinds famlies under their Care and mad answer to yᵉ Queries

---

At a monthly meeting of friends held at our meeting House In **Dartmouth**
on yᵉ 18 Day of yᵉ 10 month 1756 **Ponaganset** meeting Called **William Sanford**
and **Henry Hedly** present **Coakset** meeting Called **Christopher Gifford** & **Ichabod
Eady** present The Friends appointed to See Into **Jedidiah Allen**s Clearness
Signify that things are not Clear therefore the matter is refered to
To the next monthly meeting the Friends appointed to attend the Quar
-terly meeting and Draw the Epistle Signify they have Done it
And Whereas **Jedidiah Allen** hath sent two papers to this meeting
Signifying his Sorrow for his Disorders In the first place for his being
In a Quarrel and wounding a man Secondly for his paying money
towards maintaining war which this meeting accepts and the first
to be read publickly on a first Day at the end of the meeting for
Worship on a first Day he being present

At a monthly meeting of friends held at our meeting House in
Dartmouth on the 15 Day of the 11 month 1756 **Ponaganset** meeting
Called **Abraham Tucker** & **John Russell** present **Coakset**
meeting Called **Peter Davel** & **John Macumber** present
The Friends appointed to See into **Jedidiah Allen**s Clearness
Signify they know nothing but that things are Clear
and **Jedidiah Allen**s paper hath been read as ordered
And **Jedidiah Allen** & **Eunice Wood** appeared at this meet
ing Desiring their answer and their answer was that they
might proceed in marriage in Some Convenient time between
this and the next monthly meeting observing the good order
Established among Friends In the performance thereof
And **Daniel Russell** & **Philip Tripp** are appointed to see

their marriage Consummated In the order aboves^d and
make rturn to the next monthly meeting and **Edward Wing**
ju^r of **Sandwich** & **Mehetabel Russell D** And **William Anthony**
ju^r & **Sarah Shearman** & **Jacob Russell** and **Phebe Willcock**
Did lay their Intentions of marriage before this meeting
and were Desired to wait until ye next monthly meeting
for their answers and **William Sanford** and **William Barker**
are appointed to Inquire into **Jacob Russell**s Clearness and
Isaac Howland & **George Smith** are appointed to See into
Wm Anthonyes Clearness & make return to the next monthly meeting
And Whereras **Abraham Thomas** of **Oblong** hath Sent a
Paper to this meeting Signifying his Sorrow for his outgoing
when amongst us Which this meeting accepts for Sattisfaction
And **Isaac Smith** is ordered to read it at the end of a meet
ing on a first Day between this & the next monthly meeting
And whereas we understand that **Benjamin Farrest** and
William Russell & **Phebe Farrest** & **Mary Chase** having been
upon a Religeous visit amongst us they being **Oblong** Friend
and Desire Certificates from this meeting to the meeting where
they belong Therefore this meeting appoints **Abraham Tucker**
and **Peleg Smith** to Draw Certificates for them & bring them
to the next monthly meeting

At a monthly meeting of friends held at our meeting House
In **Dartmouth** the 20 Day of ye 12 month 1756
And this meeting adjournd until the 29 Day of this instant
At a monthly meeting held by adjourment on the 29 day
of ye 12 month 1756 **Ponaganset** meeting Called **Abraham**
Tucker & **John Russell** present for **Coakset Ichabod Eady**
And **Edward Wing** and **Mehetabel Russell** & **Jacob Russell** and
Phebe Willcock & **William Anthony** and **Sarah Shearman**
appeared at this meeting for their answers and nothing
appearing to hinder they had their answers that they might
might proceed to marry in the good order Established
among Friends in Some Convenient time between this
and the next monthly meeting And **Niolas Howland**
and **Daniel Russell** are appointed to See their marriage
that is **Jacob Russell** & **Phebe Willcocks** consummated
And **William Sanford** & **William Barker** are appointe
upon the Same account for **Edward Wing** and **Mehetabel**
Russell and **George Smith** and **Barnabas Howland** for

William Anthony and **Sarah Shearman** and all make
returns to the next monthly meeting
And **Daniel Russell** gives this meeting an account that
Jedidiah Allen and **Eunice Woods** marriage was Consum
-mated in good order and **Abraham Tucker** and **Peleg Smith**
hath Drawn the Certificates for our **Oblong** Friends
Which this meeting approves and orders they should be Signed
There was Collected at this meeting and paid to **Jonathan Hussey** for the
Last halfe years keeping the meeting House and Some other small business
about yᵉ meeting House 11 pound 3 shillings **Rhoad Island** money
And whereas the women Desires assistance of this meeting upon that account
account of **Peleg Huddlestone**s Daughter and **William Sanford**s Daughter
Therefore **Adam Mott** & **Joseph Tucker** are apointed upon that account
And this meeting is adjourned until yᵉ next Sixth Day come week
This meeting being mett according to adjournment this 7ᵗʰ Day of
the first month 1757 The Paper that **Abraham ~~Tuck~~ Thomas**
Sent in hath been read as ordered and is as followeth
Oblong the 9ᵗʰ of yᵉ 10ᵗʰ month 1756 To the monthly meeting
of Friends In **Dartmouth** Whereas I have through unwatch
-fulness violated my own Consience & Dishonoured the
Profession Which I have made by falling Into that Grie
-vous Sin of fornication also in keeping Loos Company
Where I have been much Exposed to Temptations Espe
-cially in the excessive use of Stron Licquor for which
above named Evils or Transgressions I have hope of for
-giveness from the Lord And Desire you my Friends to pass
by my offences against the Church and receive me into
your Christian Care and Charity again which is much
Desired by me your Friend　　　　　**Abraham Thomas**
and here follows **Jedidiah Allen**s paper
To the monthly meeting of Friends In **Dartmouth** on the
18 Day Day of the 10 month 1756 These are to inform Friends
of my misfortune in not keeping to Truth & my Education in
Days past in my youth I Strayed away with the People of the
World in the Customs & fashions thereof and further at
Certain time I hapned to fall in with bad Company & had a
Shameful Quarrel with one of them and in sᵈ Quarrel
I wounded him much tho not mortal which Cace was Lament
-able to me when past and to my Friends Which Evils I Can
Truly Say I am Sorry for and I Desire I may never fall into

the like again And I Desire Friends to allow me to remain under
their Care While found in they way of well Doing as witness
my hand   **Jedidiah Allen**
And the visitters have been Called upon to make answer to the
Queries which they have Done in Wrighting and this meeting orders
that they Should be sent to yᵉ Quarterly meeting
Ichabod Eady Adam Mott Nicolas Howland and **Caleb Russell**
are appointed to attend the Quarterly meeting and Draw an
Epistle to yᵉ Same and this meeting thinks propper that this
munite of the monthly meeting be perused in order that they
may go on Record And **Joseph Tucker** and **Abraham Tucker**
With **Isaac Smith** are appointe upon that account

At a monthly meeting of Friends held at our meeting House
In **Dartmouth** on the 17 Day of the first month 1757 **Ponaganset**
Meeting Called **Abraham Tucker** & **John Russ** yᵉ 3ᵈ present
Coakset meeting Called **Joseph Tripp** & **Jshua Cornell** present
The Friends appointed see the three mariages Consummated
Signify that they were accomplished in good order and nothing
being Done as to assisting yᵉ women mentioned at the last
monthly meeting it is refered to yᵉ next
The friends appointed to attend yᵉ Quarterly meeting have
Done it all except **Caleb Russell** and Drawn yᵉ Epistle as ordered

---

At a monthly meeting of Friends held at our meeting House
In **Dartmouth** on the 21 day of the 2 month 1757 **Ponaganset**
meeting Called **James Shearman** & **Abraham Tucker** present
for **Coakset William Gifford** present and Whereas **Benjamin
Howland** the Son of **Isaac Howland** hath Sent in a paper
to this meeting Signifying his Sorrows for paying money upon
The account of his being impressed but this meeting thinks
thinks it not full enough therefore **Paul Russell** and
Daniel Russell are to advise with him & bring in their judg
meent in the matter to yᵉ next monthly meeting
And it is thought proper by this meeting that we have an
accoun of the Suffering of friends upon the account of mile
tary Servises therefore all friends who have been Sufferers
belong to this meeting ar Desired to bring in their accounts
to **Peleg Smith John Shepherd** & **David Smith** of **Ponaganse**
or to **Thomas Hathaway** and **Bartholomew Taber** of **Cushnot**
or to **John Mosher** and **Peter Davel** of **Coakset**

---

3 At a monthly meeting of Friends held at our meeting House In **Dartmouth**
1757 on the 21 Day of the 3 month 1757 **Ponanset** meeting Called **Caleb**
Russell present for **Coakset John Mosher** and & **Joseph Tripp**
The matter Concerning **Benjamin Howland** is Refered to next
Monthly Meeting And this meeting hath Received a Paper Signed
by **John Davis ju**ʳ Signifying his Sorrow for his Disorderly marriage
Which this meeting accepts Ther was a Certificate Signed athis
meeting for **Adam Mot** he being about to visit Friends at
Sandwich And **William Macumber ju**ͬ hath Sent in a pa
-per to this meeting Condemning his breach of order In paying
money towards military affairs Collected at this meeting 3£–2ˢ–6ᵈ
Rhoad Island old Tenor The Friends appointed to attend the
Quarterly meeting and Draw yᵉ Epistle are **Joseph Tucker Peleg**
Smith Adam Mott & **Caleb Russell** and to Draw an Epistle to
the Same And yᵉ visitters of **Coakset** have given in their
account of their Service in visitting Friends families
And this meeting is adjourned till yᵉ first Sixth Day in yᵉ next month
at a monthly meeting of Friends held by adjournment
on the first Day of yᵉ 4ᵗʰ month 1757 we have an account
at this meeting that there hath been 12£–15shillings Province
old tenor gathered and Sent to **Pembook** according the advice
of yᵉ Quarterly meeting Ther was an account of the
Sufferings of friends upon account of yᵉ Malitia Which
amounts to 1982£-18ˢ-0ᵈ Province money
and there hath been a Paper presented to this meeting Signed
by **Christopher Slocum** Condemning his paying money towards military
affairs the Quries have been read and answers made to them
Which are ordered to be sent to yᵉ Quarterly meeting
and **Christopher Slocum**s Paper is refered to yᵉ next monthly
meeting

At a monthly meeting of Friends held at at our meeting House
In **Dartmouth** on the 18ᵗʰ Day of the 4 month 1757 **Ponaganset**
Meeting Called **Abraham Tucker** & **Peleg Smith** present
for **Coakset Ichabod Eady** and & **John Macumber** The Friends
appointed to attend the Quarterly meeting ~~are~~ Have Done
it and Drawn the Epistle as ordered and this meeting hath
Received the Quarterly meetings Epistle which was read and
well accepted
And **Christopher Slocum**s Paper hath been read in this meet
-ing & Considered and accepted The Friends appointed to take

The accounts of Friends Sufferings are Still Continued upon
the Same account there was a Paper brought into this
meeting Signed by **Abigail White** Condemning her outgoings
Which is refered to yᵉ next monthly meeting
And Friends of **Cushnot** have Desired to have a Week Day meet
-ing Settled among them therefore this meeting agreas there
may be a meeting kept there on the first and fourth fourth
Day In each month from this time till our next Fall meeting
And this meeting orders **Adam Mott** & **Joseph Tucker** to
assist the women in Drawing up **Mary Huddlestone**s Denyal
the Friends appointed to Discourc With **Benjamin Howland**
ar Still Continued to Do it

At a monthly meeting of Friends held at our meetin House
In **Dartmouth** on the 16 Day of yᵉ 5 month 1757 **Ponaganset**
meeting Called **Caleb Russell** & **John Russell** yᵉ 3ᵈ present
Coakset meeting Called **Jonathan Wood** & **Joseph Tripp** present
And **Abigail White**s Paper hath been read at this meeting and
accepted and **Jonathan Wood** is ordered to take it and let her
know it that She may be present Whe tis read and to be
read at **Coakset** meeting House on a first Day at the end of a
meeting for worship between this and the next monthly meet
-ing & there was a Certificate read at this meeting Directed
from the monthly meeting at **Portsmouth** on **Rhoad Island**
Concerning **Benjamin Tripp** & his wife & famly of their
orderly Conversation whilest among them recommending
them to our Care which this meeting accepts
Daniel Russell are Still Continued to Discource with **Benjamin**
Howland there was a paper of Denyal read at this meeting
against **Mary Huddlestone** which is approved and **Isaac Smith**
hath Signed it by order of this meeting and is ordered to
read it on a first Day at the end of the meeting for Worship
between this and the next monthly meeting
There was an account of Friends sufferings by reason of their
fines that was taken upon the account of their being impres
-sed and **Isaac Howland Peleg Smith** & **William Anthony** are
appointe to view them and where there is need to Correct
them and bring them to the adjornment of this meeting
And this meeting is adjourned till yᵉ first fourth Day in yᵉ next month
At a monthly meeting of friends held by adjournment on the first
Day of yᵉ 6 month 1757 There was an account of Friends Sufferings

by Reason of their fines taken from upon the account of their being
impressed In the years 1755 and 1756 and 1757 which amounts three
hundredred and eighty pound and four pence Lawful money
Which this meeting hath Considred and allowed

At a monthly meeting of Friends held at our meeting House in
Dartmouth on the 20 Day of the 6 month 1757 **Ponaganset** meet
-ing Call **James Shearman** & **George Smith** present for **Coakset**
Jonathan Wood & **Abiagail White**s Paper hath been read as
ordered We received a Certificate at this meeting from the
monthly meeting at **Sandwich** Concerning **Joseph Wing** and his
Wife of their orderly Conversation amongst them Recommend
-ing them to our Care Which this meeting accepts and whereas
Mary Huddlestones Paper hath not been read **Isaac Smith** is
Still Continued to Do it between this & yᵉ next monthly meeting
And whereas **John Macumber** Son of **William Macumber ju**ʳ
hath Desired a Certificate from this meeting to the monthly
meeting at the **Oblong** therefore **John Mosher** and **Othniel Tripp**
are appointed to Inquire into his sircumstances & Draw one
if they find things clear and bring it to the next monthly
meeting The Friends appointed to attend the Quarterly meeting
and Draw the Epistle are **Jonathan Wood Caleb Russell**
William Barker & **Benjamin Tripp** and whereas we under
-stand that **Abraham Thomas** Desires a Certificate from this
monthly meeting to the monthly meeting at the **Oblong** or
Nine Partners therefore this meeting appoints **Isaac Smith**
to Draw one and bring it to yᵉ next monthly meeting
And whereas it is thought Propper at this meeting that
there might be a Comᵗᵗᵉ Chosen to take an account of
Frinds Sufferings upon the account of miletary affairs
if they think propper and Consider whither it may be
Propper to Exhibit a Petition to yᵉ Generl Cort or to the
Superior Cort and to Do as they think propper in the affair
Therefore this meeting appoints **Peleg Smith Thomas Hathaway**
Bartholonew Taber Jethro Hathaway Jabez Barker Joseph
Tucker Joseph Gifford David Smith Daniel Russell and **Giles Slocum**
A comᵗᵗᵉ in that affair At a monthly meeting of Friends held at
our meeting House In **Dartmouth** on the 18 Day of the 7 month 1757
Ponaganset meeting Called **James Shearman** & **John Russell** present
And for **Coakset Ischabod Eady** & **Joseph Tripp** and **Mary Huddlestone**s
Denyal hath been read as ordered and is as followeth

Whereas **Mary Huddlestone** Daughter of **Peleg Huddlestone** and **Mary** his wife of **Dartmouth** In the **County of Bristol** In the **Province of the Massachusets Bay** In **New England** hath had her Education among us the People Called Quakers yet for want of keeping to that pure Principle the Spirit of Truth to be her Director hath fallen into that foul Sin of fornication as is Evident by her being Delivered of a bastard Child & Consealing who is the father of it so that wee Can Do no less than give this forth as a publick Testimony against her Denying her the s^d **Mary Huddlestone** to be one in unity Desiring that if it be the Will of ye Lord that she may Come to a sight & Sence of her outgoings and through unfeined repentance find mercy with The Lord and So come into unity with us his peopla again Given forth at our monthly meeting held In **Dartmouth** on the 16 Day of the 5 month 1757 And Signed by order and In s^d meeting
by Isaac Smith Clerk

And there was a Certificate Signed at this meeting for **John Macumber** The friends appointed to attend the Quarterly meeting and Draw the Epistle have Done it all Except **Caleb Russell** there was two Epistles from **London** yearly meeting read at this meeting to good Sattisfaction And the Epistle from ye Quarterly meeting hath been read to good Sattisfaction

And this meeting hath Signed a Certificate for **Abraham Thomas** We understand that the Com^tte hath Drawn a Petition to the General Cort at **Boston** & the Same Com^tte are Still Continued to Proceed in the affair as occation may require

And whereas **Seth Allen** Lies under a Scandalous report of being father to a bastard Child This meeting appoints **Nicolas Howland** and **Daniel Russell** to Discouce with him to See if he Can Clear him selfe or Condemn What he has Don amiss

And whereas we understand that **John Lawton** hath paid money towards military Services This meeting appoints **Christopher Giffor** and **Peter Davel** to Show him how that he had gone Con -trary to our profession and ought to Condemn ye Same

and there was Collected at this meeting 3 pond 9 Shillings and 4 pence And this meeting orders ye treasur to pay to ye overseer two Dollars for ye last halfe years keepin the meeting House

And **Isaac Smith** is ordered to Settle ~~their~~ the accounts of the monthly meeting with **James Shearman** and **James Shearman** hath paid ye two Dollars

---

At a monthly meeting of Friends held at our meeting House In **Dartmouth**

<u>8</u> on the 15th Day of the 8 month 1757 **Ponaganset** meeting Called **Nicholas Howland**
1757 and **Daniel Russell** present for **Coakset John Mosher** and **Ichabod Eady**
The Friends appointed to Discource with **Seth Allen** not having had opper
-tunity to Do it ar still Continued to Do it & make return to ye next monthly meeting
And the matter Concerning **John Lawton** is refered to ye next
monthly meeting And **Isaac Smith** hath made up this meetings accounts
With the Tresurer and there remains In ye Stock 7 Shillings & 11 pence
Province old Tenor the Chosing Visitters is refefer until the next
monthly meeting

At a monthly meeting of Friends held at our meeting House in
Dartmouth on the 19 Day of ye 9 month 1757 **Ponaganset** meeting
Called **Jonathan Hussey** & **Daniel Russell** present for **Coakset**
Christopher Gifford & **Peter Davel** present The Friends appointed
to Discource With **John Lawton** have Done it and Signify that
he Doth no ways Condemn what has done in paying money towards
Waring and fighting Therefor **John Mosher** is ordered to let S^d
Lawton know that if he Doth persist in the thing it being Con
-trary to our Principles that friends must proceed to Denye
him And **William Anthony ju** and his Wife have sent a paper in to
this meeting Signifying their Sorrow for their outgoings In particular
their having a Child Soon after marriage which is refered to the
next monthly meeting And **Peace Wood** hath sent a paper to this
Meeting Signifying her Sorrow for her breaking unity with
Friends Which is refered to the next monthly meeting
And the Choosing of vissiters is refered till ye next monthly
Meeting And this meeting is adjourned till the ~~next monthly~~ youths Meeting
This meeting being mett according to adjourment this 7th
of the 10 month 1757 **Abraham Tucker Ichabod Eddy** and
Job Russell are appointed to attend the Quarterly meeting
and Draw an Epistle to the Same and there hath been
Some answer made to the Queries which are ordered to be
Sent to the Quarterly meeting

And At a monthly meeting held at our meeting House in
Dartmouth on the 17 Day of the 10 month 1757 **Ponaganset** meeting
Called **Calep Russell** and **William Barker** present for **Coakset**
John Macumber and **Benjamin Tripp** and **Henry Howland**
and **Abigail Goddard** Did lay their their intentions of marriage
before this meeting and were Desired to wait till ye next
monthly meeting for their answer and **Barnabas Howland** &
Willium Anthony are appointed to inquire into the young mans

Clearness and make return to the next monthly meeting
And **Peace Wood**s papper hath been read again at this meeting
and Considered which this meeting accepts for Sattisfaction
The Friends appointed to attend the Quarterly meeting have
Done it and Drawn an Epistle to the Same
And the Quarterly meetings Epistle hath been read in this
meeting and Well accepted And **Abraham Tucker Adam Mott**
William Barker and **Job Russell** are Chosen visitters for
Ponaganset And **John Mosher** & **John Macumber** for **Coakset**
and for **Cushnot** it is refered until yᵉ next monthly meeting
And whereas **John Lawton** doth no ways incline to make any
acknowledgment for what he hath been under Dealing that
is the upholding Warring and fighting this meeting therfore
Doth Deny him to be a Friend in unity with us till he make
Sattisfaction And **William Anthony** & his wives paper is refered
until the next monthly meeting and **Isaac Howland** and **George**
Smith are appointed to talk with **William Anthony juᵣ** to know
his Sincerity and make return to the next monthly meeting

At a monthly meeting of Friends held at our meeting House
in **Dartmouth** on the 21 Day of the 11 month 1757 **Ponaganset**
meeting Called **Abraham Tucker** & **John Russell** present for
Coakset Christopher Gifford present And Choosing visitters for
Cushnot is refer till next monthly meeting the Friends appointed
to Discource with **William Anthony juʳ** Signify that they have Done it
and he hath given them good Sattisfactions therfor this meeting
accepted of him and his wives papar for Sattisfactions Provided that
he will read it or git Some friend to read it at the end of a meet
-ing for worship on a first Day he being present between this and
the next monthly meeting The Friends appointed to make Inspection
what Friends have been out of the way in military affairs are
Still Continued for the Same Service
There was Collected at this meeting 6 pound 9 Shillings & four pence

At a monthly meeting of Friends held at our meeting House
In **Dartmouth** on the 19 Day of yᵉ 12 month 1757 **Ponaganset**
meeting Called **William Barker** & **John Russell the 3ᵈ** present
Coakset meeting Called **Icahabod Eddy** and **Joseph Tripp** present
Henry Howland and **Abigail Goodard** came to this meeting for
their answer and their answer was that they might proceed to
take each other in marriage in Some Convenient time between this
and the next monthly meeting observing the good order Establishe

among Friends in the accomplishing thereof and **Abraham
Tucker** and **Isaac Smith** are appointed to See their marriage
Consumated in s^d order and make return to the next monthly meeting
And **Benjamin Shearman** and **Elisabeth Lapham** Did lay their Intentions
of marriage before this meeting and were Desired to wait till ye next month
-ly meeting for their answer and **George Smith** & **Jonathan Smith** are
appointed to to make Inquiry into the young mans Clearnedd & make
return to ye next monthly meeting
And **Joseph Tucker Abraham Tucker John Mosher** and **Abraham Russell**
are appointed to attend the Quarterly meeting and Draw an Epistle to
the Same And whereas **Othniel Allen** Desires a Certificate of his Clearness
as to marriage & Conversation to the monthly meeting at **Rhoad Island**
Therefor this meeting appoints **Nicholas Howland** and **Daniel Russell**
to make Inquiry and Draw one if they think propper and bring it to
the next monthly meeting There was Collected at this meeting
three pound five Shillings old Tenor and this meeting orders
The Tresurer to pay to **Antipas Hathaway** 2£=11s–10^d old tenor for mend
-ing Glass about the meeting house and 4 pound ten Shillings to
Jonathan Hussey for y^e last halfe years keeping y^e meeting House

At a monthly meeting of Friends held at our meeting House in
Dartmouth on the 16 Day of y^e 1 month 1758 **Ponaganset** meeting
Caleb Russell present for **Coakset** none appeard
The Friends appointed to See **Henry Howland**s marriage Consummated
Signify that it was orderly accomplished and the Quarterly meeting
Epistle hath been read at this meeting and well accepted
Joseph Tucker & **John Mosher** have attended the Quarterly meeting
And Drawn an Epistle to ye Same
And **Thomas Hix** Son of **Samuel Hix** of **Tiverton** and **Deborah Smith**
Daughter of **Benjamin Smith** Did lay their Intentions of taking
Each other In marriage before this meeting and were Desired
to wait till the next monthly meeting for their answer and
this meeting is adjourned till the next fourth Day come Week
This meeting being met according to adjournment this 25 Day of the
first month 1758 And **William Anthony** & his wives paper hath
been read and is as followeth
To the monthly meeting of Friends held In **Dartmouth** on th 19 Day
of the 9 month 1757 These are to inform the meeting that for
Want Watchfulness we have given way to the Enemy as to Commit
the Sin of fornication as appears by our having a Child born so
Soon after marriage which hath brought Grief to our Parents and

And a Scandal to the Profession we make which Sin we Condemn
and are heartily Sorry for Desireing Friends would pass it by so as
Suffer us to remain under their care and hope by repentance
to find forgiveness with God given under our hands by us

William Anthony

Sarah Anthony

And the Tresure hath paid 2£–11ˢ–10ᵈ old Tenor to **Antipas Hathaway**
for mending Glass about the meeting House and also 2 Dollers to **Jonathan
Hussey** for keeping the meeting House and **Benjamin Shearman**
and **Elizabeth Lapham** appeared at this meeting for their answer
and their answer was that they might proceed to take each other
In marriage in Some Convenient time between this and the
next monthly meeting opserving the good order Established among
Friends in the ~~good order Good order~~ In the Performance thereof
And **George Smith** and **Jonathan Smith** ~~and~~ are appointed to see
Their marriage Consummated and make return to the next month-
-ly meeting And there was a Certificate Signed at this meeting
for **Othniel Allen** Directed to the monthly meeting at **Rhoad Island**

At a monthly meeting of Friends held at our meeting House in
Dartmouth on the 20ᵗʰ day of the 2 month 1758 **Ponaganset** meet
-ing called **Abraham Tucker** and **Peleg Smith** present & for **Coak
-set John Macumber** and **Philip Tripp** The Friends appointed to
See **Benjamin Shearman** & **Elizabeth Laphams** marriag Consumma
-ted Signify that it was orderly accomplished and **Thomas Hix** and
Deborah Smith appeared at this meeting Desiring their answer
and their answer was that they might proceed to take each
other In marriage in Some Convenient time between this and
the next monthly meeting observing the good order established
~~In the~~ among Friends in the Performance thereof and **William
Anthony** and **John Russell the 2ᵈ** are appointed to see their marriage
Sollemnized in sᵈ order & make return to the next monthy meeting
And **Abraham Shearman** and **Mary Howland** Widow of
Benjamin Howland Late of **Dartmouth** Deces,d Did lay their inten
-tions of marriage before this meeting and were Desired to
wait till the next monthly meeting for their answer
And also **Benjamin Butler** & **Esther Kempton** and **Israel Wood**
and **Hannah Tripp** Did lay their Intentions of marriage before this
meeting and were Desired to wait for their answers till the
next monthly meeting and **William Anthony** and **Humphry
Smith** and **James Shearman** are appointed to see into **Mary**

Howlands Sircumstances and endeaver to have things Settled
that the Children may not be liable to be wronged by her second
marriage and **Caleb Russell** & **Job Russell** are appointed to Inquire
Into **Abraham Shearmans** Clearness and make return to the
next monthly meeting and **Ichabod Eddy** and **Christopher Gifford**
are appointed to inquire into **Israel Woods** Clearness and **Abraham**
Russell & **Caleb ssell [Russell]** for **Benjamin Butler** and make return to
the monthly meeting
And Whereas **Daniel Shepherd** and **John Merihew** being about to go to the
Oblong or **Nine Partners** to stay some time and Desire Certificates this meeting
Therefore appoints **Nathanil Howland** & **Nathaniel Bowdish** to mak inquiry
and Draw their Certificates if they find things Clear
And Whereas **Peace Wood** being about visit Friends at **Sandwich** at their
annual meeting and Desires a few lines by way of Certificate from this
meeting to Friends there Therefore **Joseph Tucker** & **Adam Mott** are
appointed to Draw one and bring it yᵉ next monthly meeting
And whereas The General Cort hath made anact as we Suppose Intend
-ed to favour frinds upon account of miletary Services Therefore
this meeting appoints **Joseph Tucker Caleb Russell Thomas Hathaway**
Humphry Smith Daniel Russell Jethro Hathaway & **Bartholomew Taber**
to Consult about the matter & Consider the thing and bring in their
Result to yᵉ next Preparitive meeting and thi meeting is adjourned
until the next Preparitive meeting

This me[eti]ng mett according to adjournment on the 15ᵗʰ Day of the
3 month 1758 The Comᵗᵗᵉ appointed to Consider the act of the
General Cort have mad return that they have Done it and find
the Consequence of the affair to be So imprortant that think propper
that it might be Communicated to the yearly meeting at **Rhoad**
Island to have the mind of Friends in General about it
They have also Drawn an address to yᵉ General Cort a Coppy Where
-of was read at this meeting and approved[23]
At a monthly meeting of Friends held at our meeting House in
Dartmouth on the 20ᵗʰ Day of yᵉ 3 month 1758 **Ponaganset**

23. In December, 1757, the Massachusetts General Court, faced with the need to contribute troops
to the Seven Years War, tried to accommodate Quaker objections. In a complicated formula, Friends in
each town would present a list of names of members liable to military duty. They would not be forced
into service, or punished for refusal to serve. Instead a poll tax for the cost of a replacement soldier was
added to the cumulative tax paid by these towns. Friends objected on the grounds that furnishing lists
of members implicated them in warmaking. See Worrall, *Quakers in the Colonial Northeast, 137-38;* and
Journals of the House of Representatives of Massachusetts, 1758-1759 (Boston: Massachusetts Historical
Society, 1963), 84.

meeting Called **Abraham Tucker** and **Daniel Russell** present
for **Coakset John Mosher** & **Peter Davel** the Friends appointed
to Inquir into yᵉ Clearness of **Abraham Shearman Benjamin
Butler** and **Israel Wood** Signify that they find nothing to hin
-der their Intended marriages and they all appearing for their
answers they had their answers that they might proceed to
marry in the good order Established amongst the Friends in Some Con
-venient time between this and the next monthly meeting
and **Abraham Russ** & **Caleb Russell** & **Isaac Smith** & **Paul Russell**
and **Ichabod Eddy** & **Christopher Gifford** are appointed to See
Their marriages Consummated in sᵈ order & make return to the
next monthly meeting The Friends appointed to See **Thomas
Hix** and **Deborah Smith**s marriae Consumated Signify that
it was performed In Good order Certificates were Drawn
and brought to this meeting for **Daniel Shepherd** and **John
Merihew** which is refered as to Signing till yᵉ next monthly meeting
There was a Paper presented to this meeting Signed by **Humphry**
Son of **Peleg Smith** and his wife Condemning their outgoings which
is Refered to the next monthly meeting and there was Some
account of Friends Sufferings brought to this meeting which is
ordered to be Sent to the Quarterly meeting And we understand
from **Coakset** that **Stoakes Potter** and **Benjamin Shaw** are
Listed Troopers and that **John Wood** hath paid Money to Save
his Son from being Impressed and that **Isaac Tripp** and
Cornelius Potter are married out of our Good order therefore
Christopher Gifford and **Joseph Tripp** are appointed to Deal fur
-ther with them and make returns to the next monthly meeting
And whereas there are Some Frends belonging to **Coakset**
That Live to the eastward of **Coakset** River that we understand
have paid money towards military Services this meeting
appoints **Peleg Huddlestone** & **Nicholas Howland** to Labour
with them to See if they Incline to Condemn it
Nicholas Howland & **Daniel Russell** have Discourced With
Seth Allen And he Desires Friends to wait till the next monthly
meeting And the Queries were Read and answers given
In wrighting which is ordered to be sent to the Quarterly
meeting and Concerning the act of the General Cort as to taking
Lists and the like it is refered to the Quarterly meeting for advice
And wheras we have been a greate Expence upon account
of Petitiong to yᵉ General Cort and also being behind hand as

to the Charg of our new meeting House at **Newton** this
meetings propper to address the Quarterly meeting for Relief
upon that account and this meeting appoints **Joseph Tucker**
Peleg Smith Christopher Gifford & **John Mosher** to attend
The Quarterly meeting & Draw an Epistle to the Same

At a monthly meeting meeting of friends held at our meet
-ing House In Dartmouth on the 17 Day of yᵉ 4 month 1758
Ponaganset meeting Called **William Barker** & **John Russell**
the 3ᵈ present for **Coakset Benjamin** and **Philip Tripp**
Caleb Russell Signifies that **Benjamin Butler** and **Esther**
Kamptons marriage wa[s] Consumated in good order in Degree
And **Isaac** Signifies that he was at the Consummation
of **Abraham Shearman** & **Mary Howland**s marriage
and that it was orderly accomplished And the Friends
appointed to See **Israel Wood** and **Hannah Tripp**s marriage
Sollemnized Reports that it was orderly performed
And **Seth Allen** hath Sent in a Paper to this meeting Signifyin his Sorrow
Which is refered to the next monthly meeting The Friends appointed to
Discource with **Stokes Potter** & **Benjamin Shaw John Wood** & **Isaac**
Tripp not having throgh Done it are Continued to Do it and bring in their
account to the next monthly meeting **Humphry Smith** & his Wives paper
is refered till yᵉ next monthly meeting And wheras **Benjamin Russell**
Carpenter William Ricketson juʳ **Jonathan Slocum** and **Job Gifford** have
paid mony upon miletary affairs not having Done anything towards
making Sattisfaction the matter is refer till yᵉ next monthly meeting
The Friends appointed to attend the Quarterly meeting have Done it
as appointed And the Quarterly meeting Epistle hath been read
and Well accepted one thing was omitted at the Last monthly meet
-ing that is the **Coakset** visitters gave in their account in wright
-ing of their Service in visitting friends families **Daniel Shepherd**
and **John Merihew** had Certificates Signed at this meeting Directed to
the monthly meetig at the **Oblong** or **Nine Partners**
And whereas we understd that the Charge upon yᵉ account **Newton**
meeting House is not Completed **Joseph Tucker James Shearman**
and**Paul Russell** are appointed to See into yᵉ matter what money there
is Due and bring in their account to yᵉ next monthly meeting
And Whereas **Edward Wing** Son of **Edward Wing** Deceased hath request
-ed a few Lines by way of Certificate from this meeting to yᵉ monthly
meeting at the **Oblong** Therefore this meetig appoints **Humphry**
Smith to Draw on and bring it tomorrow in the afternoon to

Which Time this meeting is adjourned
This meeting being mett according to adjournment this 18th of
the 11 month 1758 And **Edward Wing** had a Certificate Signed
at this meeting in behalfe of the meeting The visitters report
to this meeting that they have Laboured with **Humphry Slocum**
but Recive no Sattisfaction therefore this meeting appoints
Paul Russell & **Daniel Russell** to talk further with him and make
report to the next monthly meeting

At a monthly meeting of Friends held at our meeting House in **Dart**
-**mouth** on the 15 Day of the 5 month 1758 D **Ponaganset** meeting Called
Abraham Tucker and **Peleg Smith** present for **Coakset** ~~Peleg Smith~~
and **Ichabod Eddy** & **Christopher Gifford** present
And **Edward Thirston** of **Freetown ju**ʳ & **Pernel Sawdry** Did lay their
Intentions of marriage before this meeting and were Desired to
wait till yᵉ next monthly meeting for their answer
as also Did **Joseph Soule** & **Dinah Tripp** who were Desire to wait
as abovsᵈ And **Christopher Gifford** & **John Macumber** are appoin
-ted to See into **Joseph Soal**es Clearness & make retur accordingly
And **Seth Allen**s Paper hath been Read and Considered at this
meeting and it is Concluded not to be Sufficient without know
-ing Whither he hath took propper measures to make the
young Womans Sattisfaction and **Eleazer Smith** & **William Rickeson**s
Paper are accepted for Sattisfaction
And **William Sisson Jonath Sisson** & **Benjamin Slocum** have sent
In Papers Condemning their paying money towards the Militia
which are refered And **Daniel Russell** & **Paule Russell** are Still
Continued to Deal further With **Humphry Slocum**
The Friends appointed to Discource with **Stokes Potter John**
Wood Benjamin Shaw Cornelius Potter & **Isaac Tripp**
have Done it & they don't find **John Wood** to be Guilty and Con
-cerng **Benjamin Shaw** the matter Is refered to the next month
-ly meeting and **Isaac Tripp Stokes Potter** & **Cornelius Potter**
not Inclining to Do any thing towards making Sattisfacti this
meeting Concludes them not under our Care for the time
to come without Reformation And Whereas **Benjamin Russell**
Carpente being under the Same Sircumstance are making
not Sattisfaction this meeting Doth also set him aside from
under our Care till there be some Reformation
And Whereas **Prince Howland** & his family being Removed to
Oblong or **Nine Partners**to Dwell Desire a Certificate from

This meeting Therefore **Joseph Tucker** & **Adam Mott** are
appointed to Draw one and bring it to the next monthly
meeting if they think Propper

At a monthly meeting of Friends held at our meeting House
In **Dartmouth** on the 19 Day of yᵉ 6 month 1758 **Ponaganset** meet
ing Called **Caleb Russell** & **John Russell** & Joh the 3ᵈ present
Coakset meeting Called **Christopher Gifford** & **John Macumber**
present **Joseph Soule** and **Dinah Tripp** appeared at this meet
-ing for their answer and it was that they might proceed to take
each other in marriage in Some Convenient time between now
and the next monthly meeting observing the good order
Established among friends in the performance therereof
and **Christopher Gifford** & **John Macumber** are appointed
to see their marriage Consummated in sᵈ order & make return
to the next monthly meeting And **Edward Thirston** & **Pernel
Sawdy** came to this meeting for their answer which was that they
might preceed to take each other in marriage in Some
convenient time between this and the next monthly meeting
and **Isaac Smith** & **Joseph Smith** are appointed to See their
marriage Consummated in sᵈ order and make return to the next month
-ly meeting And whereas the abovesᵈ **Edward Thirston** not prducing any Cer
-tificate that he was under the Care of any monthly meeting yet had a
good Character from **Swansey** monthly meeting Concerning him we have
permitted him to have his answer and marry amongst us yet it is
the mind of this meeting ought not to be allowed and so not to be made
a president fo the Time to Come And Friends not having an opportunity
to go through with that affar od **Seth Allens** it is refered till yᵉ next
monthly meeting And **Benjamin Slocum** & **William Sisson** & **Jonathan
Sisson**s papers have been Considered & accepted by this meeting and
Job Gifford hath Sent in a paper to this meeting which is refered
to the next monthly meeting The Friend that was to talk with **Hum
-phry Slocum** Signify that he Desires that Friends would not be hasty
abou Denying him therefore the matter is refered till yᵉ next
monthly meeting
~~At a monthly meeting of Friends held at our meeting House in
Dartmouth on the~~ And we understand that **Peleg Cornell Silas Kerby**
and **Robert Kerby** have paid money towards Supporting military
Services and have been Laboured With and they no ways Inclining
to Condemn it yet this meeting hath refered it to yᵉ next
monthly meeting and there was a Certificate Signed at this meet

-ing for **Prince Howland** and his famly and this meeting is adjourned
untill the first fourth Day In yᵉ next month

This meeting being mett according to adjournment this 7ᵗʰ Day
of yᵉ 7ᵗʰ month 1758 The matter Concerning **Humphry Smith**
and his wife is refered till next monthly meeting And **Joseph
Tucker Stephen Willcock & Henry Hedly** are appointed to
attend the Quarterly meeting & Draw an Epistle to yᵉ Same
and this meeting hath agread to Come to a Subscription of ten
Dollars to finnish the Charge of **New Town** meeting House

At a monthly meeting of Friends held at our meeting House In **Dart**
-**mouth** on yᵉ 17 Day of the 7 month 1758 **Ponaganset** meeting ~~House in
Dartmouth on the~~ Called **William Barker & Caleb Russell** present
Coakset meeting Called **Christopher Gifford & John Macumber** present
The Friends appointed to See **Joseph Soule & Dinah Tripp**s marriage
Consummated Signify And also The Friends that was appointed to See
Edward Thirston and **Pernel Sawdy**s marriage Consummated Signify
That they wer accomplished in good order And yᵉ matter Concer
-ning **Seth Allen** And the matter Concerning **Humphry** ~~Slocum~~ **Smith**
is refered until yᵉ next meeting
The matter Concerning **Peleg Cornell Silas Cirby** and **Robert
Kerby** is refered to yᵉ next monthly meeting as is also yᵉ matter
Concerning **Jonathan Slocum** The Friends appointed to attend the
Quarterly meeting have Done it & Drawn an Epistle to the Same
And the Quarterly meetings Epistle hath been read & well accep
-ted And whereas we are Desired by the Quarterly meeting to
Come to a Subscription towards **Providence** meeting House the
matter is refered till yᵉ next monthly meeting
And whereas **Bejamin Shaw** not making any Sattisfaction
uppon account of his paying mony upon yᵉ account of military
Services nor Inclining to Do any thing as we Can Learn this
meeting thinks Propper to Set him aside And Conclude him
not in unity nor under our Care for the time to Come
Without Reformation And whereas **Peace Wood** and **Keziah
Wood** have Signified that they have a Concern to visit Friends at
the **Oblong** & thereaway & Desire Some lines by way of Certi
-ficate Therefore **Abraham Tucker & Joseph Tucker** are appoin
-ted to Draw them if think Propper & bring them to the next
monthly meeting
There Was Collected at this meeting three pound Sixteen Shil
-lings & four pence Province old Tenor

The matter Concerning **Humphry Smith** Son of **Peleg Smith**
And his wives paper is refered until yᵉ next monthly meeting
And whereas there is a great Charge arisen upon **Samuel
Craw** by reason of his Lameness & Docters Charge And we
think it our Duty to See into the affair and order **Abraham
Tucker Isaac Smith** & **Paul Russell** to See What yᵉ Charge is
and What way he is in to pay it

At a monthly meeting of Friends held at our meeting
House in **Dartmouth** on the 21 Day of yᵉ 8ᵗʰ month 1758
Ponaganset meeting Called **James Shearman** & **Abraham
Tucker** present **Coakset** meeting Called present **Joseph Tripp
Thomas Cook** of **Tiverton** And **Susannah Cornell** widow of
Edward Cornell of Did lay their Intentions of marriage before
This meeting & were desired to wait till yᵉ next monthly
meeting for their answer And **Joseph Tripp** & **Philip Tripp**
are appointed to Inquire into the widows Sircumstances
And make report to the next monthly meeting
This meeting orders the Tresurer to pay 2 Doller & ½
to **Jonathan Hussey** for the Last halfe year keeping the
Meeting House
The matter Concerning **Seth Allan** & **Humphry Slocum** is
Refered until the next monthly meeting as is also the matter
Concerning **Robert Kerby**
And Whereas **Silas Kerby** not Doing any thing towards making
Sattisfaction and also **Peleg Cornell** being under yᵉ Same Sircumstance
This meetink propper to Set them aside & Do denie them both
To be in unity with us until Some Reformations
There was Certificates Signed at this meeting for **Peace** & **Heziah Wood**
Humphry Smith juʳ & his & **Stephen Russell** have sent in Papers to
to this meeting which are refered till yᵉ next monthly meeting
We Cannot Learn that **Samuel Craw** can Do any thing
valuable towards paying the Docters for Curing his Legg
Which Charge is 15 -14 Shillings Lawful money which this
meeting hath Concluded to pay
This meeting Concludes to Come to a Subscription towards
Providence Meeting House
also this meeting orders **David Smith** to take in the Subscrip
-tions to pay the Charge of yᵉ Docters upon account of yᵉ abovsᵈ
Samuel Craw & to pay it out as he hath oppertunity
Daniel Russell is appointed take Care of yᵉ burying Ground (viz) to

to Cut all yᵉ Trees & brush and keep them Down and keep the
fence in repair

At a monthly meeting of Friends held at our meeting House
In **Dartmouth** on the 18 Day of yᵉ 9 month 1758 **Ponaganset**
meeting Called **Caleb Russell** & **Paul Russell** present **Coakset**
meeting Called **Christopher Gifford** & **John Macumber** present
The Tresurer hath paid the 2 Dollers & ½ as ordered
William Tripp & **Mariah Hammond** Did lay their Intentions of
marriage before this meeting as also Did **David Russell** &
Susannah Soule & **Levi Smith** and **Silvester Allen** and
were Desired to wait until the next monthly meeting
for their answers and **Barnabas Mosher** and **Nathll Mosher**
are appointed to Inquire into **Wᵐ Tripp** & **David Russells** Clear
-ness & and **Nicholas Howland** & **Daniel Russell** are appointed
to See into **Levi Smiths** Clearness & make returns to yᵉ next
monthly meeting
Seth Allen not Doing any thing so as to Sattisfy Friends it is
Thought proppe that a Paper of Denyal should go forth against
And **Isaac Smith** is ordered to Draw one & bring it to yᵉ next
monthly meeting
The matter Concerning **Robert Kerby** is refered
And **Joseph Tucker** is Still Continued to Labour With him
Stephen Russells paper hath been read at this meeting
Which is accepted for Sattisfaction
And **Humphry Smith** & his Wives Paper is to be Returned
to them and & they to git Some body to read it at the end
of a meeting on a first Day they being present between
this & yᵉ next monthly meeting
Isaac Smith & **Paul Russell** are appointed to mak up
accounts with the Tresurer
Abraham Tucker Peleg Smith and **Humphry Smith**
are appointed to attend the Quarterly meeting and Draw
an Epistle to the Same
And this meeting is adjourned till the first 5ᵗʰ day in yᵉ next month
This meeting being met according to adjournment
This fifth Day of yᵉ 10 month 1758
Abraham Tucker is appointed to See what mony is Raised
toward yᵉ Charge of **Providence** Meeting House and to
See that it be Carried to yᵉ Quarterly meeting
And this meeting hath an account that there is

Subscribed and paid toward the Charge of Petetioning to
the General Cort 4^l -18^s -6^d lawful money
Thomas Cook & **Susannah Cornell** appeared at this meet
-ing for their answer and their answer was that they
might proceed to take each other in marriag in Some
Convenient time between this & the next monthly
meeting observing the good ord Established among Friends
In the performance thereof and **Christopher Gifford**
and **Philip Tripp** are appointed to See their marriage Con
-summated & make return to ye next monthly meeting

m^o
16:10:
1758

At a monthly meeting of friends held at our meeting
House in **Dartmouth** on the 16 Day of ye 10 month 1758
Ponaganset meeting Called **Caleb Russell** & **Job Russell**
present **Coakset** meeting Called **John Cornell** & **Philip
Tripp** present
The three Cupples that Laid their Intentions of mar
-riage before the Last monthly meeting Came to this
for their answers that they might proceed to marry
In Some Convenient time between this and the next
monthly meeting observing the good order Established
among Friends in the performance thereof
and **Isaac Smith** & **Paul Russell** are appointed to See
William Tripp & **Mariah Harmond**s marriage Consummated
And **Barnabas Mosher** & **Nathaniel Mosher** are appointed upon the
Same account for **David Russell** & **Susannah Soule**
And **Holder Slocum** & **Nicholas Howland** for **Levi Smith** &
Silvester Allen There was a paper of Denyal Signed at this
meeting against **Seth Allen** & **Isaac Smith** is ordered to
read it at the end of a first Day meeting at **Ponaganset**
meeting House
Philip Shearman & **Mary Russell** Did Lay their Intentions
of Taking each other in marriage before this meeting &
Were Desired to wait till the next monthly meeting
for their answer And **William Sanford** & **Nathaniel
Bowdish** are appointed to see into ye young mans Clearness
And make return to the next monthly meeting
Jonathan Slocum hath Sent in a paper to this meeting
Condemning ~~th~~ his paying money toward military affairs
Which this meeting accepts
Obadiah Gifford hath Sent in a paper which is refered to the

next monthly meeting **Humphry Smith** & his wives paper
hath been read as ordered and is as followeth
To the monthly meeting of Friends at **Dartmouth**
Esteamed Friends These Lines may inform that whereas we by
not keeping to our Education & the Testimony of Truth in
our own hearts have given way to our Inclinations and
the Temptaion So far as to fall into the Sin of fornication
and had a Child before marriage all which we are now
very Sorry for and Do Condemn all our above mentioned
out goings Hoping God will forgive us our Sins and Desire
friends to pass by our offences and let us remain under
their Care which we have a great value foe

Dartmouth yᵉ 14 of yᵉ 8 month 1758   **Humphry Smith**
                                  Edith Smith

The Friends appointed to attend yᵉ Quarterly meeting
Have Done it & Drawn an Epistle to the Same as ordered
The Quarterly meeting Epistle hath been read & well accepted
The Sum that been Subscribed and paid towards **Providence**
Meeting House is 36ˡ -11ˢ -6ᵈ **Rhad Iland** old Tenor
Peace Wood & **Keziah Wood** was at this meeting and Returned
their Certificates. **Peace Wood** and **Elizabeth Gidley** being
about to visit **Rochester** Quarterly meeting Desired a few lines
of friends Concurrance in the affair which was granted
The Friends appointed to See **Thomas Cook** & **Susannah Cornell**s
marriage Consummated Signify that it was orderly Compleated
And this meeting appoints **Job Russell** to assist the Clerk
in wrighting for the meeting as there may be occation
This meeting hath Chosen **Abraham Russell** & **Thomas
Hathaway** visitters for **Cushnot**

20-11ᵐᵒ At a monthly meeting of Friends held at our meeting House in
1758 **Dartmouth** on the 20ᵗʰ Day of yᵉ 11 mᵒ 1758 **Ponganset** meeting
Called **Joseph Tucker** & **Abraham Tucker** present for **Coakset Christopher
Gifford** and **John Macumber** The friends appointed to Enquire
into **Phillip Shermans** Clearness Signifie they find nothing to
hinder his Intended marriage The friends appointed to See
the three marrages Consomated Signifie that they were
present at the Sollomising thereof and Saw nothing but
they performed in good order – **Phillip Sherman** and **Mary
Russel** appeared at this meeting for their answer & their
answer was that they might proceed to take Each other in

marrage in Sum Convenient time between this & the next
monthly meeting observing yᵉ good order Established a
mong friends In the proformance thereof and **William Sanford
& Nathaniel Bowdish** are appointed to See their marriage –
Consomated in good order & make Return to yᵉ next monthly
meeting – And where as **Seth Allen**s paper of Denial hath not
ben Read and his Father haveing Sent a paper to **Peleg Smith**
which was Read in this meeting Signifying that he think
Friends have delt hardly by his Son the matter as to
Reading his Denial is Refered to yᵉ Consideration of yᵉ next
monthly meeting – and **Christopher Gifford** and **Daniel
Rusel** are appointed to Discourse With **Increas Allen** upon
the affare – And whereas **Robert Kerby** hath been Dealt
with in Love and waited Long upon to See if he Could
Do any thing to make Satisfaction upon yᵉ account of
his paying money to military affares but nothing to
Satisfaction hath been Done by him therefore this meeting
thinks proper to Let him aside & Do Deny him the sᵈ
Robert to be one in Unity with us
Isaac Smith & **Paul Rusel** hath maid up the meeting
accounts with treasurer & there Remains in Stock
£1-4 & 3-3/4 old tener – And where as Friends Liveing
near the head of **Noquechuck River**²⁴ have Signefied to
They Desired Leave to have a meeting Set up there
aboughts which this meeting agrees to and that it
Should be held at **John Cornell**s on every first Day
the three winter mᵒˢ Insuing – –
And where as the friends in **Allens Neck** Signifie that
thay Desier to have a meeting Settled at **Susannah
Gifford**s or at Some Convenient House near there a
boughts for this winter Season
And where as **John Merethew** Desired a Certificate
of his Clearness as to marriage & Conversation to the
To the monthly meeting at yᵉ **Oblong** or **Nine Parteners** and
Nathaniel Bowdish & **Nathaniel Howland** are appointed to Draw
one and Bring it to the next monthly meeting or to yᵉ adjourn
ment of this meeting – And **Joseph Tucker Isaac Smith** &
Paul Russel are appointed to See into the Sircomstances of

24. The East Branch of the Westport River used to be called the Noquochoke, so the "head of the
Noquechuck" is now the area known as the Head of the Westport, although the actual place of the meeting was about a mile further west.

Samuel Craw Deceased & See Whither there be any thing
Left to Defray the Charge arisen upon his account – –
And **Humphry Slocum** Hath made Satisfaction upon the
account of his paying money towards military affaires and
also for his Disorderly marrage – – – – –

At a monthly meeting of friends Held at **Dartmouth** on the

18: 12ᵐᵒ 18 Day of yᵉ 12 mᵒ 1758 **Ponaganset** Called **Willᵐ Barker** &

1758 **Job Russel** present **Coxet**] meeting Called and none present
by appointment the Friends appointed to See **Phillip Shermins**
and **Mary Russels** marrage Consummated Signifies that it was
orderly performed – –
The Visitters Chose for **Aponaganset** are **Abraham Tucker** &
Adam Mott and **Willᵐ Barker** and **Job Russel** & for **Coxet**
the matter is Refared till the next monthly meeting **Peace**
Wood & **Keziah Wood** haveing performed their Service at
the **Oblong** and there aways there Certificates from the
Oblong were Read at this meeting to good Satisfaction – –
The friends appointed to See into yᵉ Sircumstances of **Saᵐˡ**
Craw Deeased have Done it and thay find that in apparell
and other things the value of £29-12:11 old tener
There was Collected at this meeting £7-1-11 province money
And this meeting is adjurned till the next 4ᵗʰ Day
This Meeting being met according to adjournment this 27 day
of the 12ᵗʰ month 1758, There was a Certificate Signed at this
Meeting for **John Merihew** to the **Oblong**, and ^this Meeting is
adjourned to the first sixth day in the next month[25]

This meeting being mett acording to adjurnment this 5ᵗʰ
Day of of yᵉ first mᵒ 1759 the Representitive of **A-**
ponaganset and **Coakset** being present at this meeting the
Queries were Read and and answered in wrighting which
are ordered to be Sent up to the Quarterly meeting the
friend appointed to attend the Quarterly meeting and
Josph Tucker Abrahan Tucker & **Willᵐ Barker** &
Draw an Epistle of the things needfull to the Same
and Sign it in behalf of Sᵈ meeting
The matter Conserning **Seth Eden** is Refered to the
next monthly meeting – there was £9-9-9 ½ province
money Subcribed and paid in towards the Charge of **Provi**

25. The preceding four lines, originally omitted at this point, are inserted here according to instructions at the end of the book.

dence meeting House and **William Barker** is ordered to
Carrie it to the Quarterly meeting – – – – –

15: of   At a monthly meeting of friends held at our meet
12 mo   ing House in Dartmouth on the 15 Day of the 1:st mo
1759   1759 **Ponaganset** meeting Called **Caleb Russel** & **John**
Rusel ye 3rd present for **Coakset Jehabud Edey** & **John**
Macumber present
Barnabas Earl and **Pernal Chase** did lay their intention of Mar
=riage before this meeting and was desird to wait til the next monthly
Meeting for their Answer and **William Sanford** and **Job Russell** are appointed
to See into **Barnabas Earl**s clearness and make Return to the next month-
-ly meeting, and **Isaac Smith** and **Paul Russell** are appointed to See into the
Circumstances of things that they may be Settle that the widows Children be
not hurt by her Second Marriage, The Friends appointed to attend the Quarterly
Meeting have done it and drawn an Epistle to the Same as appointed, and
the Quarterly Meeting Epistle hath been Read at this Meeting and well accepted
we understand that there was 7 Shillings Province mony lacking towards
paying for keeping the Meeting House which our Treasurer is ordered pay and
hath paid it And there was a paper of Denial Signed at this meeting against
Mary Wood Widow of **Daniel Wood ju**r and **Isaac Smith** is order.d to Read it
and the Matter Concerning **Seth Allen** is Refered

19th of   At a monthly Meeting of Friends held at our Meeting House in **Dart**=
2nd mo: =**mouth** on the 19th day of the 2.d month 1759 **Ponigasett** meeting called
Abraham Tucker present, **Coakset** Meeting Called and none Present
The friends appointed to See into **Barnabas Earl**s Clearness Signifie
that they find nothing to hinder his intended Marriage and also the friends
that was to See into the affair Concerning the widows Children Signify
that matters are well Settled according to their Judgment, And **Barnabas**
Earl and **Pernal Chase** Came to this meeting for their Answer and their Answer
was that they might proceed to take each other in Marriage in Some Conveni=
=ent time between now and the next Monthly Meeting Observing the good
order Established amongst friends in the performance thereof, and **William**
Sanford and **Job Russell** are appointed to See it performd accordingly
And **Seth Russel** and **Mary Mosher** did Lay their intentions of taking
each other in Marriage before this Meeting, and was desir,d to wait til
the Next Monthly Meeting for their Anser and **Paul Russell** and **Joseph**
Smith are appointed to See into **Seth Russell**s Clearness and make
Return to the next Monthly Meeting, **Mary Wood**s paper of denial
hath been Read as ordered, And **Seth Allen** hath Sent a paper into
this Meeting which is Refer,d to the Next Monthly Meeting

E Bowen **Elisha Bowen** hath Signified to this Meeting that he desires to Come under
Requests our Care therefore this Meeting appointed **Abraham Tucker** and **Caleb Russel**
to Come to discourse with him and make Return to the Next monthly Meeting
under our **Nicholas Howland** and his wife hath Sent in a paper to this Meeting Condemning
Care their Making Provision and inviting Some to a dinner after the Marriage
of their Daughter who was Married out of the order of friends, which this
Meeting accepts.

The friends on **Allens Neck** desires to have the meeting Continued there
one month longer which is Granted, the friends appointed to view the
Minutes not having done it are desired to do it between this and the
Next Monthly Meeting and **David Smith** and **Job Russell** are added to
the Comittee on that account

19: 3d mo At a Monthly Meeting of Friends held at our Meeting House in
1759 **Dartmouth** on the 19ᵗʰ day of the 3,ᵈ month 1759 **Poniganset** Meeting
Called **Joseph Tucker** and **Abraham Tucker** present for **Coakset Christopher
Gifford,** The friends appointed to See into **Seth Russells** Clearness
Signify that they find nother to hinder his intended Marriage, **William
Sanford** makes Report to this Meeting that he was at **Barnabas Earl**
and **Pernal Chases** Marriage and Saw nothing but that it was orderly
Consumated, And **Seth Russell** and **Mary Mosher** appered at this Meeting for
their answer, and their answer was that they might Proceed to take each
other in Marriage in Some Conveniant time Between this and the Next
monthly Meeting Observing the good Order established amongst Friends in the
performance thereof, And **Paul Russell** and **Joseph Smith** are appointed to
See their Marriage Consumated in Said order and Make Return to the Next
monthly Meeting, and **Seth Allens** paper is refered to the next monthly meeting
Elihu Bowens paper hath been read and Considered at this Meeting and
the matter is Refered to the next monthly Meeting
And whereas the Set time being up for the holding a meeting at the upper part
of **Coakset**, they desire that it may be held there Some time Longer
therefore this meeting agreas that there be a meeting held there as
heretofore for 2 months Longer
The friends appointed to view the Minutes have done it as ordered
And **Isaac Smith** and **Paul Russell** have Sold the things that was
Samuel Craws Deceased to his Brother **John** who has Given a note
for the Mony, And **Isaac Smith** is orderd to Record the Minutes
And whereas **Deborah Wilbour** wife of **George Wilbour** Signifies
that She hath a mind to visit her friends and Relations at the **Oblong**
and **Nine Partners** and Desires a Certificate, therefore this meeting
appoints **Gideon Gifford** and **Phillip Allen** to Enqure of the woman

into her Circumstances and draw one if they think proper

And this meeting hath Considered the Matter Concerning **Elihu Bowen**
and find freedom to Receive him and Concludes him under our Care
for the time to come

And whereas **James Macumber** Son of **William Macumber Ju.**ʳ doth
desire a Certificate from this Meeting to the monthly Meeting at
Oblong or **Nine Partners,** this Meeting appoints **Joseph** and
Philip Tripp to make Enquiry and draw one if they think proper
and Bring it to the Next monthly Meeting

Joseph Tucker hath brought in an account that he hath had 25
Sheep taken from him for 6£16S demand. It was done in the month
Called January 1758 by **Seth Williams,** and **David Ball Ebenezer**
Willisses Clark of **Dartmouth,** Said Sheep valued at 8£. it was taken
upon account of a fine for his Sons not appearing at the General Muster

And **Peleg Smith William Sanford** and **Paul Russell** are appointed
to attend the Quarterly Meeting and draw an Epistle to the Same
Collected at this Meeting 3£4S10d Province tenor and this Meeting
is adjourned to Youths meeting

This Meeting being mett according to adjournment this 6ᵗʰ day of
the 4ᵗʰ month 1759 the Queries was read and Answers Given by **Ponigan=**
-set visitors at this Meeting which is ordered to be Sent to the Quarter
-ly Meeting, but no answer from **Coakset**

16th of 4th At a monthly Meeting of friends held at our Meeting in **Dartmouth**
mo on the 16.ᵗʰ day of the 4ᵗʰ month 1759 **Poniganset** meeting Called **James**
1759 **Shearman Caleb Russell** for **Coakset Othniel Tripp** and **Philip Tripp**

The friends appointed to See **Seth Russell,** and **Mary Moshers** Marriage
Consumated Signify that it was performed in Good order

E. Bowen And this Meeting hath Consider.d the matter Concerning **Elihu Bowen**
Received and find freedom to Receive him and he to be under our Care for the time to Come

And the matter Concerning **Seth Allen** is Refered till the next monthly Meeting

And whereas we understand that there has a Practice been of late
Advice amogst our younger Sort of People of making Lotteries which we think to
not to be of a very hurtful Consequence, Therefore it is the advice of this Meeting
make for all under our Care to be Careful not to be in Said Practice, and
Lotteries that all friends Belonging to this Meeting Endeavour to Suppress the Same

Peleg Smith and **Paul Russel** hath attended the Quarterly Meeting and
drawn an Epistle to the Same as appointed, and we have Received an
Epistle from the Quarterly Meeting which hath been Read and well accepted

And there hath been two Certificates Signed in and by order of this Meeting
one for **James Macumber** and the other for **Deborah Wilbour [Wilbur]** directed to

the **Oblong** or **Nine Partners**

F. Trip And we understand that **Francis Tripp** hath been disorderly in Mar-
denied -rying out of the order of friends, therefore this Meeting orders **Othniel**
Tripp and **Philip Tripp** to Labour with Said **Francis** to See if he doth any
way incline to make Satisfaction

And **Abraham Tucker** and **Adam Mott** are appointed to Enquire into
the Conversation of **Seth Allen** and make Report to the Next monthly Meeting

---

5th mo: At a monthly Meeting of friends held at our Meeting
1759 House in **Dartmouth** on the 21.st day of the 5.th Month 1759 **Ponaganset**
Meeting Called **Joseph Tucker** and **Abraham Tucker** present for
Coakset Petter Davil and **Christopher Gifford**, The friends that
was appointed to Enquire Concerning **Seth Allens** Conversation
not having throughly Gone through the matter are Continued to do it and
make Report to the Next monthly Meeting

And whereas **Francis Tripp** hath Married out of the Good order
F. Tripp Eshablished amongst us, we Cannot find that he doth incline to
Denied make Satisfaction, Therefore **Isaac Smith** is ordered to draw up
a paper of Denial against him and bring it to the next
monthly Meeting

And whereas Some friends Seem not to be So Careful about keep-
-ing the time of day in Meeting together for worship, it is the mind
of this Meeting that friends be Careful for the time to Come and
meet togather by 12 a Clock on first days and fourth days and
by Eleven on monthly meeting days

And **Samuel Howland Ju.r** hath sent in a paper Signifying his Sorrow for
his disorderly Marriage therefore the visitors are desires to talk with him
and make Report to the Next monthly meeting

Benjamin Butlar and his wifes paper Concerning their having a Child So
Soon after Marriage hath been Read in this meeting and ordered to be
read at the End of a meeting on a first day

And **Peter Davil** and **Joseph Tripp** are Chosen visitors for **Coakset**

And whereas it is thought of Service that the meeting be Settled at the
head of **Noquechuck River** for Some time Longer, therefore this meeting
agrees that it be held there as in time past till our fall meeting next

---

6th mo: At a monthly Meeting of friends held at our Meeting House in
1759 **Dartmouth** on the 18.th day of the 6.th month 1759 **Poniganset** meeting Called
Caleb Russel present and **John Russel the 3.d**, for **Coakset Christopher Gifford**
and **Othniel Tripp**

The matter Concerning **Seth Allen** is Refered to the next monthly Meeting

Francis Tripps paper of denial was Read in this meeting and **Isaac Smith**

hath Signed it by order of this Meeting

the visitors not having had oppertunity to discourse with **Samuel Howland ju.**[r]

it is refered to the next monthly Meeting and they Continued for the Service

Benjamin Butlar and his wives paper not being read as ordered it is

ordered to be done accordingly Between this and the next monthly meeting

John Our worthy Friends **John Storer** from **Nottingham** in **Old England** and **Benajah**

Storer **Andrews** from **Berlinton [Burlington]** in **West Jersey** was at this Meeting and

from　　their Labour

O.E of Love and Religious visit was kindly accepted and their Certificates was

Read to good Satisfaction

And this Meeting agrees to Come to farther Subscription towards the Charge of

Providence Meeting House

And **Joseph Tucker Abraham Tucker John Russell** y[e] 3.[d] **Humphry Smith**

John Mosher Jethro Hathaway are appointed to attend the Quarterly Meeting

and draw an Epistle to the Same, And **Caleb Russel** and **Paul Russell** are

added to attend the Quarterly meeting

It is the mind of this Meeting that all the Books belonging to the Meeting be brought

to the Next monthly Meeting, And this meeting is adjourn.d til the youths

Meeting

This Meeting being met according to adjournment this 6.th day of the 7 mo 1759

the Queries have been Read and Answers Given at this Meeting which is

order,d to go to the Quarterly Meeting

There hath been Subscribed and brought into this Meeting £22=17[s]=7[d]

province old tenor towards the Charge of Providence Meeting House

---

7 mo: At a monthly Meeting of friends held at our Meeting House in **Dartmouth**

1759 on the 16.th day of the 7.th month 1759 **Poniganset** meeting Called **Nathaniel**

Bowdish, and **William Barker** present **Coakset** meeting Called **Peter Davil**

and **Philip Tripp** present

Benjamin Butlar and his wives paper hath been read as ordered

This meeting hath accepted of **Seth Allens** paper provided that he read it or

get Some [person?] ~~body~~ to Read it he being present at the end of a meeting for

worship on a first day between this and the next monthly meeting

The friends appointed to attend the Quarterly meeting and draw the Epistle

have done it as ordered

There were five yearly Meetings Epistles read at this Meeting which

was to Good Satisfaction

The Quarterly meeting Epistle hath been read and well accepted

we have an account that **George Lawton** Son of **John Lawton** hath

Married out of our Good order and hath been dealt with by the

visitors and Seems not to Incline to make any Satisfaction Therefore

this meeting appoints **Benjamin** and **Philip Tripp** to Labour farther
with him

John Craw hath Answered the note that he Gave to this meeting which
hath defrayed the Remaining Charge of the Doctors upon the account of
his Brothers Lameness, and Six pounds Nine Shillings and eleven pence old tenor
over which is put in with the Colection which is £4=14ˢ=11ᵈ old tenor

There are Several papers that have been given in, one from **Solomon
Lapham** one from **Samuel Howland ju.ʳ** one from **Obadiah Gifford** which are
Refer,d to the next monthly Meeting

James Shearman is ordered to pay Six pounds three Shillings and nine
pence to **Jonathan Hussey** for the Last half years keeping the meeting House

---

8 mo: At a monthly Meeting of friends held at our Meeting House in **Dartmouth**
1759 on the 20ᵗʰ day of the 8ᵗʰ month 1759, **Poniganset** Called **Joseph Tucker**
and **Abraham Tucker** present, for **Coakset Peter Devol** and **Joseph Tripp,** present

Whereas **George Lawton** hath Married out of the Order of friends and
he hath been dealt with, and Refuses to make any Satisfaction, this
Meeting Concludes him not to be under the Care of friends

James Shearman hath paid £6=3ˢ=9ᵈ old Tenor as ordered to **Jonathan Hussey**

This Meeting accepts of **Samuel Howland Ju,ʳ** his paper for Satisfation
for his Marrying Contrary to the order of friends

I Andrews **Isaac Andrews** and **William Foster**s Certificates were Read at this
& W Fosters Meeting and well accepted

Visit This Meeting accepts of **Solomon Lapham**s paper for Satisfaction for his
out=goings in Marrying Contrary to the order of friends, and in paying
his fine when Impressed to go to war

Obediah Giffords paper is Refer,ᵈ to the next monthly Meeting

There was a Complaint Brought to this Meeting by **Jonathan Sisson**
against his Brother **William Sisson**, This Meeting appoints
Peleg Huddlestone John Gifford and **Phillip Tripp** to Labour with
him and hear and determine the Contrversy between them, any two
agreeing make a Judgment and make Return to the next monthly
Meeting, **Solomon Lapham** hath Requested a Certificate from this meeting
Therefore this Meeting appoints **Daniel Russell** and **Humphry Smith**
to make Enquiry and draw one and Bring to the next monthly Meeting
if they think fit

---

9 mo: At a monthly meeting of friends held at our meeting House in
1759 **Dartmouth** on the 17ᵗʰ day of the 9ᵗʰ month 1759 **Poniganset** meeting Called
Caleb Russell present, for **Coakset Philip Tripp** present

Timothy Davis and **Hiphzibah Hathaway** did Lay their Intention of Marrige

before this Meeting, and were desir,d to wait for their Answer til the
next monthly Meeting

S. Allen   And whereas **Seth Allen** having neglected or Refused Reading his paper

Set aside   according to the order of the monthly Meeting, and there hath another
Scandulous Report happened of the Like tenor as the former, and we have good
Grounds to believe it to be true, Therefore this Meeting Concludes Said paper
Shall not be read Seeing things are So, And this Meeting Concludes it propper
to Set him aside, and **Isaac Smith** is ordered to draw up a paper of
Denial against him and bring it to the next monthly Meeting

The Committee appointed to determine the Contraversy between **William
Sisson** and his Brother **Jonathan** have done it and brought in their Judgment
to this Meeting which is accepted and is as followeth

we the Subscribers being a Committee appointed by the Last monthly meeting to
hear and
determine the difference between **Jonathan Sisson** and his Brother **William**,
after hearing their pleas and duly Considering the affair, and having Reference to
the
last will and Testament of their deceased father, Conclude that **William Sisson**
pay to his Brother **Jonathan** the Sum of one pound fourteen Shillings two
pence one farthing Lawfull mony per annum, for and toward the Support
of their Sister **Hannah Sisson**, until by Law they are acquitted from
that Charge

> **Philipp Tripp**
> **Peleg Huddelstone**
> **John Gifford**

Othniel Allen being Removed to the **Oblong** or **Nine partners** to dwell
Desires a Certificate from this Meeting to the monthly Meeting there
Therefore this Meeting appoints **Phillip Allen** and **John Gifford** to make
Inquiry, and draw one if they think propper and bring it to the next monthly
Meeting, **Job Russell** hath desir,d a Certificate from this Meeting to the
monthly meeting at **Salem** of his Clearness as to Marriage and Conversation
This meeting appoints **William Sanford** and **David Smith** to make Inquiry and
draw one if they think propper

And whereas it is thought propper that Some Friends be appointed to See that
good order
be Observed in the Galleries in full Meetings, and to place themselves where it may
be most Convenent for that Service, Therefore this Meeting appoints **Caleb
Russel, William Sanford,** and **John Russell the 2,ᵈ** for that Service

There was Collected at this Meeting five Pounds four Shillings and 2 pence province
money, The treasurer is Ordered to pay to **David Smith** one Shilling and

four pence Lawful Money which makes up the Sum in full of the Doctors
Charge upon the account of **Samuel Craws** Lameness
And this Meeting is adjourn'd till the Youths Meeting
This Meeting being mett according to adjournment this 5th day of the
10th month 1759, **Adam Mott, Stephen Wilcox, Abraham Tucker Caleb
Russell** and **Philip Tripp** are appointed to attend the Quarterly Meeting
and draw an Epistle to the Same and Sign it in behalf of this Meeting
The visitors of **Coakset** Signifie that they have visited the families of
friends under their Care and find things for the most part Midling well
and they have also made Answers to the Queries which are ordered to be
Sent by the Representatives to the Quarterly Meeting

10 mo: At a monthly Meeting of friends held at our Meeting
1759 House in **Dartmouth** on the 15th day of the 10th month 1759, **Poniganset**
Meeting Called **Peleg Smith** and **John Russell the 3d** present, for **Coakset
Joseph Tripp,**
Timothy Davis and **Hephzibah Hathway** appeared at this Meeting desiring
their answer, and their answer was that they might proceed to take Each
other in Marriage in Some Convenient time between this and the next
monthly Meeting Observing the Good order Established amongst friends
in the accomplishment thereof, And **Adam Mott** and **Abraham
Tucker** are appointed to See it accomplished accordingly
The friends appointed to attend the Quarterly Meeting, have done it and
drawn an Epistle to the Same as appointed
There was a paper of denial Read at this Meeting against **Seth Allen**
which this Meeting approves, and **Isaac Smith** hath Signed it by order of
the Meeting and is Ordered to Read it on a first day at the End of the meeting
of worship Between this and the next monthly Meeting
And whereas there was a Complaint brought into this Meeting by
William Woddel against **Christopher Gifford** that he is about to wrong
him in Several things, Therefore this Meeting appoints **Humphry Smith
Abraham Shearman** and **Paul Russell** a Committee in that afair to
hear and determine the matter and make Return to the next monthly Meeting
There was a Certificate Signed at this Meeting for **Othniel Allen**
There was also another signed for **Job Russell**
And the Quarterly Meeting Epistle hath been Read and well accepted
And whereas the Friends near the head of **Noquechuk River** desires
the Meeting might be Continued as it hath been which is Granted

11 mo: At a monthly Meeting of friends held at our Meeting
1759 House in **Dartmouth** on the 19th day of the 11th month 1759
Poniganset Meeting Called **Joseph Tucker** and **Abraham Tucker**

present for **Coakset Othniel Tripp** and **Ichabod Kerby**

The friends appointed to See **Timothy Davis** and **Hiphzibah Hathway**s

Marriage Solemnized Signify that it was done in good order

Seth Allens Denial hath been Read as Ordered

The Committee not having fully determin'd the affair between **William Woddel**
and **Christopher Gifford** the matter is Refered to the next monthly Meeting and
Said Com-ᵗᵗ Still Continued

Friends have accepted of **Ruth Hathway**s paper for having a Child So Soon after
Marriage, provided that She read it or get Some friend to do it She being present
at the End of a first day Meeting for worship on a first day between this and the
next monthly Meeting

12 *mo:* At a monthly Meeting of friends held at Our Meeting House in **Dart=**
1759 **-mouth** on the 17ᵗʰ day of the 12ᵗʰ month 1759 **Poniganset** Meeting Called
William Sanford present for **Coakset Ichabod Eddy**

Ruth Hathways paper hath not been Read as ordered, therefore this Meeting
orders that it be done between this and the next monthly Meeting

The Committee apointed to Judge ~~between~~ on the Case Between **William Woddel**
and **Christopher Gifford** have done it and their Judgment hath been Read in
this Meeting and accepted, But Said **Woddel** doth not accept, but desires
an apeal to the Quarterly Meeting which is Granted, and also Said **Christopher**
Gifford being dissatisfied Concerning the Judgment doth desire an apeal like=
=wise which is Granted

The visitors Chosen this year for **Poniganset** are **Abraham Tucker William Barker**
and **Caleb Russell,** and for **Quitionut [Cushnet] Thomas Hathway Abraham Russell**
and **Bartholomew Taber**

The friends appointed to attend the Quarterly Meeting are **Joseph Tucker Abraham**
Tucker Humphry Smith and **William Barker,** and they to draw an Epistle to the
Same and Sign it; There was Collected at this Meeting 4£=14ˢ=10ᵈ province mony
The Treasurer is ordered to pay to **Jonathan Hussey** £6=3=9ᵈ for the Last half
years keeping the Meeting House

And **Isaac Smith** and **Joseph Barker** are appointed to make up accouts with
the Treasurer and make Return to next monthly Meeting

And as to doing anything towards **Providence** Meeting House, we do not find
Ourselves in a way for it, being in debt here upon the account of petitioning to
the General Court and other things

1 *mo:* At a monthly Meeting of friends held at our Meeting House in
1760 **Dartmoth** on the 21ˢᵗ day of the first month 1760, **Poniganset** Meeting Called
Job Russell and **William Barker** present, for **Coakset James Cornel** and
Joshua Cornel

Ruth Hathways paper hath been Read as ordered

The friends appointed to attend the Quarterly Meeting have done it and drawn
an Epistle to the Same as appointed

The Treasurer hath paid to **Jonathan Hussey** £6:3ˢ:9ᵈ as order,d

The Quarterly Meeting Epistle hath been Read and well accepted

the friends appointed to make up accounts with the Treasurer not having done
it are Still Continued to do it between this and the next monthly Meeting

And whereas **Stephen Potter** hath Gone Contrary to our Profession in
takeing up arms and going to war, and also hath of Late been published
out of our Good order, Therefore **James Cornell** and **Benjamin Tripp**
are appointed to discourse with Said **Potter** to See if he would make
make any Satisfaction and make Return to the next monthly Meeting

2,ᵈ mo:	At a monthly Meeting of friends held at our meeting
1760	House in **Dartmouth** on the 18ᵗʰ day of the 2.ᵈ month 1760, **Poniganset**

meeting Called **Joseph Tucker** and **Abraham Tucker** present, for
Coakset Benjamin Tripp

The friends appointed have made up accompts with the Treasurer and
there Remains 9ˢ=2ᵈ old tenor in the Stock

S. Potter The friends appointed to discourse with **Stephen Potter** Signify they
disown'd have done it and he Gives no Satisfaction therefore this Meeting thinks
propper to Set him aside, And doth deny him the Said **Stephen Potter**
to be one in Unity with us till Satisfaction be made

This Meeting appoints **James Shearman** and **Daniel Russell** to See about
the Charge that hath arisen about petitioning to the General Court, and
bring in an account to the next monthly Meeting

William Taber Son of **Joseph Taber** hath Sent a paper to this Meeting
Signifying his Sorrow for his Marrying out of Our Good order which is
Refer,d to the next monthly Meeting

And whereas **Adam Mott** Signifies that he hath thoughts of going to **Sandwich**
upon a Religious visit, and desires a few lines from this Meeting, Therefore
this Meeting orders **Joseph** and **Abraham** to draw up Something if
J. Russell they think propper and bring it to the next monthly Meeting
Chosen And whereas **James Shearman** doth decline being Treasurer to this
Treasurer Meeting, This Meeting doth Chuse **Job Russell** to Supply in that office

3 mo=	At a monthly Meeting of friends held at out Meeting House
1760	in **Dartmouth** on the 17 day of the 3.ᵈ month 1760, **Poniganset** meeting

Called **William Barker** and **Job Russell** present, for **Coakset Philip Tripp**
and **Peter Davel**

James Shearman and **Daniel Russell** not having done any thing in the
affair that the Last monthly Meeting ordered are Still Continued to do it
between this and the next monthly Meeting

C. Huddle=   And we understand that **Catharine Huddlestone** hath Married out of our
=stone Set   Good order, and also had a Child Soon after Marriage, and She hath
Aside   been Laboured with in order to bring her to a Sight of her outgoings but
             nothing to Satisfaction hath been by her, Therefore this Meeting thinks
             propper to Set her aside, and appoints **Isaac Smith** to draw up a paper
             of Denial against her and bring it to the next monthly Meeting
             Williams Tabers paper is Refer,d to the next monthly Meeting
             There was a Certificate Signed at this Meeting for **Adam Mott** and
             another for **Samuel Chase**
             The friends appointed to attend the Quarterly Meeting and draw the Epistle
             are **Joseph Tucker, Peleg Smith, Caleb Russell,** and **Peter Davel** and they
             to Sign the Epistle
             The **Coakset** visitors have Given in an account in writing of their Service
             in visiting friends families and also their Answer to the Queries
             there was Collected at this Meeting £3=2ˢ=2ᵈ old tenor
             And this Meeting is adjourn,d til the youths Meeting
             This Meeting being met by adjournment the 4ᵗʰ day of the 4ᵗʰ month 1760, none
             of the Representatives present but **Job Russell**
             The Queries was Read and Answered by the visiters
             Whereas **Christopher Gifford** & **William Woddel** did not prosecute their apeal
             as intended, Do Still Desire an appeal to the next Quarterly Meeting which
             is Granted,
             This Meeting is adjourned again to the 14ᵗʰ day of the 4ᵗʰ month 1760
             This Meeting being mett according to adjournment this 14ᵗʰ day of the 4 mo: 1760
             There was 79 Dollars with what hath been Delivered to **Benjamin Akin** Contri=
             =buted at this Meeting, and Delivered to **Humphry Smith** in order for the
             Distressed people at **Boston** who have met with a Great Loss by fire, and
             to be Delivered to the Select men or overseers of the **Town of Boston**²⁶

4ᵗʰ mo: At a Monthly Meeting of friends held at our Meeting House in
1760   **Dartmouth** on the 21 day of the 4 month 1760, **Poniganset** Meeting Called
           Daniel Russell and **Caleb Russell** present, for **Coakset Icabud Eddy**
           Isaac Smith not having drawn any thing as ordered against **Catharine**
           Huddlestone, is Still Continued to do it and bring it to the next monthly Meeting
           The Friends appointed to attend the Quarterly Meeting have all attended it
           Except **Peleg Smith** and drawn an Epistle to the Same as appointed
           This Meeting hath accepted of **William Taber**s paper for Satisfaction
           Humphry Smith makes Report that he hath Delivered the Mony that
           was Contributed for the poor people at **Boston**, to **Benjamin Akin** to be

26. A great fire swept over Boston on the evening of March 20, 1760, destroying much of the South
End and leaving over one thousand people homeless.

Deliverd at **Boston** for the use of the above Said
And **Luke Hart Joseph Smith William Mosher** and **Joseph Mosher ju.**ʳ
are appointed to take the whole oversight of the Burying Ground at **Newtown**
and **Daniel Russell** Son of **James Russell** having gone out of the way in
his Marriage and other things, Therefore this Meeting orders **Stephen
Willcocks** and **Daniel Russel** to talk with him and bring in their account
to the next monthly Meeting
This Meeting orders **Daniel Russell** to pay to **Peleg Smith** 6ˢ=4ᵈ Lawfull
Mony which Compleats the Charge of Petitioning to the General Court
And also to pay to **Isaac Smith** two Dollars and a half for Recording the
Minutes of the Monthly Meeting, and to pay the Remainder of the money
into the Treasurers hands
The Quarterly Meeting Epistle hath been Read at this Meeting and
Well accepted
Whereas it was Signified in the Epistle that there was Considerable mony
Wanting toward Defraying the Charge of **Providence** Meeting House
This Meeting therefore appoints **Humphry Smith, Christopher Gifford**
and **Adam Mott** and **Bartholomew Taber,** to draw up Something
in order for Friends to Subscribe to as they find freedom – –
John Russell 3ᵈ hath Signified that he and his wife are about
to put out their Son **John Williams** to a friend at **Sandwich,** and
Desires Some lines to the monthly Meeting there of his being under
our Care, and **Joseph Tucker** and **Abraham Tucker** are appointed
in that affair – – – – –

5th mo: At a Monthly^ ᴹᵉᵉᵗⁱⁿᵍ of Friends held at our Meeting House in
1760 **Dartmouth** on the 19ᵗʰ day of the 5ᵗʰ month 1760, **Poniganset** meeting
Called **Joseph Tucker** and **Abraham Tucker** presend, for **Coakset
Joshua Cornell**
Samuel Shove and **Abigail Anthony** did Lay their Intentions of
taking each other in Marriage before this Meeting and were desird
to wait till the next monthly Meeting for their answer – –
Daniel Russell hath Answered the Mony that he was to pay to **Peleg
Smith** and **Isaac Smith**
This Meeting hath Received a Receipt form [from] **Boston** Signed **John
Phillips** of 24 pounds Lawful Mony that we have Sent for the use of
the Sufferers in the Late fire – –
we understand that **Daniel Russell** Son of **James** Desires that friends would
wait til the next monthly Meeting therefore the matter is Refer'd
There was a paper of Denial against **Catharine Huddlestone** brought
to this Meeting and **Isaac Smith** hath Signed it by order of the Meeting

and is also appointed to Read it on a first day at end of the Meeting
of Worship between this and the next monthly Meeting – –
Daniel Russell hath the Remainder part of the mony that was
in his hands to the Treasurer as ordered, which is 7ᶠ=7ˢ=10ᵈ old tenor
We understand that **Benjamin Wing juʳ** being Removed with his family
to **Smithfield** to dwell, Desires a Certificate, therefore this Meeting
appoints **Peleg Huddlestone** and **Ichabud [Ichabod] Eddy** to draw one if thy find
things Clear and bring it to the next monthly Meeting – – – – –

6ᵗʰ month At a monthly Meeting held in **Dartmouth** on the 16ᵗʰ day
1760 of the 6ᵗʰ month 1760, **Benjamin Shearman** and **Jonathan Hussey**
present, And this Meeting is adjourned till this day week
At a monthly Meeting of friends held at our Meeting house
in **Dartmouth** by adjournment on the 23ᵈ day of the 6ᵗʰ month 1760,
Poniganset Meeting Called **Joseph Tucker** and **Abraham Tucker**
present, for **Coakset James Cornel[l]** and **Peter Davel [Davol]** – –
Samuel Shove and **Abigail Anthony** appeared at this Meeting
for their Answer, and their Answer was that they Might proceed to
take each other in Marriage in the Good order Established among
Friends, in Some Convenient time between this and the next monthly
Meeting, And **Peleg Smith** and **Humphry Smith** are appointed to
See their Marriage Consumated and make Return the next monthly Meeting
Benjamin Russell Son of **Benjamin Russell** and **Elisabeth Slocum** Daughter
of **Holder Slocum** Deceased, have laid their Intentions of Marriage before this
Meeting, and were desired to wait till the next monthly Meeting for their Answer
and **Jonathan Hussey** and **Stephen Willcocks [Wilcox]** are appointed to Enquire
into the
young mans Clearness and make Return to the next monthly Meeting – –

[quarter page of blank space]

Whereas **Daniel Russell** Son of **James Russell** having Signified or Given
Ecouriagement of making Satisfaction but not having done anything in
that nature this Meeting thinks proper that **Stephen Willcocks** and **Daniel
Russell** talk further with him and if he make no Satisfaction as they may
Judge Reasonable then they to draw a paper of denial against him and
bring it to the next monthly Meeting – –
Catharine Huddlestones paper of denial hath been read as ordered
There was a Certificate Signed at this Meeting for **Benjamin Wing juʳ** and
Wife and Child directed to the monthly Meeting in **Smithfield** – –
This Meeting is Adjourned to the youths Meeting
This Meeting being met according to adjournment this 4ᵗʰ day of the 7ᵗʰ month 1760

The Representatives have been Called upon and all present but **Peter Davel** [**Davol**]
Poniganset visitors have made Answers to the Queries in writing which is
ordered to be Sent to the Quarterly Meeting – –
The Friends appointed to attend the Quarterly Meeting are **Adam Mott**
Humphry Smith and **Caleb Russell**, and they to draw an Epistle to the
Same and Sign it in behalf of this Meeting – –
There was one hundred Sixty & three pounds Eleven Shillings in **Rhod Island**
Mony Subscribed toward the Charge of **Providence** Meeting House which
this Meeting orders to be Sent to the Quarterly Meeting – – – – –

7 mo:　At a monthly Meeting of Friends held at our Meeting House in
1760　**Dartmouth** on the 21 day of the 7th 1760, **Poniganset** Meeting Called **Caleb**
　　Russell and **John Russell the 3d** present, for **Coakset Ichabud** [**Ichabod**] **Eddy** and
　　John Mosher present
　　Benjamin Russell jur and **Elisabeth Slocum** did appear for their answer
　　and their Answer was that they might pr[o]ceed to take each other in Marriage
　　in Some Convenient time between this and the next monthly Meeting
　　observing the good order Established amongst us in the performance
　　thereof, and **Humphry Smith** and **Jonathan Hussey** are appointed to See
　　their Marriage Consumated in Good order and make Return to the next
　　monthly Meeting – –
　　The Friends appointed to See **Samuel Shove**s and **Abigail Anthony**s
　　Marriage Consumated Make Return that it was accomplished in good order
　　Whereas **Stephen Willcocks** [**Wilcox**] and **Daniel Russell** Were appointed
　　last monthly Meeting to draw a paper of deniel against **Daniel Russel**[l]
　　Son of **James Russell,** if they thought proper, accordingly they have
　　drawn a paper of deniel against him and brought it to this Meeting

D: Russel　and it was Signed by ~~of~~ order of this Meeting and **Daniel Russell**
disown　is appointed to Read it or get it Read between this and the next monthly
　　Meeting, The Friends appointed to attend the Quarterly Meeting and
　　draw an Epistle the Same make Report that they have attended the
　　Said Meeting and drawn an Epistle as ordered
　　There was a paper Sent to this Meeting Signed by **Nicholas Lapham**
　　Signifying his Sorrow for Marrying out of the Good order Established
　　amongst us which is Refer'd to the next monthly meeting – –
　　It hath been agitated whether or no it is warrantable for friends to take
　　up land lately Improved by the French near **Noviscocia** [**Nova Scotia**] which is Refer'd
　　to the next monthly Meeting
　　It is the mind of this Meeting that it is Inconsistant with our Principles to pay
　　the tax Said to be Laid upon friends in Lieu of Personal Service in Carry=
　　=ing on the present war – – This Meeting Received two Printed Epistles

and Three Written Epistles, One printed and one written from **London**
one printed and one written one from **Philadelphia**, and one written
Epistle from **Flushing**, And this Meeting Received an Epistle from the
last Quarterly Meeting and it was Read and the Contents thereof
Recomended to friends Observation
This Meeting orders the Treasurer to pay **Jonathan Hussey** 3 Dollars – – – – –

8th mo: At a monthly Meeting of Friends held at our meeting house in
1760 **Dartmouth** on the 18th day of the 8th month 1760, **Poniganset** Meeting
Called **Joseph** and **Abraham Tucker** present, for **Coakset Peleg Huddle=
=stone** and **Joseph Tripp** – – present
Humphry Smith and **Jonathan Hussey** Signifies to this Meeting that
they was at the Solomnising of **Benjamin Russell** and **Elisabeth
Slocum**s Marriage and Saw nothing but that it was done in Good Order
Daniel Russell Son of **James** his paper ~~hath~~ of Denial hath been Read
as ordered – –
Mary Akin wife of **Benjamin Akin ju**r hath Sent in a paper
Signifying her Sorrow for her outgoings, in paticular her having a Child So
Soon after Marriage, which this Meeting accepts, provided She read it or
get Some friend to do it at the End of a first day Meeting between this and
the next monthly Meeting
Nicholas Laphams paper hath been Read in this Meeting and accepted, and
he Still to Remain under our Care
And as to the matter Referd to this Meeting Concerning whether it might
be warrantable for Friends to take up Land near **Noviscocia** [**Nova Scotia**] lately
Inhabited by the French, This Meeting thinks proper to Refer it to the
Quarterly Meeting for Advice – –
The Treasurer hath paid **Jonathan Hussey** 3 Dollars as ordered – –
J: Case And wheras **Job Case** hath made application to Come under our Care,
Requests which is Refer'd to the next monthly Meeting, and **Peleg Smith** and
to Come **Philip Allen** are Appointed to talk with Said **Case** upon that account
under and make Return to the next monthly Meeting
our Care And whereas we understand that **Jedidiah Wood** hath made a purchase
near **NovaScotia,** and also Sold a Couple of Servants to a man in them
parts, which is Refer'd to the next monthly Meeting
This Meeting hath Agreed to Come to a Subscription toward the Building
a Meeting House for Friends at **Boston** – –
And we understand that **Peleg Slocum ju**r is under Scandulous Report
of Committing fornication, therefore this Meeting appoints **Joseph Tucker**
and **John Russell the 3**d to talk with him and make Return to the next
monthly Meeting

Othniel Tripp is Chosen visitor for **Coakset** in the room of **Joseph Tripp**
who hath Desired to be Excused – – – – –

9 mo: At a monthly Meeting held at our Meeting House in **Dartmouth**
1760 on the 15th day of the 9th month 1760 **Poniganset** Meeting Called **Peleg**
Smith and **Joseph Tucker** present for **Coakset John Mosher** and **Ichabud** [Ichabod]
Eddy present – –
Joseph Slade and **Deborah Howland** have Laid their Intentions of
Marriage before this Meeting and were desired to wait for their
Answer till the next monthly Meeting
Mary Akins paper hath been Read as ordered
The matter Concerning **Job Case** is Refer'd to the next monthly Meeting
The matter Concerning **Peleg Slocum ju**r is Refer d to the next monthly Meeting
and **Joseph Tucker** and **John Russel the 3**d are Still Continued to talk with
him and make Report the next monthly Meeting
This Meeting appoints **Joseph Tucker** and **Abraham Tucker** to See things Settled
with **Deborah Howland**, So that her Children be not hurt by her
Marriage, and make Report the next monthly Meeting

10th mo: At a monthly Meeting of friends held at our Meeting House in
- 1760 **Dartmouth** on the 20th day of the 10th month 1760: **Poniganset** Meeting
Called **John Russell the 3**d and **William Barker** present, for **Coakset John**
Mackumber [Macomber] and **Peter Davil** [Davol]
The friends Appointed to See into the affairs of the Widow **Deborah**
Howlands Estate, Signify that they have made Enquiry, and find
nothing as they apprehend but that She may Marry without danger
of wronging her Children
Joseph Slade and **Deborah Howland** appear'd at this Meeting for
their Answer, and their Answer was that they might proceed to take
each other in Marriage in Some Convenient time between this and
the next monthly meeting, Observing the Good order Established
amongst Friends in the performance thereof, and **Joseph Smith** and
Barnabas Mosher are appointed to ~~attend~~ See their Marriage
Consumated and make Return to the next monthly Meeting ~ ~ ~
The matter Concerning **Job Case** is Refer'd to the next monthly Meeting
The matter Concerning **Peleg Slocum ju**r is Refer'd to the next monthly Meeting
Joseph Tucker and **Peleg Smith** hath attended the Quarterly Meeting
and drawn an Epistle to the Same as appointed
The Quarterly Meetings Epistle hath been Read in this Meeting
and well accepted
Whereas we that is the monthly Meeting hath accepted mony of
Jedidiah Wood, which we Cannot be easy to keep by Reason that he

hath not made Satisfaction in Relation to his Exposing to Sail two Indian Children to **NovaScotia**, which action we Can have no unity with, nor with him till done, and **Peter Davil** [**Davol**] is appointed to deliver the Mony to him again and let him know upon what Account, Whereas **Mary Potter** hath Signified that She is about makeing a visit to the **Oblong** to her friends and Relations there and desires a few lines by way of Certificate to the monthly Meeting there and **Peter Davil** and **Philip Tripp** are appointed to Enquire into the affair and draw one as they Shall think proper and bring it to the next monthly Meeting And this Meeting ap[p]oints **Daniel Russell, Joseph Smith, William Sanford,** and ~~Jos~~ **Paul Russell** to Endeavour to keep the people Orderly in the Galleries and Else where at this fall Meeting Coming on at **Poniganset** and **Peter Davel** [**Davol**], **Ph[i]lip Tripp** and **Joshua Cornel**[l] are appointed for the Same business at **Coakset** – –
Job Russell hath brought a Receipt to this Meeting Signed by **Ebenezer Pope** of **Boston** that he hath Received £10=1ˢ=8ᵈ Lawful Mony toward the Charge of Building Friends Meeting House at **Boston,** Said Mony being Contributed by our monthly Meeting

---

11 mo: At a monthly Meeting of friends at our Meeting House in
1760   **Dartmouth** on the 17ᵗʰ day of the 11ᵗʰ month 1760 **Poniganset** Meeting Called **William Barker** and **Caleb Russell** present, for **Coakset Philip Tripp** and **Israel Wood** ~

The Friends appointed to See **Joseph Slade** and **Deborah Howland**s Marriage Consumated, Signify, that they being there, Saw nothing but that it was performed in good order

J: Case   Whereas it hath been Some time Since **Job Case** hath made application to Come
Received   under our Care, and Still Continuing S⌃teady in his mind upon that account, we find freedom to accept of him and he to be under our Care for the time to Come

P.   And whereas **Peleg Slocum jur** not having done any thing to make Satisfaction
Slocum   this Meeting thinks proper to Set him aside, and **Isaac Smith** is Order'd to
Set aside   draw up a paper of denial against ~~me~~ him and bring it to the next monthly Meeting; There was a Certificate Signed at this Meeting for **Mary Potter** The matter Concerning **Jedediah Wood** is Refered to the next Monthly Meeting And whereas **Benjamin Rider** Son of **William Rider,** hath Signified his desire of Coming under our Care Therefore this Meeting Appoints **Adam Mott** and **Joseph Smith** to talk furder [*sic*] with him and make Enquiry into his Conversation and make Return to the next monthly Meeting

---

12 mo: At a monthly Meeting of friends held at our Meeting House in **Dartmouth**
1760   on the 19ᵗʰ day of the 12ᵗʰ month 1760, **Poniganset** Meeting Called **Joseph Tucker**

and **Abraham Tucker** present, for **Coakset John Mosher** & **Joseph Tripp** ~ ~
There was a paper of denial Read in this Meeting Against **Peleg Slocum** Son
of **Holder Slocum** deceased, which this Meeting Orders **Isaac Smith** to Read
publickly at the End of a first day Meeting between this and the next monthly
Meeting,

J. Potter **John Potter** Son of **Aaron Potter** hath made Application to ~~Come~~ this Meeting
& wife both he and his Wife to Come under Our Care which is Refer'd to the next monthly Meeting
Requests The matter Concerning **Jedidiah Wood** is Refered to the next monthly Meeting
to Come And this Meeting having Received the Committees account Concerning **Benjamin**
under **Rider** (which was very Satistisfactory) therefore this Meeting accepts and he
our Care to be under Our Care for time to Come
B. Rider Whereas friends and friendly people[27] dwelling near **Gideon Allen**s being at
Recei^d a great distance from any Settled Meeting of friends, they desire to have
have a Meeting Settled at **Gideon Allen**s for this winter Season, Therefore
this Meeting agrees that there be a Meeting Settled there for the three months
to Come, that is two days in a month the first first days in Each month and
the Sixth day following Our Preparative Meeting, which is the Second Sixth
day; The Friends Appointed to attend the Quarterly Meeting are **Joseph**
Tucker, **John Mosher**, **Abraham Tucker**, and **John Russell 3**^d, and **William**
Barker, and they to draw an Epistle to the Same, and Sign it in Behalf
of this Meeting
There was Collected at this Meeting £6:15ˢ old tenor, And this Meeting
Orders the Treasurer to pay 3 dollars to **Jonathan Hussey** for keeping the meeting
House

---

1 mo: At a monthly Meeting of Friends held at Our Meeting House in
1761 **Dartmouth** on the 19th day of the first month 1761, **Poniganset** meeting
Called **Caleb Russell** and **John Russell the 3**^d, present, for **Coakset** none present
Peleg Slocums paper of denial hath been Read as Ordered
The Matter Concerning **John Potter** and wife is Refer'd to the next Monthly
    Meeting
The Matter Concerning **Jedidiah Wood** is Refered to the next Monthly Meeting
The Friends appointed have attended the Quarterly Meeting and drawn
an Epistle to the Same as appointed
The Quarterly Meeting Epistle hath been Read in this Meeting and
well accepted
The Chusing of Visitors is Refered to the next monthly Meeting
There was a Certificate Signed at this Meeting for **Benjamin Rider**
to the monthly Meeting at **RhodeIsland**

27. The reference to "friendly people" is one of the few bits of evidence we have of people not in
membership attending Quaker worship.

Books   There was 23 Books brought into this Meeting, 14 of **William Dell**s works
Given   and nine of **John Rutlys**, which was Bestowed upon us by the yearly
to the   Meeting of **Pensylvania**, and we have also Received an Epistle from the
Meeting   Same which was Read to Good Satisfaction ~ ~ ~ ~ ~ ~

2ᵈ *mo:*   At at a monthly Meeting of Friends held at Our Meeting House
1761   in **Dartmouth** on the 15ᵗʰ day of the 2ᵈ month 1761, **Ponaganset** Meeting
    Called **Abraham Tucker** and **Peleg Smith** present, for **Coakset Peleg**
    Huddlestone & Philip Tripp ~
    Wesson [Weston] Briggs and **Phebe Russell** did lay their Intentions of taking
    each other in Marriage before this Meeting, and were desired to
    wait till the next monthly Meeting for their Answer and **Peleg Smith**
    and **Stephen Wilcox** are appointed to Enquire into the young mans Clearness
    and make Return to the next monthly Meeting
W: Wood   **William Wood**, Glaiser, hath Signified to this Meeting that he hath a
Requests   desire to be under Our Care, Therefore **Thomas Hathway [Hathaway]** and
to Come   **Bartholomew Taber** are appointed to talk with him and make Enquiry
under   Concerning his Conversation and make Return to the next monthly Meeting
our Care   **John Potter** Son of **Aaron,** and his Wife having in time past declared their
J: Potter   desire of Coming under Our Care, and due Enquiry hath been Made and
& wife   nothing Appearing to hinder, we find freedom to accept, and they to be under
Received   our Care for the time to Come
    Adam Mott, Abraham Tucker, Caleb Russell, and **William Barker,**
    are Chosen visitors for **Poniganset,** and **Thomas Hath[a]way** and **Bartholomew**
      Taber
    for **Quitionet**[28]
M. Kerby   Whereas **Mary Kerby [Kirby]** now **Wilbour [Wilbur]** Daughter of **Nathaniel**
disownd   **Kerby** deceased
    hath Married Out of Our Good order, and doth nothing to make Satisfaction
    altho friends have done their duty in advising her, Therefore this Meeting
    doth Conclude to Set her aside and doth deny her to be in unity with us
    Whereas Friends near the head of **Noquechuck River** have petitioned this
    Meeting that they may Build a Meeting House near thereabouts, Therefore
    this Meeting appoints **Joseph Tucker, Abraham Tucker, John Mosher,**
    Caleb Russell, Philip Tripp and **Paul Russell,** a Committee to go and
    See where it may be most Convenient, and Consider all Necessary Circum=
    =stances, and to allow or disallow as they may think proper in that affair
    and make Return to the next monthly Meeting
    Whereas it hath been advised by Epistle from the Quarterly Meeting

28. I.e., Acushnet.

that there be some meet persons or persons Appointed to take an account
of things Remarkable Occuring among Friends from time to time, as
[dying?] Sayings, or other things as may be for the promotion of Truth

3 mo: At a monthly Meeting of Friends held at Our Meeting
1761 House in **Dartmouth** on the 16ᵗʰ day of the 3ᵈ month 1761, **Ponaganset**
Meeting Called **Abraham Tucker** and **Peleg Smith** present, for **Coakset**
Peter Davil [Davol] and **Philip Tripp** – –
The Friends appointed to See into **Wesson** [Weston] **Briggs**s Clearness Signifie
they find nothing to hinder his proceeding in his Intended Marriage
Wossen [Weston] **Briggs** and **Ph[e]be Russell** Appeared at this meeting for their
Answer, and their Answer was that they might proceed to take each
other in Marriage in Some Convenient time between this and the next
monthly Meeting, Observing the good order Established amongst friends
and **Peleg Smith** and **Stephen Willcox** are appointed to See their
Marriage Solemnized in Sᵈ order, and make Return to the next monthly Meeting,
W: Wood This Meeting having Received a good Report of **William Wood** Glaiser
Received do Conclude to Receive him, and he to be under our Care for the time to Come
in Unity The Committee appointed to See about the Building a Meeting House
near the head of **Noquechuck River** have Signified that they think
John Cornells Ground upon the West Side of the highway against **Philip**
Howlandes is the most Suitable place to Build it, all Circomstances
Considered, And the Com.ᵗᵗ thinks it proper that the petitioners have
Liberty to Build one agreable to their Request, and think a House 28
feet wide and 30 feet Long and one Story high Should be the Dimentions
of Said House
And this Meeting appoints **Philip Tripp, Lemuel Sisson, John**
Davis ju.ʳ Daniel Wood and And **Abiel Macumber,** to take a Deed
of the Land that Said House is to be Set upon – –
And whereas the Limitted time is up Concerning the keeping a Meeting
at **Gideon Allens,** It is thought proper that it may be kept there
for two months longer as heretofore
The Treasurer is Ordered to pay to **Jonathan Hussey** for work and
Nails, and a gate for the Grave yard One pound fifteen Shilligs Old tenor;
Collected at this Meeting £3:15:5 Old tenor
The Friends appointed to attend the Quarterly Meeting are **Peleg**
Smith, Paul Russel, Peter Davil and **Philip Tripp,** and they to draw
an Epistle to the Same and Sign it in behalf of this Meeting
Thomas Hathway, Daniel Russells and **Philip Tripp** are appointed
to Get all the accounts of Friends Sufferings upon the account of
the militia, and Exhibit them to the adjournment in order to go to

the Quarterly Meeting – –

And this meeting is adjourned to the first Sixth day in the next monthly

This Meeting being met according to adjournment this 3.ᵈ day of
the 4ᵗʰ month 1761 the Representatives being present

The visitors of **Poniganset** and **Coakset** have Signified, that they
have make a pretty thorough visit throughout friends families under
their Care – –

And the Queries have been Read and Answer'd and the Representatives
are ordered to Carry them to the Quarterly Meeting

The accounts of friends Sufferings upon the account of the Military
affairs were br^ought to this Meeting, which was allowed, and order'd
to go to the Quarterly Meeting

Mary Akin wife of **William Akin,** hath Sent in a paper to this Meeting
which is Refer'd to the next monthly Meeting

The Treasurer hath paid £1=15ˢ Old tenor to **Jonathan Hussey** as order'd

---

4ᵗʰ mo: At a monthly Meeting of Friends held at our Meeting House
1761   in **Dartmouth** on the 20ᵗʰ day of the 4ᵗʰ month 1761 **Ponaganset** meeting
Called **William Barker,** and **Caleb Russell** present, for **Coakset Icabod
Eddy,** The Friends appointed to See **Wesson Briggs** and **Phebe Russell**s
Marriage Consumated Signify that it was done in good order

The Friends appointed to attend the Quarterly Meeting have done it Except
Paul Russell, and drawn an Epistle to the Same as Appointed

The Quarterly Meeting Epistle hath been Read in this Meeting and well accepted

Almy Russells paper Concerning her Sorrow for her outgoings hath been Read
as Ordered

287£   And the Quarterly Meeting hath Desired in their Epistle that this Meeting
Paid   Raise the Sum of 278£ **Rhode Island** old tenor to defray the Charge
Prov   of **Providence** Meeting House and yard which this Meeting agrees to
Meetg   and this Meeting appoints **David Smith** and **Jonathan Hussey** to get in
House   the Subscriptions, and **Joseph Mosher** and **Joseph Merihew** for **New=
=town** and **Philip Tripp** for **Coakset** upon the Same account and make
Return to the next monthly Meeting

and this Meeting hath accepted of **Mary Akin**s paper and She to
Remain under our Care

And whereas it is Ordered that each monthly Meeting be Supplyed
with a Book of Disipline Transcribed, Therefore this Meeting
appoints **Joseph Tucker Peleg** and **Humphry Smith** to procure
a Blank Book and agree with Some Suitable person to Transcribe
~~them~~ it

5th mo: At a monthly Meeting of Friends held at our Meeting
1761 House in **Dartmouth** on the 18th day of the 5th month 1761 **Poniganset**
Meeting Called **Peleg Smith** and **Abraham Tucker** present for
Coakset John Mosher -
Daniel Russell and **Mary Russell** and **Joseph Gifford** and **Hannah
Howland** and **Samuel Smith** and **Mary Anthony** Did all Lay their
Intentions of Marriage before this Meeting, and were Desired to
wait till the next monthly Meeting for their Answers and
Abraham Tucker and **Joseph Tucker** are apointed to see
into **Joseph Gifford**s Clearness, and **James Shearman** and **Isaac
Smith** are appointed upon the Same account with **Daniel Russell**
and **Peleg Smith** and **Barnabas Howland** for **Samuel Smith** and
all to make Return to the next monthly Meeting
we understand that a blank Book is procured according to the
order of Last monthly Meeting, and the Same Comittee are Still
Continued to agree with Some Suitable person to Transcribe the

P.Gifford Book of disipline
and wife Whereas **Peleg Gifford** and his wife hath Signified that they
Requests desire to Come under the Care of Friends, Therefore this
to Come meeting appoints **James Shearman** and **Paul Russell** to talk
under with him and make Enquiry Concerning his Conversation, and
our Care make Return to the next monthly Meeting

6th mo: At a monthly Meeting of Friends held ~~by~~
1761 on the 22 day of the 6th month 1761 **Poniganset** Meeting Called
Paul Russell and **Caleb Russell** present, for **Coakset William
Macumber** and **Peter Davil**
The Friends appointed to Enquire into the three Couples
Clearness, Signify they find nothing to hinder their intended
Marriages, And they all had their Answers that they might
Proceed to Marry in Some Convenient time between this
and the next monthly Meeting, Observing the good order
Established amongst Friends in the performance thereof,
And **James Shearman** and **Isaac Smith** are appointed to See **Daniel
Russell** & **Mary Russell**s Marriage Consumated in Said order, and
Joseph Tucker and **Abraham Tucker** and **Peleg Smith** & **Barnabas
Howland** are appointed to upon the Same account for the other
two couples, And all to make Return to the next monthly Meeting
And we understand that the Committee have Employed a friend to
Transcribe the Book of disipline

P. Gifford The Friends appointed to Enquire Concerning **Peleg Gifford** and his
and wife wife Signify that they find nothing but that we may accept, and this
Received Meeting doth accept them and they to be under our care for the time to Come

J.Gifford **Jonathan Gifford** Signifies that he desires to be under the Care of Friends
Requests and **Jonathan Hussey** and **David Smith** are appointed to talk with him
to Come And whereas **Job Anthony** and his family being Removed to **Rhode Island**
under to dwell and desires a Certificate, Therefore this Meeting appoints
our care **Humphry Smith** and **Daniel Russell** to make Enquiry and draw one if
they think proper and make Return to the next monthly Meeting, and
likewise they to make Enquiry Concerning **Frances Barker** and draw one
if they think proper for him – –

H Stanton Our Friend **Henry Stanton** from **N. Carolinia** was at this Meeting and
fomN.Car: his Labour in the Truth well accepted and his Certificate Read and well
accepted;[29] And whereas **Susannah Gifford** doth desire some assistance being
in difficulty Therefore this Meeting appoints **Nicholas Howland** and his wife
to take Care and assist her in what they think Necessary

**Peleg Smith, Joseph Tucker, Abraham Tucker, Thomas Hathway, Philip
Tripp** are appointed to attend the Quarterly Meeting, and draw an Epistle
to the Same and sign it in behalf of the monthly Meeting
And this Meeting is Adjourned to the youths Meeting – –
This Meeting being met according to adjournment the 3,^{d} dy of the 7th month 1761
This meeting hath Raised the money to defray the Charge of **Providence**
Meeting House all but £46=4^s=1^d **Rhode Island** old tenor and **Joseph Tucker**
is ordered to Cary it and pay it to the Quarterly Meeting – – – – –

[sideways, in pencil]
£287 0 0 46 4 1
paid. £240 15 11

7th mo: At a monthly Meeting held at **Dartmouth** the 20th day of the 7th
1761 month 1761 **Ponaganset** Meeting Called **Abraham Tucker** and **Joseph
Tucker** present, for **Coakset John Mosher** and **Peleg Huddlestone** present
The Friends appointed to see **Daniel Russells** and **Mary Russells**
Marriage and **Joseph Giffords** and **Hannah Howlands** Marriage, and
Samuel Smiths and **Mary Anthonys** Marriage Consumated, make
Report that the Said Marriages was accomplished in Good order;
The matter Concerning **Jonathan Gifford** is Refered the next monthly
Meeting, and **Jonathan Hussey** and **David Smith** Still Continued to
make furder Enquiry into his conversation and make Report
to the next monthly Meeting,
Joseph Tucker and **Peleg Smith** make Report that they attended
the Quarterly Meeting and drawn an Epistle to the Same and
Signed it in behalf of the monthly Meeting as appointed,

29. Henry Stanton (1719-1777), a native of Newport, Rhode Island, had moved to North Carolina with
his parents as a youth. See Hinshaw, *Encyclopedia*, I, 166; and William Henry Stanton, *A Book Called Our
Ancestors, the Stantons* (Philadelphia: William H. Stanton, 1922), 32-33.

This Meeting Received an Epistle from the Quarterly ^Meeting of **Rhod Island**
which was Read and the Contents Recommended to friends obser:
=vation; Whereas **Humphry Smith** and **Daniel Russell** was
appointed last monthly Meeting to Enquire into **Job Anthony**s
and his wives Life and Conversation, and they to draw a Certificate
for them to the monthly Meeting of **Rhode Island** and also to Enquire
into **Frances Barker** and his wives Life and Conversation and
draw a Certificate for them if they thought proper, which hath
been Neglected, therefore they are still continued to proceed as
above said, and make Report to the next monthly Meeting
The visitors have Informed this meeting that **Jonathan Smith ju.**r
hath been overtaken by Spirituous Liquors, therefore this
Meeting appoints **Daniel Russell** and **William Sanford** to Labour
with him and make Report to the next monthly Meeting
David Smith and **Jonathan Hussey** are appointed to make up
accompts with the Treasurer and make Report to the next
monthly Meeting
There was Collected at this Meeting £6=18s=3d old tenor, and the
Treasurer is ordered to pay three Dollars to **David Smith** for
keeping the Meeting House half a year

At a monthly Meeting of Friends held at our Meeting
8th mo: House in **Dartmouth** on the 17th of the 8th month 1761 **Ponaganset**
1761 Meeting Called **Peleg Smith** and **Abraham Tucker** present for
Coakset Peter Davel – –
The matter Concerning **Jonathan Gifford** is Refer,d to the next
monthly Meeting
Job Anthony, and **Frances Barkers** Certificates were brought to
this Meeting and the Signing of them is Refer,d to the next monthly Meeting
Christopher Gifford we understand hath fulfiled the yearly Meeting,
Judgment in the Case between hm and **William Woddel** – –
William Sanford and **Daniel Russell** not having talked with **Jonathan
Smith ju.**r are still Continued to do it and make Return to the
next monthly Meeting
The Friends appointed to make up accompts with the Treasurer
have done it and find that there Remains in the Stock £6=9s=8d old tenor
Whereas **Daniel Russell** Signifies to this Meeting that **Stephen Willcock**
hath Liv,d in one of his Houses for Some Considerable time, and
Willcocks Circomstaces is Such that he cannot well pay the Rent
Therefore Said **Russell** is desir,d to bring in his account Regular to
the next monthly Meeting

9ᵗʰ mo:　At a monthly Meeting of Friends held at our Meeting

1761　House on the 21 day of the 9ᵗʰ month 1761 **Poniganset** Meeting Called
Daniel Russell present, for **Coakset James Cornel** and **Philip Tripp**

J.Gifford　The Friends appointed to discourse with **Jonathan Gifford** son of

Receiv,d　**Benjamin Gifford** Concerning his Coming under the Care of friends
Signify, they have done it and find nothing to hinder therefore this
Meeting finds freedom to accept, and he to be under our care for
the time to Come

This Meeting hath Received a Certificate from the Monthly Meeting
at **Rhode Island** Concerning **Thomas Hicks** son of **Samuel Hicks** his
orderly Conversation whilst with them, Recommending him to
our Care which this Meeting doth accept

And this Meeting hath Received two Certificates from the monthly
Meeting at **Nantucket** one for **Benjamin Taber** and the other for
his wife which were Read and accepted by this Meeting

Frances Barker and **Job Anthony**s Certificates were read and
Approved in this Meeting, and Signed in and by order of this Meeting

This Meeting hath Received a Certificate from the monthly Meeting
at **Sandwich** Concerning **Abigail Shepherd** wife of **John Shepherd**
Recommending her to our care which is accepted

Whereas **Elnathan Eldridge** and **Lathan Wood** having Signified
their desire of coming under the Care of Friends, Therefore this
Meeting appoints **Humphry Smith** and **Peleg Huddlestone** to talk
with **Lathan Wood** to understand his Sincerity and make Report
to the next monthly Meeting, and **Jonathan Taber** and **John Russell**
the 3,ᵈ are appointed upon the Same account for **Elnathan
Eldridge**;

Joshua Davil hath Signified to this Meeting that he hath a desire
to come under our Care. Therefore **Joseph Tripp** & **Icabod Eddy**
are appointed to talk with Said **Joshua Davil**, and bring in their
account to the next monthly Meeting

The matter Concerning **Jonathan Smith** ju.ʳ is Continued till the next
monthly Meeting and **Daniel Russell** and **William Sanford** are Continued
to watch over and advise him as they may think proper – –

James Shearman and **Joseph Smith** are appointed Overseers of the
Poor among Friends of **Ponaganset** and to Give advice as they think
Proper, and for **Cushnet Jonahan Taber** and **Thomas Hathway,** and
for **Coakset Peleg Huddlestone** and **Philip Tripp** – –

E. Bowen　We understand that **Elihu Bowen** hath took a distaste Against Friends
Principles and is Joined to the Baptists, or is about to Join with them

[sideways, in pencil **Benjᵃ Taber House**]

Therefore **James Shearman** and **Paul Russell** are appointed to talk
with Said **Bowen,** if they think proper to know his Reasons for Leaving
Friends, and make Return to the next monthly Meeting – –
and this Meeting is Adjourn,d till the youths Meeting day
At a Monthly Meeting held by adjournment in **Dartmouth** on the 2,ᵈ
day of the 10ᵗʰ month 1761 **Ichabod Eddy, Humphry Smith** and ~~Cabe~~
Caleb Russell are appointed to attend the Quarterly Meeting, and
draw an Epistle to the Same, and Sign it in behalf of the monthly Meeting
The Queries have been Read and Answers Given by the Visitors
of **Coakset** and **Ponaganset,** and ordered to be Sent to the Quarterly Meeting
This Meeting orders **Daniel Russell** to pay the mony that this
Meeting was order,d to Send to the Quarterly Meeting upon account of
the Charge of Providence Meeting House, which sum is 45 pounds
with Interest till paid

Business The overseers of the poor among Friends are to Inform themselves
of the into the Circumstances of things among them and make Return how
overseers they find things to each monthly Meeting for the time to Come
of the Whereas **Daniel Russell** hath brought an account to the monthly
poor Meeting that **Stephen Willcock** is Considerably in debt to him for
Houserent, Therefore this Meeting appoints **Peleg Huddlestone**
William Barker and **John Potter** to Enquire into the matter, and
See that things are done Regular and See whether Said **Willcock**
Cannot do Something himself, and to Consider Whether it may be
proper that wood may be Sold off of the Meeting House Lot
to pay that Debt, and make Return to the next monthly Meeting

---

10 mo: At a monthly Meeting held in **Dartmouth** on the 19ᵗʰ day
1761 of the 10ᵗʰ month 1761 **Ponaganset** Meeting Called **Daniel Russell** – –
and **Joseph Smith** present, for **Coakset Israel Wood** present – –
L.Wood The Friends appointed to Enquire into **Lathan Wood**s Life and Conver=
Received =sation make a Satisfactory Report, Therefore this Meeting Concludes to accept
of him to be under our Care for the time to come
The Matter Concerning **Elnathan Eldredge** is Refered to the next monthly
Meeting, and the Friends are Contnued to take Care to talk with him
and make Report to the next monthly Meeting
Lathan Wood and **Sarah Tucker** did Lay their Intentions of Marriage
Before this Meeting and was desir,d to wait till the next Monthly
Meeting for their Answer, and **Humphry Smith** and **Peleg Huddlestone**
are appointed to Enquire into the young mans Clearness, and make
Report to the next monthly Meeting
The matter Concerning **Joshua Davil** is Refer,d to the next Monthly Meeting

The Matter Concerning **Jonathan Smith ju.**ʳ is Refered to the next Monthly Meeting
and the Friends appointed to talk with Said **Smith** are still Continued on
the Same account – –

E - Bowen The matter Concerning **Elihu Bowen** is Refer,d to the next Monthly Meeting
The Friends appointed to attend the Quarterly Meeting Signified they
have done it and drew an Epistle and Signed it in behalf of the Meeting
as Appointed
We Received an Epistle from the Quarterly Meeting which was Read
and well accepted

Money **Humphry Smith** has paid the mony for the Charge of Repairing **Providence**
Paid Meeting House and yard, and brought a Receipt for the same, and
Providence Likewise Said **Smith** has paid 2 ½ Dollars for to be put in the yearly Meeting Stock
Mg The Friends appointed to talk with **Stephen Willcox** and to see if he
House Can not pay **Daniel Russell** his demand; and also to see of it is proper
to sell wood off the meeting House Lot, Signified they had done nothing
therefore the matter is Refer,d to the next monthly Meeting, and they
Continued upon the Same account
And this Meeting appoints **Job Russell** to draw two Certificates
one for **Peace Wood** and **Elisabeth Gidley** and bring them
to the adjournment – –
Whereas **David Merihew** desires a few lines by way of Certificate
therefore this Meeting appoints **Joseph Smith** and **Barnabas Mosher**
to Enquire into his Life and Conversation, and draw a Certificate
for him if they think proper and bring it to the next monthly Meeting,
The Meeting Appoints. **Peleg Smith** and **Humphry Smith** to draw
a paper of Denial agaist **Lusannah Russell** for her outgoings and
bring it to the next monthly Meeting – –
The Meeting appoints **William Sanford John Potter William Barker**
and **Jonathan Hussey,** Overseers to take notice that the people in
the Galleries behave orderly, or other where at our fall Meeting,
And this Meeting appoints **Joseph Tripp** and **Philip Tripp** and **William
Gifford** to oversee they yearly Meeting at **Coakset** that the people
behave orderly
And this Meeting is adjourn,d to the 2ʲᵈ day after our yearly Meeting
at the 12ᵗʰ hour of the day
At a Monthly Meeting of Friends held by adjournment in **Dartmouth**
on the 26ᵗʰ day of the 10ᵗʰ month 1761 The Representatives being present
Our Esteemed Friends **Robert Willis** from **Woodbridge** in **New Jersey**
and **Lot Tripp** from the **Oblong** were at this Meeting, and their
visits well accepted, and their Certificates read to Good Satisfaction

There was two Certificates Signed at this Meeting, one for **Peace
Wood,** and another for **Elizabeth Gidley** directed to the Quarterly
Meeting next to be held at the **Long Plane**[30]
Our worthy Friends **Susanna Hatton** from **Waterford** in **Ireland**
and **Susanna Brown** from **Pensylvania** were at this Meeting
and their Labour and Service in the Truth well accepted, and
Their Certificate have been Read in this Meeting to Good Satisfaction[31]
This Meeting hath Received a Certificate from Friends of the **Oblong**
Concerning **Deborah Wilboour** of her Good Conversation whilst
among them in her late visit which was to our Satisfaction

---

11 mo=   At a monthly Meeting of Friends held at our Meeting
1761   House in **Dartmouth** on the 16th day of the 11th month 1761 **Ponaganset**
Meeting Called **Abraham Tucker** and **Peleg Smith** present, for
Coakset Ichabod Eddy – –

E. El=   The Friends appointed to talk with **Elnathan Eldridge** Signify
=dridge   that he hath Given them Good Satisfaction, And this Meeting finds
Received   freedom to accept of him and he to be under our Care for the time to Come
The Matter Concerning **Elihu Bowen** is Refer,d to the next Monthly Meeting
The Friends appointed to Enquire and talk with ~~Jonathan Smith~~ ju,r

J.Davil   **Joshua Davil** have Given in a Good Report Concerning him,
Received   therefore this Meeting accepts, and he to be under our care;
The matter Concerning **Stephen Willcox** is Refer,d to the next Monthly Meeting
The Friends appointed to Enquire into **Luthan Wood**s Clearness, Signify
they find nothing to hinder his Intended Marriage
Luthan Wood and **Sarah Tucker** come to this Meeting for their Answer
and their Answer was, that they might proceed to take Each other in
Marriage in Some Convenient time between this and the next monthly
Meeting, Observing our Good order in the performance thereof, and **Joseph
Smith** and **Daniel Russell** are appointed to See their Marriage Consumated,
and make Return to the next monthly Meeting
Whereas we have heard Something of **John Merihew**s misconduct at the
Oblong, this Meeting thinks it proper to Send a letter to Friends there -
to acquaint them in what Circumstance he was under here in
Relation to Truth, which this Meeting orders to be sent there.
There was a Certificate Signed at this Meeting for **David Merihew**
This Meeting is adjourned till next fourth day come week

30. The Long Plain Meeting House in Acushnet was built in 1759.
31. Susanna (Hudson) Hatton Lightfoot (1720-1781) traveled widely as a minister. See Larson, *Daughters of Light*, 327; and *Collection of Memorials*, 400-09. Several women named Susanna Brown were members of Philadelphia Yearly Meeting.

At a monthly Meeting held by adjournment on the 25th day of the 11th
month 1761 the Representatives being present;
There was a paper of deniel Signed at this Meeting against
Lusannah Russell, and **Isaac Smith** is ordered to Read it on a first
day at proper Season
Whereas we understand that the widow **Rebecah Slocum** doth
Refuse to Give her Consent that her Daughter **Rebecah** should Marry
with **Humphry Smith ju,r.** Therefore **Joseph Tucker** and **Daniel Russell**
are appointed to talk with her to know her Reasons, and also with
with the young man as they think proper, and make Report to our
next monthly Meeting

J.Akin We understand that **John Akin** son of **James Akin** hath a desire
Requests to Come under the care of Friends, Therefore this Meeting
to come appoints **Nathaniel Bowdish Henry Hedly** and **William**
under **Barker** to talk with him and make Enquiry Concernig his Conversation
our Care and Bring in their account to the next Monthly Meeting
It was also Signified to this Meeting that **Henry Russell** and **Mary**
Brayton hath a desire to Lay their intentions of Marriage
before the monthly Meeting which this Meeting allows if nothing
appears to hinder

12th month At a monthly Meeting held at our meeting House in
1761 **Dartmouth** on the 21st day of the 12th month 1761, **Poniganset**
Meeting Called **Abraham Tucker** and **William Barker** present
for **Coakset Joseph Tripp** and **John Mosher** Present
Nicholas Davis and **Sarah Williams** did appear for their answer
and their answer was that they might Proceed to take each other
in Marriage in Some Convenient time between this and the next
monthly Meeting observing the Good order Established among us
in the performance thereof, and **Caleb Russell** and **Thomas Hathway**
are appointed to See their Marriage Consumated and make Report
to the next monthly Meeting
The matter Concerning **Elihu Bowen** is Refered to the next monthly
Meeting, The matter Concerning **Stephen Willcox** is Refer,d to
the next monthly Meeting and **James Shearman Joseph Tucker**
and **Abraham Tucker** are appointed to talk with him and make
Report to the next monthly Meeting
The Friends appointed to See into **Luthan Wood** and **Sarah Tucker**s
Marriage make Report that it was accomplished in Good order
The Friends appointed to talk with **John Akin** Concerning his Desire
desire of coming under the Care of friends make Report that he

Gave them Satisfaction, therefore the mattere is Refer,d to the
next monthly Meeting – –

This Meeting appoints **Abraham Tucker Isaac Smith David
Smith** and **Joseph Tucker** to Peruse the monthly Meeting minutes
to see what part of them they think Proper to be put on Record
The Friends appointed to attend the Quarterly Meeting are
Caleb Russell John Mosher Jonathan Hussey and **Ichabod Eddy**
and they to draw an Epistle to the Same and Sign it in behalf
of this Meeting, There was Collected at this Meeting 7ᶫ:6ˢ:7ᵈ old
tenor, and the Treasurer is ordered to pay **David Smith** three Dollars
for keeping the Meeting House – – – – –

1ˢᵗ mo At a monthly Meeting held at our Meeting House in
1762 **Dartmouth** the 18ᵗʰ of the first month 1762, **Ponaganset** Called **Joseph
Tucker** and **Abraham Tucker** present, for **Coakset Peleg Huddlestone**
and **Christopher Gifford** present

Elnathan Eldridge and Ann Allen did appear to Lay their
Intentions of Marriage and were desired to wait till the next monthly
Meeting for their answer, and **Caleb Russell** and **Thomas Hathway**
are appointed to make Enquiry into his Clearness of Marriage, and
make Report to the next monthly Meeting

The friends appointed to see **Nicholas Davis** and **Sarah Williams**'s
Marriage Consumated, make Report that it was accomplished in Good order

whereas **Elihu Bowen** hath Gone out from among us and joyned
himself to Baptists, and a Great d̶ much Labour hath been bestowed
on him and there appearing no hopes of his Return, therefore this
Meeting doth Conclude to set him aside, and do Disown him to be
one in unity with us

Lusanna Russells paper of Denial hath been Read as order,d

This Meeting Received a Certificate from **Nantucket** Concerning
our friend **Silvanus Allen** Recomending him to be one in
unity while among them which this Meeting accepts

The matter Concerning **Stephen Willcox** is Refer,d to next monthly Meeting
and **Joseph Tucker Abraham Tucker** and **James Shearman** are Still
Continued to talk with him and Enquire into his Circumstances
Relating to his debts and Procure as Just account as they can and
make Report to the next Monthly Meeting

This Meeting doth Conclude to accept of **John Akin** to be one under
our Care and in unity with us – –

whereas **Susanna Davil** hath Requested to Come under the Care of
friends and the friends appointed to treat with her make Report

that She Gave them Good Satisfaction, therefore this Meeting
doth Conclude to accept of her to be one in unity with us and
under our Care;

We understand **Elizabeth Russell** Daughter of **Joseph Tripp**
hath Gone Contrary to Good order in Marrying the worlds way
and She hath been timely Laboured with, but She Continuing Obsti=
=nate, this Meeting doth Conclude to deny her the Sd **Elizabeth**, and
do set her aside as one not in unity with use – –

The friend, appointed to peruse the Minutes to see what
part they should think proper to put on Record make
Report that they have done it as appointed;

The Friend, appointed to attend the Quarterly Meeting, and
draw an Epistle, Signify that they have done it as appointed
we Received an Epistle from the Quarterly Meeting of **Rhod Island**
which was Read and well accepted.

This Meeting appoints **Daniel Russell** overseer of the Burying
yard in.stead of his father **John Russell**

The Treasurer hath paid **David Smith** 3 Dollars for half a years
keeping the Meeting House

This Meeting appoints **Peter Davil** and **Philip Tripp** Visitors
for **Coakset** for the year Ensuing

This Meeting appoints **Adam Mott Abraham Tucker Caleb
Russell** and **William Barker** Visitors for the year Ensuing

This Meeting appoints **William Sanford** and **Henry Hedly** to
Enquire into **David Barker**s clearness as to Conversation and
Marriage and to draw a Certificate for him to the Monthly
Meeting of **Swanzey** if they think proper and bring it to the
next monthly Meeting

This Meeting appoints **Thomas Hathway** and **Bartholomew
Taber** Visitors for the year Ensuing; – – – – –

---

2 mo: 1762   At a monthly Meeting held at **Dartmouth** the 15ᵗʰ of
the 2 month 1762, **Ponaganset** Meeting Called **Peleg Smith**
and **Abraham Tucker** present, for **Coakset William Macumber**
and **Israel Wood** present,

Elnathan Eldridge and **Ann Allen** did appear for their answer
and their answer was that they might proceed to take each
other in Marriage in Some Convenient time between this and the
next monthly Meeting Observing the Good order Established
amongst us in the performance thereof, and **Caleb Russell** and
John Russell the 3,ᵈ are appointed to see their Marriage Consumated

in Said order and make Report to the next monthly Meeting
Humphry Smith ju.ʳ and **Rebekah Slocum ju.**ʳ and **John Akin**
and **Peace Russell** and **Ignatius Dillingham** and **Deborah
Gifford** did all apear ^and Laid their Intentions of Marriage
and were desired to wait for ther answers till the next
monthly Meeting and **William Anthony** and **Benjamin
Howland the 2**ᵈ are appointed to see ~~their M~~ into **Humphry Smith j.**ʳ
Clearness as to Marriage and Conversation and make Report to
the next monthly Meeting, and **Henry Hedly** and **William Barker**
are appointed to see into **John Akin**s Clearness as to Marriage and
Conversation and make Report to the next monthly Meeting – –
The Friends appointed to make Enquiry into **Stephen Willcox**'s
affairs make Report that he Cant pay **Daniel Russell** his demand
for House Rent, Therefore this Meeting doth Conclude to pay it
for him this present year out. and **Daniel Russell** is desired to
bring his account to the next monthly Meeting;
There was a Certificate Signed for **David Barker** to ^the monthly
Meeting of **Swanzey** Certifying his Clearness as to Marriage & Conversation
Whereas we understand that Going to Horse Raceing is a prevail=
=ing Practice, therefore this Meeting doth Conclude to make a
minute against all Such Practices; And if any Friends are
found Guilty of any Such practice they are liable to be dealt with
as offenders
David Smith is appointed to take Charge of the Books
belonging to this Meeting, and to take them home with him
and distribute them out as he shall think proper – –
And this Meeting is adjourned to next Second day at the
House of **John Russell the 2,**ᵈ at **Meshoam** at ^Eleven ~~ten~~ o clock in the morning
At a monthly Meeting held by adjournment at the
House of **John Russells the 2,**ᵈ at **Meshoam** in **Dartmouth**
the 22'ᵈ day of the 2,ᵈ month 1762, the Representatives for **Pona=
=ganset** were **Abraham Tucker** and **Peleg Smith** present
for **Coakset** none present – –
Henry Russell and **Mary Brayton** did Lay their
Intentions of taking each other in Marriage, and were
Desired to wait till the next monthly Meeting for their
answer; And **Peleg Smith** and **Humphry Smith** are
appointed to make Enquiry into the young mans Clearness
as to Marriage and Conversation and make Report thereof
to the next monthly Meeting.

3ᵈ mo: At a monthly Meeting held in Dartmouth

1762 the 15ᵗʰ of the 3ᵈ month 1762, **Ponaganset** Called **William Barker** and **Nathaniel Bowdish** present; for **Coakset Christopher Gifford** and **Peleg Huddlestones** present; The Friend, appointed to Enquire into **Humphrey Smith ju.ʳˢ** Clearness as to Marriage and Conversation make Report that they don't find anything to hi^nder his Proceeding in Marrige and also the friend, appointed to make Enquiry into **John Akins** Clearness make Report that they don't find anything to hender his Proceeding in Marriage This Meeting Received a Certificate from the Monthly Meeting of **Sandwich,** Concerning **Ignatuis Dillingham,** Certifying his Clearness as to Marriage and Conversation and also that he has his parents Consent in taking in Marriage **Deborah Gifford;** – –

Humphry Smith j,ʳ and **Rebeckah Slocum j,ʳ,** and **John Akin** and **Peace Russell** And **Ignatuis Dillingham** and **Deborah Gifford** did appear for their answers ~~was that they~~ and their answer was that they might Proceed to take each other in Marriage in Some Convenient time between this and the next monthly Meeting, observing the Good order Established amongst us in the performance thereof; The friend, appointed to make Enquiry into **Henry Russells** Clearness make Report that they find nothing to hender his Proceeding in Marriage;

Henry Russell and Mary Brayton did appear for th^eir answer and their answer was that they might Proceed to take each other in Marriage in Some Convenient time between this and the next monthly Meeteing observing the Good order Established amongst us in the performance thereof and **Peleg Smith** and **Humphry Smith** are appointed to see their Marriage Consumated and make Report to the next monthly Meeting; and **William Anthony** and **Benjaⁿ Howland 2,ᵈ** are appointed to see **Humphry Smiths** and **Rebeckah Slocums** Marriage Consumated and make Report to the next monthly meeting; And **Henry Hedley** and **William Barker** are appointed to see **John Akin** and **Peace Russells** Marriage Consumated and make Report to the next monthly Meeting, And **Joseph Tucker** and **Joseph Smith** are appointed to ^see **Ignatius Dillingham** and **Deborah Giffords** Marriage Consumated and make Report to the next monthly Meeting, **George Sanford** and **Rachel Gifford** did Lay their Intentions of Marriage and were desired to wait till the next monthly Meeting for their answer

and **William Barker** and **David Smith** are appointed to make
Enquiry into **George Sanford**s Clearness as to Marriage and
Conversation and make report to the next Monthly Meeting;
the friend, appointed to see **Elnathan Eldridge** and **Ann Allen**s
Marriage Consumated make Report that it was Consumated
in Good order; **Caleb Russell** is appointed to desire Doctor
Tobey to Send his accompt to the next Monthly Meeting
of Doctering of **Samuel Craw;** – –
whereas **Samuel Howland** desires a Certificate to the
Oblong therefore this Meeting appoints **Joseph Gifford** and
Nathaniel Howland to make Enquiry into his Conversation
and affairs and draw one if they think proper and bring it to
the next monthly Meeting
whereas **Increas Allen** ^j,r hath Married out of the Good order
of Friend, and having been timely Laboured with by the Visitors
and neglecting to make Satisfaction therefore this Meeting
doth appoint **Christopher Gifford** and **Benjamin Tripp** to
treat furder with him and make Report to the next Monthly Meeting
There was Collected at this Meeting £3=15ˢ=8ᵈ old tenor.
This Meeting is adjourned to the 2,ᵈ day of next month
This Meeting being met according to adjournment this 2,ᵈ day
of the 4ᵗʰ month 1762 **Ponaganset** Called **William Barker** present
for **Coakset**] none present by appointment
The Queries have been re^ᵃd and answered and the answers are to
be sent up to the Quarterly Meeting by the Representatives
The Friends appointed to attend the Quarterly Meeting are
Joseph Tucker Humphry Smith and **Caleb Russell** and they
to draw an Epistle to the Same and Sign it in behalf of this Meeting
Henry Hedley signified to this meeting that he is about to remove
with his family to live at **Rhode Island** and desires a Certificate
for himself and family therefore this Meeting appoints **Abraham
Tucker** and **Joseph Tucker** to make Enquiry into his affairs and
~~Desires~~ Draw one for himself and famaly if they think
proper and bring it to the next monthly Meeting
We understand that **Jonathan Smith j.**ʳ still continues
to take too much Spirituous Liquor, Therefore this
Meeting appoints **William Sanford** and **William Barker**
to discourse with him and make Report to the next
monthly Meeting – –

4ᵗʰ mo:　At a monthly Meeting held in **Dartmouth** the 19

　1762　of the 4ᵗʰ month 1762, **Ponaganset** Called **Joseph Smith** and
　　　　William Barker present, for **Coakset Joseph Tripp** and
　　　　Peter Devil present;
　　　　George Sanford and **Rachel Gifford** appeared for their
　　　　Answer, and their Answer was, that they might proceed
　　　　to take each other in Marriage in Some Convenient time
　　　　between this and the next monthly Meeting, observing
　　　　the Good order Establish,d among us in the performance
　　　　thereof, and **Joseph Smith** and **William Mosher** are Appointed
　　　　to see their Marriage Consumated in Said order and make
　　　　Report to the next Monthly Meeting;
　　　　The friend, Appointed to see **Humphry Smith j,ʳ** and **Rebeckah**
　　　　Slocums Marriage Consumated make Report that is was
　　　　accomplished in Good order, and also the Friend, Appointed
　　　　to see **John Akin** and **Peace Russell**s and **Ignatius Dillingham**
　　　　and **Deborah Gifford**s **Henry Russell** and **Mary Brayton**s
　　　　Marriages Consumated make Report that the Said Marriages
　　　　was accomplished in Good order;
　　　　Caleb Russell is appointed to desire **Doctor Tobey** to send his
　　　　accompt to the next Monthly Meeting for Doctering **Samˡˡ Craw**
　　　　Whereas the Friend, appointed to make Enquiry into **Samˡˡ**
　　　　Howlands Conversation make Report that they think it not
　　　　proper to Grant him a Certificate untill Some Reports be
　　　　Cleared up; Therefore this Meeting doth appoint **Joseph Tucker**
　　　　and **Joseph Gifford** and **Abraham Tucker** to make Enquiry into
　　　　his Conversation and Affairs and draw a Certificate for him if
　　　　they think proper and bring it to the next monthly Meeting
　　　　This Meeting Concludes to accept of **Phebe Hussey**s paper of Condemna=
　　　　=tion for Satisfaction She to Read it or Get Some Friends to read it
　　　　on a first day of the week after Worship, and She to be present
　　　　between this and the next monthly Meeting
　　　　The matter Concerning **Increas Allen j,ʳ** is Refer,d to the next Monthly
　　　　Meeting; The Friends appointed to attend the Quarterly Meeting
　　　　make Report that they have attended the above s,d Meeting
　　　　and drawn an Epistle as appointed; This Meeting Received an ^Epistle
　　　　from our Quarterly Meeting which was read and well accepted
　　　　The Friends appointed to make Enquiry into **Henry Hedley**s
　　　　Conversation and Affairs, and to draw a Certificate for him
　　　　and his Family makes Report that they have ^not done it, Therefore

they are still Continued to do as appointed and make Report
to the next monthly Meeting;

The matter concerning **Jonathan Smith junor** if Refer,d to the
next monthly Meeting

The matter Concerning **Samuel Howland**s Desire for Certificate
is Refer,d to the next monthly Meeting

We understand that **Daniel Cornel** hath gone Contrary to Good
order in Marriage, and he hath been dealt with by the Visitors
and neglects to make Satisfaction; therefore this Meeting
appoints **John Mosher** and **Joseph Tripp** to discourse further
with him and make Report to the next monthly Meeting

Daniel Russell doth acquit the monthly Meeting from any
further Rent for **Stephen Wilcox** living in his House

We Received a few lines of Recommendation from the Monthly
Meeting of women held at **Portsmouth** Concerning **Kaziah
Allen** wife of **Othniel Allen,** Concerning her being under their
Care when She Came here to live which this Meeting accepts;

Whereas **Tily Wilcox** hath trangressed the Good orders of
Friends in Marriage, and also in having a child soon after
Marriage, and the visitors hath Laboured with him, and he
doth not incline to make any Satisfaction, this Meeting doth
appoint **Daniel Russell** and **Nicholas Howland** to discourse furder
with him and make RepᵽReport to the next Monthly Meeting; – –

5 mo: At a Monthly Meeting held in **Dartmouth** the 18th of the
1762 5th month 1762; **Ponaganset** Meeting Called **Humphry Smith** &
Joseph Smith present, for **Coakset Philip Tripp** and **Israel Wood** present

The Friends appointed to See **George Sanford** and **Rachel Gifford**s Marriage
Consumated make Report that it was accomplished in Good Order,

Caleb Russell hath desired **Doctor Tobey** to send his accompt as app=
=ointed and accordingly he hath sent it, which this Meeting accepts
which is Eighteen Shillings Lawfull Money, for Doctering **Samuel Craw**
in his Last Illness;

The matter Concerning **Samuel Howland** is Refer,d ^to the next Monthly Meeting

Phebe Husseys Paper of Condemnation hath been Read as Ordered

The matter Concerning **Increas Allen** is Refer,d to the next Monthly Meeting

This Meeting hath Given **Henry Hedly** and his family a Certificate
to the Monthly Meeting of **RhodIsland;**

The matter Concerning **Jonathan Smith j,**ʳ is Refer,d to the next monthly
Meeting; and this Meeting appoints **Job Russell** to Enform Said

Smith that this Meeting desires him to draw a paper of Condem=
=nation and bring it to the next monthly meeting, and the
Paper must be Read Publickly at the Close of a first day Meeting;
Whereas **Nathaniel Howland** desires a Certificate for himself
and Family, therefore this Meeting doth appoint **Joseph Smith**
and **Barnabas Mosher** to make Enquiry into his Conversation
and affairs, and draw a Certificate for him and his Family if they
think proper, and bring it to the Monthly Meeting;
The Matter Concerning **Daniel Cornel** is Refer,d to the next
Monthly Meeting, and **John Mosher** and **Joseph Tripp** are still
Continued to treat with him if they have an oppertunity and
make Report to the next monthly Meeting;
The matter Concerning **Tiley Willcox** is Refered to the next
Monthly Meeting, and **Daniel Russell** & **Nicholas Howland** are
still Continued to discours with him if they have an oppertu=
nity and make Report to the Monthly Meeting;
This Meeting appoints **Isaac Smith** to draw up a Paper of denial
against **Deborah Willcox,** and bring it to the next Monthly Meeting

6 mo: At a monthly Meeting of Friends held in **Dartmouth** on
1762 the 21 of the 6 month 1762, **Ponaganset** Called **James Shearman**
and **Peleg Smith** present, for **Coak[set] Othniel Tripp** and **Philip
Tripp** present; The matter Concerning **Samuel Howland** is
Refered to the next Monthly Meeting;
Whereas **Increas Allen junor** hath Married out of the order
Established among us, and also in marrying his first Cousen, and
he hath been timely Laboured with, and he not Regarding the
Care of Friends, therefore this Meeting doth appoint **Isaac Smith**
to draw a paper of Denial against him and bring it to the
next monthly Meeting;
Whereas **Jonathan Smith juner** hath for some Considerable time
been in the practice of takeing too much Spiritous Liquor, and
he hath been admonished from time to time, and there appear
=ing no hopes of his amendment, therefore this Meeting, for the
Clearing of our Testimony doth appoint **Joseph Tucker** and
Abraham Tucker to draw up a paper of Denial against him
and bring it to the next monthly Meeting;
The matter Concerning **Daniel Cornel** is Refered to the next
monthly Meeting, and **John Mosher** and **Joseph Tripp** are Still
Continued to discourse with him if they have an oppertunity

and make Report to the next Monthly Meeting;
Whereas **Tiley Willcox** and his wife hath trasgressed and
gone contrary to the order established amongst us in Marry=
=ing out from among us, and they have been sufficiently Laboured
with, and there appearing no signs of sorrow for their outgo=
=ings, therefore this Meeting doth appoint **Isaac Smith** to
draw up a paper of denial against them and bring it to
the next monthly Meeting; **Peleg Smith** and **Humphry Smith**
are appointed to draw an Epistle to the Quarterly Meeting
next to be held at **Rhode = Island** and bring it to the Adjourn=
=ment, and this Meeting is adjourned to the first sixth day
in next month;
This Meeting being mett according to to adjornment the 2,ᵈ
day of the 7ᵗʰ month 1762; The Representatives are Called, for
Ponaganset Peleg Smith present, **Coakset Phiplip Tripp** present.
The Visitors of **Coakset** have made Answers to the Queries;
The Friends appointed to attend the Quarterly Meetings are
Peleg Smith, Philip Tripp & **Ichabod Eddy,**
This Meeting hath sent an Epistle to the Quarterly Meeting
signed in this Meeting

7ᵗʰ *mo*   At a monthly Meeting held at our Meeting House in
1762   **Dartmouth** the 19ᵗʰ day of the 7ᵗʰ month 1762; **Ponaganset** ~~Cl~~
called **Paul Russell** and **William Barker** present, for **Coakset**
John Mosher and **Philip Tripp** present,
whereas **Samuel Howland** hath transgressed and Gone Contrary
to Good order in a Scandalous manner in uttering Several
unbecoming Speeches, and he hath been Laboured with, and he
Denied the fact proved against him, and neglected to make
Satisfaction; Therefore this Meeting (for the Clearing of ^ᵒᵘʳ Testimony)
doth appoint **Isaac Smith** to draw a Paper of denial against
him and bring it to the next monthly Meeting;

Increase   There hath been a Paper of Denial read and Signed against
Allen   **Increase Allen j,ʳ** for Marrying his first Cousens and also in Marry=
Disowned   =ing out of the order established amongst us;
This Meeting hath drawn up a Paper of denial against **Jonathan**
Smith j,ʳ for his outgoings, **Job Russell** is appointed to read it at
the end of a first day Meeting for worship,
The matter Concerning **Daniel Cornel** is Refer,d to the next monthly
Meeting, and **John Mosher** and **Joseph Tripp** are still Continued

to discourse with him and make Report to the next Monthly Meeting

T.Wilcox This meeting hath Read and Signed a Paper of Denial against

Disown,d **Tiley Willcox** and wife for their outgoings, and **William Anthony**

and his is appointed to Read it at the End of a first day Meeting of worship,

wife The Friends appointed to attend the Quarterly Meeting Signify

that they have attended it as appointed;

The Treasurer has paid **Doctor Tobey** for doctering **Sam,ll Craw**

in his Last Illness, which is Three dollars;

Whereas **Isaac Howland j,r** hath married out of the order of

Friend., and never hath been Dealt with, by the monthly

Meeting, therefore this Meeting doth appoint **Peleg Smith** and

Humphry Smith to treat with him, and make Report to the

next monthly Meeting;

This Meeting Received an Epistle from the Quarterly Meeting of

Rhode Island, which was Read in this Meeting and well accepted;

This Meeting Likewise Received two Epistles from London, one Printed

and the other written; We also Received two more ^written Epistles, one from

the yearly Meeting of **Philadelphia,** and the other from the yearly

Meeting of **Flushing** and **Long Island;** and Likwise one Epistle from

the yearly Meeting of **Rhode - Island,** which was all Read in this

Meeting to Good Satisfaction;[32]

Whereas **Peleg Smith j,r** hath Married out of the order Establish

=ed among us, and also Married without his Parents Consent

and the Visitors hath dealt with him and he neglects to mak

Satisfaction, therefore this Meeting appoints **Joseph Tucker**

and **Isaac Howland** to discourse with him and make Report

to the next monthly Meeting;

Jacob Whereas **Jacob Chase** hath married out of the order of Friend;

Chase and he hath been timely dealt with by the Visitors, and hes

not Regarding the Care of Friends. Therefore this Meeting doth

appoint **Paul Russell** and **Joseph Smith** to discourse with him

and make Report to the next Monthly Meeting;

There was Collected at this Meeting £ 3-15s-9d old tenor, the

Treasurer is ordered to pay **Jonathan Hussey** thirty Shillings

for Shoeing a traveling Friends Horse – –

8th mo: At a monthly Meeting held in **Dartmouth** on the 16th

1762 of the 8th month 1762, **Ponagamset** Called **Joseph Tucker** present

for **Coakset Peter Devil** and **Israel Wood** present;

32. New York Yearly Meeting was often referred to as the yearly meeting held at Flushing.

Sam,ˡˡ **Samuel Howland** paper of denial hath been Signed in this
Howland Meeting; and **Isaac Smith** is appointed to Read it at the end of a
disowned first day Meeting for worship, and make Report to the next
monthly Meeting;

Whereas **Jonathan Smith j,ᵘʳ** hath had his Education among
friends Nevertheless through unwatchfullness by not keeping
to that unerring Guide the Spirit of truth hath fallen into that
Scandalous Practice of taking too much Spirtuous Liquor to
the Grief and trouble of friends, and although much Labour
hath been taken with him in order to bring him off from so
evil a practice, yet all seems to be of little or no Effect,
therefore for the Clearing of truth we think we can do no less than
Give this forth as a Publick Testimony against him the the said
Jonathan Smith Denying him to be one in unity with use the
People Called Quakers, Yet sincerely Desiring that if it
be the will of God that he may Come to a sight & Sense of his
outgoing, and through unfeigned Repentence find Mercy;
Given forth at our Monthly Meeting held in **Dartmouth** the 19ᵗʰ
day of the 7ᵗʰ month 1762,

Whereas **Tyley Wilcock** son of **Stephen Wilcock** & **Mary** his
wife of and **Deborah** the wife of the s.ᵈ **Wilcock** & Daughter of **Benj,ᵃ Russell**
all of **Dartmouth** in the County of **Bristol** in the Province of the
Massachusetts Bay in **New England,** the s,ᵈ **Wilcock** and wife being
both under the Care of Friends (the People Called Quakers) yet for
want of keeping to the Spirit of Truth in themselves have Given
way to a lo^ose & vain Conversation as Plainly appears by her
having a child so soon after Marriage, they being married
out of the Good order Established amongst us, and they having been
duly dealt with in order to bring them to a sight of their outgoings
but nothing appearing to friends Satisfaction of their Repentence
Therefore for the Clearing of the Blessed Truth of such Scandulous
Practices, we can do no less but Give forth this as a Publick de=
=nial against them the s,ᵈ **Tyley Wilcock** and **deborah** his Wife, denying
them to be in Unity with us the above s,ᵈ People. Yet Truly desiring
if it be the will of God, they may Come to a sight of their outgoings &
unfeigned Repentance, Given forth at out Monthly Meeting held
in **Dartmouth** on the 19ᵗʰ day of the 7ᵗʰ month 1762 and signed in &
by order of sd meeting by – –   **Isaac Smith** Clerk[33]

33. The previous thirty-three lines inserted here were omitted on page 324 of the original text, but are included here following instructions written on the final page of the book.

Jonathan Smith ju,ʳ his Paper of denial hath been Read as
Appointed; and Likewise **Tiley Willcox** and his wifes Paper of
denial hath been Read as appointed;

D Cornel Whereas **Daniel Cornel** hath Gone Contrary to Good order
Disowned Established amongst us in Marriage and he hath been dealt
with by the Visitors and Refuses to make Satisfaction, therefore
this Meeting doth Deny the Said **Daniel Cornel** to be one in unity
with us;

P Smith Whereas **Peleg Smith ju.r** hath Gone Contrary to the Good order
jun,ʳ Established among us in Marring out the worlds way, and also in
Disownd Marrying without his Parents Consent, and he hath been
Sufficiently dealt with, and Refuses to make Satisfaction;
therefore this Meeting doth deny the S,d **Peleg** to be one in Unity

Jacob with us; The Matter Concerning **Jacob Chase** is Refered
Chase to the next Monthly Meeting, and **Joseph Smith** and **Paul
Russell** are still Continued to discourse with him and make
Report to the next monthly Meeting;

The Treasurer has paid **Jonathan Hussey** 30 Shillings as ordered
whereas **Ruth Soul** daughter of **Benj.ⁿ Tripp** has Married out of
the Good order Established among us, and she hath been dealt with
Sufficiently and Refuses to make Satisfaction, therefore this

R.Soule Meeting doth deny the Said **Ruth Soule** to be one in Unity with us;
Disowned Whereas **Joseph Tucker ju,ʳ** desires a few lines by way of
Certificate, to the Monthly Meeting of **Sandwich**, Certifying
his Clearness as to Marriage and Conversation, therefore this
Meeting doth appoint **Joseph Smith** and **Barnabas Mosher**
to make Inquiry and draw one if they think proper and bring
it to the next Monthly Meeting;

E Mosher Whereas **Ebenezar Mosher** Requests to Come under the Care
Requests to to of Friends, therefore this Meeting doth appoint **Joseph Smith**
Come under and **Barnabas Mosher** to discource with the Said **Mosher**
our Care and make Report to the next monthly Meeting;
there was Collected at this Meeting £3=16ˢ old tener
The Treasurer is ordered to pay to **Jonathan Hussey** three
Dollars for half a year, keeping the Meeting House:

9 mo: At a monthly Meeting held in **Dartmouth** on the 19ᵗʰ
1762 of the ☉ 9ᵗʰ month 1762, **Ponaganset** Called **Thomas Smith** and
Joseph Tucker present, for **Coakset Philip Tripp** and **Peter Devil**

present, **Samuel Shove** and **Rebeckah Tucker ju,**ʳ did Lay their
Intentions of Marriage, and were desired to wait till the
next monthly Meeting for their answer,

S.Howland **Samuel Howland**s paper of Denial hath been Read is appoint[ed]

disowned The matter Concerning **Jacob Chase** is Refer,d ^to the next Monthly Meeting

J. Chase → There was a Certificate Signed for **Joseph Tucker ju,**ʳ Certifying his
Clearness as to Marriage and Conversation to the Monthly Meeting
of **Sandwich;** The matter Concerning **Ebenezer Mosher** is
Refered. to the next monthly Meeting,

The Treasurer hath paid **Jonathan Hussey** 3 Dollars as ordered

J. This Meeting appoints **Job Russell** Clerk instead of **Isaac Smith**
Russell according to **Isaac Smith**s Request – –
Clerk Whereas it hath been the practice of Friend, to Record the

Children, Births and Deaths of their Children, we understand the Said practice
Births hath been very much neglected, therefore it is the advice
& Deaths of this Meeting that all Friends be Carefull to Get the Births
to be and Deaths of their Children Recorded in the Friends Book
Recorded of Records;[34] The the Queries have been Read and answered in this

L.Trip Meeting; Whereas, **Lydia Tripp** Daughter of **John Lawton**
disownd has Married out of Unity of Friends, and she hath been
Sufficiently dealt with, and Refuses to Make Satisfaction,
therefore this Meeting doth Deny the s,d **Lydia Tripp** to be one
in unity with us and not under our care;
Whereas **Archapas Hart** hath for some time past neglected to
attend Meeting, for Worship and Discipline, and hath been
dealt with by visitors, and he Refuses to Comply to order
and Good advice, therefore this Meeting doth appoint
Joseph Smith and **Barnabas Mosher** to deal furder with
him and make Report to the next Monthly Meetg;
This Meeting doth appoint ☨ **Joseph Tucker Abraham
Tucker, Humphry Smith** and **Peter Davil** to attend the
Quarterly Meeting, and draw an Epistle to the same, and
Compile the Queries into a General answer for this Meeting
and bring the Epistle and answers to the adjournment;
This Meeting is adjourned to the youths meeting next
This meeting being met according to adjournment

34. This admonition is significant for two reasons. First, it is evidence that the recorder of births and deaths depended on families to provide information. Second, it explains why many births and deaths were not recorded.

the first day of the 10 month 1762, the Representatives for
Ponaganset both present, for **Coakset** none present;
The Friends appointed to draw an Epistle to the Quarterly Meeting
and Compile the ^ answers to the Queries, have done it as appointed, and the Epistle
was Signed by the Clerk in this Meeting, and is Sent up to the
Quarterly Meeting by the Representatives

[bottom third of page is torn]

BOOK III: 1762–1785

Note:
Minutes for 10th mo. 1762 through 1 mo. 1773 follow here,
balance will continue in Volume 2.

13

At a monthly Meeting held in Dartmouth the 18
day of the 10ᵗʰ Month 1762, Ponaganset Meeting Called
James Shearman & Caleb Russell present, for Coakset Joshua Deuel
present, Samuel Shove & Rebecah Tucker jr did appear
for their Answer, and their Answer was that they might
proceed to take each other in Marriage in Some Convenient
time between this and the next Monthly Meeting Observing
the Good order Established amongst us in the performance
thereof, and Joseph Smith & Paul Russell are appointed to
see their Marriage Consumated & Make Report to the next
Monthly Meeting.

Adam Mott junr and Rachel Rider did lay their Intentions
of Marriage, and were desired to wait till the next Monthly
Meeting for their Answer, and Joseph Tucker Joseph Smith
are appointed to Enquire into the young mans Clearness as
to Marriage and Conversation and make Report to the next
Monthly Meeting;

the Matter Concerning Jacob Chase is refered to the next
monthly Meeting;

this Meeting doth Conclude to accept of Ebenezar Mosher
to be one in unity with us and under our Care—

Whereas Archapus Hart hath declined attending Meeting
for Religious Worship and Discipline, and he hath been Suffici-
ntly dealt with by the Visiters and Monthly Meeting, and he
Still Continues in the above Said disorder; therefore we can
do no less than bear a Testimony against him therefore this
Meeting doth appoint Joseph Smith and Barnabas Mosher
to draw a paper of Denial against him and bring it to
the next Monthly Meeting;

The Friends appointed to attend the Quarterly Meeting
Signify that they attended it, and Conveyed the Epistle and
Queries as appointed, This Meeting Received an Epistle from the
Quarterly Meeting which was Read and well accepted;

This Meeting doth appoint Caleb Russell, Wm Sanford, Joseph
Smith, Danl Russell, and Barnabas Mosher to have an Inspection over the Galleries & Seats at our fall Meeting; and Joshua
Deuel, Othniel Tripp, Joseph Tripp and Philip Tripp are appointed
for the Same Service at Coakset Meeting

[margin notes:]
10ᵗʰ Mo: 1762
Samuel Shove Answer
Adam Mott Proposal of Marriage
Jacob Chase Case Refered
E Mosher accepted
Complaint against Archapus Hart a Testimony to be drawn against him
Report from Quarterly meeting
Friends to over see yearly meeting

FIG. 7: *Apponegansett Friends Monthly Meeting Records, Book III, 1762–1785, opening page. Courtesy of the Dartmouth at Smith's Neck Monthly Meeting.*

[This volume starts with page 13]

10th mo. 1762	At a monthly Meeting held in **Dartmouth** the 18 day of the 10th month 1762, **Ponaganset** Meeting Called

10th mo. 1762 — At a monthly Meeting held in **Dartmouth** the 18
day of the 10th month 1762, **Ponaganset** Meeting Called

Samuel Shove — James Shearman & Caleb Russell present, for **Coakset Joshua Devel [Davol]**

Answer — present, **Samuel Shove** & **Rebecah Tucker jr** did appear
for their Answer, and their Answer was that they might
proceed to take each other in Marriage in some Convenient
time between this and the next Monthly Meeting observing
the good order Established amongst us in the performance
thereof, and **Joseph Smith** & **Paul Russell** are appointed to
see their Marriage Consumated & make Report to the next
Monthly Meeting;

Adam Mott's Proposel of Marriage — **Adam Mott** ju^r. and **Rachel Rider** did lay their Intentions
of Marriage, and were desired to wait till the next Monthly
Meeting for their Answer, **and Joseph Tucker Joseph Smith**
are appointed to Enquire into the young mans Clearness as
to Marriage and Conversation and make Report to the next
Monthly Meeting;

Jacob Chases Case Refer'd — the Matter concerning **Jacob Chase** is refer'd to the next
monthly Meeting;

E. Mosher accepted — this Meeting doth Conclude to accept of **Ebenezar Mosher**
to be one in unity with us and under our Care – –

Complaints against Archapas Hart a Testimony to be drawn against him — Whereas **Archapas Hart** hath declined attending Meetings
for Religious worship and Discipline, and he hath been Sufficien
tly dealt with by the Visitors and Monthly Meeting, and he
Still Continues in the above said disorder, therefore we Can
do no less than bear a Testimony against him, therefore this
Meeting doth appoint **Joseph Smith** and **Barnabas Mosher**
to draw a paper of Denial against him and bring it to
the next Monthly Meeting;

Reporting from Quarterly meeting — The Friends appointed to attend the Quarterly Meeting
Signify that they attended it, and Conveyed the Epistle and
Queries as appointed, This Meeting Received an Epistle from the
Quarterly Meeting which was Read and well accepted;

Friends to over see yearly meeting — This Meeting doth appoint **Caleb Russell, Wm Sanford, Joseph
Smith, Danl. Russell,** and **Barnabas Mosher** to have an Inspecti
=on over the Galleries & Seats at our fall Meeting; and **Joshua
Devel [Davol], Othniel Tripp, Joseph Tripp** and **Philip Tripp** are appointed
for the Same Service at **Coakset** Meeting

11 mo.
1762 At a monthly Meeting Held in **Dartmouth** the 15th
of the 11th m°, 1762, **Ponaganset** Meeting Called **Paul Rus
sell** and **W,ᵐ Barker** present, for **Coakset Philip Tripp** and
Israel Wood present;

Thomas Russell **Thoˢ Russell** and **Edith Shearman** did lay their Intentions
proposal of of Marriage, and were desired to wait till the next monthly
marriage Meeting for their Answer, and **Joseph Smith** and **Paul Russell**
are appointed to make Inquiry into the young mans Clearness
as to Marriage and Conversation, and make Report to the
next monthly Meeting;

Report of The friends appointed to See **Samˡˡ Shove** and **Rebeckah Tucker**
Samuel Shove Marriage Consumated, make Report that they attended the
marriage Marriage and Saw nothing but that it was accomplished in
Good Order, – –

Adam Mott's **Adam Mott** and **Rachel Rider** not appearing for their
answer Refer'd Answer, the matter is Refer'd to the next Monthly Meeting

Case of Jacob the matter Concerning **Jacob Chase** is Refered to the next Mon[thly] Meeting;
Chase refered There was a paper of Denial brought to this Meeting aga[inst]

Archapas Hart **Archapas Hart** which is Refered to the next monthly Mee[ting]
paper Refered The Friends appointed to See that the people behave order[ly]

yearly meetg in the Galleries and Seats, Signified that they have discharge[d]
overseers report their trust;

Natˡˡ Howland Whereas, **Nathˡˡ Howland** hath Returned his Certificate to
Certificate this Meeting from the **Oblong**, therefore this Meeting hath
Signed another for him

12th Mo At a monthly Meeting held in **Dartmouth** on the [10?]
1762 day of the 12ᵗʰ month 1762; **Ponaganset** Meeting Called
Peleg Smith and **Abraham Tucker** present, for **Coakset** non[e]

Adam Mott present; the Friends Appointed to Enquire into **Adam Mo[tt's]**
Clearness Clearness, Make Report that they do not find anything to
hinder his Proceeding in Marriage

Thomas Russell's The friends appointed to make Enquiry into **Thoˢ Russell's**
Clearness Clearness, make Report that they do not find any thing to
hinder his proceeding in Marriage

Adam Mott's **Adam Mott** and **Rachel Rider**, did appear for their
Answer Answer, and their answer was, that they might proceed
in Marriage, in Some Convenient time between this and the
next monthly Meeting, observing the Good Order Esta
=blished amongst us in the performance thereof, and
Paul Russell and **Joseph Smith** are appointed to See their

Marriage Consumated in Said order and make report
to the next monthly Meeting,

Thos Russell's **Thos Russell** and **Edith Shearman** did appear for their
Answer answer and their answer was that they might prceed
in Marriage in Some Convenient time between this and
the next monthly Meeting Observing the Good order Esta=
=blished among us in the performance thereof, and **W^m**
Sanford and **David Smith** are appointed to See their Mar=
=riage Consumated in Said Order and make Report to the
next monthly Meeting;

Ebenezzar **Ebenezar Mosher** and **Jane Craw** did lay their intentions
Mosher of Marriage, and were desired to wait till the next Monthly
Proposal of Meeting for their Answer, and **Barnabas Mosher** and
marriage **David Shepherd** are appointed to make inquiry into the
young mans Clearness, as to Marriage and Conversation and
make Report to the next monthly Meeting;

The matter Concerning **Jacob Chase** is Refer'd to the next
Case of monthly Meeting;
Archapus Hart The matter Concerning **Archapus Hart** is Refered to the
refer'd next monthly Meeting;

Thos Smith To whereas **Thos Smith Ju^r** Requests a few lines by way of
request a Certificate to the monthly Meeting at **Nantucket,** Certify=
Certificate =ing his Clearness as to Marriage and Conversation, therefor
this Meeting doth appoint **Wm Sanford** and **Wm Barker**
to make inquiry into his Clearness and draw a Certificate
for him if they think proper and bring it to the next monthly Meeting;

Adjourn This Meeting doth Adjourn to the 10th Hour tomorrow in the
fore noon;

This Meeting met according to adjournment the 21^s of
the 12th month 1762, the Representatives being Called for
Ponaganset Abraham Tucker present, for **Coakset** none pres[ent]
whereas the Friends appointed at **Coakset** preparative
Meeting to attend this Meeting hath neglected to attend as
appointed, therefore this Meeting doth appoint **Philip Trip**
and **Christopher Gifford** to treat with them to know the
Reasons why they did not attend and make report to the
next monthly Meeting;

D. Devels Request Whereas **David Devel [Davol]** Requests to Come under friends Care
to Come under which this Meeting thinks proper to Refer to the next monthl[y]
friends Care Meeting, and **Christopher Gifford** and **Philip Tripp** are appoint[ed]

to treat with him and make Report to the next Monthly
Meeting;

Elders **Peter Devel [Davol]** & **Philip Tripp** are appointed Elders in the
appointed Church by this Meeting

Request of Whereas **Sandwich** Monthly Meeting Requests of this Meetin[g]
Sandwic[h] to Give a List of all the friends living to the Eastward of
Monthly Meeting. **Quitionnet River** Set off by the yearly Meeting (and also
if there be any under transgression before Set off by the above
Said Meeting [∧ that] this Meeting deal with them) which we
think to be out of our Jurisdiction and therefore Refer to the
Friends to Quarterly Meeting for advice in that particular – –
attend Quar **Joseph Tucker, Abraham Tucker, Humphrey Smith,**
terly meet **Caleb Russell** and **Philip Tripp** are Appointed Represen
ings =tatives to attend our Quarterly Meeting, and they to dr[aw]
an Epistle to the Same and bring it to the adjournment of the Meeting;

To Settle **David Smith** and **Wᵐ Barker** are appointed to mak[e]
with Trea up Accounts with the Treasurer, and make Report to
surer the next monthly Meeting;

D. Smith **David Smith** is Appointed Treasurer in the place of the
Treasurer former Treasurer

overseers of the **Seth Shearman** and **John Potter** are Appointed to have the
meeting House Care of the Meeting House, and also to Agree with Somebod[y]
apointed. to keep the House, and make fires when Necessary;

L. Barkers **Lydia Barker** wife to **David Barker** hath brought a
Certificate Certificate to this Meeting from the monthly Meeting of
Swanzey which was read and Accepted;
This Meeting is adjourned to the 7ᵗʰ day of next month
This Meeting being Met according to adjournment the 7ᵗʰ
day of the First Mᵒ 1763, **Ponaganset** Called **Abraham
Tucker** and **Peleg Smith** present, for **Coakset** none present
Queries the Queries have been read, and Answers made by the
Answered Visitors, and they are ordered to be Sent up by the Representative
Job Russell Req **Job Russell** Enforms this Meeting that he desires a few lines
uest a Certi by way of Certificate to the monthly Meeting of **Swanzey**
ficate Certifying his Clearness as to Marriage and Conversation,
therefore this Meeting doth Appoint **Caleb Russell** and **David
Smith** to make Enquiry, and draw a Certificate for him if they
think proper and bring it to the next monthly Meeting;
Epistle to Quar This Meeting hath Sent up an Epistle to the Quarterly Meeting
terly meeting by the Representatives which was Signed in this Meeting

1 month At a monthly Meeting held in **Dartmouth** the 17ᵗʰ

1763 of the first month 1763, **Ponaganset** Called **Paul Russell** s present

for **Coakset   Joseph Tripp** present, the Friends appointed to

Ebenezer make Enquiry into **Ebenezer Mosher**s Clearness make

Mosher Report that they do not find anything to hinder his proceed-

Clearness ing in Marriage,

Eben Mosher **Ebenezer Mosher** and **Jane Craw** did Appear for their

answer Answer and their Answer was, that they might proceed

to take each other in Marriage in Some Convenient times

between this and the next Monthly Meeting, (~~Observing the~~

and **Joseph Smith** and **Barnabas Mosher** are apointed to

See their Marriage Consumated in Good order, and make

Report to the next Monthly Meeting;

[R]eport of the friends Appointed to See **Adam Mott** and **Rachel Riders**

Adam Motts Marriage Consumated, make Report, that they attended the

marriage the Marriage and Saw nothing but that it was Acom=

Report of plished in Good order; Likewise the friend, Appointed to see

Thoˢ Russells **Thoˢ Russell** and **Edith Shearman**s Marriage Consumated

marriage make Report that they Attended the Marriage and Said

nothing but that it was accomplished orderly – –

The matter Concerning **Jacob Chase** Refered to the next

Case of Ar= monthly Meeting;

=chapas Hart The matter Concerning **Archapas Hart** is Refer'd to

refer'd the next monthly Meeting; – –

Certificate for There was a Certificate Signed in this Meeting for **Thoˢ. Smith jr.**

Thomas Smith Certifying his Clearness as to Marriage and Conversation to the -

Monthly Meeting of **Nantucket**;

Report of Whereas there was five friends Appointed to attend the Quarterly

Quarterly Meeting, they being Called upon at this Meeting, three make

meeting Report that they attended as Appointed, and the other two

make Satisfactory Excuses;

This Meeting Received an Epistle from the Quarterly Meeting

which was read to Good Satisfaction;

Quishnet The Quarterly Meeting hath Concluded that this Meeting Give

friends to be a List of all the Friends Living at the Eastward Side of

Set off by List **Quishnet River**, and also that this Meeting deal with the

Transgressers, therefore **Abraham Tucker** and **Caleb Russell**

are appointed to prepare a List of the above sᵈ friends that

they find to stand Clear, and also to deal with those friends

that they find under transgression

D. Cornels Request to Come under friends Care	Whereas **Daniel Cornel** Requests to be taken under friends Care and also his Children, therefore this Meeting doth Appoint **Joseph Tucker** and **Peleg Smith** and **Daniel Russell** to discourse with him, and make Report to the next monthly Meetin[g]
adjourn	This Meeting Adjourns to the last fourth day in this Month – –
mett	This ∧[Meeting][inserted] being met according to Adjournment the 26 of the first month 1763; the Representatives being Called for **Ponaganset Paul Russell** and **James Shearman** present, for **Coakset Israel Wood** present – –
about frinds not attending	The friends Appointed to treat with **Joseph Tripp** and **Wm Macumber** (for not attending the monthly Meeting when appointed by the preparitive Meeting) not being both present to make report, therefore this Meeting doth appoint **Othniel Tripp** and **Philip [∧Tripp]** to talk with them and make report to the next monthly Meeting;
The Case of David Devel referd	The mtter Concerning **David Devel [Davol]** is Refer'd to the next monthly Meeting, and **Othnial Tripp** and **Philip Tripp** are appointed to talk with him and make report to the next monthly Meeting
Settling with Treasurer refer^d	The Friends that was Appointed to make up accounts with the Treasurer not being present therefore the matter is Refered to the next monthly Meeting;
Certificate for Job Russell	there was a Certificate signed in this Meeting for **Job Russell** to the monthly Meeting of **Swanzey** Certifying his Clearness as to Marriage and Conversation;
To Revise the minutes	This Meeting Appoints **Abraham Tucker, Joseph Tucker, David Smith** and **Job Russell** to peruse the monthly Meeting Minutes to see what they think proper to be put on Record and make Report to the next monthly Meeting

2·^d mo: 1763	At a Monthly Meeting held in **Dartmouth** the 21 of the 2·^d month 1763, **Ponaganset** Called **Joseph Smith** & **Caleb Russell** present, for **Coakset Peter Dewel [Davol]** and **Philip Tripp** present,
John Diling= hams proposal of marriage	**John Dillingham** and **Ruth Gifford** did lay their Intentions of Marriage before this Meeting, and were desired to wait til the next monthly Meeting for their Answer
[R]eport of Eben Mosher's marriage	the friend, Appointed to See **Ebenezer Mosher** and **Jean Craws** Marriage Consumated, make Report that they attended the Marriage and Saw nothing but that it was Accomplished in Good order;

Jacob Chase	the matter of **Jacob Chase**s is Refered to the next monthly Meeting
	the matter of **Archapas Harts** is Referd to the next monthly Meeting;
List of frinds [sent?] of to Sand= wich not accom [p]lished	whereas the friends Appointed to prepare a List of the friends Living to the Eastward Side of **Quitionet River** that they Shall find Stand Clear, and also to deal with those under transgression, have Signified to this Meeting that they have not done it, therefore this Meeting doth Appoint **Joseph Tucker Caleb Russell** and **Joseph Smith** for the Same purpose and they to make Report to the next monthly Meeting
Daniel Cornel & Children received	The friends Appointed to talk with **Daniel Cornel** make a Satisfactary Report to this Meeting, therefore this me[eting] doth accept of **D. Cornel** to be under our Care and also all his Children now under age
S. Wood and E. Slocum Rec'd	The monthly, Meeting of women friends Inform us that the[y] have Received **Sinthia wood** and **Elizabeth Slocum** to be under their Care and this Meeting doth Concur with the Same
David Devel Case referd	The matter Concerning **David Devel [Davol]** is Refer'd to the next monthly Meeting;
Settled with Treasurer	the friends Appointed to Make up Accounts with the Treasu[rer] make Report that they have done it and there Remai[n] in the Stock 12^s.1^d old tener
minutes Revised	The Friends Appointed to Review the monthly [∧ meeting] Minutes in order for them to Go to Record, make Report that they have done According to Appointment;
Order to pay Jonath Hussey	This Meeting has Collected £8=10^s:10^d Old tener and this Meeti[ng] orders the Treasurer to pay **Jonathan Hussey** three Dollars for keeping the Meeting House half a year, and make Report to the next monthly Meeting;
Visitors appointed	This Meeting Appoints **Peter Devel [Davol]** and **Philip Trip** Visi[tors] for **Coakset** the year Ensuing and **Caleb Russell** for the Same Service in **Ponaganset**
Elihu Russell proposal of marriage	**Elihu Russell** and **Elizabeth Slocum** did Lay their Intention of Marriage before this Meeting and were desired to wait till the next monthly Meeting for their Answer and **Humphr[ey] Smith** and **Paul Russel** are Appointed to make Inquiry into the young mans Clearness as to Marriage and Conver =sation and make Report to the next monthly Meeting
[3]^d mo: 1763	At a monthly Meeting held in **Dartmouth** the 25th of the 3^d mo: 1763, **Ponaganset** meeting Called **Joseph Smith** &

Wm Anthony ju. present, for Coakset Joseph Tripp &
Israel Wood present – –

Jn Dillingham John Dillingham produced a Certificate to this Meeting from
[C]ertificate Sandwich monthly meeting which was read and accepted -

Jn Dillingham John Dillingham and Ruth Gifford did appear for their answer
[a]nswer and their answer was that they might proceed to take each
other in Marriage in some Convenient time between this
and the next monthly meeting observing the Good order
Established among us, in the performance thereof, and
Joseph Tucker and Joseph Smith are appointed to see there
Marriage Consumated in Said order, and make Report thereof

[E]lihu Russells to the next monthly Meeting; Elihu Russel, Clearness was Reported as usual
answer Elihu Russell and Elizabeth Slocum did likewise appear for
their answer, and their answer was in like manner with the
former, and, Humphrey Smith and Paul Russell are appointed
to see their ~~th~~ Marriage Consumated in like order and make
Report thereof to the next monthly Meeting – –

~~Henry Smith and Sinthia wood did likewise appear for~~
~~their Answer and their Answer was likewise the~~
~~Same with the former.~~

Henry Smiths Henry Smith and Sinthia wood did lay their Intention
proposal of of Marriage before this Meeting, and were Defered, to wait
marriage untill the next monthly Meeting for their Answer.
and John Russell and W.ᵐ Anthony ju: are apointed to [?]
Inquiry in‸[to] the young mans Clearness as to Marriage and
Conversation and make Report to the next monthly Meeting

J. Chases paper This meeting doth Conclude to accept of Jacob Chases paper
Accepᵗ: of Condemnation for Satisfaction for his outgoing Provided he
Read it or Get Some friend to Read it at the Close of a first
day meeting for worship and be present
The matter Concerning Archapas Hart is Refered to the
next monthly Meeting

List of friends The friends appointed to prepare a list of those friends
Sandwich Living at the eastward Side of Quishnet River that they
Quarter prepard Shall find Stand Clear have prepared Sd So List and it hath
been Signed in this meeting by the Clerk – –

D. Daval & This Meeting doth Conclude to Accept of David Davel and his
Children accepted Children to be in Unity with us under our Care – –

Case of Eber The matter Concerning Eber Davis is Refer'd to next monthly Mee[ting]
Davis referd
John Gifford whereas John Gifford Requests a Certificate for himself and fami[ly]

request a
Certificate therefore this meeting Appoints **Daniel Russell** and **Nichols [Nicholas]
Howland** to make Enquiry into his Conversation and Circumst[an-]
=ces and draw one if they think proper and bring it to the nex[t]
monthly Meeting

Friends ap **Joseph Tucker, Humphry Smith, Peter Deval,** and **Philip Tripp**
pointed to
Quarl meet- appointed to attend the Quarterly Meeting and draw an
ing Epistle to the Same and bring it to the adjournment of this

Queries Meeting —— the Queries was Read and Answered in this Mee[ting]
answerd

adjourn This Meeting is adjourned to the first day of next month.

mett This Meeting being met according to Adjournment the first da[y]
of the 4th mo: 1763, the Representatives being Called **William
Anthony ju**: present – –

Isaac Sanford whereas **Isaac Sanford** hath Married out of the unity of friend
disorderly and he hath been timely Cautioned, therefore this meeting doth
marriage Appoint **Caleb Russell** & **Wᵐ Barker** to Labour with him and
make Report to the next monthly Meeting – –

Chusing Visitors the matter Concerning Chusing Visitors is Refered to the next
refer'd monthly Meeting

Epistle to This Meeting hath Signed and Sent an Epistle to the Quart[erly]
Quarterly
meeting Meeting by the Representatives

4ᵗʰ mo: At a Monthly Meeting held in **Dartmouth** the 18ᵗʰ of
1763. the 4ᵗʰ mo:1763, **Ponaganset** meeting Called **Daniel Russell**
and **William Barker** present, for **Coakset James Cornel** and
Joshua Davel present, **Henry Smith** Clearness was Reported as usual

Henry Smith **Henry Smith** and **Sinthia Wood** did appear for their Answer
answer and their Answer was that they might proceed to take each
other in Marriage in some Convenient time between this and

[pages 23 and 24 of text are missing]

[?] month 1763
[?] Allen **Debrah Allen** to be one in unity with us and under our Care
[a]nd Edith which this Meeting Concurs with, They also Inform that they
[T]ripp have Concluded to accept of **Edith Tripp**, paper of Condemna-
Received =tion for Satisfaction, Provided She Read it or Get some friend
to Read it at the end of a first day meeting for worship She
being present, which this meeting likewise Concurs with.

[C]omplaint Whereas there has been a Complaint brought against
against [?] **Joshua Barker** by one of the Visitors in three Repsects, First
Barker in Declining to make friend,[s] Satisfaction Concerning a Scan-
=dulous Report about he and **Catherine Russell** a married
woman in their too frequently keeping Company, and Secondly

in Declining to pay the Constable his Demand, for a Tax,
Thirdly, in Neglecting to Comply with a Verdi[c]t brought Against
him for burning Some Rails belonging to **Henry Tucker, Paul
Russell,** and **Joseph Smith** a Committee to Labour with him
and make Report to the next monthly Meeting – –

*Nath^ll
Bowdish [R]
equest a Certi=
ficate* **Nathaniel Bowdish** Informs this Meeting that he is About
to Remove to the **nine-parterners,**and Requests a few lines
by way of Certificate for himself and family, therefore
Joseph Gifford and **Jonathan Hussey** are Appointed to make
Enquiry [ₐinto] his Conversation and affairs, and draw one if they
think proper and bring [ₐit] to the next monthly Meeting – –

*[T]homas
Potter
[?]nder dealing* whereas **Thos Potter** Son of **John Potter** hath Gone Contrary
to Good order in Marrying out of the unyty of friends, and in
having a Child Soon after Marriage, for which disorders he
hath been Laboured with and declines to make Satisfaction
therefore this Meeting doth appoint **Wm Sanford** and **Jonathan
Hussey** to Labour with him and make Report to the next
monthly Meeting

*5th mo.
1763* At a monthly Meeting of friends held at our Meeting H[ouse]
in **Dartmouth** on the 16th day of the 5th mo: 1763, **Ponaganset**
Meeting Called **James Shearman** and **Peleg Smith** present, for
Coakset Peter Daval [Davol] and **John Mosher.**

*Abner Shep=
=herds clear=
=ness* the friends Appointed to See into **Abner Shepherd**s Clearness Sig[nify]
that they find nothing to hinder his Intended Marriage.

*Abner Shep=
Shepherd
Answer* **Abner Shepherd** and **Hannah Gifford** appear'd at this Meeting
their Answer, and their Answer was that they might proceed to
take Each other in Marriage in Some Convenient time betwe[en]
this and the next monthly Meeting, Observing our Good order
in the Confirmation thereof, and **Wm Sanford** and **David Smith**
are appointed to See their Marriage Consumated and make
Return to the next monthly Meeting

*Report of
Henry Smith
marriage* The friends Appointed to See **Henry Smith,** and **Synthia wood,**
Marriage Consumated, Signify that it was accomplished in Good order

*Archapas
Hart's [?]* And whereas **Archapas Hart** hath Given Some Incouragement
Concerning keeping to meeting, therefore the matter is Suspended

*John
Taber
disowned* Whereas, **John Taber jur** having been Married and of our Good ord[er]
and [ₐhe] no wise Showing any Desire to make Satisfaction having been
Laboured with we think Sufficiently, therefore this Meeting doth
Conclude to Set him aside and do deny him from being in unity
with us – –

Isaac Smith Hath Read **Abigail Macumber**s and **Zilphian Davel**s
papers of Denials as ordered, and

Abigail Macumbers Denial is as followeth – –

Testimony against Abigail Macumber

Whereas **Abigail Macumber** of **Dartmouth** in the Count[y]
Bristol in the Province of the Massachusetts Bay in New England, w[ife]
of **Joseph Macumber** & Daughter of **Benj**ᵃ **Allen** and **Deborah** [?]
both deceased of **Dartmouth** afore sd, Being one who hath been in
Care of us the People Called Quakers but for want of keep[ing?]
to her Education hath Gone from our Good order and married in [the?]
Common way of ~~th~~ other people and not only so but since her
Marriage her Conversation hath not been agreable to our holy
proffesion, in particular She not living with her husband, and
friend, [s] having Laboured with her in love in order to bring her
to a Sense of her outgoing, but nothing appearing to friends
Satisfaction of any time Repentence, we Can do no less for the
Clearing of the Blessed truth but to Set her [*blot*] and do Give
this forth as a publick denial against her [*blot*] the said
Abigail Macumber to be one in unity with [*blot*] Said people
Sincerely Desiring She may Come to a Sight and [*blot*] of her out-
=going, and find mercy, Given forth at our Monthly Meeting
held in **Dartmouth** on the 18ᵗʰ day of the 4th month 1763, and
Signed in and by order of said meeting by **Job Russell** Clerk -

Zilphia Davels Denial is as follows   Viz,

[T]estimony [a]gainst [Zi]lphia Davel

Whereas **Zilphia Davel** Daughter of **Reuben Davel** and **Mary**
his wife of **Dartmouth** in the County of **Bristol**, in the province
of the **Massecthusett Bay** in New-England being one that hath
been under the Care of friend, the People Called Quakers, yet
by disregarding the Principle of truth in herself, and Giving way
to the Information of the evil one hath fallen into the Reproach for
Sin of fornication, for which She hath been Laboured within
Love to bring her to a Sense of her evil action but nothing Seeming
to appear of true Repentence we think it our duty to Set
her aside and do Publickly deny the Said **Zilphia Davel** to
be one in unity with us the above Said people, yet truly
desiring She may Come to a Sight and Sense of this her Great Evil
and find mercy;
Given forth at our monthly meeting held in **Dartmouth**
on the 18ᵗʰ day of the 4ᵗʰ mo: 1763 and Signed in and by
order of S[ai]d meeting by – –   **Job Russell** Clerk

The Case of John Gifford refered

the matter Concerning **John Gifford** Certificate is Refered
the next monthly Meeting – –

[E]ber Davis [pa]per accepted — Friends do Conclude to accept of **Eber Davis** his paper for Satisfaction.

Isaac Sanford case referd — The matter concerning **Isaac Sanford** is Refer'd to the next monthly Meeting – –

Edith Tripps paper not Read — **Edith Tripp**s paper not having been read, is Refer'd in order that it may be accomplished between this and the next monthly Meeting

Choosing Visitors refered — The matter Concerning Chusing Visitors is Refered to next month[ly] [Mee]ting

The [*blot*] [p]aper of Denial brought and Signed in this meeting

Testimony signed against Lydia Potter — In [*blot*] [?]ce [concurence?] with the womens Meeting Against **Lydia Potter** And [*blot*] **Russell** is appointed to read it at **New-town** meeting on a first day at the end of the meeting for worship – –

Case of Joshua Barker refer^d — The Matter Concerning **Joshua Barker** is Refer'd to the next monthly Meeting, and the Com^{tte} Still Continued that hath alre[ady] had the matter in hand – –

Nathl Bowdish Certificate — There was a Certificate Signed at this Meeting for **Nathaniel Bowdish** and his wife, they being Going to Settle at the **Nine =parterners**

Thos Potter disowned — The friend appointed to deal with **Thomas Potter** Signify they hav[e] done it, and he Gave them no Satisfaction, therefore this Meeting thinks Proper to deny him, and **Wm Sanford** and **Jonathan Hus[sey?]** are appointed to draw up a paper of denial against him and bring it to the next monthly Meeting

The Transcrib the Book of Discipline — There was £18:10s old tenner Gathered by this meeting to pay for transcribing our Book of Discipline, which is paid – –

Nic Howlands paper ace=pted — **Nicholas Howland ju^r** hath Given in a paper to this Mee[ting] Signifying his Sorrow for his disorderly Marriage, which the Meeting accepts – –

Elihu Rus sell request Certificate — whereas **Elihu Russell** and his wife being Removed to the **Oblong** live and desires a few lines from this Meeting to the monthly mee[ting] there, and **Humphry Smith** and **Wm Anthony ju:** are app[ointed] to draw a Cerificate and bring it to the next monthly Meeting if they think proper – –

Complaint against Wm Smith — There was a Complaint brought to this Meeting that **William Smith** hath been addicted to take too much Spirituous Liqu[or?] therefore this Meeting appoints **Humphry Smith** & **Jonathan Hussey** to talk with him upon that account and ~~bring~~ make Return to the next Monthly meeting

[Danl] Russells to [cu]t Wood on [mee]ting land — Whereas there is a Considerable due from this Meeting to **Daniel Russell** upon **Stephen Wilcox** his account therefore this meeting doth Give leave that he Cut wood at 15^s per

Cord old tener, Except any body doth appear that will Give
more until the debt is paid, on the meeting House Lot

B. Tucker,
Request
[t]o Come
under the
[C]are of friends

Benjn Tucker hath Signified his desire of Coming
under the Care of Friends, therefore **Joseph Gifford** and **Paul
Russell** are appointed to Enquire Concerning his Conversati[on]
and talk with him and bring in their account to the next
monthly Meeting

6th mo:
1763,

At a monthly Meeting held in **Dartmouth** the 20th of the
6th mo: 1763, **Ponaganset** Meeting Called **Peleg Smith** and
Abraham Tucker present, for **Coakset Joseph Tripp** present

[Joh]n
Ricketson Jr
[P]roposal of
marriage

John Ricetson jr: and **Patience Tucker** did Lay their Intenti-
=ons of Marriage before this Meeting, and were desired to wait
til the next monthly Meeting for their answer, and **W^m
Barker** and **Job Russell** are appointed to make Enquiry into
the young mans Clearness as to Marriage and Conversation
and make Report to the next monthly Meeting

[Re]port of
Abner
[She]pherds
[m]arriage

The friends appointed to See **Abner Shepherd** and **Hannah Gifford**
Marriage Consumated make Report that they attended the
marriage and Saw nothing but that it was accomplished in
Good order

[Case?] of John
[Gi]fford referd

The matter Concerning Giving **John Gifford** a Certifica[te]
is Refer'd to the next monthly Meeting

Case of Isaac
Sanford referd
[illegible]

The matter Concerning **Isaac Sanford** is Refer'd to the
next monthly Meeting – –

[E]dey Tripp
[pa]per of [re]
pent:
[?]e

Edith Tripps Paper of Condemnation hath been Read
as Appointed by the last monthly Meeting
and is as follows – –

To the monthly Meeting of friends to be held in **Dartmouth**
on the 20th day of the 12th mo: 1762,
Whereas I by letting my mind out became weak and So Ga[ve]
way to the temtation of the enemy in the Lust of the flesh so f[ar?]
as to Commit the Shamefull Sin of fornication which was m[?]
manifest by ^[my] having a Child Soon after Marriage and also m[arriage]
out of the unity of friend, all which I do Condemn and am S[orry?]
for therefore I desire that God may forgive me my Sins
that friends would pass it by and Suffer me to Remain under
their ~~Care~~ Christian Care – –   **Edey Tripp** – –

Wm How=
land dis=
order

William Howland hath Sent a paper into this Meeting Signif[ying]
his Sorrow for his disorder in takeing too much Spirituous Liquo[r]
which matter is Refer'd to the next monthly Meeting – –

Abr^m Tucker
Visitor **Abraham Tucker** is appointed Visitor for the Ensuing year

Queries an
swered The Queries have been Read and Answers have been made by
Coakset preparitive meeting – –

Friends to
Qur meeting The friends Appointed to attend the Quarterly Meeting are
Peleg Smith, Caleb Russell Paul Russell and **Philipp Tripp**
and they to draw an Epistle to the Same and bring it to the
adjournment of this Meeting – –

adjourn This Meeting adjourns to the first day in next month – –

mett This Meeting met according to adjournment the first day of th[e]
7th mo:1763, the Representatives being Called for **Aponagans**[et]
and **Coakset** all present

L. Potter
disownd **Paul Russell** makes Report that **Lydia potter,** paper of
Denial hath been Read as order'd

[Certi]ficate for
[Eli]hu Russell
Wife There was a Certificate Signed at this Meeting for
Elihu Russell and his wife – –

[Pape]r of denial
[signe?]d against
Tom^s Potter There was a paper of Denial brought to this meeting
and Signed against **Thomas Potter,** and **Jonathan
Hussey** is appointed to Read it at the End of a first day
Meeting for worship Between this and the next Monthly Meeting – –

[Case?] of W^m
Smith [re]fer'd The matter Concerning **William Smith** is Refer'd to
the next monthly Meeting and **Humphry Smith** and
Jonathan Hussey are Still Continued to Treat furder
with him – –

Tucker Rce^d The Friend Appointed to talk with **Benjn Tucker**
Make Report that he Gave them Good Satisfaction
and this meeting Concludes him to be under our Care
for the time to Come – –

[frie]nds
appointed [?]
meeting **Peleg Smith** ~~and Humphry Smith~~ **Caleb Russell** and
Paul Russell are Appointed to Sign the Epistle to the
Quarterly Meeting in behalf of this Meeting

[answ]ers to
Queries **Peleg Smith** & **Humphry Smith** are appointed to Compil[e]
the answers to the Queries

[Jona]than
Clark [R]equest We understand that **Jonathan Clark** hath Signified
that he hath a desire to Come under our Care, therefore
this Meeting Appoints **Joseph Gifford** and **Paul Rus=
=sell** to treat with him and make Report to the
next monthly Meeting

7th month
1763 At a monthly Meeting held in **Dartmouth** the
18th of the 7th month 1763, **Ponaganset** Called **Caleb
Russell** and **Wm Barker** present, for **Coakset Peter**

Devol [Davol] present – –

John Ricket= The friends appointed to Inquire into **John Ricetsons** Clear-
=son Clearness ness as to Marriage and Conversation make Report that th[ey]
don't find anything to hinder his proceeding in Marriage

Epistle Received an Epistle from the yearly meeting held in **Lon[don?]**
Received the 5th month 1762 which was Read to Good Satisfaction

John Rick= **John Ricketson** and **Patience Tucker** did appear for th[eir]
=etsons answer and their answer was that they might proceed
answer take each other in Marriage in Some Convenient time
between this and the next monthly Meeting Observing the
Good order Established among us in the Performance there
and **Abraham Tucker** and **Wm Barker** are appointed
to see their marriage Consumated in Sd order and make
Report to the next monthly Meeting

Case of John The matter Concerning Giving **John Gifford** a Certificate
Gifford Refered to the next monthly meeting – –
referd

Case of Isaac The matter Concerning **Isaac Sanford** is Referd to the nex[t]
Sanford monthly meeting ~~as is also~~ the matter Concerning **Wm H[owland?]**
referd

Report from The Friends appointed to attend the Quarterly Meeting
Quar. meetg make Report that they have attended it and prod[?]

Eps Receivd an Epistle from the Same which was Read & well accept[ed]

Joshua Barker The Comittee appointed to Labour with **Joshua Barker** M[?]
disowned Report that he Refused to Comply with their advice, and
that he Gave them no Satisfaction, therefore this meeting do[?]
Set him aside, and appoints **Wm Sanford** and **Jonathan
Hussey** to draw a paper of Denial against him and bring it
to the next monthly Meeting if they think proper

Tho Potter. **Thomas Potters** paper of denial hath been Read accordin[g]
paper read to the appointment of last monthly meeting
And is as followeth

[Test]imony Whereas **Thos Potter** Son of **John Potter** & **Margaret** his wife
[ag]ainst he the said **Thomas Potter** having been one under our Care, yet
Potter through unwatchfulness Gave way to the temtation of the Enemy
So as to fall into that Shamefull Sin of Fornication, which appears
by his wife having a Child Soon after Marriage, and he hath
been Laboured with from time to time for his Misconduct hoping
he may See his Outgoings and make friends Satisfaction, but he Still
Remains Obstinate and Refuse to make friends Satisfaction, there-
=fore for the Clearing of truth we Can do no less than Give this forth, as
a Publick Testemony against him the Said **Thomas Potter** Denying

him from being in membership with us the People Called Quakers
yet we Sincerely desire that he may Come to a Sense of his Outgoings, and
through unfeigned Repentence find Mercy, Given forth at our monthly
Meeting held in **Dartm**º. the 1ᵗ day of the 7 mo: 1763.

Signed in and by order of Said Meeting by – – ⎧ **Abraham Tucker**
⎨ **Peleg Smith**
⎩ **Peter Devel [Davol]**

[Ca]se of Jonathan [C]lark referd   The matter Concerning **Jonathan Clark** is Refered to the next monthly Meeting – –

Coakset preparative meeting Informs this meeting that

[Da]vid Kirbys [Kerby] [diso]rderly [m]arriage   **David Kerby** hath Married out of the Unity of friends and that they have Laboured with him and he Gave them no satisfaction therefore the matter is Refered to the next monthly Meeting

[8]ᵗʰ mo: 1763   At a monthly Meeting held in **Dartmouth** the 15ᵗʰ of the 8ᵗʰ month 1763 **Ponaganset** meeting Called **Peleg Smith** and **Caleb Russell** present **Coakset** meeting Called **John Mosher** and **Philip Tripp** presents

[Rep]ort of John [Ri]cketsons [m]arriage   The Friends appointed to See **John Ricketsons** Marriage Consumated make Report that they attend[ed] the Marriage and Saw nothing but that it was accom= =plished in Good order.

Received Divers Certification   This Meeting Received an Epistle from the yearly Meeting held at **Newport** on the 10ᵗʰ of the 8ᵗʰ[?] mo 17[63?] which was Read to Good Satisfaction;

This meeting lik[e]wise Read an Epistle from the yearly meeting for Sufferings in **London**, and one from the yea[rly] Meeting held at **Philadelphia**, and one from the yearly Meeting held at **flushing**, and one from our friends **John Woolman** and **Samuel Estburn [Eastburn]**[1], all of which bei[ng] Read in this meeting to Good Satisfaction and as they Contain Good advice, and many Good Exhortations the Contents are Recommended to friends Observation;

John Giffords Case refer^d   The matter Concerning Giving **John Gifford** a Certificate is refer'd to the next monthly meeting;

1. John Woolman (1720–1772), an intinerant minister and early opponent of slavery, traveled extensively throughout the colonies and was the author of *Considerations on Keeping Negores* and a *Journal*, published posthumously, that became a classic text of early American religious literature. Samuel Eastburn (1702–1785) preached more locally in Pennsylvania, but was a close ally of Woolman in the cause of abolition. See Amelia Mott Gummere, *The Journal and Essays of John Woolman* (Philadelphia: Friends' Book Store, 1922), 538

Isaac San= *fords Case refer^d*	The matter Concerning **Isaac Sanford** is Refer'd to the next monthly Meeting;
Wm How *=lands paper* *accepted*	This Meeting doth accept of **Wm Howlands** paper of Conde[m]- nation for Satisfaction Provided that he Read it or Get Some friend to read it at the end of a first day meeting for worship and he be present between this and the next mont[hly] Meeting;
Joshua *Barkers* *Case refer^d*	The matter Concerning **Joshua Barker** is Refered to the ne[xt] monthly Meeting
Case of Jona *Clark refer^d*	The matter Concerning **Jonathan Clark** is Referrd to the next monthly Meeting ~
David Kirby *Case refer^d*	the matter Concerning **David Kerby [Kirby]** is likewise Referd to the next monthly Meeting and **John Mosher** and **Othnial Tripp** ~~is~~ are appointed to Labour with him, and make report to the next monthly Meeting
Order to pay *Jonathan* *Hussey*	This Meeting hath Collected £5=17ˢ:8ᵈ old tenor and **Davi[d]** **Smith** is ordered to pay **Jonathan Hussey** three Dollars fo[r] keeping the Meeting House half a year
Inspection *of the poor* *(to report)*	This Meeting ∧appoints **Nicholas Howland** and **Paul Russell** ove[r] =seers of the poor to have an Inspection into their Circ[um] stan[ces] and to make Report once a Quarter ~
[Com]plaint *against* *[Reuben] Devel*	There hath been ∧a Complaint brought against **Reuben** **Devil [Davol]** by one of the Visitors in Several Respects in not attending meetings, and in his Conduct which appears Scandulous [scandalous], therefore this meeting doth appoint **Christopher Gifford** and **Velantine [Valentine] Huddlestone** to Labour with him if they have an opportunity and make Report to the next monthly Meeting;
[Sub]scription *for [Step]hen* *Wilcox*	This Meeting hath Come to a subscribtion for the Relief of **Stephen Wilcox** and family;

9ᵗʰ mo.ᵗʰ 1763	At a monthly Meeting held in **Dartmouth** on the 19ᵗʰ of the 9 mo. 1763 **Ponaganset** meeting Called **Thomas Smith** and **James Shearman** present, for **Coak=** =set **Peleg Huddlestone** & **Peter Devil [Davol]** present
[Benj]ᵃ Tuckers *[pro]posal of* *[m]arriage*	**Benjᵃ Tucker** and **Surviah [Zerviah] Ricketson** Declared their Intentions of Marriage to this Meeting and were desired to wait til next monthly Meeting for their Answer and **Caleb Russell** and **Joseph Gifford** are Appointed to Enquire into the young mans Clearness as to Mar= =riage and Conversation and makes Report to the

next monthly Meeting ~

[acknow?]legment   [W]illiam Howlands paper being Read as ordered, is as follows – viz [To?]
of *Wm Howland*   the monthly meeting of friends to beholden at **Dartmo:** the 16: 9 month 1763
[W]orthy friends, Whereas I have through unwatchfulness some times been Guilty of
[drin]king too much Spirituous Liquor to the Reproach of truth and Grief of the friends
[wh]ereof, for which outgoings of mine they have in Love Labour^d with me, which
[d]ealings I do Gratefully acknowledge as a Sure mark of their tender Regard for my
[go]od, which Causes me the more freely, not only to Confess, but also to Condemn my
[w]eakness in the above S^d Respect, but as I have a Great Regard for friends and
[the] Good order Established among them, and a desire to Refrain from the Above
[?] Evil for the future, So I desire friends to pass by my offence for the time past (and
[co]ntinue me under their Care) Hoping for the future with Divine Assistance to be
[m]ore watchful over my Self, that my life & Conversation may be Such as may
[n]ot bring the like trouble on friends   ;   **William Howland**

Certificate   There was a Certificate Signed at this Meeting for
for John Gifford   **John Gifford** and his Wife and Children to the
& fam: Signed   monthly Meeting at **Oblong**; ~

Joshua Barker   The matter Concerning **Joshua Barker** is Refer'd to th[e]
Case referd   next monthly Meeting as is likewise the matter

David Kirbys   Concerning **David Kirby**; ~
Case refer^d

Jona Hussey   **David Smith** has paid **Jonathan Hussey** three Dollars
paid   According to the order of Last monthly Meeting; ~

Jonathan Clark   This Meeting doth Conclude to accept of **Jonathan**
accepted   **Clark** to be one under our Care; ~

Isaac Sanfords   This Meeting doth likewise accept of **Isaac Sanfords**
paper accepted   paper Condemning his outgoings for Satisfaction and
he to Remain under Our Care

Friends to attend   This Meeting doth appoint **Humphry Smith, W^m**
Quart[er]   **Anthony ju:** and **Philip Tripp** to attend the Quarterly
=ly meeting   Meeting and to draw an Epistle to the Same and Compile
the Answers to the Queries and bring them to the adjou[rn]
=ment of this Meeting, The Queries have been Read and
Answered by the preparitive meetings

adjourn   This Meeting adjourns to the first Sixth day in the next
[mett?]   month at the tenth Hour in the forenoon ~

This Meeting being met according to Adjournmen[t]
the Representatives being Called but none present

no report   The friends appointed to treat with **Reuben Devel [Davol]** have
of Ruben Devel   made no report to this Meeting therefore the matter is
Case   Refer'd to the next monthly Meeting;

Joseph How
=lands request | **Joseph Howland** Requests to Come ₍under₎ friends Care, therefo[re] this Meeting doth appoint **Wᵐ Sanford** and **Jonathan Hussey** to treat with him and make Inquiry into his Conversation and make Report to the next monthly

[Jon]athan
Clark
[re]quest a
[Ce]rtificate | Meeting; ~ **Jonathan Clark** Requests a Certificate to the monthly Meeting of **Sandwich** Certifying his Clearness as to Mar-=riage and Conversation, therefore this Meeting doth appoint **Joseph Tucker** and **Joseph Smith** to make Inquiry into the Above Said particulars, and to draw a Certificate for him if they think proper and bring it to the next monthly Meeting; ~

[Epi]stle &
answers
[to?] Queries | The Friends Appointed to draw an Epistle to the Quarterly Meeting and Compile the Answers to the Queries have done it and the Epistle was Signed in this Meeting and Sent to the Quarterly Meeting by the Representatives

---

10ᵗʰ mo:
1763 | At a monthly Meeting held in **Dartmouth** the 17th of the tenth month 1763 **Ponaganset** meeting Called **Joseph Smith** and **Wᵐ Sanford** present, for **Coakset Ichabod Eddy** and **Josua [Joshua] Deval [Davol]** present, – –

[Be]njᵃ Tuckers
[c]learness | The Friends Appointed to Enquire into **Benjᵃ Tuckers** Clear=ness make Report that they don't find anything to hinder his proceeding in Marriage; ~

[Be]nj Tuckers
answer | **Benjᵃ Tucker** and **Surviah [Zerviah] Ricketson** did appear for their Answer, and their Answer was that they might proceed to take each other in Marriage in Some Conveni==ent time Between this and the next monthly Meeting Observing the Good order Established Amongst us in the performance thereof, and **Caleb Russell** and **Joseph Gifford** are Appointed to See their Marriage Consumated in Said order and make Report thereof to the next monthly Meeting. ~

Joshua Bar
=ker case
refer'd | The matter Concerning **Joshua Barker** is Refer'd to the next monthly Meeting, by the Request of his brother **Abraham Barker**

David Kirby
Case referd | The matter Concerning **David Kerby [Kirby]** is Refer'd to the next monthly Meeting ~

Report from
Quarterly
Meeting | The Friends Appointed to attend the Quarterly Meetin[g] make Report that they have attended Accordingly and have produced an Epistle from the Same which w[as] Read in this Meeting and well accepted ~

Joseph Howland accepted — The Friends Appointed to Discourse with **Joseph Howland** make a satisfactory Report therefore this Meeting doth Accept of him to be one under our Care

Certificate for Jonathan Clark — This Meeting signed a Certificate for **Jonathan Clark** to the monthly Meeting of **Sandwich** Certifying his Clearness as to Marriage and Conversation, ~

overseers for meeting house lofts — This Meeting doth Appoint **Jonathan Hussey, Wᵐ Antho[ny] jʳ David Smith, Wᵐ Barker, Joseph Smith** and **Benjᵃ Howland 2ᵈ** overseers to have an Inspection over the lofts[?] and other seats to see that the people Behave orderly at our yearly meeting, And **Joshua Daval [Davol] Daniel Wood**

overseers for Accoaxet meeting [?] — **Ichabod Eddy** and **Benjᵃ Tripp** are appointed for the Same purpose at **Coakset** Meeting ~

Elihu Bowen Request the Second Time — This Meeting understands that **Elihu Bowen** Desires to Come into Un[i]ty with friends Again therefore this Meeting doth Appoint **Abraham Tucker** and **Peleg Smith**, to discourse with him and make Report to the next Monthly Meeting

---

[1]1ᵗʰ mo. [17]63 — At a Monthly Meeting held in **Dartmouth** on the 21 day of the 11ᵗʰ month 1763, **Ponaganset** Meeting Called **Joseph Tucker** present for **Coakset Joseph Tripp** and **Israel Wood** present ——— The friends appointed to See **Benjᵃ**

[Rep]ort of [Benj?] Tucker [ma]rriage — **Tucker**s Marriage Consumated, make Report that they attended the Marriage and Saw nothing but that it was Accomplished in Good order ~

[Jos]hua [Ba]rker [dis]owned — This Meeting hath Signed a paper of Denial Against **Joshua Barker** for his outgoings, and **Jonathan Hussey** is Appointed to read it or Get Some friend to read it between this and the next monthly Meeting at the end of a frist [first?] day meeting for worship

[Dav]id Kerby [cas]e referd — The matter Concerning **David Kerby [Kirby]** is Refer'd to the next monthly Meeting ~

[Re]port of [ov]erseers of [meet]ting [ho?]use — The major part of the friends that was Appointed overseers at our yearly meeting make Report that they think they have discharged their duty in that Respect and they hope there is a Service in it ~

[?]se of Elihu [Bo]wen referd — The matter Concerning **Elihu Bowen** is Refer'd to the next monthly Meeting, and the same friends are Still Continued in the Same Service – –

The women friends Inform that they have Received a Re=

Anne Russells [certific?]ate [r]eceived =moval Certificate for **Anne Russell** which they have accepted and She to be under their Care which this Meeting Concurs with

[Caleb?] Russell purchase book for [re]cords whereas this Meeting is destitute of a Book to Record the minutes of this meeting in, therefore this meeting doth Imploy **Caleb Russell** to Purchase one and bring it to the next monthly Meeting ——— If he Can Conveniently ~

[Reu]ben [Deva]lls [Ca]se whereas there was a Complaint brought Against **Reuben Devil [Davol]** Some months past and he hath not been Sufficiently Laboured with, therefore **Christopher Gifford** and **Ichabod Eddy** are appointed to Labour with him if they have an opportunity and make Report to the next monthly Meeting – –

Meetings Granted in Allens neck The friends in **Allens neck** Requests the liberty to hold a meeting there Some part of this winter therefore this meeting Grants them the liberty to hold a meeting for the three winter months on first days Except the las[t] first days preceding each monthly meeting in Each month This Meeting hath Collected £4=10ˢ:6ᵈ old Tenor – –

Comᵗᵉᵉ to revise the minutes This meeting doth appoint **Peleg Smith, Humphry Smith Joseph Tucker, Philip Tripp** and **Samuel Smith** a Com =mittee to Inspect into the monthly meeting minutes that are put on Record and Correct them where they Shall find it Necessary, and also to form a new minute

Concerning Abig[ail] Kerby or an Addition to the former Concerning **Abigail Kerby [Kirby]** There hath been a Complaint brought against **Benjᵃ**

Complaint against Ben Shearman **Shearman** for his outgoing in Marrying out of the Unity of friends, therefore this meeting doth appoint **Davi[d] Smith** and **Jonathan Hussey** to treat with him and make Report to the next monthly Meeting ~

12ᵗʰ mo: 1763 At a monthly Meeting held at our Meeting House in **Dartmouth** the 19ᵗʰ of the 12ᵗʰ month 176[3] **Ponaganset** meeting Called **Peleg Smith** and **Caleb Russell** present for **Coakset Philip Tripp** and **James Cornel [Cornell]** present

Joshua Barkers paper not Read The Reading [of] **Joshua Barker**s paper hath been Omitte[d] last month therefore **Isaac Smith** is apointed to Be[?] [him?] Some Convenient times between this and the next monthly meeting ~

[Cal]eb Russell [pu]rchased a [boo]k for Records **Caleb Russell** has purchased a Book according to the appointment of last monthly meeting and the price is two Dollars

The women friends Inform that they have Concluded to

[Cloe] Bowen
[R]eceived
accept of **Cloe Bowen** to be under their Care which
which [*sic*] this meeting Concurs with

[Reuben]
Devil
[dis]owned
whereas **Reuben Devil [Davol]** hath been one under our Care, and
he hath Declined attending Meetings for worship and
Discipline, for which he hath been Sufficiently Labour'd
with and declines to make Satisfaction, therefore this
Meeting doth Conclude to Deny him from being under
our Care

[David] Kerby
[d]isowned
whereas **David Kerby [Kirby]** hath Married out of the Unity of
friends for which he hath been Sufficiently Labour'd with
and declines to make Satisfaction, therefore this Meeting
doth Deny him from being under our Care

[Eli]hu Bowens
[c]ase referd
The matter Concerning **Elihu Bowen** is Refer'd to the
next monthly Meeting – –

[B]enj
Shearmans
[C]ase referd
The friends appointed to treat with **Benjª Shearman**
Signify they have not done it therefore they are Still
Continued in the Same Service and to make Report to
the next monthly meeting – –

[pot?] Ink and
[Lo]ck required
This meeting doth appoint **David Smith** to purchase a
Quire of paper and an Ink pot and a Lock to lock the
drawer to put them in for the use of this Meeting
This Meeting has Collected £7=5ˢ=6ᵈ old tenor, and the

[O]rder to pay
[Jo]na Hussey
Treasurer is orderd to pay **Jonathan Hussey** three Dollars
for keeping the Meeting House half a year which he
has accordingly paid

Comᵗᵉᵉ to
Revise the
minuts
This Meeting doth appoint **Peleg Smith, Humphry Smith**
Abraham Tucker Joseph Tucker and **Samuel Smith**
a Committee to peruse the monthly Meeting minutes to
See what part they Shall think proper to be put on
Record, and make Report to the next monthly Meeting

Coakset
meeting
House to
be Enlargᵈ
Coakset prepar[a]tive meeting Signify to this Meeting that
they think it will be Convenient to make Some additi[ons]
to their little meeting House, and also to build a Chimny
Therefore this meeting doth appoint **Paul Russell Barn[abas?]**
Mosher and **Joseph Smith** to Consider how big to build
and also to Compute the Cost as near as they Can and when
to build at all or not, and to make Report to the next
monthly Meeting ~

Queries
answer'd
The Queries have been read, and answers made by
both preparative Meetings

Representatives **Philip Tripp, Humphry Smith** and **Wᵐ Anthony** jᵘⁿ
in Quarter
=ly mee[t]ing are appointed to attend the Quarterly Meeting and
to Compile the answers to the Queries and draw an Epistl[e]
to the Same and bring them to the Adjournment

adjourn And this Meeting is Adjourned to the first Sixth day in
next month – –

mett   This Meeting being met according to adjournment
The Representatives being Called, for **Aponaganset** meeti[ng]
Caleb Russell present for **Coakset** none present –

answer to The friends appointed to Compile the Answers to the
Queries & Queries and to draw an Epistle to the Quarterly Meetin[g]
Epistle
[procured?] have done it according to Appointment, and this
Meeting hath Signed and Sent the Epistle by the
Representatives

---

[1]ˢᵗ mo: At a monthly Meeting held in **Dartmouth**
1764 on the 16: of the first month 1764, **Ponaganset**
Meeting Called **Caleb Russell** and **Daniel Russell**
present, for **Coakset Joshua Devil [Davol]** and **Israel Wood**
[Fr]ancis Coffins present, **Francis Coffin** and **Anne Hussey** Declared their Intentions
[pr]oposal of of Marriage and were desired to wait till the next
[m]arriage monthly Meeting for their Answer

Joshua Barkers Paper of Denial hath been read According
to the Appointment of last monthly Meeting ~
       And is as followeth (viz)

[?], Barkers Whereas **Joshua Barker** Son of **James Barker** Deceased
Denial and **Elizabeth** his wife, he the Said **Joshua Barker**
having been one under our Care and had his Education
among friends, yet he through unwatchfullness Gave
way in three Respects, firstly, in too frequently being
in Company with **Catharine Russell** that brought a
Scandulous Report on the Society, Secondly in declining
to pay the Constable his Tax, Thirdly, in Refusing to
Comply with a Verdi[c]t brought Against him for burning
Some Rails belonging to **Henry Tucker**, and he hath
been Labour'd with in love from time to time for his
misconduct hoping he may make friends Satisfaction
but he Still Remains Obstinate, therefore for the
Clearing of truth we can do no less than Give this
forth as a Publick Testimony Against him the S'ᵈ
Joshua Barker, Denying him to be one in Unity with us
the people Called Quakers, Yet we do Sincerely desire

that he may Come to a Sight and Sense of his Ongoing
and through unfeined Repentance find Mercy
Given forth at Our monthly Meeting held in **Dart**
=**mouth** the 21 of the 11 month 1763, And Signed in
and by order of Said Meeting by **Job Russell** [Clerk?]

Elihu Bow^{en} Case refer^d The matter Concerning **Elihu Bowen** is Refer'd to the next monthly Meeting,

Benj Sher man Ju^r Paper **Benj^a Shearman j^{ur}** hath Sent a paper to this Meeting Condemning his Marrying out of the Unity of friends which hath been taken notice of, and do Refer the matter to the next monthly Meeting for furder Consider[ation]

minuts not revised The Comittee Appointed to peruse the monthly Meeting minutes Signify they have not done it, therefore they are Continued in the Same Service and to make Report to the next monthly Meeting

Report on acoakset meeting house The Com^{ttee} Appointed to Consider about Enlarging the meeting House at **Coakset** and also to Compute the Cost, make Report that they think it will be proper to build a Side flush with the old part and also to Build a Chimny, and they have Computed the Cost as near as they Can which is thirty three Dollars, therefore this meeting Grants Liberty that **Coakset** friends Go on and Build as Above Said

Report from Quar =terly meet =ing The friends appointed to attend the Quarterly meeting make Report that two of them attended the other Sent a Sufficient Excuse, and they have produced an Epistle from the Same which hath been Read in this Meeting and well accepted

M: Wilkerson and R [W]ilbour [d]isowⁿd The women friends Inform that they have Deny'd **Mary Wilkerson** and **Ruhamah Wilbour** for their Marrying out of the Unity of friends which this ^{meeting} Concurs with, and do deny the Same from under our Care

[P]. Allen [R]equests [t]o Come under [f]riends Care [w]ith his [C]hildren, **Prince Allen** Requests to Come under friends Care with his Children, therefore this Meeting doth appoint **Daniel Russell** and **Phillip Allen** and **Humphry Smith** to Confer with him and make Report to the next monthly Meeting

[M]eetings [G]ranted at New Swanzey The friends at **New=Swanzey** desire the Liberty to hold a Meeting among them as often as friends Shall think proper therefore this Meeting doth Grant them the Liberty to hold a meeting two days in a month for two months, one

on the first first day in the month, the other on the third
first day of the month;

Timothy Shear
[m]an Ju^r
[dis order?]

The Visitors Inform that **Timothy Shearman Ju^r** hath
Set up a Publishment, by which we Conclude he Intends to
Marry out of the Good order of friends, and he hath been
Labour'd with and declines to Retracts his Intentions
therefore **Joseph Gifford** and **Wm Barker** are Appointed
to tell him if he Shall Continue in his proceedings that he
may Expect to be denied and they to Labour with him
as they Shall find freedom

[?] Printing
[G]eorge Foxes
[Jo]urnal refer'd

Proposals of Printing **George Fox**es Journals in **London**
by way of Subscription hath been Presented to this Meeting
which is Refer'd to the next monthly Meeting for
furder notice²

[Ca]leb Russell
[is?] paid for the
[Bo]ok for records

This Meeting hath Collected and Paid **Caleb Russell**
two Dollars for the Book for Records; ~

2^d mo:
1764

At a monthly meeting held in **Dartmouth** the 20th
of the 2^d month 1764, **Ponaganset** meeting Called **Wm Bar[ker?]**
and **David Smith** present, for **Coakset Joseph Tripp** and
Peter Devil [Davol] present;

Francis
Coffins
Certificate

Francis Coffin hath Produced a Certificate from the monthly
Meeting of **Nantucket**, Certifying him to be of an Orderly
life and Conservation and Clear from any Entanglement
Relating marriage which this Meeting accepts

Francis
Coffins
answer

Francis Coffin and **Ann Hussey** did appear for their answer
which was that they might Proceed to take each other in
Marriage in Some Convenient time between this and th[e]
next monthly Meeting Observing the Good order Establis[hed]
among us in the Performance ther[e]of and **Caleb Russell** an[d]
David Smith are appointed to see their Marriage Consumat[ed]
in Said order and make Report to the mext [*sic*] monthly Meeting

E. Bowen Rec^d

This Meeting doth accept of **Elihu Bowen** to be under our Ca[re]

Jacob Motts
paper accep=
=ted

This Meeting doth accept of **Jacob Mott**s paper Condemning his
outgoings in taking too much Spirituous Liquor, hoping h[e]
may Conduct better for time to Come – –

Prince Allen

The matter Concerning **Prince Allen**s Request to Come und[er]

2. *A Journal or Historical Account of the Life, Travels, Sufferings, Christian Experiences, and Labour of
Love in the Work of the Ministry of That Ancient, Eminent and Faithful Servant of Jesus Christ*, George Fox
was first published in London 1694. The third edition was printed in London by Richardson and Clark
in 1765.

request refer'd friends Care with his Children is Refer'd to the next month[ly]
Meeting, and the Same friends are Still Continued in that
Service and to make Report to the next monthly Meeting – –

Timothy Sher =man Ju^t Case referd The matter Concerning **Timothy Shearman ju^r** is Refer'd
to the next monthly Meeting; – –

The women friends Inform that they have accepted of

R. Cornel Rec'd **Rebeccah Cornel [Cornell]** to be under their Care which this Meeting
Concurs with

meetings Granted in Allens Neck This Meeting Grants the friends in **Allens neck** th[e]
Liberty to hold a meeting there one month longer as heretofore

John Potter overseer of the poor This Meeting doth appoint **John Potter** overseer of the poor ([?]
Nicholas Howland) in lieu of **Paul Russell** and they to make
Report once a Quarter – –

[Ca]se of Benj [She]arman Ju^r refer'd The matter Concerning **Benjamin Shearman ju^r** is Referd
to the Next monthly Meeting;

[3?] mo 1764 At a monthly Meeting held in **Dartmouth** on the
19th day of the 3^d month 1764, **Ponaganset** meeting Called
David Smith and **William Anthony ju^r** present, for **Coakset**
Peter Devil [Davol] and **Philip Tripp** present

[Jos]eph Howland [pro]posal of mar[ri]age [D]aniel Smith proposal of [m]arriage **Joseph Howland** & **Bershebe Shearman** and **Daniel Smith** and
Rebecca Cornel [Cornell] declared their Intentions of Marriage and
were desired to wait till the next monthly Meeting for their
answer, and **Benjamin Howland ju^r** and **John Potter** are
appointed to make Inquiry into the young mens Clearness
as to Marriage and Conversation and make Report to the
next monthly Meeting – –

[Re]port of ~~Fran~~ [F]rancis Coffins marriage The friends appointed to See **Francis Coffin** and **Ann Hussey**s
Marriage Consumated make Report that they attended the
Marriage and Saw nothing but that it was accomplished
in Good order

[Pr]ince Allen [R]equest refer^d The matter Concerning **Prince Allen**s Request to Come
under friends Care with his Children is Refer'd to the next
monthly meeting and the Same friends that were appointed
to discourse with them two months ago are still Continued in
the Same Service & to make Report to the next monthly Meeting,

T. Shear= man dis= own'd whereas **Timothy Shearman ju^r** hath Married out of the order
of friends, and he hath been Sufficiently Labour'd with, and
he Refusing to adhere to friends Cautions and Labour of love
therefore this Meeting doth deny him the Said **Timothy**
Shearman to be one in Unity with us and from under our Care

[Ca]se of Benj Shearman Ju^r referd	The matter Concerning **Benj^a Shearman ju**: is Refer'd to the next monthly Meeting;
[Jo?]ne Soule Receiv'd	The women friends Inform that they have Concluded to accept of **Jone Soule** to be under the Care of friends which this Meetin[g] Concurs with;
Building at coakset meeting house	This Meeting appoints **Ichabod Eddy** and **Josep[h] Tripp** ~~are~~ to Carry on the Rebuilding of **Coakset** meeting Hou[se]
To collect account of Publick friends deceased	This meeting appoints the Elders of **Aponaganset** and **Coakse[t]** a Committee to Collect an Account of the deaths of Public friends that have happened ~~from~~ for Some time past and bring them to the Adjournment;
Complaint against Benj Tripp	**Coakset** friends Preparitive meeting Inform that **Benj^a Tripp** hath Gone Contrary to friends orders in Opposin[g] the Constable in Distraining for a Tax and he hath been Labo[ured] with by the Visitors and has not made Satisfaction therefore this meeting doth appoint **Peleg Smith Humphry Smith** and **William Anthony ju**: a Committee to Labour furder with h[?] and make Report to the next monthly Meeting ~
Queries Answer^d	The Queries have been Read and answers prepar'd from both preparitive Meetings and Read in this Meeting,
Representa=tives	**Joseph Tucker Peleg Smith Philip Tripp Samuel Smith** and **Peter Devil [Davol]** are appointed to attend the Quarterly Meeting and Compile the Answers to the Queries and draw an Epistle to the Same,_^^{& bring them to the} Adjournment
Complaint against Benj Devil	**Benjamin Devil [Davol]** hath Married out of the order of friends and hath also had a Child Soon after Marriage and hat[h] been Labour'd with and Declines to make Satisfaction Therefore this Meeting doth appoint **Christopher Gifford** a[nd] **Ichabod Eddy** to labour furder with him and make Report to the next monthly Meeting, This Meeting hath Colle[cted]
order to pay Antipas Hathaway	£3–11^s–8^d old tenor and the Treasurer is orderd to pay **An[tipas] Hathaway** 10 Shillings Lawfull money for mending Glass a[t?] the meeting House; This Meeting adjourns to the Sixth day
adjourn	of next month ~
mett	This Meeting being met according to Adjournment the Sixth day of the 4th month 1764 the Representatives
[ep]istles & [an]swers to [qu]eries Sent	all present, This meeting hath Signed and Sent an Epistle to the Quarterly Meeting and also hath Sent the Answers to the Queries by the Representatives
death of Publick Friends	The Elders brought the Account of the deaths of Publick friends to this Meeting

4th month
1764

At a monthly Meeting held in **Dartmouth** b/y on the 16ᵗʰ
of the 4ᵗʰ mo: 1764 **Ponaganset** meeting Called **Caleb Russell**
and **William Anthony ju**ʳ present, for **Coakset Peleg Hud=**
=dlestone present,

[Jo]seph
Howland
Daniel Smith
[C]learness

The friends appointed to Enquire into **Joseph Howland**s and
Danil [Daniel] Smiths Clearness as to Marriage and Conversation
make Report that they do'nt find anything to hinder
their Proceeding in Marriage; – –

[Jos]eph
Howlands
Daniel Smiths
answer

Joseph Howland and **Bershebe Shearman Danil [Daniel] Smith** and
Rebecca Cornel [Cornell] did appear for their Answer and their
Answer was that they might Proceed to take each other
in Marriage in Some Convenient time between this
and the next monthly Meeting observing the Good order
used amongst us and **John Potter** and **Benj**ᵃ **Howland ju**ʳ
are appointed to See **Joseph Howland**s and **Barshebe [Bershebe] Shearman**s
Marriage Consumated in Sᵈ order and make Report to the
next monthly meeting, and **William Anthony ju**ʳ
and **Samuel Smith** are appointed for the Same Service
at the Marriage of **Daniel Smith** and **Rebecca Cornel [Cornell]** and
they to make Report to the next monthly meeting

[Pr]ince Allen
[&?]Children
Received

This Meeting doth accept of **Prince Allen** and his Children
to be under our Care for time to Come

[Ca]se of Benj
Shearman Ju
refereᵈ

the matter Concerning **Benj**ᵃ **Shearman ju**ʳ is Refer'd to
the next monthly Meeting

Benj Tripp
Case Suspen
=ded

The Comm[i]ttee appointed to Labour with **Benj**ᵃ **Tripp**
make Report that he ought to Condemn his Opposing the
officer in the manner he did and he Cannot find freedom to
Comply with their Judgment at present Therefore the matter
is Suspended ~

Report from
Quarterly
meeting

The friends appointed to attend the Quarterly Meeting make
Report that they ˄ᵃˡˡ attended it and have produced an Epistle from
the Same which was Read in this Meeting and well Accepted

Benj Deval
refer'd

The matter Concerning **Benj**ᵃ **Deval [Davol]** is Refered to the next mont[hly]
Meeting and the same friends are Still Continued in the Same Servi[ce]
and they to draw up a paper of Denial against him if they think
Necessary and bring it to the next monthly meeting;

Antp⁽ᵗ⁾ *Hath=*
=away is paid

The treasurer has paid **Antipas Hathaway** ten Shillin[gs]
for mending Glass;

Wᵐ Sanford
& David
Smith acompt

William Sanford and **David Smith** has Brought in an
account to this meeting for Repairing the Stable belong[ing to?]

this Meeting and the lock the drawer and one Quire of Pap[er]
and one Ink Stand; all £27=16ˢ–6ᵈ Old tenor which this
meeting accepts

Philip Trafford
request for
his Children
accepted

Philip Trafford Requests that his Children that he had by
his first wife be taken under friends Care which this meet[ing]
Grants and accepts them to be under Our Care for the time to Com[e]

L. Cornel
Rec'd

The women friends Inform that they have Accepted of **Lyd[ia?]**
Cornel [Cornell] to be under their Care which this Meeting Concurs with

---

5 mo:
1764

At a monthly Meeting held in **Dartmouth** the 21 of [?]
5ᵗʰ month 1764 **Ponaganset** Meeting Called **Joseph Smith** and
Samuel Smith present for **Coakset Daniel Wood** present,
John Potter and **Benjamin Howland ju**: make report that h[e]

Report of
Jos[?] Howland
marriage

attended the Marriage of **Joseph Howland** and **Barshebe [Bershebe] Shea[rman]**
and Saw nothing but that it was Accomplished in Good order
William Anthony juʳ and **Samuel Smith** Report that they

Report of
Dan Smiths
Marriage

attended the marriage of **Daniel Smith** and **Rebecca Cornel [Cornell]**
and Saw nothing but it was likewise Accomplished in
Good Order – –

[Ca]se of Benj
[She]arman Juʳ
[r]eferd

The matter Concerning **Benjamin Shearman juʳ** is Refer'd
to the next monthly Meeting and **Peleg Smith** and **William**
Anthony juʳ are Appointed to discourse with him Concerning his
not attending meetings and make Report to the next
monthly Meeting, The matter Concerning **Benjamin Devil [Davol]** is
Refer'd to the next monthly meeting; – –

[?] take Sub=
[=sc]riptions
for [Geo]rg Foxes
[Jo]urnals

Samuel Smith is appointed to take the Subscribtions [subscriptions] for
George Fox's Journals and Endeavour to Collect the Money
and Send it up to the Yearly Meeting; – –

N. Sisson
Rec'd &
L. Shear=
[=]man denied

the women friends Inform that they have accepted of **Naomy**
Sisson to be Under their Care and that they have denied
Lydia Shearman from being one under their Care both which
this Meeting Concurs with;

Complaint
[a]gainst
Wilcox

There hath been a Report brought to this Meeting that **Stephen**
Wilcox hath So Conducted in time past that he hath very
much fallen Short of discharging many of his debts which
hath been due, which Seems to be of an attendency to bring
a Reproach on friends therefore **Peter Devil [Davol] Philip Tripp**
Peleg Huddlestone Joseph Gifford and **Joseph Tucker** are
Appointed a Comittee of Enquiry and to discourse with him
and make Report to the Adjournment of this Meeting

adjourn

This Meeting Adjourns to the 30ᵗʰ of this month

mett This Meeting being mett according to Adjournment the 30ᵗʰ
of the 5th month 1764 the Representatives being Called for
Ponaganset Samuel Smith present, for **Coakset** none present

[C]ase of Stephen the Committee make Report that **Stephen Wilcox** desires that
[W]ilcox referᵈ friends would wait untill the next monthly meeting therefore
the matter is Refer'd to Sᵈ meeting; – –

[Co]mplaint **Lusana Russell** has Exhibited a Complaint against **Job How=**
[ag]ainst Job =**land** for Refusing to Leave a Contr,ᵒversy Subs,ⁱˢting Between them
Howland to Arbitration, therefore **Barnabas Mosher** and **Luke Hart** are
appointed a Committee of Enquiry and they to advise **Job Howland**
to leave it to men if they think Necessary and make
Report to the next monthly meeting;

---

6 mo: At a monthly Meeting held in **Dartmouth** the
1764 18ᵗʰ of the 6ᵗʰ month 1764 **Ponaganset** meeting Called

~~*Stephen*~~ **Peleg Smith** and **Joseph Smith** present for **Coakset** for
~~*Wilcox case*~~ **Joshua Devil [Davol]** present – –
~~*referᵈ*~~

Stephen **Stephen Hathaway** and **Abigail Smith** did lay their
Hathway Intention of Marriage and were desired to wait till the
proposal of next monthly Meeting for their Answer
marriage

Case of Ben The matter Concerning **Benjaⁿ Shearman juʳ** is Refer'd
Shearman to the next monthly meeting, as is likewise that of **Benjᵃ**
refered

Case of Ben **Devil [Davol]** – –
Devil referd

Money Collec **Samuel Smith** has answered the Appointment of last
=ted for 12 monthly meeting and Collected money Enough for twelve
Books mo of **Fox**'s Journals – –

meetings It is the advice of this Meeting that if **Stephen Wilcox** Can't
advice to discharge his debts no otherwise he ought to deliver up his
Stephen Estate to his Creditors and Notify them all as Soon as may
Wilcox be, and the Same Committee is Still Continued to Notify him
of the Conclusion of this Meeting and assist him in advice
and make Report to the next monthly Meeting; –

Henry Our Esteemed friend **Henry Stanton** has Visited this
Stantons Meeting with a Certificate from **Carterite [Carteret]**
Visit In **North Carolina** dated the 18ᵗʰ of the 4ᵗʰ mo: 1764 which being Read
was kindly accepted.

Friends **Peleg Smith Humphry Smith Philip Tripp** are Appointed
appointed to attend the Quarterly meeting and draw an Epistle to the
for Quarter Same and bring it to the adjournment; – –
=ly meeting

Case of The ^ᶠʳⁱᵉⁿᵈˢ appointed to Inquire into the Controversey between
Job How= **Job Howland** and **Lusanna Russell** make Report that they
=land

think it Necessary to Leave it to men and that they
advised them to do it which ∧ʰᵉ Refused therefore **Joseph
Smith** and **Joseph Gifford** are appointed to Labour
furder with him and make Report to the next
monthly Meeting;

[words crossed out for last two lines]

[or]der to pay
[Jon]athan
Hu]sey
This Meeting has Collected 4ᵉ–4ˢ–11ᵈ old tenor and the
Treasurer is order'd to pay **Jonathan Hussie [Hussey]** three Dollars
for keeping the Meeting House half a year

[adj]ourn
[m]ett
This meeting adjourns to the first Sixth day in next month
This meeting being met according to adjournment the 6 of the 7ᵗʰ
month 1764 the Representatives being Called for **Ponaganset**
Peleg Smith and **Joseph Smith** present for **Coakset** none pre==sent

[ans]wrs
[to] the
[Que]ries
The Queries have been Read and answers prepared from both
preparitive meetings and **Peleg Smith Humphry Smith** and
Wᵐ Anthony juʳ are appointed to Compile the answers to the
Queries and Deliver them to the Representatives
This meeting has Signed and ordered to be Sent an Epistle to the
Quarterly meeting by the Representatives

[Ru]th
[Ed]dy
[de]nied
The women friends Inform that they have Concluded to deny
Ruth Eddy therefore **david Smith** is appointed to draw a paper
of Denial against her and bring it to the next monthly meeting

---

7ᵗʰ mo:1764
At a monthly Meeting held at **Dartmouth** the 16ᵗʰ of the
7ᵗʰ month 1764 **Ponaganset** meeting Called **David Smith** and **Samˡˡ [Samuel]**
Smith present for **Coakset Joseph Tripp** and **Ichabod Eddy** present

Stephen
Hathaway
certifi=
[=ca]te
Stephen Hathaway produced a Certificate from **Sandwich** monthly meet=
=ing Certifying his Clearness as to Marriage and Conversation in a
degree Clear – –

Stephen
Hathaways
[an]swer
Stephen Hathaway and **Abigail Smith** did appear for their answer
which was that they might proceed to take each other in marriage
in Some Convenient time between this and the next monthly Mee=
=ting Observing the Good order Established Amongst us in the perfor=
=mance thereof and **William Anthony** and **Daniel Russell** are
appointed to See their Marriage Consumated in S,ᵈ order and make
Report to the next monthly Meeting

Jemima
Hoxie
Receivd
Jemima Hoxie has Produced a Certificate from the monthly meeting
of **Sandwich** dated the 29 of the 6ᵗʰ mo: 1764 Informing of her being of
an orderly life and Conversation and under their Care and that
She has Settled her outward affairs which this meeting accepts and She
to be under our Care

Mary Tuc=
=ker
Received   **Mary Tucker** hath Produced a Certificate from **Sandwich**
monthly Meeting held the 29th of the 6 mo: 1764 which Informs
her being in a Good degree of an orderly life and Conversation
which this meeting accepts and She to be under our Care for
the time to Come – –

Ben Sher   The matter Concerning **Benjª Shearman ju:** is Refer'd to the
=man case
referd   next monthly meeting

Jos Taber Ju   **Joseph Taber ju:** has produced a paper to this meeting Condem[n]ing
his paper   his falling into the Sin of fornication which this meeting
appoints **Caleb Russell** to See that it be Red [read] at the end of a first day
meeting for worship at **Quishnet** and he to be present and make
Report to the next monthly Meeting, and when Said paper be
Read as afforesaid this meeting Concludes to accept of it for

Case of   Satisfaction;   The matter Concerning **Benjª Deval** [**Davol**] is
Benj Deval
referd   Refer'd to the next monthly meeting; – –

The case   the Committee appointed to have the Care of **Stephen Wilcox**'s
of Stephen
Wilcox   affair make Report that he did not fully Comply with the Conclu:
=sion of last monthly meeting therefore the Same Committee are
Still Continued to Repeat the Same advice to him and also to Inform
him that this Meeting desires him Imediately to Comply with
the above Said advice and if he do'nt he must Expect to be
dealt with as an offender

Report   The friends appointed to attend the Quarterly meeting being
from
Quarterly   Called upon make Report that they did all attend it and have
meeting   produced an Epistle from the Same which was Red to Good Satisfaction

Epistles   This Meeting Received two Epistles from **London** one written
received   the other Printed which was Read to Good Satisfaction, and
as they Contain many wholsome Exhortations and advices, they
are Recommended to friends Observation; – –
This meeting likewise Received an Epistle from the yearly mee=
=ting at **Philadelphia** dated the 9th mo: 1763 and one from our
last yearly meeting held at **Newport** on **Rhode Island**
This ₍meeting₎ adjourns to the 25th day of this Instant
This meeting being Met According to Adjournment the
Representatives being Called for **Ponaganset** meeting **David
Smith** and **Samuel Smith** present for **Coakset** none present

Testimony   This meeting has Signed a paper of Denial against **Ruth Eddy**
[a]gainst
Ruth Eddy   for falling into the Sin of fornication which is Evident by her
having a Child Soon after Marriage and **Peleg Huddlestone**
is appointed to Read it or Get Some body to Read it at the end

of a first day meeting of worship at **Coakset** meeting house
and make Report to the next monthly meeting;

[C]ase of
Job How=
[=]land

The Committee appointed last monthly meetyng to Labour with
Job Howland make Report that he declines to leave the Contro=
=versey to men therefore **Jonathan Hussie [Hussey] Joseph Smith** and **Wᵐ**
Anthony ju: are appointed a Committee to have them face to face
and to Labour to Reconcile them and if they Can't to advise
them to leave their Controversy to men [*word crossed out*] if they think pro=
=per and make Report to the next monthly meeting

8ᵗʰ mo:
1764

At a monthly Meeting held in **Dartmouth** the 20th of the 8ᵗʰ 1764
Ponaganset meeting Called **James Shearman** and **Caleb Russell**
present, for **Coakset Peter Devil [Davol]** present and the other friend that
was appointed at **Coakset** Sent an Excuse which this meeting

report of
Stephen
Hathaways
marriage

thinks Sufficient
the friends appointed to See **Stephen Hathaway** and **Abigail Smith**s
marriage Consumated make Report that they attended the
marriage and Saw nothing but that it was accomplished in Good Order

Benj Sher
man Juʳ
paper
accepted

This ^meeting doth accept of **Benjᵃ Shearman ju:** his paper for Satisfaction
Condeming his misconduct in marriage and he to be under our Care
for the time to Come

Caleb Russell makes Report that **Joseph Taber ju:**'s paper has
been Read According to the Appointment of last monthly meeting
which is as followeth (viz)

Dartmouth the 22 of the first month 1764

J. Taber
Repen:

dear friends;

Whereas I **Joseph Taber juʳ** of **Dartmouth** have had my Educati=
=on among Friends in a Sober manner and am also fully persuaded
and Confirmed in my mind of the Truth of the Doctrines and
Principles held forth by them; have notwithstanding through
unwatchfullness and not taking that heed which I ought to have
done to that Divine Principle of Light and Grace fallen into
the Sin of Fornication which is Evident by my wive's having
a Child Soon after Marriage, also my being married out of
the Unity of friends, all which I do hereby Condem, and am
heartily Sorry for, and desire the Lord may forgive me and
friends pass it by and let me Remain Under their Care
their Labour of love with me I do Gratefully acknowledge
and hope it may not prove Labour lost

from your friend **Joseph Taber juʳ**

Case of Ben
Devil
referd

The matter Concerning **Benjamin Devil [Davol]** is Refered to next

monthly meeting and **Christopher Gifford** and **Ichabod Eddy** are
appointed to have the Care of the affair and make Report to the
next monthly meeting; – –

Peleg Huddlestone makes Report that **Ruth Eddy**s paper of
Denial hath been Read according to the appointment of last

R. Eddy monthly Meeting;   which is as follows,
disowned

Whereas **Ruth Eddy** Daughter of **William Gifford** [d?] and
Patience his wife was Educated in the profession of us the people
Called Quakers in **Dartmouth** and did Some times frequent our
Religious meetings, but for want of faithfull adherence to the
dictates of that Divine Principal which was Sufficient to have
preserved her, hath been prevailed on to Give way to the tem=
=tation of the enemy So far as to be Guilty of the Sin of Fornicatio[n]
as doth appear by her having a Child Soon after marriage
and Notwithstanding She hath been duly admonished & advised
in order to bring her to a Sight of her misconduct, but She
Still Remaining Obstinate, we do therefore hereby disown
the Said **Ruth Eddy** to be of our Society until She Come to
witness that Godly Sorrow which worketh true Repentance
which that the Lord may mercifully Grant her is our Sincere
desire;   Signed by order and in behalf of the above S'ᵈ people
in their monthly meeting held in **Dartmouth** by adjournment
the 25ᵗʰ of the 7ᵗʰ month 1764 by   **Job Russell** Clerk
                                              Elisabeth Smith Clerk

Affair of   for this day – –
[Stephen?]
Wilcox referd The affair Concerning **Stephen Wilcox** is Refer'd to the next
monthly meeting; – –

The Committee appointed to Inspect into the Controversy Subsisting
between **Job Howland** and **Lusanna Russell** make Report that
it was their advice that he ought to leave to men the Controversey
which he Refuses to do therefore he is looked upon as an offender and
John Russell 2ᵈ **John Potter** **Wᵐ Barker** are appointed to Inform
him of the Judgment of this meeting, and to Labour with him as

[V]isitors they Shall find freedom and make Report to the next monthly meeting
It is the Conclusion of this meeting that the Visitors do Still Continue
[Elijah?] Russel in the Same Service for one month longer · –
request a
[Cer]tificate **Elijah Russell** Desires a Certificate to the monthly meeting of
Swanzey Signifying his Clearness Respecting Marriage and
Conversation, therefore **Humphry Smith** and **Benjᵃ Howland** 2ᵈ
are appointed to Inspect into his Conversation and draw one for him

[Be]nj Tripps
Case

if they think proper and bring it to the next monthly meeting
The matter Concerning **Benjᵃ Tripp** hath Laid Several months
and nothing done therefore **Peleg Huddlestone** and **John Mosher**
are appointed to treat with him on that matter and make
Report to the next monthly meeting; ~

9 mo:⎫
1764⎭

At a monthly Meeting held in **Dartmouth** the 17ᵗʰ of the 9ᵗʰ
month 1764 **Ponaganset** meeting Called **Joseph Smith** and
Daniel Russell present, for **Coaset Christopher Gifford** and

Benj Devil
Case referᵈ

David Devil [**Davol**] present;
The matter Concerning **Benjᵃ Devil** [**Davol**] is Refer'd to the next monthly
meeting and **Christopher Gifford** is Still Continued according to the
appointment of last monthly meeting ~
the matter Concerning **Stephen Wilcox** is Refer'd to next monthly

Ann Coffin
Certificate

meeting; This Meeting has Signed and Sent a Certificate to the
monthly meeting of **Nantucket** ₍ᶠᵒʳ **Ann Coffin** Certifying her being in a

[Job?] Howland
[Case] referᵈ

Good degree of an orderly life and Conversation and under our Care
the matter Concerning **Job Howland** is Refer'd to the next

[Elij?] Russel
[certi]fi=
[=cate]

monthly meeting
This meeting has Signed a Certificate for **Elijah Russell** to the
monthly meeting of **Swanzey** Certifying his Clearness from any
Entanglement Respecting Marriage and in a degree of an

Joseph
Mosher
request

orderly Conversation – –
Joseph Mosher and his wife Requests to Come under friends Car[e]
therefore **Christopher Gifford** and **David Devil** [**Davol**] are Appointed to
take an Opportunity of Conference with him on that account

B. Tripp
accepted

and make Report to the next monthly meeting;
Benjamin Tripp hath appeared in this meeting and made

Certificate
requested
for Giles
Russell

friends Such Satisfaction as they have taken up with
Daniel Russell Requests a Removal Certificate for his Son
Giles to the **Oblong**, therefore **Jonathan Hussey** and **David**
Smith are Appointed to draw one if they think proper and to
make Enquiry into his life and Conversation and bring it to the

Queries
answered

next monthly meeting ~
The Queries have been Read and Answers prepared by ~~both~~
Ponaganset preparative meeting, **Joseph Tucker** and his Son

Job Howland
Case Sent to
Quar meet=ing

Barziller Tucker are Appointed to draw an Epistle to the Quarterl[y]
meeting and bring it to the adjournment – –
The like Case of **Job Howland**, is to be Sent up to the Quarterly

adjournᵈ

meeting for advice – –

mett

This meeting Adjourns to the first Sixth day in next month

This meeting being met according to Adjournment the
Representatives being Called **Daniel Russell Joseph Smith**

[R.?]Willis Visit and **David Devil [Davol]** present,

Our Esteemed friend **Robert Willis** hath Visited this meeting
with a Certificate from the monthly meeting of **Woodbridge**
in **New=Jersey** dated the 16th 5 mo: 1764 which was Read and

Chusing Visitors referᵈ well Accepted

the matter Concerning Chusing Visitors and Overseers is Refer['d]
to the next monthly meeting

Friends for Quar- meeting **Joseph Tucker, Abraham Tucker, Philip Tripp** are Appointed
to attend the Quarterly meeting and present the Epistle and
make Report to the next monthly meeting

This meeting hath Signed and Sent an Epistle to the Quarterly

Collection referᵈ Meeting by the Representatives

10ᵗʰ mo ⎱ the Quarterly Collection is Refer'd to the next monthly meeting
1764 ⎰

At a monthly Meeting held in **Dartmouth** the 15th of the 10th
Month 1764, **Ponaganset** Meeting Called **Joseph Smith** and **Benja
=min Howland** juʳ present, for **Coakset Ichabod Eddy** and **Israel**

[Benj Wings proposal of marriage?] **Wood** present,

Benjᵃ Wing and **Mary Potter** declared their Intentions of Marriage
and were desired to wait til the monthly meeting for their
answer and **Peleg Huddlestone** and **Joseph Tripp** are appointed
to make Enquiry into **Benjᵃ Wing**, Clearness as to Marriage and
Conversation and likewise to see if **Mary Potters** Estate be Settled
So that her Children be not hurt by her Said Marriage and make

[Ca]se of [B]enj Deval [re]ferᵈ Report to the next monthly meeting

The affair of **Benjᵃ Deval [Davol]** is Refer'd to the next monthly meeting
and **Philip Allen** and **Adam Gifford** are appointed to have an
Inspection over him and his Conduct and make Report to

[Step?] Wilcox Case refereᵈ the next monthly Meeting

[Job?] How- [-]lands [Case?] referd **Stephen Wilcox**s Case is Refer'd to the next monthly meeting

The Case of **Job Howland** is Refer'd to the next monthly meeting
on the account of Informing him of the Result of the Quarterly
meeting and **Peleg Smith** is appointed to Inform him of Said

Giles Russells certificate Result and make Report to the next monthly Meeting;

This Meeting hath Signed a Removal Certificate for **Giles
Russell** Certifying him to be in a degree of an orderly Conversation
and under our Care directed to the monthly meeting of the **Oblong**

a Comᵗᵉᵉ to advise with[?] in Lawsuits **Humphry Smith Joseph Tucker William Barker** are
appointed a Standing Comittee pursuant to the direction

overseers of meeting house of the late Book of Discipline in page 138
Jonathan Hussie [Hussey], David Smith, Samuel Smith, Benjamin Howland ju: William Mosher, Israel Wood, Joshua Cornel [Cornell] David Devil [Davol] are Apointed to have the oversight of the people in the Galleries and other Seats at our next Annual Meeting both here & at **Coakset** and to make Report to the next monthly meeting

Joseph Moshers Case The friends Appointed to Confer with **Joseph Mosher** make Report that they have not both Confer'd with him by reas[on?] of Indisposion, therefore **Ichabod Eddy** and **David Devil [Davol]** are Appointed for the Same Service and they to make Re:

Wᵐ Hath= [=]away request =port to the next monthly Meeting;
William Hathaway Requests to Come under Care of friends, therefore **Joseph Smith** and **Luke Hart** are Appointed a Committee to Confer with him on that account and make Report to the next monthly Meeting

H. Mosher Recᵈ The [*word crossed out*] women friends Inform that they have minuted **Hannah Mosher** wife to **Wᵐ Mosher** under their Care which this Meeting Concurs with

11 mo: 1764 At a monthly meeting held in **Dartmouth** on the 19ᵗʰ day of the 11ᵗʰ month 1764 **Ponaganset** Meeting Called **Joseph Smith** and **William Anthony ju:** present

Benj Wing Clearness for **Coakset John Mosher** and **Joseph Tripp** present, The friends appointed to Inspect into **Benjamin Wing**s Clear =ness as to Marriage and Conversation make Report that they have made Enquiry and do not find any thing to hinder his Proceeding in Marriage and also that the widows Estate

B. Wings answer is Settled according to friends orders;
Benjamin Wing and **Mary Potter** appeared for their Answer, which was that they might proceed to take each other in Marriage in Some Convenient time between this and the next monthly meeting, Observing the Good order Established amongst us in the performance thereof and **Peleg Huddlestone** and **Joseph Tripp** are appointed to See their Marriage Consumated in Said order and make

[Benj Devil case?] referd Report to the next monthly meeting
The matter Concerning **Benjamin Devil [Davol]** is Refer'd to the next monthly Meeting; and the Same Committees are Still Continued in the Same Service and to Return the paper to him and Inform him that there is a deficiency and make Report to the next

[*M. Kerby And M. Mosher Rec'd?*] monthly meeting;

The women friends Inform that they have minuted **Mary Kerby** [**Kirby**] and **Meribah Mosher** under their Care which this Meeting Concurs with

The Case of **Stephen Wilcox** is Refer'd to the next monthly meeting

[*J. How: =land denied*] Whereas, there hath been a Complaint Exhibited against **Job Howland** by **Lusanna Russell** for Refusing to leave a Contro= =versey Subsisting between them to Arbitration, and he hath been Sufficiently Laboured with and he appears Obstinate and Refuses friends Advice, therefore this Meeting for the Clearing of the Blessed truth doth deny the S,ᵈ **Job Howland** from being one under our Care

adjourn This Meeting Adjourns till tomorrow at the tenth hour in

mett the fore noon

This Meeting being met according to Adjournment the 20ᵗʰ 11:ᵐᵒ: 1764 the Representives being Called for **Ponaganset** meeting both present for **Coakset Joseph Tripp** present the other Repre:ᵗⁱᵛᵉ

[*overseers of meetg house report?*] has made an Excuse for his absence which this meeting accepts

The friends Appointed to have the oversight of the people in the Galleries and other Seats at our Annual Meeting being Called upon make Report that they attended Agreeable to

[*J.*] *Mosher Rec'd* appointment and that the people behaved in a Good degree orderly; The Committee Appointed to Confer with **Joseph Mosher** make Report that he Gave them Good Satisfaction Therefore this Meeting doth accept and minute him under

over= seers our Care

Chosen This Meeting appoints **Joshua Devel** [**Davol**] and **Israel Wood** Overseers for **Coakset**, and also appoints **William Anthony ju:** and **Job Russell** Overseers for **Ponaganset**, and also appoints **Luke**

Visitors **Hart and Barziller Tucker** overseers from **Newtown**

This Meeting Appoints **Abraham Tucker** and **Caleb Russell** Visitors for **Ponaganset** , and **Peter Deuel** [**Devol**]

Wᵐ Hathway Recᵈ and **Philip Tripp** Visitors for **Coakset**

The Comittee Appointed to Confer with **Wᵐ Hathaway** make Report that he Gave them Good Satisfaction

Meetings Granted therefore this Meeting Minutes him under our Care

This Meeting Grants the friends living in **Allens neck** Liberty to hold a Meeting down there at some friends House three first days in a month for three winter Months and the first Spring Month, Excepting the first days that precede

Complaint against Isaac Howland the monthly Meetings

Whereas, **Isaac Howland ju:** hath Married out of the Unity

of friends, and hath been in the Practice of the Slave
Trade, and hath never Condemned them to friends Satisfaction

Nat Sowle Jr   which is Refered to the next Monthly Meeting;
Request

Nathaniel Soule ju: Requests to Come under friends Care
Therefore **Ichabod Eddy** and **Israel Wood** are Appointed to
take an Oppertunity of Conference with him, and make

Jos Mosher   Report to the next Monthly Meeting
requesta
Certificate **Joseph Mosher** desires a Removal Certificate to **Smithfield**
Therefore **Isael [Israel] Wood** and **Philip Tripp** are Appointed to make
Enquiry into his Outward Affairs, and draw one for him

To draw a if they think proper and bring it to the next Monthly Meeting
Certificate
for Mathew This Meeting Appoints **Humphry Smith** and **William**
Franklin **Anthony ju**ⁿ to draw a Certificate for **Matthew Franklin**
and bring it to the next Monthly Meeting;

12 mo 1764

At a Monthly Meeting held in **Dartmouth** the 17ᵗʰ of the
12ᵗʰ month 1764, **Ponaganset** Meeting Called **David Smith** and
Wᵐ Anthony ju: present, for **Coakset, Philip Tripp** and **Israel**

[?]the **Wood** present,
[?]
[?] of **William Hathaway** and **Ruth Barker** Declared their Intentions of
[MA]rriage Marriage, and were desired to wait until the next monthly Meet=
=ing for their Answer and **Caleb Russell** and **Joseph Smith** are
Appointed to Make Enquiry into the young mans Clearness as to

[B] Marriage and Conversation and Make Report to the next Monthly
[Da]vil
[di]sowned meeting; Whereas **Benjᵃ Davil [Davol]** hath fallen into the Sin of
fornication and he hath been Sufficiently dealt with and Refuses to
make friends Satisfaction; therefore this Meeting thinks best for the
Clearing of the Blessed truth to disown him, and do Appoint **Isaac**
Smith to draw up a paper of denial Against him and bring it to the

[report?] of next Monthly Meeting;
[?] Wings
[Mar]riage The friends Appointed to See **Benjᵃ Wing**, and **Mary Potters** Marriage
Consumated Make Report that they attended the Marriage, and that

[?] of Step it was Consumated in tolerable good order;
[Wil]cox
referd The Case of **Stephen Wilcox** is Refered to the next monthly Meeting As is

[?] of Isaac likewise the Matter Concerning **Isaac Howland ju**ⁿ – – and the Represen=
[How]land
[?] =tatives to the Quarterly Meeting are Appointed to treat with Said **howland**
on that account and Inform him that his Accknowledgment is too

N. Sowle short and wherein;
[?]
The friends Appointed to Conferr with **Nathaniel Sowle yᵉ 2ᵈ** Make
Report that he Gave them Good Satisfaction, therefore this Meeting

[Certi]ficat doth Minute him under friends Care.
[?] Mosher
This Meeting has Signed and Sent a Removal Certificate to the Monthly

Certificate [for] Matthew Franklin Meeting of **Smithfield** for **Joseph Mosher** and family;
This Meeting has Signed and sent a Certificate for **Matthew Franklin** to
Flushing on **long Island**;

[Request] for [M]eeting [?] Swanzy The friends at **New Swanzy** Requests Liberty to hold a Meeting there
on first days till the last of the 4th month 1765 which this Meeting
Grants Exceptt the holding a Meeting on them first days that
John HowLand's request precedes our Monthly Meeting,
John Howland Requests to Come under friends Care, therefore this
Meeting doth appoint **Wm Bowdish** and **Joseph Gifford** to Confer
John Smith's request & Certificate with him on that Act and Make Report to the next Monthly Meeting
John Smith the 3d Requests a Certificate to the monthly Meeting
of **Sandwich** Respecting his Clearness as to Marriage and Conversation
Therefore **Luke hart** and **Barzillear Tucker** are Appointed to Inspect
into the Above Sd. particulars and draw one for him if they think
proper, and bring it to the next Monthly Meeting;

order to pay Jonan Hussey This Meeting has Collected £7:17s–2d old tener, and the Treasurer
is ordered to pay **Jonathan Hussey** three Dollars for keeping the
To Settle with Treasurer Meeting House half a year; **Wm Sanford** and **Jonathan Hussey** are
Appointed to make up Accompts with the Treasurer and Make Report
meeting house Overseers to the next monthly Meeting;
The Treasurer has paid **Jonathan Hussey** According to order. – –
Friends for Quart meeting The overseers of the Meeting House are Still Continued for one year more
**Humphry Smith, Samuel Smith, Wm Anthony ju. Caleb Russell
Philip Tripp** are Appointed to Attend the Quarterly
meeting and Compile the Answers to the Queries and draw
an Epistle to the Same and bring them to the Adjourn=
J Howland appeals =ment of this Meeting.
Job Howland Requests an Appeal from the Judgment
adjourn of this Meeting to the Quarterly Meeting which is Granted
mett This Meeting Adjourns to the 26 day of this Month
This Meeting being mett According to Adjournment this
26 day of the 12th month 1764, the Representation being
Called for **Ponaganset David Smith** and **Wm Anthony ju.**
D Smith Clerk this day present, for **Coakset** None present; – –
This Meeting Appoints **David Smith** Clark of this
Meeting for this day – –
Queries answered Epistle Signed The friends Appointed to attend the Quarterly Meeting have
drawn an Epistle and Compiled the Answers to the Queries which
was brought to this Meeting and the Epistle Signed by the
Clark and ordered to be Sent up by the Representatives;

1ˢᵗ mo. 1765 At a Monthly Meeting held at **Dartmouth** the 21 of the
first Month 1765, **Ponaganset** Meeting Called **Joseph Smith**
and **Caleb Russell** Present, for **Coakset John Mosher** present

Wᵐ Hathaway's The friends Appointed to make Enquiry into **Wᵐ Hathaway**'s
Clearness Clearness as to Marriage and Conversation Make Report
that they do not find Anything to hinder their proceeding
in Marriage.

Wᵐ Hathaways **William Hathaway** and **Ruth Barker** did appear for their
proposal of Answer which was that they might Proceed to take Each
marriage other in Marriage in Some Convenient time between this
and the next monthly Meeting Observing the Good Order
Established among us in the performance thereof and **Caleb
Russell** and **Joseph Smith** are appointed to see their Marriage
Consumated in Sᵈ order and make Report to the next Monthly Meeting.

Benjᵃ Davil This Meeting has Signed a paper of denial Against **Benjᵃ**
disowned **Davil** [Davol] for the Sin of Fornication but the Reading of it is Referd
to the next monthly Meeting, and **Philip Allen** is Appointed
to Inform him of the Judgment of this Meeting and make
Report to the next monthly meeting.

*Case of **Stephen*** The Case of **Stephen Wilcox** is Refered to the next Monthly Meeting
Wilcox refer'd as is likewise the Case Concerning **Isaac Howland juⁿ**
*Case of **Isaac*** And likewise the Case Concerning **John Howland** is Refered to
Howland Ju. & the next Monthly Meeting.
John Howland
refer'd

Certificate for This Meeting has Signed a Certificate for **John Smith**, **Joseph**'s
John Smith Son, to the monthly meeting of **Sandwich** Certifying his Clearness
as to Marriage and Conversation

Settled with The friends Appointed to make up Accompts with the Treasurer
Treasurer make Report that they have answer'd their Appointment
and there is due to this Meeting £4–10ˢ–1ᵈ old Tener

Report from The Friends Appointed to attend the Quarterly Meeting
Quarterly Make Report that three of them attended agreeable to
Meeting Appointment and one of the other made an Excuse which the
Quarterly Meeting took up with and **Caleb Russell** [*4-5 letters crossed out*] has
made an Excuse to this Meeting, and the Said friends have
produced an Epistle from the Sad [Said] Meeting which was Read in
this Meeting and Well Accepted

Obediah **Obediah Allen** has sent a paper to this Meeting Condeming
Allen's his falling into the Sin of Fornication which Was Read in
offence this Meeting and Refer'd to the next Monthly Meeting for
furder Consideration.

P. Snell denied The Women friends Inform that they have denied **Phebe Snell** for Marrying Contrary to the order of Friends which this Meeting Concurs With

T. Wings Whereas **Thomas Wing** has Married Contrary to the Order of friends, and also has Removed Without a Certificate, and

P. Davel under dealing also **Philip Davel [Davol]** has Removed without a Certificate and without friends Advice, Therefore **Daniel Russell** is Appointed to Labour with both of them for the affores[d] offences in behalf of this Meeting when he Goes to **Oblong**, and Make Report to this Meeting as Soon as he Can.

2[d] mo: 1765 At a Monthly Meeting held in **Dartmouth** on the 18th of the 2[d] Month 1765 the Representatives for **Ponaganset** are **Joseph Smith** and **Caleb Russell** present, for **Coakset Philip Tripp** and **Israel Wood** present;

Ezekiel Comstock proposal of marriage **Ezekiel Comstock** and **Mary Russell** declared their Intentions of Marriage at this Meeting and were desired to ∧wait till the next Monthly Meeting for their Answer.

Report of W[m] Hath away mar riage The friends Appointed to oversee the Marriage of **W[m] Hathaway** and **Ruth Barker** Report that they both attended the Marriage and Saw nothing but that it was Accomplished in Good order

Benj Davil disowned There was a paper of denial Signed Against **Benj[a] Davel [Davol]** at the last Monthly Meeting, and was Presen'd to this Meeting to let him know the Conclusion of S[d] Meeting, and Report being Made that he Still Refuses to Condemn his outgoings, therefore **Philip Tripp** is Appointed to Read it at **Coakset** Meeting after the Meeting of Worship on a first day between this and the next Monthly Meeting, and Make Report to the next Monthly Meeting.

Case of Stephen Wilcox & Isaac How- land refer'd The Case of **Stephen Wilcox** and likewise that of **Isaac Howland ju[n]** are both Refer'd to the next Monthly Meeting The Case of **John Howland** is Refer'd to the next Monthly Meeting under the Same Care as heretofore

Obediah Allen's case continued **Obediah Allen's** Reference is Still Continued till next Monthly Meeting, and **Peleg Huddlestone** and **Job Case** are Appointed to discourse with the young man, and also with the young Woman that Accused of∧ him of the Afores[d] Crime, and Endeavor to have them face to face and see if the young Woman be fully Satisfied and make Report to the next Monthly Meeting.

G. Handy Requests to Come among friends **George Handy** Requests to Come Under the Care of friends therefore **Joseph Smith** and **W[m] Mosher** are appointed to [fo] Confer with him on that Account and make Report to the next Monthly Meeting.

D. Smith under dealing Whereas **Daniel Smith (Isaac's** Son) hath been ~~of~~ Accused of the Sin of Fornication for which offence he hath been discoursed with by the overseers and declines to Condemn the Same, therefore this Meeting doth Appoint **Joseph Tucker** and **James Shearman** to discourse furder with him, and Inform him that it is the mind of this Meeting that if he do not Condem his offence nor Endeavour to make friends Satisfaction That they are Appointed to draw a paper of denial Against him and to bring it to the next Monthly Meeting and Make Report to the Said Meeting. – –

C Slocum under dealing Whereas **Christopher Slocum** hath been Accused of the Sin of Fornica= =tion and hath been Laboured with by one of the overseers and the visitors and Gave them no Satisfaction, Therefore this Meeting doth appoint **Daniel Cornel** and **Samuel Smith** to Labour furder with him and also Inform him that it is the Mind of this Meeting that they Should draw a paper of denial Against him if he don't Incline to Condemn his Offence and make friends Satisfaction and bring it to the next Monthly Meeting.

Order to draw a Certificate for Robert Willis **Humphry Smith** and **Wm Anthony jun** are Appointed to draw a Certificate for our Worthy friend **Robert Willis**, and bring it to the next Monthly Meeting **Peleg Smith, Samuel Smith, Wm Anthony jun, Job Russell, Joseph Tucker**

Order to Revise Minutes are Appointed to Peruse the Monthly Meetings Minutes to see what part they Shall think proper to Go on Record, and they also to Inspect into the Affair Relating to **Abigail Kerby** and prepare a Minute

Affair of Abigail Kirby for that purpose if they think proper and Make Report to the next Monthly Meeting

---

3ᵈmo 1765 At a Monthly Meeting held at **Dartmouth** the 18ᵗʰ day of the 3ᵈ Month 1765 **Ponaganset** Meeting Called **John Potter** and **Wm Anthony jun** present, for **Coakset Joseph Tripp** and **Joshua Davel [Davol]** present,

Ezekiel Comstock's Certificate **Ezekiel Comstock** hath produced a Certificate from the Monthly Meeting of **Smithfield**, Certifying him to be in some good degree of an orderly life and Conversation and Clear from Any Intanglement Respecting Marriage Among them, which this Meeting Accepts

Ezekiel Comstock's Answer **Ezekiel Comstock** and **Mary Russell** Appeared for their Answer which was that they Might Proceed to take each other in Marriage in Some Convenient time between this and the next Monthly Meeting Adviseing with the overseers for the purpose – – and **Peleg Smith** and **Wm Anthony jun** are Appointed to See their Marriage Consumated in Good order and Make Report to the next Monthly Meeting – – **Philip Tripp** Makes Report that **Benjᵃ Devels [Davol]** Denial hath

been Read According to the Appointment of last Monthly Meeting
and is as follows – –

B. Davel　Whereas **Benjᵃ Davel** [**Davoll, Devol**] Son of **Reuben Davel** and **Mary** his wife
Denial　of **Dartmouth** in the County of **Bristol** in the Province of the
Masachusets Bay in **New England**, being one Under the Care of friends
the People Called Quakers, yet for want of keeping to the Spirit of
Truth hath Given way to the Insinuations of the Evil one So as to
fall into the Sin of Fornication as is Manifest by his Wives
having a Child Soon after Marriage, and all Proper Endeavors
in love having being Used to bring him to a Sense of his outgoings, yet
no Sign of Repentance Appearing we Can do no less but to Set
him aside, Denying him the Said **Benjᵃ Davel** [**Davol, Devol**]to be one Under
the Care of us the People Called Quakers. Yet Sincerely desiring
that he May Come to a Sense of his Outgoings and find Mercy
　　　Given forth at our Monthly Meeting held in **Dartmouth**
the 21 of the first month 1765 And signed in and by order of
Said Meeting by – –　　　　　　　　　**Job Russell** Clerk

Case of　The Case of **Stephen Wilcox** is Refer'd to the next Monthly Meeting
Step Wilcox
Case [?] Howland　and likewise the Matter Concerning **Isaac Howland juⁿ** is Refer'd to
and　the next Monthly Meeting – –

[Ob]ediah　The Case Concerning **Obediah Allen** is Refer'd to the next Monthly
Allen refer'd　Meeting Under the same Care as heretofore, and they to make
Report to the next Monthly Meeting – –

Case of　The Matter Concerning **George Handy** is Refer'd to the next Month=
[George] Handy　=ly Meeting – –

Daniel Smith　The Case Concerning **Daniel Smith** is Refer'd to the next Monthly
and　Meeting Under the Same Care as heretofore – –
Christopher
Slocum　The Matter Concerning **Christopher Slocum** is Refer'd to the next Month=
Refer'd　=ly Meeting – –
[?] to

The friends Appointed to Peruse the Monthly Meetings Minutes Make
put on Rec　Report that they have Perused said Minutes and left them with **Samᵉˡ**
ord　**Smith** to be put on Record, and have prepared a minute Respecting
Abigail Kerby which is Approved by this Meeting, and ordered to be
Recorded, and is as follows – –

[**Job Howl** Crossed out] Whereas, **Abigail Kerby** was Some years past Under
A Minute　dealing as appears by our Records, but there being no Mention
about　made therein that She Made friends Satisfaction, by Reason
A. Kerby　as we Apprehend of the Deficiency of the Record (there being
the Minutes of Several Monthly Meetings omitted) and it
appearing now by living Evidence that She did make friends

Satisfaction by Sending a paper into the Monthly Meeting which
was Accepted, Therefore this Minute is Made and Recorded
for a Memorandum thereof – –

J. Howland apeal [?] **Job Howland** Requests a hearing at the next Quarterly Meeting
and hath Sent his Reasons of his not Prosecuting his Appeal at the
last Quarterly Meeting which this Meeting Grants and the Rea=
=sons to be Sent to the aforesaid Meeting – –

Queries answer'd The Queries have been Read in this Meeting and Answers prepared by
both preparative Meetings.

Friends to attend Quarterly Meeting **Peleg Smith, Caleb Russell, Humphry Smith, Wm Anthony jun,
Peter Davil [Davol, Devol]** are Appointed to Attend the Quarterly Meeting and
Compile the Answers to the Queries and draw an Epistles to the Same
and bring them to the Adjournment. – –

adjourn ment This Meeting Adjourns to the first 6th day in next Month,
This Meeting being Mett According to Adjournment the 5th day
of the 4th Month 1765, the Representatives being Called, for **Ponaganset [Aponaganset]**
both present, for **Coakset Joseph Tripp** present – –

Case of John How= land refer'd The Case of **John Howland** is Refer'd to the next Monthly Meeting
and **Wm Sanford** and **Jonathan Hussie [Hussey]** are Appointed to take an
oppertunity of Conference with him on Account of his desire of
being taken Under friends Care and Make Report to the next
Monthly Meeting – –

E. Cornel accepted The Women friends Inform that they have Accepted of **Elizabeth Cornel**
to be under the Care of friends, Which this Meeting Concurs with – –
and they also Inform that they have So far Accepted **Catherine**

Catherine Russell Acceptence **Russell**'s paper Condemning her outgoings in Keeping Company
with **Joshua Barker**, with the Provisal that She Read Said Paper
or Get Some friend to Read it at the End of a Meeting for Worship
She being present at **Ponaganset** Meeting House between this
and the next Monthly Meeting which this Meeting Concurs With,

Accompts Settled with D. Russell This Meeting Appoints **Jonathan Hussey, David ˄Smith Samuel Smith**
to Settle Accompts with **Daniel Russell** and Make Report to
the next Monthly Meeting – –

Epistle & Answers to Queries The friends Appointed to draw an Epistle and Compile the Answers
to the Queries have Answer'd their Appointment, and the Epistle
has been Read and Signed in this Meeting by the Clerk and Sent
with the Answers to the Queries to the Quarterly Meeting by the
Representatives

4th mo: 1765 At a Monthly Meeting held in **Dartmouth** the 15th of the 4th
Month 1765 **Ponaganset** Meeting Called **David Smith** and **Jonathan**

Hussey present, for **Coakset Peleg Huddlestone** present – –

Report of The friends Appointed to See **Ezekiel Comstock** and **Mary Russell**s
Ezekiel Marriage Consumated Make Report that they attended the Mar=
Comstock
Marriage =riage and Saw nothing but that it was Accomplished in Good order

Friends **Peleg Smith**, **Peleg Huddlestone** and **Wm Anthony jun** are Appoint=
Advice to =ed a Committee to advise with **Stephen Wilcox** in behalf of this Mee=
Stephen
Wilcox =ting on the Account of his debts he now Labours Under and they
to advise him to deliver all this Estate up to his Creditors if he
Can't answer them some other way before the next Monthly meeting

[Case] of [Is]aac The Case of **Isaac Howland jun** is Refer'd to the next Monthly Meeting
How[lan]d [r?]

[Ob]ediah The friends Appointed to discourse with **Obediah Allen** Make Report
[A]llen that they have Answer'd the Appointment and they don't find things
Quite Clear, therefore the Matter is Refer'd under their Care and they to
make Report to this Meeting when they shall have opportunity to
treat furder with him – –

[G?] Handy The Case of **George Handy** is Refer'd to the next Monthly Meeting.
Danil Smith The Case of **Daniel Smith** is Refer'd to the next Monthly Meeting by the
and Request of **James Shearman** – –
Christopher
Slocum Refer'd The Case of **Christopher Slocum** is Refer'd to the next Monthly Meet=
=ing Under the Care of **Humphry Slocum** – –

Report The friends Appointed to attend the Quarterly Meeting Make Report
from Quarly that they all Attended Agreeable to Appointment and have produced
Meeting an Epistle from the same which was Read in this Meeting & well Accepted

[J.] Howland The friends Appointed to discourse with **John Howland** Make Report that
received he Gave them Good Satisfaction, therefore this Meeting Accepts him
among
friends to be Under friends Care.

Settled with The friends Appointed to Make up Accompts with **Daniel Russell**
[?] Russell Make Report that they have Made up Accounts and there Remains
due £4–11s–9d old tener which he ^is to take in Wood – –

P. Slocum **Peleg Slocum juner** Requests to Come Under friends Care and has Given
Request in a paper to this Meeting Condeming his former outgoings which is
Refered to the next Monthly Meeting and **Benja Howland** and **Samel**
Smith are Appointed to discourse with him on that Account, and to
See if he has Made Satisfaction to the Young Woman that Accused him
and they to Make Report to the next Monthly Meeting – –

Tho Wilcox Whereas **Thos Wilcox** hath Gone Contrary to friends Orders in times
accepted past in Inlisting into the Kings Service and took up Arms for which
he hath Given in a paper Condemning his afore said offences which this
Meeting Accepts for Satisfaction, and he to Remain Under friends Care
The Women friends Inform that they have Accepted **patience Sowle** to be

P. Sowle
Received &
C. Soule
Denied

under friends Care and also that they have denied **Charity Sowle** from Un=
=der friends Care both which this Meeting Concurs with – –
This Meeting has collected Three Dollars

5ᵗʰ mo:
1765

At a monthly meeting held in **Dartmouth** the 20ᵗʰ of the 5ᵗʰ mo: 1765,
Ponaganset Meeting Called **David Smith** and **Samuel Smith** present,
for **Coakset John Mosher** and **Peleg Huddleston[e]** present,

Case of Step
Wilcox
refer'ᵈ

The Committee appointed to treat with **Stephen Wilcox** make
Report that he desires longer time to try to discharge his Debts
in some other way; therefore the Matter is Refer'd to the next
Monthly Meeting – –

Isaac
Howland Jᵘ
to be informᵈ

Whereas **Isaac Howland juʳ** hath been in the Practice of the
Slave trade and lik[e]wise Married out of the Unity of friends and
he hath been Sufficiently Labour'd with and Neglects to Make
Satisfaction, therefore **Wᵐ Anthony juʳ** is Appointed to Inform
him that this Meeting hath Come to a Conclusion to deny him
if he do not Endeavour to Make friends Satisfaction at the
next monthly Meeting – –

Case of
Geo Handy
refer'ᵈ

The Case of **George Handy** is Refer'd under the same Care as heretofore

Dan Smith
disownd

This Meeting hath Signed a paper of denial against **Daniel**
Smith for the Sin of Fo[r]nication and **Wᵐ Anthony juʳ** is ap=
=pointed to Read ᴧⁱᵗ at the End of a Meeting for Worship Between
this and the next monthly Meeting and make Report to S,ᵈ meeting

S. Clark
Certifica
=te

The women friends Inform that **Susanna Clark** hath Produced a
Removal Certificate from **Sandwich** monthly meeting which
they accepted, and this meeting Concurs therewith

Christophr
Slocum
disownᵈ

This Meeting hath signed a Paper of Denial Against **Christopher**
Slocum for the Sin of Fornication and **Job Russell** is Appointed
to Read it at the End of a first day meeting of worship between
this and the next monthly meeting and he to make Report
to Said meeting

Case of
Peleg
Slocum
refer'ᵈ

The Committee appointed to treat with **Peleg Slocum juʳ**
make Report that he hath made the young woman Satisfac=
=tion that accused him of the Sin of Fornication, and also that
he Gave them Good Satisfaction; which is Refered to the next
monthly meeting – –

Eben Allen
request to
come under
frien[d]s care

Ebenezer Allen (James Son) Requests to Come Under friends Care.
There ᴧ=fore **Peleg Smith** and **Samuel Smith** are appointed to
take an Opportunity of Conference with him on that account
and Make Report to the next Monthly Meeting – –

[Ste]phen
Russell

Stephen Russell Requests a Removal Certificate to the month

request Certificate =ly Meeting of **Sandwich** therefore **Caleb Russell** and **Wᵐ Sanford** are appointed to Enquire into his Conversation and draw one for him if they think Proper and bring it to the next monthly meeting

Weston Briggs request a Certificate **Weston Briggs** and his Wife Requests a Removal Certificate to the monthly Meeting of **Sandwich**, Therefore **James Shearman** and **Paul Russell** are Appointed to Enquire into his Conversation and the Circumstance of his outward affairs, and they to joyn with the women friends, to draw a Certificate for them if they think Proper and bring it to the next monthly meeting

6ᵗʰ mo: 1765 At a monthly meeting met the 17ᵗʰ of the 6ᵗʰ Month 1765 **Ponaganset** Called **James Shearman** and **Paul Russell** present, for**Coakset Benjᵃ Tripp** and **David Davil** [Davol] present whereas this Meeting happening while the yearly meeting of **Rhod-Island** is in being, therefore this Meeting thinks Proper

adjourn to adjourn and do adjourn to the 24ᵗʰ of this Instant at the Usual
mett hour of the day on other monthly meetings– –

    This Meeting being mett according to adjournment this 24ᵗʰ of the 6ᵗʰ month 1765, The Representatives being Called and all

Case of S. Wilcox referʳᵈ present; —— The Case of **Stephen Wilcox** is Refer'd to the next monthly meeting Under the Care of **Joseph Tucker**, **Joseph Gifford** and **Humphry Slocum** and they to make Report to the next monthly Meeting - -

I. Howlanᵈ Juʳ gave in a papeʳ **Isaac Howland** juʳ hath Given in a paper Signifying in Sorrow for his outgoings in Using the Slave Trade and in Marrying out of the Unity of friends, which is Refer'd to the next Monthly Meeting

G. Handy Received The Reports brought in Concerning **George Handy** being to Satisfaction Therefore this Meeting Accepts the Said **George Handy** to be in Membership and Under friends Care.

    Wᵐ Anthony juʳ makes Report that **Daniel Smith**s paper of denial hath been Read According to the Appointment of last Monthly Meeting, which paper is as follows – –

D. Smith's denial Whereas **Daniel Smith** Son of **Isaac Smith** and **Mary** his wife hath had his Education among friends the People Called Quakers Nevertheless not keeping to that unerring Guide the Spirit of Truth, hath fallen into that Scandulous sin of Fornication as - he hath been accused, and not Clearing himself, nor writing to Condem it to friends Satisfaction, altho' there hath been Consi= =derable pains taken with him in order for his Recovery. Therefore for the Clearing of Truth, we can well do no less than Give this forth as a Publick Testimony Against him the S,ᵈ **Daniel Smith**, denying him˄ᵗᵒ be one in Unity with us the afores,ᵈ

People and from Under our Care, yet desiring if it be the Will
of God, that he May Come to a Sight and Sense of his outgoings
and through Unfeigned Repentence find Mercy – –

Given forth at our monthly Meeting held in **Dartmouth**
the 20ᵗʰ day of the 5ᵗʰ mo: 1765, And signed by order and in said
Meeting by – –   **Job Russell** Clerk

Job Russell makes Report that **Christopher Slocum**'s paper
of denial hath been Read according to the appointment of last
monthly meeting,   which paper is as follows (viz) – –

C. Slocum's denial   Whereas **Christopher Slocum** of **Dartmouth** in the County
of **Bristol** in **New England** having had his Education, and
made Profession with us the People Called Quakers, Yet through
unwatchfulness and a disregard to the Testimony of Truth in
himself, hath Given Occasion for a Scandulous Report that
he hath Committed the Reproachful Sin of Fornication,
and he not Clearing himself of the Crime, but after due
Inquiry we have Reason to believe it is true, and friends
having Laboured with him in a Spirit of Love and Meekness in
order to bring him to a Sight of his Error, but their Care and
Labour Proving Ineffectual, Therefore for the Clearing of Truth
and friends from such Enormities, This Meeting is Concerned
to Give this forth as a Publick Testimony Against him
disowning him the Said **Christopher Slocum** from being a member of
our Community, and from under our Care, Sincerely desiring if it be
the Will of God that he may yet Come to a true Sight of his Great
Evil, and thro' unfeigned Repentance find acceptance with him
Given forth at our monthly Meeting held in **Dartmouth**, on the
20ᵗʰ day of the 5ᵗʰ Month 1765
Signed in and by order of said meeting by – **Job Russell** Clerk

Case of Pe Slocum referd   The Case of **Peleg Slocum** 2ᵈ is Refer'd to the next monthly meeting

E. Allen & wife Re'd   The Committee appointed to Confer with **Ebenezer Allen** 2ᵈ Make Report
that he Gave them Good Satisfaction, therefore this Meeting accepts
him into Membership and Under friends Care, and the women friends
Inform that they have Minuted his wife Under friends Care which
this Meeting Concurs with; – –

Case of Wes Briggs referd   The friends appointed to Inquire into the Circumstance of **Weston Briggs**
and draw a Certificate for him, make Report that things is not Quite
Clear, therefore the Same friends are Continued for the Same Service
and to make Report to the next monthly meeting

Whereas **Thomas Akin** hath Gone Contrary to friends orders in

T. Akin denied Several Respects, and friends not having an opportunity to labour with him until lately and he not Inclining to make Satisfaction, Therefore this Meeting denies the said **Thomas Akin** from Under friends Care ~

Philip Davil paper **Philip Davel** [**Davol**] and his wife have sent a Paper to this Meeting from **Oblong** Condeming their Removing without a Certificate the Unity of friends, and they desire a Certificate to the monthly meeting of **Oblong**, therefore **Isaac Smith** and **Paul Russell** are appointed to Enquire into his Conversation and Circumstances in Regard to his outward affairs, and they to join the women friends to draw a Certi= =ficate for them if they think Proper and bring it to the next monthly meeting – –

Tho Wing paper **Thomas Wing** hath Sent a paper to this Meeting Condeming his Mar= =rying out of the Unity of friends, and desires a Certificate to the monthly meeting of **Oblong**, which this Meeting so far accepts as to Appoint **Peter Davel** [**Davol**] and **Philip Tripp** to Inquire into his other Conversation and draw a Certificate for him if they think proper and bring it to the next monthly Meeting – –

Queries answer^d the Queries have been Read in this meeting and Answers prepared by **Ponaganset** Preparitive Meeting –

Represen= tatives to Quarterly meeting **Peleg Smith, Humphry Smith, Peter Davel** [**Davol**] and **Joshua Davel** are Appointed to attend the Quarterly Meeting and to draw an Epistle to the Same and bring it to the Adjournment.

adjourn This Meeting Adjourns to the first sixth day of next month

mett This Meeting being mett according to Adjournment the 5th day of the 7th Month 1765, The Representatives being Called **Paul Russell, Benj^a Tripp** and **David Davel** [**Davol**] present – –

Epistle This Meeting has signed an Epistle and Sent it with the Answers to the Queries to the Quarterly Meeting by the Representatives

Paper to be drawn against P. Wilbor The women Friends Inform that they have discharged themselves in Labouring with **Phebe Wilbour** for the Sin of fornication and She declines to make friends Satisfaction, therefore this meeting doth Appoint **Samuel Smith** to draw a paper of Denial against her and bring it to the next monthly meeting – –

The Treasurer has paid **Jonathan Hussey** five Dollars for Keeping the Meeting House half a year – –

J. Hicks Rec'd The women friends Inform that they have Minuted **Judith Hicks** Daughter of **Thos Hicks** under friends Care which this Meeting Concurs with

7th mo: 1765 At a monthly Meeting held in **Dartmouth** the 15th

day of the 7ᵗʰ month 1765, **Ponaganset** Meeting Called **Joseph
Smith** and **Samuel Smith** present, for **Coakset Daniel Wood**
and **Joseph Tripp** present

Zephaniah Anthony proposal of marri= =age **Zephaniah Anthony** and **Waite Allen** Declared their Intentions
of Marriage at this Meeting and were desired to wait till
the next monthly Meeting for their answer, and **Peleg Smith**
and **Humphry Smith** are Appointed to Inquire into the young mans
ˏClearness as to Marriage and Conversation and make Report to the next
monthly meeting – –

[Case] of Ste Wilcox & Isaac Howland referd The Case of **Stephen Wilcox** is Referd to the next monthly Meeting
This meeting Cannot find freedom to accept of **Isaac Howland**s paper
by Reason of his Apparrel and some friends Questioning his Sincerity
Therefore the Matter is Refer'd to the next monthly meeting – –

P. Slocum paper accepted This Meeting Accepts of **Peleg Slocum**s the 2ᵈ paper Provided he will
Read it or get Some body to read it at the End of a first day meeting for
worship he being present between this and the next monthly meeting
and make Report to the next monthly meeting – –

Certificat for Sibil Sisson This Meeting has signed a Removal Certificate to the monthly meeting
of **Oblong** for **Sibil Sisson** – –

Certifiᵉ for Weston Briggs & wife This Meeting has signed a Removal Certificate for **Weston Briggs** &
his Wife to the monthly meeting of **Sandwich** – –

Certificate to be given The friends Appointed to draw a Certificate for **Philip Davel** [**Davol**] & his wife
have drawn one too short, therefore the same friends are Still
appointed to draw one fuller and bring it to the next monthly meeting
The friends Appointed to draw a Certificate for **Thoˢ Wing** make Report
that they have not drawn one, therefore they are Still Continued
to draw one and bring it to the next monthly meeting if they think proper – –

Report from Quar meeting The friends Appointed to attend the Quarterly Meeting make
Report that they all attended Except **Peleg Smith** and he sent
an Excuse which was accepted and they have Produced an Epistle
from the S,ᵈ meeting which hath been Read in this Meeting and
well accepted – –

Epistles Receiv'd This Meeting hath Received three Printed Epistles from **London**
one written Epistle from **flushing** on **Long Island** and one Epistle
from the yearly meeting of **New-port** on **Rhod-Island** all of which
was Read to Good Satisfaction.

Denial of Phebe Wilbor This Meeting has signed a Paper of Denial against **Phebe Wilbor**
for the Sin of Fornication, and **Job Russell** is appointed to Read
it at the End of a Meeting for worship on a first day between this &
the next monthly meeting and make Return of S,ᵈ Paper to the

next monthly meeting,

Minute from Rhod-Island Received the following Minute from **Rhod-Island** Monthly Meeting Respecting **John Gifford**.

From our Monthly Meeting held at **Portsmouth** on **Rhod-Island** the 30th of the 4th month 1765.

This Meeting Gives their Approbation that **Dartmouth** Monthly

J. Gifford Rec'd Meeting Receive into Unity **John Gifford** if they think him worthy Notwithstanding his place of Abode is within the Varge [verge] of this Monthly Meeting, True Coppy of the minute.

Test . **Thos Gould** Clerk

This Meeting Accepts of **John Gifford** to be in membership with friends and under the Care of this Meeting

---

8 mo: 1765 At a Monthly Meeting held in **Dartmouth** the 19th day of the 8th month 1765, **Ponaganset** Called **Wm Anthony jun** present, for **Coakset Philip Tripp** and **Joshua Davel[Davol]** present

Zep Anthony Clearness The friends Appointed to Inquire into **Zephaniah Anthony**'s Clearness Make Report that they do'nt find anything to hinder his Proceedings in Marriage. – –

Zephaniah Anthony Answer **Zephaniah Anthony** and **Wait Allen** Appeared for their Answer which was that they Might proceed to take Each other in Marriage in some Convenient time between this & the next Monthly Meeting Advising with the Overseers for that Purpose – And **Peleg Smith** and **Humphry Smith** are appointed to see their Marriage Consumated in Good order and Make Report to the next Monthly Meeting – –

Benj Davil's proposal of marriage **Benjamin Davil[Davol]** and **Patience Sowle** Declared their Intentions of taking Each other in Marriage. And were Desired to wait till next Monthly Meeting for their Answer and **Benja Tripp** and **Israel Wood** are Appointed to Inquire into the Young Man's Clearness, Respecting Marriage and Conversation and Make Report to the next Monthly Meeting – The Case of

Isaac Howland's Case refer'd **Isaac Howland** ju: is Refered to the next Monthly Meeting – –

Certificate [?]Davil The friend Appointed to draw a Certificate for **Philip Davil[Davol]** and his Wife have drawn one which is Signed in this Meeting and Sent to the

Certificate T. Wing **oblong**. The friends Appointed to draw a Certificate for **Thos Wing** have done it, which was Signed and Sent to the **Oblong–**

P. Wilber, denial **Phebe Wilber[Wilbur]**'s paper of Denial hath been Read According to the Appointment of last Monthly Meeting, which is as follows

Whereas **Phebe Wilber[Wilbur]** Daughter of **Samuel** and **Mary**

Chase, and Now Wife to **Henry Wilbor[Wilbur]**, having had her education
Among friends and Under the Care of this Meeting, but through
Unwatchfulness and disregarding the Testimony of Truth, hath fallen
into the Reproachful Sin of Fornication, as Appears by her being
Delivered of a Child soon after Marriage, and this Meeting
having Labour'd with her in Love in order for her Recovery, but
She proving Obstinate, and Regardless of the tender Counsel to
her Given, Therefore for the Clearing of the precious Truth that
we profess from such Enormities, this Meeting is Concerned to
Give this forth as a Publick Testimony Against her, disowning
her the Said **Phebe Wilbor[Wilbur]** from being a member of our Society
and from Under the Care of this Meeting, Desiring if it be
Consistent with Divine pleasure, that She may yet be Convin=
=ced of the Error of her ways, and by a Sincere Repentance
find favour with the Lord, Given forth at our Monthly
Meeting held in **Dartmouth** on the 19th day of the 7th month 1765.
And signed in and in behalf of Said Meeting by **Job Russell** Clerk

　　　Lilless Beard's paper Condeming her outgoing hath been
Read According to the Appointment of the women's Monthly Meeting
And is as follows – –

L. Beard To the Monthly Meeting of friends in **Dartmouth**
paper Esteemed friends; This May Inform you that Through Unwatchful=
=ness I have Gave way so far to the Enemy as to go Contrary to the
Good order of the Church which Appears by My having a Child born so soon
after Marriage for which I am Sorry, and Condemn My
out goings, I hope God will forgive me. And desire friends so
far to pass it by as to let me Remain Under their Care – –
Given under My hand the 13th of the 7th Month 1765

　　　　　　　　　　　　　　　　Lillis Beard

Catherine Russell's Paper hath been Read According to the
Appointment of the Monthly Meeting tho' not so soon as the
former Minutes Expressed, which this Meeting overlooks
which said paper is as follows – –

C. Russell's To the Monthly Meeting of friends at **Dartmouth** to be held the
Confession 19th of the 11th Month 1764, Esteemed friends – –
I heartily Acknowledge My outgoings in Keeping Company
with **Joshua Barker** in too free and frequent a Manner,
to the dishonour of Truth and the Grief of friends, but tho' my
offences have been Great, yet through the Goodness of God I have
been favoured with a Sight and Sense of my outgoings, for which

my outgoings I am heartily Sorry and do Condemn, hoping God will forgive Me My Offences and Receive me Again into favour and desire friends would pass by my disorderly walking, and let me Remain under their Care, which I value highly, hoping through Divine Assistance for the time to Come to be preferred in a State of Circumspect Walking, from your friend **Catherine Russell**

D. Briggs Request   **David Briggs** Requests to come under friends Care therefore this Meeting doth Appoint **Wm Sanford** and **Wm Barker** to take an opportunity of Conference with him on his Request and Make Report to the next Monthly Meeting – –

The women friends Inform that they have Minuted **Elizabeth White** wife to **Wᵐ White**, and also **Elizabeth Macumber** wife to **Zebudee Macumber** under friends Care which this Meeting Concurs with, – –

J. Wood put Under dealing   The overseers Inform that there is a bad Report Concerning **Josiah Wood** and **William Wilcox** their Salting up Beef and Exposing it to Sale which was not Merchantable, and they have Made Some Inquiry and do not find things Clear, therefore this Meeting doth Appoint **Daniel Cornel**, **Seth Shearman**, **John Potter** a Comittee to Make furder Inquiry into the particular Circum= =stances between them in the Aforementioned Report, and they to Make Report to the next Monthly Meeting – –

P. Slocum's Confession   **Peleg Slocum**s Paper hath been Read According to the Order of last Monthly Meeting, and is as followeth (viz)

To the Monthly Meeting of friends held in **Dartmouth**;
Whereas I **Peleg Slocum** Son of **Holder Slocum** (deceased) having been Educated Amongst friends, but in My youthful days through Unwatchfulness so far gave way to the Enemy as twice to fall into the Sin of Fornication, as Appears first by My wife's having a child before Marriage, and Secondly with **Phebe Hussey**, for which I was justly disowned by friends; Now these are to Testify to friends and openly declare to all People that I do utterly Condemn and am Heartily Sorry for the Above said Crimes, with all other my outgoings, and I hope the Almighty will forgive mee all my offences, and I desire friends would so far pass them by as to Receive me Again Under their Care.

Given forth under My hand
this 15 day of the 6ᵗʰ month 1765   **Peleg Slocum**

9 mo. 1765   At a Monthly Meeting held in **Dartmouth** the 16ᵗʰ day of the 9ᵗʰ month 1765, **Ponaganset** Meeting Called **Caleb Russell** and **Humphry**

Smith present, for **Coakset David Davel[Davol]** and **Ichabod Eddy** present, The friends Appointed to Inquire into the Clearness of **Benjᵃ Davels [Davol]** ~~Clear~~ make Report that they don't find anything to hinder his proceeding in Marriage – –

Benjamin Davil's Answer **Benjᵃ Davel[Davol]** and **Patience Sowle** Appeared for their Answer which was that they Might proceed to take each other in Marriage in Some Convenient time between this and the next Monthly Meeting advising with the overseers for the purpose, And **Benjᵃ Tripp** and **Israel Wood** are Appointed to See their Marriage Consumated in Good order and Make Report to the next Monthly meeting;

[Record] of Z. Anthony Marriage The friends Appointed to see **Zephaniah Anthony** and **Wait Allen**'s Marriage Consumated make Report that they attended the Marriage and saw nothing but that it was Accomplished in Good order.

Case of S. Wilcox refer'd The case of **Stephen Wilcox** is Refer'd to the next Monthly Meeting

I. How: land accepted **Isaac Howland** juⁿ hath sent a paper to this Meeting Some Months ago, Signifying his Sorrow for his outgoings in Marrying out of the Unity of friends and also his Using the Slave trade which this Meeting accepts – –

David Briggs Received The Committee Appointed to Confer with **David Briggs** on ~~this~~ his Request to Come Under friends Care Make Report that he Gave them Good Satisfaction, therefore this Meeting doth Minute the Said **David Briggs** into Membership and under friends Care – –

Josiah Wood & Wᵐ Wilcox Cases refer'd The Committee Appointed to Make Inquiry into the Circum= =stances of the affair Concerning **Josiah Wood** and **Wᵐ Wilcox** Make Report that they have not had an opportunity to speak with both of them, therefore the Same Com:ᵗᵉᵉ are Still Continued in the Same Service, and they to Make Report to the next Monthly Meeting;

Thirty Cords of Wood Sold to pay part of S. Wilcox Debts This Meeting hath Sold Thirty Cord of Wood to **Doctor Hathaway** at two Shillings Lawful mony[money] per Cord, to discharge part of his Demand, for Doctoring of **Stephen Wilcox**'s family and **Thoˢ Hicks** ju: is Appointed to see the Wood Measured and Make Report to this Meeting as soon as he Can Conveniently

E. Max: field's Request **Edmond Maxfield** Requests to Come under friends Care therefore this Meeting doth Appoint **Joseph Tucker** and **Abraham Tucker** to Make Inquiry into his Conversation and to Confer with him on the Account of his Request and make Report to the next Monthly Meeting – –

Queries Answered The Queries have been Read in this Meeting and Answers prepared by both preparative Meetings and Read in this Meeting –

William Anthony ju: and **Samuel Smith** are Appointed to Compile the Answers to the Queries and draw an Epistle to the Quarterly Meeting and bring them to the Ajournment [Adjournment]–

This Meeting hath collected £8:4:5 old tener – –

adjourns This Meeting adjourns to the first Sixth day in next Month

mett This Meeting being Met According to Adjournment the 4ᵗʰ day of the 10ᵗʰ Month 1765, the Representatives being Called for **Ponagan= =set Humphry Smith** & **Caleb Russell** present, for **Coakset** none present

Answers to Queries and Epistle Sent by Representatives Wᵐ **Anthony** ju: and **Samuel Smith** have drawn the Epistle and Compiled ~~the~~ the Answers to the Queries and the Epistle has been signed in this Meeting and Sent up to the Quarterly Meeting by the Representatives with the Answers to the Queries, the Representa= =tives are **Peter Daval[Davol] Israel Wood** & **Caleb Russell** – –

Certificate for Rebecca Shove This Meeting hath signed a Certificate for **Rebecca Shove** to the Monthly Meeting of **Swanzey**, and likewise signed one for **Mary**

Certificate for Mary Comstock **Comstock** to the Monthly Meeting of **Smithfield** – –

John Sisson removed **John Sisson** hath Removed to the **Nine partners** without friends Advice and without a Certificate, therefore **Joseph Smith** and **Luke Hart** are Appointed to Enquire into his CerCumstances [Circumstances] and also Labour with him if they have an opportunity and Make Report to the next Monthly Meeting

M. Wing removed Whereas **Mary Wing** hath Removed without a Certificate Some years ago to **Rhod-Island**, and She not Standing Clear as Appears by our former Minutes. therefore **Humphry Smith, Samuel Smith, Wᵐ Anthony** ju: are Appointed to

a letter to be sent draft a letter to the Monthly Meeting of **Rhod-Island** as they shall think proper and bring it to the next Monthly Meeting

---

10ᵗʰ mo: 1765 At a Monthly Meeting held in **Dartmouth** the 21 day of the 10ᵗʰ Month 1765 **Ponaganset** Meeting Called **Caleb Russell** and **Joseph Smith** present, for **Coakset Joseph Tripp** and **Ichabod Eddy** present

Epistle Received This Meeting hath Received an Epistle from the yearly Meeting held at **Philadelphia** for **Pensilvania** and **New-jersey** dated the 9ᵗʰ month 1764 which was Read in this Meeting to Good Satisfaction.

John Howland's pro= =posal of marriage **John Howland** and **Hannah Smith** Declared their Intentions of Marriage at this Meeting and were desired to wait till the next Monthly Meeting for their Answer and

Jonathan Hussey and Caleb Russell are Appointed to Make
Inquiry into the young man's Clearness Respecting Marriage
and Conversation and Make Report to the next Monthly Meeting
The friends Appointed to see Benjᵃ Davel[Davol] and Patience Sowle
Marriage Consumated Make Report that they attended
the Marriage and saw nothing but that it was Accomplished
in Good order

S. Wilcox
Case Refered The Case of Stephen Wilcox is Refer'd to the next Monthly Meeting

Hannah Russell
Certificate Hannah Russell wife of Elijah Russell hath Produced a
Removal Certificate from the Monthly Meeting of Swanzey
which this Meeting Accepts

List of
Friends This Meeting has Signed a list (for the Monthly Meeting
of Sandwich) of the friends that [live?] the Eastward Side
of Quishned River that was Under Transgression when
the former List was Given who has Since Made this
Meeting Satisfaction.

The Committee Appointed to Enquire into the Circumstances

J. Wood &
Wᵐ Wilcox
Case of Josiah Wood and Wᵐ Wilcox's Salting and Exposing Beef
to Sale not Merchantable Make Report that they
they think they are neither of them Clear therefore John
Potter, Daniel Cornel, Seth Shearman, Thoˢ Hicks ju: Paul
Russell, David Smith, Samuel Smith are Appointed a Committee
to hear and Determine Upon the Complaint brought Against
them and Make Report to the next Monthly Meeting – –

Edmond
Maxfield
Case
refer'd The friends Appointed to Confer with Edmond Maxfield make
Report that he Gave Good Satisfaction, therefore this Meeting
doth Refer the Matter till the next Monthly Meeting – –

The friends Appointed to attend the Quarterly Meeting being Called

Report
from Quaterly
Meeting Upon Make Report that two of them attended and the other Made
a Satisfactory Excuse, and they have Produced an Epistle from
the Same which was Read to Good Satisfaction

Proposal
to Enlarge
little
Meeting
House It has been Proposed at this Meeting for friends to Enlarge the
little Meeting House which is Refer'd to the next Monthly Meeting
Jonathan Hussey, John Potter, Caleb Russell, Samuel Smith,
Berzillia Tucker, Daniel Cornel, David Smith, are Appointed
to oversee the Yearly Meeting, to prevent any indecency that
May happen at that time, and also Benjᵃ Tripp, David Daval[Davol],
John Mosher, Daniel Wood are Appointed for the Same Service at
Coakset Meeting, and they to make Report to the next Monthly
Meeting

Abigail States paper accepted **Abigail States[Slade?]** has Given in a paper to this Meeting Condem= =ning her falling into the Sin of fornication which this Meeting accepts Provided She Read it or Get Somebody to Read it at the End of a first day Meeting for Worship between this and the next Monthly Meeting She being present

11ᵗʰ mo: 1765 At a Monthly Meeting held in **Dartmouth** the 18ᵗʰ day of the 11ᵗʰ Month 1765, **Ponaganset** Meeting Called **Joseph Smith** and **Caleb Russell** present, for **Coakset David Davel** and **John Mosher** present,

J. Howland Clearness The friends Appointed to Make Enquiry into **John Howland**'s Clear= =ness, Make Report that they Don't find Any thing to hinder his Proceeding in Marriage.

John Howland's Answer **John Howland** and **Hannah Smith** did Appear for their Answer which was that they Might Proceed to take Each other in Marriage in Some Convenient time between this and the next Monthly Meeting, Advising with the Overseers for the Purpose and **Jonathan Hussey** and ~~David Smith~~ **Joseph Smith** are Appointed to see their Marriage Consumated in Good order and Make Report to the next Monthly Meeting; – –

Seth Russell proposal of marri= =age **Seth Russell** and **[Kaziah?] Walker** Declar'd their Intentions of Marriage and were desired to wait till the next Monthly Meeting for their Answer, and **Joseph Smith** and **Luke Hart** are Appointed to Make Enquiry into the Young Man's Clear= =ness Respecting Marriage and Conversation and Make Report to the next Monthly Meeting

Case of S. Wilcox refer'd The Case of **Stephen Wilcox** is Refer'd Under the Same Care as heretofore – –

Josiah Wood's, Paper accepted The Comittee Appointed to hear and Determine Upon the Complaint brought Against **Josiah Wood** and **Wᵐ Wilcox** Make Report that they have had a Conference With **Josiah Wood** and they think he ought to Condemn his Misconduct in that Affair Publickly and the Said **Wood** hath Accordingly Given in a Paper to this Meeting, Condemning his Selling Beef to **Wᵐ Wilcox** that was not Merchantable, which this Meeting Accepts Provided he will Read Sᵈ paper or Cause it to be Read at the End of a first day Meeting for Worship between this and the next Monthly Meeting he being present And the Same Comittee are Still Continued to Also Confer with Said **Wilcox** and Make Report to the next Monthly Meeting

E. Max Field rec'd This Meeting Minutes **Edmond Maxfield** Under friends care.

Amey Hart hath Given in a Paper to this Meeting Condemning

Amey Hart's her falling into the Sin of Fornication with the Rest of her
paper'
[?][refer'd] Misconduct in that Case, which this Meeting Refers to the
next Monthly Meeting,

Enlarging The Proposal for Enlarging the little Meeting House is Refer'd
Meeting House
refer'd to the next Monthly Meeting;

[?][report] of The friends Appointed overseers at the Yearly Meeting to Endea=
Overseers =vour to prevent Any Indecency that may happen at that time
Yearly Meeting Make Report that they attended the meeting and that the People
behaved in a Good degree Orderly, and they think the Practice
of Appointing Overseers for that Purpose has a Good Attendency

P. Shearman's **Philip Shearman** hath Given in a Paper to this Meeting Condem=
paper =ning his disorder in falling into a Bodily Strife with **Daniel Pabody**;

Meeting The friends down in **Allens Neck** Requests the Liberty to
Granted hold a Meeting there for four months from this time on first
in Allen
Neck days which is Granted, and **Philip Allen** and **Daniel Cornel**
are Appointed to see that the Meeting be held Agreable to Good
order and they to Make Report thereof at the Expiration
of the four Months

Meeting at The friends at **New Swanzey** Request the Liberty to hold a Meeting
New
Swanzey at Some Convenient Place up there for four Months on first days
granted which this Meeting Grants and **Elihu Bowen** and **Abraham
Russell** are Appointed to See that the Meeting beheld According
to Good order and they to Make Report at the End of the four Months

J. Sisson **John Sisson** Requests a Certificate to the Monthly Meeting at the
request a
Certificate **Nine Partners**, therefore **Joseph Smith** and **Luke Hart** are Appointed
to draw a Certificate for him if they think Proper and bring it to
the next Monthly Meeting – –

Abigail States' Paper hath been Read According to the
Appointment of the last Monthly Meeting, and is as follows;

A. States To the Monthly Meeting of Women friends held in **Dartmouth**
Confession the 21 day of the 10th Month 1765 –
This May Enform you that by Unwatchfulness I have
fallen into the Sin of Fornication which I do Condemn and
hope that God will forgive me, and Desire that friends
would forgive and pass by my offences and let me Remain
under their Care as before.   **Abigail States**

12 mo: At a Monthly Meeting held at **Dartmouth** the 16th day of the 12th month
1765 1765, **Ponagansett** Meeting Called **Paul Russell** and **Caleb Russell**
present, for **Coakset Peter Davel[Davol]** and **Benjᵃ Tripp** present;

S.Russell The friends Appointed to Enquire into **Seth Russells** Clearness
Clearness

make Report that they don't find Any thing to hinder his
Proceeding in Marriage – –

Seth Russell answer   **Seth Russell** & **Kaziah Walker** Appear'd for their Answer
which was that they might proceed to take Each other in
Marriage in Some Convenient time between this and the
next Monthly Meeting Advising with the overseers for
that Purpose and **Joseph Smith** and **Luke Hart** are Ap=
=pointed to see their Marriage Consumated in Good order
and Make Report to the next Monthly Meeting –

Report of John How= =land's Marriage   **Jonathan Hussey** and **Joseph Smith** make Report that
they attended the Marriage of **John Howland** and
Hannah Smith and Saw nothing but that it was Accomplish=
=ed in good order – –

Case of Ste= =ven Wilcox refer'd   The Case of **Stephen Wilcox** is Refer'd to the next Monthly Meeting
Josiah Woods Paper hath been Read According to the
Appointment of last Monthly Meeting, which Paper
is as follows(viz)

Wood's Confession   To the Monthly Meeting of friends held in **Dartmouth** on the
18th day of the 11th month 1765, through Unwatchfulness I
have Sold Beef to **William Wilcox** that was not Merchan=
=table for which I am Sorry and do Condemn, hoping that God
will forgive me, and I desire that friends would pass it
by.~~and let me R~~ – – **Josiah Wood**

Case of Wᵐ Wilcox   The Comᵗᵗᵉ Appointed to Confer with **Wᵐ Wilcox** Report that they
have not had an Opportunity to Speak with him, therefore the
same Committee are Still Continued in the Same Service and also
to Labour with him for Inlisting into the Kings Service and taking
up Arms, and also to Treat With him About his Marrying out of
the Unity of friends, and they to make Report to the next Monthly Meeting;

Case of A. Hart   The Case of **Amey Hart** is Refer'd to the next Monthly Meeting –
It hath been proposed at this Meeting to Enlarge the little Meeting

Comᵗᵉᵉ in Little Meeting House   House, therefore this Meeting doth Appoint **Joseph Gifford, Wᵐ
Sanford, Humphry Smith, Prince Allen, Barnabas Mosher,**
a Comittee to Consider the Advantages and disadvantages that
May Attend the Enlargment, and also Compute the Cost as near
as they Can, and make Report to the Adjournment – –

P. Sher= =man paper accepted   This Meeting doth so far Accept of **Philip Shearman**'s Paper Condem=
=ning his disorder as for him to Read it or Cause it to be Read at
the End of a first day Meeting for Worship between this and the
next Monthly Meeting and he to be present – –

G. Smith *Confession*	**George Smith ju:** hath Given in a Paper to this Meeting Condem= =ning his disorder in Listing[enlisting] on board of a Privateer with all the Rest of his Conduct in Supporting of War, Which this Meeting Accepts and he to Remain Under friends Care.
I.How= *=lands* *request*	**Isaac Howland ju:** Requests A Certificate to the Monthly Meeting of **Rhode-Island,** Therefore **Samuel Smith** and **Wm Anthony ju:** are Appointed to draw one for him if they think Proper and bring it to the next Monthly Meeting – – The Queries have been Read and Answer'd in this Meeting and **Wm Anthony** ju: and **Humphry Smith** are Appointed to draw an Epistle to the Quarterly Meeting and Compile the Answers to the Queries and bring them to the Adjournment
Coakset *friends Re-* *-quest to* *to have* *a Monthly* *Meeting*	**Coakset** Meeting Requests to have a Monthly Meeting Granted them, which this Meeting so far Concurs with as to Refer the Matter to the next Monthly Meeting for Consideration.
	This Meeting hath collected £6:15 – –
adjourn	This Meeting Adjourns to the first sixth day in next Month
mett	This Meeting being Met According to Adjournment this 3rd day of the first month 1766 – – The Representatives being Called, for **Ponaganset Caleb Russell** present, for **Coakset Benja Tripp** present,
Report *on little* *meeting* *house*	The friends Appointed to consider the Advantages and disad= =vantages of Enlarging the little Meeting House Make Report in writing, which is Refer'd to the Monthly Meeting to be holden in the fourth Month Next and the Report to be kept upon file till then – –
Answers *to Queries* *Epistle* *Sent*	The friends Appointed to Compile the Answers to the Queries, and draw an Epistle to the Quarterly Meeting have done it, and the Epistle was Signed in this Meeting and order'd to be Carried up to the Quarterly Meeting by the Representatives together with the Answers to the Queries, the friends Appointed
Represen *Tatives*	to attend the Quarterly Meeting are **Caleb Russell, Joseph** **Smith, Benja Tripp.**

1st mo: *1766*	At a Monthly Meeting held in **Dartmouth** the 20 day of the first month 1766, **Ponaganset** Meeting Called **Caleb Russell** and **Wm Anthony** ju: present, for **Coakset Philip Tripp** present
Report of *Seth Russell* *Marriage*	The friends Appointed to see **Seth Russell** and **Kaziah Wal=** =kers Marriage Consumated make Report that they attended the Marriage which was Accomplished in Good order –
S. Wilcox	The Case of **Stephen Wilcox** is Refer'd to the next Monthly Meeting

and
Wm Wilcox
case refer'd
The friends Appointed to Labour With **Wᵐ Wilcox** Make Report that they Labour'd with him and he desires one Month More to Endeavour to Make friends Satisfaction. Therefore the Matter is Refer'd to the next Monthly Meeting;

P. Shea:
rman
[?]
Philip Shearman's Paper hath been Read According to the Appointment of last Monthly Meeting, And is as follows,
To the Monthly Meeting of friends to be held in **Dartmouth**, the 18ᵗʰ day of the 11ᵗʰ Month 1765,
These Are to Inform that I some time past through Unwatch= =fulness unhappily fell into a Bodily Strife with **Daniel Pabody**, Whereby Blows were Passed between Us, for Which I am heartily Sorry and do Condemn, and I hope friends will pass by My Offence and let me Remain Under their Care. Given forth Under My Hand this 15ᵗʰ day of their 11ᵗʰ mo 1765

Philip Shearman

Certificate
for I. How
land
This Meeting hath Signed a Removal Certificate for **Isaac Howland** ju: To the Monthly Meeting of **Rhod-Island**

adjourn This Meeting Adjourns to the 29ᵗʰ Instant

mett This Meeting being Mett According to Adjournment the 29ᵗʰ day of the first month 1766. The Representatives being present

report
from
Quart
meeting
The friends Appointed to attend the Quarterly Meeting Make Report that they all attended Sᵈ Meeting, and have produced an Epistle from the same which was Read and well Accepted in this Meeting.

Coakset
request for a
mo meeting
Coakset friends Request to have a Monthly Meeting set off to them, is Refer'd to the next Monthly Meeting;

B. Potter
paper
accepted
Bridget Potter wife to **Stephen Potter** hath Given in a paper to this Meeting Condemning her outgoings in Marrying out of the Unity of friends with all the Rest of her outgoings, which this Meeting Accepts, and this Meeting hath signed

Certificate for
B.P.
a Certificate for her to the Monthly Meeting at the **Nine Partners**

Case of
Obediah
Allen
The Committee Appointed some months ago to Treat with **Obediah Allen** on the Account of his Sincerity in Giving in a Paper to the Meeting Condemning his outgoings in falling into Fornication, together with the Rest of the Circumstance Relating to that Case, make Report that (they not having an Opportunity to treat with him till lately) that they do not find him Clear in all the Above mentioned Circumstances therefore this Meeting doth Appoint **Daniel Russell** and **Nicholas Howland** to Join with the Aforesaid Committee to

treat furder with him for all the offences that May Appear
Against him, and they to make Report to the next Monthly Meeting

J. Russell **Joseph Russell**s Requests to Come under friends Care with
Request his wife and family which is Refer'd to the next Monthly Meeting.

2: mo: At a Monthly Meeting held in **Dartmouth** the
1766 17 day of the 2ⁿᵈ Month 1766, **Ponaganset** Meeting Called
Caleb Russell and **Samuel Smith** present, for **Coakset**
Joseph Tripp and **Israel Wood** present,

Case of The Case of **Stephen Wilcox** is Refer'd to next Monthly Meeting.
S. W. refer'd The Committee Appointed to treat with ~~Stephen~~ **Wm**

Wᵐ Wilcox **Wilcox** make Report that they have Laboured with
disowned him for Inlisting into the King's Service and taking up
Arms, and also Marrying out of the Unity of friends, and
Neglecting to attend Meetings for Worship, which disorders
he Gave them Encouragment of Condemning at this Meeting
tho' he still Neglects it, therefore this Meeting finding
themselves Clear in Labouring with him, and do Conclude
to deny the Said **Wᵐ Wilcox**, and do Appoint **David Smith**
and **Samuel Smith** to draw a Paper of denial Against
him and bring it to the next Monthly Meeting, and **Timothy**
Russell is Appointed to Inform him of the Conclusion of this Meeting
and Make Report to the next Monthly Meeting;

Coakset friends **Coakset** friends Still Request to have a Monthly Meeting Set
Request to off to them, and also desire a Committee to determine where
have a month to prefix the Boundaries between this and that Meeting
ly meeting and all Circumstances Relating thereto, Therefore **Hum=**
=phry Smith, Philip Tripp, Samuel Smith, Daniel Wood,
Joseph Tucker are Appointed a Comittee for that purpose
and Make Report to the next Monthly Meeting

O. Allen The Committee Appointed to Treat with **Obediah Allen**
case refer'd make Report that they have discoursed with him and
he Gave them Encouragment that he would write to the next
Monthly Meeting which is Refer'd to the Said Meeting Under
their Care.

J. Russell & **Joseph Russell**s and his wife's Requests to Come Under friends
Wife request Care is Refer'd to the next Monthly Meeting;

S. Howland **Samuel Howland** juⁿ Hath Given in a Paper to this Meeting
Removed Condemning his outgoing in Removing without friends Ad=
Said Howland =vice, which this Meeting Accepts, and the **Sᵈ Howland** Re=
request a =quests a Removal Certificate to the Monthly Meeting of
certificate

Smithfield in **Rhod-Island** Colony, for himself and Children
therefore this Meeting doth Appoint **Peleg Huddlestone**
and **Philip Tripp** a Committee to Inquire into his Circumstances, and
draw a Certificate for him if they think proper and bring it to
the next Monthly Meeting;

miniuts to be Revised This Meeting doth Appoint **Joseph Tucker, Humphry Smith,**
Job Russell, Samuel Smith a Com'ttee to peruse the Monthly
Meeting; Minutes to see what part they Shall think proper to
be put on Record, And Make Report to the next Monthly Meeting;

To Settle with over seers of the poor. **Jonathan Hussey** and **William Sanford** are Appointed a Committee
to Make Up Accounts with the Overseers of the Poor and make
Report to the next Monthly Meeting,

Paul Mo sher's dis orderly marriage **Coakset** Preparative Meeting Informs that **Paul Mosher**
hath Married out of the Unity of friends, and hath been
dealt with by the Overseers, and declines to Condemn his
Offence, therefore **Benj^a Tripp** and **Joseph Tripp** are Appoi=
=nted to Labour furder with him and Make Report to the
next Monthly Meeting;

Amey Hart paper acceted **Amey Hart** Hath Given in a Paper to this Meeting, Condemning
her outgoings, in falling into the Sin of Fornication which this
Meeting Accepts with the Provisal that She Read it or Cause
it to be Read at the Close of a first day Meeting for worship
at **Newtown** between this and the next Monthly Meeting
She being present, and Return the paper to the S^d Meeting.

F. Allen & Benj Allen hath alowd Fiddleing & dancing in their houses The Overseers Inform this Meeting that **Francis Allen**
and **Benj^a Allen** hath Allowed of fidling and dancing
in their Houses for which the S^d Overseers have Laboured
with them and they decline to Condemn the Offence to
friends Satisfaction therefore this Meeting doth Appoint
Joseph Gifford and **Berzillia Tucker** to Labour furder
with them, and make Report to the next Monthly Meeting.

---

3 mo: 1766 At a Monthly Meeting of friends held in **Dartmouth**
the 17th day of the 3^d Month 1766, the Representatives
are for **Coakset Philip Tripp** and **Daniel Wood** present,
for **Ponaganset Caleb Russell** and **Samuel Smith** present,

Davi Briggs Edm Maxfield & Wm Hart's proposal of marriage **David Briggs** and **Rebecca Howland** and **Edmond Max**=
=**field** and **Rachel Russell**, and **William Hart** ju^n and **Esther**
Slade declared their Intentions of Marriage at this
Meeting and were desired to wait till the next Monthly
Meeting for their Answers, and **John Potter** and Jon**athan Hussey**

are Appointed to Make Inquiry into **David Briggs'** Clearness Re=
=specting Marriage and Conversation and Make Report to the next
Monthly Meeting; And **Joseph Smith** and **Barnabas Mosher** are Appoin=
=ted for the same service with **Edmond Maxfield** and **William Hart** ju:
and to Make Report to the next Monthly Meeting;

Timothy Russell Reports that he hath Informed **Wᵐ Willcox** Agre=
=able to the Appointment of last Monthly Meeting and Also
David Smith and **Samuel Smith** hath drafted a denial against

Wᵐ Wilcox denial to be read Sᵈ **Willcox**, and presented it to this Meeting which hath been Red
and Signed by the Clerk, and the Sᵈ Clerk is order'd to Read Sᵈ
Denial Publickly, at the Close of a first day Meeting for wor=
=ship between this and the next Monthly Meeting and Make
Report to Sᵈ Meeting;

Case of W refer'd The Case of **Stephen Wilcox** is refer'd to the next Monthly Meeting

R. Tripp, R. Tripp and L. Tripp recei'd The women friends Inform that they have Minuted **Ruth Tripp**,
Rebecca Tripp, and **Lydia Tripp** under their Care, which this
Meeting Concurs with;

O. Allen's case refer'd Thee Committee Appointed to discourse with **Obediah Allen**
Make Report that he hath not [writ?] anything to this Meeting
agreeable to his talk some time past, therefore his Case is
Refer'd (on the Request of his Father) unto the next Monthly
Meeting.

J. Russell & wife & children request to be Read **Joseph Russell** and his Wife hath Given in a paper to this
Meeting Condemning their disorder in Marriage, and also
they desire to Come under friends Care with their Children
which this Meeting so far Accepts as to Appoint **Joseph Tucker**
and **Joseph Gifford** to Treat with them and their Children
that have Attained to the years of understanding, and
make Report to the next Monthly Meeting;

Wᵐ Brown Certificate **William Brown** hath Produced a Removal Certificate
from the Monthly Meeting of **Nantucket** to this Meeting
which hath been Read and Accepted

Certificate for Samuel Howland This Meeting hath signed a Removal Certificate to the
Monthly Meeting of **Smithfield** for **Samuel Howland** juⁿ
and his Children – –

Miniuts not Revised The Committee Appointed to peruse the Monthly Meeting
Minutes, Make Report that they have not perused Sᵈ
Minutes, therefore they are still continued in the Same
Service and to make Report to the next Monthly Meeting.

Settled with overseers of The Committee Appointed to Adjust Accompts with the overseers

the Poor   of the poor Make Report that all accounts are Balanced
between this Meeting and the S^d overseers – –

Case of Paul The Committee Appointed to Treat with **Paul Mosher** Make
Mosher   Report that they have not had an opportunity with S^d **Mosher**
therefore the S^d Committee are Still Continued in the Same
Service and to Make Report to the next Monthly Meeting

Amie **Amey Hart**'s Paper hath been Read According to the order
Harts   of last Monthly Meeting – –
paper read

Benj Allen's **Benjamin Allen** hath Given in a Paper Condemning his
paper accepted Allowing of fidling and dancing in his House at the time
of Husking, which this Meeting Accepts

F. Allen's The friends Appointed to treat with **Francis Allen** Report
Case   that they have not had an opportunity to Speak with him, therefore
Continued they are Still Continued in the Same Service and to Make
Report to the next Monthly Meeting;

adjourns This Meeting Adjourns to the 26 day of this Instant;

mett This Meeting being met According to Adjournment the 26 day of the
3^d Month 1766, the Representatives being Called **Caleb Russell**,
Samuel Smith, **Philip Tripp** and **Daniel Wood** present;
The Committee Appointed to fix the Boundaries between this
and the Monthly Meeting Requested to be sett off at **Coakset**, Make
Report that they have agreed Upon the Boundaries and other
things relating to **Coakset** being set off as a Monthly Meeting
which Report is as follows (viz)

Boundries   According to the Appointment of last Monthly Meeting, we
of Acoakset have Described a line for the boundaries between the Monthly
of month Meetings of **Ponaganset** and **Coakset** as follows, Beginning at the
ly meeting South Eastermost Corner of **Benjamin Wing**'s Homstead farm, from
thence to **Coakset River** as the line of Said **Benj^a** Land goes,
Thence Southerly by Said River to the Sea, Again from Said
Corner first Mentioned thence Northerly in the line between
Said Villages until it comes to the Country Road, Thence on
a Straight line to the nearest part of the Westermost Branch
of **Noquechuck River**, thence by said branch of Said River
Till it comes to **Freetown** line – –

Concerning We have likewise Concluded for **Coakset** friends to have About
the books one third part of the Books belonging to the Monthly Meeting,
and likewise that they be supplied with A Transcript of the
Book of Discipline at the Cost of the Whole, And also that
the Monthly Meetings debts be paid in the same proportion

that Shall be due when the Meeting is Divided, But the
friends that are now under Relief are to be Supported when
they are, and **Coakse** friends, to Quit their Claim of the Meeting
House Land, in **Ponaganset**; dated the 26th of the 3rd mo. 1766.

$$\left. \begin{array}{ll} \text{Joseph Tucker} & \text{Philip Tripp} \\ \text{Humphry Smith} & \text{Daniel Wood} \\ & \text{Samuel Smith} \end{array} \right\}$$

Joseph Roach accepted — **Joseph Roach** jun hath Produced a Removal Certificate from
the Monthly Meeting of **Nantucket** to this Meeting which hath
been Read and Accepted

The Queries have Been Read and Answer'd in this Meeting

Representatives to Quar Meet= =ing — **Caleb Russell, William Anthony** jun, **Samuel Smith, Thomas
Hicks** jun are Appointed to attend the Quarterly Meeting and
Compile the Answers to the Queries and draw an Epistle to the
Same, and bring them to the Adjournment of this Meeting.

Wm Smith's disorderly marriage — The overseers Inform that **William Smith** the 2d has gone
Contrary to Good order in Marrying out of the Unity of friends,
for which he hath been Labour'd with by the Overseers, and
declines to Make Satisfaction, therefore **John Potter**
and **William Barker** are Appointed to Labour furder
with him, and Make Report to the next Monthly Meeting.

Complaint against Lemuel Smith — The overseers also Inform that **Lemuel Smith** hath
fallen into the Sin of fornication, and hath been La=
=bour'd with by them and he Neglects to Condemn his out=
=goings, therefore **Paul Russell** and **Luke Hart** are
appointed to Labour furder with him, and Make Report
to the next Monthly Meeting;

adjourn — This Meeting adjorns to the first Sixth day of next month

mett — This Meeting being met According to Adjournment
the 4th day of the 4th Month 1766, the Representatives
being Called, **Caleb Russell, Samuel Smith** and **Philip
Tripp** present

[?][Queries] [?][answer'd] Epistle sent — The friends Appointed to Compile the Answers to the Queries
and draw an Epistle to the Quarterly Meeting have fulfilled their
Appointment and the Epistle has been Signed in this Meeting
and sent up by the Representatives to the Quarterly Meeting
with the Answers to the Queries

This Meeting hath signed and sent a Letter to the Monthly
Meeting of **Oblong**, Signifying that this Meeting hath Re=
=ceived their letter Concerning **Daniel Tripp**, which is as

followeth;

Letter from Oblong concerning Daniel Tripp From our Monthly Meeting held at **Oblong** the 20th of the 2nd Mo. 1766, To the Monthly Meeting of Friends at **Dartmouth**, Dear Friends, we herby Acquaint you, that whereas **Daniel Tripp** Resides sometime Amongst us, and was for some years a Member of our Society, But by Marrying out from Among= us, Contrary to the Advice of Friends, for which he was dealt with, but Proving Refractory, after some time he was Testified Aagainst, Soon after which he ~~was Testified Against~~ ˄ Set up a Seperate Meeting, which he kept for a Conside= =rable time, to the Great Dissatisfaction of Friends, And Since he has Moved to your parts we Understand he frequents friends Meetings, and Publickly Appears as a Minister Amongst you, therefore we send you the Above lines to let you know the Circumstance he Stood in at the time when he Removed from these parts. Signed in and on behalf of our Sd Meeting by

Zebulon Ferriss Clerk

D. Briggs E.Maxfield & Wm Hart Ju answers At a Monthly Meeting held in **Dartmouth** the 21 of the 4th Month 1766, **Ponaganset** Meeting Called **John Potter** and **W,m Anthony ju,r** present, for **Coakset** **Peleg Huddlestone** and **Joseph Tripp** present, **David Briggs** and **Rebecca Howland**, and **Edmond Maxfield** and **Rachel Russell**, and **William Hart ju:** and **Esther Slade** Appeared for their Answers, which was that each Couple Might Proceed to take Each other in Marrage [*sic*] in some Convenient time between this and the next Monthly Meeting Advising with the Overseers for that Purpose. And **John Potter and Jonathan Hussey** are Appointed to see **David Briggs** and **Rebecca Howland**s Marriage Consumated in Good order, and make Report to the next Monthly Meeting. And **Paul Russell** and **William Mosher** are Appoin= =ted to see **Edmond Maxfield** and **Rachel Russell**'s Marriage Consumated in Good order and Make Report to the next Month =ly Meeting; And **Joseph Smith** and **Barnabas Mosher** are Appointed for the Same ˄Service with **William Hart ju:** and **Esther Slade** and ˄to make Report to the next Monthly Meeting **William Wilcox**'s Paper of Denial hath been Read According to the Appointment of last Monthly Meeting, and is as follows; – – Whereas **William Wilcox** Son of **W,m Wilcox** Deceased and

W^m
Wilcox
disowned

Dorithy his Wife, having been under the Care of this Meeting, yet through unwatchfulness and disregarding the Testimony of Truth, has So far deviated from our Holy Profession as to fall into Several Reproachful things, and disorders, Parti= =cularly in Inlisting and Going into the Milatary [military] Service, and Marrying out of the order of Friends, likewise in Selling Such Beef as was not Merchantable to the Defrauding of the Buyer, and also in Neglecting to attend our Religious Meetings of Publick Worship, and Friends having Repeated their Labour of Love and advice ~~and~~ toward him in order to disco=^{(ver} to him the Evil of his ways, but their Labour not obtaining it's desired Effect to the Satisfaction of this Meeting, Therefore for the Clearing of the precious Truth and Friends from the Reproach thereof, this Meeting Gives this forth as a Publick Testimony against him, Disowning him the Said **Will,^m** **Wilcox** from being one of our Community, and from u[n]der the Care of this Meeting, Yet desiring his Return from the way of Error and that by the door of true Repentance he may find Mercy.

Given forth at our Monthly Meeting of friends held in **Dartmouth** on the 17th day of the 3.^d mo: 1766, And Signed In and on behalf of S.^d Meeting by – – **Job Russell** Clerk

O. Allens
case refer^d

Whereas **Obediah Allen** hath been in the Practice of Gaming and hath been dealt with, and declines to make friends Satis= =faction, therefore friends Canst find freedom to Accept of his Condemning his falling into the Sin of Fornication, therefore the matter is Refer'd to the next Monthly Meeting under the Same Care as heretofore

M. Smith;
Certifi:

Meriah Smith hath Produced a Removal Certificate from the Monthly Meeting of **Sandwich** to this Meeting which hath been Red [*sic*] and Accepted.

R. Russell
Receivd

The women friends Inform that they have minuted **Rebecca Russell** ~~wife~~ Daughter of **Joseph Russell** under their Care which this Meeting Concur's with

J. Russell
& family
Rec^d

The Com,^{tee} appointed to treat with **Joseph Russell** his wife and Family on their Request to Come under friends care, Make a Satisfactory Report, therefore this Meeting Accepts them un= =der friends Care

The friends Appointed to Review the Monthly Meetings Minutes to see what part must go on Record, make Report that

Minutes
recorded
by S.S.

they have fulfilled their Appointment and left S.^d minutes with **Samuel Smith** to be Recorded – –

Report of   The friends Appointed overseers in the Meeting held in
overseers of
mee[t]ing   **Allen's Neck**, Report that they attended the Meeting
Allens Neck   and saw nothing but that it was Carried on decently and
in Good order – –

Report from   The ‸friends appointed to attend the Quarterly Meeting Report that
Qtr meeting   they all attended S[d] meeting, and have Produced an Epistle
from the Same which hath been Read and well accepted

Coakset   And the Quarterly Meeting hath Granted our Request to
meeting
set off   have a monthly Meeting of men and women Friends Sett
off at **Coaksett**
according to the Boundaries prefixt, and
this meeting Concludes for **Coakset** friends to hold their Monthly
Meeting the Seventh day before the third Second day in
Each month;

W.ᵐ Smith   The friends Appointed to Treat with **W.ᵐ Smith** ye 2[d][?] Make
denied   Report that he Gave them no Satisfaction, therefore
friends finding themselves Clear in Labouring with him
do deny the S.[d] **W.ᵐ Smith** from under friends Care – –

Lamu Smith   The friends Appointed to Labour with **Lemuel Smith** Report
case refer'd   that both have not had an Oppertunity with, him, but the friend
that had an Oppertunity Reports that he Gave him Good
Satisfaction, And he hath Sent a Paper to this Meeting Con=
=demning his offence which is Refer'd under the Care of the
Afore Said Committee – –

S. Wilcox   Whereas **Stephen Wilcox** having Appeared in this Meeting
his Trans=
=gresion   in a very Passionate Manner, Casting heavy Reflections on
us, Saying that he believed we Should have fewer Testimones
Amongst us, And that it was Pitty we Shou[l]d have any
Except it be Some to Reprimand us for our Wickedness, and
Stamping on the floor in a Passionate Manner, to the Great
Grief and Sorrow of the Sincere in heart, Therefore this
Meeting doth Appoint **Tho,ˢ Hicks**, **Peleg Smith**, **Joseph Gifford**
Barzillia Tucker to Labour with him and Make Report there=
=of to the next Monthly Meeting; – They are likewise to
Inform him that we desire him to desist from Appearing in Publick – –

adjourn   This Meeting Adjorurns to the 7ᵗʰ day of next Month

mett   This Meeting being met according to Adjournment ye 7ᵗʰ day of the
5ᵗʰ mo. 1766, the Representatives being Called, **John Potter** and
Peleg Huddlestone present

Paul   Wher[e]as **Paul Mosher** hath Married out of the Unity of friends
Mosher

denied and hath been dealt with Agreeable to Good order, and he de=
=clines to Condemn his offence therefore this Meeting finding them=
=Selves Clear in Labouring with him, do deny the S.ᵈ **Paul
Mosher** from under the Care of this Meeting

Case of The Case of **Francis Allen** is Refer'd to the next Monthly Meeting
F. Allen under the Same Care as heretofore – –
refer'd

Proposal for Inlarging the little Meeting House is Refer'd to the
next Monthly Meeting;

---

5 mo: At a Monthly Meeting held in **Dartmouth** the 19ᵗʰ day of the
1766 5ᵗʰ month 1766, **Ponaganset** Meeting Called **Joseph Smith** and
Tho,ˢ Hicks ju.ʳ present, for **Coakset Joshua Davil** [Davol]
and **Israel Wood** present,

E. Wing Ju **Edward Wing ju:** of **Sandwich** and **Edith Tucker** declared their
proposal of Intentions of Marriage, and were desired to wait till next
marriage Monthly Meeting for their Answer,

Tho Smith Ju And **Tho,ˢ Smith ju:** and **Rebecca Howland** likewise declared
proposal of their Intentions of Marriage & were desired to wait till the
marriage next Monthly Meeting for their Answer, and **Luke Hart** and
Wᵐ Mosher are Appointed to Inquire into S.ᵈ **Smith**'s Clearness
Respecting Marriage and Conversation and to Make Report
to the next Monthly Meeting; – –

Report of **John Potter** and **Jonathan Hussey** Report, that they attended
D. Briggs the Marriage of **David Briggs** and **Rebecca Howland**
marriage and that it was Accomplish'd in Good order – –

Report of **Paul Russell** and **W,ᵐ Mosher** Report that they attended
E. Maxfield the Marriage of **Edmond Maxfield** and **Rachel Russell**
marriage which (they say) was Accomplished in Good order – –

Report of **Joseph Smith** and **Barnabas Mosher,** likewise Report
Wᵐ Hart Ju that they attended the Marriage of **W.ᵐ Hart ju:** and
marriage **Esther Slade** and that it was Accomplished in Good order

Meeting Whereas **Obediah Allen** Some time past fell into the
concluds Sin of Fornication, and also Since hath been in the Practice
to deny of Gaming, for which he hath been dealt with by this
O. Allen Meeting and declines to Condem[n] his offences to friends
Satisfaction, therefore this Meeting being Clear in Labour=
=ing with him, do Conclude to deny him from under the Care
of this Meeting, and do Appoint **Samuel Smith** to draw
a Paper of denial Against the S,ᵈ **Obediah Allen**, and bring
it to the next Monthly Meeting. – –

Case of
S. Wilcox
Referd   The friends Appointed to Labour with **Stephen Wilcox** for his Misconduct at the last Monthly Meeting, Report that he did not Condem his S,^d offence in full therefore the matter is Refer'd till next monthly Meeting under the same Care as heretofore and they to make Report to the next Monthly Meeting – –

F. Allen
Paper   **Francis Allen** hath Given in a paper to this Meeting Con= demning his Giving way to too much Liberty in Allowing of fidling and dancing at the time of his Husking, which this Meeting Accepts – –

Case of little
meeting
house
dr^apt   This Meeting Concludes to drop the Proposal for Enlarging the little Meeting House for the present – –

to Receive
accompts
of poor   This Meeting doth Appoint **Jonathan Hussey** and **David Smith** to Receive in Accounts for doing for the poor of this Meeting and also Endeavour to Inform themselves into the Validity of S^d Accounts, and also S^d friends, to Join with **Philip Tripp** to Divide the Books that belongs to this Meeting; – –

To Collect
[Ac?]count of
[Pu?]blick
Friend
deceased   This Meeting doth Appoint **Samuel Smith** and **Wm Anthony** ju: to Collect the Birth, place of abode, time of publick Ministry and death of **Elizabeth Gidley**, and bring the account to the next Monthly Meeting – –

Order to
pay Tim
Russell   This Meeting hath Collected £$_9$-$_7$^s-$_6$^d old tener [tenor] and the Treasure[r] hath paid **Timothy Russell** five Dollars for Keeping the Meeting House half a year – –

To Settle
with
Treasurer   And **Jonathan Hussey** and **Wm Sanford** are Appointed to Adjust accompts [accounts] with the Treasurer and make Report to the next Monthly Meeting

Wm Anthony
Jr. to Rece
Subscrip
tions   This Meeting doth appoint **W,^m Anthony ju^r** to Receive the Subscriptions that are Subscribed to defray the Charges of this Meeting and also to pay out the money as this Meeting Shall order

---

6 mo:
1766   At a Monthly Meeting Met the 16th of the 6th Month 1766 The Representatives are **Abraham Tucker** & **John Potter** present; Whereas the yearly Meeting is now in being, therefore this Mee= =ting doth adjourn to the 23^d Instant This Meeting being met According to adjournment the 23^d of the 6th month 1766 The Representatives being Called both present

Edw Wing
Certificat   **Edward Wing** hath Produced a Certificate from the monthly Meeting of **Sandwich**, Certifying his Clearness Respecting Marriage and Conversation which hath been Read & Accepted

Edw Wings **Edward Wing ju:** and **Edith Tucker** Appeared for their Answer
answer which was that they might Proceed to take Each other in
Marriage in Some Convenient time between this and the
next Monthly Meeting Advising with the Overseers for that
purpose, And **Abraham Tucker** and **Joseph Gifford** are Appoin=
=ted to see their Marriage Consumated in Good order and make
Report to the next Monthly Meeting; – –

Tho Smith Ju **Thomas Smith ju:** and **Rebecca Howland** Appear'd for their
Answer Answer, which was that they might Proceed to take Each other
In Marriage in Some Convenient time between this and the next
Monthly Meeting, Advising with the overseers for that purpose
and **Luke Hart** and **William Mosher** are Appointed to See
their Marriage Consumated in Good order and make Report
to the next Monthly Meeting; – –

Wᵐ Ricket **William Ricketson** and **Elisabeth Smith** declared their
=sons Intentions of taking Each other in Marriage, and were desired
proposal to wait till the next Monthly Meeting for their Answer, and
of marriag **Caleb Russell** and **Job Russell** are appointed to make Inquiry
Into **W,ᵐ Ric[k]etson**'s Clearness Respecting Marriage and
Conversation and make Report to the next Monthly Meeting

This Meeting hath Signed a paper of Denial Against
O. Allen **Obediah Allen** for the Sin of Fornication & Gaming, and
disownd the Clerk of this Meeting is appointed to read it at the Close
of a first day Meeting for worship between this and the next
Monthly Meeting and make Report to Said Meeting.

S. Wilcox' **Stephen Wilcox** hath Given in a Paper to this Meeting
paper Condem[n]ing his Reflecting Speeches, which was Expressed
in our Monthly Meeting two Months ago, which this Mee=
=ting doth accept, and Said **Wilcox**'s former References are
Still Continued under the Same Regulation as heretofore

This Meeting hath signed a Paper of Denial against **Su**=
=**sanna Brightman** for the Sin of fornication and the Clerk
is Appointed to Read Said paper at the Close of a first day
Meeting for Worship between this and the next Monthly
Meeting, and make Report to Said Meeting. – –

John⎰ Our Esteemed friend **John Griffith** hath Visited this Meeting
Griffith⎱ with a Certificate from **Chelmsford** [Essex Co England] Monthly
Visit Meeting in **Essex** dated the 25ᵗʰ of the 2ᵈ month 1765 and also from the
Quarterly Meeting held at **Coggoshall** in **Essex** the 12.ᵗʰ of the 3.ᵈ mo: 1765
and also from the Yearly Meeting of Ministers & Elders held in

London by Adjorunments from the 25.th of the 5.th Month to the 3.^d of the 6.th month 1765 which was Read to Good Satisfaction[3]

T. Ross Visit — Our Esteemed friend **Thos Ross** hath Visited this Meeting, and pro= =duced a Certificate from the Monthly Meeting held in **Write-Town [Wrightstown]** in **Bucks Country Pen[n]sylvania**, bearing date the 6th day of the 5th month 1766 which hath been Read to Good Satisfaction[4]

Queries Answerd — The Queries have been Read & Answer'd in this Meeting and **Peleg Smith** & **Humphry Smith** are Appointed to draw an Epistle to the Quarterly Meeting & bring it to the Adjornment

adjou'n — This Meeting Adjorns to the first Sixth day in next month

mett — The Meeting being Met according to Adjournment the 4th day of the 7th mo: 1766 the Representatives being Called both present

acco^mpts Receiv'd — The friends Appointed to Receive accompts [accounts] and Approbate them= Report that they have Received them and allowed to the amount of -

	£	S	d
amount of	16	6	4
Coakset Meeting paying one third part of S.^d Sum	5	8	9
Remains for this Meeting to pay – – Lawful mony	10	17	7

Elis: Gidley to go on Record — The Committee appointed to Collect the Birth & C. of **Elisabeth Gidley** have Answer'd their Appointment, and the Account thereof is order'd to be put on Record – –

[Repre]sentatives Quart meeting — **Humphry Smith, Abraham Tucker, Caleb Russell** are Ap= =pointed to attend the Quarterly Meeting. This Meeting hath Signed an Epistle to the Quarterly Meeting and Sent it up by the Representatives

7 mo: 1766 — At a Monthly Meeting held in **Dartmouth** the 21 of the 7th month 1766, The Representatives are **Samuel Smith** and **Barzillia Tucker** present;

The friends appointed to Enquire into the Clearness of **Wm Ricetson [Ricketson]** make Report that they have made proper Inquiry, and don't find anything to hinder him from Proceeding in Marr[i]age

Wm Ric^ket answer — **William Rictson [Ricketson]** and **Elisabeth Smith** appear'd for their An= =swer, which was that they might Proceed to take Each other in Marriage in Some Convenient time between this and the next monthly meeting, A[d]vising with the Overseers for that purpose, and **Caleb Russell** & **Benj,^a Howland ju:** are

3. John Griffith (1713–1776) was one of the most influential Friends of the eighteenth century. See *A Journal of the Life, Travels, and Labours in the Work of the Ministry, of John Griffith* (London: James Phillips, 1779).

4. Thomas Ross (1708–1786), a minister from Bucks County, Pennsylvania, died on a visit to England. See *Memorials of Deceased Friends: Being a Selection from the Records of the Yearly Meeting for Pennsylvania, Etc., from the Year 1788 to 1878, Inclusive* (Philadelphia: Friends' Book Store 1879), 8–19.

appointed to See their Marriage Consumated in Good order
and make Report to the next Monthly Meeting – –

Report of Ed Wing's marriage **Abraham Tucker** Reports that he attended the Marri[a]ge
of **Edward Wing ju:** and **Edith Tucker** which was Accomplish'd
in Good order – –

Luke Hart & **W.ᵐ Mosher** Reports that they attended the
Report of Tho Smith's Marriage Marriage of **Thoˢ Smith ju:** and **Rebecca Howland** which was
Accomplish'd in Good order – –

O. Allen disowned **Obediah Allen**'s Paper of Denial hath been Read Accor=
=ding to the Appointment of last Monthly Meeting – –
And is as follows (viz) – –

Whereas **Obediah Allen**, Son of our friends **Prince** and
Deborah Allen, having been under the Care of this Meet=
=ing, yet he has So far Gone astray from our Profession as to
fall into the Reproachful Sin of Fornication, and also
been found in the Practice of Gaming, And friends having
Repeated their Labour of Love with him in order for his
Recovery, but our Labour of Love not obtaining the de=
=Sired Effect to the Satisfaction of this Meeting, Therefore
we being desirous that the Truth of our Holy Profession may
be preserved from the Reproach of ˄Such Enormities, do Give
this forth as a Publick Testimony against him, disowning
him the Said **Obediah Allen** from being one of our Society
and from being in Membership With us, yet we desire if
it be Consistant with Divine Pleasure, that he May yet
find a place of Repentence (and by an Unfeigned acknow=
=ledgement of the Error of his way) Return to ~~th~~ the way
of Truth

　　　Given forth and Signed in and on behalf of our Monthly
Meeting held in **Dartmouth** by Adjournment on the 23ᵈ
day of the 6ᵗʰ month 1766 by – – – **Job Russell** Clerk

Susanna Brightman's Paper of Denial hath been read according
to the appointment of last Monthly Meeting, and is as follow's

S. Bright man's denial 　　　Whereas **Susanna Brightman** Daughter of **Joshua** and **Hannah**
Shearman having had her Education among friends and under the Care
of this Meeting, but through unwatchfulness & disregarding the
Testimony of Truth hath fallen into the Reproachful Sin of
Fornication, as appears by her having a Child Soon after Marriage
and this Meeting having Labour'd with her in Love in order for her
Recovery, but She proving obstinate, and Regardless of the ten=

=der Council to her Given, Therefore for the Clearing of the precious
Truth that we Profess, from Such Enormities, this Meeting is
Concerned to Give this forth as a Publick Testimony against her
disowning her the S^d **Susanna Brightman** from being a Member
of our Society, and from under the Care of this Meeting, desiring
if it be Consistant with Divine pleasure, that She may yet be Convin=
=ced of the Error of her ways, and by a Sincere Repentance, find fa=
=vour with the Lord – –

    Given forth at our Monthly Meeting of Friends held in **Dart**=
=**mouth** by adjournment on the 23.^d day of the 6.th month 1766
    Signed In, by order & in behalf of S.^d Meeting by **Job Russell** Clerk
                                        Apphia Mott Clerk

S. Wilcox This Meeting hath Come to a Conclusion that **Stephen Wilcox** ought
not to   to desist from Appearing in Publick untill his affairs be better
preach   Settled in Regard to his debts, and the S^d **Stephen Wilcox**'s Case is
Refer'd under the Same Regulation as heretofore to the next
Monthly Meeting

    The friends Appointed to attend the Quarterly Meeting
Report that they all attended Agreeable to Appointment
and have Produced an Epistle from the same which hath
been Read to Good Satisfaction

Epistles Received Epistles one from **London** Printed & one written one
also one Epistle from **Philidelphia**, and one from **Flushing**
Also we have Received an Epistle from our Yearly Meeting
of **Rhode-Island** held the 12th of the 6th month 1766 All which
have been read in this Meeting to Good Satisfaction, and as
they Contain a great deal of wholesome advice and Good Ex=
=hortation, they are Earnestly Recommended to friends Notice
and Observation,

Settled The friends Appointed two months ago to adjust Accounts with
With   the Treasurer Report that they have Settled accounts and
Treasurer there Remains in the Stock – – £2 – S8 – d1
Old tenner –

Coakset Monthly Meeting has paid their Proportion of the
Monthly Meeting Debts which is – – £5 – S8 – d9
Lawful Money

Care of twenty four Books belongs to this Meeting, and **Timothy Rus**=
books to =**sell** is appointed to have the Care of Said Books to lend them
T. Russell out and take them in once a month.

This Meeting hath signed a Removal Certificate of

Deb Slade Certificate	**Deborah Slade** (wife to **Joseph Slade**) and her Children to the Monthly Meeting of **Swanzey** – – – – –

8 mo: 1766	At a Monthly Meeting held in **Dartmouth** the 18 of the 8th month 1766 The Representatives are **William Mosher** and **Benjamin Smith** ju: present
Report of Wm. Ricket sons marriage	The friends Appointed to See **Wm Ricketson** and **Elizabeth Smith**'s Marriage Consumated Report that they attended the Marriage which was Consumated in Good order
Certificate for Abigail States	This Meeting hath Signed a Removal Certificate for **Abigail States** (wife of **Peter States**) to the Monthly Meeting of **South Kings-town[Perryville, South Kingstown]**, – –
Case of S. Wilcox Refer'd	The Case of **Stephen Wilcox** is Refer'd under the Care of **Thomas Hicks** 2d and he to ~~make report~~ Inform Said **Wilcox** that his Meeting Requests that he Inform friends at the next Monthly Meeting what Progress he hath made in Regard to paying his debts – –
Overseers appointed	**Luke Hart, Paul Russell, William Anthony** ju: **Benja Howland** 2d, **Samuel Smith** and **Daniel Cornel [Cornell]** are Chosen overseers
Zephaniah Anthony & Wife's paper	**Zephaniah Anthony** and his wife have Given in a Paper to this Meeting, Signifying their Sorrow for their falling into the Sin of Fornication, which is Refer'd unto the next Monthly Meeting under the Care of **Peleg Smith** & **Benjamin Smith** ju: and they to make Report to next Monthly Meeting;
Fox's Journal	This Meeting Hath received one of **George Fox**'s Journals and 7s/6d Sterling overplus Money, which is Lodged with the Treasurer

9th mo: 1766	At a Monthly Meeting held in **Dartmouth** the 15th day of the 9th month 1766,
	William Anthony ju: and to[?] **Samuel Smith** are the Representatives both present~~atives~~
To draw Epistle	This Meeting doth Appoint **Humphry Smith** and **Samuel Smith** to draw an Epistle to the Quarterly Meeting and bring it to the Adjournment of this Meeting;
	This Meeting Adjourns to the first Sixth day in next Month This Meeting being Met According to ~~Appointment~~ adjornment the 3rd of the 10th month 1766. The Representatives being Called both presents;
S. Wilcox Case refer'd	The Case of **Stephen Wilcox** is Refer'd under the Care of **Daniel Russell** and **Thomas Hix** 2d – –
Z. Anthony Case refer'd	**Peleg Smith** and **Benja Smith** ju: Report that they have Treated with **Zephaniah Anthony** in Regard to his Paper that he Gave in last Monthly Meeting, in which they think him to be Sincere,

which is Refer'd to the next Monthly Meeting;

Repre sentatives **Joseph Tucker, Humphry Smith, Caleb Russell** are Appointed to attend the Quarterly Meeting, and present the Epistle (which was Signed in this Meeting) with the Answers to the Queries, and Make Report to the next Monthly Meetings; – –

to pay [?] [Coak [?] [set]6-2-6 This Meeting orders the Treasurer to pay **Coakset** Monthly Meeting half a Crown Sterling, it being one third part of the overplus Money for **George Fox's** Journals

10 mo: 1766 At a Monthly Meeting held in **Dartmouth** the 20th of the 10th month 1766, The Representatives are **Samuel Smith** and **Benjᵃ Howland** the 2ᵈ Presents

Case of Z. Anthony refer'd The Case of **Zephaniah Anthony** is Refer'd under the Care of his Brother **Wᵐ Anthony** unto the next Monthly Meeting

Elihu Bow en requests a Certificate **Elihu Bowen** Requests a Removal Certificate for himself and Family to the Monthly Meeting of **Swanzey**. Therefore **Luke Hart** & **Paul Russell** are appointed to Make proper Enquiry into his Circumstances, and draw one for them if they think proper & bring it to the next Monthly Meeting

Report from Quarterly meeting The friends Appointed to attend the Quarterly Meeting Report that they all attended Agreeable to Appointment, and have produced an Epistle from the Same, which hath been Read in this Meeting to Good Satisfaction

R. Soule **Rachel Soule** hath been Represented under Necessituous Circumstances, and Liable to become one of this Meetings poor, Therefore **Humphry Smith** & **Jonathan Hussey** are Ap= =pointed to make Inquiry into her Circumstances & Estate and make Report to the next Monthly Meeting;

Jonaⁿ Gifford desires a Certificate **Jonathan Gifford** desires a Certificate to the Monthly Mee= =ting of **Nantucket**, Certifying his Clearness Respecting Marriage & Conversation, Therefore **Jonathan Hussey** and **David Smith** are Appointed to make Inquiry into his aforeSᵈ Circumstances, and draw a Certificate for him if they think proper, and bring it to the next Monthly Meeting;

Overseers for yearly meeting This Meeting doth Appoint **John Potter, Daniel Russell Timothy Russell Samuel Smith, Thoˢ Hicks 2ᵈ Prince Allen James Tucker** overseers at the yearly Meeting to Endeavour to prevent any Indecency that May happen at that time, and Make Report of their Service to the next Monthly Meeting

11ᵗʰ mo: 1766 At a Monthly Meeting held in **Dartmouth** the 17th of the 11th Month 1766, The Representatives are **Daniel Cornel** and **Thomas**

Hicks 2ᵈ present

Timothy **Timothy Howland** and **Lucey Allen** Declared their Intentions of
Howland taking each other in Marriage, and were desired to wait till
proposal
of marri the next Monthly Meeting for their Answer, and **Daniel Cornel**
age and **Thomas Hicks 2d** are appointed to Make Inquiry into the young
Man's Clearness Respecting Marriage & Conversation, and make Report
to the next Monthly Meeting,

Z. Anthony The Case of **Zephaniah Anthony** is Refer'd under the Same Care as
Case refer'd heretofore – –

Certificate for This Meeting hath Signed a Removal Certificate for **Elihu Bowen**
Elihu
Bowen and his family to the Monthly Meeting of **Swanzey**;

Case of The Case of **Rachel Soule** is Refered under the Same Regulation
R. Soule
refer'd as heretofore

Certificate This Meeting Hath Signed a Certificate for **Jonathan Gifford** to the
for Jonat. Monthly Meeting of **Nantucket**, Respecting his Clearness in Regard
Gifford
to Marriage & his Conversation – –

Tim Russell This Meeting allows of **Timothy Russell**'s account for Clearing the
acompt Burying yard & Repairing the fence & Bars, which is   £4   13ˢ
old tener

David Smith hath paid **Coakset** Monthly Meeting 2 / 6d Sterling agreeable
to Appointment

J. Sisson **John Sisson** Requests a Removal Certificate for himself and Children
desires a
Certifi to the Monthly Meeting of **Oblong**, therefore **Paul Russell** & **Luke**
cate **Hart** are Appointed to draw one for him if they shall think Proper
after due Inquiry into his Circumstances, and make Returns to the
next Monthly Meeting;

Report of The friends Appointed Overseers at the yearly Meeting, Report
Overseers that they attended Agreeable to Appointment & discover'd
of Yearly
meeting nothing but what was in a degree orderly, and they think that
friends Care in that Respect answers a Good Purpose – –

Meetings This Meeting Grants the friends Living in **Allen's Neck** the
granted Liberty to hold a Meeting down there at Some friends House
in Allen's
Neck for four Months to Come on first days, Excepting the first day
preceding the Monthly Meeting in Each Month, and **Daniel**
Cornel [Cornell] and **Prince Allen** are Appointed to have the oversight
of the Meeting, and to Make Report to this Meeting at the
Expiration of the four Months

12 Mo: At a Monthly Meeting held in **Dartmouth** the 15ᵗʰ
1766 of the 12ᵗʰ month 1766, the Representatives are **Paul Russell**
and **David Smith** Present;

Timothy Howland answer **Timothy Howland** and **Lucey Allen** Appeared for their Answer which was, that they Might proceed to take Each other in Marriage in Some Convenient time between this and the next Monthly Meeting, Avising with the overseers for that Purpose and **Daniel Cornel** and **Thomas Hicksⁿ** are Appointed to See their Marriage Consumated in Good order and Make Report to the next Monthly Meeting;

This Meeting hath Collected £11 – 7s – 6d old tener, and the

Tim Russell paid Treasurer has paid **Timothy Russell** the Above S^d Sum

Humphry Smith and **Jonathan Hussey** Report that they have

Rachel Sowle Case Inspected into the Circumstances of **Rachel Soule** and they find due to her by Bond and Note £12 – 16s – 9d Lawful money

John Sisson Certificates refer'd The friends Appointed to draw a Certificate for **John Sisson** and his Children have drawn one for them, but things not ap= =pearing Quite Clear, the Signing of it is Refer'd to the next Monthly Meeting

John Williams Certificate Accepted **John Williams** and his wife have Produced a Removal Certificate from the Monthly Meeting of **Sandwich**, which this Meeting accepts;

Stephen Smith hath given a paper which is accepted **Stephen Smith** hath Produced and Given in a Paper to this Meeting, Condeming his Marrying out of the Unity of friends which this Meeting Accepts;

Representatives **Caleb Russell**, **Joseph ~~Russ~~ Smith**, **William Barker** are Ap= =pointed to attend the Quarterly Meeting and Make Report to the Next Monthly Meeting;

overseers of Poor accompt The overseers of the poor hath Brought an Account for doing for the poor to the Amount of £3 – 6s – 6d old Tener, which this Meeting allows,

Case of Zep Anthony refer'd The Case of **Zephaniah Anthony** is Refer'd

Compaint against James Allen The Overseers Inform that **James Allen** hath fallen into the Sin of Fornication, for which they have Labour'd with him, and he declines to Make Satisfaction, therefore this Meeting doth Appoint **Caleb Russell** & **Job Russell** to Labour with him & make Report to the next Monthly Meeting

The Queries have been Read in this Meeting and Answer'd

This Meeting hath signed an Epistle to the Quarterly Mee= =ting, and Sent it up with the Answers to the Queries by the Representatives.

first mo: 1767 At a Monthly Meeting held in **Dartmouth** the 19th of the first Month 1767, the Representatives are **Samuel**

Smith and **William Anthony ju:** present;

Daniel Cornel and **Tho****s**** Hicks** 2ᵈ Report that they attended

Tim Howland's marriage the Marriage of **Timothy Howland** & **Lucey Allen**, which was Consumated in Good order,

John Sisson's Case The Signing of **John Sisson**'s Certificate is Refer'd to next Monthly Meeting;

James Allen Case The friends Appointed to Labour with **James Allen** Report that he declines to Condem his offence to friends Satisfaction, therefore this Meeting doth Appoint **Joseph Gifford** and **Job Russell** to draw a paper of denial Against Said **Allen** and also Inform him of the Conclusion of this Meeting and Labour with him as they shall find free= =dom, and Make Report to the next Monthly Meeting

Report from Quarterly meeting The friends Appointed to attend the Quarterly Meeting, Report that neither of them attended by Reason of the Severity of the weather; but we Received an Epistle ~~an~~ from the Quarterly Meeting which hath been Read and well accepted,

S. Dennis Request **Shadrach Dennis** Requests to be taken under friends Care, therefore this Meeting doth Appoint **Abraham Tucker** and **Peleg Smith** to Inquire into the young mans Life and Conversation, and also take an opportunity of Solid Conference with him and Make Report to the next Monthly Meeting;

E. Russell Recev'd The women friends Inform that they have Minuted **Elisabeth Russell** wife of **Isaac Russell** under friends Care, which this Meeting Concurs with;

Zeph. Anthony & Wife paper accepted **Zephaniah Anthony** and his wife have Given in a Paper to this Meeting Signifying their Sorrow for their falling into the Sin of fornication, which hath lain on file for Some Months and now friends being fully Satisfied, do Accept of Sᵈ Paper Provided they Cause it to be read at the Close of a first day Meeting for Worship, between this and the next Month= =ly Meeting they being present, and also Return Said Paper to the next Monthly Meetings –

Testimony of E. Gidley This Meeting hath Given forth a Testimony Concerning Our Well Esteemed friend **Elizabeth Gidley** deceased which was Signed in this Meeting by a Number of friends

2ᵈ month 1767 At a Monthly Meeting of friends held in **Dartmouth** the 16ᵗʰ of the 2d month 1767 The Representatives are **Paul**

Russell and **William Anthony ju:** present,

James Allen denied This Meeting hath Signed a Paper of denial against **James Allen** Son of **Francis Allen** for Fornication, and the Clerk is order'd to read S^d Paper at the Close of a first days Mee= =ting for worship, between this and the next Monthly Meeting and Make Report to the next Monthly Meeting;

Shadrich Dennis Case The friends Appointed to Inquire into the Conversation of **Shadrach Dennis**, and to Confer with him on his Request to Come under friends Care not being able to Make a Satisfac= =tory Report, therefore they are Still Continued in the Same Service, and to Make Report to the next Monthly Meeting

Certificate for John Sisson This Meeting hath Signed a Removal Certificate for **John Sisson** to the Monthly Meeting of **Oblong**; – –

Z. Anthony paper read **Zephaniah Anthony's** and his wife's Paper hath been read According to the Appointment of last Monthly Meeting

Z. & W. Anthony's Confession And is as followeth; (viz)

To the Monthly Meeting of friends held in **Dartmouth**
Esteemed friends, – –
These are to Inform that we were Educated and
Married Amongst friends, But we Acknowledge that we
have fallen into the Sin of Fornication, as Appears evident
by the Birth of our Child, the which Sin we do Condemn and
are Sorrowful for, But we hope the Almighty will forgive
us, and we desire friends would so far pass it by as to Suffer
us Still to Remain under your Care
Given under our Hands the 18th of the 8th
Month 1766 – –   **Zephaniah Anthony**
                                              Waite Anthony

Lem^l Smith paper accep =ted Whereas **Lemuel ~~Sisson~~ Smith** hath Given in a Paper to this Meeting Some Months ago, and not accepted by Reason of his Absence, Therefore this Meeting being Satisfied do accept of S^d Paper, Provided that he Cause it to be Read at the Close of a first day Meeting for worship between this and the next Monthly Meeting he being present, and Return S^d Paper to the Clerk –

Miniuts to be revised This Meeting doth Appoint **Peleg Smith, Humphry Smith, Samuel Smith, William Anthony ju^r & Job Russell** to Peruse the Monthly Meetings Minutes, to See what part they Shall think Proper to be put on Record and make Report to the next Monthly Meeting

Edith Wing's Paper Accept. **Edith Wing** hath Given in a Paper to this Meeting Condeming her falling into the Sin of fornication, which this Meeting doth Accept with the Provisal that She Cause S^d Paper to be read at the Close of a first day Meeting for worship She being present, and Make Report to the next Monthly Meeting and Return the Paper to the Clerk – –

To Settle with Treasurer **William Sanford** & **Jonathan Hussey** are Appointed to ad= =just Accounts with the Treasurer & Report to the next Monthly Meeting

Overseers This Meeting doth Appoint **John Potter**, **Prince Allen** & **Joseph Gifford** overseers of the Poor for one year – –

A. Hathaway Certificate This Meeting hath Signed a Removal Certificate for **Abigail Hathaway** to the Monthly Meeting of **Sandwich**

3^d month 1767 At a Monthly Meeting held in **Dartmouth** the 16th of the 3^d Month 1767, the Representatives are **Daniel Cornel** and **Samuel Smith** Present,

Tho Akin's proposal of marriage **Thomas Akin** and **Rebecca Russell** Declar'd their Inten= =tions of Marriage and were desired to wait until the next Monthly Meeting for their Answer, and **Thomas Hicks ju^r** and **Samuel Smith** are Appointed to Inquire into the young man's Clearness Respecting Marriage and Conversation and Make Report to the next Monthly Meeting – –

James Allen's Paper of denial hath been Read Accor= =ding to the Appointment of last Monthly Meeting – – and is as followeth – –

James Allen disowned   Whereas **James Allen** Son of **Francis Allen** & **Rebecca** his Wife deceased, having been Under the Care of this Meeting yet he has So far Gone astray from our Profession as to fall into the Reproachful Sin of Fornication and Friends having Repeated their Labour of Love with him in order for his Recovery, but our Labour of Love, not obtaining the desired Effect to the Satis= =faction of this Meeting, Therefore we being desirous that the Truth of our Holy Profession May be Preferred from the Reproach of Such Enormities do Give this forth a Pubclick Testimony against him, disowning the S^d **James** from being one of our Society, and from being under our Care, Yet Sincerely desiring if it be Consistent with Divine Pleasure that he May yet find a place of Repentance, & by an Unfeigned ~~Repentance~~ acknowledgement of the Error of his way Return to the way of Truth – –

     Given forth and Signed in and on behalf of our Monthly

Meeting held in **Dartmouth** on the 16th day of the 2d month
1767 By

Job Russell Clerk

Shadrich The friends Appointed to Inquire into the life & Conversation of
Dennis **Shadrac Dennis**, and also to take an Opportunity of Conference
Case on his Request to Come under friends Care not being able to make
a Satisfactory Report, therefore the Case is Refer'd under
their Care until the next Monthly Meeting and then to Make
Report,

Lemuel Smith's Paper hath been Read According to the App=
=ointment of last Monthly Meeting, and is as follows

Lemvuel To the Monthly Meeting of Friends to be held in **Dartmouth**
Smith's on the 21 of ye 4th month 1766 – –
Confession
Loving Friends, whereas I through the Insinuation of the Evil
one, I have fallen into the Sin of Fornication, for which Evil
Action I Can Truly Say I am Sincerely Sorry for, and pray that
God may forgive me and all my others Sins, and that you would
pass it by So as to let me Remain under you Care for I have a
Great Value for Friends, So no more at present but I Remain
your well Wishing Friend

Lemuel Smith

Miniutes The Committee Appointed to peruse the Monthly Meetings
to be recorded Minutes Report that they have perused Sd Minutes and left
them with **Samuel Smith** to Record – –

  Edith Wing's paper hath been Read According to the Appoin=
=tment of last Monthly Meeting and is as follows—

E. Wing's   To the Monthly Meeting of friends to be holden at **Dartmouth**
Confession the 16th day of the 2 Month 1767 – –
Well Esteemed friends, these May Inform altho' I have had my
Education among friends, yet through unwatchfulness I have
fallen into the Sin of Fornication, which is S̶ Known by my
having a Child So Soon after Marriage which Sin I Condemn
and am very Sorry for and pray God to forgive me and friends pass
it by So far as to let me Remain under their Care

Settled with The friends Appointed to Adjust accompts ⎫ **Edith Wing**
Treasurer with the Treasurer, Report that there is   ⎭
Remaining in the Treasury 7s – 7d old Tener – –

Ann Gifford **Anna Gifford** Informs this Meeting that She hath a Con=
[?] to =cern on her Mind to Visit **Sandwich** Quarterly Meeting, which
Sandwich this Meeting Concurs with – –

Order to pay Antipas Hathway	**Antipas Hathway** hath Sent an Accompt for Mending our Meeting House windows to the Amount of £0 –1s –6 ½ d Lawful Money which this Meeting orders the Treasurer to pay, and also to pay the overseers of the poor £3–6s–6d old Tener This Meeting hath Collected £7–18s–3d old tener
Complaint against Thoˢ Wilcox	The Overseers Inform This Meeting that **Thomas Wilcox** hath Married out of the unity of friends, for which they have Labour'd with him and he declines to Make friends Satisfaction therefore **Job Case** and **Daniel Russell** are Appointed to Labour further with him and Make Report to the next Monthly Meeting
Complaint against Holder Slocum	The Overseers Inform that **Holder Slocum** hath been in the prac= =tice of Gaming for which they have Laboured with him and he declines to Make friends Satisfaction therefore **Abraham Tucker** & **Joseph Tucker** are Appointed to Labour with Sᵈ **Slocum** and Make Report to the next Monthly Meeting –
Answers to Queries & Epistle Sent	The Queries have have been read and Answer'd in this Meeting and this Meeting hath Signed an Epistle to the Quarterly Meeting which is Sent up to the Quarterly Meeting by the Representatives with the Answers to the Queries – –
Representa= =tives	**Humphry Smith**, **Samuel Smith** and **William Mosher** are Appointed to attend the Quarterly Meeting and they to make Report to the next Monthly Meeting

4ᵗʰ mo: 1767	At a Monthly Meeting held at **Dartmouth** the 20ᵗʰ of the 4ᵗʰ month 1767 – –
	The Representatives are **Thomas Hicks 2ᵈ** and **Samuel Smith** present – The friends Appointed to Inquire into **Thomas Akin**'s Clearness Report that upon Inquiry they find nothing to hinder his proceeding in Marriage – –
Tho Akin's answer	**Thomas Akin** and **Rebecca Russell** Appeared for their Answer which was that they Might proceed to take Each other in Marriage in Some Convenient time between this and the next Monthly Meeting Advising with the overseers for that purpose, and **Humphry Smith** and **Thomas Hicks** are appointed to See their Marriage Consumated in Good order and make Report to the next Monthly Meeting – –
Tim Russell proposal of marriage	**Timothy Russell** and **Hanna Briggs** declar'd their Inten= tion of Marriage and were desired to wait till the next Monthly Meeting for their Answer and **Humphry Smith** and **Jonathan Hussey** are Appointed to Inspect into **Timothy**'s Clear= =ness Respecting Marriage and Conversation and also they

are Appointed to See that the widow's Estate be Settled So that [her]
Children be not Ronged by her Marriage and make Report
to the next Monthly Meeting – –

The friends Appointed to Inquire into the Conversation of **Shadriac**

S. Dennis **Dennis** Make a Satisfactory Report therefore this meeting
Accepted minutes him under friends Care – –

~~The overseers for the poor Report~~

The Treasurer Reports that he has paid the overseers of the
poor According to the Appointment of last Monthly Meeting

The friends Appointed to treat with **Thomas Wilcox** not Making
a Satisfactory Report they are still Continued in the Same
Service and to make Report to the next Monthly Meeting,

Holder The friends Appointed to Treat with **Holder Slocum** Report that they
Slocum's have not discharged themselves in that Respect, therefore they
case are Still Continued in the Same Service and to make Report
to the next Monthly Meeting; – –

Reprent. The Representatives to the Quarterly Meeting Report that
for Qrt. they all attended Except **Wᵐ Mosher**, and he sent an Excuse which
Meeting was Accepted, and they produced an Epistle from the same which
hath been Read and well Accepted

[Report] of The friends Appointed overseers of the Meeting held in **Allen's**
Meetings **Neck** Report that they have attended According to Appoint=
in Allen's =ment and Saw nothing but that it was Carried on in Good order
Neck

5ᵗʰ mo: At a Monthly Meeting held at **Dartmouth** the 18ᵗʰ of the 5ᵗʰ
1767 month 1767 the Representatives are **Caleb Russell** & **Daniel Russell**
both present;

Humphry Smith & **Jonathan Hussey** Make Report that they have made
Inquiry into **Timothy Russell**'s Clearness Respecting Marriage and Con=
=versation, and do not find anything to hinder his proceeding in Mar=
=riage, and they also Report that the widow's Estate is Settled
Acgreeable to Good order

Tim Russell **Timothy Russell** and **Hannah Briggs** Appeared for their Answer
Answer which was that they might proceed to take Each other in Marriage
in Some Convenient time between this and the next Monthly
Meeting, Advising with the oversers for that purpose, and **Humphry**
Smith and **Jonathan Hussey** are Appointed to See their Marriage
Consumated in Good order and Make Report to the next Monthly
Meeting – –

Report of The friends Appointed to See **Thomas Atkin**'s and **Rebecca Russell**'s
Tho Akin's Marriage Consumated Make Report that they attended the
Marriage

S^d Marriage which was Accomplished in Good Order

Thomas Wilcox Case   The friends Appointed to treat with **Thomas Wilcox** Report that they have not had a Convenient Opportunity to discharge themselves therefore they are Still Continued in the Same Service until Opportunity affords and then to make Report

P. Sisson denied   The women friends Inform that they have denied **Phebe Sisson** Daughter of **Joseph Barker** for Marrying out of the Unity of friends which this Meeting Concurs with – –

Phebe Allen's paper accepted   **Phebe Allen** hath Given in a Paper to this Meeting Condemning her falling into the Sin of Fornication which this Meeting Accepts Provided She Cause said paper to be Read publickly at the Close of a first day meeting for worship between this & the next Monthly Meeting She being present and Make Return of S^d paper to S^d Meeting

Holder Slocum's Case   The friends Appointed to treat with **Holder Slocum** Report that he declines to Condemn his offence to Satisfaction therefore his Case is Refer'd under the Same Care as heretofore and they to Make Report to the next Monthly Meeting

B. Taber Requested a Certificate   **Benjamin Taber** Requests a Certificate to the Monthly Meeting of **Nantucket**, Certifying his Clearness Respecting Marriage & Conversation therefore **Joseph Gifford** and **Joseph Russell** are Appointed to Make proper Inquiry and to draw one for him if they think proper and bring it to the next Monthly Meeting

R. Russell's affair   Whereas **Rose Russell** hath Removed out of the verge of **Coak= =set** Monthly Meeting where this Meeting Apprehends She belongs, and makes Application for assistance, therefore **Joseph Tucker** & **Humphry Smith** are Appointed to Inform **Coakset** Meeting that this Meeting desires them to take Care of her and S^d Com^{tee} to make Report to the next Monthly Meetings

---

6th mo: 1767   At a Monthly Meeting met the 15th of the 6th mo: 1767 The Representatives are **Daniel Russell** and **John Williams** present; – – The yearly Meeting being now in being, for which Reason This Meeting Adjourns to the 22^d Instant,

      At a Monthly Meeting Met and held by Adjournment the 22^d of the 6th mo: 1767

The Representatives being Called and both presen

Timothy Russell Marriage   **Humphry Smith** and **Jonathan Hussey** Report that they attended the Marriage of **Timothy Russell** and **Hannah Briggs** which was Consumated in Good Order – –

Phebe **Allen**'s Paper hath been read According to the Appoint=
=ment of last Monthly Meeting and is as follows – –

P. Allen's Confession   To the Monthly Meeting of friends to be held in **Dartmouth** the
20th day of the 4th month 1767 – –

     dear Friends

I through unwatchfulness have fallen into the Sin of Fornica=
=tion which Appears by my having a Child So Soon after Mar=
=riage, for which I am heartily Sorry and do Condemn, hoping
that God will forgive me and friends pass it by so far as to let
me Remain under their Care.   **Phebe Allen** – –

H. Slocum Case   The Case of **Holder Slocum** is Refer'd under the Same Care as heretofore

B. Taber Certificate   This Meeting hath Signed a Certificate for **Benjᵃ Taber** to the Monthly
Meeting of **Nantucket** Certifying his Clearness Respecting Marriage
and Conversation – –

Rose Rus= =sell Case   The friends Appointed to Treat with **Coakset** Monthly Meeting on
behalf of **Rose Russell** Report that they have not had an opportunity
Conveniently to discharge themselves, therefore they are still
Continued in the Same Service and to make Report to the next
Monthly Meeting;

A. Hathway is paid   The Treasurer has paid **Antipas Hathaway** 11 / 8d old tener

Queries Answer'd   The Queries have been Read and Answer'd in this Meeting,

Represen tatives   **Peleg Smith, Humphry Smith, Joseph Tucker, Samuel Smith
Caleb Russell** are appointed to attend the Quarterly Meeting
and to present the Answers to the Queries with the Epistle to the
Same, which hath been Signed in this Meetings – –
This Meeting Collected £8 – 7s – 3d old Tenner – –

Tim. Russell is paid   The Treasurer has paid **Timothy Russell** five dollars for
keeping the Meeting House half a year

7th mo: 1767   At a Monthly Meeting held in **Dartmouth** the 20th of the 7th
month 1767, Called **Joseph Smith** & **Jonathan Hussey** present

Clerk for this day   **William Anthony juʳ** Chosen Clerk for this day, – –

Hol. Slocum Case   The Case of **Holder Slocum** is Refer'd to the next Monthly Mee=
=ting under the Same Case as heretofore, and he is desired to attend
Meetings more diligently for the future; – –

To Treat with Coak= =set Meeting   The friends Appointed to Treat with **Coakset** Monthly Meeting
Report that they have not discharged their Trust by reason of one
of Sᵈ friends being unwell therefore 'tis Refer'd Still under [their care]

Report from Quar: meeting   the friends Appointed to attend the Quarterly Meeting Report
that they all attended but **Humphry Smith** and he Sent an
Excuse which was Accepted – –

Epistles Received This Meeting Received an Epistle from the yearly Meeting of **London** which was read in this Meeting, and the Good and wholsome advice therein Recommended to friends Observation also Received an Epistle of the yearly meeting of **Rhod Island** also one from the Quarterly Meeting which were read in this Meeting and Kindly accepted;

8th mov: 1767 At a Monthly Meeting held in **Dartmouth** the 17th of the 8th Month 1767

The Representatives are **Caleb Russell** & **Samuel Smith** both present, – –

R. Wilbor Received The women friends Inform that they have minuted **Rachel Wilbor [Wilbur]** under their Care which this meeting Concurs with,

Holder Slocum paper accepted **Holder Slocum** hath Given in a Paper to this Meeting Condemning his being in the Practice of Gaming, which this Meeting Accepts Provided the Cause Sd paper to be read Publickly at the Close of a first day meeting for worship be= =tween this and the next monthly meeting he being present and Return Sd Paper to the next monthly Meeting – –

Rose Russell case The Comittee Appointed to Treat with **Coakset** Monthly Mee= =ting on the Account of **Rose Russell** Report that they [have] discharged their Trust in that Case, and **Coakset** Meeting hath promised to Give this Meeting an Answer as soon as they Can Conveniently

Eunice Kirby accpt. The women friends Inform that they have accepted: of **Eunice Kirby**'s Acknowledgement for Marrying out of the Unity of friends which this Meeting Concurs with

9th mo: 1767 At a Monthly Meeting held in **Dartmouth** the 21 of ye 9th month 1767 The Representatives are **Wm Sanford** and **Daniel Cornel[Cornell]** present

David Anthony proposal of marriage **David Anthony** and **Judith Hicks** declared their Intentions of Marriage and were desired to wait till the next Monthly Mee= =ting for their Answer, and **George Smith** and **Benja Howland** are Appointed to Inquire into the young Man's Clearness Respect= =ing Marriage & Conversation and Make Report to the next Month= =ly Meeting **Holder Slocum**'s Paper hath been read According to the Appointment of last Monthly Meeting, and here follows

H. Slocum's Paper To the Monthly Meeting of Friends next to be held in **Dartmo** on the 20th of the 7th mo: 1767 – – Esteemed friends, Whereas I through unwatchfulness and by Keeping Unnecessary Company have fallen into the bad Prac=

=tice of Gaming, which I am heartily Sorry for and do Condemn
hoping God will forgive me, and I desire friends would pass
it by So far as to let me Remain under their Care, hoping
I shall walk More Agreeable for the time to come

Holder Slocum

Answer
from Coakset
Concerning
Rose Russ
[ell]not
accepted
Whereas this Meeting hath Received an Answer from **Coakset**
Monthly Meeting Respecting **Rose Russell**, which this Meeting
Apprehends is too Short and not to Satisfaction, therefore **Joseph
Gifford William Anthony ju**: & **Samuel Smith** are Appointed to
Make Sufficient Inquiry to know whether Said **Rose Russell**
properly belongs to **Coakset** Meeting or not, and if upon Inquiry
they ~~her~~ think her to belong to **Coakset**, to Inform them that this
Meeting desires them to Appoint a Committee to Confer with them
on the Case and Make a final Settlement between the two Meetings
and if they Cannot Agree to a Settlement, then for the two Com^{ttees}
to Chuse friends to Settle the Case belonging to Some other Monthly Meeting

Overseers
appointed
This Meeting doth Appoint **Daniel Cornel[Cornell], Luke Hart,
Paul Russell, Benj^a Howland 2^d William Anthony ju: Samuel
Smith** Overseers for the year Ensuing – –

Conclude
to repair
the meeting
house
This Meeting hath Come to a Conclusion to Repair our Meeting
House, therefore **George Smith, Daniel Russell, & Timothy
Russell** are Appointed to Consider what they shall think Ne=
=cessary to be done and also to Imploy Some body to do Said
business and Make Report to the next Monthly Meeting

Answers
to Queries
and
Epistle
sent by
Represen=
=tatives
The Queries have been read & Answer'd in this Meeting
and we have Signed an Epistle and Sent it up to the Quar=
=terly Meeting by the Representatives who are as follows
**Peleg Smith Abraham Tucker, Nicholas Howland, Benj^a
Howland 2^d** who are Appointed to attend the Quarterly Meeting
and present the Epistle with the Answers to the Queries and to
Make Report to the next Monthly Meeting

10th mo:
1767
At a Monthly Meeting held in **Dartmouth** the 19th of the
10th Month 1767 The Representatives are **David Smith**
and **Jonathan Hussey** present – –

The friends Appointed to Inspect into the Clearness of **David
Anthony**'s Report that they have Made Inquiry and find nothing
to hinder his Proceeding in Marriage – –

David
Anthony
answer
David Anthony and **Judith Hicks** Appear'd for their Answer
which was that they Might proceed to take Each other in Mar=
=riage in Some Convenient time between this and the next

Monthly Meeting Advising with the overseers for that purpose
and **George Smith** and **Benj^a Howland** are Appointed to
See their Marriage Consumated in Good Order, and Make
Report to the next Monthly Meeting

Shadach Dennis proposal to marriage **Shadrac Dennis** and **Abial Hussey** declared their Inten=
=tions of Marriage and were desired to wait till the next
Monthly Meeting for their Answer and **Wm Sanford** and **David
Smith** are Appointed to Inquire into the young man's Clearness
Respecting Marriage & Conversation and Make Report to the
next Monthly Meeting

Repairing Meeting House The Comittee Appointed to Repair our Meeting House Report
that they are on their way to accomplish S^d business therefore
they are desired to do it as soon as may be and make Report to
the next Monthly Meeting; – –

Report from Quar^{ly} Meeting The friends Appointed to attend the Quarterly Meeting Report
that they all attended Agreeable to Appointment and have
Produced an Epistle from the Same which hath been read and
Kindly Accepted – –

B. Chase desires a Certificate **Benj^a Chase** Requests a Certificate to the Monthly Meeting of
Swanzey Certifying his Clearness Respecting Marriage & Conversa=
=tion therefore **Paul Russell Russell** and **Luke Hart** are Ap=
=pointed to make proper Inquiry and draw a Certificate for him
if they think Proper and Make Report to the next Monthly
Meeting

Rotche's Certif. Whereas **Joseph Rotch** hath Resided Among us for a Considera=
=ble time & Agreeable to Good order hath Produced a few lines
by way of Certificate from the Monthly Meeting of **Nantucket**
Signifying his being a friend in Unity Among them which this
Meeting Accepts:[5] – –

Overseers for yearly Meeting **Daniel Russell, Timothy Russell, Jonathan Hussey, Thomas
Hicks Ju^r David Smith** are Appointed to have the Oversight of
the Galleries and other Seats to Endeavour to prevent any
Indecency that may happen at our yearly Meeting, and to
Make Report to the next Monthly Meetings; – –

Complaint against Henry Russell **Henry Russell** hath Married out of the Unity of friends and
hath been Labour'd with by the Overseers, and he declines

---

5. Joseph Rotch (1704–1784), a native of Salem, moved to Nantucket in 1725, where he grew wealthy
as a whaling merchant. He expanded to Dartmouth in 1764 and established a shipyard. His first ship
was the *Dartmouth*, one of the three tea ships boarded in the Boston Tea Party in 1773. See Barbara K.
Wittman, *Thomas and Charity Rotch: The Quaker Experience of Settlement in Ohio in the Early Republic
1800–1824* (Newcastle upon Tyne, Eng.: Cambridge Scholars Publishing, 2015), 72

to Condemn his offence to Satisfaction, Therefore **Jonathan Hussey** and **Barzillai Tucker** are Appointed to Treat far=ther with him and Make Report to the next Monthly Meeting

11ᵗʰ mo: 1767 At a Monthly Meeting held in **Dartmouth** the 16ᵗʰ 11ᵗʰ Mon: 1767
The Representatives are **William Sanford** and **Jonathan Hussey** both present – –
The friends Appointed to Inquire into **Shadrac Dennises** Clearness Report that they have Made Inquiry and find nothing to hinder his proceeding in Marriage –

Sha: Dennis answer **Shadric Dennis** and **Abial Hussey** Appeared for their Answer which was that they Might proceed to take each other in Marriage in Some Convenient time between this and the next Monthly Meeting Advising with the overseers for that purpose, and **William Sanford** and **David Smith** are appointed to See their Marriage Consumated in Good order & Make Report to the Next Monthly Meeting

Report of David Anthony's Marriage The friends Appointed to See **David Anthony** and **Judith Hicks** Marriage Consumated in Good order Report that they attended the Marriage, which was Accomplished in Good order – –

Bill for repairing meeting house The friends Appointed to Repair our Meeting House Report that they have Repared Sᵈ House Agreeable to Appointment, and have brought in their Bill which is two pounds Lawful Money

Certifiate for B. Chase This Meeting hath Signed a Certificate for **Benjᵃ Chase** to the Monthly Meeting of **Swanzey**, Certifying his Clearness Respec=
=ting Marriage and Conversation;

Wᵐ Hunt & T.Thorn=brough's Visit Our friends **William Hunt** and **Thoˢ Thornbrough** have Visited this Meeting with their Certificates from the Monthly Meeting held at **New-garden** in **Rowan Country North Carolina** dated the 25ᵗʰ 4ᵗʰ month 1767 which have been Read to Good Satisfac=
=tion and their Visit Kindly accepted[6]

Henry Russell's case The friends Appointed to Treat with **Henry Russell** for Mar=
=rying out of the Unity of friends Report that they Labour'd with him, and he Neglects to Make friends Satisfaction for his offence Therefore this Meeting being Tender of him do Refer the Matter under the Care of **Peleg Smith** & he to Treat with him as he shall find freedom and Report to the next Monthly Meeting

Report of Overseers of Yearly Meeting The Committee Appointed to have the oversight of the people that they behave orderly at our yearly Meeting Report that they all

6. William Hunt (1733–1772) died on a visit to England. *Memoirs of William and Nathan Hunt, Taken Chiefly from Their Journals and Letters* (Philadelphia: Uriah Hunt, 1858).

attended According to Appointment and Saw nothing but what
was tolerable orderly – –

Meeting in Allen's Neck Granted The friends living in **Allen's Neck** Request Liberty to hold a Meeting
there four Months from now on first days Excepting the day preceding
the Monthly Meeting in Each Month which this Meeting Grants
and do Appoint **Daniel Cornel[Cornell]**and **Philip Allen** and **Prince Allen**
to have the oversight of the Same and they to Make Report to
the Monthly Meeting at the Expiration of S^d 4 Months – –
This Meeting Adjorns to the 23^d Instant at the 11th hour in ye fore noon

Certificates to be [?] ted for our Esteemed Visiting Friends This Meeting being Mett according to Adjournment this 23rd of 11th mo: 1767
The Representatives being Called **Jonathan Hussey** present
Whereas **William Hunt** and **Thos Hornbrough** from **Newgarden** in **North
Carolina**, and **Aaron Veal** from the **Nine partners**, have Visited Sever'l
Meetings in these parts and being About to Return Home, This Meeting
finds freedom to Give Each of them a Certificate, therefore **Abraham Tucker**,
Jonathan Hussey and **David Smith** are Appointed to draw them and bring them

adjourn to the Adjournment of this Meeting,

mett This Meeting Adjourns to the 25th Instant after the Meeting of Worship
This Meeting being Mett by Adjournment the 25th of the 11th month 1767
the Representatives being Called **Jonathan Hussey** present

Complaint against Hum. Smith & Hol. Slocum The Overseers Inform this Meeting that **Humphry Smith** (son of **Humphry**)
and **Holder Slocum** have been Concerned in Horse Racing, and that
said **Slocum** has lately been in the practice of Gaming, for which
the Overseers have Labour'd with them but they decline to make friends
Satisfaction therefore **Jonathan Hussey Thomas Hicks** 2^d **Barzillai Tuc=
=ker** and **David Smith** are appointed to Treat with them and also to advise them to
be More frequent in attending Meetings.

Certificates for Visiting friends This Meeting hath Signed Three Certificates, One for **Wm Hunt**, one
for **Thomas Thornbrough** and one for **Aaron Veal**, (The overseers Inform that

Complaint against D. Russell **Daniel Russell** hath Suffered too much Liberty in his tavern, which tend to bring
reproach on Truth, there
fore **Joseph Tucker** & **Abraham Tucker** are appointed to Labour with him, &
make Report next Monthly Meeting

12 mo: 1767 At a Monthly Meeting held in **Dartmouth** ye 21 of the 12 Month 1767
The Representatives are **William Anthony** ju^r and **Samuel Smith**
both present,

Shadrch Dennis Marriage **William Sanford** and **David Smith** Report that they attended the
Marriage of **Shadrach Dennis** and **Abial Hussey** According to
Appointment which was Consumated in Good order – –

Henry Russell Case **Peleg Smith** Reports that he Spoke with **Henry Russell** Concerning his
disorderly Marriage, and he desires friends to wait a while Longer
with him, therefore his Case is Refer'd to the next Monthly Meeting
under the Care of **Thomas Hicks** 2ᵈ

The Case of Hum. Smith Son of Hum. and Holder Slocum The friends Appointed to Treat with **Humphry Smith** (son of **Humphry**)
and **Holder Slocum**, Report that they have Laboured with them
and that **Humphry Smith** desires friends friends to wait a while longer
with him therefore his Case is Refer'd to the next Monthly Meeting, they also
Report that **Holder Slocum** declines to make friends Satisfaction and doth
not desire friends to wait any Longer on him, therefore this Meeting
doth Conclude to deny him and do Appoint **Daniel Cornel[Cornell]**, **Samᵉˡ
Smith** and **Wᵐ Anthony juʳ** to draw a Paper of Denial Against
him and to Inform him of the Conclusion of this Meeting and bring Sᵈ
Paper to the next Monthly Meeting – –

advise of friends is that Dan. Russell to forbear Selling Spirituous Liquors The Friends Appointed to Labour with **Daniel Russell** for
allowing too Much Liberty in his Tavern Report that they have
discharged themselves in that Respect, and it is the Sense and
Judgment of this Meeting that he throw up Selling Spirituous Liquor – –
This Meeting hath Collected £8 – 10S – 8D old Tener – –

adjourn This Meeting Adjourns to the 28ᵗʰ day of this Instant at the 11ᵗʰ Hour
in the fore noon

mett This Meeting being met by Adjournment this 28ᵗʰ of yᵉ 12ᵗʰ month
1767, The Representatives being Called **Wᵐ Anthony juʳ**
and **Samuel Smith** present
This Meeting Adjourns to Tomorrow after the Meeting of worship
This Meeting being Met by Adjournment the 29ᵗʰ of the 12ᵗʰ month 1767
The Representatives being Called **Wᵐ Anthony juʳ** and **Samuel Smith**
Both present – –
The Queries have been read and Answer'd in this Meeting, and the

Answers with the Epistle to be sent up by Representatives Answers order'd to be Sent up to the Quarterly Meeting by the Repre=
=sentatives with the Epistle which hath been read And Signed in this
Meeting, **Caleb Russell**, **Benjᵃ Howland** the 2ᵈ & **Nicolas Howland**
are Appointed to attend the Quarterly Meeting and make Report
to the next Monthly Meeting – –
This Meeting hath Collected £9 – 17s – 6d old Tennor – –
This Meeting Adjourns to the first fourth day in next Month after
the Meeting of worship – –
This Meeting being Met by Adjournment the 6ᵗʰ of the first month 1768
The Representatives being Called both present,
The Overseers of the poor hath brought an Accompt to this Meeting

a debt to pay for Ste. Wilcox   for doing for **Stephen Wilcox** which is £3 – 10s – od Old Tener which this David Briggs; which he Saith he hath paid Accordingly – –

Joᵘ Williams and wife desires a Certificate   **John Williams** and his wife Requests a Removal Certificate to the Monthly Meeting of **Sandwich**, therefore **Joseph Tucker** and **Paul Russell** are Appointed to make proper Inquiry and Join with the womens Committee Appointed for the Same purpose and draw a Certificate for them if they think proper and bring it to the next Monthly Meeting

Geo. Smith's paper accepted   **George Smith** ju: hath Given in a Paper to this Meeting Signifying his falling into the Sin of Fornication and Condemning the Evil [?][there] of which this Meeting Accepts, Provided he Cause Sᵈ paper to be Read at the Close of a first day Meeting for worship between this and the next Monthly Meeting he being present and Make Return of Said paper to the next Monthly Meeting

---

first mo: 1768   At a Monthly Meeting held in **Dartmouth** the 18ᵗʰ of the first Month 1768 The Representatives are **Thoˢ Hicks 2ᵈ** and **Barzillai Tucker** present – –

Henry Russell Case   **Thoˢ Hicks 2ᵈ** Reports that he hath Spoke with **Henry Russell** and that he desired longer time to Endeavour to Make friends Satisfaction therefore his Case is Refer'd under the Same Care as heretofore – –

Case of Hum. Smith   The Case Concerning **Humphry Smith** Son of **Humphry** is Refer'd under the Care of **Samuel Smith**, and he to Make Report as Soon as oppertunity will Afford – –

Hold. Slocum   This Meeting hath Signed a paper of Denial Against **Holder Slocum** and **Wᵐ Anthony juʳ** is Appointed to Read Sᵈ Paper at the End of a first day Meeting for worship between this and the next Monthly Mee= =ting, and Return Sᵈ Paper to Sᵈ Meeting – –

J. Craw's paper accepted   **John Craw** hath Given in a Paper to this Meeting Condemning his Marrying out of the Unity of friends which this Meeting Accepts,

Report from Quarterly Meeting   The friends Appointed to attend the Quarterly Meeting Report that they all attended According to appointment and have Produced an Epistle from the Same which hath been Read & Kindly Accepted,

John Williams Case   The friends Appointed to draft a Certificate for **John Williams** [?] Report that all things are not Quite Clear therefore the Same friends are Continued for the Same Service and to Make Report to the next Month= =ly Meeting – –

George Smith juʳ his Paper hath been Read According to order of last Monthly Meeting & Return'd to this Meeting, which is as follows

      To the Monthly Meeting of **Dartmouth**

G. Smith ju: Confession   Whereas I **George Smith juʳ** having been Educated Among friends but through unwatchfulness So far Gave way to the Enemy as to fall into the

Sin of Fornication which Appears by my wife having a Child So Soon
After Marriage, Now these are to Testefy to all whom it may
Concern, that I am heartily Sorry for the Above said Evil, and do
Condemn the Same, with all other My outgoings, hoping God will
forgive me my offences and Receive me into favour, and I desire
friends So far to pass them by as to let me Remain under their Care
Given forth this 10ᵗʰ day of yᵉ 11ᵗʰ month 1767 by your friend

George Smith jur

Step. Wilcox Case The friends Appointed Some time past to have the Care of **Stephen Wilcox**'s
Affairs Respecting his discharging his debts, Make Report that he has
not discharged them all yet, and this Meeting thinks proper to discharge
Daniel Russell he being one of the Comᵗᵉᵉ, and to Appoint **Joseph Gifford**
and **Paul Russell** to join the afore Sᵈ Committee to have the whole over=
=sight of **Stephen Willcox**'s aforementioned Circumstances

2ᵈ mo: 1768 At a Monthly Meeting held in **Dartmouth** the 15ᵗʰ of the 2d month
1768. The Representatives are **Wᵐ Anthony jur** and **Samuel Smith**
both present , – –

Daniel Ricketson proposal of marriage **Daniel Ricketson** and **Rebecca Russell** declared their In=
=tentions of Marriage and were desired to wait till the next Monthly
Meeting for their Answer, and **Daniel Cornel[Cornell]** and **Thoˢ Hicks 2ᵈ**
are Appointed to Inquire into the Young Man's Clearness Respecting
Marriage and Conversation and Make Report to the next Monthly Meeting

H. Russell disown'd Whereas **Henry Russell** hath Married out of the Unity of friends, and
friends having discharged themselves in Labouring with him, and
he disregarding their Labour, therefore for the Clearing of Truth this
Meeting do deny the Said **Henry Russell** from being under the Care
of this Meeting

William Anthony jur Reports that he hath Read **Holder Slocum**'s
Paper of denial according to the Appointment of last Monthly
Meeting and has Returned the same to this Meeting, which is a follows

H. Slocum's denial Whereas **Holder Slocum** the Son of **Holder Slocum** deceased
and **Rebecca** his wife, having been under the Care of this Meeting
Yet through unwatchfulness and disregarding the Testimony of
Truth, has So far Deviated from our Religious Profession as to
be found in the practice of Gaming, and in Supporting of
Horseracing, and also in the Neglect of that Indispensable
duty of attending Religious Meetings of Divine worship, And friends
having Repeatedly Labour'd with him in Love in order to Shew unto
him his Errors and Reclaim him from his outgoings, But he Continu=
=ing Obstinate, and not adhering to our tender advice and Council,

Therefore for the preservation of the precious Truth and Friends from the Reproach thereof this Meeting is Concerned to Give this forth as a Testi= =mony Against him, Hereby Publicly disowning him the S^d **Holder Slocum** from being one of our Religious Community and from under the Care of this Meeting, Yet Sincerely desiring (if it be Consistant with Divine pleasure) that he may yet Return from the Evil of his ways, and by Sincere Repentance Return to the way of Truth & Salvation. Given forth & Signed in and on behalf of our Monthly Meeting held in **Dartmouth** the 18th day of the first month A.D. 1768 by

Job Russell Clerk

John Williams Case The friends Appointed to draft a Certificate for **John Williams** & his wife Report that his affairs are not all settled to Satisfaction, therefore the Case is Refer'd under the Care of the S^d Committee, and they to make Report to the next Monthly Meeting – –

Chusing Visitors refer'd This Meeting hath Made Trial for a Choice of Visitors, and finding the work of Great Importance, but no friend finding the weight of that Service laid on them at present, therefore the Chusing them is Refer'd to the next Monthly Meeting;

Com^{tee} to Review Miniuet **Humphry Smith, Benj^a Howland** the 2^d **Samuel Smith, Caleb Russell** and **Job Russell** are Appointed to Review the Monthly Meeting's Minutes to see what part they Shall think proper to go on Record, and Make Report to the next Monthly Meeting

Overseers of poor **John Potter, Joseph Gifford** and **Prince Allen** are Appointed Overseers of the poor for the year Ensuing – –

Rose Rus sell case **Joseph Tucker** & **Humphry Smith** are Added to the former Committee Appointed to Confer with **Coakset** Meeting Respecting **Rose Russell**

Thomas Rusell[sic] paper **Thos Willcox** hath Given in a Paper to this Meeting, Condemning his disorder in Marrying out of the order of friends, which is Refer'd to next Monthly Meeting under the Care of **Job Case** and **Jonathan Hussey** and they to Make Report to the next Monthly Meeting – –

Daniel Russell case This Meeting being Informed that **Daniel Russell** hath Proceeded Contrary to the Advice and Judgment of this Meeting in Selling of Spiritous Liquor, and this Meeting Reconsidering a former Minute Respecting Said **Russell** and do think it is Rather too Extensive in that part which debars him from Selling Spiritous Liquor by the Large Quantity therefore do Reverse that part of S^d Minute Nevertheless this Meeting Continuing of the Same Judgment in Re= =spect to his Selling Liquor by the small Quantity and do Appoint **Prince Allen** and **Thomas Hicks** 2^d to Labour with him and make Report to the next Monthly Meeting

3ᵈ mo:
1768

At a Monthly Meeting held in **Dartmouth** the 21
of the 3d Month 1768 – The Representatives are **Thoˢ**
Hicks and **Barzillai Tucker** both present; – –
The Friends Appointed to Enquire into **Daniel Ricketson**'s
Clearness Respecting Marriage and Conversation Report

Daniel
Recketson
answer

that they find nothing to hinder their Proceeding in Marriage
Daniel Ricketson and **Rebecca Russell** Appeared for their
Answer which was that they Might Proceed to take Each
other in Marriage in Some Convenient time between this
and the next Monthly Meeting and **Joseph Gifford** and **Job**
Russell are Appointed to See their Marriage Consumated in
Good order and Make Report to the next Monthly Meeting

Benj Wing's
proposal of
marriage

Benjamin Wing of **Sandwich** and **Peace Gifford** declar'd their
Intention of Marriage and were desired to wait till the
next Monthly Meeting for their Answer, The Sᵈ **Wing**
having Produced a Certificate Certifying his Clearness Respecting
Marriage & Conversation which is Accepted and ~~also~~ hath Pro=
=duced his Parents Consent – –

Chusing
Visitors
omitted

Chusing of Visitors was Refer'd to this Meeting, and no friend
finding the weight of that Service, laid upon them at [present?][present]
Therefore this Meeting thinks fit to Omitt any furder Trial
in that Matter – –

Miniutes
perused

The friends Appointed to Peruse the Monthly Meetings Minutes
Report that they have discharged their Trust in that Respect.

Case of
Coakset friends
Respecting
Rose Rus=
=sell

The Committee Appointed to Confer with **Coakset** Monthly Meeting
Respecting **Rose Russell** Report that they have had Several Confe=
=rences on that Account, but Could not Come to an Accomidation
without Submitting the Case to Friends of another Monthly Meeting
and have Made Choice of **Edward Upton**, **Philip Chase** and
William Buffinton whose Judgment is as followeth – –

The Coakset
Judgment
about
Rose Russell

　　　Coakset the 16ᵗʰ of the 3ᵈ Month 1768,
To the two Committees of the Monthly Meetings of **Dartmouth**
We the Subscribers by your Appointment, have heard your
Allegations and Consider'd them weightily, and upon the whole
our Judgment is that **Ponaganset** Meeting be at yᵉ two thirds of
the Charge that may Acrue by **Rose Russell** for the future
and **Coakset** the one third part for the future
　　　　　　　　　　　　　　　Edward Upton
　　　　　　　　　　　　　　　Philip Chase
　　　　　　　　　　　　　　　William Buffinton

Case of Thomas Wilcox The Friends Appointed to Treat with **Thomas Wilcox** Report
that he desires one Month Longer to Endeavour to Make friends
Satisfaction, Therefore the Case is Refer'd under the Same Care
as heretofore and they to Make Report to the Next Monthly Meeting

Report of meetings in Allen's Neck The Friends Appointed to oversee the Meeting in **Allensneck**
Report that they have attended the Meetings According to
appointment which was orderly and to Satisfaction – –
The Queries have been Read & Answer'd in this Meeting, and an
Epistle Signed and Sent to the Quarterly Meeting by the Representa=
tives who are **Caleb Russell**, **Nicholas Howland** and **William
Barker** who are to present the Same and to Make Report to
the next Monthly Meeting – –

The Case of Daniel Russell The Friends Appointed to Labour with **Daniel Russell**
Report that they have Labour'd with him and he declines
to Retract his Proceedings in Selling of Spirituous Liquor
And this Meeting having been Informed from time to time
of the undue Liberty that **Daniel Russell** Suffers in
his Tavern, which Tends to bring a Reproach on Truth
and Friends, his House not being in a fit Place to keep
a Tavern in because of the Great Report of Town's people
Therefore do Appoint, **John Potter, Prince Allen** and
Thomas Hicks 2ᵈ, to Labour with him for the Above
Sᵈ disorder and to desist from Keeping Tavern and Make
Report to the next Monthly Meeting
This Meeting hath Collected £9 – 9s – 9d Old Tenor,

Case of JohnWilliams Refer'd **John Williams** and Wife's Certificate not drafted by the
Same Reason as heretofore which is Refer'd to the next
Monthly Meeting

4ᵗʰ mo: 1768 At a Monthly Meeting held in **Dartmouth** the
18ᵗʰ of the 4ᵗʰ Month 1768, The Representatives are **David
Smith** and **Jonathan Hussey** both Present – –

Benj Wings answer **Benjᵃ Wing** & **Peace Gifford** appeared for their Answer
which was that they Might Proceed to take each other in
Marriage in Some Convenient time between this & the
next Monthly Meeting advising with the overseers for
that Purpose, and **Joseph Tucker** and **Joseph Mosher** are
Appointed to See their Marriage Consumated in Good order
and Make Report to the next Monthly Meeting – –

David Allen's proposal of marriage **David Allen** and **Hannah Ricketson** declared their Inten=
=tion of Marriage and were desired to wait until next Month=

=ly Meeting for their Answer, and **Caleb Russell** & **Job Russell** are Appointed to Inspect into the young Man's Clearness Re= =specting Marriage & Conversation and Make Report to the next Monthly Meeting

Daniel Ricketson's marriage **Joseph Gifford** and **Job Russell** Report that they attended the Marriage of **Daniel Ricketson** and **Rebecca Russell** which was Consumated in Good order – –

Tho.ˢ Wilcox paper **Thomas Wilcox** hath Given in a Paper to this Meeting Condem= =ning his falling into the Sin of Fornication which is Refer'd to

Report from Quarterly Meeting the next Monthly Meeting under the Same Care as heretofore The friends Appointed to attend the Quarterly Meeting Report that ~~they~~ two of them attended According to Appointment & the other Sent a reasonable Excuse which was ~~Exce~~ Accepted, and they have Produced an Epistle from S.ᵈ Meeting which hath been read and Kindly accepted – –

[?] of friends Dan. Russell The ~~appointed~~ ˄Appointed to Labour with **Daniel Russell** Report that he declines to Make friends Satisfaction, Therefore **Joseph Tucker Caleb Russell** and **Daniel Cornell** are Appointed to let him know the Mind of this Meeting that is if he do not make friends Satis= =faction he may Expect to be denied, and they to make Report to the next Monthly ~~Monthly~~ Meeting

Treasurer paid Tim. Russell The Treasurer hath paid **Timothy Russell** the whole of his demand, on this Meeting, and also **Daniel Russell**'s demand, which is £2 – 2[S?] Lawful Money – –

J. Williams & wife Certificate This Meeting hath Signed a Certificate for **John Williams** & his wife to **Sandwich** Monthly Meeting;

5ᵗʰ mo: 1768 At a Monthly Meeting held in **Dartmouth** the 16ᵗʰ of the 5ᵗʰ Month 1768, The Representatives are **Thomas Hicks** & **Barzilai Tucker** both Present; – –

Caleb Russell & **Job Russell** Report that they have made Suffi= =cient Inquiry into **David Allen**'s Clearness in Respect to Marriage and Conversation & do not find anything to hinder his Proceeding in Marriage – –

David Allen's proposal of marri= =age **David Allen** & **Hannah Ricketson** appeared for their Answer which was that they Might Proceed to take each other in Marriage in Some Convenient time between this & the next Monthly Meeting, advising with the overseers for that purpose and **Caleb Russell** and **Job Russell** are Appointed to See their Marriage Consumated in Good order and Make Report to the next Monthly Meeting

Joseph Tucker & Joseph Mosher Report that they attended the

Benj Wing's Marriage Marriage of **Benjᵃ Wing** and **Peace Gifford** which was Consum= =ated in Good order – –

Case of Tho Wilcox refer'd The Case of **Thoˢ Wilcox** is Refered under the Same Care as hereto[heretofore?] and they to Make Report to the next Monthly Meeting,

The case of Daniel Russell refer'd The friends Appointed to Enform **Daniel Russell** of the Sense of this Meeting Report that they have discharged their Trust in that Respect, and that he declines to desist from keeping of Tavern until his year is up that he has taken out Licenses to sell Liquor and also **Daniel Russell** hath Given in a Paper to this Meeting which is nowise to Satisfaction, Therefore his Case is Refer'd at the Request of his Brother, **John Russell**, and he to Inform him how his Paper was received, and also to Labour with him as he shold find freedom and Make Report to the next Monthly Meeting,

F. Rotch his Certi= =ficate Reᵈ **Francis Rotch**, Son of **Joseph Rotch** hath Removed into the verge of this Meeting, and hath Produced a Removal Certificate from the Monthly Meeting of **Nantucket** which hath been read & Accepted

R. Sowl's affair whereas the Committee Appointed to Give a List of those friends living at the Eastward Side of **Quishnet River** report that they have Given in **Rachel Sowle** to **Sandwich** Monthly Mee= =ting which they decline to accept, therefore this Meeting doth Appoint **Humphry Smith, Job Russell William Mosher** & **Prince Allen** to join with Sᵈ Comᵗᵉᵉ to Confer with **Sandwich** Monthly Meeting on that account, and also to make a final Settlement about the Sᵈ **Rachel Sowle** in behalf of this Mee= =ting & they to make report to the next monthly Meeting

6 mo: 1768 At a Monthly Meeting held in **Dartmouth** the 20ᵗʰ of the 6ᵗʰ Month 1768. The Representatives are **Caleb Russell & David Smith** both present

Barnabas Kirby & Allen's proposal of marriage **Barnabas Kirby** & **Elizabeth Allen** declared their Intentions of taking each other in Marriage & were desired to wait till yᵉ next Monthly Meeting for their Answer and **Philip Allen** and **Nicolas Howland** are Appointed to Inspect into the young Man's Clearness Respecting Marriage & Conversation & Make Report to the next Monthly Meeting

David Allen's Marriage **Caleb Russell & Job Russell** Report that they attended the Marriage of **David Allen & Hannah Ricketson** & that it was Consumated in Good order – –

Case respecting Thoˢ Wilcox The friends Appointed to have the Care of **Thoˢ Wilcox** Respecting Receiving his paper that he Gave into this Meeting some months

past Report that he declines to attend Meetings for Religious
Worship therefore this Meeting Cannot find freedom to Accept
his paper, and do Appoint **Abraham Tucker** to Join the former
Committee to Labour farther with him for his Several disorders
and draw a paper of denial against him if he Gives them no
Satisfaction, and bring it to next Monthly Meeting

D. Russell **Daniel Russell** hath Given in a paper to this Meeting Condemning
accepted his former disorder in Indulging too Much Liberty in his Tavern
which this Meeting accepts, and it is the desire of this Meeting
that he would desist from keeping a Tavern after the year is Expired
that he has Engaged for, and it is Recommended that the overseers
have a particular Inspection over him in his Conduct Respecting
his Tavern.

Case with The Committee Appointed to Treat with **Sandwich** Monthly
Sandwich Meeting Respecting **Rachel Sowle** Report that they have
respecting had a Conference with Said Meeting and that they have Appoint^d
Rachel a Com^{tee} to Confer with them, therefore they are Continued in
Sowle in the Same Service and to Make Report to the next Monthly Meeting – –

Visits Our Esteemed friends **Thomas Carleton, Aaron Lancaster**[7] and
of Travel **Joshua Shearman** hath Visited this Meeting with their
ling Respective Certificates, The first from **Chester County** in the
friends Province of **Pensylvania** bearing date the 12th of the 5th mo: 1768
The Second (viz **Aaron Lancaster**) from the **Purchase** in the
County of **westchester** in the Province of **New York** whose Cer=
=tificate bears date the 5th month 1768 The ~~first~~ third from
the **Nine Partners** in **dutches County** in S^d Province of **New-**
-york bearing date the 19th of the 5th Month 1768 – all of
which were read in this Meeting and their Visits well accepted
The Queries have been read and Answer'd in this Meeting

adjourn This Meeting Adjourns to our next youth's Meeting after
the Meeting of worship – –

mett This Meting being met according to Adjournment the
first of the 7th month 1768 The Representatives being Called
both Present; – –

7. Thomas Carleton (1699–1792), a native of Ireland, was a member of Kennett Monthly Meeting,
Chester County, Pennsylvania. See Martha Reamy, ed., *Early Church Records of Chester County,
Pennsylvania* (3 vols., Westminister, Md.,: Willow Bend Books, 1999), 8. Aaron Lancaster (1744–1786)
was a native of Bucks County, Pennsylvania, who moved to Purchase Monthly Meeting, New York, as a
young man. See Harry Fred Lancaster, *The Lancaster Family: A History of Thomas and Phebe Lancaster,
of Bucks County, Pennsylvania, and Their Descendants, from 1711 to 1902. Also a Sketch on the Origin of the
Name and Family in England* (Huntington, Ind.: A. J. Hoover, 1902), pp. 143–44. Joshua Sherman (1730–
1770) died at Oblong Monthly Meeting in Westchester County, New York. See James Hazard, comp.

Friends to attend Quar. meeting **Joseph Tucker**, **Caleb Russell**, **William Anthony** and **Humphry Smith** are Appointed to Attend the Quarterly

Epistle & answers to Queries sent up Meeting and Present the Epistle with the Answers to the Queries which have been read & signed in this Meeting and they to make Report to the next Monthly Meeting

To Settle with Treasurer **William Sanford** and **Jonathan Hussey** are Appointed to adjust Accounts with the Treasurer and Make Report to the next Monthly Meeting – –

Order to pay Jos Tucker This Meeting orders the Treasurer to pay **Joseph Tucker** one dollar that this Meeting borrowed some time past ~~which~~ he has done Accordingly; – –

case of Hump Smith son of Hump. Whereas **Humphry Smith** Son of **Humphry Smith** hath been under dealing sometime past under the Care of **Samuel Smith**, who now Informs this Meeting that the S^d **Humphry** Neglects to Make friends Satisfaction Therefore This Meeting doth Appoint **Abraham Tucker** & **Joseph Tucker** to Labour farther with him as they may find freedom and make Report to the next Monthly Meeting

This Meeting hath Collected £6 – 6s – 9d old Tener

7th mo: 1768 At a Monthly Meeting held in **Dartmouth** the 18th of the 7th Month 1768, The Representatives are **Samuel Smith** and **Thomas Hicks 2^d** both Present.

The friends Appointed to Inspect into the Clearness of **Barnabas Kirby** Report that they have made Sufficient Enquiry and find nothing to hinder his Proceeding in Marriage – –

[Barn]Kirby answer **Barnabas Kirby** & **Elizabeth Allen** Appear'd for their Answer which was that they Might Proceed to take each other in Marriage in Some Convenient time between this and the next Monthly Meeting Advising with the overseers for that Purpose, And **Nicholas Howland** & **Philip Allen** are Appointed to See their Marriage Consumated in Good order and make Report to the next Monthly Meeting

Wm Tripp proposal of marriage **William Tripp** & **Elizabeth Maxfield** declared their Intentions of Marriage & were desired to wait till the next Monthly Mee= =ting forthar Answer – –

Case of Thomas Wilcox The Committee Appointed to Labour with **Thomas Wilcox** Report they have not had a Convenient Oppertunity to Treat with him, therefore they are Continued in the Same Service and to Make Report to the next Monthly Meeting,

[Report] of the Com^tee to Treat with Sandwich meeting The Com^tee Appointed to Treat with **Sandwich** Monthly Meeting Report that they have met with **Sandwich** Meeting's Committee and Could not Settle the Affair, and have Refered the Matter Till next fall, therefore they are Still Continued in the Same Service and to Make Report when they have Settled the Affair, The Committee ~~Com~~ Appointed to Adjust Accounts with the Treasurer

Treasury not Settled Report they have not done it therefore they are Still Continued in S^d Service and to make Report to the next Monthly Meeting

Weston Briggs Certi: **Weston Briggs** and his wife have Returned into these parts Again and have Produced a Removal Certificate from the Monthly Meeting of **Sandwich** which hath been Read and Accepted – –

James Davis Certifi: **James Davis** hath Produced a Removal Certificate from the Monthly Meeting of **Sandwich** which hath been Read and Accepted

Report from Quarterly Meeting The friends Appointed to attend the Quarterly Meeting Report that they all attended According to Appointment and have brought an Epistle from the same but it is not Come to hand therefore they are desired to take Care and bring it to the next Monthly Meeting

Humphry Smith 3rd paper **Humphry Smith** the 3^d hath Given in a Paper to his Mee= =ting Condeming his Runing Horses and Keeping Loose Company which is Refered to the next Monthly Meeting and he is desired to attend at that time – –

David Anthony & wife's paper **David Anthony** and his wife have Given in a paper to this Meeting Condemning their falling into the Sin of Fornication which is Refered to the next Monthly Meeting and **Joseph Gifford** and **Barzillia Tucker** are appointed to take an oppertunity of discourse with him and Make Report to the Next Monthly Meeting

T. Almy Request **Thomas Almy** Requests to Come under friends Care and **Daniel Cornel[Cornell]** & **Prince Allen** are Appointed to Inquire into the young Man's Conversation & take an oppertunity of Sollid Conference and Endeavour to understand if his Motive be from the bottom of True Conviction and they to Make Report to the next Monthly Meeting

Wm Brown request of Certi: **William Brown** Informs this Meeting that he is About to Remove to **Nantucket** and desires a Removal Certificate, Therefore **Caleb Russell** & **Job Russell** are Appointed to draw one for him if they think proper after they have made Sufficient Inquiry into

his Life & Conversation And bring it to next Monthly Meeting
This Meeting hath Collected £9 – 13s – 7d old Tener

Treasurer paid Tim. Russell The Treasurer has paid **Timothy Russell** five Dollars for Keeping the Meeting House half a year

---

8ᵗʰ mo: 1768 At a Monthly Meeting held in **Dartmouth** the 15ᵗʰ 8 mo: 1768
The Representatives are **David Smith** and Samuel **Smith** present
William Tripp hath Produced a Certificate from **Coakset** Monthly Meeting Certifying his Clearness in Respect to Marriage and Conversation which hath been read and accepted

Wᵐ Tripp answer **William Tripp** & **Elizabeth Maxfield** Appeared for their Answer which was that they might Proceed to take each other in Marriage in Some Convenient time between this and the next Monthly Meeting advising with the overseers for that Purpose, and **Luke Hart** & **Wᵐ Mosher** are Appointed to see their Marriage Consumated in Good order and Make Report to the next Monthly Meeting

Barnab Kirby's ~~answer~~ marriage The friends Appointed to See **Barnabas Kirby**'s & **Elizabeth Allen**'s Marriage Consumated Report that they attended According to Appointment which was Consumated in Good order

Tho Wilcox case The Committee Appointed to Confer with **Thoˢ Wilcox** Report that they have had a Conference with him and they desire to have the Matter defered one Month Longer, which is accordingly under their Care who are to make Report to next Monthly Meeting

Settled with Treasurer The friends Appointed to Adjust accounts with the Treasurer Report that they Settled Accounts with him and there Remain £2 – 2s – 8d old Tener in the Treasury

Epistles receiv'd The Epistle from the last Quarterly Meeting now Came to hand and hath been read and Kindly accepted
Likewise the **London** Printed Epistle and one from **Philadelphia**, and as they Contain a Great deal of Counsel and Good Advice the Contexts are Earnestly Recommended to friends Notice and Observation – –

David Anthony's Case The friends Appointed to Confer with **David Anthony** ~~An~~ make Report that he Gave them Satisfaction but we not having any account from the women the matter is Refered to the next Monthly Meeting – –

Thoˢ Almy The friends Appointed to Confer with **Thomas Almy** make a Satisfactory Report and the matter is Still Continued under Their Care who are to Make Report to the next Monthly Meeting

Wᵐ Brown removed   This Meeting hath Signed a Removal Certificate for **William Brown** to the Monthly Meeting of **Nantucket**

Humph Smith 3ᵈ case   This Meeting doth Refer the Case of **Humphry Smith** the 3ᵈ under the Care of **Abraham Tucker** & **Joseph Tucker** and they to make Report to the next Monthly Meeting

P. Russell & D. Cornel dismist   This meeting Excuses **Paul Russell** from having having the Care of **Stephen Wilcox**'s affair, and also Excuses **Paul Russell** and **Daniel Cornel[Cornell]** from being overseers.

Stephen Wilcox's affair   **Prince Allen, Benjᵃ Howland 2ᵈ Samuel Smith** and **Barzillai Tucker** are added to the former Comittee to have the Care of Stephen **Wilcox**'s affair in Regard to his paying his debts and they to make Report to the next monthly meeting

---

9ᵗʰ mo 1768   At a Monthly Meeting held in **Dartmouth** the 19 of the 9ᵗʰ month 1768, The Representatives are **Benjᵃ Howland 2ᵈ** and **Thomas Hicks 2ᵈ** both present – –

Caleb Macumber's proposal of marriage   **Caleb Macumber** & **Rachel Wilbour** declared their Intentions of Marriage and were desired to wait Till next Monthly Meeting for their Answer

Wᵐ Tripp marriage   **Luke Hart** & **William Mosher** Report that they attended the Marriage of **William Tripp** & **Elizabeth Maxfield** which was Consumated in Good order

Thoˢ Wilcox paper accepted   The friends Appointed to Treat with **Thoˢ Wilcox** Report that they think best to accept of his Paper therefore this Meeting accepts it accordingly with the Provisal that he Cause Sᵈ paper to be read at the Close of a first day meeting of worship between this and the next Monthly Meeting he being present and Return Sᵈ Paper to the next monthly meeting

David Anthony & wife's paper   This Meeting Likewise accepts of **David Anthony** & his wife's paper provided they Cause it to be read at the Close of a first day Meeting for worship they being present and return Sᵈ paper to the next Monthly Meeting

T. Almy accepted   The friends Appointed to Confer with **Thomas Almy** on his Request to Come under friends Care, Make a Satisfactory Report, Therefore This Meeting doth accept him a Member under friends Care

Case of Humph. Smith 3   The friends Appointed to have the Care of **Humphry Smith** yᵉ 3ᵈ Report that they think it not best to Receive his paper and that he desires friends to Defer the Matter one Month longer, Therefore his Case is Refered Ɇ under the Same Care as heretofore and they to Make Report to next Monthly Meeting; – –

Ste. Wilcox affair   The friends Appointed to have the Care of **Stephen Wilcox**'s affair in Regard to his discharging his debts Report that they are not ready for

an Answer, Therefore the Matter is Refered to the next
Monthly Meeting under their Care who are then to make Report

Paul Russell intends a visit **Paul Russell** Informs this Meeting that he hath it on his
Mind to visit Some Meetings in the Circuit of the Quarterly
Meeting of **Sandwich** which this Meeting Approves of – –

P Russel & Daniel Cornel approv^d ministers This Meeting hath Recommended **Paul Russell** and **Danil Cornel[Cornell]**
as Ministers in Unity to the Quarterly Meeting of Ministers
and Elders at **Rhode-Island** – –

Overseers chosen **Luke Hart, Benj^a Howland 2^d William Anthony ju:** and
Samuel Smith are Appointed overseers for the year Ensuing

Rotches Certificate **Joseph Rotch** hath Produced a Removal Certificate from the
Monthly Meeting of **Nantucket** which hath been read and accepted – –

Answers to Queries sent up The Queries have been Read in this Meeting and Answer'd
and the Answers Sent up to the Quarterly Meeting by the Repre=

Represent atives =sentatives who are **Paul Russell, Caleb Russel Nicolas Howland**

Epistle Sent and **Jonathan Hussey.** This Meeting hath Signed an Epistle to
the Quarterly Meeting and Sent it up by the Representatives,
Nicolas Howland hath brought an Account to this Meeting

Covering Fox's Journal &c for Covering **Fox**'s Journal and Mending the Bellow's to
to the Amount of four Shilling Lawful Money which this
Meeting Approves, and the Treasurer has paid it by order of
the Meeting
This Meeting hath Collected £6 – 0s – 9d old Tener

10th mo 1768 At a Monthly Meeting held in **Dartmouth** the 17th of
the 10th Month 1768 The Representatives are **David Smith**
and **Benjamin Howland** [2^d] both present – –

Caleb Macumber Clearness **Caleb Macumber** hath produced a Certificate from the
Monthly Meeting of **Coakset** Certifying his Clearness Respect=
=ing Marriage & Conversation – –

C. Mac umber's answer **Caleb Macumber** and **Rachel Wilborr** Appeared for their Answer
which was that they Might Proceed to take Each other in
Marriage in Some Convenient time between this & the next Month=
=ly Meeting and **Philip Allen** and **Daniel Cornel[Cornell]** are Appointed
to See their Marriage Consumated in Good order and Make Report
to the Next Monthly Meeting – –
Thomas Wilcox's Paper hath not been read According to the Appoint
Ment of last Monthly Meeting by Reason of a Mistake, therefore
he is desired to Cause S^d paper to be read between this & the next Mont=
=hly Meeting and Return Said Paper to S^d Meeting
David Anthony and his wife's paper hath been read and Return'd

to this Meeting According to the Appointment of last Monthly Meeting
　　And is as followeth

David &　To the Monthly Meeting of **Dartmouth**
Judith
Anthony's　　　These Comes with Sorrow to Inform that through weakness and the
Confession　Insinuation of the Adversary, we have fallen into the Reproachful
Sin of Fornication, as Appears by our having a Child So Soon after
Marriage for which we are heartily and Sincerely Sorry and do Con=
=demn the Same hoping forgiveness from Almighty God and desire
to take the Reproach thereof upon ourselves, and [?][Clear] friends
and the Truth from the same and desire friends so far to pass
it by as to let us Remain under their Care
　　　　Given forth this 13ᵗʰ of the 7ᵗʰ month 1768 by your friends
　　　　　　　　　　　　　David Anthony
　　　　　　　　　　　　　Judith Anthony

Case of　The Committee Appointed to have the Care of **Humphry Smith** yᵉ 3ᵈ
H. Smith 3　Report that they have not had an oppertunity with him and that
he desires that friends would wait on him one month[longer] therefore
the Matter is Refered under the Same Care as heretofore and they
to Make Report to the Next Monthly Meeting – –

S. Wilcox　The friends Appointed to Assist **Stephen Wilcox** Report that the Mat=
case　=ter Remains not Settled therefore the Case is Refered under the Same
Care and they to Make Report to the next Monthly Meeting

Report　The friends Appointed to attend the Quarterly Meeting Report that
from Quar　they all attended According to Appointment and have produced an
terly Meeting　Epistle from the Same which hath been read & Kindly Accepted

Susanna　The Women friends Inform that they have Minuted **Susanna**
Howland　**Howland** under friends Care, which this Meeting Concurs with
Received

overseers of　**Joseph Gifford, William Anthony ju: Berzillai Tucker, Prince**
yearly　**Allen, Timothy Russell, Samuel Smith, Jonathan Hussey &**
meeting　**John Potter** are Appointed to have the oversight of the Gallery
and other Seats at our yearly Meeting to Endeavour to prevent
any Indecency that may be liable to happen at that time
and they to Make Report of their Service at the next Monthly Meeting,

---

11 mo: }　At a Monthly Meeting held in **Dartmouth** the 21
1768 }　of the 11ᵗʰ mo: 1768, The Representatives are **Benjᵃ Howland**
the 2ᵈ and **Samuel Smith** both present

Caleb　**Daniel Cornel** and **Philip Allen** Report that they
Macumber　attended the Marriage of **Caleb Macumber** and **Rachel**
marriage　**Wilborr [Wilbur]** which was Consumated in Good order
Thomas Wilcox's paper hath been read According to the

appointment of last monthly Meeting, and is as follows

Dartmouth 18th day 11th [4th?]mo: 1768

Wilcox's To the Monthly Meeting of friends – –
Confession
  Whereas Through unwatchfulness have I falled
Into the Sin of Fornication as Manifestly hath Appeared by
my wife having a Child Soon after Marriage, for which
Evil I am Sorry for, hoping for the future to be more Carful, &
I beg that God will forgive me for the Above S^d Evil and all
my misconduct, and friends would pass it by, and I Remain
under their Care, from your friend – **Thomas Wilcox**

Hum. Smith' 3^d Whereas **Humphry Smith the 3^d** Some time past hath been in the
case Practice of Horse racing and hath been Laboured with for
the Same and Neglects to Condemn the Above S^d practice to
friends Satisfaction and Since hath Kept a Great deal of loose
Company, and hath fallen into a Bodily Strife with **Sam^el**
Macumber ju: Therefore this Meeting doth Appoint **Benj^a**
Howland the 2^d and **William Anthony ju**: to Labour with him for
the aforeS^d offences as they Shall find freedom and draw a paper
of denial if he do not Give them Satisfaction, and to Inform him of
their Appointment from this Meeting and Make Report to y^e
next Monthly Meeting – –

The friends Appointed to Assist **Stephen Wilcox** Report as follows

Wilcox's   Agreeable to Appointment we have made Inspection into
affair the affairs of **Stephen Wilcox** in Regard to his debts (which the
Meeting hath long held in Suspense) and we think he is very Much
Involved in debt, & in low Circumstances, and Neglects the
payment of his Just debts as Appears to us by the Complaints
of his Creditors, Some of whom appear to be long Kept out of their
Just dues, and he not in a way to discharge them to the Honour
and Credit of Friends, and the Pro[fession ?]we bear, wherefore we
having Seriously and weightily Considered the Same it is our
united Sense and Judgment that he ought to pay & Satisfy his
Said Creditors or Imediately deliver up his Estate to [them?]
Notifying them Respectively to Come and take it in proportion
to their Several dues, which Method we have Repeatedly advised
him to Proceed in, and which he now promises Imediately to
Comply with – – Given forth this 21 of the 11th mo: 1768 by
      your friends   **Benja Howland**
               Samuel Smith
               Thomas Hicks
               Barzillai Tucker

And the afore S^d Com^{tee} are Still Continued to See that the
Said **Stephen Wilcox** fulfils his Promise and make Report to
the Monthly Meeting as soon as the Matter Can be Accomplished

Report of overseers of yearly Meeting The Comittee Appointed to have the oversight of ^the yearly Mee=
=ting Several of them Report that they attended the Service to
Satisfaction and that People behaved tolerable orderly, but
Several of the Committee hath Neglected to Make Report
therefore **Samuel Smith** is Appointed to Call on them for
the reasons of their Neglect & make Report next Monthly Meeting

Meetings in Allen's Neck Granted The friends living in **Allen's Neck** Request the Liberty
to hold a Meeting down there on each first in the four
following Months which this Meeting Grants, and do
Appoint **Philip Allen** & **Daniel Cornel** to See the
Meeting Carried on agreable to Truth and Make Report
to the Monthly Meeting at the Expiration of Said Time

Meetings in Smith's Neck granted And the Friends living in **Smith's Neck** Request the
Liberty to hold a Meeting among them on two first days
in Each Month for the winter Season, which this Meeting
Grants, and they are to hold it on Every other first
day as Comes in Course for the winter Season and **Benj^a
Howland 2^d** and **Samuel Smith** are appointed to See
that the S^d Meeting be held According to Truth and
they to Make Report to the Monthly Meeting at
the Expiration of the Afore S^d time – –

E. Baker Certifi: Whereas Our Esteemed friend **Ephraim Baker**
hath Visited our Meeting and desired our Certificate
Therefore, **Joseph Tucker** and **Barzillai Tuker** [Tucker]
are appointed to draw one for him and bring it to
the next Monthly Meeting – –

H. Slocum's Certfi: Whereas **Humphry Slocum** now Resides at **Rhode Island**
and desires a few lines to Recommend him to the Monthly
Meeting there, Therefore **Joseph Tucker** & **Barzillai Tucker** are
Appointed to draw a Certificate for him and bring it to the
next Monthly Meeting – –

Rotch's Certfi: Whereas **Joseph Rotch** desires a Certificate to the Monthly
Meeting of **Rhode Island** Certifying his Clearness in Respect
to Marriage and Conversation, therefore **Caleb Russell** and
Job Russell are Appointed to draw one for him if they
think proper after they have made Sufficient Enquiry
in his afore S^d Clearness, and bring it to next Monthly Meeting

B. to be Transcri^bed for [?] This Meeting Appoints **Samuel Smith** to Join with **Coakset** friends to Transcribe the the Book of Discipline as reasonably as they can & make Report when it is Accomplished

---

12: mo:} 1768} At a Monthly Meeting held in **Dartmouth** the 19th of the 12th month 1768, The Representatives are **David Smith** and **Barzillai Tucker** both present

Peleg Slocum's proposal [of] marriage **Peleg Slocum Ju:** and **Susanna Howland** declared their Intention of Marriage and were desired to wait Till next Monthly Meeting for their Answer and **Nicolas Howland** & **Prince Allen** are Appointed to Enquire into **Peleg Slocum**'s Clearness Respecting Marriage & Conversation and Make Report to the next Monthly Meeting – –

Barnabas Wing's proposal of marriage And **Barnabas Wing** and **Jane Merihew** declared their Inten= =tion of Marriage and were desired to wait till the next Month= =ly Meeting for their Answer – –

Humphry Smith 3 Case The Friends Appointed to Labour with **Humphry**ˏ ˢᵐⁱᵗʰ yᵉ 3 Report that they have Laboured with him, and that he desires friends to wait on him one month longer which is Granted, and they Still Con= =tinued in the Same Service and to Make Report to the next Monthly Meeting – –

Overseer yearly meeting Report Whereas three friends were deficient last Monthly Meeting in Making Report of their Service in the oversight of the yearly Meeting now make Report that they all attended the Service to pretty Good Satisfaction, and they have assigned the Reasons of their Neglect to the Satisfaction of this Meeting

B: Certifi: This Meeting hath Signed a Certificate directed to the Monthly Meeting of friends held at the **Nine partners** in the Province of **Newyork** for our friend **Ephraim Baker** – –

H. S: Certifi: And this Meeting hath also Signed a Certificate for our friend **Humphry** ~~Smi~~ **Slocum** to the Monthly Meeting of **Rhod Island** Certifying his being under the Care of this meeting, and his Conversation in a Good degree orderly – –

R: Certi: And this Meeting hath also Signed a Certificate for **Joseph Roch** to the Monthly Meeting of **Rhod Island** Certifying his Clearness in Respect to Marriage & Conversation – –

Queries & Epistle The Queries have been Read and Answer'd in this Meeting – – This Meeting hath Signed an Epistle to the Quarterly Meeting The Friends Appointed to attend the Quarterly Meeting are

Represen= tatives **William Anthony ju:, William Mosher, Samuel Smith,** and **Benjamin Howland the [2?]ᵈ** and they to present the Epistle

with the Answers to the Queries and to Make Report to the next
Monthly Meeting;

This Meeting hath Collected £10 – 16ˢ – 8ᵈ old Tener – –

Tim Russel and the Treasurer has paid **Timothy Russell** five Dollars
paid for Keeping the Meeting House half a year According to order

---

1: mo:} At a Monthly Meeting hold in **Dartmouth** the 16ᵗʰ
1769} of the first month 1769 The Representatives are **Caleb Russell**
and **Jonathan Hussey** both Present

Bar Wing **Barnabas Wing** hath Produced a Certificate from the
Certificat Monthly Meeting of **Sandwich**, Certifying his Clearness in
Respect to Marriage and Conversation which hath been Read
and Accepted – –

Peleg Slocum ᴶᵘ **Peleg Slocum ju:** and **Susanna Howland**, and **Barnabas**
& Barna **Wing** and **Jane Merihew** Appeared for their Answers which
Wing's was that Each Couple Might Proceed to take each other in
answer Marriage in Some Convenient time between this and the
next Monthly Meeting Advising with the overseers for that
purpose and **Joseph Gifford** & **Job Russell** are Appointed to
see **Peleg Slocum**'s and **Susanna Howland**s Marriage Con=
=sumated in Good order and make Report to the next Monthly
Meeting, And **Joseph Smith** and **William Mosher** are appointed
for the Same Service with **Barnabas Wing** & **Jane Merihew**
and to Make Report to the next Monthly Meeting

Batho: Taber **Bartholomew Taber** and **Mercy Bowdish** and **Thomas**
and **Almy** and **Deborah Allen** Declared their Intentions of
Thoˢ Almy Marriage and were desired to wait Till next Monthly
proposal of Meeting for their Answers And **Daniel Cornel** & **Prince**
marriage **Allen** are Appointed to ~~wait till~~ Make Enquiry into
Thomas Almy's Clearness Respecting Marriage & Conver=
=sation and Make Report to the next Monthly Meeting

H. Smith's **Humphry Smith** the 3ᵈ hath Given in a Paper to this
paper Meeting Condemning his offences in horse Racing, Gaming
And in having a Bodily Strife with **Samuel Macuᴧᵐber**
with all the Rest of his Misconduct which is Continued
under the Care of **William Anthony juʳ** until the next
Monthly Meeting – –

Report The Friends Appointed to attend the Quarterly Meeting
[from]Quar Report that they all attended According to Appointment
[M]eeting and have Produced an Epistle from the same which hath
been read & well accepted – –

Books [to]be Printed   Proposals for Printing two Sorts of Primers and a Book of **Samuel Fuller**'s works has been Sent down from the Quarterly Meeting[8]. Therefore this Meeting doth Appoint **Caleb Russell, Jonathan Hussey Wm Anthony ju^r Samuel Smith, Prince Allen Daniel Cornel, Thos Hicks, William Mosher, Peleg Gifford** and **Benj^a Russell the 4th** to Collect Subscriptions for the afore Said Books and Make Report to the next Monthly Meeting – –

Certificate for Thos Wilcox- [prop]osed   The overseers Inform this Meeting that **Thomas Willcox** hath Re= =moved out of the verge of this Meeting without a Certificate therefore **Humphry Smith Samuel Smith** and **William Anthony ju^r** are Appointed to draw a Certificate for him and bring ~~bring~~ it to the next Monthly Meeting

Rachel Sowle's affair   the Committee Appointed Some time past to Settle the Affair Respec =ting **Rachell Sowle** with **Sandwich** Monthly Meeting Report that they have had two Conferences with S^d Meetings Com'ttee and that they Could not ~~not~~ settle that affair therefore the Matter is Refered to next Monthly Meeting

---

2^d mo: 1769   At a Monthly Meeting held in **Dartmouth** the 20th of the 2^d month 1769, The Representatives are **Samuel Smith** and **William Anthony ju^r** Both Present, – –

Bart Taber Certificat   **Bartholomew Taber** hath Produced a Certificate from the Monthly Meeting of **Sandwich**, Certifying his Clearness in Respect to Marriage and that he is under the Care of that Meeting and also Signifying his Parent's Consent – –

Tho Almy Clearness   The friends Appointed to Inquire into the Clearness of **Thomas Almy** Respecting Marriage and Conversation Report that they have Made Inquiry and do not find anything to hinder his Proceeding in Marriage – –

Bart Taber and Thos Almy answer   **Bartholomew Taber** and **Mercy Bowdish** and **Thomas Almy** and **Deborah Allen** Appeared for their Answers which was that Each Couple Might Proceed to take Each other in Marriage in Some Convenient time between this and the next Monthly Meeting Advising with the overseers for that Purpose and **Thomas Hicks** and **Prince Allen** are Appointed to See **Thomas Almy** and **Deborah Allen**'s Marriage Consu=

---

8. Samuel Fuller (died 1736) was an Irish Quaker schoolmaster, and the author of *Some Principles and Precepts of the Christian Religion, by Way of Question and Answer. Recommended to Parents and Tutors for the Use of Children* (Dublin: Samuel Fuller, 1736). It was reprinted by S. Southwick in Newport in 1769. For the primers see below, p. 749 below.

=mated in Good order and make Report to the next Monthly Meeting
and **Caleb Russell** and **Joseph Gifford** are Appointed to See
Bartholomew Taber and **Mercy Bowdish**'s Marriage Consumat[ed]
in Good order & Make Report to the next Monthly Meeting

Peleg Slo =cum's marriage The friends Appointed to See **Peleg Slocum**'s and **Lucy Howland**
Marriage Consumated Report that they attended the Marriage
and that it was Accomplished in Good order – –
and also the friends Appointed on the Same Account with
Barnabas Wing and **Jane Merihew** Make the like Report
that their Marriage was Consumated in Good order – –

on Printg Books The friends Appointed to Collect Subscriptions for the
Printing the Primers and Books Report that they ˄are in the
Progress of their Service but have not Accomplished it yet
Therefore they are Still Continued in the Same Service and
to make Report to the next Monthly Meeting – –

The Matter Concerning **Humphry Smith the 3ᵈ** is Refer'd to the
next Monthly Meeting – –

T. Wilcox's Certificate This Meeting hath Signed a Certificate for **Thomas Wilcox**
to the Monthly Meeting of **Coakset** – –

The Matter Concerning **Rachel Sowle** is Refered to the
next Monthly Meeting – –

Minutes to be review'd **Humphry Smith, Samuel Smith, Benjᵃ Howland Job
Russell** are Appointed to Review the Monthly Meeting's
Minutes to See what part they may think proper to be
put on Record and Make Report to the next Monthly Meeting

[3ᵈ] mo: 1769 At a Monthly Meeting held in **Dartmouth** the 20ᵗʰ of
3ᵈ month 1769 – The Representatives are **Caleb Russell**
and **Samuel Smith** both Present – –

James Davis proposal [of] marriag **James Davis** & **Patience Russell** declared their Intentions of
Marriage, and were desired to wait Till next Monthly Meeting
for their Answer, and **William Sanford** & **David Smith** are Appointed
to Enquire into the young Man's Clearness Respecting Mareriage
and Conversation & Make Report to yᵉ next Monthly Meeting

Thoˢ Almy & [Bart]. Taber marriage The friends Appointed to See **Thoˢ Almy** & **Deborah Allen**'s Marriage
Consumated in Good order Report that they both attended the Marriage
which was Consumated in good order, and likewise the friends
Appointed on the Same Account for **Bartholomew Taber** & **Mercy
Bowdish** make the Like Report that their Marriage was
Consumated in Good order –

The friends Appointed to Collect Subscriptions for **Fox's** Primers

Subscrip=
tions

and **Fuller**'s Books Report ~~as followeth~~ they have taken them in as followeth (viz)

	Small Primers	Fox's Primers	Fuller's Books
Caleb Russell	23	24	21
Prince Allen	22	16	16
Peleg Gifford	12	5	3
Willm Mosher	60	24	26
Daniel Cornell	10	5	5
Benj^a Russell 4th	41	20	8
Thomas Hicks	11	3	2
Samuel Smith	31	[13?]	6
Wm Anthony ju^r	15	10	00
Jonathan Hussey	6	6	00
Whole of Each Sort Subscribed for – – }	231	126	87

Hum Smith 3
case

The Matter Concerning **Humphry Smith** y^e 3^d is Refer'd to the under the Care of **Joseph Gifford, Wm Sanford & Barzillai Tucker** and they are desired to Visit the young man and make Report to the adjournment of this Meeting – –

Dinah Ric=
=ketson's
paper
Received

The women friends Inform that **Dinah Ricketson** hath Given in a Paper to their Meeting Some Months past Condemning her falling into the Sin of Fornication, which they have Concluded to Accept Provided She Cause S^d paper to be Read Publickly at the Close of a first day Meeting for worship She being present, and Return Said paper to the Next Monthly Meeting which this Meeting Concurs with – –

The affair
of Rachel
Sowle

Whereas **Rachel Sowle** was Set off to **Sandwich** Monthly Meeting Some time past, and the S^d Meeting Refusing to Accept her, and this Meeting having Appointed a Committee to hear the Reasons of their Refusal and also to Settle the Matter Concerning her, and they have Some Months past Made Report that they have had Several Conferences with **Sandwich** Monthly Meeting and Could not Settle the matter in Controversey, their Reasons as we Apprehend not being Sufficient therefore this Meeting doth Appoint a Committee to Settle ^the matter the best way that they may think proper in behalf of this Meeting whose Names are **Humphry Smith, Prince Allen, Thos Hicks, Joseph Gifford, James Tucker** or Either two of them and they to Make Report to this Meeting when they have Made full Trial for a Settlement – –

Overseers of poor accompts   The overseers of the Poor have brought an Accompt for doing for the poor to the amount of £6 – 11ˢ – 10ᵈ old Tener, and the Treasurer has paid the Same by the order of this Meeting – – This Meeting hath Collected £8 – 4 – 2ᵈ old Tener – –

adjourns   This Meeting adjourns to the 29ᵗʰ Instant – –

mett   This Meeting being mett According to Adjournment yᵉ 29ᵗʰ of the 3d Month 1769 – The Representatives being Called both Present – –

Miniuts Review'd   The Committee Appointed to Review the Meeting's Minutes Report they have Reviewed Sᵈ Minutes and Left them with **Samuel Smith** to be Recorded – –

[Que]ries   The Queries have been Read and Answered in this Meeting and
[E]pistle   This Meeting hath Signed an Epistle to the Quarterly Meeting and
[Rep]resen= [ta]tives   **Jonathan Hussey, Thoˢ Hicks** and **Wᵐ Barker** are Appointed to attend the Quarterly Meeting, and to Present the Epistle with the Answers to the Queries & Make Report to the next Monthly Meeting – –

[H.] Smith 3 [pa]per [ac]cepted   The friends Appointed to have the Care of **Humphry Smith** yᵉ 3ᵈ Report that he Gave them Tolerable Good Satisfaction therefore This Meeting Concludes to Accept his paper that he Gave in to this Meeting Some Months past if he will Cause it to be Read at the Close of a first day Meeting of worship he being present between This and the next Monthly Meeting and Return Said paper to next Monthly Meeting – –

[Ch]using [El]ders referd   Chusing of Elders is Refered to the next Monthly Meeting **Prince Allen, Joseph Gifford, Barzillai Tucker, Thoˢ Hicks** 2ᵈ and **Caleb Russell** are appointed overseers of the Poor – –

[Re]port of [M]eeting in Allen Neck   The friends Appointed to have the Care of the Meetings held in **Allen's** Neck and in **Smith's Neck** Report that they attended the Meetings Respectively, which were held to Good Satisfaction

---

4ᵗʰ mo: 1769   At a Monthly meeting held in **Dartmouth** the 17:ᵗʰ 4ᵗʰ Month 1769 – The Representatives are **David Smith** & **Barzillai Tucker** both Present – – The friends Appointed to Enquire into the Clearness of

James Davis Clearness   **James Davis** in Respect to Marriage & Conversation Report that they have Made Inquiry & do not find anything to hinder his Proceeding in Marriage – –

James Davis answer   **James Davis** & **Patience Russell** Appeared for their Answer which was that they Might Proceed to take each other in Marriage in Some Convenient time between this & the next

Monthly Meeting advising with the overseers for that Purpose
and **Wᵐ Sanford** and **Joseph Gifford** are Appointed to See their
Marriage Consumated in Good order, and Make Report to the
next Monthly Meeting – –

Dinah Ric
=ketson paper
Read

Dinah Ricketson's Paper hath been Read & Returned to this
Meeting According to the Direction of Last Monthly Meeting

Report
of the
Judgment
about
R. Sowle

The friends Appointed to Settle the Controversey between this and
Sandwich Monthly Meeting Concerning **Rachel Sowle**, Report
that they have Settled the Matter by Referring it to Indifferent
friends, and their Judgment is that the Said **Rachel Sowle**
belongs to this Meeting – –

Dinah Ricketson's paper Above mentioned is as followeth

Dinah
Ricketson's
Confession

To the Monthly Meeting of friends to be held the 21 of the
11ᵗʰ Month 1768 – –

Esteemed friends, Whereas I through unwatchfulness
have fallen into the ₄Reproachful Sin of Fornication which plainly
appears by my having a Child So Soon after Marriage & gone
Contrary to the Good order of friends all which I am Sorry
for, hoping God will forgive me, and I desire friends would
pass it by, So far as to Let me Remain under their Care

Dinah Ricketson

Rachel Sowle
affair

Jonathan Hussey & **David Smith** are Appointed to Make
Inquiry to find what Estate belongs to the above Sᵈ **Rachel
Sowle** and also to Settle accounts with her Creditors, and to
Make Report to the next Monthly Meeting – –

Report from
Quar meeting

The friends Appointed to attend the Quarterly Meeting Report
that they all attended According to Appointment, and have
Produced an Epistle from the Same which hath been Read
and well Accepted – –

Humphry Smith the 3ᵈ his paper hath been Read Agree=
=able to the Appointment of Last Monthly Meeting –
and is as follows – –

H. Smith's
Acknow=
ledgement

To the Monthly Meeting of **Dartmouth**

These Comes with Sorrow to Acknowledge my outgoings in Horse-Ra=
=cing, Gaming & falling into a bodily Strife with **Samuel
Macumber ju:** all which I do heartily & Sincerely Condemn with
all other my outgoings, and hoping forgiveness from the Lord, I
desire friends So far to pass them by as to let me Remain under
your Care, desiring that I may for the time to Come be preserved from
the like evil or any others, dated this 15ᵗʰ of yᵉ first mo: 1769

Humphry Smith the 3ᵈ

[Chus]ing [El-ders] referd Chusing of Elders is Refered to the next Monthly Meeting

[J] Mosher Joseph Mosher Informs this Meeting that he is about to Remove
[desire?] with his family to the **Nine partners**, and desires a Removal
[Ce]rtificate Certificate, Therefore **Luke Hart** & **Barzillai Tucker** are
appointed to Make Inquiry into his Life & Conversation, and to
See that his outward affairs be Settled to Satisfaction, and draft
a Certificate for himself & family if they think Proper, and
bring it to the next Monthly Meeting

Complaint William Wilcox hath Exhibited a Complaint against **Benj^a Smith** for Refu=
against sing to pay him an award brought in by Arbitrators Indifferently Chosen
Benj. Smith between them, Therefore **Abraham Tucker** & **Joseph Tucker** are
appointed to Treat with the Said **Benjamin Smith** for his Neglect
and to Make Report to the next Monthly Meeting

5 mo:} At a Monthly Meeting held in **Dartmouth** the 15: 5th month
1769 } 1769 – The Representatives are **David Smith** & **Barzillai**
Tucker both Present – –

James Davis The friends appointed to See **James Davis** and **Patience**
marriage **Russell**'s Marriage Consumated Report that their S^d Mar-
not accom -riage is not accomplished by Reason the young woman
plished has been Sick, therefore they are Still Continued in S^d
Service and to Make Report to the next Monthly Meeting

Rach Sowle The friends Appointed to Inquire into **Rachel Sowle**'s affairs
Case and to Settle accounts with her Creditors Report that they
have made Some Progress therein & desire one month longer
to Accomplish S^d business which is Granted them & they to make
Report next Monthly Meeting

This Meeting hath Signed a Removal Certificate for
Certifi} Joseph Mosher & his family to the Monthly Meeting at the
for J. Mosher} **Nine- partners** in **Douches [Dutchess] County** in the Province of **Newyork**

The friends Appointed to Treat with **Benjamin Smith** for Ne-
-glecting to fulfil an award brought in ~~by~~ between him and
Benj Smith's William Wilcox Report that the S^d. **Benjamin** Informed the[m]
Case that the arbitrators were not Chosen between them according
to Rule, & therefore ye Case was not brought to the Meeting according to
the Rule of Discipline, therefore this meeting doth add **Joseph Giffor[d]**
to the former Committee on that Case, and they Treat with the S^d.
Benj^a Smith & to make Inquiry into Every particular Circumstance Relat[ing?]
to the Controversey & to Labour as they find freedom to Settle the S^d· Controv[ersey]
and to make Report to ye next Monthly Meeting – –

Chusing Elder refered Chusing of Elders is Refered to the next Monthly Meeting

Obediah Allen request **Obediah Allen** hath Given in a Paper to this Meeting
Condemning his former Outgoings, for which he was denied,
and desiring to be Received Again under friends Care, which
is Refered to Next Monthly Meeting under the Care of
Thomas Hicks & **Barzillai Tucker**, and they to Make Report
to the next Monthly Meeting

6th Month 1769 At a Monthly Meeting held in **Dartmouth** the 19ᵗʰ
of the 6ᵗʰ month 1769, ˄ᵀʰᵉ ᴿᵉᵖʳᵉˢᵉⁿᵗᵃᵗⁱᵛᵉˢ are **Caleb Russell** & **Jonathan Hussey**
both present – –

James Davis marriage **William Sanford** & **Joseph Gifford** Report that they
attended the Marriage of **James Davis** & **Patience Russell**
which was Consumated in Good order – –

Rachel Sowle's Estate The friends Appointed to Settle Accompts with **Rachel Sowle**['s]
Creditors, & to See what Money Remains due to her Report
that there Remains due to the Sd, **Rachell** £6 – 5ˢ – 10ᵈ ½ Lawful
Money – –

Benj Smith affare Settled The Committee Appointed to Treat with **Benjamin Smith** ~~for~~
on account of a Complaint Exhibited against him by
William Wilcox Report, that the Matter is Settled to
Satisfaction Between the Said **Benja Smith** & **Wm Wilcox**

Removal Certificates for E. Tripp R. Macumbr & M. Taber This meeting hath Signed Three Removal Certificates
one for **Elizabeth Tripp** & one for **Rachal Macumber** both
to the Monthly Meeting of **Coakset**, and one for
Mercy Taber to **Sandwich** Monthly Meeting – –

The Visits of Foreign Friends Our Esteemed friend **Rachel Wilson** hath Visited us
with her Certificate from the Monthly Meeting at
Kendal in **Westmorland** in old **England** bearing date
the 24ᵗʰ of the 6ᵗʰ month 1768, With a Concurrance from the
Quarterly Meeting held at **Kendal** for **Westmorland** the
8ᵗʰ of the 7ᵗʰ month 1768, Which were Read in this Mee-
=ting to Good Satisfaction - in Company with whom Came
our Esteemed friend **Sarah Hopkins** with her Certificate
from the Monthly Meeting held at **Haddonfield** in the
County of **Gloucester** the 8ᵗʰ of the first month 1769
and her Visit Kindly accepted, And likewise our Esteemd
friend **John Pemberton** hath Visited This Meeting with
his Certificate from the Monthly Meeting held in **Phi-
-ladelphia** by Adjournment from the 26ᵗʰ 5 ᵐᵒ to the 30ᵗʰ

of the Same 1769, which hath been Read & well accepted[9]

This meeting hath Signed a Removal Certificate for

Certificate **Thomas Wilcox** to the Monthly Meeting of **Coakset**
for T. Wilcox This Meeting hath Collected 19ˢ – 2ᵈ Lawful money

adjourn This Meeting Adjourns to the Last fourth day of this Month

mett This Meeting being Mett by Adjournment the 28ᵗʰ of the
6ᵗʰ mo: 1769, The Representatives being Called, **Caleb
Russell** Present, but **Jonathan Hussey** not Present by
Reason he is gone to **Nantucket** yearly Meeting

Chusing Elders The Matter Concerning Chusing Elders is Refered to the
Refered Next Monthly Meeting – –

Obediah Allen The Matter Concerning **Obediah Allen** is Refered to next
Case referd Monthly Meeting under the Same Care as heretofore and they
then to make Report – –

E. Potter The women friends have brought a Paper to this Meeting
accepted from **Elisabeth Potter**, Condemning her disorerly Marriage
which they have Accepted, & this Meeting Concurs therewith

Representatives **Joseph Tucker**, **Caleb Russell**, & **William Barker** are
appointed to attend the Quarterly Meeting and Present
the Epistle to the Same which this Meeting hath Signed
and make Report to the next Monthly Meeting

Time of **Humphry Smith** & **Samuel Smith** are appointed to Collec[t]
Publick an Account of ^the Several Publick friends decease that have
fr'ds decease Lately been Removed, and Put them in order Agreeable
to be to the Book of Discipline, and bring them to this Meeting
Collected as Soon as they Conveniently Can

[7]th mo: At a Monthly Meeting held in **Dartmouth** the 17ᵗʰ
1769 of the 7ᵗʰ month 1769, The Representatives are **Samuel
Smith** and **Benja, Howland 2** both Present

Obedi Allen **Obediah Allen** hath Given in a Paper to this Meeting
paper accep Some time past, and now this Meeting Concludes to Accept of
it, Provided he Cause Sᵈ paper to be Read Publickly at the
Close of a first day Meeting for worship he being present [and ?]
Return Sᵈ paper to the next Monthly Meeting – –

9. Rachel (Wilson) Wilson (1720–1775) made an extended visit to America in 1768–1769, preaching before the students at Princeton and visiting Patrick Henry in Virginia. See Geoffrey Braithwaite, *Rachel Wilson and Her Quaker Mission in Eighteenth-Century America* (York, Eng.: Sessions, 2012). Sarah Hopkins (ca. 1744–1812) was an elder in Haddonfield Monthly Meeting. See Philadelphia Yearly Meeting Men's Minutes, 1813, p. 226, Philadelphia Yearly Meeting Archives (Friends Historical Library, Swarthmore College, Swarthmore, Pa.). John Pemberton (1727–1795) was one of the leaders of the "reformation" among Friends. He died on a ministerial journey to Germany. See William Hodgson, *The Life and Travels of John Pemberton, a Minister of the Gospel of Christ* (London: C. Gilpin, 1844).

Report from Quar meeting The friends Appointed to attend the Quarterly Meeting Report that they all attended According to Appointment and have

their Epistle returnd back Produced an Epistle from the Same which hath been Read in which it Appears there is a Mistake, therefore this Meeting Concludes to Return S^d Epistle to the Quarterly meeting again – –

*Treasurer paid **Tim Russel*** The Treasurer Reports that he hath paid **Timothy Russell** five Dollars for keeping the Meeting house half a year

Epistles Rece =ved This Meeting hath Received the **London** Epistle for the year 1768, as likewise a Transcript of our Last yearly Meetings Epistle and likewise a Transcript of the Judgment of the

Respecting Tenth Query yearly Meeting Committee Respecting the tenth Query – –

Peace Shear- -man paper accepted **Peace Shearman** hath Given in a paper to this Meeting which Came from the womens Meeting and they Inform this Meeting that they have Concluded to accept of the same which this this Concurs with Provided She Cause it to be Read Publickly at the Close of a first day Meeting of worship & She be present, and Re- turn Sd paper to next monthly meeting – –

[Chu]sing Elders [re]ferd The Matter Concerning Chusing of Elders is Refered to the next Monthly Meeting

8ᵗʰ mo: 1769 At a Monthly Meeting held in **Dartmouth** the 21 of the 8ᵗʰ month 1769 – The Representatives are **Caleb Russell** and **Jonathan Hussey** both present – –

Abraham Smith proposal of marriage **Abraham Smith** & **Suruiah Ricketson** declared their Inten- tions of Marriage and were desired to wait till next monthly Meeting for their Answer and **Caleb Russell** & **Joseph Gifford** are Appointed Enquire into the young man's Clearness Respecting marriage and Conversation and make Report to the next monthly meeting – –

O. Allen's Confession **Obediah Allen's** paper hath been Read According to the appointment of Last Monthly Meeting and is as follows – – To the Monthly Meeting of **Dartmouth** – –
    Loving friends Whereas I through weakness and the Insinuation of the Adver- -Sary have twice fallen into the Sin of Fornication, and Likewise in Gaming, for which Evils I Can Truly Say I am Sorry for, and do Sincerely Condemn the Same with all other my outgoings, hoping forgiveness from Almighty God, I desire friends to Receive me Again under their Care, and would hereby take the Reproach of my outgoings on myself and Clear friends and the Truth from the Same

Given for the this 15ᵗʰ day of the 5ᵗʰ month 1769

By your friend **Obadiah Allen**

P. Shearman's **Peace Shearman**'s paper hath been Read & Returned to
Confession this meeting According to the Appointment of Last Monthly
meeting, and is as followeth – –

      Dartmouth the 12th of the 1 month 1769

To the Monthly Meeting of friends to be holden in
Dartmouth the 16th Instant – –

Dear friends, These may Inform that Notwithstanding
I had my Education Amongst Friends. I have by Giving
way to the Temtation of the Adversary, been Guilty of
the Sin of Fornication, as Appears by my having a
Child So Soon after Marriage, which Sin I do hereby
Condemn, with all other my offences and am heartily
Sorry for, hoping that God in his Abundant Mercy
will forgive me, and I do desire that friends will So far
pass by my offences as to Suffer me Still to Remain
under Their Care – –**Peace Shearman** – –

Remo: This Meeting hath Signed two Removel Certificates
Certifi: to the Monthly Meeting of **Sandwich** one for **Edith Wing**
for E. W. wife of **Edward wing ju**: the other for **Jane Wing** wife
& J. W of **Barnabas wing** – –

J. Russel This Meeting doth Appoint **Job Russell** an Elder in
an Elder addition to our former Elders – –

Letter from **Smithfield** Monthly Meeting hath writ to this Meeting
Smithfield Informing us that **Samuel Howland Ju**: hath omitted
respecting to Deliver his Removal Certificate ~~till~~ to them till
Saml How= three years after the date, and also they discover a
=land Shortness in the Certificate Respecting the Settlement
of his owtward Affares, Therefore **Wᵐ Anthony Juʳ**
and **Samuel Smith** are Appointed to write the Said
Howland in behalf of this Meeting as they Shall think
Proper, and also to Enquire into his Affairs Above mentioned, and to make Report as Soon as they Conveniently
Can to this Meeting – –

Danˡ Cornel **Daniel Cornel** Desires a Certificate to the Monthly
desires a Meeting of **Coackset** Concerning his Clearness in
Certificate Respect to Marriage & Conversation. Therefore This Meeting doth
appoint **Nicolas Howland** and **Philip Allen** to Enquire
into the Above Mentioned Respects and draft a Certifi;

cate for him if they think proper and Make Report to
next Monthly Meeting – –

Wᵐ Sanford Ju **William Sanford ju**: hath Given in a paper to this Meeting
paper Condemning his disorder in Marrying out of the unity of
friends, which is Refer'd to the next Monthly Meeting;

9ᵗʰ mo: At a Monthly Meeting held in **Dartmouth** the 18ᵗʰ of the
1769 9ᵗʰ mo: 1769, The Representatives are **Samuel Smith** and
Barzillai Tucker both present – –
Caleb Russell & **Joseph Gifford** Report that they have
made Inquiry into the Clearness of **Abraham Smith** in
Respect to Marriage & Conversation and find nothing to
hinder his Proceeding in Marriage – –

Abraham **Abraham Smith** & **Surviah [Zeruiah] Ricketson** Appeared for their
Smith answer Answer which was that thy might Proceed to take Each
other in Marriage in Some Convenient time between now
and next Monthly Meeting Advising with the overseers
for that Purpose, and **Caleb Russell** & **John Potter** are Ap:
pointed to See their Marriage Consumated in Good order, and
make Report to the next Monthly Meeting – –

John Tucker **John Tucker** & **Rhoda Wing** declared their Intentions of
proposal of Marriage, & were desired to wait till next monthly Mee:
marriage ting for their Answer, and **Luke Hart** & **Wᵐ Mosher** are
Appointed to Inquire into **John Tucker**'s Clearness in Respect to Marriage & Conversation and Make Report to the
next Monthly Meeting

Certificate for This Meeting hath Signed a Certificate for **Daniel Cornel**
Dan: Cornel to **Coakset** Monthly Meeting Certifying his Clearness in
Respect to Marriage & Conversation – –

Case of Wᵐ The Case of **Wᵐ Sanford jur** is Refered to next monthly
Sanford Ju Meeting under the Care of **Jonathan Hussey** & **David Smith**
referd & they to make Report to the next Monthly Meeting – –

Rhoda **Rhoda Wing** hath Produced a Removal Certificate from
Wings the monthly Meeting of **Coakset** which hath been read
Certificate in this Meeting and Accepted – –

Chusing It hath been moved at this Meeting for a new Choice
Overseers of Overseers, and the matter Labouring Somewhat hard
refered the matter is Refered to next monthly meeting, and
the Same friends that were in that Service are Continued
in the Same Service one month Longer – –

writ to Smithfield about S. Howl'd   This Meeting hath Signed a few Lines to **Smithfield** Monthly Meeting in Answer to their Request Respecting a deficiency in **Samuel Howland ju:r** Certificate

Phebe Sisson paper accepted   The women friends Inform that they have accepted of **Phebe Sisson**'s paper, which this meeting Concurs with

This meeting hath Collected £12 - 5ˢ - 6ᵈ old tener

adjourn   This Meeting Adjourns to the first Sixth day in next month

mett   This Meeting being mett by adjournment the 6ᵗʰ day of the 10ᵗʰ month 1769 – –The Representatives being Called, both Present – –

Answers to Queries   The Queries have been read & Answer'd in this Meeting and the Answers are order'd to be Sent up to the Quarterly Meeting by the Representatives with the Epistle to the Same which hath been Signed in this meeting

Representa =tives   **Joseph Tucker, Nicholas Howland & Wᵐ Sanford** are Appointed to attend the Quarly Meeting and Present the Said Epistle & Answers as aforesaid, and Make Return to the next Monthly Meeting

J Russel Recomendᵈ an Elder   This meeting hath Signed a few Lines to the Quarterly Meeting of Ministers & Elders, Signifying our Appointing of **Job Russell** an Elder

1847-10 mᵒ 5ᵗʰ Examined by S. R. Gifford   { It appears that **Job Russell** was Clark at this time }

10ᵗʰ mo: 1769   At a Monthly Meeting held in **Dartmouth** the 16ᵗʰ of the 10ᵗʰ month 1769, The Representatives are **Jonathan Hussey & Wᵐ Anthony juʳ** both Present – –

The friends Appointed to Enquire into **John Tucker**'s Clearness Respecting Marriage & Conversation Report that they have Made Inquiry & find nothing to hinder his Proceeding in Marriage

John Tucker answer   **John Tucker & Rhoda Wing** Appeared for their Answer which was that they Might Proceed to take Each other in Marriage in Some Convenient time between this & the next Monthly Meeting, Advising with the overseers for that Purpose, and **Luke Hart & William Mosher** are Appointed to See their Mar--riage Consumated in Good order, and Make Report to the next Monthly Meeting

Wᵐ Taber pro posal of marri age   **William Taber** (Son of **Joseph Taber**) and **Martha Hart** declared their Intentions of Marriage, and were desired to wait until the next Monthly Meeting for their Answer – –

Caleb Russell and **John Potter** Report that they attended the

Abraham Smith marriage	Marriage of **Abraham Smith & Zeruiah [Surviah]** ~~Howland~~ **Ricketson** which was Consumated in Good order – –
Wm Sanford Ju Case referd	**Jonathan Hussey & David Smith** Report that they have had no oppertunity to Treat with **Wm Sanford ju^r**, therefore that Case is Refer'd to next monthly Meeting under the Care of the Same friend & they then make Report – –
Chusing Over= seers referd	A New Choice of overseers is Refered to next Monthly Meeting, and the former overseers Still Continued one month Longer The friends Appointed to attend the Quarterly Meeting
Report from Quart meeting	Report that they all Attended According to Appointment & have Produced an Epistle from the Same which hath been Read and well Accepted – –
Epistles from the meetings of Suffering	This meeting hath Received two Printed Epistles, one from the meeting of Sufferings in **London** dated in the 3^d Month 1769, the other from the Meeting of Sufferings in **Philadelphia** dated in the 9th month 1769
Certificate for Elisa: Gifford	This meeting hath Signed a Removal Certificate to the Monthly Meeting of **Coakset** for our friend **Elisabeth Gifford**
Overseers of yearly meeting	This Meeting doth Appoint **Joseph Gifford, John Potter, Wm Barker, Caleb Russell, Barzillai Tucker, Prince Allen, & James Tucker** to have the oversight of the Lofts and other Seats at our yearly meeting to Prevent any disoreder at that time, and to Make Report to the next Monthly Meeting

11th mo: 1769	At a Monthly Meeting held in **Dartmouth** the 20th of the 11th month 1769 The Representatives are **Caleb Russell & Jonathan Hussey** both Present
Wm Taber Certificate	**William Taber** (Son of **Joseph Taber**) hath Produced a Certi--ficate from the monthly meeting of **Sandwich**, Certifying his being under the Care of friends there, and Clear from Any Entanglement Respecting Marriage, and he hath also Produced the Consent of his Parents to Proceed in Marriage
Peter Bar= =neds Certificate	**Peter Barnard** hath Produced a Certificate from the Monthly Meeting of **Nantucket** , Certifying his being under the Care of that Meeting, and Clear from Any Entanglement in Respect to Marriage, and he hath also Produced his Parent's Consent that he may Proceed in Marriage with **Rebecca Hussey** – –
Peter Bar= =ned proposal of marriage	**Peter Barnard** with **Rebeccca Hussey**, and **John Wood** with **Dinah Hussey**, and **Increase Smith** with **Elisabeth Barker** Declared their Intentions of Marriage, and

each Couple were desired to wait until the next Monthly
Meeting for their Answer, and **William Anthony ju**[r] and
Samuel Smith a[re] appointed to Inquire into the S[d] **Increase
Smith**'s Clearness Respecting ~~Res~~ Marriage and Conversation
and to Make Report to the Next Monthly Meeting

John Tucker marriage **Luke Hart** & **W**[m] **Mosher** Report that they attended the Marriage of **John Tucker** & **Rhoda Wing**, and that it was Consu-
mated in Good order – –

Wm Sanford Jur case referd **Jonathan Hussey** & **David Smith** Report that they have not
yet had an opportunity to Speak with **Wm Sanford ju**[r] by
Reason of his being Absent, therefore the matter is Refered
under their Care as heretofore, and they to make Report
to the next monthly meeting – –

Certifi for M. Hamond This Meeting hath Signed a Removal Certificate to the
Monthly Meeting at **Oblong** for our friend **Mary Hammond**

This Meeting doth Adjorn to the 29th day of this Instant

At a Monthly Meeting met by Adjornment in **Dartmouth**
the 29th 11[mo] 1769—the Representatives being Called
Caleb Russell Present the other not Present: **William**

Wm Tabers proposal of marriage **Taber** Son of **Joseph Taber** and **Martha Hart** appeared
for their Answer, which was that they mought Proseed
to take Each other in Marriage in Some Convenient
Time between this and the next Monthly Meeting Advising
with the Overseers that we Shall appoint for that Purpose
William Mosher and **Barzillaj Tucker** are appointed to
See their Marriage Consomated in Good order and make
Report to the next monthly meeting

Chsing overseers referd A New Choice of Overseers is Refered to the next Monthly
Meeting

Report of Overseers of yearly meeting The Friends appointed to have the oversight of the Lofts
and other Seats at the yearly meeting Report that they
Mostly attended the Said meeting and Saw nothing but
what was Tolerable orderly – –

Meetings Granted in Allens Neck The Friends Living in **Allen's Neck** Request Liberty to
hold a Meeting for worship in Said neck as heretofore
which is Granted them Agreeable to their Request, and
Philip Allen & **Daniel Cornel[Cornell]** are appointed to have the
oversight of the Same to See that it be Kept in Good
order, & to make Report to the monthly Meeting in
the fourth Month Next – –

Meetings granted in Smiths Neck The friends Living in **Smith's Neck** do also Request Liberty to hold a Meeting of worship in their neck on Each first day of the week for the three Ensuing winter Months, Which is Granted them, and **William Anthony & Samuel Smith** are Appointed to See that the Same be Kept orderly, and to Make Report to the Monthly Meeting in the fourth Month next

12 mo: 1769 At a Monthly Meeting held in **Dartmouth** the 18th of the 12th month 1769; The Representatives are **Jonathan Hussey** and **William Anthony ju**: both Present – –

John Wood Certificate **John Wood** hath Produced a Certificate from **Coakset** Monthly Meeting, Certifying his Clearness Respecting Marriage & that he hath the Consent of his near Relations to Proceed in Marriage – –

Increase Smiths Clearness **Wm Anthony Jur & Samuel Smith** Report that they have made Inquiry into **Increase Smith**'s Clearness, and find nothing to hinder his Proceeding in Marriage – –

Peter Barned John Wood and Increase Smith proposals of marriage **Peter Barnard & Rebecca Hussey**, and **John Wood & Dinah Hussey**, and **Increase Smith** and **Elisabeth Barker**, all Appeared for their Answers, Which Was that Each Couple Might Proceed to take Each other in Marriage in Some Convenient time between this and the Next Monthly Meeting Advising with the overseers for that purpose, and **Abraham Tucker & David Smith** are Appointed to See that the Marriages of the two first Mentioned Couples are Consumated in Good order and Make Report to the next Monthly Meeting – – and **Wm Anthony ju: & Samuel Smith** are Appointed to See that the Marriage of **Increase Smith & Elisabeth Barker** be Consumated in Good order and Make Report to the next Monthly Meeting

Case of Wm Sanford jur referd **Jonathan Hussey & David Smith** Report that they have not had an opportunity to Treat with **Wm Sanford jur** Therefore the Matter is Refered under their Care, and they to make Report to the Monthly Meeting as Soon as they Conveniently Can – –

Wm Taber marriage **Wm Mosher & Barzillai Tucker** Report that they attended the Marriage of **Wm Taber & Martha Hart**, and that it was Consu= -mated in Good order – –

Chusing overseers refered A new Choice of overseers is Refer'd to next Monthly Meeting This meeting hath Collected £7–15s–2d old Tener – –

Treasurer paid Tim Russell The Treasurer hath paid **Timothy Russell** five Dollars for keep- -ing the meeting House half a year by the direction of this Meeting

adjourn This Meeting adjourns to the 27th Instant – –

mett At a Monthly Meeting hld by Adjournment the 27th of
the 12th month 1769 The Representatives being Called both
Answers to Queries present; The Queries have been read and Answered
& Epistles Sent up This meeting hath Signed an Epistle to the Quarterly Mee-
Representatives ting, And **Caleb Russell** & **William Mosher** are Appointed
to attend the Quarterly Meeting & Present the Epistle with
the P. Answers, and to make Report to yᵉ next Monthly Meeting
To Collect money for Books **Jonathan Hussey, Wᵐ Anthony juʳ** & **Samuel Smith** are Ap-
pointed to Collect the Money for the Books, and to Send it to
John Dockry as Soon as May be, According to the Request of the
Last Quarterly Meeting;

---

first mo: 1770 At a Monthly Meeting held in **Dartmouth** the 15th of
the first Month 1770, The Representatives are **Jonathan Hussey**
and **Wᵐ Barker** both Present – –
Benj Howland 2ⁿᵈ proposal of marriage **Benjᵃ Howland 2ᵈ** and **Silvester Smith** Declared Their
Intentions of Marriage at this Meeting, and were desired
to wait till next Monthly Meeting for their Answer, and
John Potter & **Thomas Hicks** are appointed to Enquire into the
Said **Benjᵃ Howland**; Clearness in Respect to Marriage &
Conversation, and make Report to next Monthly Meeting
Abraham Tucker & **David Smith** Report that they Attended
Peter Barnad marriage the Marriages of **Peter Barnard** & **Rebecca Hussey**, and **John**
John Wood **Wood** & **Dinah Hussey** which were Consumated in Good order
& Increase Smith's and **Wᵐ Anthony juʳ** & **Samuel Smith** Make the Like Report
marriage Respecting the Marriage of **Increase Smith** & **Elisabeth Barker**
M. Cornell's Certificate **Mary Cornell** wife of **Daniel Cornell** has Produced a Removal
Certificate from the Monthly Meeting of **Coakset** which hath
been Read and Accepted – –
C. Brigg accepted The women friends Inform that they have accepted of **Catherine**
Briggs's Paper Condemning her Marrying out of unity of friends
which This Meeting Concurs with – –
Chusing Over seers Refer'd A New Choice of overseers is Refer'd to the next Monthly Meeting
and the following friends are Chosen as a Committee for that
Service for one Month, /viz/ **Daniel Cornell, Jonathan Hussey**
Wᵐ Barker, & **Nicolas Howland**, and they to Make Report
to the next Monthly Meeting; – –
Report from Quar meeting **Caleb Russell** and **Wᵐ Mosher** Report that they attended the
~~Marriage~~ Quarterly Meeting Agreeable to Appointment, and they
have Produced an Epistle from the Same, which hath been
read & Kindly Accepted – –

State of Trea sury The friends Appointed have Adjusted Accompts with the
Treasurer, and there Remains in the Stock £10-6-2 d old Tener

money Sent to pay for Books and they also Report that they have fulfilled their Appointment in Regard to the Books, and that they have Sent all the
money in the Stock to pay for Sᵈ Books

Complaint against S. Wilcox **William Smith** hath Exhibited a Complaint against **Stephen
Wilcox** for Neglecting to pay him his due, which the overseers
hath brought to this Meeting with a Scandulous Report Re-
-Specting the Sᵈ **Wilcox**'s deceiving of **Benjᵃ Gifford** of **Falmouth**
by taking Money of him to Convey to **William Smith** & Converted
it to his own use, and also that he Neglects to attend Meetings
both for Worship & discipline, for all which offences the overseers
have Labour'd with him, and this Meeting doth Appoint **Abraham
Tucker, Joseph Gifford & Barzillai Tuker[Tucker]** to Labour further with
the Sᵈ **Wilcox** in order to Convince him of the Above Sᵈ offences &
to make Report to the next Monthly Meeting

David Shepherd request a Certificate **David Shepherd** desires a Certificate to the Monthly Meeting of
Rhod-Island of his Clearness in Respect to Marriage & Conversation
Therefore **Caleb Russell & Job Russell** are Appointed to Make Inquiry
& draw one for him if they think Proper, and bring it to the next
Monthly Meeting – –

Complaint against Elihu Mosher One of the overseers with another friend have Exhibited a
Complaint against **Elihu Mosher** for Marrying out of the unity of
friends, for which they Labour'd with him, and he declines to make
Satisfaction, Therefore **Joseph Gifford** and **Barzillai Tucker** are ap-
-pointed to Labour farther with him, and to Make Report to
the next Monthly Meeting;

---

2 mo: 1770 At a Monthly Meeting held in **Dartmouth** the 19ᵗʰ
of the 2ᵈ Month 1770, The Representatives are **Caleb
Russell & Jonathan Hussey** both Present – –

Friends app appointed reprt The friends Appointed to Enquire into **Benjᵃ Howlands**
Clearness Report that they don't find him Quite Clear
and they also Report that the widows Estate is not Settled

Benja Howland 2ᵈ case not Clear According to Good order, Therefore **John Potter & Thoˢ Hicks**
are Still Continued in the Same Service, And they are
also Appointed with **Jonathan Hussey & Benjᵃ Slocum** to
See that the widows Estate be Settled According
to Good order, and to make Report to the next Monthly Meeting

Choosing overseers refer'd friends appoint- ed to assist them continued a New Choice of overseers is Refer'd to the next Monthly Meeting
The friends Appointed as overseers Last month Report that they
have been in a Progress to discharge their Trust, and have

found tolarable Good Satisfaction, Therefore they are Still
Continued in the Same Service one month Longer, and to
make Report to the next Monthly Meeting – –

The meeting conclude to deny Step Wilcox The friends appointed to Labour with **Stephen Wilcox** Report
that they have discharged their Trust in that Respect, and
that he Gave them Some Encouriagement to Appear at this
Meeting, which he hath failed of, and hath not Sent any
Excuse for his offence, and their Report not being Satisfactory
and this Meeting being Clear of any further Labour with
him, have Concluded to deny the Said **Stephen Wilcox**, and
do Appoint **Joseph Gifford, Daniel Cornell & Samuel Smith**
to draft a paper of Denial Against him, Agreeable to
his offences, and to bring it to next Monthly Meeting, and they
to Inform Said **Stephen** of the Conclusion of this Meeting – –

Certification for David Shepherd This Meeting hath Signed a Certificate for **David Shepherd**
to the Monthly Meeting of **Rhode-Island** Certifying his Clear-
in Respect to Marriage & Conversation – –

minutes to be reviewed **Abraham Tucker, Joseph Tucker, Samuel Smith, Job Russell**
and **Barzillai Tucker** are Appointed to Review the Meeting
Minutes, to See what part they think Proper to go on Record
and to make Report to the next Monthly Meeting – –

E. Mosher paper **Elihu Mosher** hath Given in a paper to this Meeting Condemning his disorderly Marriage, which is Refer'd under
the Care of the friends Appointed Last Monthly Meeting to
Labour with him – –

E. Gifford paper **Elihu Gifford** hath Given in a paper to this Meeting
Condemning his disorderly Marriage, which is Refer'd
under the Care of **William Barker**

Wm Anthony Ju^r [pa]per accepted **William Anthony ju^r** hath Given in a Paper to this Mee-
-ting Condemning his falt Against **John Russell**, which
this Meeting hath Concluded to Accept, Provided he Cause it
to be Read at the Close of a first day Meeting of worship he being
Present, and Make Report to the next Monthly Meeting, and
then to Return Said Paper – –

This meeting adjourns to the 28th Instant
At a Monthly Meeting mett According to adjornment the
28th of the 2^d month 1770, The Representatives being Called
both Present – –

Hepzabah Shearman disowned The women friends Inform that they have denied **Hephzi-**
bah Shearman for Marrying out of the unity of friends
which this Meeting Concurs with – –

James Davis and Wife gave in a paper **James Davis** and his wife have Given in a paper to this
this Meeting, Signifying their Sorrow for their falling into
the Sin of Fornication which is Refer'd under the Care of
Paul Russell and **Daniel Cornell**, and they are desired to
Treat with them Respecting the above S^d offence, and to make
Report to the next Monthly Meeting

3^d mo: 1770 At a monthly meeting held in **Dartmouth** the 19th 3rd mo
1770 The Representetives are **Thomas Hicks 2nd** & **Samuel Smith**
Both Present The Friends appointed to inspect into **Benj^ni-**
Benj Howland 2nd Clearness **Howland** the 2nd Clearness Respecting marriage & Conversation Repoart
that they have made inquiery and don^t find any thing
Benj Howland^2 proposal of marriage Material to hinder his proceeding in marage **Benj^m Howland** 2nd
& **Selvester Smith** appeared for their answer which was that
they might Proceed to Take Each other in marrage in Some
Convenant Time between this & the next monthly meeting
advising with the overseors for that purpose and **Thomas
Hicks** & **Samuel Smith** are appointed to See their marrage
Consomated in good order & make Report to the next monthly meeting
Caleb Russell Ju^r proposal of marriage **Caleb Russell Ju^r** & **Content Gifford** declared thire intention
marrage at this meeting and was Desired to wate untill the
next monthly meeting for Their answer & **William Barker** &
Berzillar Tucker are appointed to Enquire into the yonug mans
Clearness Respecting marrage & Conversation and make Report to
Friends added to overseers continued to the next monthly meeting, The Friends appointed as overseers
at the Last monthly meeting Report that they have in a good
Degree Discharged their Trust Reposed in them and they are still
Continued in the Same Cervise one month Longer and to make
Report to the Next monthly meeting and **Wil^m Mosher** &
Samuel Smith are aded to the [?]afore Sd Committe of oversee[rs]
Paper of denial of Stphen Wilcox Signed The Friends appointed to Draw a paper of denial against **Stephe[n]
Wilcooks[Wilcox]** and to inform him of the Conclusion of Last monthly
Meeting Report that they have Discharged their Trust in the respect
And that the Sd **Stephen** gave them Some incoragement of
Trying to make Friends Satisfaction at this meeting which
He hath failed off therefore the Clark hath Signed Sd paper by
order of this meeting and he is appointed to Read Sd paper at
the Close of a first day meeting for Worship between this & the
Next monthly meeting & he then to make Report
Minutes Reviewed The Committee appointed to purruse the monthly meetings minutes
Report that they have done it and have Left them with **Saml**

P. Wings Certificate	**Smith** to be Reccorded, This meeting hath Signed a Removel Certificate for **Peace Wing** wife of **Benjⁿ Wing** to the monthly
Rebecca Cornal Received	meeting of **Sandwich**, The women Friends inform that they have Minuted [**Cornell**] under ~~Friends~~ their Care which this meeting
Wm Anthony jr paper read	Conkirs[Concurs] with, **Wilᵐ Anthony Junior** hath Reported to this meeting that his paper hath been Read and returned to the meeting According to the apointment of Last monthly meeting Which S[?]
Jame Davis Case referd	The Friends apointed to treat with **James Davis** and his wife Report that they have not had an opertunity to discharge their Trust therefore they are Still Continued in the Same Servis & to make Report to the Next monthly meeting,
report of meetings in Allen & Smiths Neck	The Friends apointed to have the Care of the meeting granted to be held in **Allins[Allens] neck** and in **Smiths neck** Report that they have Attended Sd meetings which hath been keept to good Satisfaction
T. Briggs Request	**Thomas Briggs** Requests be taken under Friends Care therefore **Seth Shearman & Wᵐ Sanford** are appointed to inquire into his Life & Conversation and make Report to next monthly meeting – – The Queries hath been Read and answered in this meeting – –
Certificate Ann Gifford	This meeting hath Signed a Certificate for our Friend **Anna Gifford** to the Quarterly meeting of **Sandwich** Certifing that her Testimony & Conversation is accepted among us
Certificate for Paul Rusel	This meeting hath Signed a Certificate for **Paul Russell** to the [care] of **Sandwich** Quarterly meeting Certifiing that his Conversation & Testemony is in unity among us – –
Epistle signd	This meeting hath Signed an Epistle to the Quarterly meeting
Representatives	to be held next at **Rhodisland** and **Abraham Tucker Joseph Tucker Samᵘˡ Smith Wiᵐ Mosher Thomas Hicks 2ᵈ** are apointed to attend the Quarterly meeting and to Present the Epistle with the answers to the Queries and they to make Report to the next
Complaint against J. Russell	Monthly meeting: The overseers hath Exhibitted a Complint against **John Russel [Russell]** for Reporting from time to time that **Wiᵐ Anthony Junir** was a false man & a Deceiver and he Refuses to Condemn it according to the Judgment of the Arbitrators therefore this meeting appoints **John Potter Prince Allin[Allen]** and **Joseph Gifford** to inspect into the Cause of Sd **Russels [Russells]** Refusing to Comply to Condemn his fault as aforesaid and to Labour with him as they may find ocation and to make report
T. Hick App: Treasurer who is dismiss	to the Next monthly meeting **Thomas, Hicks 2ᵈ** is appointed Treasurer for this meeting in Stead of **David Smith** ~~which the Request~~ This meeting doth appoint **Joseph Gifford & Barzᵉʳ**

Stephen Wilcox to have a copy of deial **Tucker** to Serve **Stephen Wilcks [Wilcox]** with a Coppy of his Denial And make Report to the next monthly meeting **Samuel Smith** &

Treasurers accompt to be compared **Benjaᵐ Slocom [Slocum]** are appointed to Compair the Treasurers accounts With the Records & make Report to the next monthly Meeting this meeting hath Colected – – £10 S8 3 old tener

---

4th mo: 1770 At a monthly meeting held in **Dartmouth** the 16th of the 4th month 1770, The Representatives are **William Barker** & **Barzillai Tucker** both Present; – – **Wᵐ Barker** & **Barzillai Tucker** Report that they have Answered Their Appointment in Regard to **Caleb Russell ju** and find nothing to hinder his Proceeding in Marriage – –

Caleb Rus= =sell Ju Proposal of marriage **Caleb Russell jur** & **Content Gifford** appear'd for their Answer which was that they minght Proceed to take each other in Marriage in Some Convenient time between this & the next Monthly Meeting, Advising with the overseers for that purpose and **Wᵐ Barker** & **Barzillai Tucker** are Appointed to See the Same Consumated in Good order & make Report to the next Monthly Meeting

Benj How= =land 2 marriage The Friends Appointed to See the Marriage of **Benjᵃ Howland the 2ᵈ** and **Silvester Smith** Consumated in good order Report that they attended their Said Marriage, and that it was Consumated in Good order

overseers continued The Friends appointed as overseers Report that have discharged Their Trust in Some degree, therefore they are Still Continued one month Longer in the Same Service, and to make Report to the next Monthly Meeting ~ ~ ~ ~ ~ ~ **Stephen Wilcox**'s paper of Denial hath been Read According to the Appointment of Last Monthly Meeting, and is as followeth

Testimo =ny Against S. Wilcox Whereas **Stephen Wilcox** of **Dartmouth** in the County of **Bristol** in the Province of the **Massachusetts Bay** in **New England**, Having been Educated under the Care of friends, and has long made Profession with us, and in times past bore a Publick Testimony which was Acceptable Among us, Yet Nevertheless with Sorrow we find that thro' the Prevailence of the Adversary, and disregarding the divine Principal of Life in his own heart, he has So deviated from the way of Truth, and the Profession he has made as to fall into Several Reproachful Evils & disorders, particularly in that he being Intrusted by a Friend of **Falmouth** to Carry Some money to **William Smith** and Converted the Same to his own use whereby he betrayed his Trust, and very Much deceived the S,ᵈ friend, for the want of which money the Said **Wᵐ Smith** hath

Exhibited his Complaint to this meeting, and likewise the
Said **Stephen** is found in the Neglect of that Indispensable duty
of attending Religious Meetings of Divine Worship and discipline
And friends having in Great love & tenderness toward him Re-
-peatedly Visited him & Labour'd with him in order to discover to
him the Evil of his ways, and Reclaim him from his outgoings
But our Labour of Love not obtaining the desired Effect to
the Satisfaction of this Meeting, Therefore for the Clearing of [~~Truth~~ *erased*]
the precious Truth and friends from the Reproach of Such Evils and
defective Members this Meeting is Concerned to Give this forth as
a Testimony Against him, and do hereby Publickly disown the
Said **Stephen Wilcox** from being a member of our Society, and
from under the Care of this meeting, Sincerely desiring (if
it be Consistant with Divine pleasure) that he may yet Return
from the Evil of his ways, and by an unfeigned Repentance
and Reformation, be Restored to the way of Truth & Salvation.

    Given forth by our Monthly Meeting of friends held in **Dartm.**ᵒ
the 19ᵗʰ of the 3,ᵈ month 1770,

    And Signed in & by order of Said Meeting by **Job Russell** Clerk

order to give S Wilcox Coppy of denial   The friends Appointed to Serve **Stephen Wilcox** with a Coppy of the forego-
-ing denial, Report that they Gave him only Coppies of the minutes
of his denial therefore they are Still Requested to Serve him with
a Coppy of the Above denial, and to make Report to the next
Monthly Meeting ~ ~ ~

Tho Brig request Continued   The Freinds Appointed to Enquire into **Thomas Briggs**'s Life and
Conversation on his Request to Come under friends Care, and to
Treat with him in that Respect, one of the Said friends Report
that but one of them has had an oppertunity to Speak with him
Therefore they are Still Continued in the Same Service, and to make
Report to the next Monthly Meeting ~ ~ ~ ~ ~ ~

Report from Quarterˡʸ meeting   The friends Appointed to attend the Quarterly Meeting Report
that they all attended According to Appointment, and have Producᵈ
an Epistle from the Same which hath been read and Kindly accepted

John Russell case continuᵈ   The Committee Appointed to Treat with **John Russell** for his
fault Cognised in the Last Monthly Meeting Report that they
desire one month longer to discharge their Trust in that Respect
Therefore they are Continued in the Same Service and to make
Report next monthly meeting – –

To compare Treasurers accompts referᵈ   The Committee Appointed to Compare the Treasurers Accompts
with the Records Report that they have not had an oppertunity
to fulfill that Service, Therefore they are Still Continued in Sᵈ

Service and to make Report to the next monthly meeting – –

Book of disci- -pline Transcrib,ᵈ for Coak- -set — meeting **Samuel Smith** Reports that he hath Joined with a friend of **Coakset** monthly meeting, and they have Transcribed the Book of Discipline According to the Appointment of this Meeting Some months past, for which he Charges this meeting £7 – 1 – 6 old Tenner which is allowed, and he is Tolerated to draw the money out of the Treasury if there be Enough in its Stock, and he to make Report next monthly meeting – –

J Potter & S. Sherman accompt **John Potter** and **Seth Shearman** hath brought an Accompt to this meeting for one Trenching Shoval which Cost – – £2   5   0 which this meeting allows

E. Mosher's Paper accepted **Elihu Mosher** hath Given in a paper to this Meeting Some months past, Condemning his Marrying out of the unity of friends, and now a Report hath been made to Tolerable Good Satisfaction Therefore his Said paper is accepted – –

Rebecca Ricketson denial This Meeting hath Signed a paper of Denial Against **Rebecca Rickeston [Ricketson]** for falling into the Sin of Fornication, and the Clerk of this Meeting is ordered to read the Same at the Close of a first day meeting for worship between this and the next monthly meeting, and then to make Report thereof – –

S. Almy denied The women friends Enform that they have denied **Sarah Almy** for Marrying out of the unity of friends which this meeting Concurs with

B. Russel's paper **Barnabas Russell** hath Given in a paper to this Meeting Condemning his disorder in taking the oath in Common form, which this meeting accepts

James Davis [&] wife [p]aper [a]cceptd **James Davis** and his wife have Given in a Paper to this Meeting Condemning their falling into the Sin of Fornication, which this Meeting Concludes to accept Provided they Cause the Same to be Read at the Close of a first day meeting for worship they being Present, and Return Said paper to the next Monthly meeting, and make Report of its being read

[Jos] Rotch [jur] requ est a certificate **Joseph Rotch Ju,ʳ** Informs that he Intends to go to **London** and desires a Certificate, therefore **Caleb Russell & Samuel Smith** are Appointed to Enquire into his Conversation and in his Clearness Respecting Marriage and to draft a Certificate for him if they find things Clear and to bring it to the next monthly meeting – –

Barnabas Request a Certificate **Barnabas Russell** likewise Informs that he Intends a Voiage [voyage] to **London** and desires a Certificate, and **Joseph Gifford & Samuel Smith** are to make the like Enquiry Concerning him, and to draft a Certificate for him if they find him Clear & to bring it to the next Monthly Meeting – –

Complaint against Hum Smith son of Humphry

The overseers have Exhibited a Complaint Against **Humphry Smith** the Son of **Humphry** for falling into the Sin of Fornication and in frequently drinking of Spirituous Liquor to Excess, and in frequently using of bad Language, for all of which Evils they have Labour'd with him and he declines to Condemn his offences to their Satisfaction, Therefore this Meeting do Appoint **John Potter** & **Thomas Hicks** to Labour with him as they may find freedom, and to draft a paper of denial against Him if he do not Give them Satisfaction, & Inform him of their Appointment, and make Report to the next monthly Meeting – – – – –

5th mo: 1770

At a Monthly Meeting held in **Dartmouth** the 21 of the 5th month 1770, The Representatives are **Samuel Smith** and **Barzillai Tucker** both Present – –

Wm Barker and **Barzillai Tucker** Report that they attend,d

Caleb Russell Ju marriage

the Marriage of **Caleb Russell Ju,r** and **Content Gifford**, and that it was Consumated in Tolerable Good order – –

oversers Continued

The friends Appointed as overseers Report that they have been in a Labour to discharge the Trust Reposed in them, therefore they are Continued in that Service one month Longer as heretofore

gave S Wilcox coppy of denial

The friends Appointed to Serve **Stephen Wilcox** with a Coppy of his denial, Report that they have fulfilled their Appointment

Case of Tho Briggs

The friends Appointed to Treat with **Thos Briggs** Respecting his Request to Come under friends Care Report that things are not Clear, and the Said friends desire to be Excused from that Service which is Granted, and do Appoint **Joseph Tucker**, **John Potter** & **Job Russell** in the Room of the afores,d friends that were Excused and they to make Report next monthly meeting – –

Ŧ Elisabeth Kirby disownd

This meeting hath Signed a paper of Denial Against **Elisabeth Kirby** daughter of **Robert Kirby**, for falling into the Sin of Fornication, and the Clerk of this meeting is ordered to read S,d paper at the Close of a first day meeting of worship between This & the next Monthly Meeting and then to make Report – –

C. Macumber - & wife's Certifi:

Caleb Macumber & his wife have Removed within the Compass of this meeting, and Each of them have Produced a Removal Certificate which have been read and Accepted – –

Certificates for Jos Rocth Jur and Barnabas Russell

This Meeting have Signed Certificates for **Joseph Roch [Rotch] jur** and **Barnabas Russell** to friends in **London** – –

Accounts Settled with the former Treasur

Benja Slocum and **Samuel Smith** Report that they have Compared the former Treasurers Accounts with the Records of This meeting as far as Seems Needful, and find no Error – –

S Smith
Rec^d money for
Tra[n]sc Book

Samuel Smith Reports that he hath Received the mon[e]y out
of the Treasury for Transcribing the Book of Discipline According
to the order of Last monthly Meeting – –

R. Ricket=
[=]son's
denial

Rebecca Ricketsons Paper of Denial hath been Read
According to the Appointment of Last Monthly Meeting
which paper is as follows – –

Whereas **Rebecca Ricketson** Daughter of **John Ricketson** and
Phebe his wife, being under friends Care having (Through the Pre-
-vailence of the Adversary, and the depravity of her own Nature)
fallen into the Reproachful Sin of Fornication, as Appears by her
being deliver,^d of a bastard Child, and friends having Suffi-
-ciently Labour,^d with her for her Recovery, and to Restore her
to the way of Truth, but friends Labour not Proving Effectuel
She Appearing obstinate, & no appearance of hearty Sorrow, there-
-fore for the Clearing of the Truth and friends from the Reproach
thereof, This meeting Gives this forth as a Publick Testimony Against
her, hereby disowning her the Said **Rebecca Ricketson** from being
one of our Society, and from under the Care of this Meeting, until
by unfeigned Repentance She Shall Return to the way of Truth
Given forth at our Monthly Meeting of friends held in **Dartmouth**
on the 16 day of the 4th month 1770 – –

Signed in & on behalf of S.^d meeting by   ⎰ **Job Russell** Clerk
                                                  ⎱ **Hephzibah Hussey** Clerk

James Davis
paper not read

James Davis hath failed of making the Report of Reading his paper
and his wife's According to the Provisal of Last Monthly Meeting
Therefore **Caleb Russell** is Appointed to Treat with with him for his
Neglect, and to make Report to the next Monthly Meeting – –

The Committee Appointed on Account of **John Russell** Report as
follows, which is Accepted in this Meeting, and is as followeth

Report on John
Russell case

Agreeable to the Minute from our monthly meeting we have
heard **John Russell**'s Reasons why he Refused to Comply with the
Judgment of the Arbitrators, which Reasons we think not Suf=
=ficient to Excuse him, Therefore it is our Judgment that **John
Russell** Publickly Condemns what the Arbitrators found him
Guilty of, Agreeable to their Judgment   **Joseph Gifford**
                                                John Potter
                                                Prince Allen

John Russell's
paper not
accepted

And the Said **John Russell** hath Given in a paper to this Meeting which
this Meeting thinks is too Short, and do not accept of it, Therefore
Peleg Gifford and **Jedidiah Allen** are Appointed to Labour with

the Said **Russell** to Condemn his fault Agreeable to the Judgment
of the afore S,ᵈ Committee, and to return him his paper and let him
Know the mind of this Meeting, and to make Report to next
monthly meeting – –

Hum: Smith   The Committee Appointed to Labour with **Humphry Smith** Son of
son of Hum   **Humphry Smith** Report that they have not had an oppertunity
case continuᵈ   to discharge themselves in that Respect, Therefore they are Still
Continued in that Service, until next monthly meeting and then to
Make Report – – – – –

---

6 mo: At a Monthly Meeting held in **Dartmouth** the 18ᵗʰ
1770   of the 6ᵗʰ month 1770 – – The Representatives are **Caleb
Russell** and **Jonathan Hussey** both Present ~ ~ ~ ~

report of   The Friends Appointed as overseers Report that they have been
overseers   in a Progress to discharge the Trust Reposed in them.
**Jonathan Hussey, Daniel Cornell, Samuel Smith, W,ᵐ Barker
W.ᵐ Mosher** are Appointed overseers for the year Ensuing ~ ~

T. Briggs   The ₐfriends Appointed to Treat with **Thomas Briggs** on his Request to Come
declines   under friends Care, Report that he declines his Request at
his Request   Present, things not being Clear – –

Elisabeth Kirby's Paper of denial hath been read According to
the Appointment of Last Monthly Meeting, and is as follows – –

E. Kirby's   Whereas **Elisabeth Kirby** Daughter of **Robert Kirby** and
Denial   **Abigail** his wife having had her Education among friends under
the care of this Meeting, yet thro' the ~~Infirmety~~ Insinuation of the
adversary, and the depravity of her own Nature hath So far
gone astray from her Education and the Profession we bear, as
to fall into the Reproachfull Sin of Fornication, as Appears by
her having a Bastard Child. And friends having Sufficiently
Labour'd with her in Love for her Recovery, but our Labour
of love not obtaining the desired Effect to the Satisfaction of
this Meeting. Therefore for the clearing of Truth and friends
from the Reproach of Such Enormities This meeting Gives this
this forth as a Testimony against her, hereby Publickly disown-
-ing the Said **Elisabeth Kirby** from being one of our Society
and from under the care of this Meeting, desiring if it be
agreeable to Divine pleasure that She may yet come to a
Sense of her outgoings and by unfeigned Repentance Return
to the way of Truth – –

Given forth and Signed in & on behalf of our Monthly Meeting
held in **Dartmouth** on the 21 of the 5ᵗʰ Month 1770 by

Job Russell Clerk

Hephzibah Hussey Clerk

James Davis paper Read **James Davis** and his wife's paper hath been read according to
the direction of the Monthly Meeting held two months ago,
which paper is as follows – –

To the Monthly Meeting of friends in **Dartmouth**

Beloved friends – –

J & P Davis's Paper whereas we thro' unwatchfulness have fallen into the
Reproachful Sin of Fornication as Appears by our having
a child So Soon after Marriage, for which we are heartily
Sorry & do condemn the Same, and hoping forgiveness from
almighty God we desire friends So far to pass it by as to let
us Remain under your care, from your friends **James Davis**

Patience Davis

dated this 16ᵗʰ: 4 mo: 1770 – –

James Davis Neglect And **Caleb Russell** Reports that he hath Treated with the S.ᵈ
Davis for Neglecting to read Said paper by the time first limitted
for which he hath Render'd a Sufficient Excuse ~

Hum Smith Son of Hump denied The friends Appointed to Labour with **Humphry Smith** Son of
Humphry Smith Report that he gave them no real Satisfaction
therefore according to Appointment they have drafted a paper
of denial against him which hath been read & Signed and
the Clerk is Appointed to Read Said paper Publickly as usual
and make Report to next monthly meeting and **William
Anthony** is Appointed to Serve him with a coppy of his denial
and to make Report next monthly meeting – –

Visits of Publck friends The Queries have been Read & Answer'd, and this meeting
hath Signed an Epistle to the Quarterly Meeting
Our Esteemed Friends **Joshua Brown** and **David Willets** having
Visited this meeting with their Respective Certificates, the first
from the Monthly Meeting held in **Nottingham** by adjournment
the 5ᵗʰ of the 5 month 1770: in **Pennsylvania**, the other from
the Monthly Meeting held at **westbury** on **Long Island** the 30ᵗʰ
of the 5ᵗʰ month 1770, whose Certificates have been read
to Satisfaction, and their Visits Kindly accepted ~ ~ ~

Wᵐ Barker, Caleb Russell, Paul Russell & Wᵐ Mosher are
appointed to attend the Quarterly Meeting, and to present the

Epistle & answers to the Queries, and to make Report to the next
Monthly Meeting ~ ~

Mary Gifford   The women friends Inform that they have minuted **Mary Gifford**
Receiv'd & wife of **Obediah Gifford** under friends care, and also that **Leah**
Leah Shrm
& Rhoda   **Shearman** & **Roda Hathway** [**Hathaway**] hath made Satisfaction for Marrying
Hathway out of the unity of friends, which this meeting concurs with

John Russel   The friends Appointed to Labour with **John Russell** Report that they
case have Labour.d with him, and he hath Given in a paper to this Meeting
refer'd condemning his disorder in Reporting that **Wm Anthony ju,^r**
was a false man & a deceiver, which this Meeting thinks is too
Short, and do Still Refer the matter under the care of the afore
Said friends and **Joseph Gifford,** and they to Inform him the mind
of this Meeting, and to Make Report to the next Monthly Meeting

money Sent   This Meeting hath collected & Sent the money due for the Books
for books to **John Dockry** by the Representatives to the Quarterly meeting
This meeting hath collected £7-13-0 old Tenner [tenor] ~ ~

7th mo: At a monthly Meeting held in **Dartmouth** the 16th of
1770 the 7th month 1770, the Representatives are **Nicolas Howland**
and **Barzillai Tucker** both present ~ ~
William Anthony Reports that he hath Served **Humphry Smith**
with a coppy of his denial According to the Appointment of Last

[H] Smith   Monthly Meeting, and Said paper hath been read as ordered by last
paper Monthly Meeting ~ which paper is Recorded at large in pages 201:202
[re]cor^d pag
[2]01:202   The friends Appointed to attend the Quarterly Meeting Report that they all

Return from   attended, and have Produced an Epistle from the same which hath been read
Quar meeting and Kindly accepted and they Report that they have deliver'd the Money to
John Dockry for the Books, and have produced a Receipt in full from S'^d **Dockry**

Epistles   This Meeting hath Received Several of the **London** Printed Epistles, and
Rec^d also a Transcript of our last yearly Meeting's Epistles & Likewise a coppy
of Several Matters concluded on by Said Meeting ~ – –

N Howl^d   **Nicolas Howland** is Appointed an Overseer to Serve with the others
[o]verser that were Appointed last Month – –

John   The committee Appointed to treat with **John Russell** Report that they
Russell have discharged the Trust Reposed in them, and **John Russell** hath Given
paper
accepte^d   in a paper to this Meeting condemning his offence in Reporting in too
Extencive a manner that **william Anthony ju·^r** was a false man and
a deceiver, which this Meeting concludes to Accept of, Provided he
cause Said paper to be read publickly, at the End of a first day Meeting
of worship he being present between this & the next Monthly Meeting
and then Return S·^d paper & make Report – –

C. Russel Condemg his Exp: [r]ession whereas Some Months past **Caleb Russell** Expressed in a Monthly Meeting that **David Smith** was not Suitable to be Appointed in business by reason that he was against the Meeting, and it was the Sense & Judgment of this Meeting that **Caleb Russell** Inconsiderately Expressed himself to[o] far, which he hath condemned to the Satisfaction of this Meeting two months past, and then begged of **David Smith** to pass it by, but we have omitted Minuting of it until this day – –

adjourn This Meeting Adjorns to the 25th day of this Instant after the Meeting of worship – –

mett   At a monthly Meeting Mett by Adjournment the 25th of the 7th mo: 1770 The Representatives being called both present – – it was proposed for a New Choise of overseers of the poor, but the former not being all present the matter is Refer'd to next Monthly Meeting.

John Potter accompt. **John Potter** hath Exhibited an Accompt to this meeting for doing for the poor, and for one Trenching Shoval, and one Pail, all Amounting ^to £4 - 1s - 3d old tenner and **Thomas Hicks** hath likewise Exhibited an Accompt for mending the Meeting House to the amount of £1 - 2[s] - 6d old tenner which this Meeting Approves and do order them to draw the money out of the Treasury, and make Report as Soon as they can conveniently – –

Com.tee to advise in cases of Sueing **William Barker, William Mosher and Barzillai Tucker** are Appointed a Standing Committee for friends to Advise with in the Intervals of monthly meetings, in Cases of Sueing at Law – –

Books to be Sold Whereas this Meeting is possessed of a Number of [**George**] **Fox**'s Large Primers and [**Samuel**] **Fuller**s Books. Therefore **Caleb Russell** & **Wm Mosher** are Appointed to take the Books, and Endeavour to Sell them at the prime Cost, and Return the Money to this Meeting as Soon as they can.

8th mo: 1770, At a Monthly Meeting held in **Dartmouth** the 20th of the 8th month 1770, the Representatives are **John Potter** & **Samuel Smith** both present

J Russell paper not returnd **John Russell**'s paper hath been read according to the Appointment of Last Monthly Meeting ^but he hath omitted Returning S.d paper to this Meeting as ordered. Therefore he ^is desired to Return Said paper to the next Monthly Meeting – –

overseers of the poor **Caleb Russell, Joseph Barker, Barzillai Tucker, & Gideon Howland** are Appointed Overseers of the Poor for the year Ensuing

J. Mosher & family Returned **Joanna Mosher** widow, and her family having Returned to live Among us again, have Produced a Removal Certificate from the monthly meeting of the **Nine partners**, which hath been read and Accepted – –

R. Barnard Removed   This meeting hath Signed a Removal Certificate for **Rebecca Barnard** to the Monthly Meeting of **Nantucket** ~ ~ ~ ~

Complaint against J Smith   The overseers Inform that **John Smith** hath Married out of the unity of friends for which they have Laboured with him but he de--clines to Make friends Satisfaction. Therefore this Meeting doth Appoint **Joseph Tucker** and **Paul Russell** to Labour with him furder [further] and to make Report to the next Monthly Meeting – –

John Potter & **Thoˢ Hicks** have taken the money out of the Treasury as ordered by last monthly meeting – –

This Meeting hath Collected £7 - 15ˢ - 6ᵈ old tener – –

Receivᵈ Resolve from yearly meeting   Whereas at the Last Monthly Meeting we Received Several Matters concluded on by our last yearly Meeting, and now this Meeting concludes to Send up to the Quarterly Meeting to Know under what head, in the Book of discipline will be most proper to place them

---

9ᵗʰ Mo: 1770   At a Monthly Meeting held in **Dartmouth** the 17ᵗʰ of the 9ᵗʰ month 1770, the Representatives are **Wᵐ Mosher** & **Barzillai** – – **Tucker** both presents – –

Lemuel Mosher Proposal of marriage   **Lemuel Mosher** & **Ruth Gifford** declared their Intentions of Marriage and were desired to wait Till next monthly Meeting for their Answer and **Paul Russel** & **Barzillai Tucker** are Appointed to Enquire into the young man's clearness Respecting Marriage & Conversation and make Report to the next monthly meeting – –

J Russell Paper returnᵈ   **John Russell** hath Returned his paper according to the Request of Last Monthly Meeting ~ ~ which paper is as followeth

J. Russell's Confession   To the Monthly Meeting of friends held this 16.ᵗʰ of the 7.ᵗʰ mo:1770 Esteemed friends – –

As I have Reported of **William Anthony ju.ʳ** that he was a false man & a deceiver, for which I am Sorry, that thro[ugh] Inadvertancy I Reported in So Extensive a manner, by which I have broke the Good order of friends – – my misconduct in So Reporting, I condemn. and I desire friends to pass by my offence and Still Continue me under their Care, as I Desire that I may be more Careful for the futer – – **John Russell**

John Smith Case   The friends Appointed to Labour with **John Smith** Report that they have Labour'ᵈ with him and he gave them Encouragement of making this Meeting Satisfaction. Therefore the matter is Referᵈ under their care until next monthly Meeting, and they are desired to make Report – –

O. Gifford Removed Request a Certificate   **Obediah Gifford** hath Removed to the **Nine-partners** with his family and Requests a Removal Certificate for himself and family therefore **Daniel Cornell** & **Philip Allen** are Appointed

to make Inquiry into his Life & Conversation, and also to See if His
Temporal affairs be Settled According to the good order of friends and
to draft a Certificate for them if they think proper, and to make
Report to the next Monthly Meeting – –

Compl.ᵗint ag against Benj Chase The overseers Inform that **Benjᵃ Chase** hath gone contrary to good
order in Striking of **Abigail Blackmer**, therefore this meeting do
Appoint **Luke Hart** and **Barnabas Mosher** to Inquire into the
Circumstance Relating to the cause of his afore said disorder, and
to Labour with him as they may find freedom, and to make
Report to the next Monthly Meeting – –

The Queries have been Read and Answered in this meeting.

Representaᵗⁱᵛᵉˢ **Abraham Tucker**, **Joseph Tucker**, **Nicolas Howland** are Ap-
-pointed to attend the Quarterly Meeting and to Present the

answers & Epistle Sent upp Epistle with the Answers to the Queries, which Epistle hath been
Signed in this Meeting, and they to Make Report to the next
Monthly Meeting – –

Paul Rus= =sell desires a Certificate Our friend **Paul Russell** desires a few Lines by way of Certificate
in order to Visit the Quarterly Meeting next to be holden at **pem-
-brook**, which hath been Read & Signed in this Meeting.

Martha Pabody paper accepᵗed The women friends Inform that **Martha Pabody** hath Given in a
paper to their Meeting condemning her falling into the Sin of
Fornication which is Accepted Provided She Cause it to be read
Publickly at the close of a first day meeting for worship between this
and next monthly meeting, She being present, and Return S'd
paper to next Monthly Meeting – –

[ˢi]lvia [S]mith accepted The women friends also Inform that **Silvia Smith** wife of **Humphy [Humphry]
Smith** the 3ᵈ hath Made them Satisfaction for marrying out of the
unity of friends. They also Inform that they have denied

[Re]becca Briggs Disownd **Rebecca Briggs** wife of **Tho.ˢ Briggs** for Keeping Company and
Marrying out of the unity of friends, which this Meeting Concurs
with – – This Meeting hath Collected £ 6 – 13ˢ – 0ᵈ old tener [tenor]

---

10 mo: 1770 At a Monthly Meeting held in **Dartmouth** the 15ᵗʰ of the 10ᵗʰ
Month 1770, The Representatives are **Wᵐ Mosher & Bazillai
Tucker** both present – –

Paul Russell & Barzillai Tucker Reports that they have Made
Inquiry into **Lemuel Mosher**'s Clearness Respecting Marriage and
Conversation, and find nothing to hinder his Proceeding in Marriage

Lemuel Mosher answer **Lemuel Mosher & Ruth Gifford** Appearᵈ for their Answer
which was that they Might Proceed to take each other in
Marriage in Some convenient time between this & the next
Monthly Meeting, advising with the overseers for that purpose

and **paul Russell** and **Barzillai Tucker** are Appointed to See
their Marriage Consumated in Good order, and make Report to
the next Monthly Meeting.

John Smith case The Committee Appointed to Treat with **John Smith** Report that
they have Treated with him, and he hath Given in a paper to
this Meeting in order to Condem[n] his disorder, which this Meeting
thinks is too Short & not to the purpose, therefore the matter is
Refer^d under the Care of afore Said Committee, to the next
Monthly Meeting; – –

O.Gifford Certificate This Meeting hath Signed a Removal Certificate for **Obediah
Gifford** and his Children to the Monthly Meeting at the **NinePartners**

Benja Chas^e case The friends Appointed to Treat with **Benj,^a Chase** Report that
matter to be Continued one month Longer under their care
which is Refer^d Accordingly, and they to make Report to the
next Monthly Meeting – –

Return from Qar meeting The friends Appointed to attend the Quarterly Meeting Report
That they all attended according to Appointment, and have
Produced an Epistle from the Same, which hath been Read &
kindly accepted – –

M. Pabody paper not read **Martha Pabody**'s Paper hath ^ not been read According to the
direction of Last monthly ^ meeting for which omission there hath
been a Reasonable Excuse made. Therefore She is directed to
Cause it to be read at the End of a first day meeting for worship
before the next monthly meeting, and She to be present and
Return Said paper to the next monthly meeting – –

Visits of Publick friends Our friends **Matthew Frankin [Franklin]** and **Richard Titus** have Visited
This Meeting with their Certificates, the first from the Monthly
Meeting held at **Newtown** on **Long Island** the 7th of the 4th mo:
1770 and the Latter from the Monthly Meeting held at
Westbury on **Long Island** the 29th of the 8th month 1770 which
have been Read to good Satisfaction, and their Visits Kindly
Accepted, and this meeting finds freedom to Give Each of them
a Certificate, Therefore we do Appoint **Samuel Smith** and
Wm Anthony ju^r to prepare Certificates for them & bring
them to the adjournment – –

Overseers of yearly meeting This meeting doth Appoint **Jonathan Hussey, Wm Mosher,
Barzillai Tucker, Samuel Smith Wm Anthony ju^r** and
Barnabas Mosher to have the oversight of the Lofts and
other Seats at our yearly meeting to prevent any Indecency
that may be liable to happen at that time ~~and to~~

make Report of their Service to the next Monthly Meeting

Lydia Potter [Dis]ownd This meeting hath Signed a paper of denial against **Lydia Potter** for the Sin of Fornication, and **Job Russell** is ordered to read S.d paper at the End of a first day meeting for worship between this and next monthly Meeting, and he then to make Report

Com.tee [?] Invite Delinquents into meeting **Joseph Tucker, Caleb Russell, W.m Mosher, Barzillai Tucker** and **Jonathan Hussey** are Appointed a Committee to have the oversight of those friends and others that attend our Religious Meetings and are frequently in the practice of Staying out of doors after the Meetings are gathered, and to Invite them into meeting when they think Necessary – –

adjourn This meeting Adjourns to the 24.th Instant after the Meeting of worship

mett At a Monthly Meeting met According to adjournment the 24.th of the 10.th month 1770. The Representatives being called both present,

Certificate for Mat= =thew Franklin Rich Titus This Meeting hath Signed two Certificates, one of our friend **Matthew Franklin** to˄ the monthly Meeting of **Newtown** on **Long Island** and the other for our friend **Richard Titus**, to the Monthly Meeting of **Westbury** on Said Island ~

11.th Mo: 1770 At a monthly Meeting held in **Dartmouth** the 19.th of the 11.th Month 1770, the Representatives are **Jonathan Hussey** and **William Barker** both present; – –

Paul Russell and Barzillai Tucker Report that they attended the

Lemuel Moshers Marriag Marriage of **Lemuel Mosher** & **Ruth Gifford** which was consumated in tolerable good order – –

John Smith Case referd The Committee Appointed to Labour with **John Smith** Report that they have Treated with him, and he Still Neglects to Condemn his disorder to the Satisfaction of this meeting, therefore the matter is Refer.d under the care of the afore said Committee, and they to make Report to the next Monthly Meeting

B Chase referd The Com.ttee appointed to Labour with **Benj,.a Chase** Report that they have made Some progress therein, and they desire one Month Longer for that Service therefore they are Still Continued in said Service Accordingly and to make Report to the next Monthly Meeting ~

M. Pabody Paper read **Martha Pabody**es paper hath been read According to the Appointment of last monthly meeting and Returned to This meeting, and is as follows – – /viz/

Mar: Pabody's paper To the Monthly Meeting to be held in **Dartmouth** the 16.th: 7.th mo: 1770; Esteemed friends These are to Inform that through unwatchfulness I have fallen

into the Reproachful Sin of Fornication, as Appears by my
having a Child So Soon after Marriage, for which I am heartily
Sorry for, and do Condemn the Same, with all the Rest of my
outgoings, hoping God will forgive me, and desiring friends
So far to pass it by as to let me Remain under your Care
from your friend – – **Martha Pabody** – –
          dated the 16th. 7·mo: – 1770 – –

Overseers of yearly meeting report The friends Appointed to have the oversight of the Lofts and
other Seats at our last yearly Meeting Report that they all
Attended According to Appointment, and that people behaved as
Still as could be Reasonably Expected – –

Lydia Potter's paper of Denial hath been Read According to
the Appointment of last monthly Meeting, and is as followeth

Lydia Potter's denial   At a monthly meeting of friends held in **Dartmouth** on the
15th of the 10th. mo:1770 – –

Whereas **Lydia Potter** having had her Education Among friend
and under the care of this Meeting but yet for want of watchful-
-ness, and by Giving Way to the Insinuations of the Evil one hath
fallen in the Reproachful Sin of Fornication which may Appear
to the world by her having a Child So Soon after Marriage
notwithstanding the Much Labour that hath been taken for to
bring her to a Sight & Sense of her outgoings proves Ineffectual
and She not having any Appearance of a disposion [*sic*] to Condemn her
S.d outgoings, and to make friends Satisfaction. Now for the
Clearing the Truth this Meeting can do no less than Give this forth
bearing their Testimony Against Such Reproachful Evils and
do deny the Said **Lydia Potter** from being under the Care of this
Meeting, yet Truly desiring that She may be brought to a Sight
and Sense of˄ all her outgoings, and come to a true Repentance and find
Mercy. Given forth and Signed in & on behalf of S.d meeting by

                                         Job Russell Clerk
                                         Hephzibah Hussey Clerk

Han Win[slow] accepted [*word crossed out*] The women friends Inform that they have Minuted **Hannah Wins-**
-low under their care, which we concur with – –

P. Thirston's Certi: This Meeting hath Signed a Removal Certificate for **Pernal Thirston** [**Thurston**]
wife of **Edward Thurston Ju·r** to the Monthly Meeting of **Swanzey** ~

Meeting in Allens & Smiths Neck granted The Friends Living in **Allen's Neck**, and also those Living in **Smith's**
Neck Request the Liberty to hold a Meeting in Each neck, the Ensu-
-ing Winter. Therefore this meeting Grants them their Request in
both Necks, and they to hold a Meeting in each neck on Each first day

of the week from now to the monthly meeting to be held in the third
Month next, and **Philip Allen** & **Daniel Cornell** are Appointed to have
the oversight of the Meeting in their s.ᵈ neck, and **Samuel Smith** &
Benjᵃ Howland the 2·ᵈ are Appointed for the Same Service in the meeting
in their neck, and all to Make Report to the S.ᵈ third month next

Weston Briggs request a Certicate **Weston Briggs** hath Removed in the Compass of **Swanzey** Monthly
Meeting, and Requests a Removal Certificate for himself & family

Jacob Chase request a Certificate and **Jacob Chase** hath likewise Removed in the Compass of the same
meeting & Requests a Removal Certificate for himself & Children
Therefore **Luke Hart & Barnabas Mosher** are Appointed to Inquire into **Jacob
Chase**'s Life & Conversation and to draft a Certificate for them if they
think proper and bring it to the next monthly meeting – –
And **Tho.ˢ Hicks** and **Wᵐ Anthony juʳ** are Appointed for the Same
Service for **Weston Briggs** and to Join the women friends to draft
a Certificate for himself & family if they think proper, and to
bring it to the next monthly Meeting

Jenaverah Gifford's paper accepted **Jenaᵥᵉrah Gifford** hath Given in a paper to this Meeting Condem-
-ning her falling into the Sin of Fornication, Which this Meeting
Concludes to Accept Provided Said paper be read at the End of
a first day Meeting for worship, and She is Excused from being
present at the reading Said paper by reason of her being at
a Great distance, and a Lame woman, and under Low Circum-
-Stances in the world, therefore the Clerk of this Meeting is order'd
to Read Said paper According to the afore sᵈ directions, and to
Make Report to the next Monthly Meeting ~ ~ ~

Proposal to build a new Meeting house This Meeting Proposes to build a new Meeting House where
our old one now Stands in **Ponaganset**, and do Appoint **Barnabas
Mosher, Prince Allen, Philip Trafford, Caleb Russell, Jonathan
Hussey, Wᵐ Anthony ju.ʳ Joseph Russell, Samuel Smith** and
Deliverence Smith, and they to consider how Large to build
Said House and also to compute the cost as near as they can
and to make Report to the next Monthly Meeting – –

Comᵗᵉᵉ to assist the over- seers of the poor **John Potter, Prince Allen, Wᵐ Anthony juʳ** are Appointed to
Join the overseers of the poor to Settle Accounts in behalf of
Alice Smith with **John Sisson,** and they to Make Report to the next
monthly Meeting; ~ ~ ~ ~ ~ ~ ~ ~

12 Mo: 1770 At a Monthly Meeting held in **Dartmouth** the 17th of the
12th Month 1770 The Representatives are **Wᵐ Barker** and
Barzillai Tucker both present ~ ~ ~ ~ ~ ~ ~ ~

[J] Gifford
[juʳ?] proposal
[of] marriage

Joseph Gifford juʳ and **Hannah Winslow** declared their Intentions of Marriage, and were desired to wait till next Monthly Meeting for their Answer, and **Wᵐ Barker** and **Barzillai Tucker** are appointed to Enquire into the young man's clearness Respecting Marriage & Conversation and make report to the next Monthly Meeting

John Smith
case

The Committee Appointed to Labour with **John Smith** Report that they have Treated, ᶠᵘʳᵗʰᵉʳ with him, and that he gave them Some Satisfaction, but S[t]ill Neglects to make this meeting Satisfaction, therefore the Matter is Still Refer'd under the Care of the afore S.ᵈ Committee, and they to Make Report to the next Monthly Meeting ~ ~ ~ ~ ~ ~

Ben Chase
Paper
accepted

The friends Appointed to Inspect into the Case of **Benj.ᵃ Chase**'s Striking of **Abigail Blackmer** Report that he hath Made the Said **Abigail** Satisfaction, therefore this meeting concludes to Accept of his paper that he gave in Some months past, Provided he Cause it to be read at the close of a first day Meeting for worship at **Newtown** between this & the next Monthly Meeting he being present, and make Report to the next monthly Meeting, and Return Said paper – –

Barnabus
Russell's
Certificat
from London

Barnabas Russell hath Produced a Certificate from the two weeks Meeting in **London** held on the 17ᵗʰ of the 9ᵗʰ month 1770 which hath been Read & well Accepted – –

Jacob Chase
Certificate

Luke Hart & Barnabas Mosher have prepared a Removal Certificate for **Jacob Chase** & Children to the Monthly Meeting of **Swanzey** which hath been Signed in this meeting, and this meeting has Likewise Signed a Removal Certificate for **Weston Briggs** & family to the abovesᵈ meeting **Jenavarah [Jenaverah] Gifford**'s paper hath been Read According to the direction of Last Monthly Meeting, and is as follows ~ ~ ~ /viz/

J. Giffords
Confession

Sandwich the 2 of the 7ᵗʰ month 1769,

To the Monthly ~~Monthly~~ Meeting of friends to be held in **Dartmouth** the 17th Instant – –

> Beloved friends, These May Inform that Notwithstanding I had my Education amongst friends, I have by Giving way to the Temtation of the enemy, been Guilty of the Sin of fornication

as appears by my having a Child So Soon after Marriage which Sin I do condemn with all other my offences and am heartily Sorry for(them) hoping that God will forgive me, and I do desire that friends will So far pass by my offences as to let me Still Remain under their care, from your friend,

Jeneverah Gifford

The Committee appointed to consider about Building a New Meeting House in **aponagaset** and to calculate the cost Report as follows

Estate of
Alice Smith
not Settled The committee appointed to Join with the overseers of the poor to
Settle the Estate of **Alice Smith** Report that the matter is unsettled
therefore they are Still continued to Endeavour to Settle the
matter as Soon as may be and then to make Report

W. Cornals
complaint **Walter Cornell** hath Exhibited a complaint against **Jedediah Allen**
for Refusing to Join with him in fulfilling the Judgment of the Arbitration
Respecting the discharging of their Mother **Wood**'s debts that she left
at her decease, therefore this meeting do Appoint **Caleb Russell**
**Wm Anthony jnr Barzillai Tucker, Joseph Barker, & Thomas
Hicks** a Committee to Inquire into the State of the case and to
Labour as they may find freedom, and to Make Report to the
next monthly meeting – –

Complaint
against [?]
H.Smith **Benjamin Shearman, Thos Shearman and Peleg Shearman** Jointly
have Exhibited a complaint against **Humphry Smith** for Refusing to
Submitt a controversey between them to men. Therefore this meeting
do Appoint **Joseph Gifford, Gideon Howland, Barzillai Tucker, Joseph
Barker & Benja Slocum** a Committee to Inquire into the State of
the Case and to Labour as they may find freedom, and to make
Report to the next Monthly Meeting

Queries
answered The Queries have been read and answer'd in this meeting and

Representatives
appointed **Joseph Tucker, Jonathan Hussey, Wm Anthony jnr** and **Samuel Smith**
are appointed to attend the Quarterly Meeting and to present the
Epistle with the Answers to the Queries which Epistle hath been
Signed in this Meeting, and they to make Report next Monthly Meeting

J.Trafford
paper **Joseph Trafford** hath Given in a paper to this Meeting Condemning
his falling into Sin of fornication therefore this meeting do
Appoint **Wm Anthony jnr** and **Benja Howland the 2d** to Inquire if
the young woman be Satisfied that Accused him, and they to make
Report to the next Monthly Meeting – –
This meeting hath Collected £ 7–10s–6 old tener

The Denial of
Hum. Smith 3d The following denial of **Humphry Smith the 3d** ought to have been
Recorded Among the minutes of the 7th month Last in page 189
but was omitted /viz/
Whereas **Humphry Smith,** Son of **Humphry Smith** having had his
Education among friends, yet thro' disregarding the Principle of
Life in his own heart hath So far followed the Variety of his own un-
-stable mind as to fall into Several Reproachful Soils, particularly
in that he being accused of being the father of a Bastard Child, and
he in no wise clearing himself therefrom to the Satisfaction of
friends and after Inspection we have Sufficient to believe the

Accusation to be Justly Grounded. Likewise he is found in the too
frequent practice of Drinking Spiritous Liquors to Excess and also
in the use of bad Language, for which friends have Repeatedly
Laboured with him in Love in order to Reclaim him from Such Vanities
but our Labour not having the desired Effect to friends Satisfaction
Therefore for the Clearing of Truth and friends from the Reproach of
Such Enormous Practices this meeting is Concerned to Give this
forth Against him, and do hereby Publickly disown him the Said
Humphry Smith from being one of our Society, and from being
in membership with us, desiring Nevertheless if it be Agree-
-able to Divine pleasure that he may yet be Restored from the
evil of his ways and by unfeigned Repentence Return to the
way of Truth – – Given forth by our Monthly Meeting of
friends held in **Dartmouth** on the 18th of the 6th month 1770
And Signed in & on behalf of Said Meeting by **Job Russell** Clerk

---

first mo:
1771   At a Monthly Meeting held in **Dartmouth** the 21st of the first
month 1771, the Representatives are **Nicolas Howland** and
Wm Anthony jnr both present

Wm Barker and **Barzillai Tucker** Report that they have Made
Inquiry into **Joseph Gifford Jur's** Clearness Respecting Marriage and
conversation, and find nothing to hinder his Proceeding in Marriage

Jos. Gifford jn   **Joseph Gifford jur** and **Hannah Winslow** Appear'd for their Answer
proposal of   which was that they might proceed to take each other in Mar-
marriage
answer   -riage before the next Monthly Meeting advising with the
overseers for that purpose and **Wm Barker** & **Barzillai Tucker**
are Appointed to See their Marriage consumated in good order
and to make Report to the next Monthly Meeting – –

J.Smith   **John Smith** hath Given in a paper to this Meeting Condemning his
accepted   disorderly Marriage which is accepted and he Stil to Remain
under the care of this meeting – –

B. Chase's   **Benja Chase's** paper hath been read According to the direction
paper   of the Last Monthly Meeting, and is as follows /viz/
Dartmouth 17th day of 9th month 1770 – –
To the Monthly Meeting of friends held at **Ponaganset**
whereas I thro' weakness and Giving way to the Temtations of the
enemy Some time past struck **Abigail Blackmer** for which I am
now Sorry for and Condemn, hoping the almighty will forgive me
desiring to be preserved from Such practices for the futer[future] and desire that
friends will pass it by and Continue me under their Care from
your friend – –   **Benjamin Chase**

Return from Quar. meeting   The friends Appointed to attend the Quarterly Meeting Report that they all attended According to Appointment and have produced an Epistle from the Same which hath been read & kindly accepted – –

Jed. Allen case referd.   The Committee Appointed to Inquire into the Complaint of **Walter Cornel [Cornell]** against **Jedidiah Allen** Request the matter to be defer'd one month Longer under their Care therefore their Request is Granted and they to make Report to the next Monthly Meeting – –

J Gifford Certifi.   This meeting hath Signed a Removal Certificate for **Jeneverah Gifford** wife of **Silvanus Gifford** to the Monthly Meeting of **Sandwich**

Humphry Smith Case   The Committee Appointed to Inquire into the Complaint of **Benjᵃ Thos** and **Peleg Shearman** against **Humphry Smith** Report that the Matter is Still unsettled, and **Humphry Smith** Requests a Coppy of the Complaint therefore the Said Complaint is Refer'd under the care of the afore said Committee and they to Consider whether it be left to Give Said **Smith** a Coppy or not and if upon Mature Consideration they think best to Give a Coppy they may, and **Job Case** and **Wᵐ Anthony jnʳ** are added to the afore sᵈ Committee, and they to Advise and Labour as they may find freedom and make Report to the next Monthly Meeting – –

Jos Trafford paper accepted   The Committee Appointed on the account of **Joseph Trafford** Make a Satisfactory Report, therefore his paper is Accepted Provided he cause it to be read Publickly at the End of a first day meeting for worship before next Monthly Meeting, he being present and Return it to next Monthly Meeting and Report of its being read

B. Howland Gives in a paper   **Barnabas Howland the 2ᵈ** hath Given in a paper to this meeting Condemning his disorderly Marriage, therefore the matter is Refer'd. under the care of **Samuel Smith** & **Wᵐ Anthony jnʳ** and they to make Report to the next Monthly Meeting – –

B. Little Produced a Removl. Certifi.   **Barker Little** hath Produced a Removal Cerificate from the Monhtly Meeting of **Pembrook** which hath been read and Accepted

I Howland Produced a Removal Certificate   **Isaac Howland jnʳ** hath Produced a Removal Certificate from the Monthly Meeting of **Rhode Island** which hath been Read and Accepted

Paul Russell Certificate   This Meeting hath Given **Paul Russell** a few Lines to the monthly Meeting of **Sandwich** Signifying our unity with his Visit

This Meeting hath collected £10-14ˢ-11ᵈ old Tenner, and the

Order on Treasurer   Treasurer is order'd to pay **Timothy Russell** five Dollars for Keeping the meeting house half a year, and Also to pay **John Sanford** half a Dollar

2d Mo:1771   At Monthly Meeting held in **Dartmouth** the 18 of the
2d month 1771, the Representatives are **Samuel Smith** and
Thos Hicks both present
Wm Barker & **Barzillai Tucker** Report that they attended

Jos Gifford jnr   the Marriage of **Joseph Gifford jnr** & **Hannah Waslow** which
marriage   was Consumated in Good order

Humphry   The Comtee appointed to Inquire into the Complaint
Smith Case   of **Benja Thos** & **Pelef Shearman** against **Humphry Smith**
Report that they have made Some progress therein and desire
one month Longer for tat Service which is Granted.

Paper for the   **Thos Hicks** hath Procured a Quire of paper for this meeting
meeting   which Cost 11/3d old Tenner
Joseph Trafford's Paper hath been Read according to the ap
pointment of Last monthly Meeting & Returned to this meeting
which paper is as followeth/viz/
to the Monthly Meeting of **Dartmouth**

J. Trafford   Respected Friend
Paper   With Sorrow I have to acknowledge my misconduct in
falling into the Reproaching Sin of Fornication for which
I am heartily and sincerely Sorry and do Condemn the
Same with all other my outgoings and Desiring forgiveness
for the almighty, and that friends would so far pass my
misconduct as to Let me Remain under their Care
given forth by yout friend this 14th of the II mo:1770
                                                Joseph Trafford

Treasurer paid   The Treasurer Reports that he hath paid **Timothy Russell** Ten
Tim Russell   Dollars for Keeping the meeting house a year but has not
J. Sanford
not paid   paid **John Sanford** as ordered therefore he is still Continued to pay
Sd Sanford & to make Report to the next Monthly Meetings
Wm Anthony jnr and **Samuel Smith** Report that they have

Case of Barna   Treated with **Barnabas Howland jnr** Respecting id disorerly Mar
Howland Jn   riage and that he Gave them some Satisfaction, therefore they
are still continued in the Same Service and to make Report
when they think Necessary

Jedidi Allen   the Greatest part of the Comtee appointed to Inquire into the Complaint
Case   of **Walter Cornel** against **Jedidiah Allen** Report as followeth which
is accepted by this Meeting
According to appointment of Last Monthly Meeting we
have Inspected into the Reason of **Jedidiah Allen**'s Refusing to Joyn
Walter Cornel in the Discharging their **Mother Woods** Debts according

to the Judgment of the arbtrators that Settled that affair & according to the
best of our understanding we have to Inform that although it falls
Somewhat hard upon sd **Allen**, yet we think **Walted Cornel** suffers Equelly
with him in said Judgment, and as they have found themselves to
perform the same we advised **P. Allen** to Comply with
Likewise we understand there is some Debts that was not brought
in to yᵉ Arbitrators to Judge on, that was made by **Jedidiah Wood** we
think them Dont belong to **Jedidiah Allen** and **Walter Cornell** to pay
unless then Arbitrators thinks it proper & Reasonable
from your Committee this 18 Day 2mo 1771 **Wm Anthony jnr Caleb Russell**
                                                    Barzillai Tucker Joseph Barker

J Allen refuse to comply The Said **Allen** Refusing to Comply with the Sd Judgment
Therefore this meeting do appoint **Abraham Tucker, Joseph**
Tucker and **John Potter** to Labour with Said **Allen** to Comply
therewith as they may find freedom and to Make Report
to the next Monthly Meeting

Prince Allen Gives in a paper **Prince Allen** hath Given in a Paper to this Meeting
Condemning his Saying that; If **Thomas Briggs** had
got Such a Receipt as he Said he had he made it,
which Paper hath been Read & Considered in this Meeting
and Accepted – –

To Review meeting minutes **Samuel Smith Job Russell, Wᵐ Anthony juʳ John Potter**
and **Thoˢ Hicks** are Appointed to Review their Meeting's Minutes
to See what part they may think proper to go on Record, and
to Make Report to the next Monthly Meeting

Complaint against D. Gifford The overseers have Exhibited a Complaint against **David**
Gifford Junʳ as Charged on Oath by **Meribah Hammond** deceased
of being the father of her Child, and also for denying a matter
of fact between himself & **Jabez Hammond**, for which they
have Labour'd with him, and he declines to Condemn
his offences, Therefore This Meeting do Appoint **Abraham**
Tucker, and **Paul Russell** to Labour with him as they
may find freedom, and to make Report to the next
Monthly Meeting;
The following paper of **Wm Anthony jur** ought to have
been Recorded in page 178 but was omitted by reason of not
coming to hand /viz/

Confession of Wᵐ Anthony juʳ To the Monthly Meeting to be held in **Dartmouth** the
19ᵗʰ 2ᵈ month 1770,   Esteemed friends & Brethren
These are to Inform that in the year 1768 I was Indebted to

John Russell for a Large Sum of Money, and the time being
Expired for payment, and he calling for his pay; I not having
near all the money to pay him, I proposed for to Answer part
of the Money due to him, by Giving Notes to his Creditors, which
he Consented to, and I being under an Engagement to Go
a Voiage to **perkipsey [Poughkeepsie]**, and being disapointed at that time
about Answering to Some of his Creditors as afore said I
Then Inconsiderately Proceeded the Voiage before there
was a full Settlement between the S^d **Russell** & I, which
Gave him cause to think hard of me, The which I am Sorry
for and do condemn, and I desire Friends to pass by my
offence in That Respect,

From your friend Wm Anthony ju^r

<table>
<tr><td>3^d
mo:
1771</td><td>At a Monthly Meeting held in Dartmouth the 18th of
the 3^d Month 1771, The Representatives are Jonathan
Hussey & Wm Anthony ju^r both present – –</td></tr>
<tr><td>J Sanford
is paid</td><td>The Treasurer Reports he hath paid John Sanford £1-2^s-6^d
old Tener According to Appointment – –</td></tr>
<tr><td>Jed Allen
refuse to
Comply</td><td>The Committee Appointed to Labour with Jedidiah Allen to
Comply with the Judgment of this meeting in Regard to his
Mother Wood's debts, Reports that the Said Allen Still
Refuses to Comply with the afore S^d Judgment, therefore they are
Still Continued in the Same Service, and to make Report to the
next Monthly – –</td></tr>
<tr><td>Anna Smith's
Certifi:</td><td>Anna Smith hath Produced a Removal Certificate from the
Monthly Meeting of Nantucket which hath been Read and Accepted</td></tr>
<tr><td>Minutes
Revie'd</td><td>The Committee Appointed to Review this meeting's minutes to See
what part they may think proper to be Recorded, Report they have
fulfill'd their Appointment and Samuel Smith hath undertook
to Record them – –</td></tr>
<tr><td></td><td>The Greatest part of the Committee Appointed to Inquire into the
Complaint of Benj^a, Thos and Peleg Shearman Against Humphry
Smith Report as followeth, which is accepted – –</td></tr>
<tr><td>Report
Respecting
H. Smith
& Shearman</td><td>According to appointment of the Monthly Meeting we had
Humphry Smith & the Shearmans together to Inspect into the Controversy
Subsisting between them, and have to Inform, that firstly S^d Smith
Queried if Gospel order had been kept to, and by Inquiring we found that
before they Entered their Complaint to the meeting one of the overseers
taking a friend with him went to S^d Smith with Thos Shearman on the</td></tr>
</table>

affair, which appear'd to us according to Good order, then S^d **Smith**
Demanded a Coppy of the Complaint which after Consideration we
thought best for him not to have without he would promise to make
no use thereof in the Law, which promise he Refused, Then we offer'd that
a friend Should wait with him as long as he thought Proper to peruse
and Consider the Complaint, and he might Call in friends to advise with
but not Suffer any Coppy to be taken, and then Give us an Answer
which offer S^d **Smith** Refused Complying with- Then we refer'd S^d
Smith to Give us Some reasons ~~why he~~ why he Refused to Leave the
the affair to men, by he declined giving us any, for we found the **Shear-**
-mans would Leave it to men by them Equally Chosen or the Meeting might
Choose them and they would be bound to abide Judgment, and the **Shearman**s
Say there is a Number of Judicious Neighbours are Ready to Say that **Smiths**
Evidence in Court Contradicts the Known matters of fact but yet they
offer'd to Settle the whole affare by friends as aforesaid, and we have
made Much Inquiry in Regard to its touching Titles of Land and find
that Said **Smith**s and **Shearman**s written Titles Jointly Concur and the dispute
is only in Settling the Line, and our Judgment is that where friends hold
Land under Vouchers not to Compel them to Leave to Arbitration, but
in this Controversy we find that the **Shearmans** are willing that a num-
-ber of Surveyors Should take Said **Smith**s Deed and by the Return
therein, Run the Line as they shall think Just & Right, and they will
be bound to abide by the Same, which Appears to us that the **Shearmans**
Contend, for no Land that S^d **Smith** holds under a Voucher, therefore our
Judgment is that Said **Smith** ought to Leave the Controversy to men
or Render Sufficient Reason why, which he declines – –

from your Committee the 18th the 3^d month 1771 – **Joseph Barker**
　　　　　　　　　　　　　　　　　　　　　　　Job Case
　　　　　　　　　　　　　　　　　　　　　　　Gideon Howland
　　　　　　　　　　　　　　　　　　　　　　　Wm Anthony jn
　　　　　　　　　　　　　　　　　　　　　　　Barziallai Tucker

Hum Smith This Meeting doth Appoint **Joseph Tucker** & **Abraham Tucker** to inform Said
Case **Smith** of the Judgment of this Meeting and to Labour as they may find a
freedom and make Report to the adjournment – –

David The Committee Appointed to Labour with **David Gifford** Report they
Gifford have discharged themselves in Labouring with Said **Gifford** and he Gave
case them no Satisfaction, therefore this Meeting being Clear of any further
Labour with him do Appoint **Wm Barker** & **Barzillai Tucker** to
draft a paper of Denial against him, and also Inform him of their
Appointment, and make Return to the next monthly meeting

report of meetings in Allen & Smith Neck	The friend Appointed to have the care of the Meetings in **Allen** & **Smiths Necks** Report that they attended the Respective Meetings which were held orderly & to Satisfaction – –
Complaint against J Barker	The overseers have Exhibited a Complaint against **Jabez Barker** for Suffering two of his children to be married in his house the world, way for which they have Labour'd with him, and he declines to Condemn his disoner[dishonor], Therefore This Meeting do Appoint **Barnabas Mosher** & **Thos Hicks** to Labour with him as they may find freedom and to Make Report to the next Monthly Meeting.
P. Shearman	The overseers likewise Inform That **Philip Shearman** hath Married Contrary to Good order, for which they timely Cautioned & Advised him
and	Therefore this Meeting do Appoint **Wm Sanford** & **Job Russell** to Labor with him as they may find freedom, and make Report to the next
A. Ricketson	Monthly Meeting, They also Inform that **Abraham Ricketson** hath been in the Practice of Running horses, for which they have
offenders	Laboured with him, and he declines to Condemn his offence therefore This meeting doth Appoint **Thos Hicks** & **Phillip Allen** to Labour with him as they may find freedom, and to make Report to the next Monthly Meeting – –
	This Meeting hath Collected in old tener – –£ 6 – 5s – 10d
adjourns	This Meeting Adjourns to the 27th Instant after the meeting of worship – –
mett	This meeting being met According to adjournment the 27 the 3d mo: 1771, The Representatives being Called both Present – – The Queries have been Read & Answer'd in this meeting – –
Request for advice to the Quarterly Meeting	This meeting taking into Consideration the Practice of diverse persons amongst us in going out of the order of friends, in marriage It is therefore Recommended to the Quarterly meeting for advice, whether it may not be Sufficient in that Case for overseers or Visitors to Pre-admonish them, and then for the meeting to proceed to disown them if they persist in their disorder, without any furder Labor with them – –
H. Smith Requests an appeal	The friends appointed to Inform **Humphry Smith** of the Judgment of This Meeting, Report that they have fulfil'd their Appointment and Labour'd with him to Comply with sd Judgment, which he declines, and Requests an Appeal to the Quarterly Meeting which is Granted
Friends to attend Quarter meeting	**Paul Russell**, **Wm Anthony jur** and **Caleb Russell** are appointed to attend the Quarterly Meeting and Present the Epistle with the Answers to the Queries, and they to ~~present~~ Represent **Humphrey Smith**'s Appeal, and to produce Such papers and minutes as Shall appear

Necessary in that case, and to make Report to the next monthly
meeting - The afore said Epistle was Signed in this meeting by the Clerk

At a Monthly Meeting held in **Dartmouth** the 15th: 4th mo: 1771

4th mo:
1771

The Representatives are **Jonathan Hussey** & **Samuel Smith**
both present – –

Jonathan
Tucker's
proposal
of mar=
=riage

Jonathan Tucker and **Mehetabel Mosher** declared their Intentions
of Marriage, and were desired to wait Till the next Monthly
Meeting for their Answer, and **Joseph Gifford** & **Barzillai Tucker**
are appointed to Inquire into the young man's clearness Respecting
Marriage and conversation, and Make Report to the next
Monthly Meeting – –

order
to draw
a denial
against
J. Allen

one of the Committee that had the care of **Jedidiah Allen**'s case
Reports that he Still declines to Comply with the Judgment of this
Meeting, therefore this Meeting believing that we are clear of
any farther Labour with him, and do Appoint **Nicolas Howland**
ans **Wm Anthony ju^r** to draft a paper of denial against S^d
Allen, and to Inform him of their Appointment and make
Report to the next Monthly Meeting – –

D. Gifford
denial

The friends Appointed to draft a paper of denial Against **David
Gifford ju**: have drafted & brought S^d paper to this Meeting which
hath been Signed by the clerk, and he is appointed to read Said
paper at the close of a first day meeting for worship, before the
next monthly meeting & then to Make Report, And **Joseph ~~Gifford~~ Tucker**
is appointed to Serve S^d **Gifford** with a Coppy of his denial, and
Make Report to the next Monthly Meeting – –

Philip
Shearman
case referd

The friends Appointed to Labour with **Philip Shearman** Report that
they have not had an oppertunity to Labour with him both together
therefore the matter is Refer'd under their care until the next
Monthly Meeting, and then make Report – –

Abraham
Ricketson
Case
referd

The Committee Appointed to Labour with **Abraham Ricketson**
Report that they have not had an opportunity fully to to discharge
themselves, therefore the matter is Refer'd under their care one
month Longer, and then to make Report – –

Report
from
Quar
meeting

The friends Appointed to attend the Quarterly Meeting Report
they all attended according to appointment, and have produced an Epistle from the Same, which hath been Read, and
the Contents are Recommended to friends Notice & observation

Hump
Smith
to be
Inform'd

and **Samuel Smith** & **Wm Anthony ju**: are appointed to In-
-form **Humphry Smith** of the above Contents Respecting his Requ-
-est or appeal to S^d Meeting, & give him a coppy of the Compt if he Comply with S^d Epistle

Jabez Barker case The Com^tee appointed to Labour with **Jabez Barker ju.** Report
that they have Labour'd with him, and he declines to Condem[n]
his fault to their Satisfaction, therefore the matter is
Refer^d under their care one month Longer, and then to make Report
The said Epistle from the Quarterly Meeting Informs us that
their Com^tee appointed to View our our meeting House made
the following Report, which was accepted by s^d Quarterly Meeting

Judgm^t of the Quar^ly meeting Respecting Meeting House   To the Quarterly Meeting of friends next to be held at **Portsmouth**
on **Rhode Island.**

We the Subscribers Agreeable to the appointment of the
Quarterly Meeting having Viewed and Examind the Meeting
house at **Apponaganset**, there being a Number of friend, belong-
-ing to **Dartmouth** Monthly Meeting then present, and it is our
Judgment that it will be best to Repair it – –
Notwithstanding we think it might be well for the Quarterly
Meeting to leave them at their Liberty to Rebuild if they
Should Still continue to prefer it, and if Rebuilt we think a house of the
following dimentions would be Sufficient (viz) Sixty feet
in Length, and thirty five feet in width and twenty feet [?],
Dartmouth 15th the 1st mo: 1771 – –   **Abraham Barker**
                                  Moses Farnum   Jacob Mott Ju^r
                                  Thos Gould Ju^r   Wm Readwood

Quarterly Meetings advice about disorderly Marriage And our Representatives from the s^d Quarterly Meeting Informing
Verbally that the s^d Meeting Concluded to leave it at the discression
of the Monthly Meeting, in Regard to disowning of persons that Mar-
-ry out of the unity of friends without dealing with them
after they have been Pre-caution^d before marriage

Complaint against Stephen Marihew   One of the overseers Informs that **Stephen Merihew** hath
Married out of the unity of friends and that he hath Labour'd with
him therefor, and he declines to condemn his offence, therefore
This Meeting doth appoint **Caleb Russell** & **James Davis** to
Labour with him as they may find freedom, and to make
Report to the next monthly meeting

5th mo. 1771 At a Monthly Meeting held in **Dartmouth** the
20th of the 5th month 1771, The Representatives are
Samuel Smith and **Wm Anthony ju^r** both present
The friends Appointed to Inquire into **Jonathan Tucker**'s Clear-
-ness Respecting Marriage & Conversation Report that they have

Jona Tucker made Inquiry & do not find anything to hinder his proceeding in
answer Marriage. And the s^d **Jonathan Tucker** appear'd for their Answer which
was that they Might proceed to take each other in Marriage in
Some Convenient time before next Monthly Meeting, advising
with the overseers that this Meeting shall appoint for that pur-
-pose, and **Joseph Gifford** & **Barziallai Tucker** are appointed to
See their Marriage Consumated in Good order & Make Report to
the next Monthly Meeting – –

Case of The friends Appointed to draft a paper of Denial against
Jedediah
Allen **Jedidiah Allen** Report they have not it, and they have Render'd
referd a Reason for their omission, Therefore the matter is Refer'd un-
-der their care until next Monthly Meeting, and they to draft
S^d paper if they think Necessary, and then to Make Report

    Joseph Tucker Reports that he hath Served **David Gifford**
D Gifford ju^r with a Coppy of his Denial, and also his denial hath been read
inform^d According to the Appointment of Last Monthly Meeting, and
is a followeth

From our Monthly Meeting of friends held in **Dartmouth** ye 15th of
D Gifford the 4th month 1771, Whereas **David Gifford ju^r** having had his
Denial Education Amongst friends, but by not Giving heed to that unerring
Guide & Teacher the Spirit of Truth in his own heart he has So far
deviated from our Christian Profession, that he has been accused
and charged on oath by **Meribah Hammond** deceast of being
the father of her Child, & also denying a matter of fact between
himself & **Jabez Hammond**, for which offences friends having
Laboured with him in order to bring him to a True Sense of his
Transgressions, but their Labour of Love in that Respect pro-
-ving Ineffectual, he not condemning the same to friends Satisfac-
-tion, Therefore for the clearing of Truth & our Christian profession
from Such Reproaches, we can do no less than Testify against
him, & do hereby disown him the S^d **David Gifford** from being
one in unity with us and under our care, Notwithstanding
desiring if it be consistant with divine pleasure that he yet may
be brought to a True Sight & Sense of his offences, & through a
true and unfeigned Repentance and Reformation which
his peace made with the Lord, and thereby be Restored to the
unity of his friends – –

    Signed in & on be half of the said Meeting by **Job Russell** Clerk

The friends Appointed to Labour with **Philip Shearman** Reports
that they have Labour'd with him, and he declines to Condem
his offence to their Satisfaction. Therefore this Meeting being

P Shearman denied Clear of any farther Labour with him to deny the s^d **Philip
Shearman** from being a member of our Society and from under
the Care of the Meeting and **Wm Sandford** is Appointed to Inform
him of his denial & make Report to the next monthly Meeting

Care of Abraham Ricketson refer'd The friends that had the care of **Abraham Ricketson**
Report that they have had no opportunity to Treat with
him by reason he is gone to Sea, therefore the matter is
Still Refer'd under their Care, and they to make Report as
Soon as they Can with Conveniency.

J Barker ju^r denied The friends Appointed to Labour with **Jabez Barker ju^r**
Report they have discharged themselves in Labouring with
him, and he declines to condemn his offences to their Satis=
=faction. Therefore this Meeting being Clear of any farther
Labour with him do deny the s^d **Jabez Barker** from being
a member of our Society & from under the Care of this Meeting
and **Peleg Gifford** is appointed to inform him of his denial
and to make Report to the next monthly Meeting-----

S. Merihew Accepted The friends Appointed to Treat with **Stephen Merihew** Report
That he hath Condemned his offense to their Satisfaction, and he
hath also Appear'd in this Meeting & Verbally Condemned the same
which is accepted – –

E Sheperd Certif. **Elisabeth Shepherd** wife of **David** hath Produced a Removal
Certificate from **Rhode Island** monthly Meeting which is Accepted
and also the women friends Inform that **Abigail Winslow** hath
Given in a paper Condemning her falling into the Sin of
fornication, which they have accepted, and this Meeting
Concurs therewith – –

6th mo: 1771 At a monthly Meeting held in Dartmouth the 17th 6th month 1771
The Representatives are **Jonathan Hussey** and **Thos Hicks** both present
whereas our yearly Meeting is now being at Rhode Island There=
fore this Meeting doth Adjourn to the 24th Instant at the 11th hour
in the Morning – –

At a monthly Meeting held by Adjournment the 24ᵗʰ 6ᵗʰ month 1771

The Representatives being called both present

The friends that were Appointed Some months past to draft a paper of

Jedidiah Allen denial Against **Jedidiah Allen** Report that they have Still omitted
Case refer'd it for the Same reasons as heretofore, therefore they are Stil Continued
in that Service & to make Report at the next monthly Meeting

Jonathan one of the friends that was appointed to see **Jonathan Tucker** and
Tucker's **Mehitabel Mosher**'s Marriage Consumated in good order Reports
marriage That he attended Said Marriage and that it was Consumated orderly
The other friend Reports that he did not attend and he hath Render'd
an Excuse for his omission – –

P. Shearmans **William Sanford** Reports That he hath Informed **Philiip Shearman** of
& J Barker's his denial, and **Peleg Gifford** also Informs That he hath Informed
denial **Jabez Barker Juʳ** of his denial according to the Appointment of
Last monthly Meeting – –

The Queries have been Read & Answer'd in This Meeting

Visits of **Henry Chase** hath Visited this meeting with a few Lines from the Month=
foreign friends =ly meeting of **Oblong**, dated the 5ᵗʰ month 1771, Certifying him to
be of an orderly Conversation & an approved Minister in unity
which hath been read to Satisfaction & his Visit Kindly accepted
Our friend **Joshua Thomson** hath Visited this meeting with a
Certificate from the monthly Meeting held at Salem in **New Jersey**
the 27ᵗʰ 5ᵗʰ month 1771, Certifying him to be in Good unity as an Elder
which hath been read to Satisfaction & his Visit Kindly accepted

Complaint The overseers have Introduced a Complaint into this meeting Sign'd
against by **George Winslow** Against **Joseph Rotch** for Refusing to Com=
J. Rotch =ply with the Judgment of the arbitrators that were Mutually
Chosen between them, therefore this Meeting do Appoint **Joseph
Gifford, Wᵐ Anthony juʳ, Barzillai Tucker, Prince Allen, Thoˢ
Hicks, Joseph Barker & Gideon Howland** to Enquire into the Grounds
& Validity of sᵈ Complaint & make Report to the Adjournmentof this
Meeting – –

Anne Sher The women friends Inform that they have denied **Anne Shearman**
man denyᵈ wife of **Philip Shearman** for Marrying out of the unity of friends
which This Meeting Concurs with – –

J Oxly's Our Esteemed Friend **Joseph Oxl[e]y** hath Visited this Meeting
Visit with his Certificate from the Monthly Meeting in **Norwich Old England**

bearing date the 23ᵈ 3ᵈ month 1770, with Concurring Certificates from
the Quarterly Meeting held at **Norwich** for the **County** of **Norfolk** the
28ᵗʰ 3ᵈ mo: 1770, And from the yearly meeting of Ministers ~~the~~ˬheld yᵉ
11ᵗʰ of the 6ᵗʰ month 1770, Certifying from whence he came that they
had Good unity with his Concern, and also his Publick and Private
Charector, and his Ministry Sound & Living, which have been
read in this meeting to Good Satisfaction and his Visit Kindly accepted[10] – –
This Meeting hath Collected £8 s8 – 2ᵈ old Tenner and the

Order to pay Tim Russell — Treasurer is orderᵈ to pay **Timothy Russell five** dollars for
Keeping the meeting house half a year and Make Report to the
next monthly meeting – –

    This Meeting Adjourns to the first Sixth day in next month after
the Meeting of worship – –
At a monthly meeting held by adjournment the 4ᵗʰ 7ᵗʰ mo: 1771
The Representatives being called both present – –

Jos Rotch case Settled — The Committee Appointed to Inquire into the Complaint of **George Winslow**
Against **Joseph Rotch** Report that said Rotch hath Complyᵈ to
fullfill the Judgment of the Arbitrators – –

J Barker's appeal — **Jabez Barker** juʳ Requests an Appeal from the Judgment of
This Meeting to the Quarterly Meeting which is granted – –

Representatives — **Samuel Smith, Wᵐ Anthony** juʳ **Barzillai Tucker & Jonathan
Hussey** are Appointed to attend the Quarterly Meeting and Convey
the Epistle with the Answers to the Queries, and present the business
from this meeting to the Quarterly Meeting, and make Report to the
next monthly Meeting. The above Sᵈ Epistle was Signed in this Meeting

Complaint against B Shearman — whereas **Benjᵃ Shearman** hath Neglected to attend Religious Meeting
both for worships & discipline for Some years past, and now Refuses
to condemn the Same, therefore this Meeting do Appoint **John Potter
Job Russell Gideon Howland, Thoˢ Hicks, & Barzillai Tucker** to Labour
with him as they may find freedom, and make Report to the
next monthly meeting

7ᵗʰ mo: 1771 — At a Monthly Meeting held in **Dartmouth** the 15ᵗʰ 7ᵗʰ Mo: 1771
The Representatives are **Wᵐ Anthony** juʳ **& Benjᵃ Howland** 2ᵈ, Sᵈ
Howland not being present by Reason of his wife being not well – –
The friends Appointed to draft a paper of denial against **Jedidiah**

---

10. Joseph Oxley (1714–1775) traveled extensively in the colonies in 1770–1771. See "Joseph Oxley's Journal of His Life, Travels, and Labours of Love, in the Faith and Fellowship of Our Lord Jesus Christ," in *The Friends' Library: Comprising Journals, Doctrinal Treatises, and Other Writings of the Religious Society of Friends*, ed. by William Evans and Thomas Evans (14 vols., Philadelphia: Joseph Rakestraw, 1837–1850), II, 415–76.

Jedidiah Allen's case continued **Allen** Report that they have not done it by Reason that Some of the Arbitrators are not fully Satisfied in their Settlement between S^d parties, therefore this Meeting do Appoint **Caleb Russell Joseph Barker, Wm Anthony Ju^r, Barzillai Tucker Thos Hicks** to Treat with monthly **Coakset** Meeting and Request said Meeting to Appoint a Com^tee to assist to bring s^d parties (as some of them below there) to a Rehearing, and to make Report as Soon as they can Conveniently

Report from Quar meeting The friends Appointed to attend the Quarterly Meeting Report that they all attended According to Appointment, and they have Produced an Epistle from the Same which hath been Read & Kindly Accepted, and likewise the **London** Printed Epistle for the year 1770 hath been Read to Good Satisfaction, and the Contents earnestly Recommended to friends Notice & Observation – –

Benja Shearman Case The friends Appointed to Labour with **Benj^a Shearman** for his Neglect of attending Religious Meetings Report they have not all of them had an oppertunity to discharge themselves in that Respect therefore they are still Continued in that Service, and to make Report to the next Monthly Meeting – –

Humph Smith case The Appeal of **Humphry Smith** is Returned to this meeting again, in order for him to Render his Reason for not Refering his Con--troversey to Arbitration if he Still declines the Same, therefore do Appoint **Wm Mosher, Caleb Russell, Job Russell, Wm Sanford** and **Adam Gifford** to hear the Reason and Judge whether they be Sufficient or not, and to make Report to the next Monthly Meeting – –

J Barker to be in= =formed **Jonathan Hussey** and **Job Russell** are Appointed to Serve **Jabez Barker ju^r** with a Coppy of his denial and Accusation, and to Make Report next monthly Meeting

To Collect money for London The Quarterly Requests of this meeting to Collect four pounds Sterling, and Send it up to the next Quarterly Meeting for the Suply of the Stock in the yearly Meeting of **London**

Overseers Continued The time being Expired that the overseers were appointed in Their Service, therefore they are Continued in that Service one month Longer.

Tim Russell is paid The Treasurer Reports that he hath paid **Timothy Russell** five Dollars for Keeping the Meeting House half a year as appointed by Last Monthly Meeting – –

T. Smith Certificate **Thos Smith** and family have Removed into the Compass of this meeting to Live, and have Produced a Certificate from the Monthly Meeting of **Nantucket** which hath been read & Accepted

8mo
1771 At a Monthly Meeting held in **Dartmouth** the 19th 8 mo 1771

The Representatives are **Caleb Russell** & **Jonathan Hussey** both present

Report on The friends appointed to Labour with **Benjᵃ Sherman** [**Shearman**] for his
the Case of Neglecting of attending Religious meetings, Report that they
B: Shear have Treated with him and he Declines to Condemn his Disorder
man their Satisfaction which is Referᵈ to the Next monthly meeting
Referᵈ for further Consideration – –

Report on The friends appointed to serve **Jabes** [**Jabez**] **Barker jᵘ** with a Coppy
J: Barker's of his Accusation & Denial, Report if they have answerᵈ their
Caser appointment

The Committee Appointed to Treat with **Humphry Smith** and hear
his Reasons on account of his appeals being Returnᵈ, back from
the Quarterly Meeting Report as followeth

Jacob Chase Whereas **Jacob Chase** had a Removal Certificate to **Rhod-Island**
Certificate Monthly meeting and now he hath Removed back again within
Returnᵈ the Compass of this meeting much Sooner than he Expected, And
Returnᵈ Said Certificate which we Except[Accept] – –

Overseers 			**Daniel Cornel** [**Cornell**] **William Mosher William Barker Jonathan Hussey**
appointed **William Anthony jᵘ** & **Thoˢ Hicks**, Are appointed Overseers for the
year Insueing

Overseers 			**Caleb Russell Barzillai Tucker Joseph Barker Gideon**
of poor Appoin: **Howland** & **Philip Allen**, are apointed overseers of the Poor for
the year Insueing

9mo
1771 At a Monthly Meeting held in **Dartmouth** yᵉ 16th 9mo 1771

the Representatives are **William Anthony jᵘ** & **Thoˢ Hicks** Present

Benja: Sherman The matter Concerning **Benjᵃ Sherman** is Referᵈ to next Monthly
Case referᵈ Meeting for Further Consideration – – – The Committee appointed

Hump Smith to Serve **Humphry Smith** with a Coppy of the Judgment of
case this meeting, And Labour with him to Comply therewith report
that they have answered their appointment and Said **Smith**
Declines to Comply therewith, therefore this Meeting Doth
appoint **Benjᵃ Smith jᵘ** and **Abraham Howland** to Inform
Said **Smith** If he Dont Comply with the Judgment of this meeting
he may Expect to be Denyᵈ And make Report to next Meeting

Committee to 		This Meeting Comes to a Conclusion to Repair our Meeting
Repair Meeting house in **Poneganset**, And do appoint **John Potter Thoˢ Hicks**
house and **William Anthony Juner**, To Shingle Sᵈ House and Repair it
as they think Proper, and they are Desired to Accomplish Said
Business as Soon as may bee and then to make Report to this meeting

The Queries hath been Read & Answered in this Meeting – –

Representatives to ye Quarterly meeting this Meeting has Signed an Epistle to the Quarterly Meeting and Appoint **Joseph Tucker William Anthony j^u William Mosher** and **Job Russell** to Attend the Quarterly Meeting and to Present the Epistle with the Answers to the Queries, & Represent the Business of this Meeting & make Report to the next Monthly Meeting

money paid for Smithfield This meeting hath collected four pounds five Shillings Lawfull money for the Use of **Smithfield** Monthly meeting and Sent up by our Representatives – –

Complaint against A: S: The Overseers hath Exhibited a Complaint against **Abraham Sherman[Shearman]** for taking too much Spirituous Liker for for which they have Labour^d, with him and he still Persists therein therefore this Meeting doth appoint **William Sanford** & **Job Russell** to Labour with him as they may find freedom & make Report to nex monthly meeting – –

Committee's Report of J: W: heirs The Committee appointed from this monthly meeting & **Coakset** meeting to Inquire into the Controversy Subsisting between the heirs of **Jedediah Wood**, Report as followeth – –

According to the appointment of the Monthly Meetings to which we belong, We having inspected into the Reasons why one of the heirs of **Jedediah Wood** Refuses to Comply with the Judgment of the Arbitrators which was mutually Chosen by them, as appear by Articles of agreement under their hands – – And have Inform as followeth – – That we had the said heirs & Arbitrators together, in order to Inquire into all Circum= =stances Relating thereto, And find there is some things brought to light that was not Laid before S^d Arbitrators to Judg upon (altho their Judgment Expreses the whole) Which since appearing to some of s^d Arbitrators, gave them Some Uneasiness therein, & we by Inspection finding those things not Consider^d, nor Judg^d upon, Give this forth as our A[d]vice and Judgment that if said Parties doth not Settle those matter & things between themselves then they Lay all those things & matters not Considered, Befor said Arbitrators in order that the Same may be fully Compleated and Settled as they shall think Just & Right, And also Rectifie what they formerly Judg^d upon if they shall find it Necessary,

Given forth this 26th Day ye 8mo 1771 by your friends

Thos Hicks	David Davel
Wm Anthony j^u	Joshua Davel
Barzillai Tucker	Joseph Barker

The above Report being Axcepted

10ᵐᵒ At a Monthly Meeting held in **Dartmouth** yᵉ 21ˢᵗ : 10ᵐᵒ: 1771
1771 The Representatives are **Caleb Russell** & **Jonathan Hussey**

Case of Benjᵃ both present, The matter Concerning **Benjᵃ Sherman** is
Sherman
referᵈ Refered to next monthly meeting for furthe[r] Consideration

This meeting hath Signed a Removal Certificate for

E: Potter **Elizabeth Potter** wife to **Benjᵃ Potter** to the monthly meeting
Certificate of the **Nine= Partners** in the Province of **New York**

M: Taber and also Signed a Removal Certificate for **Marthew Taber** to
Certificate the Monthly Meeting of **Sandwich** – –

J: Rotch **Joseph Rotch Jᵘ** hath Returned from **London** and hath Produced a
Certificate Certificate from the two weeks meeting held in **London** yᵉ 10ᵗʰ: 6ᵐᵒ: 1771
which hath been Read to yᵉ Satisfaction of this meeting – –

The friends appointed to Inform **Humphry Smith** of the Judgment
of the last monthly meeting & also to Inform him if he Dont Comply
therewith he may Expect to be Denied, Report that they have
Answered their appointment and Said **Smith** Requests an Appeal

H: Smith's from the above Sᵈ Judgment, to the Quarterly Meeting which
appeal this Meeting grants – –

The friends appointed to Labour with **Abraham Sherman**
Report, that they took an opertunity and Treated with Said
Sherman and he Gave them Some Satisfaction therefore the
matter is Referᵈ, under the Cair of the afore Sᵈ friends & they
to make Report to the next monthly meeting – –

The friends appointed to attend the Quarterly Meeting Report
that they all Attended according to appointment and have
Produced an Epistle from the Same which hath been Read
to good Satisfaction, also Received two Transcrips of Yearly meet:

Received Epistles one from the yearly Meeting held in **Philadelphia**
Epistles from yᵉ for **Pennsylvania** & **New=Jersey** by Ajournments from the
yearly meeting 22ⁿᵈ yᵉ 9ᵐᵒ 1770 to the 28 of the same Inclusive

The other from the yearly Meeting held in **Newport** on **Rhod=
Island** by Adjournments from the 14ᵗʰ: 6ᵐᵒ 1771 to yᵉ 17 of the
Same Inclusive, Which hath been Read to good Satisfaction
and the Contents thereof are Earnestly Recommended to
friends observation – –

Certificates The Women friends Inform, they have Received two Removel
received Certificates from the Monthly Meeting of **Rhod Island**
for
R .Michel & one for **Rhodey Mitchel** wife of **James Mitchel** – The othe
M. Spencer for **Mary Spencer**, which this Meeting Excepts – –

H: Allen
Deni^d

The Women Likwise Inform that they have Denied **Hope Allen**
wife of **John Allen** for marring the the Unity of friends
which this meeting Concurs with

Whereas **Jabez Barker Juner** hath been Denied Some months
past, for suffering two of his Children to be Married in this house

J: Barker
acknowledg
=ment --

and now the said **Barker** appearing in this meeting and
verbally Desired friends, & this Meeting to pass it by – –
and after a space of Silence this Meeting finds freedom to
pass by his afore Said fault, And to Receive him under friends
Care again – –

Report on
the case of
B. Howland
Juner

The friends that was appointed Some time past to treat with
Barnabus [Barnabas] Howland J^u on the account of his Disorderly marr[i]age
now Report that he gave them no Satisfaction and they also
Report that he hath fallen into the Sin of Fornication as
appears by his wives having a Child So Soon after Marrage
therefore this Meeting do appoint **William Anthony J^u** & **Samuel**
Smith to Labour further with him and make Report to
the next monthly meeting – –

friends to
oversee
ye Lofts

John Potter Barzillai Tucker Thos Hicks Joseph Barker
Gideon Howland William Anthony J^u are Appointed to have
the over sight of the Lofts & the Seets [seats] at our Insueing yearly
Meeting to Indeavour to Prevent any Indecent Behaviour that
may be liable to happen at that time and to make Report
to the next monthly meeting – –

Complaint
against
B. Howlan^d
Sadler

The Overseers hat[h] Brought a Complaint against **Benj^a**
Howland Sadler for abusing **Benj^a Smith** in Threting [threatening] words
and Expressions and Cut[t]ing Down his fruit trees, And also S^d
Howlands Cre[a]tures Tresspas[s]ing on him, for which Disorders
the Overseers hat Laboured with him for and he Refuses to
indeavour to Settle it to their Satisfaction therefore this

Committee
appointed

Meeting Doth appoint **Joseph Barker** & **Wm Sandford** to
Labour with him & to Judge & Detirmine and make Report
to the next Monthly Meeting

11mo
1771

At a Monthly Meeting held in **Dartmouth** the
18th of ye 11mo 1771 – The Representatives are **Caleb Russell**
and **Jonathan Hussey** both present

Report on
the case of
B. Howland
Juner

The friends appointed to Labour with **Barnabus [Barnabas] Howland**
Juner Report, that they have Laboured with him
and he Declines to Condemn his Disorder therefore
the above Said friends are appointed to Draw a paper of Denial

against S^d **Howland** and inform him of their appointment
and make Report to the next Monthly Meeting – –

Report of frinds The friends appointed to have the oversight of the Lofts &C [etc]
oversee the
Lofts at our yearly Meeting, Report that most of them attended
the three Days, and that the People behaved in a Degree orderly

Report on the The friends Intrusted with the care of the Case of **Abraham Sherma**^n
case of Abra^m Report that they hant had an opportunity to Discharge their
Shearman
trust therefore the Case is Referd as heretofore and to make
Report to next meeting

Case of Benj^a   The friends appointed to Labour with **Benj^a Howland** S^d [S^adler]
Howland
Sadler and to Judge and Determine in a matter between S^d **Howland**
and **Benj^a Smith** Report that they have made some progress
but have not gone through, therefore they are Still Continued
in the Same Service and to make Report to next meeting

Wm Russells **William Russell** Requests to be taken under friends Care
Request
therefore **Caleb Russell** & **James Davis** is appointed to Inquire
into his Conversation & to m̶take an oppertunity of Sollid
Conferrance with him in order to Discover wheather his
motive be from the bot[t]om of true Conviction and make
Report to next meeting,

Selling not[e]s   It hath been brought to this meeting from the Preparative
of hand Confir,^d
wheather it be Consistant with friends Discipline for
a friend to sell a note of hand which he had from a
friend Payable to him or his order. Therefore this meeting
Do appoint, **Sam^ll** [Samuel] **Smith Barzillia Tucker Wm Anthony ju**
James Davis Joseph Gifford John Potter Jonathan Hussey
to Consider of the above S^d matter and bring in their Judgment
in behalf of this Meeting and make Report to next meeting

M: and Ann   The women friends inform that they have minuted
Howland
admitted **Mehetable** & **Ann Howland** Daughters of **Isaac Howland J**^u
memb: under their Care which this meeting Concurs with

Coaket request   **Acoakset** monthly meeting Requests this meeting
a Com^tee
to appoint a Committee to Join them to Labour
with the Heirs of **Jedediah** & **Keziah Wood** to Comply with
the advice of the Committee which was appointed Some
adjourn months past,   This meeting adjourns to the 27 Day of this
month after the meeting for Worship – –

mett   This Meeting met According to Adjornment ye 27: 11mo 1771
Jorment
the Representatives being called one Present ye othe[r] not by
Reason of his being gone to **Nantucket**, This meeting appointed

Committee appointed a Committee agreeable to the above Said minute who are **William Anthony jᵘ Barzillai Tucker Job Russell** and they to Labour and a[d]vise as they think best and make Report to the next Meeting

B: S: Condemna: **Benjᵃ Sherman** hath given in a paper to this meeting Condemning his Disorder in not attending meeting Several years Past which is Referᵈ to next meeting – –

Complaint against L. Smith   The Overseers hath Exhibited a Complaint against **Lamuel Smith** for Marr[y]ing out of the Unity of Friends for which they have timely Precautioned him and he Persisted therein therefore this meeting do appoint **Abraham Tucker** and **Barzillai Tucker** to Labour with him as Soon as they can Conveniently & make Report

Request for a meet: house in Allens Neck   The Friends in **Allens Neck** Request some Assistance or advise in Regard to their holding a meeting in said **Neck** they being under some Difficulty in Regard to a house to hold their meeting in Therefore this meeting doth Appoint **John Potter William Anthony jᵘ Thoˢ Hicks Caleb Russell** to pay them a Visit and Consider wheather it may be best for them to build themselves a Meeting house or not and also to Consider wheather they Continue to hold a Meeting there or not & make Report to next Meeting

J. Barker under[?] Dealing   Whereas **Jabez Barker jᵘ** appearᵈ in our Monthly meeting at the tenth month past and made an acknowledgement which was then Accepted and he appearing in the monthly meeting held the 11ᵐᵒ 1771 in the first Sitting of Said meeting and would not own what he had done in Regard to Suffering his Children to be married in his house was a Breach of order which Causes this meeting to be Dissatisfied with his Sᵈ acknowledgment therefore this meeting do appoint **Samuel Smith Barzillia Tucker Prince Allen** to Labour with him in order to show him his mistake and make Report to next meeting

12ᵐᵒ 1771   At a Monthly Meeting held in **Dartmouth** yᵉ 16: 12ᵐᵒ 1772 the Representatives are **Wᵐ Anthony Jᵘ** and **Samˡˡ [Samuel] Smith** both Present. This meeting hath Signed a paper of

B: H: paper of Denial   Denial against **Barnabus [Barnabas] Howland Juner** for the sin of fornication and the Clark is appointed to Read said paper at the close of a First day meeting for Worship before the next Monthly meeting and at Said meeting to make Report of its being Read – –

Case of   The Friends that had the Care of the Case of **Abraham**
Abraham
Sherman   **Sherman** Report that they Desire one month Longer time
Refer^d   which is granted them and then they to make Report

Report of   The friends that was appointed to Joine **Acoakset** Monthly
frinds
that Joynd   meetings Committee to Labour & advise with the heirs of
accoakset **Jedidiah Wood** Report that they have Join^d S^d Committee
friends   and bestowed Some labour and advice, And the matter
             Remains unsett[l]ed – –

                  The Committee appointed to Labour with **Benj^a Howland**
Case of Benj^a Sadler and to Judge & Determine a matter between Said
Howland]   **Howland** and **Benj^a Smith** Report as followeth
Benj Howland which is accepted & S^d **Howland** hath made an acknoledgment
acknoledgment to this meeting which is Excepted

friends to   The friends appointed to treat with **Wm Russell** on account
treat with
W: Russel   of his Request Report that they have Discharg^d themselves
             in that Respect, and that he gave them a Degree of Satisfaction
             therefore it was Refer^d to the Adjournment – –

To build   The Committee appointed to Consider on Account of the friends
a meeting
not grant   Request, in **Allens Neck** to build a Meeting house there and
ed   also to hold a meeting there this wintter, Report that they
             think best not to build a meeting house there at Present
             but in Regard to holding a meeting they think it may be well
             with the Provisal that they can accomadate themselves with a
meeting   House Su[i]table Therefore their Request is Granted in Regard to holding
in Allen
neck   a meeting As Usual and **Daniel Cornel** [**Cornell**] & **Philip Allen** is
granted   appointed to see the meeting held agreeable to Good order and
             to make Report to next   third month

                  The Women friends inform this meeting that they have
W: Spen[cer] minuted **Welthan Spencer** a member under their Cair [care] which
Receivd
adjourn   this meeting Concurs with – – This meeting Adjorns to
             the 25 Instant after the meeting of worship – –

mett   This Meeting meet by adjournment the 25th of 12mo 1771
             the Representatives both Present **Samuel Smith** is Chosen
W: Russel Clark [Clerk] for this Day.   **William Russell** is Received under the
Received   Care of this meeting – –

                  The friends appointed to Judge and Determine Respecting
Committee the Sel[l]ing Notes of hand Report as followeth which is Exceped
Respecting
Selling   According to the appointment of the monthly meeting we have meet
Note of hand and Consid[e]red the matter Respecting friends Selling of notes of hand
             payable to them or their order; and as on the one hand we do not

think it Reasonable to prohibit friends from Selling all or any
Kind of Such Securities in a way Just Commerce – –
So on the other hand we think it not Consistant with
the Discipline of friends, for any friend to Sell
Such a Note to an at[t]orney or any Else that he
hath on a friend with Intention for the said friend to be
Prosecuted in the Law, of which Said Intention the Circumstance
of Such particular Case (if any such happen) will Sufficiently
Demonstrate and friends & the monthly meeting are the
proper Judges thereof according as the wisdom of truth shall Direct

     Given forth and Dated This 23 Day of the 12ᵐᵒ 1771

by	**Jonathan Hussey**	**William Anthony Jʳ**
	Joseph Gifford	**Samuel Smith**
	John Potter	**Barzillai Tucker**

Comᵗᵉᵉ on the
Heirs of
Jedediah Woods
case
The Committee appointed to give **Coakset** Committee in Labouring
with the heirs of **Jedidiah** & **Kᵉᶻⁱᵃʰ Wood** are Continued and to make Report
as Soon as Conveniency will admitt – –

Ben Sherman
paper
Benjᵃ Sherman hath Given in a paper to this meeting
Condemning his Declining to attend meetings also his
pretending to prophecy which this meeting accepts provided
he Cause Sᵈ paper to be Read Publickly at the Close of a first
Day meeting for worship at any convenient time before the next
Monthly meeting he being Present,   Said paper is as followeth

     To the Monthly Meeting of Friends to be held in

     Dartmouth the 16 of yᵉ 12ᵐᵒ 1771

B: S paper
of Confession
Dear Friends whereas I have been Missled through
Imagination so far as not to attend Religious meetings for
Several years past which is Contrary to the good Order
of friends and also in Pretending to Provesy or aforetell
future things all which I am fully perswaded was wrong
and I am hertely [heartily] Sorry for and do Condemn and I Desire
friends would pass it by with all the Rest of my outgoings
So far as to let me Remain under their Care
from your friend – –

            Benjamin Sherman

The friends appointed to Labour with **Jabez Barker juʳ** Report
as followeth which is Excepted

     According to appointment of Last Monthly Meeting we

Committee
to Labour
with J: B
have Discoursed with **Jabez Barker juʳ** on the account of his
Suffering his Daughters to be married in his house, And had

a Long Conferrance with him on that subject. Endeavouring
(according to our Abilities) to Convince him of his Error therein
we likewise Shew^d him a Coppy of part of a minute made
in our yearly meeting in the year 1708. Which we think
is very Clear against Such Conduct as his, yet he would
by no means Condemn the Same, nor yet own that he had
broaken any order of Friends, but used many words tending to
Justifie himself therein – –

        Given forth this 16th of ye 12mo 1771 by your friends

                    Sam,^ll [Samuel] Smith
                    Prince Allen
                    Barzillia Tucker

And the matter is Refer^d to the next monthly meeting and
the Same Committee are Still Continued in the Same Service
and **Abraham Tucker** & **Caleb Russell** are ad[d]ed to them & they
to make Report to the next meeting – –

B: R^ls
paper

Barnabus [Barnabas] Russell hath Given in a paper to this meeting
Condemning his Assisting in a tumultuous Riot which is
Accepted Provided he Cause the Same to be Read Publickly
at the Close of a first Day meeting for worship between this
& the next monthly meeting he being Present and Return S^d
paper to next meeting – –

B. Russel
Intention of
marrage

Barnabus [Barnabas] Russell Proposes his Intention of Marraige [marriage] with
Anna Howland at the Preparative meeting but he having fallen
into the aforesaid disorder it is Refer^d to the next Monthly meeting

Bedford
friends
Request
to build a
meet house

The friends at **Bedford**[11] Request this meeting to Consider
wheather it may not be Needfull to build a meeting House
in or near Said place therefor this meeting do appoint
Abraham Tucker Wm Sanford Wm Mosher Barzillia Tucker
Sam^ll [Samuel] Smith Prince Allen Jonathan Hussey to Consider
of Said matter and bring in their Judgment to the meeting as
soon as they ^can Conveniently – –

G: Howland
paper

Gideon Howland hath Given in a paper Condemning his unbe=
=coming Expressions & falling into a bodily Strife with **Zephaniah**
Anthony which this meeting accepts Provided he Cause the Same
to be Read Publickly as Usual and Return the Same to next meeting

Representatives
to the Quarter

The Queries have been Read and Answer^d and the answers
approved, Likewise ~~the~~ an Epistle prepared and Sign,^d all which

---

11. The present city of New Bedford, Massachusetts was first known simply as Bedford or Bedford Village. This change from the original name will not be further noted.

are Sent up to the Quarterly meeting by our Representatives who
are **Caleb Russell Wᵐ Mosher Job Russell** & **Wᵐ Anthony jʳ** and
Report of ᵗʰᵉⁱʳ Doings to next monthly meeting – –

John Williams
Certificate
　　John Williams hath Produced a Removal Certificate from the
Monthly meeting of **Sandwich** Certif[y]ing him to be in unity with
friends and his outward affairs Sett[l]ed to Satisfaction which
is accepted – –

Bill for repair
=ing meeting
house
　　The friend appointed to Repair the meeting house have
given in their bill which is £10 " 14ˢ " 6ᵈ Lawfull money – –
This Meeting hath Collected 5ᵉ – 2ˢ – 10ᵈ old tennor and
the Collection is Referᵈ to next monthly meeting – –

order to pay
Tim Russell
　　The Treasurer is orderᵈ to pay **Timothy Russell**
five Dollars for Keeping the meeting house half a year

1ᵐᵒ 1772　At a Monthly meeting held in **Dartmouth** 20ᵗʰ 1ᵐᵒ 1772
the Representatives are **William Mosher** & **Barzillia**

Barᵈ⁽ᵗ⁾ Howland
paper read
Tucker both present, the Clerk Reports that **Barnabus** [**Barnabas**]
Howlands Jᵘ Paper of Denial hath been Read according
to the appointment of Last monthly meeting – –

Abra: Shearman
case referᵈ
　　The matter Concerning **Abraham Sherman** is Referᵈ
under the same Care as heretofore and **Barzillia Tucker**
and **William Mosher** and **David Smith** are ad[d]ed to the
fo[r]mer Committee to Labour with said **Sherman**
and make Report to next monthly meeting – –

Ben Shearman
paper read
　　Benjᵃ Shermans paper hath been Read and Returⁿd to
this meeting according to appointment of Last monthly
meeting, **Barnabus** [**Barnabas**] **Russell**s paper hath been read
and Returned to this meeting as ordered. – –

Jabez
Barker
case
　　The Committee appointed to Treat with **Jabez Barker Juner**
Report that they hant had an oppertunity to Discharge themselves
in that Respect Therefore they are Still Continued in that
Service and to make Report to next monthly meeting – –
Gideon Howlandˢ Paper hath been Read and Returnᵈ to this
meeting as orderᵈ　　and is as followeth – –

Confession
of G: H
　　To the Monthly meeting of friends to be held in **Dartmouth**
the 16ᵗʰ of the 12ᵐᵒ 1771
　　Beloved friends whereas I through unwatchfulness got into
a Passion and uttered Some unbecoming Expressions and fell
into a bodily Strife with **Zepheniah Anthony** all which
I am hertily Sorry for and do Condemn and Desire friends
would pass by my offence and Let me Remain under their

Care hoping through Divine Assistance I shall be more
Carefull for the time to come, from your friend

Gideon Howland

Report of Represen: to the Quar meeting　　The friends appointed to attend the Quarterly meeting
Report that they all Attended S^d meeting and have Produced
an Epistle from the same which hath been Read to Good
Satisfaction and the Contents are Earnestly Recommended

Hum: Smith & Shearman to be inform　to friends notice and Observation, **Jonathan Hussey** and
William Barker are appointed to take the Epistle of Last
Quarter and show that Parragraff to **Humphry Smith** and
Benj^a Thos & Peleg Sherman that Respects the appeal
of S^d **Smith** from this meeting to the Quarterly – And the above
Said friends are Desired to advise the above said Parties to
Comply therewith and to make Report to next monthly
meeting – –

money paid for London Stock　　**Caleb Russell** informs this meeting that he hath paid
Wm Redwood Four pounds Sterling in order to recruit
the yearly meeting Stock in **London** & Produc^d S^d **Readwood**[?]

meeting adjornd　Rece[i]pt for the Same – –.This meeting adjorns
to the 29th Instant after the meeting for Worship

mett　This Meeting meet according to Adjornment
the 29th 1st mo 1772 – The Representatives both Present

Wm Russ- parents' Consent　**Jonatha[n] Russell** & Wife of **Nantucket** Gave their Consent
in Writing to this meeting that their Son **Wm Russell**
Shall Proceed in marr[i]age with **Welthan Spencer**

W: R Intention of marrage　**William Russell** and **Welthan Spencer** Declar,d their
Intentions of marr[i]age at this meeting and were Desir^d
to wait untill next monthly meeting for their answer

B: R Intention of marrage　**Barnabus [Barnabas] Russell** and **Anna Howland** Declar^d their
Intentions of marriage and were Desir^d to wait untill
next monthly meeting for their answer. And **Jon^a Hussy [Hussey]**
and **Job Russell** is appointed to mak[e] Inquiry into **William
Russell^s** and **Barnabus [Barnabas] Russell^s** Clearness Respecting marr[i]age
and Conversation and make Report to next meeting

Tim Russell paid　　The Treasurer Reports that he hath paid **Timothy
Russell** five Dollars for keeping the meeting house half
a year -

accompts for repairing meet house to be viewed　**Caleb Russell & James Davies[Davis?]** is appointed to Inspect
into the accounts of the Committee that was to Repair
our meeting house and make Report to next monthly meeting

John: A Request Certificate	**John Allen** Requests a Certificate to the monthly meeting of **Sandwich** Certifying his Clearness Respecting marr[i]age & Conversation therefore **Prince Allen** & **Barzillia Tucker** are appointed to make inquiry into his Clearness and Conversation and Draught a Certificate for him If they find things Clear and make Report to the next meeting
Complaint against Danl Smith Ju^r	This Meeting is inform^d that **Daniel Smith Ju** hath Abused a Tranchent [Transient?] man named **Morrison** with blows for which Disorder he hath been Laboured with and Declines to Condemn it therefore **Abraham Tucker** and **Joseph Tucker** are appointed to Labour with him and make Report to next monthly meeting – –
Complaint against Zebelon Cornel	This Meeting is also inform^d that **Zebulon Cornal** [Cornell?] hath fallen into the Sin of fornication as appears by his Wives having a Child So Soon after marr[i]age for which Disorder he hath been Labour^d with by the overseers and Declines Condemning it therefore **Paul Russell** and **Joseph Tucker** and **Job Russell** are appointed to Labour with him and make Report to next monthly meeting
Complaint against A: Russell	This meeting is Inform^d that **Abner Russell** hath been accused on Oath of being guilty of Fornication for which Disorder the overseers hath Labored with him and he Declines to Condemn it therefore **Wm Sandford** and **Barzillia Tucker** is appointed to Labour with S^d **Russell** and Report to next monthly meeting
Elihu Gifford & David Chase papers	**Elihu Gifford** and **David Chase** hath given in papers to this meeting Condemning their marriing [marrying] out of the Unity of friends which is Refer^d under the care of **Caleb Russell Job Russell** and **Barzillia Tucker** and they to make Report to next monthly meeting – –
money order^d to pay for repairing meetg house	This Meeting is inform^d that there was 24 Pounds old tennor overplush money which was Rais^d to Recrute [recruit] the yearly meeting Stock in **London** Said money is Lodg^d in **Wm Anthony Ju** hands to pay to those that have Demands on the Committee for Repairing the meeting house
	This meeting Collected 7^£ – 0^[s] – 4^d old tennor – –
Bill on Alice Smiths acc^t	The Overseers of the Poor hath given in an account of Doing for **Alice Smith** 3^£ " 15^s " 0^[d] old tennor and the treasurrer is order^d to pay the money to **John Potter** and Report to next meeting

2mo 1772	At a Monthly Meeting held in **Dartmouth** ye 17th: 2mo 1772 The Representatives are **Wm Mosher** & **Barzillia Tucker** Present

Joseph Russell and Wife hath Given their Consent that their Son
Should Proceed in marr[i]age with **Anna Howland**

Wᵐ Russel
and
Bar Russel
Clearness

The fri[e]nds appointed to Inquire into **Wᵐ Russell**s
and **Barnabus** [Barnabas] **Russell**s Clearness Respecting marraige
and Conversation, Report that they have made inquiry
according to appointment and Dont find anything

Wᵐ Russel
and
Bar Russels
answer

to hinder their Proseeding **William Russell** & **Welthan**
Spencer, and **Barnabus** [Barnabas] **Russell** & **Anna Howland** appearᵈ
at this meeting for their answer which was that Each
Couple might Proceed to take Each other in Marraige
in Some Convenient time before next monthly meeting
Advising with the overseers that this meeting shall appoint for that
Purpose, and **Caleb Russell** & **James Davis** are appointed to see

W: R: answer

William Russells and **Welthan Spencer** marraige Consomated in
good order and make Report to next monthly meeting, And
Jonathan Hussey & **Job Russell** are appointed to see **Barnabus** [Barnabas]

B: R answer

Russells and Anna **Howland**s marriage Consomated in good
order and make Report to the next monthly meeting – –

Caleb Russell and **James Davis** Reports that they have
inspected into the Committee Accounts that was appointed to
Repair the Meeting House and find Sᵈ Accounts to be Just
which this meeting approveth – –

J: Allen
Certificate

This meeting hath signed a Certificate for **John Allen**
to the monthly meeting of **Sandwich** Certifiing his Clearness
Respecting marraige & Conversation – –The friends appointed

Abraham
Shearman
Case

to Labour with **Abraham Sherman** Report that they have Treated with
him and he gave them no Real incouragment [encouragement] of Reforming from
his Disorder in taking too much Spiritous Licquor. therefore the
above Said Committee is appointed to Draw a paper of Denial against
Sᵈ **Sherman** and to Shew [show] Sᵈ paper to him and to Labour with him
as they may find freedom and make Report to the next meeting

Jabez Barkers
Case

The Committee appointed to Labour with **Jabis** [Jabez] **Barker Jᵘ** Report
that they hant had an oppertunity to Discharge themselves with
him though they went to his house & Did not find him at home
Therefore they are still Continued in that Service & to make Report
to next meeting

Hum Smith
informed
respecting
his appeal

The friends appointed to Inform **Humphry Smith** of the Judgment
of the Quarterly meeting Respecting his Appeal Report that they
have fulfilled their Appointment – –

The friends Appointed to Labour with **Daniel Smith** for his

Dan Smith
paper

Disorder Report that he gave them a Degree of Satisfaction
and the S^d **Daniel Smith** hath Given in a paper to this
meeting Condemning his Disorder which is Referd to next
meeting under the Care of the afore Said Committee and then
they to make Report.

Zebulon
Cornels
case continued

The friends appointed to Labour **Zebulon Cornal** [**Cornell**] Report
Report that they hant had an oppertunity to Discharge themselves
in that Respect therefore they are Continued in that Service and to
make Report to next monthly meeting – –

Abner Russel
case continued

The friends appointed to Labour with **Abner Russell** Report
that they hant had an oppertunity to treat with him therefore
they are Continued in that Service and to make Report to
next monthly meeting – –

Elihu Gifford
&
David Chase
papers

The friends appointed to have the Cair [care] of the matter Concerning
Elihue Gifford and **David Chase** Report, that they have Labour^d
with Said **Gifford** for being in Company with Some People
that was Shuting [shooting?] Cakes[cocks?] at the time Called Crismus [Christmas]
and they have Given in Papers Condem[n]ing their marriing [marrying] outt
of the Unity of Friends and **David Chase**^s is Refer^d under the same
fri[e]nds

J. Potter
paid

The Treasurer Reports that he hath paid **John Potter**
£3 – ^s15 old Tennor According to Appointment

D: Allen
Confession

David Allen hath Given in a Paper to this meeting Condemning
his being in Company with the Rabble at the time Called
Crismus and Shot a Goos[e] for which he hath Condemn^d
in writing which is accepted – –

To Revise
minutes

Samuel Smith Job Russell Wm Anthony J^u Thos Hicks
are appointed to Revise and Correct this meeting[s] minutes
and papers in order to be Recorded and make Report to the
next monthly meeting

women
want
assistance
about D: W:

This Meeting being Informed that there is a Report about
Deborah Willbur which is of such a Gross & Scandalous Nature
that the women friends desire assistance from us therefore
this meeting appoints **Job Russell Jon^a** [**Jonathan**] **Hussey** and **Prince**
Allen for that Service

3mo
1772

adjourn

At a Monthly meeting held in **Dartmouth** ye 16: 3mo 1772
the Representatives are **Wm Barker** & **Samuel Smith** both Request
this meeting Adjourns to the Last forth Day in this month
it being the 25 Instant – –

mett by Adjornment   At a Monthly meeting meet According to Adjournment this 25th of 3mo 1772 the Representatives being Called both Present Whereas a Committee of the Quarterly meeting Requests this meeting to Adjorn till the third Day of next month which this meeting Concurs

Adjornment   with and Doth Adjourn to Sd 3rd Day and to meet at the usual hour

mett by Adjornment   This Meeting being meet by Adjornment the 3rd of ye 4mo 1772 the Representatives being Called **Wm Barker** present, This meeting Adjorns to the 4 Instant – –

met by adjornm   This meeting meet by Adjornment the 4 Day of ye 4mo 1772 the Representatives being Called are **William Barker** & **Saml [Samuel] Smith** both present

Barnas: Russell marriage   The friends appointed to See **Barnabus [Barnabas] Russell**s and **Anna Howland**s marr[i]age Consomated Report that they both attended the marrage which was Consomated in a Degree orderly Except the young mans apparel – –

This meeting hath Signed a paper of Denial against

Paper of Denial Signd against Abram Shearman   **Abraham Sherman** for a Disorder mentioned in the former minutes and the Clerk is appointed to Read Said paper at the Close of a first Days meeting for worship and to make Report to next monthly meeting, Said paper Recorded in next page

The Committee appointed to Labour with **Jabiz [Jabez] Barker Ju** Report as followeth, which is Excepted

Committee Report about J: Barker   According to Appointment of Las[t] monthly meeting we have Disco[u]rsed with **Jabez Barker jur** on the account of his Suffering his Daughters to be married in his House, and had a Long Conference with him on that Subject, Endea= =vouring (according to our Abilities) to Convince him of his Error therein, We likewise Shewed him a Coppy of part of a minute made in our yearly Meeting in the year 1708, which we think is very Clear against Such Conduct as his yet he would by no means Condemn the Same, not yet own that he had broaken any Good order of friends but used many words tending to Justify himself therein

Given forth this 26th of ye 12mo 1771 by your friends-   ⎧ **Saml Smith** and this meeting being Clear of further Labour with him do   ⎨ **Prince Allen** Deny the said **Jabez Barker** from being a member of our Society   ⎩ **Barzillia Tucker** & from under our Cair & **Paul Russell** is to Inform him of his Denial & make Report to next monthly meeting

A: Shermans Denial ought to been Record: in ye forgoing page   From our Monthly Meeting of friends held in **Dartmouth** by Adjornment the 4th Day of ye 4mo 1772

Whereas **Abraham Sherman Seanor [Senior]** being under the Care of our Said meeting, But he not giving heed to that Divine

Power to wit the Spirit of Truth in his heart, has so far
Deviated from our Christian profession as to be in the
frequent practice of Drinking Spiritous Liquor, in an Exce=
=ssive manner, for which Transgressions friends having from
time to time in Love and tenderness Labour,[d] with him
in order thereby to be Instrumental to Reclaim him from
the Error of his ways, But their Labour of Love in that
Respect not having its Desired affect therefore for the
Clearing of Truth and our Christian Profession from such
Reproachfull Practices we think we Can do no Less than
to Deny him, And do hereby Disown the said **Abraham
Sherman** from being a member of our Society Nevertheless
Desiring if it be Consistant with Divine Preasure [pleasure?]
that he may through an Unfeigned Repentance and
Reformation witness his peace to be made with the
Lords,   Signed in and on behalf of Said meeting by

Job Russell Clerk

Miniutes Revised
The Committee appointed to Revise and Correct
the Monthly Meeting minutes and Papers Report, that they
have fulfilled their appointment and have Left said minutes
and papers with **Samuel Smith** to Record – –

Denial of Zeb. Cornel
The Greater part of the Committee appointed to Labour with
Zebulon Cornal [Cornell] Report that they have Discharg,[d] themselves
in Labouring with him, And now this meeting being Clear
of any further Labour with the Said **Cornal** have Concluded
to Deny him and do appoint **Sam[el] Smith** to Draught [draft] a paper
of Denial and bring it to next monthly meeting – –

Complaint against David Smith
The Overseers hath handed a Complaint to this meeting
against **David Smith** for Refusing to Submit a Controversy
to arbitration, Subsisting between him Self and **Abner
Russell** and **Daniel Russell**, And this meeting hath Given
Said **David** a Coppy of Said Complaint agreeable to his Request
but this meeting being Small by reason of the Extremity of
of the weather, the appointing a Committee on that account is Refer[d]
to the Adjornment of this meeting – –
The Queries hath been Read and Answer[d] in this meeting

mett
This Meeting adjorns to the Seventh Day of this Instant at the
Eleventh hour in the forenoon – –

met by Adjornment
This Meeting met according to adjournment the 7 Day 4[mo] 1772
The Representatives being Called **William Barker** and **Samuel Smith** Present

Report of W[m] Russells marriage not made
The friends appointed to see **W[m] Russell**s & **Welthan Spencer** marraige
Consomatted have not made any Report therefore **Abraham Tucker** and

Joseph Tucke[r] are appointed to Call on them to know the Reason of their not making Report – –

Dan Smith case refer^d
This Meeting has not had a Return Respecting **Daniel Smith** it is Refer,^{d} under the Same Care as heretofore and they to make report to next monthly meeting – –

Case of David Chase refer^d
The friends appointed to Treat with **David Chase** Report that they hant [haven't] had an oppertunity since Last month therefore it is Refer,^{d} under their Care and they to make Report to next meeting

Case of Abner Russell refer^d
The Friends appointed to Treat with **Abner Russell** Report that they hant had any Oppertunity with him therefore the matter is Refer,^{d} under the Same Cair [care] as heretofore and they to make Report to next monthly meeting

To Visit those possesed of Slavees
The Friends appointed to visit those that Pos[s]ess Slaves Report, That they have not Discharg,^{d} themselves in that Respect therefore they are Continued

According to the Referrance of the former Sitting of this Meeting Do appoint **Joseph Tucker Abraham Howland**

Complaint against D: Smith
Benjamin Howlands 2nd **Barnabus [Barnabas] Mosher** to Inquire into the above Complaint Respecting **David Smith** and Labour as they may find accation [occasion] and make Report as Soon as Conveniency will admitt – –

Quar meeting Collectio refer^d
Our Quarterly Collection is Refer,^{d} to next monthly meeting

Jos Rotch Ju^r request a Certificate to London
Joseph Rotch j^{ur} informs this meeting that he Intends to **London** and Desires a few Lines as ^{a} Certificate therefore **Samuel Smith** & **William Anthony J^u** is appointed to make inquirey into his Conversation and Draught [draft] Draught a Certificate if they find things Clear on his Behalf and bring it to the Monthly Meeting as Soon as they Can

One of the Overseers Informs this meeting that he hath

Wm Smith Complain^d of
taken two friends with him and Labour,^{d} with **William Smith** for Taking two [*sic*] much Spirittous Licqour for which he Niglects to Condemn and Likewise this Meeting is Inform,^{d} that the Said **Smith** has Purchased Land under such Ministeral incombrances [encumbrances] as is not Consistant with our Profession therefore this meeting Do appoint **Samuel Smith** & **John Potter** & **Philip Trafford** to Labour with the Said **William Smith** and make Report to next monthly Meeting

This Meeting hath Signed an Epistle to the Quarterly meeting to be held next at **Porthmouth**, And **Joseph Tucker Wm Barker**

Representatives to the Quar
Samuel Smith and **Wm Anthony j^{ur}** are appointed to attend the

Above Said Meeting and to Present the Epistle with the Answers
to the Queries and to make Report next monthly Meeting —

4ᵐᵒ 1772   At a Monthly Meeting held in **Dartmouth** 20: 4ᵐᵒ 1772
the Representatives are **Caleb Russell** & **William Anthony jᵘʳ**
both Present, The Clerk Reports that he hant Read
Abraham Sherman,ˢ Paper of Denial, as Appointed, by Reason
of his Wives Request and said Clerk is Still under appointment
to Read Said ˄ᴾᵃᵖᵉʳ at the Close of a first Day meeting for Worship before
next Monthly meeting and then make Report – –

    Paul Russell Reports that he hath inform,ᵈ **Jabez Barker jᵘʳ**
of his Denial according to the appointment of Last monthly meeting
    This Meeting hath Signed a Paper of Denial against

Z: Cornel **Zebulon Cornal** [**Cornell**] for the Sin of Fornication and the Clerk is
Deni[e]d appointed to Read said paper at the Close of a first Day meeting
for Worship befor next monthly meeting and then make Report

    Caleb Russell Reports the Reason that he and **James Davis** Did
not make Report at the Adjornment of the said meeting of their attending
of the Marraige of **Wᵐ Russell** & **Welthen** [**Welthan**] **Spencer** was by Reason of
the Extremity of the weather, And they Now have made Report
that they attended Said Marraige which was Consomatted in tolerable
Good order – –

D: Smith 3ᵈ **Daniel Smith yᵉ 3ʳᵈ** hat[h] Given in a Paper to this meeting Condemning
paper his falling into a bodily strife with **Michel Morriss** which this meeting
Concludes to Except with Provisal that he Cause Said paper to ˄ᵇᵉ Read
at the Close of a first Days meeting for Worship before next monthly meeting
he being Present, and then ~~the~~ Return Said paper to Said meeting and
make Report of its being Read – –

Case of David The Friends appointed to Treat with **David Chase** Report that
Chase Con- they hant had an opportunity to Discharge themselves in that Respect.
tinued therefore they are Still Continued in the Same Service and to make
Report as Soon as they have an Oppertunity to Discharge their trust

Case of Abner The Friends appointed to Labour **Abner Russell** Report that they have
Russell referᵈ made Some Progress in that Respect and Desire the matter to be Referᵈ
which is Referᵈ under their Cair [care] untill next monthly meeting and then
to make Report – –

R: M This Meeting is Inform,ᵈ that **Rachel** [**Merithew?**] is about to Remove
Request a within the Compass of **Sandwich** monthly meeting and Desires a
Certifiate Certificate therefore **Joseph Tucker** & **Paul Russell** & **Wᵐ Mosher** are
appointed to Joine the Women friends to make Inquirey into her Circum=
=stances and Consider whether it may be best for her to Remove and

If they think it Necessary to Draught [draft] a Certificate for her and bring it
to the next monthly meeting – –

Case of Wᵐ Smith referᵈ

The friends appointed to Labour with **William Smith** Report that they
have Labour,ᵈ with him and he Condemn,ᵈ his taking two [*sic*] much Spiritous
Licquors Therefore the matter is Referd under their Cair and they to make
Report when they had an oppertunity fully to Discharge themselves
in that Respect – –

Representatives to the Q: meeting

The Friends appointed to attend the Quarterly meeting
Report that they all Attended according to appointment
and have Produced an Epistle from the same which hath
been Read and kindly Accepted – –

Report consern= =ing building a meeting house at Bedford

The Committee appointed to Consider about the
Request of the friends at **Bedford** building a Meeting
house; Report as followeth which is accepted

According to appointment of the Monthly Meeting,
we have Confer,ᵈ with the friends at **Bedford** and weightily
Consid[e]red their Requse [Request?] in Regard to building a meeting house
there, and altho we look favoura[b]ly on their Sᵈ Request
yet we think it would be better for them to make Some Trial
of holding a meeting in a Private House before they build
a House for that purpose in order for Some Degree of Experance [Experience?]
of Keeping up their meeting in the Authority of truth, which
would be a farther Satisfaction to us in that matter, we not
being so fully Satisfied wholly to Grant their Request before some
Such Trial be made, Given forth this 20ᵗʰ day yᵉ 4ᵐᵒ 1772

by your friends　　　　**Jonathan Hussey : Wᵐ Sandford**

　　　　　　　　　　　Prince Allen　　: Wᵐ Mosher

　　　　　　　　　　　Samᵘˡ Smith　　: Barzillia Tucker

Concerning Reprinting Wᵐ Sewels History

This Meeting is Inform,ᵈ that friends at **Philidelphia** are about to
Reprint **Wᵐ Sewel**s History, And this Meeting Conclud[e]s to Subscribe
for one Book,¹² and **Samuel Smith** & **Barzillia Tucker** & **Caleb Russell**
are appointed to Receive Subscriptions – –

　　　　There was Collected 2ᵉ-19ˢ-5ᵈ old Tenno[r] and the Collection is Referᵈ
to the next monthly meeting This meeting Adjorns to the 29 Instant

adjourn after the meeting of Worship – –

mett This Meeting meet According to Adjournment the

---

12. William Sewel (ca. 1650–ca. 1725) was a Dutch Friend. His *The History of the Rise, Increase, and Progress of the Christian People Called Quakers, Intermixed with Several Remarkable Occurrences. Written Originally in Low-Dutch by William Sewel, and by Himself Translated into English. Now Revis'd and Published'd with Some Amendments* (London: J. Sowle, 1722) The edition referenced here is printed in Burlington, New Jersey, by Isaac Collins in 1774.

29th 4mo 1772 – The Representatives being Called **Caleb Russell**
and **William Anthony J**ur both present, This meeting hath Sign,d

Jos Rotch Ju
Certificate
a Certificate for **Joseph Roach [Rotch] j**ur to friends in the Citty of
London Old England

5mo
1772
At a Monthly Meeting held in **Dartmouth** ye 18th : 5mo 1772
The Representatives are **Caleb Russell & Tho**s **Hicks** both Present
Daniel Smiths paper ~~of Denial~~ hath been Read according
to the appointment of Last monthly meeting, and is as followeth

D: Smith
paper
To the Monthly Meeting of friends in **Dartmouth**, Esteemed friends
whereas I being of my watch and got into a bodily Strife with
Mikel morris whereby I have transgrees d [*sic*] the good orders of friends
notwithstanding the agravation was great yet taking into Consideration
the bad Effect of Passion, Which transgression I Due [Do] not Justifie
but am sorry for & do Condemn & Desire that friends would pass
by my offence and Still Continue me under their Care
hoping to be more Car[e]full for the futur in such Respects
from your well wishing friend – –   **Daniel Smith** – –
     the 17 of ye 2nd month 1772

~~Da~~ **Zebulon Cornal**,s paper of Denial hath been Read as order,d
and is as followeth

Z Cornel
paper of
Denial
Whereas **Zebulon Cornell** Son of our friends **Daniel Cornell** and
his Deceas,d wife **Elisabeth**, having had his Education Amongst
friends & under the care of this meeting, yet he hath so for [far?] departed
from the Simplicity of Truth and the Testimony thereof in this own heart
as to fall into the Sin of Fornication as appears by his wifes having a
Child So Soon after Marraige and friends having Labour,d with him
in Love in order to Convince him of the Evil thereof, and that he
may be Restor,d to the way of Truth, but our Labour & Cair [care] therein
not Obtaining the Desired Effect to the Satisfaction of this meeting
and friends beleiving they are clear of him in that Respect do
hereby publickly disown him ye Sd **Zebulon C** from under the Care of this meeting
the 20 ye 4mo 1772 by – –   **Job Russell** Clerk

Case of David
Chase Continued
The friends appointed to Labour with **David Chase**
Report that they hant had on oppertunity to Treat with
him therefor they are Still Continued in that Service
and **Adam Gifford** is ades [added?] to them and they to make Report
to next monthly Meeting

Case of Abner
Russell
*Continu*d
The friends appointed to Labour with **Abner Russell**
Report that he is gone from home and they have not
had an oppertunity to Treat with him and they are Still

Continued in that Service and to make Report when they
have an oppertunity to Discharge themselves in that Respect

Case of Rachel
Merithew
Continued
The friends appointed to Inquire into **Rachel Marithew**s
Request for a Removal Certificate, Report that Inquiry hath
been made, and her affairs not being all Settle,ᵈ they are
Continued in that Service and make Report to the next monthly
meeting

Abra:
Shearman
denial not read
The Clerk Reports that he hant Read **Abraham Sherman**s
Paper of Denial by Reason of some hopes of a Reformation
and now this meeting se[e]ing no real sign of Reformation to Continue
the Clerk to Read Said paper before next monthly meeting
and then make Report

C: Green
Certificate
Accepted
Caleb Green hath Removed within the Compass of this meeting
and hath Produced a Removal Certificate from the Monthly
Meeting held at **East Greenwich** which is Accepted –

The friends appointed to have the Cair of thee meeting held in
Allen's Neck (So Called) Report that they attended the Meeting which
was held Somewhat Satisfactory – –

Complaint
against
J:A and
D: Gifford
The Overseers hath Exhibited a Complaint against **Jedidiah
Allen** for Striking **Samuel Gifford** Son of **Daniel Gifford** –
And they also have Exhibited a Complaint against the Sᵈ **Daniel
Gifford** for Prosecuting the Said **Jedediah Allen** in the [Law?] for
Striking his Son. Therefore this meeting do Appoint **Wᵐ Sandford
Caleb Russell** & **Samuel Smith** to Inquire into the whole matter
Respecting the two above said Complaints and Labour as they may
find freedom and make Report to next monthly meeting
This Meeting hath Collected £5=8ˢ=6ᵈ old Tennor

6ᵐᵒ
1772
At a Monthly Meeting held in **Dartmouth** the 15ᵗʰ 6ᵐᵒ 1772
the Representatives are **Jonathan Hussey** & **Seth Sherman** both Present
Whereas the yearly meeting at **Rhod Island** is now in being for
which Reason this meeting Doth Adjourn to the 22 day of this

Adjourn Instant after the Meeting for Worship which meeting of worship
begins at the Eleventh hour – –

mett At a Monthly Meeting meet by Adjournment 22:6ᵐᵒ 1772
the Representatives being Called both Present. The Committee

David Chase
give in a paper
appointed to Labour with **David Chase** for marring[marrying] out of the
Unity of friends, Report that he gave them a Degree of
Satisfaction & the Said Chase has given in a Paper Condemning
his manning[marrying] out of the Unity of friends which is Referᵈ under
under the care of sᵈ Committee and they to make Report to next
monthly meeting

Rachel Merithew Certificate not prepar^d The friends appointed to Prepare a Removal Certificate for **Rachel Merithew** Report that they have not Prepar^d Said Certificate for the Same Reson as was last monthly meeting therefore S^d Committee are Still Continued in that Service and to make Report to the next monthly meeting – –

Abra Shear= =man's paper read The Clerk Reports that he hath Read **Abraham Sherman**'s paper of Denial according to the appointment of Last monthly meeting ·

Jededi Allen Case Continued The Committee appointed to Labour with **Jedidiah Allen** last monthly meeting Report that they Labour^d with S^d **Allen** and the matter is not fully setted[settled] to their Satisfaction therefore they are Still Continued in that Service and **Prince Allen** aded to them and they to mak Report next monthly meeting – –

Women Inform y^t they accept H: Bennet's paper The Women friends inform this meeting that **Hannah Bennitt** hath Given in a Paper to their meeting Condemning her Disorder in falling into the Sin of fornication as appears by her having a Child so soon after marriage which hath been Read & Accepted by their meeting which this meeting Concurs with, and the Women friends also Inform that **Mary Howland** wife of **Luthan Howland** hath Condemned her marring [marrying] out of the Unity of friends, to the Satisfaction of their meeting which this meeting

Alice Philips Received Concurs with, And the women friends Likewise Inform that they minited **Alice Philips** a Member under their Cair which this meeting Conkers[Concurs] with – –

Case of Daniel Gifford continu^d The Committee appointed to Labour with **Daniel Gifford** for Prosicuting **Jedidiah Allen** in the Law, Reports that they have treated with him, and the matter is not fully made up to their Satisfaction therefore the Said friends are still Continued in that Service and make Report to next monthly meeting

L: Mosher Request to betaken under friend's Care **Lemuel Mosher** Requests to be Admitted under friends Cair therefore **Paul Russell** & **Barzillia Tucker** & **Joseph Gifford** and **Adam Gifford** are appointed to Inquire into the Said **Mosher**s Life and Conversation and take an Oppertunity of [Solled?][Solid] Conference with him and make Report to next Monthly meeting – –

Joseph Russell Dan Gifford Tim Gifford Isaac Howland in practice of runing goods This meeting is Informed from the Preparative meeting that **Joseph Russell Daniel Gifford Timothy Gifford** [?] **Isaac Howland** hath been in the Practice of Runing Goods for which Disorder the Overseers have Laboured with them for, And they Decline to Condemn it, Therefore **Samuel Smith Joseph Gifford Prince Allen John Potter** & **Philip Allen** are appointed to Labour with them in order to show them the Error of Such Practices and make Report to next Monthly meeting

Queries answer^d The Queries hath been Read and Answered in this meeting This meeting hath Collected £7:12^s:10 Old tennor

Adjourn This Meeting Ajourns to the 24ᵗʰ of this Instant after
the meeting for Worship

mett At a Monthly Meeting met According to Adjornment the
24: 6ᵐᵒ 1772 the Representatives being Called both present
This meeting Adjourns to the 3ʳᵈ Day of next month after the
meeting of worship – –

· At a Monthly Meeting met According to Adjournment
this 3ʳᵈ Day 7ᵐᵒ 1772 the Representatives being Called both present

Order to The Treasurer is Ordered to pay **Timothy Russell** five Dollars for
pay Tim. keeping the Meeting House half a year & Report to next mᵒ Meeting

Ben Allen The Overseers of the poor hath brought an Account from **Benj:**
Accomᵗ. **Allen** for helping **Rachel Sole** 155 weeks at 3/ [?][p] week which [?][amounts]
to £23–5ˢ Which account this meeting Approveth – –

The friends Appointed to Assist the Women friends in Labouring
Committee with **Deborah Willbur** Report that the matter Labours very
to Assist Difficuld and they Desire Some more Assistance, therefore Do
the Women appoint **Caleb Russell** & **Samuel Smith** to Join them in that
to Labour Case and they to make Report as Soon as they are Ready.
with D: W:

This Meeting hath Signᵈ an Epistle to the Quarterly meeting
Represent: Next to be held at **Newport** – And our friends **Caleb Russell**
to yᵉ Quarterly **Jonᵃ Hussey Paul Russell Wᵐ Sandford** & **Wᵐ Mosher** are
appointed to attend the above Sᵈ Quarterly meeting and to
Present the Epistle with yᵉ Answers to the Queries and make
Report to next monthly meeting – Our Quarterly Collection
is Referᵈ to next monthly meeting

7ᵐᵒ At a Monthly meeting held in **Dartmouth** yᵉ 20: 7ᵐᵒ 1772
1772 the Representatives are **Wᵐ Anthony jᵘʳ** and **Samˡˡ Smith** both Present
Thoˢ Philips & his Wife hath given their Consent in writing that their
Daughter **Allice** Should Should Proceed in Marriage with **Elisheb Smith**
Elisheb **Elisheb Smith** & **Elice Philips** Declared their Intentions of
Smith pro Marriage and were Desirᵈ to wait untill the next monthly meet:
=posal of For their Answer And **Adam Gifford** & **Wᵐ Mosher** are
marriage appointed to Inquire into the young mans Clearness Respecting
marriage & Conversation and make Report to next monthly meeting

The friends appointed to have the Care of the matter Respecting
Case of **David Chase** Report that they hant anything new to Inform this
David Chase meeting – And sᵈ **Chase** is not Present therefore the matter is Referᵈ
Referᵈ under the Same cair as heretofore and they to make Report to next
monthly meeting – –

The friends Intrusted with the Cair of **Rachel Mearithew** Certificate

Report that they have not prepair^d one, therefor they are
Continued in that Caire and to make Report to next monthly meeting

L: M matter Refer^d   The friends Appointed to treat with **Leamuel Mosher** on account
of his Request Report that they have made Some Progress in
that matter and they think it best to Refer the matter
for the Present, therefore it is Refer^d under the same friends
Cair and they to make when they think necessary – –

Tim Russell paid   The Treasurrer Reports that he hath paid **Timothy Russell** five
Dollars as Ordered – The Committee appointed to Labour

D:G & J:A setled their Controversy   and Advise with **Daniel Gifford** and **Jedediah Allen** Report
that the Controversy is made up between them to Satisfaction and
the [?][S^{d]} **Gifford** hath Given in a paper Condemning his Prosecuting the

Jede^h: Allen paper refer^d   Said **Allen** in the Law Contrary to the Advice of the Overseers advice
which paper is Accepted, and the S^d **Allen** not being Present his
paper is not Accepted but is Refer^d to next monthly meeting

Report of those that run goods   The Committee appointed to Labour with those friends that
hath been in the Practice of Runing of Goods Report that
they have made Some Progress in that matter and have
found Some Satisfaction, tho none of them have fully
Condemned S^d Disorder – –

Reports from Qly meeting   The friends Appointed to attend the Quarterly Meeting Report
that they all Attended According to Appointment

L: Mosher Denied   The Women friends inform that they have Denied **Elisabeth Mosher**
wife of **Leamuel Mosher** for Marr[y]ing out of the Unity of
friends which this meeting Concurs with – –

Com^{tee} Report on those that posses Slaves   The Committee appointed to labour with those friends that
Possess Slaves Report as followeth which is Accepted
Agreable to the Appointment of ye M^{o.} Meeting, We have
Visited those Friends that Possess Slaves belonging to this
meeting and have had much Conference with them
on that account Endeavoring (according to our abilities) to

[?]
Since ^{ye} above account some of us have been with Isaac Howl who gave some of Compliance   Convince them of the Evil of that Iniquitous Practice of Keeping
our fellow Creatures in Bondage but Several of them yet Refuses
to Comply with the advice of friends in that matter; who are
Joseph Russell who has Two Negroes in Bondage & Refuses to set them at
Liberty **Isaac Howland** y^e [2nd] one Negro in bondage & Refuses to free him
    Rebecca [?] [**Slocum**]
widow, three Negroes in Bondage of full age (& one or two under age) and Refuses
to free any of them yet But has (as she saith) order^d them to be free in her
will, **John Russell** we think complies with friends Advice who has

let one goe at Liberty & has one under age that he says he Intends to
free, and have order^d it So in his will, **Wm Sandford** one Negroe but
he fully complies with friends advice by frankly Setting her at Liberty
Peleg Slocum having Negroes one of full age to be free & has So far Complies as
to free them at Six & twenty] Laying up five Dollars yearly after that
for Security wherefore upon the whole we find that **Joseph Russell** [**I Howland**]
& **Rebecca Slocum** widow are offenders in this matter by keeping their Negroes
in bondage when they are fit for freedom after they have been Repeatedly admonis
to Comply with ye order of friends in that Case. Neith **Peleg Slocum** so fully comply
as could be desired but upon further Labour in a Spirit of Love we are in some hope
he will more fully Comply therewith – by your Comittee this 20th 4mo 1772

Job Russell   **Caleb Russell**

Barzillai Tucker   **Benj^a Howland**

friends to Labour with Negro masters & those that Run goods
And the above s^d Committee are Appointed to Labour with
the above Said friends that appear Difficient Respecting of
keeping Slaves in Bondage, And also to Labour with those
friends that appear Difficient in Regard to the Clandestand
Trade in the foregoing Minutes And make Report when ready

Epistles Receiv^d
This Meeting hath Received a Number of **London** printed
Epistles with a Transcrip of the last Epistle from the yearly
held at **RhodIsland** – –

D: Wilbor Denied
This Meeting hath Signed a paper of Denial Against
Deborah Willbur for ye Offences therein mentioned And the
Clerk is appointed to Read Said Paper at the Close of a first Day
Meeting before the next monthly meeting and then make
Report Said paper is as followeth

Complaint against Daniel Russell
Josep Rotch and Sons hath Exhibited a Complaint against **Daniel**
Russell for Neglecting to pay them their Due, And the Overseers inform
that they have bestowed much Labour in order for him to Comply with
their Request which hath Proved inaffectual therfore this meeting
Do appoint **Philip Allen** & **Prince Allen David Shepherd** & **James Davile**
to Labour with the Said **Daniel Russell** and to make Report to next mon: meeting –

Report of the Com^{tee} on Jedidi Wood's Heirs
The Committee appoint to joine with **Coakset** Committee to
Labour with heirs of **Jedediah** & **Keziah Wood** Report as followeth which
is Accepted

To the Monthly Meetings of **Dartmouth** and **Accoakset**
We the Subscribers being a Committee appointed by the monthly meeting
to Labour with the Heirs **Jedidiah** and **Keziah Wood** to bring them
to a Settlement of the Estate Left them by S^d **Jedediah** & **Keziah Wood**
And we having meet together with S^d heirs from time to time, and Labour^d

in Love with them to Compose and finally Settle S^d Estate among them
Selves, or Submitt to friends as Arbitrators to Settle the Same, but
our Labour proving Ineffectually with them, And it is our Advice
and Judgment that S^d Heirs apply to the Judge of Pro[?][Probate] in order to
have the Estate Setted, Or Compose a Settlement among themselves
for we find the Circumstances of the affair to be such we think best not
to Compell S^d heirs to Arbitration

from your Committee the 29 ye 6mo 1772

> **Pelleg Huddlestone**
> **Joseph Tripp**
> **Wm Anthony Juner**
> **Barzillia Tucker**
> **Abial Maccomber**
> **Job Russell**

This Meeting is Inform^d by the Preparative meeting that **Jacob Mott** hath fallen into Several Disorders Particularly in taking
too much Spirittous Liquors & in Using bad Language & in
Abusive behavour & in Niglecting attending for Worship and

Committee to labour with J.M. Discipline for which Several Disorders he hath been Treated with
and gave no Satisfaction therefore **Joseph Tucker Wm Sandford** and
Abraham Tucker are appointed to Labour with the S^d **Moot** as they
may find Accation and make Report to next monthly meeting

To Collect account of friends Sufferings This Meeting is Informed that **Pelleg Smith** hath in his Cair
Some Accounts of the Sufferings of Friends therefore **Samuel Smith**
and **Wm Anthony j^u** are Appointed to Inspect the Accounts and
make Report the next monthly meeting

Received Transcrip from ye ye^a meeting This Meeting hath Received a Transcript of Several matters
Concluded on as Rules of our Society at our Last yearly meeting
at **Rhod Island** & **Samuel Smith** & **William Anthony j^u** Are appointed
to Place the Above Said Rules under Proper heads in our Book of
Discipline and make Report to the next monthly meeting

To collect money for repairing meet. house **Benjamin Howland David Shepherd Barnabus Mosher Prince Allen**
are Appointed to Collect money by way of Subscription for to
Defray the Charges of Repairing our Meeting house and to
make Report as Soon as they Can

24 books Subscribed for This Meeting hath Subscribed for Twenty four Books of [Sewl?]
Histories and **Caleb Russell** is appointed to Send the money for
Said Books to **Wm Redwood** or **Joseph Jacobs** and make Report
as Soon as he Can – The Treasurer hath paid one Dollar
to **Caleb Russell** for to Send for one of Sd books for this meeting

8mo 1772 At a Monthly Meeting held in **Dartmouth** ye 17 ye 8 mo 1772

The Representatives are **Wm Mosher** & **Barzillia Tucker** Present

Joseph Smith hath Given his Consent that his Son **Elishep Smith**

may Proceed in Marraige with **Alice Philips** – The friends [appointed?]

to Inquire into **Elishep Smith**'s Clearness Respecting marriage and

Conversation Report that they have made Inquiry, And Don't

find anything to hinder his Proceeding in marraige –

E:S & E:P
come for **Elishep Smith** & **Alice Philips** Appeard for their Answer which was
their Answer

that they might Proceed to take Each other in Marriage in Some

Convenient time before the next monthly meeting Advising with

the Overseers that this meeting shall appoint for that Purpose

and **Adam Gifford** & **Wm Mosher** are appointed to see their marriage

Consomated in good order and make Report to next mo meeting

Report Re= The Report Respecting **David Chase** not appearing to good Satisfaction
=specting
David Chase by reason of his neglecting of Attending of meetings, And this

meeting not being fully Satisfied about Receiving his Acknowledgment

therefore the matter is Referd Under the Cair of the Same friends

that was appointed in that Case Same months past & **Paul Russell** is aded

to them and they to make Report when they think proper –

Deb: Wilbur The Clerk Reports that he hath Read **Deborah Willbur**s paper of
denial read
Denial According to Appointment –

Jedidi Allen The Paper that **Jedediah Allen** gave into this meeting Some
paper accepd
months past Condemning his Striking **Samuel Gifford** has been

now read, and Considred, which is Accepted provided he Cause Sd paper

to be Read at the Close of a first Day meeting for Worship before next mo meeting

he being Present and Return sd paper to sd meeting and make Report of its

being read sd paper is as followeth

J. Allens   To the Monthly Meeting of Friends to be held in **Dartmouth** 18th 9mo 1772
paper
Whereas I through unwatchfulness have Struck **Samuel Gifford** Son of **David**

Gifford, Which I am hertily Sorry for and do Condemn, hoping God will

forgive me, and friends So perhaps by mine offence as to let me Remain

under their Care hoping for time to Come I shall be more Carefull

Jedediah Allen

This meeting hath signed a Removal Certificate for our friend

H. Bennet **Hannah Bennitt** wife of **Robert Bennitt** to the Monthly meeting
Certificate
Rhod Island The friends appointed to Labour with **Jacob Mott** Report that

Jacob Mott they have taken an Oppertunity and treated with him and he gave
Case
them no Satisfaction therefore **Samuel Smith** is aded to the Committee

and they to inspect into his Disorders and Labour as they may find

Accation and make Report to next monthly meeting –

Report on inspec= =ting friend's Sufferings	**Samuel Smith** & **Wᵐ Anthony jᵘ** Reports that they have made Some Progress in Inspecting of the Accounts of friends Sufferings as Appointed but have not gone through, therefore they are still Continued in that Service and to make Report when Ready
Placing matters In book of Dis =cipline	And the above Sᵈ friends Report that they have Answerᵈ their Appointment in Placing the Several matters Concluded on as Rules in our Society under proper heads in the book of Discipline – –
Red wood Recept	**Caleb Russell** hath producᵈ a Receipt from **Wᵐ Read Wood** that he Delinᵈ the money According to appointment of last Mᵒ Meeting
S: Russell Condemᵈ his Disorder	**Seth Russell** hath appearᵈ in this meeting and Verbally Condemned his Disorder in Suffering a Couple to be married ~~in~~ before a Justis of peace in his House which is Accepted
Dan Russel's Case	The Committee Appointed to Labour with **Daniel Russell** for Neglecting to pay **Joseph Rotch** & Sons their Demands, Report that they have Labourᵈ with him and **Daniel** hath made Some proposals to Said **Rotch** to Satisfy him but it not being Setled the Said Committee are appointed to Judge & Determine of Sᵈ Proposals and make Report to next monthly meeting
Overseers appointed	**Daniel Cornal[Cornell] William Anthony Jᵘ Jonathan Hussey Thoˢ Hicks William Mosher William Barker** are appointed Overseers in the meeting for the year Insewing [Ensuing]
Overseers of yᵉ poor appointed	**Caleb Russell Joseph Barker Barzillea Tucker Philip Allen Abraham Howland** are Appointed Overseers of the Poor for the year Insuing
9ᵐᵒ 1772	At a Monthly Meeting held in **Dartmouth** 21: 9ᵐᵒ 1772 the Representatives are Called **Caleb Russell** & **Jonathan Hussey** both Present
[Elishib] Smith marriage	The friends appointed to see **Elishib Smith** and **Allice Philips** marriage Consomated Report that they attended Said marraige which was Consomated in good order
J: Allen's paper Read	**Jedediah Allen**'s Paper hath been read and Returnᵈ to this meeting According to the Appointment of last monthly meeting
Jacob Mott Case	The Committee appointed to Labour with **Jacob Mott** Report that they have Dischargᵈ themselves in that Respect, therefore the Said committee is Still Continued to Draught a paper of Denial against the Sᵈ **Jacob Mott** and make Report to next monthly meeting
Dan Russell Case	The Committee Appointed to Judge & Determine between **Daniel Russell** & **Joseph Rotch** & Sons, Report that the matter in that Service & to make Report to next monthly meeting

David Shepherd
James Davis
Overseers of poor

David Shepherd and **James Davice [Davis]** are appointed Overseers of the poor whereas **David Smith** and **Jonathan Hussey** was appointed to

Wm Sanford J^u
case

Labour with **Wm Sandford j^u** for marring[marrying] out of Unity of friends Some time past and S^d **Sandford** has been much from home and nothing hath been Done to the Satisfaction of this meeting therefore **Wm Barker** is appointed in the Room of **David Smith** and they to Labour with S^d **Sandford** and make Report to next monthly meeting – The Queries hath been Read and Answered in this meeting

Received
Transcrips

Received Several Transcrips (viz)
one written Epistle from the yearly meeting in **London**
one from the yearly meeting held in **Philidelphia**
one from the yearly meeting held in **Flushing** on **Long Island**
all Which were read to good Satisfaction

William Barker Wm Anthony J^u Benjamin Smith J^u are appointed

Representa^s
for ye Quarter^y
meeting

to attend the Quarterly meeting and to present the Epistle with the Answers to the Queries which Epistle hath been sign^d in this meeting – And they to make Report to next m^o meeting This meeting hath Sign^d a Removal Certificate fo[for] **Rachel**

R. Mertihew
Certificate

Merithew to the monthly meeting of **Sandwich**
There was collected at this meeting £11 – 2^s – 9^d old tennor

Order on Trea
=surer

The Treasurrer is Ordered to pay the above seem[?] to the Overseers of the poor for the use of the poor
S^d Treasurer Reports that he hath now paid S^d money as ordered

---

10ma 1772

At a Monthly Meeting held in **Dartmouth** the 19th y^e 10mo 1772 the Representatives are **Caleb Russell** & **Jonathan Hussey** Present

Jos Russell Ju^r
proposal of
marriage

Joseph Russell j^ur and **Mehetable Howland** Declar^d their Intentions of marraige and were Desir^d to wait untill the next Monthly meeting for their Answer, And **David Shepherd** & **John Williams** are Appointed to make Inquirey into the young man's Clerness[Clearness] Respecting marraige & Conversation and make Report to next Monthly Meeting

J: Mott
Denied

This meeting hath Signed a Paper of Denial against **Jacob Mott** (for the Offences [Cognis^d] against him some months past) And the Clerk is appointed to Read Said paper at the Close of a first Day's meeting for Worship befor next monthly meeting and then make Report Said paper is as followeth

Whereas **Jacob Mott** of **Dartmouth** in the **County of Bristol** in the **Provence of the Massachusetts Bay** in **New England** – – Having been

Educated Amongst friends, under the Cair [care] of this meeting, yet by
Departing from his Education, and the Principal of Truth in his own br[??]t
hath so far gone astray as to be found Guilty of Diverse Disorderly practi-

Testimony against J: Mott

-ces highly Inconsistant with the Piety and Gravity of our Profession
Particularly in Absenting himself from our Religious meetings, And
in taking too much Spirittous Licquor, and Using bad Language, and
in Abusive behaviour, For which Reproachful Conduct this meeting hath
Treated with him and admonished him in love & Moderation in order
to Convince him of the Evil thereof, and Reclaim him therefrom, but
our Admonition & Labour not being Effectual So as to obtain the desir^d
End Therefore for the Clearing of truth and the Professors thereof
from such Reproachful behav[i]our, This Meeting is Concern^d Publickly
To Testify against him, And do hereby Disown him the Said **Jacob
Mott** from being a Member of our Religious Society Untill by
Unfeigned Repentance he Shall Return to the way of truth, Which y^t [that?]
he may is our Sincear [sincere] desire – Given forth & Signed in & on behalf
of our monthly Meeting held in **Dartmouth** the 19th 10mo 1772

By – –**Job Russell** Clerk

Case of Dan [R]ussell & Rocths [Rotch] Settled

The Committee Appointed to labour with **Daniel Russell** for
Neglecting to pay **Joseph & Sons** their Demands Report, that the Matter
is made up to the Said **Rotch**es Satisfaction for the Present – –

Case of Wm Sanford Ju Continu^d

The Committee appointed to Labour with **Wm Sandford J^u** Report that
they hant had an Oppertunity to Labour with him, (both together) tho they
have Labour^d with Seperate & Rec[e]iv^d Some Incouragment, therefore they
are Still Continued in that Service untill next m^o Meeting and then to
make Report – –

The friends Appointed to Attend the Quarterly Meeting Report

Represent^t Report

that they all attended Except **Benj^a Smith J^u** & he Render^d a Reasonable
Accuse [excuse?] for his not attending, And the [he?] produced an Epistle from S^d
Quarterly meeting which hath been Read to Good Satisfaction
and they have Produced a Coppy of an Epistle from the
Quarterly Meeting held in **Newport** on **Rhodisland** the
9th & 10th Days of ye 7 ^{mo} 1772, Said Epistle informs that

money [call^d?] for

its Concluded to ~~be~~ Lay^d out thirty pounds Lawfull money
on a Meeting House belonging to the Monthly Meeting [at?]

this ^{meeting} desires to be excus^d by reason of debt for their own meet house

South Kingston and Each monthly meeting is Desir^d to Contribute
according to their freedom, But we think this meeting may bee
Excused by Reason that we are Considerably in Debt for Repairs
of our Meeting house in **Aponeganset** and for Supporting of our poor

yearly meeting
reverst
Judgment of
Qr meeting
against
Humphry Smith And also S^d Epistle informs that the yearly meeting of **Rhodisland**
hath Reversed the Judgment of the Quarterly ^meeting Respecting
Humphry Smith

Jonathan Hussey Samuel Smith Prince Allen Wm Sandford

friends to
oversee y^e
Lofts **Thos Hicks** & **William Mosher**, are Appointed to have the Oversight
of the People in the Lofts & Other Seets [seats] at our insuing yearly
Meeting to Indeavour to Prevent Any indeacency that may
be Liable to happen at that time and make Report of their
Service at the next monthly meeting, This Mee^[n?] hath Conclude^d

Monthly Collec
tions Conclud
ed to alter our Quarterly Colle[c]tion to a Monthly Collection
and Conclude to Collect Every month as nead [need] may Appear

Order on Trea=
=surer The Treasurer is Ordered to pay **William Anthony J^u** two Dollars
which he Distributed for this meeting to Purchase Extracts

    And Said Treasurer is Likewise Ordered to pay **Ant^ipas
Hathaway** one Dollar for Glasing the Meeting House

    This Meeting hath Collected 4^£ – 6^s – 11^d old tennor [tenor]

11mo 1772 At a Monthly Meeting held in **Dartmouth** 16th the 11mo=
1772 the Representatives being Called which are **Joseph
Barker** & **Barzillia Tucker** Both Present

Barz Tucker
Clerk for this
day **Barzillia Tucker** is Chosen Clerk for this Day – –

The friends appointed to Inquire into the Clearness of **Joseph
Russell j^ur** Report that they find nothing to hinder
his proceeding in marraige [marriage]

J:R: & M:H
appear^d for
their answer **Joseph Russell j^ur** and **Mehetable Howland** appear^d for
their Answer which was that they might Proceed in to
take Each Other in Marraige between this & next monthly
meeting Advising with the Ove[r]seers that this meeting
shall appoint for the purpose and **David Sheepherd** [Shepherd] and **John Williams**
    are Appointed to See
their Marriage Consomated in Good order and make Report to
the next monthly meeting

Jacob Mott
denial not read   By Reason of the Clerk^s being Sick he has not Read **Jacob
Mott**s denial as Ordered therefor he is Continued in that Service
and to make Return to next monthly meeting – –

Report of
Overseers
of yerly
meeting refer^d   The friends appointed last monthly meeting to have the oversight
of the People in the Lofts and Other Seets [seats] at our yearly meeting
not being all Present therefore their Report is Refer^d to next
monthly meeting

Case of W^m
Sanford Ju^r
continu^d   The friends appointed on the Case of **Wm Sandford j^ur** not
fulfilling their Appointment by Reason of Sickness therefore

FIG. 8: The interior of the Apponegansett Meeting House showing "the lofts."
© *Copyright Jean Schnell*

they are Still Continued in that Service and **Abraham Tucker** is
ad[d]ed to them & they are Desired to do Somthing in that Case before
next monthly meeting and then make Report – –

Wᵐ Jones visited this meeting   Our friend **William Jones** hath Visited this meeting with his
Certificate from the monthly meeting of **Burlington** in the **Provence
of New=jersey** the 7ᵗʰ of the 9ᵐᵒ 1772 whose Visit and Service in the
Truth is Kindly Accepted – –

Friends at **Bedford** Request to have a Meeting for Worship
held there two Days in a week, the Week Day meeting to be held
on the Sixth Day of the week (Except those weeks of our Mᵒ
meeting & Preparative & youths meetings are held in) untill
meeting granted at Bedford   the Last of the third month next, Which Request is Granded [Granted]
and **David Shepherd** and **James Davis** are appointed to have the
oversight thereof and to see if it be held in the Authority of truth
and to make Report at the Expiration thereof – –

Treasurer report   The Treasurer Reports that he has paid **Antipas Hathaway**
one Dollar as Ordered

this Meeting hath Collected 7ᵉ – 17ˢ – 10ᵈ Old Tennor [Tenor]

12ᵐᵒ 1772   At a Monthly Meeting held in **Dartmouth** 21ˢᵗ: 12ᵐᵒ 1772
the Representatives are **Thoˢ Hicks** and **Samuel Smith** [?; Juʳ?]
John Williams Reports that, by reason of Sickness he did not
attend the marraige of **Joseph Russell** & **Mehitible Howland**
and we Understand **David Shepherd** could not attend this meeting
by Reason of his family being unwell therefore his Reporting is
Referᵈ to next monthly meeting

Jacob Mott   The Clerk Reports that he hath Read **Jacob Mott**s paper of Denial
denial read   According to the Appointment of last mᵒ meeting – –

Overseers of   The friends appointᵈ to have the Oversight of the ᴾᵉᵒᵖˡᵉ ⁱⁿ ᵗʰᵉ Lofts and
yearly meeting   at our yearly meeting Report that most of them attended
report   all the meetings and that the People behaved in Some Degree
orderly – –

Case of Wᵐ   The Committee Appointed to Labour with **Wᵐ Sanford** ʲᵘ
Sanford Ju   Report that they have not Dischargᵈ their trust in that
Continued   Respect by reason of Some Disappointment therefore [*two words crossed out*]
they are Still Continued in that Service and they to make Report
to next monthly meeting

money from   This meeting hath Received from **David Shepherd** by the hand
D Shepherd Recᵈ   of **John Howland** the Sum of 1ᵉ – 9ˢ – 3ᵈ [?] Lawfull money which
he Raised by way of Subscription Acording to Appointment of
this meeting, And the Same is Deliverᵈ to **Wᵐ Anthony Jᵘʳ**
this meeting Collected 7ᵉ – 7ˢ – 8ᵈ Old tennor – –

Adjourn   This meeting Adjourns to the first Sixth day in next month
after the meeting for Worship – –

mett   This Meeting meet According to Adjournment the first Sixth
Day of the first mᵒ 1773 the Representatives being Called both Present
The Overseers of the Poor hath brought an Account
to this meeting for doing for the Poor therefore we do

Comᵗᵗᵉᵉ to   Appoint **Samuel Smith Job Russell Prince Allen** and
examin   **William Mosher** a Committee to Exammine Said Accounts
accompts   and Also to Collect the whole Accounts that this meeting
is in Indebt and make Repor[t] as Soon as they Can
with Conveniency

Order on Trea=   The Treasurer is ordered to pay **Timothy Russell** 5 Dollars
=surer   for keeping the meeting House half a year – –
The Queries hath been read and Answerᵈ and an Epistle
to the Quarterly Meeting was read and Signed, & **Joseph Tucker**
Representˢ   and **William Sanford** are Appointed to Attend the Quarterly
to attend   Meeting and Convey the Answers & Epistle to Sᵈ Quarterly meeting
yᵉ Quarterly
meeting

and make Report to next monthly meeting

This Meeting Received 8ᵉ – 10ˢ – 9ᵈ old Tennor of **Barnabus** [**Barnabas**]

money Recᵈ
of Bar Mosher **Mosher** which he Collected by way of Subscription which is

Deliverᵈ to **Wᵐ Anthony Jᵘʳ**

1ᵐᵒ 1773 At a Monthly Meeting held in **Dartmouth** 18ᵗʰ 1ᵐᵒ 1773

the Representatives are **William Mosher** & **Barzillai Tucker** Present

Report of **David Sheepherd** [**Shepherd**] hath not made Report of his attending **Josʰ** [**Joseph**]
Jos Russell **Russells** marraige according to Referrance of Last monthly
not made
meeting therefor **James Davice** [**Davis**?] is appointed to Call upon

him to know the reason of his not making report and to Desire

him to make Report to next monthly meeting

Tim Russell The Treasurer Reports that he hath paid **Timothy Russell**
paid five Dollars as Ordered

Wᵐ Sanford Ju The friends Appointed to Labour with **William Sandford jᵘʳ**
give in a
paper is for marriing [marrying] out of the Unity of friends Report that he gave
accepted them a Degree of Satisfaction and Sᵈ **Sandford** hath given

in a Paper Condemning his Disorder which is Accepted and

is as followeth

Wᵐ Sanford To the monthly meeting of friends in **Dartmouth**
Confession
beloved friends these are to inform you that I have

gone Conterary [Contrary] to the good order Established among friends

in Marriage which breach of Unity after I have

meturly [maturely] Considered it am sorrow for and should be glad

that friends would So far pass it by as to let me Remain

under their Care given forth and Dated this – –

18ᵗʰ Day of the 1ᵐᵒ 1773　　–　　**William Sandford Jᵘ**

Report from The friends appointed to attend the Quarterly Meeting
Quart meeting
Report that they all attended according to appointment and

have Produced an Epistle from the Same which hath been

Read to good Satisfaction and the Contents thereof Earnestly – –

Recommended to friend notice and Observation

Whereas this meeting Requested of the Quarterly meeting that

on the subject there may bee an Alteration in our yearly meeting as it is
of holding our now held in two Branches, to have the same held in two
yearly meeting
in two places Destinct [Distinct] yearly meetings, and this meeting is informᵈ by an
a Comᵗᵉᵉ Epistle from the Quarterly meeting that Sᵈ Quarterly meeting Desires
appoᵢnted
this meeting to Consult with **ACoakset** monthly meeting about

the Alteration, And we Appoint **Joseph Tucker Abraham Tucker**

Paul Russell Job Russell Jonathan Hussey and **Samuel Smith** a

Committee to Confer with **Acoakset** monthly meeting on that

and make Report So as to have Sᵈ matter Sent up to next Quarter

Sh: Craw
Dealt with

Two of the Overseers Informes this meeting that **Sherman Craw**
hath married out of the Unity of friends Although they
Precautioned him before marraige therefore we do appoint
Barnabus Mosher & **Wᵐ Wood** to Labour with him as they
may find freedom and make Report to next monthly meeting
The Committee appointed to treat with **David Smith** Report
as followeth which is Accepted

Agreable to the Appointment of the Monthly Meeting
We have made Inquiry into the Complaint Against **David Smith**
and have Labourᵈ with him to Leave the matter to Indifferant
men in order to Settle the Controvercy which was then Subsisting

Report
Concerning
David Smith

between him and **Daniel Russell** & **Abner Russell**, which was [*faded word*]
So far Complied with as to Choose the Arbitrators, but the other
parties not Appearing to proceed in the Matter in order for
Settlement, therefore we think **David Smith** may be Dismised
from Sᵈ Complaint at Present – –
Given forth by your Committee this 18ᵗʰ yᵉ 1ˢᵗ ᵐᵒ 1773

> **Joseph Tucker**
> **Abraham Howland**
> **Barnabas Mosher**
> **Benjᵃ Howland 2ⁿᵈ[?]**

Thomas
Almy
request a
Certificate

Thomas Almy hath Removed within the Compass of **ACoakset**
Monthly Meeting to Live and Desires a Removal Certificate
Do appoint **Prince Allen** & **Nicholass Howland** to Inquire into
his life & Conversation and to see ~~that his Life & Conversation~~
that his outward affairs be settled to Satisfaction and Draw a
Certification for him if they think proper and make Report to next meeting

Complaint
against
David
Smith

William Barker and **Daniel Cornal [Cornell]** hath Exhibeted a Complaint
against **David Smith** for Reporting that Some of the Overseers were
fals [false?] men, in Perticularly **Wᵐ Barker** & **Daniel Cornal** to their
Diffimation [defamation?], Therefore this meeting do appoint **Benjᵃ Taber**
Nicholass Howland John Ricketson Benjᵃ Howland 2ⁿᵈ Wᵐ Wood
a Committee to inquire into and to Judge and Determine the
matter between them in behalf of this meeting and make
Report to next mᵒ meeting.

Money col=
=lected for
repairing
meeting
house

Prince Allen hath Collected by way of Subscription –– 7ᵉ : 12ˢ: 9ᵈ O[ld] [Tennor?]
also **Benjᵃ Howland 2ⁿᵈ** hath Collected by way of Subscription 19 - 4 : 0 o:T:
and said money is Deliverᵈ to **Wᵐ Anthony Jᵘ** for Repairing Meeting house
the collection is Referᵈ to next monthly meeting